University of Southern Colorado Library

UNIVERSITY OF SOUTHERN COLORADO

3 3040 00473 0245

D0534883

DISCARDED BY
CSU-PUEBLO LIBRARY

Contemporary Authors®

NEW REVISION SERIES

ISSN 0275-7176

Contemporary Authors®

A Bio-Bibliographical Guide to Current Writers in Fiction, General Nonfiction, Poetry, Journalism, Drama, Motion Pictures, Television, and Other Fields

NEW REVISION SERIES
volume 102

GALE GROUP

THOMSON LEARNING

Detroit • New York • San Diego • San Francisco
Boston • New Haven, Conn. • Waterville, Maine
London • Munich

Staff

Scot Peacock, *Managing Editor, Literature Product*

Mark W. Scott, *Publisher, Literature Product*

Frank Castronova, Lisa Kumar, *Senior Editors*; Katy Balcer, Sara Constantakis, Kristen A. Dorsch, Marie Lazzari, Thomas F. McMahon, *Editors*; Alana Joli Foster, Arlene M. Johnson, Jennifer Kilian, Michelle Poole, Thomas Wiloch, *Associate Editors*; Karen Abbott, Madeline Harris, Anita Sundaresan, Maikue Vang, Denay L. Wilding, *Assistant Editors*; Anna Marie Dahn, Judith L. Pyko, *Adminstrative Support*; Joshua Kondek, Mary Ruby, *Technical Training Specialists*

Dwayne Hayes, Joyce Nakamura, *Managing Editors*

Susan M. Trosky, *Content Director*

Victoria B. Cariappa, *Research Manager*

Tamara C. Nott, *Research Associate*; Nicodemus Ford, *Research Assistants*

While every effort has been made to ensure the reliability of the information presented in this publication, Gale Group neither guarantees the accuracy of the data contained herein nor assumes any responsibility for errors, omissions, or discrepancies. Gale Group accepts no payment for listing; and inclusion in the publication of any organization, agency, institution, publication, service, or individual does not imply endorsement of the editors or publisher. Errors brought to the attention of the publisher and verified to the satisfaction of the publisher will be corrected in future editions.

This publication is a creative work copyrighted by Gale Group and fully protected by all applicable copyright laws, as well as by misappropriation, trade secret, unfair competition, and other applicable laws. The authors and editors of this work have added value to the underlying factual material herein through one or more of the following: unique and original selection, coordination, expression, arrangement, and classification of the information.

Gale Group will vigorously defend all of its rights in this publication.

Copyright © 2002 by Gale Group, Inc.
27500 Drake Rd.
Farmington Hills, MI 48331-3535

Gale Group and Design is a trademark used herein under license.
All rights reserved including the right of reproduction in whole or in part in any form.

Library of Congress Catalog Card Number 81-640179
ISBN 0-7876-4611-3
ISSN 0025-7176
Printed in the United States of America

10 9   367111

R
PN771
C75$
v. 102

University of Southern Colorado Library

Contents

Indexing note: All *Contemporary Authors* entries are indexed in the *Contemporary Authors* cumulative index, which is published separately and distributed twice a year.

As always, the most recent *Contemporary Authors* cumulative index continues to be the user's guide to the location of an individual author's listing.

Preface

Contemporary Authors (*CA*) provides information on approximately 100,000 writers in a wide range of media, including:

- Current writers of fiction, nonfiction, poetry, and drama whose works have been issued by commercial publishers, risk publishers, or university presses (authors whose books have been published only by known vanity or author-subsidized firms are ordinarily not included)

- Prominent print and broadcast journalists, editors, photojournalists, syndicated cartoonists, graphic novelists, screenwriters, television scriptwriters, and other media people

- Authors who write in languages other than English, provided their works have been published in the United States or translated into English

- Literary greats of the early twentieth century whose works are popular in todays high school and college curriculums and continue to elicit critical attention

A *CA* listing entails no charge or obligation. Authors are included on the basis of the above criteria and their interest to *CA* users. Sources of potential listees include trade periodicals, publishers' catalogs, librarians, and other users.

How to Get the Most out of *CA*: Use the Index

The key to locating an author's most recent entry is the *CA* cumulative index, which is published separately and distributed twice a year. It provides access to *all* entries in *CA* and *Contemporary Authors New Revision Series* (*CANR*). Always consult the latest index to find an authors most recent entry.

For the convenience of users, the *CA* cumulative index also includes references to all entries in these Gale literary series: *Authors and Artists for Young Adults, Authors in the News, Bestsellers, Black Literature Criticism, Black Literature Criticism Supplement, Black Writers, Children's Literature Review, Concise Dictionary of American Literary Biography, Concise Dictionary of British Literary Biography, Contemporary Authors Autobiography Series, Contemporary Authors Bibliographical Series, Contemporary Dramatists, Contemporary Literary Criticism, Contemporary Novelists, Contemporary Poets, Contemporary Popular Writers, Contemporary Southern Writers, Contemporary Women Poets, Dictionary of Literary Biography, Dictionary of Literary Biography Documentary Series, Dictionary of Literary Biography Yearbook, DISCovering Authors, DISCovering Authors: British, DISCovering Authors: Canadian, DISCovering Authors: Modules* (including modules for Dramatists, Most-Studied Authors, Multicultural Authors, Novelists, Poets, and Popular/Genre Authors), *Discovering Authors 3.0, Drama Criticism, Drama for Students, Feminist Writers, Hispanic Literature Criticism, Hispanic Writers, Junior DISCovering Authors, Major Authors and Illustrators for Children and Young Adults, Major 20th-Century Writers, Native North American Literature, Novels for Students, Poetry Criticism, Poetry for Students, Short Stories for Students, Short Story Criticism, Something about the Author, Something about the Author Autobiography Series, St. James Guide to Children's Writers, St. James Guide to Horror, Ghost, and Gothic Writers, St. James Guide to Science Fiction Writers, St. James Guide to Young Adult Writers, Twentieth-Century Literary Criticism, Twentieth-Century Romance and Historical Writers, World Literature Criticism,* and *Yesterday's Authors of Books for Children.*

A Sample Index Entry:

Name (parentheses denote parts of name not used for publication)	Birth date (and death date, if applicable)	Volume containing most recent sketch (*CA/CANR* entries come first if they exist; no acronym means *CA* volume)

Kinnell, Galway 1927- CANR-66
Earlier sketches in CA 9-12R, CANR-10, 34
Interview in CANR-34
See also CLC 1, 2, 3, 5, 13, 29
See also DLB 5
See also DLBY 87
See also MTCW

Volumes containing previous *CA* and *CANR* sketches	Volumes of *CA/CANR* containing unique interviews with the author

Volumes of *Dictionary of Literary Biography* and *DLB Yearbook* containing entries on author	Volumes of *Contemporary Literary Criticism* containing entries on author

	Major Twentieth Century Writers contains entry on author

How Are Entries Compiled?

The editors make every effort to secure new information directly from the authors; listees' responses to our questionnaires and query letters provide most of the information featured in *CA*. For deceased writers, or those who fail to reply to requests for data, we consult other reliable biographical sources, such as those indexed in Gale's *Biography and Genealogy Master Index,* and bibliographical sources, including *National Union Catalog, LC MARC,* and *British National Bibliography*. Further details come from published interviews, feature stories, and book reviews, as well as information supplied by the authors' publishers and agents.

An asterisk (*) at the end of a sketch indicates that the listing has been compiled from secondary sources believed to be reliable but has not been personally verified for this edition by the author sketched.

What Kinds of Information Does An Entry Provide?

Sketches in *CA* contain the following biographical and bibliographical information:

- **Entry heading:** the most complete form of author's name, plus any pseudonyms or name variations used for writing

- **Personal information:** author's date and place of birth, family data, ethnicity, educational background, political and religious affiliations, and hobbies and leisure interests

- **Addresses:** author's home, office, or agent's addresses, plus e-mail and fax numbers, as available

- **Career summary:** name of employer, position, and dates held for each career post; resume of other vocational achievements; military service

- **Membership information:** professional, civic, and other association memberships and any official posts held

- **Awards and honors:** military and civic citations, major prizes and nominations, fellowships, grants, and honorary degrees

- **Writings:** a comprehensive, chronological list of titles, publishers, dates of original publication and revised editions, and production information for plays, television scripts, and screenplays

- **Adaptations:** a list of films, plays, and other media which have been adapted from the author's work

- **Work in progress:** current or planned projects, with dates of completion and/or publication, and expected publisher, when known

- **Sidelights:** a biographical portrait of the author's development; information about the critical reception of the author's works; revealing comments, often by the author, on personal interests, aspirations, motivations, and thoughts on writing

- **Interview:** a one-on-one discussion with authors conducted especially for *CA*, offering insight into authors' thoughts about their craft

- **Autobiographical Essay:** an original essay written by noted authors for *CA*, a forum in which writers may present themselves, on their own terms, to their audience

- **Photographs:** portraits and personal photographs of notable authors

- **Biographical and critical sources:** a list of books and periodicals in which additional information on an author's life and/or writings appears

- **Obituary Notices** in *CA* provide date and place of birth as well as death information about authors whose full-length sketches appeared in the series before their deaths. The entries also summarize the authors' careers and writings and list other sources of biographical and death information.

Related Titles in the *CA* Series

Contemporary Authors Autobiography Series complements *CA* original and revised volumes with specially commissioned autobiographical essays by important current authors, illustrated with personal photographs they provide. Common topics include their motivations for writing, the people and experiences that shaped their careers, the rewards they derive from their work, and their impressions of the current literary scene.

Contemporary Authors Bibliographical Series surveys writings by and about important American authors since World War II. Each volume concentrates on a specific genre and features approximately ten writers; entries list works written by and about the author and contain a bibliographical essay discussing the merits and deficiencies of major critical and scholarly studies in detail.

Available in Electronic Formats

GaleNet. *CA* is available on a subscription basis through GaleNet, an online information resource that features an easy-to-use end-user interface, powerful search capabilities, and ease of access through the World Wide Web. For more information, call 1-800-877-GALE.

Licensing. *CA* is available for licensing. The complete database is provided in a fielded format and is deliverable on such media as disk, CD-ROM, or tape. For more information, contact Gale's Business Development Group at 1-800-877-GALE, or visit us on our website at www.galegroup.com/bizdev.

Suggestions Are Welcome

The editors welcome comments and suggestions from users on any aspect of the *CA* series. If readers would like to recommend authors for inclusion in future volumes of the series, they are cordially invited to write the Editors at *Contemporary Authors*, Gale Group, 27500 Drake Rd., Farmington Hills, MI 48331-3535; or call at 1-248-699-4253; or fax at 1-248-699-8054.

Contemporary Authors Product Advisory Board

The editors of *Contemporary Authors* are dedicated to maintaining a high standard of excellence by publishing comprehensive, accurate, and highly readable entries on a wide array of writers. In addition to the quality of the content, the editors take pride in the graphic design of the series, which is intended to be orderly yet inviting, allowing readers to utilize the pages of *CA* easily and with efficiency. Despite the longevity of the *CA* print series, and the success of its format, we are mindful that the vitality of a literary reference product is dependent on its ability to serve its users over time. As literature, and attitudes about literature, constantly evolve, so do the reference needs of students, teachers, scholars, journalists, researchers, and book club members. To be certain that we continue to keep pace with the expectations of our customers, the editors of *CA* listen carefully to their comments regarding the value, utility, and quality of the series. Librarians, who have firsthand knowledge of the needs of library users, are a valuable resource for us. The *Contemporary Authors* Product Advisory Board, made up of school, public, and academic librarians, is a forum to promote focused feedback about *CA* on a regular basis. The five-member advisory board includes the following individuals, whom the editors wish to thank for sharing their expertise:

- **Barbara C. Chumard,** Reference/Adult Services Librarian, Middletown Thrall Library, Middletown, New York.

- **Eva M. Davis,** Teen Services Librarian, Plymouth District Library, Plymouth, Michigan.

- **Adam Janowski, Jr.,** Library Media Specialist, Naples High School Library Media Center, Naples, Florida.

- **Robert Reginald,** Head of Technical Services and Collection Development, California State University, San Bernadino, California.

- **Barbara A. Wencl,** Media Specialist, Como Park High School, St. Paul, Minnesota.

International Advisory Board

Well-represented among the 100,000 author entries published in *Contemporary Authors* are sketches on notable writers from many non-English-speaking countries. The primary criteria for inclusion of such authors has traditionally been the publication of at least one title in English, either as an original work or as a translation. However, the editors of *Contemporary Authors* came to observe that many important international writers were being overlooked due to a strict adherence to our inclusion criteria. In addition, writers who were publishing in languages other than English were not being covered in the traditional sources we used for identifying new listees. Intent on increasing our coverage of international authors, including those who write only in their native language and have not been translated into English, the editors enlisted the aid of a board of advisors, each of whom is an expert on the literature of a particular country or region. Among the countries we focused attention on in 2000 are Mexico, Puerto Rico, Germany, Luxembourg, Belgium, the Netherlands, Norway, Sweden, Denmark, Finland, Taiwan, Singapore, and Japan, as well as England, Scotland, Wales, Ireland, Australia, and New Zealand. The nine-member advisory board includes the following individuals, whom the editors wish to thank for sharing their expertise:

- **Lowell A. Bangerter**, Professor of German, University of Wyoming, Laramie, Wyoming.

- **David William Foster**, Regent's Professor of Spanish, Interdisciplinary Humanities, and Women's Studies, Arizona State University, Tempe, Arizona.

- **Frances Devlin-Glass**, Associate Professor, School of Literary and Communication Studies, Deakin University, Burwood, Victoria, Australia.

- **Hosea Hirata**, Director of the Japanese Program, Associate Professor of Japanese, Tufts University, Medford, Massachusetts.

- **Linda M. Rodríguez Guglielmoni**, Associate Professor, University of Puerto Rico—Mayagüez, Puerto Rico.

- **Sven Hakon Rossel**, Professor and Chair of Scandanvian Studies, University of Vienna, Vienna, Austria.

- **Steven R. Serafin**, Director, Writing Center, Hunter College of the City University of New York, New York City.

- **Ismail S. Talib**, Senior Lecturer, Department of English Language and Literature, National University of Singapore, Singapore.

- **Mark Williams**, Associate Professor, English Department, University of Canterbury, Christchurch, New Zealand.

CA Numbering System and Volume Update Chart

Occasionally questions arise about the *CA* numbering system and which volumes, if any, can be discarded. Despite numbers like "29-32R," "97-100" and "194," the entire *CA* print series consists of only 224 physical volumes with the publication of *CA* Volume 195. The following charts note changes in the numbering system and cover design, and indicate which volumes are essential for the most complete, up-to-date coverage.

CA First Revision
- 1-4R through 41-44R (11 books)
  Cover: Brown with black and gold trim.
  There will be no further First Revision volumes because revised entries are now being handled exclusively through the more effcient *New Revision Series* mentioned below.

CA Original Volumes
- 45-48 through 97-100 (14 books)
  Cover: Brown with black and gold trim.
- 101 through 195 (95 books)
  Cover: Blue and black with orange bands.
  The same as previous *CA* original volumes but with a new, simplified numbering system and new cover design.

CA Permanent Series
- *CAP*-1 and *CAP*-2 (2 books)
  Cover: Brown with red and gold trim.
  There will be no further Permanent Series volumes because revised entries are now being handled exclusively through the more efficient *New Revision Series* mentioned below.

CA New Revision Series
- CANR-1 through CANR-102 (102 books)
  Cover: Blue and black with green bands.
  Includes only sketches requiring significant changes; **sketches are taken from any previously published *CA*, *CAP*, or *CANR* volume.**

If You Have: You May Discard:

If You Have:	You May Discard:
CA First Revision Volumes 1-4R through 41-44R and *CA Permanent Series* Volumes 1 and 2.	*CA* Original Volumes 1, 2 ,3, 4 Volumes 5-6 through 41-44
CA Original Volumes 45-48 through 97-100 and 101 through 195	**NONE:** These volumes will not be supeseded by corresponding revised volumes. Individual entries from these and all other volumes appearing in the left column of this chart may be revised and included in the various volumes of the *New Revision Series*.
CA New Revision Series Volumes *CANR*-1 through *CANR*-102	**NONE:** The *New Revision Series* does not replace any single volume of *CA*. Instead, volumes of *CANR* include entries from many previous *CA* series volumes. All *New Revision Series* volumes must be retained for full coverage.

A Sampling of Authors and Media People Featured in This Volume

John Ashbery

Ashbery is recognized as one of the leading lights of American letters. Although even his strongest supporters admit that his poetry is often difficult to read and willfully difficult to understand, Ashbery has become, as James Atlas noted in the *New York Times Sunday Magazine*, "the most widely honored poet of his generation." Ashbery's position in American letters is confirmed by his unprecedented sweep of the literary "triple crown" in 1976, when *Self-Portrait in a Convex Mirror* won the Pulitzer Prize, the National Book Award, and the National Book Critics Circle Prize.

Lynda Barry

Barry is perhaps most widely known as the creator of the comic strip "Ernie Pook's Comeek," which can be found in alternative newspapers throughout the United States. In such works as "Ernie Pook" and the illustrated novel-turned-play *The Good Times Are Killing Me*, Barry ranges over the whole comic/tragic experience of growing up, from dirt bombs to divorced parents to the strains that pull friendships apart. Her earlier comic strips, collected in the volumes *Big Ideas* and *Everything in the World*, satirize dating and the illusions of romance. Barry is also the author of the dark work *Cruddy: An Illustrated Novel*, published in 1999.

Eric Bogosian

Bogosian is an actor and writer who has garnered acclaim for his stage productions, including such solo works as *Drinking in America*, in which he performed as a fatuous hippie, a manic, substance-abusing Hollywood agent, a young vandal, and a pathetic wino. In his review of *Sex, Drugs, and Rock 'n' Roll*, another solo stage work by Bogosian, Frank Rich observed that the author/performer is "a great talent, a chameleon actor and penetrating social observer." Several of Bogosian's plays have been adapted as films, including *Talk Radio* and *SubUrbia*. He is also the author of the novel *Mall*, published in 2000.

Ramsey Campbell

Campbell, a British author of horror fiction, writes of the terrors that lurk in modern life. His work has been singled out for its unsettling, dreamlike prose and convincing attention to detail (many of Campbell's stories are set in his native Liverpool and involve the real people who live there). Although his early work was heavily influenced by the weird fiction of H. P. Lovecraft, Campbell has since struck out in new directions, creating more believable characters and adding a veneer of everyday life to his stories. Campbell is the winner of the 1998 Bram Stoker Life Achievement Award and numerous British Fantasy awards.

Mary Higgins Clark

Clark, a prolific author of bestselling mystery novels, began her writing career as a newly widowed mother of five. Her first novel, *Where Are the Children?*, became a bestseller in 1975, and was followed by the thriller *A Stranger Is Watching*, which earned more than $1 million in paperback rights and was filmed by Metro-Goldwyn-Mayer in 1982. Clark's stories have proven so popular that her publisher has continually signed her to multi-million dollar contracts. By 2000, Clark had over fifty million titles in print and enjoyed bestseller status around the world. In 2001, she issued the novel *On the Street Where You Live*.

Adam Gopnik

An editor and contributor to the *New Yorker* magazine, Gopnik has written frequently about art. In 1995, after the *New Yorker* offered him the opportunity to serve as the publication's Paris correspondent, Gopnik began a series of personal essays that not only reflect on daily life in Paris, but comment on what it's like for an American couple to raise a young child in the city. The essays, published regularly in the *New Yorker*, were later collected in the volume *Paris to the Moon*.

Edna O'Brien

Irish author O'Brien is an accomplished novelist, short story writer, playwright, and screenwriter. Her works include such award-winning titles as *Lantern Slides*, a collection of short fiction, and the novel *Time and Tide*. O'Brien is known for using her personal experiences, especially her childhood in Ireland, as sources for many of her works, drawing on her memories to evoke the emotions of her readers. Her first novel, *The Country Girls,* broke new ground in Irish literature, giving a frank speaking voice to women characters. The subject matter and especially the daringly graphic sexual scenes caused this book, and the six that followed, to be banned in Ireland.

William Trevor (Cox)

Short-story writer, novelist, and playwright William Trevor Cox is an Irish-born English writer better known to his readers as William Trevor. Considered by many critics to be one of the finest living short story writers in English, Trevor is equally renowned as a novelist, and is widely known in England for the television adaptations of his novels. Having lived in both Ireland and England, Trevor has written about people in both countries, often focusing on ordinary people who lead tragic, lonely lives. He is the recipient of numerous awards and honors, including the 2001 *Irish Times* Literary Award for Fiction for the short story collection *The Hill Bachelors*.

Acknowledgments

Grateful acknowledgment is made to those publishers, photographers, and artists whose work appear with these authors' essays. Following is a list of the copyright holders who have granted us permission to reproduce material in this volume of *CA*. Every effort has been made to trace copyright, but if omissions have been made, please let us know.

Photographs/Art

Louis Althusser: Althusser, photograph. UPI/Corbis-Bettmann. Reproduced by permission.

Kevin J. Anderson: Anderson, photograph. Reproduced by permission.

John Ashbery: Ashbery, photograph by Jerry Bauer. © Jerry Bauer. Reproduced by permission.

Lynda Barry: Barry, photograph by Jim Sulley. AP/Wide World Photos. Reproduced by permission.

Marvin Bell: Bell, photograph. James Morgan. Reproduced by permission.

Ted Berrigan: Berrigan, photograph by Layle Silbert. Reproduced by permission.

Eric Bogosian: Bogosian, photograph. The Kobal Collection. Reproduced by permission.

Betsy Byars: Byars, photograph by Ed Byars. Reproduced by permission of Betsy Byars. © Bozi/Corbis. Reproduced by permission.

Ramsey Campbell: Campbell, photograph by Jerry Bauer. © Jerry Bauer. Reproduced by permission.

Mary Higgins Clark: Clark, photograph by Jerry Bauer. © Jerry Bauer. Reproduced by permission.

Christopher Darden: Darden, photograph. AP/Wide World Photos. Reproduced by permission.

Ken Follett: Follett, photograph. AP/Wide World Photos. Reproduced by permission.

Charles de Gaulle: de Gaulle, photograph. Getty Images. Reproduced by permission.

Roy Hattersley: Hattersley, photograph. Getty Images. Reproduced by permission.

Larry King: King, photograph. Archive Photo/Lee. Reproduced by permission.

Dalai Lama: Dalai Lama, photograph. AP/Wide World Photos. Reproduced by permission.

Kyoko Mori: Mori, photograph by Katherine McCabe. Reproduced by permission of Kyoko Mori.

Vladimir Nabokov: Nabokov, photograph by Jerry Bauer. © Jerry Bauer. Reproduced by permission.

James Stevenson: Stevenson, photograph. Reproduced by permission.

A

Indicates that a listing has been compiled from secondary sources believed to be reliable, but has not been personally verified for this edition by the author sketched.

AARON, Chester 1923-

PERSONAL: Born May 9, 1923, in Butler, PA; son of Albert (a grocer and farmer) and Celia (Charleson) Aaron; married Margaurite Kelly (a jeweler), April 17, 1954 (divorced, 1973); children: Louis Daniel Segal (stepson). *Education:* Attended University of California, Los Angeles; University of California, Berkeley, B.A., 1966; San Francisco State University, M.A., 1972. *Avocational interests:* Garlic farming.

ADDRESSES: Home—P.O. Box 388, Occidental, CA 95465. *E-mail*—cgar@sonic.net.

CAREER: Educator, author, and farmer. St. Mary's College, Moraga, CA, assistant professor, 1972-82, then professor of English, 1983-94; freelance writer, 1967—. Kaiser Permanente, San Francisco, CA, X-ray technician, 1957-58; Alta Bates Hospital, Berkeley, CA, chief X-ray technician, 1957-75; MKI Engineering, San Francisco, technical writer, 1971-72; California Marine Mammal Center, Marin County, volunteer. *Military service:* U.S. Army Armored Infantry, 1943-46.

AWARDS, HONORS: Grants from Huntington Hartford Foundation, 1950, 1951, Chapelbrook Foundation, 1970, and National Endowment for the Arts, 1976; *Duchess* was named a notable children's trade book in the field of social studies by a joint committee of the National Council for the Social Studies and the Children's Book Council, 1982.

WRITINGS:

YOUNG ADULT FICTION

Better than Laughter, Harcourt (New York, NY), 1972.

An American Ghost, illustrations by David Lemon, Harcourt (New York, NY), 1973.
Hello to Bodega, Atheneum (New York, NY), 1976.
Spill, Atheneum (New York, NY), 1978.
Catch Calico!, Dutton (New York, NY), 1979.
Gideon, Lippincott (Philadelphia, PA), 1982.
Duchess, Lippincott (Philadelphia, PA), 1982.
Out of Sight, out of Mind, Lippincott (Philadelphia, PA), 1985.
Lackawanna, Lippincott (Philadelphia, PA), 1986.
Alex, Who Won His War, Walker (New York, NY), 1991.

Author's works have been translated into French.

OTHER

The Cowbank (play), produced at University of California, Berkeley, 1955.
About Us (autobiographical novel), McGraw (New York, NY), 1967, reprinted, Ten Speed Press (Berkeley, CA), 2001.
Garlic Is Life: A Memoir with Recipes, Ten Speed Press (Berkeley, CA), 1996.
The Great Garlic Book, Ten Speed Press (Berkeley, CA), 1997.

Also author of unpublished novel *Axel.* Contributor of short stories to periodicals, including *Amistad, Coastlines, Highlights for Children, New York Times, North American Review, San Francisco Chronicle,* and *Texas Quarterly.*

ADAPTATIONS: Cougar, based on *An American Ghost,* was produced by ABC-TV as a weekend special in 1984, and produced as a video recording, 1991;

Lackawanna was optioned for a feature film by Moonlight Productions/ITC Productions.

SIDELIGHTS: While Chester Aaron has traveled a number of career paths as an adult—from X-ray technician to college professor to garlic farmer—his desire to become a writer originated in his childhood and has been the thread that unites Aaron's varied life experiences. An early and avid reader, Aaron remembered the incident that would shape his ultimate career. For his eleventh birthday, he received a copy of Jack London's *White Fang* from one of his brothers. After rushing through the book, the young Aaron rendered an exciting account of it to a spellbound group of his friends. "But as good as my story was," he recalled in an essay in *Something about the Author Autobiography Series* (*SAAS*), "its impact did not approach the impact the original writing, the words and the sentences Jack London had composed, had had on me. . . . 'Someday,' I promised the kids as well as myself, 'I'm going to write stories.' " Although he wrote throughout his life, Aaron was in his mid-forties before he published his first book, the autobiographical novel *About Us,* which recounts growing up in a coal-mining town in Pennsylvania. In his books for younger readers, he has also drawn strongly upon the experience of his youth, earning critical praise for his realistic characters and suspenseful storylines. While the critical reception of Aaron's work has often surpassed its popular success, his books "belong to the sterling old adventure genre, though with more inner subtleties," according to *St. James Guide to Children's Writers* essayist Naomi Lewis.

Aaron's parents, Jews from Poland and Russia, emigrated from eastern Europe at the turn of the twentieth century to settle in the Pennsylvania mining town of North Butler where they operated a small grocery store. Aaron's five brothers and one sister were nearly adults when he was born in 1923. While the Great Depression of the 1930s would throw the Aaron family into upheaval, Chester's parents refused food to no one, even those who had no money for groceries. Their philanthropy, which included preparing and delivering packages of meat, vegetables, and bread to the poorest of the unemployed at Christmas, eventually caused problems. "Before long we were as impoverished as the poorest worker's family," recalled Aaron. "We had no food. I went, with other kids, to trail along behind the occasional coal trains, gathering fallen lumps of coal for our stove. I hiked many miles with my father to pick wild mushrooms and nuts and berries to supplement the potatoes that composed our meals." Unlike many hard-pressed families in their town, Chester's father refused to accept government assistance, and when taxes were due he took on extra work digging ditches in order to pay them. With the onset of World War II came a cultural clash; the generosity of the Jewish grocer was forgotten as Aaron and his family were suddenly at the receiving end of a barrage of ethnic slurs: insensitive childish remarks and pranks as well as Nazi swastikas painted on their store. "The jokes and curses I received from the kids could no longer be forgiven so easily," recalled Aaron. "I was driven not just to fight back but to fight and hurt, and even, if necessary, to maim. Driven by a mix of fear and anger, I earned the reputation of being a kid it was no longer wise to tease with epithets suggesting Jews were stingy and biblically convicted Christ-killers."

After graduating from Butler High School in the spring of 1941, Aaron was deferred from the military draft since four of his brothers were already in the service and his parents were both old and ill. Although he got a job at a local steel mill for several months, burning inside him was the desire to join the Army and go overseas. "Fighting ignorant and insensitive kids for their stupid little epithets was no longer enough. I had to kill Germans," he admitted. After enlisting and training, Aaron was stationed in southern Germany from 1943 to 1945. There, in 1945, he experienced something that changed him as a human being. As his military unit approached the town of Dachau, they saw a hovering gray-orange cloud suspended over the area. Marching closer, they detected a stench in the air, which was later discovered to emanate from burning human flesh. "We stormed the gates of Dachau and overwhelmed the few remaining German troops," Aaron recalled. "I helped open the doors of the various gray wooden barracks that contained the living and the dead, one indistinguishable from the other. We remained at Dachau two days. Those two days changed whatever direction my life, up until then, might have been traveling. I was never the same man. I still dream about those two days at Dachau. I have struggled to convince myself that I am more than a Jew, I am a man, a human being, like Catholic and Protestant and Moslem men. But it doesn't work. I find myself listening to words of Gentiles, even of those I love, waiting to hear the denunciation that might precede a fist or a rifle butt or knocks at my door in the middle of the night."

Aaron was twenty-two when he returned from the war, and during the three years he was in Germany his parents had died. He moved to California and worked at odd jobs while studying creative writing at the University of California, Los Angeles, on the G.I. Bill. Although the stories he submitted for publication usually were rejected, the budding writer was encouraged by professors who felt his powerful writer's voice needed to be heard. With the help of a Hartford Foundation grant he began work on a praised, but ultimately unpublished novel; discouraged, Aaron set aside his plans to write full-time and trained instead as an X-ray technician—a profession he worked at for nearly fifteen years while continuing to write part-time. Finally, in the late 1960s, he published his first book, the critically acclaimed autobiographical novel *About Us.*

Calling *About Us* "a beautiful and original book," *Nation* contributor Donald Fanger praised it as being "lyrical without mushiness and tough without posing, full of a truth that cannot be abstracted from the words that carry it." Reviewing Aaron's debut in the *Los Angeles Times Calendar,* Richard G. Lillard described the novel as "a rich cross-section of attitudes and conflicts in America during the Depression and World War II," and concluding: "Its radiant insight illuminates a wide circumference of human joy and suffering." Describing *About Us* as a novel about the disintegration of a family, Fanger noted that the plot follows "the scarcely perceptible stages through a pure present tense that becomes gradually complicated with a past and with intimations of a future." As the critic concluded, "It is a remarkable first novel, able in its authenticity to hear comparison with the best of its kind."

Shortly after the publication of *About Us,* Aaron began teaching at Saint Mary's College in Moraga, California, which gave him more time to pursue writing. Realizing that many of his students were ignorant of the Nazi concentration camps, he knew the time had come to write about the Holocaust. In 1982's *Gideon,* which Lewis labeled a "powerful and important book" in *St. James Guide to Children's Writers,* a brave fourteen-year-old boy survives the Warsaw Ghetto and later the death camp at Treblinka through his own resourcefulness. A contributor to *Bulletin of the Center for Children's Books* praised the novel as a "moving and terrible story, written with craft and conviction."

Since publishing *Gideon,* Aaron has written several other well-received novels for younger readers. In *Out of Sight, out of Mind,* twin teen psychics find themselves orphaned and their efforts to present a talk on world peace thwarted by an aggressive foreign government. *Lackawanna* finds six homeless orphans bonding together as a family during the Great Depression of the 1930s, their sense of invulnerability shattered when one of them becomes lost while jumping a freight train. *An American Ghost* draws readers back to 1850, as young Albie and his home are washed down river during a flood, his only companion a female cougar seeking shelter so she can give birth to her cubs. Noting the "lasting quality" of these novels, Lewis praised Aaron's work for young readers as containing "an unquenchable spark of optimism, a hopeful energy, [that is] always to be found in the central youthful characters."

Aaron once explained in *SAAS* that he makes no distinction between writing for children and writing for adults. "I use the same vocabulary, the same reliance on clear prose, the same insistence on direct narrative (with as little complexity as possible in the structure) that I learned from Jack London." However, Aaron has grown to respect young readers as a unique and challenging audience—"readers who not merely expressed their enthusiasm for my own work but expressed as well that voracious hunger for literature (stories) that adds depth and color to their world." Pointing out that "they admit to an unrestrained thrill, they do not censor or sublimate, they yield to the writer, they willingly suspend disbelief and accept what the writer offers them," Aaron added that "if the writer stumbles, or deceives, or concocts lies to describe truths, the young readers will quietly but surely turn away, put the book down, shrug off the writer."

Since retiring from teaching in 1993, Aaron has continued to live in California, where he now spends much of his time cultivating over eighty different varieties of garlic from all over the world. His 1996 book, *Garlic Is Life: A Memoir with Recipes,* focuses on his successful attempt to make the transition from retired college professor to garlic farmer, and includes forty recipes. *The Great Garlic Book* is a guide to the many varieties of garlic, and features pictures and growing information. His promotion of garlic and its uses has led to invitations from television and radio shows, and Aaron has also been actively involved with the farming of garlic through California's "Garlic Is Life" festival, which was named after his memoir.

BIOGRAPHICAL/CRITICAL SOURCES:

BOOKS

Sixth Book of Junior Authors and Illustrators, H. W. Wilson, 1989.
Something about the Author Autobiographical Series, Volume 12, Gale (Detroit, MI), 1991.
St. James Guide to Children's Writers, 5th edition, St. James Press (Detroit, MI), 1999.

PERIODICALS

Bulletin of the Center for Children's Books, November, 1977; June, 1982, review of *Gideon.*

English Journal, September, 1986, review of *Lackawanna,* p. 69; October, 1986, review of *Out of Sight, out of Mind,* p. 85.

Horn Book, December, 1977; January-February, 1992, Ann A. Flowers, review of *Alex, Who Won His War,* p. 78.

Instructor and Teacher, May, 1982, Allan Yeager, review of *Gideon,* p. 105; November-December, 1982, A. Yeager, review of *Duchess,* p. 151.

Nation, June 26, 1967, Donald Fanger, review of *About Us.*

Los Angeles Times Calendar, July 16, 1967, Richard G. Lillard, review of *About Us.*

Publishers Weekly, June 4, 1982, review of *Gideon,* p. 67; October 28, 1983; May 30, 1986, review of *Lackawanna,* p. 69.

School Library Journal, April 15, 1982, review of *Gideon,* p. 78; February, 1983, Sylvie Tupacz, review of *Duchess,* p. 72; November, 1985, Ruth Vose, review of *Out of Sight, out of Mind,* p. 93; April, 1996, Dvid A. Lindsey, review of *Lackawanna,* p. 94; October, 1991, Curtis Klause, review of *Alex, Who Won His War,* p. 119.

Wilson Library Bulletin, April, 1986, Patty Campbell, review of *Lackawanna,* p. 48; May, 1992, Cathi Dunn MacRae, review of *Alex, Who Won His War,* p. 107.

OTHER

Garlic Is Life Web site, http://www.garlicislife.com/ (August 29, 2001), "Chester Aaron."*

*   *   *

AFFRON, Charles   1935-

PERSONAL: Born October 16, 1935, in Brooklyn, NY; son of Maurice B. (a salesman) and Toby (Lebow) Affron; married Mirella Jona (a university teacher), September 3, 1961; children: Matthew, Beatrice. *Education:* Brandeis University, B.A., 1957; Yale University, Ph.D., 1963. *Avocational interests:* Opera, theater, and films.

ADDRESSES: Home—180 Park Row, New York, NY 10038. *Office*—Department of French and Italian, New York University, New York, NY 10003.

CAREER: Brandeis University, Waltham, MA, assistant professor of French, 1962-65; New York University, New York, NY, 1965—, began as assistant profes-

sor, became professor of French. Director of Italian branch, Classrooms Abroad.

MEMBER: Modern Language Association of America.

WRITINGS:

Patterns of Failure in "La Comedie humaine," Yale University Press (New Haven, CT), 1966.

A Stage for Poets: Studies in the Theatre of Hugo and Musset, Princeton University Press (Princeton, NJ), 1971.

Star Acting: Gish, Garbo, Davis, Dutton (New York, NY), 1976.

Cinema and Sentiment, University of Chicago Press (Chicago, IL), 1982.

Divine Garbo, Ramsay (Paris, France), 1985.

(Editor and translator) *8 1/2: Federico Fellini, Director* (screenplay), Rutgers University Press (New Brunswick, NJ), 1987.

(With wife, Mirella Jona Affron) *Sets in Motion: Art Direction and Film Narrative,* Rutgers University Press (New Brunswick, NJ), 1995.

(Editor with Robert Lyons and Peter Lehman) *Defining Cinema,* Rutgers University Press (New Brunswick, NJ), 1997.

Lillian Gish: Her Legend, Her Life, Scribner (New York, NY), 2001.

SIDELIGHTS: Charles Affron, a professor of French at New York University, has written extensively about film studies. He is the editor and translator of the first English version of Federico Fellini's *8 1/2* screenplay, which *New Republic* critic Stanley Kauffmann considered "lively," and "more limber and helpful" than the subtitled version. In addition, Kauffmann noted that Affron "shows that the picture couldn't have been begun without a fairly detailed map and . . . that the result diverged from that map." Comparing the continuity script and the shooting script, Affron identifies changes Fellini made while the film was in production.

Among Affron's books on film history and theory are *Cinema and Sentiment* and *Sets in Motion: Art Direction and Film Narrative,* a volume he wrote with his wife. Linda C. Ehrlich in *Film Quarterly* wrote that *Sets in Motion* "is the first examination of art direction to provide a precise framework within which to analyze the role a particular set might play in a film's overall effect." Ehrlich added that the authors consider a film's overall design "according to its relative transparency or opacity in relation to the narrative," and "underline the rigor, excitement, and dignity of this versatile art form."

Affron has also written studies of film stars, including Greta Garbo, Bette Davis, and Lillian Gish. *Lillian Gish: Her Legend, Her Life* received several positive reviews. Critics noted the book's focus on the great discrepancies between myth and reality regarding the film icon, who began acting in 1902 at age nine and rose to fame in silent films under the direction of the controlling D. W. Griffith. As Jay Carr put it in a *Boston Globe* review, Gish "recycled vulnerability, heartbreak, and endurance in melodramatic roles" but was really "a wisp of steel." Carr admired Affron's balanced assessment of Gish's career, noting that the author "completes the picture by restoring details Gish routinely omitted," including her naive involvement with isolationist politics and her failure to get plum roles—including that of Blanche DuBois in *A Streetcar Named Desire*—later in her career. Richard Schickel made a similar point in the *New York Times Book Review,* writing that Affron "consistently refutes Gish's line, remaining unfailingly generous to his subject's art and indomitability, all the while fastidiously and expertly devastating the fairy tale in which she wrapped herself. If we are ever to rescue silent film from its status as a dwindling cult's enthusiasm and restore it as a vital part of our cultural heritage, we need more work of this balanced and balancing kind."

BIOGRAPHICAL/CRITICAL SOURCES:

PERIODICALS

American Film, June 1983, review of *Cinema and Sentiment,* p. 67.
Boston Globe, June 15, 2001, Jay Carr, review of *Lillian Gish: Her Legend, Her Life,* p. C3.
Choice, June 1978, review of *Star Acting: Gish, Garbo, Davis,* p. 556; May 1983, review of *Cinema and Sentiment,* p. 1298; December 1995, review of review of *Sets in Motion: Art Direction and Film Narrative,* p. 626.
Criticism, summer 1983, review of *Cinema and Sentiment,* p. 288.
Entertainment Weekly, March 23, 2001, Charles Winecoff, review of *Lillian Gish: Her Legend, Her Life,* p. 106.
Film Criticism, fall 1996, review of *Sets in Motion,* p. 91.
Film in Review, May 1996, review of *Sets in Motion,* p. 85.
Film Quarterly, summer 1978, review of *Star Acting,* p. 57; summer 1983, review of *Cinema and Sentiment,* p. 28; fall 1996, Linda C. Ehrlich, review of *Sets in Motion,* p. 62.

Kirkus Reviews, January 15, 2001, review of *Lillian Gish,* p. 87.
Knight-Ridder/Tribune News Service, March 28, 2001, Roger Moore, review of *Lillian Gish: Her Legend, Her Life,* p. Y3.
National Post, March 10, 2001, Robert Cushman, review of *Lillian Gish: Her Legend, Her Life,* p. B9.
New Republic, August 31, 1987, Stanley Kauffmann, review of *8 1/2: Federico Fellini, Director,* p. 26.
New York Times Book Review, October 16, 1977, review of *Star Acting,* p. 24; March 4, 2001, Richard Schickel, review of *Lillian Gish: Her Legend, Her Life.*
Publishers Weekly, December 11, 2000, review of *Lillian Gish,* p. 69.
Quarterly Journal of Speech, May 1986, review of *Cinema and Sentiment,* p. 204.
Quarterly Review of Film Studies, fall 1984, review of *Cinema and Sentiment,* p. 333.
Rocky Mountain News (Denver, CO), March 25, 2001, Greg Moody, review of *Lillian Gish: Her Legend, Her Life,* p. 3E.
Sight and Sound, November 1995, review of *Sets in Motion,* p. 37.
Variety, February 26, 2001, Wendy Smith, review of *Lillian Gish: Her Legend, Her Life,* p. 50.
Washington Post, March 18, 2001, Jeanine Bastinger, review of *Lillian Gish: Her Legend, Her Life,* p. T5.
West Coast Review of Books, May 1978, review of *Star Acting,* p. 16; May 1983, review of *Cinema and Sentiment,* p. 26.*

* * *

AGNON, S(hmuel) Y(osef Halevi)   1888-1970

PERSONAL: Original name, Shmuel Yosef Halevi Czaczkes; born July 17, 1888, in Buczacz, Galicia, Austria-Hungary (now Poland); immigrated to Palestine (now Israel); died February 17, 1970, in Tel Aviv, Israel; son of Shalom Mordecai (an ordained rabbi, merchant, and scholar) and Esther (Farb-Hacohen) Czaczkes; married Esther Marx, May 6, 1919; children: Emuna (daughter), Shalom Mordecai Hemdat. *Education:* Spent six years in various private hadarim and a short period at the Baron Hirsch School. *Religion:* Jewish.

CAREER: First secretary of the Jewish court in Jaffa, Palestine, and secretary of the National Jewish Council; went to Germany, 1913, and was a lecturer in Hebrew literature, 1920-24, and a tutor in Hebrew; helped found journal *Der Jude* ("The Jew"); returned to Palestine in 1924.

MEMBER: Hebrew Language Academy, Mekitzei Nirdanim (society for the publication of ancient manuscripts; president, 1950-70).

AWARDS, HONORS: Bialik Prize for Literature, 1934, for *Bi-levav Yamin,* c. and 1950s; D.H.L., Jewish Theological Seminary of America, 1936; Hakhnasat Kala, 1937; Ussishkin Prize, 1950, for *Tmol Shilshom;* Israel Prize, 1958; Honorary Ph.D., Hebrew University, Jerusalem, 1959; named an honorary citizen of Jerusalem, 1962; Nobel Prize for Literature, 1966; fellow, Bar Ilan University.

WRITINGS:

Ve-Hayah he-'Akov le-Mishor, Y. H. Brener (Yafo, Israel), 1912, Juedischer (Berlin, Germany), 1919.

(Editor, with Ahron Eliasberg) *Das Buch von den Polnischen Juden* (folk tales), Juedischer (Berlin, Germany), 1916.

(Editor) *Moaus Zur: Ein Chanukkahbuch,* Juedischer (Berlin, Germany), 1918.

Giv 'at ha-Hol, Juedischer (Berlin, Germany), 1919.

Sipur ha-Shanim ha-Tovot (II Title: *Ma'aseh ha-Rav Veha-Orah*), [Tel Aviv, Israel], c. 1920.

Be-Sod Yesharim, Juedischer (Berlin, Germany), 1921.

Sipur Me-Hamat ha-Metsik, Juedischer (Berlin, Germany), 1921.

'Al Kapot ha-Man'ul (novellas and short stories), Juedischer (Berlin, Germany), 1922.

Polin (fiction), Hedim (Tel Aviv, Israel), c. 1924.

Ma'aseh ha-meshulah me-erets ha-Kedosha, Kupat Ha-sefer (Tel Aviv, Israel), 1925.

Ma'aseh rabi Gadiel ha-Tinok, [Berlin, Germany], 1925.

Ha-Nidah, 1926.

Agadat ha-sofer, Omanut (Tel Aviv, Israel), 1929.

Laylot, [Tel Aviv, Israel], c. 1930.

Be-shuvah va-nahat, Schocken (Berlin, Germany), 1935.

Bi-levav Yamim, Schocken (Berlin, Germany), 1935, translation by Israel Meir Lask published as *In the Heart of the Seas: A Story of a Journey to the Land of Israel,* Schocken (New York, NY), 1948, reprinted, 1980.

Sipur Pashut, Schocken (Berlin, Germany), 1935, translation by Hillel Halkin published as *A Simple Story,* Syracuse University Press (Syracuse, NY), 1985.

Kovets Sipurim, [New York, NY], 1937.

Yamim Nora'im, Schocken (Jerusalem, Israel), 1938, 4th edition, Schocken (New York, NY), 1956, translation by Maurice T. Galpert, revised by Jacob Sloan, published as *Days of Awe: Being a Treasury of Traditions, Legends, and Learned Commentaries concerning Rosh ha-Shanah, Yom Kippur, and the Days between, Culled from Three Hundred Volumes, Ancient and New,* condensed and edited by Nahum N. Glatzer, Schocken (New York, NY), 1948, published as *Days of Awe: A Treasury of Jewish Wisdom for Reflection, Repentance, and Renewal on the High Holy Days,* 1995.

Oreah natah la-lun, Schocken (Jerusalem, Israel), 1939, translation by Misha Louvish published as *A Guest for the Night,* Schocken (New York, NY), 1968.

Pi Shenaim o me-Husar Yom, [Tel Aviv, Israel], 1939.

Shevu'ath Emunim, [Jerusalem, Israel], 1943, translation by Walter Lever published as "Betrothed" in *Two Tales: Betrothed* [and] *Edo and Enam,* Schocken (Tel Aviv, Israel), 1966.

'Al Berl Kazenelson, Schocken (Tel Aviv, Israel), 1944.

Tmol Shilsom, Schocken (Jerusalem, Israel), 1945, translation by Barbara Harshav published as *Only Yesterday,* Princeton University Press (Princeton, NJ), 2000.

Edo ve-Enam, Schocken (Jerusalem, Israel), 1950, translation by Walter Lever published as "Edo and Enam" in *Two Tales: Betrothed* [and] *Edo and Enam,* Schocken (Jerusalem, Israel), 1966.

Ad olam, 1954, translated as *Forever More,* 1961.

Sifrehem shel Anshe Butshatsh reprinted from "Sefer Butsats," [Tel Aviv, Israel], 1956.

(With others) *Tehilla, and Other Israeli Tales,* Abelard, 1956.

(Editor) *Atem re'item,* Schocken (Jerusalem, Israel), 1959.

Pen-ishom ha-mavet, [Tel Aviv, Israel], c. 1960, translation edited by Alan Mintz and Anne Golomb Hoffman published as *A Book That Was Lost and Other Stories,* Schocken (New York, NY), 1995.

Kelev Hutsot, Sifre Tarshish (Jerusalem, Israel), 1960.

Elu ve-elu, Schocken (Jerusalem, Israel), 1960.

(Compiler) *Sifrehem shel Tsadikim,* [Jerusalem, Israel], 1961.

Ha-Esh ve-Ha'etsim, Schocken (Jerusalem, Israel), 1962.

Ad henah, (short stories), Schocken (Jerusalem, Israel), 1966.

Sipurim (short stories), edited by Ginaton, [Israel], 1967.

Sipure Yom ha-Kipurim, edited by Ginaton, [Israel], 1967.

Hakhnasat Kalah, Schocken (New York, NY), 1967, translation by I. M. Lask published as *The Bridal Canopy,* Syracuse University Press (Syracuse, NY), 2000.

Selected Stories of S. Y. Agnon (Hebrew text), edited, with introduction, interpretations, and vocabulary by Samuel Leiter, Tarbuth Foundation, 1970.

Twenty-one Stories, edited by Nahum N. Glatzer, Schocken (New York, NY), 1970.

Shirah, Schocken (Jerusalem, Israel), 1971, translation by Zeva Shapiro published as *Shira,* Schocken (New York, NY), 1989, reprinted, Syracuse University Press (Syracuse, NY), 1996.

Ir u-Melo'ah, [Israel], 1973.

Ma'asmey 'el 'smi, Schocken (Jerusalem, Israel), 1976.

Pithe devarim, Schocken (Jerusalem, Israel), 1977.

Present at Sinai: The Giving of the Law, English edition, Jewish Publication Society (Philadelphia, PA), 1994.

Agnon's Alef bet: Poems, translated by Robert Friend, Jewish Publication Society (Philadelphia, PA), 1998.

Contributor to books, including *A Golden Treasury of Jewish Literature,* edited by Leo W. Schwarz, Farrar & Rinehart (New York, NY), 1937; *The Purim Anthology,* edited by Philip Goodman, Jewish Publication Society (Philadelphia, PA), 1949; *A Treasury of Jewish Humor,* edited by Nathan Ausubel, Doubleday (New York, NY), 1952; *The Bar Mitzvah Treasury,* edited by Azriel Eisenberg, Behrman (Springfield, NJ), 1952; *Sabbath: The Day of Delight,* edited by Abraham E. Millgram, Jewish Publication Society (Philadelphia, PA), 1952; *Yisroel,* edited by Joseph Leftwich, Behrman (Springfield, NJ), 1952; *The Confirmation Reader,* edited by Azriel Eisenberg, Behrman (Springfield, NJ), 1953; *Sound the Great Trumpet,* edited by M. Z. Frank, Whittier Books, 1955; *Tehilla and Other Israeli Tales,* Belard Schuman, 1956; *A Whole Loaf: Stories from Israel,* edited by Sholom J. Kahn, Vanguard (New York, NY), 1962; *Israeli Stories,* Joel Blocker, Schocken (New York, NY), 1962; *Great Jewish Short Stories,* Saul Bellow, Dell (New York, NY), 1963; *A Treasury of Jewish Sea Stories,* edited by Samuel Sobel, Jonathan David, 1965; *The Jewish Caravan,* edited by Leo W. Schwarz, Farrar, Straus (New York, NY), 1965; *Hebrew Short Stories,* Volume 1, edited by S. Y. Penueli and A. Ukhmani, Institute for the Translation of Hebrew Literature, and Megiddo Publishing Co. (Tel Aviv, Israel), 1965.

Contributor to *Haaretz* (daily newspaper), *Palestine Review, Commentary, Gazith, Congress Bi-Weekly,* and other publications.

SIDELIGHTS: "I am not a modern writer," S. Y. Agnon once commented. "I am astounded that I have even one reader. I don't see the reader before me. . . . I never wanted to know the reader. I wanted to work in my own way." It is true that, though Agnon was the dominant figure among Hebrew fiction writers for many years, he was virtually unknown outside the Jewish reading community until he won the Nobel Prize. Yet his advent as a writer early in the twentieth century turned Jewish literature from what Menachem Ribalow in his book *Dichter und Shafer für neu-Hebraish* called "the general European spirit. . . . [Agnon] reversed the trend from Europe homeward again, from alien ways back to the native road. . . . He said not a single word *pro* or *contra.* He simply began to write in a different manner, different from all other Hebrew writers of that time. His novelty lay in his old-fashionedness. His uniqueness consisted in his return to the old sources, to the folk-character and its traits of simplicity and sincerity, purity and piety."

Agnon had sensed the alien aspects of European culture and initiated a return to Jewish folk material, to Medieval Hebrew, and to the traditions and laws that he found in ancient sources. His prose, which is lyrical, ironic, humorous, and deceptively simple, reads as though it was written ages ago. "With Agnon," wrote Ribalow, "the Hebrew short story reaches artistic heights. He has the secret of the perfect blend of content and form, style and rhythm, inner beauty and outer grace. He has tapped new sources of Jewish ethical and esthetic values, revealing the spiritual grandeur in Jewish life. He has done what others have sought in vain to do: to convert simplicity and folk-naïveté into a thing of consummate art and beauty. To the jangled nerves of this troubled generation, Agnon's stories bring balm and comfort."

Agnon revived ancient forms of storytelling, forms unlike those of the modern Hebrew "realistic" story. Rueben Wallenrod, in *The Literature of Modern Israel,* said that "because of its [apparent] lack of frame, Agnon's story flows without effort, and events follow one another in loose sequence. The time of the events is very seldom indicated. In the continuous shift of his relationships, he lives mainly within his memories, and the boundary between the actual and the imaginary has become blurred to such an extent that the confines of time are gone." According to David Patterson, author of *Tradition and Trauma: Studies in the Fiction of S. J. Agnon,* "The first impressions of apparent simplicity soon give way to a realization of the overtones, references and allusions arising from the author's complete familiarity with the whole vast corpus of Hebrew literature. The ancient vocabulary of Hebrew is pregnant with associations of all kinds, and the skillful juxtaposition of words and phrases can be made to yield a variety of nuances. Linguistically, as well as thematically, Agnon's writings can be read at different levels."

Arnold J. Band wrote in *Nostalgia and Nightmare: A Study in the Fiction of S. Y. Agnon:* "For some readers, Agnon is the epitome of traditional Jewish folk-literature; for others, he is the most daring of modernists. For the older reader, Agnon conjures up memories of Jewish life in Eastern Europe; for the younger reader, he wrestles with the central universal problems of our agonized century." Band took issue with those who saw Agnon as merely a reviver of Jewish folk material and techniques. He pointed out that Agnon read widely in German and Scandinavian literatures, and also read Russian and French novelists in German translation. "To attribute Agnon's literary technique to Jewish folk-literature alone, as many tend to do, is sheer nonsense; Agnon was well-acquainted with the best in modern European literature at a relatively early age."

Agnon's characters are the pious and the humble men of faith whom he endowed "with divine qualities without making an effort to emphasize the mystical," wrote Ribalow. He, as well as his characters, believed that righteousness will ultimately triumph and that the cruel aspects of reality can be transcended by pity and love. He wrote about the dispossessed of the earth, he himself having twice lost his home to fire. Robert Alter, author of *After the Tradition,* wrote that in 1924 Agnon's house in Hamburg burned down, "and everything he owned went up in the flames, including his library of four thousand books and the manuscript of an autobiographical novel (which he never attempted to begin again)." Other manuscripts, all unpublished, were also destroyed. In 1929, Arab rioters ravaged his home in Jerusalem, and a good part of his library was lost. In 1948, during the Israeli liberation, Agnon had to evacuate his home in Talpiot. He returned after the end of the hostilities.

Agnon took his pen name, which later became his legal name, from the title of his first published story, "Agunot," which was published in Jaffa, Israel, in 1909. Baruch Hochman, author of *The Fiction of S. Y. Agnon,* explained that the Hebrew word *agunah* refers to a Jewish grass widow, i.e., a woman who is separated from her husband. "It would seem no accident that Agnon took his name from the tale. The very word is redolent of loss, but also of the infinite yearning and ineffable tenderness elicited by loss. All of Agnon's work was to pivot on such feeling. First there was the sort of loss

rendered in this tale: of loved ones torn away in the midst of life. . . . [and] historical loss: the submergence of the world of origins to which one's feelings are bound, in the abyss of history. Finally, there was metaphysical loss: of transcendent objects of desire in the bewilderment of modernity."

His work has been compared to that of Miguel de Cervantes and, even more frequently, to Franz Kafka's, though his relation with the former is tenuous, and Agnon had reportedly denied any knowledge of Kafka. Alter noted that Agnon was not unlike Kafka in that he possessed "something of the same sense of a world where terrible things are waiting to spring out from the shadows of experience. Also . . . his Hebrew has much the same unexcited, deliberately restrained tone of narration as Kafka's German." But Agnon's world, unlike Kafka's, was moral, and there was a clear distinction between good and evil.

Agnon once stated his reasons for writing in Hebrew: "Out of affection for our language and love of the holy, I burn midnight oil over the teachings of the Torah and deny myself food for the words of our sages that I may store them up within me to be ready upon my lips. If the Temple were standing, I would take my place on the platform with my fellow choristers and would recite each day the song that the Levites used to say in the Holy Temple. [Agnon traced his ancestry to the tribe of Levi.] But since the Temple is destroyed and we have neither Priests in their service nor Levites in their chorus and song, I devote myself to the Torah, the Prophets, the latter Scriptures, the Mishnah, Halachah and Aggada, the Tosefta, rabbinical commentaries and textual glosses. When I look at their words and see that of all our precious possessions in ancient times only the memory is left us, I am filled with sorrow. And that sorrow makes my heart tremble. And from that trembling I write stories, like a man banished from his father's palace who builds himself a small shelter and sits there telling the glory of his ancestral home." Alter noted that "like generations of Jews before him, Agnon regards Hebrew as the Jew's indispensable means of entrance into the sphere of sanctity." For Agnon, the Hebrew characters comprised "the alphabet of holiness."

Although Agnon's stories reflect the tragedy and death that lurk in the background, Patterson wrote that "one positive element alone remains constant—Jerusalem herself, which in Agnon's stories is endowed with a personality of her own, and becomes a symbol for all that is meaningful and permanent and harmonious in life. It is as though the holy city alone contains the seeds which might restore that wholeness of spirit and oneness [with the world] that are slipping through the nerveless fingers of our unhappy generation."

After his immigration in 1924 until his death, Agnon wrote about life in Israel. The style remained the same, wrote Ribalow, "epically quiet and midrashically wise. But more and more do present realities play a part, together with all of their difficulties and sufferings, their problems and contradictions." And Wallenrod observed that "the new form of Agnon's stories has not changed the former content. The criterion for the human being is still his humaneness."

Agnon's entire life had been devoted to writing, and, with a permanent annual stipend from his publisher, Schocken Books, he was able to support himself on his writings alone. (In 1916 Salman Schocken promised to find a publisher for Agnon, and he redeemed this promise by becoming a publisher in order to issue Agnon's writings). He was known to be a perfectionist who sometimes set aside a story for as long as fifteen years before he felt ready to rework it and submit it for publication. Agnon revised stories he had published more than thirty years previously. He described his writing habits for the *New York Times:* "When I was healthy I used to work standing. I felt myself fresh and good and sometimes worked that way all day and into the night. I recommend it to every writer. But now I must sit to work and keep this [nitroglycerine] for the heart condition I have had for fifteen years." The street in Talpiot on which he lived was closed to traffic, and a sign at the head of the street read: "Quiet. Agnon is Writing." The house, which later became a museum and memorial to Agnon, has several rooms that are preserved as they were used by the writer and his family—including the podium-style desk he used.

Before he was awarded the Nobel Prize in 1966, Agnon was not well known outside Israel. Afterwards, however, his works began to be widely translated into English. Agnon's *Two Tales: Betrothed and Edo and Enam,* for example, "show how difficult it is to convey to those not versed in Hebrew, or east European Jewish folklore, his strange medley of realism and mysticism, but [the stories] also give an indication of what a fascinating story-teller he is," noted a *Times Literary Supplement* reviewer. While "Betrothed" tells the story of a scholar's discovery of the woman to whom he is fated to be married, "Edo and Enam" relates a much darker and (some argue) more compelling tale of the supernatural. With *In the Heart of the Seas* Agnon turned to a more recognizable adventure tale, creating a vivid sea voyage from Galicia to Palestine. "We have the rabbis versed in the legends of the land of Israel, the wives

tearfully abandoning their worldly goods, and in their midst Hananiah, the archetypal humble saint," observed a commentator for the *Times Literary Supplement.*

The picaresque form and the folk tradition informed several of Agnon's novels, such as *The Bridal Canopy* and *A Guest for the Night.* Set in the early nineteenth century in eastern Europe, *The Bridal Canopy* portrays a Jewish man who travels widely in search of dowries for his daughters. Much of the narrative concerns the incidental events and stories that take place during his journey. Originally published in Hebrew in 1939, *A Guest for the Night* depicts a man's struggle to cope with the changes that have taken place in his native village in Poland during his absence in Palestine. Considering Agnon's digressive style in the works, a reviewer for *Times Literary Supplement* commented: "The effect of Agnon is elusive, cumulative and worth an effort to catch." Richard Elman of *New York Times Book Review,* however, regarded *A Guest for the Night* as one of those "works of literature, especially in translation, that one is asked to love entirely as an act of good faith." While acknowledging Agnon's eminence as a writer of Hebrew literature, Elman faulted the "tedium" of the author's works in English translation, concluding that "[s]peaking to us in translation, out of his commitment to the Jewish nation, Agnon cannot help seeming irrelevant."

Originally published in Hebrew in 1935, Agnon's novel *A Simple Story* was posthumously translated into English. The book portrays Hirshl Hurvitz, who is forced to marry the daughter of wealthy farmers, a fate that thwarts his obsessive love for his cousin Blume Nacht. Hirshl's obsession with Blume continues even after his marriage, leading to his depression and, ultimately, his psychosis. At the novel's conclusion, however, Hirshl eschews his romantic wishes and resigns himself to the responsibilities of his married life. Robert Alter of *New York Times Book Review* detected the influence of Flaubert in the novel, pointing to the story's juxtaposition of bourgeois values with romantic longings. Critics have offered varied interpretations of the novel's ending, viewing the work as both "antimodernist" and conservative, or, as Alter suggested, "painfully aware of the terrible price Hirshl pays for his final normality." Explaining the difficulty of summarizing the meaning of the work, Nicholas Spice commented in the *London Review of Books:* "*A Simple Story* is a masterpiece of the shifting perspective, of shiftiness and wile. As well gather moonbeams in a jar as attempt to trap the meaning of such a work in a thesis. Its elusiveness has much to do with its mock innocence. From behind the persona of an unsophisticated, wide-eyed and open-minded narrator, Agnon multiplies the perspectives of his story without ever having to come into view."

A Book That Was Lost and Other Stories, originally published in Hebrew in the 1960s, presents a collection of Agnon's short fiction. Reviewers have emphasized the literary range evidenced by the collection, which encompasses coming-of-age tales, such as "The Kerchief"; magical fables, such as "Pisces" and "Buczacz"; and accounts of modern alienation, such as "A Whole Loaf" and "At the Outset of the Day." The significance of Judaism in relation to political turmoil and exile endured throughout history is also addressed, for example, in "The Tale of the Menorah." "What remains so impressive, even in these English renditions, is the seductive melody of [Agnon's] voice," observed Susan Miron in *New York Times Book Review.* "Whatever material he chooses, he seems able to tease out an enticing tale."

Agnon worked on his novel *Shirah* (translated into English as *Shira*) for more than twenty years, and the book was still incomplete and in need of revision at the time of the author's death, as evidenced by some occasionally awkward transitions in the narrative and an inconclusive ending to the story. The main character is Manfred Herbst, a history professor who is residing in Jerusalem, due to his political exile from Germany. Set in the 1930s, the narrative suggests the rise of volatile political forces in the form of rising Nazi power and Arab terrorism. Early in the novel, Manfred has a love affair with a nurse named Shira (whose name in Hebrew signifies poetry), and his feelings toward her become increasingly conflicted, passionate, and troubling. Writing in the *Times Literary Supplement,* David Aberbach emphasized Agnon's treatment of relationships between the sexes in the novel: "Herbst's sadomasochistic impulses, his thoughts and much of his behaviour with Shira make little sense unless Shira is understood to be the mother-figure for whom he is searching. . . . Herbst is looking for the certainty of a mother's affection, and this he cannot obtain in an adult relationship." In one of two alternate concluding chapters to the book (both are published), a later reunion occurs between Manfred and Shira in a lepers' colony, with Shira emerging as an image of salvation—a "Dostoyevskian reunion," commented Beverly Fields in Chicago *Tribune Books,* through which, "presumably, [Manfred] will achieve poetic redemption through suffering."

Agnon read less in his later years, his vision failing, but when he did he turned to the Talmud. He apologized to one American interviewer for not being able to speak English, and added: "I made a contract with the Almighty, that for every language I did not learn he would give me a few words in Hebrew. . . . [Also], in order that I shouldn't have to go many places, I don't learn English." One place he wanted to, and did, visit, however, was Stockholm to receive the Nobel Prize from the Swedish king. It would be a rare pleasure, Agnon said beforehand, "because there is a special benediction one says before a king, and I have never met a king."

Works that have been translated into English after Agnon's death include the collection *Agnon's Alef bet: Poems* and *Only Yesterday,* a translation of his novel *Tmol Shilshom.* In an essay for the *NJ Jewish News,* Susan Dworkin commented that while Agnon is among the writers she "most admire[s]," he is little known in the United States. "The key . . . is in the translation. . . . [Agnon] is the acknowledged master of modern Hebrew fiction and his works are taught to Israelis in their schools as we are taught Mark Twain, but they have been only rarely translated into English. And even when translated, Agnon's layered, nuanced work, with its many references to religious texts and European literature, often comes across as obscure and hard to fathom," she reflected.

Agnon's Alef bet: Poems offers English-language readers translations of twenty-two poems, one for each letter of the Hebrew alphabet, and illustrations by Arieh Zeldich. The *Jewish Journal* described it as a collection of interest to all ages and noted that adults will appreciate Robert Friend's notes on his translations and the Hebrew originals given at the end of the volume.

Only Yesterday is a translation of the work that many consider to be Agnon's masterpiece as a novelist. The picaresque novel became available in English fifty-five years after its original publication. While the book is considered one of Agnon's best works, it is also one of his longest and most convoluted. The central character, Isaac Kumer, comes to Palestine during the Second Aliya, a wave of Jewish immigration spanning 1904-1914 that was inspired by Zionist fervor. Like Agnon, Kumer comes to the Holy Land from Galicia, but this is where the similarity between the character and the author ends. Kumer is a rather bumbling young man who faced the worst poverty in his homeland. Urged by his father, he immigrates with the hope of working on a farm, but finds that the wealthy Jewish landowners mostly use cheaper Arab laborers. He eventually finds work as a house and sign painter. Like much of the young man's experiences, this happens almost by accident.

Kumer's subsequent adventures serve to show the extremes of political and religious attitudes amongst his fellow Jews. He first settles in Jaffa, where he becomes part of a secular, cosmopolitan set of companions. Under this influence, he abandons religious observances. He has an affair with Sonya, a modern, liberated woman from Russia, who later leaves him. Devastated, Kumer departs for Jerusalem, where he meets a religious extremist from Hungary, Reb Fayesh, and his daughter Shifra. When Kumer impulsively paints the words "Crazy Dog" on the back of a stray, he sets off a panic among those who read them. Here, the novel makes a dramatic shift as the dog, named Balak, takes over the narrative. He realizes that Kumer has made him a despised object and sets out to take revenge on the painter.

The novel and its translation won praise from a number of critics. A *Publishers Weekly* reviewer remarked that *Only Yesterday* "has a folkloric quality analogous to the bold simplifications of Chagall, locating the archaic residue lurking just below the surface disenchantment of modernity." Writing for the *Washington Post,* Tova Reich commented, "This is a work so rich and allusive, so real and yet so strange . . . it's not surprising that no one had undertaken until now the formidable challenge of translating it into English." Reich marveled at the author's creation of the dog Balak as "the more vivid and reflective of the novel's two main characters." She noted how he "dominates the novel and pitches it into a surreal realm. . . . it is probably most useful to think of him as the uninhibited physical projection of the desires and fury that Isaac with all his limitations is unable to express." Reich also found the novel to be an outstanding achievement even without considering the section narrated by Balak. In her judgment, the novel would remain "the classic evocation of the Second Aliya . . . [and] a model of the universal struggle of an ordinary soul torn between the earthly and the spiritual, between exile and home, as embodied in the juxtaposition of Jaffa and Jerusalem."

Critic Alan Mintz's comments in *Forward* also included praise for the use of Balak's character and the polarity of the two cities. He remarked, "The considerable achievement of *Only Yesterday* rests on two strokes of genius: Agnon declines to make the protagonist . . . a version of himself as a young man. And he has the further good sense, in view of the human material at hand, to give a hefty chunk of the novel over to a talking dog." Mintz confessed that he was at first bothered by the Balak passages, but then found that "the descriptions of Balak's world became increasingly compelling as the novel progressed, and I soon realized

that this dog stood—and sniffed and growled—at the book's center." Mintz concluded, "It is in the contrastive analogy between Jaffa and Jerusalem . . . that *Only Yesterday* comes closest to realizing its epic ambitions." The critic found new insight into the lives of those who took part in the Second Aliyah: "The defining experience of the generation, as Agnon sees it, is a kind of double orphanhood. Whether by choice or by circumstance, these young Jews have lost the nurturing support of both their biological families and the Judaic religious tradition."

Thus, the publication of *Only Yesterday* gives English-language readers another glimpse of Agnon's consistent approach to writing. As Mark Shechner summarized in the Chicago *Tribune Books,* "The enduring subject behind the immediate subject of any story [of Agnon's] was the sacred dimension of Judaism; the method was allusion, a thick veining of Biblical echoes and Talmudic citations in even the most secular of stories, and the audience was the community of pioneers who had settled in Palestine."

BIOGRAPHICAL/CRITICAL SOURCES:

BOOKS

Agnon: Texts and Contexts in English Translation: A Multi-disciplinary Curriculum, Biographies, and Selected Syllabi, M. Wiener Publishers (New York, NY), 1988.

Alter, Robert, *After the Tradition,* Dutton (New York, NY), 1969.

Aphek, Edna, *Word Systems in Modern Hebrew: Implications and Applications,* E. J. Brill (New York, NY), 1988.

Band, Arnold J., *Nostalgia and Nightmare: A Study in the Fiction of S. Y. Agnon,* University of California Press (Berkeley, CA), 1968.

Ben-Dov, Nitza, *Agnon's Art of Indirection: Uncovering Latent Content in the Fiction of S. Y. Agnon,* E. J. Brill (New York, NY), 1993.

Contemporary Literary Criticism, Gale (Detroit, MI), Volume 4, 1975, Volume 8, 1978, Volume 14, 1980.

Hochman, Baruch, *The Fiction of S. Y. Agnon,* Cornell University Press (Ithaca, NY), 1970.

Hoffman, Anne Golomb, *Between Exile and Return: S. Y. Agnon and the Drama of Writing,* State University of New York Press (Albany, NY), 1991.

Hojman, B., *The Fiction of S. Y. Agnon,* Cornell University Press (Ithaca, NY), 1970.

Hurwicz, Elias, *Aus Agnons dichterischen Schaffen,* [Berlin, Germany], 1936.

Kaufmann, Fritz Mordechai, *Vier Essais Über ost-juedische Dichtung und Kultur,* [Berlin, Germany], 1919.

Kimhi, Dob, *Soferim,* J. Sreberk (Tel Aviv, Israel), 1953.

Kurzweil, Baruch, *Masekhet ha-Roman,* [Tel Aviv, Israel], 1953.

Malachi, Eliezer Raphael, *Dr. Sh. Y. Agnon,* Hadoar (New York, NY), 1935.

Ohaokaok, Lev, *Equivocal Dreams: Studies in Modern Hebrew Literature,* Ktav (Hoboken, NJ), 1993.

Patterson, David, *Tradition and Trauma: Studies in the Fiction of S. J. Agnon,* Westview Press (Boulder, CO), 1994.

Penuell, S. I., *Yetsirato shel Sh. Y. Agnon,* [Tel Aviv, Israel], 1960.

Ribalow, Menachem, *Dichter und Shafer für neu-Hebraish,* 1936, translation by Judah Nadich published as *The Flowering of Modern Hebrew Literature,* Twayne (New York, NY), 1959.

Roshwald, Miriam, *Ghetto, Shtetl, or Polis?: The Jewish Community in the Writings of Karl Emil Franzos, Sholom Aleichem, and Shemuel Yosef Agnon,* Borgo Press (San Bernadino, CA), 1995.

Sadan, Dob, *Al Shai Agnon,* [Tel Aviv, Israel], 1959.

Seh-Lavan, Yosef, *Shmuel Yosef Agnon,* [Tel Aviv, Israel], 1947.

Shaked, Gershon, *Shmuel Yosef Agnon: A Revolutionary Traditionalist,* New York University Press (New York, NY), 1989.

Wallenrod, Rueben, *The Literature of Modern Israel,* Abelard, 1956.

Zoref, Ephraim, *Sh. Y. Agnon,* [Tel Aviv, Israel], 1957.

PERIODICALS

Adam International Review, numbers 307-309, 1966.

Ariel (Jerusalem), number 11, 1965; number 17, 1966-67.

Commentary, August, 1961, Robert Alter, "The Genius of S. Y. Agnon"; December, 1966; February, 1986, Robert Alter, "Kafka's Father, Agnon's Mother, Bellow's Cousin," p. 46; February, 1990, Alan Mintz, "Agnon without End," p. 57.

Commonweal, April 5, 1996, p. 36; April 5, 1996, Carolyn Cohen, review of *A Book That Was Lost and Other Stories,* p. 36.

Congress Bi-Weekly, November 7, 1966, Curt Leviant, "Mirror of the Jewish Past," pp. 20-21.

Daedalus, fall, 1966.

Jerusalem Post, July 13, 1998, Allan Rabinowitz, "The House That Agnon Built."

Jewish Journal, March 26, 1999, review of *Alef bet: Poems.*

Kirkus Reviews, October 15, 1985, p. 1094.

Library Journal, November 15, 1985, Marcia G. Fuchs, review of *A Simple Story,* p. 108; May 1, 1995, Molly Abramowitz, review of *A Book That Was Lost and Other Stories,* p. 132.

London Review of Books, September 4, 1986, p. 22.

Nation, December 12, 1966.

New Republic, November 20, 1989, Hillel Halkin, review of *Shira,* p. 42.

New Statesman, December 9, 1966.

New Yorker, March 3, 1986, review of *A Simple Story,* p. 104.

New York Review of Books, March 29, 1990, Gabriele Annan, review of *Shira,* pp. 14-16.

New York Times, October 21, 1966.

New York Times Book Review, September 18, 1966; April 28, 1968, p. 5; July 20, 1980, review of *The Bridal Canopy* and *A Guest for the Night,* p. 23; December 22, 1985, Robert Alter, "Blind Beggars and Incestuous Passions," p. 8; October 19, 1986, Patricia T. O'Conner, review of *In the Heart of the Seas* and *A Simple Story,* p. 50; December 24, 1989, Grace Schulman, review of *Shira,* p. 6; May 21, 1995, Susan Miron, review of *A Book That Was Lost and Other Stories,* p. 37; July 20, 1998, p. 23; September 24, 2000, Jonathan Rosen, "You Can't Go Home Again: In a Novel from 1945, S. Y. Agnon Explores the Harsh Realities of Jewish Settlement in Palestine," p. 28.

Partisan Review, fall, 1989, Robert Alter, "On S. Y. Agnon," p. 619.

Publishers Weekly, October 11, 1985, p. 58; August 25, 1989, Sybil Steinberg, review of *Shira,* p. 50; March 13, 1995, review of *A Book That Was Lost and Other Stories,* p. 59; March 27, 2000, review of *Only Yesterday,* p. 50.

Tikkun, January-February, 1991, Evan Zimroth, review of *Shira,* p. 27; July, 2000, review of *Only Yesterday,* p. 81.

Times Literary Supplement, October 27, 1966; July 27, 1967; January 18, 1968; October 31, 1968; April 20, 1990, p. 428; September 1, 2000, Morris Dickstein, review of *Only Yesterday,* p. 12.

Tribune Books (Chicago), December 31, 1989, p. 4; July 30, 1995, p. 3.

Village Voice Literary Supplement, July, 1995, p. 20.

Washington Post, August 2, 2000, Tova Reich, "For Israel's Forebears, a Dog's Life," p. C3.

OTHER

Forward, http://www.forward.com/ (September 20, 2000), Alan Mintz, "A 'Crazy' Dog Has His Say in Agnon's Surreal Epic."

NJ Jewish News, http://www.njjewishnews.com/ (February 17, 2000), Susan Dworkin, "Israel's S. Y. Agnon—A Writer One Dares Not Forget."*

*   *   *

ALIKI
   See BRANDENBERG, Aliki (Liacouras)

*   *   *

ALTHUSSER, Louis   1918-1990
   (L. Althusser)

PERSONAL: Born October 16, 1918, in Birmandreis, Algeria; died of heart failure, October 22, 1990, near Paris, France; son of a bank manager; married Hélène Rytmann Legotier (a sociologist), 1976 (died, November, 1980). *Education:* Received agrège de philosophie and docteur des lettres from École Normale Supérieure.

CAREER: Philosopher and educator. École Normale Supérieure, Paris, France, maitre assistant de philosophie and secretary, 1945-80; writer. Member of Catholic youth organizations, beginning in 1937, and of French Communist Party, 1948-80. *Military service:* Served in military, 1939-40; prisoner of war in Germany, 1940-45.

WRITINGS:

Montesquieu: La Politique et l'histoire, Presses Universitaires de France (Paris, France), 1959, 4th edition, 1974, translated by Ben Brewster as "Montesquieu: Politics and History," in *Politics and History: Montesquieu, Rousseau, Hegel, and Marx,* New Left Books (London, England), 1972, Shocken (New York, NY), 1978, published as *Montesquieu, Rousseau, Marx: Politics and History,* Verso (New York, NY), 1982.

Pour Marx, Maspero (Paris, France), 1965, translated by Ben Brewster as *For Marx,* Pantheon (New York, NY), 1969.

(With Jacques Ranciere and Pierre Macherey in Volume I; with Étienne Balibar and Roger Establet in Volume II) *Lire "Le Capital,"* two volumes, Maspero (Paris, France), 1965, selections by Althusser and Balibar published under the same title, 1968, selections translated by Ben Brewster as *Reading "Capital,"* New Left Books (London, En-

Louis Althusser

gland), 1970, Pantheon (New York, NY), 1971, 2nd edition, New Left Books, 1977.

Lénine et la philosophie, Maspero (Paris, France), 1969, translated by Ben Brewster as *Lenin and Philosophy, and Other Essays,* New Left Books (London, England), 1971, Monthly Review Press (New York, NY), 1972, reprinted, 2001, French edition expanded as *Lénine et la philosophie: suivi de Marx et Lenine devant Hegel,* Maspero (Paris, France), 1972.

(Under name L. Althusser; with J.-M. Domenach, M.-D. Chenu, M. Marechal, and others) *L'Eglise aujourd'hui,* Lumiere et Vie (Lyon, France), 1969.

Réponse à John Lewis, Maspero (Paris, France), 1973.

Philosophie et philosophie spontanée des savants, 1967, Maspero (Paris, France), 1974, translated by Ben Brewster as *Philosophy and the Spontaneous Philosophy of the Scientists, and Other Essays,* edited with an introduction by Gregory Elliott, Verso (New York, NY), 1990.

Éléments d'autocritique, Hachette (Paris, France), 1974, translated by Grahame Lock as "Elements of

Self-Criticism," in *Essays in Self-Criticism,* Humanities, 1976.

Positions, 1964-1975, Sociales (Paris, France), 1976.

Vingt-deuxième Congres, Maspero (Paris, France), 1977.

Ce qui ne peut plus durer dans le Parti communiste (essays; originally published in *Le Monde,* 1978), Maspero (Paris, France), 1978.

Essays on Ideology, translated from the French by Grahame Lock and Ben Brewster, Verso (New York, NY), 1984.

Journal de captivité: Stalag XA, 1940-1945: Carnets, correspondances, textes, edited by Olivier Corpet and Yann Moulier Boutang, Stock/IMEC (Paris, France), 1992.

Avenir dure longtemps, edited by Olivier Corpet and Yann Moulier Boutang, Stock/IMEC (Paris, France), 1992, translated by Richard Veasey as *The Future Lasts Forever: A Memoir,* Norton (New York, NY), 1993.

Écrits sur la psychanalyse: Freud et Lacan, edited by Olivier Corpet and François Matheron, Stock/IMEC (Paris, France), 1993, translated by Jeffrey Mehlman as *Writings on Psychoanalysis: Freud and Lacan,* Columbia University Press (New York, NY), 1999.

Sur la philosophie, Gallimard (Paris, France), 1994.

Écrits philosophiques et politiques, edited by François Matheron, Stock/IMEC (Paris, France), 1994.

Althusser: A Critical Reader, edited by Gregory Elliott, Blackwell (Cambridge, MA), 1994.

Sur la reproduction, introduction by Jacques Bidet, Presses Universitaires de France (Paris, France), 1995.

The Spectre of Hegel: Early Writings, edited with an introduction by François Matheron, translated by G. M. Goshgarian, Verso (New York, NY), 1997.

Machiavelli and Us, edited by François Matheron, translated by G. M. Goshgarian, Verso (New York, NY), 1999.

Also author of *Manifestations philosophiques de Feuerbach.* Contributor to *La Pensée* and *La Nouvelle Critique.* Editor of "Theorie" series for Maspero, beginning in 1965.

SIDELIGHTS: Louis Althusser, an educator, author, and prominent French philosopher, was known for his structuralist interpretation of the writings of Karl Marx, the nineteenth-century German political philosopher who inspired twentieth-century communism. The publication of Althusser's *Pour Marx* and *Lire "Le Capital,"* published in English as *For Marx* and *Reading "Capital,"* brought the relatively unknown Marxist philosopher international acclaim as the leading intellectual in the French Communist Party. *For Marx* and *Reading "Capital"* stirred considerable controversy among Marxists because they opposed the humanistic interpretations of Marx's works that became increasingly popular after the 1953 death of Soviet leader Joseph Stalin. Because Marxist humanists claimed that Marx's philosophy addressed the concerns of individual workers, they opposed Althusser's emphasis on examining the overall structure of society rather than the needs of individuals. While many were shocked to find Althusser admitting in a posthumously published memoir that he had read little of Marx's writing, the French philosopher's theories nonetheless significantly impacted twentieth-century Marxism and resulted in a new school of Althusserian theorists.

Althusser's *For Marx* and *Reading "Capital"* incorporate structuralist ideas. Developed in France near the beginning of the twentieth century by anthropologist Claude Levi-Strauss, structuralism is a multidisciplinary philosophy based on the conviction that all societies have one fundamental structure. It is opposed to humanism, which views individual humans, or subjects, as the initiators of change, and instead claims that humans themselves are shaped by societal structures. Althusser's structuralist reading of Marx in *For Marx* and *Reading "Capital"* has several key points. His overall thesis is that, beginning in 1845, Marx abandoned the humanistic ideology characteristic of his early works and developed a "science of history," as Althusser terms it, that explained societal change. Humanistic concerns over individuals' suffering from alienation became less important to Marx than understanding the structure that caused this alienation. The resulting science of history, according to Althusser, consists of tracing the causes of social phenomena to economic, political, ideological, and theoretical factors which often act independently of one another. Moreover, structural change is rooted in an "overdetermination"—a term borrowed from psychoanalyst Sigmund Freud—of events from these four factors. Specifically, change occurs through an "overdetermination of contradiction," which means that when a society's structural components include opposing forces, the contradiction is resolved through a change in the structure. Hence, change arises not from individual achievement but from large-scale struggle and contradiction, an idea Althusser derived in part from Marx's concept of history as class struggle.

These ideas prompted as much criticism as praise. Althusser initially drew favorable attention for offering a genuinely new approach to Marx, and gained a reputation as a prominent French intellectual. However, his sudden rise to fame in the mid-1960s was credited by some as the result of timing rather than intellectual talent; it was a time when rebellious young communists, tired of antiquated Stalinism, were insufficiently inspired by the new humanistic Marxism and looking for something new. "A new generation of rebels requires a new version of revolutionary ideology, and [Althusser] is essentially an ideological hard-liner, challenging the political and intellectual softening around him," explained a *Times Literary Supplement* reviewer. The critic went on to praise Althusser's contributions to Marxism, saying, "One reads him with attention, even with excitement" and later adding that "the net effect of his irruption into Marxist theoretical debate will undoubtedly be positive."

Subsequent reviewers disputed the "positive" aspects of Althusser's "net effect." Humanist Marxists, for example, objected to Althusser's lack of concern for the individual, bolstering their arguments by showing where the French philosopher's first two books neglect or even contradict Marx's own words. Althusser later countered these arguments by saying that since Marx was ahead of his time, he must be given a "symptomatic reading": the modern reader must understand the structure under which Marx wrote and then supplement Marx's nineteenth-century texts with twentieth-century terminology. Althusser used this principle to reconcile the differences between his own theories and Marx's words. In addition, *Spectator* contributor David McLellan dubbed *Reading "Capital"* largely "unintelligible." "The parts of the book that are intelligible," McLellan commented, "constitute the greatest deformation of Marx's thought yet perpetrated." It bothered him that Althusser imposed Freudian concepts and French structuralism on the works of Marx and then called his version the true Marx, a criticism echoed by other reviewers. "Althusser's book is an anti-Marx [book]," McLellan concluded, "which sets out to combat systematically all Marx's leading insights into historical development, the alienation of man in capitalist society and the possibilities of developing the manifold capacities of each individual under communism."

Other criticisms focused on the consistency of Althusser's theories. Some felt that the concept of "overdetermination of contradiction" could only trace causal factors after the fact; it could not predict future change, which these detractors deemed essential to a scientific theory. Althusser's critics also thought his structural theories were unscientific because they could not be verified. Althusser dismissed these arguments in his critique of empirical scientists, claiming that these sci-

entists fool themselves when they think they attain knowledge of the world through the five senses. According to Althusser's "theory of theoretical practice," knowledge of reality comes through a mixture of sensory data and theory. Yet this argument was criticized for the same reason Althusser rejected empiricism: it purports to reveal the essence of reality.

Althusser was also faulted for his silence regarding separate events in Czechoslovakia (now the Czech Republic) and France in 1968, when Soviet troops occupied Czechoslovakia and French students and workers staged massive protests and strikes to express their dissatisfaction with French President Charles de Gaulle's administration. While the use of force in Czechoslovakia represented a return to Stalin's hard-line communism, the turmoil in France represented an opportunity for a new form of communism to emerge. The French Communist Party and French trade unions enjoyed unprecedented support, but the opposition to de Gaulle never unified and the president was reelected. By most accounts, 1968 was a momentous year for communists, yet Althusser, as a leading intellectual of the French Communist Party, neither denounced Soviet communists nor supported French communists. In 1969 George Lichtheim suggested in the *New York Review of Books* that Althusser may have been "privately critical of the illusions entertained by the students." While his silence resulted in a loss of popularity, he nevertheless maintained his influence among intellectuals in the years following 1968.

The French Marxist philosopher continued to refine his science of Marxism in his later works, beginning in 1969 with *Lenine et la philosophie,* later translated as *Lenin and Philosophy, and Other Essays.* A *Times Literary Supplement* reviewer observed that the volume revealed that Althusser is basically "at loggerheads with Marx." Still, the critic went on to say that the book is "the work of an acute intellect and contains flashes, indeed extended passages, of originality and brilliance." The opinion that Althusser's Marxism contradicts Marx was also echoed by several other reviewers. However, *Lenin and Philosophy* was considered significant because it contains Althusser's first reference to his new view of philosophy: "1/ philosophy is not (a) science; 2/ it has no object, in the sense in which a science has an object of study; 3/ it has no history (in the sense in which a science has a history); 4/ philosophy is politics within theory. I now add, with greater precision: philosophy is, in the last instance, the class struggle within theory."

Several reviewers found these new distinctions more vague than helpful. *Biographical Dictionary of Neo-Marxism* contributor Jennifer Daryl Slack stated: "In one of the most controversial and ambiguous moments in his work, Althusser . . . impl[ied] a kind of privileged position for the science of Marxism." That is, Althusser's science of Marxism now claimed to be outside of philosophy and the all-encompassing system it posits. Karel Williams, in *Makers of Modern Culture,* also questioned the success of Althusser's revisions, concluding, "This post-1967 position neither resolves nor transcends the problems posed by the failure of the earlier differentiations."

Throughout Althusser's controversial career he led an equally tumultuous private life. After spending five years in a German prison camp during World War II, Althusser went to the prestigious École Normale Supérieure to complete his doctorate in philosophy and begin teaching. During his academic career, though, the philosopher was hospitalized several times for manic depression. In 1976 he married sociologist Hélène Legotier, a woman he met through the French Communist Party who lived with him for several years while serving as his private nurse. Their relationship ended tragically in 1980 when Althusser strangled her to death. Because of his history of mental instability, he was not held criminally responsible for killing his wife; in 1981 a Paris court judged him insane and consigned him to an asylum, where he remained until his release in 1984.

Althusser died in 1990, and his autobiographical work, *Avenir dure longtemps* (published in English as *The Future Lasts Forever: A Memoir*), was published a few years later. In this book, reported Gilbert Adair in London's *Independent Sunday* newspaper, "Althusser related how little he had read of the great philosophers, not excluding Marx himself, and went on to admit that he filched most of his revolutionary theories from others." Adair described the work as "an absolutely unparalleled example of what might be called 'posthumous suicide.' " The critic, however, deemed the book "a masterpiece, unlike any other ever written, and . . . the only one of [Althusser's] liable still to be read in a hundred years." *Avenir dure longtemps* also seeks to explain the forces behind Althusser's mental illness and the murder of his wife; at one point he claims she wanted him to kill her. A *Kirkus Reviews* contributor found the book "a disturbing, demanding memoir that illustrates the alliance of genius and madness, the delusive clarity of which the insane are capable, and the enormous influence they can acquire over the thinking of others." Another posthumous publication was *Machiavelli and Us,* a collection of lectures Althusser delivered in 1972 on the Italian nobleman, author, and political philosopher whose name has become synonymous with scheming and ruthlessness, although in reality his ideas were more complex. While not immune to the tendency of some Marxists to claim Niccolò Machiavelli, who lived in the fifteenth and sixteenth centuries, as one of their own, "Althusser reveals himself to be an independent and searching questioner," remarked Sebastian de Grazia in the *Times Literary Supplement.* The book "make[s] one feel that the author has tried hard to meet Niccolò and converse with him *tu per tu,*" De Grazia added.

Though some critics claim Althusser's influence on philosophy to be negative, others maintain his writings have had a positive influence on philosophy as well as other academic disciplines. Simon Evans, reviewing re-issues of *For Marx* and *Reading "Capital"* for the *Birmingham Post,* observed that "Althusser has gradually been rehabilitated, intellectually at least, in the years since his death." Evans maintained that Althusser's "effective denial of free will . . . can be seen as contributing to the eventual collapse of Western Marxism in the 1980s. . . . That Althusser should contribute much to its demise and then collapse into psychosis was somehow tragically appropriate." Jameson commented that the British can be grateful to Althusser for providing "a powerful weapon against the dominant tradition of empiricism." The critic also noted the French philosopher's influence on such Althusserians as Pierre Macherey, who transferred Althusser's concept of "symptomal reading" to the field of literary criticism, and Maurice Godelier, who used Althusser's ideas to develop anthropological theories concerning capitalist and precapitalist societies. Finally, Jameson suggested that after removing Marx from Althusser's system, "we may well want to . . . preserve, in a post-individualistic age, his rejection of humanism and of the categories of the subject." In short, while many of his theories have been attacked, Althusser nevertheless significantly contributed to twentieth-century philosophy.

BIOGRAPHICAL/CRITICAL SOURCES:

BOOKS

Althusser, Louis, *Lenin and Philosophy, and Other Essays,* Monthly Review Press (New York, NY), 1972.

Assiter, Alison, *Althusser and Feminism,* Pluto Press (Winchester, MA), 1990.

Clarke, Simon, and others, *One-Dimensional Marxism: Althusser and the Politics of Culture,* Allison & Busby (New York, NY), 1980.

Elliott, Gregory, *Althusser: The Detour of Theory,* Verso (New York, NY), 1987.

Elliott, Gregory, editor, *Althusser: A Critical Reader,* Blackwell (Cambridge, MA), 1994.

Glucksmann, Miriam, *Structuralist Analysis in Contemporary Thought: A Comparison of the Theories of Claude Levi-Strauss and Louis Althusser,* Routledge & Kegan Paul (Boston, MA), 1974.

Majumdar, Margaret A., *Althusser and the End of Leninism?,* Pluto Press (Boulder, CO), 1995.

Payne, Michael, *Reading Knowledge: An Introduction to Barthe, Foucault, and Althusser,* Blackwell (Malden, MA), 1997.

Resch, Robert Paul, *Althusser and the Renewal of Marxist Social Theory,* University of California Press (Berkeley, CA), 1992.

Smith, Steven B., *Reading Althusser: An Essay on Structural Marxism,* Cornell University Press (Ithaca, NY), 1984.

Wintle, Justin, editor, *Makers of Modern Culture,* Facts on File (New York, NY), 1981.

PERIODICALS

Birmingham Post, March 25, 2000, Simon Evans, review of *For Marx* and *Reading "Capital,"* p. 61.

Commonweal, December 10, 1971.

Independent Sunday, May 2, 1999, Gilbert Adair, "The Guillotine: No. 17: Louis Althusser," p. 14.

Kirkus Reviews, November 15, 1993, review of *The Future Lasts Forever: A Memoir.*

Newsweek, December 1, 1980.

New York Review of Books, January 30, 1969.

Spectator, January 23, 1971.

Time, December 1, 1980.

Times Literary Supplement, December 15, 1966; December 3, 1971; June 15, 1973; August 22, 1975; August 4, 2000, Sebastian de Grazia, "The Candid Secretary," pp. 27-28.

OBITUARIES:

PERIODICALS

Chicago Tribune, October 25, 1990.

Los Angeles Times, October 30, 1990.

New York Times, October 24, 1990.*

ANCONA, George   1929-

PERSONAL: Born Jorge Efrain Ancona, December 4, 1929, in New York, NY; son of Efrain Jose (an accountant and amateur photographer) and Emma (a seamstress; maiden name, Diaz) Ancona; married Patricia Apatow, March 4, 1951 (divorced, 1966); married Helga Von Sydow (a journalist), June 20, 1968; children: (first marriage) Lisa, Gina, Tom; (second marriage) Isabel, Marina, Pablo. *Education:* Attended Academia San Carlos, 1949-50, Art Students League, 1950-51, and Cooper Union, 1951-52.

ADDRESSES: Home—Route 10, Box 94-G, Santa Fe, NM 87501.

CAREER: Esquire magazine, New York, NY, art director, 1951-53; *Seventeen* magazine, New York, NY, head of promotion department, 1953-54; Grey Advertising, New York, NY, art director, 1954-57; Daniel & Charles, New York, NY, art director, 1957-61; George Ancona, Inc., New York, NY, photographer and filmmaker, 1961—. Instructor at Rockland Community College, School of Visual Arts, and Parsons School of Design in New York, NY; lecturer on film, design photography, and books.

AWARDS, HONORS: Art Director's Show awards, 1959, 1960, 1967; Cine Golden Eagle Awards, Council on Non-Theatrical Events, 1967, for film *Reflections,* and 1972, for film *Cities of the Web;* awards from American Institute of Graphic Arts, 1967, 1968, 1974; Cindy Award, Industry Film Producers Association, 1967; Nonfiction Younger Honor, Science Book Awards, New York Academy of Sciences, 1975, for *Handtalk: An ABC of Finger Spelling and Sign Language,* and 1988, for *Turtle Watch;* Golden Kite Award, Society of Children's Book Writers and Illustrators, 1980, for *Finding Your First Job;* Junior Literary Guild selection, c. 1984, for *Monster Movers;* American Library Association Notable Book, and Notable Children's Book in the Field of Social Studies, 1986, for *Sheepdog;* Best Illustrated Children's Books of the Year citation, *New York Times,* 1987, for *Handtalk Birthday;* Carter G. Woodson Book Award for Outstanding Merit, National Council for the Social Studies, 1987, for *Living in Two Worlds;* Junior Literary Guild selection and New York Academy of Sciences Children's Science Book Award, c. 1988, both for *Turtle Watch;* Notable Trade Book in the Field of Social Studies, Children's Book Council, c. 1989, for *Spanish Pioneers of the Southwest;* Texas Blue Bonnet Award, c. 1989, for *The American Family Farm;* Notable Children's Book in the Field of Social Studies, c.

1990, for *Riverkeeper* and *Mom Can't See Me;* Pick of the Lists citation, American Booksellers Association, 1991, for *The Aquarium Book;* Children's Book of the Year citation, Bank Street College, 1993, for *Pablo Remembers;* Best 100 children's books citation, New York Public Library, 1993, for *Powwow;* Parents' Choice Award, 1994, for *The Piñata Maker/El piñatero;* Child Study Children's Book Committee Children's Book of the Year, 1994, for *Twins on Toes;* Golden Duck Award for excellence in children's science fiction, 1994, for *Richie's Rocket;* Outstanding Science Trade Book for Children citation, National Science Teachers Association and Children's Book Council, 1995, for *The Golden Lion Tamarin Comes Home;* Pura Belpe Illustrator Award, 2000, for *Barrio.*

WRITINGS:

AND PHOTOGRAPHER

Monsters on Wheels, Dutton, 1974.
And What Do You Do?, Dutton, 1975.
I Feel: A Picture Book of Emotions, Dutton, 1977.
Growing Older, Dutton, 1978.
It's a Baby!, Dutton, 1979.
Dancing Is . . . , Dutton, 1981.
Bananas: From Manolo to Margie, Clarion, 1982.
Teamwork: A Picture Essay about Crews and Teams at Work, Crowell, 1983.
Monster Movers, Dutton, 1984.
Freighters, Crowell, 1985.
Sheepdog, Lothrop, 1985.
Helping Out, Clarion, 1985.
Turtle Watch, Macmillan, 1987.
Riverkeeper, Macmillan, 1990.
The Aquarium Book, Clarion, 1991.
Man and Mustang, Macmillan, 1992.
My Camera, Crown, 1992.
Pablo Remembers: The Fiesta of the Day of the Dead, Lothrop, 1993.
Powwow, Harcourt, 1993.
Ser util, Scholastic, 1993.
Ricardo's Day/El día de Ricardo, Scholastic, 1994.
The Golden Lion Tamarin Comes Home, Macmillan, 1994.
The Piñata Maker/El piñatero, Harcourt, 1994.
Fiesta U.S.A., Dutton, 1995.
Stone Cutters, Carvers, and the Cathedral, Lothrop, 1995.
Earth Daughter: Alicia of Acoma Pueblo, Simon & Schuster, 1995.
Mayeros: A Yucatec Maya Family, Lothrop, 1996.
The American Family Farm, Turtle Books, 1997.
Let's Dance!, Morrow/Avon, 1998.

Fiesta Fireworks, Lothrop, 1998.
Barrio, Harcourt Trade Publishers, 1998.
Carnaval, Harcourt Children's Books, 1999.
Charro, Harcourt Trade Publishers, 1999.
Cuban Family Book, Lothrop, 2000.
Cuban Kids, Marshall Cavendish, 2000.
The Fiestas, Marshall Cavendish, 2001.
The Folk Arts, Marshall Cavendish, 2001.
Harvest, Marshall Cavendish, 2001.
The Past, Marshall Cavendish, 2001.
The People, Marshall Cavendish, 2001.

Turtle Watch was published in Portuguese as *Tartarugas marinhas: uma especie em extincao,* Salamandra Consultoria Editorial, 1987; *Pablo Remembers: The Fiesta of the Day of the Dead* was published in Spanish as *Pablo recuerda,* Lothrop, 1993; *Fiesta U.S.A.* was published in Spanish under the same title, Lodestar, 1995.

"HANDTALK" SERIES; AND PHOTOGRAPHER

(With Remy Charlip and Mary Beth Miller) *Handtalk: An ABC of Finger Spelling and Sign Language,* Parents' Magazine Press, 1974.
(With Remy Charlip and Mary Beth Miller) *Handtalk Birthday: A Number and Story Book in Sign Language,* Four Winds Press, 1987.
(With Mary Beth Miller) *Handtalk Zoo,* Four Winds Press, 1989.
(With Mary Beth Miller) *Handtalk School,* Four Winds Press, 1991.

PHOTOGRAPHER

Barbara Brenner, *A Snake-Lover's Diary,* Scott Young Books, 1970.
Barbara Brenner, *Faces,* Dutton, 1970.
Barbara Brenner, *Bodies,* Dutton, 1973.
Louise Jackson, *Grandpa Had a Windmill, Grandma Had a Churn,* Parents' Magazine Press, 1977.
Jean Holzenthaler, *My Feet Do,* Dutton, 1979.
Louise Jackson, *Over on the River,* Lothrop, 1980.
Sue Alexander, *Finding Your First Job,* Dutton, 1980.
Howard Smith, *Balance It,* Four Winds Press, 1981.
Maxine B. Rosenberg, *My Friend Leslie,* Lothrop, 1982.
Joan Anderson, *First Thanksgiving Feast,* Clarion, 1984.
Maxine B. Rosenberg, *Being Adopted,* Lothrop, 1984.
Maxine B. Anderson, *Christmas on the Prairie,* Clarion, 1985.
Maxine B. Rosenberg, *Being a Twin, Having a Twin,* Lothrop, 1985.

Joan Anderson, *The Glorious Fourth in Prairietown,* Morrow, 1986.

Maxine B. Rosenberg, *Making a New Home in America,* Lothrop, 1986.

Maxine B. Rosenberg, *Living in Two Worlds,* Lothrop, 1986.

Joan Anderson, *Pioneer Children of Appalachia,* Clarion, 1986.

Floreva G. Cohen, *My Special Friend,* Board of Jewish Education, 1986.

Sam and Beryl Epstein, *Jackpot of the Beagle Brigade,* Macmillan, 1987.

Joan Anderson, *Joshua's Westward Journal,* Morrow, 1987.

Maxine B. Rosenberg, *Artists of Handcrafted Furniture at Work,* Lothrop, 1988.

Maxine B. Rosenberg, *Finding a Way: Living with Exceptional Brothers and Sisters,* afterword by Stephen Greenspan, Lothrop, 1988.

Joan Anderson, *From Map to Museum: Uncovering Mysteries of the Past,* introduction by David Hurst Thomas, Morrow Junior Books, 1988.

Joan Anderson, *A Williamsburg Household,* Clarion, 1988.

Joan Anderson, *The American Family Farm: A Photo Essay,* Harcourt, 1989.

Marcia Seligson, *Dolphins at Grassy Key,* Macmillan, 1989.

Joan Anderson, *Spanish Pioneers of the Southwest,* Dutton, 1989.

Joan Anderson, *French Pioneers,* Lodestar, 1989.

Shirley Climo, *City! New York,* Macmillan, 1990.

Shirley Climo, *City! San Francisco,* Macmillan, 1990.

Joan Anderson, *Harry's Helicopter,* Morrow, 1990.

Sally Hobart Alexander, *Mom Can't See Me,* Macmillan, 1990.

Anderson, *Pioneer Settlers of New France,* Dutton, 1990.

Maxine B. Rosenberg, *Brothers and Sisters,* Clarion, 1991.

Joan Anderson, *Christopher Columbus: From Vision to Voyage,* Dial, 1991.

Shirley Climo, *City! Washington, D.C.,* Macmillan, 1991.

Christine Loomis, *My New Baby-Sitter,* Morrow, 1991.

Bonnie Larkin Nims, *Just Beyond Reach and Other Riddle Poems,* Scholastic, 1992.

Sally Hobart Alexander, *Mom's Best Friend,* Macmillan, 1992.

Joan Anderson, *Earth Keepers,* Gulliver Green/Harcourt, 1993.

Mildred Leinweber Dawson, *Over Here It's Different: Carolina's Story,* Macmillan, 1993.

Joan Anderson, *Richie's Rocket,* Morrow, 1993.

Joan Anderson, *Twins on Toes: A Ballet Debut,* Lodestar, 1993.

Joan Anderson, *Sally's Submarine,* Morrow, 1995.

Joan Anderson, *Cowboys: Roundup on an American Ranch,* Scholastic, 1996.

Faces was translated into Spanish by Alma Flor Ada as *Caras,* 1977.

OTHER

Also author of filmscripts, including "Doctor" and "Dentist," two short films for *Sesame Street; Faces* and *The River,* for children; *Getting It Together,* a documentary film about the Children's Television Workshop and Neighborhood Youth Corps; *Cities of the Web,* produced by Macmillan; *Looking for Pictures, Looking for Color,* and *Seeing Rhythm,* a series; *Reflections,* produced by American Crafts Council; *The Link,* produced by Orba Corporation; and *Expansion,* produced by Diamond International Corporation.

WORK IN PROGRESS: Migrants.

SIDELIGHTS: George Ancona is renowned for his vivid photo essays that allow children to immerse themselves in new ideas and cultures, to appreciate labor that so often goes unnoticed behind the scenes of daily life, and to accept themselves as well as others. Ancona's more recent photo essays and writings also celebrate his own Mexican heritage and the Spanish language. Ancona keeps the interests of his readers in mind while he works. As he wrote in *Something about the Author Autobiography Series (SAAS),* he attempts to convey "the same feeling I had when my father would show me . . . big ships. It's like seeing something awe-inspiring and you just have to say, 'WOW.' "

Ancona once said of his childhood: "My parents had come from Yucatan in Mexico and I was raised a Mexican, learning to speak Spanish first. My father wanted me to grow up in the American way so we never lived in a Latin barrio. Instead I grew up the only Latin in an Italian neighborhood. There I acquired my English, work skills, street wisdom and a godfather.

"Growing up in Coney Island, my world consisted of the contrast between the fantasies of the amusement rides and the limitless space of the sea. Summers were spent in a bathing suit running with a pack of boys through the streets to the beach, swimming out beyond the third barrel, straining the sands for coins and sneaking into the amusement parks. From the age of twelve I worked weekends and summers for a variety of craftsmen. An auto mechanic, a carpenter, and in the amusement parks. I would, also, make money with a friend by collecting junk and scrap paper in an old push cart. When loaded with newspaper it took both of us to raise it on its two big wheels and push it to the junk dealer. This way we always had money for the movies and a hot dog."

Ancona began to express his creativity as an artist while he was still young. "My father's hobby was photography and it was my first introduction to the making of images. . . . It was at home that I began to draw by copying photographs." Later, at Mark Twain Junior High School, Ancona began "to take an active interest in drawing and design. It was the sign painting teacher who got me interested in lettering and painting the sets for the dramatic performances. When I graduated I was given the Sign Painting Medal. In Lincoln High School I had the good fortune of studying design with Mr. Leon Friend, who had organized an extra-curricular group called the Art Squad," Ancona recalled. He excelled under the direction of the Art Squad and its alumni, and won a scholarship to the Art Students League in New York City. He also met Rufino Tamayo, a renowned Mexican artist, who invited Ancona to visit him in Mexico.

Ancona accepted Tamayo's invitation, and Tamayo arranged for Ancona to spend six months painting at the Academy of San Carlos in Mexico. There, Ancona met Jose Clemente Orozco, a famous Mexican muralist; Igor Stravinsky, the composer; Diego Rivera, another great Mexican muralist; and Rivera's wife Frida Kahlo, a painter and artist in her own right. Ancona also journeyed to Merida, in the Yucatan, to meet relatives from both sides of his family. Traveling further into the Yucatan, he spent the night at the Mayan ruins of Chichen Itza.

When his money ran out, Ancona returned to the United States to attend the Art Students League. He stayed for the duration of his scholarship, nine months, and then went to work as an artist's apprentice. Although he tried to attend school at Cooper Union at night, a new job in the promotion department at the *New York Times* left him exhausted. He decided to forgo school and concentrate on work. Around the same time, he also decided to marry his first wife, Patricia Apatow. Ancona went on to work as a staff designer at *Esquire* magazine, as an art director for *Apparel Arts* magazine, and then as art director of the promotion department for *Seventeen* magazine. Ancona recalled in his *SAAS* essay that the job at *Seventeen* "gave me my first taste of advertising.

I enjoyed the challenge of blending images with words to create forceful messages."

Ancona moved on again to become an art director for the NBC television and radio networks, to work in fashion photography, and to try his hand at filmmaking. "The film experiences and my early attempts at photography seemed to be leading me into a different career direction. Having started out as someone who loved to draw and paint I was spending more and more time with film and still cameras." At thirty years old, Ancona felt he had to make a decision about his career: "It was now or never so I took the plunge," he wrote in *SAAS*. He quit his job and began his career as a freelance photographer by taking photographs for *Vogue Children*. In addition, he made a film for *Sesame Street* and filmed the children's series *Big Blue Marble*. As he worked, he traveled to Brazil, Pakistan, Hong Kong, Japan, Iceland, Tunisia, and Switzerland. It was during this time that Ancona and his first wife divorced. Ancona's three children—Lisa, Gina, and Tomas—stayed with him, and he later married Helga Von Sydow. With Von Sydow, Ancona had three more children: Isabel, Marina, and Pablo.

Ancona created his first children's book photographs in 1970. "My introduction to children's books was totally unexpected," Ancona revealed. Barbara Brenner, Ancona's friend and an established writer, asked Ancona if he would be interested in making photographs to illustrate one of her books. "Since I had never done a children's book I said yes." *Faces, Bodies,* and *A Snake-Lover's Diary* resulted. Later, when the editor of Brenner and Ancona's books suggested that he write the text as well as illustrate a book, Ancona "gulped hard" and said he "would try." Ancona's interest in "watching construction sites and huge machinery" and "several months photographing" led to the creation of his first book, *Monsters on Wheels*. This detailed book describes machines that "push, lift, crush and haul," from cranes to the Lunar Roving Vehicle that explored the moon. John S. Radosta, in the *New York Times Book Review*, characterized the book as "excellent."

Monster Movers features sixteen machines, from a walking dragline to a clamshell bucket loader, that move mountains of coal, grain, and cargo over land, onto ships, and off ships. One of these machines, a crawler-transporter, is pictured moving the Space Shuttle. "Once again Ancona has mixed striking photographs, a lucid text and a fascinating subject with winning results," Connie Tyrrell Burns of *School Library Journal* commented. Like *Monsters on Wheels* and *Monster Movers, Freighters* presents various machines that help people work. Yet in *Freighters* Ancona focuses on the people who control the machines as well as on the machines; with his camera, Ancona follows the qualifications, training, and daily routine of a freighter crew. Many of Ancona's books are entirely devoted to workers and the jobs they perform. Even *Sheepdog,* which features a very intelligent breed of dogs, is about an important kind of work: guarding and herding sheep.

According to a reviewer in *School Library Journal, And What Do You Do?* presents twenty-one jobs, including carpenter, costume designer, dental assistant, barber, and nurse with "outstanding photographs" and a "lucid writing style." Denise M. Wilms of *Booklist* noted that the photographs feature "men and women of varying racial and ethnic backgrounds" and that there is a "conscious attempt to avoid stereotyping." *Teamwork: A Picture Essay about Crews and Teams at Work* follows the team efforts of mountain climbers, a nursing crew, a sailing crew, a film crew, and other workers. Like *And What Do You Do?,* women and men in *Teamwork* are not cast in stereotypical roles.

Ancona has also made photo essays on specific jobs. *Man and Mustang* shows how feral horses are captured, transported, and tamed by prison inmates for the Bureau of Land Management. *Stone Cutters, Carvers and the Cathedral* illuminates an esoteric and fascinating profession. With black and white photographs and text, *Riverkeeper* follows John Cronin, the riverkeeper of the Hudson River in New York who protects the water, plants, and wildlife. Ancona demonstrates that Cronin cannot protect the water from pollution from the seat of his powerboat, named *Riverkeeper;* as a representative of the Hudson River Fishermen's Association, he must deal with corporate polluters and a host of government agencies to ensure its cleanliness. According to Mary M. Burns in *Horn Book,* Ancona provides a "balanced, rational presentation" which "speaks directly to our times in a manner as informative as it is appealing." Betsy Hearne of *Bulletin of the Center for Children's Books* concluded that *Riverkeeper* "will energize kids" to view its subject "in the light of ecological responsibility."

Looking forward to a satisfying career and an understanding of the world of work is just one aspect of childhood. Ancona has dealt with a variety of other childhood concerns and interests in his work. *Helping Out,* according to a *Publishers Weekly* critic, is based on a "stimulating" idea—children can help out (washing cars, planting seeds, doing chores) to the satisfaction of all. The children featured in Ancona's black and white pictures smile and, as the reviewer noted, "show clearly that they like what they're doing."

Children are fascinated with babies, as the nursery school teachers who told Ancona that they needed a book that would discuss babies and explain how they grow must have known. Ancona met this need by staying home to photograph the first twelve months in the life of Pablo, his third child with Helga. Ancona said in a *Junior Literary Guild* article that the text of *It's a Baby!* "grew out of the questions children would ask" about Pablo when they saw him. This book shows Pablo nursing, playing, climbing, and taking his first steps. In *Horn Book* Kate M. Flanagan described the black and white photographs as "exquisite."

Ancona's photographs have also helped children learn to accept themselves and others by bringing life to books featuring physically challenged children and adults. *Mom Can't See Me* and *Mom's Best Friend,* both by Sally Hobart Alexander, show how a blind woman lives a fulfilling life; *Finding a Way: Living With Exceptional Brothers and Sisters* by Maxine B. Rosenberg, demonstrates how children can help physically challenged siblings in a caring, positive manner. The "Handtalk" series has been especially popular. In *Handtalk Zoo,* the third book by Ancona and Mary Beth Miller, children visit the zoo and communicate in sign language. Ancona's color photographs clearly show the signs the children make, as well as capturing hands in rapid movement. As Hanna B. Zeiger observed in *Horn Book,* some "photos of signs capture very clearly the essence of the animal" the children are viewing. In the words of *School Library Journal* contributor Susan Nemeth McCarthy, *Handtalk Zoo* introduces children to sign language vocabulary in a "creative and exuberant manner."

Ancona's travels to countries around the world have provided him with alternate settings to explore his favorite topics—machines, working and occupations, and nature. Ancona was inspired to write *Bananas: From Manolo to Margie* while visiting a Honduran village. This book demonstrates how the bananas are cultivated on a Honduran plantation, picked by plantation workers, and sent on a two-week trip to a grocery store in the United States, where Margie and her mother buy some. The mostly black and white photos focus on the equipment used in the process of picking and transporting as well as on the people who operate it. They also feature the families of the plantation workers. These photos in *Bananas* are "fair: workers live poorly and work hard," as Terry Lawhead noted in *School Library Journal.* Zena Sutherland of the *Bulletin of the Center for Children's Books* observed that information about the plantation workers is offered, although the text does not really discuss the "personal lives" of Margie and the transportation and marketing workers.

Turtle Watch follows the efforts of oceanographers attempting to replenish the sea turtle population in northeastern Brazil. During nesting season, oceanographers and the people of Praia do Forte alike have important responsibilities. The local people, especially fishermen, must encourage one another to leave the eggs and turtles they find instead of selling them. Oceanographers must observe female turtles laying eggs, recover the eggs for safe hatching, and then, after the baby turtles emerge from their eggs, help them make their way to the ocean. According to Karey Wehner in *School Library Journal,* "Ancona conveys some of the excitement and wonder scientists must feel when observing animals firsthand, in the field." Ancona said in *Junior Literary Guild* that photographing the turtles was difficult. "We would arrive either too early or too late to see them emerge from the sea." Although it took a long time for Ancona to finally get his photos, he remarked that he didn't mind much. "Brazil is a wonderful place to be stranded in." Ancona returned to Brazil to research and take photos for a book on the Golden Lion Tamarin monkey.

Pablo Remembers: The Fiesta of the Day of the Dead features a Mexican family as they prepare for and enjoy the festival of the Day of the Dead. As Ancona wrote in *SAAS,* "It is a time for family reunions, meals, and an evening spent in the cemetery among flowers and candles on the decorated tombs of departed relatives." He continued, "In the streets people parade in costume and recite satiric poems in front of their neighbors' houses." During the festival's three days (All Hallows Eve, All Saints Day, and All Souls Day), which honor the dead in a combination of Aztec and Catholic traditions, altars are decorated, children eat candy skulls, and Pablo takes time to remember his deceased grandmother. According to *Bulletin of the Center for Children's Books* contributor Roger Sutton, the "photography has the intimacy of high-quality family snapshots." Margaret A. Bush concluded in *Horn Book* that the "beautiful book" serves as a fitting "tribute to Mexican home life."

The Piñata Maker/El piñatero also focuses on life in Mexico, but its text is written in both Spanish and English. Ancona follows Don Ricardo Nuñez Gijon, better known as Tio Rico in the village, as he carefully crafts fantastic, delightful piñatas. Ancona's photos demonstrate how Tio Rico makes a paste out of old newspa-pers and paper bags, and then shapes the paste into the form of a carrot, swan, star, or other figure. The next series of photos demonstrates how Daniela, a young girl, chooses a piñata for her birthday party, and how her guests crack it open and spill the candy. "Ancona has created an authentic, detailed account of one aspect of Mexican culture which has particularly wide appeal to children," wrote Maeve Visser Knoth in *Horn Book.* According to Ann Welton in *School Library Journal,* the "balance between text and illustration is masterful."

One problem Ancona had once he had created *Pablo Remembers* and *The Piñata Maker,* as he wrote in *SAAS,* was saying good-bye to the friends he had made. "The departure is very sad for me because these people have become part of my life and I don't know if I will ever see them again. . . . Someday I would like to take as much time as it would take to visit all the people I have gotten to know through my travels and books."

Ancona did not have to travel far to meet the people he photographed for *Powwow.* With color photographs and a thoughtful introduction, Ancona provides what *School Library Journal* reviewer Lisa Mitten described as an "exquisite kaleidoscope of Native American music, customs, and crafts." The Crow Fair in Montana provides an opportunity for people from various tribes, including the Crow, Lakota, Cheyenne, Cree, and Ojibwa, to dance Traditional, Fancy, Grass, and Jingle-dress dances competitively. Ancona follows the celebration as it progresses from parade to dance; he focuses his camera on the people watching the dances as well as the dancers themselves. As Bush noted in *Horn Book,* Ancona's camera records "the ironies of traditional cultural practice in the modern setting." Objects like Diet Pepsi, cars, and telephone wires, according to Sutton in another *Bulletin of the Center for Children's Books* article, "[give] the old ways—in new forms—the breath of continuing relevance." Importantly, as Bush concluded, Ancona "conveys the universal appeal of spectacle and celebration" in *Powwow.*

Aspiring photographers who admire Ancona's work may enjoy *My Camera,* which demonstrates how to use a 35mm camera like the one Ancona uses. He describes how to compose pictures, how to use the flash, and how to put together albums, photo essays, and storyboards. Ancona also includes a diagrammatic and textual explanation of how a camera works. "Evidence of Ancona's photographic talent and teaching ability radiates from every page," remarked Nancy E. Curran in *School Library Journal.*

Fiesta Fireworks shows the work of a Mexican family of fireworks experts as they prepare for a festival honoring their town's patron saint. In *Horn Book,* Margaret A. Bush wrote that "readers of all ages will be drawn to the splash of the fireworks and the experience of carnival." In *Carnaval,* Ancona presents an "ebullient" photo essay, according to Chris Sherman in *Booklist.* The book describes the pre-Lenten Carnaval celebration in Olinda, Brazil, with photos of preparations for the festival as well as the actual event. Sherman wrote that Ancona's "artfully arranged, riotously full-color photographs . . . fairly dance across the pages." *Charro,* another photoessay, depicts the life of the "Mexican cowboy." In *Booklist,* Isabel Schon called Ancona's color photographs "stunning."

Barrio, described as "a striking photoessay" by a reviewer in *Booklist,* describes a year in the life of eight-year-old Jose, who lives in the Mission District of San Francisco. Annie Ayres wrote in *Booklist* that the book is "a fond and fascinating photo-essay focusing on the richness of the Latino experience." The book won the Pura Belpe Illustrator Award for 2000.

Ancona explored Cuban culture in *Cuban Kids* and *Cuban Families.* For *Cuban Kids,* he traveled to Cuba and visited families in rural and urban areas, and depicts work, play, sports, farming, doctor's office, music making, and dance. In *School Library Journal,* Marilyn Long Graham commented that the text avoids discussing the political differences between the United States and Cuba, and "suggests a life with few problems," but she also noted that the photos "add balance" by showing some of the difficulties of life in Cuba. However, Denia Hester wrote in *Booklist* that the "well-written" text does comment on the effects of communism and the influence of Fidel Castro and other revolutionary leaders. She called the book "a very fine portrait of modern Cuba."

A thorough understanding of the technical issues involved in photography is just one aspect of any photographer's success. Ancona once revealed the character trait that has stimulated his achievements: "Curiosity is the biggest element in my work. . . . I think people are fascinating and I love to find myself in strange places, meeting people, getting to know them and learning about them. This helps me to learn about myself. Photographing, filming or writing about someone or someplace is my way of feeling alive and in touch with the world around me. I believe that work does this for many people. Whether it is baking bread, building a house, driving a truck or singing a song, people reach each

other each in their own way. I think that's what living is all about."

BIOGRAPHICAL/CRITICAL SOURCES:

BOOKS

Something About the Author Autobiography Series, Volume 18, Gale (Detroit, MI), 1994, pp. 1-18.
St. James Guide to Children's Writers, 5th ed., St. James Press (Detroit, MI), 1999.

PERIODICALS

Booklist, July 1, 1976, p. 1525; April 15, 1982, p. 1091; December 1, 1994, p. 670; March 1, 1995, p. 1236; October 15, 1995, p. 397; March 15, 1996, p. 1261; April 15, 1997, p. 1420; April, 1998, p. 1323; December 1, 1998, p. 662; May 15, 1999, p. 1689; November 15, 1999, p. 617; January 1, 2000, p. 928, 929; March 15, 2000, p. 1354; December 15, 2000, p. 811.
Bulletin of the Center for Children's Books, January, 1983, p. 81; November, 1989, p. 49; July-August, 1990, p. 259; May, 1993, p. 276; December, 1993, p. 114.
Horn Book, February, 1980, p. 71; November-December, 1989, p. 775; May-June, 1990, p. 345; spring, 1992, p. 100; May-June, 1993, p. 343; March-April, 1994, pp. 213-14; July-August, 1994, p. 469; May-June, 1995, p. 339; November-December, 1995, pp. 728-29; May-June, 1996, p. 347; May-June, 1998, p. 353.
Junior Literary Guild, September, 1979; October, 1987-March, 1988, p. 25.
Kirkus Reviews, May 1, 1976, p. 537.
New York Times Book Review, January 19, 1975, p. 8; November 14, 1993, p. 42.
Publishers Weekly, July 19, 1985, p. 53; February 19, 1996, p. 216; June 7, 1999, p. 85.
School Library Journal, September, 1976, p. 109; November, 1977, p. 43; January, 1983, pp. 69; February, 1984, p. 65; October, 1987, p. 131; October, 1989, pp. 99; April, 1992, p. 128; February, 1993, p. 95; April, 1993, pp. 125; April, 1994, p. 116; April, 1995, p. 97; September, 1995, p. 204; November, 1995, p. 136; December, 1995, p. 94; March, 1996, p. 199; January, 2001, p. 112.*

ANDERSON, Kevin J(ames) 1962-

PERSONAL: Born March 27, 1962, in Racine, WI; son of Andrew James (a banker) and Dorothy Arloah (a homemaker; maiden name, Cooper) Anderson; married Mary Franco Nijhuis, November 17, 1983 (divorced June, 1987); married Rebecca Moesta (a technical editor and writer), September 14, 1991; children: Jonathan Macgregor Cowan (stepson). *Education:* University of Wisconsin—Madison, B.S. (with honors), 1982. *Avocational interests:* Hiking, camping, reading, astronomy.

ADDRESSES: Office—Lawrence Livermore National Laboratory, P.O. Box 808, L-11, Livermore, CA 94550.

CAREER: Writer. Lawrence Livermore National Laboratory, Livermore, CA, technical writer/editor, 1983-95; Materials Research Society, Pittsburgh, PA, columnist, 1988—; International Society for Respiratory Protection, Salem, OR, copy editor, 1989—.

MEMBER: Science Fiction Writers of America, Horror Writers of America.

AWARDS, HONORS: Dale Donaldson Memorial Award for lifetime service to the small-press field, 1987; Bram Stoker Award nomination for best first novel, Horror Writers of America, 1988, for *Resurrection, Inc.;* Writers of the Future honorable mention citations, Bridge Publications, 1985, 1988, and 1989; Nebula award nomination for best science-fiction novel, 1993, for *Assemblers of Infinity; Locus* magazine award for best science-fiction paperback novel of 1995, for *Climbing Olympus.*

WRITINGS:

NOVELS; WITH DOUG BEASON

Lifeline, Bantam (New York, NY), 1991.
The Trinity Paradox, Bantam (New York, NY), 1991.
Assemblers of Infinity, Bantam (New York, NY), 1993.
Ill Wind, Forge (New York, NY), 1995.
Virtual Destruction, Ace Books (New York, NY), 1996.
Ignition, Forge (New York, NY), 1997.
Fallout, Ace Books (New York, NY), 1997.
Lethal Exposure, Ace Books (New York, NY), 1998.

NOVELS; WITH KRISTINE KATHRYN RUSCH

Afterimage, Roc (New York, NY), 1992.

Kevin J. Anderson

Afterimage/Aftershock, Meisha Merlin (Decatur, GA), 1998.

Also coauthor of *Aftershock,* Roc (New York, NY).

"X-FILES" SERIES

Ground Zero, HarperPrism (New York, NY), 1995.
Ruins, HarperPrism (New York, NY), 1996.
Antibodies, HarperPrism (New York, NY), 1997.

SCIENCE FICTION

Resurrection, Inc., Signet (New York, NY), 1988, tenth anniversary limited edition, Overlook Connection Press (Woodstock, GA), 1998.
Climbing Olympus, Warner (New York, NY), 1994.
Blindfold, Warner (New York, NY), 1995.
(Editor) *War of the Worlds: Global Dispatches* (anthology), Bantam (New York, NY), 1996.
Dogged Persistence (short stories), Golden Gryphon Press (Urbana, IL), 2001.
Hopscotch, Bantam (New York, NY), 2002.

"GAMEARTH" SERIES

Gamearth, Signet (New York, NY), 1989.
Gameplay, Signet (New York, NY), 1989.
Game's End, Roc (New York, NY), 1990.

FOR YOUNG ADULTS

(With John Gregory Betancourt) *Born of Elven Blood,* Atheneum (New York, NY), 1995.
Bounty Hunters, Bantam (New York, NY), 1996.

"STAR WARS" SERIES

Darksaber, Bantam (New York, NY), 1995.
(With Rebecca Moesta) *Delusions of Grandeur,* Boulevard (New York, NY), 1997.
(With Rebecca Moesta) *Diversity Alliance,* Boulevard (New York, NY), 1997.
Dark Lords, D. I. Fine (New York, NY), 1997.
(With Rebecca Moesta) *Jedi Bounty,* Boulevard (New York, NY), 1997.
(With Daniel Wallace) *Star Wars: The Essential Chronology,* Ballantine (New York, NY), 2000.

"STAR WARS: JEDI ACADEMY" TRILOGY

Jedi Search, Bantam (New York, NY), 1994.
Dark Apprentice, Bantam (New York, NY), 1994.
Champions of the Force, Bantam (New York, NY), 1994.
Jedi Academy Trilogy (includes *Jedi Search, Dark Apprentice,* and *Champions of the Force*), Doubleday (New York, NY), 1994.

"STAR WARS: YOUNG JEDI KNIGHTS" SERIES

(With Rebecca Moesta) *Heirs of the Force,* Boulevard (New York, NY), 1995.
(With Rebecca Moesta) *Shadow Academy,* Boulevard (New York, NY), 1995.
(With Rebecca Moesta) *The Lost Ones,* Boulevard (New York, NY), 1995.
(With Rebecca Moesta) *Lightsabers,* Boulevard (New York, NY), 1996.
(With Rebecca Moesta) *Darkest Knight,* Boulevard (New York, NY), 1996.
(With Rebecca Moesta) *Jedi under Siege,* Boulevard (New York, NY), 1996.
(With Rebecca Moesta) *Shards of Alderaan,* Boulevard (New York, NY), 1997.
(With Rebecca Moesta) *Crisis at Crystal Reef,* Boulevard (New York, NY), 1998.
Young Jedi the Lost, Boulevard (New York, NY), 1998.
Jedi Trilogy, Bantam (New York, NY), 1998.
(With Rebecca Moesta) *Trouble on Cloud City,* Boulevard (New York, NY), 1998.
(With Rebecca Moesta) *Return to Ord Mantell,* Boulevard (New York, NY), 1998.
(With Rebecca Moesta) *The Emperor's Plague,* Boulevard (New York, NY), 1998.

"STAR WARS" ANTHOLOGIES

(Editor) *Star Wars: Tales from the Mos Eisley Cantina,* Bantam (New York, NY), 1995.
(Editor) *Star Wars: Tales from Jabba's Palace,* Bantam (New York, NY), 1995.

"STAR WARS: TALES OF THE JEDI" SERIES

Dark Lords of the Sith, Dark Horse Comics (Milwaukee, OR), 1996.
The Sith War, Dark Horse Comics (Milwaukee, OR), 1996.
Golden Age of Sith, Dark Horse Comics (Milwaukee, OR), 1997.
Fall of the Sith Empire, Dark Horse Comics (Milwaukee, OR), 1998.

"DUNE" SERIES

(With Brian Herbert) *Dune: House Atreides,* Bantam (New York, NY), 1999.
(With Brian Herbert) *Dune: House Harkonnen,* Bantam (New York, NY), 2000.
(With Brian Herbert) *Dune: House Corrino,* Bantam (New York, NY), 2001.

NONFICTION

The Illustrated Star Wars Universe, illustrated by Ralph McQuarrie, with additional art by Michael Butkus and others, Bantam (New York, NY), 1995.
(With Rebecca Moesta) *Star Wars: The Mos Eisley Cantina Pop-up Book,* illustrated by Ralph McQuarrie, Little, Brown (Boston, MA), 1995.
(With Rebecca Moesta) *Jabba's Palace Pop-up Book,* illustrated by Ralph McQuarrie, Little, Brown (Boston, MA), 1996.

OTHER

(With L. Ron Hubbard) *Ai! Pedrito!: When Intelligence Goes Wrong,* Bridge Publications (Los Angeles, CA), 1998.
(With Harlan Ellison) *The Outer Limits: Armageddon Dreams,* Quadrillion Media (Scottsdale, AZ), 2000.
(With Gregory Benford and Marc Scott Zicree) *Science Fiction Theater,* edited by Brian Forbes, Quadrillion Media (Scottsdale, AZ), 2000.
(With Rebecca Moesta) *Supernova,* Quadrillion Media (Scottsdale, AZ), 2000.
(With Rebecca Moesta) *Star Trek—The Next Generation: The Gorn Crisis* (comic book), painted by

Igor Kordey, WildStorm/D.C. Comics (La Jolla, CA), 2001.

Work represented in anthologies, including *Full Spectrum,* volumes I, III, and IV; *The Ultimate Dracula;* and *The Ultimate Werewolf.* Contributor of short stories, articles, and reviews to periodicals, including *Analog, Amazing,* and *Fantasy and Science Fiction.* Also author of several comic-book series. Over two dozen of Anderson's books have been translated for foreign publication.

ADAPTATIONS: The X-Files: Ground Zero was recorded as an audiocassette, read by Gillian Anderson, Harper Audio, 1995.

WORK IN PROGRESS: The first three books of a science-fiction series, "The Saga of Seven Suns," chronicling an interstellar war, tentatively titled *Hidden Empire, An Ocean of Stars,* and *Fire and Night,* for Warner Books.

SIDELIGHTS: Kevin J. Anderson, the author of a daunting array of science-fiction books for young adults, has emerged as one of the most successful writers in the genre's history. Over ten million copies of books by Anderson were in print by the late 1990s, and in 1998 he set a world record for the largest single-author book signing while promoting his spoof-filled spy thriller, *Ai! Pedrito!: When Intelligence Goes Wrong,* in Los Angeles. In addition to creating original novels with themes of space exploration and new frontiers, Anderson has written many books in the "Star Wars" series for teen readers under the auspices of Lucasfilm. For a 1999 prequel to the science-fiction classic *Dune,* Anderson set another record when he was signed to the most lucrative book publishing contract yet drawn up for a science-fiction author.

Anderson was born in 1962 and grew up in a small town in Wisconsin. He recalled in a biography published on his Web site that a television movie of the H. G. Wells classic *War of the Worlds* made a tremendous impression on his five-year-old mind. Originally a radio play, *War of the Worlds* caused a stir when first broadcast in the late 1930s, sending many Americans into a panic after convincing them that the Earth was being attacked by Martians. The television movie, based on the radio play, made such an impression on Anderson that, still too young to read or write well, he began drawing pictures of the movie scenes the next day.

Anderson wrote his first short story at the age of eight, and two years later he bought a typewriter with savings

from his allowance. The year he entered high school, he began submitting short stories to science-fiction magazines, but received nothing but peremptory rejection letters. By the time he entered the University of Wisconsin, Madison, he had begun to enjoy minor success with his fiction. After he graduated from college with an honors degree in 1982, he began working for the Lawrence Livermore National Laboratories in Livermore, California. As a technical writer at the important defense-industry complex, Anderson was exposed to ideas and technologies that fired his imagination. He also met his future wife and coauthor, Rebecca Moesta, and another future collaborator, physicist Doug Beason.

Anderson's first published book was *Resurrection, Inc.,* which appeared in 1988. Its protagonist is François Nathans, founder of a company that recycles human corpses. Nathans owns technology that can animate the cadavers with a microchip, and, since their human memory has been erased, these "Servants" are used to free the living from difficult, drudge-like, or dangerous labor. When some of the Servants begin to recover their memories, they rebel. One of them possesses inside knowledge about the company because his father, once the greedy Nathans's partner, had been ousted from the partnership. "Although familiar in outline, this first effort is well plotted and lively in the telling," wrote Barbara Bannon in *Publishers Weekly.* As testament to its appeal, *Resurrection, Inc.* was published in a tenth-anniversary edition in 1998.

Anderson's next project was a series of novels based on the fantasy role-playing games popular with teenagers and young adults in the late 1980s. *Gamearth* introduced Melanie, David, Tyrone, and Scott, a quartet of students deeply involved in a Dungeons-and-Dragons-style fantasy game. David begins to think that the others are taking the plotted movements and created characters too seriously, and he wants to quit. To extricate himself, he creates a monstrous character that will destroy the other players' characters. His strategy backfires, however, and the book's ending is a cliffhanger. Tom Whitmore of *Locus* wrote that "the characters within the game are rather humorously limited by their dice-given powers."

In the sequel, *Gameplay,* the four teens and their two-year-long role-playing game continues. Baffled by some occurrences, they come to realize that some of the created characters have begun to make their own moves. The forces of good and evil meet in battle, aided by a new character who speaks only in advertising and pop culture platitudes. "Anderson adds a delightfully fresh sense of humor in his character of Journeyman, the clay golem Melanie sends to save the day," noted a reviewer in *Kliatt.*

Beginning in the early 1990s, Anderson found success with several titles co-authored with his Livermore colleague, Doug Beason. The first of these books, 1991's *Lifeline,* posits a futuristic scenario of an American base on the Moon, a corporate satellite called Orbitech, and a Soviet counterpart that is viewed with some suspicion. At the beginning of the story, the U.S. government has agreed to a deal with the Philippines: in order to extend the leases for their military bases on the Pacific archipelago, the government has provided the Philippines with a space station, called Aguinaldo. There, scientist Luis Sandovaal and his team of 1,500 researchers are creating groundbreaking new scientific products, including wall-kelp, a quick-growing edible that provides all necessary nutrients for humans. Aguinaldo is also home to experimental prototypes of fantastic flying creatures that can be transformed into sails for the satellites.

Lifeline's action starts with the space settlers observing nuclear mushroom clouds on Earth. The United States and the Soviet Union have attacked one another, and all space stations are stranded. The Russians on Kibalchick put themselves into suspended animation, while the Americans on Orbitech attempt to find a more immediate solution. When Brahms, the director of Orbitech, turns tyrannical and ejects 150 "under-performing" personnel, Duncan McLaris flees to the moon base Clavius. Then the Soviets unexpectedly awaken, and tensions mount. "The posing and solving of apparently insuperable problems keeps the reader involved in that classic way," stated Tom Easton in *Analog Science Fiction and Fact,* who nonetheless faulted Anderson's pacing and his rapid introduction of technological innovations that come to the rescue. "At the same time, the characters are real enough to engage the reader's sympathy. . . . and at the end there is a very real sense of resolution and satisfaction," Easton concluded.

Anderson and Beason's second collaboration, *The Trinity Paradox,* "demonstrates their collaborative storytelling powers . . . effectively," wrote Dan Chow in *Locus.* This time the protagonist is Elizabeth Devane, a radical anti-nuclear activist. She and her boyfriend plan to disable a nuclear weapon sitting unguarded in the desert of the American Southwest, but a mishap occurs. Her boyfriend dies, and she is catapulted back in time to Los Alamos, New Mexico, during World War II, when that locale was the primary research site for U.S. nuclear weapons technology. Finding herself in the midst of a feverish race to master nuclear technology at the top-secret national laboratory, Devane realizes that through her actions she might be able to change history and sabotage the invention of the atomic bomb.

Instead of stopping the future Cold War, however, Devane's actions set in motion a new version of Cold War history: the outcome of World War II is affected, and nuclear technology heads in an entirely new direction. Realizing that she possesses the power to change the world, she becomes as dangerous as the scientists she considers traitors to humankind. "Hers is the most chilling of revolutionary beliefs, that with a constituency of one," noted Chow in *Locus. The Trinity Paradox* includes several real scientists in its plot, such as Robert Oppenheimer and Edward Teller, and the "Trinity" of the title takes its name from the site of the first successful test explosion.

Anderson and Beason continued their successful collaboration in *Assemblers of Infinity.* Set in the early decades of the twenty-first century, the plot centers around a group of scientists who believe an alien invasion is imminent. A team of investigators is sent to a suspicious site at the Earth's base on the moon, but they mysteriously die shortly after landing. Back on Earth, other researchers are positing that the relatively new field of nano-technology—machines run by microprocessors—may have something to do both the deaths and the threat of invasion. Erika Trace, one of the Earth's leading nano scientists, is enlisted to help.

Assemblers of Infinity won praise from reviewers, *Kliatt* reviewer Bette D. Ammon noting that "The premise is riveting and the technology is fascinating," and adding that Anderson and Beason create a situation "utterly plausible and frightening—the stuff of which good SF is made." In a review for *Voice of Youth Advocates,* Rosie Peasley praised its "sophisticated science fiction concepts," declaring that "the plot hums along at high speed." In a *Booklist* critique, Roland Green compared it to "the techno-thriller, sort of a Tom-Clancy-meets-space-advocacy effort."

Ill Wind was Anderson's fourth collaboration with Beason, an eco-thriller involving a massive oil spill in San Francisco Bay. The large corporation responsible for this disaster, eager to clean up both the spill and its corporate image as quickly as possible, unleashes an untried new microbe to do the job. Soon the uncontrollable organism begins eating everything made from petroleum products, such as gasoline and plastic. When martial law is declared and the electricity fails, a scientist and two pilots try to save the world.

In *Virtual Destruction,* Anderson and Beason move the action closer to home: the story is set at the Livermore Labs and shows how large national defense labs were forced to refocus their missions after the end of Cold War tensions. After decades of relying heavily on federal funding to develop new weapons technology, Livermore and other facilities were challenged to find consumer and private-sector applications for their patents. The conflicts presented by this new era—specifically between profit-minded management and the more altruistic scientists—is the focus of *Virtual Destruction.* The plots revolves around a virtual reality chamber that produces devastatingly real effects; Livermore executive Hal Michaelson is discussing with the government possible uses for this chamber in the dangerous realm of nuclear-weapons surveillance. One of Michaelson's researchers, Gary Lesserec, who has been involved with the Virtual Reality Lab from its conception, knows that this is not feasible, that even sound recordings can trick entrants. Lesserec is about to be fired when Michaelson is found dead inside the chamber. FBI agent Craig Kreident investigates and uncovers nefarious industrial espionage links to the computer-gaming industry. While the introduction of Kreident changes the novel's genre from sci-fi thriller to detective fiction, but as Tom Easton noted in *Analog,* "There's not much detecting going on here. The tale exists to give us a tour of Livermore, explicate some interesting technology, and discuss the problems the end of the Cold War has given the national labs."

For help with the details in his next book with Beason, Anderson was able to make an insider's visit to Kennedy Space Center in Florida. *Ignition* chronicles the planning and sabotage of a joint U.S.-Soviet mission on the space shuttle *Atlantis.* The first commodore, Colonel Adam "Iceberg" Friese, suffers an accident that cancels his participation. He becomes vitally involved, nevertheless, when a band of terrorists, organized by a famous Wall Street criminal, takes the crew hostage. The pilot's former paramour, Nicole Hunter, an astronaut-turned-launch controller, is also held hostage, but manages to help Friese battle the gang, some of whom have unusual personal quirks. The realistic details pertaining to the launch pad and pre-launch tensions, somewhat altered for security reasons, make *Ignition* "a nail biter" of a book, according to *Library Journal* reviewer Grant A. Frederickson.

Intrepid FBI agent Kreident reappears in Anderson and Beason's next thriller, *Lethal Exposure.* This work is set at another government-funded research facility, the Fermi National Accelerator Laboratory in Illinois. Kreident arrives to investigate the mysterious radiation death of renowned physicist Georg Dumenco. A reviewer for *Publishers Weekly* observed that the authors' familiarity with the subject matter and lab environment "gives their latest [book] plenty of scientific authenticity."

Anderson is also the author of several books in the "Star Wars" series. The plots, aimed at young-adult readers but popular with "Star Wars" fans of all ages, help provide panoramic details of the factions, clans, and worlds in this classic saga of good and evil. The first series is set at the Jedi Academy and begins with *Jedi Search.* Heroic Han Solo is married to Princess Leia, and they have three small children. Other characters from the original 1977 film make appearances, including Luke Skywalker and Chewbacca, and a new one is introduced, the teenager Kyp Durron. Spice mines and a space battle lead to a "rollicking SF adventure," reported Ingrid von Hausen in a review for *Kliatt.* Together with the Anderson-penned sequels *Dark Apprentice* and *Champions of the Force,* were published under the collective title *Jedi Academy Trilogy.*

Anderson has written several other "Star Wars" books that are not part of a definitive series. In *Darksaber* the Empire is again attempting to resurrect its former glory, aided by a new leader of the Hutt group named Durga. Luke Skywalker is in love with a Jedi named Callista, whose special powers have vanished. Many other successful science-fiction writers have authored titles for various "Star Wars" series, but "Anderson leads the pack in both overall popularity and sheer storytelling power," in the opinion of Carl Hays in *Booklist.* Hays further remarked that Anderson's well-developed characters add greatly to their appeal, giving readers a far more in-depth treatment than is possible in the film plots.

Anderson has coauthored most of the books for the "Young Jedi Knights" series with his wife, Rebecca Moesta. In this series, the heroes are teen twins Jacen and Jaina, the offspring of Han Solo and Princess Leia. Series debut *Heirs of the Force* finds the two at the fabled Jedi Academy founded by their uncle, Luke Skywalker. When the teens are captured by a fighter pilot from the evil Empire, they are threatened with being stranded on a jungle moon. In *The Lost Ones,* Anderson and Moesta again place Jacen and Jaina in danger. As expected, the fourteen-year-olds ably extricate from danger both themselves and a friend who has been lured astray by the malevolent Dark Jedi Master, Brakiss.

The Dark Jedi Force is attempting to revive the empire, creating a Second Imperium that will rule the galaxy. Hugh M. Flick, reviewing *The Lost Ones* in *Kliatt,* called it, along with its two series predecessors, "well written and . . . interesting for *Star Wars* fans of all ages."

Lightsabers, another book in the series, features the maimed Tenel Ka, a friend of Jacen and Jaina. Tenel Ka's arm was destroyed when her lightsaber misfired, and out of shame she has exiled herself to the planet Hapes, where she is now the crown princess. Jacen and Jaina help her attempt to maintain political stability on her home planet, and convince her to return to the Jedi Academy despite her accident. In the fifth book in the "Young Jedi Knights" series, *Darkest Knight,* Jacen and Jaina travel to Kashyyk, home of Lowbacca and the Wookies. The Dark Jedis of the Shadow Academy steal vital computer technology to help build the Second Imperium, but Jacen and Jaina save the galaxy once again.

Anderson has authored several solo titles outside the young adult market that have garnered him definitive praise. Among these is the short-story collection *Dogged Persistence,* which includes eighteen stories which range from "Scientific Romance," a tale of H. G. Wells as an earnest young student, to "Final Performance," wherein lumber from the demolished Globe Theatre brings with it the ghosts of long-dead actors when it is used to construct a new stage. Praising the collection, a *Publishers Weekly* contributor noted that the collection "provide[s] solid entertainment, and reveal[s] depths not evident in Anderson's more commercial fiction," while *Booklist* reviewer Roland Green dubbed *Dogged Persistence* "pretty good reading."

Climbing Olympus is set on a planet Mars inhabited by three types of humans. Rachel Dycek, the United Nations commissioner there, is in charge of Lowell Base. She is the famous surgeon who created *adins* (Russian for "first"), surgically modified prisoners from Soviet labor camps whose physiology was altered to enable them to survive on Mars and construct a colony.

After the adins rebelled and fled to another part of the planet, Dycek created the *dva* (Russian for "two"), much less monstrously engineered and in possession of a higher degree of intelligence. The dvas were sent to Mars to prepare an infrastructure that would allow average, non-modified humans to survive there. As their work nears completion, both the dvas and Dycek are being phased out. When a landslide kills a large number of dvas, Dycek learns that, although adins and dvas were sterilized, the partner of an escaped adin named

Boris is now expecting a child. On the mountain Pavonis Mons, Dycek finds the unbalanced Boris ruling over the remaining adins and she attempts to right her past wrongs and direct the planet toward a more harmonious future. Reviewers praised Anderson's vividly drawn portrayals, and Russell Letson in *Locus* called Dycek and Boris "characters as compelling as the technological widgetry of survival augmentation or the extremities of the Martian landscape and climate."

Anderson's rank as a leading American science-fiction writer was reinforced by his selection as coauthor in creating companion works to Frank Herbert's classic sci-fi novel, *Dune,* and its five sequels. Anderson first teamed with Herbert's son, Brian Herbert, to write *Dune: House Atreides,* and received for it the most lucrative contract ever signed by a science-fiction author. *House Atreides* has since been followed by several other "Dune" novels.

House Atreides and the subsequent *Dune: House Harkonnen* and *Dune: House Corrino* serve as a "prequel" trilogy to *Dune.* As such, the coauthors' first task was to explain some of the relationships and feuds behind the extremely intricate plot of the original book. Central to all characters and subplots is the vast wasteland of Dune, where nothing except "Spice" lives. Authors Anderson and Herbert won praise from a *Publishers Weekly* critic for their creation of a complex groundwork for lovers of the original *Dune.* The critic wrote, "The attendant excitement and myriad revelations not only make this novel a terrific read in its own right but will inspire readers to turn, or return, to its great predecessor." *New York Times Book Review* contributor Gerald Jonas thought Anderson and Herbert "fall far short of their model when describing action," but allowed that "the new work captures the sense of seriousness that distinguished the earlier works." Jonas added that *Dune* enthusiasts "will rejoice in this chance to return to one of science fiction's most appealing futures."

Of *Dune: House Harkonnen,* a *Publishers Weekly* reviewer stated, "Although myriad plot lines abound and plans are afoot in every Great House to bring down the Kwisatz's enemies, very little actually happens for much of the book." However, Jackie Cassada in *Library Journal* highly recommended the novel, stating that it offers "strong characterizations, consistent plotting, and rich detail" that allow for "the same evocative power of the original novels." Jonas remarked that *House Harkonnen* "succeeds admirably in setting the stage for the epic conflicts recounted" in Herbert's original "Dune" volumes.

In the concluding volume of the trilogy, *Dune: House Corrino,* a weak-willed emperor, head of the ruling House Corrino, is threatened by the devious Count Fenring, who learns of the location of a synthetic spice operation. In a *Booklist* review of the work, Roberta Johnson noted that the coauthors "draw emotional power from every character to fuel the complex political tale they tell."

BIOGRAPHICAL/CRITICAL SOURCES:

BOOKS

St. James Guide to Science-Fiction Writers, 4th edition, St. James Press (Detroit, MI), 1996.

PERIODICALS

Analog Science Fiction and Fact, May, 1991, Tom Easton, review of *Lifeline,* pp. 178-180; November, 1992, p. 161; January, 1995, p. 301; December, 1995, p. 162; August, 1996, Tom Easton, review of *Virtual Destruction,* p. 146; October, 1996, p. 145.

Booklist, August, 1992, p. 2028; February 15, 1993, Roland Green, review of *Assemblers of Infinity,* p. 1041; June 1, 1995, p. 1736; September 15, 1995, Carl Hays, review of *Darksaber,* p. 144; March 15, 1996, p. 1244; May 15, 1996, p. 1573; December 15, 1996; May 15, 2001, Roland Green, review of *Dogged Persistence,* p. 1738; August, 2001, Roberta Johnson, review of *Dune: House Corrino,* p. 2051.

Booktalker, November, 1990, p. 7.

Book Watch, December, 1995, p. 11; January, 1996, p. 10.

Kirkus Reviews, May 1, 1995, p. 570.

Kliatt, January, 1990, review of *Gameplay,* p. 16; May, 1993, Bette D. Ammon, review of *Assemblers of Infinity,* p. 12; May, 1994, Ingrid Von Hausen, review of *Jedi Search,* p. 13; July, 1994, p. 54; January, 1996, p. 12; March, 1996, p. 13; p. 51; spring, 1996, p. 55; May, 1996, Hugh M. Flick, review of *The Lost Ones,* p. 12; July, 1996, p. 16; November, 1996, p. 11.

Library Journal, December, 1990, p. 167; May 1, 1992, p. 133; June, 1995, p. 128; October 15, 1995, p. 91; May 15, 1996, p. 86; January, 1997, Grant A. Frederickson, review of *Ignition,* p. 141; October 15, 1999, Jackie Cassada, review of *Dune: House Atreides,* p. 109; June 1, 2000, p. 228; September 15, 2000, Jackie Cassada, review of *Dune: House Harkonnen,* p. 118.

Locus, February, 1989, p. 21; November, 1989, p. 53; October, 1990, p. 50; November, 1990, p. 21; December, 1990, p. 19; January, 1991, p. 54; February, 1991, p. 36; December, 1991, Dan Chow, review of *The Trinity Paradox,* p. 31; January, 1993, p. 27; July, 1993, p. 39; April, 1994, p. 47; August, 1994, Russell Letson, review of *Climbing Olympus,* p. 27.

Magazine of Fantasy and Science Fiction, November, 1988, p. 28; March, 1991, p. 18.

Monthly Review, October, 1996, p. 43.

Necro, fall, 1995, p. 25; spring, 1996, p. 26.

New York Times Book Review, November 28, 1999, Gerald Jonas, review of *Dune: House Atreides;* October 1, 2000, review of *Dune: House Harkonnen.*

Publishers Weekly, June 3, 1988, Barbara Bannon, review of *Resurrection, Inc.,* p. 83; February 7, 1994, p. 85; March 14, 1994, p. 69; May 15, 1995, p. 60; September 4, 1995, p. 54; February 12, 1996, p. 75; April 22, 1996; p. 63; May 13, 1996, p. 30; February 3, 1997, p. 25; February 10, 1997, p. 67; June 15, 1998, review of *Lethal Exposure,* p. 57; January 11, 1999, p. 20; August 30, 1999, review of *Dune: House Atreides,* p. 57; October 2, 2000, review of *Dune: House Harkonnen,* p. 63; May 21, 2001, review of *Dogged Persistence,* p. 86.

Quill & Quire, March, 1994, p. 7.

School Library Journal, December, 1994, p. 38.

Science Fiction Chronicle, September, 1988, p. 64; March, 1989, p. 38; September, 1990, p. 38; March, 1991, pp. 28, 30; May, 1991, p. 32; April, 1993, p. 30; February, 1994, p. 5; October, 1995, p. 45; December, 1995, p. 59; February, 1996, p. 46.

Voice of Youth Advocates, February, 1990, p. 369; August, 1993, Rosie Peasley, review of *Assemblers of Infinity,* p. 159; December, 1995, p. 283; October, 1996, p. 214.

Wilson Library Bulletin, November, 1990, p. 7.

OTHER

Kevin J. Anderson Web site, http://www.wordfire.com/ (June 7, 2001).*

*   *   *

ANDERSON, Martin 1936-

PERSONAL: Born August 5, 1936, in Lowell, MA; son of Ralph and Evelyn Anderson; married Annelise Graebner, September 9, 1965. *Education:* Dartmouth College, A.B. (summa cum laude), 1957, M.S., 1958; Massachusetts Institute of Technology, Ph.D., 1962.

ADDRESSES: Office—Hoover Institution, Stanford University, Stanford, CA 94305.

CAREER: Columbia University, Graduate School of Business Administration, New York, NY, assistant professor of finance, 1962-65, associate professor of business, 1965-68; special assistant and consultant to President Nixon, 1969-71; Stanford University, Hoover Institution, Stanford, CA, senior fellow, 1971—. Director of research for Nixon presidential campaign, 1968; senior advisor to Reagan presidential campaign, 1976 and 1980. Public interest director, Federal Home Loan Bank of San Francisco, 1972-79. Member of Commission on Critical Choices for America, 1973-75, Council on Trends and Perspectives, 1974-76, and 1981—, Defense Manpower Commission, 1975-76, Committee on the Present Danger, 1977—, President's Economic Policy Advisory Board, 1982—, and President's Foreign Intelligence Advisory Board, 1982—. Assistant to President Reagan for policy development, 1981-82. *Military service:* U.S. Army, Security Agency; became second lieutenant.

MEMBER: American Finance Association, American Economic Association, Phi Beta Kappa.

WRITINGS:

The Federal Bulldozer: A Critical Analysis of Urban Renewal, 1949-1962, Massachusetts Institute of Technology Press (Cambridge, MA), 1964.

(Editor) *Conscription,* Hoover Institution (Stanford, CA), 1976.

Welfare: The Political Economy of Welfare Reform in the United States, Hoover Institution (Stanford, CA), 1978.

(Editor) *Registration and the Draft,* Hoover Institution (Stanford, CA), 1982.

(Editor) *The Military Draft,* Hoover Institution (Stanford, CA), 1982.

An Economic Bill of Rights, Stanford University (Stanford, CA), 1984.

An Insurance Missile Defense, Stanford University (Stanford, CA), 1986.

Revolution, Harcourt (New York, NY), 1988, expanded and updated as *Revolution: The Reagan Legacy,* Stanford University (Stanford, CA), 1990.

Impostors in the Temple: A Blueprint for Improving Higher Education in America, Simon & Schuster (New York, NY), 1992.

The Ten Causes of the Reagan Boom, 1982-1997, Stanford University (Stanford, CA), 1997.

(Editor, with Kiron K. Skinner and wife, Annelise Graebner Anderson) *Reagan, in His Own Hand: The Writings of Ronald Reagan That Reveal His Revolutionary Vision for America,* foreword by George P. Schultz, Free Press (New York, NY), 2001.

SIDELIGHTS: Economist Martin Anderson, who served in both the Nixon and Reagan administrations, has written several books on economic and political issues, as well as authored a critique of higher education in the United States. In *Welfare: The Political Economy of Welfare Reform in the United States,* Anderson outlines various government attempts at welfare reform and undertakes to explain the reasons for the failure of these efforts. Writing in *National Review,* M. S. Evans called attention to Anderson's "diligence in research and gift for clarifying issues." An *Atlantic* reviewer wrote that *Welfare* is "clearly written and patiently argued. Anyone who can make economic analysis accessible to general readers, regardless of his doctrinal bias, deserves a respectful reading."

Anderson's books on President Reagan and his administration also drew significant interest. *Revolution* is his assessment of the Reagan years, which in his view strengthened world capitalism against socialism and communism. The book includes comments on campaign tactics, the Strategic Defense Initiative (SDI, commonly known as "Star Wars"), and the Iran-Contra affair. *Reagan, in His Own Hand: The Writings of Ronald Reagan That Reveal His Revolutionary Vision for America* presents a collection of radio scripts that Reagan wrote for broadcast between 1976 and 1980. Critics felt that the collection, which Anderson coedited with Kiron K. Skinner and his wife, Annelise Anderson, revealed Reagan as a skilled and thoughtful writer on a broad range of topics. Commenting on the intellectual level of the writings, *New York Times Book Review* contributor David Brooks observed "These are earnest policy sermons. Reagan covered everything from bilingual education to the Panama Canal to the political situation in Equatorial Guinea, engrossing himself in a level of detail that frankly surpasses that of almost all op-ed columnists today. . . . One of the things these commentaries do is blow apart the notion that Reagan was a flighty actor who floated through the presidency on the basis of charm and communication skills." Jay Nordinger, in *National Review,* commented that the book "proves that Reagan, in addition to the many other things he was, was a writer." *Washington Post Book World* reviewer Lou Cannon expressed a similar view, suggesting that the volume "drives a stake into the heart of the notion that the president was any kind of dunce."

Impostors in the Temple: A Blueprint for Improving Higher Education in America, Anderson's analysis of systemic flaws in the American higher education system, provoked considerable controversy. Some critics agreed with Anderson's assessment that elite universities are marked by corruption and emphasize frivolous research over quality teaching. Others considered his argument to be a politically motivated conservative attack on intellectual freedom as it is practiced on American campuses. *Reason* reviewer Charles K. Rowley, however, deemed *Impostors in the Temple* a "well documented, scholarly, and well written" analysis that is "persuasive concerning the decline and fall of the American academy." Helle Bering-Jensen, in *Insight on the News,* found *Impostors in the Temple* a forceful and persuasive book, and added that Anderson's "disgust with academic pretense and hypocrisy comes across . . . strongly." *Change* contributor Rosemary Park commented that "If it takes a book like this to catch the impostors, then so be it."

BIOGRAPHICAL/CRITICAL SOURCES:

PERIODICALS

American Political Science Review, September, 1989, Charles O. Jones, review of *Revolution: The Reagan Legacy,* p. 98.

American Spectator, July, 1991, Robert D. Novak, review of *Revolution,* p. 34; January, 1993, D. G. Myers, review of *Impostors in the Temple,* p. 94.

Atlantic, September, 1978.

Booklist, June 1, 1992, Gilbert Taylor, review of *Impostors in the Temple,* p. 1734.

Change, January-February, 1993, Rosemary Park, review of *Impostors in the Temple,* p. 53.

Christian Science Monitor, August 31, 1992, Laurel Shaper Walters, review of *Impostors in the Temple,* p. 14.

Chronicle of Higher Education, July 29, 1992, Peter Monaghan, review of *Impostors in the Temple,* p. A5.

Fortune, November 16, 1992, David R. Henderson, review of *Imposters in the Temple,* p. 196.

Insight on the News, September 21, 1992, Helle Bering-Jensen, review of *Impostors in the Temple,* p. 22.

Journal of American History, September, 1993, Jon Wiener, review of *Impostors in the Temple,* p. 757.

Monthly Review, April, 1990, Wassily Leontiff, "We Can't Take More of This 'Reagan Boom,' " p. 32.

National Review, July 23, 1978; November 10, 1978; August 17, 1992, Thomas Short, review of *Impostors in the Temple,* p. 50; February 19, 2001, Jay Nordinger, review of *Reagan, in His Own Hand: The Writings of Ronald Reagan That Reveal His Revolutionary Vision for America.*

New York Times Book Review, July 9, 1978; May 15, 1988, Garry Wills, review of *Revolution,* p. 3; August 9, 1992, Paul Starr, review of *Impostors in the Temple,* p. 10; January 28, 2001, David Brooks, review of *Reagan, in His Own Hand.*

Publishers Weekly, June 1, 1992, review of *Impostors in the Temple,* p. 44; January 8, 2001, review of *Reagan, in His Own Hand,* p. 62.

Reason, October, 1992, Charles K. Rowley, review of *Reagan, in His Own Hand,* p. 70.

Wall Street Journal, August 19, 1992, Richard K. Armey, review of *Impostors in the Temple,* p. A10.

Washington Monthly, September, 1992, Stanley Fish, review of *Impostors in the Temple,* p. 53.

Washington Post Book World, February 4, 2001, Lou Cannon, review of *Reagan, in His Own Hand,* p. 1.

* * *

ANTHONY, Piers   1934-
(Robert Piers, a joint pseudonym)

PERSONAL: Full name Piers Anthony Dillingham Jacob; born August 6, 1934, in Oxford, England; came to United States, 1940, naturalized U.S. citizen, 1958; son of Alfred Bennis and Norma (Sherlock) Jacob; married Carol Marble, June 23, 1956; children: Penelope Carolyn, Cheryl. *Education:* Goddard College, B.A., 1956; University of South Florida, teaching certificate, 1964. *Politics:* Independent. *Religion:* "No preference." *Avocational interests:* Tree farming, archery.

ADDRESSES: Office—c/o Tor Books, 175 Fifth Ave., New York, NY 10010.

CAREER: Novelist. Electronic Communications, Inc., St. Petersburg, FL, technical writer, 1959-62; freelance writer, 1962-63, 1966—; Admiral Farragut Academy, St. Petersburg, FL, teacher of English, 1965-66. *Military service:* U.S. Army, 1957-59.

MEMBER: Authors Guild, Authors League of America, National Writers Union.

AWARDS, HONORS: Nebula Award nomination, Science Fiction Writers of America, 1966, for short story "The Message"; Nebula Award nomination, 1967, and Hugo Award nomination, World Science Fiction Convention, 1968, both for *Chthon;* science fiction award, Pyramid Books/*Magazine of Fantasy and Science Fiction*/Kent Productions, 1967, and Hugo Award nominations, 1969, both for *Sos the Rope;* Hugo Award nomination, 1969, for novella *Getting through University,* and 1970, for *Macroscope;* Nebula Award nominations, 1970, for short story "The Bridge," and, 1972, for novelette *In the Barn;* British Fantasy Award, 1977, and Hugo Award nomination, 1978, both for *A Spell for Chameleon.*

WRITINGS:

SCIENCE FICTION

Chthon, Ballantine, 1967.
(With Robert E. Margroff) *The Ring,* Ace Books, 1968.
Macroscope, Avon, 1969.
(With Margroff) *The E.S.P. Worm,* Paperback Library, 1970.
Prostho Plus, Berkley, 1973.
Race against Time, Hawthorne, 1973.
Rings of Ice, Avon, 1974.
Triple Detente, DAW Books, 1974.
Phthor (sequel to *Chthon*), Berkley Publishing, 1975.
(With Robert Coulson) *But What of Earth?,* Laser (Toronto, Ontario, Canada), 1976, corrected edition, Tor Books, 1989.
(With Frances T. Hall) *The Pretender,* Borgo Press, 1979.
Mute, Avon, 1981.
Ghost, Tor Books, 1986.
Shade of the Tree, Tor Books, 1986.
(Editor with Barry Malzberg, Martin Greenberg, and Charles G. Waugh) *Uncollected Stars* (short stories), Avon, 1986.
Total Recall, Morrow, 1989.
Balook, illustrated by Patrick Woodroffe, Underwood-Miller, 1990.
Hard Sell, Tafford, 1990.
(With Roberto Fuentes) *Dead Morn,* Tafford, 1990.
MerCycle, illustrated by Ron Lindahn, Tafford, 1991.
(With Philip Jose Farmer) *Caterpillar's Question,* Ace Books, 1992.
Killobyte, Putnam, 1993.
The Willing Spirit, Tor Books, 1996.
Volk Internet 1996, Xlibris, 1997.
(With Clifford Pickover) *Spider Legs,* Tor, 1998.
(With J. R. Goolsby and Alan Riggs) *Quest for the Fallen Star,* Tor, 1998.
(With Julie Brady) *Dream a Little Dream,* Tor, 1999.
(With Jo An Taeusch) *The Secret of Spring,* Tor, 2000.
(With Ron Leming) *The Gutbucket Quest,* Tor, 2000.
Realty Check Pulpless, Xlibris, 2000.

"OMNIVORE" SERIES; SCIENCE-FICTION NOVELS

Omnivore, Ballantine, 1968.
Orn, Avon, 1971.
Ox, Avon, 1976.

"BATTLE CIRCLE" SERIES; SCIENCE-FICTION NOVELS

Sos the Rope, Pyramid, 1968.
Var the Stick, Faber, 1972.
Neq the Sword, Corgi, 1975.
Battle Circle (omnibus volume; contains *Sos the Rope, Var the Stick,* and *Neq the Sword*), Avon, 1978.

"CLUSTER" SERIES; SCIENCE-FICTION NOVELS

Cluster, Avon, 1977, published as *Vicinity Cluster,* Panther (London, England), 1979.
Chaining the Lady, Avon, 1978.
Kirlian Quest, Avon, 1978.
Thousandstar, Avon, 1980.
Viscous Circle, Avon, 1982.

"TAROT"; SCIENCE-FICTION TRILOGY

God of Tarot, Jove, 1979.
Vision of Tarot, Berkley Publishing, 1980.
Faith of Tarot, Berkley Publishing, 1980.
Tarot (contains *God of Tarot, Vision of Tarot,* and *Faith of Tarot*), Ace Books, 1988.

"BIO OF A SPACE TYRANT" SERIES; SCIENCE FICTION NOVELS

Refugee, Avon, 1983.
Mercenary, Avon, 1984.
Politician, Avon, 1985.
Executive, Avon, 1985.
Statesman, Avon, 1986.

FANTASY

Hasan, Borgo Press, 1977.
(With Robert Kornwise) *Through the Ice,* illustrated by D. Horne, Underwood-Miller, 1989.
(With Mercedes Lackey) *If I Pay Thee Not in Gold,* Baen, 1993.

"MAGIC OF XANTH" SERIES; FANTASY NOVELS

A Spell for Chameleon, Del Rey, 1977.
The Source of Magic, Del Rey, 1979.
Castle Roogna, Del Rey, 1979.
The Magic of Xanth (omnibus volume; contains *A Spell for Chameleon, The Source of Magic,* and *Castle*

Roogna), Doubleday, 1981, published as *Piers Anthony: Three Complete Xanth Novels,* Wings Books, 1994.
Centaur Aisle, Del Rey, 1982.
Ogre, Ogre, Del Rey, 1982.
Night Mare, Del Rey, 1983.
Dragon on a Pedestal, Del Rey, 1983.
Crewel Lye: A Caustic Yarn, Del Rey, 1985.
Golem in the Gears, Del Rey, 1986.
Vale of the Vole, Avon, 1987.
Heaven Cent, Avon, 1988.
Man from Mundania, Avon, 1989.
(With Jody Lynn Nye) *Piers Anthony's Visual Guide to Xanth,* illustrated by Todd Cameron Hamilton and James Clouse, Avon, 1989.
Isle of View, Morrow, 1990.
Question Quest, Morrow, 1991.
The Color of Her Panties, Avon, 1992.
Demons Don't Dream, Tor Books, 1993.
Harpy Thyme, Tor Books, 1994.
Geis of the Gargoyle, Tor Books, 1995.
Roc and a Hard Place, Tor Books, 1995.
Yon Ill Wind, Tor Books, 1996.
Faun and Games, Tor Books, 1997.
Zombie Lover, Tor Books, 1998.
Xone of Contention, Tor Books, 1999.
The Dastard, Tor Books, 2000.
Swell Foop, Tor Books, 2001.
Up in a Heaval, Tor Books, 2001.

"INCARNATIONS OF IMMORTALITY" SERIES; FANTASY NOVELS

On a Pale Horse, Del Rey, 1983.
Bearing an Hourglass, Del Rey, 1984.
With a Tangled Skein, Del Rey, 1985.
Wielding a Red Sword, Del Rey, 1986.
Being a Green Mother, Del Rey, 1987.
For Love of Evil, Morrow, 1988.
And Eternity, Morrow, 1990.

"DRAGON'S GOLD" SERIES; FANTASY NOVELS

(With Robert E. Margroff) *Dragon's Gold,* Tor Books, 1987.
(With Robert E. Margroff) *Serpent's Silver,* Tor Books, 1988.
(With Robert E. Margroff) *Chimaera's Copper,* Tor Books, 1990.
(With Robert E. Margroff) *Orc's Opal,* Tor Books, 1990.
(With Robert E. Margroff) *Mouvar's Magic,* Tor Books, 1992.

(With Robert E. Margroff) *Three Complete Novels* (contains *Dragon's Gold, Serpent's Silver,* and *Chimaera's Copper*), Wings Books, 1993.

"APPRENTICE ADEPT" SERIES; SCIENCE-FICTION/FANTASY NOVELS

Split Infinity, Del Rey, 1980.
Blue Adept, Del Rey, 1981.
Juxtaposition, Del Rey, 1982.
Double Exposure (omnibus volume; contains *Split Infinity, Blue Adept,* and *Juxtaposition*), Doubleday, 1982.
Out of Phaze, Ace Books, 1987.
Robot Adept, Ace Books, 1988.
Unicorn Point, Ace Books, 1989.
Phaze Doubt, Ace Books, 1990.

"MODE" SERIES; SCIENCE FICTION/FANTASY NOVELS

Virtual Mode, Putnam, 1991.
Fractal Mode, Putnam, 1992.
Chaos Mode, Putnam, 1993.
DoOon Mode, Tor Books, 2001.

"JASON STRIKER" SERIES; MARTIAL ARTS NOVELS

(With Roberto Fuentes) *Kiai!,* Berkley Publishing, 1974.
(With Roberto Fuentes) *Mistress of Death,* Berkley Publishing, 1974.
(With Roberto Fuentes) *The Bamboo Bloodbath,* Berkley Publishing, 1974.
(With Roberto Fuentes) *Ninja's Revenge,* Berkley Publishing, 1975.
(With Roberto Fuentes) *Amazon Slaughter,* Berkley Publishing, 1976.

"GEODYSSEY" SERIES; HISTORICAL SCIENCE FICTION

Isle of Woman, Tor Books, 1993.
Shame of Man, Tor Books, 1994.
Hope of Earth, Tor Books, 1997.
Muse of Art, Tor Books, 1999.

Also author of *Climate of Change,* in progress.

OTHER

Steppe (science fiction/history), Millington, 1976, Tor Books, 1985.
Anthonology (short stories), Tor Books, 1985.
Bio of an Ogre: The Autobiography of Piers Anthony to Age Fifty, Ace Books, 1988.
Pornucopia (erotic fantasy), Tafford, 1989.

Firefly (novel), Morrow, 1990, Avon, 1992.
Tatham Mound (historical fiction), Morrow, 1991.
Alien Plot (short stories), Tor Books, 1992.
Letters to Jenny (nonfiction), Tor Books, 1993.
(Editor with Richard Gilliam) *Tales from the Great Turtle,* Tor Books, 1994.
How Precious Was That While (memoir), Tor Books, 2001.

Contributor to *Science against Man,* edited by Anthony Cheetham, Avon, 1970; *Nova One: An Anthology of Original Science Fiction,* edited by Harry Harrison, Delacorte Press, 1970; *Again, Dangerous Visions,* edited by Harlan Ellison, Doubleday, 1972; *Generation,* edited by David Gerrold, Dell, 1972; and *The Berkley Showcase,* edited by Victoria Schochet and John Silbersack, Berkley Publishing, 1981. Also contributor, with Robert E. Margroff under joint pseudonym Robert Piers, of a short story to *Adam Bedside Reader.* Contributor of short stories to periodicals, including *Analog, Fantastic, Worlds of If, Worlds of Tomorrow, Amazing, Magazine of Fantasy and Science Fiction, SF Age, Vegetarian Times, Twilight Zone, Books and Bookmen, Writer, Gauntlet, Chic, Far Point, Starburst, Vertex,* and *Pandora.*

ADAPTATIONS: Macroscope, A Spell for Chameleon, The Source of Magic, Castle Roogna, Through the Ice, Virtual Mode, and *Fractal Mode* have been adapted to audio cassette.

SIDELIGHTS: Within a childhood affected by illness and isolation, prolific science fiction and fantasy author Piers Anthony escaped by immersing himself in books. "From the time I was 13, I had been hooked on science fiction," Anthony recalled in an interview with the *Science Fiction Radio Show* (*SFRS*) published in *The Sound of Wonder.* "It's what I did for entertainment. It was a whole different world, multiple worlds, each one of them better than the one I knew. And so when I thought about writing [science fiction], I thought I could be original because I had read everything in the field." He began to write at age twenty, deciding in college to make writing his career. As an adult, Anthony's escape became his livelihood. His many popular series—including the ongoing "Magic of Xanth" novels—and his various novels and collections add up to more than one hundred books since 1967. "I am an SF writer today," he told Cliff Biggers in a *Science Fiction* interview, "because without SF and writing I would be nothing at all today."

Among the traumatic events of Anthony's youth were his family's moves to Spain when he was five and to

the United States the next year, the loss of his cousin to cancer at fifteen, and his parents' divorce at eighteen. As members of the Quaker faith, his parents were involved with the British Friends Service Committee during the Spanish Civil War, and Anthony spent the first years of his life in England under the care of his grandparents and a nanny. When he and his sister joined his parents after the war, they "seemed like acquaintances rather than close kin," the author recounted in his *Something about the Author Autobiography Series* (*SAAS*) entry. The family soon moved to the United States, where Anthony found it difficult to fit in. He often had to deal with bullies at school, and this compounded the alienation he suffered because of his parents' divorce. "The dominant emotion of my later childhood was fear," he recalled in his essay. "Fear of bigger kids at school, of a monster in the forest, and fear of the corpse. Fear, really, of life. I hated being alone, but others neither understood nor cared, so I was alone a lot. That is, often physically, and almost always emotionally. Today when I get a letter from a reader who feels almost utterly alone, I understand, because I remember."

In addition, the young Anthony had difficulty at school. "Everyone in my immediate family was academically gifted except me," he continued in *SAAS.* "I was the dunce who made up for it all, pulling the average down." It wasn't until he was an adult that he discovered his academic problems had been due to some type of learning disability; "in my day things like learning disabilities or dyslexia didn't exist, just stupid or careless children." Nevertheless, encouraged by his parents, who read and told stories to him, Anthony became a regular reader. "I think that nightly reading, and the daytime storytelling when we worked together outside, was the most important influence on my eventual choice of career. I knew that books contained fascinating adventures, and those stories took me away from my dreary real life."

After eight years of submitting stories to magazines, Anthony sold his first piece, "Possible to Rue," to *Fantastic* in 1962. In the next several years, he worked variously as a freelance writer and English teacher, but finally decided to devote all of his time to writing. *Chthon,* Anthony's first novel, was published in 1967, received numerous award nominations, and caught the attention of both critics and readers in the science fiction genre. The next year brought a prize from a contest jointly sponsored by Pyramid Books, Kent Productions, and the *Magazine of Fantasy and Science Fiction* for *Sos the Rope,* the first entry in the "Battle Circle" series.

Chthon traces the escape efforts of Aton Five, imprisoned on the planet Chthon and forced to work in its garnet mines. A *Publishers Weekly* reviewer commented on the many elements of the book, including language, myth, suspense, and symbolism, "a bursting package, almost too much for one book, but literate, original and entertaining." Those elements—and Anthony's liberal use of them—would become his trademark. In a detailed analysis of *Chthon* and its sequel, *Phthor,* in his study *Piers Anthony,* Michael R. Collings noted Anthony's liberal references to mythological symbols. Literary references are present as well, exemplified by the resemblance of the prison caverns of Chthon to Dante's depiction of Hell in *The Inferno.* In *Chthon,* "Anthony has created a whole new world, a dream universe which you find yourself living in and, after a while, understanding," Leo Harris declared in *Books and Bookmen.* "Very poetic and tough and allegorical it all is, and it will rapidly have thee in thrall." While *Chthon* focuses on Aton's life, *Phthor* follows Aton's son, Arlo, who symbolizes Thor of Norse mythology. "The mythologies embedded in *Chthon* and *Phthor* go far beyond mere ornamentation or surface symbolism," Collings noted. "They define the thematic content of the novels. Initially, there is a clear demarcation between myth and reality. Yet early in *Chthon* Anthony throws that clear demarcation into question."

Anthony's first trilogy begins with *Sos the Rope,* based on a chapter of his 1956 B.A. thesis novel titled "The Unstilled World." The first installment of the "Battle Circle" books, *Sos the Rope* explores the efforts of a group of radiation survivors led by Sos as they attempt to rebuild their society after the Blast. Yet the resulting Empire soon becomes a destructive force and Sos sets out to destroy it. The novel speaks against the dangers of centralized civilization and overpopulation: millions of shrews, like the Biblical plague of locusts, invade the area and consume every living creature within their reach. Eventually the horde destroys itself with its enormity and its wholesale pillaging. The shrews' rampage and ultimate demise serve as a metaphor for man's overcrowding and abuse of the environment. Humankind, like the shrews, will be decimated when it outgrows the Earth's ability to sustain it. In *Var the Stick* and *Neq the Sword,* the "Battle Circle" story is completed. The books' titles are actually characters' names; the trilogy's warriors are named after their weapons. Collings observed similarities to the epic works of Homer, Virgil, and John Milton in "Battle Circle," which "investigates the viability of three fundamental forms of epic: the Achilean epic of martial prowess; the Odyssean epic of wandering; and the Virgillian/Miltonic epic of self-sacrifice and restoration."

The "Omnivore" trilogy provided a forum for Anthony to further his exploration of the dangers humankind continues to inflict upon itself, and introduced his support of vegetarianism. "Like *Battle Circle, Chthon,* and *Phthor,*" Collings observed, "*Omnivore* deals with control—specifically, with controlling the most dangerous omnivore of all, man." Three interplanetary explorers, the herbivorous Veg, carnivorous Cal, and omnivorous Aquilon, play out Anthony's views. The three journey to the planet Nacre, reporting back to investigator Subble and subsequently revealing to readers their adventures and clues to the secret threatening to destroy Earth. In the sequel, *Orn,* the three explorers venture to the planet Paleo, which resembles the Earth of sixty five million years past, and encounter Orn, a creature whose racial memory endows it with the knowledge of its ancestors and enables it to survive the changes bombarding its planet. In *Ox,* the final volume of the trilogy, Veg, Cal, and Aquilon gradually uncover the existence of a sentient super-computer while exploring alternate worlds. As with other Anthony books, reviewers noted that the "Omnivore" volumes contain substantial discussions of technical and scientific issues. A *Publishers Weekly* reviewer described *Ox* as "a book for readers willing to put a lot of concentration into reading it." The similarly complex *Macroscope,* described by Collings as "one of Anthony's most ambitious and complex novels," seeks to place man in his proper context within the galaxy. The book increased Anthony's reputation but, due to a publisher's error, was not submitted for consideration for the important Nebula Award and lost one crucial source of publicity. Nevertheless, *Macroscope* was a milestone in Anthony's career. In a *Luna Monthly* review, Samuel Mines declared, "*Macroscope* recaptures the tremendous glamour and excitement of science fiction, pounding the reader into submission with the sheer weight of its ideas which seem to pour out in an inexhaustible flood."

Beginning with the "Cluster" series, Anthony began writing "trilogies" that expanded past the usual three books. "Cluster" became a series of five, and the still-active "Magic of Xanth" has been supplemented by the companion book *Piers Anthony's Visual Guide to Xanth.* The "Apprentice Adept" series, with seven entries published between 1980 and 1990, was also originally planned as a trilogy. In the case of the "Xanth" books, Anthony attributed his decision to continue the series to reader response. "We did a third [Xanth novel], and said, 'Let's wrap it up as a trilogy and not do any more,' " Anthony remarked to *SFRS.* "Then the readers started demanding more, and more, and more, and finally both the publisher and the author were convinced. It's hard to say 'No' when the readers are begging for more."

Anthony branched out from science fiction into fantasy writing with *A Spell for Chameleon,* the first of the "Xanth" books, published in 1977. Although one early work, *Hasan,* was fantasy, it was his second fantasy novel, *Chameleon,* that established Anthony in the genre. The switch to fantasy came as a result of Anthony's much-publicized split with his first publisher, Ballantine Books. As the author related to *SFRS,* Ballantine "was sending me statements-of-account that were simply not true. I sent a letter demanding a correct statement and correct payments. Rather than do that, they blacklisted me for six years." Anthony moved to Avon Books; six years later, with a new administration at Ballantine, the author found himself invited back and wanted to give Ballantine another chance. His contract at Avon, however, prohibited him from writing science fiction for another publisher, so he decided to try fantasy. Luckily, Anthony knew and liked the fantasy editor at Ballantine, Lester del Rey; Ballantine's Del Rey imprint went on to publish the first nine "Xanth" novels as well as the early "Apprentice Adept" and "Incarnations of Immortality" entries. Anthony differentiates between his science-fiction and fantasy works in their content as well as their popularity. "For the challenge and sheer joy of getting in and tackling a difficult problem and surmounting it, science fiction is better," Anthony remarked to *SFRS.* "But if I need money, fantasy is better." He later added, "I talk about writing fantasy in the sense of doing it for the money, but I also enjoy it. If I didn't enjoy it, I wouldn't do it for the money."

The "Xanth" series is still continuing, over two decades after its first book. The "Xanth" stories are generally less complex and easier to read than Anthony's earlier works, appealing to younger readers as well as adults. *A Spell for Chameleon,* a 1978 Hugo Award nominee, introduced Bink, who tackles another recurring topic in Anthony's novels: maturity and control. The first "Xanth" installment chronicles Bink's growing-up; later volumes feature his son, Dor. The land of Xanth, which closely resembles the state of Florida, is a place where everyone and everything—even a rock or tree—has a magical talent, except Bink. *Chameleon* follows Bink on his quest to discover his talent or face exile to the boring, powerless land of Mundania. In the process, Bink gains not only knowledge of his talent but emotional maturity as well. Bink sets out on another adventure in *The Source of Magic,* assigned to discover the source of all magic in Xanth. In *Castle Roogna,* Bink's son Dor travels eight hundred years back in time to rescue his nurse's boyfriend. Throughout each book, Bink

and Dor encounter innumerable illusions and feats of magic. "Piers Anthony apparently decided to invest his magical land of Xanth with every fantastical conception ever invented," a reviewer for *Isaac Asimov's Science Fiction Magazine* remarked. "It has quests, enchanted castles, riddles, unicorns, griffins, mermaids, giants (not to mention invisible giants), zombies, ghosts, elves, magicians, man-eating trees, enchantresses, and a host of inventions from Anthony's own fertile mind."

"The Magic of Xanth" continued with *Centaur Aisle, Ogre, Ogre,* and *Night Mare,* the next "trilogy" of "Xanth" books. The first of these finds Dor filling in for Xanth's King Trent while he and Queen Iris take a trip to Mundania, good experience for Dor since he will one day become king. When the king and queen fail to return, Dor sets out on another adventure. Anthony once again explores the process of maturing, as Dor leads a search party through Xanth and into Mundania, and falls in love with Princess Irene. In *Ogre, Ogre,* the half-human, half-ogre Smash must protect the half-human, half-nymph Tandy. A stupid, insensitive creature at the beginning of the tale, Smash gradually acquires more human traits until he finally realizes that he is in love with Tandy.

Later entries in the series added to Anthony's portrait of the fantastic land of Xanth, with storylines including the rescue of the kingdom by a creature responsible for delivering bad dreams (*Night Mare*), the adventures of three-year-old Princess Ivy, lost and wandering in the forest with newfound friends Hugo and the Gap Dragon (*Dragon on a Pedestal*), the diminutive Golem's quest to rescue a lost baby dragon and prove himself worthy of attention (*Golem in the Gears*), Prince Dolph's protest against the Adult Conspiracy that keeps children ignorant of adult matters (*Heaven Cent*), Princess Ivy's trip to Mundania in search of Good Magician Humfrey (*Man from Mundania*), and the search of Gloha, Xanth's only half-harpy/half-goblin, for advice from Magician Trent to further a quest for her true love (*Harpy Thyme*). Richard Mathews applauded the "Xanth" series in *Fantasy Review,* asserting that it "ranks with the best of American and classic fantasy literature."

Anthony's use of puns and other language tricks is a hallmark of the "Xanth" novels. "In Xanth," Collings noted, Anthony "incorporates much of this interest in language in furthering the plot and in establishing the essence of his fantasy universe. In Xanth, language is literal, especially what in Mundania would be called metaphors." As a result, the critic continued, "breadfruit bears loaves of bread; shoetrees bear shoes in varying sizes and styles; nickelpedes are like centipedes, only five times larger and more vicious; and sunflowers are flowers whose blossoms are tiny suns blazing at the top of the stalk—a potent weapon if an enemy looks directly at them." In a *Voice of Youth Advocates* review of *Ogre, Ogre,* Peggy Murray found that Anthony's stories, "full of sophomoric humor and bad puns, have tremendous appeal with YA fantasy readers." In fact, some of the puns in *Harpy Thyme* were sent to Anthony by his readers.

In the *Sarasota Herald Tribune,* Cindy Cannon commented, "I can't think of a better place to meet up with centaurs, merfolk, zombies, ghosts, magically-talented humans and assorted half-breeds of every shape and kind than in one of Piers Anthony's many Xanth novels." She also noted that since the beginning of the series in 1977, the "original characters have seen several generations of their offspring star in their own tales (or tails, if they be centaurs)." And, she notes, "Where else will you hit an imp ass, eat pun-kin pies, see a river bank lien or meet a character named Ann Arky?" Amusingly, Anthony, who lives in Inverness, Florida, has made Xanth the same size and shape as his home state, and place names in Xanth are often wittily twisted versions of Floridian ones.

Cluster, the first novel in the series of the same name, was published in the same year as the first "Xanth" book. Intergalactic travel and adventure are again the subjects in the "Cluster" books, in which Anthony introduces the concept of Kirlian transfer, a type of out-of-body travel that requires much less energy than the outmoded "mattermission." The Kirlian transfer and other innovations are fundamental to the outcomes of the First and Second Wars of Energy, described in the first two volumes, and to the battle of an intergalactic force against the space amoeba in *Kirlian Quest.* "More than anything, the Cluster series is an exercise in enjoyment" for Anthony, Collings remarked. The author relishes the opportunity to create bizarre beings and situations unlike any the reader has experienced. The original "Cluster" trilogy led to *Tarot,* published in three volumes as *God of Tarot, Vision of Tarot,* and *Faith of Tarot.*

From the ending of *Kirlian Quest,* Anthony created *Tarot,* which he had intended for publication as one volume. Anthony emphasized in his interview with *SFRS* that *Tarot* is not a trilogy, but "a quarter-million-word novel." The novel was published not only in three parts, but in two different years. "It bothered me because I feel that this is the major novel of my career," Anthony remarked in the *SFRS* interview published in

1985. "Split into three parts and published in two years—it washed me out totally. I had no chance to make a run for any awards or anything like that. It was simply gone." He resents referrals to the book as a trilogy because they imply that each volume is a full novel, when in fact they are each one-third of a novel. Brother Paul, a character introduced in the "Cluster" trilogy and featured in *But What of Earth?,* is the central figure in *Tarot,* in which Anthony attempts to develop a definition of God. Collings acknowledged that the "brutality, horror, and disgust" present in the book were not unlike those of many other Anthony novels, but combined with religious references proved controversial and offensive to many readers. *Tarot* "is certainly not for the squeamish, nor is it altogether for those who enjoyed the first installment of Tarot civilization in the Cluster novels. Anthony himself admits this," Collings noted.

Anthony returns to pure fantasy in the "Incarnations of Immortality" series, which begins with *On a Pale Horse* and is set in "a world very much like ours, except that magic has been systematized and is as influential as science," a *Publishers Weekly* reviewer commented. The abstract concepts of Time, War, Nature, Fate, and Death are all real people—the Incarnations—and all are involved in the battle of Satan against God. In *Bearing an Hourglass,* a grief-stricken man agrees to take on the role of Chronos, the Incarnation of Time, and soon finds himself locked in a battle with Satan. *Booklist* reviewer Roland Green noted the religious and ethical content of the series that "even people who may disagree with [Anthony's] ideas will recognize as intelligently rendered." Subsequent volumes feature the Incarnations of Fate (*With a Tangled Skein*), War (*Wielding a Red Sword*), Nature (*Being a Green Mother*), Evil (*For Love of Evil*), and finally, Good (*And Eternity*). "This grand finale showcases Anthony's multiple strengths" including his humor, characterizations, and themes, a *Library Journal* reviewer declared.

Virtual Mode is a novel "to which teens relate well," Anthony remarked to *Authors and Artists for Young Adults (AAYA).* Published in 1991, *Virtual Mode* introduced the "Mode" series, in which characters traverse the universe through the use of "skew paths" anchored by other people. As the anchors change, the paths and destinies of the travelers are affected and new stories are presented. In *Virtual Mode,* Darius of Hlahtar ventures to Earth to bring the girl he loves, the suicidal Colene, back to his universe. Together Darius and Colene discover that they must build a skew path to complete the journey. *Publishers Weekly* writer Sybil Steinberg described Colene as "a clearly defined character, virtues, flaws and all" who is "brought fully to life in this skillful, enjoyable book."

Similarly, YA readers will enjoy *MerCycle,* Anthony's story about five people recruited to pedal bicycles under the waters of the Gulf of Mexico on a secret mission to save the Earth from collision with a meteor. The novel was originally written in 1971 but then shelved after it was unable to find a publisher. After establishing his reputation as a best-selling author, Anthony returned to the manuscript, revised it extensively, and added it to his oeuvre. The story deals heavily with themes of human nature and survival: the bicyclists experience being "out of phase" and "phased in" to other Earth life, are kept unaware of their mission, and meet up with Chinese mermaids. "The result," wrote a critic in *New York Times Book Review,* "is an engaging tall tale, spun out of the most unpromising raw material."

According to *AAYA,* Anthony noted that, like *Virtual Mode, Tatham Mound* is another of his works most likely to appeal to young adults. The story of fifteen-year-old Throat Shot, a sixteenth-century Florida Indian, *Tatham Mound* is based on an actual Indian burial mound discovered in North Florida and features historically accurate reconstructions of Spanish explorer Hernando de Soto's march across Florida and his battles with the Indian tribes of the area. A *Library Journal* reviewer described *Tatham Mound* as a "heartfelt tribute to a lost culture" and a "labor of both love and talent."

Also based on history, but spanning eight million years, are the works in the "Geodyssey" series—*Isle of Woman* and *Shame of Man. Isle of Woman* is comprised of a series of vignettes that center on the lives of two prehistoric families who are reborn into succeeding centuries up to twenty-first century America. According to Jackie Cassada in a *Library Journal* review, *Isle of Woman* is Anthony's "most ambitious project to date." *Shame of Man* explores evolution one generation at a time, beginning with families of gorillas and chimpanzees on through the Homo Sapiens of 2050 A.D. Called "speculative fiction" by *Voice of Youth Advocates* reviewer Kim Carter, *Shame of Man* encompasses more than twenty-five years of Anthony's research in "history, archaeology, anthropology, and human nature," as well as showcasing some of the author's own theories on these subjects.

In *How Precious Was That While,* a sequel to his earlier autobiography, *Bio of an Ogre,* Anthony noted that the response of his readers means far more to him than any comments made by literary critics. He is devoted to his many readers, and often spends two days a week answering their letters.

Virtual Mode, Tatham Mound, and *Shame of Man* exemplify Anthony's desire to produce works of lasting value along with those written simply for entertainment. While he wants readers to enjoy his work, the author hopes also to provoke contemplation of the serious issues he presents. "I'd like to think I'm on Earth for some purpose other than just to feed my face," Anthony remarked to *SFRS.* "I want to do something and try to leave the universe a better place than it was when I came into it." He commented in the *St. Petersburg Times,* "Today, I am turning back to serious writing with direct comment on sexual abuse in *Firefly* and on history in novels like *Tatham Mound.*"

BIOGRAPHICAL/CRITICAL SOURCES:

BOOKS

Authors and Artists for Young Adults, Volume 11, Gale (Detroit, MI), 1993, pp. 9-19.
Collings, Michael R., *Piers Anthony,* Starmont House, 1983.
Contemporary Literary Criticism, Volume 35, Gale (Detroit, MI), 1985, pp. 34-41.
Lane, Daryl, William Vernon, and David Carson, *The Sound of Wonder: Interviews from "The Science Fiction Radio Show,"* Volume 2, Oryx, 1985.
Something about the Author Autobiography Series, Volume 22, Gale (Detroit, MI), 1996.

PERIODICALS

Analog, January, 1989, p. 182; August, 1992, pp. 165-166.
Booklist, July, 1984, p. 1497; October 15, 1999, p. 424; April 15, 2000, p. 1527; October 15, 2000, p. 426; March 1, 2001, p. 1232.
Books and Bookmen, April, 1970, pp. 26-27.
Fantasy and Science Fiction, August, 1986, pp. 37-40.
Fantasy Review, March, 1984, pp. 24-25.
Horn Book, October 6, 1989, p. 84.
Isaac Asimov's Science Fiction Magazine, September, 1979, p. 18.
Kirkus Reviews, August 15, 1993, p. 1034.
Kliatt, November, 1992, p. 13.
Library Journal, December, 1989, p. 176; August, 1991, p. 150; October 15, 1998, p. 104; September 15, 1993, p. 108; January, 1999, p. 166; October 15, 1999, p. 111; May 15, 2000, p. 129; October 15, 2000, p. 108; April 15, 2001, p. 137.
Luna Monthly, September, 1970, p. 22.

New York Times Book Review, April 20, 1986, p. 27; September 13, 1992, p. 28.

Publishers Weekly, June 5, 1967, p. 180; July 26, 1976, p. 78; September 2, 1983, p. 72; July 25, 1986, p. 174; August 29, 1986, p. 388; May 29, 1987, p. 73; February 10, 1989, p. 58; August 11, 1989, p. 444; August 25, 1989, p. 58; April 20, 1990, p. 61; May 11, 1990, p. 251; August 10, 1990, p. 431; December 21, 1990, p. 57; January 4, 1991, p. 61; October 18, 1991, p. 55; July 20, 1992, p. 237; November 29, 1993, pp. 57-58; September 5, 1994, p. 96; September 21, 1998, p. 79; December 14, 1998, p. 61; April 26, 1999, p. 61; September 27, 1999, p. 78; March 6, 2000, p. 88; May 1, 2000, p. 55; October 2, 2000, p. 64; March 5, 2001, p. 66; July 23, 2001, p. 59.

Sarasota Herald Tribune, November 26, 2000, p. E4; July 23, 2001, p. 59.

Science Fiction, November, 1977, p. 60.

St. Petersburg Times, July 13, 2001, p. P5.

Voice of Youth Advocates, April, 1983, p. 44; December, 1992, p. 290; August, 1994, p. 152; February, 1995, p. 343.

Writer, August, 1989, pp. 11-13, 35.

Writer's Digest, January, 1991, p. 32.

OTHER

Piers Anthony's Web site, http://www.hipiers.com/ (August 20, 2001).*

* * *

John Ashbery

ASHBERY, John (Lawrence) 1927-
(Jonas Berry)

PERSONAL: Born July 28, 1927, in Rochester, NY; son of Chester Frederick (a farmer) and Helen (a biology teacher) Ashbery. *Education:* Deerfield Academy, graduated 1945; Harvard University, B.A., 1949; Columbia University, M.A., 1951; graduate study at New York University, 1957-58.

ADDRESSES: Office—Department of Languages & Literature, Bard College, P.O. Box 5000, Annandale-on-Hudson, NY 12504-5000. *Agent*—Georges Borchardt, Inc., 136 East 57th St., New York, NY 10022.

CAREER: Writer, critic, and editor. Worked as reference librarian for Brooklyn Public Library, Brooklyn, NY; Oxford University Press, New York, NY, copywriter, 1951-54; McGraw-Hill Book Co., New York,

NY, copywriter, 1954-55; New York University, New York, NY, instructor in elementary French, 1957-58; *Locus Solus,* Lans-en-Vercors, France, editor, 1960-62; *New York Herald-Tribune,* European Edition, Paris, France, art critic, 1960-65; *Art International,* Lugano, Switzerland, art critic, 1961-64; *Art and Literature,* Paris, France, editor, 1963-66; *Art News,* New York, NY, Paris correspondent, 1964-65, executive editor in New York, NY, 1965-72; *New York Magazine,* art critic, 1975-80; *Partisan Review,* poetry editor, 1976-80; *Newsweek,* art critic, 1980-85. Brooklyn College of the City University of New York, Brooklyn, NY, professor of English and codirector of M.F.A. program in creative writing, 1974-90, distinguished professor, 1980-90, distinguished emeritus professor, 1990; Harvard University, Cambridge, MA, Charles Eliot Norton Professor of Poetry, 1989-90; Bard College, Annandale-on-Hudson, NY, Charles P. Stevenson, Jr. Professor of Languages and Literature, 1990—. Has read his poetry at the Living Theatre, New York, NY, and at numerous universities, including Yale University, University of Chicago, and University of Texas. Has conducted special research on the life and work of Raymond Roussel.

MEMBER: American Academy and Institute of Arts and Letters, American Academy of Arts and Sciences; Academy of American Poets (chancellor, 1988-99).

AWARDS, HONORS: Discovery Prize co-winner, Young Men's Hebrew Association, 1952; Fulbright scholarships to France, 1955-56 and 1956-57; Yale Series of Younger Poets Prize, 1956, for *Some Trees;* Poets' Foundation grants, 1960 and 1964; Ingram-Merrill Foundation grants, 1962 and 1972; Harriet Monroe Poetry Award, *Poetry,* 1963; Union League Civic and Arts Foundation Prize, *Poetry,* 1966; National Book Award nomination, 1966, for *Rivers and Mountains;* Guggenheim fellowships, 1967 and 1973; National Endowment for the Arts grants, 1968 and 1969; National Institute of Arts and Letters Award, 1969; Shelley Memorial Award, Poetry Society of America, 1973, for *Three Poems;* Frank O'Hara Prize, Modern Poetry Association, 1974; Harriet Monroe Poetry Award, University of Chicago, 1975; Pulitzer Prize, National Book Award, and National Book Critics Circle Award, all 1976, all for *Self-Portrait in a Convex Mirror;* Levinson Prize, *Poetry,* 1977; Rockefeller Foundation grant in playwriting, 1978; D.Litt., Southampton College of Long Island University, 1979; Phi Beta Kappa Poet, Harvard University, 1979; English-Speaking Union Poetry Award, 1979; American Book Award nomination, 1982, for *Shadow Train;* Academy of American Poets fellowship, 1982; Mayor's Award of Honor for Arts and Culture, City of New York, 1983; Charles Flint Kellogg Award in Arts and Letters, Bard College, 1983; National Book Critics Circle award nomination, and *Los Angeles Times* Book Award nomination, both 1984, both for *A Wave;* named Poet of the Year, Pasadena City College, 1984; Bollingen prize (corecipient), 1985, for body of work; Wallace Stevens fellowship, Yale University, 1985; MacArthur Foundation fellowship, 1985-90; *Los Angeles Times* Book Award nomination, 1986, for *Selected Poems;* Common Wealth Award, 1986; Lenore Marshall award, *Nation,* 1986, for *A Wave;* Creative Arts Award in Poetry, Brandeis University, 1989; Ruth Lilly Poetry Prize, *Poetry* magazine, 1992; Robert Frost medal, Poetry Society of America, 1995; Grand Prix des Biennales Internationales de Poesie, 1996; Gold Medal for Poetry, American Academy of Arts and Letters, 1997; Walt Whitman citation of merit, New York State Writers Institute; Signet Society Medal for Achievement in the Arts, Harvard University, 2001; named New York state poet, 2001-02.

WRITINGS:

Turandot and Other Poems (chapbook), Tibor de Nagy Gallery, 1953.

Some Trees (poems), foreword by W. H. Auden, Yale University Press (New Haven, CT), 1956, Ecco Press (Hopewell, NJ), 1978.

The Poems, Tiber Press (New York, NY), 1960.

The Tennis Court Oath (poems), Wesleyan University Press (Middletown, CT), 1962.

Rivers and Mountains (poems), Holt (New York, NY), 1966.

Selected Poems, J. Cape (London, England), 1967.

Sunrise in Suburbia, Phoenix Bookshop (New York, NY), 1968.

Three Madrigals, Poet's Press, 1969.

(With James Schuyler) *A Nest of Ninnies* (novel), Dutton (New York, NY), 1969.

Fragment (poem; also see below), Black Sparrow Press (Santa Barbara, CA), 1969.

Evening in the Country, Spanish Main Press, 1970.

The Double Dream of Spring (includes "Fragment," originally published in book form), Dutton (New York, NY), 1970.

The New Spirit, Adventures in Poetry, 1970.

(With Lee Hawood and Tom Raworth) *Penguin Modern Poets 19,* Penguin (New York, NY), 1971.

Three Poems, Viking (New York, NY), 1972.

The Serious Doll, privately printed, 1975.

(With Joe Brainard) *The Vermont Notebook* (poems), Black Sparrow Press (Santa Barbara, CA), 1975.

Self-Portrait in a Convex Mirror (poems), Viking (New York, NY), 1975.

Houseboat Days (poems), Viking (New York, NY), 1977, reprinted, Farrar, Straus (New York, NY), 1999.

As We Know (poems), Viking (New York, NY), 1979.

Shadow Train: Fifty Lyrics, Viking (New York, NY), 1981.

(With others) *R. B. Kitaj: Paintings, Drawings, Pastels,* Smithsonian Institution (Washington, DC), 1981.

(With others) *Apparitions* (poems), Lord John Press (Northridge, CA), 1981.

Fairfield Porter: Realist Painter in an Age of Abstraction, New York Graphic Society (New York, NY), 1983.

A Wave (poems), Viking (New York, NY), 1984.

Selected Poems, Viking (New York, NY), 1985.

April Galleons, Penguin (New York, NY), 1987.

The Ice Storm, Hanuman Books, 1987.

Reported Sightings: Art Chronicles, 1957-1987 (art criticism), edited by David Bergman, Knopf (New York, NY), 1989.

Three Poems (different text than 1972 volume with same title), Ecco Press (New York, NY), 1989.

Haibun, illustrations by Judith Shea, Collectif Génération (Colombes, France), 1990.

Flow Chart (poem), Knopf (New York, NY), 1991.

Hotel Lautreamont, Knopf (New York, NY), 1992.

Three Books (poems), Penguin (New York, NY), 1993.

And the Stars Were Shining, Farrar, Straus (New York, NY), 1994.

Can You Hear, Bird, Farrar, Straus (New York, NY), 1995.

Pistils (essays), photographs by Robert Mapplethorpe, Random House (New York, NY) 1996.

Wakefulness, Farrar, Straus (New York, NY), 1998.

The Mooring of Starting Out: The First Five Books of Poetry, Ecco Press (Hopewell, NJ), 1998.

Girls on the Run, Farrar, Straus (New York, NY), 1999.

Other Traditions: The Charles Eliot Norton Lectures, Harvard University Press (Cambridge, MA), 2000.

Your Name Here: Poems, Farrar, Straus (New York, NY), 2000.

As Umbrellas Follow Rain, Qua Books, 2001.

PLAYS

The Heroes (one-act; also see below; produced Off-Broadway, 1952, produced in London, England, 1982), in *Artists' Theater,* edited by Herbert Machiz, Grove (New York, NY), 1969.

The Compromise (three-act; also see below; produced in Cambridge, MA, at the Poet's Theater, 1956), in *The Hasty Papers,* Alfred Leslie, 1960.

The Philosopher (one-act; also see below), in *Art and Literature,* no. 2, 1964.

Three Plays (contains *The Heroes, The Compromise,* and *The Philosopher*), Z Press (Calais, VT), 1978.

EDITOR

(With others) *The American Literary Anthology,* Farrar, Straus (New York, NY), 1968.

(With Thomas B. Hess) *Light* (art), Macmillan (New York, NY), 1969.

(With Thomas B. Hess) *Painters Painting* (art), Newsweek (New York, NY), 1971.

(With Thomas B. Hess) *Art of the Grand Eccentrics,* Macmillan (New York, NY), 1971.

(With Thomas B. Hess) *Avant-Garde Art,* Macmillan (New York, NY), 1971.

Penguin Modern Poets 24: Ken Ward Elmslie, Kenneth Hoch, James Schuyler, Penguin (New York, NY), 1974.

Richard F. Sknow, *The Funny Place,* O'Hara (Chicago, IL), 1975.

Bruce Marcus, *Muck Arbour,* O'Hara (Chicago, IL), 1975.

(Translator from the French) Max Jacob, *The Dice Cup: Selected Prose Poems,* SUN (New York, NY), 1979.

(With David Lehman) *The Best American Poetry, 1988,* Scribner (New York, NY), 1989.

(Translator, with others) Pierre Reverdy, *Selected Poems,* Wake Forest University Press (Winston-Salem, NC), 1991.

CONTRIBUTOR TO ANTHOLOGIES

New American Poetry, 1945-1960, Grove (New York, NY), 1960.

Paris Leary and Robert Kelly, editors, *A Controversy of Poets,* Doubleday/Anchor (New York, NY), 1964.

L'Avant-Garde aujourd'hui, [Brussels, Belgium], 1965.

Anthology of New York Poets, Random House (New York, NY), 1969.

The Voice That Is Great within Us: American Poetry of the Twentieth Century, Bantam (New York, NY), 1970.

Contemporary American Poetry, Houghton Mifflin (Boston, MA), 1971.

Louis Untermeyer, editor, *Fifty Modern American and British Poets, 1920-1970,* McKay (New York, NY), 1973.

Shake the Kaleidoscope: A New Anthology of Modern Poetry, Simon & Schuster (New York, NY), 1973.

OTHER

(Translator) Jean-Jacques Mayoux, *Melville,* Grove (New York, NY), 1960.

(Translator, as Jonas Berry, with Lawrence G. Blochman) *Murder in Montmarte,* Dell (New York, NY), 1960.

(Translator, as Jonas Berry, with Lawrence G. Blochman) Genevieve Manceron, *The Deadlier Sex,* Dell (New York, NY), 1961.

(Translator) Marcel Allain and Pierre Souvestre, *Fantomas,* Morrow (New York, NY), 1986.

(Translator) Pierre Martory, *Every Question but One,* Groundwater Press/InterFlo Editions, 1990.

(Translator) Pierre Martory, *The Landscape Is behind the Door,* Sheep Meadow Press (Riverdale-on-Hudson, NY), 1994.

Collaborator with Joe Brainard on C Comic Books; collaborator with Elliott Carter on the musical setting *Syringa,* first produced in New York, NY, at Alice Tully Hall, December, 1979; verse has been set to music by Ned Rorem, Eric Salzman, Paul Reif, and James Dashow. Poetry recordings include *Treasury of 100 Modern American Poets Reading Their Poems,* Volume 17, Spoken Arts; and *Poetry of John Ashbery,* Jeffrey Norton. Translator, from the French, of the works of Raymond Roussel, Andre Breton, Pierre Reverdy, Arthur

Cravan, Max Jacob, Alfred Jarry, Antonin Artaud, Noel Vexin, and others. Contributor of poetry to periodicals, including *New York Review of Books, Partisan Review, Harper's,* and *New Yorker;* contributor of art criticism to periodicals, including *Art International* and *Aujourd'hui;* contributor of literary criticism to *New York Review of Books, Saturday Review, Poetry, Bizarre* (Paris, France), and other periodicals. Coeditor, *One Fourteen,* 1952-53. Recordings of Ashbery reading his works include *John Ashbery* ("Voice of the Poet" series), Random Audio, 2001.

SIDELIGHTS: Poet John Ashbery, winner of a MacArthur Foundation "genius grant," is recognized as one of the leading lights of American letters. Ashbery's poetry challenges its readers to discard all presumptions about the aims, themes, and stylistic scaffolding of verse in favor of a literature that reflects upon the limits of language and the volatility of consciousness. In *New Criterion,* William Logan noted: "Few poets have so cleverly manipulated, or just plain tortured, our soiled desire for meaning. [Ashbery] reminds us that most poets who give us meaning don't know what they're talking about." *Dictionary of Literary Biography* contributor Raymond Carney likewise contended that Ashbery's work "is a continuous criticism of all the ways in which literature would tidy up experience and make the world safe for poetry." *New York Times Book Review* essayist Stephen Koch characterized Ashbery's voice as "a hushed, simultaneously incomprehensible and intelligent whisper with a weird pulsating rhythm that fluctuates like a wave between peaks of sharp clarity and watery droughts of obscurity and languor."

Ashbery's style, once considered avant-garde, has since become "so influential that its imitators are legion," Helen Vendler observed in the *New Yorker.* Although even his strongest supporters admit that his poetry is often difficult to read and willfully difficult to understand, Ashbery has become, as James Atlas noted in the *New York Times Sunday Magazine,* "the most widely honored poet of his generation." Ashbery's position in American letters is confirmed by his unprecedented sweep of the literary "triple crown" in 1976, when *Self-Portrait in a Convex Mirror* won the Pulitzer Prize, the National Book Award, and the National Book Critics Circle Prize. However, as Nicholas Jenkins suggested in the *New York Times Book Review,* Ashbery has been resistant to his canonization. "For him," the critic contended, "prizes and fame seem little more than sweetly scented warning signs that his strategies have become too easily legible, that his poems are in danger of being embalmed. . . . Certainly no other poet has been more diligent about finding new ways of 'starting out'

again—of continuously emerging from the shadow of his own previous work."

A key element of Ashbery's success is his openness to change; it is both a characteristic of his development as a writer and an important thematic element in his verse. "It is a thankless and hopeless task to try and keep up with Ashbery, to try and summarize the present state of his art," Carney observed, adding, "He will never stand still, even for the space (or time) of one poem. Emerson wrote that 'all poetry is vehicular,' and in the case of Ashbery the reader had better resign himself to a series of unending adjustments and movements. With each subsequent book of poetry we only know that he will never be standing still, for that to him is death." In a *Washington Post Book World* review of *Shadow Train,* David Young noted: "You must enjoy unpredictability if you are to like John Ashbery. . . . We must be ready for anything in reading Ashbery because this eclectic, dazzling, inventive creator of travesties and treaties is ready to and eager to include anything, say anything, go anywhere, in the service of an esthetic dedicated to liberating poetry from predictable conventions and tired traditions." And in the *New York Times Book Review,* J. M. Brinnon maintained that *Self-Portrait in a Convex Mirror* is "a collection of poems of breathtaking freshness and adventure in which dazzling orchestrations of language open up whole areas of consciousness no other American poet has even begun to explore. . . . The influence of films now shows in Ashbery's deft control of just those cinematic devices a poet can most usefully appropriate. Crosscut, flashback, montage, close-up, fade-out—he employs them all to generate the kinetic excitement that starts on the first page of his book and continues to the last."

As Brinnon's analysis suggested, Ashbery's verse has taken shape under the influence of films and other art forms. The abstract expressionist movement in modern painting, stressing nonrepresentational methods of picturing reality, is an especially important presence in his work. "Modern art was the first and most powerful influence on Ashbery," Helen McNeil declared in the *Times Literary Supplement.* "When he began to write in the 1950s, American poetry was constrained and formal while American abstract-expressionist art was vigorously taking over the heroic responsibilities of the European avant garde. . . . Ashbery remarks that no one now thinks it odd that Picasso painted faces with eyes and mouth in the wrong place, while the hold of realism in literature is such that the same kind of image in a poem would still be considered shocking."

True to this influence, Ashbery's poems, according to Fred Moramarco, are a "verbal canvas" upon which the poet freely applies the techniques of expressionism. Moramarco, writing in the *Journal of Modern Literature,* felt that Ashbery's verse, "maligned by many critics for being excessively obscure, becomes less difficult to understand when examined in relation to modern art. *The Tennis Court Oath* is still a book that arouses passions in critics and readers, some of whom have criticized its purposeful obscurity. For me it becomes approachable, explicable, and even downright lucid when read with some of the esthetic assumptions of Abstract Expressionism in mind. . . . [Jackson] Pollock's drips, Rothko's haunting, color-drenched, luminous, rectangular shapes, and Gottlieb's spheres and explosive strokes are here, in a sense, paralleled by an imagistic scattering and emotional and intellectual verbal juxtaposition."

In the same article, Moramarco reviewed "Self-Portrait in a Convex Mirror," a long poem inspired by a painting by the Renaissance artist Francesco Parmigianino, and was "struck by Ashbery's unique ability to explore the verbal implications of painterly space, to capture the verbal nuances of Parmigianino's fixed and distorted image. The poem virtually resonates or extends the painter's meaning. It transforms visual impact to verbal precision." And Jonathan Holden believed that "Ashbery is the first American poet to successfully carry out the possibilities of analogy between poetry and 'abstract expressionist' painting. He has succeeded so well for two reasons: he is the first poet to identify the *correct* correspondences between painting and writing; he is the first poet to explore the analogy who has possessed the *skill* to *produce* a first-rate 'abstract expressionist' poetry, a poetry as beautiful and sturdy as the paintings of Willem de Kooning." In the *American Poetry Review,* Holden added that "it is Ashbery's genius not only to be able to execute syntax with heft, but to perceive that syntax in writing is the equivalent of 'composition' in painting: it has an intrinsic beauty and authority almost wholly independent of any specific context."

Ashbery's experience as an art critic in France and America has strengthened his ties to abstract expressionism and instilled in his poetry a sensitivity to the interrelatedness of artistic media. As he once commented in an essay on American artist and architect Saul Steinberg: "Why shouldn't a painting tell a story, or not tell it, as it sees fit? Why should poetry be intellectual and nonsensory, or the reverse? Our eyes, minds, and feelings do not exist in isolated compartments but are part of each other, constantly crosscut-

ting, consulting and reinforcing each other. An art constructed to the above canons, or any others, will wither away since, having left one or more of the faculties out of account, it will eventually lose the attention of the others." Ashbery's poetry is open-ended and multivarious because life itself is, he told Bryan Appleyard in the London *Times:* "I don't find any direct statements in life. My poetry imitates or reproduces the way knowledge or awareness come to me, which is by fits and starts and by indirection. I don't think poetry arranged in neat patterns would reflect that situation. My poetry is disjunct, but then so is life."

Ashbery's verbal expressionism has attracted a mixed critical response. James Schevill, in a *Saturday Review* article on *The Tennis Court Oath,* wrote: "The trouble with Ashbery's work is that he is influenced by modern painting to the point where he tries to apply words to the page as if they were abstract, emotional colors and shapes. . . . Consequently, his work loses coherence. . . . There is little substance to the poems in this book." In the *New York Times Book Review,* X. J. Kennedy praised the same title: " 'I attempt to use words abstractly,' [Ashbery] declares, 'as an artist uses paint'. . . . If the reader can shut off that portion of the brain which insists words be related logically, he may dive with pleasure into Ashbery's stream of consciousness." Appleyard related the view of some critics that, "however initially baffling his poetry may seem, it is impossible to deny the extraordinary beauty of its surface, its calm and haunting evocation of a world of fragmentary knowledge." And Moramarco believed Ashbery's technique has an invigorating effect: "We become caught up in the rich, vitalized verbal canvas he has painted for us, transported from the mundane and often tedious realities of our daily lives to this exotic, marvelous world. . . . Literature and art can provide these moments of revitalization for us, and although we must always return to the real world, our esthetic encounters impinge upon our sensibilities and leave us altered."

Many critics have commented on the manner in which Ashbery's fluid style has helped to convey a major concern in his poetry: the refusal to impose an arbitrary order on a world of flux and chaos. In his verse, Ashbery attempts to mirror the stream of perceptions of which human consciousness is composed. His poems move, often without continuity, from one image to the next, prompting some critics to praise his expressionist technique and others to accuse him of producing art that is unintelligible, even meaningless.

"Reality, for Ashbery, is elusive, and things are never what they seem to be. They cannot be separated from one another, isolated into component parts, but overlap, intersect, and finally merge into an enormous and constantly changing whole," Paul Auster suggested in *Harper's.* "Ashbery's manner of dealing with this flux is associative rather than logical, and his pessimism about our ever really being able to know anything results, paradoxically, in a poetry that is open to everything."

In the *American Poetry Review,* W. S. Di Piero stated that Ashbery "wonders at the processes of change he sees in people, in the seasons, in language, but his perception of the things about him also persuades him that nothing has ever really changed. If all things, all thought and feeling, are subject to time's revisions, then what can we ever know? What events, what feelings can we ever trust? In exploring questions such as these, Ashbery has experimented with forms of dislocated language as one way of jarring things into order; his notorious twisting of syntax is really an attempt to straighten things out, to clarify the problems at hand." David Kalstone, in his book *Five Temperaments,* commented: "In his images of thwarted nature, of a discontinuity between past and present, Ashbery has tuned his agitation into a principle of composition. From the start he has looked for sentences, diction, a syntax which would make these feelings fully and fluidly available." "Robbed of their solid properties, the smallest and surest of words become part of a new geography," Kalstone wrote of *The Double Dream of Spring* in the *New York Times Book Review.* To explore this "new geography," Kalstone added, the reader must immerse himself in Ashbery's language and "learn something like a new musical scale."

Closely related to Ashbery's use of language as a "new musical scale" is his celebration of the world's various motions and drives. Under the poet's care, the most ordinary aspects of our lives leap into a new reality, a world filled with the joyous and bizarre. In his book, *The Poem in Its Skin,* Paul Carroll found that "one quality most of Ashbery's poems share is something like the peculiar excitement one feels when stepping with Alice behind the Looking Glass into a reality bizarre yet familiar in which the 'marvelous' is as near as one's breakfast coffee cup or one's shoes. His gift is to release everyday objects, experiences and fragments of dreams or hallucinations from stereotypes imposed on them by habit or preconception or belief: he presents the world as if seen for the first time." In a review of *Self-Portrait in a Convex Mirror* for *Harper's,* Paul Auster contended that "few poets today have such an uncanny ability to undermine our certainties, to articu-

late so fully the ambiguous zones of our consciousness. We are constantly thrown off guard as we read his poems. The ordinary becomes strange, and things that a moment ago seemed clear are cast into doubt. Everything remains in place, and yet nothing is the same." Edmund White, appraising *As We Know* in *Washington Post Book World,* observed: "As David Shapiro has pointed out in his critical study, all [of Ashbery's] long poems tend to end on a joyful note, though one harmonized with doubt and anguish." In the conclusion of "Litany" he "rejects the equation of life and text in order to acknowledge the rich messiness of experience."

Several critics have suggested that this joyful quality is sometimes contradicted by an intellectualism and obscurity present in Ashbery's verse. Victor Howes, reviewing *Houseboat Days* for the *Christian Science Monitor,* recognized the rich diversity of the poet's work, but asked, "does he touch the heart? Does he know the passions? My dear. My dear. Really, sometimes you ask too much." J. A. Avant of *Library Journal* argued that in *The Double Dream of Spring,* "emotion has been intellectualized to the extent that it is almost nonexistent." And Pearl K. Bell commented in the *New Leader:* "Long stretches of 'Self-Portrait' read like the bland prose of an uninspired scholar, complete with references and quotations. Bleached of feeling and poetic surprise, the words gasp for air, stutter, go dead." In a *New York Review of Books* article on *The Double Dream of Spring,* Robert Mazzocco asserted that "in Ashbery there has always been a catlike presence, both in the poems themselves and in the person these poems reveal: tender, curious, cunning, tremendously independent, sweet, guarded. Above all, like a cat, Ashbery is a born hunter. . . . But the one prime act of the cat—to spring, to pounce, to make the miraculous leap—Ashbery, for me, has yet to perform."

In *The Poem in Its Skin,* Carroll examined Ashbery's "Leaving the Atocha Station," and felt that "several close readings fail to offer a suspicion of a clue as to what it might be all about." Carroll admitted his annoyance: "The poem makes me feel stupid. . . . [The] narrative skeleton is fleshed out by skin and features made from meaningless phrases, images and occasional sentences. In this sense, 'Leaving the Atocha Station' out-Dadas Dada: it is totally meaningless. . . . The most obvious trait is the general sense that the reader has wandered into somebody else's dream or hallucination." After suggesting several ways to read the poem, Carroll concluded that "the reader should feel free to do whatever he wants with the words in this poem. . . . I also suspect some readers will respond to Ashbery's invitation that the reader too become a poet as he re-reads [the poem]." As Ashbery explained in an essay on Gertrude Stein in *Poetry,* a poem is "a hymn to possibility . . . a general, all-purpose model which each reader can adapt to fit his own set of particulars." In the *New York Review of Books,* Irvin Ehrenpreis commented on Ashbery's assessment of the participatory nature of poetry: "The poem itself must become an exercise in re-examining the world from which the self has become alienated. We must confront its language with the same audacity that we want when confronting the darkened world within us and without. To offer a clear meaning would be to fix the reader in his place, to turn him away from the proper business of poetry by directing him to an apparent subject. . . . The act of reading must become the purpose of the poem."

Calling the poet a "late Romantic," Adam Kirsch declared in *New Republic:* "Ashbery, like God, is most easily defined by negatives. His poems have no plot, narrative, or situation; no consistent emotional register or tone; no sustained mood or definite theme. They do not even have meaningful titles. So complete is Ashbery's abandonment of most of what we come to poetry for that his achievement seems, on first acquaintance, as though it must be similarly complete: a radical new extension of poetry's means and powers, or an audacious and wildly successful hoax." In a review of *As We Know* for the *Chicago Tribune Book World,* Joseph Parisi granted that Ashbery's " 'subject matter' remains incomprehensible, to be sure," but the critic nevertheless insisted: "As these streams of everyday and extraordinary objects flow past us in no apparent order, but always in wondrously lyrical lines, the poems make their own curious kind of sense. After all, isn't this how we perceive 'reality'? . . . Ashbery's poems imply the improbability of finding ultimate significance amid the evanescence and transience of modern life. If, however, in the process of these poems the old order is lost or irrelevant, the longing for it or some kind of meaning is not." Reflecting upon the critical response to his poem, "Litany," Ashbery once told *CA,* "I'm quite puzzled by my work too, along with a lot of other people. I was always intrigued by it, but at the same time a little apprehensive and sort of embarrassed about annoying the same critics who are always annoyed by my work. I'm kind of sorry that I cause so much grief."

Di Piero described the reaction of critics to Ashbery's style as "amusing. On the one hand are those who berate him for lacking the Audenesque 'censor' (that little editing machine in a poet's head which deletes all superfluous materials) or who accuse him of simply being willfully and unreasonably perverse. On the other hand are those reviewers who, queerly enough, praise the difficulty of Ashbery's verse as if difficulty were a positive literary value in itself, while ignoring what the poet is saying." Vendler offered this summary in the *New Yorker:* "It is Ashbery's style that has obsessed reviewers, as they alternately wrestle with its elusive impermeability and praise its power of linguistic synthesis. There have been able descriptions of its fluid syntax, its insinuating momentum, its generality of reference, its incorporation of vocabulary from all the arts and sciences. But it is popularly believed, with some reason, that the style itself is impenetrable. . . . An alternative view says that every Ashbery poem is about poetry." Kirsch commented: "Ashbery proves, better than any other poet, that a certain style of 'difficulty' is not at all as difficult as it may seem. . . . Difficulty is only possible within a system of conventions, including the convention of meaning. . . . When a poet leaves conventions behind (which is not the same thing as playing with them or transcending them), a vast territory of verbiage is opened up, and he can journey anywhere."

This alternative view emphasizes Ashbery's concern with the nature of the creative act, particularly as it applies to the writing of poetry. This is, Peter Stitt noted, a major theme of *Houseboat Days,* a volume acclaimed by Marjorie Perloff in *Washington Post Book World* as "the most exciting, most original book of poems to have appeared in the 1970s." Ashbery shares with the abstract expressionists of painting "a preoccupation with the art process itself," Stitt maintained in the *Georgia Review.* "Ashbery has come to write, in the poet's most implicitly ironic gesture, almost exclusively about his own poems, the ones he is writing as he writes about them. The artist becomes his own theoretical critic, caught in the critical lens even at the moment of conception." Roger Shattuck made a similar point in the *New York Review of Books:* "Nearly every poem in *Houseboat Days* shows that Ashbery's phenomenological eye fixes itself not so much on ordinary living and doing as on the specific act of composing a poem. Writing on Frank O'Hara's work, Ashbery defined a poem as 'the chronicle of the creative act that produces it.' Thus every poem becomes an ars poetica of its own condition." Ashbery's examination of creativity, according to Paul Breslin in *Poetry,* is a "prison of self-reference" which detracts from the poet's "lyrical genius." *New Leader* reviewer Phoebe Pettingell commented that Ashbery "carries the saw that 'poetry does not have subject matter because it is the subject' to its furthest limit. Just as we feel we are beginning to make sense of one of his poems, meaning eludes us again. . . . Still, we are somehow left with a sense that the conclusion is satisfactory, with a wondering delight at what we've heard. . . . *Houseboat Days* is evidence of the transcendent power of the imagination, and one of the major works of our time."

Ashbery's poetry, as critics have observed, has evolved under a variety of influences besides modern art, becoming in the end the expression of a voice unmistakably his own. Among the influences seen in his verse are the Romantic tradition in American poetry that progressed from Whitman to Wallace Stevens, the so-called "New York School of Poets" featuring contemporaries such as Frank O'Hara and Kenneth Koch, and the French surrealist writers with whom Ashbery has dealt in his work as a critic and translator. In *The Fierce Embrace*, Charles Molesworth traced Ashbery's development: "The first few books by John Ashbery contained a large proportion of a poetry of inconsequence. . . . Subject matter, or rather the absence of it, helped form the core of his aesthetic, an aesthetic that refused to maintain a consistent attitude toward any fixed phenomena. The poems tumbled out of a whimsical, detached amusement that mixed with a quizzical melancholy. . . . Slowly, however, it appears as if Ashbery was gaining confidence for his true project, and, as his work unfolds, an indulging reader can see how it needed those aggressively bland 'experiments' in nonsense to protect its frailty." Ashbery's "true project," Molesworth believed, is *Self-Portrait in a Convex Mirror*. Many reviewers agreed with Molesworth that this volume, especially the long title poem, is Ashbery's "masterpiece."

Essentially a meditation on the painting "Self-Portrait in a Convex Mirror," the narrative poem focuses on many of the themes present in Ashbery's work. "I have lived with John Ashbery's 'Self-Portrait in a Convex Mirror' as with a favorite mistress for the past nine months," Laurence Lieberman declared in his *Unassigned Frequencies*. "Often, for whole days of inhabiting the room of its dream, I have felt that it is the only poem—and Ashbery the only author—in my life. It is what I most want from a poem. Or an author." Lieberman enthused that "when I put this poem down I catch myself in the act of seeing objects and events in the world as through different—though amazingly novel other eyes: the brilliantly varied other life of surfaces has been wonderfully revivified, and I take this transformation to be an accurate index of the impact of Ashbery's poetry upon the modus operandi of my perception." Like Molesworth, Lieberman believed that Ashbery's early work, though "unreadable," was an "indispensable detour that precipitated, finally, the elevated vision of Ashbery's recent work. . . . Following his many years of withdrawal and seclusion, a period of slow mellowing, this exactly appointed occasion has been granted to him."

Like other critics, Lieberman felt that Ashbery was once overly concerned with examining the nature of art and creativity, with escaping into his poems and "producing forms that achieved a semblance of ideal beauty." In "Self-Portrait," Lieberman contended, "Ashbery forecloses irrevocably on the mortgage of an *ars poetica* which conceives the poem as 'exotic refuge,' and advances to an aesthetic which carries a full burden of mirroring the age's ills." Unlike Parmigianino, who retreated into his hermitage, Ashbery ventures out from "the comfortable sanctuary of the dream" to confront the world. "His new art achieves a powerful re-engagement with the human community," Lieberman concluded. "That is his honorable quest."

Ashbery's second epic poem, *Flow Chart*, was published in 1991. One might assume, as Alfred Corn noted in *Poetry*, that "such a poet might . . . [now] reflect the golden serenity that comes in the latter years of a life that has achieved its aims. No. Or not simply, yes. In fact, *Flow Chart* shows us a John Ashbery at his most achingly vulnerable." Corn continued, "It is impossible to be certain this early on, but the reach of *Flow Chart* suggests that it is Ashbery's most important book, and certainly his most human." Lawrence Joseph declared in *Nation* that the poem, "more than any of his other books, portrays the essence of Ashbery's process. . . . *Flow Chart* is a catalogue, which Ashbery presents as endlessly expansive and open to interpretation, encompassing within its subject matter—well, as much as the poet may imagine." Helen Vendler, writing in *New Yorker*, attempted to capture the poem in its entirety: "What is John Ashbery's . . . *Flow Chart*? A two-hundred-and-fifteen-page lyric; a diary; a monitor screen registering a moving EEG; a thousand and one nights; Penelope's web unraveling; views from Argus' hundred eyes; a book of riddles; a ham-radio station; an old trunk full of memories; a rubbish dump; a Bartlett's *Familiar Quotations;* a Last Folio; a vaudeville act. . . . It makes Ashbery's past work (except for those poems in *The Tennis Court Oath* . . .) seem serenely classical, well ordered, pure, shapely, and above all, *short*."

As with Ashbery's other poetry, his volume, *Hotel Lautreamont*, was met with mixed critical response. In the *National Review*, James Gardner qualified his criticism by noting: "The appreciation of a poem by John Ashbery requires an act of faith, a surrender of the ordinary faculties of judgment. What you are to admire is a certain deposit of psychic life in each of these poems, a shifting, disengaged record of the poet's spiritual state at the moment of setting the words down on paper." Gardner concluded: "There was a time when I had more patience for this sort of thing than I now have. It is no longer enough." As Nicholas Everett noted in the *Times Literary Supplement,* "Those who expect poetry to evoke a specific experience or event, real or fictional, will always find Ashbery's work frustrating or just dull." He added, "Besides, the essential subjects of Ashbery's poetry—subjectivity and time . . .—are themselves general and elusive; and though in passing it says a good deal about them, its means are in the end mimetic rather than discursive." Tom Sleigh in the *New York Times Book Review* found Ashbery "extremely forgiving, a poet, like Wordsworth, of superb passages who doesn't insist that one dig out the gold in every line." However, Sleigh admitted, "This isn't to say that he's wired like other poets."

Can You Hear, Bird was Ashbery's seventeenth volume of poetry. According to John Boening in *World Literature Review,* "The poems in *Can You Hear, Bird* range across all manner of forms and styles, moods and voices. Some are more engaging than others (almost all Ashbery poems, even those which 'do' nothing for us or leave us disoriented, are engaging)." Stephen Yenser raved in the *Yale Review:* "There is nowhere that Ashbery's poetry can't sail, one feels, and nothing it can't do, apart of course from 'doing' anything." Yenser continued, "Reading Ashbery—like reading the Gertrude Stein of *Tender Buttons*—is a continually surprising, exciting venture that proves the endlessness of the resources that we call language.' " Mark Ford, writing in the *Times Literary Supplement,* compared Ashbery's poetry to Walt Whitman's. "Like Whitman's, it is essentially a means of involving the reader in the poem on what Whitman calls 'equal terms'. . . . Ashbery's evasions might be seen as motivated by a similar desire to achieve a greater—and more democratic—intimacy by short-circuiting conventional modes of address."

The poems in *Girls on the Run* were inspired by the art work and writings of Henry Darger (1892-1973), a mentally ill recluse whose fantastic sketches and paintings of little girls only came to light after his death. Once again, Ashbery uses Darger's work only as a point of departure for his own vivid and free-flowing imaginings, described by David Kirby in the *New York Times Book Review* as "a tank of literary laughing gas that exhilarates and confounds in roughly equal measures." The "characters" in *Girls on the Run* include Tidbit, Rags the Dog, Uncle Margaret, and Dimples, but these creations come and go through the pieces with no discernable plot or motivation to compel them on-

ward. As *Art in America* contributor Raphael Rubinstein saw it, *Girls on the Run* "is, in an odd way, closer in spirit to Ashbery's earlier work. . . . Despite expressing a degree of nostalgia for childhood diversions, this new poem is perhaps more radical in its unpredictability than anything Ashbery has yet written." Calling the volume "beautiful, comic, and mysterious" in his review for *World Literature Today,* Michael Leddy cited references to Homer and classical myth that runs through both Darger's work and Ashbery's poem, and notes that the work's "large cast gives a good sense of the poem's many dimensions." *Booklist* reviewer Donna Seaman felt that the work in *Girls on the Run* "has captured the peculiar energy of Darger's disturbing creation" in "a virtuoso interpretative performance."

In more recent Ashbery works, such as *Girls on the Run* and *Wakefulness* critics have noted an infusion of elegy as the poet contemplates aging and death. In *Nation,* Calvin Bedient stated: "For all his experimentation, Ashbery writes (as the important writers have always done) about happiness and woe. If the woe he knows is treated comically, it's still woe." The critic added: "Ashbery's brilliantly eccentric images are bees released to find a hidden (mythic) hive. His humor is the knowledge that they will perish en route. . . . Even if his pathos is by now well worn, it's no fuzzy pair of slippers. His poetry is almost as full of strange voices as Caliban's island, and as full of magic, a gracefully humorous pathos, a pathetic humor like no other shuddering laughter in the world."

In an online review for *MensJournal,* Mark Levine contended that Ashbery "remains the most outrageously daring verbal mapmaker of the modern imagination. Bawdy, feverish, irreverent, and beset by melancholy, his poems inhabit a range of textures and emotions you won't find in another living writer." Nicholas Jenkins concluded in the *New York Times Book Review* that Ashbery's poetry "appeals not because it offers wisdom in a packaged form, but because the elusiveness and mysterious promise of his lines remind us that we always have a future and a condition of meaningfulness to start out toward." Jenkins characterized Ashbery's work as "a poetry whose beauties are endless."

BIOGRAPHICAL/CRITICAL SOURCES:

BOOKS

Ashton, Dore, *The New York School: A Cultural Reckoning,* Viking (New York, NY), 1973.
Blasing, Mutlu Konuk, *Politics and Form in Postmodern Poetry: O'Hara, Bishop, Ashbery, and Merrill,*

Cambridge University Press (New York, NY), 1995.

Bloom, Harold, *John Ashbery*, Chelsea House (New York, NY), 1985.

Carroll, Paul, *The Poem in Its Skin*, Follett (New York, NY), 1968.

Cazé, Antoine, *John Ashbery*, Belin (Paris, France), 2000.

Contemporary Literary Criticism, Gale (Detroit, MI), Volume 2, 1974, Volume 3, 1975, Volume 4, 1975, Volume 6, 1976, Volume 9, 1978, Volume 13, 1980, Volume 15, 1980, Volume 25, 1983, Volume 41, 1988, Volume 77, 1993.

Contemporary Poets, 6th edition, St. James Press (Detroit, MI), 1996.

Dictionary of Literary Biography, Gale (Detroit, MI), Volume 5: *American Poets since World War II*, 1978, Volume 165: *American Poets since World War II, Fourth Series*, 1996.

Dictionary of Literary Biography Yearbook, 1981, Gale (Detroit, MI), 1982.

Herd, David, *John Ashbery and American Poetry: Fit to Cope with Our Occasions*, St. Martin's Press (New York, NY), 2001.

Hoeppner, Edward Haworth, *Echoes and Moving Fields: Structure and Subjectivity in the Poetry of W. S. Merwin and John Ashbery*, Bucknell University Press (Lewisburg, PA), 1994.

Howard, Richard, *Alone with America: Essays on the Art of Poetry in the United States since 1950*, Atheneum (New York, NY), 1969.

Kalstone, David, *Five Temperaments: Elizabeth Bishop, Robert Lowell, James Merrill, Adrienne Rich, John Ashbery*, Oxford University Press (New York, NY), 1977.

Kelly, Lionel, editor, *Poetry and the Sense of Panic: Critical Essays on Elizabeth Bishop and John Ashbery*, Rodopi (Atlanta, GA), 2000.

Kermani, David K., *John Ashbery: A Comprehensive Bibliography*, Garland Publishing (New York, NY), 1976.

Koch, Kenneth, *Rose, Where Did You Get That Red?*, Random House (New York, NY), 1973.

Kostelanetz, Richard, editor, *The New American Arts*, Horizon Press (New York, NY), 1965.

Kostelanetz, Richard, *The Old Poetries and the New*, University of Michigan Press (Ann Arbor, MI), 1979.

Leary, Paris and Robert Kelly, editors, *A Controversy of Poets*, Doubleday (New York, NY), 1965.

Lehman, David, editor, *John Ashbery*, Cornell University Press (Ithaca, NY), 1979.

Lehman, David, editor, *Beyond Amazement: New Essays on John Ashbery*, Cornell University Press (Ithaca, NY), 1980.

Lehman, David, *The Last Avant-Garde: The Making of the New York School of Poets*, Doubleday (New York, NY), 1999.

Lieberman, Laurence, *Unassigned Frequencies: American Poetry in Review, 1964-1977*, University of Illinois Press (Champaign, IL), 1977.

Meyers, John Bernard, editor, *The Poets of the New York School*, University of Pennsylvania Press (Philadelphia, PA), 1969.

Molesworth, Charles, *The Fierce Embrace: A Study of Contemporary American Poetry*, University of Missouri Press (Columbia, MO), 1979.

Packard, William, editor, *The Craft of Poetry*, Doubleday (New York, NY), 1964.

Perloff, Marjorie, *Poetic License: Essays on Modernist and Postmodernist Lyric*, Northwestern University Press (Evanston, IL), 1990.

Ross, Andrew, *The Failure of Modernism: Symptoms of American Poetry*, Columbia University Press (New York, NY), 1986.

Schultz, Susan M., editor, *The Tribe of John Ashbery and Contemporary Poetry*, University of Alabama Press (Tuscaloosa, AL), 1995.

Shapiro, David, *John Ashbery: An Introduction to the Poetry*, Columbia University Press (New York, NY), 1979.

Shaw, Robert B., editor, *American Poetry since 1960: Some Critical Perspectives*, Carcanet Press, 1973.

Shoptaw, John, *On the Outside Looking Out: John Ashbery's Poetry*, Harvard University Press (Cambridge, MA), 1994.

Stepanchev, Stephen, *American Poetry since 1945: A Critical Survey*, Harper (New York, NY), 1965.

Sutton, Walter, *American Free Verse: The Modern Revolution in Poetry*, New Directions (New York, NY), 1973.

Ward, Geoff, *Statutes of Liberty: The New York School of Poets*, St. Martin's Press (New York, NY), 1993.

PERIODICALS

American Poetry Review, August, 1973; September, 1978; July, 1979; July, 1981; May-June, 1984, pp. 29-33.

Architectural Digest, June, 1994, p. 36.

Art in America, February, 2000, Raphael Rubinstein, review of *Girls on the Run*, p. 37.

Booklist, May 1, 1981; March 15, 1999, Donna Seaman, review of *Girls on the Run*, p. 1271; October 1, 2000, Donna Seaman, review of *Your Name Here*, p. 313.

Chicago Tribune Book World, January 27, 1980; July 26, 1981.

Christian Science Monitor, September 6, 1962; March 9, 1970; October 12, 1977; December 3, 1979.

Commentary, February, 1973.

Confrontation, fall, 1974, pp. 84-96.

Contemporary Literature, winter, 1968; spring, 1969; summer, 1992, pp. 214-242.

Encounter, April, 1980.

Esquire, January, 1978.

Georgia Review, winter, 1975; winter, 1978; summer, 1980.

Harper's, April, 1970; November, 1975.

Hudson Review, spring, 1970; autumn, 1975; autumn, 1976; spring, 1978; autumn, 1980; winter, 1981.

Journal of Modern Literature, September, 1976.

Library Journal, January 1, 1970; August, 2000, Graham Christian, review of *Your Name Here,* p. 109; August, 2001, Laurie Selwyn, review of *John Ashbery,* p. 186.

Listener, August 18, 1977.

London Review of Books, April 23, 1992, p. 20.

Michigan Quarterly Review, summer, 1981, pp. 243-255.

Nation, December 12, 1966; April 14, 1969; September 3, 1977; November 11, 1978; May 29, 1989; April 20, 1992, p. 531; June 1, 1998, Calvin Bedient, review of *Wakefulness,* p. 27.

National Review, February 15, 1993, p. 50.

New Criterion, June, 1998, William Logan, "Soiled Desires," p. 61.

New Leader, May 26, 1975; November 7, 1977; January 29, 1981.

New Republic, June 14, 1975; November 29, 1975; November 26, 1977; December 29, 1979; October 16, 1989; June 17, 1991; September 28, 1998, Adam Kirsch, review of *Wakefulness,* p. 38; January 1, 2001, Mark Ford, "Life without End," p. 30.

New Statesman, June 16, 1967; January 4, 1980; April 24, 1981.

New Statesman & Society, July 22, 1994, p. 45.

Newsweek, September 26, 1977.

New York, May 20, 1991, pp. 46-52.

New York Arts Journal, November, 1977.

New Yorker, September 1, 1956; March 24, 1969; March 16, 1981; August 3, 1992; December 13, 1993; February 14, 1994; February 28, 1994.

New York Quarterly, winter, 1972.

New York Review of Books, April 14, 1966; December 14, 1973; October 16, 1975; March 23, 1978; January 24, 1980; July 16, 1981.

New York Times, April 15, 1956.

New York Times Book Review, July 15, 1962; February 11, 1968; May 4, 1969; June 8, 1969; July 5, 1970; April 9, 1972; August 2, 1975; November 13, 1977; January 6, 1980; September 6, 1981; May 23, 1993; October 23, 1994, p. 3; January 4, 1998, Nicholas Jenkins, review of *The Mooring of Starting Out: The First Five Books of Poetry;* April 11, 1999, David Kirby, review of *Girls on the Run,* p. 24; November 12, 2000, Taylor Antrim, review of *Other Traditions.*

New York Times Sunday Magazine, May 23, 1976; February 3, 1980.

Observer (London, England), December 9, 1979; December 16, 1979.

Paris Review, winter, 1983, pp. 30-59.

Parnassus, fall-winter, 1972; fall-winter, 1977; spring-summer, 1978; fall-winter, 1979.

Partisan Review, fall, 1972; summer, 1976.

Poet and Critic, Vol. 11, no. 3, 1979.

Poetry, July, 1957; September, 1962; December, 1966; October, 1970; August, 1972; October, 1980; May, 1988; December, 1991, p. 169; October, 1994, p. 44.

Poetry Review, August, 1985, pp. 20-25.

Publishers Weekly, March 28, 1994; September 25, 1995, p. 49.

Saturday Review, June 16, 1956; May 5, 1962; August 8, 1970; July 8, 1972; September 17, 1977.

Sewanee Review, April, 1976; April, 1978; July, 1980.

Southern Review, April, 1978.

Spectator, November 22, 1975.

Time, April 26, 1976.

Times (London, England), August 23, 1984.

Times Literary Supplement, September 14, 1967; July 25, 1975; September 1, 1978; March 14, 1980; June 5, 1981; October 8, 1982; February 12, 1993, p. 10; May 17, 1996, p. 26.

Twentieth-Century Literature, summer, 1992, pp. 125-151.

Verse, spring, 1991, pp. 61-72.

Village Voice, January 19, 1976; October 17, 1977; December 26, 1977.

Village Voice Literary Supplement, October, 1981.

Virginia Quarterly Review, autumn, 1970; winter, 1973; spring, 1976; spring, 1979; spring, 1980.

Washington Post Book World, May 11, 1975; October 30, 1977; December 11, 1977; November 25, 1979; June 7, 1981; December 10, 1995, p. 8.

Western Humanities Review, winter, 1971.

World Literature Review, autumn, 1996, p. 961.

World Literature Today, autumn, 1999, Michael Leddy, review of *Girls on the Run,* p. 740.

Yale Review, October, 1969; June, 1970; winter, 1981; spring, 1990; April, 1993; January, 1996.

OTHER

MensJournal, http://www.mensjournal.com/agenda/ 0010/ (November 6, 2000), Mark Levine, "Lingo Here Awhile."

Entry reviewed by David K. Kermani, assistant to John Ashbery.

*   *   *

ATHILL, Diana   1917-

PERSONAL: Born December 21, 1917, in London, England; daughter of Lawrence Francis Imbert and Katharine (Carr) Athill. *Education:* Lady Margaret Hall, Oxford, B.A., 1939.

ADDRESSES: *Home*—7 Elsworthy Ter., London, England.

CAREER: British Broadcasting Corp. (BBC), London, England, research worker, 1941-46; Allan Wingate Publishers Ltd., London, England, editor, 1946-51; André Deutsch Publishers Ltd., London, England, director, 1952-92.

AWARDS, HONORS: Short story prize, *London Observer,* 1958.

WRITINGS:

(Translator) Berthe Grimault, *Beau Clown,* André Deutsch (London, England) 1957.
(Translator) Christine Arnothy, *Women of Japan,* André Deutsch (London, England), 1959.
(Translator) Jacques Valentin, *The Monks of Mount Athos,* André Deutsch (London, England), 1960.
An Unavoidable Delay, and Other Stories, Doubleday (New York, NY), 1962.
Instead of a Letter (memoir), Doubleday (New York, NY), 1962.
(Translator) Christine Rivoyre, *The Sultans,* André Deutsch (London, England), 1967.
Don't Look at Me like That (fiction), Viking (New York, NY), 1967.
(Translator) Pia Paoli, *Atoms at Tea-Time: The Story of a Cure,* André Deutsch (London, England), 1968.
(Translator) Liane de Pougy, *My Blue Notebooks,* Harper (New York, NY), 1979.
After a Funeral (memoir), Ticknor & Fields (New York, NY), 1986.
Make Believe: a True Story (memoir), Steerforth Press (Royalton, VT), 1993.
Stet: An Editor's Life (memoir), Granta Books (London, England), 2000, Grove Press (New York, NY), 2001.
Yesterday Morning, Granta Books (London, England), 2002.

Contributor to *Short Story One,* Hutchinson, 1961. Also contributor of short stories to *London Magazine, Evergreen Review, Harper's, Harper's Bazaar, Glamour, Gentleman's Quarterly,* and other magazines.

SIDELIGHTS: As an editor at the London publishing company of André Deutsch, Diana Athill worked with some of the most notable writers of the twentieth century. Her four volumes of memoirs detail her many relationships with literary figures, and offer what critics found to be a fascinating look behind the scenes of the publishing world.

After working for the BBC during World War II, Athill met Hungarian émigré André Deutsch and accepted an editing job in his first publishing house, Allan Wingate. As recounted in *Stet: An Editor's Life,* she began a brief affair with Deutsch and was his partner in founding the company that bore his name. Though Athill admits she had no special qualifications for her job, she went on to work successfully with such major authors as V. S. Naipaul, Jack Kerouac, Molly Keane, Brian Moore, Mordecai Richler, Norman Mailer, Philip Roth, Jean Rhys, Margaret Atwood, and John Updike. "She had near impeccable editorial judgment," observed Evelyn Toynton in the *New York Times Book Review.*

In the opinion of many critics, she also had considerable literary talent of her own. Noel Perrin, in a *Washington Post Book World* assessment of her memoir, *Instead of a Letter,* called her a "gifted writer" capable of the rare achievement of writing about oneself without any egotistical illusions. The book, written when Athill was forty-three, chronicles her privileged childhood and her adolescent love affair with Paul, an Oxford student who was her brother's tutor. After Paul rejected her, Athill began her career, but, according to Perrin, "led a kind of half-life" devoid of real joy. At age forty-one, however, her life reached a turning point when she began to write fiction and entered into a new and more rewarding romantic relationship. Noting that the book contains "the plot of many a romance novel," Perrin went on to praise its exceptional honesty and "overwhelming sense of female life," which he linked to Athill's talent for observation and detail. "I sighed with pleasure at how well this woman writes," he wrote.

Perrin expressed equal enthusiasm for Athill's second memoir, *After a Funeral,* an account of her five-year relationship with "Didi" (Waguih Ghali), a penniless Egyptian aristocrat living in London and ten years Athill's junior. In the book, which Perrin describes as "completely uncensored," Athill describes Didi as a reckless, brilliant romantic with whom she fell in love, who finally killed himself in her apartment. Didi was reluctant to make their relationship anything more than intellectual; though he lived with her for three years, he didn't want anyone to consider him Athill's lover. Perrin marveled at the author's ability to admit this embarrassing truth with such honesty. He also admired her insight. "Here a subtle woman is depicting the gradual self-destruction of an equally subtle man," he wrote. "The book reads like a first-rate psychoanalysis without the jargon and without the theories."

Another tumultuous relationship is at the heart of *Make Believe: A True Story.* In 1969 Athill met a radical African American writer, Hakim Jamal, fourteen years her junior. In *Make Believe,* Athill writes that when Jamal approached her with the idea for a book project about his relationship with Malcolm X, she and Jamal were immediately attracted to each other. Jamal, who grew up in Boston, had struggled with alcoholism and drug addiction and had been in prison for attempted murder. He was also notorious for the brutal treatment of his wife and children, lovers, and friends; he allowed his British companion, Gail Benson, to be murdered by the followers of Trinidadian racial extremist Michael X. A year after Benson's death, Jamal was murdered in an unrelated incident in the United States.

Critical response to *Make Believe* was mixed. Sean French, in *New Statesman & Society,* discerned an "elusive racism" in its theme of "attraction by whites to blackness and black culture, to its supposed air of primitive vitality, danger and primal sexuality." Finding a large element of "escape, experimentation and fantasy" in the relationship, French observed that Athill "writes honestly and painfully" about its ambiguities but in the end has written "a deeply disturbing book . . . that . . . vividly enacts a racist fantasy." A reviewer for *Publishers Weekly,* however, found the book "occasionally compelling," while *Booklist* contributor Mary Ellen Sullivan appreciated its depiction of a "life-altering" relationship that is "ultimately less about political upheaval than about how personal histories shape personal futures."

Stet met with more consistent praise. Critics enjoyed its mix of gossip and insight and its candid detail. "Athill's own forte is describing people," commented Gabriele Annan in *Times Literary Supplement,* who found the author's insights often "wickedly comical . . . but not

unkind." Some of Athill's portraits, Annan observed, are "so perceptive as to be almost shocking." Critics particularly admired her insights on American writer Alfred Chester and on Jean Rhys, whose chapter Toynton considered "a miniature masterpiece." In the *Boston Globe,* Jules Verdone wrote that "What's exceptional [about *Stet*] is the way in which Athill tells stories, in utterly personal terms, about tantrums and trysts and drug use and poor judgment and unseemly behavior, presenting them with a matter-of-factness that can camouflage what they often are: gossip. It's a rare individual who can dish that kind of dish without suggesting that what she knows makes her special, without melodrama or apparent malice. Her tone says that she is merely passing along a bit of history."

BIOGRAPHICAL/CRITICAL SOURCES:

PERIODICALS

Antioch Review, winter, 1987, review of *After a Funeral,* p. 114.
Best Sellers, November 15, 1967.
Booklist, March 15, 1994, Mary Ellen Sullivan, review of *Make Believe: A True Story,* p. 1323.
Books & Bookmen, February, 1986, review of *After a Funeral,* p. 15.
Boston Globe, March 26, 2001, Jules Verdone, review of *Stet: An Editor's Life,* p. D18.
British Book News, May, 1986, review of *After a Funeral,* p. 315; 1987, review of *After a Funeral,* p. 691.
Economist (U.S.), September 9, 2000, review of *Stet.*
Kirkus Reviews, January 1, 1994, review of *Make Believe,* p. 26.
Library Journal, March 15, 1994, Wilda Williams, review of *Make Believe,* p. 78.
Listener, March 6, 1986, review of *After a Funeral,* p. 26.
London Review of Books, July 3, 1986, review of *After a Funeral,* p. 11.
Ms., June, 1985, review of *Instead of a Letter,* p. 58.
New Statesman, December 17, 1982, review of *Instead of a Letter,* p. 29; March 21, 1986, Gillian Wilce, review of *After a Funeral,* p. 29; January 22, 1988, Paul Hallam, review of *After a Funeral,* p. 32.
New Statesman & Society, January 15, 1993, Sean French, review of *Make Believe,* p. 39.
New York Times Book Review, September 25, 1994, Bruce Allen, review of *Make Believe,* p. 24; April 1, 2001, Evelyn Toynton, review of *Stet.*
Observer, February 23, 1986, review of *After a Funeral,* p. 29; January 17, 1993, review of *Make Believe,* p. 49.

Publishers Weekly, January 17, 1994, review of *Make Believe,* p. 386; December 18, 2000, review of *Stet.*

Punch, May 14, 1986, review of *After a Funeral,* p. 60.

Rapport, January, 1994, review of *Make Believe,* p. 35.

Small Press, spring, 1994, review of *Make Believe,* p. 76.

Spectator, March 1, 1986, review of *After a Funeral,* p. 26; January 9, 1993, review of *Make Believe,* p. 21.

Times Educational Supplement, February 28, 1986, review of *After a Funeral,* p. 22.

Times Literary Supplement, February 28, 1986, review of *After a Funeral,* p. 212; January 15, 1993, review of *Make Believe,* p. 27; November 8, 2000, Gabriele Annan, review of *Stet.*

Vogue, November, 1986, Susan Bolotin, review of *After a Funeral,* p. 240.

Washington Post Book World, January 27, 1985, review of *Instead of a Letter;* February 1, 1987, Noel Perrin, review of *After a Funeral,* p. 8.

B

BAKER, Jeannie 1950-

PERSONAL: Born November 2, 1950, in England; daughter of Bernard Victor (a welder) and Barbara Joan (a tracer; maiden name, Weir) Baker. *Education:* Attended Croydon College of Art, 1967-69; Brighton College of Art, B.S. (with honors), 1979. *Politics:* "Left."

ADDRESSES: Home and Office—42 Cross St., Double Bay, Sydney, New South Wales 2028, Australia.

CAREER: Freelance artist and illustrator, 1972—. *Exhibitions:* Exhibitor at group shows, including Royal Academy Summer Exhibition, 1974, 1975; Portal Gallery, London, 1975; Crafts Council of Australia Gallery, Sydney, Australia, 1977-79; Hogarth Gallery, Sydney, 1978; Robin Gibson Gallery, Sydney, 1979; and Interiors State Gallery of New South Wales, Sydney, 1981. Exhibitor at one-woman shows, including Brettenham House, Waterloo Bridge, London, 1975; Gallery One, Hobart, Australia, 1977; Bonython Gallery, Adelaide, Australia, 1980; Crafts Council of Australia Gallery, Sydney, 1980; and Newcastle Regional Art Gallery, New South Wales, 1980. Permanent collections: Australian National Gallery; State Gallery of Queensland; Droomkeen Museum of Children's Literature, Riddall, Victoria, Australia.

AWARDS, HONORS: Visual arts grants, Australia Council, 1977-78, 1978-79; commended picture book of the year, Children's Book Council of Australia, 1985, for *Home in the Sky;* Picture Book honor from *Boston Globe,* Picture Book Honour from Children's Book Council of Australia, Earthworm Award from Reading Magic Award, and Picture Book award from Young Australian Best Book, all 1988, illustration/Australia category award from International Board on

Books for Young People, and primary category award from KOALA, both 1990, all for *Where the Forest Meets the Sea;* picture book award from Children's Book Council of Australia, and Young Australian Best Book, both 1992, both for *Window.*

WRITINGS:

SELF-ILLUSTRATED; FOR CHILDREN

Grandfather, Dutton, 1977, revised edition, 1980.
Grandmother, Dutton, 1978, revised edition, 1980.
Millicent, Dutton, 1980.
One Hungry Spider, Deutsch, 1982.
Home in the Sky, Greenwillow, 1984.
Where the Forest Meets the Sea, Greenwillow, 1987.
Window, Greenwillow, 1991.
The Story of Rosy Dock, Greenwillow, 1995.
The Hidden Forest, Greenwillow, 2000.

ILLUSTRATOR

Elaine Moss, *Polar* (picture book), Deutsch, 1975, Dutton, 1979.

Also contributor of illustrations to periodicals, including *New Scientist, Nova, Observer,* and London *Times.*

SIDELIGHTS: Picture-book author and illustrator Jeannie Baker has gained international attention with a unique style she calls "relief collage." As she once remarked, this method of illustration "is very painstaking and detailed. I use such natural materials as stone, veneer, paint peeled from old doors and windowsills, and plaster from old walls. I collect grass and leaves. For hair on my characters I use real hair. If they are to wear woolen jumpers, I knit them myself." Baker explained that when her relief collages are "photographed for reproduction, shadows will be cast, often in strange places, giving the reproduction a slightly three-dimensional effect." She noted on her Web site, "I don't know any other way of achieving the results that collage can give me. I've always loved texture and started as a painter trying to reproduce textures using paint. Then I thought, why not use the actual textures and that is what I do now."

Baker is best known for the application of her illustrative talents to ecological themes in books like *Where the Forest Meets the Sea* and *Window.* Some critics have appreciated her ability to present powerful messages about the environment with conviction as well as subtlety. *Horn Book* critic Mary M. Burns, for one, proclaimed that *Where the Forest Meets the Sea* is an "uncanny and unforgettable experience" that "represents a truly notable achievement in the picture-book genre, breaking new ground, adding new dimensions."

Baker began her career by providing the illustrations for *Polar,* a story written by Elaine Moss about a tobogganing teddy bear. She then began to write and illustrate her own picture books. In *Grandfather,* the first of these, Baker portrays a girl sitting on her grandfather's lap. The girl's hair looks real, and the textures of her sweater and skirt and of grandfather's tweed cap stand out. In *Grandmother* Baker presents a girl visiting the home of her grandmother. The illustrations for this book, as one *Bulletin of the Center for Children's Books* reviewer noted, show the Grandmother's "cozy, cluttered" home and "lush overgrown garden." Baker hinted at the inspiration for these stories when she said that "eccentrics (especially old people)" fascinate her, and that she appreciates "wild overgrown places and houses and textures—the crumbling erosion of decay."

Baker's *Home in the Sky* demonstrates her love of wild places and textures in an urban setting. Kristi Thomas Beavin remarked in *School Library Journal* that the details of the "busy city-scape" featured in this work "form a visually pleasing and intriguing jumble." The story begins when Light, a white pigeon, flies away from its flock and its coop on top of an abandoned building. Light's adventures in the city include an encounter with street pigeons and a ride on a subway car. *Horn Book* contributor Gertrude Herman especially enjoyed the way one particular illustration captures an arresting "moment in time" when a boy and a man see Light on the subway. According to Herman, Baker brings "stereotypic patterns of New York City life" to "conscious recognition. Textured surfaces, stretched tightly, pulsate with imagery and resonate with life." A

Junior Bookshelf critic concluded that *Home in the Sky* is the work of a "poet of the city streets and sky."

Baker moved toward nature as her subject with *One Hungry Spider,* a counting book that features collages made from embroidered and stuffed insects and natural materials. The book's protagonist, a hungry spider, awaits a meal in a web she has constructed between two branches; she avoids the three birds and nine wasps she sees, but she catches baby spiders and flies. Children may learn more about the spider Baker portrays, the Orbweb Eriophora, by reading the information included after the story. A *Bulletin of the Center for Children's Books* reviewer described this work as a "functional and attractive counting book." And a critic for *Junior Bookshelf* commented that the pictures were accurate and "remarkably beautiful."

The collages in *Where the Forest Meets the Sea* consist of paper, clay, paint, leaves, and other natural materials. According to Ilene Cooper in a *Booklist* review, the "pages are masterworks of both technical skill and artistic endeavor." In this book, a boy tells how he travels on a boat named *Time Machine* through a reef with his father to get to an ancient rain forest. As *School Library Journal* critic Judith Gloyer wrote, the "visual treat moves from beautiful sandy beaches inland along a creek into the densely tangled primordial forest." As the father and son explore the forest, the boy imagines, and the double-page collages represent the dinosaurs, animals, and even aboriginal children he might have seen in those long-ago times. He wonders if the forest will survive. The illustrations demonstrate how the forest would look with a modern resort on it as the boy asks, "Will the forest still be here when we come back?" A note on the Daintree Wilderness, in North Queensland, Australia, in which the story is set, and a map, are included.

Like *Where the Forest Meets the Sea, Window* carries a message about the environment. In *Window,* which has no text to accompany the illustrations, Baker's double-page illustrations focus on one man and a window over the course of twenty years. When the man is just a baby in his mother's arms, the view outside is relatively pristine Australian bush, but as he grows older an urban world replaces the natural one. "Development becomes suburb, then city, complete with billboards, high-rises, noise pollution, litter, and overpopulation," related Susan Scheps in *School Library Journal.* As a critic for *Kirkus Reviews* pointed out, the boy begins to litter and trap "creatures," and his toys begin to include "plastic dinosaurs" and "rockets." Finally, when the man has his own house in the country, he shows his infant child the view out another window where the countryside is already being prepared for development. Ann A. Flowers praised the work in *Horn Book,* asserting that it "presents an artistically unique examination of a pressing world-wide problem."

In *The Hidden Forest,* Baker depicts the mysterious underwater world of the kelp forest, featuring an encounter with a whale and what Susan Dove Lempke called in *Booklist,* "Baker's fascinating sea collages." The illustrations, she wrote, "combine pressed seaweed, sponges and sand to luminous effect." In the London *Times,* Sarah Johnson wrote that the images are "staggering," and commented, "I have rarely seen a picture book offer such a breathtaking trip into the natural world."

As she wrote in the author's note in *Window,* Baker hopes to help children understand how people change the environment. She once said, "I am inspired by my surroundings, and I feel the occasional need for personal new adventures into my surroundings to nurture my creative growth."

On her Web site, she commented that when she finishes a book, she finds it hard to think about it any more. "My favourite book is the 'new' book I'm working on, still working out and trying to make better than the books I made before it!"

BIOGRAPHICAL/CRITICAL SOURCES:

BOOKS

St. James Guide to Children's Writers, 5th edition, St. James Press (Detroit, MI), 1999.

PERIODICALS

Booklist, June 15, 1988, p. 1733; September 1, 2000, p. 112.
Bulletin of the Center for Children's Books, May, 1979; January, 1983.
Horn Book, March, 1985, p. 211; July-August, 1988, pp. 475-76; May, 1991, pp. 312-13; July, 2000, p. 431.
Independent Sunday, April 30, 2000, p. 32.
Junior Bookshelf, February, 1985, p. 10; October, 1988, p. 227.
Kirkus Reviews, March 1, 1991, p. 315.
Los Angeles Times Book Review, August 25, 1991, p. 9.
New York Times Book Review, December 30, 1984, p. 19.

Observer (London, England), April 12, 1998, p. 17; April 23, 2000, p. 12.
Publishers Weekly, April 17, 1995, p. 59.
School Library Journal, January, 1985, pp. 62-63; June-July, 1988, p. 83; March, 1991, p. 166; May, 1995, p. 98.
Teacher Librarian, June, 2000, p. 50.
Times (London, England), February 14, 1998, p. 15.
Vogue Living, June, 1980.

OTHER

Jeannie Baker's Web site, http://www.jeanniebaker. com (August 20, 2001).*

*   *   *

BAKER, Will(iam Edwin)   1935-
(Victoria Webb)

PERSONAL: Born May 10, 1935, in Council, ID; son of Waldo E. (a logger) and Bessie Mae (a teacher; maiden name, Savage) Baker; married Patricia Cooper (a zoologist), December 20, 1962 (died, January, 1987); married Malinda Penn; children: (first marriage) Willa Blythe; (second marriage) Dylan Cole, Montana Bess. *Education:* Attended College of Idaho, 1952-54; University of Washington, Seattle, B.A., 1956; Sorbonne, University of Paris, Certificat de la Langue, 1958; University of Hawaii, M.A., 1960; University of California, Berkeley, Ph.D., 1964. *Ethnicity:* "Mostly white." *Politics:* Independent. *Religion:* Buddhist. *Avocational interests:* Farming, music (folk and bluegrass), horses, fishing.

ADDRESSES: Home—14845 CR 42/Highway 16, Guinda, CA 95637. *Agent*—Sobel-Weber, 146 East 19th St., New York, NY 10003-2404. *E-mail*—webaker@ucdavis.edu.

CAREER: Free Press, Nampa, ID, reporter, 1957-58; Reed College, Portland, OR, assistant professor of English literature, 1964-68; University of California, Davis, CA, began as associate professor, became professor of English, 1969-95. Peace Corps Project, assistant director, 1966, director, 1967. Member of Yolo County general plan advisory committee, 1980-82; National Endowment for the Arts panelist, 1986.

AWARDS, HONORS: Rockefeller humanities grant, 1968; Fulbright grant, 1979; Associated Writing Programs award, 1985; Silver Spur Award, Western Writers Guild, 1990.

WRITINGS:

NONFICTION

Jacques Prevert, Twayne (New York, NY), 1967.
Syntax in English Poetry, 1870-1930, University of California Press (Berkeley, CA), 1967.
(Editor) *Critics on George Eliot,* Allen & Unwin (Australia), 1973.
Backward: An Essay on Indians, Time, and Photography, North Atlantic Books (Berkeley, CA), 1983.
Mountain Blood, University of Georgia Press (Athens, GA), 1985.
Tony and the Cows: A True Story from the Range Wars, Confluence (Lewiston, ID), 2000.

NOVELS

Chip, Harcourt (New York, NY), 1979.
(Under pseudonym Victoria Webb) *A Little Lady-Killing,* Dial (New York, NY), 1982.
Track of the Giant, Doubleday (New York, NY), 1990.
Shadow Hunter, Simon & Schuster (New York, NY), 1993.
Star Beast, Hodder & Stoughton (London, England), 1996.
The Raven Bride, Hodder & Stoughton (London, England), 1998.

STORY COLLECTIONS

Hell, West, and Crooked, Confluence (Lewiston, ID), 1993.
What a Piece of Work, University of Missouri Press (Columbia, MO), 1993.

SIDELIGHTS: Will Baker has written both nonfiction and fiction about the American West. Baker's novels include *Track of the Giant,* the story of 1880s Boston scientist Willard Evans and his quest for the Missing Link in the wilds of Idaho, and *Shadow Hunter,* a futuristic tale in which the southern hemisphere has become a vast desert inhabited by the mutant Ginks, a part-human species. A critic for *Publishers Weekly* described *Shadow Hunter* as a "complex and ambitious" story that was "intricately plotted and competently written."

Some of Baker's stories are gathered in the collection *What a Piece of Work,* including "Gorepac," in which a couple try to wean their teenaged son from his violent video games, "Chiquita Banana Muy Bonita," about Andean natives fleecing naive tourists, and "Jogger's Reef," which tells of a new cult of suburban joggers. A

critic for *Publishers Weekly* described Baker as "a quietly lethal satirist of popular culture" whose stories "paint a terrifying picture of an America without a moral center."

In *Tony and the Cows: A True Story from the Range Wars,* Baker follows the real-life case of a former Sierra Club officer who committed suicide after being suspected of killing over thirty cows. Driven by radical environmental beliefs, Tony Merten launched a one-man crusade against ranchers in his New Mexico community and may have shot their cattle. In the course of telling this story, Baker, according to a *Publishers Weekly* reviewer, presents a "tough-minded, philosophically grounded critique" of many popular environmentalist positions.

Baker told *CA:* "Writing is now a habit, based originally I suppose on an addiction to the scatter of thrills that comes from imagining exotic, self-indulgent, and forbidden scenes and then shaping these fantasies into a string of black ink-ants across a paper tundra, which magically transforms itself into an interior movie. Of course there's an element of exhibitionism, a joy in the power of compelling attention, but eventually a more practical motive materializes: I write in order to find out what I really think and feel. Ideas mate and metamorphose, are incarnated or transfigured, in their expression. So it's a process of discovery—at once passionate, personal, and universal—as I alternately take possession of language, or am possessed by it.

"I like all kinds of writing, and have had a shot at most forms, from sportswriting to sonnets. Poets are my heroes, and I fervently wish I was one, but I think my best work has been in novels, memoirs, and long essays. I am a plodder by nature, a prospector, and I prefer to chip away at something big for a long time. That way I know where I am every day, can see the piles of good ore and dross, measure the depth of the shaft, and pack my lunch without worrying about where my next inspiration is coming from.

"Influences? Zane Grey, Milton, Conrad, Walt Kelly, Woolf, McPhee, Dostoevsky, and Bob Dylan."

BIOGRAPHICAL/CRITICAL SOURCES:

PERIODICALS

Publishers Weekly, July 27, 1992, review of *What a Piece of Work,* p. 48; May 10, 1993, review of *Shadow Hunter,* p. 49; April 24, 2000, review of *Tony and the Cows: A True Story from the Range Wars,* p. 78.

BARRY, Lynda (Jean) 1956-

PERSONAL: Born January 2, 1956, in Richland Center, WI. *Education:* Graduated from Evergreen State College c. 1978.

ADDRESSES: Agent—c/o Author Mail, Sasquatch Books, Suite 260, 615 Second Ave., Seattle, WA 98104.

CAREER: Artist, author, and playwright. Commentator for National Public Radio; guest on television programs, including *Late Night with David Letterman.* Exhibitions include "Naked Ladies! Naked Ladies! Naked Ladies!," Linda Farris Gallery, Seattle, WA, 1984, and "The Good Times Are Killing Me," Linda Farris Gallery, 1986.

WRITINGS:

COMICS

Girls + Boys, Real Comet Press (Seattle, WA), 1981.
Big Ideas, Real Comet Press (Seattle, WA), 1983.
Naked Ladies! Naked Ladies! Naked Ladies!, Real Comet Press (Seattle, WA), 1984.
Everything in the World, Perennial Library (New York, NY), 1986.
The Fun House, Perennial Library (New York, NY), 1987.
Down the Street, Perennial Library (New York, NY), 1988.
Come over, Come Over, Harper Perennial (New York, NY), 1990.
My Perfect Life, Harper Perennial (New York, NY), 1992.
It's So Magic, HarperCollins (New York, NY), 1994.
The Freddie Stories, Sasquatch Books (Seattle, WA), 1999.
The Greatest of Marlys, Sasquatch Books (Seattle, WA), 2000.

Contributor of cartoon strips "Girls and Boys," "Ernie Pook's Comeek," and "Modern Romance" to periodicals, including *Esquire,* 1984-89, *Village Voice, New York Times,* and *Raw.*

OTHER

The Last House (play), produced by Pioneer Square Theater, Seattle, WA, 1988.
The Good Times Are Killing Me (novel), Real Comet Press (Seattle, WA), 1988, with new illustrations, Sasquatch Books (Seattle, WA), 1998.

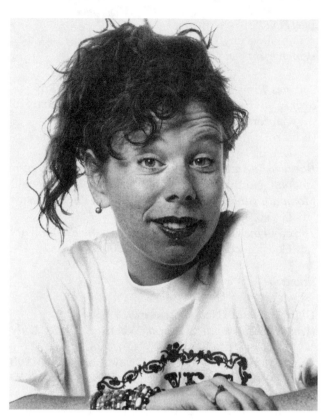

Lynda Barry

(With Arnold Aprill) *The Good Times Are Killing Me* (play; adapted from her novel), first produced in Chicago, IL, 1989, produced Off-Broadway, 1991.
Cruddy: An Illustrated Novel, Simon & Schuster (New York, NY), 1999.

Contributor of articles and book reviews to periodicals, including *American Film, Life, Los Angeles Times, Newsweek,* and *New York Times.* Contributor of short stories to periodicals, including a monthly fiction column for *Mother Jones,* 1989—.

WORK IN PROGRESS: A sequel to the novel *The Good Times Are Killing Me,* showing Edna from ages twelve to thirteen; plans for a screenplay adaptation of *The Good Times Are Killing Me* and for a musical.

SIDELIGHTS: "Imagine having a job like mine where you sit around all day and think about dirt bombs!," commented Lynda Barry in the *San Jose Mercury News.* In such writings as her "Ernie Pook" comic strip and the novel-turned-play, *The Good Times Are Killing Me,* Barry ranges over the whole comic/tragic experience of growing up, from dirt bombs to divorced parents and record-player nightclubs, to the strains that pull friendships apart. The lives of young people, Barry suggests, offer major insights about life in general. "I think about my own childhood all the time," she told the *Los Angeles Times.* "It's the only place to go if you're looking for answers. It's where all our motivations, feelings and opinions come from."

While many adults prefer to remember their youth as a "simpler" time, Barry grew up knowing that life is complicated. She was born in a small Wisconsin town into a multicultural family, daughter of a Filipino mother and a Norwegian-Irish father. Her mother soon felt out of place in the Midwest, so the family moved to Seattle, Washington, where her father felt out of place—surrounded by Filipino in-laws who couldn't speak English. Though Barry inherited her father's European looks—"Norwegian blood," she told the Chicago *Sun-Times,* "can suck the color out of anything"—she was received as a fellow Filipino by her mother's relatives, who talked to her routinely about "white" people. "I never felt completely Filipino and I never felt completely white," she told the *San Jose Mercury News.* "I felt completely different. I didn't even feel like a girl; I didn't feel like a boy, either. I could not find a peer."

Barry settled as best she could into her new neighborhood—the multiracial, working-class south end of Seattle, where dozens of her Filipino relatives lived. Music became one of the joys of her life. "Filipinos are really cool people. They have a tradition of a lot of dancing, a lot of group activity," Barry recalled in the Chicago *Sun-Times.* "The radio's always going, there's always music playing. We had our record player in the kitchen, which was the center of where people sat around and hung out. They were always listening to the hippest things. Still, to this day, my aunts and uncles listen to Top 40. They listen to the same music kids do." Also in the kitchen was her "exuberant" Filipino grandmother, who served up delicious potfuls of chicken *adobo,* boiled in vinegar and soy sauce. "I worship and adore her," Barry wrote in the *Los Angeles Times,* "because she has made my life incredibly rich."

Despite the vitality exhibited by her family, life was never easy. Money was tight; Barry's parents bought a run-down house where the faucets ran brown with rust; so many relatives came to stay that she made a "bedroom" for herself in the basement. Sometimes Barry would escape for a few hours by hopping on a city bus and touring Seattle. Her parents eventually broke up. She started to realize that society wasn't very equitable, and that her family had to struggle more than most. Finally, she told the Chicago *Sun-Times,* "when I was in high school, I arranged a transfer to a different school

as an Asian student. I made sure they didn't see me until I actually got the form. I switched to a white school because I wanted to know what a white school was like." At the time, affluent white teenagers were dressing in ragged jeans and were claiming to reject the fruits of capitalism, a trend less fortunate kids sometimes found hard to understand. "All the things my [white] girlfriends were rejecting," Barry continued, "I wanted to say, 'No. You have it good.' "

Barry, the first in her family to attend college, enrolled at Evergreen State, where her goal, as she told the *New York Times,* was "to be the best, the most depressed, bohemian in the world and make the most serious paintings." Being cast off by a boyfriend changed her life. "I couldn't sleep, going through my first heartbreak, and I drew a lot of comics about women and men," she told *Mother Jones.* "The men were cactuses who would talk to women and say, you know, 'Come to bed with me' and stuff. And a lot of them were friendly, too. It was just that they would be really bad to lay [sic] on top of." She called her drawings "Spinal Comics" and, for all the pointy spines, men seemed to like them as well as women. Eventually her work would become known as "Ernie Pook's Comeek," in honor of her little brother, who liked to call everything he owned by that name.

One of Barry's earliest fans was the editor of the Evergreen school paper, Matt Groening, who went on to fame as the creator of "Life in Hell" comics and *The Simpsons* television series. "Lynda's stuff," he told the *Washington Post,* "was funny, wild, had a very strong point of view, and it was obviously what *Lynda* thought was funny." Soon Barry's work was appearing in the papers at Evergreen State and the University of Washington.

Barry had qualms about switching her focus from painting to cartoons, and at first she hid the fact that she was drawing comics. Both she and Groening doubted it was possible to make a living at such work, especially doing the kind of quirky, personal humor they both enjoyed. However, a nasty boss made up Barry's mind for her. "I had a job selling popcorn in a movie theater when I was 21," she told the New York *Daily News,* "and then they found out I could draw and so I started doing paste-up for their little ads. I worked really hard. One day my boss came in—he was an alcoholic, I hated him—and his highball breath was blowing on me and he told me I was skating on thin ice. And I thought, 'This is what having a job is all about. That you can be alone in a room working hard on something you don't care about and a complete ass can come in and blow his nasty breath on you and tell you you're skating on thin ice.' " She promptly quit and, on the bus home, wrote a pledge to herself: "I will never work for anyone ever again as long as I live. Signed, Lynda Barry."

Barry's letter of independence was a brave and perilous gesture. Fresh out of college in the late 1970s, she didn't have much of a cartooning career except continued appearances in the University of Washington *Daily* and ten dollars a week from the Seattle *Sun*—a struggling alternative paper that finally went out of business. Just as she was ready to give up, her friendship with Groening helped to save her. Groening, himself a struggling cartoonist/writer in Los Angeles, wrote an article describing his friends in the "Evergreen mafia" that came to the attention of Bob Roth, publisher of the thriving alternative weekly the *Chicago Reader*. Roth liked Barry's work. "She was drawing a hipper kind of strip that you couldn't find anywhere else," he told the *San Jose Mercury News.* "She was addressing adult concerns in a way that comic strips almost never do." Barry liked Roth's offer of eighty dollars a week—at last she could live. "I had a telephone answering machine," she observed, "and for the next year, whenever Roth called I wouldn't pick up the phone because I was too scared he would fire me."

By the early 1980s Barry's comic strip was ensconced in alternative weeklies nationwide. She had stopped drawing men as spiny plants, but she remained interested in male-female relationships—"the whole luuuv thang," as she was quoted in the *Seattle Times.* In strips that were later collected in the volumes *Girls + Boys, Big Ideas,* and *Everything in the World,* she satirized dating, parties, fashions, two-faced boyfriends, and the illusions of romance. She became known for quips such as "Cupid is a monster from hell" and "Love is an exploding cigar which we willingly smoke"; interviewers likened her live delivery to that of a stand-up comedian. "Cupid *is* a monster," Barry explained in *Interview,* "because he shoots you and then you suddenly have to do all these things that you ordinarily wouldn't do. To operate a car you must have a driver's license. Love is a hundred times more dangerous than driving a car and you do it completely unprepared. You can fall in love with anybody, even people who hit you or steal your money or make you feel like you have a giant butt."

To satirize popular culture, Barry studied it avidly, poring through magazines, catalogs, and even junk mail. "Basically there is no idea *too* small," she told *Interview.* She became an accomplished eavesdropper: overheard conversations were not only a source of subject matter, but a way to understand how people actually talk. She visited singles bars a lot—for business reasons. "I go there with my boyfriend," she explained, "who is very good at making me look occupied, but not saying much, so I can eavesdrop." By 1984 Barry was supplementing her weekly newspaper strip with a monthly "Modern Romance" strip she wrote especially for *Esquire* magazine. "Her screwy depictions of the mating game," wrote Margot Sims in *Mother Jones,* "are so dead-on they make you cringe."

A favorite target of Barry's barbs became what sociologists call "women's body image": specifically, the difference between the glamour that society expects women to exude and their actual appearance. Her pop culture studies gave her plenty of ammunition. "Magazines like *Cosmopolitan* . . . really capitalize on women feeling horrible about themselves," Barry told *Interview.* "They resemble porno magazines. . . . You're supposed to look at the pictures of models standing around with no clothes on trying to look as sexy as possible and think to yourself, 'Oh, that's me looking like that for so-and-so.' Women yell about *Playboy* for its sexist treatment of women, while *Glamour* and *Mademoiselle* slip under the rug, no sweat. Women's magazines are as guilty, if not more so, of creating an image of how women think they should be." False expectations were deeply entrenched, going back all the way to childhood. "Girls have an idea of how their bodies should be," said Barry in *Ms.* "They don't play with their Barbie dolls because they are looking for intellectual idols."

Barry created her own gallery of more authentic women. In *Naked Ladies! Naked Ladies! Naked Ladies!* she uses a coloring-book format to present cartoon portraits of dozens of different (undressed) women, including fashionable women, fat women, anorexic women, and a groggy woman with curlers in her hair wearing "Foxy Lady" underwear. Along with the pictures is a first-person narrative in which an adolescent girl describes the uneasy blossoming of her own sexuality. "We got Bras and they got Jock Straps," the narrator recalls of her school days. "Like everything was suddenly going out of control and your mom had to buy you something to stop it."

The book was another daring move for Barry. Friends warned her against it; some feminists criticized it; some pornographers liked it. "I couldn't figure out who was going to kill me—the Moral Majority or the lesbian separatists," Barry told *Ms.* "But the thing that surprised me most was that it seemed to work on enough levels that everyone saw it totally differently, and most found a reason to like it." Wrote B. Ruby Rich in the

Voice Literary Supplement: "Barry stakes her position not on the good or bad essence of sexuality, but rather on the tragicomic inevitability of it all, traumas and yearnings included. It is a testimony to her skill that she confronts so complicated a subject in so simple a format."

Meanwhile, Barry had mixed feelings about her work for *Esquire,* even if it did help her become more widely known. Unlike her usual comic strips, in which she followed her own creative instincts, "Modern Romance" was made to order for a particular audience—*Esquire's* affluent, young, male readers. The stories weren't supposed to be whimsical or darkly satirical, and they had to be quick, lively, and unambiguously funny. At first Barry tried to take the assignment in stride, viewing it as chance to develop her versatility. "I really like being in *Esquire* because it *is* a man's magazine," she told *Mother Jones.* "It makes me feel just like the girls in high school who would take electronics or machine shop. You know, you would take those classes not only because you wanted to learn about machines, but mostly because you wanted to be in there with the guys, and just kind of messing up their act, too." Eventually, though, the need to conform to someone else's ideas took its toll, and Barry discontinued the *Esquire* strip. "I had to work with an editor, whose job it was to make sure my cartoons conformed to the 'Esquire Man' way of looking at things," she told the *Los Angeles Times.* "Thing is, I don't see the world through the eyes of a successful, 30-year-old white guy."

Instead of quips about modern romance, Barry increasingly wanted to express the concerns of growing up. The adolescent narrator of *Naked Ladies!* was her inspiration. "That was my first character, my first encounter with the fact that you can take a character and then they'll do all the work and you just sit behind them and jot down everything they're saying," she told the *San Jose Mercury News.* "To me it is simply a marvel that you could have various characters that speak in different voices!" By the time Barry produced the comic strips that appear in *Down the Street,* she had settled on four elementary schoolers for her focus: Arna, the sensitive, observant narrator; Arnold, her rowdy brother; Marlys, a cousin who is smart, self-assured, even bratty; and Freddie, brother of Marlys, who lives with the humiliating knowledge that his parents had him "by accident." "With those four characters," she told the Chicago *Sun-Times,* "you can pretty much tell any story."

Barry's work wasn't as predictably funny anymore. Along with Freddie's bug collection, Marlys's beauty makeovers, and Arnold's chewing-gum map of South America came narratives about child abuse, poverty, and the man at the candy store who hadn't said much to anyone since his wife left him. Some readers thought Barry was saying that childhood unhappiness was funny; some thought she was too depressing; others assumed the traumas were all autobiographical. The last assumption especially troubled Barry ("My God, what kind of life would I have had?" she remarked in the *Seattle Times*), and she ran disclaimers at the front of several of her books. A few papers canceled the strip. For a while Barry was worried. "You always have fears of pushing your audience away," she told the *San Jose Mercury News.* "If you made your reputation doing these sorts of snappy jokes about relationships and then you move into some other field, you're going to definitely lose a lot of people who feel there's something wrong with you. And then I'm going to wonder whether there's something wrong with me. But there's really no choice," she said. "When I found a story that I thought was so good and so authentic, I wasn't going to write one about somebody eating hot dogs just because I was scared to send the stronger one out."

Why should a comic strip about children be painful at times? "Pain for kids is much sharper," Barry explained to the *Chicago Tribune.* "As a kid, you're stuck, no matter what's going on. As an adult, if you're at your friend's house and she and her boyfriend have a wild fight, you can leave. As a kid you can't." Wouldn't it be better to just forget about it? "It's important to go back and decide what happened back then," she said in the *St. Paul Pioneer Press-Dispatch.* "Making an adult decision about it really works wonders. . . . [As a child] when you're not invited to a party, you figure it's because you're a jerk, when really maybe the other kids just needed someone to boast to or you just lived in the wrong neighborhood. People do go through their lives hurt by these things. There's a beauty about reconciling it. It's like music; it has the same kind of power." Barry likened her strips to short stories, and increasingly observers agreed, describing her less as a cartoonist than as an author. "This isn't just a smart cartoon," wrote Katherine Dieckmann in the *Voice Literary Supplement.* "It's strong writing." In the long run Barry's bold move to change her comic strip was amply rewarded. Fewer than twenty papers carried her work in 1983; five years later the number had grown to nearly fifty; she topped sixty in the early 1990s.

Meanwhile Barry had begun another ambitious project, inspired by a vision she had while driving through a pineapple field during a Hawaiian vacation. "I saw a series of portraits," she told the *Los Angeles Times,* "in funky metal frames, of my favorite musicians—most of them black, most of them dead. Suddenly, I knew what my next project would be." Using the bright, flat, multi-colored style of American folk art, Barry created eighteen portraits of American musicians, ranging from pioneering blues singer Gertrude ("Ma") Rainey to soul singer Otis Redding. The paintings were exhibited at a Seattle gallery, which asked Barry to write a short introduction for the exhibition catalog.

She read up on the musicians, many of whom endured poverty and racial discrimination, and began to ponder how thoroughly racism had saturated American society. Determined to explain how closely the history of American music was intertwined with the history of American racism, Barry struggled with her essay for months without success. "[I] was telling instead of showing," she explained in the New York *Daily News*. Instead of finishing the essay she decided to dramatize her concerns in a work of fiction, using the setting she knew best: the poor, interracial neighborhood where she had grown up. In particular, she told the *New York Times,* "I wanted to paint a picture of adolescence, because one of the things that's incredible about adolescence is that you start to see the problems of the world, and when they first hit, you think you know how to fix things."

The resulting novel, *The Good Times Are Killing Me,* is set in the 1960s and narrated by Edna Arkins, a white junior high school student looking back on her last year in elementary school. Edna's downscale neighborhood exemplifies the interracial tensions of the Sixties: while the ideals of the civil rights era preached a new interracial harmony, whites were fleeing from the racially mixed inner cities as quickly as they could. "In the beginning of this street it was a mainly white street," Edna recalls. "The houses went White, White, White, Japanese, White, White. . . . Then it seemed like just about everybody kept moving out until now our street is Chinese, Negro, Negro, White, Japanese, Filipino." As the novel progresses, Edna describes her abortive friendship with Bonna Willis, a hip, assertive black girl from the nearby housing projects. The bridge between the two girls is music: Bonna has records she wants to play, and Edna is lucky enough to have a battered old record player. Their friendship blossoms as Bonna teaches Edna about black singers like James Brown and dances like the Tighten Up while the girls cavort in Edna's Record Player Nightclub—actually Edna's basement, redone in a sixth grader's notion of glamour and style.

The girls' friendship is never free of tension. Edna's aunt, reeking with condescension, takes Bonna along on a family camping trip to acquaint her with the finer things in life (Bonna has been camping many times). Edna is utterly afraid when Bonna starts taking her on a tour of the housing projects. Things deteriorate further when Edna attends a slumber party from which black girls have been excluded, and the two girls start avoiding each other. Then comes the more grown-up, hostile world of junior high, where "from the second we walked through the doors we all automatically split apart into groups of who was alike. . . . This was our new main rule of life even though it wasn't us who created it. It just grew there, like big permanent teeth after baby teeth." Fights erupt. Edna gets pushed around in the girl's bathroom by one of Bonna's friends, then Edna blames Bonna, and Bonna smacks Edna. The friendship is over. "In the vice principal's office we acted like we had never met," Edna concludes. "Like all it was was any black girl slapping any white girl who had mouthed off to her, something that happened every single day and would just keep on happening world without end." "I really wanted to show how the problem of racism affects people for their entire lives," Barry told the *New York Times.* "Edna and Bonna are a couple of kids who became friends at a time when they each really needed a friend. And that need isn't about to stop. I wanted to make them the first casualties. Because it is a war. To me [*Good Times* is] a tragedy—or perhaps a feel-bad comedy."

Barry's novel brought her a new level of fame, including her first major critical notice. Writing in the *New York Times Book Review,* Deborah Stead praised Barry's "impeccable ear" for Edna's way of speaking and declared: "This funny, intricate and finally heartbreaking story exquisitely captures an American childhood." *The Good Times Are Killing Me* also piqued the interest of the theater world, particularly Arnold Aprill, head of Chicago's City Lit Theater Company. After meeting with Barry he roughed out a dramatic adaptation of the novel, and then Barry joined him to work with the cast and write a final script. The play debuted in Chicago in 1989, and then, after further rewriting by Barry, it was produced Off-Broadway in 1991 and became a hit with audiences and theater critics alike. A writer for the *New York Post* praised its "masterly sense of progression, construction, and dramatic form." *The Good Times Are Killing Me,* the reviewer concluded, "hits us in places we had forgotten, and tells us things we never knew we knew." Some reviewers suggested that the play had too many short scenes—the result, they surmised, of Barry's comic-strip background—but they nonetheless lauded her as an acute observer of human nature. Edith Oliver of the *New Yorker* called Edna Arkins "the most enchanting heroine of the Off-Broadway season."

The Good Times Are Killing Me ends as Edna and Bonna enter junior high school, and Barry prepared to follow them, writing about their further adventures in short stories for *Mother Jones,* beginning in 1989. She also moved her weekly comic strip into the world of adolescence, changing its focus from four elementary schoolers to Marlys and her fourteen-year-old sister Maybonne. "I've pretty much exhausted what I know about [childhood]," she told the Chicago *Sun-Times.* Writing about adolescence was a new gamble. "It's hard because people hate that time of their lives. And in general, I think society does not like adolescence. It's really hard to find the right voice of the narrator." As part of her search Barry explored yet another aspect of popular culture: the diaries of teenage girls. Spotlighted in cartoon collections beginning with *Come over, Come Over,* Maybonne's adventures include coping with her overburdened, inadequate parents, getting snubbed by girlfriends, and acting out the role of the small intestine for science class ("I swear to God I hate my life"). She confides in her diary frequently, and Marlys, of course, reads it. Somehow Maybonne survives all the emotional ups and downs. "Life," she declares, "can magically turn cruddy then turn beautiful . . . and then back to cruddy again." *The Freddie Stories* and *The Greatest of Marlys* collect more adventures of Maybonne, Marlys, and Freddie. In the former, Freddie suffers indignities that include sexual abuse, name-calling, and incarceration for a crime he did not commit, but he manages to weather it all. *The Freddie Stories* is "a foray into the perceptions of children growing up in a callous and destructive culture" and "Barry's newest testimony of genius," commented Inga Muscio in *Lambda Book Report.* A *Mother Jones* reviewer added that "Freddie's charm is the sense he makes of the bleak, adult-infested world." *The Greatest of Marlys* shows how "simple pleasures" allow the siblings to cope in a world of "callous teachers, ruthless classmates, and vicious dogs," related Gordon Flagg in *Booklist.* A *Publishers Weekly* critic noted that the book displays Barry's talent for "the very nearly poetic invocation of moments of pubescent joy and humiliation."

Horror rather than joy is at the center of *Cruddy: An Illustrated Novel.* The year is 1971, and the protagonist, Roberta Rohbeson, is a sixteen-year-old living a "cruddy" life with her mother, sister, and misfit friends. Five years earlier, Roberta was the only survivor of a mass murderer's attack on a group of people in a motel in the Nevada desert. Roberta had arrived at that motel with her father, who had gone on a cross-country crime spree after the breakup with her mother. Roberta narrates this harrowing story in flashback. A *Publishers Weekly* reviewer thought "Barry goes over the top with alarming details," and felt readers may have trouble following this "labyrinthine" story. *Booklist* contributor Donna Seaman, however, praised Barry's "galvanic prose" and "daredevil literary wizardry"; mixed in with the story's darker aspects, Seaman wrote, is a "stubborn affection for our seriously flawed species." *Library Journal* reviewer Reba Leiding commented that "Roberta's wacky, irrepressible outlook makes her story fresh, compelling, and sometimes hilarious." And Alanna Nash, writing in the *New York Times Book Review,* called *Cruddy* "a work of terrible beauty," marked by Barry's "ability to capture the paralyzing bleakness of despair, and her uncanny ear for dialogue."

BIOGRAPHICAL/CRITICAL SOURCES:

PERIODICALS

Booklist, January 1, 1987, p. 674; June 1, 1988, p. 1635; October 1, 1988, p. 185; April 15, 1994, p. 1496; August, 1999, Donna Seaman, review of *Cruddy: An Illustrated Novel,* p. 2020; August, 2000, Gordon Flagg, review of *The Greatest of Marlys,* p. 2093.

Chicago Tribune, August 9, 1987; April 19, 1989, sec. 5, p. 1.

Daily News (New York, NY), April 14, 1991.

Denver Post, February 12, 1989.

Interview, November, 1985, p. 119.

Lambda Book Report, July-August, 1999, review of *The Freddie Stories,* p. 20.

Library Journal, March 1, 1999, Stephen Weiner, review of *The Freddie Stories,* p. 78; September 15, 1999, Reba Leiding, review of *Cruddy,* p. 110.

Los Angeles Times, October 18, 1990, p. H13; April 28, 1991.

Los Angeles Times Book Review, October 21, 1990, p. 10.

Mother Jones, December, 1984, p. 17; March, 1999, review of *The Freddie Stories,* p. 75.

Ms., October, 1983, p. 106; April, 1985, p. 23.

New Straits Times, July 9, 2001, review of *Cruddy.*

Newsweek, August, 19, 1991, p. 54.

New York, April 29, 1991, p. 84.

New Yorker, May 6, 1991, p. 81.

New York Post, April 19, 1991.

New York Times, November 27, 1988; August 14, 1991, p. C11.

New York Times Book Review, November 20, 1988, p. 53; September 5, 1999, Alanna Nash, "Bad Trip."

Oregonian (Portland, OR), April 21, 1991.

People, March 30, 1987, p. 109; September 27, 1999, Anne-Marie O'Neill, review of *Cruddy,* p. 53.

Philadelphia Inquirer, September 27, 1991.

Publishers Weekly, March 15, 1999, review of *The Freddie Stories,* p. 48; July 12, 1999, review of *Cruddy,* p. 72; August 28, 2000, review of *The Greatest of Marlys,* p. 57.

St. Paul Pioneer Press-Dispatch, April 2, 1988.

San Jose Mercury News, May 22, 1988.

Sassy, November, 1991, p. 43.

Seattle Times, November 6, 1988; April 25, 1991.

Sun-Times (Chicago, IL), April 30, 1989.

Time, August 26, 1991, p. 63.

Voice Literary Supplement, July, 1985, p. 13; January, 1989, p. 5.

Washington Post, December 12, 1988.

Washington Post Book World, December 20, 1987, p. 12; October 30, 1988, p. 16.

OTHER

Salon, http://www.salon.com/ (May 21, 1999), Pamela Grossman, "Barefoot on the Shag: An Interview with Cartoonist, Novelist Lynda Barry."*

*   *   *

BELL, Marvin (Hartley) 1937-

PERSONAL: Born August 3, 1937, in New York, NY; son of Saul and Belle (Spector) Bell; married Mary Mammosser, 1958 (marriage ended); married Dorothy Murphy; children: Nathan Saul, Jason Aaron. *Education:* Alfred University, B.A., 1958; attended Syracuse University, 1958; University of Chicago, M.A., 1961; University of Iowa, M.F.A., 1963.

ADDRESSES: Home—1416 East College St., Iowa City, IA 52245; (May through August) P.O. Box 1759, Port Townsend, WA 98368. *Office*—Writers' Workshop, University of Iowa, Iowa City, IA 52242. *E-mail*—marvin-bell@uiowa.edu.

CAREER: Poet and educator. University of Iowa, Writers' Workshop, Iowa City, IA, visiting lecturer, 1965, assistant professor, 1967-69, associate professor, 1969-75, professor of English, 1975—; University of Iowa, Flannery O'Connor Professor of Letters, 1986—.

Visiting lecturer, Oregon State University, 1969, Goddard College, 1972, University of Hawaii, 1981, and University of Washington, 1982; University of the Redlands, Lila Wallace-*Reader's Digest* writing fellow, 1991-92, 1992-93; Woodrow Wilson visiting fellow,

Marvin Bell

St. Mary's College of California, 1994-95, Nebraska-Wesleyan University, 1996-97, Pacific University, 1996-97, Hampden-Sydney College, 1999, West Virginia Wesleyan College, 2000-01; Birmingham-Southern College, 2000-01, and Illinois College, 2001-02. Judge for various writing competitions. *Military service:* U.S. Army, 1964-65; first lieutenant.

AWARDS, HONORS: Lamont Award, Academy of American Poets, 1969, for *A Probable Volume of Dreams;* Bess Hokin Award, *Poetry,* 1969; Emily Clark Balch Prize, *Virginia Quarterly Review,* 1970; Guggenheim fellowship, 1976; National Book Award finalist, 1977, for *Stars Which See, Stars Which Do Not See;* National Endowment for the Arts fellowships, 1978, 1984; *American Poetry Review* prize, 1981; Senior Fulbright Scholar to Yugoslavia, 1983, to Australia, 1986; LH.D., Alfred University, 1986; Literature Award, American Academy of Arts and Letters, 1994.

WRITINGS:

POETRY

Two Poems, Hundred Pound Press (Iowa City, IA), 1965.

Poems for Nathan and Saul (pamphlet), Hillside Press (Mount Vernon, IA), 1966.

Things We Dreamt We Died For, Stone Wall Press (Iowa City, IA), 1966.

A Probable Volume of Dreams, Atheneum (New York, NY), 1969.

Woo Havoc (pamphlet), Barn Dream Press (Somerville, MA), 1971.

The Escape into You, Atheneum (New York, NY), 1971.

Residue of Song, Atheneum (New York, NY), 1974.

Stars Which See, Stars Which Do Not See, Atheneum (New York, NY), 1978.

These Green-Going-to-Yellow, Atheneum (New York, NY), 1981.

(With William Stafford) *Segues: A Correspondence in Poetry,* David Godine (Boston, MA), 1983.

Drawn by Stones, by Earth, by Things That Have Been in the Fire, Atheneum (New York, NY), 1984.

New and Selected Poems, Atheneum (New York, NY), 1987.

(With William Stafford) *Annie-Over,* Honeybrook Press (Rexburg, ID), 1988.

Iris of Creation, Copper Canyon Press (Port Townsend, WA), 1990.

A Marvin Bell Reader: Selected Poetry and Prose, Middlebury College Press/University Press of New England (Hanover, NH), 1994.

The Book of the Dead Man, Copper Canyon Press (Port Townsend, WA), 1994.

Ardor: The Book of the Dead Man, Volume 2, Copper Canyon Press (Port Townsend, WA), 1997.

Poetry for a Midsummer's Night, Seventy-fourth Street Productions (Seattle, WA), 1997.

Wednesday: Selected Poems, 1966-1997, Salmon Publishing (Cliffs of Moher, County Clare, Ireland), 1998.

Nightworks: Poems 1962-2000, Copper Canyon Press (Port Townsend, WA), 2000.

OTHER

Old Snow Just Melting: Essays and Interviews, University of Michigan Press (Ann Arbor, MI), 1983.

(Author of introduction) Earl S. Braggs, *Hat Dancer Blue,* Anhinga (Tallahassee, FL), 1992.

(Author of preface) David H. Bain and Mary S. Duffy, editors, *Whose Woods These Are: A History of the Bread Loaf Writers' Conference, 1926-1990,* Ecco Press (New York, NY), 1993.

Also contributor of poems to various anthologies, including *Contemporary American Poets,* edited by Mark Strand, New American Library (New York, NY), 1969; *New Yorker Book of Poems,* Viking (New York, NY), 1969; *The Major Young Poets,* edited by Al Lee, World Publishing, 1971; *New Voices in American Poetry,* edited by David Allan Evans, Winthrop Publishing, 1973; *Preferences,* edited by Richard Howard, Viking (New York, NY), 1974; *The American Poetry Anthology,* edited by Daniel Halpern, Avon (New York, NY), 1975; *Fifty Poets,* edited by Alberta Turner, McKay (New York, NY), 1977; *Fifty Years of American Poetry,* Academy of American Poets/Abrams (New York, NY), 1984; *The Vintage Book of Contemporary American Poetry,* edited by J. D. McClatchy, Random House (New York, NY), 1990; *Poems for a Small Planet: Contemporary American Nature Poetry,* edited by Robert Pack and Jay Parini, Middlebury College Press/University Press of New England, 1993; *Voices on the Landscape,* edited by Michael Carey and Bob Neymeyer, Loess Hills Press, 1996; *The Invisible Ladder,* edited by Liz Rosenberg, Holt (New York, NY), 1996; and *Contemporary American Poetry,* edited by A. Poulin, Jr. and Michael Waters, Houghton Mifflin, 1985, 1991, 1996, 2000. Editor of *Iowa Workshop Poets 1963.*

Author of column, "Homage to the Runner," *American Poetry Review,* 1975-78, 1990-92. Editor and publisher, *Statements,* 1959-64; poetry editor, *North American Review,* 1964-69, and *Iowa Review,* 1969-71.

SIDELIGHTS: American poet and critic Marvin Bell "is a poet of the family. He writes of his father, his wives, his sons, and himself in a dynamic interaction of love and loss, accomplishment, and fear of alienation. These are subjects that demand maturity and constant evaluation. A complete reading of Bell's canon shows his ability to understand the durability of the human heart. Equally impressive is his accompanying technical sophistication," commented William M. Robins in the *Dictionary of Literary Biography.* The son of a Jew who immigrated from the Ukraine, Bell has written frequently of distance and reconciliation between people, often touching on his complex relationship to his heritage.

His *A Probable Volume of Dreams* opens with a poem addressed to the poet's father, initiating a dialogue that continues throughout Bell's works. "Although Bell is never narrowly confessional, it is important to note just how much the death of the father—his profound absence and presence—helps shape Bell's poetry and create possible worlds. *The* father: Bell's own dead father, and his growing sense of himself as a father who has sons and who, like him, will someday die," wrote Arthur Oberg in *American Poetry Review*. In addition to this motif, the poems "tell how unlinear life and art are, how 'progress' is a deception of the nineteenth century, how increasingly distant the finishing line for the poet-runner proves to be," Oberg observed. *A Probable Volume of Dreams* won the Lamont Award from the Academy of American Poets in 1969.

Bell's concern with the self and its relationships, a focus of his earlier poetry, gradually gave way to reflections on the self in relation to nature in books such as *Stars Which See, Stars Which Do Not See*. Speaking of this development to Wayne Dodd and Stanley Plumly in an *Ohio Review* interview, Bell noted that attention to nature has always been an integral part of his life. He grew up among farmers, so the rural life that so fascinated other writers during the 1960s back-to-nature movement was not Bell's inspiration. His first work came from his interest "in what language could make all by itself. . . . And I was interested in relationships between people. I wrote one whole book of poems-in-series about the relationships between a couple of people, or among several people. But now, for whatever good reasons, I *am* interested in allowing nature to have the place in my poems that it always had in my life."

For Bell, the change in subject matter signaled a change in attitude, both personal and cultural. He once explained, "Contemporary American poetry has been tiresome in its discovery of the individual self, over and over and over, and its discovery of emotions that, indeed, we all have: loneliness, fear, despair, ennui, etcetera. I think it can get tiresome when the discovery of such emotions is more or less all the content there is to a poem. We know these things. . . . So I sort of write poetry nowadays from some other attitudes, I think, that came upon me without my ever really thinking about them. I think, for example, that it's ultimately pleasanter and healthier and better for everyone if one thinks of the self as being very small and very unimportant. . . . And I think, as I may not always have thought, that the only way out of the self is to concentrate on others and on things outside the self."

Bell has sometimes referred to this development as an achievement of poetic modesty. He told Dodd and Plumly, "There is a kind of physical reality that we all share a sense of. I mean, we might argue about what reality is, but we all know how to walk across a bridge—instead of walking across the water, for instance. And it seems to me that one definition of modesty in poetry would be a refusal to compromise the physical facts of what it is that is showing up in one's poems," Bell explained.

Speaking of his personal aesthetic, he told the interviewers, "I would like to write poetry which finds salvation in the physical world and the here and now and which defines the soul, if you will, in terms of emotional depth, and that emotional depth in terms of the physical world and the world of human relationships." Regarding style, he added, "I'd like to write a poetry which has little if any insistence about it, as little as possible. I would like to write a poetry which doesn't seem either to button-hole the reader, or demand too much allegiance, or demand that too much of the world be given up for the special world of the poem."

Reviewers have commented that Bell's more recent poems fulfill these aspirations. G. E. Murray, writing in the *Georgia Review,* remarked, "I am impressed by this poet's increasing ability to perceive and praise small wonders. There is life and health in . . . [his verse], and if sometimes Bell's expression is quiet and reserved, his talent is not. Altogether, *Stars Which See, Stars Which Do Not See* demonstrates an important transitional phase for the poet—a subdued, graceful vein that enables him to 'speak of eyes and seasons' with an intimacy and surehandedness that informs and gratifies. . . . I believe Marvin Bell is on a track of the future—a mature, accessible and personalized venture into the mainstream of contemporary American verse." Of the same book, David St. John wrote in *Parnassus,* "Many poets have tried to appropriate into their poems a gritty, tough-talking American character, and to thereby earn for themselves some . . . 'authenticity'. . . . In *Stars Which See, Stars Which Do Not See,* Bell has found within his *own* voice that American voice, and with it the ability to write convincingly about the smallest details of a personal history."

Bell's subsequent works have elicited from critics an appreciation of the poet's blending of precise descriptive powers with deceptively simple grammar and syntax. In reviewing *These Green-Going-to-Yellow,* Richard Jackson commented in the *American Book Review* that Bell's strategy of deploying words and phrases in unusual contexts has resulted in "an increasingly expansive and colloquial language that is willing to gather in larger fragments of the world without the 'new critical' necessity of neatly tying each bit together on the surface of the text." The poet's linguistic maturity has also been singled out in discussions of the 1987 anthology, *New and Selected Poems.* For several critics, the less private and self-referential later poetry contained in this volume has made Bell one of the most arresting of contemporary writers. A *Poetry* reviewer noted that Bell "is a discreet master of withheld information. His writing has a distinctive enough flavor to make us feel we know him well after turning the last page of this book; but . . . of the events and circumstances of his life the poems say very little directly." And a contributor to *American Poetry Review* related: "It is Bell's later poetry, far less private and solipsistic, and far more abundantly intelligent and astonishing [than his earlier poetry,] that has made him one of the best poets now working."

The subsequent collection, *Nightworks: Poems 1962-2000,* further allows readers to trace Bell's growth, remarked a *Publishers Weekly* reviewer, who said, "This selection shows a poet progressing to the peak of his powers." The text, which contains selections from *A Probable Volume of Dreams, The Escape into You,* and *Stars Which See, Stars Which Do Not See,* among others, highlights subjects consistent throughout Bell's body of work. Poems included in this collection touch on the death of Bell's father, his identity as a Jew, his experiences in the military, as well as his relationships with his wives and children. In an article for the *North Stone Review,* James Naiden noted that *Nightworks* places Bell in the more comprehensive context of poetic tradition. "While the 'father poems' and poems otherwise exhuming the past, as it were, illustrate the incantatory ghosts in Bell's oeuvre," wrote Naiden, "there are also acknowledgments to his prolific forebears, such as William Stafford . . . and, of course, Emily Dickinson." These and other "kindred poets . . . provide clarity to [Bell's] voice by their own leave-taking, the offering of a poet to give voice where otherwise there is silence." In addition, the poems in the collection strike a balance between what Naiden termed "common experience" and Bell's personal history, as well as his connections to others. In her *North Stone Review* assessment of Bell's *The Book of the Dead Man,* Carol Ellis similarly remarked that in the interplay between Bell's "Odysseus," the dead man, and nature, "communion creates community," emphasizing that "the dead man is in a state of constant knowing because he is never out of touch with the world."

Bell's use of humor has continued to develop over the years. "Humor in the fifteen new poems contained in *New and Selected Poems* is of the sort that deflates our facile reductions of experience," observed an essayist for *Contemporary Poets.* "Marvin Bell's work satisfies a need for every kind of laugh and reminds us that com-

edy is at least as tough as tragedy. From the outset, however, he has been modulating the balance of amusement and profundity in his poetry. Early on his wit was, by turns, clever and probing, tending at one moment to trivialize his work, at another to deepen it. But over the long haul he has exerted mature control."

In 1994 Bell published what some reviewers regard as his most radical work, *The Book of the Dead Man,* which consists of a sequence of thirty-three poems on various facets of life, narrated by the anonymous title character. Stan Sanvel Rubin wrote in *Prairie Schooner* that Bell has fashioned in this work "a dazzling linguistic Chinese box, at once alluring and elusive, which shows up for once and for all (maybe) the emptiness of 'Language Poetry' and, in fact, much recent experimental and postmodern writing." Bruce Murphy averred in *Poetry* that "Bell is really out there—trying to invent a new kind of poetry, something like an epic with only one character." Richard Jackson, in an appraisal for the *North American Review,* termed *The Book of the Dead Man* "one of the most complex, most original books in a long time." Jackson added that Bell deals with both internal and external forces but does not see them as necessarily separate: "The counterpointed vision also means that to talk about the cosmos is to talk about the self and its tiniest sensations, to talk about government is to talk about the self 's needs—one thing is always seen in contrast to several other things." The critic concluded, "What *The Book of the Dead Man* does, by its verbal pyrotechnics, is redefine sensibility, and this is the most essential thing any poetry can do. . . . This is an astounding feat. There's not a greater gift any poet or poetry can bring." In *Ardor: The Book of the Dead Man, Volume Two,* Bell continues in an similar mode, darkly rendering what a *Publishers Weekly* contributor described as "the thin line that separates the real from the unreal, the illuminated from the dim, the living from the dead."

Bell's volume of essays, *Old Snow Just Melting: Essays and Interviews,* is concerned with themes typical of the author's poetic works, particularly mutability and decay. *Virginia Quarterly Review* contributor Thomas Swiss commended Bell's prose, saying Bell "writes with style: clean, metaphoric prose that's readable and instructive. He writes simply without condescending and without ignoring the complexity of the issues he examines." The volume also presents valuable insights into the author's poetic process. Bell writes, as quoted by Swiss, "I'll tell you right now the secrets of writing poetry. . . . First, one learns to write by reading. . . . Number two, I believe that language, compared to the materials of other art forms, has only one thing going for it: the ability to be precise. . . . And the third and most important secret is that, if you do anything seriously for a long time, you get better at it."

BIOGRAPHICAL/CRITICAL SOURCES:

BOOKS

Contemporary Literary Criticism, Gale (Detroit, MI), Volume 8, 1978, Volume 31, 1985.
Contemporary Poets, 6th edition, St. James Press (Detroit, MI), 1996.
Dictionary of Literary Biography, Volume 5: *American Poets since World War II,* Gale (Detroit, MI), 1980.
Malkoff, Karl, *Crowell's Handbook of Contemporary American Poetry,* Crowell (New York, NY), 1973.

PERIODICALS

American Book Review, September, 1982, p. 20.
American Poetry Review, May-June, 1976; September, 1985; January-February, 1989.
Antaeus, spring-summer, 1982.
Antioch Review, spring, 1982; spring, 1995, Daniel McGuiness, review of *The Book of the Dead Man,* p. 246.
Booklist, March 15, 1994, p. 1322; October 15, 2000, Donna Seaman, review of *Nightworks: Poems 1962-2000,* p. 411.
Chicago Review, Vol. 28, no. 1, 1976.
Georgia Review, fall, 1982, pp. 675-679; summer, 2001, Judith Kitchen, review of *Nightworks.*
Hudson Review, August, 1985.
Iowa Review, winter, 1981; Volume 30, number 2, 2000, pp. 3-22.
Missouri Review, summer, 1982.
Nation, February 2, 1970.
New Republic, March 29, 1975.
New York Times Book Review, April 8, 1984; November 11, 1984.
North American Review, January-February, 1995, Richard Jackson, "Containing the Other: Marvin Bell's Recent Poetry," p. 45.
North Stone Review, number 13, 2001, Carol Ellis, "History and Renaissance: Marvin Bell;" number 14, 2002, James Naiden, "The Work of Marvin Bell."
Ohio Review, Volume 17, number 3, 1976.
Parnassus, fall-winter, 1972.
Poetry, March, 1985, p. 349; April, 1988, pp 35-37; August, 1991, pp. 280-295; December, 1995, pp. 159-161; August, 1998, David Yezzi, review of *Ardor: The Book of the Dead Man, Volume 2,* p.

288; November, 2001, John Taylor, review of *Nightworks,* pp. 112-114.
Prairie Schooner, spring, 1996, pp. 181-184.
Publishers Weekly, September 22, 1997, review of *Ardor,* p. 77; August 28, 2000, review of *Nightworks,* p. 79.
Shenandoah, summer, 1971.
Stand, Vol. 13, no. 4, 1972.
Virginia Quarterly Review, summer, 1982, p. 94; winter, 1986, pp. 173-185; spring, 1988, p. 62; spring, 1998, review of *Ardor: The Book of the Dead Man, Volume 2.*

OTHER

The Poetry Kit, http://www.poetrykit.org (October 31, 2001).

*   *   *

BERRIGAN, Edmund Joseph Michael, Jr.   1934-1983
(Ted Berrigan)

PERSONAL: Born November 15, 1934, in Providence, RI; died July 4, 1983, in New York, NY; son of Edmund (an engineer) and Margaret (Dugan) Berrigan; married Sandra Alper, 1962 (marriage ended); married Alice Notley (a poet), 1971; children: (first marriage) Kate, David; (second marriage) Anselm, Edmond. *Education:* Attended Providence College, c. 1952; University of Tulsa, B.A., 1959, M.A., 1962.

CAREER: Poet, publisher, and educator. Editorial assistant, *Art News;* "C" Press and *C* Magazine, New York, NY, founder, editor, and publisher, beginning 1964. St. Mark's Poetry Project, New York, NY, organizer and instructor, beginning 1966; visiting lecturer for Writer's Workshop at University of Iowa, Iowa City, IA, 1968-69; also taught at Yale University, University of Michigan, the Kerouac School, Boulder, CO, and Essex University, Essex, England. Poet-in-residence, Northeastern Illinois University, 1969-76, and City College of the City University of New York. *Military service:* U.S. Army, 1954-57.

AWARDS, HONORS: Poetry Foundation award, 1964, for *The Sonnets.*

Ted Berrigan

WRITINGS:

ALL UNDER NAME TED BERRIGAN; ALL POETRY, UNLESS INDICATED

A Lily for My Love: 13 Poems, privately printed, 1959.

Galileo: Or Finksville (play), privately printed, 1964.

The Sonnets, "C" Press (New York, NY), 1964, expanded and with introduction by Alice Notley, Penguin (New York, NY), 2000.

(With Ron Padgett) *Seventeen* (plays), "C" Press (New York, NY), 1965.

(With Ron Padgett and Joe Brainard) *Some Things* (drawings and poems), privately printed, 1965.

Living with Chris, Boke Press, 1966.

Many Happy Returns to Dick Gallup, Angel Hair (New York, NY), 1967.

(With Ron Padgett and Joe Brainard) *Bean Spasms* (poetry and art), Kulchur Press (New York, NY), 1967.

Many Happy Returns: Poems, Corinth Books (New York, NY), 1969.

Fragment: For Jim Brodey, Cape Goliard Press (London, England), 1969.

(With Anselm Hollo) *Doubletalk,* T. G. Miller (Iowa City, IA), 1969.

(With Ron Padgett) *Noh,* privately printed, 1969.

(With Tom Clark, Allen Kaplan, and Ron Padgett) *Guillaume Apollinaire ist tot: Gedichte, Prosa* (German-English text), Maerz (Frankfurt, Germany), 1970.

In the Early Morning Rain, Cape Goliard Press (New York, NY), 1970.

(With Anne Waldman) *Memorial Day,* Poetry Project (New York, NY), 1971.

Train Ride, Vehicle Editions (New York, NY), 1971.

(With Tom Clark and Ron Padgett) *Back in Boston Again,* Telegraph Books (New York, NY), 1972.

The Drunken Boat, Adventures in Poetry (New York, NY), 1974.

A Feeling for Leaving, Frontward Books (New York, NY), 1975.

Red Wagon, Yellow Press (Chicago, IL), 1976.

Nothing for You, Angel Hair (New York, NY), 1977.

Clear the Range, Adventures in Poetry/Coach House South (New York, NY), 1977.

(With Kenneth Koch) *ZZZZZZ,* edited by Kenward Elmslie, 1978.

(With Harris Schiff) *Yo-Yo's with Money,* United Artist Books (Henniker, NH), 1979.

So Going around Cities: New and Selected Poems, 1958-1979, Blue Wind Press (Berkeley, CA), 1980.

In a Blue River, Little Light Books (New York, NY), 1981.

A Certain Slant of Sunlight, O Books (Oakland, CA), 1988.

Selected Poems, edited by Aram Saroyan, Penguin (New York, NY), 1994.

Joel Lewis, editor, *On the Level Everyday: Selected Talks on Poetry and the Art of Living,* Talisman House (Jersey City, NJ), 1997.

Contributor to anthologies, including *Young American Poets,* edited by Paul Carroll, Follett, 1968, *The American Literary Anthology I,* Farrar, Straus, 1968, and *Sparklers,* Random House, 1969. Contributor to *Poetry, Art News, Art and Literature, Angel Hair, Mother,* and *World.*

EDITOR

(With Ron Padgett) Tom Veitch, *Literary Days: Selected Writings,* L. and E. Gude (New York, NY), 1964.

Kenward Elmslie, *The Power Plant Poems,* "C" Press (New York, NY), 1965.

Ron Padgett, *In Advance of the Broken Arm,* "C" Press (New York, NY), 1965.

Dick Gallup, *Hinges: Poems,* "C" Press (New York, NY), 1965.

Joe Ceravolo, *Fits of Dawn,* "C" Press (New York, NY), 1965.

Michael Brownstein, *Behind the Wheel: Poems,* "C" Press (New York, NY), 1967.

SIDELIGHTS: Poet Ted Berrigan's work grew out of the American Expressionist movement, "which grounds literary authority in the personality of the writer rather than, say, a political creed or traditional aesthetics," explained essayist Edward Halsey Foster in the *Dictionary of Literary Biography.* Writers who were part of the Expressionist tradition include Ralph Waldo Emerson, Walt Whitman, Gertrude Stein, William Saroyan, William Faulkner, and Thomas Wolfe. Beat Generation writers Allen Ginsberg and Jack Kerouac also built on the Expressionist foundation, and, as Foster related, "Berrigan considered himself a 'late beat.' " Foster continued, "Berrigan argued that the world as presented in his poetry was a projection of his self." As Libbie Rifkin noted in *Contemporary Literature,* "Berrigan's poetry is at the place where the institutional and the aesthetic meet."

In a separate *Dictionary of Literary Biography* entry on Berrigan, Alice Smith Haynes noted that the poet was preoccupied with style, was "consciously concerned with form and with his role as the creator; this emphasis is sometimes looked upon as playing 'games with the craft of poetry.' " Noting his tendency to switch around lines and sections of his poems, she commented, "These characteristics of artistic creation place Berrigan loosely within the modern art movement of abstract expressionism. Berrigan, in fact, likens his poetry to the paintings of Willem de Kooning, whose forceful, even violent, brush strokes show his unmistakable presence within his work, a unity of artist and canvas that abstract expressionists seek. In much the same way, Berrigan's presence in his poetry is illustrated by the unusual placement of lines."

Berrigan sometimes married traditional structures, such as the sonnet, to untraditional content. This and some other aspects of his work are seemingly contradictory yet frequently effective, in the opinion of some critics. In a review of the posthumously published *Selected Poems* for *World Literature Today,* Michael Leddy wrote that Berrigan "created a poetry that melded wit, feeling, and intelligence in unexpected ways, a poetry that encompassed both painterly abstractions and an attention to daily human details, a poetry of radical formalism (the sonnet as a series of fourteen one-line units) and open-field composition, a poetry by turns opaque and utterly clear, a poetry of unabashed imitation (of Frank O'Hara, among others) and singular originality." Foster remarked, "Berrigan owes much to O'Hara's 'I do this, I do that' style," describing mundane occurrences of day-to-day living, but also noted that the poet sometimes parodied this style. "There are characteristic O'Hara phrasings in many Berrigan poems, particularly in the early work, but the sensibility they express is unmistakably Berrigan's," Foster added. "He borrowed procedures and even lines from other poets but fused them with a persona that was distinctly his own."

For example, Foster observed, Berrigan's *The Sonnets* shows the influence of T. S. Eliot's 1922 work, *The Waste Land.* "In particular, the disjunctive structure and the mixture of cadences and voices in *The Sonnets* is modeled on Eliot's example," Foster noted. "What did not interest Berrigan was Eliot's wearied tone and sensibility, and in its place one finds Berrigan's distinctive Irish-American temper, his own blend of humor and grace. Instead of Eliot's allusions to, and quotations from, canonical works of high culture, Berrigan employed a great range of references from popular as well as serious works." *Los Angeles Times Book Review* critic Peter Clothier observed that in *So Going around Cities: New and Selected Poems, 1958-1979,* "many of the lines or phrases in the sonnets (as in other poems) are interchangeable, repeated in new contexts, an old piece of cloth stitched back into a new quilt. . . . Similarly, large and small chunks of poems from sources as various as Rilke and Rimbaud are picked up and dropped into the text, becoming a part of the texture of the whole."

Berrigan found subject matter for his poems in all facets of his life. His second wife, poet Alice Notley, wrote in the introduction to *Selected Poems* that Berrigan "believed that being a poet was a 24-hour-a-day job" and that his work utilized "everything we did or said." This aspect of his poetry has not pleased all critics. *Contemporary Literature* contributor Libbie Rifkin, after quoting a poem from *The Sonnets* in which Berrigan meditates on his friends' careers and personal ambitions as he awaits delivery of the mail, remarked, "There's a persistent sense in *The Sonnets* that writing poetry of communal experience is something to do while waiting, for the mail, or—more ominously—for posterity. . . . It seems worth noting that the experience Berrigan records in these poems is often falsified, or at least pureed by the cut-up procedure until it is no longer autobiographical. Treating his own life as a 'ready-made,' the poet anticipates an afterlife on the bookshelves and syllabi of secure canonicity." Ray Olson, reviewing *Selected Poems* for *Booklist,* felt Berrigan created an idealized and "corny" view of life in the 1960s counterculture and termed Berrigan a "pop" poet. Some other critics, though, have maintained that Berrigan's poetry is of high and enduring quality. A *Publishers Weekly* commentator, discussing a new edition of *The Sonnets,* called the contents "first and foremost wonderful poetry." Foster praised Berrigan's "ability to create subtly shifting evocations of meaning and tone," and Leddy commended the poet for "mining the possibilities of the language that comes one's way." Foster added, "Above all, his absolute dedication to poetry in a culture that has only a marginal interest in that art was virtually heroic."

BIOGRAPHICAL/CRITICAL SOURCES:

BOOKS

Berrigan, Ted, *On the Level Everyday: Selected Talks on Poetry and the Art of Living,* edited by Joel Lewis, Talisman House (Jersey City, NJ), 1997.

Clark, Tom, *Late Returns: A Memoir of Ted Berrigan,* Tombouctou (Bolinas, CA), 1985.

Dictionary of Literary Biography, Gale (Detroit, MI), Volume V: *American Poets since World War II, First Series,* 1980, Volume 169: *American Poets since World War II, Fifth Series,* 1996.

Fischer, Aaron, *Ted Berrigan: An Annotated Checklist,* Granary Books (New York, NY), 1998.

Foster, Edward, *Code of the West: A Memoir of Ted Berrigan,* Rodent Press (Boulder, CO), 1994.

MacBeth, George, *Interview with Ted Berrigan,* Ignu Publications, 1971.

Padgett, Ron, *Ted: A Personal Memoir of Ted Berrigan,* The Figures (Great Barrington, MA), 1993.

Ratcliffe, Stephen, and Leslie Scalapino, editors, *Talking in Tranquility: Interviews with Ted Berrigan,* O Books (Oakland, CA), 1991.

Waldman, Anne, editor, *Nice to See You: Homage to Ted Berrigan,* Coffee House Press (Minneapolis, MN), 1991.

PERIODICALS

Booklist, January 15, 1994, Ray Olson, review of *Selected Poems,* p. 895.

Contemporary Literature, winter, 1997, Libbie Rifkin, " 'Worrying about Making It': Ted Berrigan's Social Poetics," pp. 640-647.

Hudson Review, summer, 1968.

Library Journal, May 15, 1997, David Kirby, review of *On the Level Everyday: Selected Talks on the Poetry and the Art of Living,* p. 76.

Los Angeles Times Book Review, June 1, 1980.

Publishers Weekly, September 18, 2000, review of *The Sonnets,* p. 105.

Village Voice, March 5, 1970.

Vort, no. 2, 1972.

Yale Review, June, 1969.

Western Humanities Review, summer, 1971.

World Literature Today, spring, 1995, Michael Leddy, review of *Selected Poems,* p. 364.

OBITUARIES:

PERIODICALS

Newsweek, July 18, 1983.
New York Times, July 7, 1983.
Washington Post, July 9, 1983.*

*   *   *

BERRIGAN, Ted
    See BERRIGAN, Edmund Joseph Michael, Jr.

*   *   *

BERRY, James   1925-

PERSONAL: Born 1925, in Jamaica; immigrated to England in 1948. *Avocational interests:* Cricket and music, especially jazz, reggae, and classical.

ADDRESSES: Office—c/o Hamish Hamilton, 27 Wright's Lane, London W8, England.

CAREER: Writer and editor. Has worked as an educator and conductor of writing workshops for children in the British school system, 1977.

AWARDS, HONORS: C. Day Lewis Fellowship, 1977-78; National Poetry Competition Award, 1981, for "Fantasy of an African Boy"; Grand Prix Smarties Prize for Children's Books, Book Trust, 1987, and Coretta Scott King award honor book, 1988, both for *A Thief in the Village and Other Stories; Signal* Poetry Award, 1989, for *When I Dance: Poems;* Order of the British Empire, 1990; Cholmondeley Award for Poetry, Society of Authors, 1991; Coretta Scott King Award Honor Book, and *Boston Globe-Horn Book* Award for fiction, 1993, for *Ajeemah and His Son.*

WRITINGS:

(Editor) *Bluefoot Traveller: An Anthology of Westindian Poets in Britain,* Limestone Publications, 1976, revised edition published as *Bluefoot Poetry by West Indians in Britain,* Harrap, 1981.

Fractured Circles (poetry), New Beacon Books, 1979.

Cut-away Feelins; Loving; [and] *Lucy's Letters,* Strange Lime Fruit Stone, 1981.

Lucy's Letters [and] *Loving,* New Beacon Books, 1982.

(Editor) *Dance to a Different Drum: Brixton Festival Poetry 1983,* Brixton Festival, 1983.

(Editor) *News for Babylon: The Chatto Book of West Indian-British Poetry,* Chatto & Windus, 1984.

Chain of Days, Oxford University Press, 1985.

A Thief in the Village and Other Stories, Hamish Hamilton, 1987, Orchard Watts, 1988.

Anancy-Spiderman, illustrations by Joseph Olubo, Walker, 1988, published as *Spiderman-Anancy,* Holt, 1989.

When I Dance: Poems, Hamish Hamilton, 1988, published as *When I Dance,* illustrations by Karen Barbour, Harcourt, 1991.

(Contributor) Grace Nichols, editor, *Black Poetry,* Blackie, 1989.

The Future-telling Lady: Six Stories, HarperCollins, 1993.

Ajeemah and His Son, HarperCollins, 1993.

Celebration Song: A Poem, illustrated by Louise Brierley, Simon & Schuster, 1994.

(Compiler) *Classic Poems to Read Aloud,* illustrated by James Mayhew, Larousse, 1995.

Rough Sketch Beginning (poems), illustrated by Robert Florczak, Harcourt, 1996.

Hot Earth Cold Earth, Dufour, 1996.

Don't Leave an Elephant to Go and Chase a Bird, illustrated by Ann Grifalconi, Simon & Schuster, 1996.

Everywhere Faces Everywhere, illustrated by Reynold Ruffins, Simon & Schuster, 1997.

First Palm Trees, illustrated by Greg Couch, Simon & Schuster, 1997.

Isn't My Name Magical? illustrated by Shelly Hehenberger, Simon & Schuster, 1999.

Also author of *The Girls and Yanga Marshall,* 1987.

SIDELIGHTS: James Berry "has acquired a considerable reputation for fusing two cultures into a sensitive understanding of both in prose and poetry," according to a *Junior Bookshelf* critic. The same reviewer went on to comment that Berry "draws upon his West Indian memories for subject matter and his wide acquaintance with the richness of English language as a means of expression." The recipient of numerous honors, Berry "is not just another fist-raising polemicist," according to *Booklist*'s James Parisi. In his poems, as in his novel and short stories for young readers, Berry paints not only a self-portrait, but also a sketch of his people, the conflicts, "injustices, and coming-to-conscious identity of a colonized race," according to Parisi.

Berry noted in his acceptance speech for a 1993 *Boston Globe-Horn Book* award that as a child he only slowly understood the legacy of slavery and oppression that touches people of all races. "Denial and exclusion easily become part of a total dispossessing," Berry noted. "What is necessary is to move beyond the world of exclusion and of denial." Kwame S. N. Dawes, in *Writers of Multicultural Fiction for Young Adults,* observed that Berry's preoccupations with race and identity questions began as a teenager in his Jamaican village where the privileged position of the whites vis-a-vis the blacks was all too apparent. The slave history of the island deeply affected the future poet as well. "Alarmed by the implication of inferiority that such a background suggested, Berry has committed his work to trying to retrieve the humanity and dignity of blacks all over the world," Dawes wrote. Berry's mission is not one of vengeance according to Dawes. "Instead, he has sought in his work to create dialogue through a two-way process of culture sharing and respect."

In story collections such as the prize-winning *A Thief in the Village and Other Stories, The Girls and Yanga Marshall,* and *The Future-telling Lady: Six Stories,* Berry has celebrated the quotidian of growing up black in Jamaica, writing of aspirations, hopes, and dreams both fulfilled and unfulfilled. In his collections of trickster tales dealing with the spiderman named Anancy, Berry has brought oral tradition to life, calling up the West African past of the peoples of the Caribbean. In his poetry, such as *When I Dance,* he introduces readers not only to the experiences of a different time and world, but also to the musical possibilities of Creole language and English. His prize-winning novel, *Ajeemah and His Son,* has also moved readers on several continents and made real and deeply personal the horrifying experience of slavery. Yet through it all, Berry maintains the light touch; his is the voice of reconciliation rather than simply condemnation. His job as a writer, as he has often noted, is to build bridges between cultures and races, to tell the stories of those whom history often ignores.

Berry was born in rural Jamaica in 1924, one of six children. A close family, the children grew up by the sea, living a subsistence lifestyle on their own crops and animals. He enjoyed "a gregarious, outdoor, rural country life," as he noted in his *Horn Book* acceptance speech. Yet always there was a great yearning in the young Berry to learn what had gone on in the world before he was born. "When I was about ten years old, I began to be truly bewildered by my everyday Jamaican rural life," Berry wrote. "I felt something of an alien and an outsider and truly imprisoned." In part this was due to the "lacks" surrounding his life: lack of information, lack of reading matter, lack of a sense of being a worthwhile person simply because of his skin color. Reading and writing came easily for the young Berry; he learned to read the Bible before he was four years old, and one school textbook was generally shared between all members of his family. "But I had an inner life that could not be shared," he noted in *Horn Book*. There were Bible stories and the Anancy traditional folktales about that spiderman trickster which helped to open his "inner seeing," but these also emphasized the lack of more formal written tales.

At age seventeen, Berry went to the United States as part of a labor scheme during the war years. He stayed for four years, but went back to his coastal Jamaican village, disillusioned by the treatment of blacks in the United States. He stayed on in Jamaica until 1948, but finally the limited opportunities of island life sent him off to London, just as many others from the West Indies had done before him. In London, Berry worked to put himself through night school in telegraphy, and stayed in that field for many years until he was ultimately made 'redundant,' losing his job to automation. Such career termination carried with it a state pension in Britain, and this redundancy came at a fortuitous moment for Berry, for he had begun to write by this time, publishing short stories and creating stage plays. Now, out of a job, he could devote himself full time to his craft.

Early chapbook publications, as well as his advocacy of black writing in Britain, led to Berry's editing of an anthology of West Indian, or Westindian, poets in Britain, *Bluefoot Traveller,* and to conducting writers' workshops in the schools. In 1977, he worked for a year as writer-in-residence in a comprehensive school in London, an experience that convinced Berry of the need

for children's books about black life. However, another decade and several adult volumes of poetry and stories intervened before Berry set himself to right that situation.

Berry had been gone from his native Jamaica for almost four decades before publication of his first book for children, *A Thief in the Village and Other Stories,* yet frequent visits had kept him in touch with his roots, allowing him to celebrate the importance of simple things in this collection. Neil Bissoondath, writing in the *New York Times Book Review,* felt that Berry's collection of stories for teens "fills a gap that has existed for years in West Indian writing." Bissoondath went on to note that in his own household, where books were treasured, there had been no stories of people like himself; nothing about the children of the West Indies. "Our daily life, it seemed, was too pedestrian to provide drama between hard covers," Bissoondath wrote. "Now James Berry, in his sprightly and realistic tales of Jamaican life, proves this to be untrue."

Berry was happy to present the story collection to Jane Nissen, an editor at Hamish Hamilton, because he saw the need for more children's books about black life. He noticed there were few books available on the subject while he was working in the British school system in 1977. "Those stories were straight out of my own childhood and later observations," Berry told a *Publishers Weekly* interviewer. "In the Caribbean, we were the last outpost of the Empire. No one has reported our stories, or the way we saw things. It's the function of writers and poets to bring in the left-out side of the human family."

A variety of boys and girls are presented in the nine short stories set mostly in a coastal town some eighty miles from Kingston. In one story, "Becky and the Wheels-and-Brakes-Boys," a girl gets a long-awaited bicycle. "I know total-total that if I had my own bike, the Wheels-and-Brake-Boys wouldn't treat me like that," Becky tells readers in this opening tale to the collection. In the title story, a Rastafarian man is wrongly accused of stealing, and the villagers allow their own prejudices to cover up the more respected member of the village who is actually guilty of the crime. There are tales of underdogs and children struggling for acceptance from their peers. The object of belonging, as Dawes pointed out, "is usually something physical," such as Becky's bike or a mouth organ in "The Mouth-Organ Boys," and even a mongoose, in "Elias and the Mongoose." A reviewer for *Publishers Weekly* noted that "Berry's prose is liquid and cool," that the stories "are musical in print, even before they are read aloud," and that Berry produced an "epiphanic" collection: the stories wrap themselves "around ordinary incidents and transforms them into lore." Writing in *Bulletin of the Center for Children's Books,* Betsy Hearne concluded that the language was "rhythmic" and that the scenes in the stories "will take readers beyond suburban America to a subsistence society that is nonetheless complex in family relationships and community dynamics." A critic in *Junior Bookshelf* called Berry's initial juvenile effort a "lovely collection," noting that they "focus on family life, of poverty, of joy and sadness, and all have the atmosphere of Jamaican life, tightly bottled and ready to fizz out on opening." Bissoondath noted in the *New York Times Book Review* that these "are simple stories of restricted possibility, but Mr. Berry delves deep, revealing and examining the dreams of the children."

Berry tells his stories in the language of the people he features, a rhythmic mixture of local dialect and more formal English. "It's so important to me to use authentic voices," Berry told *Publishers Weekly.* "Readers need to learn to appreciate black people's voices. Sounds are community. We may damage children by putting down something so closely knitted to their early years. Life has given us a rich variety of language. And if we celebrate one language over the many, we are deprived. When people share, they are joyful and enriched."

A Thief in the Village and Other Stories won the Grand Prix Smarties Prize in 1987 and was named a Coretta Scott King award honor book in 1988. Berry feels his success is partly due to changing attitudes about cultural and ethnic differences. People of all cultures are more accepting and appreciative of the ethnic differences that exist between people, especially in the larger nations. As more and more writers celebrate their ethnic heritage, such as their language, in poems and stories, the entire world benefits, he said in *Publishers Weekly.* He believes this is especially important for Caribbeans since language plays such a central role in the preservation of their culture, with dialect or "national language" being taught as well as traditional history in stories and poems spoken or performed for children by their elders. Eva Gillies comments in the *Times Literary Supplement* that the language in *A Thief in the Village* makes it "ideal for reading aloud. Both language and stories form a good introduction to West Indian culture."

More such linguistic enrichment has come with Berry's other works for young readers, including *The Girls and Yanga Marshall,* a further collection of four tales from the Caribbean, built around the central theme of the de-

sire to resolve conflicts. The title story, about a young man's adventures at school and on the streets, brings another aspect of Caribbean life into focus. Readers can perceive the two kinds of history he learns and the difference between how he feels about others and the way they regard him. In another story of identity, a young man endures a conflict with the traditional ways of his father by strengthening his relationship with his sister. Each of the four stories in the book says something about the desire to resolve conflicts, which is not a quick or easy task.

The Future-telling Lady: Six Stories, geared toward middle-grade readers, combines five contemporary Caribbean tales with one African-American folktale featuring "young people between the ages of ten and fourteen who, in the course of the story, learn something about themselves," according to Lyn Miller-Lachmann writing in *School Library Journal.* The "Future-telling Lady" is Mother Eesha, who can see into the future and helps a boy who at first is skeptical of her special ability. "The Cotton-Tree Ghosts" tells of a young girl's encounter with a family who has been dead for hundreds of years. All the stories are told from the child's point of view, and also capture the rhythmic Jamaican language. The provocative "Mr. Mongoose and Mrs. Hen" is about a hen who seeks justice for a mongoose who has eaten her children. The case is brought to trial, and the hen finds that all the court officials and the judge are mongooses.

"Berry's poetic, often onomatopoeic, style captures the language and daily rhythms of rural and small-town Jamaica," noted Miller-Lachmann, who also said that his "sense of humor will attract readers." *Booklist*'s Hazel Rochman commented that "Berry tells his stories of contemporary Jamaica with a joyful exuberance, rooted in the oral tradition, that demands they be read aloud," while *Horn Book*'s Ellen Fader observed that the "strikingly original stories . . . show tremendous range in subject matter and mood" and that "Berry's language sings with grace, beauty, and respect."

With his *Anancy-Spiderman,* Berry introduced that West African trickster into the literature. This particular clever character is supposed to outwit his opponents and even whisper stories into children's ears at night, tales told in a mixture of Creole and English. Reviewing the American publication of the collection, a contributor in *Bulletin of the Center for Children's Books* concluded that there was "no question that this is a living tradition." Berry has written two further Anancy tales, *Don't Leave an Elephant to Go and Chase a Bird* and *First Palm Trees.* These picture books reveal different aspects of the trickster. In the former title, Anancy receives a corncob from Skygod. Giving this gift to a hungry woman, he receives a gourd in exchange. Anancy continues to trade up all day until greed leads to his undoing by a herd of elephants. In *First Palm Trees,* Anancy desperately wants to win the king's reward for creating the first palm trees in the world. When he tries to bribe the Spirits into making such a tree and then splitting the reward with him, Anancy learns a lesson of cooperation as each Spirit in turn rejects his offer in favor of working together. A *Kirkus Reviews* critic noted that "Berry uses a lovely West Indian lilt" in this "rollicking, original read-aloud."

While writing his second collection of short stories, Berry suddenly realized that there was a missing aspect to his tales. Only as an adult had he come to see the irony of how he and his siblings and friends would play on the ruins of an old slave plantation sugar mill in Jamaica. Growing up he heard bits and pieces of the slave history of his island; as an adult he brought himself to read of this ignoble past. The missing element from his story collection was the ingredient of slavery—connecting Jamaica with Africa and the slave trade. "Then the full idea struck me," Berry wrote in *Horn Book.* "I was excited. I'd come to know in my writing that whenever the spark of an idea so struck and heated me that sweat instantly poured down my armpits, I was really onto something."

What Berry was onto was the story of a father and his son kidnapped in the early nineteenth century from their African home and shipped into slavery. *Ajeemah and His Son* is a short but hard-hitting book. *Horn Book*'s Gail Pettiford Willett noted that in "eighty-three pages James Berry has given us a most powerful book that will leave the reader with many of the same intense feelings as its characters" Ajeemah and his son. Dawes commented that *Ajeemah and His Son* is Berry's "most ambitious children's book to date," and that it "is telling evidence that Berry is a writer of children's literature to be contended with."

Ajeemah and his son, Atu, are en route to present the bride price—two pieces of gold hidden in Ajeemah's sandals—for Atu's bride-to-be, Sisi. Suddenly set upon by slave traders, they are shipped like cattle to Jamaica. Berry captures the emotions that overcome Ajeemah and Atu as they are taken away, Willett wrote. Once in Jamaica, the father and son are separated, never to see one another again. Both work the Jamaican sugar plantations, but each has a different fate. The father learns to survive, leaving his African roots behind and marrying again, siring a daughter, and ultimately living to be

a free man again once the West Indian slaves are freed. But Atu, turned bitter and brutal by the experience, ends his life in suicide. Hearne, writing in *Bulletin of the Center for Children's Books,* called Berry's prose "hypnotic," noting that he "telescopes a story covering thirty-three years" into a mere eighty-three pages. "The pace achieves a kind of poetic momentum," observed Hearne. "Intense scenes and rhythmic dialogue punctuate the narrative and focus the characters as singular individuals pinioned by history." In a starred *Booklist* review, Rochman wrote that Berry is "a fine poet, and he tells his story with the rhythm, repetition, and lyricism of the oral tradition, tells his story as passionately as the personal account of capture, journey, sale, and toil." Award committees agreed with the critics on this book, and Berry suddenly found himself a well-known writer on this side of the Atlantic.

In an interview with Brian Merrick of *Children's Literature in Education,* Berry explained that he first became interested in the sound of poetry through listening to the Bible, and started to write poetry as a young boy just to satisfy himself. As a young man, living in the United States, Berry carried a notebook around with him, and wrote down his impressions to fill the need to express himself. He later moved to England and became a telegraphist, a job that he worked at for twenty-three years. While working in England, Berry started to write short stories, and met his future wife, who happened to be a secretary for a poetry group run by Bob Cobbing, the sound poet and artist. "They were studying T. S. Eliot, *Four Quartets.* I was never more moved! And it was most strange, because I'd never studied poetry. That was how I started." Berry continues, "About a fortnight later, I was vacuuming my sitting room and I felt this poem in my head. This voice, you know, with this poem. And it was in dialect. It was a funny thing because I hadn't been writing in dialect but this was in my Jamaican dialect."

The poems in *When I Dance* are in Berry's Caribbean dialect, "but they exclude noone," John Mole observed in a *Times Educational Supplement* review. Critics liked its insights into teen life as well as its language, which is rhythmic and energetic. A reviewer for *Junior Bookshelf* called the poems "relaxed and humorous as well as wise," adding that the poet's control of rhythm teaches that "it's the ear, not the eye, that governs understanding" for the Jamaican. These are balanced poems that tell much about daily life, regarding both injustice and goodness "with more warmth than anger." They celebrate the possibility of fun and discovery even in difficult times, Jan Mark and Aidan Chambers related in *Signal.* Many of them delight in the uniqueness of individuals, as one poems states: "Nobody can get into my clothes for me / or feel my fall for me, or do my running. / Nobody hears my music for me, either." Matching this awareness of personality is the invitation to reach out and make connections to the rich opportunities in the world—even though some poems acknowledge that racial barriers exist and not all reaching out is rewarded. Further enriching the prize-winning volume is a section of Jamaican proverbs, expressed in both the difficult-to-understand Creole and English translations. For example, "De tick wha flog de black dog wi whip de white" becomes "The same stick that flogs the black dog will also flog the white one."

When I Dance won the *Signal* Poetry Award in 1989. Mark and Aidan concluded, "If Berry did nothing more than give us a voice for our times, his book would be worthy of the [*Signal*] award, but it seems to me that he is also offering a lifeline back to a language that most of his readers will never have seen, and all the vigour and frankness that went with it." Deborah Fenn noted in the *Times Literary Supplement* that these "poems in Creole surprise, excite and engage by the unfamiliar appearance of words on the page, which, written more phonetically than standard English, create the immediacy of a particular voice." Fenn concluded that the poems, divided into eight sections, explore interests and preoccupations of young children as well as probe their private thoughts, and that Berry "brilliantly" achieves the adolescent perspective.

Berry has also written a lyrical poem of the birth of Jesus for the picture book *Celebration Song,* and three further collections: *Rough Sketch Beginning, Everywhere Faces Everywhere,* and *Isn't My Name Magical.* In *Rough Sketch Beginning,* he creates a poem about an artist sketching ideas for a landscape painting while the illustrator of the book mirrors that experience in the artwork. Michael Cart, writing in *Booklist,* called this book "beautifully written, lavishly designed, and ingeniously illustrated." A popular collection of forty-six poems, *Everywhere Faces Everywhere* is "lyrical, sometimes topical," according to Cart. "Berry speaks with wit and warmth in a variety of poetic voices, including narrative and dramatic. And as always, he demonstrates an extraordinary gift for richly imaginative simile and metaphor." A reviewer for *Voice of Youth Advocates* called this collection "delightful," and commented that it "will appeal to young adults who enjoy poetry." A critic in *Kirkus Reviews* called *Everywhere Faces Everywhere* "a mosaic-like collection," with poems in styles from haiku to ballad. There is rap, graffiti language and proverb here as well, all in Berry's unmistakable "lyrical" voice.

In an interview in *Young Writer,* Berry commented that when he first begins a new poem, it sometimes first manifests as "a wrapped up excitement that will soon reveal a part of its content. . . . Usually I go to my idea notebook, pick out an idea, think about it, find its meaning and rhythm, then start writing it." He advised young people who want to write to "find stories that engage you and read, read, read," and "Write every day, if at all possible."

With his poetry, short stories, and one novel, Berry has filled in that "lack" he felt as a youngster growing up in Jamaica, creating a world of literature which celebrates the black Caribbean experience, both in language and culture. He has given voice to those previously left out of that world which exists between hard covers. Berry wrote in his acceptance speech in *Horn Book* that: "To unify ourselves into one human family with an expanded and harmonious human spirit in any kind of abundant one-world is a millions-of-years job. I believe that the sharing of experience through stories is a great contribution towards that. Wanting to share an experience through a story is this wonderful saving grace that we possess."

BIOGRAPHICAL/CRITICAL SOURCES:

BOOKS

Authors and Artists for Young Adults, Volume 30, Gale (Detroit, MI), 1999.
Berry, James, *When I Dance,* illustrations by Karen Barbour, Harcourt, 1991.
Black Authors and Illustrators of Children's Books, second edition, Garland, 1992.
Children's Literature Review, Volume 22, Gale (Detroit, MI), 1989, pp. 7-11.
Seventh Book of Junior Authors and Illustrators, H. W. Wilson, 1996.
St. James Guide to Children's Writers, 5th edition, St. James Press (Detroit, MI), 1999.
Writers of Multicultural Fiction for Young Adults, edited by M. Daphne Kutzer, Greenwood Press, 1996, pp. 43-51.

PERIODICALS

Booklist, December 1, 1985, pp. 524-25; October 1, 1992, p. 315; February 15, 1993, p. 1061; May 1, 1996, p. 1500; May 1, 1997, p. 1496.
Bulletin of the Center for Children's Books, July-August, 1988, p. 223; December, 1989, p. 78; November, 1992, p. 65, 66; April, 1997, pp. 273-74.
Children's Literature in Education, Volume 27, number 4, 1996, pp. 195-208.

Horn Book, March-April, 1993, pp. 207, 210; January-February, 1994, pp. 50-52.

Junior Bookshelf, October, 1987, p. 229; April, 1989, p. 78; April, 1992, pp. 68-69.

Kirkus Reviews, March 15, 1997, p. 458; November 15, 1997, p. 1704.

New York Times Book Review, May 8, 1988, p. 30; April 25, 1993, p. 24; December 3, 1995, p. 68; May 15, 1998, p. 23.

Publishers Weekly, January 29, 1988, p. 429; December 23, 1988, pp. 27-28; January 18, 1993, p. 470; October 10, 1994, p. 69; December 11, 1995, p. 70; November 24, 1997, p. 73.

School Library Journal, February, 1993, p. 92; May, 1995, p. 111; March, 1996, p. 185; June, 1997, p. 131; December, 1997, p. 105.

Signal, May, 1989, pp. 75-92.

Times Educational Supplement, June 3, 1988, p. 48; November 11, 1988, p. 51; December 6, 1991, p. 32; February 14, 1997, p. 7.

Times Literary Supplement, July 8, 1988, p. 765; March 3, 1989, p. 232.

Voice of Youth Advocates, October, 1997, p. 258.

OTHER

Young Writer, http://www.mystworld.com/young writer/authors/jamesberry.html (August 20, 2001).*

*   *   *

BERRY, Jonas
See ASHBERY, John (Lawrence)

*   *   *

BLAU, Herbert   1926-

PERSONAL: Born May 3, 1926, in Brooklyn, NY; son of Joseph (a plumber) and Yetta Blau; married Beatrice Manley (an actress; divorced); married Kathleen Woodward (director of Walter Simpson Center for the Humanities at the University of Washington), December 29, 1980; children: (first marriage) Richard, Tara, Gwyneth, Jonathan; (second marriage) Jessamyn. *Education:* New York University, B.Ch.E., 1947; Stanford University, M.A., 1949, Ph.D., 1954.

ADDRESSES: Office—Department of English, University of Washington, Box 354330, Seattle, WA 98195-4330. *E-mail*—hblau@u.washington.edu.

CAREER: San Francisco State College (now University), San Francisco, CA, began as assistant professor, became professor of English and world literature, 1950-65; Repertory Theater of Lincoln Center, New York, NY, co-founder and co-director, 1965-67; City College of the City University of New York, New York, NY, professor of English, 1967-68; California Institute of the Arts, Valencia, CA, professor of theater, provost, and dean of School of Theater and Dance, 1968-71, vice president of institute, beginning 1968; Oberlin College, Oberlin, OH, professor of arts and director of inter-arts program, 1972-74; University of Maryland—Baltimore County, Baltimore, MD, professor of English, 1974-78, dean of Division of Arts and Humanities, 1974-76; University of Wisconsin—Milwaukee, WI, professor of English, 1978-84, Distinguished Professor of English, 1984-2000, senior fellow at Center for Twentieth-Century Studies, 1981; University of Washington, Seattle, WA, Distinguished Professor of English and Byron W. and Alice L. Lockwood Professor of the Humanities, 2000—. Co-founder and co-director of Actor's Workshop of San Francisco, CA, 1952-65; founder and artistic director of KRAKEN, 1971-81.

Member of National Humanities Faculty, 1969—; visiting research professor at University of Wisconsin—Milwaukee, 1976; visiting professor at University of Giessen, 1979, and New York University, 1982; Collins Lecturer at Indiana University; lecturer at colleges and universities in the United States, France, Germany, England, and Sweden, including Columbia University, Yale University, Stanford University, and University of California, Los Angeles. Has delivered lectures and presented papers at numerous meetings and conferences. Director of Salzburg Seminar in American Studies, 1962, Rocky Mountain Writers Conference, 1963, and National Theater Center at University of Wisconsin—Madison, 1964 and 1969. Host of dramatic reading series on KQED-TV; guest on television programs. Member of board of directors of Re-Cher-Chez: Studio for Experiment in the Avant-Garde, New York, NY; past member of board of directors of theaters, including Theater X, Milwaukee, WI, Theater Project, Baltimore, MD, Modern Theater, Boston, MA, and Theater at St. Clement's, New York, NY; charter member, Institute for Theater Culture, New York, NY; member of International Council of Fine Arts Deans and Shakespeare Convocation at the White House, 1964. Designer, with Jules Fisher, of Modular Theater, California Institute of Arts, 1971, and Caliper-Thrust Theater, California Institute of the Arts. Adviser to Festival of Alternatives in the Arts, State University of New York at Binghamton, 1982; consultant to World

Theater Festival, Ford Foundation's Theater Communications Group, and various university presses. *Military service:* U.S. Army, 1944-46.

MEMBER: Modern Language Association of America, American Theater Association.

AWARDS, HONORS: Ford Foundation fellowship, 1959; Guggenheim fellowship, 1962, 1977; President's Distinguished Service Award, California State University System, 1965; Design in Steel Award, American Iron and Steel Institute, 1973, for designing the Modular Theater at California Institute of the Arts; National Endowment for the Humanities grant, 1981, 1983, 1985, and senior fellowship, 1984; George Jean Nathan Award for Dramatic Criticism, 1984; Camargo Foundation fellowship, 1984; *Kenyon Review* Prize, 1993.

WRITINGS:

The Impossible Theater: A Manifesto, Macmillan (New York, NY), 1964.
(Translator) Georg Buechner, *Danton's Death* (play), produced in New York, NY, at Vivian Beaumont Theater, 1965.
Blooded Thought: Occasions of Theater, Performing Arts Journal, 1982.
Take up the Bodies: Theater at the Vanishing Point, University of Illinois Press (Urbana, IL), 1982.
The Eye of Prey: Subversions of the Postmodern, Indiana University Press (Bloomington, IN), 1987.
The Audience, Johns Hopkins University Press (Baltimore, MD), 1989.
To All Appearances: Ideology and Performance, Routledge (New York, NY), 1992.
Nothing in Itself: Complexions of Fashion, Indiana University Press (Bloomington, IN), 1999.
Sails of the Herring Fleet: Essays on Beckett, University of Michigan Press (Ann Arbor, MI), 2000.
The Dubious Spectacle: Extremities of Theater, 1976-2000, University of Minnesota Press (Minneapolis, MN), 2002.

PLAYS

A Gift of Fury (three-act), produced in San Francisco at Actor's Workshop, 1958.
Telegraph Hill (three-act), produced in San Francisco at Actor's Workshop, 1963.
Seeds of Atreus, produced in Oberlin, OH, at Oberlin College, 1973.
The Donner Party: Its Crossing, produced in Oberlin, OH, at Oberlin College, 1974.
Elsinore, produced in Baltimore, MD, at New Theater Festival, 1976.

Crooked Eclipses: A Theatrical Essay on Shakespeare's Sonnets, and Derived from the Sonnets, produced in Baltimore, MD, at New Theater Festival, 1977.

OTHER

Contributor to books, including *The Noble Savage,* Meridian, 1962; *The Innocent Party,* New Directions, 1967; *The Writer's World,* McGraw, 1969; *Julius Caesar: A Selection of Critical Essays,* Macmillan, 1969; *Performance in Postmodern Culture,* Coda, 1977; *Modern Theater: A Reflection of Twentieth-Century Man and Society,* Department of Theater, Loyola University (Chicago, IL), 1980; *Innovation/Renovation: New Perspectives on the Humanities,* University of Wisconsin Press (Madison, WI), 1983; *The Play and Its Critic: Essays for Eric Bentley,* University Press of America, 1986; and *Memory and Desire: Aging, Literature, Psychoanalysis,* Indiana University Press (Bloomington, IN), 1986.

Also author of program notes for play productions, 1952-67. Contributor of articles and reviews to numerous periodicals, including *Saturday Review, Salmagundi, Educational Theater Journal, Daedalus, Performing Arts Journal, American Quarterly,* and *Journal of Aesthetics and Art Criticism.* Member of editorial board, *Performing Arts Journal, Theater Journal, Modern International Drama, New Literary History,* and *Journal of Beckett Studies;* past member of editorial board, *Drama Review* and *Arts in Society.*

SIDELIGHTS: Herbert Blau has written and directed plays and written books on such subjects as the theater and fashion. Among his titles are *Nothing in Itself: Complexions of Fashion* and *Sails of the Herring Fleet: Essays on Beckett. Nothing in Itself* is an examination of the paradoxical role of fashion in contemporary society. Using a philosophical approach to his subject, Blau explores how fashion reflects and influences many other aspects of society while managing to be both frivolous and profound at the same time. He notes fashion's role in defining gender and class, its relationship to theater and performance, and its ultimately transitory nature. B. B. Chico in *Choice* found *Nothing in Itself* to contain "a lifetime of thoughts, analyses, and critiques on the mysteries of fashion." Chico also found that Blau possesses "an expansive mind" and "a wide, interdisciplinary exposure to history, literature, the arts, sociology, and anthropology."

In *Sails of the Herring Fleet: Essays on Beckett,* Blau gathers twelve of his essays written over forty years on the works of playwright Samuel Beckett. "Blau directed Beckett's plays," wrote Susan L. Peters in *Library Journal*, "when they were practically unknown, including the now legendary production of *Waiting for Godot* that was given in San Quentin Prison." According to J. Schlueter in *Choice*, some of Blau's essays "are required reading for anyone interested in the influence of Beckett—and, for that matter, Blau—on the direction and definition of theater."

A theater director for many years, Blau once told *CA:* "My activity in theater has been divided into two major phases—the work done with large companies in San Francisco and New York and, starting in 1971, the more intensive research and performances developed with the experimental group KRAKEN. Work in San Francisco and New York included, as director and/or producer, nearly a hundred plays performed at the Actor's Workshop and the Repertory Theater at Lincoln Center."

Blau explained: "KRAKEN was a small itinerant group. The investigative process was central to its idea of theater, and each work took about a year or more to generate through the collective inquiry, after which it was widely toured. KRAKEN also did workshops and lecture/demonstrations at numerous colleges and universities. It was in residence at Roger Williams College in 1972, Oberlin College from 1972 to 1974, and University of Maryland's Baltimore County campus from 1974 to 1978."

BIOGRAPHICAL/CRITICAL SOURCES:

PERIODICALS

Back Stage, January 14, 1983, George L. George, review of *Take up the Bodies: Theater at the Vanishing Point,* p. 103.

Bookwatch, December, 1999, review of *Nothing in Itself: Complexions of Fashion,* p. 1.

Choice, February, 1993, S. Golub, review of *To All Appearances: Ideology and Performance,* p. 975; May, 2000, B. B. Chico, review of *Nothing in Itself,* p. 1700; May, 2001, J. Schlueter, review of *Sails of the Herring Fleet: Essays on Beckett,* p. 1638.

Christian Science Monitor, January, 1965.

Drama Review, spring, 1983, reviews of *Blooded Thought: Occasions of Theater* and *Take up the Bodies,* p. 118.

Journal of Popular Culture, summer, 1993, review of *To All Appearances,* p. 214.

Kenyon Review, summer, 1994, Bonnie Marranca, review of *To All Appearances,* p. 155.

Library Journal, September 1, 2000, Susan L. Peters, review of *Sails of the Herring Fleet,* p. 210.

New Performance, Volume 2, number 2, 1981.

Performing Arts Journal, September, 1992, Bonnie Marranca and Gautam Dasgupta, "The Play of Thought: An Interview with Herbert Blau," p. 1.

Publishers Weekly, August 16, 1999, review of *Nothing in Itself,* p. 75.

Theater Journal, May, 1974; March, 1979; October, 1992, Philip Auslander, review of *The Audience,* p. 411.

Theater Research International, spring, 1992, Michael L. Quinn, review of *The Audience,* p. 73.

Theater Survey, May, 1991, Reed Whittemore, review of *The Audience,* p. 106.

Village Voice, November 1, 1976.*

*   *   *

BOGOSIAN, Eric   1953-

PERSONAL: Born April 24, 1953, in Boston, MA; son of Henry and Edwina Bogosian; married Jo Anne Bonney (a graphic designer and theater director), October, 1980; children: Harris Wolf. *Education:* Attended University of Chicago; Oberlin College, B.A., 1976.

ADDRESSES: Home—New York, NY. *Agent*—George Lane, William Morris Agency, 1325 Avenue of the Americas, New York, NY 10013.

CAREER: Actor and writer. Cofounder of Woburn Drama Guild, Woburn, MA; director and founder of dance program at the Kitchen in New York, NY. Actor in stage productions, including *Careful Moment, Drinking in America, Talk Radio,* and *Sex, Drugs, and Rock 'n' Roll;* in television series, including *The Twilight Zone, Miami Vice,* and *Crime Story;* in other television productions, including *The Caine Mutiny Court Martial, Eric Bogosian Takes a Look at Drinking in America, Witch Hunt,* and *Bright Shining Lie;* and in motion pictures, including *Talk Radio, Under Seige 2,* and *Deconstructing Harry.* Co-creator of television series *High Incident.*

AWARDS, HONORS: Obie Award for playwriting, *Village Voice,* and Drama Desk Award for outstanding solo performance, both 1986, both for *Drinking in America;* Silver Berlin Bear for Outstanding Single Achievement, Berlin International Film Festival, 1989, for *Talk Radio;* Obie Award special citation, 1990, for *Sex, Drugs, and Rock 'n' Roll;* Obie Award for play-

Eric Bogosian

writing, 1994, for *Pounding Nails in the Floor with My Forehead.*

WRITINGS:

STAGE PLAYS

Careful Moment, produced in New York, NY, 1977.

Men Inside [and] *Voices of America* (double bill), produced Off-Broadway, 1982.

FunHouse, produced Off-Broadway, 1983.

Drinking in America (produced Off-Broadway, 1986; also see below), Vintage (New York, NY), 1987.

Talk Radio (produced Off-Broadway, 1987; also see below), Samuel French (New York, NY), 1988.

Sex, Drugs, and Rock 'n' Roll (produced Off-Broadway, 1988; also see below), HarperCollins (New York, NY), 1991.

Pounding Nails in the Floor with My Forehead (produced Off-Broadway, 1994; produced on CD, Blackbird, 1998), Theatre Communications Group (New York, NY), 1994.

SubUrbia (produced at Lincoln Center, 1994; also see below), Theatre Communications Group (New York, NY), 1995.

(With others) *Love's Fire: Seven New Plays Inspired by Shakespearean Sonnets* (produced at Public Theater, New York, NY, 1998), Morrow (New York, NY), 1998.

Griller, produced at Goodman Theatre, Chicago, IL, 1998.

Wake up and Smell the Coffee (produced Off-Broadway, 2000), Theatre Communications Group (St. Paul, MN), 2001.

Author of numerous other plays, including *Men in Dark Times, Sheer Heaven, The Ricky Paul Show,* and *The New World.*

OTHER

Eric Bogosian Takes a Look at Drinking in America (television production; adapted from *Drinking in America*), HBO/Cinemax, 1986.

(With Oliver Stone) *Talk Radio* (screenplay; adapted from Bogosian's play), Universal, 1988.

Sex, Drugs, and Rock 'n' Roll (screenplay; adapted from Bogosian's play), Avenue Entertainment, 1991.

Notes from Underground (contains novella, *Notes from Underground,* and play, *Scenes from the New World*), Hyperion (New York, NY), 1993.

The Essential Bogosian, Theatre Communications Group (New York, NY), 1994.

SubUrbia (screenplay; adapted from Bogosian's play), Castle Rock Entertainment, 1997.

(Author of introduction) *Physiognomy: The Mark Seliger Photographs,* Little, Brown (Boston, MA), 1999.

Mall (novel), Simon & Schuster (New York, NY), 2000.

Contributor to periodicals, including *New York Times* and *Esquire.*

WORK IN PROGRESS: A play, *Humpty Dumpty,* to be produced at McCarter Theater, Princeton, NJ, 2002.

SIDELIGHTS: Eric Bogosian is an actor and writer who has garnered acclaim for his various stage productions, including several solo works. After graduating from Oberlin College in 1976, he worked as a gofer at a Westside theatre in New York City and then went on to direct dance productions at the Kitchen, a forum for avant-garde productions in New York. In 1977 he made his acting and writing debut with *Careful Moment,* a one-man show in which he played a range of characters, including a game-show host and a dancer. Throughout the next several years and into the 1980s, Bogosian developed and performed in similar works, each featuring him as a number of different characters. Among the more memorable of his characterizations, according to some critics, is his portrait of Ricky Paul, a particularly obnoxious comedian who harangues and humiliates his audience.

Bogosian eventually grew weary of performing in his solo, multicharacter works, particularly those featuring the exhaustingly abusive Ricky Paul. In the early 1980s he wrote and directed *The New World,* a play in which he appeared, for the first time, with other actors and actresses. Bogosian followed *The New World* with another one-man production, *Men Inside,* featuring entirely new characters. That show, in which Bogosian plays a carnival barker and a success-seminar conductor among others, was his first work to draw substantial attention from the New York press.

In 1983 Bogosian created *FunHouse,* in which he played such characters as a bum, a man with a rubber fetish, and a convicted killer awaiting execution. With this work Bogosian drew further recognition from reviewers. *New York* critic John Simon, though harboring reservations about *FunHouse,* observed that Bogosian possesses "imagination, wit . . . and a good ear for the rumblings of society's underbelly and the burblings of our brain-damaged media." *Dance* reviewer Kevin Grubb noted that Bogosian manages the difficult task of producing "an engrossing, though difficult-to-digest, brand of performance art." Grubb added that Bogosian's unsparing vision—which is sometimes horrific, sometimes humorous—makes him "one of our most important performing artists."

Bogosian impressed critics once again with *Drinking in America,* a fast-paced examination of life's more sordid denizens. Here he performed as a fatuous hippie; a manic, substance-abusing Hollywood agent; an empty-headed young vandal; and a pathetic wino. Frank Rich, in his *New York Times* review, described *Drinking in America* as "a breakneck, hair-raising comic tour of the contemporary American male psyche," while *New York*'s Simon praised the production as "sardonic and uncompromising social commentary." Most of the skits, Simon added, "are precise, sharp, witty, and disturbing." This work, among Bogosian's most popular, ran Off-Broadway for sixteen weeks and was published in 1987. In addition, it was adapted by Bogosian and broadcast on cable television as *Eric Bogosian Takes a Look at Drinking in America.*

In his next work, the play *Talk Radio,* Bogosian limited himself to one characterization, that of a misanthropic,

hyper-energetic radio talk-show host who regularly degrades those listeners foolhardy enough to phone questions and comments to the show. Though *Talk Radio* failed to match the acclaim of *Drinking in America,* it drew the attention of filmmaker Oliver Stone, who collaborated with Bogosian on the script for a broader, multicharacter film version that retained Bogosian in the lead role. Some reviewers thought the adaptation overwhelming in nature but unenlightening in effect, but other critics found it a bold, invigorating portrait of haywire America. *Washington Post* reviewer Michael Wilmington, for instance, deemed it a "savagely audacious" work that "makes you laugh, makes you mad, and keeps you edgily watching for the killers in the shadows."

Sex, Drugs, and Rock 'n' Roll, Bogosian's next solo stage work, features the actor-writer's familiar gallery of street people and introduces several others, notably a blowhard rock star who seems to be exploiting the save-the-rainforest groundswell to further his own stardom, and a spiteful old man railing against the industrial revolution's repercussions of widespread, life-threatening pollution. Bogosian ended the performance with what *New York Times* reviewer Frank Rich described as a "chilling soliloquy," one in which a former hippie argues that the United States has become a nation enslaved by computers and other technological devices. Rich called *Sex, Drugs, and Rock 'n' Roll* a "brilliant show, [Bogosian's] funniest and scariest yet," and he praised Bogosian as "a great talent, a chameleon actor and penetrating social observer." With *Sex, Drugs, and Rock 'n' Roll,* Rich commented, Bogosian "has crossed the line that separates an exciting artist from a cultural hero."

Pounding Nails in the Floor with My Forehead was another solo work, with Bogosian again playing several bizarre and disturbing characters, including a drug dealer, a bigoted suburbanite, a platitude-mouthing pop psychologist, an arrogant doctor, and an ordinary man whose complacency is shattered by televised images of people starving in Africa. The production, like many of Bogosian's works, was directed by his wife, Joanne Bonney, who also served as dramaturge, with input into "what actually happens in the tone of the show," Bogosian told *Back Stage* interviewer Hettie Lynne Hurtes. William A. Henry, III, reviewing the show for *Time,* called Bogosian "the subtlest and most daring" of solo performers and commended him for creating risky material. *Back Stage* critic David Lefkowitz praised Bogosian's "enthralling stage presence," but saw a "creeping familiarity" in the script. "Are Bogosian's losers all starting to sound the same?" he asked. Nevertheless, he termed the show "powerful." In addition to being performed on stage and published, *Pounding Nails in the Floor with My Forehead* was Bogosian's first performance work to be produced in a CD version.

Bogosian did not appear in his play *SubUrbia,* about aimless young people in a blue-collar suburb who spend most of their time hanging out in a convenience-store parking lot, eating junk food, drinking beer, and using recreational drugs. The promise of some excitement, however, comes with the return to town of a friend who has achieved some degree of fame, if not the top echelon of success, as a rock musician. When he arrives, the characters are drawn into sexual power games and violent struggles. *New Republic* contributor Robert Brustein found "structural imperfections" in the play, but called it "a considerably more ambitious effort" than Bogosian's one-man shows. Bogosian is a "potentially strong, gritty playwright," Brustein added. *Back Stage's* David Sheward deemed Bogosian's work "promising," although he thought the characters were underdeveloped. The film version of *SubUrbia* was released in 1997; John Simon, critiquing it for *National Review,* termed the material "theatrical, not cinematic." He explained, "Transposed to the screen, it works about as well as a poem in a prose translation." *Nation* commentator Stuart Klawans, though, praised Bogosian's screenplay as "well constructed in plot and frequently sharp in its dialogue."

Bogosian returned to solo performance work with *Wake up and Smell the Coffee,* portraying characters that include a self-help guru, an unscrupulous film producer, and a fawning actor while also reflecting on his discomfort with being a celebrity. The show is "a commentary on two recent trends in American culture, a taste for pop spirituality and the quest for lots and lots of money, and it's strongest when it's tackling those two subjects directly and making connections between them," remarked Charles Isherwood in *Variety.* Isherwood found "plenty of bitter truth" in the monologues, but thought "the unremitting bleakness of Bogosian's work here grows somewhat monotonous." Isherwood added that no matter what the material, "Bogosian is an amazingly magnetic live performer." *New Criterion* contributor Mark Steyn did not care for the show, calling Bogosian "an observational satirist who can no longer observe so well and is blaming it on the tinted windows." *Back Stage* critic David A. Rosenberg, however, maintained that Bogosian offers a "bitingly funny vision."

Bogosian's first novel, *Mall,* features the quirky characters one might expect from the playwright, such as a businessman with a penchant for voyeurism, a home-maker looking for sexual fulfillment, and a drug-addled teenager. One night at their local mall, they experience no ordinary shopping trip, but events of shocking violence as a gunman roams the building. In the *New York Times,* Janet Maslin claimed that the book's characters "feel as if they need actors to make them complete," while allowing that Bogosian "manages to sketch, propel, and intermingle them with a satirist's sure hand." *Entertainment Weekly* reviewer L. S. Klepp praised Bogosian's "merciless, satirical vision" but saw the plot as lacking in credibility. *Mother Jones* contributor Ben Ehrenreich felt Bogosian's subject matter was overly familiar and his writing often cliched, "despite a few sharp, satiric moments." A *Publishers Weekly* critic, though, commended the author for his "droll remarks and dramatic pacing" and termed *Mall* "a typically Bogosian experience—lively and unique." *Library Journal's* Jeff Ayers called the book "an entertaining success," with well-conceived characters and effective flashes of humor even in terrifying scenes. Ted Leventhal, writing in *Booklist,* described Bogosian's writing style as "clever, vivid, and infused with very dark humor," and called the novel an "impressive, frightful work." Leventhal also compared Bogosian to a well-regarded literary predecessor: "If John Cheever lived in America today, watched MTV, and shopped at the mall, he'd probably write like Eric Bogosian."

BIOGRAPHICAL/CRITICAL SOURCES:

BOOKS

Contemporary Literary Criticism, Volume 45, Gale (Detroit, MI), 1987.
Newsmakers 90, Gale (Detroit, MI), 1990.

PERIODICALS

Art in America, April, 1986, pp. 189-190.
Back Stage, October 29, 1993, Hettie Lynne Hurtes, "Eric Bogosian Hits Hard by 'Driving Nails,' " p. 6W; February 25, 1994, David Lefkowitz, review of *Pounding Nails in the Floor with My Forehead,* p. 48; May 27, 1994, David Sheward, review of *SubUrbia* (play), p. 32; May 12, 2000, David A. Rosenberg, review of *Wake up and Smell the Coffee,* p. 44.
Booklist, October 1, 2000, Ted Leventhal, review of *Mall,* p. 323.
Chicago Tribune, May 8, 1987; June 28, 1987; December 20, 1988; December 22, 1988.
Dance, January, 1984, pp. 78-83.
Entertainment Weekly, December 1, 2000, L. S. Klepp, review of *Mall,* p. 92.

Library Journal, September 15, 2000, Jeff Ayers, review of *Mall,* p. 111.

Listener, June 16, 1988, p. 34.

Los Angeles Times, April 10, 1985; December 21, 1988.

Los Angeles Times Book Review, July 19, 1987, p. 3.

Mother Jones, November, 2000, Ben Ehrenreich, review of *Mall.*

Nation, March 3, 1997, Stuart Klawans, review of *SubUrbia* (film), p. 35.

National Review, March 10, 1997, John Simon, review of *SubUrbia* (film), p 53.

New Criterion, June, 2000, Mark Steyn, "Waddling toward the Edge," p. 41.

New Republic, June 27, 1994, Robert Brustein, review of *SubUrbia* (play), p. 28.

Newsweek, March 24, 1986, p. 69; February 16, 1997, Jack Kroll, review of *SubUrbia* (film), p. 66.

New York, October 31, 1983, p. 60; February 3, 1986, p. 57; December 12, 1988, pp. 50-56.

New Yorker, February 3, 1986, p. 85.

New York Times, July 8, 1983; September 30, 1983; January 21, 1986, p. 15; July 30, 1987; December 21, 1988; February 4, 1990; February 9, 1990; November 20, 2000, Janet Maslin, "Attention, Shoppers: Gallows Humor."

New York Times Magazine, May 24, 1987.

Publishers Weekly, October 2, 2000, review of *Mall,* p. 57.

Rolling Stone, February 9, 1989, pp. 95-97.

Time, February 15, 1994, William A. Henry III, review of *Pounding Nails in the Floor with My Forehead,* p. 67; March 7, 1994, W. A. Henry III, "One and Only," p. 66.

Tribune Books (Chicago), January 6, 1991.

Variety, May 8, 2000, Charles Isherwood, review of *Wake up and Smell the Coffee,* p. 88.

Washington Post, December 20, 1988; December 21, 1988; December 23, 1988.

OTHER

Eric Bogosian's Home Page, http://www.ericbogosian.com/ (June 5, 2001).

Entry reviewed by Amanda Moran, assistant to Eric Bogosian.

* * *

BOWERS, Neal 1948-

PERSONAL: Born August 3, 1948, in Clarksville, TN; son of Floyd E. and Willine (Tigart) Bowers; married Nancy Brooker (a writer), 1979. *Education:* Austin Peay State University, B.A., 1970, M.A., 1971; University of Florida, Ph.D., 1976.

ADDRESSES: Home—1507 Carroll Ave., Ames, IA 50010. *E-mail*—nbowers@iastate.edu.

CAREER: Iowa State University, Ames, IA, assistant professor, 1977-83, associate professor, 1983-87, professor of creative writing and modern poetry, 1987—, distinguished professor of liberal arts and sciences, 1997—.

AWARDS, HONORS: Poetry prize, Iowa Arts Council Literary Awards, 1985, 1989; Rainmaker Award, *Zone 3,* 1989; poetry fellow, National Endowment for the Arts, 1989; Frederick Bock Prize, *Poetry,* 1991; best poem published in *Yankee* during 1993; Union League Civic and Arts Poetry Prize, *Poetry,* 1995.

WRITINGS:

Theodore Roethke: The Journey from I to Otherwise, University of Missouri Press (Columbia, MO), 1982.

The Golf Ball Diver, New Rivers Press (St. Paul, MN), 1983.

James Dickey: The Poet as Pitchman, University of Missouri Press (Columbia, MO), 1985.

Lost in the Heartland, Cedar Creek Press (Mason City, IA), 1990.

Night Vision, BkMk Press (Kansas City, MO), 1992.

Words for the Taking: The Hunt for a Plagiarist, Norton (New York, NY), 1997.

Loose Ends (novel), Random House (New York, NY), 2001.

Out of the South (poetry), Louisiana State University Press (Baton Rouge, LA), 2002.

Also contributor to poetry anthologies, including *Modern American Poets,* 2nd edition, McGraw-Hill (New York, NY), 1994; *Sweet Nothings: An Anthology of Rock and Roll in American Poetry,* Indiana University Press (Bloomington, IN), 1994; and *The Art and Craft of Poetry,* Writer's Digest Books (Cincinnati, OH), 1994. Contributor of articles and poems to periodicals, including *New Yorker, American Poetry Review, Sewanee Review, Harper's, Hudson Review, North American Review,* and *Modern Poetry Studies.* Former editor of *Poet and Critic.*

WORK IN PROGRESS: As Good as Dead, novel; *Hazards of the Heart,* poetry; *After Sarah,* novel.

SIDELIGHTS: Poet and teacher Neal Bowers endured one of the most frustrating battles a writer can face: his work was plagiarized by an unknown man who made minimal changes and got it published under pseudonyms in reputable poetry journals. Bowers discovered the crime in 1992 when a fellow poet contacted him and faxed him a copy of one of the plagiarized works. In the ensuing years Bowers became a detective of sorts in order to track down his plagiarizer and put an end to the activity. Bowers chronicled his difficulties, first in a magazine piece published in *American Scholar,* and more recently in his book, *Words for the Taking: The Hunt for a Plagiarist. Words for the Taking* covers more than just Bowers's search for a criminal. It also reveals the level of indifference he encountered both in academic circles and among the editors and publishers of poetry magazines. *Booklist* correspondent Gilbert Taylor wrote that the work is "courageous for Bowers to publish and important to read for all who work in creative spheres."

In his *Washington Post* review, Jonathan Yardley called *Words for the Taking* "a thoughtful book that is about a good deal more than the theft of one man's words." Yardley further stated: "Looking back on the case, Bowers finds that he must offer 'not merely a defense of my creative worth but also of poetry's worth.' This obviously should not be necessary—it puts the victim rather than the plagiarist on trial—but it is perhaps inevitable in a culture where the word is of minimal value. This book should be a bracing corrective for that culture, but only the naïve can imagine that it will get the attention it deserves."

Los Angeles Times reviewer, Mark Rozzo, called Bowers's debut novel, *Loose Ends,* "a low-key psychodrama, . . . all about half-states: between truth and lies, life and death, health and sickness."

Bowers told *CA:* "At the beginning of the twenty-first century, I made two significant decisions: to stop writing poetry, and to leave the university.

"While there are some good poets writing and publishing in America today, poetry at large has become a diluted commodity hawked by writer's workshops and hustled through various contests. To speak plainly, I grew weary (after thirty years) of feeling like part of the problem. Having no solution to offer, I chose to withdraw.

"Likewise, universities in America have become empty, desolate places. In my own academic area, literature has been supplanted by the text of the moment— often something contemporary, sometimes a grab-bag of letters or journal entries rummaged from another century's attic. Theory has replaced texts, and blab has eliminated meaningful discussion.

"With no significant readership and no possibility of generating an income from what they write, poets wrestle and race one another in an empty arena in competitions that determine book publication. But the world of the novelist is purified by money. If an agent takes an interest in a novel, it's because he thinks he can sell it to a publisher who also thinks it will sell. The trick is to find an agent and an editor who care about language and good writing as an aspect of marketability. Where 'po-biz' is characterized by in-bred stroking and bickering, novel writing offers the pragmatics of a real audience in a much larger world of readers.

"My movement from poetry to fiction has been personally invigorating. The novel presents challenges that are new and exciting to me, and I do not regret leaving poetry behind. The volume of poems that will appear in the coming years—*Hazards of the Heart* (which has not been offered for publication yet)—will conclude my career as a poet. Soon, I will officially sever my connection with the crumbling university. In however many years I have left, I intend to write as many novels as I can."

BIOGRAPHICAL/CRITICAL SOURCES:

PERIODICALS

Baltimore Sun, March 11, 2001, review of *Loose Ends.*
Booklist, January 1, 1997, Gilbert Taylor, review of *Words for the Taking,* p. 806.
Des Moines Register, October 21, 1984.
Georgia Review, spring, 1986.
Los Angeles Times, March 18, 2001, Mark Rozzo, review of *Loose Ends,* p. 10.
Nashville Tennessean, July 1, 1984.
New Yorker, January 20, 1997, James R. Kincaid, review of *Words for the Taking,* p. 93.
New York Times Book Review, March 25, 2001, review of *Loose Ends.*
Publishers Weekly, December 18, 2000, review of *Loose Ends,* p. 52.
Sewanee Review, spring, 1986.
Washington Post, January 1, 1997, Jonathan Yardley, "The Word on Plagiarism," p. D3.

OTHER

Cortland Review, http://www.cortlandreview.com/ issuefive/ (March 19, 2001), "Neal Bowers, Interview."

*   *   *

BRANDENBERG, Aliki (Liacouras) (Aliki)

PERSONAL: Born September 3 in Wildwood Crest, NJ; daughter of James Peter and Stella (Lagakos) Liacouras; married Franz Brandenberg (an author), March 15, 1957; children: Jason, Alexa Demetria. *Education:* Graduated from Philadelphia Museum School of Art (now Philadelphia College of Art), 1951. *Avocational interests:* Macrame, weaving, music, baking, traveling, reading, gardening, theater, films, museums.

ADDRESSES: Home—17 Regent's Park Terrace, London NW1 7ED, England.

CAREER: Muralist and commercial artist in Philadelphia, PA, and New York City, 1951-56, and in Zurich, Switzerland, 1957-60; commercial artist, writer, and illustrator of children's books in New York, NY, 1960-77, and London, England, 1977—. Has also taught art and ceramics.

AWARDS, HONORS: The Story of Johnny Appleseed, 1963, and *The Story of William Penn,* 1964, were named Junior Literary Guild selections; Junior Book Award, Boys' Clubs of America, 1968, for *Three Gold Pieces: A Greek Folk Tale; At Mary Bloom's* was chosen by the American Institute of Graphic Arts for the Children's Book Show and as a Junior Literary Guild selection, 1976, and by the Children's Book Council for the Children's Book Showcase, 1977; Children's Science Book Award, New York Academy of Sciences, 1977, for *Corn Is Maize: The Gift of the Indians;* Silver Slate Pencil Award, Dutch Children's Book Council, and Garden State (NJ) Children's Book Award, both 1981, for *Mummies Made in Egypt;* Omar's Book Award (Evansville-Vandeburgh), 1986, for *Keep Your Mouth Closed, Dear;* Prix du Livre pour Enfants (Geneva, Switzerland), 1987, for *Feelings;* World of Reading Readers' Choice Award (Silver Burdett & Ginn), 1989, for *The Story of Johnny Appleseed;* Drexel University/Free Library of Philadelphia citation, 1991; Pennsylvania School Librarians Association Award, 1991, in recognition of outstanding contributions in the field of literature; Garden State Children's Book Award, 1996, for *My Visit to the Aquarium;* Honor Book Award, *Boston Globe-Horn Book,* 1999, for *William Shakespeare and the Globe;* Jane Addams Peace Prize, 1999, for *Marianthe's Story.*

WRITINGS:

AUTHOR AND ILLUSTRATOR; UNDER NAME ALIKI

The Story of William Tell, Faber & Faber (London, England), 1960, A. S. Barnes, 1961.
My Five Senses, Crowell, 1962.
My Hands, Crowell, 1962.
The Wish Workers, Dial (New York, NY), 1962.
The Story of Johnny Appleseed, Prentice-Hall, 1963.
George and the Cherry Tree, Dial (New York, NY), 1964.
The Story of William Penn, Prentice-Hall, 1964.
A Weed Is a Flower: The Life of George Washington Carver, Prentice-Hall, 1965.
Keep Your Mouth Closed, Dear, Dial (New York, NY), 1966.
Three Gold Pieces: A Greek Folk Tale, Pantheon (New York, NY), 1967.
New Year's Day, Crowell, 1967.
(Editor) *Hush Little Baby: A Folk Lullaby,* Prentice-Hall, 1968.
My Visit to the Dinosaurs, Crowell, 1969, 1985, HarperCollins (New York, NY), 1994.
The Eggs: A Greek Folk Tale, Pantheon (New York, NY), 1969.
Diogenes: The Story of the Greek Philosopher, Prentice-Hall, 1969.
Fossils Tell of Long Ago, Crowell, 1972.
June 7!, Macmillan (New York, NY), 1972.
The Long Lost Coelacanth and Other Living Fossils, Crowell, 1973.
Green Grass and White Milk, Crowell, 1974.
Go Tell Aunt Rhody, Macmillan (New York, NY), 1974.
At Mary Bloom's, Greenwillow, 1976.
Corn Is Maize: The Gift of the Indians, Crowell, 1976.
The Many Lives of Benjamin Franklin, Prentice-Hall, 1977.
Wild and Woolly Mammoths, Crowell, 1977.
The Twelve Months, Greenwillow, 1978.
Mummies Made in Egypt, Crowell, 1979.
The Two of Them, Greenwillow, 1979.
Digging up Dinosaurs, Crowell, 1981.
We Are Best Friends, Greenwillow, 1982.
Use Your Head, Dear, Greenwillow, 1983.
A Medieval Feast, Harper (New York, NY), 1983.
Feelings, Greenwillow, 1984.

Dinosaurs Are Different, Crowell, 1985.

How a Book Is Made, Crowell, 1986.

Jack and Jake, Greenwillow, 1986.

Overnight at Mary Bloom's, Greenwillow, 1987.

Welcome, Little Baby, Greenwillow, 1987.

Dinosaur Bones, Crowell, 1988.

The King's Day: Louis XIV of France, Crowell, 1989.

My Feet, Crowell, 1990.

Manners, Greenwillow, 1990.

Christmas Tree Memories, HarperCollins (New York, NY), 1991.

I'm Growing!, HarperCollins (New York, NY), 1992.

Milk: From Cow to Carton, HarperCollins (New York, NY), 1992.

Aliki's Dinosaur Dig: A Book and Card Game, Harper-Collins (New York, NY), 1992.

My Visit to the Aquarium, HarperCollins (New York, NY), 1993.

Communication, Greenwillow, 1993.

Gods and Goddesses of Olympus, HarperCollins (New York, NY), 1994.

Tabby: A Story in Pictures, HarperCollins (New York, NY), 1995.

Best Friends Together Again, Greenwillow, 1995.

Hello! Good-bye!, Greenwillow, 1996.

My Visit to the Zoo, HarperCollins (New York, NY), 1997.

Those Summers, HarperCollins (New York, NY), 1997.

Marianthe's Story (contains *Painted Words* and *Spoken Memories*), Greenwillow, 1998.

William Shakespeare and the Globe, HarperCollins (New York, NY), 1999.

All by Myself, HarperCollins (New York, NY), 2000.

One Little Spoonful, HarperCollins (New York, NY), 2000.

Ah, Music!, HarperCollins (New York, NY), 2002.

Aliki's books have been translated into Chinese, Portuguese, Spanish, Catalan, Danish, Dutch, Finnish, French, German, Hebrew, Japanese, Norwegian, Swedish, and Braille.

ILLUSTRATOR; UNDER NAME ALIKI

Pat Witte and Eve Witte, *Who Lives Here?,* Golden Press, 1961.

Joan M. Lexau, *Cathy Is Company,* Dial (New York, NY), 1961.

Paul Showers, *Listening Walk,* Crowell, 1961.

Margaret Hodges, *What's for Lunch, Charley?,* Dial (New York, NY), 1961.

Mickey Marks, *What Can I Buy?,* Dial (New York, NY), 1962.

Dorothy Les Tina, *A Book to Begin On: Alaska,* Holt (New York, NY), 1962.

James Holding, *The Lazy Little Zulu,* Morrow (New York, NY), 1962.

Joan M. Heilbronner, *This Is the House Where Jack Lives,* Harper (New York, NY), 1962.

Vivian L. Thompson, *The Horse That Liked Sandwiches,* Putnam (New York, NY), 1962.

Arthur Jonas, *Archimedes and His Wonderful Discoveries,* Prentice-Hall, 1962.

Bernice Kohn, *Computers at Your Service,* Prentice-Hall, 1962.

Arthur Jonas, *New Ways in Math,* Prentice-Hall, 1962.

Eugene David, *Television and How It Works,* Prentice-Hall, 1962.

Eugene David, *Electricity in Your Life,* Prentice-Hall, 1963.

James Holding, *Mister Moonlight and Omar,* Morrow (New York, NY), 1963.

Joan M. Lexau, *That's Good, That's Bad,* Dial (New York, NY), 1963.

Judy Hawes, *Bees and Beelines,* Crowell, 1964.

Arthur Jonas, *More New Ways in Math,* Prentice-Hall, 1964.

James Holding, *Sherlock on the Trail,* Morrow (New York, NY), 1964.

Bernice Kohn, *Everything Has a Size,* Prentice-Hall, 1964.

Bernice Kohn, *Everything Has a Shape,* Prentice-Hall, 1964.

Bernice Kohn, *One Day It Rained Cats and Dogs,* Coward, 1965.

Helen Clare, *Five Dolls in a House,* Prentice-Hall, 1965.

Rebecca Kalusky, *Is It Blue as a Butterfly?,* Prentice-Hall, 1965.

Mary K. Phelan, *Mother's Day,* Crowell, 1965.

Betty Ren Wright, *I Want to Read!,* A. Whitman, 1965.

Sean Morrison, *Is That a Happy Hippopotamus?,* Crowell, 1966.

Bernice Kohn, *Everything Has a Shape and Everything Has a Size,* Prentice-Hall, 1966.

Helen Clare, *Five Dolls in the Snow,* Prentice-Hall, 1967.

Helen Clare, *Five Dolls and the Monkey,* Prentice-Hall, 1967.

Helen Clare, *Five Dolls and Their Friends,* Prentice-Hall, 1968.

Helen Clare, *Five Dolls and the Duke,* Prentice-Hall, 1968.

Wilma Yeo, *Mrs. Neverbody's Recipes,* Lippincott (New York, NY), 1968.

Esther R. Hautzig, *At Home: A Visit in Four Languages,* Macmillan (New York, NY), 1968.

Polly Greenberg, *Oh Lord, I Wish I Was a Buzzard,* Macmillan (New York, NY), 1968.

Roma Gans, *Birds at Night,* Crowell, 1968.

Jane Jonas Srivastava, *Weighing and Balancing,* Crowell, 1970.

Joanne Oppenheim, *On the Other Side of the River,* Watts, 1972.

Philip M. Sherlock and Hilary Sherlock, *Ears and Tails and Common Sense: More Stories from the Caribbean,* Crowell, 1974.

Jane Jonas Srivastava, *Averages,* Crowell, 1975.

Joanna Cole, *Evolution,* Crowell, 1987.

Alice Low, *Mommy's Briefcase,* Scholastic (New York, NY), 1995.

ILLUSTRATOR OF BOOKS BY HUSBAND, FRANZ BRANDENBERG; UNDER NAME ALIKI

I Once Knew a Man, Macmillan (New York, NY), 1970.

Fresh Cider and Pie, Macmillan (New York, NY), 1973.

No School Today!, Macmillan (New York, NY), 1975.

A Secret for Grandmother's Birthday, Greenwillow, 1975.

A Robber! A Robber!, Greenwillow, 1976.

I Wish I Was Sick, Too!, Greenwillow, 1976, published in England as *I Don't Feel Well,* Hamish Hamilton, 1977.

What Can You Make of It?, Greenwillow, 1977.

Nice New Neighbors, Greenwillow, 1977.

A Picnic, Hurrah!, Greenwillow, 1978.

Six New Students, Greenwillow, 1978.

Everyone Ready?, Greenwillow, 1979.

It's Not My Fault!, Greenwillow, 1980.

Leo and Emily, Greenwillow, 1981.

Leo and Emily's Big Idea, Greenwillow, 1982.

Aunt Nina and Her Nephews and Nieces, Greenwillow, 1983.

Aunt Nina's Visit, Greenwillow, 1984.

Leo and Emily and the Dragon, Greenwillow, 1984.

The Hit of the Party, Greenwillow, 1985.

Cock-a-Doodle-Doo, Greenwillow, 1986.

What's Wrong with a Van?, Greenwillow, 1987.

Aunt Nina, Good Night!, Greenwillow, 1989.

Home: A Collection of Thirty Distinguished Authors and Illustrators of Children's Books to Aid the Homeless, edited by Michael J. Rosen, HarperCollins (New York, NY), 1992.

ADAPTATIONS: Digging up Dinosaurs was released as an audiocassette, HarperAudio, 1991.

SIDELIGHTS: In her hundred-plus publications for children, the Greek-American author-illustrator Aliki Brandenberg has demonstrated a rare talent in imparting information to children and young readers in manifold ways. Employing at times comic book-style illustration and word bubbles, at others elaborate frieze pictures or a faux illuminated manuscript, Aliki (who writes and illustrates under her first name) is well known for adapting illustration to content. As both author and illustrator she works in fiction and nonfiction formats. In the former she tells generational tales in books such as *The Two of Them, At Mary Bloom's,* and *Marianthe's Story;* with picture books, such as *We Are Best Friends, Best Friends Together Again,* and *Hello! Good-bye!,* she details the emotional lives of young children; and in *Christmas Tree Memories* and *Those Summers,* she focuses on family memories.

In nonfiction Aliki has produced award-winning titles in biography, from the life of William Tell to Benjamin Franklin and King Louis XIV of France. She has also written books of folktales, particularly those of Greece, which reflect her heritage. Additionally, Aliki has produced over two dozen information books on subjects from dinosaurs to natural history and anatomy. Accompanying the many stories she has written herself, Aliki has also illustrated dozens of books written by others, including her husband, Franz Brandenberg. Gearing her works to a preschool-to-middle grade audience, Aliki fills her books with warmth, humor, and enthusiasm. As she once commented, "I write fiction out of a need to express myself. I write nonfiction—out of curiosity and fascination. And I draw in order to breathe."

Aliki was born in Wildwood Crest, New Jersey, where her parents, who lived in Philadelphia, were vacationing at the time. She attended school in Philadelphia and Yeadon, Pennsylvania, starting to draw during her preschool years. While in kindergarten she exhibited her first two portraits—one of her family and another of Peter Rabbit's family. Aliki continued to draw and attend art classes on Saturdays and also took piano lessons. After she graduated from high school, she enrolled in the Philadelphia Museum School of Art.

When Aliki graduated from college in 1951, she took a job working in the display department of the J. C. Penney Company in New York City. After a year she moved back to Philadelphia and worked as a freelance advertising and display artist. She also painted murals, started her own greeting card company, and taught classes in art and ceramics. Aliki, whose parents were natives of Greece and had taught her to speak Greek before she learned to speak English, decided in 1956 to visit that country and other places in Europe—especially Italy—traveling, painting, sketching, and learning about her heritage.

While on her tour she met Franz Brandenberg, and in 1957 the two married, settling in his native Switzerland. Aliki continued her freelance art career there. While in Switzerland she learned that William Tell was Swiss, and she and Franz visited the territory where he lived. That experience inspired her to write and illustrate her first book, *The Story of William Tell,* which was published in 1960. Reviewing this debut book in *School Librarian and School Library,* H. Millington reacted with praise: "Aliki has taken [the old tale] and dressed it up as fresh as the daisies with some of the most gorgeous illustrations I have seen." The characters "jump off the page," Millington continued, "with the sheer audacious simplicity of their representation."

Later that year Aliki and her husband moved to New York City, where she was asked to illustrate several books written by other authors. That gave her the idea to write a second book of her own, *My Five Senses.* Since then, she has published dozens more nonfiction titles, many of them in association with the "Let's Read and Find out Science Books" series for Crowell, as well as engaging, simplified biographies. Of the former, some of her most popular titles deal with dinosaurs, a topic with intrinsic interest to young children. Reviewing *My Visit to the Dinosaurs,* a writer for *Kirkus Reviews* commented that "what this dinosaur book has that others don't is what might be called human interest—also a sense of humor." Aliki followed this with *Digging up Dinosaurs,* whose "main text and energetic drawings will appeal to any child who hungers for extra information on those endlessly fascinating 'bags of bones,'" according to Susan Bolotin writing in the *New York Times Book Review.* Aliki has continued with a personal fascination for the ancient reptiles in *Dinosaurs Are Different, Dinosaur Bones,* and *Aliki's Dinosaur Dig.*

Aliki's nonfiction books start with a fascination for a certain subject, which she researches over an extended period of time. "The pleasure of these [nonfiction] books," she once wrote, "is writing complicated facts as clearly and simply as possible, so readers (and I) who know nothing about a subject learn a great deal by the time we are finished." *Publishers Weekly* reviewer Dulcy Brainard observed that "these science primers inform, entertain and delight in a way that is particularly Aliki's, using script and different typefaces, with frieze frames and borders. One doesn't have to be a kid to devour each page, intent on not missing a single bit of in-

formation it contains." Aliki spoke about her science books with Margaret Carter in *Books for Your Children,* remarking, "It's best for me to know nothing about a subject when I begin . . . that way I have to get it right. Because I am not a scientist I can perhaps approach the subject with fresh eyes."

Other popular nonfiction works from Aliki's pen include writings on fossils, on natural cycles and manufacturing, and on history. Reviewing *Fossils Tell of Long Ago,* Mary Neale Rees commented in *School Library Journal* that this "factually accurate, clearly written text will be welcomed by primary graders who are usually captivated by fossils and dinosaurs." Aliki has developed a text-within text style by employing dialogue or thought bubbles for characters as well as a main text explicating pictures. Combining both science and history, she looked at the significance of corn in America in *Corn Is Maize: The Gift of the Indians,* an "engaging description" and a "successful blend of social studies, science, and history," according to Diane Holzheimer in *School Library Journal.*

Food is also the subject of her *Green Grass and White Milk* and *Milk: From Cow to Carton,* and informs the inspired tableaux of her popular *A Medieval Feast.* This latter was another blending of history and sociology to recreate what such a feast of the year 1400 must have been like. The fruit of two years labor, *A Medieval Feast* "seems to spring from the copy," noted Brainard. Employing a style reminiscent of illuminated manuscripts and a lush prose style, "Aliki has provided us with a veritable feast of a book," concluded Patricia Dooley in *School Library Journal.* More history was at the heart of the popular *Mummies Made in Egypt,* with "stunning" art "adapted from the real article and rendered frieze-style," according to Nora Magid in the *New York Times Book Review,* and text that "is uncompromisingly informative and clear."

Aliki tackled manufacturing processes in *How a Book Is Made,* in which she employed a comic strip format and step-by-step illustrations to "make the information easily accessible," according to Zena Sutherland in *Bulletin of the Center for Children's Books.* "Yes, there are other good books on how a book is made," noted Sutherland, "but probably none better for younger readers." Emotional states were the focus of *Feelings,* in which Aliki again uses the comic strip format to create a "lighthearted mood," according to *Booklist*'s Denise M. Wilms, who concluded that Aliki's "fresh, colorful execution lends grace beyond what often passes for bibliotherapy." With *Manners* Aliki presented a short course in etiquette, a book useful for both parents and teachers, according to Cathryn A. Camper writing in *The Five Owls.* "The playful cartoon dialogue and the funny 'good manners' quiz on the endpapers help keep the tone of the book non-didactic and lighthearted," concluded Camper.

Aliki is also known for her popular biographies. Indeed it was such a book, *The Story of William Tell,* that launched her career. She has continued to produce simplified versions of the lives of the famous ever since. Her award-winning *The Story of Johnny Appleseed* and *The Story of William Penn* were lauded for their relaxed style and humor. Reviewing Aliki's rendition of Johnny Appleseed, Millicent J. Taylor commented in *Christian Science Monitor* that "Aliki has a remarkable way of capturing the spirit of a small child's paintings and lighting them up with the genius of the adult painter of true primitives." The life of George Washington Carver was profiled in *A Weed Is a Flower,* "a simplified biography true both to its subject and the interests of early childhood," according to *Kirkus Reviews.*

Aliki has gone further afield for her biographies, as well. In *The King's Day,* she details the life of King Louis XIV of France in a book full of fascinating details and fine artwork recreating the royal court at Versailles. "Color is the most striking element in Aliki's drawings," observed Shirley Wilton in a *School Library Journal* review of the book. "The richness of the king's costumes, his wigs, lace, red stockings, and high-heeled shoes are echoed by the attire of his courtiers." Shakespeare also gets the Aliki treatment in *William Shakespeare and the Globe,* "one of the most appealing and responsible biographies of Shakespeare" for the middle grades, according to Sally Margolis in *School Library Journal,* as well as "a history of the Globe of the 17th century and the recently completed facsimile of the theater." Margolis concluded that Aliki's book is a "thoroughly enjoyable and reliable introduction to the Bard." *Kirkus Reviews* noted that "Aliki creates a cascade of landscapes, crowd scenes, diminutive portraits, and sequential views, all done with her trademark warmth and delicacy of line."

Aliki's story of the Greek philosopher in *Diogenes* underlines her interest in her Greek heritage. Adapting the style of the Greek fresco for this biography, she introduces young readers to someone they might not otherwise know. In her retelling of Greek myth and folktales, she also has introduced new and less typical information to young readers. In her award-winning *Three Gold Pieces,* she retold the story of a submissive Greek peasant and the meager pay he receives for ten years work. Eleanor Dienstag noted the "almost Biblical quality" of

the story in the *New York Times Book Review,* as well as Aliki's "rich, Oriental illustrations." More folktales were presented in *The Twelve Months* and *The Eggs.* With her 1994 *The Gods and Goddesses of Olympus,* Aliki moved to Greek myth, presenting a winning introduction to that endlessly fascinating subject.

Aliki and her family moved to England in 1977, where she and Franz have since continued their careers as children's book writers. "I'm one of those lucky people who love what they do," Aliki commented. "I also love my garden, music, theater, museums, and traveling. But I'm happiest when I'm in my studio on the top floor of our tall house in London, alone with the book I'm working on, and Mozart."

In addition to her information picture books and illustrations for other writers, Aliki is also noted for storybooks or fiction picture books written from "a lifetime of experiences" as she once commented—sometimes her own and sometimes the experiences of her two children. "A word can trigger a story that has been somewhere in my mind for years," she continued. From her very first picture book, *The Wish Workers,* in 1962, Aliki carved out territory in fiction uniquely her own. "The theme is old, but the simple text and gaily imaginative illustrations by the author in lovely colors have modern charm," noted Allie Beth Martin in *School Library Journal* of this title. Comedy of the anatomy is the central joke of *Keep Your Mouth Closed, Dear,* an "altogether winning creation," according to Richard Kluger in *Book Week.* The absent-minded alligator from this tale was reprised in *Use Your Head, Dear.*

Family memories are gathered in several books, including *Christmas Tree Memories, June 7!,* and *Those Summers.* Reviewing the birthday party book, *June 7!,* Edward Hudson noted in *Children's Book Review* that Aliki "has a simplicity of line and an eye for detail that children seek out," while Judith Gloyer observed in *School Library Journal* that Aliki's *Those Summers* "offers vivid memories of childhood summers spent at the ocean with her cousins, parents, aunts, and uncles." Gloyer concluded that the book provided a "delightful glimpse of a cherished childhood."

Babies—both mouse and human—beckon in *At Mary Bloom's* and *Welcome, Little Baby.* The former title is also a generational story, about a little girl and an older neighbor, a book that is "great fun," in the words of Zena Sutherland writing in *Bulletin of the Center for Children's Books.* Another powerful generational tale is *The Two of Them,* inspired by Aliki's own father, which tells of the mutual love between an old man and his granddaughter. *Publishers Weekly* called the tale "a moving but unsentimental story," and concluded that it was a book "parents who read to their children will probably appreciate even more than will the young." In *Marianthe's Story* a young immigrant girl learns a new language sufficiently to tell her school class the story of how her family came to this new land. "The words and illustrations combine to tell a powerful story of growth, acceptance and overcoming adversity," commented Kristi Steele in *Children's Book Review Service*. A writer for *Kirkus Reviews* concluded that the "storytelling is vivid and exquisitely emotional, making Aliki's story painfully personal, yet resonant, in very few pages."

It is such conciseness, both in her fiction and nonfiction, that has helped to make Aliki a staple in books for preschool to middle grade readers. Yet such simplicity belies the fact of the years of experience or months of research that go into each title. As Aliki once commented, "Much of my work involves intricate and time-consuming research—made doubly difficult because I both write and illustrate. I spend long hours at my desk. Some books take three years to complete. That is why I call what I do 'hard fun.' But I love the challenge of a new idea, and finding out something I don't know about a subject—or even myself."

BIOGRAPHICAL/CRITICAL SOURCES:

BOOKS

Children's Literature Review, Volume 9, Gale (Detroit, MI), 1985.
Children's Books and Their Creators, edited by Anita Silvey, Houghton, 1995.
St. James Guide to Children's Writers, 5th edition, St. James Press (Detroit, MI), 1999.

PERIODICALS

Book Week, October 30, 1966, Richard Kluger, "Crocodile Smiles," pp. 4-5, 8.
Booklist, December 1, 1994, Denise M. Wilms, review of *Feelings,* p. 520; August, 1995, p. 94; May 1, 1996, p. 1511; July, 1996, p. 1827; June 1, 1999, Carolyn Phelan, review of *William Shakespeare and the Globe,* p. 1824; March 15, 2000, review of *William Shakespeare and the Globe,* p. 1359; November, 2000, Carolyn Phelan, review of *All by Myself,* p. 544; July, 2001, Hazel Rochman, review of *One Little Spoonful,* p. 2022.
Books for Your Children, spring, 1984, Margaret Carter, "Cover Artist—Aliki," p. 9.

Bulletin of the Center for Children's Books, November, 1976, Zena Sutherland, review of *At Mary Bloom's,* p. 37; November, 1986, Zena Sutherland, review of *How a Book Is Made,* p. 41.
Children's Book Review Service, summer, 1975, Edward Hudson, review of *June 7!,* p. 55; October, 1998, Kristi Steele, review of *Marianthe's Story,* p. 19.
Christian Science Monitor, November 14, 1963, Millicent J. Taylor, "Peopling the Past," p. 7B.
Five Owls, February, 1991, Cathryn, A. Camper, review of *Manners,* p. 53.
Horn Book, May-June, 1993, p. 342; March-April, 1994, p. 198; July-August, 1995, p. 446; September-October, 1997, p. 589; September-October, 1998, p. 595; January, 2000, review of *William Shakespeare and the Globe,* p. 50; September, 2000, review of *All by Myself,* p. 545.
Kirkus Reviews, October 1, 1965, review of *A Weed Is a Flower: The Life of George Washington Carver,* p. 1039; September 1, 1969, review of *My Visit to the Dinosaurs,* pp. 930-931; September 1, 1998, review of *Marianthe's Story,* p. 1282; May 1, 1999, review of *William Shakespeare and the Globe,* p. 718.
New York Times Book Review, April 30, 1967, Eleanor Dienstag, review of *Three Gold Pieces,* p. 26; November 18, 1979, Nora Magid, review of *Mummies Made in Egypt,* pp. 30-31; March 8, 1981, Susan Bolotin, review of *Digging up Dinosaurs,* p. 30; October 16, 1983.
Publishers Weekly, September 10, 1979, review of *The Two of Them,* p. 65; July 22, 1983, Dulcy Brainard, interview with Aliki Brandenberg, pp. 134-135; August 8, 1994, p. 434; June 3, 1996, p. 82; August 19, 1996, p. 66; August 11, 1997, p. 402; July 20, 1998, p. 219; May 31, 1999, review of *William Shakespeare and the Globe;* p. 91; August 21, 2000, review of *All by Myself,* p. 71.
Reading Today, October, 2000, Lynne T. Burke, review of *Marianthe's Story,* p. 32.
School Librarian and School Library, December, 1961, H. Millington, review of *The Story of William Tell,* p. 567.
School Library Journal, November, 1962, Allie Beth Martin, review of *The Wish Workers,* p. 39; September, 1972, Mary Neale Rees, review of *Fossils Tell of Long Ago,* p. 111; April, 1976, Diane Holzheimer, review of *Corn Is Maize,* p. 58; September, 1983, Patricia Dooley, review of *A Medieval Feast,* p. 114; October, 1989, Shirley Wilton, review of *The King's Day: Louis XIV of France,* p. 99; April, 1993, p. 104; August, 1996, Judith Gloyer, review of *Those Summers,* p. 115; October,

1998, Diane S. Marton, review of *Marianthe's Story,* p. 86; May, 1999, Sally Margolis, review of *William Shakespeare and the Globe,* p. 134; September, 2000, Sharon R. Pearce, review of *All by Myself,* p. 184.

OTHER

Aliki (publicity sheet), Greenwillow Books, 1986.

* * *

BREGER, Louis 1935-

PERSONAL: Born November 20, 1935, in Los Angeles, CA; son of Leo I. (a social worker) and Lillian (a nursery school teacher) Breger; married Gail Heller (a teacher), January 27, 1957; children: Lisa, Samuel, Josie. *Education:* University of California, Los Angeles, B.A., 1957; Ohio State University, M.A., 1959, Ph.D., 1961.

ADDRESSES: Office—Division of Humanities and Social Sciences, California Institute of Technology, 1200 East California Blvd., Pasadena, CA 91125.

CAREER: University of Oregon, Eugene, OR, assistant professor of psychology, 1961-66; Langley Porter Neuropsychiatric Institute, San Francisco, CA, staff psychologist, 1966-70; California Institute of Technology, Pasadena, CA, associate professor, then professor emeritus of psychoanalytic studies, beginning 1970. Founder, Institute of Contemporary Psychoanalysis. Psychoanalyst in Los Angeles, CA.

MEMBER: American Psychological Association, Association for the Psychophysiological Study of Sleep, American Academy of Psychoanalysis, Southern California Psychoanalytic Institute.

WRITINGS:

(Editor) *Clinical-Cognitive Psychology,* Prentice-Hall (Englewood Cliffs, NJ), 1969.
(With Ronald W. Lane and Ian Hunter) *The Effect of Stress on Dreams,* International University Press (Madison, CT), 1971.
From Instinct to Identity: The Development of Personality, Prentice-Hall (Englewood Cliffs, NJ), 1974.
Dostoevsky: The Author as Psychoanalyst, New York University Press (Albany, NY), 1989.
Freud: Darkness in the Midst of Vision: An Analytical Biography, Wiley (New York, NY), 2000.

Contributor to psychology journals.

SIDELIGHTS: Louis Breger is a psychoanalyst who applies psychoanalytic techniques in his unique biography, *Freud: Darkness in the Midst of Vision.* Using the techniques developed and advocated by Sigmund Freud to examine and explain Freud's own life, Breger creates a biography that is a "groundbreaking work," according to Michael Spinella in *Booklist.* Breger finds that events in Freud's own life influenced his creation of psychoanalysis and the assumptions about the human mind that lie behind it. E. James Lieberman in *Library Journal* called *Freud* a "masterly biography and cultural history" as well as a "landmark work." A critic for *Publishers Weekly* concluded that Breger's biography is "a provocative, well-written and up-to-date account of the life and career of one of the 20th century's most influential intellectual figures."

BIOGRAPHICAL/CRITICAL SOURCES:

PERIODICALS

Booklist, September 15, 2000, Michael Spinella, review of *Freud: Darkness in the Midst of Vision,* p. 189.
Library Journal, September 1, 2000, E. James Lieberman, review of *Freud,* p. 233.
Publishers Weekly, September 4, 2000, review of *Freud,* p. 98.*

* * *

BRODER, David S(alzer) 1929-

PERSONAL: Born September 11, 1929, in Chicago Heights, IL; son of Albert I. (a dentist) and Nina M. (Salzer) Broder; married Ann Creighton Collar, June 8, 1951; children: George, Joshua, Matthew, Michael. *Education:* University of Chicago, B.A., 1947, M.A., 1951.

ADDRESSES: Home—4024 North 27th St., Arlington, VA 22207. *Office*—*Washington Post,* 1150 15th St. N.W., Washington, DC 20007. *Agent*—Elizabeth McKee, McIntosh, McKee & Dodd, Inc., 22 East 40th St., New York, NY 10016.

CAREER: Pantagraph, Bloomington, IL, reporter, 1953-55; *Congressional Quarterly,* Washington, DC, reporter, 1955-60; *Washington Star,* Washington, DC, reporter, 1960-65; *New York Times,* New York, NY, reporter in Washington, DC, 1965-66; *Washington Post,*

Washington, DC, reporter, columnist, and associate editor, 1966—. Participant, *Meet the Press* and *Washington Week in Review* television programs. Fellow of Institute of Politics at Harvard University, 1969-70; Poynter fellow at Yale University and Indiana University, 1973; fellow of Institute of Policy Science and Public Affairs, Duke University. Regular commentator on CNN's *Inside Politics*. *Military service:* U.S. Army, 1951-53.

MEMBER: American Political Science Association (member of advisory board for Conglomerate Fellows Program, 1964—), American Newspaper Guild, Gridiron Club.

AWARDS, HONORS: American Newspaper Guild award, 1961, 1973, and 1974; Pulitzer Prize in journalism for distinguished commentary, 1973; White Burkett Miller Presidential Award, 1989; Common Wealth award, 1990; Elijah Parrish Lovejoy award, Colby College, 1990; National Press Foundation, recipient of 4th Estate Award, 1990, and Distinguished Contributions to Journalism Award, 1993; National Society of Newspaper Columnists Lifetime Achievement Award, 1997; William Allen White Foundation's medal for distinguished achievement in journalism, University of Kansas, 1997; elected to Sigma Chi's Hall of Fame; named "Best Newspaper Political Reporter" by *Washington Journalism Review*.

WRITINGS:

(With Stephen Hess) *The Republican Establishment,* Harper (New York, NY), 1967.
The Party's Over: The Failure of Politics in America, Harper (New York, NY), 1972.
Changing of the Guard: Power and Leadership in America, Penguin (New York, NY), 1981.
Behind the Front Page: A Candid Look at How the News Is Made, Simon & Schuster (New York, NY), 1987.
(With Bob Woodward) *The Man Who Would Be President: Dan Quayle,* Simon & Schuster (New York, NY), 1992.
(With Haynes Johnson) *The System: The American Way of Politics at the Breaking Point,* Little, Brown (Boston, MA), 1996.
Democracy Derailed: Initiative Campaigns and the Power of Money, Harcourt (New York, NY), 2000.

Contributor to books, including *The Pursuit of the Presidency 1980,* edited by Richard Harwood, Berkley Books (New York, NY), 1980. Syndicated columnist; contributor to *Atlantic*.

SIDELIGHTS: David Broder is a veteran reporter whose long career as a political columnist for the *Washington Post* has earned him the reputation among his colleagues as "the country's best-informed political journalist," according to the *New York Times Book Review*'s Thomas Griffith.

In addition to writing his column, Broder has written several books on American politics. *Behind the Front Page* is a behind-the-scenes look at the making of political news in America. Broder explores how the news is shaped and manipulated by public officials and journalists, but primarily focuses on the flaws of this process. As a critic for *Kirkus Reviews* explained, "Broder . . . exposes failures and triumphs of the press and the political entities it covers." *Behind the Front Page,* the critic concluded, is a "compelling account of how political news is made, notable for both its insight and brutal candor." Griffith pointed out that Broder "writes in a sprightly, anecdotal fashion, but a melancholy awareness of ordinary pleasures sacrificed to work suffuses this honest work."

In 1992 a series of articles on then-vice president Dan Quayle appeared in the *Washington Post*. Co-authored by Broder and fellow journalist Bob Woodward, these pieces were later published as *The Man Who Would Be President: Dan Quayle*. The articles, primarily drawn from interviews—including twenty with Quayle himself—discuss such topics as Quayle's campaign for the vice presidency, his stint in the National Guard in lieu of serving in Vietnam, and his golf game. Max Boot of the *Christian Science Monitor* found that "the ace *Washington Post* reporters make a compelling case that the vice president isn't nearly as dumb as some people think he is." However, Jefferson Morley, in the *Los Angeles Times Book Review,* called *The Man Who Would Be President* "a dismally disappointing biography," accusing the authors of having "joined the ranks of the Quayle revisionists." Morley did note their willingness to point out some of Quayle's flaws, but concluded: "Dan Quayle has proven to be a skillful player of the political game with a competitive drive that has been underestimated repeatedly by his rivals." James K. Glassman of the *New York Times Book Review* criticized the authors for not having a thesis: "This is after all, a book, and a book requires its authors to have, if not a strong moral position, then at least a discernible point of view."

With co-author Haynes Johnson, Broder next published *The System: The American Way of Politics at the Breaking Point*. In this study, Broder and Johnson examine the failure of President Bill Clinton to successfully push through his much-touted health care reform bill. David Frum in the *Wall Street Journal* noted that "two of Washington's most eminent journalists lay the blame squarely on a corrupt and dysfunctional system of national politics." Although Frum did not agree with their placement of blame, he found that "it is among the many merits of this intensely reported book that it presents most of the information a reader will need to reach precisely the opposite conclusion." Richard Bernstein of the *New York Times* pointed out that the authors had not accounted for other successes that had made their way through the "clunkiness" of the system, such as NAFTA and the crime bill. Matthew Dallek in the *Washington Post Book World* contended that although "there is little new in their explanation of why the system failed, . . . in the growing literature on why Americans hate politics, it is an important publication." J. Anthony Lukas, also of the *New York Times,* stated that "with this reporting and analysis, Mr. Johnson and Mr. Broder make a valuable contribution to the debate over the state of our public life. *The System* will be a useful casebook in political science courses across the land."

Democracy Derailed: Initiative Campaigns and the Power of Money attacks the use in America of ballot initiatives. In twenty-four states, plus the District of Columbia, citizens are allowed to place their measures before the voters via these initiatives. Hundreds of municipalities also allow this practice, which arose out of the well-intentioned ideals of the Populist and Progressive movements. In Broder's opinion, this bypasses the established legislative process. He asserts that this "is alien to the spirit of the Constitution and its careful system of checks and balances," and "threatens to challenge or even subvert the American system of government in the next few decades."

Broder initially tackles the history of ballot initiatives. He quickly moves forward to recent and sometimes controversial initiatives, exploring not only the initiatives themselves, but the business of how they function. A substantial amount of the book is devoted to an analysis of the 1998 election cycle, in which over a quarter of a billion dollars was spent on promoting initiatives and counter-initiatives, including pro-casino gambling, anti-hunting, and anti-abortion measures. Broder also focuses in great detail upon California's Proposition 226, the so-called "paycheck-protection initiative," whose intention was to limit the ability of labor unions to spend members' dues on political donations—a measure that, ultimately, failed to pass. In Broder's opinion, lack of spending limits allow big-money, special interest groups to buy media advertising, thereby promoting their own selfish interests. He laments the growth of the "lucrative initiative industry," comprised of paid signature gatherers, consultants, pollsters, and public-relations firms.

Robert T. Nelson, writing in *Seattle Times,* wrote in regard to *Democracy Derailed: Initiative Campaigns and the Power of Money:* "Missing is that moment of revelation when the reader discovers something he or she didn't already know or suspect." And Nelson said of Broder, "smart as he is, good as he is, he can put you to sleep in a heartbeat if the subject isn't riveting. . . . And in *Democracy Derailed: Initiative Campaigns and the Power of Money* . . . Broder has provided a sure cure for sleepless nights." A *Mother Jones* reviewer noted that "Alarmed by the growing impact of state ballot initiatives, the *Washington Post*'s Broder—the 'dean of American political journalism,' according to Brill's Content—takes a thorough look at the phenomenon and pronounces it a bad thing." Mary Carroll concluded in her *Booklist* review: "Despite public cynicism about legislatures, Broder offers solid evidence that the initiative process, with its up-or-down simplicity and potential for manipulation by deep-pocket funders, is no solution to the nation's problems." A *Publishers Weekly* reviewer termed the book a "well-argued and often chilling study," and deemed the book's "centerpiece . . . a balanced but tough-minded analysis of Proposition 226."

In *New York Times,* David Brooks described *Democracy Derailed: Initiative Campaigns and the Power of Money* as a "lucent and fair book." He commented: "All pundits are egomaniacs, but the best pundits are humble egomaniacs. They assume that their own opinions are important enough to publish and broadcast, but they also make a second and rarer assumption—that other people's opinions are worth listening to as well. So decade after decade the best of them—like the *Washington Post*'s David S. Broder and the columnist Robert Novak—go out and ask questions, even though they know more about politics than 99 percent of the people they interview." Brooks proceeded to observe, "watching David Broder polemicize against direct democracy is a bit like watching a bunch of Unitarians trying to start the Spanish Inquisition. The guy can't stop bending over backward to give the other side a fair hearing."

BIOGRAPHICAL/CRITICAL SOURCES:

BOOKS

Downs, Robert B., and Jane B. Downs, *Journalists of the United States: Biographical Sketches of Print and Broadcast News Shapers from the Late Seven-*

teenth Century to the Present, McFarland & Company, Inc. (Jefferson, NC).

Grauer, Neil A., *Wits and Sages: Jack Anderson, Russell Baker, Erma Bombeck, Jimmy Breslin, David Broder, Art Buchwald, William F. Buckley, Jr., Ellen Goodman, James J. Kilpatrick, Carl T. Rowan, Mike Royko, George F. Will,* Johns Hopkins University Press (Baltimore, MD), 1984.

PERIODICALS

American Spectator, March, 1992, p. 50.

Booklist, May 1, 1996, p. 1474; March 15, 2000, Mary Carroll, review of *Democracy Detailed: Initiative Campaigns and the Power of Money,* p. 1290.

Business Week, May 27, 1996, p. 19.

Chicago Tribune, November 13, 1996.

Chicago Tribune Magazine, March 6, 1994, p. 6.

Choice, October, 1988, p. 278.

Christian Science Monitor, October 23, 1992, p. 13.

Editor & Publisher, July 5, 1997, p. 32.

Insight on the News, February 3, 1992, p. 14.

Kirkus Reviews, February 15, 1987, p. 272.

Lancet, May 11, 1996, p. 1316.

Library Journal, May 1, 1996, p. 113; Philip Young Blue, review of *Democracy Detailed: Initiative Campaigns and the Power of Money,* p. 110.

Los Angeles Times Book Review, June 14, 1992, p. 4.

Mother Jones, May, 2000, review of *Democracy Detailed: Initiative Campaigns and the Power of Money,* p. 81.

National Review, July 29, 1996, p. 46.

New England Journal of Medicine, August 22, 1996, p. 602.

New Leader, June 1, 1992, p. 5.

New York Review of Books, June 6, 1996, p. 11.

New York Times, May 5, 1996; May 10, 1996, p. C31.

New York Times Book Review, April 26, 1987, p. 14; May 24, 1992, p. 5; May 5, 1996, p. 34; April 16, 2000, David Brooks, review of *Democracy Detailed: Initiative Campaigns and the Power of Money,* p. 38.

Progressive, December, 1992, p. 36.

People, June 22, 1992, p. 32.

Publishers Weekly, March 25, 1996, p. 70; March 13, 2000, review of *Democracy Detailed: Initiative Campaigns and the Power of Money,* p. 71.

Seattle Times, March 31, 2000, Richard T. Nelson, "David Broder's 'Democracy Derailed' Is Informative, but Lacks Punch."

U.S. News and World Report, April 16, 1990, p. 25.

Village Voice, November 3, 1992, pp. 66-67.

Wall Street Journal, May 7, 1996, p. A20.

Washingtonian, August, 1996, p. 23.

Washington Post Book World, April 21, 1996, pp. 1, 14.

OTHER

Washington Post Web site, http://www.washington post.com/ (October 22, 2001), "David S. Broder Biography."*

*   *   *

BROWN, Rebecca
   See ORE, Rebecca

*   *   *

BURLEIGH, Michael   1955-

PERSONAL: Born April 3, 1955, in London, England; son of B. G. S. Bennet-Burleigh (in business); married Linden Mary Brownbridge (a writer), November, 1990. *Education:* University of London, B.A. (with first class honors), 1977, Ph.D., 1982.

ADDRESSES: *Agent*—c/o David Godwin Associates, 55 Monmouth St., London WC2H 9DG, England. *E-mail*—mandlburleigh@aol.com.

CAREER: Oxford University, Oxford, England, research fellow at New College, 1984-87; British Academy, research fellow, 1987-88; University of London, London School of Economics and Political Science, London, England, reader in international history, 1988-95; Cardiff University, Wales, distinguished research professor of history, 1999-2000; Washington and Lee University, Lexington, VA, William R. Kenan professor of history, 2000—. Raoul Wallenberg Chair of Human Rights; writer.

MEMBER: Royal Historical Society (fellow).

AWARDS, HONORS: British Film Institute award for archival achievement, 1991; bronze medal, New York Film and Television festival, 1994; Samuel Johnson prize for nonfiction, 2001, for *The Third Reich.*

WRITINGS:

Prussian Society and the German Order: An Aristocratic Corporation in Crisis c. 1410-1466, Cambridge University Press (New York, NY), 1984.

Germany Turns Eastwards: A Study of "Ostforschung" in the Third Reich, Cambridge University Press (New York, NY), 1988.

(With Wolfgang Wippermann) *The Racial State: Germany, 1933-1945,* Cambridge University Press (New York, NY), 1991.

Death and Deliverance: Euthanasia in Germany, 1900-1945, Cambridge University Press (New York, NY), 1995.

Confronting the Nazi Past: New Debates on Modern German History, Trafalgar Square (North Pomfret, VT), 1996.

Ethics and Extermination: Reflections on Nazi Genocide, Cambridge University Press (New York, NY), 1997.

The Third Reich: A New History, Hill & Wang (New York, NY), 2000.

Burleigh's books have been translated into Italian, Japanese, German, Spanish, Polish, French, and Hungarian. Also a writer for television. Contributor to periodicals, including *Times Literary Supplement, Financial Times, Sunday Times,* and *Literary Review.*

WORK IN PROGRESS: Politics and religion since the French revolution, for Knopf.

SIDELIGHTS: Michael Burleigh has written extensively on various aspects of the Weimar Republic and Nazi Germany. In two of his books, *Death and Deliverance: Euthanasia in Germany, 1900-1945* and *Ethics and Extermination: Reflections on Nazi Genocide,* he focuses on the highly organized killing programs set up by the Nazi regime. *The Third Reich: A New History,* for which Burleigh won Britain's prestigious nonfiction literary award, the Samuel Johnson prize, covers all aspects of that period in Germany's history. Although the story has been told many times before, *Booklist* reviewer Jay Freeman stated that Burleigh's *The Third Reich* is a significant addition to the literature on the subject, providing a "brilliant and unique view of a great tyranny."

In *Death and Deliverance,* Burleigh carefully details the escalation of the Nazi killing programs, beginning with the move for "mercy killing" of terminally ill patients. Soon mentally and physically handicapped people were being sterilized and killed without the consent of their families. Although these euthanasia programs were kept secret for a long while, the German public was simultaneously being bombarded with propaganda about the need to save food and resources for those who could contribute to the building of a better society. Patients deemed unworthy of life were gassed, poisoned, and starved to death by medical personnel, and the techniques used were later put to work in death camps for Jews and others deemed "undesirable" by the Nazis.

"This is one of those books that no reader will ever forget," reported Jonathan Steinberg in *History Today,* one that offers "profound insights into the heart of darkness that was Hitler's Reich."

Burleigh's *The Third Reich* is a wide-ranging work, but at its core is the idea that the Nazi regime was able to rise to power because of the economic and social conditions in Europe following World War I. The devastation of that war led to a spiritual and moral void which made the moral certainties proclaimed by the Nazis, along with their pseudo-religious trappings, very appealing to many Europeans. Burleigh "demonstrates the extent to which Hitler came to reflect the frustrations, the aspirations, and the impulses of growing numbers of Germans," noted Omer Bartov in a *New Republic* article. "Similarly, although he outlines the intellectual, religious, and political sources for opposition to Hitler's regime, he simultaneously traces the deep roots of support for Hitler along with the more opportunistic collaboration with specific policies such as 'euthanasia,' territorial expansion, or anti-Semitism. And even as he dismisses the idea of collective guilt, Burleigh paints a depressing picture of a society that acquiesced in the establishment of a brutal dictatorship and facilitated the unfolding of its increasingly murderous policies."

A *History Today* reviewer stated that Burleigh "draws a picture of Germany that combines the political and economic evidence with a portrayal of the colourful, pseudo-religious mass movements that seemed to offer salvation to the German people." William D. Rubinstein, in another *History Today* review, called the work "a central contemporary account of the Nazi regime." Freeman maintained that *The Third Reich* is a "comprehensive and majestic work" that reminds readers of "the costs we still pay for the worship of false gods." *Contemporary Review*'s Edward Bradbury concluded that *The Third Reich* "is a refreshing return to the writings of earlier historians who combined scholarship, breadth and moral outrage."

Burleigh told *CA:* "I am very relieved to not be writing about Nazi Germany any more."

BIOGRAPHICAL/CRITICAL SOURCES:

PERIODICALS

American Historical Review, June, 1996, Michael H. Kater, review of *Death and Deliverance: Euthanasia in Germany, 1900-1945,* p. 865; April, 1998, Frank Dikotter, review of *Death and Deliverance,* p. 470.

Booklist, August, 2000, Jay Freeman, review of *The Third Reich: A New History,* p. 2103.

Canadian Journal of History, December, 1998, Paul Weindling, review of *Ethics and Extermination: Reflections on Nazi Genocide,* p. 462.

Commonweal, September 8, 1995, Daniel Callahan, review of *Death and Deliverance,* p. 20.

Contemporary Review, January, 2001, Edward Bradbury, review of *The Third Reich,* p. 59.

History Today, February, 1994, Dick Geary, review of *The Racial State: Germany, 1933-1945,* p. 54; January, 1997, Jonathan Steinberg, *Death and Deliverance: Euthanasia in Germany, 1900-1945,* p. 51; November, 1997, Stuart Woolf, review of *Confronting the Nazi Past: New Debates on Modern German History,* p. 58; July, 2001, William D. Rubinstein, review of *The Third Reich,* p. 59; August, 2001, review of *The Third Reich,* p. 2.

Journal of the American Medical Association, July 5, 1995, review of *Death and Deliverance,* p. 80.

Library Journal, August, 2000, Frederic Krome, review of *The Third Reich,* p. 123.

New England Journal of Medicine, June 22, 1995, Harry Yeide, Jr., review of *Death and Deliverance,* p. 1722.

New Republic, November 20, 2000, Omer Bartov, review of *The Third Reich,* p. 29.

New Statesman & Society, January 24, 1992, David Herman, review of *The Racial State,* p. 37.

New York Review of Books, May 29, 1997, Gordon A. Craig, review of *Confronting the Nazi Past,* p. 7.

New York Times Book Review, February 5, 1995, Robert N. Proctor, review of *Death and Deliverance,* p. 3.

Publishers Weekly, January 13, 1992, review of *The Racial State,* p. 44; August 28, 2000, review of *The Third Reich,* p. 64.

Sunday Times, June 17, 2001, Stuart Wavell, "Paying the Price for Studying Adolf Hitler," p. NR4.

Times Literary Supplement, February 22, 1985, p. 206; April 13-19, 1990, p. 393.

*   *   *

BYARS, Betsy (Cromer) 1928-

PERSONAL: Born August 7, 1928, in Charlotte, NC; daughter of George Guy and Nan (Rugheimer) Cromer; married Edward Ford Byars (a professor of engineering and a writer), June 24, 1950; children: Laurie, Betsy Ann, Nan, Guy. *Education:* Attended Furman Univer-

Betsy Byars

sity, 1946-48; Queens College, B.A., 1950. *Avocational interests:* Flying (licensed pilot).

ADDRESSES: *Home*—26 Riverpoint, Clemson, SC 29631.

CAREER: Writer.

AWARDS, HONORS: America's Book of the Year selection, Child Study Association, 1968, for *The Midnight Fox,* 1969, for *Trouble River,* 1970, for *The Summer of the Swans,* 1972, for *The House of Wings,* 1973, for *The Winged Colt of Casa Mia* and *The 18th Emergency,* 1974, for *After the Goat Man,* 1975, for *The Lace Snail,* 1976, for *The TV Kid,* and 1980, for *The Night Swimmers;* Notable Book Award, American Library Association, 1969, for *Trouble River,* 1970, for *The Summer of the Swans,* 1972, for *The House of Wings,* 1977, for *The Pinballs,* and 1996, for *My Brother Ant;* Lewis Carroll Shelf Award, 1970, for *The Midnight Fox;* John Newbery Medal, American Library Association, 1971, for *The Summer of the Swans;* Best Books for Spring selection, *School Library Journal,* 1971, for *Go and Hush the Baby;* Booklist, *Library Journal,* 1972, and National Book Award finalist, 1973, both for *House of Wings; New York Times* Outstanding Book of the Year, 1973, for *The Winged Colt of Casa Mia* and *The 18th Emergency,* 1979, for *Good-bye Chicken Little,* and 1982, for *The Two-thousand-Pound Goldfish;* Dorothy Canfield Fisher Memorial Book Award, Vermont Congress of Parents and Teachers, 1975, for *The 18th Emergency;* Woodward Park School

Annual Book Award, 1977; Children's Book Award, Child Study Children's Book Committee at Bank Street College of Education, 1977; Hans Christian Andersen Honor List for Promoting Concern for the Disadvantaged and Handicapped, 1979; Georgia Children's Book Award, 1979; Charlie May Simon Book Award, Arkansas Elementary School Council, 1980 and 1987; Surrey School Book of the Year Award, School Librarians of Surrey, British Colombia, 1980; Mark Twain Award, Missouri Library Association, 1980, William Allen White Children's Book Award, Emporia State University, 1980, Young Readers Medal, California Reading Association, 1980, Nene Award runner-up, 1981 and 1983, and Golden Archer Award, Department of Library Science, University of Wisconsin—Oshkosh, 1982, all for *The Pinballs;* Best Book of the Year, *School Library Journal,* 1980, and American Book Award for Children's Fiction, 1981, both for *The Night Swimmers;* Children's Choice, International Reading Association, 1982, Tennessee Children's Choice Book Award, Tennessee Library Association, 1983, and Sequoyah Children's Book Award, 1984, all for *The Cybil War;* Parent's Choice Award for Literature, Parent's Choice Foundation, 1982, Best Children's Books, *School Library Journal,* 1982, CRABbery Award, Oxon Hill Branch of Prince George's County Library, 1983, Mark Twain Award, 1985, all for *The Animal, the Vegetable, and John D. Jones;* Notable Book of the Year, *New York Times,* 1982, for *The Two-thousand-Pound Goldfish;* Regina Medal, Catholic Library Association, 1987; Charlie May Simon Award, 1987, for *The Computer Nut;* South Carolina Children's Book Award, William Allen White Award, and Maryland Children's Book Award, all 1988, all for *Cracker Jackson;* Edgar Alan Poe Award, Mystery Writers of America, 1992, for *Wanted . . . Mud Blossom;* Texas Bluebonnet Award and Sunshine State Young Readers Award, both 1998, both for *Tornado;* Nevada Young Readers Award, 1998, for *Tarot Says Beware.*

WRITINGS:

FOR CHILDREN

Clementine, illustrated by Charles Wilton, Houghton (Boston, MA), 1962.

The Dancing Camel, illustrated by Harold Berson, Viking (New York, NY), 1965.

Rama, the Gypsy Cat, illustrated by Peggy Bacon, Viking (New York, NY), 1966.

(And illustrator) *The Groober,* Harper (New York, NY), 1967.

The Midnight Fox, illustrated by Ann Grifalconi, Viking (New York, NY), 1968.

Trouble River, illustrated by Rocco Negri, Viking (New York, NY), 1969.

The Summer of the Swans, illustrated by Ted CoConis, Viking (New York, NY), 1970.

Go and Hush the Baby, illustrated by Emily A. McCully, Viking (New York, NY), 1971.

The House of Wings, illustrated by Daniel Schwartz, Viking (New York, NY), 1972.

The 18th Emergency, illustrated by Robert Grossman, Viking (New York, NY), 1973.

The Winged Colt of Casa Mia, illustrated by Richard Cuffari, Viking (New York, NY), 1973.

After the Goat Man, illustrated by Ronald Himler, Viking (New York, NY), 1974.

(And illustrator) *The Lace Snail,* Viking (New York, NY), 1975.

The TV Kid, illustrated by Cuffari, Viking (New York, NY), 1976.

The Pinballs, Harper (New York, NY), 1977.

The Cartoonist, illustrated by Cuffari, Viking (New York, NY), 1978.

Good-bye Chicken Little, Harper (New York, NY), 1979.

The Night Swimmers, illustrated by Troy Howell, Delacorte (New York, NY), 1980.

The Cybil War, illustrated by Gail Owens, Viking (New York, NY), 1981.

The Animal, the Vegetable, and John D. Jones, illustrated by Ruth Sanderson, Delacorte (New York, NY), 1982.

The Two-thousand-Pound Goldfish, Harper (New York, NY), 1982.

The Glory Girl, Viking (New York, NY), 1983.

The Computer Nut, illustrated with computer graphics by son Guy Byars, Viking (New York, NY), 1984.

Cracker Jackson, Viking (New York, NY), 1985.

The Not-Just-Anybody Family, illustrated by Jacqueline Rogers, Delacorte (New York, NY), 1986.

The Golly Sisters Go West, illustrated by Sue Truesdale, Harper (New York, NY), 1986.

The Blossoms Meet the Vulture Lady, illustrated by Rogers, Delacorte (New York, NY), 1986.

The Blossoms and the Green Phantom, illustrated by Rogers, Delacorte (New York, NY), 1987.

A Blossom Promise, illustrated by Rogers, Delacorte (New York, NY), 1987.

Beans on the Roof, illustrated by Melodye Rosales, Delacorte (New York, NY), 1988.

The Burning Question of Bingo Brown, illustrated by Cathy Bobak, Viking (New York, NY), 1988.

Bingo Brown and the Language of Love, illustrated by Bobak, Viking (New York, NY), 1988.

Hooray for the Golly Sisters, illustrated by Truesdale, Harper (New York, NY), 1990.

Bingo Brown, Gypsy Lover, Viking (New York, NY), 1990.

The Seven Treasure Hunts, Harper (New York, NY), 1991.

Wanted . . . Mud Blossom, Delacorte (New York, NY), 1991.

Bingo Brown's Guide to Romance, Viking (New York, NY), 1992.

Coast to Coast, Delacorte (New York, NY), 1992.

McMummy, Viking (New York, NY), 1993.

The Golly Sisters Ride Again, illustrated by Truesdale, HarperCollins (New York, NY), 1994.

The Dark Stairs: A Herculeah Jones Mystery, Viking (New York, NY), 1994.

(Compiler) *Growing up Stories,* Kingfisher (New York, NY), 1995.

Tarot Says Beware, Viking (New York, NY), 1995.

My Brother, Ant, illustrated by Marc Simont, Viking (New York, NY), 1996.

The Joy Boys, illustrated by Frank Remkiewicz, Yearling First Choice Chapter Book (New York, NY), 1996.

Tornado, illustrated by Doron Ben-Ami, HarperCollins (New York, NY), 1996.

Dead Letter, Viking (New York, NY), 1996.

Ant Plays Bear, illustrated by Simont, Viking (New York, NY), 1997.

Death's Door, Viking (New York, NY), 1997.

Disappearing Acts, Viking (New York, NY), 1998.

Me Tarzan, HarperCollins (New York, NY), 2000.

(With Betsy Duffey and Laurie Myers) *My Dog, My Hero,* illustrated by Loren Long, Holt (New York, NY), 2000.

Little Horse, illustrated by David McPhail, Holt (New York, NY), 2001.

OTHER

(Author of afterword) Margaret Sidney, *The Five Little Peppers and How They Grew,* Dell (New York, NY), 1985.

(Author of preface) Margaret M. Kimmel, *For Reading out Loud,* Dell (New York, NY), 1987.

The Moon and I (autobiography), J. Messner (New York, NY), 1991.

(Author of introduction) *A Newbery Zoo: A Dozen Animal Stories by Newbery Award-winning Authors,* Delacorte Press (New York, NY), 1995.

Contributor of "Taking Humor Seriously," to *The Zena Sutherland Lectures,* Clarion (New York, NY), 1983-92. Contributor of articles to numerous magazines, including *Saturday Evening Post, TV Guide,* and *Look.*

Byars's works have been translated into nine languages.

ADAPTATIONS: The following books have been adapted for ABC-TV and broadcast as episodes of the *ABC Afterschool Special: The 18th Emergency,* broadcast as "Psst! Hammerman's after You," 1973; *The Summer of the Swans,* broadcast as "Sara's Summer of the Swans," 1974; *The Pinballs,* 1977; and *The Night Swimmers,* broadcast as "Daddy, I'm Their Mamma Now," 1981. *Trouble River,* 1975, and *The Winged Colt of Casa Mia* (adapted as "The Winged Colt"), 1976, were broadcast as *Saturday Morning Specials,* ABC-TV; *The Lace Snail* was adapted as a filmstrip and cassette by Viking; *The Midnight Fox, The Summer of the Swans, Go and Hush the Baby,* and *The TV Kid* were adapted as record/audio cassette recordings by Miller-Brody; *The Pinballs* was adapted as a play, published in *Around the World in 21 Plays: Theatre for Young Audiences,* edited by Lowell Swortzell, Applause (New York, NY), 1997.

SIDELIGHTS: Over the course of her long and productive career, Betsy Byars has received extensive critical praise for her insightful portrayals of adolescents suffering from feelings of isolation and loneliness. "In a succession of psychologically-sound stories," wrote a *New York Times Book Review* critic, "she has developed her theme: that the extreme inward pain of adolescence lessens as a person reaches outward." Byars has produced books for children of several different ages, including chapter books for beginning readers and novels aimed at an early adolescent audience. Though her works are intended for children, Byars does not shy away from controversial subjects. Mental retardation, teenage sexuality, and physical abuse are among the volatile topics considered in Byars's work, and her skillful handling of the material has helped convince critics that such issues can be effectively portrayed in juvenile literature.

Raised in North Carolina, Byars entered college as a math major but soon found English more to her liking. After marrying and starting a family, she turned to writing. She got her start by penning magazine articles, but eventually devoted her talents to children's literature. Her first published book, *Clementine,* appeared in 1962, but the negative reviews it received caused Byars to turn away from the personal material she had included in the book. "I went back to writing books that anyone could have written," Byars related in an interview for *Children's Literature in Education,* "like *Rama the Gypsy Cat*—very impersonal." Though she continued to publish regularly throughout the 1960s, it was not until she wrote *The Midnight Fox* that Byars again returned to events from her own life as a source of her fiction.

The Summer of the Swans, Byars's next effort, was drawn from the author's work with mentally retarded children. *The Summer of the Swans* tells the story of Sara, an awkward adolescent who struggles both with doubts about herself, and with the mixed feelings she has for her mentally impaired brother, Charlie. When Charlie wanders away from the house and becomes lost in a forest, Sara understands how valuable her brother is to her. In the end, Sara locates Charlie, and in the process, gains a new and positive sense of herself.

In a *Horn Book* review of *Summer of the Swans,* Ethel L. Haines stated: "Seldom are the pain of adolescence and the tragedy of mental retardation presented as sensitively and unpretentiously as in the story of Sara and Charlie." A *Top of the News* reviewer also lauded the book: "Betsy Byars, a sensitive writer with an ear and heart attuned to the subtleties of growing up, has created a story of extraordinary understanding and warmth." Barbara H. Baskin and Karen H. Harris, writing in *Notes from a Different Drummer: A Guide to Juvenile Fiction Portraying the Handicapped,* attributed the book's strengths, in part, to the way in which Byars handled the sentimental aspects of the story. "The descriptions of behavior are both tender and accurate," the authors wrote. "[Byars] can describe scenes revealing limitations in ways that reflect reality and avoid maudlin pity."

Byars's ability to avoid an overly sentimental treatment of her subjects has been praised frequently by reviewers of her work. Another factor contributing to the author's critical success is her appealing use of comedy. In *Children and Books,* Zena Sutherland, Dianne L. Monson, and May Hill Arbuthnot wrote that Byars's writing exhibits a "quiet, understated sense of humor that children quickly recognize and enjoy." *Times Literary Supplement* reviewer Diane Moss seconded this opinion, pointing out Byars's use of funny situations to soften her books' serious messages. "There are many ways in which the author can distance the agonies children endure," Moss wrote. "Humor is Betsy Byars's chosen path."

An example of this process comes from a more recent Byars work, *Cracker Jackson.* In the course of the book, eleven-year-old Jackson discovers that his former

baby sitter, Alma, is being physically abused by her husband. When the abuse spreads to Alma's baby, Jackson and a friend take action. Their attempt to drive Alma to a shelter for battered women is related as a humorous adventure, and the comedy of Jackson's day-to-day mischief is also woven throughout the story.

A *Horn Book* reviewer noted that this combination "would be an audacious undertaking in the hands of a less-skilled storyteller," but found Byars's effort to be an "expert blend of humor and compassion." Patricia Craig, writing in the *Times Literary Supplement,* found the book's subject "grim indeed; yet the atmosphere in which the events of the story are located is full of bounce." In addition to Byars's use of humor, Craig also credited the author's skill at "keeping the reprehensible actions of one of her characters very much in the background." *New York Times Book Review* contributor Mary Louise Cuneo registered a minor complaint about the characterization of Goat, Jackson's friend. "Goat regularly acts so much like a standard free spirit," Cuneo wrote, "that a reader could tire or disbelieve him." However, Cuneo also cited Byars's ability to "write low-key humor deftly."

Such criticism of Byars's characterization is rare. Her books have often been hailed for containing vivid characters that appeal to young readers. Critic Jane Langton of the *New York Times Book Review* wrote that "there is something uncanny about the way that Betsy Byars transcends the book in your hand and gives you living, feeling people instead." Jean Fritz, also writing in the *New York Times Book Review,* noted that Byars "has always had the capacity to create unique and believable characters." This ability is ably demonstrated in her series of novels featuring the Blossom family. Junior Blossom has a knack for unsuccessful inventions such as his subterranean hamster resort. Junior's sister, Maggie, wants to be a trick horseback rider like her mother and deceased father, and Vicki, the mother, occasionally leaves her children to rejoin the professional rodeo circuit. The family's acquaintances are also unusual, including Ralphie, a boy with an artificial leg, and Mad Mary, who lives in a cave and makes her dinner from the dead animals that she finds on the road.

In her review of *A Blossom Promise,* *Los Angeles Times Book Review* contributor Kristiana Gregory wrote that Byars's "perception of kids' feelings is keen." She also praised the author for creating a "cast so memorably quirky that you hate to say good-bye." Elizabeth-Ann Sachs's review of *Wanted . . . Mud Blossom* in the *New York Times Book Review* sounded a cautionary note regarding the bizarre characters. "The adults are

University of Southern Colorado Library

atypical," Sachs wrote, "more flawed than it is comfortable to think about—indeed somewhat alarming in their eccentricity." Despite this reservation, Sachs found that "Ms. Byars's dialogue rings true. She captures the whining and the teasing and the playfulness of children."

The Blossom series also demonstrates Byars's attempt to create a detailed view of her protagonists by devoting several books to their adventures. She has applied this approach to other characters as well, including Bingo Brown. In the first installment of this series, *The Burning Questions of Bingo Brown,* the title character grapples with uncertainty by writing down his questions about various adolescent concerns. Many of Bingo's questions deal with the three girls he has fallen in love with simultaneously. There are also questions regarding Bingo's English teacher, Mr. Markham, who has begun to give the class strange lectures on suicide and the woman that he loves. When Mr. Markham is involved in a motorcycle crash, Bingo wonders if the teacher was attempting to take his own life.

Ellen Fader, reviewing the book in *School Library Journal,* called *The Burning Questions of Bingo Brown* a "humorous and poignant novel," but also warned readers about the book's consideration of suicide. "Byars's light handling of a serious subject may disturb some adults," the critic wrote. Despite this reservation, Fader ultimately judged the book a success: "Accurate characterization developed through believable dialogue and fresh language, give this tremendous child appeal and read-aloud potential." A *Publishers Weekly* reviewer also praised the book. "Byars relays Bingo's questions and his answers in a way that is so believable," the critic wrote, "that readers may wonder if there isn't a Bingo Brown in their classrooms."

In 1994 Byers published the first of the Herculeah Jones mysteries, *The Dark Stairs.* The well-received series revolves around thirteen-year-old Herculeah, whose father is a police officer and whose mother is a private investigator. A *Publishers Weekly* reviewer called Herculeah a "distinctive and engaging heroine," and a *Booklist* reviewer lauded the "delightful middle-grade" mystery. Byers continued the series with *Dead Letter, Death's Door, Tarot Says Beware,* and *Disappearing Acts.* Critics have been largely positive in assessing the series. *Tarot Says Beware* garnered the Nevada Young Readers Award in 1998.

Over the course of her career Byars has gained a great respect for her young readers. "Boys and girls are very sharp today," Byars told Rachel Fordyce in an inter-

view for *Twentieth-Century Children's Writers.* "When I visit classrooms and talk with students I am always impressed to find how many of them are writing stories and how knowledgeable they are about writing." Her personal contact with children has also affected the way she shapes her stories. "Living with my own teenagers has taught me that not only must I not write down to my readers," Byars said, "I must write up to them."

BIOGRAPHICAL/CRITICAL SOURCES:

BOOKS

Baskin, Barbara H., and Karen H. Harris, *Notes from a Different Drummer: A Guide to Juvenile Fiction Portraying the Handicapped,* Bowker (New York, NY), 1977.
Children's Literature Review, Volume 1, Gale (Detroit, MI), 1976.
Contemporary Literary Criticism, Volume 32, Gale (Detroit, MI), 1985.
Rees, David, *Painted Desert, Green Shade: Essays on Contemporary Writers of Fiction for Children and Young Adults,* Horn Book (Boston, MA), 1984.
Something about the Author Autobiography Series, Volume 1, Gale (Detroit, MI), 1986.
Sutherland, Zena, Dianne L. Monson, and May Hill Arbuthnot, editors, *Children and Books,* sixth edition, Scott Foresman (New York, NY), 1981.
Twentieth-Century Children's Writers, edited by D. L. Kirkpatrick, St. Martin's Press (New York, NY), 1978.
Usrey, Malcolm, *Betsy Byars,* Twayne (New York, NY), 1995.

PERIODICALS

Book, September, 2000, Kathleen Odean, review of *Me Tarzan,* p. 86.
Booklist, April 1, 1994, p. 1465; August, 1994, p. 2042; July, 1995, p. 1878; January 1, 1996, p. 828; September 15, 1996, p. 238; March 1, 1997, p. 1162; September 1, 1997, p. 116; February 15, 1998, p. 1027; March 1, 1998, p. 1134; March 15, 2000, Hazel Rochman, review of *Me Tarzan,* p. 1376; January 1, 2001, Ellen Mandel, review of *My Dog, My Hero,* p. 954.
Book Week, October 10, 1965.
Bulletin of the Center for Children's Books, November, 1972; September, 1973; March, 1974; March, 1975; September, 1976; April, 1977.
Children's Book Review, September, 1973; April, 1979.
Children's Literature in Education, winter, 1982.

Christian Science Monitor, November 4, 1965; May 7, 1970; October 3, 1973; November 7, 1973; June 10, 1975; May 3, 1978.

Commonweal, November 22, 1968.

Horn Book, February, 1971; May-June, 1985; May-June, 1998, p. 341; May, 2000, review of *Me Tarzan,* p. 309.

Language Arts, October, 1978; September, 1980; October, 1982.

Los Angeles Times Book Review, January 31, 1988, p. 7.

New York Review of Books, December 14, 1972.

New York Times, December 4, 1979; December 5, 1980; November 30, 1982.

New York Times Book Review, June 14, 1969; February 28, 1971; April 23, 1972; June 4, 1972; November 5, 1972; May 6, 1973; June 10, 1973; August 19, 1973; November 4, 1973; October 13, 1974; November 3, 1974; December 15, 1974; May 2, 1976; October 7, 1979; November 25, 1979; May 4, 1980; August 4, 1980, p. 21; July 19, 1981; May 30, 1982; November 28, 1982; January 2, 1983; November 27, 1983; August 4, 1985; December 15, 1991, p. 29.

Observer (London, England), September 25, 1977.

Psychology Today, January 10, 1974.

Publishers Weekly, September 16, 1971; April 17, 1978; April 8, 1988, p. 95; July 19, 1991, p. 56; April 20, 1992, p. 58; May 18, 1992, p. 71; October 12, 1992, p. 79; August 16, 1993, p. 105; July 18, 1994, p. 246; May 22, 2000, review of *Me Tarzan,* p. 93.

Saturday Review, September 18, 1965; November 9, 1968; March 20, 1971; May 20, 1972; November 29, 1975.

School Library Journal, May, 1988, pp. 95-96; April, 1992, p. 112; January, 1998, review of *Bingo Brown, Gypsy Lover;* March, 1998, Linda L. Plevak, review of *Disappearing Acts,* p. 211; June, 1999, Fritz Mitnick, review of *My Brother, Ant* (audio book), p. 77; July, 2000, Janet Gillen, review of *Me Tarzan,* p. 68; January, 2001, Pat Leach, review of *My Dog, My Hero,* p. 92.

Times Literary Supplement, July 2, 1970; July 20, 1970; April 6, 1973; March 29, 1974; April 4, 1975; September 19, 1975; July 16, 1976; October 21, 1977; July 7, 1978; December 14, 1979; July 18, 1980; July 24, 1981; July 23, 1982; November 25, 1983; February 1, 1985; October 11, 1985, p. 1154.

Top of the News, April, 1971.

Washington Post Book World, May 7, 1972; April 10, 1977; May 13, 1979; April 11, 1980; May 10, 1981; July 12, 1981; October 11, 1981; April 11, 1982; October 10, 1982; October 9, 1983; January 13, 1985.

Young Reader's Review, January, 1967.*

C

CAMPBELL, Keith 1938-

PERSONAL: Born December 19, 1938, in Wellington, New Zealand; son of Ian Drummond (a professor of law) and Emily (a teacher; maiden name, Kennedy) Campbell; married Julianne Joan McKenzie (a college professor), January 30, 1960; children: Helen, Andrew, Kirsten. *Education:* Victoria University of Wellington, B.A., 1959, M.A., 1961; Oxford University, B.Phil., 1963.

ADDRESSES: Home—Sydney, Australia. *Office*—Department of Traditional and Modern Philosophy, University of Sydney, Darlinghurst, Sydney, New South Wales 2006, Australia.

CAREER: Writer. University of Melbourne, Melbourne, Australia, lecturer, 1963-64, senior lecturer in philosophy, 1964-65; University of Sydney, Sydney, Australia, senior lecturer, 1966-71, associate professor of philosophy, 1972—. Visiting fellow at Victoria University of Wellington, 1981, and Australian National University, 1982-84.

MEMBER: Australasian Association of Philosophy (president, 1980-81).

AWARDS, HONORS: Fellow of the Australian Academy of the Humanities, 1978.

WRITINGS:

Body and Mind, Doubleday (Garden City, NY), 1970, 2nd edition, University of Notre Dame Press (Notre Dame, IN), 1984.

Metaphysics: An Introduction, Wadsworth Publishing (Belmont, CA), 1976.

A Stoic Philosophy of Life, University Press of America (Lanham, MD), 1986.

Abstract Particulars, Basil Blackwell (Cambridge, MA), 1990.

(Editor, with John Bacon and Lloyd Reinhardt) *Ontology, Causality, and Mind: Essays in Honor of D. M. Armstrong,* Cambridge University Press (New York, NY), 1993.

Contributor to philosophy journals. Member of editorial board of *Australasian Journal of Philosophy.*

SIDELIGHTS: Keith Campbell once commented in *CA:* "*A Stoic Philosophy of Life* is designed to bring philosophy, especially the moral philosophy of the Stoics, back into the consciousness of contemporary civilization. I am motivated by the conviction that our culture needs a return to old-fashioned virtue without the supernatural machinery of religion." He added that this conviction leads, on the nonacademic level, to his pursuit of "self-reliance and retreat from the consumer life."

BIOGRAPHICAL/CRITICAL SOURCES:

PERIODICALS

British Journal for the Philosophy of Science, September, 1996, Fraser MacBride, review of *Ontology, Causality, and Mind: Essays in Honour of D. M. Armstrong,* p. 463.

Mind, January, 1991, Bob Hale, review of *Abstract Particulars,* p. 142.

Philosophical Quarterly, January, 1991, E. J. Lowe, review of *Abstract Particulars,* p. 104.*

CAMPBELL, (John) Ramsey 1946-
(Montgomery Comfort, Carl Dreadstone, Jay Ramsay, Errol Undercliffe)

PERSONAL: Born January 4, 1946, in Liverpool, England; son of Alexander Ramsey and Nora (Walker) Campbell; married Jenny Chandler (a teacher), January 1, 1971; children: Tamsin Joanne, Matthew Ramsey. *Education:* Educated in Liverpool, England. *Politics:* "Leftist: But I become progressively more cynical about political generalizations!" *Religion:* Agnostic.

ADDRESSES: Home and Office—31 Penkett Rd., Wallasey, Merseyside L45 7QF, England. *Agent*—Kirby McCauley, 425 Park Avenue S., New York, NY 10016.

CAREER: Novelist. Inland Revenue, Liverpool, England, tax officer, 1962-66; Liverpool Public Libraries, Liverpool, England, library assistant, 1966-73, acting librarian in charge, 1971-73; writer, 1973—. Lecturer on films and horror fiction; film critic, BBC Radio Merseyside, 1969—.

MEMBER: British Film Institute, Science Fiction Writers of America, British Fantasy Society (president).

AWARDS, HONORS: British Fantasy Awards for best short story, 1978, for "In the Bag," for best novel, 1981, for *To Wake the Dead,* 1985, for *Incarnate,* 1988, for *The Hungry Moon,* 1989, for *The Influence,* 1991, for *Midnight Sun,* 1994, for *The Long Lost,* and for best anthology/collection, 1991, for *Best New Horror* (with Stephen Jones), and 1999, for *Ghosts and Grisly Things*; World Fantasy Awards for best short fiction, 1978, for "The Chimney," 1980, for "Mackintosh Willy," for best anthology, 1991, for *Best New Horror* (with Stephen Jones), and for best collection, 1994, for *Alone with the Horrors*; Bram Stoker Award, 1993, for *Alone with the Horrors,* and 1998, for lifetime achievement; International Horror Guild Award, 1997, for "The Word."

WRITINGS:

HORROR FICTION

The Inhabitant of the Lake, and Less Welcome Tenants, Arkham (Sauk City, WI), 1964.
Demons by Daylight, Arkham (Sauk City, WI), 1973.
The Height of the Scream, Arkham (Sauk City, WI), 1976.
The Doll Who Ate His Mother, Bobbs-Merrill (New York, NY), 1976.
(Under house pseudonym Carl Dreadstone) *The Bride of Frankenstein,* Berkley (New York, NY), 1977.

Ramsey Campbell

(Under house pseudonym Carl Dreadstone) *The Wolfman; Dracula's Daughter,* Berkley (New York, NY), 1977.
The Face That Must Die, Star Books, 1979.
The Parasite, Macmillan (New York, NY), 1980, published as *To Wake the Dead,* Millington (London, England), 1980.
Through the Walls (booklet), British Fantasy Society, 1981.
The Nameless, Macmillan (New York, NY), 1981.
Dark Companions, Macmillan (New York, NY), 1982.
(As Jay Ramsay) *Night of the Claw,* St. Martin's Press (New York, NY), 1983.
Incarnate, Macmillan (New York, NY), 1983.
Obsession, Macmillan (New York, NY), 1985.
Cold Print (short stories), Scream/Press (Santa Cruz, CA), 1985.
The Hungry Moon, Macmillan (New York, NY), 1986.
(With Lisa Tuttle and Clive Barker) *Night Visions 111,* 1986.
Scared Stiff: Tales of Sex and Death, 1986.
The Influence, Macmillan (New York, NY), 1987.
Dark Feasts: The World of Ramsey Campbell, Robinson (London, England), 1987.

Ancient Images, Scribner (New York, NY), 1989.

Midnight Sun, Tor Books (New York, NY), 1990.

(Editor, with Stephen Jones) *Best New Horror,* Carroll & Graf (New York, NY), 1990.

Needing Ghosts, 1990.

The Count of Eleven, Tor Books (New York, NY), 1991.

(Editor, with Stephen Jones) *Best New Horror 2,* Carol & Graf (New York, NY), 1991.

Waking Nightmares, Tor Books (New York, NY), 1991.

Alone with the Horrors: The Great Short Fiction of Ramsey Campbell, 1991, Arkham (Sauk City, WI), 1993.

Two Obscure Tales, 1993.

(Editor with Stephen Jones) *Best New Horror 4,* Carol & Graf (New York, NY), 1993.

Strange Things and Stranger Places, Tor Books (New York, NY), 1993.

(Editor) *Deathport,* Pocket Books (New York, NY), 1993.

The Long Lost, Tor Books (New York, NY), 1993.

The One Safe Place, Forge (New York, NY), 1995.

Far Away and Never: The Fantasy Tales of Ramsey Campbell, Necronomicaon Press (West Warwick, RI), 1996.

Nazareth Hill, Forge (New York, NY), 1996, published as *The House on Nazareth Hill,* [England], 1996.

The Last Voice They Hear, Tor Books (New York, NY), 1998.

Ghosts and Grisly Things, Tor Books (New York, NY), 1998.

Silent Children, Forge (New York, NY), 2000.

Pact of the Fathers, Forge (New York, NY), 2001.

EDITOR AND CONTRIBUTOR

Superhorror, St. Martin's Press (New York, NY), 1976, published as *The Far Reaches of Fear,* Star Books (England), 1980.

New Terrors, two volumes, Pan Books, 1980.

New Tales of the Cthulhu Mythos, Arkham (Sauk City, WI), 1980.

The Gruesome Book, Piccolo, 1982.

Meddling with Ghosts: Stories in the Tradition of M. R. James, British Library (Boston Spa, England), 2001.

Work represented in anthologies, including *Travellers by Night,* edited by August Derleth, Arkham (Sauk City, WI), 1967; *Nameless Places,* edited by Gerald W. Page, Arkham (Sauk City, WI), 1975; *The Year's Best Horror Stories 9,* DAW Books, 1981; and *The Year's Best Horror Stories 10,* DAW Books, 1982. Author of column, "Layouts," *British Fantasy Society Bulletin,* 1974-77. Contributor of short stories to fantasy magazines.

Campbell's works have been translated into Italian, Spanish, French, German, Japanese, Dutch, Danish, and Swedish. A collection of his manuscripts is housed at the Liverpool Local History Library.

SIDELIGHTS: Ramsey Campbell's horror stories are often set in contemporary Merseyside, England, and involve quite ordinary characters. His unsettling, dreamlike prose, however, transforms his work into very effective horror fiction. Stephen King stated in *Danse Macabre* that Campbell "writes a cool, almost icy prose line, and his perspective on his native Liverpool is always a trifle offbeat, a trifle unsettling. In a Campbell novel or story, one seems to view the world through the thin and shifting perceptual haze of an LSD trip that is just ending. . . . or just beginning." Gary William Crawford also found a drug-like sensation in Campbell's prose. "Campbell remains most sensitive," Crawford wrote in *Horror Literature,* "to a culture obsessed with alienation, Dharma psychology, strange states of consciousness, and sexual and moral anarchy. He renders this world in some of the most effective prose of modern terror fiction: As in a 'bummer,' minute elements of the environment convey a potent, terrifying meaning; news headlines of mass murder, suicide, and rape, snatches of radio dialogue, and flashes of television images are pregnant with subversive meaning; statues, automobiles, neon signs collude as in a psychotic state; and the images that Campbell creates can be labeled quite simply those of paranoia." T. E. D. Klein also found Campbell's style unsettling. Campbell's world, Klein wrote in *Nyctalops,* is "a world in which anything can happen. Expect anything. Expect the worst. What this leads to, of course, is a kind of dreamlike paranoia that affects his characters' perceptions—not a new thing for horror stories, it's true, except that Campbell does it so much better."

Although he had long enjoyed horror literature—he claims that a horrific scene in Victorian children's book author George MacDonald's *The Princess and the Goblin* first drew his attention to the genre at the age of six—Campbell was not inspired to write fiction until reading the work of 1930s horror writer H. P. Lovecraft. His first collection of stories, in fact, is based on the Cthulhu Mythos, a malignant pantheon of Elder Gods invented by Lovecraft for use in his fiction. Campbell borrowed the Mythos from Lovecraft as well as the use of rural settings and characters, placing his early stories in the English countryside. But as Campbell's writing matured, his style became less imitative of Lovecraft's work and more expressive of his own perceptions. "When I began to feel that the Cthulhu Mythos was growing too restrictive," he wrote in *The Fantasy Reader's Guide to Ramsey Campbell,* "too explicit as a structure, to function in the way Lovecraft wanted (as a means to imply the indescribable) . . . I decided to strike off into the unknown without Lovecraft's map." David Sutton noted in *Shadow* that this change was "not a rejection of Lovecraft in essence. It is only a rejection of the art of employing the technique of another writer."

An important part of this development was that Campbell began writing stories set in his native Liverpool, and involving the real people who live there. This authenticity has been especially praised. Speaking of *Demons by Daylight,* Klein wrote: "At last we have a collection of tales in which the hero is convincingly human, not a neurasthenic antiquarian or a gentleman of leisure or a mad scientist or an eccentric sculptor. We have instead a fellow who works in a boring office or library." Speaking of his work in an interview with *Fantasy Macabre,* Campbell stated: "I feel I've at least tried to be honest about the terrors I write about, particularly to be honest about their sources. . . . By contrast, my Lovecraftian tales . . . were a matter of involving myself with someone else's horrors, an attempt to pass on some of the imaginative appeal they had for me."

Elaborating further on this subject, Campbell once told *CA:* "Most of my terrors are rooted in modern life, contemporary psychology, often in cities. Some writers believe that horror fiction is a way of concealing oneself or one's feelings—they've said so—but I'm trying to be honest. I don't view my stories as escapism, exactly the opposite. I believe that horror fiction cannot be too frightening or too disturbing." "Campbell's two great strengths as a writer of horror fiction," commented Michele Slung in the *Washington Post,* "are his talent for not quite describing the monstrous forces and events that propel his plots and his ability to blast any of the reader's lurking complacency when he does go into detail."

Campbell has proven his versatility, inspiring a *Publishers Weekly* writer to credit him as "the most protean of horror writers," one capable of producing "quiet terror in the classic tradition . . . eccentric horror that plays for laughs, [or] fiction that uses the genre as a staging ground for deft psychological and sociological commentary," such as his 1994 novel, *The Long Lost.* That story turns on a modern British couple's rescue of a dying old woman from a strange, deserted town in Wales. After welcoming her into their home, they begin to experience chaos in their neighborhood. The old woman seems to rejuvenate as a result of the mayhem around her, but the supernatural element of the story seems almost secondary to "the tracing of what happens when conscience gives way to license," commented a *Publishers Weekly* reviewer of the novel.

Campbell does away with the supernatural altogether in *The One Safe Place,* described as "his grimmest novel yet," by a *Publishers Weekly* contributor. The book is a thriller that indicts the judicial system for failing to protect victims. The Travis family is targeted by criminal Phil Fancy and his family in an escalating series of events that culminates with the kidnaping of twelve-year-old Marshall Travis, who is drugged and tortured by Phil's son, Darren. The *Publishers Weekly* reviewer concluded that "ultimately, Campbell persuades the reader that the loss of innocence that Darren embodies and that he inflicts upon Marshall is more horrifying than any supernatural menace."

Campbell enters the mind of a serial child killer in *Silent Children,* another suspenseful thriller, singled out as the author's "best in nearly a decade," in a *Publishers Weekly* evaluation. The story concerns Leslie Ames and her son Ian, who move into a house with a grisly past. When they rent a room to a writer of horror stories, they have no idea of the man's connection to the house's terrible history. "Campbell establishes his characters in sharp, precise slashes of chapters," said the *Publishers Weekly* reviewer, who found the book's climax "a tour-de-force of suspense."

Critical evaluations of Campbell usually judge him to be one of the best horror writers of his generation. "Good horror writers are quite rare," King stated, "and Campbell is better than just good." Jack Sullivan of the *Washington Post Book World* maintained that although Campbell is "still not as well known as he deserves to be, [he] is surely the most sophisticated stylist in modern horror." Klein simply declared: "I think Campbell reigns supreme in the field today."

BIOGRAPHICAL/CRITICAL SOURCES:

BOOKS

Ashley, Michael, editor, *The Fantasy Reader's Guide to Ramsey Campbell,* Cosmos, 1980.
King, Stephen, *Danse Macabre,* Everest House (New York, NY), 1981.

PERIODICALS

Booklist, November 1, 1980; September 1, 1992, Elliott Swanson, review of *Best New Horror 3,* p. 30; February 1, 1993, Ray Olson, review of *Alone with the Horrors: The Great Short Fiction of Ramsey Campbell, 1991,* p. 969; October 15, 1993, Elliott Swanson, review of *Best New Horror 4,* p. 417; June 1, 1998, David Pitt, review of *The Last Voice They Hear,* p. 1731; June 1, 2000, David Pitt, review of *Silent Children,* p. 1852.

Delap's F and SF Review, April, 1977.

Fantastic Stories, June, 1977.

Fantasy Macabre, April, 1981.

Fantasy Newsletter, April, 1980; December, 1980.

Kirkus Reviews, April 15, 1997, review of *Nazareth Hill,* p. 570; May 1, 1998, review of *The Last Voice They Hear,* p. 599.

Library Journal, February 15, 1982, James B. Hemesath, review of *Dark Companions,* p. 472; October 15, 1982, review of *New Terrors,* p. 2004; September 1, 1983, Keith W. McCoy, review of *Incarnate,* p. 1719; February 15, 1985, Eric W. Johnson, review of *Obsession,* p. 179; July 16, 1986, James B. Hemesath, review of *The Hungry Moon,* p. 105; February 1, 1988, Marylaine Block, review of *The Influence,* p. 75; June 1, 1992, Marylaine Block, review of *The Count of Eleven,* p. 172; October 15, 1994, Eric W. Johnson, review of *The Long Lost,* p. 86; July, 1996, Robert C. Moore, review of *The One Safe Place,* p. 154; May 15, 1997, John Noel, review of *Nazareth Hill,* p. 98.

Liverpool Daily Post, March 31, 1964.

Los Angeles Times Book Review, January 18, 1981.

Magazine of Fantasy and Science Fiction, December, 1973; May, 1986, Algis Budrys, review of *The Face That Must Die,* p. 46.

Necrofile, summer, 1998, review of *The Last Voice They Hear,* p. 1; spring, 1999, review of *Ghosts and Grisly Things,* p. 3.

New Statesman, April 3, 1987, Kim Newman, review of *The Hungry Moon,* p. 31; March 25, 1988, Kim Newman, reviews of *The Influence, Cold Print, Night Visions, Cutting Edge,* and *Dark Feasts,* p. 28.

New Statesman & Society, December 7, 1990, Elizabeth J. Young, review of *Best New Horror,* p. 35.

New York Times Book Review, November 21, 1976.

Nyctalops, May, 1977.

Publishers Weekly, August 26, 1983, Barbara A. Bannon, review of *Incarnate,* p. 369; October 28, 1983, review of *The Face That Must Die,* p. 59; December 21, 1984, review of *The Nameless,* p. 86; February 8, 1985, review of *Obsession,* p. 67; May 3, 1985, review of *Cold Print,* p. 67; December 13, 1985, review of *Obsession,* p. 52; May 30, 1986, Sybil Steinberg, review of *The Hungry Moon,* p. 56; March 6, 1987, Sybil Steinberg, review of *Scared Stiff: Tales of Sex and Death,* p. 105; January 15, 1988, Sybil Steinberg, review of *The Influence,* p. 77; April 28, 1989, Sybil Steinberg, review of *Ancient Images,* p. 66; October 19, 1990, Sybil Steinberg, review of *Best New Horror,* p. 48; December 21, 1990, Sybil Steinberg, review of *Midnight Sun,* p. 43; October 4, 1991, review of *Best New Horror 2,* p. 78; May 11, 1992, review of *The Count of Eleven,* p. 55; December 14, 1992, review of *Alone with the Horrors,* p. 40; May 3, 1993, review of *Strange Things and Stranger Places,* p. 294; August 16, 1993, review of *Deathport,* p. 98; October 18, 1993, review of *Best New Horror 4,* p. 64; September 12, 1994, review of *The Long Lost,* p. 84; July 1, 1996, review of *The One Safe Place,* p. 42; May 19, 1997, review of *Nazareth Hill,* p. 67; April 27, 1998, review of *The Last Voice They Hear,* p. 43; June 26, 2000, review of *Silent Children,* p. 55; September 25, 2000, review of *Ghosts and Grisly Things,* p. 92.

Rapport, January, 1997, review of *The One Safe Place,* p. 20.

School Library Journal, October, 1992, review of *Best New Horror 2,* p. 155.

Shadow, fall, 1972; October, 1973.

Washington Post, November 20, 1981.

Washington Post Book World, August 23, 1981; April 25, 1982.

Whispers, March, 1982.

Wilson Library Bulletin, May 15, 1989, review of *Ancient Images,* p. 87; November, 1989, Gene LaFaille, review of *Ancient Images,* p. 98; March, 1994, Gene LaFaille, review of *Alone with the Horrors,* p. 102.

*   *   *

CARD, Orson Scott 1951-
(Brian Green, Byron Walley)

PERSONAL: Born August 24, 1951, in Richland, WA; son of Willard Richards (a teacher) and Peggy Jane (a secretary and administrator; maiden name, Park) Card; married Kristine Allen, May 17, 1977; children: Michael Geoffrey, Emily Janice, Charles Benjamin (deceased), Zina Margaret, Erin Louisa (deceased). *Education:* Brigham Young University, B.A. (with distinction), 1975; University of Utah, M.A., 1981. *Politics:*

Moderate Democrat. *Religion:* Church of Jesus Christ of Latter-Day Saints (Mormon). *Avocational interests:* Computer games.

ADDRESSES: Agent—Barbara Bova Literary Agency, 3951 Gulf Shore Blvd. North #PH1B, Naples, FL 34103-3639.

CAREER: Mormon missionary in Brazil, 1971-73; operated repertory theater in Provo, UT, 1974-75; Brigham Young University Press, Provo, editor, 1974-76; *Ensign,* Salt Lake City, UT, assistant editor, 1976-78; freelance writer and editor, 1978—; Compute! Books, Greensboro, NC, senior editor, 1983; Lucasfilm Games, game design consultant, 1989-92. Instructor at Brigham Young University, University of Utah, University of Notre Dame, Appalachian State University, Clarion West Writers' Workshop, Cape Cod Writer's Workshop, and Antioch Writers' Workshop. Has served as local Democratic precinct election judge and Utah State Democratic Convention delegate.

AWARDS, HONORS: John W. Campbell Award for best new writer of 1977, World Science Fiction Convention, 1978; Hugo Award nominations, World Science Fiction Convention, 1978, 1979, 1980, for short stories, 1986, for novelette *Hatrack River,* and 1988, for *Seventh Son;* Nebula Award nominations, Science Fiction Writers of America, 1979, and 1980, for short stories; Utah State Institute of Fine Arts prize, 1980, for epic poem "Prentice Alvin and the No-Good Plow"; Hamilton-Brackett Award, 1981, for *Songmaster;* Nebula Award, 1985, and Hugo Award and Hamilton-Brackett Award, both 1986, all for *Ender's Game;* Nebula Award, 1986, and Hugo Award and Locus Award, both 1987, all for *Speaker for the Dead;* World Fantasy Award, 1987, for *Hatrack River;* Hugo Award, and Locus Award nomination, both 1988, both for novella "Eye for Eye"; Locus Award, World Fantasy Award nomination, and Mythopoeic Society Fantasy Award, all 1988, all for *Seventh Son;* Locus Award, 1989, for *Red Prophet;* Hugo Award for nonfiction, 1991, for *How to Write Science Fiction and Fantasy;* Israel's Geffen Award for Best Science Fiction book, 1999, for *Pastwatch: The Redemption of Christopher Columbus;* Grand Prix de L'Imaginaire, 2000, for *Heartfire.*

WRITINGS:

PLAYS

(And director) *Tell Me That You Love Me, Junie Moon* (adaptation of novel by Marjorie Kellogg), produced in Provo, UT, 1969.
The Apostate, produced in Provo, UT, 1970.

In Flight, produced in Provo, UT, 1970.
Across Five Summers, produced in Provo, UT, 1971.
Of Gideon, produced in Provo, UT, 1971.
Stone Tables, produced at Brigham Young University, Provo, UT, 1973.
A Christmas Carol (adapted from the story by Charles Dickens), produced in Provo, UT, 1974.
Father, Mother, Mother, and Mom (produced in Provo, UT, 1974), published in *Sunstone,* 1978.
Liberty Jail, produced in Provo, UT, 1975.
Fresh Courage Take, produced in Salt Lake City, UT, 1978.
Elders and Sisters (adaptation of novel by Gladys Farmer), produced in American Fork, UT, 1979.

Also author, under pseudonym Brian Green, of *Rag Mission,* published in *Ensign,* July, 1977. Author of *Wings* (fragment), produced in 1982.

SCIENCE FICTION AND FANTASY

Capitol (short stories), Ace (New York, NY), 1978.
Hot Sleep: The Worthing Chronicle, Baronet, 1978.
A Planet Called Treason, St. Martin's Press (New York, NY), 1979, revised edition, Dell (New York, NY), 1980, published as *Treason,* St. Martin's Press (New York, NY), 1988.
Songmaster, Dial (New York, NY), 1980.
Unaccompanied Sonata and Other Stories, Dial (New York, NY), 1980.
(Editor) *Dragons of Darkness,* Ace (New York, NY), 1981.
Hart's Hope, Berkley (New York, NY), 1983.
(Editor) *Dragons of Light,* Ace (New York, NY), 1983.
The Worthing Chronicle, Ace (New York, NY), 1983.
Ender's Game (first novel in "Ender" series; also see below), Tor (New York, NY), 1985.
Speaker for the Dead (second novel in "Ender" series; also see below), Tor (New York, NY), 1986.
Ender's Game [and] *Speaker for the Dead,* Tor (New York, NY), 1987.
(With others) *Free Lancers,* Baen (New York, NY), 1987.
Seventh Son (first novel in "Tales of Alvin Maker" series), St. Martin's Press (New York, NY), 1987.
Wyrms, Arbor House (New York, NY), 1987.
Red Prophet (second novel in "Tales of Alvin Maker" series), Tor (New York, NY), 1988.
Folk of the Fringe (short stories), Phantasia Press (Huntington Woods, MI), 1989.
The Abyss (novelization of screenplay by James Cameron), Pocket Books (New York, NY), 1989.
Prentice Alvin (third novel in "Tales of Alvin Maker" series), Tor (New York, NY), 1989.

Eye for Eye (bound with *The Tunesmith* by Lloyd Biggle, Jr.), Tor (New York, NY), 1990.

Maps in a Mirror: The Short Fiction of Orson Scott Card (includes stories originally published under pseudonym Byron Walley), Tor (New York, NY), 1990.

Worthing Saga, Tor (New York, NY), 1990.

(Editor) *Future on Fire,* Tor (New York, NY), 1991.

Xenocide (third novel in "Ender" series), Tor (New York, NY), 1991.

The Changed Man, Tor (New York, NY), 1992.

Cruel Miracles, Tor (New York, NY), 1992.

Flux, Tor (New York, NY), 1992.

The Memory of Earth (first novel in "Homecoming" series; also see below), Tor (New York, NY), 1992.

The Call of the Earth (second novel in "Homecoming" series; also see below), Tor (New York, NY), 1993.

Monkey Sonatas, Tor (New York, NY), 1993.

The Ships of Earth (third novel in "Homecoming" series; also see below), Tor (New York, NY), 1993.

(With Kathryn H. Kidd) *Lovelock* (first novel in "Mayflower" trilogy), Tor (New York, NY), 1994.

Earthfall (fourth novel in "Homecoming" series), Tor (New York, NY), 1994.

Homecoming: Harmony (contains *The Memory of Earth, The Call of Earth,* and *The Ships of Earth*), Science Fiction Book Club, 1994.

Alvin Journeyman (fourth novel in "Tales of Alvin Maker" series), Tor (New York, NY), 1995.

Earthborn (fifth novel in "Homecoming" series), Tor (New York, NY), 1995.

Children of the Mind (fourth novel in "Ender" series), Tor (New York, NY), 1996.

Pastwatch: The Redemption of Christopher Columbus, Tor (New York, NY), 1996.

Heartfire (fifth novel in "Tales of Alvin Maker" series), Tor (New York, NY), 1998.

Future on Ice (companion volume to *Future on Fire*), Tor (New York, NY), 1998.

Ender's Shadow, Tor (New York, NY), 1999.

Shadow of the Hegemon (sequel to *Ender's Shadow*), Tor (New York, NY), 2000.

Also author of novelette *Hatrack River,* 1986. Contributor to *The Bradbury Chronicles: Stories in Honor of Ray Bradbury,* edited by William F. Nolan and Martin H. Greenberg, New American Library (New York, NY), 1991. Contributor to numerous anthologies.

OTHER

Listen, Mom and Dad, Bookcraft (Salt Lake City, UT), 1978.

Saintspeak: The Mormon Dictionary, Signature Books (Midvale, UT), 1981.

Ainge, Signature Books (Midvale, UT), 1982.

A Woman of Destiny (historical novel), Berkley (New York, NY), 1983, published as *Saints,* Tor (New York, NY), 1988.

Compute's Guide to IBM PCjr Sound and Graphics, Compute (Greensboro, NC), 1984.

Cardography, Hypatia Press, 1987.

Characters and Viewpoint, Writer's Digest (Cincinnati, OH), 1988.

(Author of introduction) Susan D. Smallwood, *You're a Rock, Sister Lewis,* Hatrack River Publications, 1989.

How to Write Science Fiction and Fantasy, Writer's Digest (Cincinnati, OH), 1990.

Lost Boys, HarperCollins (New York, NY), 1992.

(Editor, with David C. Dollahite), *Turning Hearts: Short Stories on Family Life,* Bookcraft (Salt Lake City, UT), 1994.

Treasure Box (novel), HarperCollins (New York, NY), 1996.

Stone Tables (novel), Deseret Book Co. (Salt Lake City, UT), 1997.

Homebody (novel), HarperCollins (New York, NY), 1998.

Enchantment, Del Rey (New York, NY), 1999.

Sarah (first novel of "Women of Genesis" series), Shadow Mountain (Salt Lake City, UT), 2000.

Rebekah (second novel of "Women of Genesis" series), Shadow Mountain (Salt Lake City, UT), 2001.

Also author of several audio plays for Living Scriptures; coauthor of animated videotapes. Contributor of regular review columns, including "You Got No Friends in This World," *Science Fiction Review,* 1979-86, "Books to Look For," *Fantasy and Science Fiction,* 1987—, and "Gameplay," *Compute!,* 1988-89. Contributor of articles and reviews to periodicals, including *Washington Post Book World, Science Fiction Review,* and *Destinies.*

Card's manuscripts are housed at Brigham Young University. His books have been translated into Catalan, Danish, Dutch, Finnish, French, German, Hebrew, Italian, Japanese, Polish, Portuguese, Romanian, Russian, Slovakian, Spanish, and Swedish.

ADAPTATIONS: Xenocide has been adapted into two audiocassettes, read by Mark Rolston, Audio Renaissance, 1991; *Seventh Son* has been adapted into five audiocassettes, read by Card, Literate Ear, Inc., 1991; dramatic rights for all of Card's works were acquired by Fresco Pictures, 1997.

WORK IN PROGRESS: The Crystal City and *Master Alvin,* the final episodes in the "Tales of Alvin Maker" series; *Shadow Puppets* and *Shadow of the Giant,* the final episodes in the Hegemon series.

SIDELIGHTS: Orson Scott Card is the award-winning author of over sixty books of science fiction, fantasy, history, and ghost stories. With the creation of Andrew "Ender" Wiggin, the young genius of *Ender's Game,* Card launched an award-winning career as a science fiction and fantasy writer. Since his debut in the field in 1977, when the short story "Ender's Game" appeared in *Analog* magazine, Card has become the first writer to win the genre's top awards, the Nebula and the Hugo, for consecutive novels in a continuing series. These two novels—*Ender's Game* and *Speaker for the Dead*—have been described by *Fantasy Review* contributor Michael R. Collings as "allegorical disquisitions on humanity, morality, salvation, and redemption"—evaluations that many critics have applied to Card's other works as well. Such thematic concerns, in part influenced by Card's devout Mormonism, are what critics feel set him apart from other writers in the science-fiction field. Beyond the "Ender" series, Card's other projects include creating the American fantasy series "Tales of Alvin Maker," a retelling of ancient scripture in the "Homecoming Saga," contemporary novels with occult and ghost themes such as *Lost Boys, Treasure Box,* and *Homebody,* and a further series with a religious theme, "Women of Genesis," begun with the novels *Sarah* and *Rebekah.* Additionally, Card is a playwright of note with a dozen plays to his credit, and his work has been produced in regional theaters.

In many of his works, Card focuses on the moral development of young protagonists whose abilities to act maturely and decisively while in challenging situations often determine the future of their communities. Card, a devout Mormon, is intrigued by the role of the individual in society, and credits his solid religious background with instilling in him both a strong sense of community and an affinity for storytelling. "I don't want to write about individuals in isolation," he told Graceanne A. DeCandido and Keith R. A. DeCandido in *Publishers Weekly.* "What I want to write about is people who are committed members of the community and therefore have a network of relationships that define who they are. I think if you're going to write about people, you have to write about storytelling." In his works Card is deeply concerned with his own unresolved moral and philosophical questions as well, and maintains that science fiction affords him the benefit of exploring these issues against a futuristic and imaginative backdrop. "In some of the best SF, you move into a universe where all moral bets are off, where you have a group of aliens, or humans in an alien setting, who live by different rules because some key aspect of life that we take for granted as human beings has been changed radically. . . . After a while we can see ourselves through their eyes and see how bizarre we are. Then you come back and you question everything."

Though he is a profoundly moral writer, Card dismisses standard black-and-white versions of good and evil. As he told Laura Ciporen of *Publishers Weekly,* such representations are "so boring." Card further explained, "When a character comes upon a case of right and wrong and chooses to do wrong, that shows you he's the kind of jerk who'd do that. My characters wrestle with real moral dilemmas where all the choices have steep prices. If they make the selfish choice, then I show the consequences. I'm not trying to teach that lesson, though it underlies everything I write."

Card was born in 1951, in Richland, Washington, the son of a teacher father and an administrator mother. Card moved often in his youth, growing up in California, Arizona, and finally Utah. As a teenager, both the theater and science fiction captured Card's attention. At only sixteen, he entered Brigham Young University and three years later saw his first play, *The Apostate,* produced in Provo, Utah. Ten plays and adaptations followed through the seventies, mostly with scriptural or historical themes, but Card's education and writing were put on hold for several years in the early 1970s when Card served as a missionary in Brazil. Returning to Provo, Card founded a theater company and earned his B.A., with honors, in 1975. Thereafter he became an editor at *Ensign* magazine, the official publication of the Church of Jesus Christ of Latter-Day Saints, and also worked for the Brigham Young Press. There was, however, little money in writing plays. "I was supporting myself on the pathetic wages paid to an editor at a university press—and BYU's wages were even more pathetic than usual," he told the DeCandidos. "I knew there was no hope of paying off my debts through my salary, so I made a serious effort to write fiction as a career."

"All the time that I was a playwright," Card once said, "these science fictional ideas that never showed up in my plays were dancing around in the back of my mind." The genre, he felt, offered him the most expedient way of getting published, since the field thrives on up-and-coming talent and fresh ideas. He also admitted that he chose science fiction because, as he noted, "I knew the genre. While it was never even half my reading, I had read enough to be aware of the possibilities within it.

It allowed the possibility of the kind of high drama that I'd been doing with religious plays for the Mormon market. . . . In order to write the kind of intense romantic drama that I wanted to write, I needed the possibilities that science fiction and fantasy offered."

Hoping to break into the field, Card sent "The Tinker," one of his first short stories, to Ben Bova, then editor of the leading science-fiction magazine *Analog*. Bova in turn rejected the work, though he did not crush the aspirations of its author. "Apparently he [Bova] saw some reason to hope that I might have some talent," Card explained to the DeCandidos. "His rejection letter urged me to submit a real science fiction story, because he liked the way I wrote." The real story became "Ender's Game," which, upon its publication, garnered Card the World Science Fiction Convention's John W. Campbell Award for best new writer.

Though Card was thrilled with his sudden success, he later admitted to a *Publishers Weekly* interviewer that he was "not so stupid as to quit my job." He retained his position as editor for *Ensign* and in 1978 began composing audio plays for Living Scriptures. He also continued honing his writing skills and released his first book, *Capitol,* during that same year. A collection of short stories, the work follows the fall of the planet Capitol and revolves in part around the drug somec, which induces a state of suspended animation in its user and allows him to live for several thousand years. At least one reviewer remarked upon Card's literary skill in *Capitol*. The collection "demonstrates a fine talent for storytelling and characterization," decided a critic for *Publishers Weekly*. Card's 1980 novel *Songmaster* generated praise as well. The lyrical tale, set in a futuristic galactic society that reveres those who sing, focuses on Ansset, a "Songbird" who is summoned to serve the emperor. The work encompasses "personal growth and exploration melded into a tale of interplanetary politics and court intrigue," asserted Richard A. Lupoff in *Washington Post Book World*. "*Songmaster* is a first-class job." Some of Card's other early works, however, including *Hot Sleep* and *A Planet Called Treason,* encountered critical censure for employing standard science fiction elements and for containing what some reviewers considered gratuitous violence. George R. R. Martin in the *Washington Post Book World* especially criticized Card's 1981 work, *Unaccompanied Sonata and Other Stories,* which he found filled "with death, pain, mutilation, dismemberment, all described in graphic detail." The volume includes such unfortunate characters as a malformed infant who is drowned in a toilet and whose body is sliced to pieces, and a woman whose breasts are chopped off and eaten.

Apart from these negative evaluations, the general critical consensus of Card's early works was that they display imagination, intelligence, literary aptitude, and promise. "Card is a young, talented, and ambitious writer," conceded Martin.

In 1985, Card released *Ender's Game*. This novel began as a short story, which Card once described as "still the most popular and the most reprinted of my stories, and I still have people tell me that they like it better than the novel. . . . When I started working on the novel that became *Speaker for the Dead,* a breakthrough for me in that story was realizing that the main character should be Ender Wiggin. That made it a kind of sequel, although its plot had nothing to do with the original plot; it was just using a character. . . . I told the publisher, Tom Doherty, that I needed to do a novel version of 'Ender's Game' just to set up *Speaker for the Dead*. That's the only reason 'Ender's Game' ever became a novel."

Ender's Game concerns the training of Ender Wiggin, a six-year-old genius who is the Earth's only hope for victory over invading "bugger" aliens. While this plot appears to be standard science-fiction fare, *New York Times Book Review* critic Gerald Jonas observed that "Card has shaped this unpromising material into an affecting novel full of surprises that seem inevitable once they are explained." The difference, asserted Jonas and other critics, is in the character of Ender Wiggin, who remains sympathetic despite his acts of violence. A *Kirkus Reviews* contributor, for example, while noting the plot's inherent weakness, admitted that "the long passages focusing on Ender are nearly always enthralling," and concluded that *Ender's Game* "is altogether a much more solid, mature, and persuasive effort" than the author's previous work. Writing in *Analog Science Fiction/Science Fact,* Tom Easton noted that Ender's Game "succeeds because of its stress on the value of empathy," and *Washington Post Book World* reviewer Janrae Frank concluded that "Card is a writer of compassion."

Following the success of *Ender's Game,* its sequel, *Speaker for the Dead,* was hailed as "the most powerful work Card has produced" by Collings in *Fantasy Review*. "*Speaker* not only completes *Ender's Game* but transcends it. . . . Read in conjunction with *Ender's Game, Speaker* demonstrates Card's mastery of character, plot, style, theme, and development." Ender Wiggin, now working as a "Speaker for the Dead," travels the galaxy to interpret the lives of the deceased for their families and neighbors; as he travels, he also searches for a home for the eggs of the lone surviving "hive queen" of the race he destroyed as a child. "Like *Game, Speaker* deals with issues of evil and empathy, though not in so polarized a way," observed Tom Easton in his *Analog* review. Some critics found an extra element of complexity in the "Ender" books; *Washington Post Book World* contributor Frank, for example, saw "quasi-religious images and themes" in the conclusions of both novels.

With the publication of 1991's *Xenocide,* Card's reputation as an unflinching explorer of both moral and intellectual issues was firmly established. In this novel, Card picks up the story of Ender as he works feverishly with his adopted Lusitanian family to neutralize a deadly virus. Many critics venture that with *Xenocide,* Card relies more on the scientific ruminations of a multitude of contemplative characters rather than on a plot. "The real action is philosophical: long, passionate debates about ends and means among people who are fully aware that they may be deciding the fate of an entire species, entire worlds," observed Gerald Jonas in the *New York Times Book Review.*

In 1996, Card published *Children of the Mind,* the final volume of the "Ender" quartet. In this novel, Ender is already moving off the stage, playing a relatively minor part in the hectic attempt to avoid destruction of the planet Lusitania by the Starways Congress. Characters who take a more active role in this episode are Peter and Young Valentine, who are copies of Ender's brother and sister, and both products of Ender's mind. Also instrumental in Ender's current bid to save his adopted planet is Jane, a rather irascible Artificial Intelligence who has the uncanny knack of transcending the light-speed barrier. Together these three must roam the galaxy to find a new home for the three races of Lusitania that may all too soon become refugees. Meanwhile, they also try and convince politicians to halt the Starways Congress from destroying the planet. "Card's prose is powerful here," commented a reviewer for *Publishers Weekly,* "as is his consideration of mystical and quasi-religious themes." The same writer went on to wonder whether this book, "billed as the final Ender novel," would in fact be the last the reader hears of Ender or his world. "[T]his story leaves enough mysteries unexplored to justify another entry."

When Card once again approached that same world it was not from Ender's point of view, but in a stand-alone parallel novel in the 1999 *Ender's Shadow.* Library Journal's Jackie Cassada noted that "Card returns to the world of his award-winning *Ender's Game* to tell the story of a child's desperate struggle for recognition and self-worth." The superhuman child in ques-

tion, Bean, is taken from the streets of Rotterdam and sent to the Battle School to learn to fight the insect-like Buggers. Bean wins selection to the Battle School by his understanding of personal motivation—a skill that kept him alive in the mean streets when he was a starving child. At Battle School he learns how to command fleets for the war with the alien Buggers. When he comes into contact with Ender, Bean wants to understand what makes this larger-than-life figure tick. "Thus Bean's story is twofold," wrote a *Publishers Weekly* contributor, "he learns to be a soldier, and to be human." Through Bean the reader learns about the formation of Ender's Dragon army and also about the last of Ender's games. "Everyone will be struck by the power of Card's children," concluded the same reviewer, "always more and less than human, perfect yet struggling, tragic yet hopeful, wondrous and strange." Cassada felt that Card's "superb storytelling and his genuine insight into the moral dilemmas that lead good people to commit questionable actions" blend together to make the novel a "priority purchase."

Questioned by Ciporen in *Publishers Weekly* about his child protagonists, Card observed that, for children, life is very real. "They don't think of themselves as cute or sweet. I translate their thoughts from the language available to children into the language available to adults." For Card, children are every bit as complex as adults, and in fact their thoughts and fears—because they have fewer such to compare with—can be even more real than those of adults. Card's ability to portray young protagonists sympathetically yet not condescendingly is part of what makes him a popular writer for adults and juveniles alike.

Shadow of the Hegemon, a sequel to *Ender's Shadow,* continues the story of Bean, now a young man. With the wars over and Ender off to colonize a new world, the children of the Battle School become increasingly important to those nations wishing to gobble up their neighbors. Bean, the second best of the Battle School children and aide to Peter Wiggin, is sought for his powers by Achilles, an unbalanced genius who wishes to conquer Earth. Both young Peter and Achilles have the same goal, though they pursue it in different ways: Achilles through might and Peter through diplomacy. Bean must decide if by helping Peter become Hegemon he will actually be helping the better cause. Bean's dilemma is thus to figure out whether Peter or Achilles—both full of themselves and delighted by power—will create a better world. "The complexity and serious treatment of the book's young protagonists will attract many sophisticated YA readers," observed a writer for *Publishers Weekly,* who further commented that Card's "impeccable prose, fast pacing and political intrigue will appeal to adult fans of spy novels, thrillers and science fiction." *Library Journal* reviewer Jackie Cassada dubbed the novel a "gripping story of children caught up in world-shaking events."

Card's storytelling techniques are further displayed in the "Tales of Alvin Maker" series. "This series began as an epic poem I was writing during graduate study at the University of Utah," Card once commented, "when I was heavily influenced by Spenser and playing games with allegory. That epic poem won a prize from the Utah State Institute of Fine Arts, but I realized that there is very little future for an epic poem in terms of reaching an audience and telling a story to real people, so I converted it and expanded it and, I think, deepened and enriched it into something much longer and larger."

The first novel in the "Tales of Alvin Maker" series, *Seventh Son,* "begins what may be a significant recasting in fantasy terms of the tall tale in America," wrote *Washington Post Book World* reviewer John Clute. Set in a pioneer America where the British Restoration never happened, where the "Crown Colonies" exist alongside the states of Appalachia and New Sweden, and where folk magic is readily believed and practiced, *Seventh Son* follows the childhood of Alvin Miller, who has enormous magical potential because he is the seventh son of a seventh son. While *Fantasy Review* contributor Martha Soukup admitted that "this could easily have been another dull tale of the chosen child groomed to be the defender from evil," she asserted that Card's use of folk magic and vernacular language, along with strongly realized characters, creates in *Seventh Son* "more to care about here than an abstract magical battle."

"Because we know it is a dream of an America we do not deserve to remember, Orson Scott Card's luminous alternate history of the early 19th century continues to chill as it soothes," Clute explained in a review of *Red Prophet,* the second volume of Alvin's story. The novel traces Alvin's kidnaping by renegade Reds employed by "White Murderer" William Henry Harrison, who wishes to precipitate a massacre of the Shaw-Nee tribe. Alvin is rescued by the Red warrior Ta-Kumsaw, however, and learns of Native American ways even as he attempts to prevent the conflict caused by his supposed capture and murder. While *"Red Prophet* seems initially less ambitious" than its predecessor, covering a period of only one year, a *West Coast Review of Books* contributor commented that, "In that year, Card creates episodes and images that stun with the power of their emotions." Sue Martin, however, believed that the set-

ting was not enough to overcome the plot, which she described in the *Los Angeles Times Book Review* as "yet another tale of Dark versus Light." She conceded, however, that while Alvin "seems almost Christlike" in his ability to heal and bring people together, the allegory is drawn "without the proselytizing." *Booklist* writer Sally Estes summarized, "Harsher, bleaker, and more mystical than *Seventh Son,*" Card's second volume displays his strong historical background, "keen understanding of religious experience, and, most of all, his mastery of the art of storytelling."

In *Alvin Journeyman,* published six years after its predecessor, *Prentice Alvin,* Card returns readers to Alvin's life following his apprenticeship. His bad but similarly talented brother, Calvin, leaves for Europe, hoping to learn the arts of manipulation and domination from Napoleon. Alvin himself is forced to leave Vigor Church after being accused of improprieties by a girl dreaming of his passion. He returns to Hatrack River, his birthplace and the location of his apprenticeship, but has to defend himself in court. Written with the input of Card's fans via online forums, the story could have descended into mediocrity, as Martin Morse Wooster noted in the *Washington Post Book World.* However, Wooster declared, "Card appears to have resisted the encroachments of his admirers because *Alvin Journeyman* is a well-written, engaging entertainment."

Heartfire, the 1998 installment to the series, sees Alvin traveling to New England during Puritan times with historical friends such as John James Audubon, seeking to put an end to anti-witch laws. Meantime Alvin's wife, Peggy, who has the ability to see into the hearts of others, tries put an end to slavery in the South and to stop Alvin's more malevolent brother, Calvin, from destroying her husband. "Card's antebellum settings, dialogue and historical figures seem authentic and thoroughly researched," according to a writer for *Publishers Weekly,* who noted however that Card "is as occasionally windy and preachy as ever." Jackie Cassada, reviewing the novel in *Library Journal,* concluded that the fifth installment to the "Tales of Alvin Maker" series "exhibits the same homespun charm of its predecessors."

In 1992 Card introduced his "Homecoming" series with *The Memory of Earth,* a novel many critics found to be a mixture of philosophy, futuristic technology, and biblical lore. Memory opens on the planet Harmony, where for forty million years humans have been controlled by Oversoul, a powerful, global computer programmed to prevent humanity from destroying itself through needless wars. David E. Jones, in Chicago's *Tribune Books,* argued that "what Card gives us [in *The Memory of Earth*] is an interaction between supreme intelligence and human mental capability that is at once an intellectual exercise, a Biblical parable and a thoroughly enjoyable piece of storytelling."

Card joined forces with a newer science fiction voice, Kathryn H. Kidd, for the publication of *Lovelock* in 1994. The title shares its name with the central character, a genetically enhanced monkey, who is trained to record the activities of important persons for posterity. Realizing his own servitude and the indifferent neglect of his masters, *Lovelock* plots his escape. The work was welcomed by several critics as a solid blending of two talents. "Masterful," commented Maureen F. McHugh in the *Washington Post Book World,* who found the character of Lovelock to be, "Clearly as nasty and clever as a genetically enhanced capuchin monkey could be expected to be." McHugh continued, "None of Card's previous tellings has possessed the satirical bite we see here, which makes for a welcome change."

Card concludes his "Homecoming" series with the fourth and fifth novels, *Earthfall* and *Earthborn.* In *Earthfall,* the wandering humans return from Harmony to Earth to continue the species when it appears Harmony is about to self destruct. They meet two new species who have evolved in the absence of humans and must make peace with them. "As in other Card novels, plotting is intricate, characters are multifaceted, and strange creatures co-exist with humans," observed Pam Carlson in *Voice of Youth Advocates. Earthborn* focuses on the three groups from *Earthfall* who are speaking a common language but who differ in their habitat. The sky people are able to fly as angels; the earth people or diggers are treated as slaves; the returned humans from Harmony are known as the middle people. As Gerald Jonas noted in the *New York Times Book Review,* "As in all Mr. Card's novels, the characters spend . . . time talking about what they are going to do and why they are going to do it." The critic continued, "these long philosophical discussions crackle with tension." While several reviewers appreciated the "Homecoming" series, the concluding volume received mixed reviews.

Card again weaves historical fact with science fiction in *Pastwatch: The Redemption of Christopher Columbus.* Here, he sends several future scientists, members of a group known as Pastwatch, back to 1592 in order to Christianize America and save the world for future generations. Tom Easton in *Analog* noted the story to be "the most explicitly Mormon science fiction novel that . . . Card has ever written" and found the ethical

and religious questions Card poses to be "especially interesting because of the characters Card uses to analyze them," including Columbus, "who believed himself to be touched by God." Roland Green, writing for *Booklist* also found Card's portrayal of Columbus to be exceptional, calling it "marvelous, enormously powerful" and pronounced *Pastwatch* to be "Another superior addition to a superior body of work." However, a reviewer for *Publishers Weekly* felt that the trio of heroes developed by Card "is just too sanctified to believe, and in their hands, the complexities of temporal mechanics are boiled down to simplistic cause and effect."

Though firmly established as a successful author of science fiction, Card has not limited himself to that genre, publishing throughout his career numerous works of nonfiction, drama, and, most notably, historical fiction. In *A Woman of Destiny* (later published as *Saints*), for example, he returns to the subject of the life of Joseph Smith, first touched upon in *Seventh Son. A Woman of Destiny* offers an account of the lives of Smith, the founder of Mormonism, and Dinah Kirkham, a (fictional) English woman who is converted to Mormonism and becomes Smith's polygamous wife. When Smith is murdered in 1844, Kirkham escapes with a group of fellow Mormons to Utah, where she becomes a staunch leader as well as one of the wives of Brigham Young, Smith's successor as president of the Mormon Church. *Los Angeles Times Book Review* critic Kristiana Gregory pronounced Saints an "engrossing epic," stressing that Card "is a powerful storyteller."

Card's *Treasure Box* is billed as his second mainstream novel, following the publication of *Lost Boys,* yet it contains elements of the supernatural. Quentin Fears loses his beloved older sister Lizzy as a young boy. However, he continues to confide in her following her death. A millionaire, following his sellout of his computer firm, he meets his true love, Madeleine, at a party and marries her. But there are gaps in her background, and when he finally meets his in-laws at a spooky mansion in upstate New York, events unravel following Madeleine's insistence that Quentin open a box supposedly containing her inheritance.

Following up *Treasure Box* and *Lost Boys,* 1998's *Homebody* is another mainstream supernatural fantasy, combining elements of spirituality, the occult, and psychological insight in a haunted house tale. Homebody tells the story of Don Lark who, grieving the death of his two-year-old daughter, sets out to renovate the Bellamy House, a grand old Victorian mansion in a terrible state of disrepair. His three elderly neighbors warn him about the house's dark powers, but he goes forward with his project and becomes attached to a squatter who lives there. She is the occult key to the violent history of the house as a brothel and speakeasy. A writer for *Kirkus Reviews* assessed the novel as "solid but undistinguished work, not high in either tension or in depth." A *Publishers Weekly* reviewer found more to like, saying that the novel has "great potential that shines through its superfluous detail," and describing it as "a powerful tale of healing and redemption that skillfully balances supernatural horrors with spiritual uplift."

Card turns from the realms of the haunted to those of fairy tales with *Enchantment,* a blending of the story of Sleeping Beauty with Russian mythology. Ten-year-old Ivan is both frightened by and attracted to a lovely woman frozen in time in the midst of a Russian forest. A decade later and now an up-and-coming track star, Ivan returns to the forest to set this bewitched woman free. Drawn back into the ninth-century world of his princess, Ivan discovers that his modern-day talents do not stand him in good stead in his desperate battle to defeat the mythical witch Baba Yaga and claim his princess. Ivan takes Princess Katerina back to the modern world for a time, and the pair learns each other's powers before returning to battle the witch. A *Publishers Weekly* reviewer felt that Card's "new look at a classic tale is clever . . . [due to] adding attractive whimsical twists and cultural confluences to a familiar story."

In *Stone Tablets* Card returns to biblical themes, telling the story of Moses and retelling Exodus in a novel "that exhibits the same profound and compassionate understanding of human nature that marks his best sf and fantasy efforts," according to a contributor to *Publishers Weekly.* Card puts the focus here on the difficult relationship between Moses and his siblings. With *Sarah* Card inaugurated a new series, "Women of Genesis." In Card's retelling, Sarah is to become a priestess of Asherah until she meets a man named Abram, a mystic and desert wanderer. Sarah realizes that her destiny is tied up with Abram's and she waits eight years for his return, only to have many more years of a childless marriage test her belief in Abram's God. "Card adds depth, understanding, and human frailty to the woman who became known as Sarah," wrote Melanie C. Duncan in a *Library Journal* review. Duncan felt the novel "will attract secular readers as well." A reviewer for *Publishers Weekly* maintained that Card's rendering of Sarah as "a wise and virtuous figure who struggles to have the unflinching faith of Abraham," and his portrait of Biblical life and times, creates a "playfully speculative novel" that "succeeds in bringing Sarah's oft-overlooked character into vivid relief."

In a critique of the author's 1990 collection, *Maps in a Mirror: The Short Fiction of Orson Scott Card, Analog* reviewer Easton characterized Card as "an intensely thoughtful, self-conscious, religious, and community-oriented writer." In spite of such critical acclaim and the numerous awards his writing has earned, Card seems to prefer a simpler description of himself; as he told the DeCandidos, "I'm Kristine's husband, Geoffrey and Emily and Charlie's dad, I'm a Mormon, and I'm a science fiction writer, in that order." Replying to a query by Ciporen of *Publishers Weekly* as to why he writes mainly in SF, Card replied: "The truth is, SF is the most powerful genre available right now. Mainstream literature is so stultifyingly rigid. I don't just want to talk to people who believed everything their English teacher told them. I want to reach people who read books for the sheer pleasure of it, because those are the people who are open to having their lives changed by what they read."

BIOGRAPHICAL/CRITICAL SOURCES:

BOOKS

Collings, Michael R., and Boden Clarke, *The Work of Orson Scott Card: An Annotated Bibliography & Guide,* Borgo Press (San Bernardino, CA), 1995.

Collings, Michael R., *Storyteller: Official Guide to the Works of Orson Scott Card,* Overlook Connection Press (Woodstock, CA), 2001.

Contemporary Literary Criticism, Gale (Detroit, MI), Volume 44, 1987, Volume 47, 1988, Volume 50, 1988.

Contemporary Popular Writers, St. James Press (Detroit, MI), 1997.

PERIODICALS

Analog, July, 1983, p. 103; July, 1985, Tom Easton, review of *Ender's Game,* p. 180; June, 1986, Tom Easton, review of *Speaker for the Dead,* p. 183; mid-December, 1987; September, 1988, p. 179; August, 1989, p. 175; January, 1990, p. 305; March, 1991, p. 184; mid-December, 1991; January, 1996, Tom Easton, review of *Pastwatch,* p. 277; June, 1996, p. 145.

Booklist, December 15, 1985, p. 594; December 15, 1987, Sally Estes, review of *Red Prophet;* December 1, 1995, p. 586; June 1 & 15, 1996, Roland Green, review of *Pastwatch,* p. 1629.

Economist, September 5, 1987, p. 92.

Fantasy Review, April, 1986, Michael R. Collings, "Adventure and Allegory," p. 20; June, 1987, Martha Soukup, review of *Seventh Son;* July/August, 1987.

Kirkus Reviews, December 1, 1980, p. 1542; November 1, 1984, p. 1021; May 1, 1994, p. 594; June 15, 1995, p. 864; June 15, 1996, p. 839; February 2, 1998, review of *Homebody.*

Kliatt, April, 1991, p. 15.

Library Journal, February 15, 1989, p. 179; November 15, 1990; September 1, 1991; October 15, 1991; January, 1994, p. 172; June 15, 1994, p. 99; May 15, 1995, p. 99; December, 1995, p. 163; July, 1996, p. 154; April 15, 1998, Jackie Cassada, review of *Stone Tablets,* p. 111; August, 1998, Jackie Cassada, review of *Heartfire,* p. 140; September 14, 1999, Jackie Cassada, review of *Ender's Shadow,* p. 115; November 1, 2000, Melanie C. Duncan, review of Sarah, p. 60; December, 2000, Jackie Cassada, review of *Shadow of the Hegemon,* p. 196.

Locus, April, 1991, p. 15; February, 1992, pp. 17, 57; May, 1994, p. 48; February, 1995, p. 17.

Los Angeles Times Book Review, September 28, 1980; March 6, 1983; July 22, 1984, Kristiana Gregory, review of *A Woman of Destiny,* p. 8; February 3, 1985; August 9, 1987; February 14, 1988, Sue Martin, "Battling the Natives along the Mississippi"; July 20, 1990.

Magazine of Fantasy and Science Fiction, January, 1980, p. 35.

New York Times Book Review, June 16, 1985, Gerald Jonas, review of *Ender's Game,* p. 18; October 18, 1987, p. 36; September 1, 1991, Gerald Jonas, review of *Xenocide,* p. 13; March 15, 1992; May 8, 1994, p. 25; July 9, 1995, Gerald Jonas, review of *Earthborn,* p. 18.

Publishers Weekly, December 4, 1978, review of *Capitol,* p. 62; January 2, 1981, p. 49; January 24, 1986, p. 64; December 25, 1987, p. 65; September 16, 1988; May 19, 1989, p. 72; August 17, 1990, p. 55; November 30, 1990, Graceanne A. DeCandido and Keith R. A. DeCandido, "PW Interview: Orson Scott Card," pp. 54-55; June 14, 1991, p. 48; June 20, 1994, p. 97; January 30, 1995, p. 89; April 10, 1995, p. 58; August 7, 1995, p. 445; January 22, 1996, review of *Pastwatch,* pp. 61-62; June 24, 1996, review of *Children of the Mind,* pp. 45, 49; August 12, 1996, p. 20; February 2, 1998, review of *Homebody,* p. 79; June 29, 1998, review of *Heartfire,* p. 40; September 28, 1998, p. 77; March 8, 1999, review of *Enchantment,* p. 52; July 5, 1999, review of *Ender's Shadow,* p. 63; November 1, 1999, p. 48; September 11, 2000, review of *Sarah,* p. 71; November 20, 2000, Laura Ciporen, "PW Talks with Orson Scott Card," p. 51; November

ber 20, 2000, review of *Shadow of the Hegemon,* p. 50.

School Library Journal, January, 1991, p. 123; November, 1991; June, 2001, Jan Tarasovic, review of *Shadow of the Hegemon,* p. 183.

Science Fiction and Fantasy Book Review, April, 1979, p. 27; December, 1979, p. 155; June, 1983, p. 21.

Science Fiction Review, August, 1979; February, 1986, p. 14.

SF Chronicle, June, 1988, p. 50.

Tribune Books (Chicago), March 1, 1990; March 1, 1992, David E. Jones, "Trapped in a Serial Universe."

Voice of Youth Advocates, October, 1992, p. 236; August, 1995, Pam Carlson, review of *Earthfall* and *Earthborn,* p. 167.

Washington Post Book World, August 24, 1980, Richard A. Lupoff, "Beasts, Songbirds, and Wizards," p. 6; January 25, 1981, George R. R. Martin, "Scanning the Stars of the Short Story," pp. 9, 11; March 27, 1983; February 23, 1986, Janrae Frank, "War of the Worlds," p. 10; August 30, 1987, John Clute, review of *Seventh Son;* February 28, 1988, John Clute, review of *Red Prophet;* March 19, 1992; September 25, 1994, Maureen F. McHugh, review of *Lovelock,* p. 14; September 24, 1995, Martin Morse Wooster, review of *Alvin Journeyman.*

West Coast Review of Books, March, 1984; July, 1986; no. 2, 1987; no. 4, 1988, review of *Red Prophet.*

Wilson Library Bulletin, February, 1994, p. 70.

Writer's Digest, October, 1986, p. 26; November, 1986, p. 37; December, 1986, p. 32; May, 1989, p. 31.

OTHER

Hatrack River, http://www.hatrack.com/ (February 9, 2001).

*   *   *

CHENEY, Margaret 1921-

PERSONAL: Born April 5, 1921, in Eugene, OR; daughter of George L. (a horse trainer) and Josie (a teacher; maiden name, Goughnour) Swisher; married Michael S. Cheney (a writer), May 29, 1952 (deceased); children: Victoria Leigh. *Education:* Attended Cornish School of Fine Arts. *Avocational interests:* Naturalist, farmer, vintner.

ADDRESSES: *Home*—California. *Agent*—c/o New Voyage Publishers, 1839 16th St. NW, Washington DC, 20009.

CAREER: Associated Press, Seattle, WA, editor, 1943-46; University of California, Berkeley, CA, writer, 1960-67; Carnegie Commission on Higher Education, Berkeley, CA, editor, 1970-71; freelance writer, 1971—.

MEMBER: National Audubon Society (president of Gabilan chapter, 1980), Feminist Writers Guild.

AWARDS, HONORS: Award from Columbus Film Festival, 1963, for *Which Campus?*

WRITINGS:

A Brief History of the University of California, University of California Press (Berkeley, CA), 1965.
Meanwhile Farm (nonfiction), Les Femmes (Millbrae, CA), 1975.
Coed Killer (nonfiction), Walker & Co. (New York, NY), 1976, revised edition published as *Why?: The Serial Killer in America,* R & E Publishers (Saratoga, CA), 1992.
Tesla: Man out of Time, Prentice-Hall (Englewood Cliffs, NJ), 1981.
Midnight at Mabel's, New Voyage (Washington, DC), 2000.

Coauthor, with Carol Levene, of *Which Campus?,* a documentary film released by University of California, 1963; coauthor, with Robert Uth, of *Tesla: Master of Lightning.* Work represented in anthologies, including *Audubon Anthology.* Editor of books published in the series, "Carnegie Commission on Higher Education." Reporter for *Aberdeen Daily World.* Contributor to *Encyclopedia Americana.* Contributor to magazines, including *Gourmet.*

SIDELIGHTS: Margaret Cheney has written two biographies of influential yet little-known individuals. Her *Tesla: Man out of Time* covers the career of Nikola Tesla, a Serbian inventor and prominent scientist of the early twentieth century whose inventions changed society worldwide. *Midnight at Mabel's* tells of Mabel Mercer, whose style of singing influenced generations of later performers.

In *Tesla* Cheney chronicles the remarkable life of the inventor of alternating current and hundreds of other electrical devices and techniques which have had an enormous impact on modern society. Among Tesla's many creations were the huge dynamos at Niagara Falls, the earliest wireless telegraph (predating that of Marconi), and a number of household appliances he sold to the young George Westinghouse and his budding company. By the 1930s, however, Tesla had begun to be obsessed with such things as death rays and the transmission of electrical power without wires. By the time of his death during World War II, he was living in poverty and was largely forgotten. Cheney's "chatty biography outlines the boom-and-bust career," according to P. Robert Paustian in *Library Journal.* The critic for *Publishers Weekly* found *Tesla* to be "a well documented, sympathetic and engaging biography."

Midnight at Mabel's focuses on cabaret singer Mabel Mercer and her long and influential career. Born in England to a biracial couple, Mercer was raised in an orphanage after her parents abandoned her. As a teenager, she began singing in Parisian clubs and soon developed a following among other performers, many of whom imitated her style. Frank Sinatra is said to have been one of those influenced by Mercer. Working with what little dependable information exists about Mercer's personal life, Cheney's biography chronicles Mercer's career "in a breezy style," according to Barry Zaslow in *Library Journal.* David Finkle in *Back Stage* found it to be "an acceptable look at the singer's life," which "seems to get right what facts are known" about the legendary performer.

Cheney once told *CA:* "I am an avid foreign traveler, having lived with my family in the Middle East and in England for several years. Most of my education has occurred outside of classrooms, where the study list is endless. A favorite interest is animal behavior.

"My writing career began at age eight with publishing of newspapers, and continued with reporting for school papers. The choice of career was never a conscious decision although it conflicted with my desire to be a painter.

"The biography of Nikola Tesla is the first comprehensive work on him since John J. O'Neill's *Prodigal Genius,* published in the 1940s, and there appears to be interest in it both in America and abroad. Tesla is a great favorite in Canada as well as a leading folk hero [in Eastern Europe]. A prodigiously gifted scientist—a naturalized American—he may well have been, as Hugo Gernsback thought, 'the greatest inventor in history.' He was a contemporary of Edison's, a friend of Mark Twain's, Anne Morgan's, and J. Pierpont Morgan's; and his alternating current patents helped launch the Westinghouse Electric Co. The idea of writing on Tesla attracted me because of the mystery surrounding his remarkable life and the patent injustices done to his memory, which I hope may be to some degree remedied by this biography. Lee Anderson, the Tesla authority, says he hopes it will at least enable people to learn to spell Tesla's name (i.e. *not* Nicola) correctly!

"With Einstein and Edison, I believe that formal education tends to have a constricting effect upon intellectual growth. Each of my books has been about a radically different subject, a reflection of my pleasure in learning. Like Tesla I find the idea of specializing abhorrent. As I grow older I find it particularly important to tackle mind-stretching subjects. A point I hope to convey with this biography is not only that the ordinary woman *can* understand science but—in view of the ubiquitous, bewildering experts to be found on both sides of every issue—must do so to survive. My use of the word wo*man* subsumes the male gender."

BIOGRAPHICAL/CRITICAL SOURCES:

PERIODICALS

Back Stage, December 1, 2000, David Finkle, review of *Midnight at Mabel's,* p. 13.
Library Journal, November 15, 1981, P. Robert Paustian, review of *Tesla: Man out of Time,* September 1, 2000, Barry Zaslow, review of *Midnight at Mabel's,* p. 210.
Publishers Weekly, October 9, 1981, review of *Tesla,* p. 57.*

*　　*　　*

CLARK, Carol Higgins 1956(?)-

PERSONAL: Born c. 1956; daughter of Warren (an airline executive) and Mary (a writer; maiden name, Higgins) Clark.

ADDRESSES: Agent—c/o Scribner, 1230 Avenue of the Americas, New York, NY 10020.

CAREER: Actress and novelist. Appeared off-Broadway, and in television films and miniseries, including *Fatal Charm, Night of the Fox,* and *A Cry in the Night.*

AWARDS, HONORS: Agatha Award nomination for *Decked.*

WRITINGS:

MYSTERY NOVELS

Decked, Warner Books (New York, NY), 1992.
Snagged, Warner Books (New York, NY), 1993.
Iced, Warner Books (New York, NY), 1995.
Twanged, Warner Books (New York, NY), 1998.
(With Mary Higgins Clark) *Deck the Halls,* Simon & Schuster (New York, NY), 2000.
Fleeced, Scribner (New York, NY), 2001.

SIDELIGHTS: Some authors have writing in their blood. Such a writer is Carol Higgins Clark, who has penned five popular mystery novels featuring sleuth Regan Reilly, including her first book, *Decked.* Clark is the daughter of best-selling suspense novelist Mary Higgins Clark, whose own titles include *A Stranger Is Watching, The Cradle Will Fall,* and *Remember Me.* Carol Higgins Clark is also an actress, and has played a starring role in the television version of one of her mother's books, *A Cry in the Night.*

Clark grew up with four siblings, all of whom, like their mother, were interested in storytelling. She recalled for Michael A. Lipton and Ann Guerin in *People* magazine: "If anyone told a boring story in my family, he or she was promptly cut off." Clark's father died when she was still a young child, and her mother began writing, eventually penning the novels that would send Carol and her brothers and sisters to college. After college, Carol Higgins Clark began acting, adding her mother's maiden name to her own at the insistence of an acting agent. She did both off-Broadway productions and television work, but between acting roles she worked typing her mother's manuscripts.

Though she learned much from her mother, most critics agree with Mary Higgins Clark that the younger Clark's novel-writing style is different, more light and humorous than her mother's. Carol agrees. "Her books are scarier," she told *Philadelphia Inquirer* interviewer Thomas J. Brady. "She's known for being the queen of suspense, as they say, whereas mine are funny. . . . I'm glad, because I'd rather have my own voice than to try and do the same thing that my mother is doing."

Decked, Carol Higgins Clark's first effort, introduces her sleuth, Regan Reilly, whose mother is a suspense writer. The story starts with Regan's return to Oxford University for a reunion with classmates who had spent a semester abroad together. During the reunion, the body of Athena, a Greek student who Regan and her comrades thought had run away years before, is discovered. Her body is found on the estate of one of Regan's professors, and in the course of Reilly's investigation, she must accompany the professor's eccentric aunt on a cruise across the Atlantic Ocean. As a *Publishers Weekly* reviewer noted, "Clark deftly ties the plot playing out on the ocean liner to Athena's murder in a suspenseful climax." Susan Toepfer in *People* hailed the book as "a sharp and satisfying mystery." She predicted that the character of Regan Reilly could "easily carry a dozen more books."

Snagged concerns possible murder attempts on a man who has invented a type of virtually indestructible pantyhose. Regan Reilly and her parents are at a hotel in Miami that is hosting two conventions—one for funeral directors (her father's profession) and one for the pantyhose industry. Clark attended a hosiery business convention in order to do research for her novel. "They kept telling me to say 'hosiery,' " she told Sarah Booth Conroy in the *Washington Post.* Stacy Pober, reviewing *Snagged* for *Library Journal,* cited the author's "fine talent for giving many of the characters distinctive voices." Glenna Whitley in *New York Times Book Review* applauded the novel as "upbeat" and "fast-paced."

In *Iced,* Clark allows Reilly to travel to Aspen, Colorado. Regan has recommended a friend (who is an ex-con) for a house-sitting job there. When her friend and some paintings disappear, others jump to conclusions, but Regan sets out to clear his name. Several other possible art thieves are on the local scene, including a mysterious figure known as the Coyote. "Clark's tone is as chipper as ever in her third Regan Reilly book," observed a *Publishers Weekly* critic. Emily Melton in *Booklist* declared the novel to be "solidly entertaining, mostly clever, occasionally funny, and always fun." *Iced* was also recommended for younger readers by Claudia Moore in the *School Library Journal,* who affirmed it as "a good choice for teens, who will enjoy the wit."

Southampton socialites are Higgins's satirical target in *Twanged.* In this novel, Regan Reilly goes to Long Island to protect up-and-coming country music star Brigid O'Neill from the clutches of Chappy Tinka, a wealthy buffoon who wants to steal Brigid's fiddle. The instrument was a gift from legendary Irish fiddler Malachy Sheerin and is believed to bring good luck to its owner; Chappy believes that, if only he possessed the magic fiddle, he could become a major star, and his efforts to get his hands on the instrument set in motion a series of events which reviewers found more zany than suspenseful. A *Publishers Weekly* contributor enjoyed the book's "promising screwball-comedy plot,"

but added that the novel suffers from some "clumsy" writing. Alice DiNizo, in *Library Journal,* considered *Twanged* a "light but well-composed" mystery.

Mother and daughter collaborated in *Deck the Halls,* a Christmas-themed mystery that critics noted would please many of their fans. Revolving around a plot to kidnap Regan Reilly's father, Luke, and featuring both Regan and Mary Higgins Clark's amateur detective, Alvirah Meehan, as investigators, the novel combines suspense and comedy in a mix that *Booklist*'s Stephanie Zvirin found seamless but "lightweight." A reviewer for *Publishers Weekly* expressed a similar opinion, deeming the book a "middling" effort that would nevertheless appeal to the Clarks' loyal readers.

BIOGRAPHICAL/CRITICAL SOURCES:

PERIODICALS

Booklist, May 15, 1995, p. 1611; November 1, 2000, Stephanie Zvirin, review of *Deck the Halls,* p. 492.
Library Journal, July, 1992, p. 131; September 1, 1993, p. 242; June 1, 1995, p. 170; February 1, 1998, Alice DiNizo, review of *Twanged,* p. 116.
New York Times Book Review, October 17, 1993, p. 42.
People, August 31, 1992, p. 31; November 2, 1992, pp. 79, 82.
Philadelphia Inquirer, April 19, 1998, Thomas J. Brady, interview with Carol Higgins Clark.
Publishers Weekly, May 18, 1992, pp. 60-61; June 14, 1993, p. 64; May 29, 1995, p. 70; December 22, 1997, review of *Twanged,* p. 41; March 6, 2000, "Move for Higgins Clark Jr.," p. 14; October 30, 2000, review of *Deck the Halls,* p. 47.
School Library Journal, January, 1996, p. 138.
USA Today, May 18, 1995, p. 14D.
Washington Post, September 28, 1993, p. C1.

OTHER

Book Reporter.com, http://www.bookreporter.com/ (January 12, 2001), interview with Carol Higgins Clark.*

*   *   *

CLARK, Mary Higgins 1929(?)-

PERSONAL: Born December 24, 1929 (some sources say 1931), in New York, NY; daughter of Luke Joseph (a restaurant owner) and Nora C. (a buyer; maiden

Mary Higgins Clark

name, Durkin) Higgins; married Warren F. Clark (an airline executive), December 26, 1949 (died September 26, 1964); married Raymond Charles Ploetz (an attorney), August 8, 1978 (marriage annulled); married John J. Conheeney (a retired Merrill Lynch Futures CEO), November 30, 1996; children: Marilyn, Warren, David, Carol, Patricia. *Education:* Attended Villa Maria Academy, Ward Secretarial School, and New York University; Fordham University, B.A. (summa cum laude), 1979. *Politics:* Republican. *Religion:* Roman Catholic. *Avocational interests:* Traveling, skiing, tennis, playing piano.

ADDRESSES: Home—Saddle River, NJ; and 210 Central Park South, New York, NY 10019. *Agent*—Eugene H. Winick, McIntosh & Otis, Inc., 475 Fifth Ave., New York, NY 10017.

CAREER: Writer. Remington Rand, New York, NY, advertising assistant, 1946; Pan American Airlines, flight attendant, 1949-50; Robert G. Jennings, radio scriptwriter and producer, 1965-70; Aerial Communications, New York, NY, vice president, partner, creative director, and producer of radio programming, 1970-80; David J. Clark Enterprises, New York, NY,

chairman of the board and creative director, 1980—. Chairman, International Crime Writers Congress, 1988.

MEMBER: Mystery Writers of America (president, 1987; member of board of directors), Authors Guild, Authors League of America, American Academy of Arts and Sciences, American Society of Journalists and Authors, American Irish Historical Society (member of executive council).

AWARDS, HONORS: New Jersey Author Award, 1969, for *Aspire to the Heavens,* 1977, for *Where Are the Children?* and 1978, for *A Stranger Is Watching;* Grand Prix de Litterature Policiere (France), 1980; Women of Achievement Award, Federation of Women's Clubs in New Jersey; Irish Woman of the Year Award, Irish-American Heritage and Cultural Week Committee of the Board of Education of the City of New York; Gold Medal of Honor Award, American-Irish Historical Society; Spirit of Achievement Award, Albert Einstein College of Medicine of Yeshiva University; Gold Medal in Education, National Arts Club; Horatio Alger Award, 1997; thirteen honorary doctorates, including Villanova University, 1983, Rider College, 1986, Stonehill College and Marymount Manhattan College, 1992, Chestnut Hill, Manhattan College, and St. Peter's College, 1993; Dame of the Order of St. Gregory the Great; Dame of Malta, Dame of the Holy Sepulcher of Jerusalem.

WRITINGS:

Aspire to the Heavens: A Biography of George Washington, Meredith Press, 1969.
Where Are the Children? (also see below), Simon & Schuster (New York, NY), 1975.
A Stranger Is Watching (also see below), Simon & Schuster (New York, NY), 1978.
(Contributor) *I, Witness,* Times Books, 1978.
The Cradle Will Fall (also see below) Simon & Schuster (New York, NY), 1980.
A Cry in the Night, Simon & Schuster (New York, NY), 1982.
Stillwatch, Simon & Schuster (New York, NY), 1984.
(With Thomas Chastain and others) *Murder in Manhattan,* Morrow (New York, NY), 1986.
Weep No More, My Lady, Simon & Schuster (New York, NY), 1987.
(Editor) *Murder on the Aisle: The 1987 Mystery Writers of America Anthology,* Simon & Schuster (New York, NY), 1987.
While My Pretty One Sleeps (also see below), Simon & Schuster (New York, NY), 1989.

The Anastasia Syndrome and Other Stories, Simon & Schuster (New York, NY), 1989.

Loves Music, Loves to Dance (also see below), Simon & Schuster (New York, NY), 1991.

All Around the Town (also see below) Simon & Schuster (New York, NY), 1992.

Missing in Manhattan: The Adams Round Table, Longmeadow Press, 1992.

Mists from Beyond: Twenty-two Ghost Stories and Tales from the Other Side, New American Library/Dutton, 1993.

I'll Be Seeing You, Simon & Schuster (New York, NY), 1993.

Remember Me, Simon & Schuster (New York, NY), 1994.

The Lottery Winner: Alvirah and Willy Stories, Simon & Schuster (New York, NY), 1994.

Silent Night: A Novel, Simon & Schuster (New York, NY), 1995.

Mary Higgins Clark: Three Complete Novels (includes *A Stranger Is Watching, The Cradle Will Fall,* and *Where Are the Children?*), Wings Books (New York, NY), 1995.

(Contributor) *The International Association of Crime Writers Presents Bad Behavior,* Harcourt Brace (San Diego), 1995.

Let Me Call You Sweetheart, Simon & Schuster (New York, NY), 1995.

Moonlight Becomes You: A Novel, Simon & Schuster (New York, NY), 1996.

Mary Higgins Clark, Three New York Times Bestsellers (includes *While My Pretty One Sleeps, Loves Music, Loves to Dance,* and *All Around the Town*) Wings Books (New York, NY), 1996.

My Gal Sunday, Simon & Schuster (New York, NY), 1996.

Pretend You Don't See Her, Simon & Schuster (New York, NY), 1997.

(Editor) *The Plot Thickens,* Pocket Books, 1997.

All Through the Night, Simon & Schuster (New York, NY), 1998.

You Belong to Me, Simon & Schuster (New York, NY), 1998.

We'll Meet Again, Simon & Schuster (New York, NY), 1999.

Before I Say Goodbye, Simon & Schuster (New York, NY), 2000.

(With Carol Higgins Clark) *Deck the Halls,* Simon & Schuster (New York, NY), 2000.

On the Street Where You Live, Simon & Schuster (New York, NY), 2001.

Work anthologized in *The Best "Saturday Evening Post" Stories,* 1962. Also author of syndicated radio dramas. Contributor of stories to periodicals, including *Saturday Evening Post, Redbook, McCall's,* and *Family Circle.*

Simon & Schuster plans to rerelease all of Clark's works in e-book format.

ADAPTATIONS: A Stranger Is Watching was filmed by Metro-Goldwyn-Mayer in 1982; *The Cradle Will Fall* was shown on CBS as a "Movie of the Week" in 1984; *A Cry in the Night* was filmed by Rosten productions in 1985; *Where Are the Children?* was filmed by Columbia in 1986; *Stillwatch* was broadcast on CBS in 1987; Ellipse, a French production company, produced *Weep No More My Lady, A Cry in the Night* (starring Clark's daughter Carol), and two stories from *The Anastasia Syndrome.*

SIDELIGHTS: "You can set your bestseller clock each spring for a new Mary Higgins Clark winner," observed *Publishers Weekly* contributor Dick Donahue in 2001. The prolific mystery author began her writing career as a newly widowed mother of five, and has instilled her passion for suspense stories in her children, including daughter Carol, also a best-selling novelist. Clark's stories have proven so popular that her publisher, Simon & Schuster, signed her to a then-record-breaking $11.4 million contract in 1989 to produce four novels and a short story collection, and a $35 million contract for five novels and a memoir in 1992. By 2000, Clark had over fifty million titles in print and enjoyed bestseller status around the world.

Clark had always intended to become a writer. "When I was fifteen I was picking out clothes that I would wear when I became a successful writer," she told *Powells.com* interviewer Dave Welch. "I was sure I'd make it." For the first nine years of her marriage, Clark wrote short stories. "The first one was rejected for six years," she confided to Welch. "Then it sold for $100." Confronted with the daunting task of supporting five young children after the early death of her husband, Clark turned to suspense novels. Her first, *Where Are the Children?,* became a bestseller in 1975, earning more than $100,000 in paperback royalties. She followed that with another thriller, *A Stranger Is Watching,* which earned more than $1 million in paperback rights and was filmed by Metro-Goldwyn-Mayer in 1982. For Clark, this meant financial security. "[The money] changed my life in the nicest way," she told Bina Bernard in *People.* "It took all the choking sensation out of paying for the kids' schools."

The key to Clark's popularity, according to several critics, is her technique. Jean M. White of the *Washington*

Post maintained that Clark "is a master storyteller who builds her taut suspense in a limited time frame," noting that *Where Are the Children?* takes place in one day and *A Stranger Is Watching* in three. Carolyn Banks, moreover, pointed out in the *Washington Post* that there is a kind of "Mary Higgins Clark formula" that readers both expect and enjoy: "There are no ambiguities in any Clark book. We know whom and what to root for, and we do. Similarly, we boo and hiss or gasp when the author wants us to. Clark is a master manipulator." Although Clark wants to provide her readers with entertainment and romance, she once told *CA:* "I feel a good suspense novel can and should hold a mirror up to society and make a social comment."

Clark's style is to write about "terror lurking beneath the surface of everyday life," observed White. "[She] writes about ordinary people suddenly caught up in frightening situations as they ride a bus or vacuum the living room," such as the characters in *Loves Music, Loves to Dance,* who encounter a murderer when they agree to participate in an experiment involving newspaper personal ads. Other stories play on readers' fears of unfamiliar or undesirable situations. For example, Clark explored mental illness in *Loves Music, Loves to Dance,* in which the killer's behavior is caused by a personality disorder, and in *All Around the Town,* in which the main character is afflicted with multiple personality disorder attributed to severe sexual abuse in her childhood. In *I'll Be Seeing You,* Clark's characters find themselves victimized by villains more knowledgeable than they in the issues of genetic manipulation and in-vitro fertilization. Many of the events and details of Clark's stories come from the lives of her friends and family, news events, and even her own experiences. Clark told *New York Times* interviewer Shirley Horner that the burglary the heroine interrupts in *Stillwatch* was based on break-ins Clark herself had endured. "Everything that a writer experiences goes up in the mental attic," she told Horner.

In her more recent novels, nice people have been vanquishing the powers of darkness with great flair. In *Moonlight Becomes You,* Maggie Holloway, a young photographer and amateur sculptor, visits her deceased stepmother's home in Newport, Rhode Island, in order to investigate the woman's mysterious death. Maggie's search leads her to a nursing home plagued by a series of sudden deaths, and she begins to suspect that she, too, is being targeted by the killer, who does not want her to expose his diabolical plot. A reviewer from *Booklist* acknowledged that "though this is not her finest book, Clark's popularity will surely put *Moonlight* on the lists."

In her collection of short stories, *My Gal Sunday,* Clark introduces a new detective team. Henry Parker Britland IV is a former U.S. president enjoying an early retirement, and his wife, Sandra (Sunday), has just been elected to Congress and appointed the darling of the media. Henry and Sunday specialize in solving crimes that occur among their friends in political society. In one story, when Henry's former secretary of state is indicted for the murder of his mistress, Henry and Sunday determine he is willing to take the fall for a crime of passion he did not commit.

In *Pretend You Don't See Her,* Clark takes on the federal witness protection program. While working as a real estate agent in Manhattan, Lacey Farrell witnesses a client's murder and has been given a new name and a new life by the government. However, merely changing her name does not protect her from the web of danger and deceit that surrounds the crime. As new clues emerge, Lacey realizes that a link exists between her family and the murder. In the meantime, romance enters her life and leads her to embark on a perilous journey to reclaim her old identity. *Booklist* found the story "briskly paced," though with few surprises. Kimberly Marlowe of the *New York Times Book Review* noted that in the author's fifteenth novel, Clark covers "a lot of ground . . . life, death threats and the perfect date."

By the late 1990s, some critics had begun to suggest that Clark's writing was growing rather stale. In a review of *You Belong to Me,* a *Publishers Weekly* contributor commented that the book gives fans "the page-flipping perils they expect without challenging them or [Clark's] art one whit." But Clark's popularity remained as strong as ever. *We'll Meet Again,* in which a greedy head of a Connecticut HMO is murdered, shot straight to the top of bestseller lists after just one week in stores. *New York Times Book Review* crime columnist Marilyn Stasio appreciated "the diabolical plot that Clark prepares so carefully and executes with such relish"; *Booklist* reviewer Jenny McLarin deemed the novel "first-rate entertainment." *Before I Say Goodbye,* also an immediate top-seller, was hailed as one of Clark's "page-turning best" by *Booklist* contributor Kristine Huntley. And *On the Street Where You Live,* Clark's third novel in a row to capture the number-one slot in its first week, intrigued critics with its premise: that a serial killer from a century past might be stalking young women in a present-day New Jersey resort town. "Clark's prose ambles as usual," commented a reviewer for *Publishers Weekly,* "but it takes readers where they want to go—deep into an old-fashioned tale of a damsel in delicious distress."

Writing has become a family affair for the Clarks. Carol Higgins Clark's first novel, *Decked,* appeared on the paperback bestseller list at the same time as her mother's *I'll Be Seeing You* was departing the hardcover list after seventeen weeks. To critics who suggest that Clark may have contributed to the writing of her daughter's books, the elder author's response is, "Not so, we have very different voices," Sarah Booth Conroy noted in the *Washington Post.* Conroy observed that Mary "writes deadly serious novels about the sort of chilling fears that come to women in the middle of the night," while Carol "spoons in a bit of bawdy, a soupcon of slapstick." Carol did, however, exert some influence on her mother's writing: she is responsible for saving two of Clark's most popular characters, Alvirah, a cleaning woman who wins the lottery, and her husband, Willy. When they first appeared in a short story, Alvirah was poisoned and Clark planned to finish her off, but Carol convinced her mother to allow Alvirah to recover. The two have since become recurring characters and are featured in *The Lottery Winner: Alvirah and Willy Stories,* published in 1994. Mother and daughter took their literary bond to a further level with *Deck the Halls,* a mystery novel they co-wrote featuring both Alvirah and Carol Higgins Clark's popular sleuth, Regan Reilly.

BIOGRAPHICAL/CRITICAL SOURCES:

BOOKS

Bestsellers '89, number 4, Gale (Detroit, MI), 1989.
Newsmakers 2000, Gale (Detroit, MI), 2000.
St. James Guide to Young Adult Writers, second edition, St. James Press (Detroit, MI), 1999.

PERIODICALS

Best Sellers, December, 1984.
Booklist, October 15, 1994, p. 371; April 15, 1996; April, 1998, Mary Frances Wilkens, review of *You Belong to Me,* p. 1277; September 15, 1998, Kathleen Hughes, review of *All Through the Night,* p. 172; April 15, 1999, Jenny McLarin, review of *We'll Meet Again,* p. 1468; April 15, 2000, Kristine Huntley, review of *Before I Say Goodbye,* p. 1500; November 1, 2000, Stephanie Zvirin, review of *Deck the Halls,* p. 492; April 15, 2001, Kristine Huntley, review of *On the Street Where You Live,* p. 1508.
Chicago Tribune, September 20, 1987; July 31, 1989.
Cosmopolitan, May, 1989.
English Journal, December, 1979, p. 80.
Good Housekeeping, November, 1996, pp. 23-24.
Kirkus Review, November 1, 2000, review of *Deck the Halls,* p. 1519.

Newsweek, June 30, 1980.
New Yorker, August 4, 1980; June 27, 1994, p. 91.
New York Times, January 22, 1982; December 6, 1989; May 18, 1997.
New York Times Book Review, May 14, 1978; November 14, 1982; May 2, 1993, p. 22; December 15, 1996; May 5, 1996; April 19, 1998, Marilyn Stasio, review of *You Belong to Me,* p. 30; June 29, 1997; May 23, 1999, Marilyn Stasio, review of *We'll Meet Again;* April 16, 2000, Marilyn Stasio, review of *Before I Say Goodbye,* p. 32.
Observer, May 7, 1978, p. 34.
People Weekly, March 6, 1978; May 9, 1994, p. 35; December 16, 1996, pp. 54-56.
Progressive, May, 1978, p. 45.
Publishers Weekly, May 19, 1989; October 14, 1996, pp. 28-29; March 30, 1998, review of *You Belong to Me,* p. 70; September 14, 1998, review of *All Through the Night,* p. 52; October 30, 2000, review of *Deck the Halls,* p. 47; April 2, 2001, review of *On the Street Where You Live,* p. 41; April 30, 2001, "Clark's Spark Marks," p. 20.
Tribune Books (Chicago), June 8, 1980.
Wall Street Journal, May 29, 1996, p. A16; December 7, 1998, Tom Nolan, review of *All Through the Night,* p. A28; December 11, 2000, Tom Nolan, review of *Deck the Halls,* p. A38.
Washington Post, May 19, 1980; July 17, 1980; October 18, 1982; August 10, 1987.

OTHER

Powells.com, http://www.powells.com/ (January 12, 2001), "Mary Higgins Clark Reveals."
Writers Write, http://www.writerswrite.com/ (January 12, 2001), "A Conversation with Mary Higgins Clark."*

*   *   *

CLARKE, Brenda (Margaret Lilian) 1926-
(Brenda Honeyman; Kate Sedley, a
pseudonym)

PERSONAL: Born July 30, 1926, in Bristol, England; daughter of Edward (an insurance agent) and Lilian Rose (Brown) Honeyman; married Ronald John Clarke (a civil servant), March 5, 1955; children: Roger Stephen, Gwithian Margaret. *Education:* Cambridge University, school certificate, 1942. *Politics:* Socialist. *Religion:* Methodist. *Avocational interests:* Theater, reading, history, music.

ADDRESSES: Home—25 Torridge Rd., Keynsham, Bristol, Avon BS31 1QQ, England. *Agent*—David Grossman Literary Agency Ltd., 118b Holland Park Ave., London W11 4UA, England.

CAREER: British Civil Service, Ministry of Labour, Bristol, England, clerical officer, 1942-55; writer, 1968—. Section leader for British Red Cross, 1941-45.

MEMBER: Society of Authors, Wessex Writers' Association.

WRITINGS:

The Glass Island, Collins (London, England), 1978.
The Lofty Banners, Fawcett (New York, NY), 1980.
The Far Morning, Fawcett (New York, NY), 1982.
All through the Day, Hamlyn Paperbacks (London, England), 1983.
A Rose in May, Hutchinson (London, England), 1984.
Three Women, Hutchinson (London, England), 1985.
Winter Landscape, Century Hutchinson (London, England), 1986.
Under Heaven, Transworld Publishers (London, England), 1988.
Riches of the Heart, Pinnacle Books (New York, NY), 1989, originally published in England as *An Equal Chance.*
Sisters and Lovers, Pinnacle Books (New York, NY), 1990.
Beyond the World, Transworld Publishers (London, England), 1991.
A Durable Fire, Bantam (London, England), 1993.
Sweet Auburn, Little, Brown (London, England), 1995.

UNDER NAME BRENDA HONEYMAN

Richard by Grace of God, R. Hale (London, England), 1968, reprinted as *Richard Plantagenet,* under name Brenda Clarke, Severn House (Sutton, England), 1997.
The Kingmaker, R. Hale (London, England), 1969, reprinted as *Last of the Barons,* under name Brenda Clarke, Severn House (Sutton, England), 1998.
Richmond and Elizabeth, R. Hale (London, England), 1970, Pinnacle Books (New York, NY), 1973.
Harry the King, R. Hale (London, England), 1971, reprinted as *The Warrior King,* Pinnacle Books (New York, NY), 1972, reprinted, Severn House (Sutton, England), 1998.
Brother Bedford, R. Hale (London, England), 1972.
Good Duke Humphrey, R. Hale (London, England), 1973.
The King's Minions, R. Hale (London, England), 1974.

The Queen and Mortimer, R. Hale (London, England), 1974.
Edward the Warrior, R. Hale (London, England), 1975.
All the King's Sons, R. Hale (London, England), 1976.
The Golden Griffin, R. Hale (London, England), 1976.
At the King's Court, R. Hale (London, England), 1977.
The King's Tale, R. Hale (London, England), 1977.
Macbeth, King of Scots, R. Hale (London, England), 1977.
Emma, the Queen, R. Hale (London, England), 1978.
Harold of the English, R. Hale (London, England), 1979.

UNDER PSEUDONYM KATE SEDLEY

Death and the Chapman, St. Martin's Press (New York, NY), 1992.
The Plymouth Cloak, St. Martin's Press (New York, NY), 1993.
The Hanged Man, St. Martin's Press (New York, NY), 1993.
The Holy Innocents, Headline (London, England), 1994, St. Martin's Press (New York, NY), 1995.
The Weaver's Tale, St. Martin's Press (New York, NY), 1994.
The Eve of Saint Hyacinth, Headline (London, England), 1995, St. Martin's Press (New York, NY), 1996.
The Wicked Winter, Headline (London, England), 1996, St. Martin's Press (New York, NY), 1999.
The Brothers of Glastonbury, Headline (London, England), 1997, St. Martin's Minotaur (New York, NY), 2001.
The Weaver's Inheritance, Headline (London, England), 1998, St. Martin's Press (New York, NY), 2001.
The Saint John's Fern, Headline (London, England), 1999.
The Goldsmith's Daughter, Severn House (Sutton, England), 2001.

A number of Clarke's books have been published in German, French, and Italian. Those adapted for audio include *Death and the Chapman, The Hanged Man,* and *The Holy Innocents.*

SIDELIGHTS: Brenda Clarke is the author of novels of both historical fiction and romantic fiction. She began her career writing historical fiction under her birth name, Brenda Honeyman, usually exploring the lives of past British royalty. In the late 1970s, however, Clarke's agent persuaded her to begin writing romantic fiction, a move that "did both herself and her readers a great service, and turned to advantage her predilection for broad canvasses and large casts of characters," wrote Judith Rhodes in *Twentieth-Century Romance and Historical Fiction.* From this point Clarke wrote under her married name.

Beginning in 1991, Clarke also began writing historical crime fiction under the pseudonym Kate Sedley. In *Death and the Chapman,* Clarke introduces the character of Roger the Chapman, a fifteenth-century monk turned peddler, who travels through the countryside solving crimes using his extraordinary powers of deduction. *Booklist* reviewer Margaret Flanagan called *The Eve of Saint Hyacinth* "an artfully crafted caper." In this novel, Roger the Chapman aids the Duke of Gloucester in identifying the traitor who would murder the Duke's brother, King Edward IV. In *The Holy Innocents,* he investigates the murder of two children in a story *Booklist*'s Flanagan called "another exemplary medieval mystery steeped in suspense and historical detail." A *Publishers Weekly* reviewer called it a "vividly colored tapestry of medieval English life."

Roger finds himself at odds with Brother Simeon, a fanatical friar who, like Roger, is heading to Cederwell Manor in *The Wicked Winter.* When they arrive, they find that Lady Cederwell has died from a fall from a tower window. Roger's task is to determine whether the death of the woman who had summoned him was an accident or whether she was pushed, possibly by her husband. A *Publishers Weekly* contributor wrote that "the mystery, though it has a tendency to turn gothic, is expertly plotted." In reviewing the book for *Crescent Blues Book Views* online, Teri Dohmen said she "enjoyed the twists and turns employed by the author to bring her readers to the ultimately satisfying conclusion."

In *The Brothers of Glastonbury,* Roger is commissioned by the Duke of Clarence to deliver the daughter of the duke's sergeant-at-arms to her husband-to-be. When Roger and Cicely arrive, they find that Peter has disappeared, and they go on a hunt to find the missing groom. Peter's brother, Mark, disappears as well, and Roger finds that both were involved with a manuscript that suggests the location of the Holy Grail. "Sedley deftly camouflages down-to-earth villainy with the magical dust of romance," wrote a *Kirkus Reviews* contributor. A *Publishers Weekly* reviewer said the author "portrays late medieval England with remarkable clarity and vividness." *BookBrowser* reviewer Harriet Klausner called *The Brothers of Glastonbury* "a wonderfully executed mystery." Protagonist Roger appears again in *The Weaver's Inheritance.* A contributor to

Kirkus Reviews noted that Roger "remains an appealingly sturdy, believable hero."

Clarke once commented in *CA:* "Acquiring an agent changed the course of my writing career. Instead of 'factional' novels about the Middle Ages and Saxon England, [my agent] persuaded me to turn my attention to romantic fiction. Several years ago, I felt the urge to return to my first love, historical fiction, but decided this time to combine it with one of my favourite forms of entertainment, the detective novel. The result has been a series of books, written under the pseudonym Kate Sedley, featuring Roger the Chapman, a lapsed Benedictine monk (which means he can read and write) now travelling late fifteenth-century England as a pedlar and solving various crimes as he goes. The background is the final years of the Wars of the Roses."

BIOGRAPHICAL/CRITICAL SOURCES:

BOOKS

Twentieth-Century Romance and Historical Novels, 3rd edition, St. James Press, 1994.

PERIODICALS

Booklist, February 15, 1995, Margaret Flanagan, review of *The Holy Innocents,* p. 1063; May 15, 1996, Margaret Flanagan, review of *The Eve of Saint Hyacinth,* p. 1573; January 1, 2001, Margaret Flanagan, review of *The Brothers of Glastonbury,* p. 926.

Kirkus Reviews, April 1, 1996, review of *The Eve of Saint Hyacinth,* p. 491; July 15, 1999, review of *The Wicked Winter,* p. 1090; December 1, 2000, review of *The Brothers of Glastonbury,* p. 1649; August 1, 2001, review of *The Weaver's Inheritance,* p. 1073.

Library Journal, May 1, 1994, p. 142; February 1, 1995, Rex E. Klett, review of *The Holy Innocents,* p. 103; May 1, 1996, Rex E. Klett, review of *The Eve of Saint Hyacinth,* p. 137.

Publishers Weekly, April 4, 1994, p. 60; January 23, 1995, review of *The Holy Innocents,* p. 64; July 26, 1999, review of *The Wicked Winter,* p. 66; December 11, 2000, review of *The Brothers of Glastonbury,* p. 67.

School Library Journal, January, 1995, Penny Stevens, review of *The Weaver's Tale,* p. 146.

OTHER

BookBrowser, http://www.bookbrowser.com/ (October 30, 2000), Harriet Klausner, review of *The Brothers of Glastonbury.*

Crescent Blues Book Views, http://www.crescentblues.com/ (March 6, 2001), Teri Dohmen, review of *The Wicked Winter.*

*   *   *

COLE, K. C. 1946-

PERSONAL: Born August 22, 1946, in Detroit, MI; daughter of Robert (in advertising) and Mary Rose (Dennebaker) Cole; married Peter A. Janssen (a writer and editor), January 20, 1974; children: Peter A., Jr. *Education:* Columbia University, B.A., 1968. *Avocational interests:* Sailing, the flute.

ADDRESSES: Home—Washington, DC. *Agent*—c/o *Los Angeles Times*/Mind Over Matter, 202 West First St., Los Angeles, CA 90012.

CAREER: Merrill Lynch, Pierce, Fenner & Smith, New York, NY, research assistant, 1967; Free Europe, Inc., New York, NY, research assistant, 1968-69; freelance reporter in Czechoslovakia, Hungary, and the Soviet Union, 1969-70; freelance magazine writer, 1970-71; *Saturday Review,* San Francisco, CA, associate editor, 1973-74; *Newsday,* Long Island, NY, feature editor and staff writer, 1974-78; freelance writer, 1978—; *Los Angeles Times,* science writer, 1994—. Writer for Exploratorium (museum), 1974; consultant to Select Panel for the Promotion of Child Health and Robert Wood Johnson Foundation.

MEMBER: National Organization for Women, Journalism and Women Symposium (JAWS), PEN West (director).

AWARDS, HONORS: All-America Award from Educational Press Association of America, 1972; American Institute of Physics Science Writing Award, 1995; Skeptics Society Edward R. Murrow Award for Thoughtful Coverage of Scientific Controversies, 1998; *Los Angeles Times* award for deadline reporting, 1998.

WRITINGS:

Vision: In the Eye of the Beholder, Exploratorium (San Francisco, CA), 1978.

Facets of Light: Colors and Images and Things That Glow in the Dark, Exploratorium (San Francisco, CA), 1980.

What Only a Mother Can Tell You About Having a Baby, Anchor Press, 1980.

Order in the Universe, Exploratorium (San Francisco, CA), 1982.

Between the Lines: Searching for the Space Between Feminism and Femininity and Other Tight Spots, Anchor Press (Garden City, NY), 1982.

Sympathetic Vibrations: Reflections on Physics as a Way of Life, foreword by Frank Oppenheimer, William Morrow (New York, NY), 1985, reissued as *First You Build a Cloud: and Other Reflections on Physics as a Way of Life,* Harcourt Brace (San Diego, CA), 1999.

The Universe and the Teacup: The Mathematics of Truth and Beauty, Harcourt Brace (New York, NY), 1998.

The Hole in the Universe: How Scientists Peered Over the Edge of Emptiness and Found Everything, Harcourt Brace (New York, NY), 2001.

Author of columns in *Newsday, Washington Post, New York Times,* and *Discover.* Contributor to magazines, including *Smithsonian, Omni, Glamour, Seventeen,* and *Cosmopolitan,* and to newspapers.

SIDELIGHTS: A small minority of science journalists, wrote physicist Robert March in the *New York Times Book Review,* manage to convey complex subject matter to their audience in an admirably clear and relevant way. Of these, March said, "K. C. Cole . . . is one of the best." Indeed, Cole has received rave reviews for her books on physics and math. Yet she did not set out to become a science writer. After majoring in political science at Barnard College she began a journalistic career, covering Eastern Europe and the Soviet Union. After joining the staff of the *Saturday Review* in San Francisco in 1972, Cole discovered Frank Oppenheimer's Exploratorium—a new kind of interactive science museum that sparked her enduring fascination with physics. Since then, Cole has devoted her writing to science and to women's issues.

Among Cole's most highly regarded books is *The Universe and the Teacup: The Mathematics of Truth and Beauty.* According to *Los Angeles Times Book Review* contributor Martin Gardner, Cole was surprised to discover she'd written a book about math; her intent had been to survey contemporary trends in science, but she found that mathematics was, in Gardner's words, "the common threat that binds it all together." Different chapters address such subjects as giant numbers, doubling and exponential growth, risk analysis, measurements, "tipping points" where sudden qualitative changes occur, data filtering, and even voting systems. In *Astronomy,* Jake Miller wrote that *The Universe and the Teacup* "is a book about the mathematics underlying everything from astrophysics and quantum mechanics to the development of systems for truly fair democracy and divorce settlement. It's not a book about numbers, though; it's about the words and images we use and the stories we tell to help ourselves understand the numbers that make the universe work." Though Miller went on to say that Cole "glosses over or omits a few key concepts," he concluded that she "helps to teach us that math is more than just a tool to balance our checkbooks. It's the key to understanding the beauty of a rainbow and to discovering our true place in the universe."

Some critics expressed disappointment that *The Universe and the Teacup* does not deal with numbers themselves in a more straightforward manner. Ann Finkbeiner, in the *New York Times Book Review,* observed that "Cole tells us only the results of the math, so we have to take her word for it. Nor is the relation between the math and its results always clear. . . . Maybe the math behind these wonderful ideas is so complex that showing it wouldn't help, but I wish Cole had tried." Yet many reviewers hailed the book as an exceptionally engaging and fascinating work. "Cole's book is a loving paean to the awesome power and beauty of mathematics," wrote Gardner. In *Publishers Weekly,* a contributor concluded that "Cole shows that truth does indeed add up to beauty, and beauty to truth."

In *First You Build a Cloud: And Other Reflections on Physics as a Way of Life,* which was first published as *Sympathetic Vibrations: Reflections on Physics as a Way of Life,* Cole explores the place of physics in modern life and explains basic physical concepts. It prompted *Booklist* reviewer Patricia Monaghan to exclaim, "If ever there were an exemplary science writer, it must be the *Los Angeles Times'* K. C. Cole." Monaghan especially admired Cole's treatment of the aesthetics of physical theory, and her explanations of relativity, quantum physics, optics, and astrophysics.

Cole tackles the subject of the vacuum in *The Hole in the Universe: How Scientists Peered Over the Edge of Emptiness and Found Everything.* She discusses the basics of various fields and forces, including the Higgs field and the Higgs boson, the cosmological constant, string theory, the Big Bang theory, and black holes. Gilbert Taylor in *Booklist* considered the book "an enthusi-

astic, companionable guide to the inner limits of the universe."

Cole once told *CA:* "My writing career has changed gear many times. I began straight out of school with a specialty in Eastern European affairs and wrote first about that; then for several years I was an education specialist; then I stumbled on the Exploratorium in 1972 and have been writing about science ever since, and about health. Lately I've been writing personal columns and essays for newspapers on politics and women's issues."

BIOGRAPHICAL/CRITICAL SOURCES:

PERIODICALS

Astronomy, June, 1998, Jake Miller, review of *The Universe and the Teacup: The Mathematics of Truth and Beauty,* p. 102.

Booklist, December 1, 1997, Gilbert Taylor, review of *The Universe and the Teacup,* p. 594; Patricia Monaghan, review of *First You Build a Cloud: And Other Reflections on Physics as a Way of Life,* p. 1373; December 1, 2000, Gilbert Taylor, review of *The Hole in the Universe: How Scientists Peered Over the Edge of Emptiness and Found Everything,* p. 683.

Boston Globe, January 25, 1998, Robert March, review of *The Universe and the Teacup,* p. F1.

Kirkus Reviews, November 1, 2000, review of *The Hole in the Universe,* p. 1527.

Library Journal, May 1, 1982, review of *Between the Lines,* p. 899; November 1, 1997, Harold D. Shane, review of *The Universe and the Teacup,* p. 110; May 1, 1999, Harold D. Shane, review of *First You Build a Cloud,* p. 104.

Los Angeles Times Book Review, February 1, 1998, Martin Gardner, review of *The Universe and the Teacup,* p. 5.

New York Times Book Review, December 2, 1984, Timothy Ferris, review of *Sympathetic Vibrations: Reflections on Physics as a Way of Life,* p. 76; February 22, 1998, Ann Finkbeiner, review of *The Universe and the Teacup.*

Publishers Weekly, March 26, 1982, review of *Between the Lines,* p. 60; November 17, 1997, review of *The Universe and the Teacup,* p. 48; March 15, 1999, review of *First You Build a Cloud,* p. 43.

Whole Earth, summer, 1998, Michael Stone, review of *The Universe and the Teacup,* p. 110.

OTHER

Santa Fe Institute, http://www.santafe.edu/ (January 12, 2001), "K.C. Cole."*

*   *   *

COLLIER, Christopher 1930-

PERSONAL: Born January 29, 1930, in New York, NY; son of Edmund (a writer) and Katharine (a teacher; maiden name, Brown) Collier; married Virginia Wright (a teacher), August 21, 1954 (marriage ended); married Bonnie Bromberger (a librarian), December 6, 1969; children: (first marriage) Edmund Quincy, Sally McQueen; (second marriage) Christopher Zwissler. *Education:* Clark University, B.A., 1951; Columbia University, M.A., 1955, Ph.D., 1964. *Avocational interests:* Trumpet playing, figure skating, ice hockey, water skiing, reading.

ADDRESSES: Home—876 Orange Center Rd., Orange, CT 06477. *Office*—Department of History, University of Connecticut, Storrs, CT 06269.

CAREER: Julian Curtiss School, Greenwich, CT, teacher, 1955-58; New Canaan High School, New Canaan, CT, teacher of social studies, 1959-61; Columbia University, Teachers College, New York, NY, instructor in history, 1958-59; University of Bridgeport, Bridgeport, CT, instructor, 1961-64, assistant professor, 1964-67, associate professor, 1967-71, professor of history, 1971-78, David S. Day Professor of History, 1978-84, chairman of department, 1978-81; University of Connecticut, Storrs, CT, professor of history, 1984—. New York University, visiting professor, spring, 1974; Yale University, visiting lecturer, 1977 and 1981; Columbia University Seminar on Early American History, chairman, 1978-79. National Endowment for the Humanities Summer Institute for College Teachers, director, 1989. Consultant to numerous public and private organizations, including museums, historical societies, law firms, public utilities, and text, trade, and scholarly publishers. Connecticut State Historian, 1985—; member of various historical committees. *Military service:* U.S. Army, 1952-54; became corporal.

MEMBER: American Historical Association, Organization of American Historians, Connecticut Historical Society, Association for the Study of Connecticut History (co-founder).

AWARDS, HONORS: Pulitzer Prize nomination and Award of Merit from Connecticut League of Historical Societies, both 1971, both for *Roger Sherman's Connecticut: Yankee Politics and the American Revolution; My Brother Sam Is Dead* was named a Newbery Honor Book and a Jane Addams Honor Book, and was a finalist for a National Book Award, all 1975; *Jump Ship to Freedom* and *War Comes to Willy Freeman* were each named a Notable Children's Trade Book in the Field of Social Studies by the National Council for Social Studies and the Children's Book Council, 1981 and 1982, respectively; Award of Merit from Connecticut League of Historical Societies, 1982; Christopher Award, 1987, for *Decision in Philadelphia: The Constitutional Convention of 1787;* Wilbur Cross Award, Connecticut Humanities Council, 1987.

WRITINGS:

HISTORICAL NOVELS FOR CHILDREN; WITH BROTHER, JAMES LINCOLN COLLIER

My Brother Sam Is Dead, Four Winds (Bristol, FL), 1974.
The Bloody Country, Four Winds (Bristol, FL), 1976.
The Winter Hero, Four Winds (Bristol, FL), 1978.
Jump Ship to Freedom, Delacorte (New York, NY), 1981.
War Comes to Willy Freeman, Delacorte (New York, NY), 1983.
Who Is Carrie?, Delacorte (New York, NY), 1984.
The Clock, Delacorte (New York, NY), 1992.
With Every Drop of Blood, Delacorte (New York, NY), 1994.

HISTORICAL WRITINGS FOR JUVENILES; WITH BROTHER, JAMES LINCOLN COLLIER

Building a New Nation, 1789 to 1803, Benchmark Books (New York, NY), 1998.
Clash of Cultures: Prehistory to 1638, Benchmark Books (New York, NY), 1998.
The French and Indian War, 1660 to 1763, Benchmark Books (New York, NY), 1998.
The Paradox of Jamestown, 1585 to 1700, Benchmark Books (New York, NY), 1998.
The Cotton South and the Mexican War, 1835 to 1850, Benchmark Books (New York, NY), 1998.
The Civil War, 1860 to 1866, Benchmark Books (New York, NY), 1998.
Reconstruction and the Rise of Jim Crow, 1864 to 1896, Benchmark Books (New York, NY), 1998.
The American Revolution, 1763 to 1783, Benchmark Books (New York, NY), 1998.

The Road to the Civil War, 1831 to 1861, Benchmark Books (New York, NY), 1998.

Pilgrims and Puritans, 1620 to 1676, Benchmark Books (New York, NY), 1998.

Andrew Jackson's America, 1824 to 1850, Benchmark Books (New York, NY), 1999.

The Rise of Industry: 1860 to 1900, Marshall Cavendish (Tarrytown, NY), 1999.

Creating the Constitution, 1787, Benchmark Books (New York, NY), 1999.

Brother Sam and All That: Historical Context and Literary Analysis of the Novels of James and Christopher Collier, Clearwater Press (Orange, CT), 1999.

The Jeffersonian Republicans, 1800 to 1823: The Louisiana Purchase and the War of 1812, Benchmark Books (New York, NY), 1999.

A Century of Immigration: 1820 to 1924, Marshall Cavendish/Benchmark Books (Tarrytown, NY), 1999.

Indians, Cowboys, and Farmers and the Battle for the Great Plains, 1865 to 1910, Benchmark Books (New York, NY), 2000.

The United States Enters the World Stage: From Alaska through World War I, 1867-1919, Benchmark Books (New York, NY), 2000.

Progressivism, the Great Depression, and the New Deal, 1901 to 1941, Cavendish/Benchmark (Tarrytown, NY), 2000.

The Rise of the Cities, Cavendish/Benchmark (Tarrytown, NY), 2000.

The Changing Face of America, 1945 to 2000, Benchmark Books (New York, NY), 2001.

The United States in the Cold War, Cavendish/Benchmark (Tarrytown, NY), 2001.

World War Two, Cavendish/Benchmark (Tarrytown, NY), 2001.

The Middle Road: American Politics, 1945 to 2000, Benchmark Books (New York, NY), 2001.

OTHER

(Editor) *The Public Records of the State of Connecticut, 1802-03,* Volume 11, State Library of Connecticut, 1967.

Roger Sherman's Connecticut: Yankee Politics and the American Revolution, Wesleyan University Press (Middletown, CT), 1971.

Connecticut in the Continental Congress, Pequot Press, 1973.

Roger Sherman: Puritan Politician, New Haven Colony Historical Society, 1976.

The Pride of Bridgeport: Men and Machines in the Nineteenth Century, Bridgeport Museum of Art, Science, and Industry, 1979.

(With wife, Bonnie Collier) *The Literature of Connecticut History,* Connecticut Humanities Council, 1983.

(With brother, James Lincoln Collier) *Decision in Philadelphia: The Constitutional Convention of 1787,* Random House (New York, NY), 1986.

Contributor to *Lyme Miscellany,* edited by George Willauer, Wesleyan University Press, 1977; and *Long Island Sound: The People and the Environment,* Oceanic Society, 1978. Author of foreword to *Connecticut: A Bibliography of Its History,* edited by Roger Parks, University Press of New England, 1986. Contributor to history and legal journals. Editor, *Monographs in British History and Culture,* 1967-72, and *Connecticut History Newsletter,* 1967-73.

ADAPTATIONS: My Brother Sam Is Dead has been adapted as a record, a cassette, and a filmstrip with cassette.

SIDELIGHTS: A scholar and teacher of American history, Christopher Collier is best known for his historical novels for young people written with his brother, James Lincoln Collier. Most prominent among their works is *My Brother Sam Is Dead,* a 1975 Newbery Honor Book that, like most of their other collaborations, is set in America's Revolutionary War period. The novel has been praised for explaining historical issues to children in a lively and entertaining manner. Christopher's motivation to write captivating books of history is due in part to his distaste for the dry textbooks often used to educate young people. His and James's stories, which blend historical facts and fictional characters, portray ordinary people who undertake heroic struggles. Presenting such complex issues as racism, sexism, and war in eighteenth-century Colonial America, the Colliers, in addition to entertaining readers, suggest that the past can provide a useful guide to understanding the present.

Born in New York City in 1930, Christopher comes from a family of writers. "My father has written scores of short stories about the West, and biographies of Annie Oakley, Kit Carson, and Buffalo Bill for teenagers," the author once commented. Many of Christopher's other family members write, and, he continued, "several ancestors dating back to the 17th century have been writers, too. . . . We all do it because we like to, but we write also as a way of earning a living that makes it possible for us to set our own schedules, take our vacations when we please, and not have to take orders from anyone."

In addition to working part-time as a writer, Christopher follows a distinguished career as historian and educator. Earning his bachelor's degree from Massachusetts' Clark University in 1951 and his master's degree from Columbia University in 1955, he began teaching history and social studies at junior and senior high schools in Connecticut. He later taught history at universities in New England, earned his doctorate degree from Columbia, and, beginning in the late 1960s, penned scholarly books on American history. "I began writing because, along with teaching, that is what historians do," Christopher once noted.

As time went on, Christopher decided that "it would be great to teach history through novels," the author was quoted by Allen Raymond in *Teaching K-8.* He approached brother James—already a successful children's writer—with the idea of working together on books of historical fiction for children. "When I tried to get [James] to do it, he said it wouldn't sell!," Collier was quoted by Raymond. "Eventually, . . . I talked him into it."

The Colliers fashioned a system of producing books wherein Christopher conceptualizes and provides historical details to the work while James creates the characters and story lines. Christopher "starts with something important, something I want to teach about," the historian was quoted by Raymond. James "is the one who makes the stories fun to read, interesting and exciting, sometimes funny. Most of all, . . . he gives the individuals in the books character and personality. That's really essential; nobody will like the books if they don't like the people in them." Christopher summarized his thoughts on working with his brother, as quoted by Hughes Moir in *Language Arts:* "Collaboration between historians and writers is necessary so that [historical fiction] can be read with enjoyment and so that history can be learned without young readers thinking that they're being taught history."

The first product of their partnership was *My Brother Sam Is Dead.* In addition to providing an accurate and entertaining rendering of the Revolutionary War, the Colliers strive to portray in the book an alternative view of history. For example, they present the Revolutionary War—a battle between Great Britain and Colonial America derived from America's desire to free itself of British rule—as an internal war fought between those Americans who were loyal and those who were hostile to British rule. In doing so, the Colliers tell the story of teenaged Tim Meeker and his family, who raise cattle in a small Connecticut town. When the war enters the Meeker's lives, Tim is torn between siding with his brother Sam, who eagerly joins the American forces to fight the British, and his father, who, fearing the safety

of his family and business, staunchly opposes the rebellion. "In the end," noted Moir, "neither Tim nor the reader can make any clear-cut commitment to either side of the conflict."

My Brother Sam Is Dead earned high praise not only for informing readers of the events surrounding the American Revolution but for demonstrating the complexities of war. "Young readers," stated Joyce Alpern in the *Washington Post Book World,* "will probably be most surprised to learn how many average people actually opposed the Revolution." The book depicts the war "not as the good guys versus the bad guys," continued Moir, "but rather as a *civil war* where families and communities were divided in public opinion. It was not an easy war to fight or to make decisions about. . . . The book might be used to help young readers understand aspects of war in general." For these reasons, noted a reviewer in *Horn Book,* "this stirring and authoritative novel earns a place beside our best historical fiction." Reviewing the audio adaptation of *My Brother Sam Is Dead* in *Publishers Weekly,* a contributor noted that the Colliers' book "does a valuable service in bringing history to life."

The Colliers followed *My Brother Sam Is Dead* with several other books set during the Revolutionary War era. *The Bloody Country* tells of the conflict between Pennsylvania and Connecticut for the ownership of the Wyoming Valley, and *The Winter Hero* presents the political and financial hardships brought upon Massachusetts during Shay's Rebellion. Among the Colliers' other books are *Jump Ship to Freedom,* about a fourteen-year-old boy who is a runaway slave, and *War Comes to Willy Freeman,* which depicts a young black girl coping with the loss of her parents. All of these works received high marks from reviewers for their fast-paced plots, faithful renderings of events, and convincing characters. According to Moir, Christopher and James "have collaborated successfully on [some of] the most compelling historical novels for young readers . . . that have been published in recent years."

In their 1994 novel, *With Every Drop of Blood,* the Colliers relate a "gripping story," according to *Horn Book*'s Elizabeth S. Watson, "of two young men caught by a cruel war." Watson felt this narrative was "played out in intensely human terms." During the Civil War, Johnny leaves his Virginia farm in the waning days of battle to earn money as a teamster, transporting food to Confederate troops. When he is captured by Cush, an African American who is serving in the Northern army, Johnny must come to terms with his own upbringing and his received knowledge of African Americans.

Slowly the two young men form an uneasy friendship in a book that paints a "strong, affecting picture of the Civil War era," according to a reviewer for *Publishers Weekly.*

While Christopher attributes their books' entertainment value to James's writing skills, the historian takes pride in his meticulous efforts to make the books factually correct. "My books for teen-agers are just as thoroughly researched as are my scholarly works," he once said. "If we say it snowed three inches on January 4, 1787 in Springfield, Massachusetts, then you can be sure that it really did. We even have dialogue in our historical novels that actually took place—words that I found in letters, diaries, eye-witness accounts, and other sources. Every episode that is found in our books actually happened exactly as we describe it; all we make up are the members of the central family, and all their experiences actually did happen to someone living at their time."

In addition to their fiction offerings for young readers, the Collier brothers have written over two dozen non-fiction works in the "Drama of American History" series, tracing American history from the settling of the America and the Revolution through the Civil War, the two World Wars of the twentieth century, the Cold War, and to the coming of the new millennium. In so doing, the Colliers have examined a large array of historical topics, including the French and Indian War, the settling of Jamestown, the framing of the Constitution, the importance of cotton in the Southern economy, the rise of industry in America, the situation of Native Americans, immigration to America, and political movements such as Progressivism.

Reviewing *The American Revolution, 1763-1783,* Carolyn Phelan noted in *Booklist* that the series as a whole is typified by "a scholarly approach, a clear writing style, and a great deal of knowledge." Phelan went on to comment that the real strength of the series "is its writers' clear perspective on what matters and what does not." Phelan concluded, "Few nonfiction series books for young people could be read one after the other with more enjoyment and enlightenment than these." In a review of *Andrew Jackson's America, 1824-1850, Booklist*'s Phelan again praised the series, noting that it was not only "useful for school reports," but also "surprisingly readable" and "engaging." Coop Renner, writing in *School Library Journal,* felt that the Colliers' *A Century of Immigration, 1820-1924* was an example of "interpretational history." Renner further commented, "By focusing on broad themes, the Colliers are able to show cause and effect over several dec-

ades and to make the sweep of time 'bite-sized' and intelligible."

Deciphering the value in the way the Colliers teach history to young people, Moir wrote: "The historical moods of James and Christopher Collier are more than just a good 'read.' They delve into our history with an eye for truth—truth that may result in contradiction and uncertainties. The stories are at the same time readable and challenging to our conception of the reality of human events and the need for faith in human values. . . . [The] combined talents [of the Colliers] offer young readers not only a story worth reading, but an opportunity, through their books, to deal with fundamental human issues in a way not possible in most literature." Christopher, as quoted by Raymond, succinctly summarized his and his brother's reasons for writing historical fiction: "Knowledge of how we got here will help us understand where we are."

BIOGRAPHICAL/CRITICAL SOURCES:

BOOKS

Authors and Artists for Young Adults, Volume 13, Gale (Detroit, MI), 1994.
Beacham's Guide to Literature for Young Adults, Volume 2, Beacham Publishing (Osprey, FL), 1990, pp. 916-922.
Contemporary Literary Criticism, Volume 30, Gale (Detroit, MI), 1984, p. 70.

PERIODICALS

Booklist, October 15, 1974, p. 241; June 1, 1976, p. 1403; December 1, 1978, p. 615; October 1, 1981, p. 233; April 1, 1983, p. 1030; April, 1, 1984, p. 1113; February 1, 1987, p. 848; April 15, 1987, p. 1300; March 1, 1990, p. 1355; December 15, 1992, p. 757; July, 1994, p. 1935; April 15, 1998, Carolyn Phelan, review of *The American Revolution, 1763-1783,* p. 1442; February 15, 1999, Carolyn Phelan, review of *Andrew Jackson's America, 1824-1850,* p. 1061; February 15, 2000, p. 1106; March 15, 2001, p. 1396.
Books for Young Readers, spring, 1984.
Bulletin of the Center for Children's Books, December, 1976; February, 1979; March, 1983; May, 1984.
English Journal, September, 1992, p. 95.
Horn Book, April, 1975, review of *My Brother Sam Is Dead,* p. 152; April, 1976, p. 132; June, 1976, p. 293; February, 1979, p. 67; February, 1982, p. 50; June, 1983, p. 308; March-April, 1992, p. 203; Jan-

uary-February, 1995, Elizabeth S. Watson, review of *With Every Drop of Blood,* pp. 57-58.

Language Arts, March, 1978, Hughes Moir, "Profile: James and Christopher Collier—More Than Just a Good Read," p. 373.

New Republic, June 29, 1987, p. 28.

New York Times Book Review, November 3, 1974, p. 26; May 2, 1976, p. 26; February 14, 1982, p. 28; May 8, 1983, p. 37; March 2, 1986, p. 19.

Publishers Weekly, November 25, 1974, p. 45; May 10, 1976, p. 84; November 27, 1978, p. 60; November 13, 1981, p. 88; April 1, 1983, p. 60; May 25, 1984, p. 59; July 5, 1985, p. 68; February 27, 1987, p. 166; January 1, 1992, p. 56; July 11, 1994, review of *With Every Drop of Blood,* p. 79; June 17, 1996, review of *My Brother Sam Is Dead,* p. 33.

School Library Journal, May, 1976, p. 67; September, 1978, p. 132; October, 1981, p. 140; May, 1982, p. 44; April, 1983, p. 121; May, 1984, p. 78; February, 1992, p. 107; February, 1993, p. 58; April, 1999, p. 145; March, 2000, Coop Renner, review of *A Century of Immigration, 1820-1924,* p. 249; July, 2001, p. 120.

Teaching K-8, January, 1988, Allen Raymond, "Jamie and Kit Collier: The Writer and The Historian," p. 35.

Washington Post Book World, January 12, 1975, Joyce Alpern, "Not a Bad Tory," p. 4.*

*   *   *

COLLIER, James Lincoln   1928-
(Charles Williams)

PERSONAL: Born June 27, 1928, in New York, NY; son of Edmund and Katharine (Brown) Collier; married Carol Burrows, September 2, 1952 (divorced); married Ida Karen Potash, July 22, 1983; children: (first marriage) Geoffrey Lincoln, Andrew Kemp. *Education:* Hamilton College, A.B., 1950. *Avocational interests:* "I have been deeply involved in jazz from youth and continue to work as a jazz musician regularly."

ADDRESSES: Home—71 Barrow St., New York, NY 10014.

CAREER: Writer. Magazine editor, 1952-58; worked a number of odd jobs, including playing trombone in a jazz band in New York City. *Military service:* U.S. Army, 1950-51; became private.

AWARDS, HONORS: Child's Study Association Book Award, 1971, for *Rock Star; My Brother Sam Is Dead* was named a Newbery Honor Book and a Jane Addams Honor Book, and was a finalist for a National Book Award, all 1975; London *Observer* Book of the Year award and American Book Award nomination, both for *The Making of Jazz: A Comprehensive History; Jump Ship to Freedom* and *War Comes to Willy Freeman* were each named a Notable Children's Trade Book in the Field of Social Studies by the National Council for Social Studies and the Children's Book Council, 1981 and 1982, respectively; National Foundation for the Humanities fellowship, 1982; Institute for Studies in American Music fellowship, 1985; Christopher Award, 1987, for *Decision in Philadelphia: The Constitutional Convention of 1787;* Phoenix Award, 1994.

WRITINGS:

FICTION FOR CHILDREN

The Teddy Bear Habit; or, How I Became a Winner, illustrations by Lee Lorenz, Norton (New York, NY), 1967.

Rock Star, Four Winds (Bristol, FL), 1970.

Why Does Everybody Think I'm Nutty?, Grosset (New York, NY), 1971.

It's Murder at St. Basket's, Grosset (New York, NY), 1972.

Rich and Famous: The Further Adventures of George Stable, Four Winds (Bristol, FL), 1975.

Give Dad My Best, Four Winds (Bristol, FL), 1976.

Planet Out of the Past, Macmillan (New York, NY), 1983.

When the Stars Begin to Fall, Delacorte (New York, NY), 1986.

Outside Looking In, Macmillan (New York, NY), 1987.

The Winchesters, Macmillan (New York, NY), 1988.

My Crooked Family, Simon & Schuster (New York, NY), 1991.

The Jazz Kid, Puffin (New York, NY), 1996.

Chipper, Marshall Cavendish/Benchmark Books (New York, NY), 2001.

NONFICTION FOR CHILDREN

Battleground: The United States Army in World War II, Norton (New York, NY), 1965.

A Visit to the Fire House, photographs by Yale Joel, Norton (New York, NY), 1967.

Which Musical Instrument Shall I Play?, photographs by Joel, Norton (New York, NY), 1969.

Danny Goes to the Hospital, photographs by Joel, Norton (New York, NY), 1970.

Practical Music Theory: How Music Is Put Together from Bach to Rock, Norton (New York, NY), 1970.

The Hard Life of the Teenager, Four Winds (Bristol, FL), 1972.

Inside Jazz, Four Winds (Bristol, FL), 1973.

Jug Bands and Hand-Made Music, Grosset (New York, NY), 1973.

The Making of Man: The Story of Our Ancient Ancestors, Four Winds (Bristol, FL), 1974.

Making Music for Money, F. Watts (New York, NY), 1976.

CB, F. Watts (New York, NY), 1977.

The Great Jazz Artists, illustrations by Robert Andrew Parker, Four Winds (Bristol, FL), 1977.

Louis Armstrong: An American Success Story, Macmillan (New York, NY), 1985.

Duke Ellington, Macmillan (New York, NY), 1991.

Jazz: An American Saga, Holt (New York, NY), 1997.

The Corn Raid: A Story of the Jamestown Settlement, Jamestown Publishers (Lincolnwood, IL), 2000.

The Worst of Times: A Story of the Great Depression, Jamestown Publishers (Lincolnwood, IL), 2000.

HISTORICAL NOVELS FOR CHILDREN; WITH BROTHER, CHRISTOPHER COLLIER

My Brother Sam Is Dead, Four Winds (Bristol, FL), 1974.

The Bloody Country, Four Winds (Bristol, FL), 1976.

The Winter Hero, Four Winds (Bristol, FL), 1978.

Jump Ship to Freedom, Delacorte (New York, NY), 1981.

War Comes to Willy Freeman, Delacorte (New York, NY), 1983.

Who Is Carrie?, Delacorte (New York, NY), 1984.

The Clock, Delacorte (New York, NY), 1991.

With Every Drop of Blood, Delacorte (New York, NY), 1994.

Clash of Cultures: Prehistory to 1638, Benchmark Books (New York, NY), 1998.

The Paradox of Jamestown, 1585 to 1700, Benchmark Books (New York, NY), 1998.

The French and Indian War, 1660 to 1763, Benchmark Books (New York, NY), 1998.

The American Revolution, 1763 to 1783, Benchmark Books (New York, NY), 1998.

Pilgrims and Puritans, 1620 to 1676, Benchmark Books (New York, NY), 1998.

Creating the Constitution, 1787, Benchmark Books (New York, NY), 1998.

Building a New Nation, 1789 to 1803, Benchmark Books (New York, NY), 1998.

Andrew Jackson's America, 1821 to 1850, Benchmark Books (New York, NY), 1998.

The Cotton South and the Mexican War, 1835 to 1850, Benchmark Books (New York, NY), 1998.

The Jeffersonian Republicans, 1800 to 1820, Benchmark Books (New York, NY), 1998.

The Civil War, 1860 to 1866, Benchmark Books (New York, NY), 1998.

The Road to the Civil War, 1831 to 1861, Benchmark Books (New York, NY), 1998.

Reconstruction and the Rise of Jim Crow, Benchmark Books (New York, NY), 1998.

The Rise of Industry: 1860 to 1900, Marshall Cavendish (New York, NY), 1999.

Creating the Constitution, 1787, Benchmark Books (New York, NY), 1999.

Brother Sam and All That: Historical Context and Literary Analysis of the Novels of James and Christopher Collier, Clearwater Press (Orange, CT), 1999.

The Jeffersonian Republicans, 1800 to 1823: The Louisiana Purchase and the War of 1812, Benchmark Books (New York, NY), 1999.

A Century of Immigration: 1820 to 1924, Marshall Cavendish/Benchmark Books (Tarrytown, NY), 1999.

Indians, Cowboys, and Farmers and the Battle for the Great Plains, 1865 to 1910, Benchmark Books (New York, NY), 2000.

The United States Enters the World Stage: From Alaska through World War I, 1867 to 1919, Benchmark Books (New York, NY), 2000.

Progressivism, the Great Depression, and the New Deal, 1901 to 1941, Benchmark/Cavendish (Tarrytown, NY), 2000.

The Rise of the Cities, Cavendish/Benchmark (Tarrytown, NY), 2000.

The Changing Face of America, 1945 to 2000, Benchmark Books (New York, NY), 2001.

The United States in the Cold War, Benchmark/Cavendish (Tarrytown, NY), 2001.

World War Two, Benchmark Books (New York, NY), 2001.

The Middle Road: American Politics, 1945 to 2000, Benchmark Books (New York, NY), 2001.

FOR ADULTS

Cheers (novel), Avon (New York, NY), 1960.

Somebody up There Hates Me (novel), Macfadden, 1962.

The Hypocritical American: An Essay on Sex Attitudes in America, Bobbs-Merrill, 1964.

(With others) *Sex Education U.S.A.: A Community Approach,* Sex Information and Education Council of the United States, 1968.

The Making of Jazz: A Comprehensive History, Houghton (Boston, MA), 1978.

Louis Armstrong: An American Genius, Oxford University Press (New York, NY), 1983, published as

Louis Armstrong: A Biography, M. Joseph (London, England), 1984.

(With brother, Christopher Collier) *Decision in Philadelphia: The Constitutional Convention of 1787,* Random House (New York, NY), 1986.

Duke Ellington, Oxford University Press (New York, NY), 1987.

Benny Goodman and the Swing Era, Oxford University Press (New York, NY), 1989.

The Rise of Selfishness in the United States, Oxford University Press (New York, NY), 1991.

Jazz: The American Theme Song, Oxford University Press (New York, NY), 1993.

Also author, under pseudonym Charles Williams, of *Fires of Youth.* Contributor of more than six hundred articles to periodicals, including *Reader's Digest, New York Times Magazine, Village Voice,* and *Esquire.*

ADAPTATIONS: *My Brother Sam Is Dead* has been adapted as a record, a cassette, and a filmstrip with cassette.

SIDELIGHTS: James Lincoln Collier is a versatile and prolific writer for both adults and children. Notable among his works for young people are volumes of nonfiction informed by his background in music, fictional works portraying young male narrators, and historical novels written with his brother, historian Christopher Collier. While his nonfiction has been hailed as educational and well written, Collier's novels are often lauded for their exciting, fast-paced plots and their depiction of characters who grapple with moral dilemmas and unpleasant parental figures.

Collier was born in 1928 into a family of writers. After serving in the army from 1950 to 1951, Collier moved to New York City and decided to earn a living from writing. He did not find instant success in the endeavor and consequently supported himself as a magazine editor. Six years passed and Collier had yet to make a sale from his writing. Finally, he realized modest prosperity by selling articles to magazines and some adult books to publishers. Collier then decided to try his hand at writing books for children, "a choice," according to Hughes Moir in *Language Arts,* "he has never regretted."

His first book for a young audience is *Battleground: The United States Army in World War II,* a work explaining important military maneuvers conducted in Europe during the Second World War. Collier went on to produce more instructional works, including *Danny Goes to the Hospital,* which outlines a typical visit to the hospital, and *The Hard Life of the Teenager,* a book providing advice to adolescents battling such common elements as acne, raging emotions, and parental authority.

Among Collier's most noted books of nonfiction for young people are those concerning music. The first on this topic is *Which Musical Instrument Shall I Play?* Collier later produced *Practical Music Theory: How Music Is Put Together from Bach to Rock; School Library Journal* reviewer Loretta B. Jones deemed the volume a "lucid, step-by-step exposition of musical theory for dedicated music students." Collier also earned praise for *Inside Jazz,* a 1973 book that Loraine Alterman in the *New York Times Book Review* called "as good a verbal explanation as I've seen about jazz and its distinguishing features." The author's other books on music include *The Great Jazz Artists, Louis Armstrong: An American Success Story,* and *Duke Ellington.*

Collier also has fared well writing novels for young audiences. His first effort, *The Teddy Bear Habit; or, How I Became a Winner,* details how teenager George Stable's obsession with his teddy bear leads to his involvement in a jewel theft. The book's suspenseful plot and comic scenes of adventure prompted Jerome Beatty, Jr., in the *New York Times Book Review* to call *The Teddy Bear Habit* "a heck of an exciting story." The novel's sequel, *Rich and Famous: The Further Adventures of George Stable,* also earned high marks from reviewers. "George is . . . consistently perceptive, and often humorous, [in his] observations of people and situations," wrote Donald A. Colberg in *School Library Journal.*

Collier has written a number of novels concerning young people struggling to overcome adversity, an element often presenting itself in the form of an unsavory parent. Among these books are *Give Dad My Best,* about a boy forced to care for his family because his father is a down-and-out musician, and *Rock Star,* which details Tim Anderson's battle to become a successful rock-and-roll guitarist despite his father's disapproval. In *Outside Looking In* Collier tells the story of Fergy, a fourteen-year-old boy who runs away after his unscrupulous father steals an expensive motor home. Collier's 1988 offering, *The Winchesters,* presents a boy caught in the middle of a dispute between his wealthy relatives and a town in economic peril. In *My Crooked Family,* set in 1910, Collier depicts a young boy's efforts to triumph over poverty and negligent parents. *The Jazz Kid* tells the story of Paulie Horvath and how his love of jazz transforms his life from a dead-end blue collar existence to the fulfillment of a career in music.

And in *The Corn Raid: A Story of the Jamestown Settlement,* Collier offers up the story of another youth's efforts to overcome the hand that life has dealt out. Twelve-year-old Richard is an indentured servant living in fear of the master who continually beats him. Discovering that the English are planning a raid on the local Indians, he warns them, only to feel guilty enough later to tell his master what he has done. When the master subsequently begins to beat Richard, the boy finally stands up to the man and begins to plan for the day when he will be free. Reviewing this title in *School Library Journal,* Shawn Brommer felt that "history takes precedence over story."

Further proving his versatility in children's literature, Collier has written highly esteemed books of historical fiction with his brother Christopher, a distinguished historian. Most popular among their novels set in the Revolutionary War era is *My Brother Sam Is Dead;* other books include *The Winter Hero, War Comes to Willy Freeman,* and *Who Is Carrie?* The success of these books rests, according to Moir, on both Christopher's ability to provide the story with historically accurate data and James's talent for fashioning "out of raw events a story that is fast-moving and highly readable." In the 1992 novel, *The Clock,* set in Connecticut in the early nineteenth century, a fifteen-year-old girl named Annie Steele is sent by her father to work in a wool mill in order to pay off his chronic debts. The story involves Annie's dealings with the villainous mill boss, and it touches on historical issues such as patriarchal power and the country's gradual change from agrarian to industrial modes of production. Reviewing the title in *Publishers Weekly,* a contributor concluded that "the novel . . . succeeds not only as historical fiction, but also as a riveting story of the tragic romance and hard-won victory of one teenaged girl." A further fiction title co-authored with Christopher Collier is *With Every Drop of Blood,* a Civil War tale about a Southern youth captured by Northern forces who comes to respect and like the black Union soldier guarding him. *Booklist*'s Hazel Rochman noted that the theme of "my enemy, my friend is at the core of this docu-novel of the Civil War." Rochman further noted that it is "the large canvas that will draw readers to the story . . . ."

In addition to their fiction offerings for young readers, the Collier brothers have written over two dozen nonfiction works in the "Drama of American History" series, tracing American history from the settling of the Americas and the Revolution through the Civil War, the two World Wars of the twentieth century, the Cold War, and to the coming of the new millennium. In so doing, the Colliers have examined a large array of historical topics, including the French and Indian War, the settling of Jamestown, the framing of the Constitution, the importance of cotton in the Southern economy, the rise of industry in America, the situation of Native Americans, immigration to America, and political movements such as Progressivism.

Reviewing one of the first titles in the series, *Building a New Nation, 1789-1801,* in *Booklist,* Carolyn Phelan called the entire series "well-written." Phelan also dubbed the series "excellent," in her *Booklist* review of *The Rise of Industry, 1860-1900.* Phelan added that the books also have "the visual appeal of colorful graphics and good layout." Writing in *School Library Journal,* Patricia Ann Owens found *Indians, Cowboys, and Farmers and the Battle for the Great Plains, 1865-1910* to be "American history at its most basic." Owens, writing again in *School Library Journal,* thought *The Rise of the Cities, 1820-1920* was a book "that focuses on the broad themes of history rather than facts and dates." *Booklist*'s Phelan found that same book to be part of a "noteworthy series . . . . [H]ighly readable and informative."

Although much of Collier's writing is devoted to adult works, he professes a deep appreciation of children's literature and prefers it to writing adult books. Expressing his fondness for the craft, Collier was quoted by Moir: "The 'real' books written today are written for children. . . . The author [of children's books] can deliver more than just a good read, but also a view of the world."

BIOGRAPHICAL/CRITICAL SOURCES:

BOOKS

Authors and Artists for Young Adults, Volume 13, Gale (Detroit, MI), 1994.
Beacham's Guide to Literature for Young Adults, Volume 2, Beacham Publishing (Osprey, FL).
Children's Literature Review, Volume 3, Gale (Detroit, MI), 1978.
Contemporary Literary Criticism, Volume 30, Gale (Detroit, MI).
Fifth Book of Junior Authors and Illustrators, edited by Sally Holmes Holtze, H. W. Wilson (New York, NY), 1983.

PERIODICALS

Booklist, February 15, 1966, p. 582; June 1, 1976, p. 1403; February 1, 1992, p. 1026; July, 1994, Hazel Rochman, review of *With Every Drop of Blood,* pp.

1935-1936; April 15, 1998, p. 1442; February 15, 1999, Carolyn Phelan, review of *Building a New Nation, 1789-1801,* p. 1061; February 15, 2000, Carolyn Phelan, review of *The Rise of Industry, 1860-1900,* p. 1106; March 15, 2001, Carolyn Phelan, review of *The Rise of the Cities, 1820-1920,* p. 1396.

English Journal, September, 1992, p. 95.

Horn Book, April, 1975, p. 152; February, 1976, p. 48; March-April, 1992, p. 203; January-February, 1995, pp. 57-58.

Language Arts, March, 1978, Hughes Moir, "Profile: James and Christopher Collier—More Than Just a Good Read," p. 373.

New York Times Book Review, March 12, 1967, Jerome Beatty, Jr., review of *The Teddy Bear Habit; or, How I Became a Winner,* p. 28; October 25, 1970, p. 38; February 25, 1973, p. 10; December 30, 1973, Loraine Alterman, review of *Inside Jazz,* p. 10; November 3, 1974, p. 26; May 2, 1976, p. 26; February 13, 1977, p. 25; February 14, 1982, p. 28; May 8, 1983, p. 37; March 2, 1986, p. 19.

Publishers Weekly, March 8, 1971, p. 71; October 16, 1972, p. 49; November 7, 1977, p. 83; May 25, 1984, p. 59; July 5, 1985, p. 67; November 28, 1986, p. 77; March 13, 1987, p. 86; October 28, 1988, p. 82; July 25, 1991, p. 55; January 1, 1992, review of *The Clock,* p. 56; July 11, 1994, p. 79; June 17, 1996, p. 33.

School Library Journal, December, 1970, Loretta B. Jones, review of *Practical Music Theory: How Music Is Put Together from Bach to Rock,* p. 58; November, 1975, Donald A. Colberg, review of *Rich and Famous: The Further Adventures of George Stable,* p. 72; March, 1976, p. 111; December, 1976, p. 53; September, 1977, p. 142; November, 1977, p. 68; September, 1978, p. 132; January, 1984, p. 73; October, 1985, p. 169; November, 1986, p. 98; January, 1989, p. 92; October, 1991, p. 142; August, 1994, p. 168; April, 1999, p. 145; April, 2000, Shawn Brommer, review of *The Corn Raid: A Story of the Jamestown Settlement,* p. 130; July, 2001, Patricia Ann Owens, review of *Indians, Cowboys, and Farmers and the Battle for the Great Plains, 1865-1910,* p. 120.

Teaching K-8, January, 1988, p. 35.*

*   *   *

COMFORT, Montgomery
   See CAMPBELL, (John) Ramsey

CONNOR, Joan   1954-

PERSONAL: Born January 21, 1954, in Holyoke, MA; daughter of Walker (a professor) and Mary (a teacher) Connor; married Nils Wessell (marriage ended); children: Kerry. *Ethnicity:* "Caucasian." *Education:* Mount Holyoke College, B.A. (cum laude), 1976; Middlebury College, M.A., 1984; Vermont College, M.F.A., 1995. *Politics:* Independent. *Avocational interests:* Cooking, reading, skiing, dancing.

ADDRESSES: Home—328 Carroll Rd., Athens, OH 45701. *Office*—Department of English, 209A Ellis Hall, Ohio University, Athens, OH 45701. *E-mail*—connor@oak.cats.ohiou.edu.

CAREER: Vermont Department of Public Health, representative of Women's Health Outreach Program, 1977-79; English teacher at schools in Woodstock, VT, 1979 and 1980, and Philadelphia, PA, 1980-83; English teacher at Northfield-Mt. Hermon School, East Northfield, MA, 1980-81; Ohio University, Athens, OH, visiting professor, 1995-96, associate professor of English, 1996—. Vermont League of Writers, leader of fiction-writing workshop, 1994-95; judge of fiction contests; gives readings from her works.

MEMBER: Associated Writing Programs, Young Writers Institute.

AWARDS, HONORS: Fellow at Vermont Studio Colony, 1990, MacDowell Colony, 1992, Virginia Center for the Creative Arts, 1993, and Yaddo Colony, 1993; Ohio Arts Fellowship recipient; Ohio Writer, First Place, fiction and nonfiction.

WRITINGS:

Here on Old Route 7, University of Missouri Press (Columbia, MO), 1997.
We Who Live Apart, University of Missouri Press (Columbia, MO), 2000.

Work represented in anthologies, including *Loss of the Ground-Note: Women Writing about the Deaths of Their Mothers,* edited by Helen Vozenilek, Clothespin Fever Press, 1992; *Women and Transitions Anthology,* 1998; *Sex and Writing Anthology,* 1998; and *Millenium Watch Anthology.* Contributor of articles, poems, and reviews to magazines, including *Kestrel, New Letters, 13th Moon, Ohio Writer, New Millennium, Rio Grande Review, Kenyon Review, TriQuarterly, Connecticut Review, Gettysburg Review, Pleiades, North Dakota Quarterly, Antietam Review, Ohio Review, North*

American Review, Southern Review, North Atlantic Review, Mississippi Valley Review, Oxford Magazine, Blueline, Shenandoah, Worcester Review, and *Journal of Irish Literature.* Assistant fiction editor, *Chelsea,* 1994-96.

SIDELIGHTS: Her native New England serves as an inspiration for much of Joan Connor's fiction. In her first collection of interconnected short stories, *Here on Old Route 7,* she explores the tensions between old-timers and newcomers along one stretch of rural highway. According to its publisher, the book is notable for its strong sense of individual and communal identity; as Kelly Cherry puts it in a quote on the publisher's Web site, "rich syntax, a defiant wit, and the vividness of the characters engage us, hold us, make us not want to leave."

Most of the thirteen stories in Connor's second collection, *We Who Live Apart,* are also set in New England; many focus on the plight of lonely and isolated women. Though a *Publishers Weekly* reviewer found the book "disjointed and lacking in cohesion," the reviewer appreciated Connor's narrative skill with various points of view and styles, as well as the resilience with which her characters face their futures. A contributor to *Kirkus Reviews* found Connor's writing "polished," and deemed the collection "an accomplished work."

Connor once told *CA:* "I write to make discoveries. To some extent, the New England landscape remains a significant source for my fiction. Usually some quirk or detail of a historical character catches my fancy and imagination."

BIOGRAPHICAL/CRITICAL SOURCES:

PERIODICALS

Kirkus Reviews, October 15, 2000, review of *We Who Live Apart,* p. 1446.
Publishers Weekly, October 2, 2000, review of *We Who Live Apart,* p. 58.

OTHER

University of Missouri Press, http://www.system.missouri.edu/upress/ (July 6, 2001), reviews of *Here on Old Route 7* and *We Who Live Apart.*

COX, William Trevor 1928-
(William Trevor)

PERSONAL: Born May 24, 1928, in Mitchelstown, County Cork, Ireland; son of James William (a bank official) and Gertrude (Davison) Cox; married Jane Ryan, August 26, 1952; children: Patrick, Dominic. *Education:* Attended St. Columba's College, Dublin, Ireland, 1941-46; Trinity College, Dublin, B.A., 1950. *Politics:* Liberal.

ADDRESSES: Office—c/o Sterling Lord Literistic Ltd., 1 Madison Ave, New York, NY 10010; c/o Peters, Fraser & Dunlop Group, 503-504 The Chambers, Chelsea Harbour, Lots Road, London SW10 0FX, England.

CAREER: Teacher in County Armagh, Northern Ireland, 1952-53; art teacher at prep school near Rugby, England, 1953-55, and in Somerset, England, 1956-59; while teaching, worked as a church sculptor; advertising copywriter for Notley's, London, England, 1960-65; writer, 1965—. Has had one-man exhibitions of his art work in Dublin, Ireland, and Bath, England.

MEMBER: Irish Academy of Letters.

AWARDS, HONORS: Winner of Irish section, "Unknown Political Prisoner" sculpture competition, 1953; second prize, *Transatlantic Review* short story competition, 1964; Hawthornden Prize, Royal Society of Literature, 1965, for *The Old Boys;* Society of Authors' traveling scholarship, 1972; Benson Medal, Royal Society of Literature, 1975, for *Angels at the Ritz, and Other Stories;* Allied Irish Bank Prize for literature, 1976; Heinemann Award for fiction, 1976; Whitbread Prize, 1978, for *The Children of Dynmouth,* and 1983, for *Fools of Fortune;* Commander, Order of the British Empire, 1979; Irish Community Prize, 1979; Giles Cooper Award for radio play, 1980, for *Beyond the Pale,* and 1982, for *Autumn Sunshine;* Jacob Award for television play, 1983; D.Litt., University of Exeter, 1984, Trinity College, Dublin, 1986, University of Belfast, 1989, and National University of Ireland, Cork, 1990; *Sunday Express* Book of the Year Award, and Whitbread Book of the Year award, Whitbread Breweries, both 1994, both for *Felicia's Journey;* Lannan Literary Award for Fiction, 1996; *Irish Times* Literary Award for Fiction, 2001, for *The Hill Bachelors.*

WRITINGS:

NOVELS; UNDER NAME WILLIAM TREVOR

A Standard of Behavior, Hutchinson (London, England), 1958.

The Old Boys (also see below), Viking (New York, NY), 1964.

The Boarding-House, Viking (New York, NY), 1965.

The Love Department, Bodley Head (London, England), 1966, Viking (New York, NY), 1967.

Mrs. Eckdorf in O'Neill's Hotel, Bodley Head (London, England), 1969, Viking (New York, NY), 1970.

Miss Gomez and the Brethren, Bodley Head (London, England), 1971.

Elizabeth Alone, Bodley Head (London, England), 1973, Viking (New York, NY), 1974.

The Children of Dynmouth, Bodley Head (London, England), 1976, Viking (New York, NY), 1977.

Other People's Worlds, Bodley Head (London, England), 1980, Viking (New York, NY), 1981.

Fools of Fortune, Viking (New York, NY), 1983.

Nights at the Alexandra, Harper (New York, NY), 1987.

The Silence in the Garden, Viking (New York, NY), 1988.

Two Lives (contains the novels *Reading Turgenev* and *My House in Umbria*), Viking (New York, NY), 1991.

Felicia's Journey, Viking (New York, NY), 1994.

Juliet's Story, Simon & Schuster (New York, NY), 1994.

After Rain, Viking (New York, NY), 1996.

The Silence in the Garden, Penguin (New York, NY), 1996.

Death in Summer, Viking (New York, NY), 1998.

STORIES; UNDER NAME WILLIAM TREVOR

The Day We Got Drunk on Cake, and Other Stories, Bodley Head (London, England), 1967, Viking (New York, NY), 1968.

The Ballroom of Romance, and Other Stories (includes "The Mark-2 Wife," "The Grass Widows," and "O Fat White Woman"; also see below), Viking (New York, NY), 1972.

Angels at the Ritz, and Other Stories, Bodley Head (London, England), 1975, Viking (New York, NY), 1976.

Lovers of Their Time, and Other Stories (includes "Matilda's England" and "Attracta"), Viking (New York, NY), 1978.

The Distant Past, and Other Stories, Poolbeg Press, 1979.

Beyond the Pale, and Other Stories, Bodley Head (London, England), 1981, Viking (New York, NY), 1982.

The Stories of William Trevor (includes "The Penthouse Apartment," "Broken Homes," "A Compli-

cated Nature," and "In at the Birth"), Penguin (England), 1983.

The News from Ireland, and Other Stories, Viking (New York, NY), 1986.

Family Sins, and Other Stories (includes "Kathleen's Field," "Events at Drimaghleen," "Coffee with Oliver," and "The Third Party"), Viking (New York, NY), 1989.

William Trevor: Collected Stories, Viking (New York, NY), 1992.

Outside Ireland: Selected Stories, Penguin (New York, NY), 1995.

Cocktails at Doney's and Other Stories, Bloomsbury, 1996.

Ireland: Selected Stories, Penguin (New York, NY), 1998.

The Hill Bachelors, Viking (New York, NY), 2000.

Nights at the Alexandra, Random House (New York, NY), 2001.

Also author of other stories, including "The Wedding in the Garden," "Mulvihill's Memorial," "Miss Smith," "The Bedroom Eyes of Mrs. Vansittart," and "The Time of Year." Stories anthologized in numerous collections, including *The Bedside Guardian,* edited by W. L. Webb, Collins, 1969, *The Bodley Head Book of Longer Short Stories,* edited by James Michie, Bodley Head (London, England), 1974, *Best for Winter,* edited by A. D. Maclean, Macmillan, 1979, *The Bodley Head Book of Irish Short Stories,* edited by Marcus, Bodley Head (London, England), 1980, and *Seven Deadly Sins,* Severn House, 1983.

PLAYS; UNDER NAME WILLIAM TREVOR

The Elephant's Foot, produced in Nottingham, England, 1966.

The Girl, S. French (London, England), 1968.

The Old Boys (adapted from his novel; produced in the West End, 1971), Davis-Poynter, 1971.

Going Home (one-act; produced in London at King's Head Islington, February 29, 1972), S. French (London, England), 1972.

A Night with Mrs. da Tanka (one-act; produced in London, 1972), S. French (London, England), 1972.

A Perfect Relationship (one-act), produced in London, 1973.

The 57th Saturday (one-act), produced in London, 1973.

Marriages (one-act; produced in London, 1973), S. French (London, England), 1974.

Beyond the Pale (radio play), broadcast in England, 1980, televised, 1989.

Scenes from an Album, produced in Dublin at the Abbey Theatre, 1981.

Also author of television and radio plays for British Broadcasting Corp. (BBC) and ITV, including *The Mark-2 Wife, O Fat White Woman, The Grass Widows, The General's Day, Love Affair, Last Wishes, Matilda's England, Secret Orchards, Autumn Sunshine, The Penthouse Apartment, Travellers,* and *Events at Drimaghleen.*

OTHER; UNDER NAME WILLIAM TREVOR

Old School Ties (memoir), Lemon Tree Press (London, England), 1976.
A Writer's Ireland: Landscape in Literature (nonfiction), Viking (New York, NY), 1984.
(Editor) *The Oxford Book of Irish Short Stories,* Oxford University Press (Oxford, England, and New York, NY), 1989.
Excursions in the Real World: Autobiographical Essays, Knopf (New York, NY), 1994.

A collection of Trevor's manuscripts is housed at the University of Tulsa.

ADAPTATIONS: *The Old Boys* was adapted as a BBC television play, 1965; *The Ballroom of Romance* was broadcast on BBC-TV, 1982; *The Children of Dynmouth* was aired on BBC-TV, 1987; a screenplay by Michael Hirst was based on *Fools of Fortune* and directed by Pat O'Connor, 1990; *Elizabeth Alone* was also produced for BBC-TV; *Felicia's Journey* was adapted as a film by Atom Egoyan, 1999.

SIDELIGHTS: Short-story writer, novelist, and playwright William Trevor Cox is an Irish-born English writer better known to his readers as William Trevor. Considered by many critics to be one of the finest living short story writers in English, Trevor is equally renowned as a novelist, and is widely known in England for the television adaptations of his novels. Having lived in both Ireland and England, Trevor has written about people in both countries, often focusing on ordinary people who lead tragic, lonely lives. "I don't really have any heroes or heroines," Trevor remarked in a *Publishers Weekly* interview with Amanda Smith. "I don't seem to go in for them. I think I am interested in people who are not necessarily the victims of other people, but simply the victims of circumstances. . . . I'm very interested in the sadness of fate, the things that just happen to people." Originally working as a sculptor, Trevor became displeased with the increasingly abstract turn his art was taking, and so he took up writing

as a means of better expressing his concern for the human condition. "I think the humanity that isn't in abstract art began to go into [my] short stories," Trevor told Smith.

Trevor's ability to empathize with a broad array of characters is among the qualities that critics most admire in his fiction. A contributor to the *Economist* praised Trevor as "piercingly sympathetic with the most socially negligible passer-by," while *Commonweal's* Suzanne Berne hailed his blend of "microscopically precise detail and cosmic insights into the human heart." A *Publishers Weekly* reviewer observed that Trevor "is equally able to inhabit the worlds of priests, restless American expatriates and quarrelsome academics, always with an acute sense of their wide range of voices and habits of mind."

In much of Trevor's fiction, the events or situations that most affect his characters occur offstage and often years in the past. Sometimes these are personal, as in *The Old Boys,* in which the public school reunion of eight octogenarians causes them to revert back to childish competitive behavior by reminding them of old grudges and rivalries. In other cases these events are historical, as in the "The Mourning," from *The Hill Bachelors,* in which a naïve young man is almost persuaded to plant a bomb for the IRA. His realization that, before him, another young man had died in this attempt gives him the strength to reject the job.

Satire is also prominent in such early Trevor books as *The Boarding House* and *The Love Department,* although the situations in which his characters find themselves are often lamentable. However, *New York Times Book Review* critic Robert Towers wrote, since "the mid-1970's there has been . . . a subtle change of tone in the stories. The harsh comedy—the gleeful misanthropy—is less in evidence, as is the stance of impartiality; in the later work one can guess rather clearly where the author's sympathies lie."

In what one *Times Literary Supplement* reviewer declared to be "a collection that is never disappointing," *The Ballroom of Romance, and Other Stories* portrays a series of characters who are caught in dreary, barren lives, but lack the necessary confidence to change. Instead, they can only reflect upon what might have been, their memories and dreams leaving them isolated and alone. "The stories may be sad, but they have about them the unmistakable ring of truth." It is with these sad stories of ordinary people that the author finds himself repeatedly concerned. They may live unhappy lives because of their unwillingness or inability to give up the past or their illusions of reality, or, as with Trevor's *Elizabeth Alone,* because they are simply victims of fate.

In *Elizabeth Alone* Trevor first proposes a possible reason for human suffering. Set in a hospital, the book presents a series of ostensibly comic situations while simultaneously probing deeper issues through its sympathetic character portrayals. The title character, Elizabeth Aidallbery, has in one way or another lost everyone who was important in her life, and has even begun to lose her sense of identity. She finds the strength to overcome her loneliness and carry on through one of her hospital mates, Miss Samson, whose religious faith has recently been shaken. Miss Samson convinces Elizabeth that the importance of caring for others, even—or perhaps especially—if the world has no God, gives people a purpose in life. A *Times Literary Supplement* reviewer complimented Trevor on his ability to execute this conclusion convincingly in a seriocomic novel, attributing this success to "the authority he has built up, as a writer, out of the sheer, detailed understanding of the characters he creates. . . . The stance of compassion which is adopted finally in *Elizabeth Alone* can now be seen to be implicit in all Mr. Trevor's best work. It gives him a place as a writer capable of handling the human comedy instead of merely manipulating comic human beings."

Collections such as *Angels at the Ritz, and Other Stories* and *Lovers of Their Time, and Other Stories* continue to illustrate Trevor's concern for average people and the importance of the effects of time. "Trevor is especially adept at making the presence of the past, the presence of people offstage, lean upon his characters," said Peter S. Prescott in a *Newsweek* review of *Angels at the Ritz.* Similarly, *New York Times Book Review* contributor Victoria Glendinning commented on the stories in *Lovers of Their Time,* "Nothing very extraordinary happens to [Trevor's] teachers, tradesmen, farmers and shop-assistants; the action is all off-stage, and they are caught and thrown off course by the wash of great and passionate events that happened in another time, another place."

With *The Children of Dynmouth,* Trevor's first Whitbread Prize-winning book, the author focuses on an unsympathetic boy named Timothy Gedge. Abandoned by his father and ignored by the rest of his family, Timothy has become a despicable character who has a crude sense of humor and is fascinated by death. Desperate for attention, he becomes convinced that he can find fame by doing an act for the variety television show, "Opportunity Knocks." But to get the props he needs,

Timothy blackmails several of the respectable citizens of Dynmouth and "by the novel's end he has come close to destroying several people," wrote Joyce Carol Oates in the *New York Times Book Review.* "Timothy's malice arises from his chronic aloneness, so that it isn't possible, as the [character of] the vicar recognizes, to see the boy as evil."

Some critics see Timothy's rescue by the vicar at the novel's conclusion to be a weak solution to an otherwise excellent book. "To imply that sooner or later the shrinks and the socialists will put an end to evil is to drag out an old chestnut indeed," wrote *Sewanee Review* contributor Walter Sullivan. Sullivan found that this flaw negates "the fine performance which leads up to this foolishness." Thomas R. Edwards commented in the *New York Review of Books* that *The Children of Dynmouth* "succeeds in being funny, frightening, and morally poised and intelligent at once." Oates similarly concluded that it is "a skillfully written novel, a small masterpiece of understatement."

In another Whitbread Prize-winning novel, *Fools of Fortune,* Trevor chronicles the years of lonely isolation of two lovers separated by a tragic turn of fate. *Washington Post Book World* critic Charles Champlin called the book a "benchmark novel against which other contemporary novels will have to be measured," one which reflects the "last seven decades of English-Irish history." The novel relates how British soldiers misguidedly destroy Willie Quinton's family and home in the year 1918, and how Willie's revenge on a British officer leads to his exile from Ireland. Forced to leave his beloved English cousin, Marianne, he is denied the chance to see her or their daughter, Imelda, for years to come. The Quintons, remarked Jonathan Yardley in the *Washington Post Book World,* "are all good, honorable people, but they—like poor Ireland—are victims of mere chance, arbitrary and random."

With other tales, such as the central story of *The News from Ireland, and Other Stories* and the novel, *The Silence in the Garden,* Trevor relates the struggles in Ireland to the misfortunes of his characters and, as Richard Eder of the *Los Angeles Times* put it, "the passing of a kind of civility that Yeats celebrated." In the case of *The Silence in the Garden,* the story of how war and terrorism ruin a once-happy and prosperous Anglo-Irish family, *Washington Post Book World* critic Gregory A. Schirmer noted that Trevor "has much to say about the attitudes and patterns that lie behind the [British-Irish] violence, and about the ways in which the present is inevitably—and, in Ireland, often tragically—shaped by the past."

Although Trevor's stories and novels often involve dramatic events, he is mainly concerned with how these events preoccupy and obsess his characters. This inner tension is subtly portrayed through the author's quiet, understated writing style. Michiko Kakutani of the *New York Times* described this style in a review of *Fools of Fortune* as "spare, lilting prose . . . delineat[ing] these melodramatic events with economy and precision." For some critics, however, Trevor's use of understatement is a drawback in his writing. Anatole Broyard, for one, wrote in a *New York Times* review of *Beyond the Pale and Other Stories,* "Though everyone regards [Trevor] as a master of understatement, I wonder whether it isn't conceited in a way to insist on writing such carefully removed stories, so breathlessly poised on the edge of nonexistence."

In 1992 sixty of Trevor's short stories were published in *William Trevor: Collected Stories.* Reviewers were generally enthusiastic about the quality of the collection. Joseph Coates wrote in the Chicago *Tribune Books,* "The stories of this modern master often hinge on a slightness and subtlety that are the last thing we think of hefting a volume of this size." Coates went on to say that "despite this massive output, the salient characteristic of his work is the careful craftsmanship that produces its deceptively transparent surfaces. . . . What gives Trevor's stories their paradoxical sparkle . . . is his fascination with the endless variety and sheer unaccountability of human life, the infinite inventiveness with which people make their odd, pathetic but always somehow dignified arrangements for getting through their days and nights, with or without satisfaction, with or without the slimmest of memories to sustain them."

Trevor's sympathy for outcasts is at the core of his 1994 novel, *Felicia's Journey.* The plot concerns a young Irish girl, Felicia, who travels to the gloomy industrial districts of England in search of the young man who seduced and then abandoned her. She is preyed upon by Mr. Hilditch, a huge, lonely man with hidden sociopathic tendencies. Cunningly he weaves his web around her, engineering "chance" meetings and making innocent-sounding offers of help to her. Felicia stays with him for a time, and then, sensing evil, turns to Mrs. Calligary, a door-to-door evangelist. But when the missionary-like retreat Mrs. Calligary offers becomes unbearable, Felicia returns to her doom at Mr. Hilditch's residence. Reviewers differed sharply in their assessment of *Felicia's Journey.* Some, such as *Spectator* contributor Peregrine Hodson, found the book's many references to brand names and other details to be pointless and tedious. "Having finished *Felicia's Journey,* I

felt I had read an extremely long short story," remarked Hodson. "Some may find, in the author's descriptions of minutiae, evidence of the artist's eye, which misses nothing. Others may feel the accumulation of trivia— 'Marlboro, it said on the packet on the table'—clogs the narrative."

Richard Eder expressed a more serious objection to the book in the *Los Angeles Times Book Review.* He praised the author's rendering of Felicia, stating that "William Trevor, who is good at a great deal, is particularly good with the meek; and most particularly with the rural Irish meek. He finds the passion in them and he finds the ruses they devise to preserve . . . their lives." But Eder dismissed Mr. Hilditch as an unconvincing authorial device, one which unfortunately dominated the book: "True, [Trevor] can do splendid bullies, tricksters and arrogant bastards; but in each case he builds on their humanity and warps it just enough. . . . A monster, on the other hand, is a kind of void. . . . A writer can portray a man with a hole—an absence—in him, but a writer needs to be a special kind of metaphysician . . . to make the hole the character. . . . Hilditch is not enough of a character to generate a moral or significant action; he is a device through which the author acts."

Trevor's collection of stories, *After Rain,* is set in the familiar setting of Irish villages; more stories of failed relationships are displayed as Trevor describes a huge range of human emotions. Kakutani remarked that Trevor writes "with such assurance that he's able to collapse entire lives into a few brief pages, showing us how a character's past connects to his future, how his fate, in short, has been constructed." Some critics thought the collection lacks humor, and Kakutani believed there is a decided "mood of resignation" that permeates the stories.

The Hill Bachelors, Trevor's tenth volume of short stories, drew consistent praise. Finding some of the weaker stories marked by too much authorial manipulation, Kakutani nevertheless noted that Trevor "always manages to give the reader a sense of the entire arc of their lives," and hailed the volume for its "masterful variations on . . . familiar melodies, demonstrating once again [Trevor's] authority and poise as a storyteller, his Chekhovian understanding of missed connections and misplaced hopes." Suggesting that the book reveals more generosity toward its characters than is evident in Trevor's earlier work, *New York Times Book Review* contributor William H. Pritchard found the collection wise and moving. "No story here," claimed Brad Hooper in *Booklist,* "is anything less than a bravura performance." Among the stories that critics singled out for special praise were "Death of a Professor," in which a university don guesses what his colleagues really think of him after his fake obituary is published as a prank; "Against the Odds," in which an enterprising older woman lures a susceptible widower into "lending" her his life savings and then disappears; and the title story, concerning a young farmer's return to the land where no young woman is inclined to follow him.

Trevor has been compared to such luminaries as Muriel Spark, Anton Chekov, and Andre Malraux, but most often to his Irish predecessor, James Joyce. *New York Times Book Review* critic Ted Solotaroff compared Joyce and Trevor this way: "Both Trevor and the early Joyce are geniuses at presenting a seemingly ordinary life as it is, socially, psychologically, morally, and then revealing the force of these conditions in the threatened individual's moment of resistance to them. This is the deeper realism: accurate observation turning into moral vision." "Yet like Joyce before him," concluded *Washington Post Book World* contributor Howard Frank Mosher, "Trevor is entirely his own writer, with his own uncompromised vision of human limitations made accessible by a rare generosity toward his characters and their blighted lives."

BIOGRAPHICAL/CRITICAL SOURCES:

BOOKS

Contemporary Dramatists, St. James Press (Detroit, MI), 1993.

Contemporary Literary Criticism, Gale (Detroit, MI), Volume 7, 1977, Volume 9, 1978, Volume 14, 1980, Volume 25, 1983, Volume 71, 1992.

Contemporary Novelists, St. James Press (Detroit, MI), 1991.

Dictionary of Literary Biography, Gale (Detroit, MI), Volume 14: *British Novelists since 1960,* 1983, Volume 139: *British Short-Fiction Writers, 1945-1980,* 1994.

Schirmer, Gregory A., *William Trevor: A Study of His Fiction,* Routledge, 1990.

PERIODICALS

Atlantic Monthly, August, 1986.

Booklist, September 1, 2000, Brad Hooper, review of *The Hill Bachelors,* p. 8.

Boston Book Review, 1998.

Boston Globe, November 15, 1992, p. 91; February 6, 1994, p. 89; February 13, 1994, p. A15; January 8, 1995, p. 47.

Chicago Tribune, November 13, 1987; September 30, 1988; April 6, 1994, section 5, p. 3; January 15, 1995, section 14, p. 3.

Chicago Tribune Book World, July 29, 1979; March 15, 1981; February 14, 1982; October 30, 1983.

Christian Science Monitor, February 26, 1970; March 10, 1994, p. 14; January 10, 1995, p. 13.

Commonweal, December 3, 1999, Jon Nilson, review of *The Collected Stories,* p. 29; June 16, 2000, Suzanne Berne, "Summer Reading," p. 20.

Economist (US), November 11, 2000, review of *The Hill Bachelors,* p. 108.

Encounter, January, 1979.

Globe and Mail (Toronto), December 31, 1983; October 24, 1987; September 17, 1988.

Harper's, October, 1983, pp. 74-75.

Hudson Review, winter, 1991, pp. 686-690.

Irish Literary Supplement, spring, 1991, p. 20.

Irish Times, May 22, 1988.

Listener, July 21, 1988, pp. 25-26.

London Magazine, August, 1968.

London Review of Books, June 23, 1988, p. 22; December 16, 1993, pp. 22-23.

Los Angeles Times, October 2, 1983; September 29, 1988; February 10, 1994, p. E10.

Los Angeles Times Book Review, January 11, 1981; March 11, 1984, p. 4; May 4, 1986, p. 3; August 6, 1989; May 20, 1990, p. 3; September 5, 1993, p. 6; February 13, 1994, p. 6; January 8, 1995, p. 3.

Nation, December 3, 1983, pp. 574-577.

New Republic, February 4, 1967; November 28, 1983, pp. 37-39; June 9, 1986, pp. 28-30; February 6, 1989, pp. 37-40; October 1, 1990, pp. 40-41.

New Statesman, October 15, 1971; July 9, 1976; September 22, 1978.

New Statesman & Society, August 27, 1993, pp. 40-41.

Newsweek, June 14, 1976; February 22, 1982; October 10, 1983.

New Yorker, July 12, 1976.

New York Review of Books, April 19, 1979; March 19, 1981; December 22, 1983, pp. 53-54; June 26, 1986, pp. 32-33, 35; May 17, 1990; September 26, 1991, pp. 29-30.

New York Times, September 31, 1972; March 31, 1979; January 17, 1981; February 3, 1982; September 26, 1983; May 14, 1986; August 27, 1988; May 11, 1990, p. C33; January 3, 1995, p. B27; November 12, 1996; October 17, 2000, Michiko Kakutani, review of *The Hill Bachelors,* p. B7.

New York Times Book Review, February 11, 1968; July 11, 1976; April 8, 1979; February 1, 1981; February 21, 1982; October 2, 1983, pp. 1, 22, 24; June 8, 1986, p. 14; January 17, 1988, p. 24; October 9,

1988, p. 12; June 3, 1990, p. 9; September 8, 1991, p. 3; February 3, 1993, p. 1; February 28, 1993, pp. 1, 25-27; February 13, 1994, p. 7; January 8, 1995, pp. 1, 22; October 22, 2000, William H. Pritchard, review of *The Hill Bachelors,* p. 11.

Observer, June 11, 1980; April 6, 1986, p. 27; June 5, 1988; November 1, 1987; February 4, 1990; May 26, 1991.

Plays and Players, September, 1971.

Publishers Weekly, October 28, 1983; September 11, 2000, review of *The Hill Bachelors,* p. 65.

San Francisco Review of Books, Volume 16, number 3, 1991, pp. 47-48.

Saturday Review, May 12, 1970, pp. 44-45.

Sewanee Review, spring, 1978, pp. 320-325.

Spectator, October 11, 1969; May 13, 1972; November 29, 1986, p. 25; June 1, 1991, p. 28; October 17, 1992, pp. 25-26; August 28, 1993, p. 32; August 20, 1994, p. 34.

Sunday Times, May 29, 1988, pp. 68-69; May 26, 1991, pp. 6-7.

Time, January 26, 1970; October 10, 1983.

Times (London), June 18, 1980; October 15, 1981; April 28, 1983; March 20, 1986; May 30, 1991, p. 12.

Times Literary Supplement, October 26, 1973; June 20, 1980; October 16, 1981; April 29, 1983; August 31, 1984; April 11, 1986; November 5, 1987; June 10, 1988; January 26, 1990, p. 87; May 31, 1991, p. 21; September 17, 1993, p. 24; August 19, 1994, p. 20.

Tribune Books (Chicago), September 10, 1989; November 22, 1992, p. 1.

Variety, May 24, 1999, Emanuel Levy, review of *Felicia's Journey* (film), p. 65.

Vogue, February 1, 1968.

Wall Street Journal, March 2, 1994, p. A9; January 26, 1995, p. A12.

Washington Post, March 11, 1995, p. A17.

Washington Post Book World, April 8, 1979; February 1, 1981; February 21, 1982; September 25, 1983, p. 3; March 4, 1984; May 25, 1986, p. 6; August 28, 1988; May 27, 1990; August 18, 1991; January 22, 1995, pp. 1, 10.

Writer, October, 1990.*

*   *   *

CRAMER, Richard Ben 1950-

PERSONAL: Born June 12, 1950, in Rochester, NY; son of A. Robert and Blossom (Lackritz) Cramer. *Education:* Johns Hopkins University, B.A., 1971; Columbia University, M.S., 1972.

ADDRESSES: Agent—Sterling Lord Literistic Inc., 65 Bleeker St., New York, NY 10012-2420.

CAREER: Sun, Baltimore, MD, reporter, 1973-76; *Philadelphia Inquirer,* Philadelphia, PA, reporter, 1976-78, foreign correspondent in Europe, Africa, and the Middle East, beginning in 1978; freelance journalist and writer. Has worked as a contributing editor for *Esquire.*

MEMBER: Pen and Pencil, Stampa Estere d'Italia.

AWARDS, HONORS: Pulitzer Prize for international reporting, 1979, for reports from the Middle East; Sigma Delta Chi award for foreign correspondence, 1980; Ernie Pyle Award, Scripps Howard News Service, 1980; Hal Boyle Award, Overseas Press Club of America, 1981, for coverage of Afghan guerrillas fighting the Russians; American Society of Newspaper Editors award for excellence in writing.

WRITINGS:

Ted Williams: The Season of the Kid, photo essays by John Thorn, Prentice-Hall (Englewood Cliffs, NJ), 1991.

What It Takes: The Way to the White House, Random House (New York, NY), 1992.

Bob Dole, Vintage (New York, NY), 1995.

Joe DiMaggio: The Hero's Life, Simon & Schuster (New York, NY), 2000.

Contributor to anthologies, including *Best Newspaper Writing,* edited by Roy Peter Clark, Modern Media Institute (St. Petersburg, FL), 1980; *The Pulitzer Prize Archive,* Volume 1, edited by Heinz-Dietrich Fischer, K. G. Saur (Munich, Germany), 1987; and *The Best American Essays 1987,* edited by Gay Talese, Ticknor & Fields (New York, NY), 1987. Also contributor to newspapers and periodicals, including the *New York Times, New York Times Book Review, Esquire,* and *Rolling Stone.*

SIDELIGHTS: During his award-winning career as a newspaper journalist, Richard Ben Cramer spent most of his time covering affairs outside the United States. As the *Philadelphia Inquirer*'s correspondent for Europe, Africa, and the Middle East, he spent many years overseas, reporting on both the civil war in Lebanon and the fighting between Soviet troops and Afghan guerrillas. In the years since he left the *Inquirer,* however, Cramer has been concerned with uniquely American subjects. *What It Takes: The Way to the White House* presents a study of six of the 1988 presidential candidates. He has also focused on the American sports world in two major biographies, *Ted Williams: The Season of the Kid* and *Joe DiMaggio: The Hero's Life.* All three books have been praised by critics for delivering an unusual glimpse of their prominent and powerful subjects.

In profiling baseball legend Ted Williams, Cramer was faced with a man who was renowned for his exploits on the field, but who was uncomfortable with his role as a superstar. As the last professional player to hold a season batting average of .400, Williams has been touted by many experts as the best hitter ever to play the game. His career was also marred by incidents in which he spit at fans and threw his bat into the crowd to silence hecklers. *Ted Williams: The Season of the Kid* opens with an account of Cramer's visit to the aging star in his Florida retirement home, and then presents a chronicle of Williams's career and personal life. *Newsweek* reviewer Charles Leerhsen proclaimed the book "a timeless piece of journalism" that results in "a brilliantly crafted profile" of Williams, a man, Cramer writes, who "wanted fame . . . but could not stand celebrity."

The celebrities in *What It Takes,* Cramer's second book, are also involved in a competitive American pastime: politics. As he confided to *Publishers Weekly* interviewer Dermot McEvoy, Cramer envisioned the book as a return to the kind of intimate journalism typical of Theodore White's writing about John F. Kennedy. "I was reading all the presidential books," he said, "but I never got a sense of these human beings who were running." Before he even knew who the 1988 presidential candidates would be, Cramer secured a contract to follow them on the campaign trail—but he was not content to present a conventional political analysis of the presidential race. "I wanted to know not about the campaign, but about the campaigners," the author notes in his introduction to the book. "Who are these guys. . . . What happened to their idea of themselves? What did *we do to them,* on the way to the White House?"

What It Takes studies candidates Gary Hart, Joseph Biden, Richard Gephardt, Michael Dukakis, Bob Dole, and George Bush. Cramer worked on the book for a total of six years, before, during, and after 1988. He conducted over 1,000 interviews with people involved in the campaign, including extensive discussions with each of the six candidates. The resulting book is over 1,000 pages in length, providing an extensive study of the men who aspired to be president.

"Cramer renders his representative men with specificity and sensitivity," judged *Dictionary of Literary Biography* contributor Robert Schmuhl. "He captures their strengths, limitations, habits, and idiosyncrasies, and even seems to empathize with them for what they are forced to endure. The politicians, in fact, have a stature just short of heroic." Devoting seven chapters to the alleged extramarital affair of Gary Hart and its effect on Hart's career, Cramer exposes "more monkey business by journalists than sexual shenanigans by the former Colorado senator," advised Schmuhl. "But the intense coverage is enough to make Hart withdraw. Hart's experience allows Cramer to focus on the importance of character and the involvement of the media in presidential politics."

Douglas Bell, reviewing the book in the Toronto *Globe & Mail,* noted that "Cramer zeroes in and with surgical precision dissects layer upon layer of his subjects' persona." These insights stem, in part, from the details the author relates about the candidates. The book pictures Biden as he shops for real estate between political rallies, discusses Hart's choice of cocktails at a campaign stopover, and describes the mysterious tune that Bob Dole continually whistles and hums throughout the primaries. "Cramer has a particularly sensitive ear for dialogue," Bell continued, "capturing not just what the candidate said but the way he said it." In addition to documenting the behavior of the candidates, *What It Takes* also provides the author's assessment of the campaign's headline stories. Cramer defends the two candidates who withdrew from the race after allegations of impropriety—Biden, who plagiarized a campaign speech, and Hart, who was accused of having an extramarital affair. In both cases Cramer feels the candidates were the victims of an overzealous news media hungry for sensational stories.

Besides the media, there are many forces that impact the candidates in Cramer's account. The author also considers the so-called "handlers"—the analysts, pollsters, and image consultants who help manage each candidate's campaign. Jack Shafer, reviewing the book in the *Washington Post Book World,* noted that "the subtext of *What It Takes* is that a candidate must maintain his vigilance lest the handlers (Cramer calls them 'the white men') take over." The author also describes the closed world that the candidates exist in, a claustrophobic environment created by their non-stop travel and carefully orchestrated appearances. This quality is made clear, according to *Time* reviewer Walter Shapiro, in the book's depiction of George Bush on the campaign trail. "Where Cramer excels," wrote Shapiro, "is in portraying Bush's sterile life inside the bubble—the Secret-Service-secure world of motorcades, advancemen, rope lines, and step-by-step schedules." Cramer argues that such elements created a campaign environment where Bush would "never see one person who was not a friend, or someone whose sole purpose it was to serve or protect him."

The epic length of *What It Takes* became an issue for some critics. Some, such as *New Statesman & Society* reviewer Boyd Tonkin, found the book excessively detailed. "No one ever stopped to think that this project might have worked better at 300 pages than at *1046*," Tonkin complained. "Few will finish it, and no skimmer can use its information, as it lacks an index." McEvoy also criticized the book's length and its "at times mind-numbing minutiae." Though Shapiro observed that "only the dust jacket is terse" in *What It Takes,* he felt that the book's significant length was justified. "Despite its heft," Shapiro wrote, "the prose is a joyous journey" that results in an "artful reworking" of the campaign.

Cramer's writing style in the book—his use of numerous exclamation points and capitalized words, for instance—was singled out by many reviewers and compared to the writing of other experimental journalists such as Tom Wolfe and Hunter S. Thompson. *Newsweek*'s Joe Klein also addressed another aspect of Cramer's technique, noting that the author doesn't cite his sources, as is the normal journalistic practice. Because of this, Klein speculated that *What It Takes* "is bound to cause a fair amount of controversy among the political and media priesthoods, as it blithely skirts the boundaries of responsibility and good taste." Despite this danger, the critic felt that the book succeeded in its quest to explain the political candidates. "Even if only semi-journalistic," Klein wrote, "this is still great fun and . . . far more insightful about pols and political tradecraft than the common run of campaign effluvia."

In the end, the book suggests that "what it takes" to be president is a willingness to give all. Shapiro, summing up Cramer's views, wrote that the president must be "so driven in his pursuit of the White House that he jettisons family, friends, any semblance of privacy or normal human existence." A similar question was addressed by the critics who reviewed Cramer's study: did the book have "what it takes" to be worthwhile reading? Bell was one of many who felt it did, citing the author's "deft mix of insight and breathtaking reportage." The critic went on to proclaim the book an

important document of the campaign, declaring that "Cramer's delightfully unexpected insights capture the tenor and the timbre of his political times."

In 1995, the minibiography of Senator Dole that made up part of *What It Takes* was published separately, as *Bob Dole.* A fifteen-page introduction also provides new information gathered during a speaking trip and an interview with Dole. According to Schmuhl, *What It Takes* and *Bob Dole* "enhanced Cramer's reputation as a detail-oriented reporter who writes with imagination and originality. The people he selects to write about are at the heart of his work, and they frequently come to life as characters in a well-wrought piece of fiction do. His willingness to test established journalistic forms yields creative approaches that a reader sees from his earliest newspaper days to his magazine articles and books. Journalism often simplifies complexity. With Cramer's in-depth probing of subjects, clear and precise explanation illumines what is complex, and the presentation is engagingly distinctive."

It wasn't much of a leap, McEvoy suggested, for Cramer to move in his next book from the saga of political personalities to the "glamour of baseball, Hollywood and the glittering personas of Joe DiMaggio and Marilyn Monroe." *Joe DiMaggio: The Hero's Life* is by most accounts a demythologizing portrait of an American sports icon. Though some critics disapproved of Cramer's negative focus, many welcomed the biography as a fascinating expose of its subject's dark side.

DiMaggio, Cramer writes, was "the first man in history to be brilliant at five out of five" tools necessary to excel in baseball: running, fielding, throwing, hitting, and power hitting. His 1941 fifty-six-game winning streak is still considered one of the sport's greatest achievements. He was voted Most Valuable Player three times, and in 1969 was named "Baseball's Greatest Living Player." But the DiMaggio whom Cramer presents was also notorious for his stinginess and self-promoting zeal, his womanizing and his violent marriage to Hollywood sex goddess Marilyn Monroe, and his connections with the Mafia. "DiMaggio, in Mr. Cramer's penetrating and unforgiving illumination of him, is a scowling, calculating and sometimes cruel phantom lurking behind the splendid image created more by collective need than by reality," wrote Richard Bernstein in the *New York Times Book Review.*

Pointing out that *Joe DiMaggio* is "more than a definitive revisionist biography of a cultural archetype," Bernstein added that Cramer "has furnished us with a grand American tale, its ingredients including struggling immigrants from Sicily, the limitless dimensions to which talent can aspire, the possibility that dreams can be realized, and baseball." Citing Cramer's thorough research, commanding prose, and vivid writing about DiMaggio's sports career and relationship with Monroe, Bernstein concluded that "Cramer never lets us forget that DiMaggio's greatness on the field was only one part of the picture. The other part was American fabulism, our need for images of imperial majesty arising out of the melting pot."

Some critics objected to the book's vilification of its subject. In the *Knight-Ridder/Tribune News Service,* Bruce Newman called the book a "560-page assault on [DiMaggio's] cloak of privacy." And both Wilfrid Sheed in the *New York Times* and Pete Hamill in the *Los Angeles Times Book Review* sharply criticized Cramer for describing DiMaggio's inner thoughts and private actions when the athlete himself never spoke to the author. "Cramer is faced with the daunting task of reading the mind of a man totally unlike himself or any of us," wrote Sheed, who added that "the author's overexposed you-are-there style only reminds you that you are not there and don't really know what these people are thinking at all. By trying to go the truth one better, the famous 'new journalism' continually undercuts it, and you can't hang a man on this kind of evidence." Observing that "we are asked to take [Cramer's assertions] on faith," Hamill complained that Cramer's lack of footnotes or other sources is a "blurry biographical strategy" that "has grievously wounded his book." Hamill also felt that this flaw "is compounded by the adoption of a semi-fictional intimacy that allows the writer to penetrate his subject's mind." This approach, according to both Hamill and Sheed, fails to illuminate DiMaggio's mystery. However, praise came from several reviewers. Terry W. Hartle in the *Christian Science Monitor* hailed *Joe DiMaggio* as "a wonderfully rich and full portrait" of its subject; Daniel Okrent in *Time* observed that Cramer's "absolutely persuasive" portrait of DiMaggio is "rendered so vividly you almost want to look away." *Entertainment Weekly* contributor Steve Wulf called the book "a devastating look at the machinery that made idols out of mere mortals"; acknowledging that some readers will object to Cramer's unflattering depiction of DiMaggio, Wulf suggested that "what [Cramer] really does is bring a statue to life."

In an online chat with *CNN.com,* Cramer summarized his thoughts on DiMaggio thus: "I think . . . that Joe made a grand and glorious sweep through the century—a big life and a fascinating life, for a guy who started in San Francisco without a lot of advantages. I have a lot of sympathy for Joe—for the pressures we

put on our gods. We gave him the Hero's Life, and he took it . . . but I'm not sure he had many happy days in it."

BIOGRAPHICAL/CRITICAL SOURCES:

BOOKS

Cramer, Richard Ben, *Joe DiMaggio: The Hero's Life,* Simon & Schuster (New York, NY), 2000.

Cramer, Richard Ben, *Ted Williams: The Season of the Kid,* Prentice Hall (Englewood Cliffs, NJ), 1991.

Cramer, Richard Ben, *What It Takes: The Way to the White House,* Random House (New York, NY), 1992.

Dictionary of Literary Biography, Volume 185: *American Literary Journalists, 1945-1995, First Series,* Gale (Detroit, MI), 1997.

PERIODICALS

Chicago Tribune, July 14, 1992, section 2, pp. 1-2.

Christian Science Monitor, October 19, 2000, Terry W. Hartle, review of *Joe DiMaggio: The Hero's Life,* p. 20.

Entertainment Weekly, November 1, 2000, Steve Wulf, review of *Joe DiMaggio.*

Esquire, October, 1984, p. 7.

Globe & Mail (Toronto), July 11, 1992, p. C5.

Houston Chronicle, November 16, 2000, Richard Hauer Costa, review of *Joe DiMaggio.*

Knight-Ridder/Tribune News Service, October 18, 2000, Bruce Newman, review of *Joe DiMaggio.*

Los Angeles Times Book Review, November 5, 2000, Pete Hamill, review of *Joe DiMaggio,* p. 1.

New Statesman & Society, July 31, 1992, Boyd Tonkin, review of *What It Takes: The Way to the White House,* p. 37.

Newsweek, October 28, 1991, Charles Leerhsen, review of *Ted Williams: The Season of the Kid,* p. 62; July 6, 1992, Joe Klein, review of *What It Takes: The Way to the White House,* p. 55.

New York Times Book Review, October 18, 2000, Richard Bernstein, review of *Joe DiMaggio: The Hero's Life;* October 29, 2000, Wilfrid Sheed, review of *Joe DiMaggio,* p. 10.

Publishers Weekly, October 23, 2000, Dermot McEvoy, "American Icon under a Spotlight," p. 54.

Time, July 13, 1992, pp. 78-80; November 6, 2000, Daniel Okrent, review of *Joe DiMaggio,* p. 114.

Wall Street Journal, October 18, 2000, Richard J. Tofel, review of *Joe DiMaggio,* p. A28.

Washington Post, July 6, 1992, pp. D1, 4.

Washington Post Book World, June 28, 1992, pp. 1, 10.

OTHER

CNN.com, http://www.cnn.com/chat (October 25, 2000), author chat.*

*   *   *

CROSSLEY-HOLLAND, Kevin (John William) 1941-

PERSONAL: Born February 7, 1941, in Mursley, Buckinghamshire, England; son of Peter Charles (a professor) and Joan Mary (Cowper) Crossley-Holland; married Caroline Fendall Thompson, 1963 (marriage ended); married Ruth Marris, 1972 (marriage ended); married Gillian Cook, 1982; children: (first marriage) Kieran, Dominic; (third marriage) Oenone, Eleanor. *Education:* St. Edmund Hall, Oxford, B.A. (with honors), 1962. *Avocational interests:* Music, archaeology, travel, architecture.

ADDRESSES: Office—Clare Cottage, Burnham Market, Norfolk PE31 8HE, England. *Agent*—Rogers, Coleridge & White, 20 Powis Mews, London W11 1JN, England.

CAREER: Writer and translator. Macmillan & Co. (publishers), London, England, editor, 1962-69; Victor Gollancz Ltd. (publisher), London, editorial director, 1972-77; Boydell & Brewer (publisher), Woodbridge, Suffolk, England, editorial consultant, 1983-91. Tufts-in-London Program, lecturer in English, 1967-78; University of Leeds, Gregory Fellow in poetry, 1969-71; University of Regensburg, English lecturer, 1978-80; Winchester School of Art, Arts Council Fellow in writing, 1983-84; St. Olaf College, Northfield, MN, visiting professor of English and Fulbright Scholar-in-Residence, 1987-88; St. Thomas College, MN, professor and endowed chair of humanities, 1991-95; visiting lecturer for British Council in Germany, Iceland, India, and Yugoslavia. BBC, London, talks producer, 1972; contributor to radio, television and musical works.

MEMBER: Eastern Arts Association (chairman, literature panel, 1986-89), Friends, Wingfield College (trustee and chairman, 1989—), Royal Society of Literature (fellow).

AWARDS, HONORS: Arts Council awards for best book for children, 1968, for *The Green Children,* 1977, and 1978; poetry award, 1972, for *The Rain-Giver;* Poetry Book Society Choice, 1976, for *The Dream-House;* Francis Williams Award, 1977, for *The Wildman;* Carnegie Medal, 1985, for *Storm;* Whitbread Award, 2000, for *Arthur: The Seeing Stone.*

WRITINGS:

FOR YOUNG ADULTS

(Reteller) *Havelok the Dane,* illustrated by Brian Wildsmith, Macmillan (London, England), 1964, Dutton (New York, NY), 1965.

(Reteller) *Kinq Horn,* illustrated by Charles Keeping, Macmillan (London, England), 1965, Dutton (New York, NY), 1966.

(Reteller) *The Green Children* (also see below), illustrated by Margaret Gordon, Macmillan (London, England), 1966, Seabury Press (New York, NY), 1968, illustrated by Alan Marks, Oxford University Press (London, England), 1994.

(Editor) *Winter's Tales for Children: No. 3,* Macmillan (London, England), 1967, St. Martin's Press (New York, NY), 1968.

(Reteller) *The Callow Pit Coffer,* illustrated by Margaret Gordon, Macmillan (London, England), 1968, Seabury Press (New York, NY), 1969.

(Reteller, with Jill Paton Walsh) *Wordhoard: Anglo-Saxon Stories,* Farrar, Straus (New York, NY), 1969.

(Translator) *Storm and Other Old English Riddles* (verse), illustrated by Miles Thistlethwaite, Farrar, Straus (New York, NY), 1970.

(Reteller) *The Pedlar of Swaffham,* illustrated by Margaret Gordon, Macmillan (London, England), 1971, Seabury Press (New York, NY), 1972.

(Reteller) *The Sea-Stranger,* illustrated by Joanna Troughton, Heinemann (London, England), 1973, Seabury Press (New York, NY), 1974.

(Reteller) *The Fire-Brother,* illustrated by Joanna Troughton, Seabury Press (New York, NY), 1975.

(Reteller) *Green Blades Rising: The Anglo-Saxons,* Deutsch (London, England), 1975, Seabury Press (New York, NY), 1976.

(Reteller) *The Earth-Father,* illustrated by Joanna Troughton, Heinemann (London, England), 1976.

The Wildman (also see below), illustrated by Charles Keeping, Deutsch (London, England), 1976.

(Editor) *The Faber Book of Northern Legends,* illustrated by Alan Howard, Faber (London, England), 1977.

(Editor) *The Faber Book of Northern Folk-Tales,* illustrated by Alan Howard, Faber (London, England), 1980.

(Editor) *The Riddle Book,* illustrated by Bernard Handelsman, Macmillan (London, England), 1982.

(Reteller) *The Dead Moon and Other Tales from East Anglia and the Fen Country,* illustrated by Shirley Felts, Deutsch (London, England), 1982.

(Reteller) *Beowulf,* illustrated by Charles Keeping, Oxford University Press (London, England), 1982, reprinted, 1999.

(Reteller, with Gwyn Thomas) *Tales from the Mabinogion,* illustrated by Margaret Jones, Gollancz (London, England), 1984, Overlook Press (New York, NY), 1985.

Storm, illustrated by Alan Marks, Heinemann (London, England), 1985, Barron's (Hauppage, NY), 1989.

(Reteller) *Axe-Age, Wolf-Age: A Selection from the Norse Myths,* illustrated by Hannah Firmin, Deutsch (London, England), 1985.

(Reteller) *The Fox and the Cat: Animal Tales from Grimm,* illustrated by Susan Varley, Andersen Press (London, England), 1985, Lothrop (New York, NY), 1986.

(Reteller) *Northern Lights: Legends, Sagas, and Folk-Tales,* illustrated by Alan Howard, Faber (London, England), 1987.

(Reteller) *British Folk Tales: New Versions,* Orchard (New York, NY), 1987, published in four volumes as *Boo!, Dathera Dad, Piper and Pooka,* and *Small-Tooth Dog,* illustrated by Peter Melnyczuk, Orchard (London, England), 1988.

(Reteller, with Gwyn Thomas) *The Quest for Olwen,* illustrated by Margaret Jones, Lutterworth Press (Cambridge, England), 1988.

(Reteller) *Wulf,* Faber (London, England), 1988.

(Reteller) *Under the Sun and over the Moon* (poetry), illustrated by Ian Penney, Putnam (New York, NY), 1989.

(Reteller) *Sleeping Nanna,* illustrated by Peter Melnyczuk, Orchard (London, England), 1989, Ideals (New York, NY), 1990.

(Reteller) *Sea Tongue,* illustrated by Clare Challice, BBC/Longman (London, England), 1991.

(Reteller) *Tales from Europe,* BBC (London, England), 1991.

(Reteller, with Gwyn Thomas) *The Tale of Taliesin,* illustrated by Margaret Jones, Gollancz (London, England), 1992.

(Reteller) *Long Tom and the Dead Hand,* illustrated by Shirley Felts, Deutsch (London, England), 1992.

(Reteller) *The Labours of Herakles,* illustrated by Peter Utton, Orion (London, England), 1993.

(Reteller) *The Old Stories: Folk Tales from East Anglia and the Fen Country,* illustrated by John Lawrence, Colt (Cambridge, England), 1997.

(Reteller) *Short! A Book of Very Short Stories,* Oxford University Press (London, England), 1998.

(Reteller) *The King Who Was and Will Be: The World of King Arthur and His Knights,* illustrated by Peter Malone, Orion (London, England), 1998, published as *The World of King Arthur and His Court: People, Places, Legend, and Lore,* Dutton (New York, NY), 1999.

(Editor) *Young Oxford Book of Folk Tales,* Oxford University Press (New York, NY), 1998.

(Reteller) *Enchantment: Fairy Tales, Ghost Stories, and Tales of Wonder,* illustrated by Emma Chichester Clark, Allen & Unwin (London, England), 2000.

Arthur: The Seeing Stone (first volume of trilogy), Allen & Unwin (London, England), 2000, Arthur A. Levine (New York, NY), 2001.

(Reteller) Hans Christian Andersen, *The Ugly Duckling,* illustrated by Meilo So, Knopf (New York, NY), 2001.

POETRY; FOR ADULTS

On Approval, Outposts (London, England), 1961.

My Son, Turret (London, England), 1966.

Alderney: The Nunnery, Turret (London, England), 1968.

Confessional, Sceptre Press (Frensham, Surrey, England), 1969.

Norfolk Poems, Academy (London, England), 1970.

A Dream of a Meeting, Sceptre Press (Frensham, Surrey, England), 1970.

More than I Am, Steam Press (London, England), 1971.

The Wake, Keepsake Press (Richmond, Surrey, England), 1972.

The Rain-Giver, Deutsch (London, England), 1972.

Petal and Stone, Sceptre Press (Knotting, Bedfordshire, England), 1975.

The Dream-House, Deutsch (London, England), 1976.

Between My Father and My Son, Black Willow Press (Minneapolis, MN), 1982.

Time's Oriel, Hutchinson (London, England), 1983.

Waterslain and Other Poems, Hutchinson (London, England), 1986.

The Painting-Room and Other Poems, Hutchinson (London, England), 1988.

East Anglian Poems, Jardine (Colchester, England), 1988.

Oenone in January, Old Stile Press (Llandogo, Wales), 1988.

New and Selected Poems: 1965-1990, Hutchinson (London, England), 1990.

Eleanor's Advent, Old Stile Press (Llandogo, Wales), 1992.

The Language of Yes, Enitharmon (London, England), 1996.

Poems from East Anglia, Enitharmon (London, England), 1997.

Selected Poems, Enitharmon (London, England), 2001.

EDITOR; FOR ADULTS

Running to Paradise: An Introductory Selection of the Poems of W. B. Yeats, Macmillan (London, England), 1967, Macmillan (New York, NY), 1968.

Winter's Tales 14, Macmillan (London, England), 1968.

(With Patricia Beer) *New Poetry 2,* Arts Council of Great Britain (London, England), 1976.

The Norse Myths: A Retelling, Pantheon (New York, NY), 1980.

(And translator) *The Anglo-Saxon World: An Anthology,* Boydell Press (Woodbridge, Suffolk), 1982, Barnes & Noble (New York, NY), 1983, reprinted, Oxford University Press (New York, NY), 1999.

Folk Tales of the British Isles, Folio Society (London, England), 1985, Pantheon (New York, NY), 1988.

The Oxford Book of Travel Verse, Oxford University Press (New York, NY), 1986.

Medieval Lovers: A Book of Days, Weidenfeld & Nicolson (New York, NY), 1988.

Medieval Gardens: A Book of Days, Rizzoli (New York, NY), 1990.

(Editor, with Lawrence Sail) *The New Exeter Book of Riddles,* illustrated by Simon Drew, Enitharmon (London, England), 1999.

General editor, "Mirror of Britain" series, Deutsch (London, England), 1975-80.

TRANSLATOR; FOR ADULTS

Bruce Mitchell, editor, *The Battle of Maldon and Other Old English Poems,* St. Martin's Press (New York, NY), 1965.

Beowulf, Farrar Straus (New York, NY), 1968, published with *The Fight at Finnsburh,* edited by Heather o'Donoghue, Oxford University Press (New York, NY), 1999.

The Exeter Riddle Book, Folio Society (London, England), 1978, revised as *The Exeter Book of Riddles,* Penguin (London, England), 1979, revised edition, Penguin (New York, NY) 1993.

The Wanderer, Jardine (Colchester, England), 1986.

The Old English Elegies, Folio Society (London, England), 1988.

Beowulf, Oxford University Press (London, England), 1998.

OTHER

Pieces of Land: Journeys to Eight Islands, Gollancz (London, England), 1972.

The Stones Remain: Megalithic Sites of Britain, photographs by Andrew Rafferty, Rider (London, England), 1989.

(Author of libretto) *The Green Children* (two-act opera; based on his work of the same title), music by Nicola LeFanu, Novello (London, England), 1990.

(Author of libretto) *The Wildman* (opera; based on his work of the same title), Boydell & Brewer (Woodbridge, England), 1995.

Different—but Oh How Like! (booklet), Daylight Press (London, England), 1998.

Crossley-Holland's poetry notebooks are housed in the Brotherton Collection, University of Leeds; manuscripts for children's books are housed at the Lillian H. Smith and Osborne Collections, Toronto Public Library, Toronto, Canada; the Kerlan Collection, Minneapolis, houses material relating to *Under the Sun and over the Moon.*

ADAPTATIONS: Crossley-Holland's *Exeter Book of Riddles* was adapted as the musical work *Riddles: For Six Solo Voices, SATB Chorus, Bells, and Piano* by William Mathias, 1991.

SIDELIGHTS: British poet and translator Kevin Crossley-Holland has introduced many a young reader to the myths, legends, and folktales of the Anglo-Saxon tradition—particularly from his native East Anglia, England—through his engaging translations and retellings. The characters and messages in these retellings are fresh and timeless, and their stories convey subtle truths about life that are as pertinent today as they were when these tales were originally told. Crossley-Holland has been repeatedly praised by critics and readers alike for his ability to bring these ancient stories sharply into the present, while preserving their mystery, richness, and texture. "All of Crossley-Holland's best work combines his storytelling skills with his mastery of the poetic elements of language," noted a *St. James Guide to Young Adult Writers* essayist. Citing *The Dead Moon and Other Tales from East Anglia and the Fen Country* and *Beowulf* as among the author's finest works, the essayist concluded that, "Combining these skills creates and maintains an appropriate tone for each story."

Born in Buckinghamshire, England, in 1941, Crossley-Holland's youth was spent learning viola. He was born into a very musical family and had little recollection of reading books, claiming to have finished less than fifteen throughout his youth. Instead, his interests were similar to other boys his age: cricket, tennis, and the outdoors. It was when he studied English literature at Oxford University that he first got bit by the writing bug, when he learned about the history of Britain. The Anglo-Saxons, an ancient people who live on the island of Britain before the Norman conquest, fascinated him, and he immersed himself in a study of their history, language, and literature. He also discovered poetry, and a love of words, and published his first book of poetry, *On Approval,* in 1961, at the age of twenty. A year later he finished up his degree at Oxford and graduated with honors.

On the strength of his academics and his first book, which was well received, Crossley-Holland got a job at the London publishing firm of Macmillan, where he worked for almost a decade as an editor. Surrounded by writers and editors and books, he was able to sustain what became a successful writing career as well, publishing his first book for children, a retelling of a medieval romance titled *Havelock the Dane,* in 1964.

Havelok the Dane was followed by several books about the Anglo-Saxon world Crossley-Holland had fallen in love with. *Wordhoard Anglo-Saxon Stories,* written with Jill Paton Walsh, paints a vivid picture of that ancient culture through the authors' translations of Old English poems and history. *Tales from the Mabinogion, The Quest for Olwen,* and *The Tale of Taliesin,* which he authored with Gwyn Thomas, are simple, lyrical retellings of Welsh legends. *The Dead Moon* focuses on more ghostly tales, "peopled" by boggarts, will-o'-the-wykes, witches, dead hands, and green children, within which the author weaves a hint of East Anglian dialect. Several of the stories included in such anthologies as *The Dead Moon* and *British Folk Tales: New Versions* were later published as picture books. One of his notable retellings from the latter, *Small-Tooth Dog,* recounts the story of a curious dog who saves the life of a man only to demand the man's only daughter as payment.

A major focus of Crossley-Holland's young adult work has been the folktales of his native East Anglia, England. *The Green Children,* one of his most acclaimed works, contains retellings of several medieval tales. As a testament to Crossley-Holland's ability to bring these age-old stories to life, Charles Causley commented in *Twentieth-Century Children's Writers* that in *The Green Children:* "Mind and imagination are continuously stimulated and fed as the tales are resolved."

The tales surrounding King Arthur figure prominently in Crossley-Holland's work, both in his translations from the Anglo-Saxon and in his original novels for young readers. 1998's *The King Who Was and Will Be: The World of King Arthur and His Court,* published in the United States as *The World of King Arthur and His Court: People, Places, Legend, and Lore,* contains not only stories of Arthur, Lancelot, Merlin, and Guinevere, but also what Carolyn Phelan described in *Booklist* as "a veritable collage of materials related to King Arthur." Containing a wealth of facts, quotes from Chaucer and other ancient texts, maps of Briton, and discussions of heraldry, jousting, castle life, art, and other aspects of everyday life during the time of Camelot, the beautifully illustrated volume "will delight young readers with a taste for history," according to a reviewer for *Publishers Weekly.* "If ever a book could ignite a passion for Camelot," the reviewer concluded of *The World of King Arthur and His Court,* "this is it."

The golden age of Camelot is also the focus of *Arthur: The Seeing Stone,* the second of Crossley-Holland's original novels and the first of a projected trilogy focusing on the life of that ancient king by linking it with that of twelve-year-old Arthur de Caldicot, who lived in the twelfth century. The two stories—that of the ancient king and the coming of age of the young man—reflect each other, beginning with Arthur de Caldicot's gift of a mysterious piece of black obsidian by an old friend of his father, named, coincidentally, Merlin. "At the very heart of Arthurian legend lies a magnetic dream," Crossley-Holland explained in an interview published on the *Allen & Unwin Web site:* "That there was a time when people formed a society more perfect than ours, a Golden Age . . . and by reading about it, reaching out to it and its ideals, each of us too will be [sprinkled] with a little gold dust, and will rededicate our own lives." The "Arthur" Trilogy covers the years 1199 to 1203, and ends when Arthur de Caldicot is eighteen; *The Seeing Stone* won Great Britain's coveted Whitbread Award in 2000.

In addition to collecting British folk tales, Crossley-Holland has also spent time searching out and documenting the age-old stories of Iceland for the collection *Northern Lights: Legends, Sagas, and Folk-Tales* and *Axe-Age, Wolf-Age.* These stories draw from the rich, often violent Icelandic sagas that are among the oldest tales in the world. *The Labours of Herakles* recounts, in picture-book format, the twelve labors performed by the Greek hero for the king of Argos. And Hans Christian Andersen's *The Ugly Duckling* also benefits from Crossley-Holland's treatment, its text praised as more abridged and "sprightlier than the original" by *Booklist* contributor Ilene Cooper. A *Publishers Weekly* contributor agreed, noting that, "The familiar sequence of events unfolds in a courtly retelling shot through with flashes of humor," in prose "as elegant as it is lyrical."

A writer and translator who is discriminating in his use of language, Crossley-Holland works methodically on his manuscripts, putting them through numerous revisions before publication. His early exposure to the rhythms of music also figures strongly; when writing about the sea, he insists on getting the cadence of the waves into his prose. In his translations, Crossley-Holland tries to be as faithful as possible to the original work, although he is not afraid of taking an innovative approach to an ancient tale. "From time to time I've stepped into a tale and told it, as it were, from the inside out . . . by allowing [the protagonist] to tell his or her own story," he related in *Magpies.* "Recently, I've been thinking further about the use of monologue, and the possibilities of giving inanimate objects the power of speech."

The real power of Crossley-Holland's folk tales have been their ability to take an ancient story and make it appeal to a modern audience. He enjoys bringing to his books some of the things he loves—the sea, Anglo-Saxons, and East Anglia. Asked to describe the basis of his work, he once commented that it was lodged in "roots, the sense of past embodied in present, [and] the relationship of person to place." In a professional life that has incorporated a varied career as a university professor, poet, translator, radio and television commentator, editor, and children's book author, Crossley-Holland has resurrected the drama, language, and culture of an ancient world and made it resonate with meaning for readers young and old, in England and abroad.

BIOGRAPHICAL/CRITICAL SOURCES:

BOOKS

De Montreville, Doris, and Elizabeth D. Crawford, editors, *Fourth Book of Junior Authors and Illustrators,* H. W. Wilson (Bronx, NY), 1979.

Dictionary of Literary Biography, Volume 40: *Poets of Great Britain and Ireland since 1940,* Gale (Detroit, MI), 1985.

St. James Guide to Young Adult Writers, 2nd edition, St. James Press (Detroit, MI), 1999.

Twentieth-Century Children's Writers, 3rd edition, St. James Press (Detroit, MI), 1989.

PERIODICALS

Booklist, May 15, 1999, GraceAnne A. DeCandido, review of *The Young Oxford Book of Folk Tales,* p. 1694; November 15, 1999, Carolyn Phelan, review of *The World of King Arthur and His Court,* p. 617; July, 2001, Ilene Cooper, review of *The Ugly Duckling,* p. 2012.

Folklore, April, 2000, Ruth Glass, review of *Different—but Oh How Like!,* p. 146.

Listener, November 14, 1968.

Magpies, July, 1991, Kevin Crossley-Holland, "The Flying Word, the Word of Life: Approaches to Norse Myth and British Folktale, Pt. II."

New Leader, May 4, 1987, Phoebe Pettingell, review of *The Oxford Book of Travel Verse,* p. 9.

Observer Review, February 26, 1970.

Publishers Weekly, October 18, 1999, review of *The World of King Arthur and His Court,* p. 85; July 16, 2001, review of *The Ugly Duckling,* p. 180.

Punch, October 23, 1968.

Saturday Review, March 15, 1969.

School Library Journal, April, 1991, Ruth K. MacDonald, review of *Sleeping Nanna,* p. 91; October, 1999, Grace Oliff, review of *The Young Oxford Book of Folk Tales,* p. 166; January, 2000, Connie C. Rockman, review of *The World of King Arthur and His Court,* p. 140.

Teacher Librarian, June, 2000, Jessica Higgs, review of *The King Who Was and Will Be,* p. 54.

Times Educational Supplement, January 19, 1990, John Mole, review of *Under the Sun and over the Moon,* p. 29; November 29, 1991, James Riordan, review of *Tales from Europe,* p. 27; May 15, 1992, J. Riordan, review of *Long Tom and the Dead Hand,* p. S13; May 29, 1992, Gillian Clarke, review of *The Tale of Taliesin,* p. 30; November 12, 1993, Charles Causley, review of *The Labours of Herakles,* p. R2; March 24, 1994, John Mole, review of *The Green Children,* p. R7.

Times Literary Supplement, March 30, 1990, Gerald Mangan, review of *Under the Sun and over the Moon,* p. 356; June 21, 1991, Virginia Rounding, *New and Selected Poems,* p. 18.

Young Reader's Review, January, 1967; June, 1968; October, 1969.

OTHER

Achuka Web site, http://www.achuka.co.uk/ (August 29, 2001), "Special Guest #38: Kevin Crossley-Holland."

Allen & Unwin Web site, http://www.allenandunwin. com/ (August 29, 2001), "Kevin Crossley-Holland."*

* * *

CZACZKES, Shmuel Yosef Halevi
  See AGNON, S(hmuel) Y(osef Halevi)

D

DALAI LAMA XIV
  See GYATSO, Tenzin

*   *   *

DARDEN, Christopher   1956-

PERSONAL: Born April 8, 1956, in Martinez, CA; son of Edward (a welder) and Jean Darden; married Marcia Carter (an executive in the entertainment industry), August 31, 1997; children: Jenee. *Education:* San Jose State University, B.A. (administrative justice), 1977; Hastings College of Law, University of California, J.D., 1980.

ADDRESSES: Office—School of Law, Southwestern University, 625 South West Moreland Ave., Los Angeles, CA 90005-3905.

CAREER: Attorney and novelist. Called to the Bar of the State of California, 1980. National Labor Relations Board, attorney, 1980-81; Special Investigations Division, Los Angeles County, Los Angeles, CA, assistant head deputy, 1981—; Los Angeles County District Attorney's Office, Los Angeles, CA, deputy district attorney; Southwestern University School of Law, associate professor of law, 1995—. Panel member of television show *Power of Attorney;* actor in movie, *One Hot Summer Night,* American Broadcasting Company (ABC), 1997.

MEMBER: National Black Prosecutors Association (member of board, 1989), California Bar Association (member of executive committee, criminal law section, 1994-97), Loved Ones of Homicide Victims (former

Christopher Darden

president; member of board, 1987—), Los Angeles County Association of Deputy District Attorneys (member of board, 1986-87).

AWARDS, HONORS: San Jose State University Department of Administrative Justice Alumnus of the Year award, 1995.

WRITINGS:

(With Jess Walter) *In Contempt* (memoir), HarperCollins (New York, NY), 1996.

(With Dick Lochte) *The Trials of Nikki Hill,* Warner (New York, NY), 1999.

(With Dick Lochte) *L.A. Justice,* Warner (New York, NY), 2000.

ADAPTATIONS: In Contempt was released as an audiobook read by Darden.

SIDELIGHTS: Attorney Christopher Darden was thrust into the national spotlight in 1995 when he replaced ailing attorney Bill Hodgman in the number-two slot of the prosecuting team in the famous O. J. Simpson murder trial. Prior to this trial, Darden worked for the Los Angeles County District Attorney's Office for fourteen years and successfully prosecuted nineteen murderers. By 1994, though, Darden had become somewhat disenchanted with the legal system and was thinking of leaving the district attorney's office, when he was chosen to work on the Simpson case. He first worked behind the scenes, investigating Al Cowlings, Simpson's friend and the driver of Simpson's white Bronco in the famous low-speed police chase that occurred following the murder. Convinced of Simpson's guilt, Darden took over Hodgman's role when it became available. Darden then became a lightning rod and target for criticism by defense attorneys, who suggested that he was a "token black" on the DA's team, placed there to influence a largely black jury. He was perceived by some as a traitor to his race for his role in the trial, and he even received death threats.

After the jury returned a not-guilty verdict, Darden was angry to the point of exploding. He needed to vent his anger. "I was full of contempt for some people, and it was easy to purge myself of all of this," Darden confessed in a *People* magazine interview. *In Contempt,* which he co-authored with Jess Walter, a journalist from Spokane, Washington, tells not only the story of the trial but of Darden's coming of age as a black man and lawyer. Darden describes his childhood, college, and law school years, dramatizes how he believes the murders of Nicole Brown Simpson and Ronald Goldman took place, portrays the various participants in the trial, and discusses his reactions to being called an "Uncle Tom" for his work for the district attorney's office.

In Contempt elicited favorable reviews. According to Michiko Kakutani, writing in the *New York Times,* Darden's work results in a "powerful and affecting new book." "In a trial peopled with glib demagogues and carefully coiffed publicity hounds, Mr. Darden stood out as an earnest, conflicted presence—alternately brooding and impassioned, introspective and acerbic.

That same voice comes through in *In Contempt,*" Kakutani added. Likewise, Adam Hochschild commented in the *New York Times Book Review:* "During the trial Mr. Darden seemed, unlike many on view, as if he might be a decent human being. *In Contempt* leaves you convinced of this." "While some of his remarks read like a rationalization of his team's mistakes . . . he is as tough on himself as he is on his colleagues," observed Kakutani, who added, "Darden's portraits of the main players in the trial are colorful and blunt."

Hochschild voiced some misgivings about celebrity books in general: "On the whole, Mr. Darden's book is disappointing, because it, too, is touched by the disease of celebrity. . . . With books like this, you never really know whose voice you're hearing." In a review for *Entertainment Weekly,* Gene Lyons assessed the work's value: "The real importance of *In Contempt* lies not in the Simpson trial, but in its powerful self-portrait of a proud, complex individual confronting racial groupthink and refusing to bow down. Chris Darden is indeed a genuine American hero."

Darden left the Los Angeles District Attorney's Office after the Simpson trial, beginning a new career as a professor of law. He also teamed up with veteran mystery writer Dick Lochte to create a new detective series featuring a smart, ambitious young Los Angeles prosecutor, Nikki Hill. The character made her debut in *The Trials of Nikki Hill,* in which she is put to work on a case involving the murder of a high-profile television journalist, Maddie Gray. Maddie's naked corpse is found in a dumpster, and a young gangster is apprehended fleeing the scene with her diamond ring. It seems to be an open-and-shut case, but Nikki soon questions the accused man's guilt. Disappearing evidence and an apparent security leak within the department complicate matters, and Nikki begins to receive harassing telephone calls reminding her of a guilty secret. *Booklist* reviewer Jenny McLarin found *The Trials of Nikki Hill* "a genuinely suspenseful crime novel with a charismatic heroine and a cast of well-drawn supporting characters." A *Publishers Weekly* writer also praised the novel, calling it "a stimulating investigation into the intersections, and racial tensions, among the dispossessed, the wealthy and a legal system that purports to dispense justice to both in equal measure."

Darden and Lochte's sequel to *The Trials of Nikki Hill,* titled *L.A. Justice,* is a "high-octane" legal thriller, according to another *Publishers Weekly* review. In *L.A. Justice,* Nikki Hill and her boyfriend, police detective Virgil Sykes, investigate the apparent suicide of Shelli Dietz, an artist and lover of wealthy Randy Bingham.

Dietz's young son was hiding upstairs in a closet at the time of the death, and his testimony implicates Bingham as Dietz's killer. Bingham's wealth is pitted against justice when paid expert testimony is introduced at the trial. Darden's "intimate knowledge of the criminal justice system" infuses the plot with "gritty realism," in the opinion of *Booklist* contributor Wes Lukowsky. The *Publishers Weekly* reviewer concluded: "This novel is just the kind of frenzied page-turner many authors aspire to and few deliver."

BIOGRAPHICAL/CRITICAL SOURCES:

PERIODICALS

Booklist, February 15, 1999, Jenny McLarin, review of *The Trials of Nikki Hill,* p. 1044; October 1, 2000, Wes Lukowsky, review of *L.A. Justice,* p. 292.

Broadcasting & Cable, January 17, 2000, Melissa Grego, "Power of Attorney," p. 47; August 14, 2000, interview with Christopher Darden, p. 18.

Entertainment Weekly, April 12, 1996, pp. 58-59; February 14, 1997, Gene Lyons, review of *In Contempt,* p. 57; April 2, 1999, review of *The Trials of Nikki Hill,* p. 88.

Essence, November, 1997, Christopher Darden, "The Trials of a Black Former Prosecutor," p. 62.

Kirkus Reviews, January 1, 1999, review of *The Trials of Nikki Hill,* p. 6.

Library Journal, November 1, 1999, Mark Pumphrey, review of *The Trials of Nikki Hill,* p. 144.

Los Angeles Times Book Review, March 28, 1999, review of *The Trials of Nikki Hill* (audio version), p. 8.

Mediaweek, November 22, 1999, "New Show Will Feature O. J. Lawyers," p. 3.

New Yorker, April 15, 1996, pp. 40-44.

New York Times, March 26, 1996, Michiko Kakutani, review of *In Contempt,* p. C18.

New York Times Book Review, April 28, 1996, Adam Hochschild, review of *In Contempt,* p. 14.

People, April 1, 1996, pp. 50, 52, 55; June 2, 1997, Chuck Arnold, "New Line of Work," p. 146; March 29, 1999, review of *The Trials of Nikki Hill,* p. 51.

Publishers Weekly, February 10, 1997, Judy Quinn, "Chris Darden, Mystery Writer," p. 19; June 2, 1997, Daisy Maryles, "Behind the Bestsellers," p. 24; January 25, 1999, review of *The Trials of Nikki Hill,* p. 70; October 9, 2000, review of *L.A. Justice,* p. 76.

Rapport, January, 2000, review of *The Trials of Nikki Hill,* p. 26.

Time, February 17, 1997, Christopher Darden, "Justice Is in the Color of the Beholder," p. 38; September 1, 1997, p. 77.*

*   *   *

DARLOW, Michael (George) 1934-

PERSONAL: Born June 13, 1934, in Wolverhampton, England; son of George Francis and Dorothy Irene Darlow; married Sophia Sipic (a teacher), February 20, 1964. *Education:* Attended Northern Theatre School, 1951-54. *Politics:* Labour. *Religion:* Humanist.

ADDRESSES: Home and Office—Leigh Grove Farmhouse, Bradford On Avon, London BA15 2RF, England. *Agent*—Andrew Mann Ltd., 1 Old Compton St., London W1V 5PH, England.

CAREER: Granada Television, London, England, producer and director, 1965-69; Derby Playhouse, Derby, England, director, 1970; freelance television producer, director, and writer, 1970—; controller of drama at Clyde Fair International, 1972; Try Again Limited, cofounder and director, 1985; Partners in Production Limited, director; Producers Creative Partnership, director; professional actor; committee member of Channel Four Group; executive producer of Channel Four's rock music magazine, *The Other Side of the Tracks;* teacher of direction, production, and other disciplines in schools in England, Ireland, and Denmark; National Film and Television School, London, England, external assessor of documentary direction. *Military service:* Royal Air Force, pilot officer, 1954-56.

MEMBER: Independent Programme Producers Association (cofounder and member of council, chair, 1989-91), Producers Alliance for Cinema and Television, Arts Council of England (member of Arts and Short Films Committee), Film Council, National Short Course Training Advisory Committee.

AWARDS, HONORS: Award from British Academy of Film and Television Arts, 1968, for best factual program, for "Cities at War"; gold award, New York Film and Television Festival, 1984, for "The Barretts of Wimpole Street"; silver medal, Royal Television Society, 2000; British Academy of Film and Television Arts award nominations for *The Sun is God (J. M. Turner)* and *Auschwitz: The Final Solution;* Emmy Award, World Jewish Film Festival, for "The World at War (Genocide and Occupation)"; Country Music award, for "Johnny Cash in San Quentin"; certificate of merit, United Nations Peace Prize, for "The Fatal Spring"; American Award for Cable Excellence, for "The Master Builder"; first prize, Baltic Film Festival, for "Betrayal"; Royal Television Society fellow.

WRITINGS:

(With Richard Fawkes) *The Last Corner of Arabia,* Namara Publications, 1976.

(With Gillian Hodson) *Terence Rattigan: The Man and His Work,* Quartet Books (London, England), 1979, revised edition (sole author), 2000.

(Author of introduction) Terence Rattigan, *The Winslow Boy,* Longman Study Texts, 1983.

TELEVISION SCRIPTS

François Truffaut, first broadcast by British Broadcasting Corp., 1974.

The Sun Is God (J. M. Turner), first broadcast by Thames Television, 1974.

Auschwitz: The Final Solution, first broadcast by Thames Television, 1975.

A Highbury Family, first broadcast by British Broadcasting Corp., 1990.

OTHER

Contributor to magazines and newspapers, including *Sight and Sound, Times, Guardian, Daily Telegraph, New Society,* and *Listener.*

WORK IN PROGRESS: Open Secret, "a study of programme makers in opposition to the broadcasting authorities and the emergence of the independent production sector in British television," for Quartet Books (London, England), 2002; (with Maxine Baker) *Documentary in the Digital Age,* for Focal Press, 2002.

SIDELIGHTS: Film director Michael Darlow wrote a biography and critical appraisal of British playwright Terence Rattigan in *Terence Rattigan: The Man and His Work.* A playwright at the mid-(twentieth)-century, and the author of such popular plays as *French without Tears* and *The Winslow Boy,* Rattigan was dismissed by later playwrights who thought of his work as outdated and even reactionary. According to Robert W. Melton in the *Library Journal,* Darlow is "a believer in Rattigan's place among the [twentieth] century's most important nonexperimental playwrights." Darlow traces Rattigan's life from childhood to successful playwright to ignored master, showing along the way how the author used elements of his own biography as the basis of his plays. "Carefully balancing discussions of the major plays and pure biography," Jack Helbig wrote in *Booklist,* "[Darlow] crafts a book to please Rattigan fanciers and general readers alike."

Darlow once told *CA:* "All my writing has been primarily concerned to correct a false impression, right a wrong, or share an enthusiasm."

BIOGRAPHICAL/CRITICAL SOURCES:

PERIODICALS

Booklist, September 15, 2000, Jack Helbig, review of *Terence Rattigan: The Man and His Work,* p. 203.

Guardian, June 9, 1970.

Library Journal, September 1, 2000, Robert W. Melton, review of *Terence Rattigan,* p. 210.

Observer, January 23, 2000, review of *Terence Rattigan,* p. 12.

Spectator, January 8, 2000, review of *Terence Rattigan,* p. 26.

*   *   *

DAVIES, Peter J(oseph) 1937-

PERSONAL: Born May 15, 1937, in Terang, Victoria, Australia; son of Thomas Hugh (a clerk) and Margaret (a homemaker; maiden name, Sutton) Davies; married Clare Loughnan (a secretary), December 21, 1960; children: Maria Eleanor. *Education:* University of Melbourne, M.B.B.S., 1961, M.D., 1991. *Politics:* Conservative. *Religion:* Roman Catholic.

ADDRESSES: Home—Melbourne, Australia. *Agent*—Greenwood Press, 88 Post Road West, Westport, CT 06881-9990.

CAREER: St. Vincent's Hospital, Melbourne, Australia, physician in internal medicine and gastroenterology, 1971-86; private practice of medicine in Melbourne, 1986—. Lecturer in the United States, England, and Australia. *Military service:* Australian Army, Royal Australian Medical Corps, medical officer, 1963-66.

MEMBER: Royal Australasian College of Physicians (fellow), Gastroenterological Society of Australia, Royal College of Physicians (Great Britain; fellow), Royal Musical Association, Royal Musicological Society.

WRITINGS:

Mozart in Person: His Character and Health, Greenwood Press (Westport, CT), 1989.
Beethoven in Person: His Deafness, Illnesses, and Death, Greenwood Press (Westport, CT), 2001.
Beethoven in Profile: The Character of a Genius, Greenwood Press (Westport, CT), 2001.

Work represented in anthologies, including *The Pleasures and Perils of Genius: Mostly Mozart,* edited by Peter Ostwald and Leonard Zegans, International Universities Press (New York, NY), 1991. Contributor to medical journals and music magazines.

WORK IN PROGRESS: Research on the effects of illness on creativity; novels.

SIDELIGHTS: Peter J. Davies once commented in *CA:* "It has been my aim to apply the skills acquired in the study and practice of medicine to a study of the health of Wolfgang Amadeus Mozart and Ludwig van Beethoven, with a view to realizing a better understanding of their music."

BIOGRAPHICAL/CRITICAL SOURCES:

PERIODICALS

Music & Letters, November, 1990, review of *Mozart in Person: His Character and Health,* p. 573.
Musical Quarterly, winter, 1990, review of *Mozart in Person,* p. 170.
New York Times, September 10, 1989.
Notes, June, 1991, review of *Mozart in Person,* p. 1129.
Opera Quarterly, winter, 1990, review of *Mozart in Person,* p. 170.
Times Literary Supplement, November 16, 1990, review of *Mozart in Person,* p. 1238.

*   *   *

de GAULLE, Charles (Andre Joseph Marie) 1890-1970

PERSONAL: Born November 22, 1890, in Lille, France; died of a ruptured aorta following a heart attack, November 9, 1970, in Colombey-les-deux-églises, France; son of Henri (a professor of literature and philosophy) and Jeanne (Maillot-Delannoy) de Gaulle; married Yvonne Vendroux, April 7, 1921; children: Philippe, Elisabeth de Boissieu, Anne (deceased).

Charles de Gaulle

Education: Ecole Militaire de St. Cyr, graduated 1911; attended École Superieure de Guerre, 1924-26.

CAREER: French general and first president of Fifth Republic. French Army, commissioned second lieutenant, 1911; served in Thirty-third Infantry Regiment during World War I; taken prisoner by the Germans, 1916; served in Poland, 1920-24; held various commands, including as leader of military missions to Near East and Egypt; promoted to colonel and commander of 507th Armored Regiment, 1937-39; promoted to brigadier-general and commander of Fourth Armored Division, 1940; appointed undersecretary of state for war and national defense by Premier Paul Reynaud, 1940; led forces against German invaders at Laon and Abbeville; moved to London, England, June, 1940, and organized Free French Forces; elected president of French National Committee government-in-exile, 1940; participated in Allied military planning and joint war efforts, 1940-45; returned to France after Allied Normandy invasion, 1944, and commanded French troops against German occupiers. Named president, with General Henri Honore Giraud, of French Committee of National Liberation, 1943; named president of Provisional Government of France, 1944-46; founder and president of Rally for the French People (political party), 1947-53; elected prime minister of France, 1958-59, then president, 1959-69. Ecole Militaire de St. Cyr, professor of history, c. 1918-20; Ecole Superieure de Guerre and Centre des Hautes Etudes, professor, 1926-36.

AWARDS, HONORS: Polish Cross of St. Wenceslas from Government of Poland.

WRITINGS:

NONFICTION

La Discorde chez l'ennemi (title means "Discord in the Enemy's House"), [France], 1924, reprinted, Plon (Paris, France), 1972.

Le Fil de l'épée, Berger-Levrault, 1932, reprinted, Livre de Poch (Paris, France), 1973, translated by Gerard Hopkins as *The Edge of the Sword,* Criterion (New York, NY), 1960, reprinted, Greenwood Press (Westport, CT), 1975.

Vers l'armée de métier, Les lettres Français (Beyrouth, France), 1943, reprinted, Plon (Paris, France), 1971, translated as *The Army of the Future,* Hutchinson (London, England), 1940, Lippincott (Philadelphia, PA), 1941, reprinted, Greenwood Press (Westport, CT), 1976.

La France et son armée, Plon (Paris, France), 1938, translated by F. L. Dash as *France and Her Army,* Hutchinson (London, England), 1945.

Discours aux Français, 18 juin 1940-18 juin 1943 (title means "Addresses to the French People, June 18, 1940-June 18, 1943"), Editions France-Levant (Beyrouth, France), 1943.

Discours et messages du general de Gaulle, Oxford University Press (London, England), 1943, translated by Sheila Mathieu and William G. Corp as *The Speeches of General de Gaulle,* Oxford University Press, 1944.

Appels et discours du general de Gaulle, 1940-1944, Imprimerie Artra, 1944.

Trois Etudes, suives du memorandum du 26 janvier 1940, Editions Berger-Levrault, 1945.

Mémoires de guerre (memoirs; also see below), Plon (Paris, France), Volume 1: *L'Appel, 1940-1942,* 1954, translated by Jonathan Griffin as *The Call to Honor, 1940-1942,* Viking (New York, NY), 1955; Volume 2: *L'Unite, 1942-44,* 1956, translated by Richard Howard as *Unity, 1942-1944,* Simon & Schuster (New York, NY), 1959; Volume 3: *Le Salut, 1944-1946,* 1959, translated by Howard as *Salvation, 1944-1946,* Simon & Schuster, 1960; translations published in one volume as *The Complete War Memoirs of Charles de Gaulle: 1940-1946,* appended documents translated by Joyce Murchie and Hamish Erskine, Simon & Schuster, 1964, reprinted, Da Capo Press (New York, NY), 1984.

Discours et messages (includes selection of speeches from 1940-1969), Plon (Paris, France), 1970.

Message de Noël aux enfants de France (picture book), illustrated by Paul Durand, Plon (Paris, France), 1970.

Mémoires d'espoir: l'esprit de la Ve République; suivi d'un choix d'allocutions et messages sur la I'Ve et la Ve République: 1946-1969 (also see below), Plon (Paris, France), 1970, translated by Terence Kilmartin as *Memoirs of Hope: Renewal, 1958-62; Endeavor, 1962—,* Simon & Schuster (New York, NY), 1971.

Pour l'avenir, Livre de Poche (Paris, France), 1973.

Presence en Normandie, Presses Universitaires de Bretagne, 1973.

The Other de Gaulle: Diaries, 1944-1954, translated by Moura Budbery and Gordon Latta, 1973.

Articles et écrits, Plon (Paris, France), 1975.

Lettres, notes et carnets (correspondence), Plon, 1980.

"Une mauvaise rencontre," L'Union fait la force (Paris, France), 1990.

Mémoires (includes *Mémoires de guerre* and *Mémoires d'espoir*), Gallimard (Paris, France), 2000.

Also author of numerous short political pamphlets and published speeches; contributor to military journals.

SIDELIGHTS: Charles de Gaulle, one of the greatest French statesmen and military leaders of the twentieth century, also ranks among the ablest historical writers of his time. De Gaulle's autobiographical three-volume *Mémoires de guerre* (translated in one volume as *The Complete War Memoirs of Charles de Gaulle: 1940-1946*) recounts his experiences as leader of the Free French Army-in-exile fighting the Axis powers during World War II, and is considered a classic of the genre for its stylistic brilliance and historical insight. De Gaulle also wrote of his extraordinary political career as president of France in *Mémoires d'espoir* (translated as *Memoirs of Hope: Renewal, 1958-1962; Endeavor, 1962—*), published in 1970. A controversial figure often perceived as arrogant and authoritarian, de Gaulle irritated many of his political associates, but few questioned his total devotion to the cause of France or his success in restoring national pride after wartime defeat and occupation.

A career military officer, de Gaulle caused a political stir in the 1930s by publishing two books boldly challenging the French High Command's national defense strategy. In *The Edge of the Sword* (1932) and *The Army of the Future* (1934) de Gaulle predicted that fixed, fortified positions—like the vaunted Maginot Line running along France's eastern border—would require support from a mobile armed force to defend France from an overland invasion. Although de Gaulle's call for a sweeping reassessment of French military doctrine annoyed his military superiors, the colonel won political support and was able to disseminate his ideas as a military academy instructor. Promoted to brigadier-general and commander of the Fourth Armored Division on the eve of Germany's invasion of France in May of 1940, de Gaulle was named undersecretary of national defense by Premier Paul Reynaud the following month. Even though de Gaulle's division distinguished itself in battle, French defenses proved inadequate against the heavily armored and mechanized German forces, and the country fell to the Nazis in just six weeks.

Celebrated for its prophetic military analysis, *The Edge of the Sword* impressed later critics for the light it shed on de Gaulle as a future statesman. Writing in *Saturday Review,* critic Alexander Werth called this slim volume "the most revealing book that de Gaulle has ever written. . . . He lays down, as it were, the rules of greatness, leadership, prestige, and authority." And *Chicago Sunday Tribune* reviewer R. M. Brie observed that "the writing is in the classic tradition—brilliant in concept, concise and clear, and full of axioms and precepts in the manner of [French philosopher Blaise] Pascal or even of [Italian political philosopher Niccolo] Machiavelli."

Following France's defeat in June of 1940, de Gaulle took exile in London in order to direct military resistance from abroad. Supported by Winston Churchill's British government, then also at war with Germany, he began radio broadcasts to France, urging his compatriots to continue fighting the foreign occupiers. An isolated figure at first, de Gaulle began to build up a Free French Army—subordinated to the British High Command—from troops stationed in the French colonies. With his forceful personality and tireless activity on behalf of France, de Gaulle earned recognition within two years as France's supreme military and political leader in exile.

De Gaulle discusses the fall of France and this first period of resistance in *The Call to Honor, 1940-1942,* the first volume of his acclaimed *Mémoires de guerre.* "The tale of tragedy and grandeur" is told "in soaring language—on a par in its finest passages with Churchill's eloquence," remarked *New York Times* critic H. W. Baldwin. Writing in *Saturday Review,* S. L. A. Marshall concurred that the author "throws fresh light on some of history's confusions with an extraordinary

economy of words." Marshall concluded, "On the shelf of military memoirs of this century there is no more moving book than this, and there is no personal story by a great man of action which has more exquisite balance." *Foreign Affairs* correspondent Stanley Hoffman cited the work for its "restrained lyricism . . . [and] classical lucidity, the gravitas of a style that was the product of . . . a powerful personality."

In 1943 de Gaulle was named co-chairman of the French Committee of National Liberation with General Henri Honore Giraud, and became commander of the French forces in North Africa. After contributing to the expulsion of Giraud from the committee, de Gaulle consolidated his position and insisted that the wartime Allies treat him as a head of state and equal partner in the Alliance. In addition, he often tried to dictate the conditions under which Allied generals could use the small French units under their commands. His singular preoccupation with defending France's national prestige and restoring the country's reputation as a major power irritated leaders of Allied countries, particularly U.S. president Franklin D. Roosevelt, through whose insistence the French leader was excluded from the major war and peace conferences at Yalta and Potsdam. Nonetheless, it was through de Gaulle's efforts that France emerged from the war as a victorious power with advantages quite disproportionate to its valiant but small-scale military effort, earning a role in drafting the final peace treaties, a zone of occupation in Germany, and a permanent seat on the United Nations Security Council.

De Gaulle's relations with his Allied partners, his triumphant return to France in the summer of 1944, and his leadership of the post-occupation French provisional government are the principal subjects of the final two volumes of *Mémoires de guerre: Unity, 1942-1944* and *Salvation, 1944-1946.* These volumes, too, earned critical praise for their lustrous prose, insightful profiles of world leaders, and displays of political wisdom. A hugely popular figure when he returned to his native land, de Gaulle acted quickly to build the foundations of France's postwar Fourth Republic government by extending suffrage to women, nationalizing some industries, and beginning economic planning. But his authoritarian style and confirmed self-image as France's savior led to friction with his political associates, particularly French communists who had played a dominant role in organizing the domestic resistance to German occupation. In January of 1946, after losing a popular referendum to reform the French constitution by shifting power from the legislature to the executive branch, de Gaulle retired from politics and moved to his country home at Colombey-les-deux-églises. There he spent the next twelve years writing *Mémoires de guerre* and directing his newly formed Rally for the French People political party.

As de Gaulle had foreseen, the Fourth Republic proved extremely unstable, the weak executive rendered all but impotent after a succession of cabinet crises. In the spring of 1958, confronted with a seemingly intractable economic crisis and a serious rebellion by French Army units and *colons* (settlers) in the North African colony of Algeria, President Rene Coty asked de Gaulle—who retained far more popularity than any other politician—to form a new government. The aging general rose to the challenge and quickly restored confidence simply by assuming power. The French people overwhelmingly approved a new constitution strengthening the presidency and elected de Gaulle to a seven-year term as the inaugural president of the Fifth Republic in December of 1958. De Gaulle granted independence to France's African colonies as one of his first major policy initiatives. He also skillfully engineered France's withdrawal from Algeria despite violent opposition from elements in the Army and rightist colons, who made four attempts on his life in the early 1960s.

De Gaulle's decade-long presidency was distinguished by an imaginative and aggressively independent foreign policy. Gaullist nationalism was built on the triad of distance from the United States, closer ties to the Soviet Union and eastern bloc countries, and efforts to achieve a unified Europe of strong nation states capable of acting independently of the two superpowers. De Gaulle anticipated a thaw in the Cold War, the breakdown of the rival superpower blocs in Europe, and European rapprochement with a liberalized Soviet Union, developments remarkably like those that eventually came to pass in the late 1980s. According to a *Times Literary Supplement* contributor, his wariness toward the United States stemmed from his belief that America aspired to world domination and wanted weak, dependent European allies. These concerns prompted him to pull France out of military operations organized by the North Atlantic Treaty Organization (NATO), develop an independent French nuclear weapons program, and inaugurate a staunchly independent policy toward the Third World, particularly China and the Arab countries. Additionally, de Gaulle's suspicions of U.S. motives influenced his desire to keep Great Britain—a close ally of the United States—out of the European Economic Community.

Domestically, de Gaulle pursued pro-business policies while permitting a significant state role in the economy.

He retained considerable popularity throughout his presidency and faced no major crisis until mass student and worker demonstrations suddenly erupted in Paris in May of 1968. De Gaulle weathered the revolt with a restrained response but later lost a popular referendum on political and economic reforms intended to meet some of the demonstrators' demands. He resigned from the presidency in April, 1969, and retired to Colombey-les-deux-églises. The French leader died of a heart attack in that picturesque village nineteen months later, mourned by many of his countrymen and President Georges Pompidou, who, as quoted in the *New York Times,* solemnly informed the nation, "General de Gaulle is dead. France is a widow."

In 2000 the texts of both *Mémoires de guerre* and *Mémoires d'esporir,* the latter about de Gaulle's political career, were collected as *Mémoires.* In the *Times Literary Supplement,* Douglas Johnson noted that some critics questioned the reprint, feeling that de Gaulle was not a natural stylist and that the voluminous secondary literature on the man and his statesmanship was of greater value to historians and general readers. Johnson stated, however, that de Gaulle's "identification with the history, intellect and culture of France . . . distinguishes him from most writers of memoirs." The critic concluded: "From all these volumes we can see that de Gaulle, born in 1890 and formed in the years before 1914, is essentially a nineteenth-century figure. The de Gaulle of the twentieth century is very present. The de Gaulle passionately devoted to scientific change and progress is undoubtedly of the twenty-first century."

BIOGRAPHICAL/CRITICAL SOURCES:

BOOKS

Alexandre, Philippe, *Duel: De Gaulle and Pompidou,* translated by Elaine P. Halperin, Houghton Mifflin (Boston, MA), 1972.

Apsler, Alfred, *Vive de Gaulle: The Story of Charles de Gaulle,* Messner (New York, NY), 1973.

Aron, Robert, *An Explanation of de Gaulle,* translated by Marianne Sinclair, Harper (New York, NY), 1966.

Banfield, Susan, *Charles de Gaulle,* Chelsea House (New York, NY), 1985.

Clark, Stanley Frederick, *The Man Who Is France: The Story of General Charles de Gaulle,* Dodd Mead (New York, NY), 1960.

Cogan, Charles G., *Charles de Gaulle: A Brief Biography with Documents,* Bedford Books (Boston, MA), 1996.

Cook, Don, *Charles de Gaulle: A Biography,* Putnam (New York, NY), 1983.

Crawley, Aidan, *De Gaulle: A Biography,* Collins (New York, NY), 1969.

Crozier, Brian, *De Gaulle,* Scribner (New York, NY), 1973.

Debre, Jean Louis, *Les Idees constitutionelles du general de Gaulle,* Librairie Generale de Droit et de Jurisprudence, 1974.

De Gaulle, Charles, *The Complete War Memoirs of Charles de Gaulle: 1940-1946,* Da Capo Press (New York, NY), 1984.

De Gaulle, Charles, *Memoirs of Hope,* Simon & Schuster (New York, NY), 1971.

De Menil, Lois Pattison, *Who Speaks for Europe? The Vision of Charles de Gaulle,* St. Martin's Press (New York, NY), 1977.

Eunson, Roby, *When France Was de Gaulle,* Franklin Watts (New York, NY), 1971.

Funk, Arthur Layton, *Charles de Gaulle: The Crucial Years, 1943-1944,* University of Oklahoma Press (Norman, OK), 1959.

Furniss, Edgar Stephenson, *De Gaulle and the French Army: A Crisis in Civil-Military Relations,* Twentieth Century Fund (New York, NY), 1964.

Gough, Hugh, and John Horne, editors, *De Gaulle and Twentieth-Century France,* Edward Arnold (New York, NY), 1994.

Grinnell-Milne, Duncan, *The Triumph of Integrity: A Portrait of Charles de Gaulle,* Macmillan (New York, NY), 1962.

Hartley, Anthony, *Gaullism: The Rise and Fall of a Political Movement,* Outerbridge & Dienstfrey, 1971.

Hatch, Alden, *The de Gaulle Nobody Knows: An Intimate Biography of Charles de Gaulle,* Hawthorn (New York, NY), 1960.

Hess, John L., *The Case for de Gaulle: An American Viewpoint,* Morrow (New York, NY), 1968.

Kersaudy, François, *Churchill and de Gaulle,* Atheneum (New York, NY), 1982.

Knapp, Andrew, *Gaullism since de Gaulle,* Dartmouth, 1994.

Kulski, W. W., *De Gaulle and the World: The Foreign Policy of the Fifth French Republic,* Syracuse University Press (Ithaca, NY), 1966.

Lacouture, Jean, *De Gaulle,* translated by Francis K. Price, American Library (New York, NY), 1966.

Lester, John, *De Gaulle: King without a Crown,* Hawthorn, 1968.

Macridis, Roy C., editor, *De Gaulle—Implacable Ally,* Harper (New York, NY), 1966.

Mahoney, Daniel J., *De Gaulle: Statesmanship, Grandeur, and Modern Democracy,* Praeger (Westport, CT), 1996.

Malraux, André, *Felled Oaks: Conversations with de Gaulle,* 1972.

Masson, Philippe, *De Gaulle,* Ballantine (New York, NY), 1972.

Mauriac, François, *De Gaulle,* translated by Robert Howard, Doubleday (Garden City, NY), 1966.

Monticone, Ronald C., *Charles de Gaulle,* Twayne (Boston, MA), 1975.

Newhouse, John, *De Gaulle and the Anglo-Saxons,* Viking (New York, NY), 1970.

Schoenbrun, David, *Three Lives of Charles de Gaulle* Atheneum (New York, NY), 1965.

Shennan, Andrew, *De Gaulle,* Longman (New York, NY), 1993.

Thompson, Robert Smith, *Pledge to Destiny: Charles de Gaulle and the Rise of the Free French,* McGraw (New York, NY), 1974.

Werth, Alexander, *The de Gaulle Revolution,* R. Hale (London, England), 1960.

Werth, Alexander, *De Gaulle: A Political Biography,* Simon & Schuster (New York, NY), 1966.

White, Dorothy Shipley, *Seeds of Discord: De Gaulle, Free France, and the Allies,* Syracuse University Press (Syracuse, NY), 1964.

PERIODICALS

Atlantic, November, 1955; May, 1959.

Chicago Sunday Tribune, May 1, 1960.

Foreign Affairs, September-October, 1997, Stanley Hoffman, review of *Mémoires de guerre,* p. 225.

History Today, April, 1999, Douglas Johnson, "Exit de Gaulle," p. 15.

New Republic, July 6, 1959.

Newsweek, January 21, 1974.

New York Review of Books, October 7, 1982.

New York Times, October 23, 1955; November 10, 1970.

New York Times Book Review, April 24, 1960; May 29, 1960; January 30, 1972; January 22, 1984.

New York Times Magazine, September 2, 1973.

Saturday Review, November 12, 1955; May 14, 1960; February 5, 1972.

Saturday Review of Literature, May 31, 1941.

Time, January 5, 1959.

Times (London), November 11, 1970.

Times Literary Supplement, November 9, 1940; September 25, 1959; April 8, 1960; July 21, 2000, Douglas Johnson, "The Caesar of Colombey," pp. 3-4.*

DELESSERT, Étienne 1941-

PERSONAL: Born January 4, 1941, in Lausanne, Switzerland; son of Ferdinand (a minister) and Berengere (de Mestral) Delessert; married Rita Marshall (a graphic designer and art director), 1985; children: Adrien. *Education:* Attended College Classique, Lausanne, 1951-56, and Gymnase Classique, Lausanne, 1957-58. *Religion:* Protestant.

ADDRESSES: Home—Lausanne, Switzerland; and Lakeville, CT. *Office*—c/o Author Mail, Creative Education, Inc., 123 South Broad St., Mankato, MN 56001.

CAREER: Painter, graphic designer, illustrator, film director, publisher, and author. Freelance graphic designer and illustrator in Lausanne, Switzerland, and in Paris, France, 1962-65; author and illustrator of children's books, 1965—; co-founder, with Herb Lubalin, Good Book (publishing house), 1969-74; co-founder, with Anne van der Essen, Societe Carabosse (animated film production company), Lausanne, 1973-84. Art director, *Record* (children's magazine), Paris, 1975-76; co-founder of Editions Tournesol, 1977. *Exhibitions:* One-man exhibitions include Art Alliance Gallery, Philadelphia, PA, 1970; California State College Gallery, 1972; Galerie Delpire, Paris, 1972; Galerie Melisa, Lausanne, 1974; Galerie Marquet, Paris, 1975; Le Musée des Arts décoratifs du Louvre, Paris, 1975; Musée des Arts décoratifs, Lausanne, 1976; Palais de l'Athenée, Geneva, Switzerland, 1976; Le Manoir, Martigny, 1985; Palazzio delle Espozizioni, Rome, 1991; Lustrare Gallery, New York, 1991; and School of Visual Arts, New York, 1999. Group exhibitions include Galeríe Wolfsberg, Zurich, Switzerland, 1970; Galeríe Pauli, Lausanne, 1976; Centre Pompidou, 1985; and Art Institute, Boston, MA, 1985.

AWARDS, HONORS: Society of Illustrators, gold medals, 1967, 1972, 1976, 1978, four others, and four silver medals; *Story Number One for Children under Three Years of Age,* 1968, and *Just So Stories,* 1972, were named to list of *New York Times* Ten Best Illustrated Books of the Year; *How the Mouse Was Hit on the Head by a Stone and So Discovered the World,* 1971, and *Just So Stories,* 1972, were both chosen among American Institute of Graphic Arts' Fifty Books of the Year, and for the Children's Book Show, 1971-72; Brooklyn Art Books for Children citations, Brooklyn Museum/Brooklyn Public Library, 1973, 1974, and 1975, for *How the Mouse Was Hit on the Head by a Stone and So Discovered the World;* Premio Europeo Prize, Trente, Italy, 1977, for *Thomas et l'infini;* Gold Plaque, Biennale of Illustration, Bratislava, 1979, for

Les sept familles du lac Pipple-Popple and *Die maus und was ihr bleibt,* and 1985, for *La belle et la bête;* Hans Christian Andersen highly commended illustrator award, 1980; Prix Loisirs-Jeunes, Paris, 1981, for *Quinze gestes de Jesus,* and for *Story Number One for Children under Three Years of Age, How the Mouse Was Hit on the Head by a Stone and So Discovered the World, Le roman de Renart,* and *L'eau;* First Graphic Prizes, International Bologna Book Fair, 1981, for "Yok-Yok" series, and 1989, for *A Long Long Song;* German Best Book of the Year awards for translations of *Story Number One for Children under Three Years of Age* and *Story Number Two for Children under Three Years of Age;* Hamilton King Award, 1996.

WRITINGS:

FOR CHILDREN

L'arbre, edited by Eléonore Schmide, Quist/Ruy Vidal (Paris, France), 1960, translated as *The Tree,* Quist (New York, NY), 1966.

(With Eléonore Schmid; and illustrator) *San fin la fête,* Quist (Paris, France), 1967, revised edition translated by Jeffrey Tabberncr as *The Endless Party,* Oxford University Press (New York, NY), 1981.

Comment la souris reçoit une pierre sur la tête ed découvre le monde, foreword by Jean Piaget, L'Ecole des loisirs, (Paris, France), translated as *How the Mouse Was Hit on the Head by a Stone and So Discovered the World,* Doubleday (Garden City, NY), 1971.

(With Anne van der Essen) *La souris s'en va-t'en en Guerre,* Gallimard (Paris, France), 1978.

(With Christophe Gallaz) *L'amour-petit croque et ses amis,* Tournesol-Gallimard (Paris, France), 1982.

(Editor with Ann Redpath) *Prince Ring: Icelandic Fairy Tale,* illustrated by Heinz Edelmann, Creative Education (Mankato, MN), 1983.

Happy Birthdays: A Notebook for Everyone's Birthday, designed by Rita Marshall, Stewart, Tabori (New York, NY), 1986.

(And illustrator) *A Long Long Song,* Farrar, Straus (New York, NY), 1988.

(And illustrator) *Ashes, Ashes,* Stewart, Tabori (New York, NY), 1990.

(With wife, Rita Marshall; and illustrator) *J'aime pas lire,* Gallimard (Paris, France), 1992, translated as *I Hate to Read!,* Creative Education (Mankato, MN), 1992.

Bas les monstres, Bayard (Paris, France), 1994.

(Adaptor) *The Seven Dwarfs,* Creative Education (Mankato, MN), 2001.

ILLUSTRATOR; FOR CHILDREN

Eugène Ionesco, *Story Number One for Children under Three Years of Age,* translated by Calvin K. Towle, Quist (Paris, France), 1968.

Betty Jean Lifton, *The Secret Seller,* Norton (New York, NY), 1968.

George Mendoza, *A Wart Snake in a Fig Tree,* Dial (New York, NY), 1968.

Eugène Ionesco, *Story Number Two for Children under Three Years of Age,* translated by Calvin K. Towle, Quist (Paris, France), 1969.

Rudyard Kipling, *Just So Stories* (anniversary edition), Doubleday (Garden City, NY), 1972.

Gordon Lightfoot, *The Pony Man,* Harper Magazine Press (New York, NY), 1972.

Joseph G. Raposo, *Being Green,* Western (Racine, WI), 1973.

Michel Deon, *Thomas et l'infini* (title means "Thomas and the Infinite"), Gallimard (Paris, France), 1975.

Anne van der Essen, *La souris et les papillons* (title means "The Mouse and the Butterflies"), Gallimard (Paris, France), 1975.

Anne van der Essen, *La souris et les poisons,* Gallimard (Paris, France), 1975, translation published as *The Mouse and the Poisons,* Middelhauve, 1977.

Anne van der Essen, *Die Maus und der Larm,* Middelhauve, 1975.

Anne van der Essen, *Die maus und was ihr bleibt,* Middlehauve, 1977, translation published as *Amelia Mouse and Her Great-Great-Grandchild,* Evans, 1978.

Oscar Wilde, *Le prince heureux* (translation of *The Happy Prince*), Gallimard (Paris, France), 1977.

Edgar Allan Poe, *Le scarabé d'or* (translation of *The Gold Bug*), Gallimard (Paris, France), 1978.

Edward Lear, *Les sept familles du lac Pipple-Popple* (translation of *The Seven Families from Lake Pipple-Popple*), Gallimard (Paris, France), 1978.

Andrienne Soutter-Perrot, *Les premiers livres de la nature* (title means "My First Nature Books"), Book 1: *La Terre,* Book 2: *L'eau,* Book 3: *L'air,* Book 4: *Le ver,* Tournesol-Gallimard (Paris, France), 1979, translated by Kitty Benedict as *The Earth, Water, Air,* and *Earthworm,* Creative Education (Mankato, MN), 1993.

Jacques Prevert, *Paroles,* Gallimard-Rombaldi (Paris, France), 1979.

Pierre-Marie Beaude and Jean Debruyne, *Quinze gestes de Jesus,* Centurion Jeunesse (Paris, France), 1981.

Jean Touvet Gallaz and François Baudier, *Petit croque et ses amis,* Tournesol (Paris, France), 1982.

Truman Capote, *A Christmas Memory,* Creative Education (Mankato, MN), 1984.

Marie Catherine D'Aulnoy, *La belle et la bête,* Editions Grasset (Paris, France), 1983, translated as *Beauty and the Beast,* Creative Education (Mankato, MN), 1985, reprinted, 2000.

Henri Des, *Chanson pour mon chien,* Script (Switzerland), 1986.

Henri Des, *La Petite Charlotte,* Script (Switzerland), 1986.

Henri Des, *On ne verra jamais,* Script (Switzerland), 1986.

Willa Cather, *A Wagner Matinee,* Redpath Press (Minneapolis, MN), 1986.

Roald Dahl, *Taste,* Redpath Press (Minneapolis, MN), 1986.

A. A. Milne, *The Secret,* Redpath Press (Minneapolis, MN), 1986.

William Saroyan, *The Pheasant Hunter: About Fathers and Sons,* Redpath Press (Minneapolis, MN), 1986.

Zora Neale Hurston, *The Gilded Six-Bits,* Redpath Press (Minneapolis, MN), 1986.

Mark Twain (pseudonym of Samuel Clemens), *Baker's Bluejay Yarn,* Redpath Press (Minneapolis, MN), 1986.

Daniel Keyes, *Flowers for Algernon,* Creative Education (Mankato, MN), 1988.

Michael E. Goodman, *Edwin Arlington Robinson,* Creative Education (Mankato, MN), 1994.

Alistair Highet, *Lucas,* Creative Education (Mankato, MN), 2000.

ILLUSTRATOR; "YOK-YOK" SERIES; WRITTEN BY ANNE VAN DER ESSEN

The Caterpillar, Tournesol-Gallimard (Paris, France), 1979, Merrill, 1980.

The Magician, Tournesol-Gallimard (Paris, France), 1979, Merrill, 1980.

The Night, Tournesol-Gallimard (Paris, France), 1979, Merrill, 1980.

The Blackbird, Tournesol-Gallimard (Paris, France), 1979, Merrill, 1980.

The Frog, Tournesol-Gallimard (Paris, France), 1979, Merrill, 1980.

The Rabbit, Tournesol-Gallimard (Paris, France), 1979, Merrill, 1980.

The Shadow, Tournesol-Gallimard (Paris, France), 1981.

The Circus, Tournesol-Gallimard (Paris, France), 1981.

The Cricket, Tournesol-Gallimard (Paris, France), 1981.

The Snow, Tournesol-Gallimard (Paris, France), 1981.

The Violin, Tournesol-Gallimard (Paris, France), 1981.

The Cherry, Tournesol-Gallimard (Paris, France), 1981.

Le grand livre de Yok-Yok, Tournesol-Gallimard (Paris, France), 1981.

AND ILLUSTRATOR; "YOK-YOK" SERIES

Best Friends, Creative Education (Mankato, MN), 1994.

At Home, Creative Education (Mankato, MN), 1994.

Dance!, Creative Education (Mankato, MN), 1994.

For the Birds, Creative Education (Mankato, MN), 1994.

Lets Play, Creative Education (Mankato, MN), 1994.

Magic Tricks, Creative Education (Mankato, MN), 1994.

Moonlight, Creative Education (Mankato, MN), 1994.

Nonsense, Creative Education (Mankato, MN), 1994.

Nuts!, Creative Education (Mankato, MN), 1994.

Snowflakes, Creative Education (Mankato, MN), 1994.

Surprises, Creative Education (Mankato, MN), 1994.

Weird?, Creative Education (Mankato, MN), 1994.

What a Circus!, Creative Education (Mankato, MN), 1994.

ILLUSTRATOR; ADULT

Joel Jakubec, *Kafka contre l'absurde,* Cahiers (Paris, France), 1960.

Maurice Chappaz, *Le Match Valais-Judee,* Cahiers (Paris, France), 1968.

Jacques Chessex, *La confession du Pasteur Burg,* Le livre du mois (Paris, France), 1970.

Le roman de Renart, Gallimard (Paris, France), 1977.

François Nourissier, *Le temps,* Le Verseau-Roth & Sauter (Paris, France), 1982.

Jacques Chessex, *Des cinq sens,* Le Verseau-Roth & Sauter (Paris, France), 1982.

Anne Morrow Lindbergh, *Hour of Lead: Sharing Sorrow,* Redpath Press (Minneapolis, MN), 1986.

Maya Angelou, *Mrs. Flowers: A Moment of Friendship,* Redpath Press (Minneapolis, MN), 1986.

Woody Allen, *The Lunatic's Tale,* Redpath Press (Minneapolis, MN), 1986.

Bob Greene, *Diary of a Newborn Baby,* Redpath Press (Minneapolis, MN), 1986.

P. G. Wodehouse, *The Clicking of Cuthbert,* Redpath Press (Minneapolis, MN), 1986.

John Updike, *A & P,* Redpath Press (Minneapolis, MN), 1986.

William Saroyan, *The Pheasant Hunter: About Fathers and Sons,* Redpath Press (Minneapolis, MN), 1986.

Sonoko Kondo, *The Poetical Pursuit of Food,* C. N. Potter (New York, NY), 1986.

Roy Finamore, editor, *Ogden Nash's Zoo,* Stewart, Tabori (New York, NY), 1987.

John Cheever, *Angel of the Bridge,* 1987.

Ernest Hemingway, *Christmas on the Roof of the World: A Holiday in the Swiss Alps,* Redpath Press (Minneapolis, MN), 1987.

Saki, *The Story-Teller,* Redpath Press (Minneapolis, MN), 1987.

Ogden Nash, *Food,* edited by Roy Finamore, Stewart, Tabori (New York, NY), 1989.

Les chats, Gallimard (Paris, France), 1998, translated as *The Cat Collection* Creative Education (Mankato, MN), 1998.

Also author of animated films and children's films. Contributor of editorial illustrations to magazines, including *Atlantic Monthly, New York Times, Fortune, Rolling Stone, Redbook, McCall's, Fact,* and *Elle.*

ADAPTATIONS: How the Mouse Was Hit on the Head by a Stone and So Discovered the World was adapted by Nathalie Nath into a play produced in Geneva, Switzerland, by the Amstramgram Theater Group and filmed by Michel Soutter for Swiss television; Delessert designed costumes and settings.

WORK IN PROGRESS: Adult books; editorial work; paintings; watercolors.

SIDELIGHTS: Award-winning Swiss children's writer, illustrator, publisher, and filmmaker Étienne Delessert has been credited by many critics as one of the fathers of the modern picture book for children. Self-taught, Delessert has channeled his artistic talent, his vivid imagination, and his understanding of children into over eighty books for children. In addition to writing and illustrating such well-respected books as *How the Mouse Was Hit on the Head by a Stone and So Discovered the World* and creating the popular character Yok-Yok, who has been featured in both picture books and animated films, Delessert has created characters for the popular *Sesame Street* television program and exhibited his work in museums and galleries around the world. Describing Delessert's illustrations for the 1993 work *I Hate to Read!,* a *Publishers Weekly* contributor characterized it as "inventive," adding that Delessert "wreaks playful havoc with perspective and scale, and features striking earthtone pastels punctuated with splashes of vibrant color."

Born in Lausanne, Switzerland, in 1941, Delessert traces his interest in storytelling to his early childhood. "I was raised by my stepmother, who was a great storyteller, and who influenced my creative development tremendously. . . . ," he once recalled. "The stories she told were of her own invention; she was best at dialogue and situation. I'm sure she would have made a fine playwright. We often acted out simple scenarios together which resembled [Samuel] Beckett plays—no sets, no props, no costumes—just long, endless monologues in which I would attempt to become a tree or animal. . . . If my stepmother had to stop this activity to run an errand, I would go on for hours by myself. It was very good training for my imagination, and as an only child, it taught me how to play by myself."

Later in childhood, Delessert became interested in the fairy tales of Northern and Eastern Europe, and the rich images conjured up by these stories have continued to influence his artistic vision. "Much like in the northern fables," he once remarked, "I have looked into the shadows and the fog for monsters and witches." Delessert worked at recapturing the mood of such stories in the late 1960s, when he co-founded the publishing house Good Book. There he collaborated with Rita Marshall, an American graphic designer and art director whom he later married, to supervise the production of a series of fairy tale books. "Many fairy tales are illustrated and interpreted too sweetly, even when the story itself is quite strong," the artist explained. "I feel it is important to use visuals which are equivalent in strength to the text. Fairy tales usually work to open the reader up, to give him a kind of psychological help; while some images of the tale may be violent or bizarre, by the end, things are resolved and open. These great stories bring out the fears, loneliness, and violence that a person must face in order to move into peace and harmony."

Delessert and Marshall recruited a group of artists to illustrate their fairy tale storylines. Commenting on one of the books in the series, Delessert observed that *Little Red Riding Hood* "ends with the girl being eaten by the wolf. I saw no reason to rewrite it, or to use other 'sweeter' versions such as the Brothers Grimm. We used the Perrault original text, and [writer] Sarah Moon set the story in Paris in the forties, using very disturbing black-and-white photographs." He further asserted that one "should not present children with sugar coated versions of reality. You have to expose them to all kinds of experiences, especially with a sense of humor and a sense of the bizarre with surrealistic situations which open them up to another kind of reality, another point of view. . . . After all, truth is not one-sided, not only what you see on T.V. or read in the papers, or what your parents tell you, or what you learn in school: truth is also what *you* see and how you perceive the unknown forces of the world, how you face birth, life, decay, and death. That has been, I believe, the essence of my books."

To assure himself that he was successfully incorporating children's views of the world into his books, at the start of his career as a children's author Delessert worked closely with noted Swiss psychologist Jean Piaget, who has investigated stages of children's mental development. Delessert worked into story form some explanations for features of the natural world—such as the sun and moon—that children had given Piaget during interviews held during the 1950s. Piaget's assistants read Delessert's story to several groups of children, and checked for comprehension of single words and concepts. The resulting finished work, *How the Mouse Was Hit on the Head by a Stone and So Discovered the World,* was written and illustrated by Delessert for the cognitive level of five-and six-year-old children. "One of the most interesting discoveries was that five-and six-year olds have their own interpretation of how the sun and moon rise and set," the author/illustrator recalled of the project, "interpretations which are somewhat similar to some ancient Mexican and African legends. Big hands, for example, throw the sun into the sky at dawn, and catch it back at sunset. We asked children to make their own drawings illustrating the story we had built together. Without knowing it, the children made drawings very similar to my own."

In addition to writing stories and illustrating both his own work and the stories of numerous other authors, Delessert branched out into animated film production in 1973, and has more recently embraced the computerized technology of graphic programs. "I'm a storyteller, and I love to tell stories," he explained of his overall body of work. "I was attracted to children's books because they are a medium in which I can develop a story through text and illustrations on several levels. Picture books are closely related to film, which also play with images and text." Together with Anne van der Essen, Delessert founded the Lausanne-based Carabosse Studios [Carabosse being the fairy who cast a spell on Sleeping Beauty], for the production of animated films. One of the studio's main projects before it closed in 1984 was *Supersaxo,* a film adaptation of a fantasy novel by Swiss writer Maurice Chappaz. Writing in *Phaedrus,* Denise von Stockar observed that "Many French-Swiss illustrators . . . started their careers at Delessert's studio." For Delessert, exposure to fresh, young talent, was inspiring; the studio "became like a school of illustration," he later recalled. "Young illustrators worked with me and slowly created their own styles. Several have become fine artists."

One of Delessert's most popular characters, Yok-Yok, had its start at Carabosse. Book adaptations of the "Yok-Yok" films, with texts by van der Essen and illustrations by Delessert, were later published by Editions Tournesol ("Sunflower"), a company Delessert and van der Essen co-founded in 1977. "The 'Yok-Yok' books were based on 150 ten-second animated films," explained Delessert. "When I first made the films for Swiss television I wanted to base them on nature. I wanted to answer such questions as 'Why does a woodpecker tap on a tree trunk?' and 'What do frogs eat?' with animation. We did pilots but felt that something was missing and created a character to link all the films."

Apart from the "Yok-Yok" book series, which Delessert eventually wrote and illustrated, Tournesol has also printed children's books by a host of other authors and illustrators, making a significant contribution to European picture books. Noting Delessert's role in establishing Tournesol, *Phaedrus* contributor von Stockar proclaimed Delessert "the catalyst for a newly born picture book activity" in Switzerland's French-speaking region.

For Delessert, each book requires between three and four months to complete. "In some ways, I get more pleasure out of conceiving an idea than executing it," he once admitted. "I love to make the little thumbnail sketches. But after that, there is a long period which is simply craft—slowly executing what you intended—which sometimes makes me impatient. The very last part of drawing—the polishing, the 'making it work'—interests me again, but I don't like that in-between, very technical and painstaking stage." While that boredom has made him experiment with computerized renderings, he continues to prefer pen and ink and pastel. "I think that one of the basic satisfactions [of making art] is just to create a little object," he explained to *MacWeek* contributor Rick LePage. "This satisfaction doesn't exist when you work on a computer because [the image] is behind a glass. You cannot own it; you cannot have it; you cannot put it into your pocket." Delessert's preference for paper and canvas will likely gratify fans of his illustrations, who flock to the showings of his work exhibited in museums from the Art Institute in Boston, Massachusetts, to the Louvre in Paris, France, as well as numerous galleries.

BIOGRAPHICAL/CRITICAL SOURCES:

BOOKS

Catalogue du Musée des Arts décoratifs du Louvre, [Paris, France], 1975.

Chessex, Jacques, *Les dessins d'Étienne Delessert,* Bertil Galland (Paris, France), 1974.

Étienne Delessert: Dessins, gravures, peintures et films, Musée des Arts décoratifs (Paris, France), 1975.

Marshall, Rita, *Étienne Delessert* (monograph), Gallimard (Paris, France), 1991, Stewart, Tabori (New York, NY), 1992.

Kingman, Lee, and others, compilers, *Illustrators of Children's Books: 1967-1976,* Horn Book, 1978.

Vassali, P., and A. Rausch, *Étienne Delessert,* Carte Segrete, 1992.

PERIODICALS

Idea (Japan), number 66, 1965; number 71, 1965.

Graphis, number 128, 1967; number 208, 1979-80; number 235, 1985.

MacWeek, December 18, 1990, Rick Le Page, "Artist Takes the Mac Back to School," p. 50.

New York Times, August 22, 1971.

New York Times Book Review, October 23, 1988.

Novum gebrauchs graphik, January 1, 1976.

Phaedrus, 1982, Denise Von Stockar, "From Töpffer to Delessert: The Picture Book Illustrators of French-speaking Switzerland," pp. 35-39.

Print, April, 1986.

Publishers Weekly, June 29, 1990, review of *Ashes, Ashes,* p. 99; June 14, 1993, review of *I Hate to Read!,* p. 71; September 26, 1994, review of *Dance!,* p. 70.

School Library Journal, July, 1990, Christine Behrmann, review of *Ashes, Ashes,* p. 75.*

*   *   *

DETZ, Joan (Marie) 1951-

PERSONAL: Born August 13, 1951, in Lancaster, PA; daughter of Vernon Gerald and Mary Jane (McLaughlin) Detz. *Education:* Millersville University, B.A., 1973; College of William and Mary, M.A., 1975.

ADDRESSES: Office—Joan Detz Speechwriting/Coaching, 73 Harvey Ave., Doylestown, PA 18901.

CAREER: Junior high school English teacher in Williamsburg, VA, 1974-76; Wells, Rich, Greene Advertising, New York, NY, in account executive training program, 1976-80; Brooklyn Union Gas, Brooklyn, NY, speechwriter, scriptwriter, and editor, 1980-84; writer and communications consultant, 1984—.

MEMBER: International Association of Business Communicators, Public Relations Society of America, National Association of Corporate Speaker Activities, American Society of Journalists and Authors.

AWARDS, HONORS: Excellence in Speechwriting Award, International Association of Business Communicators, 1982, for "The Economic and Social Responsibilities of a Public Utility"; Award of Merit in Publications, 1983, for redesigning and producing a newspaper for retirees.

WRITINGS:

How to Write and Give a Speech, St. Martin's Press (New York, NY), 1984, revised edition, 1992.
You Mean I Have to Stand up and Say Something? (for children), Atheneum (New York, NY), 1986.
Can You Say a Few Words?, St. Martin's Press (New York, NY), 1991.
It's Not What You Say, It's How You Say It, St. Martin's Press (New York, NY), 2000.

Contributor to periodicals, including *Savvy, Learning, Instructor,* and *Lutheran.*

SIDELIGHTS: Joan Detz is a speechwriter and public-speaking consultant who has authored several books on the subject of giving successful speeches. She also runs a consulting business offering private coaching in speaking, persuasion techniques, media presentation, and interpersonal skills. Her clients have included Citibank, the *New York Times,* Xerox, and other major corporations.

How to Write and Give a Speech was written as a source of practical instruction for those with little experience in public speaking. The book provides guidelines on important steps in preparing and delivering a public address, including audience analysis, research, organization, delivery, and overcoming nervousness. Detz's common sense approach in *How to Write and Give a Speech* has received endorsements from many places, from advertising and media executives to Governor Mario Cuomo of New York, a highly praised public speaker. Stuart Towns, reviewing Detz's book for *Communication World* magazine, recommended *How to Write and Give a Speech* for anyone "in the market for an easy-to-follow handbook on public speaking," and noted that Detz's "admonition to choose the correct word and avoid jargon-loaded language is worth the price of the book." Speaking of the 1992 revised edition of the book, John Rosser in *Kliatt* found that "the tone throughout is very commonsensical" and judged the book to be "something of a classic." Michael Rogers in

Library Journal called *How to Write and Give a Speech* "a valuable title."

In *It's Not What You Say, It's How You Say It* Detz again focuses on speechmaking, giving tips and advice on the proper delivery of a good speech. She also helps readers to develop the confidence required to speak in front of an audience. Writing in the *Library Journal,* Denise S. Sticha noted that Detz's book provided "guidance to make the experience [of public speaking] successful."

Detz told *CA:* "I wrote *How to Write and Give a Speech* for a few reasons. First, I happen to love writing speeches, and I get a kick out of sharing the 'tricks of my trade' with anyone who's interested. Second, executives give more than a million speeches each year, but most of these are forgotten as soon as the audience leaves the room—if not sooner. Why? Because most executives don't know how to prepare speeches that get a message across, that make a lasting impression, and that are irresistably quotable. Finally, the typical public speaking book focuses on delivery—an approach that I consider short-sighted. Sure, eye contact and gestures are important, but they can never substitute for a well researched and powerfully written speech—they can only reinforce it. After all, the actual delivery of a speech might be over in fifteen minutes, but a carefully prepared manuscript can yield valuable publicity that lasts forever.

"My goal was to write a practical book that would show people how to make every word count. When they read my book, they will learn in a few hours what it took me God-knows-how-many speechwriting assignments to learn the hard way."

BIOGRAPHICAL/CRITICAL SOURCES:

PERIODICALS

Communication World, May 5, 1985, Stuart Towns, review of *How to Write and Give a Speech.*
Kliatt, March, 1993, John Rosser, review of *How to Write and Give a Speech,* p. 23.
Library Journal, October 15, 1992, Michael Rogers, review of *How to Write and Give a Speech,* p. 105.

OTHER

Joan Detz Web site, http://www.joandetz.com/ (July 10, 2001).*

DEUTERMANN, P(eter) T(homas) 1941-

PERSONAL: Born December 27, 1941, in Boston, MA; son of Harold T. (a naval officer) and Dorothy (Tinan) Deutermann; married Susan Cornelia Degenhardt (a horse trainer), July 25, 1968; children: Daniel Thomas, Sarah Laffan. *Education:* U.S. Naval Academy, B.S., 1963; University of Washington, M.A., 1970; Royal College of Defense Studies, graduated, 1987. *Politics:* "Conservative Republican." *Religion:* Episcopalian. *Avocational interests:* Breeding ponies, carriage driving, gardening, computer science.

ADDRESSES: Home—Georgia. *Agent*—Nicholas Ellison, Ellison & Co., 55 Fifth Ave., New York, NY 10003.

CAREER: U.S. Navy, 1963-89, became captain; gunboat commander during Vietnam War, 1966-67; missile destroyer commander during Lebanon Crisis, 1981-84; commander of a squadron of destroyers, 1985-86; technical delegate to United Nations and arms control negotiator with Soviet Union, both 1988-89. MiTech, Inc., senior engineer, 1990-92; senior consulting engineer for Unisource Systems, Inc.

MEMBER: Authors Guild, U.S. Naval Institute, Dartmoor Pony Society of America, Retired Officers Association.

AWARDS, HONORS: Nineteen military decorations.

WRITINGS:

The Operations Officer's Manual (textbook), Naval Institute Press, 1980.
Scorpion in the Sea: The Goldsborough Incident (novel), George Mason University Press, 1992.
The Edge of Honor (novel), St. Martin's (New York, NY), 1994.
Official Privilege (novel), St. Martin's (New York, NY), 1995.
Sweepers: A Novel of Suspense, St. Martin's (New York, NY), 1997.
Zero Option: A Novel of Suspense, St. Martin's (New York, NY), 1998.
Train Man (novel), St. Martin's (New York, NY), 1999.
Hunting Season: A Novel, St. Martin's (New York, NY), 2001.

Contributor to U.S. Naval Institute's periodical *Proceedings.*

WORK IN PROGRESS: Darkside: A Novel, for St. Martin's, expected 2002; *The Last Man,* a novel set in contemporary Israel, that "deals with the Zealots' last stand on the mountaintop fortress of Masada."

SIDELIGHTS: A former naval officer who retired from the service in 1989, P. T. Deutermann has realized considerable success as a novelist. In 1992 he published *Scorpion in the Sea: The Goldsborough Incident,* a military thriller about an outmoded naval destroyer that suddenly finds itself pitted against a Libyan submarine off the Florida coast. In his review of *Scorpion in the Sea* for the *Florida Times-Union,* Bill Roach affirmed that "the characters are interesting and dialogue is fast-paced," and added that the novel achieves "a crashing, pounding climax." A critic for *Publishers Weekly* stated that "Deutermann tells a convincing naval detective story."

Deutermann's successive thrillers have met with similar praise. A writer for *Publishers Weekly* called his second novel, *The Edge of Honor,* "a lot more than the standard military thriller" and an "exciting genre standout." The book's action takes place in 1969 and centers around weapons officer Lt. Brian Holcomb, assigned to the U.S.S. *John Bell Hood* in the Gulf of Tonkin during the height of the Vietnam War. *Official Privilege,* which features a murder investigation after the mummified body of a navy officer is found on a decommissioned ship in Philadelphia, was also commended in *Publishers Weekly* as a "fine suspense novel enhanced by solid background detail." *Sweepers,* which a *Publishers Weekly* reviewer deemed a "gripping new addition to [Deutermann's] line of naval mysteries," returns to the legacy of the Vietnam War, as Admiral Tag Sherman must confront the man he left for dead in the Mekong Delta years before. In *Zero Option,* a container of deadly nerve gas disappears from a Georgia Army base; military investigator David Stafford encounters FBI agents and bureaucrats, as well as a psychic young girl, in his quest to retrieve the terrifying weapon. Noting that the story "fits nicely between *The X Files* and the reality of what could be tomorrow's headlines," *Booklist* writer Budd Arthur hailed the book as an "engrossing" thriller. A contributor to *Publishers Weekly* added that the book is "also something else: an unexpectedly resonant portrait of people, good and bad, who have been chewed up and spit out by military and government bureaucracies."

This sensitivity to character was also praised in *Train Man,* in which FBI shortcomings are showcased when a military train is caught in a dangerous race against a psychotic bomber of railroad bridges. Calling the book

Deutermann's "most accomplished thriller yet," a *Publishers Weekly* writer hailed the novel as "intelligent, expertly detailed and highly suspenseful." FBI flaws are again exposed in *Hunting Season,* in which retired agent Edwin Kreiss defies the Agency to find his kidnapped daughter. "The author exceeds his near-perfect *Train Man* with this ripped-from-the-headlines plot," observed a contributor to *Publishers Weekly,* who concluded that Deutermann "never sounds a wrong note in this nonstop page-turner." *Booklist* writer Budd Arthur, praising *Hunting Season*'s expert plotting, hailed the book as "a solid read from an author whose own tradecraft is every bit as good as that of his characters."

Deutermann once commented in *CA:* "My writing career began at the Naval Academy, where I wrote short stories and poetry for the school's monthly magazine. During my active duty career in the Navy I continued to write, publishing *The Operations Officer's Manual,* which is a textbook on naval operations, and nineteen professional articles. I wrote *Scorpion in the Sea* in hopes of initiating a career as a novelist, and so far, so good. *Scorpion in the Sea* has been classified as a techno-thriller, but I tried to differentiate it from many books of that genre by developing realistic, three-dimensional characters whose personal fates become as important as the resolution of the underlying 'thriller.'"

BIOGRAPHICAL/CRITICAL SOURCES:

PERIODICALS

Booklist, April 1, 1994, Dennis Winters, review of *The Edge of Honor,* p. 1423; June 1, 1995, Gilbert Taylor, review of *Official Privilege,* p. 1734; August 1997, Gilbert Taylor, review of *Sweepers,* p. 1884; August 1998, Budd Arthur, review of *Zero Option,* p. 1962; January 1, 2000, Budd Arthur, review of *Hunting Season,* p. 924.
Florida Times-Union, January 31, 1993.
Library Journal, April 15, 1994, Elsa Pendelton, review of *The Edge of Honor,* p. 111; May 15, 1995, Elsa Pendleton, review of *Official Privilege,* p. 94; June 1, 1997, Marylaine Block, review of *Sweepers,* p. 146; September 1, 1998, Edwin B. Burgess, review of *Zero Option,* p. 212.
New York Times Book Review, October 11, 1992; June 25, 1995, Newgate Callendar, review of *Official Privilege,* p. 34.
Publishers Weekly, August 31, 1992; Marcy 28, 1994, review of *The Edge of Honor,* p. 82; May 8, 1995, review of *Official Privilege,* p. 287; July 7, 1997, review of *Sweepers,* p. 52; July 13, 1998, review of *Zero Option,* p. 63; July 12, 1999, review of

Train Man, p. 75; December 18, 2000, review of *Hunting Season,* p. 52; March 5, 2001, review of *Hunting Season* (audiobook), p. 42.

*   *   *

DEVALLE, Susana B(eatriz) C(ristina)   1945-

PERSONAL: Born May 31, 1945, in Buenos Aires, Argentina; daughter of Juan Jose P. (a naval engineer) and Lilia C. B. B. (a professor of literature) Devalle. *Education:* Buenos Aires National University, Licentia, 1967, Certificate in American Ethnology, 1967; El Colegio de Mexico, M.A., 1973; London School of Oriental and African Studies, London, D.Phil., 1989.

ADDRESSES: Home—Mexico City, Mexico. *Office*—Center for Asian and African Studies, El Colegio de Mexico, Camino al Ajusco, No. 20, Mexico City, DF 01000, Mexico; fax: 525-6450464. *E-mail*—sdevalle@colmex.mx.

CAREER: Buenos Aires National University, Buenos Aires, Argentina, researcher at Institute of Anthropology, 1966-67; El Colegio de Mexico, Mexico City, Mexico, researcher at Center for Asian and African Studies, 1970-72, professor and researcher of Asian and African studies, 1973—, director of research group on ethnicity and nationalisms in Asia, Africa, and Latin America, and coordinator of research group on the culture of violence, coexistence, and human rights, both 1994—. Australian National University, visiting fellow in Asian studies, 1983, 1984; University of Hawaii at Manoa, visiting fellow in ethnic studies, 1990; lecturer at Universidad Iberoamericana. Mexican Ministry of Education, national researcher in the social sciences, Sistema Nacional de Investigadores, 1987—; consultant to the Australian Parliament (foreign affairs).

MEMBER: International Union of Anthropological and Ethnological Sciences, Asociacion Latinoamericana de Asia y Africa (international and Mexican organizations), Association for Asian Studies, American Anthropological Association.

AWARDS, HONORS: Grants from British Council, Canadian Ministry of External Relations, Mexican Ministry of Education, International Rural Sociology Association, Indian Council for Social Sciences Research, and UNESCO.

WRITINGS:

(With P. Mukherjee, C. Aguero, and others) *Movimientos Agrarios y Cambio Social en Asia y Africa* (title means "Agrarian Movements and Social Change in Asia and Africa"), El Colegio de Mexico, 1974.

La Palabra de la Tierra: Protesta Campesina en India, siglo XIX (title means "The Word of the Land: Peasant Protest in India, Nineteenth Century"), El Colegio de Mexico, 1977.

(Editor with C. Aguero and M. Tanaka, and contributor) *Peasantry and National Integration,* El Colegio de Mexico, 1981.

(Editor and contributor) *La Diversidad Prohibida: Resistencia Etnica y Poder de Estado* (title means "Forbidden Diversity: Ethnic Resistance and State Power"), El Colegio de Mexico, 1989.

Discourses of Ethnicity: Culture and Protest in Jharkhand, Sage Publications, 1992.

Saadath Hasan Manto: Antologia de cuentos (*Saadat Hasan Manto: Tales Anthology's*), El Colegio de Mexico, 1996.

(Compiler) *Poder y Cultura de la Violencia* (*Power and the Culture of Violence*), El Colegio de Mexico, 1999.

Work represented in anthologies, including *Aspects of Ecological Problems and Environmental Awareness in South Asia,* edited by W. Werner, Manohar (Delhi), 1993; *Asia's Environmental Crisis,* edited by M. Howard, Westview, 1993; and *Bhakti Religion in North India: Community, Identity, Theology, and Political Action,* edited by D. Lorenzen, State University of New York Press, 1994. Contributor of more than thirty articles to academic journals. Member of editorial board, *Estudios de Asia y Africa,* 1973—, *Revista de Sociologia,* Universidad Autonoma de Barcelona, 1977-80, *South Asian Anthropologist,* 1979—, and *Comunicacion e Informatica,* 1981-85.

WORK IN PROGRESS: Two books, *Augustus Cleveland and Colonialism in India,* and *Etnicidad e Identidad: Continuidad y Cambio* (*Ethnicity and Identity: Continuity and Change*). Also research on ethnicity, nation, and the state, on cultural production and social consciousness, and on conceptions of peace and security in the world today.*

DONOGHUE, Denis   1928-

PERSONAL: Born December 1, 1928, in Tullow, Ireland; son of Denis (a policeman) and Johanna (O'Neill) Donoghue; married Frances P. Rutledge (a guidance counselor), December 1, 1951; children: David, Helen, Celia, Hugh, Mark, Barbara, Stella, Emma. *Education:* National University of Ireland, B.A., 1950, M.A., 1953, Ph.D., 1956. *Religion:* Roman Catholic.

ADDRESSES: Office—New York University, 19 University Place, New York, NY 10003.

CAREER: Irish government, Department of Finance, Dublin, Ireland, administrative officer, 1950-54; National University of Ireland, Dublin, Ireland, college lecturer, 1954-65; Cambridge University, Cambridge, England, fellow of King's College, 1965; University College, Dublin, Ireland, professor of English and American literature, 1966-79; New York University, New York, NY, Henry James Professor of Letters, 1979—. Visiting scholar, University of Pennsylvania, 1963-64; teacher of courses at Harvard University, University of California—Los Angeles, and University of Edinburgh; director of Yeats International Summer School, 1960. Member of board of Abbey Theatre, Dublin. Radio lecturer, British Broadcasting Corp. (BBC), 1982.

AWARDS, HONORS: American Council of Learned Societies fellowship, 1963-64.

WRITINGS:

The Third Voice, Princeton University Press (Princeton, NJ), 1959.

(Editor) *The Integrity of Yeats,* Mercier Press (Cork, Ireland), 1964.

Connoisseurs of Chaos, Macmillan (New York, NY), 1965.

(Editor, with J. R. Mulryne) *An Honoured Guest,* Edward Arnold (London, England), 1965.

Jonathan Swift: A Critical Introduction, Cambridge University Press (Cambridge, England), 1967.

(Editor) *Swift Revisitied,* Mercier Press (Cork, Ireland), 1968.

The Ordinary Universe, Macmillan (New York, NY), 1969.

Jonathan Swift: A Critical Anthology, Penguin (Harmondsworth, England), 1971.

William Butler Yeats, Viking Press (New York, NY), 1971.

Yeats, Fontana (London, England), 1971.

(Editor and transcriber) *Memoirs: W. B. Yeats,* Macmillan (New York, NY), 1972.

Thieves of Fire, Oxford University Press (Oxford, England), 1974.

Imagination, University of Glasgow Press (Glasgow, Scotland), 1974.

(Editor) *Seven American Poets from MacLeish to Nemerov: An Introduction,* University of Minnesota Press (Minneapolis, MN), 1975.

The Sovereign Ghost, University of California Press (Berkeley, CA), 1976.

(With Robert W. Burchfield and Andrew Timothy), *The Quality of Spoken English on BBC Radio: A Report for the BBC,* British Broadcasting Corporation (London, England), 1979.

Emily Dickinson, University of Minnesota Press (Minneapolis, MN), 1969.

Ferocious Alphabets, Little, Brown (Boston, MA), 1981.

The Arts without Mystery, Little, Brown (Boston, MA), 1984.

(Editor, with Desmond Guinness) *Ascendancy Ireland: Papers Read at a Clark Library Seminar, 28 September 1985,* William Andrews Clark Memorial Library, University of California, Los Angeles (Los Angeles, CA), 1986.

(Editor and author of introduction) *Selected Essays of R. P. Blackmur,* Ecco Press (New York, NY), 1986.

We Irish: Essays on Irish Literature and Society, Knopf (New York, NY), 1986.

Reading America: Essays on American Literature, Knopf (New York, NY), 1987.

(Editor, with Louis Menand) *America in Theory,* Oxford University Press (New York, NY). 1988.

England, Their England: Commentaries on English Language and Literature, Knopf (New York, NY), 1988.

Warrenpoint (memoir), Knopf (New York, NY), 1990.

Being Modern Together, introduction by Ronald Schuchard, Scholars Press (Atlanta, GA), 1991.

The Pure Good of Theory, Blackwell (Cambridge, MA), 1992.

The Old Moderns: Essays on Literature and Theory, Knopf (New York, NY), 1994.

Walter Pater: Lover of Strange Souls, Knopf (New York, NY), 1995.

The Practice of Reading, Yale University Press (New Haven, CT), 1998.

Words Alone: The Poet, T. S. Eliot, Yale University Press (New Haven, CT), 2000.

Adam's Curse: Reflections on Religion and Literature, University of Notre Dame Press (Notre Dame, IN), 2001.

Music critic, *Irish Times,* 1957. Author of *The Scandal of T. S. Eliot* (audio tape of lecture), 1988; author of introduction to *The Stories of J. F. Powers,* New York Review Books (New York, NY), 2000. Contributor to *New Statesman, Hudson Review, Sewanee Review,* and other journals in the United States, England, and Ireland.

SIDELIGHTS: "To those of us who take the professor-journalist as an inspiring ideal," wrote *New York Times Book Review* contributor Michael H. Levenson, "Denis Donoghue is our dashing elder brother." Over his four-decade career, the Irish-born critic has written several highly praised works on British, Irish, and American literature and culture. Much like the New Critics, Donoghue is skeptical of what he considers the "ideologically opportunistic" criticism that came into vogue after Deconstruction, and argues for the importance of readers' direct experience of literary texts. Though this stance has drawn some negative response, it has caused others to welcome Donoghue's work as bracing and corrective. *Boston Globe* writer Mark Feeney, praising Donoghue's work as "scrupulous, authoritative, [and] common-sensical," called him "one of our finest literary critics," and Alfred Kazin in the *New Republic* hailed him as "one of the ablest critics writing today."

The Arts without Mystery is a series of "complex but wittily incisive essays" that attack the tendency of contemporary societies to reduce art to a commodity, writes Christopher Lehmann-Haupt in the *New York Times.* In Lehmann-Haupt's review, Donoghue is quoted as saying: "One of the strongest motives in modern life is to explain everything and preferably to explain it away. . . . The typical mark of modern critics is that they are zealots of explanation, they want to deny the arts their mystery and to degrade mystery into a succession of problems . . . but the effort is perverse." *The Arts without Mystery* include the texts of six lectures Donoghue presented over the British Broadcasting Corporation radio network in 1982. Richard Gilman's *New York Times Book Review* article criticizes Donoghue's "gingerly presentation" of his arguments, stating, "It's not that one wishes for the kind of bare-knuckle assault French intellectuals are so given to making on one another; one can respect Mr. Donoghue's tacit belief that literary polemics ought to be respectful and humane. But humaneness is one thing and pussyfooting another. . . . How much stronger [the book] would have been had Mr. Donoghue shed his caution and allowed his remarkable qualities of mind their full play." However, Gilman concedes that parts of the book are "supple and revelatory," and that it is "in many respects a splendid work, full of erudition, wit and high intelligence."

In three subsequent volumes of essays, Donoghue explores the literary legacies of Ireland, the United States, and England. *We Irish* focuses in particular on Yeats and Joyce, though it also includes essays on such writers as Sean O'Casey, Maud Gonne, George Moore, and Flann O'Brien. The book received generally respectful reviews. Though *New York Times Book Review* contributor Robert Boyers suggested that the book does not entirely succeed in distinguishing the Irish spirit from that of other groups, he noted that Donoghue "is ever alert to questions of memory and identity," and felt that the essays "are not only a pleasure to read and to argue with; they also provide valuable testimony that tradition remains very much alive even for the most cosmopolitan Irish writers and thinkers." John Gross in the *New York Times* praised the scholarship and "intimate knowledge of Irish life" with which the book is imbued, and *National Review* contributor Thomas P. McDonnell hailed it as a "fascinating study of a highly individualistic culture that still confronts the dilemma of having to write in the language of another." Julian Moynahan, however, in an otherwise highly positive *New Republic* review, pointed out that Donoghue's writing on recent Irish poetry is relatively weak; he also expressed puzzlement that *We Irish* scarcely mentions Samuel Beckett.

Reading America: Essays on American Literature, which *New York Times Book Review* critic Lawrence Graver hailed as a "mixture of discriminating intelligence, vigor, civility and acidulousness," includes ten essays and seventeen book reviews on such writers as Emerson, Thoreau, Dickinson, Henry James, T. S. Eliot, Allen Tate, Sylvia Plath, and Wallace Stevens. "Imagination has long been the cardinal term in Mr. Donoghue's criticism," wrote Graver, "and *Reading America* is more a book about the many ways our writers transform experience—real or imagined—into poetry, essays and fiction than it is about an essentially American imagination. . . . What emerges most powerfully from Mr. Donoghue's book is not a theory of American literature but a kind of continuous drama of American literary creation, heightened by the critic's receptivity and fine habits of attention." In *National Review,* Thomas P. McDonnell found Donoghue's essays "well-focused" and intelligent, but added that the author fails to address fully the issue of Christianity and anti-Christianity in American letters.

England, Their England: Commentaries on English Language and Literature, is, as Michael H. Levenson observed in the *New York Times Book Review,* a book that contains two parallel histories: the chronological history of English literature, and the story of Donoghue's "passage through those scenes of carnage we know as contemporary criticism." His essays on such subjects as Shakespeare's sonnets, the politics of the English language, the importance of Oscar Wilde, or the fascism of Wyndham Lewis—all of which Levenson considered "little gems"—are interspersed with Donoghue's responses to other critics. "The result," wrote Levenson, "is that his work becomes . . . not simply a commentary on literary tradition but a commentary on commentaries. The tension between the two perspectives creates the unacknowledged drama of his book." John Gross, in the *New York Times,* deemed *England, Their England* a "fairly orthodox, fairly miscellaneous gathering of literary studies . . . [that] might just as well have been written by an Englishman." Nevertheless, though Gross expressed disappointment that the book lacks the thematic unity of its predecessor, he considered it "always intelligent and usually illuminating."

Donoghue challenges new trends in critical thought in *The Old Moderns: Essays on Literature and Theory.* The book is Donoghue's defense of modernism against such detractors as Lionel Trilling, Fredric Jameson, Leo Bersani, and Michel Foucault, who have argued that modernist art is elitist and narcissistic. In essays about such writers as Poe, Wordsworth, Joyce, Eliot, Yeats, Wallace Stevens, and Henry James, Donoghue insists on the value of aesthetics in art and advocates the patient reading of, rather than political reaction to, literary texts. Bill Marx, in the *Nation,* criticized the book for some vagueness, but emphasized that "Donoghue's attempt to intuit ethics in the dynamics of aesthetic form is a welcome alternative to the banalities to his left and the pieties to his right. . . . Respectful of literature's sense of anarchy as well as order, Donoghue stands for a sensitive—and supple—middle ground. His belief in the constants of human experience is a welcome rebuke to deconstructionist cliches about the opacity of language, the illusion of continuity and the abolition of the self."

This engagement with new literary theories is expanded in *The Practice of Reading,* in which Donoghue argues that we are losing the capacity to read texts with the close attentiveness that literature requires. "If we taught English as a second language and a second literature," he suggests, "we would become more responsive to the mediating character of the literary language." Donoghue disagrees with the "ideologically opportunistic" criticism that treats literature as a socially constructed product without any special meaning, and argues for, in the words of *New York Times Book Review* contributor Peter Brooks, "the rehabilitation of the esthetic." Though he expressed much admiration for *The Practice of Reading,* however, Brooks pointed out that Donoghue does not sufficiently develop issues that are "crucial and complex." Though he found Donoghue's ideas often "bracing," Brooks added that "they can also confuse and even trivialize important issues now much debated. . . . The result is a book that is somehow less than the sum of its parts."

Terry Eagleton in the *Times Literary Supplement* also found Donoghue's arguments flawed. In particular, he challenged Donoghue's view that theorists do not read texts with close attention; he also commented that "Donoghue seems not to recognize that what he means by 'imaginative sympathies' is what some radical theorists mean by politics." Eagleton acknowledged that "few literary critics since F. R. Leavis have matched Donoghue's own skill in tracking the complex sense of a poem," and felt that *The Practice of Reading* contains "some fascinating criticism," but he nevertheless faulted Donoghue for not accepting the importance of theoretical approaches to literary study. "There is no need," Eagleton concluded, "for theory and this kind of critical practice to be at odds."

Donoghue's study of T. S. Eliot generated much critical debate. Some found *Words Alone: The Poet T. S. Eliot* to be conservative and too defensive about the poet's reactionary political views and anti-Semitism. *New York Times Book Review* contributor Adam Kirsch acknowledged the book's scope, intelligence, and "respectful seriousness toward Eliot's poetry," but complained that Donoghue's "interventions in the debate over Eliot's anti-Semitism do not do justice to the complexity of the issue, and at moments are simply querulous." *New Leader* critic Phoebe Pettingell noted that Donoghue "argues that Eliot's detractors misread and caricature his intellectual positions." Conceding that "the book's defense [of Eliot's anti-Semitism] will doubtless fail to persuade those who passionately condemn attitudes that once seemed merely unenlightened," Pettingell pointed out that "Donoghue himself dislikes many of Eliot's comments" and that his book shows how it is possible to appreciate the poetry without accepting all of the poet's beliefs. "Donoghue's passionate readings make Eliot sound fresh, lyrical and exciting," she concluded. "Best of all, *Words Alone* reminds us what it was like to discover poetry and be transformed by its song."

In *Walter Pater: Lover of Strange Souls,* Donoghue explores the life and art of a subject many considered rather unlikely: Victorian critic and essayist Walter Pater, who led an uneventful life as an Oxford don and wrote most memorably about art of the Italian Renaissance. Donoghue takes the unconventional view that Pater was a stylistic precursor of modernism, arguing that Pater's writing influenced Joyce, Eliot, Woolf, and other modern authors. The book drew mixed reviews. A *Publishers Weekly* reviewer considered it an "interesting and informed contribution to literary studies," but *National Review* contributor James Gardner commented that Donoghue "has little new material to reveal about his subject, and his treatment is perfunctory in the extreme." Richard Jenkyns, in the *New Republic,* found the book difficult to follow and "strange," as if the author were actually more interested in writing about someone else. Nevertheless, Jenkyns pointed out that "Donoghue . . . is too perceptive and intelligent a critic . . . for his book not to contain good things," in particular an "admirable" chapter on Pater's style.

Among Donoghue's most admired works is his memoir, *Warrenpoint.* The book recounts the author's early home life in Northern Ireland in the family barracks of the Royal Ulster Constabulary, in which his father—a Catholic—served. Though Donoghue writes about Protestant bigotry against Catholics and the frustrations of growing up in a cultural backwater, the book most impressed critics as a tribute to Donoghue's beloved father. As Mark Feeney wrote in the *Boston Globe,* "*Warrenpoint* . . . is far from the standard Irish memoir of the 'how I escaped the tyranny of Church and family and so gained my intellectual freedom' variety. . . . This fine and various book reminds us . . . that the child is father to the mind." Alfred Kazin in the *New Republic* observed that "The son's feeling for the father is the great thing about the book." Though Kazin appreciated Donoghue's asides on Irish history and literature, he found them sometimes underdeveloped; nevertheless, he concluded that "*Warrenpoint* is a fascinating personal document. As an unexpected story of total love between a father and son, it is wonderful that the son could write it."

BIOGRAPHICAL/CRITICAL SOURCES:

PERIODICALS

Boston Globe, October 5, 1990, Mark Feeney, review of *Warrenpoint,* p. 98.
Christian Century, September 22, 1999, Richard Rosengarten, review of *The Practice of Reading,* p.

911; April 11, 2001, John Ottenhoff, review of *Words Alone: The Poet T. S. Eliot,* p. 27.

Commonweal, February 26, 1988, Peter LaSalle, review of *Reading America: Essays on American Literature,* p. 125; February 22, 1991, Elizabeth Shannon, review of *Warrenpoint,* p. 138.

Economist, March 24, 2001, review of *Words Alone: The Poet T. S. Eliot,* p. 4.

Esquire, July 1989, "Denis Donoghue: Literary Critic," p. 65.

Independent (London, England), January 27, 2001, Lachlan Mackinnon, review of *Words Alone: The Poet T. S. Eliot,* p. 9.

Insight on the News, June 26, 1995, Hilton Kramer, review of *Walter Pater: Lover of Strange Souls,* p. 24; December 21, 1998, William H. Pritchard, review of *The Pleasure of the Book,* p. 36.

Library Journal, September 15, 1986, Michael Hennessy, review of *We Irish: Essays on Irish Literature and Society,* p. 88; September 15, 1987, Richard Kuczkowski, review of *Reading America,* p. 81; October 15, 1988, Richard Kuczkowski, review of *England, Their England: Commentaries on English Language and Literature,* p. 91; August 1990, John P. Harrington, review of *Warrenpoint,* p. 118; March 1, 1994, Gene Shaw, review of *The Old Moderns: Essays on Literature and Theory,* p. 88; April 1, 1995, Robert L. Kelly, review of *Walter Pater,* p. 95; October 15, 2000, Denise J. Stankovics, review of *Words Alone: The Poet T. S. Eliot,* p. 68.

Nation, April 25, 1994, Bill Marx, review of *The Old Moderns,* p. 571.

National Review, December 31, 1986, Thomas P. McDonnell, review of *We Irish,* p. 60; June 24, 1988, Thomas P. McDonnell, review of *Reading America,* p. 53; July 31, 1995, James Gardner, review of *Walter Pater,* p. 61; July 9, 2001, Jeffrey Hart, review of *Words Alone: The Poet T. S. Eliot.*

New Criterion, May, 2001, Paul Dean, review of *Words Alone: The Poet T. S. Eliot,* p. 78.

New Leader, June 5, 1995, John Simon, review of *Walter Pater,* p. 22; November 2000, Phoebe Pettingell, review of *Words Alone: The Poet T. S. Eliot,* p. 45.

New Republic, January 5, 1987, Julian Moynahan, review of *We Irish,* p. 38; September 24, 1990, Alfred Kazin, review of *Warrenpoint,* p. 44; May 22, 1995, Richard Jenkyns, review of *Walter Pater,* p. 34.

New Statesman and Society, March 22, 1991, Owen Dudley Edwards, review of *Warrenpoint,* p. 42.

New York Review of Books, March 31, 1988, Thomas Flanagan, review of *We Irish,* p. 46; October 25,

1990, John Banville, review of *Warrenpoint,* p. 48; November 2, 1995, John Gross, review of *Walter Pater,* p. 48.

New York Times, July 9, 1981, March 9, 1984; September 15, 1986, John Gross, review of *We Irish,* p. 16; October 28, 1988, John Gross, review of *England, Their England,* p. 33.

New York Times, November 26, 2000, Adam Kirsch, review of *So Elegant, So Intelligent,* p. 17.

New York Times Book Review, October 11, 1981, May 20, 1984; June 8, 1986, Harry Marten, review of *Selected Essays of R. P. Blackmur,* p. 29; September 21, 1986, Robert Boyers, review of *We Irish,* p. 13; September 27, 1987, Lawrence Graver, review of *Reading America,* p. 11; December 25, 1988, Michael H. Levenson, review of *England, Their England,* p. 13; October 14, 1990, William H. Pritchard, review of *Warrenpoint,* p. 13; May 14, 1995, Valentine Cunningham, review of *Walter Pater,* p. 15; November 8, 1998, Peter Brooks, review of *The Practice of Reading;* November 26, 2000, Adam Kirsch, review of *Words Alone.*

New Yorker, October 27, 1986, review of *We Irish,* p. 146; May 15, 1995, Peter Ackroyd, review of *Walter Pater,* 87.

Publishers Weekly, August 1, 1986, review of *We Irish,* p. 63; July 31, 1987, review of *Reading America,* p. 61; July 13, 1990, review of *Warrenpoint,* p. 46; February 7, 1994, review of *The Old Moderns,* p. 79; February 27, 1995, review of *Walter Pater,* p. 95; October 16, 2000, review of *Words Alone,* p. 62.

Review of Contemporary Fiction, fall, 1999, review of *The Practice of Reading,* p. 181.

Southern Review, summer, 2001, James Olney, review of *Words Alone: The Poet T. S. Eliot,* p. 614.

Sunday Telegraph (London, England), December 31, 2000, Jonathan Bate, review of *Words Alone: The Poet T. S. Eliot,* p. 15.

Sunday Times (London, England), March 25, 2001, review of *Words Alone: The Poet T. S. Eliot,* p. 38.

Times (London, England), February 14, 2001, Robert Nye, review of *Words Alone: The Poet T. S. Eliot,* p. 11.

Times Literary Supplement, February 5, 1982; January 29, 1999, review of *The Practice of Reading,* p. 27.

Wall Street Journal, January 2, 1987, George V. Higgins, review of *We Irish,* p. 13; October 10, 1990, James Bowman, review of *Warrenpoint,* p. A16; May 12, 1995, Roger Kimball, review of *Walter Pater,* p. A11.

Washington Post, November 26, 2000, Steven Moore, review of *Words Alone: The Poet T. S. Eliot,* p. X8.

Wilson Quarterly, autumn, 1994, review of *The Old Moderns: Essays on Literature and Theory,* p. 95; spring, 1995, review of *Walter Pater: Lover of Strange Souls,* p. 88.

World Literature Today, autumn, 1994, William Pratt, review of *The Old Moderns: Essays on Literature and Theory,* p. 817; William Pratt, review of *The Practice of Reading,* p. 251.

Yale Review, January 2000, Willard Spiegelman, "Criticism at Century's End," p. 133.*

* * *

DORE, Ronald Philip 1925-

PERSONAL: Born February 1, 1925, in Bournemouth, England; son of Philip Brine and Elsie Constance Dore; married Nancy Macdonald, 1957; children: Sally, Jonathan, Julian (with Maria Paisley). *Education:* School of Oriental and African Studies, London, B.A., 1947. *Avocational interests:* Daydreaming.

ADDRESSES: Home—157 Surrenden Rd., Brighton, East Sussex, England. *Office*—Jeirc Imperial College, London SW7 2BX, England.

CAREER: University of London, School of Oriental and African Studies, London, England, lecturer in Japanese institutions, 1951-56; University of British Columbia, Vancouver, Canada, professor of Asian studies, 1956-60; University of London, London, England, School of Economics and Political Science, reader, 1961-65, professor of sociology, 1965-69; University of Sussex, Brighton, England, fellow of Institute of Development Studies, 1969-81; Technical Change Center, London, England, assistant director, 1981-85; Harvard University, Cambridge, MA, adjunct professor of sociology, 1986-91; Massachusetts Institute of Technology, Cambridge, MA, adjunct professor of political science, 1991-96; London School of Economics, London, England, Centre for Economic Performance, senior research fellow, 1992—.

AWARDS, HONORS: Commander of the British Empire, 1989.

WRITINGS:

City Life in Japan: A Study of a Tokyo Ward, Routledge, 1958, reprinted, University of California Press (Berkeley, CA), 1967.

Land Reform in Japan, Oxford University Press (Oxford, England), 1959.

Education in Tokugawa, Japan, University of California Press (Berkeley, CA), 1965, reprinted, Center for Japanese Studies, University of Michigan (Ann Arbor, MI), 1992.

(Editor) *Aspects of Social Change in Modern Japan,* Princeton University Press (Princeton, NJ), 1967.

British Factory, Japanese Factory: The Origins of National Diversity in Industrial Relations, University of California Press (Berkeley, CA), 1973, revised edition, 1990.

Deschool? Try Using Schools for Education First: The Educational Impasse in the Developing World, Institute of Development Studies at the University of Sussex (Brighton, England), 1974.

The Diploma Disease: Education, Qualification, and Development, University of California Press (Berkeley, CA), 1976.

Shinohata: A Portrait of a Japanese Village, Pantheon, 1978.

(With Chris Deraniyagala and Angela Little) *Qualifications and Employment in Sri Lanka,* Institute of Development Studies (Brighton, England), 1978.

(Editor, with Zoe Mars) *Community Development: Comparative Studies in India, the Republic of Korea, Mexico, and Tanzania,* Croom Helm, 1981.

Industrial Policy and Structural Adjustment in Japan, 1970-1980, ILO, 1985.

Taking Japan Seriously: A Confucian Perspective on Leading Economic Issues, Athlone, 1987.

(Editor) *Japan and World Depression Then and Now: Essays in the Memory of E. F. Penrose,* St. Martin's (New York, NY), 1987.

(With Mari Sako) *Talent and Training: How Japanese Learn to Work,* Routledge & Kegan Paul (London, England), 1988; revised edition published as *How the Japanese Learn to Work,* Routledge (New York, NY), 1998.

(With Colin Crouch) *Corporatism & Accountability: Organized Interests in British Public Life,* Clarendon, 1990.

(With Fukada Yusuke) *Nihon-gata shihon shugi nakushite nan no Nihon ka,* Kobunsha (Tokyo, Japan), 1993.

(Editor of translation and author of introduction, with Hugh Whittaker) *Business Enterprise in Japan: Views of Leading Japanese Economists,* edited by Kenichi Imai and Ryutaro Komiya, MIT Press (Cambridge, MA), 1994.

(Editor, with Masahiko Aoki) *The Japanese Firm: The Sources of Competitive Strength,* Oxford University Press (New York, NY), 1994.

(Editor, with Robert Boyer) *Les politiques des revenus en Europe,* Editions La Découverte (Paris, France), 1994.

Fushigi na kuni Nihon, Chikuma Shobo (Toyko, Japan), 1994.

Nihon to no taiwa: fufuku no shoso, Iwanami Shoten (Toyko, Japan), 1994.

(Editor, with Robert Boyer and Zoe Mars) *The Return to Incomes Policy,* Pinter Publishers (New York, NY), 1994.

(Editor, with Susanne Berger) *National Diversity and Global Capitalism,* Cornell University Press (Ithaca, NY), 1996.

Japan, Internationalism, and the U.N., Routledge (New York, NY), 1997.

"Oyake" o "watakushi" subekarazu: yappari fushigi na kuni Nihon, Chikuma Shobo (Toyko, Japan), 1997.

(With William Lazonick and Henk W. de Jong) *The Corporate Triangle: The Structure and Performance of Corporate Systems in a Global Economy,* edited by P. J. Admiraal, Blackwell Publishers (Malden, MA), 1997.

Stock Market Capitalism: Welfare Capitalism: Japan and Germany versus the Anglo-Saxons, Oxford University Press (New York, NY), 2000.

(With D. H. Whittaker) *Social Evolution, Economic Development and Culture: What it Means to Take Japan Seriously,* Edward Elgar Publishers (Northampton, MA), 2001.

Also author of *Rhodesia: The Settlement and After.*

SIDELIGHTS: Of Ronald Philip Dore's book, *Shinohata: A Portrait of a Japanese Village, New York Times Book Review* contributor Thomas P. Rohlen wrote: "When the master of a seemingly exotic discipline writes for the general public . . . [and also] creates a work of value to his fellow experts, it is cause for celebration. *Shinohata,* an intimate account of a Japanese hamlet observed over several decades . . . is just such an accomplishment. The sweep of modern Japanese social history—particularly the spectacular changes that have occurred since World War II, occupation and the achievement of industrial parity—is meshed with marvelously revealing portraits of how the hamlet is structured, how it works and what it means to live in this most elemental and formative of all Japanese social entities."

Dore, a sociologist who has specialized in Japanese social and economic affairs, has written extensively about Japanese capitalism and foreign policy. Many of his arguments are considered controversial, such as his belief, articulated in *Japan, Internationalism, and the U.N.,* that Japan should assume a leading role in modernizing and strengthening the United Nations. Donald

Zagoria, in *Foreign Affairs,* found the book stimulating but flawed by Dore's "excessive faith in the United Nations" and his evident bias against American global power. *Pacific Affairs* contributor Robert E. Bedeski admired the combination of realism and idealism in the book, but added that it remains questionable whether a U.N.-centered foreign policy would really be feasible for Japan. Several reviewers pointed out that comments from Japanese readers, included in the second section of the book, indicate some resistance to Dore's thesis.

Dore also challenges conventional thinking in *Stock Market Capitalism: Welfare Capitalism: Japan and Germany versus the Anglo-Saxons.* The book argues that, economic slumps notwithstanding, Japan should adhere to its own type of capitalism and resist the encroachments of Anglo-American capitalism, which Dore finds morally and economically flawed. This thesis, observed *Times Literary Supplement* reviewer Geoffrey Owen, runs counter to much thinking that blames Japanese business habits for that country's major economic troubles in the 1990s. Though Dore admits the imperfections in the Japanese system, he points out that Japan has created efficient companies as well as a high standard of living and a unified society. As Owen explained, Dore identifies four factors in this success: "a corporate ethos that favours employees rather than shareholders; a sense of mutual obligation between firms and their suppliers; a 'tilt towards co-operation' in the competition/co-operation balance between market competitors; and an active role for government in promoting economic growth and arbitrating between private interests." Though Owen considered the book's disapproval of Anglo-American capitalism to be rather biased, he had much praise for Dore's analysis. "Backward looking he may be," wrote Owen, "but he has written a provocative and stimulating book. . . . Informed by a deep understanding of Japanese business and society, Ronald Dore's book also serves as a salutary antidote to the prevailing mood of Anglo-American triumphalism."

BIOGRAPHICAL/CRITICAL SOURCES:

PERIODICALS

British Journal of Industrial Relations, December 1994, Oliver Clarke, review of *The Return to Incomes Policy,* p. 612.

Business History, October 1995, Paul Stewart, review of *The Japanese Firm: Sources of Competitive Strength,* p. 145; April 1997, Etsuo Abe, review of *Business Enterprise in Japan: View of Leading Japanese Economists,* p. 149; October 1997, Stephen Broadberry, review of *National Diversity and Global Capitalism,* p. 201.

Economic Journal, January 1996, Allan Hutton, review of *The Japanese Firm,* p. 222.

Foreign Affairs, May-June 1998, Donald Zagoria, review of *Japan, Internationalism and the U.N.,* p. 153.

Journal of Comparative Economics, December 1996, Tatsuro Ichiishi, review of *The Japanese Firm,* p. 322.

Journal of Economic Literature, September 1997, Menzie David Chinn, review of *National Diversity and Global Capitalism,* p. 1379.

New York Times Book Review, January 28, 1979.

Pacific Affairs, summer 1999, Robert E. Bedeski, review of *Japan, Internationalism, and the U.N.,* p. 270.

Perspectives on Political Science, spring 1999, Jerold Adams, review of *Japan, Internationalism, and the U.N.,* p. 112.

Times Literary Supplement, September 22, 2000, Geoffrey Owen, review of *Stock Market Capitalism: Welfare Capitalism: Japan and Germany versus the Anglo-Saxons,* p. 28.

Washington Post Book World, January 7, 1979.

*   *   *

DREADSTONE, Carl
   See CAMPBELL, (John) Ramsey

*   *   *

DUBOFSKY, Melvyn 1934-

PERSONAL: Born October 25, 1934, in Brooklyn, NY; son of Harry (a projectionist) and Lillian (Schneider) Dubofsky; married Joan S. Klores (a speech pathologist), January 16, 1959; children: David Mark, Lisa Sue. *Education:* Brooklyn College (now Brooklyn College of the City University of New York), B.A., 1955; University of Rochester, Ph.D., 1960.

ADDRESSES: Home—23 Devon Blvd., Binghamton, NY 13903. *Office*—Department of History, State University of New York, Binghamton, NY 13902; fax: 607-777-2896. *E-mail*—dubof@binghamton.edu.

CAREER: Northern Illinois University, DeKalb, IL, assistant professor of history, 1959-67; University of Massachusetts—Amherst, Amherst, MA, associate professor of history, 1967-69; University of Wisconsin—Milwaukee, Milwaukee, WI, professor of history, 1970-71; State University of New York at Binghamton, Binghamton, NY, professor of history, 1971-79, professor of history and sociology, 1979-91, distinguished professor of history and sociology, 1991—. Senior lecturer in the history of American labor at the University of Warwick, England, 1969; Fulbright senior lecturer, Tel Aviv University, Israel, 1977-78; University of Salzburg, Austria, Fulbright Distinguished Professor of History, 1988-89; guest professor, 1993; University of Amsterdam, John Adams Professor in U.S. History, 2000.

MEMBER: American Historical Association, Organization of American Historians, New York State Labor History Association (vice president, 1978-79; president, 1979-80), Phi Beta Kappa.

AWARDS, HONORS: Grants from American Philosophical Society and American Council of Learned Societies, both 1965; research fellowships from SUNY Research Foundation, 1972, 1973; National Endowment for the Humanities senior fellow, 1973-74, research fellow, 1985; Chancellor's Award, and University Award, for excellence in teaching, 1996.

WRITINGS:

When Workers Organize: New York City in the Progressive Era, University of Massachusetts Press (Amherst, MA), 1968.

We Shall Be All: A History of the Industrial Workers of the World, Quadrangle (New York, NY), 1969, paperback edition with new preface, 1974, 2nd edition with new bibliographical essay, University of Illinois Press (Champaign, IL), 1988, abridged paperback edition, University of Illinois Press (Champaign, IL), 2001.

(Editor) *American Labor since the New Deal,* Quadrangle (New York, NY), 1971.

Industrialism and the American Worker, 1865-1920, Crowell (New York, NY), 1975, 2nd edition, edited by John H. Franklin and Abraham Eisenstadt, Harlan Davidson, 1985, 3rd edition, 1996.

(With Warren W. Van Tine) *John L. Lewis: A Biography,* Quadrangle (New York, NY), 1977, abridged edition, University of Illinois Press (Champaign, IL), 1986.

(With Daniel Smith and Athan Theoharis) *The United States in the Twentieth Century,* Prentice-Hall (Englewood Cliffs, NJ), 1978.

(With Athan Theoharis) *Imperial Democracy: The United States since 1945,* Prentice-Hall, 1983.

(With Foster R. Dulles) *Labor in America: A History,* 4th revised edition (Dubofsky was not associated with earlier editions), Harlan Davidson, 1984, 5th edition, 1993.

(Editor) *Technological Change and Worker's Movements,* Sage Publications (Beverly Hills, CA), 1985.

"Big Bill" Haywood, St. Martin's Press (New York, NY), 1987.

(Editor, with Warren W. Van Tine) *Labor Leaders in America,* University of Illinois Press (Champaign, IL), 1987.

(Editor, with Stephen Burwood) *The Great Depression and the New Deal,* 7 volumes, Garland Publishing (New York, NY), 1990.

(Editor) *The New Deal: Conflicting Interpretations and Shifting Perspectives,* Garland Publishing (New York, NY), 1992.

The State and Labor in Modern America, University of North Carolina Press (Chapel Hill, NC), 1994.

Industrialism and the American Worker, 1865-1920, 3rd edition, Harland Davidson, 1996.

Hard Work: The Making of Labor History, University of Illinois Press (Champaign, IL), 2000.

(Editor, with Paul S. Boyer, Ronald L. Numbers, and Eric H. Monkkonen) *The Oxford Companion to United States History,* Oxford University Press, 2001.

Contributor to books, including *The Carter Presidency: Policy Choices in the Post-New Deal Order,* edited by Gary Fink and Hugh Davis Graham, University Press of Kansas (Lawrence, KS), 1998, and *The Pullman Strike and the Crisis of the 1890s: Essays on Labor, Politics, and the State,* edited by Richard Schneirov and Nick Salvatore. Contributing editor, *Radical Periodicals in the United States,* edited by J. R. Conlin, Greenwood Press (Westport, CT), 1974. Consulting editor, *Biographical Dictionary of American Labor Leaders,* edited by Gary Fink, Greenwood Press (Westport, CT), 1974. General editor, Research Collections on Labor Studies, University Publications of America (Frederick, MD). Member of editorial board, *Labor History.* Contributor of articles and reviews to periodicals, including *American Historical Review, Labor History, Nation, Commentary,* and *Journal of Economic History.*

SIDELIGHTS: Melvyn Dubofsky's books provide information on the history of labor in America. One of his first major works was *We Shall Be All: A History of the Industrial Workers of the World,* described by Thomas Brooks of the *New York Times Book Review* as "the de-finitive history of the I.W.W. It's a fine fat book that gets behind the romanticism to the gut experience of the men and women who tackled a tough job in tough times."

John L. Lewis: A Biography, which Dubofsky co-authored with Warren W. Van Tine, was praised as "definitive" by *Progressive* reviewer Ward Sinclair. The story of labor leader John L. Lewis "has never been told in such detail or with such objectivity before," claimed *Newsweek* reviewer Raymond Sokolov. Sinclair concurred that the authors' research "is impressive; their sources in many instances new and previously untapped; their organization skillful." Sokolov explained that Dubofsky and Van Tine "are labor historians who have drawn on hitherto unpublished [United Mine Workers] archives and various oral accounts to produce a vivid history of Lewis's rise from obscurity in a humble Iowa mining town to power and wealth." A *Best Sellers* critic observed that *John L. Lewis: A Biography* "was clearly intended to be a scholarly effort, seeking to distinguish fact from the alleged hearsay and gossip of earlier books." While warning that "there is tedium in the text and documentation (71 pages of footnotes)," the reviewer added, "let the graduate student wrestle with the infinite detail while the general reader sifts for the romance of the greatest force American labor has ever known." Sinclair concluded that the book "contributes vastly to our understanding of a man who was one of the titanic figures of the American century."

In *The State and Labor in Modern America,* Dubofsky traces the relationship between labor and government from the 1870s to the 1970s. He demonstrates that labor unions and their members have prospered most when they have had the support of the federal government. He also makes the claim that modern liberalism is a direct result of union actions, and that unions have been a powerful force for the rights of American workers. "Mr. Dubofsky is cynical about the attitudes of most Presidents and politicians toward labor," remarked Jordan A. Schwarz in *New York Times Book Review.* He "presents a history without a hero—although Frank P. Walsh, the chairman of the United States Commission on Industrial Relations under President Woodrow Wilson and the co-chairman with William Howard Taft of the National War Labor Board during World War I, is close to being one because he demonstrates Mr. Dubofsky's point that labor needs friends in government." Christopher L. Tomlins, a writer for *Business History Review,* found much to praise in *The State and Labor in Modern America.* He wrote: "Dubofsky's narrative has in it much from which working historians and their students, undergraduate and graduate, can learn. It is admirably succinct. . . . It is clearly written and tightly focused, dwelling throughout on business's persistent antagonism to labor organization as a defining fact of American economic life. And it is thoughtfully organized."

Hard Work: The Making of Labor History is a collection of ten essays by Dubofsky, on subjects ranging from the impact of technology on workers' movements to the working-class radical movement in the western United States. Describing the author as one of a handful of historians who "laid the groundwork for labor history" with seminal writings during the 1950s and 1960s, *Booklist* reviewer Mary Carroll went on to rate *Hard Work* as "a gracefully written, enlightening volume."

BIOGRAPHICAL/CRITICAL SOURCES:

PERIODICALS

American Historical Review, June, 1995, Daniel Nelson, review of *The State and Labor in Modern America,* p. 950.
Best Sellers, November, 1977.
Booklist, June 1, 2000, Mary Carroll, review of *Hard Work: The Making of Labor History,* p. 1811.
Book World, November 9, 1969.
Business History Review, winter, 1994, Christopher L. Tomlins, review of *The State and Labor in Modern America,* p. 593.
Historian, November, 1979.
Journal of American History, June, 1995, Nick Salvatore, review of *The State and Labor in Modern America,* p. 289.
Library Journal, April 15, 1994, Clay Williams, review of *The State and Labor in Modern America,* p. 90; July, 2000, Harry Frumerman, review of *Hard Work,* p. 111.
Monthly Labor Review, July, 1995, Michael Wald, review of *The State and Labor in Modern America,* p. 81.
Newsweek, August 8, 1977.
New York Times Book Review, November 23, 1969; February 1, 1970; May 8, 1994, review of *The State and Labor in Modern America,* p. 21.
Progressive, February, 1978.
Times Literary Supplement, July 16, 1970.
Washington Post, November 28, 1969.

DWORKIN, R. M.
See DWORKIN, Ronald M(yles)

*   *   *

DWORKIN, Ronald M(yles) 1931-
(R. M. Dworkin)

PERSONAL: Born December 11, 1931, in Worcester, MA; son of David and Madeline Dworkin; married Betsy Celia Ross, July 18, 1958; children: Anthony Ross, Jennifer. *Education:* Harvard University, B.A., 1953, LL.B., 1957; Oxford University, B.A., 1955, M.A.

ADDRESSES: Home—39 Hallsey Lane, Woodbridge, CT 06525.

CAREER: Admitted to the Bar, 1959; Sullivan & Cromwell (law firm), New York, NY, associate, 1958-62 Yale University, New Haven, CT, assistant professor, 1962-65, professor, 1965-68, Wesley N. Hohfeld Professor of Jurisprudence, 1968-69; Oxford University, Oxford, England, professor of jurisprudence, 1969—, fellow of University College, 1969—; New York University, New York, NY, professor of law, 1975—. Harvard Law School clerk for Judge Learned Hand, 1957-58. Princeton University, Princeton, NJ, visiting professor of philosophy, 1963, 1974-75, Gauss seminarian, 1965-66; Stanford University, Stanford, CA, visiting professor of law, 1967; Western Reserve University (now Case Western Reserve University), Cleveland, OH, Case Lecturer, 1967; delegate to the Democratic National Convention, 1972, 1976; Northwestern University, Evanston, IL, Rosenthal Lecturer, 1975; University of Witwatersrand, Witwatersrand, South Africa, Academic Freedom Lecturer, 1976; Cornell University, Ithaca, NY, professor-at-large, 1976-82; Harvard University, Cambridge, MA, visiting professor of philosophy and law, 1977, visiting professor of philosophy, 1979-82; University of Nebraska, Lincoln, Roscoe Pound Lecturer, 1979. Member of Democratic Charter Commission and Ditchley Foundation (member of program committee).

MEMBER: Democrats Abroad (chairman, 1972-74), Oxford American Democrats, Garrick Club.

AWARDS, HONORS: Honorary degree from Yale University, 1965; LL.D. from Williams College, 1981, and John Jay College of Criminal Justice, 1983; fellow of the British Academy; fellow of the American Academy of Arts and Letters.

WRITINGS:

UNDER NAME RONALD DWORKIN, EXCEPT AS NOTED

(With Herbert W. Titus; under name Ronald M. Dworkin) *The Perils of Decriminalization* (sound recording), Center for the Study of Democratic Institutions, 1976.

Taking Rights Seriously, Harvard University Press (Cambridge, MA), 1977.

(Editor under name R. M. Dworkin) *The Philosophy of Law,* Oxford University Press (New York, NY), 1977.

Political Judges and the Rule of Law (lectures), Longwood, 1977.

(Editor with Karl Miller and Richard Sennett) David Rieff, general editor, *Humanities in Review: Volume I,* Cambridge University Press, 1982.

A Matter of Principle, Harvard University Press, 1985.

Law's Empire, Belknap Press (London, England), 1986.

A Bill of Rights for Britain, Chatto & Windus (London, England), 1990.

Justice and the Good Life, University of Kansas, 1990.

Life's Dominion: An Argument about Abortion, Euthanasia, and Individual Freedom, Knopf (New York, NY), 1993.

The Rise of the Imperial Self: America's Culture Wars in Augustinian Perspective, Rowman & Littlefield (Boston, MA), 1996.

Freedom's Law: The Moral Reading of the American Constitution, Harvard University Press (Cambridge, MA), 1996.

Sovereign Virtue: The Theory and Practice of Equality, Harvard University Press (Cambridge, MA), 2000.

(Editor with others) *The Legacy of Isaiah Berlin,* New York Review of Books (New York, NY), 2001.

Also author of *Life's Dominion: An Argument about Abortion, Euthanasia, and Individual Freedom,* 1993. Contributor, under name Ronald M. Dworkin, to *The Role and Rule(s) of Law in Contemporary America,* Antioch Press, 1970; contributor, *Equality and Preferential Treatment,* edited by Marshall Cohen, Thomas Nagel, and Thomas Scanlon, Princeton University Press, 1977. Contributor to periodicals, including *Philosophy and Public Affairs* and *New York Review of Books.*

SIDELIGHTS: Political philosopher Ronald M. Dworkin is highly regarded as an expert in jurisprudence, the science of law. A professor of law at New York University and of jurisprudence at Oxford University, Dworkin advanced his own controversial theory of legal principles in several books, including *Taking Rights Seriously, A Matter of Principle,* and *Law's Empire.* Critics have praised his works for their clarity, soundness of logic, and accessibility to the general reading public.

Dworkin's first book, a collection of essays titled *Taking Rights Seriously,* was deemed "the most sophisticated contribution to [jurisprudence] yet made by an American writer" by Marshall Cohen in the *New York Review of Books.* In the volume Dworkin rejects two prevailing models of law: legal positivism and utilitarianism. Legal positivism holds that individuals possess only those rights that have been granted by political decision or social practice. Utilitarianism maintains that the law should provide for the happiness of the greatest number and, in so doing, subordinates the individual moral rights of a minority to the desires of a majority. Finding both theories inadequate, Dworkin developed an alternative view of rights based on a distinction between legal rules and legal principles.

Dworkin's "major contribution to jurisprudence," wrote Cohen, is his attempt to "show that even in a hard case one of the parties has a legal right to win." Dworkin readily admits that different judges might decide the same case in different ways, but he proposes that a strict adherence to his tenets could increase the consistency of judges' verdicts. In a difficult case that lacks precedent or involves ambiguous or conflicting rules, a judge must exercise judicial discretion based on principle, the origin of which, explained Cohen, lies "in a sense of appropriateness—often . . . moral appropriateness—developed in the legal profession and in the public during a considerable period of time." The judges, in effect, take on legislative responsibilities, making new rights when issues cannot be decided on the basis of preexisting rights.

Dworkin exemplifies his theory in *Taking Rights Seriously,* applying the logic of his principles to several court cases. One essay in the volume cites *Riggs v. Palmer,* the 1889 case that questioned an heir's right to inherit his grandfather's estate after murdering the grandfather. Statutory law would yield the property to the murderer. But the court noted, as cited in the *New York Review of Books,* that "all laws as well as all contracts may be controlled in their operation and effect by general, fundamental maxims of the common law." The court's decision that "no one shall . . . profit by his own . . . crime" reflected, in Dworkin's terms, the invocation of a principle. According to positivist doctrine, the murderer was denied his property. Dworkin contends, however, that because the law includes both principles and rules, the murderer had no right to the property under the law.

Alluding to several historic court cases, including *Bakke v. the Regents of the University of California* and the *DeFunis* discrimination case, Dworkin, as quoted by David Beckwith in *Time,* theorized that "the right to be treated as an equal" does not necessarily mean "the right to equal treatment." In both the *Bakke* and *DeFunis* cases, white males claimed that their right to equal protection of the law was violated by an educational institution's admissions policy favoring minority groups—Bakke was denied admission to the University of California's Davis medical school and DeFunis was denied admission to the University of Washington's law school. Dworkin argues that no individual has a right to a medical or legal education. Any admissions policy will place some group, be it the less intelligent, the more intelligent, a racial minority, or a racial majority, at a disadvantage. But because, as Cohen related, the policy in question "displays no lack of respect for those it disadvantages," it does not violate any student's right to be treated as an individual.

Michael Walzer asserted in the *New Republic* that under Dworkin's model "the rights that belong to all of us are ultimately entrusted to some of us, judicial Guardians, an elite of judges." But Dworkin counters the fear that such a system could be easily abused and sets up a broad scenario—which was cited by Walzer—to explain his theory: if a judge when confronted with a difficult case refers to a political theory that encompasses the convictions of a society then "the judge discovers rather than invents the rights that he enforces: his decision is really a 'finding.' Whether he likes what he finds or not, he is bound by it."

Despite the controversy it incited, Dworkin's first book was highly acclaimed. Roger Errera, writing in the *Times Literary Supplement,* echoed the majority of reviewers when he called *Taking Rights Seriously* "a tightly packed, energetic and profound book, the result of deep study and teaching . . . [that] is also well written and easy to read." Dworkin's second collection of essays, *A Matter of Principle,* was published in 1985 and also fared well with the critics. Hailed as "a philosophical feast" by Steven Shiffrin in the *New York Times Book Review,* the book expanded on Dworkin's notion of principle in relation to the law. The author makes a distinction between arguments of principle, which are based on individuals' rights, and arguments of policy, which are based on the promotion of the public good. He suggests in one essay, as excerpted by Shiffrin, that liberalism, "an authentic and coherent po-

litical morality," revolves around an argument of principle: that "government must be neutral on what might be called the question of the good life." Dworkin emphasizes throughout the book that fair interpretations of the law are rooted in a moral framework and must expose and defend the fundamental principles relevant to each specific case.

Dworkin's 1986 book, *Law's Empire,* dubbed "a jurisprudential epic" by Bill Blum in the *Los Angeles Times Book Review,* offers perhaps the deepest explication of Dworkin's previously established philosophy. It presents another Dworkinian alternative to the conventional and pragmatic view of the law. Conventionalist doctrine is based on tradition and sees established authority as the source of the law. The pragmatist view of the law is more flexible, allowing individuals to interpret the law to their own advantage. With "elegance and power," wrote Edwin M. Yoder, Jr., in *Washington Post Book World,* Dworkin argues his alternative, "law as integrity." As quoted by Yoder, Dworkin claims in his book that the law as integrity "begins in the present and pursues the past only so far as and in the way that its contemporary focus dictates. It does not aim to recapture . . . the ideals or practical purpose of the politicians who first created it. It aims rather to justify what they did . . . to provide an honorable future."

Commenting on the controversy and criticism that Dworkin's theories have set off among scholars of jurisprudence in recent years, Beckwith noted that the author "has succeeded in stimulating his colleagues": editors of the *Georgia Law Review* seeking articles for an issue on jurisprudence "found that virtually every contribution [from scholars to the journal] addressed the challenging thoughts of the Yank at Oxford." Graham Hughes, a professor of law at New York University and colleague of the author, noted in the *New Republic* that Dworkin "is more honored among philosophers and political scientists than among lawyers." He called Dworkin's "partial exile" to England "unfortunate" because "Dworkin speaks with a specially American voice, bearing a hopeful gospel that the parched community of American lawyers and law professors needs to hear and debate."

Dworkin has continued to tackle the thorniest legal and moral questions of the modern era. His 1993 book, *Life's Dominion: An Argument about Abortion, Euthanasia, and Individual Freedom,* delves into the religious, biological, and deeply held personal beliefs surrounding the sanctity of life. Dworkin arrives at the theory that people's views on the matter differ so greatly that they become a set of religious beliefs in and of themselves. Therefore, for the government to regulate such matters, such as overturning the 1973 U.S. Supreme Court decision that guarantees the right to abortion, creates a veritable establishment of religion itself—which the First Amendment's guarantee of religious liberty for all expressly prohibits. A *Kirkus Reviews* critic's assessment of *Life's Dominion* called it "an original contribution to the abortion debate, as well as a stimulating discussion of our contradictory feelings about the meaning of human life."

While at Harvard Law School in the late 1950s, Dworkin clerked for Judge Learned Hand, a New York state federal judge who was sometimes referred to as the Supreme Court's "tenth justice." Hand wrote extensively about the Constitution and the High Court, most famously in his 1952 book, *The Spirit of Liberty,* in which he asserted that, ideally, it is a spirit that "is not too sure that it is right." Dworkin's own body of writing has diverged from that view in favor of a moral-based interpretation of the Constitution. Hand and his ideas are discussed in the last chapter of Dworkin's 1996 book, *Freedom's Law: The Moral Reading of the American Constitution,* a collection of essays that were previously published in the *New York Review of Books* between 1987 and 1994. Other chapters analyze the constitutional theories of Robert Bork, a rejected Supreme Court nominee in 1987, and Justice Clarence Thomas, who claimed to have formed no constitutional philosophy at all. The first two sections of the book are given over to discussions on abortion and freedom of speech. These essays discuss the Constitution and how judges should interpret a document that was written more than two centuries before in a far different era with different customs and morals; Dworkin argues against strict historical interpretation in favor of a moral interpretation. The Framers of the Constitution, he asserts, deliberately set down abstract moral principles that could stand the test of time. "Complex and compelling, learned and readable, it goes to the heart of what it means to live in a democracy," stated a *Publishers Weekly* reviewer. Cass R. Sunstein, writing in the *New Republic,* called the essay on Learned Hand "the most intriguing chapter in the book, largely because of the tension between Dworkin's evident affection for Hand and Dworkin's equally evident antipathy to Hand's views."

Freedom's Law incited debate within the legal community. *Michigan Law Review* writer Thomas D. Eisele disagreed with Dworkin's assertion that the Constitution speaks in a moral voice. "Dworkin's recommended 'moral reading' of the Constitution is based upon an assumption that he, Dworkin, knows or understands what kind of a document the Constitution is," Eisele stated.

"At the most basic level, Dworkin seems to think that he knows how the Constitution works and, in particular, that he knows how it speaks." Eisele compared it with other "statements of moral absolutes" from past philosophers and concluded that the Constitution fails to measure up as the moral document that Dworkin terms it. In contrast, Eisele argued, its language is similar to a corporate charter. In a lengthy *California Law Review* article, Edward J. McCaffery discussed the criticism of Dworkin's writings and theories. "We should stop arguing at or against Ronald Dworkin and start arguing with him," McCaffery concluded. "Dworkin has consistently stood up for what is best in liberal society," he said. "*Freedom's Law* amply demonstrates that he is still doing so with considerable skill, at precisely a time when our public political culture, liberal no less than conservative, is most in need of principles."

In Dworkin's *Sovereign Virtue: The Theory and Practice of Equality,* published in 2000, he discusses, over the course of several essays dating back to 1981, the slippery political ideal of "equality" and its vital importance to democracy. "No government is legitimate that does not show equal concern for the fate of all those citizens over whom it claims dominion and from whom it claims allegiance," Dworkin writes. In a line of reasoning leading from this assertion, Dworkin argues in favor of legislation that recognizes that not all citizens are created or born equal, and he concludes that a government should ensure that all have equal access to resources. With this in mind, he explores some contemporary political issues such as universal health care, cloning, and campaign finance reform. Dworkin judges the 1996 Welfare Reform Act harshly and also condemns the lack of universal health-care coverage in the United States as "a national disgrace." In the final chapters of *Sovereign Virtue,* Dworkin argues in favor of the idea that all human life should flourish, but that each person, on the other hand, is also responsible for his or her own flourishing. *National Review* essayist Peter Berkowitz disagreed with Dworkin's reasoning. "Dworkin is a powerful and persuasive advocate of the view that law and politics do indeed at crucial junctures depend on moral philosophy's services. At the same time, exposing the subtle maneuvers and clever obfuscations he employs to advance his particular derivation of law and public policy from morality is a powerful reminder that we have good reason to limit our dependence on philosophers." A *Publishers Weekly* reviewer termed it an "ambitious investigation into the very bedrock of a democratic society," and said its author is "one of our leading legal thinkers."

BIOGRAPHICAL/CRITICAL SOURCES:

BOOKS

Dworkin, Ronald, *Law's Empire,* Belknap Press, 1986.

Dworkin, Ronald, *A Matter of Principle,* Harvard University Press (Cambridge, MA), 1985.

Dworkin, Ronald, *Taking Rights Seriously,* Harvard University Press (Cambridge, MA), 1977.

Thinkers of the Twentieth Century, St. James Press (Detroit, MI), 1987, pp. 195-197.

PERIODICALS

Booklist, June 1, 2000, Bryce Christensen, review of *Sovereign Virtue,* p. 1811.

California Law Review, July 1997, Edward J. McCaffery, review of *Freedom's Law,* pp. 1043-1086.

Commonweal, December 15, 2000, David McCabe, "How Equal Can We Be?," p.21.

Independent Review, spring, 2001, Daniel Choi, review of *Sovereign Virtue,* p. 618.

Kirkus Reviews, April 1, 1993, review of *Life's Dominion.*

Los Angeles Times Book Review, May 11, 1986, Bill Blum, review of *Law's Empire.*

Michigan Law Review, May 1997, Thomas D. Eisele, review of *Freedom's Law,* pp. 1799-1838.

National Review, April 28, 1978; August 28, 2000, Peter Berkowitz, "Easy Virtue."

New Republic, June 25, 1977; July 29, 1985; May 13, 1996, Cass R. Sunstein, review of *Freedom's Law,* p. 35.

New York Review of Books, May 26, 1977; February 14, 1985.

New York Times Book Review, June 9, 1985; May 25, 1986.

Observer, June 8, 1986.

Publishers Weekly, March 11, 1996, review of *Freedom's Law,* p. 47; May 1, 2000, review of *Sovereign Virtue,* p. 57.

Reason, October 2000, Richard A. Epstein, "Impractical Equality," p. 60.

Spectator, August 17, 1985.

Theological Studies, June, 2001, David E. Decosse, review of *Sovereign Virtue,* p. 433.

Time, September 5, 1977, David Beckwith, review of *Taking Rights Seriously.*

Times Literary Supplement, August 19, 1977; October 25, 1985; August 22, 1986.

Washington Post Book World, June 15, 1986, Edwin M. Yoder Jr., review of *Law's Empire.*

Yale Law Journal, October 1996, Noah R. Feldman, review of *Freedom's Law,* pp. 229-234.*

E

EGAN, Desmond 1936-

PERSONAL: Born July 15, 1936, in Athlone, County Westmeath, Ireland; son of Thomas (a shopkeeper) and Kathleen (a teacher; maiden name, Garland) Egan; married Vivienne Abbot (a lecturer and writer), August, 1981; children: Kate, Bebhinn. *Ethnicity:* "White Caucasian." *Education:* Maynooth University, B.A.; University College, Dublin, M.A., 1965. *Religion:* Catholic. *Avocational interests:* Landscape, people, political events, travel, music (traditional Irish, classical, progressive jazz), painting, sculpture, tennis.

ADDRESSES: *Home*—Great Connell, Newbridge, County Kildare, Ireland. *Agent*—Mrs. Ann Burke, The Goldsmith Press Ltd., Newbridge, County Kildare, Ireland.

CAREER: Teacher and poet. Editor and founder of the literary magazine, *Era,* 1974-84; Newbridge College, County Kildare, Ireland, teacher, 1972-87; writer, 1987—. Juror, Neustadt Prize, 1996; appointed to Cultural Relations Committee by Department of Foreign Affairs, 1998; artistic director, Gerard Manley Hopkins International Summer School; invited readings, lectures and workshops in various countries, including Unites States, Germany, France, Spain, Switzerland, Latvia, Sweden, Hungary, Great Britain, Denmark, Czech and Slovak Republics, Russia, Italy and Belgium; and at various festivals and conferences, including American Conference for Irish Studies, International Association for the Study of Irish Literature, European Poetry Festival, International Poetry Festival of Malmo, World Poetry Congress, and international conferences on T. S. Eliot, Ezra Pound, W. B. Yeats, G. M. Hopkins, Patrick Kavanagh, and James Joyce.

MEMBER: Amnesty International.

AWARDS, HONORS: National Poetry Foundation of America Award, 1983; Muir Award, 1983; American Society of Poetry Award, 1984; Osaka University (Japan) citation, 1986; Chicago Haymarket Literary Award, 1987; Farrell Literary Award, 1988; Pilgrim's Progress Prize, Stanford University, 1993; D.Litt., Washburn University, 1996; Bologna Literary Award, Italy, 1998.

WRITINGS:

POETRY

Midland, Goldsmith Press (Dublin, Ireland), 1972.
Leaves, Goldsmith Press (Dublin, Ireland), 1974.
Siege!, Goldsmith Press (Newbridge, County Kildare, Ireland), 1977.
Woodcutter, Goldsmith Press (Newbridge, County Kildare, Ireland), 1978.
Athlone?, Goldsmith Press (Newbridge, County Kildare, Ireland), 1980.
Seeing Double, Goldsmith Press (Newbridge, County Kildare, Ireland), 1983.
Collected Poems, National Poetry Foundation, 1983.
Snapdragon, 1983, reprinted, Milestone Press (Little Rock, AK), 1993.
Poems for Peace, introduction by Séan MacBride, Afri Publications (Newbridge, County Kildare, Ireland), 1986.
A Song for My Father, Peterloo Poets, 1989.
Peninsula: Poems of the Dingle Peninsula, with photographs by Liam Lyons, Kavanagh Press, 1992.
Selected Poems, edited by Hugh Kenner, Creighton University Press (Omaha, NE), 1992.
In the Holocaust of Autumn, Goldsmith Press (Newbridge, County Kildare, Ireland), 1994.
Poems for Eimear (sequence), Milestone Press (Little Rock, AK), 1994.

Poems/Gedichte, Karl Stutz (Munich, Germany), 1995.

Famine, Goldsmith Press (Newbridge, County Kildare, Ireland), 1997.

Elegies (selected poems), Goldsmith Press (Newbridge, County Kildare, Ireland), 1997.

Music, Goldsmith Press (Newbridge, County Kildare, Ireland), 2000.

OTHER

(Editor, with Michael Hartnett) *Choice* (poetry anthology), Goldsmith Press (Dublin, Ireland), 1973.

The Death of Metaphor: Collected Prose, Barnes and Noble, 1986.

(Translator) Medea, *Euripides,* St. Andrews Press (Laurinburg, NC), 1991.

(Translator) Philoctetes, *Sophocles,* 1998.

The Hill of Allen, 2001.

Also contributor to numerous magazines and anthologies, including *Review of Irish Literature, Feathers and Bones, Wearing of the Black, Poetry Wales, Aquarius, Times Literary Supplement, Irish Times, Europa Studies, Artes,* and *A Rage for Order.* Selected poems have been published in a variety of languages, including French, Dutch, Italian, German, Japanese, Czech, Hungarian, Russian, Greek, and Bulgarian.

SIDELIGHTS: Although Desmond Egan often focuses on uniquely Irish topics in his poetry, the tone and style of his verse was said to resemble such American poets as Walt Whitman, Ezra Pound, William Carlos Williams, and John Berryman. Egan employs punctuation sparingly and avoids the use of capital letters in poems that explore issues of identity and emotions with an energy and informality that critics either praise as genuine or fault as too straightforward. In his collection entitled *Woodcutter,* Egan includes a long tribute to Pound as well as shorter poems drawing on political events and contemporary debates on the proper subjects for poetry and the role of the poet in society. Peter Lewis wrote in the *Times Literary Supplement:* "Most of these poems are emotionally tentative and exploratory, and this is achieved by a fluid, telescoped and ambiguous syntax . . . that permits hesitation, repetition, backtracking and dislocation." Lewis concluded that Egan's poems are refreshingly free of the "formal strait-jacket" of style found in some other examples of Anglo-Irish poetry.

The poems in *Athlone?* center on Egan's small, rural hometown in County Kildare, Ireland. As in James Joyce's collection of short stories *Dubliners,* to which *Athlone?* has been compared, Egan delineates the drab,

evocative sights, smells, and sounds of the everyday world in which his identity was formed. However, Hugh Haughton in the *Times Literary Supplement* pointed out that it would be inaccurate to view the work as "another strand in the rambling delta of Irish autobiographical writing about childhood." Calling the verse "curiously selfless," he noted that the narrative voice "has a low profile." Although Haughton faulted a lack of intensity in some of the poems, he also remarked that Egan's syntax flows "in an oddly weightless, apparently aimless way through the town's 'twisty lanes,' conjuring up old walks, odd corners, local characters, bottled-up smells and specific mysteries, in a carefully controlled drift through precise commonplaces."

With *Seeing Double,* Egan returned mainly to political subjects for his poetry, commenting on the inability of politics to effect change and mourning the violence and loss of life in Northern Ireland. *Times Literary Supplement* contributor Michael O'Neill commented: "For all its modernist packaging . . . Egan's erratic but exuberant collection . . . opts for a cards-on-the-table straightforwardness." Egan's *A Song for My Father* features both political and personal works presented with the syntactical and stylistic flourishes critics have lauded in his poetry. According to William Scammell, who reviewed the collection in the *Times Literary Supplement,* Egan's "most memorable poem . . . is 'Have Mercy on the Poet,' " a piece with a "wry, downbeat lament."

Egan has also edited, with Michael Hartnett, an anthology of Irish poetry titled *Choice.* In this collection, poets ranging from the revered to the obscure were requested by the editors to select their favorite poem to be included in the work, along with a brief commentary about the piece. A *Times Literary Supplement* reviewer observed that although this selection process allowed for the inclusion of some lesser verse, *Choice* provides "as good a cross-section of contemporary Irish poetry as one could get."

BIOGRAPHICAL/CRITICAL SOURCES:

BOOKS

Kenner, Hugh, editor, *Desmond Egan,* Northern Lights, 1990.

Arkins, Brian, *Desmond Egan: A Critical Study,* Milestone Press (Little Rock, AR), 1992.

PERIODICALS

Times Literary Supplement, July 27, 1973, p. 864; November 3, 1978, p. 1291; April 10, 1981, p. 416; May 11, 1984, p. 516; May 18, 1990, p. 522.
World Literature Today, spring, 1996, Jose Lanters, review of *Poems/Gedichte,* p. 414; fall, 1996, William Pratt, review of *Elegies,* p. 962; autumn, 2000, William Pratt, review of *Music,* p. 830.

OTHER

Peace and Poetry Web site, http://irishpoems.com.*

*   *   *

ELKINS, James P.   1955-

PERSONAL: Born October 13, 1955, in Ithaca, NY; married Margaret MacNamidhe, August 20, 1994. *Education:* Cornell University (cum laude), B.A., 1977; M.A., 1984; M.F.A., 1983; University of Chicago, Ph.D., 1989.

ADDRESSES: Office—School of the Art Institute of Chicago, 37 South Wabash, Chicago, IL 60603; fax: 312-899-1431. *Agent*—Barbara Braun, 230 Fifth Ave., New York, NY 10001. *E-mail*—j.elkins@artic.edu.

CAREER: School of the Art Institute of Chicago, Chicago, IL, associate professor of art history, theory, and criticism, 1989—; University of California at Berkeley, 1996, visiting associate professor; Duke University, 2000, visiting research scholar.

WRITINGS:

The Poetics of Perspective, Cornell University Press (Ithaca, NY), 1994.
The Object Stares Back: On the Nature of Seeing, Simon & Schuster (New York, NY), 1996.
(Contributor) *The Macmillan Dictionary of Art: Thirty-four Volumes,* edited by Jane Shoaf Turner, Macmillan, 1996.
Our Beautiful, Dry, and Distant Texts: Art History as Writing, Pennsylvania State University Press (University Park, PA), 1997.
Pictures, and the Words That Fail Them: How Images Resist Description, Cambridge University Press (Cambridge, England), 1998.
Pictures of the Body: Pain and Metamorphosis, Stanford University Press (Stanford, CA), 1998.

What Painting Is: How to Think about Oil Painting, Using the Language of Alchemy, Routledge (New York, NY), 1999.
Why Are Our Pictures Puzzles?: On the Modern Origins of Pictorial Complexity, Routledge (New York, NY), 1999.
The Domain of Images, Cornell University Press (Ithaca, NY), 1999.
How to Use Your Eyes, Routledge (New York, NY), 2000.
Why Art Cannot Be Taught: A Handbook for Art Students, University of Illinois Press (Urbana, IL), 2001.
Pictures and Tears: A History of People Who Have Cried in Front of Paintings, Routledge (New York, NY), 2001.

Contributor of more than sixty articles to academic journals.

WORK IN PROGRESS: Streams into Sand: Links between Renaissance and Modern Painting, for Gordon & Breach (New York, NY); *Chinese Landscape Painting as Western Art History,* to be published in Chinese translation, China National Academy of Arts (Hangzhou, China); *What Heaven Looks Like: Comments on a Strange Book concerning the Universe, God, and Painting; On Teaching Art; Things and Their Places: The Concept of Installation from Prehistoric Tombs to Contemporary Art; The Surface of the Body, Based on the Work of Michelangelo; The Meaning of the Studio: Art History and the Labor of Painting; Logic and Its Loss: How the Arts Avoid Making Sense, and the Sciences Make Too Much of It; Stories of Art; The Drunken Conversation of Science and Painting; Concepts of Art.*

SIDELIGHTS: James P. Elkins is considered one of the most original art historians of the 1990s and early 2000s. His books analyze the processes of seeing and of creating paintings, and explore major questions regarding postmodern approaches to art.

The Object Stares Back: On the Nature of Seeing established Elkins as a writer able to engage both artists and a broader readership as well. In the book, which *Washington Post Book World* contributor Robert Storr deemed "curious and curiosity-provoking," Elkins argues that the act of seeing is far more complex than we might assume. Using Lacanian philosophical theory as well as evidence from such fields as neurobiology, literature, and psychology, Elkins insists that, in Storr's words, "by the act of looking we reveal ourselves to the world . . . as surely as the objects we examine are revealed to us in turn." Elkins discusses such matters as the power of the image of the face; our ambivalence about viewing nakedness, deformities, pain and death; and visual pathologies, including glaucoma and blindness. "Elkins argues that seeing is neither passive nor comprehensive," commented Storr, "but is, instead, an aggressive, catalytic and highly selective activity predicated on our screening out far more than our eyes take in."

Critical response to *The Object Stares Back* was emphatically positive. *Booklist* reviewer Donna Seaman considered it "almost unnervingly accurate and gratifyingly frank about our habits of sight," and a contributor in *Publishers Weekly* hailed it as "a remarkable tour de force." A writer for the *Economist* observed that Elkins writes well, and that the book's "constantly fascinating details . . . challenge readers to look more closely and to notice what happens when they do. His book sets all sorts of inquiries into motion." Storr emphasized the broad relevance of Elkins's ideas, noting that his thesis "resonates well beyond the disciplines of art or science and focuses attention on a willful turning away from troubling realities that is in ever-increasing demand for correction."

The fact that Elkins trained as a painter before moving toward theory is, in the view of some critics, central to his freshness of approach. His intimate knowledge of the painting process is particularly evident in *What Painting Is: How to Think about Painting, Using the Language of Alchemy.* This book, which *Art Journal* contributor David Carrier considered Elkins's most deeply original, describes the physical action of painting and relates it to the process of alchemy. "Painting is alchemy," Elkins asserts. "Its materials are worked without knowledge of their properties, by blind experiment, by the feel of the paint." He looks as the composition of oils and pigments, and the various methods by which they are applied to a canvas to create a finished painting. *Booklist* reviewer Veronica Scrol praised *What Painting Is* as "an original and insightful book that is sure to transform the reader's understanding of painting." Similar enthusiasm

Marked Barbara Fisher's review in the *Boston Globe,* in which she pronounced the book "strange and original," "fascinating," and bound to make readers "look at paintings differently and think about paint differently." *What Painting Is* sold more than 10,000 copies in its first year of publication, and was embraced by artists themselves as a unique and useful study.

In *Why Are Our Pictures Puzzles?: On the Modern Origins of Pictorial Complexity,* Elkins tackles the question of why and how paintings, once seen as relatively straightforward images of recognizable things, became more difficult to understand during the twentieth century. Part of the problem, as Carrier explained, is that the discipline of art history continues to produce numbers of scholars who are expected to continue to increase their writing and teaching; also implicated is the twentieth-century reverence for visual complexity as well as public insecurity regarding artistic meaning. Given many different analyses of a work of art, we become frustrated because, Elkins suggests, "we sense a very simple, unanswerable property that pictures have always had: in the end, after all the interpretations have failed, they reveal themselves to be utterly meaningless." In *Publishers Weekly,* a reviewer called *Why Are Our Pictures Puzzles?* a "cogent, conversational, and lucid" book that "provides a useful, nuanced understanding" of its subject. Hailing Elkins as a "true alchemist of ideas," Scrol, in a *Booklist* review, commended the book as an original, insightful, and transformative work.

How to Use Your Eyes further articulates Elkins's ideas on seeing. Using images as diverse as X-rays, postage stamps, tree twigs, and Chinese calligraphy, he suggests ways in which readers can enhance their ability to derive pleasure and meaning from looking carefully at objects they might otherwise take for granted. Though the book received less attention than *The Object Stares Back,* reviews in both *Publishers Weekly* and *Booklist* hailed it as an insightful and enjoyable work. *Why Art Cannot Be Taught: A Handbook for Art Students* is, as its title indicates, an expose of the shortcomings in art education—among them Elkins's belief that "most artists do not make interesting art" and that students are taught mediocrity. "Art students and teachers might find a grim sort of gallows accuracy in this deadly portrait of their activities," commented a *Publishers Weekly* reviewer.

Continuing his exploration of subjects not usually discussed among art historians, Elkins published a query in the *New York Review of Books* to research people's emotional responses to paintings. In the query, he asked readers to describe paintings that had made them cry and to explain this reaction. He received 400 replies; in addition, he posed the question to thirty art historians, ten of whom admitted to this emotional reaction to art. From these responses, Elkins produced *Pictures and Tears: A History of People Who Have Cried in Front of Paintings.* As with much of his previous work, the book asks unusual questions. The discipline of art history, Elkins explained to *Chronicle of Higher Education* writer Scott Heller, trains viewers away from emotional responses. "For the most part, the discipline [of art history] is resolutely tearless," he says, "and this seems very serious to me." Another project which Elkins is planning is tentatively titled *Failure in Twentieth Century Painting* and, according to Heller, is a "sweeping history" that "will cover styles that have fallen out of fashion but continue in other parts of the world: Czech Cubism, Hungarian post-Impressionism, and regional painting from Thailand, Bangladesh, and Azerbaijan," as well as "bad Picasso, old-barn watercolors, and paintings by Hollywood celebrities."

Such projects, in Carrier's view, make Elkins's books "the most ambitious and fully realized body of work by any younger art historian." Noting that Elkins "reads and looks with great human sympathy," Carrier concludes that "Elkins's best writing teaches you how to look more closely and see more. Few authors aspire to do that—and even fewer succeed."

BIOGRAPHICAL/CRITICAL SOURCES:

PERIODICALS

Art Journal, summer, 2000, David Carrier, "Close Reading and Looking: Some Recent Books by James Elkins," p. 114.

Atlantic Monthly, November 1, 1998, Phoebe-Lou Adams, review of *What Painting Is,* p. 137.

Booklist, March 1, 1996, Donna Seaman, review of *The Object Stares Back,* p. 1106; January 1, 1999, review of *What Painting Is,* p. 774; August, 1998, Veronica Scrol, review of *What Painting Is,* p. 1950; April 1, 1999, Veronica Scrol, review of *Why Are Our Pictures Puzzles?,* p. 1376; November 1, 2000, Veronica Scrol, review of *How to Use Your Eyes,* p. 509.

Boston Globe, October 25, 1998, Barbara Fisher, review of *What Painting Is,* p. N2.

British Journal of Aesthetics, July, 2000, G. Kemp, review of *The Domain of Images,* p. 400.

Chronicle of Higher Education, June 25, 1999, Scott Heller, "A Maverick Art Historian Examines His Field's Idiosyncrasies and Blind Spots," p. A17.

CIRCA Art Magazine, winter, 2000, Margaret Corcoran, "Open to Criticism, an Interview with James Elkins," pp. 26-29.

Economist, April 30, 1996, review of *The Object Stares Back,* p. S12.

New York Times, November 27, 2000, Christopher Lehmann-Haupt, review of *How to Use Your Eyes,* p. E7.

New York Times Book Review, December 3, 2000, Christopher Benfey, review of *How to Use Your Eyes,* p. 20.

Publishers Weekly, January 22, 1996, review of *The Object Stares Back,* p. 53; March 8, 1999, review of *Why Are Our Pictures Puzzles?,* p. 59; October 30, 2000, review of *How to Use Your Eyes,* p. 65; June 4, 2001, review of *Why Art Cannot be Taught,* p. 73.

Times Literary Supplement, November 1, 1996, Joseph Rykwert, review of *The Macmillan Dictionary of Art.*

Washington Post Book World, March 24, 1996, Robert Storr, review of *The Object Stares Back,* p. X10.*

*   *   *

ENTMAN, Robert M(athew) 1949-

PERSONAL: Born November 7, 1949, in Brooklyn, NY; son of Bernard (an administrator) and Rose (an artist; maiden name, Jacobson) Entman; married Francie Seymour (a hospital administrator), June 1, 1979; children: Max, Emily. *Education:* Duke University, A.B. (magna cum laude), 1971; Yale University, Ph.D., 1977; University of California, Berkeley, M.P.P., 1980.

ADDRESSES: Office—North Carolina State University, Department of Communications, P.O. Box 8104, Raleigh, NC 27695-0001.

CAREER: Dickinson College, Carlisle, PA, instructor in political science, 1975-77; Duke University, Durham, NC, assistant professor of public policy and political science, 1980-89; Northwestern University, Evanston, IL, associate professor of communication studies and journalism, 1989-94; University of North Carolina, Chapel Hill, NC, adjunct professor of public policy, 1995—; North Carolina State University, professor of communication, 1994—, interim department head, 1996-97; Harvard University, Cambridge, MA, Lombard visiting professor, 1997. Program manager in National Telecommunications and Information Administration, U.S. Department of Commerce, 1984-85; consultant to U.S. House of Representatives subcommittee on telecommunications.

MEMBER: International Communications Association, American Political Science Association, Association for Education in Journalism and Mass Communication; Phi Beta Kappa.

AWARDS, HONORS: Graduate fellow of National Science Foundation, 1971-74; fellow of National Institute of Mental Health, 1978-80; grants from Markle Foundation, 1984, 1986, and 1988-89; guest scholar at Woodrow Wilson International Center, 1989; Alumnae Professor Award, Northwestern University, 1991; McGannon Award for community policy research, 1993.

WRITINGS:

(With David Paletz) *Media Power Politics,* Free Press, 1981.

Telecommunications Regulation and Deregulation: Early Policy Perspectives from the States, Program on Information Resources Policy, Harvard University (Cambridge, MA), 1985.

The Impacts of Media Messages on the Attitudes of the Public toward Welfare-State Liberalism, University of Wisconsin—Madison (Madison, WI), 1985.

Democracy without Citizens: Media and the Decay of American Politics, Oxford University Press (New York, NY), 1989.

Local Competition: Options for Action: A Report on the Eighth Annual Aspen Conference on Telecommunications Policy, Aspen Institute (Washington, DC), 1993.

Competition, Innovation, and Investment in Telecommunications: A Report of the Twelfth Annual Aspen Institute Conference on Telecommunications Policy, Aspen Institute (Washington, DC), 1998.

(With others) *Television, Radio, and Privatization: Ownership, Advertising, and Programming Policies for the Changing Media Marketplace,* Aspen Institute (Queenstown, MD), 1998.

Residential Access to Bandwidth: Exploring New Paradigms: A Report of the Thirteenth Annual Aspen Institute Conference on Telecommunications Policy, Aspen Institute (Washington, DC), 1999.

Six Degrees of Competition: Correlating Regulation with the Telecommunications Marketplace: A Report of the Fourteenth Annual Aspen Institute Conference on Telecommunications Policy, Aspen Institute (Washington, DC), 2000.

(With Andrew Rojecki) *The Black Image in the White Mind: Media and Race in America,* University of Chicago Press (Chicago, IL), 2000.

(Editor, with W. Lance Bennett) *Mediated Politics: Communication in the Future of Democracy,* Cambridge University Press (New York, NY), 2001.

Also contributor to political science and communication journals, and to popular magazines, including *Nation.*

SIDELIGHTS: Communications scholar Robert M. Entman has written extensively about the social influences of media in the United States. His work on race has elicited particular interest. In *The Black Image in the White Mind: Media and Race in America,* which he coauthored with Andrew Rojecki, he shows how media images continue to perpetuate negative stereotypes about African Americans. Much of the book examines the depiction of blacks on television. Despite the fact that many television programs have added roles for African American actors, Entman finds that these roles are often unrealistic and misleading; many put these characters in positions of authority that, in effect, distance them from real interactions with other characters. On TV commercials, black actors have fewer speaking parts than whites, and seldom touch another person; by contrast, white actors frequently speak to and touch others. And on TV news programs, blacks are disproportionately featured as criminals. Entman's evidence shows that when newscasts report on crimes perpetrated by blacks, the programs show the accused in custody 38 percent of the time; when programs report on crimes committed by whites, however, the perpetrator is shown in custody only 15 percent of the time. Similar discrepancies exist in other media coverage, including magazines and newspapers.

The Black Image in the White Mind drew serious critical attention. *Columbia Journalism Review* contributor Lawrence K. Grossman appreciated the authors' wealth of evidence and their understanding of the complex motivating factors driving media decisions. Their findings, he concluded, "suggest . . . that television journalists need to be more aware of and sensitive to the cumulative effects of news reports that focus disproportionately on the bad things that minorities do." Susan Douglas in the *Progressive* deemed *The Black Image in the White Mind* an "important book" that "prompts us to see portrayals of race—including allegedly positive ones—with new insight and concern." *New Leader* reviewer Ben Yagoda, however, who praised the book's analysis of content, considered its analysis of the television, advertising, film, and news industries to be oversimplified. *America* contributor Kathy O'Connell expressed a similar view, noting that "What Entman and Rojecki utterly fail to take into consideration in their study are the variables of exposure and intellectual and emotional compatibility" among various groups. O'Connell objected to the authors' statement that "at the minimum, the news media's focus on Blacks as entertainers and athletes registers a lost opportunity for Whites to learn more important things about African Americans than that they can sing a song or dunk a basketball," and added that "the authors say nothing about the seepage up of hip-hop culture, which is predominantly black, into the edges of middle-class and mostly white teen mainstream, nor do they address the very real democratizing forces of jazz and rock 'n' roll." Toni Lester, however, in *Black Issues Book Review*, hailed *The Black Image in the White Mind* as a book serving "an invaluable purpose," and a contributor to *Publishers Weekly* commended it as "convincingly argued" and "a probing and useful addition to media studies."

Entman told *CA:* "My central concern has been the unintentional contributions of the mass media to irrationality and cynicism in American politics. I attempt to understand the influence that the media wield without implying, as do many critical observers, that the impacts of the media are the products of conscious choice and bias. It is the process and culture of news gathering and reporting that create the media effects so many decry, and these are what I explore in my writings."

BIOGRAPHICAL/CRITICAL SOURCES:

PERIODICALS

America, November 18, 2000, Kathy O'Connell, review of *The Black Image in the White Mind: Media and Race in America,* p. 25.

American Political Science Review, December 1991, Doris A. Graber, review of *Democracy without Citizens: Media and the Decay of American Politics,* p. 1443.

Black Issues Book Review, September 2000, Toni Lester, review of *The Black Image in the White Mind: Media and Race in America,* p. 56.

Columbia Journalism Review, July 2001, Lawrence K. Grossman, review of *The Black Image in the White Mind,* p. 55.

Emerge, June 2000, Mark Anthony Neal, review of *The Black Image in the White Mind,* p. 67.

Journal of Communication, spring 1991, review of *Democracy without Citizens,* p. 236.

Los Angeles Times Book Review, March 19, 1989.

New Leader, May 2000, Ben Yagoda, review of *The Black Image in the White Mind,* p. 27.

Political Science Quarterly, spring 1990, Michael X. Delli Carpini, review of *Democracy without Citizens,* p. 139.

Progressive, January 2001, Susan Douglas, review of *The Black Image in the White Mind,* p. 38.

Publishers Weekly, May 22, 2000, review of *The Black Image in the White Mind,* p. 89.

Quarterly Journal of Speech, May 1991, review of *Democracy without Citizens,* p. 236.

Social Science Quarterly, spring 1990, review of *Democracy without Citizens,* p. 212.

Washington Post, March 2, 1981.*

F

FELLOWS, Richard A(stley)   1947-

PERSONAL: Born January 21, 1947, in Dudley, England; son of Frank I. A. (a clerk) and Minnie (a homemaker; maiden name, John) Fellows; married Jane Gray (an administrator), January 25, 1975; children: Rosalind Jane, William Edward Astley. *Ethnicity:* "White." *Education:* Kingston upon Hull Regional College of Art, diploma in architecture, 1972; University of York, 1980. *Avocational interests:* Singing, opera.

ADDRESSES: Home—4 Almondbury Close, Fenay Lane, Huddersfield, West Yorkshire HD5 8XX, England. *Office*—Department of Architecture, University of Huddersfield, Queensgate, Huddersfield, West Yorkshire, England; fax 01-48-447-2440. *E-mail*—r.a.fellows@hud.ac.uk.

CAREER: Architectural assistant at architecture firms in Leeds, Gloucester, and Bath, England; University of Huddersfield, Huddersfield, England, lecturer in architecture, 1974—, head of department, 1996—. Open University, lecturer in history of architecture, summers, 1981-83; Architecture Workshops Ltd., Leeds, England, members of council of management, 1985—; Calderdale Architecture Workshop, consultant director; NCUK/ITM Programme, Malaysia, tutor/lecturer. Halifax Civic Trust, member of executive committee, 1979-81.

MEMBER: Royal Institute of British Architects, Society of Architectural Historians of Great Britain, West Yorkshire Society of Architects (member of Bedford Scholarship Panel, 1989—).

WRITINGS:

Sir Reginald Blomfield: An Edwardian Architect, Zwemmer (London, England), 1985.
(With wife, Jane Fellows) *Buildings for Hospitality: Principles of Care and Design for Accommodation Managers,* Pitman (London, England), 1990.
Edwardian Architecture: Style and Technology, 1995.
Edwardian Civic Buildings and Their Details, 1999.

Contributor to *The Dictionary of Art,* Macmillan (New York, NY). Contributor to magazines, including *Period Home, Yorkshire Architect,* and *Landscape Design.*

SIDELIGHTS: Richard A. Fellows examines the life and work of British architect Reginald Blomfield in his 1985 book, *Sir Reginald Blomfield: An Edwardian Architect.* A staunch opponent of the modern movement in architecture, Blomfield designed mainly large country houses and gardens reflecting his preoccupation with the "Grand Manner" style. Most notable among his works in civic architecture are London's Regent Street Quadrant and the fronts to Piccadilly Circus as well as the World War I memorial Menin Gate in Ypres, Belgium. According to *Times Literary Supplement* critic Andrew Saint, Fellows's book provides "a crisp, efficient and admirably succinct account" of the architect's career.

Fellows once told *CA:* "My study of Blomfield was, to some extent, a vehicle for investigation into a complex and fascinating period of British architecture—an attempt to sort out the various strands of design in the late nineteenth and early twentieth centuries."

BIOGRAPHICAL/CRITICAL SOURCES:

PERIODICALS

British Book Notes, June, 1985, p. 356.
Times Literary Supplement, February 22, 1985, p. 195.*

* * *

FERRELL, Robert H(ugh) 1921-

PERSONAL: Born May 8, 1921, in Cleveland, OH; son of Ernest Henry (a banker) and Edna Lulu (a homemaker; maiden name, Rentsch) Ferrell; married Lila Esther Sprout (a homemaker), September 8, 1956; children: Carolyn Irene. *Education:* Bowling Green State University, B.S. in Ed., 1946, B.A., 1947; Yale University, M.A., 1948, Ph.D., 1951. *Politics:* Democrat. *Religion:* Methodist.

ADDRESSES: Home—512 South Hawthorne, Bloomington, IN 47401. *Office*—Department of History, Indiana University, Bloomington, IN 47405.

CAREER: U.S. Air Force, intelligence analyst, 1951-52; Michigan State University, East Lansing, lecturer in history, 1952-53; Indiana University at Bloomington, Bloomington, assistant professor, 1953-58, associate professor, 1958-61, professor, 1961-74, distinguished professor of history, 1974-87. Visiting professor, Yale University, 1955-56, American University at Cairo, 1958-59, University of Connecticut, 1964-65, Catholic University of Louvain (Belgium), 1969-70, Naval War College, 1974-75, Eastern Illinois University, 1985, 1989, Doshisha University, 1986, United States Military Academy, 1987-88, and Texas Christian University, 1988. *Military service:* U.S. Army Air Force, 1942-45.

MEMBER: American Historical Association, Society for Historians of American Foreign Relations, Phi Beta Kappa.

AWARDS, HONORS: John Addison Porter Prize, Yale University, 1951; George Louis Beer Prize, American Historical Association, 1952; grants from Carnegie Foundation, 1955-56, Social Science Research Council, 1956 and 1961-62, Smith-Mundt, 1958-59, and Fulbright, 1969-70, 1986; distinguished teaching award, Indiana University, 1969, 1980, 1983.

WRITINGS:

Peace in Their Time: The Origins of the Kellogg-Briand Pact, Yale University Press (New Haven, CT), 1952.
American Diplomacy in the Great Depression: Hoover-Stimson Foreign Policy, 1929-1933, Yale University Press (New Haven, CT), 1957.
American Diplomacy: A History, Norton (New York, NY), 1959, 4th edition published as *American Diplomacy: The Twentieth Century,* 1987.
Frank B. Kellogg and Henry L. Stimson, Cooper Square (New York, NY), 1963.
(With Maurice G. Baxter and John E. Wiltz) *The Teaching of American History in High Schools,* Indiana University Press (Bloomington, IN), 1964.
George C. Marshall, Cooper Square (New York, NY), 1966.
(With Richard Brandon Morris and William Greenleaf) *America: A History of the People,* Rand McNally (Chicago, IL), 1971.
(With others) *Unfinished Century,* Little, Brown (Boston, MA), 1973.
(With Samuel F. Wells and David F. Trask) *The Ordeal of World Power: American Diplomacy since 1900,* Little, Brown (Boston, MA), 1975.
Harry S. Truman and the Modern American Presidency, Little, Brown (Boston, MA), 1983.
Truman: A Centenary Remembrance, Viking (New York, NY), 1984.
Woodrow Wilson and World War I: 1917-1921, Harper (New York, NY), 1985.
(With Richard Natkiel) *Atlas of American History,* Bison Books (London, England), 1987, Facts on File (New York, NY), 1988.
Harry S. Truman: His Life on the Family Farms, High Plains (Worland, WY), 1991.
Ill-Advised: Presidential Health and Public Trust, University of Missouri Press (Columbia, MO), 1992.
Choosing Truman: The Democratic Convention of 1944, University of Missouri Press (Columbia, MO), 1994.
Harry S. Truman: A Life, University of Missouri Press (Columbia, MO), 1994.
The Strange Deaths of President Harding, University of Missouri Press (Columbia, MO), 1996.
The Dying President: Franklin D. Roosevelt, 1944-1945, University of Missouri Press (Columbia, MO), 1998.
The Presidency of Calvin Coolidge, University Press of Kansas (Lawrence, KS), 1998.
Truman and Pendergast, University of Missouri Press (Columbia, MO), 1999.

EDITOR

(With Howard H. Quint) *The Talkative President: The Off-the-Record Press Conferences of Calvin Coolidge,* University of Massachusetts Press (Amherst, MA), 1964.

History of American Diplomacy, Harper and Row (New York, NY), Volume I: *Foundations of American Diplomacy, 1775-1872,* 1968, Volume II: *America as a World Power, 1872-1945,* 1971, Volume III: *America in a Divided World, 1945-1972,* 1975.

Off the Record: The Private Papers of Harry S. Truman, Harper and Row (New York, NY), 1980.

The Autobiography of Harry S. Truman, Colorado Associated University Press (Boulder, CO), 1980.

The Eisenhower Diaries, Norton (New York, NY), 1981.

The Diary of James C. Hagerty: Eisenhower in Mid-Course, 1954-1955, Indiana University Press (Bloomington, IN), 1983.

Dear Bess: The Letters from Harry to Bess Truman, 1910-1959, Norton (New York, NY), 1983.

The Twentieth Century Almanac, World Almanac Publications (New York, NY), 1984.

Joseph Douglas Lawrence, *Fighting Soldier: The A.E.F. in 1918,* Colorado Associated University Press (Boulder, CO), 1986.

Banners in the Air: The Eighth Ohio Volunteers and the Spanish-American War, Kent State University Press (Kent, OH), 1988.

Monterrey Is Ours!: The Mexican War Letters of Lieutenant Dana, 1845-1847, University Press of Kentucky (Lexington, KY), 1990.

Truman in the White House: The Diary of Eben A. Ayers, University of Missouri Press (Columbia, MO), 1991.

(With Lawrence E. Wikander) *Grace Coolidge: An Autobiography,* High Plains (Worland, WY), 1992.

Flavel C. Barber, *Holding the Line: The Third Tennessee Infantry, 1861-1864,* Kent State University Press (Kent, OH), 1994.

(With Joan Hoff) *Dictionary of American History: Supplement* (two volumes), Scribner (New York, NY), 1996.

Harry S. Truman and the Bomb: A Documentary History, High Plains (Worland, WY), 1996.

FDR's Quiet Confidant: The Autobiography of Frank C. Walker, University Press of Colorado (Niwot, CO), 1997.

The Kansas City Investigation: Pendergast's Downfall, 1938-1939, University of Missouri Press (Columbia, MO), 1999.

William S. Triplet, *A Youth in the Meuse-Argonne: A Memoir of World War I, 1917-1918,* University of Missouri Press (Columbia, MO), 2000.

William S. Triplet, *A Colonel in the Armored Divisions: A Memoir, 1941-1945,* University of Missouri Press (Columbia, MO), 2000.

William S. Triplet, *In the Philippines and Okinawa: A Memoir, 1945-1948,* University of Missouri Press (Columbia, MO), 2001.

Coeditor of "American Secretaries of State and Their Diplomacy" series, Volumes XI-XX, Cooper Square (New York, NY), 1963-80.

SIDELIGHTS: Robert H. Ferrell is a "prolific diplomatic historian," noted Geoffrey Ward in the *New York Times Book Review,* and he has written extensively about Harry S. Truman. In addition to books about Truman's presidency, Ferrell has edited Truman's autobiography as well as his private papers. *Truman: A Centenary Remembrance* marks the one-hundredth anniversary of his birth, "and it does so in a straightforward, informed and affectionate manner," remarked Daved R. Jones in the *New York Times Book Review.* "While not pretending to break new ground or to offer the insights of a full-scale biography, *Truman* will be useful for those seeking a brisk, well-illustrated overview of the man, his life and his Presidency."

Of the more than twelve hundred letters written by Truman to his wife during the course of their courtship and marriage, about half were selected and edited by Ferrell for *Dear Bess: The Letters from Harry to Bess Truman, 1910-1959. Dear Bess* "is at once a love story, an astonishing record of what one industrious man managed to accomplish, and an intimate look into the heart and mind of the 33rd President," wrote Ward. "The letters in themselves are not much more than the cataloguing of the doings of day after day," observed Abigail McCarthy in the *Washington Post Book World.* "What makes the letters absorbing is the way in which, in their consummate ordinariness and matter-of-factness, they give us a detailed and vivid picture of the world in which Harry Truman lived, the world and time which molded him and most Americans in the era just before our own."

Although Ward felt that "there are probably too many letters" in the collection, he found Ferrell's notes helpful. "But there are too few annotations; the reader often wishes for a fuller explanation of people and events mentioned only in passing," said Ward. While Charles Kaiser noted in *Newsweek* that Ferrell "wisely chose to present Truman warts and all," Cleveland Amory objected in the *Detroit News* to "evidence after evidence of his clerk-sized mind, his pettinesses and even his provincial prejudices." Amory wished more of Truman's "personal growth" had been shown and found that Ferrell's "between-the-letters comments are far more interesting than the letters themselves." Nevertheless, Kaiser believed that, given the length of time which these letters span, "there has rarely been such a comprehensive record of how a modern statesman thought."

In *Truman and Pendergast,* Ferrell examined Truman's relationship with corrupt political boss Thomas J. Pendergast. The two met in 1927, when Truman was a county judge and Pendergast was at the helm of a powerful Kansas City political machine. Pendergast helped Truman reach many of his goals, but his shady reputation threatened Truman's career as the future president began to rise to national prominence. Ultimately, Truman sought to distance himself from the man who helped him reach the top. "This fine work sheds light on a part of Truman's past full of conflict and contradictions," commented Michael A. Genovese in *Library Journal.* And Mary Carroll in *Booklist* wrote, "Ferrell brings to life the political battles of another era and adds nuance to the portrait of the redoubtable Harry Truman."

In addition to Truman, Ferrell has written about other presidents and their eras. *Woodrow Wilson and World War I: 1917-1921* is an "admirable contribution to the 'New American Nation' series," wrote Edward Berenson in the *Los Angeles Times Book Review,* and it "tells the whole frustrating story, from the country's extraordinary mobilization of men and money in 1917 to the politicians' tragic inability to endorse the League of Nations three years later." Ferrell explores the effect of Wilson's decision to enter the war and a new era of internationalism in a book that David M. Kennedy in the *Atlantic* called "richly informative and often moving." Kennedy agreed with Ferrell's premise that Wilson's decision "effectively upset the balance of power that had ensured a precarious but enduring peace in Europe for a century before 1914 . . . [and that] the arrival of the fresh and huge American Army nullified any prospect of a negotiated peace." Steve Neal suggested in the *Chicago Tribune Book World* that "this superb volume is the best account yet of Wilson's performance as commander-in-chief and as the architect of the Versailles Treaty."

Ferrell has written about other United States presidents as well. Calvin Coolidge has gained a reputation as one of the dullest, least effective presidents in American history, one whose passivity gave momentum to the events causing the Great Depression. Ferrell provides a more flattering portrait in *The Presidency of Calvin Coolidge.* In addition, he gives a picture of the 1920s and the complex issues faced by the government at that time. Thomas J. Baldino, writing in *Library Journal,* said: "Ferrell's research is solid and his writing graceful, making this a very informative and accessible volume."

Ferrell exposed the hidden secrets of Franklin D. Roosevelt's last year in office in *The Dying President: Franklin D. Roosevelt, 1944-1945.* Roosevelt's death on April 12, 1945, was presented to the world as an unexpected, tragic event, but in fact he had been increasingly debilitated by heart disease for more than a year, leading him to work as little as two hours a day during the time when World War II was reaching its climax. Ferrell explores the cover-up and speculates on how the course of world history might have been changed if Roosevelt's health had not been so poor during his last year. "As mystery and history, steeped in medicine, this is a book to sit down with," recommended William H. Barker in *Journal of the American Medical Association.* Ferrell looked at other instances of concealed information regarding the health of American leaders in *Ill-Advised: Presidential Health and Public Trust.*

Ferrell told *CA:* "My interest in history, American and otherwise, came out of participation in World War II, initially through a year in Cairo, Egypt, with the antiquities nearby, then from fascination with the cathedral and other architecture of Western Europe. In college and graduate school courses I pursued study of American foreign relations under—for graduate instruction—a master historian and teacher, the late Samuel Flagg Bemis. Then late in the 1970s, through chance discovery of President Harry S. Truman's newly opened private papers at the Truman Library in Independence, Missouri, I turned to what is now known as presidential history, and have sought to combine the two subdisciplines since then."

BIOGRAPHICAL/CRITICAL SOURCES:

PERIODICALS

American Historical Review, October, 1993, review of *Ill-Advised: Presidential Health and Public Trust,* p. 1315; April, 1996, Richard M. Freeland, review of *Harry S. Truman: A Life,* p. 1670; June, 1999, Donn C. Neal, review of *The Presidency of Calvin Coolidge,* p. 929.
American Spectator, March, 1995, Victor Gold, review of *Harry S. Truman: A Life,* p. 67; December,

1996, Florence King, review of *The Strange Deaths of President Harding*, p. 72; August, 1998, review of *The Dying President: Franklin D. Roosevelt, 1944-1945*, p. 72.

Atlantic, April, 1985, David M. Kennedy, review of *Woodrow Wilson and World War 1: 1917-1921;* April, 1990, Phoebe-Lou Adams, review of *Monterrey Is Ours!: The Mexican War Letters of Lieutenant Dana, 1845-1847*, p. 109.

Booklist, February 15, 1994, Gilbert Taylor, review of *Choosing Truman: The Democratic Convention of 1944*, p. 1054; November 15, 1994, Margaret Flanagan, review of *Harry S. Truman: A Life*, p. 576; June 1, 1996, Gilbert Taylor, review of *Harry S. Truman and the Bomb: A Documentary History*, p. 1670; November 1, 1996, review of *Dictionary of American History: Supplement*, p. 534; November 15, 1996, Iva Freeman, review of *The Strange Deaths of President Harding*, p. 568; February 15, 1998, Gilbert Taylor, review of *The Dying President*, p. 971; June 1, 1999, Mary Carroll, review of *Truman and Pendergast*, p. 1778.

Chicago Tribune Book World, June 16, 1985, Steve Neal, review of *Woodrow Wilson and World War 1.*

Christian Century, March 15, 1995, Myron A. Marty, review of *Harry S. Truman: A Life*, p. 303.

Civil War History, Willard Carl Kludner, *Monterrey Is Ours!*, p. 166.

Detroit News, October 16, 1983, Cleveland Amory, review of *Dear Bess: The Letters from Harry to Bess Truman, 1910-1959.*

History Today, March, 1989, review of *Atlas of American History*, p. 50.

Journal of American History, September, 1991, John K. Mahon, review of *Monterrey Is Ours!*, p. 666; March, 1995, Kenneth C. Martis, review of *Atlas of American History*, p. 1889; June, 1995, review of *Choosing Truman: The Democratic Convention of 1944*, p. 339; September, 1995, James N. Giglio, review of *Harry S. Truman: A Life*, p. 819; September, 1997, review of *Harry S. Truman and the Bomb*, p. 609; December, 1999, review of *The Presidency of Calvin Coolidge*, p. 1378.

Journal of the American Medical Association, November 24, 1993, Oglesby Paul, review of *Ill-Advised*, p. 2497; August 5, 1998, William H. Barker, review of *The Dying President*, p. 482.

Journal of Southern History, February, 1992, Wayne Cutler, review of *Monterrey Is Ours!*, p. 138; December, 1993, Herbert Abrams, review of *Ill-Advised*, p. 1116; August, 1995, review of *Choosing Truman*, p. 636; August, 1996, article by Russell D. Buhite, p. 615.

Kirkus Reviews, October 1, 1994, review of *Harry S. Truman: A Life;* February 1, 1998, review of *The Dying President.*

Library Journal, January, 1988, James Moffet, review of *Atlas of American History*, p. 76; October 1, 1991, review of *Truman in the White House: The Diary of Eben A. Ayers*, p. 118; March 15, 1994, review of *Choosing Truman*, p. 86; December, 1994, Robert F. Nadini, review of *Harry S. Truman: A Life*, p. 102; August, 1996, Don Wismer, review of audio version of *Harry S. Truman: A Life*, p. 132; September 1, 1996, p. 192; November 1, 1996, review of *The Strange Deaths of President Harding*, p. 88; March 1, 1998, Richard P. Hedlund, review of *The Dying President*, p. 100; May 15, 1998, Thomas J. Baldino, review of *The Presidency of Calvin Coolidge*, p. 99; May 15, 1999, Michael A. Genovese, review of *Truman and Pendergast*, p. 110.

Los Angeles Times Book Review, August 14, 1983; June 17, 1984; December 23, 1984; May 19, 1985.

National Forum, fall, 1995, Robert H. Ferrell, review of *Harry S. Truman and the Bomb*, p. 22.

Newsweek, August 22, 1983.

New York Times, August 22, 1983.

New York Times Book Review, August 7, 1983; September 18, 1983; June 10, 1984.

Publishers Weekly, October 18, 1991, review of *Truman in the White House*, p. 47; February 14, 1994, review of *Choosing Truman*, p. 73; September 19, 1994, review of *Harry S. Truman: A Life*, p. 59; May 18, 1998, review of *The Presidency of Calvin Coolidge*, p. 63.

RQ, spring, 1988, R. David Weber, review of *Atlas of American History*, p. 421.

Times Literary Supplement, November 17, 1966; June 3, 1983.

Wall Street Journal, April 27, 1998, review of *The Dying President*, p. A20; July 19, 1999, review of *Truman and Pendergast*, p. A13.

Washington Monthly, September, 1992, review of *Ill-Advised*, p. 57.

Washington Post Book World, September 18, 1983, Abigail McCarthy, review of *Dear Bess;* September, 1992, Charles Peters, review of *Ill-Advised*, p. 57.

*   *   *

FINCKE, Gary (William) 1945-

PERSONAL: Born July 7, 1945, in Pittsburgh, PA; son of William A. and Ruth (Lang) Fincke; married Elizabeth Locker (an elementary teacher), August 17, 1968; children: Derek, Shannon, Aaron. *Education:* Thiel College, B.A., 1967; Miami University, Oxford, Ohio, M.A., 1969; Kent State University, Ph.D., 1974.

ADDRESSES: Home—3 Melody Ln., Selinsgrove, PA 17870. *Office*—Susquehanna University, Selinsgrove, PA 17870; fax: 570-372-2274. *E-mail*—gfincke@ susqu.edu.

CAREER: Freedom Area High School, Freedom, PA, English teacher, 1968-69; Pennsylvania State University, Beaver Campus, Monaca, instructor in English, 1969-75; LeRoy Central School, LeRoy, NY, chairperson of the English department, 1975-80; Susquehanna University, Selinsgrove, PA, professor of English and director of Writers Institute, 1980—, tennis coach, 1981—. Tennis instructor, 1970—; tennis professional, 1976-80.

MEMBER: Poetry Society of America, Associated Writing Programs, Poets and Writers.

AWARDS, HONORS: Fellowships for poetry and fiction, Pennsylvania Arts Council, 1982, 1985, 1987, 1991, 1995, and 2000; syndicated fiction prize, PEN, 1984; Bess Hokin Prize, *Poetry* magazine, 1991; Pushcart Prize, 1995 and 2000; Rose Lefcowitz Prize, *Poet Lore,* 1997.

WRITINGS:

POETRY

Victims, Windy Row Press, 1974.
Emptied, Branden Press (Brookline Village, MA), 1974.
Permanent Season, Branden Press (Brookline Village, MA), 1975.
Breath (poetry chapbook), State Street, 1984.
The Coat in the Heart (poetry chapbook), Blue Buildings, 1985.
The Days of Uncertain Health, Lynx (Amherst, MA), 1988.
Handing the Self Back (poetry chapbook), Green Tower, 1990.
Plant Voices, Yardbird, 1991.
The Public Talk of Death (poetry chapbook), Two Herons, 1991.
The Double Negatives of the Living, Zoland, 1992.
Inventing Angels, Zoland, 1994.
The Technology of Paradise, Avisson, 1998.
The Almanac for Desire, BkMk Press, University of Missouri-Kansas City, 2000.
Blood Times, Time Being, 2001.

OTHER

For Keepsies (stories), Coffee House, 1993.
Emergency Calls (stories), Missouri, 1996.

Contributor of short stories, articles, and poems to periodicals, including *Paris Review, Harper's, DoubleTake, Poetry, American Scholar, North American Review,* and *Kenyon Review.*

SIDELIGHTS: Gary Fincke told *CA:* "Although I began by writing poems after I received a Ph.D. in 1974, I have become a 'writer'—that is, I now write poems, short stories, novels, and creative nonfiction, usually concentrating on one genre for six to nine months. I think this is what makes the books I've published or have recently completed distinctly different from each other. Likewise, there are three months each year (tennis season) when I do no writing at all. I used to read exclusively poetry and fiction; now I read almost exclusively nonfiction—all of the sciences that I once ignored. The fact that I'm self-taught is a blessing, although my current job is teaching aspiring writers. I hope that the mix of my essentially 'blue-collar, jock' upbringing with the eventual professional educator's life proves interesting enough to sustain whatever distinctive voice I have."

*   *   *

FITZ-SIMON, Christopher   1934-

PERSONAL: Born June 9, 1934, in Belfast, Northern Ireland; son of Christopher O'Connell (an army officer) and Gladys Elliott (Killen) Fitz-Simon; married Anne Makower (an opera and television director), May 15, 1965; children: Vanessa Una, Adrian Christopher. *Ethnicity:* "Caucasian." *Education:* Trinity College, Dublin, Mod.B.A., 1957, M.A., 1959.

ADDRESSES: Home and Office—8 Richmond Hill, Monkstown, County Dublin, Ireland. *E-mail*— fitzmak@eircom.net.

CAREER: Radio Telefis Eireann (RTE), Dublin, Ireland, television drama director, 1961-79; Irish Theatre Company, Dublin, artistic director, 1979-83; Abbey Theatre, Dublin, Ireland, script editor and artistic director, 1983-95. Visiting lecturer at universities in Ireland, England, Italy, Brazil, Argentina, Australia, the United States, and Canada. Founding member of board of directors, Tyrone Guthrie Centre (Annaghmakerrig, Ireland) and Siamsa Tire (Ireland's national folk theater); Irish representative on European Community (EC) Cultural Commission (theater group); board member, Lyric Theatre (Belfast).

MEMBER: Irish Actors Equity Association, Irish Georgian Society, Irish Association for Political and Economic Development, Friends of the Monaghan Museum, Association of Drama Adjudicators, Shareholders of the National Theatre Society.

WRITINGS:

PLAYS

But Still and All, broadcast by British Broadcasting Corp. (BBC), 1962.
April Fool, broadcast by BBC, 1963.
Remembrance Sunday, broadcast by RTE, 1968.
The Pool, broadcast by RTE, 1974.
A Bed in the Nettles, broadcast by RTE, 1983.
Vina, broadcast by RTE, 1990.
Johnny Sheehy, broadcast by BBC, 1994.
Ballylenon, broadcast by BBC, 1994.
Raskolnikov's Axe, broadcast by BBC, 1995.
A Snowman in July, broadcast by RTE, 1997.
Spangles and Tights, broadcast by BBC, 1998.
Faithful Departed, broadcast by BBC, 2000.

OTHER

The Arts in Ireland, Gill & Macmillan (Dublin, Ireland), 1982.
The Irish Theatre, Thames & Hudson (London, England), 1983.
The Boys: A Biography of Micheal MacLiammoir and Hilton Edwards, Nick Hern Books, 1994, Heinemann, 1995.
(Coeditor, and author of introduction) *New Plays from the Abbey Theatre, 1993-1995,* Syracuse University Press, 1996.
The Most Beautiful Villages of Ireland, Thames & Hudson (London, England), 2000.

Also author of several dramatized documentaries, 1987—, and dramatizations of Jean Giraudoux, James Joyce, Forrest Reid, Elizabeth Bowen, and others.

WORK IN PROGRESS: A Hundred Years of the Abbey Theatre, for Thames & Hudson (London, England), 2004.

SIDELIGHTS: Christopher Fitz-Simon once told *CA:* "I am best known in Ireland as a theater and television director. If I had to describe my own work I suppose I would say that I am a theater practitioner and have been so since leaving Dublin University in the late 1950s. There is no common theme in my plays or short stories, except that all are set in contemporary Ireland and in the traditional Irish manner are comic in spite of non-comic themes.

"*The Arts in Ireland* was commissioned by the Anglo-Irish publishers Gill & Macmillan after I had complained (in an office conversation) about the difficulty of finding chronological references to events and personalities in the arts in Ireland. Michael Gill said, 'You write it.' It took several years to compile, and it covers the period from 2,500 B.C. to 1970.

"*The Irish Theater* was a commission for the Anglo-American publisher Thames & Hudson. The objective was to show how central the Irish theatrical tradition has been to the development of Western theater, from 1690 to Samuel Beckett, and to formulate a consistent view of the 'Irishness' of writers like Goldsmith, Shaw, Wilde, and Beckett.

"The arts in Ireland at present are bedeviled by a well-meaning, ill-funded, and largely scatterbrained bureaucracy, but professional artists still manage to emerge in spite of this. The theater is very strong here at present, particularly on account of the diversity and energy of playwrighting.

"*The Boys,* though first published in the U.K., was among the top five Irish best-sellers for five weeks in the spring of 1994. The hardback edition sold out in four months. It was republished in the U.S. by Heinemann in 1995."

*   *   *

FLEMING, Thomas (James) 1927-

PERSONAL: Born July 5, 1927, in Jersey City, NJ; son of Thomas James (a politician) and Katherine (a teacher; maiden name, Dolan) Fleming; married Alice Mulcahey (a writer), January 19, 1951; children: Alice, Thomas, David, Richard. *Education:* Fordham University, A.B., 1950, graduate study in social work, 1951. *Politics:* Democrat.

ADDRESSES: Home—315 East 72nd St., New York, NY 10021. *Agent*—Ted Chichak, Suite 175, 1040 First Ave., New York, NY 10022.

CAREER: Yonker's Herald Statesman, Yonkers, NY, reporter, 1951; *Reader's Digest,* Pleasantville, NY, assistant to Fulton Oursler, 1951-52; Oursler Estate, literary executor, 1952-54; *Cosmopolitan,* New York, NY, associate editor, 1954-58, executive editor, 1958-61; writer, 1961—. Consultant on U.S. Bicentennial to Corporation for Public Broadcasting. *Military service:* U.S. Navy, 1945-46.

MEMBER: Society of American Historians, American P.E.N. (president, 1971-73), Society of Magazine Writers (president, 1967-68), American Revolution Round Table (chairman, 1970-81), Century Association, University Club, Dutch Treat Club, History News Network, board member, 2001.

AWARDS, HONORS: Brotherhood award of National Conference of Christians and Jews, for article "Religious Abuse," published in *Cosmopolitan,* 1963; Achievement Award, 1961, and Encaenia Award, 1966, both from Fordham University; Annual Book Awards for best history book, Colonial Dames of America, 1970, for *The Man from Monticello: An Intimate Life of Thomas Jefferson,* and 1972, for *The Man Who Dared the Lightning: A New Look at Benjamin Franklin;* Christopher Award, The Christophers, 1970, for *The Man from Monticello; The Man from Monticello* was named one of the outstanding books of the year by *New York Times,* 1970; award of merit, American Association for State and Local History, 1973, for *The Forgotten Victory: The Battle for New Jersey;* Religious Book Award, Catholic Press Association, 1974, for *The Good Shepherd;* named distinguished fellow, New Jersey Historical Society, 1975; *1776: Year of Illusions* was named one of the outstanding books of the year by American Library Association, 1975; New Jersey Historical Commission Award, 1975, for "unique contributions to the expansion of public knowledge about New Jersey history through the complementary roles of historian and novelist"; Annual Book Award, American Revolution Round Table, 1976, for *1776;* citations for writing from American Foundation of Religion and Psychiatry and from Family Service Association; awarded ARRT prizes, 1997, for *Liberty: The American Revolution,* and 1999, for *Duel: Alexander Hamilton, Aaron Burr, and the Future of America;* Distinguished Article award, Army Historical Foundation, 2000, for "From the Hudson to the Halls of Montezuma," *MHQ,* spring 1999; American Revolution Roundtable of Philadelphia's Thomas Fleming book award instituted in author's name, 2001.

WRITINGS:

NONFICTION

Now We Are Enemies: The Battle of Bunker Hill, St. Martin's Press (New York, NY), 1960.

Beat the Last Drum: The Siege of Yorktown, St. Martin's Press (New York, NY), 1963.

One Small Candle: The Pilgrims' First Year in America, Norton (New York, NY), 1964.

(Editor) *Affectionately Yours, George Washington: A Self-Portrait in Letters of Friendship,* Norton (New York, NY), 1967.

First in Their Hearts: A Biography of George Washington, Norton (New York, NY), 1968.

(With editors of *American Heritage*) *Battle of Yorktown,* American Heritage (New York, NY), 1968.

The Man from Monticello: An Intimate Life of Thomas Jefferson, Morrow (New York, NY), 1969.

West Point: The Men and Times of the United States Military Academy, Morrow (New York, NY), 1969.

The Man Who Dared the Lightning: A New Look at Benjamin Franklin, Morrow (New York, NY), 1971.

(Editor) *Benjamin Franklin: A Life in His Own Words,* Newsweek Books (New York, NY), 1972.

The Forgotten Victory: The Battle for New Jersey, Reader's Digest Press (New York, NY), 1973.

1776: Year of Illusions, Norton (New York, NY), 1975.

New Jersey: A History, Norton (New York, NY), 1977.

The First Stroke: Lexington and Concord and the Beginning of the American Revolution, Division of Publications (Washington, DC), 1978.

(Editor) *The Living Land of Lincoln,* Reader's Digest Press (New York, NY), 1980.

New Jersey: A History, with a historical guide, Norton (New York, NY)/American Association for State and Local History (Nashville, TN), 1984.

The Spoils of War, Putnam (New York, NY), 1985.

Cowpens: "Downright Fighting," Division of Publications (Washington, DC), 1988.

Harry S. Truman, President, Walker (New York, NY), 1993.

Liberty!: The American Revolution (companion to PBS television series of the same name), Viking (New York, NY), 1997.

Lights along the Way: Great Stories of American Faith, Morehouse Publications (Harrisburg, PA), 1999.

Duel: Alexander Hamilton, Aaron Burr, and the Future of America, Basic Books (New York, NY), 2000.

The New Dealers' War: FDR and the War within World War II, Basic Books (New York, NY), 2001.

FICTION

All Good Men, Doubleday (New York, NY), 1961.
The God of Love, Doubleday (New York, NY), 1963.
King of the Hill, New American Library (New York, NY), 1966.
A Cry of Whiteness, Morrow (New York, NY), 1967.
Romans, Countrymen, Lovers, Morrow (New York, NY), 1969.
The Sandbox Tree, Morrow (New York, NY), 1970.
The Good Shepherd, Doubleday (New York, NY), 1974.
Liberty Tavern, Doubleday (New York, NY), 1976.
Rulers of the City, Doubleday (New York, NY), 1977.
Promises to Keep, Doubleday (New York, NY), 1978.
A Passionate Girl, Warner (New York, NY), 1979.
The Officers' Wives, Doubleday (New York, NY), 1981.
Dreams of Glory, Warner (New York, NY), 1983.
Time and Tide, Simon & Schuster (New York, NY), 1987.
Over There, HarperCollins (New York, NY), 1992.
Loyalties: A Novel of World War II, HarperCollins (New York, NY), 1994.
Remember the Morning, Forge (New York, NY), 1997.
The Wages of Fame, Forge (New York, NY), 1998.
Hours of Gladness, Forge (New York, NY), 1999.

Also author of numerous "Keepsake" issues of *This Week* magazine. Author of scripts for television. Contributor of articles to magazines and periodicals, including *Reader's Digest, American Heritage,* and *New York Times Magazine.* Consultant for the television movie *The American Revolution,* History Channel, 1994. Principal commentator for documentary *The Long Journey Home: The Irish in America,* 1998. Script writer for the narrative film, *We The People,* at the National Museum of the Civil War, which opened in Harrisburg, PA, 2001.

WORK IN PROGRESS: Conquerers of the Sky, a novel set in California, exploring the sixty-year history of the Buchanan Aircraft Company, will be forthcoming from Forge in early 2003, a year in which the United States will celebrate the 100th anniversary of the Wright Brothers flight at Kitty Hawk. Also *Argonne Ring,* a nonfiction book that describes the impact of the return of a ring Fleming's father gave him on his deathbed. The book is the story of Fleming's relationship with his father, which progresses from antagonism to profound love and understanding.

SIDELIGHTS: "For a long time Americans thought history happened to other people," Thomas Fleming once commented in *CA.* "The main thrust of my work . . . has been to explode this idea." The well-known novelist, historian, and biographer has explored a wide variety of subject matter in his work, with an emphasis on two disparate but important segments of American history: the Revolutionary War and the twentieth-century immigrant experience—particularly that of Irish Catholics. More recently he has expanded his interest to American's national and international political experience, particularly, in *Time and Tide, Over There, Loyalties* and *The New Dealer's War.* Here he displayed a strong revisionist bent, arguing in dramatic terms against conventional accounts of major events and historical outcomes.

Fleming has been praised by critics for his ability to present not only the facts of history but also the emotions. Through the use of quotations from diaries and letters written during the American Revolution, Fleming has been able to convey the thoughts of the men and women who fought on both sides of the American War for Independence. Fleming, commented *Publishers Weekly* interviewer Barbara A. Bannon, is "a respected interpreter of the history of this country. . . . He has acquired an insider's interest in little-known characters and events of the Revolution that reveal much about the real temper of those times." In a *Christian Science Monitor* review of *Beat the Last Drum: The Siege of Yorktown,* R. M. Hallett wrote that Fleming "has a deep feeling for the human drama of war—not only in the horrendous decisions that must be made by generals but in the more earthy feelings of the common soldiers."

"When I first came to American history I thought I was going to play 'Yankee Doodle' all the way," Fleming said in the *Publishers Weekly* interview with Bannon. "I started reading letters and diaries of the time to try and find out what the average guy thought about things, not just Washington, Franklin, Jefferson. What the private thoughts were is very hard to find. I trudged through the archives of historical societies and found myself getting into the politics of the Revolution. There was plenty of corruption, the politics of self-interest, those who were in it for the cushy contracts they could get, who were ready to steal everything not nailed down."

The Battle of Bunker Hill suppled prime material for Fleming's technique of combining individual experience and large historical drama. The first major clash of the colonial rebellion against the British, the Battle of Bunker Hill galvanized the Americans into action and divided them—father against son, brother against brother, neighbor against neighbor, friend against friend—according to their political loyalties. It is that tension that Fleming tries to capture in *Now We Are Enemies: The Battle of Bunker Hill.* "The most interesting thing about Mr. Fleming's book is the emphasis he places on friendships and old attachments broken in this the beginning of the Revolutionary War," stated E. H. Smith in *New York Herald Tribune Book Review.*

Three of Fleming's other historical inquiries, *Beat the Last Drum: The Siege of Yorktown, The Battle of Yorktown,* and *The Forgotten Victory: The Battle for New Jersey,* cover territory similar to that in *Now We Are Enemies.* In all three books, Fleming combines detailed descriptions of the military campaigns with added insights culled from personal papers. George F. Scheer in *New York Times Book Review* considered *The Battle of Yorktown* to be "a smart, orderly account of that most dramatic and decisive moment in American Revolutionary and military history." In *Beat the Last Drum,* noted Hallett, "people walk through [Fleming's] pages and make history glow." Again in *The Forgotten Victory* Fleming characteristically places his emphasis on the thoughts and feelings of the battle's participants. Thomas Fleming "reminds us that the American Revolution was a civil war," commented Lawrence A. Howard in *Best Sellers.* "Sons such as William Franklin fought fathers such as Benjamin Franklin. . . . Through adept characterizations of researched and resurrected men and women, Mr. Fleming has written, successfully, a bona fide history." Of that same book Scheer, again in *New York Times Book Review,* observed that "Thomas Fleming's full-length account of the political machination and battlefield actions that made up the Springfield affair, replete with colorful details and characterizations, makes both compelling reading and a convincing case for the lasting significance of the victory."

1776: Year of Illusions explores the events of the central year of the American Revolution—which included the Revolutionists' disastrous invasion of Canada, numerous losses by an ill-trained and poorly supplied colonial army, and, finally, George Washington's victories in New Jersey—and the illusions that spurred on the colonial fighters, which were quickly dispelled when they came in contact with the hard realities of war. "Fleming writes on two levels—the year 1776 as narrative history and as a period in which the aims of the Revolution were articulated and, to a degree, institutionalized through the Continental Congress," stated Alden Whitman in the *New York Times.* "In the process, he peels away the layers of myth and legend that, like verdigris, have formed an obscuring patina over that crucial year."

Chief among these illusions, says Fleming, were the beliefs that moderation of British rule could be obtained short of actual independence, and the belief that the British were a military pushover and so independence, as Edmund S. Morgan summed up in *New York Review of Books,* "could be won by a few bold strokes." Further, as Whitman described Fleming's contentions, "there were enough examples of incompetence, stupidity, cravenness and disorganization to raise the suspicion that the American revolutionaries were a clutch of inept and inglorious bunglers." "Reduced . . . to its simplest terms, [*1776* demonstrates] that for the greater part of the glorious year of our country's birth nobody on either side really knew what he was doing," Phoebe Adams commented in the *Atlantic.* "The wonder of '76 was not that stupidity, uncertainty, self-interest, and dishonesty existed, but that so much was accomplished in spite of them."

Fleming's *Liberty!: The American Revolution,* a companion volume to the 1997 PBS Television series of the same title, offers a less analytical and more general interpretation of the same era, concentrating, as a writer for *Publishers Weekly* noted, on "dramatic events and colorful personalities." The same reviewer stated: "Shaped but not constrained by the TV format, the book highlights the role of African Americans, women and Indians whenever possible." *Liberty!* also provides an overview of the adoption of the U.S. Constitution and the conflicting ideas, such as individual liberty versus public responsibility, that had to be reconciled in determining its content. Reviewing *Liberty!* in *Booklist,* Gilbert Taylor praised the volume's "extravagant two-page color spreads" and its numerous sidebars "on topics that interest people." However, Taylor found these secondary to the central thrust of Fleming's text, "the military course of the war." "Fleming's . . . condensation of seven years of war," Taylor concluded, "is the picture of precision for those reading about America's Book of Genesis for the first time."

With the 1999 historical account *Duel: Alexander Hamilton, Aaron Burr, and The Future of America,* Fleming shifts the focus to a period after the Revolutionary War. The 1804 duel between Hamilton and Burr, which left the former fatally wounded, remains one of the most famous duels in history. Fleming portrays the era as one of heated political maneuvering and conflicting ambitions, both for the new nation and the men who would set its course. The immediate cause of the duel, remarks made by Hamilton at a dinner party, was merely an offshoot of a bitter rivalry that already existed between the two men. Burr had successfully mobilized New York City's Tammany Hall, defeating

Hamilton and assuring Republican victories throughout the city. When the 1800 presidential election was thrown into the House of Representatives, Hamilton conspired against Burr to assure Jefferson's victory. Although popular history casts Burr as the instigator of the duel, Fleming shows that in an exchange of letters between the two men, Hamilton was just as guilty as Burr in escalating the conflict. "To be as masterfully concise as Fleming manages to be," stated Katherine Whittemore of *Salon.com,* "is an achievement in itself, for this epic would have challenged Tolstoi." Whittemore went on to conclude that "*Duel* does a scintillating job of restoring salient edges that decades of historical buffing have rounded."

The New Dealers' War takes Fleming into World War II—territory he had not hitherto explored in nonfiction, though he had done extensive research on the subject for his novels *Time and Tide* and *Loyalties.* The book's theme is captured in the subtitle, *FDR and the War within World War II.* In *Washington Post Book World,* Richard Pearson called it "a gripping controversial, informative and at times infuriating look at FDR's leadership as the nation entered and fought World War II. . . . Fleming paints a devastating portrait of a Roosevelt whose health and powers were in steep and terminal decline after 1940." Other reviewers waxed indignant at Fleming's refusal to view FDR as a sacred icon. In *Wall Street Journal,* Michael Ybarra stated: "Roosevelt haters will love this book" but admits even admirers will find themselves "frequently disconcerted" by the evidence Fleming accumulates of Roosevelt's wartime blunders. In *Flint Journal,* David Forsmark praised Fleming for realizing it was time to "cut through the wartime propaganda and take a clear-eyed look at FDR." Some critics found especially compelling Fleming's argument that FDR embodied both the tension between the idealism of the Declaration of Independence and the often brutal realism that Americans have shown in times of crisis. Pragmatists, most of them conservatives, took control of the global conflict (World War I) and in the first postwar election the Republican Party won both houses of Congress.

Fleming's biographies reflect his interest in the impact of the political on the personal and the effects of personal convictions on public actions, as well as his concern with the individual personality in history. Just as his other books quote liberally from diaries and documents, his biographies also make ample use of the personal correspondence and papers of his subjects. As a result, Fleming's books take an intimate view of his subjects' lives rather than simply showing them as a part of a historical panorama. "What Fleming has

done," noted Marshall Smelser in a *New York Times Book Review* article on *The Man from Monticello: An Intimate Life of Thomas Jefferson,* "is to look at life from Jefferson's point of view rather than looking from the orchestra seats at Jefferson on stage. This is not a 'Life and Times,' although it tells the public story too."

Fleming's biographical skill lies in his ability to cut away the legend surrounding these early American heroes and to ferret out the personalities upon which those legends were built. Commenting on *First in Their Hearts: A Biography of George Washington, Washington Post Book World* contributing critic Bernard A. Weisberger wrote that "to Thomas J. Fleming's credit, this good short biography makes that love [of the common people for George Washington] understandable without the author's typewriter transforming itself into a chisel for cutting a new marble bust. In fact, Fleming's theme is that Washington was a man of exultant energy, impetuous will, fiery passions and wicked temper. . . . [When] confronted with examples of greatness through self-discipline, youngsters like to kid themselves that yesterday's heroes were neither as lively nor as tempted as they themselves. This fine little tale could even convince some hard juvenile heads otherwise."

In Thomas Lask's *New York Times* review of *The Man from Monticello* he claimed that "one of the virtues of partisan biography at its best—and Mr. Fleming's is a splendid example of the kind—[is] that some of the author's own passion rubs off on the reader. . . . The author warns what he is about in the subtitle. What we have is a personal portrait drawn from inside the home: Jefferson as wooer, husband, parent, grandfather, squire of Monticello and bibliophile—a man of the widest intellectual interests and skills, and of a Cato-like integrity and morality. . . . Mr. Fleming has humanized [Jefferson], substituted the buff coat for a silk one, the fireside for the halls of debate. But in any guise, his central greatness remains."

Lask, in another *New York Times* review, also praised Fleming for cutting through the legend but not sensationalizing his material by debunking a hero. In his review of *The Man Who Dared the Lightning: A New Look at Benjamin Franklin,* Lask stated, "By cutting away the years when Franklin was getting through by pluck and luck, [Fleming] has avoided the story of economic progress and tidy resourcefulness that grates so on the modern reader. And by subordinating the salon figure to the political activist, the man of sagacity to the cunning negotiator, he has created a tough-minded, hard-headed colonial radical who does not quite jibe with the author of *Poor Richard's Almanac.* . . . Mr. Fleming has not changed the portrait beyond recognition. . . . What is different is the radical pamphleteer, the colonial agitator, the relentless advocate of independence."

While most critics view Fleming's biographies as excellent examples of scholarship and popular history, some have also found that his presentations of his subjects tend to be one-sided. "The book's chief flaw is that Franklin is portrayed as all but flawless," a *Time* magazine reviewer noted regarding *The Man Who Dared the Lightning*. In a review of that same book for the *Boston Herald Traveler,* Richard D. Brown stated, "The only major drawback to Fleming's story of the achievement of American independence is that it is so heavily centered on Franklin and always apologetic for Franklin's behavior. Moreover Franklin's opponents are Fleming's enemies. Thus he simplifies his analysis of British politics so that the English are divided into 'pro' and 'anti' Americans, the former being good, far-sighted, and noble, while the latter are corrupt, stupid, and arrogant. This sort of interpretation hinders rather than advances understanding." Lask reported in *New York Times* that "in such a book [as *The Man from Monticello*], opponents are likely to be not only men of differing ideas but also a little detestable. Jefferson's great rival, Alexander Hamilton, is scarcely treated with even-hefted justice. . . . It is not that Mr. Fleming is wrong in the facts but that he assigns to Hamilton a Machiavellianism, in the vulgar sense, that does not really fit Hamilton's frank aims in doing what he considered best for the country. Jefferson's acquisition of the Louisiana territory was a great act of statesmanship, but Mr. Fleming does not emphasize the fact that the action did not lie well with Jefferson's earlier strict constructions of the powers allowed the Federal Government."

Fleming's interest in American history extends beyond the Revolutionary War period and into the modern era. His continued interest in the individual's place in history is evident in all his works of fiction. "More and more, as my research into American history became deeper and more extensive, I began to graft a sense of history on my fiction," Fleming once commented in *CA*. "This has now become my central preoccupation, to use fiction to focus on human beings at flash points in history, where crises entangle both public and private lives. I remain intensely interested in the historical development of private lives, especially as they emerge from private ghettos—ethnic or economic—to participate in the larger American society."

Such "flashpoints in history" can be found in Fleming's multi-novel saga of the Stapleton family, which ranges from colonial days throughout the history of America. *Remember the Morning* opens in 1721 when two young girls, the Dutch Catalyntie Van Vorst and her African slave, Clara, are captured by Seneca natives. The girls are raised by the Seneca for twelve years before they are returned to a white settlement in a prisoner exchange. Enter the settler Malcolm Stapleton, a man who seeks to build an American consciousness. A love triangle, with its consequent jealousies and betrayals, ensues over the next thirty years between Stapleton and the two women. Meanwhile, Catalyntie becomes a shrewd businesswoman, trading with the native tribes, while Clara spends most of her life caring for the sick and indigent. A *Publishers Weekly* reviewer characterized *Remember the Morning* a "sad intricately plotted book . . . a grim compelling tale of historical adventure amid rapacious imperialism and wholesale treachery." Barbara Conaty of *Booklist* offered a different take on the novel, praising Fleming's "stereotype-smashing insights into the psychology of ambitious, conflicted young people." and his "marvelously fresh interpretation of an era."

Fleming followed *Remember the Morning* with *The Wages of Fame,* which traces the fortunes and travails of the Stapleton clan from 1827 to the beginning of the Civil War. By this time the Stapletons are wealthy and own land in the Hudson Valley. In a gender reversal of the love triangle depicted in *Remember the Morning,* young George Stapleton and his considerably less well-to-do friend John Sladen fall in love with the same woman, Caroline Kemble. George marries Caroline while John Sladen goes on to become a U.S. senator. Yet the ambitious Caroline soon coerces her own husband into politics while at the same time carrying on an affair with Sladen. Numerous historical figures play a part in the drama as Caroline and Sladen manipulate George Stapleton to their own ends. When the United States is drawn into a war with Mexico, Caroline and Sladen try to enlist George, who becomes a brigadier general, in a campaign to seize all of Mexico and make it an American colony. George's refusal ruptures his relationship with Caroline and they remain at loggerheads as America stumbles toward civil war between the North and South. In a final confrontation, George blocks her attempt to declare New Jersey neutral on the eve of war. Margaret Flanagan in *Booklist* found *The Wages of Fame* to be a "fiery sequel to *Remember the Morning* . . . [and a] riveting narrative." However, a *Publishers Weekly* reviewer felt that Fleming the historian overshadowed Fleming the novelist and the novel suffered from "too much history, and not enough fiction."

The son of a first-generation Irish-American politician, Fleming first became interested in American history as a result of his inquiries into his own ethnic heritage. He then came to believe that the strong sense of ethnic identity possessed by many Irish-American Catholics isolated them from the broader American experience. His novels that revolve around the Irish-American "ghetto," as he refers to it, reflect the drama that occurs when these tight-knit Irish-American communities are faced with pressures from the outside. Thus Fleming also tries to incorporate the Irish Catholic experience into the wider spectrum of American life. "The immigrant experience lasts for at least three, probably four generations," he told *CA*. In his *Publishers Weekly* interview with Barbara A. Bannon, Fleming explained, "What I am trying to write about is a kind of 'Roots' in reverse, about people who have a sense that they do have family and ethnic roots still pushing up into their lives from the past. They must either cut them or let them grow back into their lives in some new ways. It is a very painful process."

In these novels about the Irish-American ghetto—or the flight from it—characters weave in and out of the stories, appearing as minor figures in one, as major figures in the next. Four of these books in particular—*All Good Men, The God of Love, King of the Hill,* and *Rulers of the City*—explore the Irish experience in urban America, viewing it from a political perspective as well as a personal one. These novels, which rely heavily on Fleming's recollections of his youth in Jersey City, examine the workings of the political machine in an Irish-dominated city and the anguish of those who are torn between their ethnic and party loyalty and their conscience. Together these books form "the continuing political history of a city," Martin Levin pointed out in *New York Times Book Review.* Fleming, continued Levin in his review of *King of the Hill,* "reveals a talent for weaving large and small corruptions into a fascinating web of municipal intrigue. . . . He has as intense an interest in his scrofulous wedge of geography as Faulkner had in his. His characters are solidly linked together by blood, tradition and old crimes—and the rich texture of their past makes their present credible."

This loose series of books traces the political career of Jake O'Connor, who enters the political machine at the behest of his father and who eventually becomes mayor of the city. Within this continuing story line, Fleming is able to reveal the uglier side of American urban politics. Reviewing *All Good Men* in the *Springfield Repub-*

lican, a critic called the book "a graphic, authentic picture of the rough-and-tumble world of demagogic party bosses, opportunistic ward-heelers, and 'the organization,' where every man has his price." Discussing Fleming's portrayal of the busing controversy (in order to desegregate the schools) in *Rulers of the City,* former New York City mayor John V. Lindsay commented that "Americans don't like their cities very much and in fact know very little about them—an information gap that includes American governments, past and present. . . . [but] Thomas Fleming has accumulated some understanding of what's wrong with today's American cities." And despite some other problems with the book, concluded Lindsay in the *New York Times Book Review, Rulers of the City* "goes quite far enough into one bleeding aspect of America's urban problem. Most any American city, perhaps even more importantly any state or even the Federal Government, could use a Thomas Fleming, or at least their rulers should read his book."

Fleming returned to the Irish-American ghetto setting in 1999 with *Hours of Gladness,* a novel that concerns a Vietnam veteran who suffers guilt for having betrayed his unit in battle. Returning to Paradise Beach, New Jersey, Mick O'Day joins the town's police force, which is controlled by his corrupt uncle. Mick finds himself involved with more than he bargained for, including illegal dealings with the Mafia and the IRA. Ultimately, Mick emergences on the side of law and justice, and in so doing manages to assuage his guilt for his past wrongs committed in Vietnam. Flanagan, again writing in *Booklist,* praised Fleming's ability to interweave several plot lines. She judged *Hours of Gladness* to be "a stunning multilayered thriller" and noted: "The tension mounts at an almost unbearable rate, exploding into a physically and emotionally violent climax."

Although many of Fleming's novels are placed in his fictional Irish-dominated city and involve many of the same characters (usually Irish-Catholic), not all of the books are concerned exclusively with the Irish-American ghetto, but instead reach deeper into the general American experience. *A Cry of Whiteness,* for example, "vividly conveys the sense of disorder in both the [African-American] ghetto and lily-white areas [in the 1960s]," Clinton J. Maguire commented in *Best Sellers.* "It also speaks with impartiality of the motives and characters of parties throughout the civil rights spectrum." *Romans, Countrymen, Lovers* effectively considers the national obsession for personal freedom and liberation that began in the 1960s.

The Officers' Wives is Fleming's powerful statement on American life during the past three decades. The novel is written from the perspectives of three women, each married to graduates of the West Point Class of 1950; the book explores their lives, their marriages, and the changing consciousness (and conscience) of a nation. *The Officers' Wives* carries its characters through two disastrous and morally devastating wars (Korea and Vietnam), as well as through the sweeping social changes brought about by the feminist movement. In telling his story, Fleming "is attentive to both the dynamics of his characters' private lives and to the wider worlds in which they develop," wrote Jane Larkin Crain in the *New York Times Book Review*. William B. Hill in a *Best Sellers* review considered Fleming to be "triumphantly successful in his depiction of the sixties and the effects of the war in Vietnam on the wives and children of army officers. The picture of American military ineptitude and North Vietnamese brutality is joined to a portrait of turbulent America and the whole disastrous era comes back to life."

Fleming is especially praised by critics for his ability to capture the growing sense of uneasiness that affected the United States in the 1960s and 1970s. This shift in the general feeling of the population is reflected in the subtly changing moods of the women in the novel. "What energizes this novel . . . is the war between the sexes," stated Peter Davison in *Atlantic*. "When each woman—as each must—is required to choose between her conscience and her husband, it is the husband who loses. The wives seem to follow the example of an entire nation by gradually withdrawing their confidence in the integrity of American might."

In his 1987 novel, *Time and Tide,* Fleming again deals with war in the twentieth century, but this time his main character is a warship, the *Jefferson City*. She is a ship that courts disaster; in the words of *New York Times Book Review* critic Walter Lord, "since no one vessel could endure as many misadventures as the Jefferson City, she is a sort of composite of several American warships beset by mishaps" in the Pacific Theater during World War II. Newly captained by Arthur McKay as a replacement for McKay's former classmate Winfield Kemble, the ship becomes a pawn in the relationships between various people on board, whose actions reflect less than sterling characters. Fleming's fictional characters flesh out the book's central premise that "World War II and a lot of the present dilemmas of the United States began in the gunboat diplomacy and the dream of empire unleashed by [U.S.] activities in China," in the words of Chicago's *Tribune Books* critic Marge Piercy. Piercy felt that the author's knowledge

of "what he is writing about on many levels, profoundly, thoroughly, sensuously," was one of *Time and Tide*'s central strengths. Fleming "created daily life on a heavy cruiser in concrete detail. He writes equally well of the officers and the men. He knows sailors and likes them with all the barnacles still attached." And while cautioning readers that Fleming has blurred the line between fact and fiction by interspersing actual historical incidents into his fictional narrative, Lord added that readers "can thank Thomas Fleming for an engrossing novel that makes the war in the Pacific live again."

Fleming has set several other novels against the military backdrop of World War I and World War II. *Over There* tells the story of a young nurse, Polly Warden, who works at the front in war-torn Europe. This is a riveting account of World War I, seen through the eyes of a disillusioned general and a feminist woman volunteer. Warden falls in love with a French doctor, Paul Lebrun, who has become cynical because of the horrors he has experienced in treating victims of the conflict. The novel, in which real-life General John J. Pershing plays a role, traces Polly's descent from idealism into a weary disillusionment that mirrors Lebrun's. Florence King in *New York Newsday* called the book "a wonderfully readable story that blends breathless action and food for thought on every fascinating page . . . a woman's novel for men and a man's novel for women." The *Publishers Weekly* reviewer commented: "Fleming traces a cast of flat, stock characters (the leader, the spy, the poet, the foot soldier) through an uninspired formulaic plot."

Flemings' book *Loyalties* is set in World War II. It traces the intertwining lives of two military couples, the U.S. Navy Captain Jonathan Talbot and his wife Annie, and German U-boat Commander Ernst von Hoffman and his wife Berthe. Talbot is captured in the North Atlantic by Hoffman and then released shortly before war is officially declared between the United States and Germany. Later, in Spain on an espionage mission, Talbot has an affair with Hoffman's wife. He also becomes involved in a plot to assassinate Hitler. A reviewer in *Library Journal* praised the book as "a thrilling story of espionage and a morality play about people forced to make compelling choices between their perceptions of good and evil." A reviewer in *The Stars and Stripes* said the book demonstrated Fleming's "powerful ability to use fiction as a way of providing readers with astonishing new perspectives on world events." "Elaborately plotted and meticulously researched," stated a reviewer in *Publishers Weekly,* "this sprawling saga of World War II offers some new political insights."

In addition to contemporary warfare and its affect on U.S. society, another dominant theme in Fleming's early fiction is the influence of the Roman Catholic Church in the lives of his characters. This interest, Fleming has stated, is an outgrowth of both his own background and of his concern with individual freedom. "I have a special interest in two fields," Fleming once commented in *CA*, "religion and politics. As I see it, politics is the area in which religious values are realized (or not realized) in our society. Religion as such, is essentially powerless and is growing more so. Of course there is also a fundamental conflict between traditional religious ideas and ideas inherent in the American experience—freedom vs. obedience, revolt in the name of self-realization. These are main themes in my work."

Although religion plays a strong role in much of Fleming's fiction, it gained him the most attention in *The Sandbox Tree*. The book was originally written in 1952 but not published until 1969, partially due to Catholic censorship in the publishing world, Fleming contends. In the intervening years he rewrote the novel eight times, making the final manuscript less harsh than the original. *The Sandbox Tree* takes the conflict between religious devotion and personal freedom as its central theme. The novel centers on a number of young Catholics who gradually reject the church in which they were raised, including Margaret Connolly, a young woman destined for the convent. Margaret is the roommate of a woman who merely goes through the motions of practicing her religion, is friends with a rebellious lapsed Catholic and, finally, falls in love with a Protestant. In the end, after much pain, Margaret turns away from her family and her church and thus becomes, as she states in the novel, "something better, I think: a free adult American."

The Sandbox Tree won praise for what many reviewers saw as its precise, albeit painful, depiction of early post-War American Catholicism. "This is Mr. Fleming's valid assessment of the year 1948," stated Charles Dollen in *Best Sellers*. "So painfully true is his novel of Catholic family life in that year that it makes it difficult to write an objective review. Irish American Roman Catholicism—a ghetto, a system, one in which the institution was much more valuable than the person. Fear put up the walls of that ghetto; inhumanity kept it firmly in place. Or so it seemed." *Tablet Magazine*'s Richard Ryan contended that "in the lives of Faith and Margaret and Judge Kilpatrick and some of the others in *The Sandbox Tree*, [Fleming] has tried to restore the grace of humor in American life, the idea of forgiveness, an idea of life that restores some of the more human things that are indeed both Catholic and American."

The Good Shepherd is another of Fleming's novels that centers on the question of faith and conscience. The "good shepherd" of the title, Archbishop Matthew Mahan, is to be appointed cardinal, but he is deeply troubled by a number of recent rulings of the Church as well as plagued by dissension within his own see. By placing the action in the tumultuous years following the Second Vatican Council, Fleming is able to introduce the concerns of the modern Church to the reader. *The Good Shepherd* is a "novel that probes deeply into problems that, like them or not, millions of Catholics must contend with today," commented Priscilla L. Buckley in *National Review*. The book, according to Francis Sweeney in *New York Times Book Review*, shows its characters "believably confronting the Church's problems and crystallizing the Church's moods." James G. Murray, writing in *Critic*, found that Fleming produced a believable portrait in Matthew Mahan. "You can accept not just the priesthood but the humanity of [the book's] central figure, Matthew Mahan," Murray said. "One likes him, finding in his very simplicity a kind of complexity, and ultimately taking his teamsmanship and gamesmanhood as the only ways possible of effecting good within the present church structure. Liberals may not like or get the point of his style, but he does genuinely wish to feed his sheep and to prove his theology and philosophy by acts rather than words. On the other hand, he knows—and knows that he knows—which side his bread is buttered on, which clause is a very free translation of *Roma locuta est, causa finita est*. In short, he is not the usual one dimensional prelate as priest or priest as man that one too often finds in novels of this type. His being different is what makes the difference."

In many ways, *The Good Shepherd* can be seen as Fleming's outline for reform in the Roman Catholic Church. In the form of a letter Mahan writes to the Pope, Fleming raises and argues issues of debate within the Church today: policies on birth control, divorce, the status of women, and clerical celibacy. However, some critics question the novel's effectiveness as ecclesiastical argumentation. For example, Sweeney observed that "true enough, *Humanae Vitae* [a papal proclamation by which Mahan was deeply disturbed] was a watershed of dissent in the Church, and there is widespread dissatisfaction with the Roman Curia. But to polarize history as Fleming does is not to write a novel but a hanging sermon."

The anger Fleming often shows toward the Catholic Church has seemed disturbing to many critics who find his treatment of Catholicism and Catholics stereotypical as well as unduly harsh. "Would Protestants be interested in a novel of this kind?" Buckley asked of *The Good Shepherd.* "Probably not, unless they are members of Protestant and Other Americans United for Separation of Church and State. . . . All they have ever wanted to believe about the Church of Rome is here, the venality, the striving for power, the cynicism in high places, every sin in the book, yea even unto fornication between priest and nun. Would Catholics be interested? Very much so, but lots of them will not like it, many will loathe it, none will feel comfortable with it." In his review of *The Good Shepherd,* James G. Murray commented: "Hard-nosed bastard of a pastor. Swinging nuns. One or two alcoholic priests. A cynical Jesuit (there's one in every crowd). A seminary rector who objects to the use of Rye-Crisp in a Eucharistic service. And so it goes, *ad infinitum* and *ad nauseam.*"

Anthony Boucher remarked in *New York Times Book Review* that he wished "the author had not depicted his many Roman Catholics [in *A Cry of Whiteness*] as stupid racial bigots." Robert Norberg noted in a *Best Sellers* review of *Romans, Countrymen, Lovers:* "This book is a fairly heavy-handed piece of anti-Catholic polemic. The author asserts about a hundred times how false are the teachings of the Church and how stupid those who believe in and propagate them, without ever troubling to document his case. Everything is conveniently arranged the way it always is in propaganda novels. The believing Catholics are all petty, hypocritical, stupid, and so on."

Other critics found Fleming's criticism of the Church not only harsh but also unnecessary. Maguire, in his *Best Sellers* review of *A Cry of Whiteness,* charged that "the interjection of Catholicism as the religion of the protagonist [is] pointless and irrelevant." Roger B. Dooley, reviewing *King of the Hill* for *Commonweal,* stated that Fleming "does a good deal of snarling, snapping and sneering himself, mostly in the direction of the Church. Those who cling to it are invariably dismissed as 'idiots,' 'morons,' and 'rosary-rattlers,' while the intelligent characters can scarcely pass a Catholic institution without choking on bitter regrets for the years wasted trying to swallow all that 'mush, ten centuries cold.' This observation is not made on grounds of prudence but of art; it seems a violation of the writer's objectivity when his tone becomes shrill with the sound of grinding axes, especially since Church and clergy play no part in the action."

Despite the negative reaction to his views on the Catholic Church, especially in Catholic journals such as *Best Sellers, Critic,* and *Commonweal,* Fleming has gained a reputation as a "Catholic writer"—a label he eschews. "Hopefully, some day I will be recognized as an American writer who happens to be Catholic," he told Richard Ryan in *Tablet Magazine.* "And this will be a sign that the Catholic Church has indeed emerged into the fullness of American life, and the freedom and responsibility will be there in the Church and also in each of us to report and reflect on the life of all Americans."

In that same article Ryan commended Fleming for his writing about Catholic issues. "Fleming has done a couple of things with the writing of *The Sandbox Tree,*" Ryan stated. "And one of the things that he may have done is to open a window on Catholic writing, with a little more light, a little more air, a little more freedom. There was a time when a man like John XXIII made a sacrament out of opening windows. Maybe, in what it can do for American Catholic writing, the liberation of Tom Fleming has done the same thing."

In his later work, Fleming moved away from his antagonistic feelings toward the Roman faith into what he has called more "widened spiritual concerns." "I have become absorbed in a much larger spiritual idea," Fleming once commented in *CA,* "the conflict between idealism and realism, or faith and disillusion, which seems to me at the heart of the American experience."

Promises to Keep, a book Fleming views as "a bridge . . . across which I traveled to the broader American experience," takes the state of being an American as its theme. This concern is revealed and summed up in the book's epigraph by George Santayana: "To be an American is of itself almost a moral condition, an education and a career." The central character of the novel, Paul Stapleton, tries to live up to the idealism inculcated in him by his parents, but has been forced by two world wars and the Depression to make some difficult compromises. Gradually the reader discovers that the source of Stapleton's spiritual strength is his wife, a Mexican Catholic whose love, rooted in her mystical faith, sustains the entire family. It is this religious element of the novel—the depiction of religious belief as a positive force rather than as something to rebel against—that Fleming considers central to an understanding of the book. In *Promises to Keep* Fleming's mix of Wasp and Irish-Catholic worlds also provides a potent symbolic moment in the evolution of his political thinking. Jim Kilpatrick, son of a corrupt judge in Fleming's fictional city's political machine, has escaped the Irish-American ghetto in *Romans, Country-*

men, *Lovers* and has now been hired by the Stapleton family to write a biography of Paul Stapleton. He discovers that in the late 1930s Stapleton paid a huge bribe to enable the family to move their textile mills from New Jersey to the labor-union free South. When Kilpatrick confronts Stapleton with the facts, the older man tells him he paid the bribe to Kilpatrick's father. "We're all in this together, Jim," Stapleton says. Stapleton is saying we are all—Wasps, Blacks, Irish and other ethnic groups—in the American experience, with its perpetually confusing mix of idealism and brutal realism.

Likewise, *The Officers' Wives* also traces the spiritual paradoxes Fleming sees in American society. With that book, Jane Larkin Crain observed in the *New York Times Book Review*, "Thomas Fleming has written a satisfying novel that illuminates matters as diverse as the changing status of women, the ordeals and consolations of marriage, the permutations of religion—or any form of idealism—that arise in a rapidly changing culture and the bitter fallout from American involvement in Vietnam. He probes the heart of the American experience over the last 30 years with subtlety and intelligence. He mourns the loss of a sometimes arrogant but undeniably heady American innocence, speculates on the promise of what endures and closes on a note of cautious affirmation."

Fleming told *CA:* "Looking back over my career, I am struck by several turning points that triggered fundamental changes in my literary and intellectual life. One of the most important was my decision to accept the offer to write a history of West Point in 1964. This carried me beyond the confines of my first historical field, the American Revolution, and put me in touch with a prime example of America's secular idealism, which in turn freed me from my conflicts with the Catholic Church and gave me access to a wider American experience. The cadets are taught to revere 'Duty, Honor, Country.' But in the real world of the army, West Point graduates encounter careerism, political pressures, and the many other flaws of a large bureaucratic organization—with the ongoing realization that the bottom line for some of them may be death on a battlefield. It creates a fascinating series of conflicts which I explored in *The Officers' Wives* and *Time and Tide*. Another important moment was a speech at a meeting of the American Revolution Round Table by historian William B. Willcox, author of a biography of Sir Henry Clinton, *Portrait of a General*. In that talk, Willcox urged the importance of 'thinking historically,' of using the events of history to ask hard questions abut policies and personalities. (His book convincingly singles out Sir

Henry Clinton as the chief reason the British lost the Revolutionary War.)

"Still another turning point was a little-known book by Ronald Knox, *Enthusiasm*. It chronicled the heresies of the Roman Catholic church, showing how they began in a burst of emotional-intellectual fervor that swept away whole communities and even countries—and then slowly ebbed into routine religions and eventually expired. The book gave me an understanding of the workings of the popular mind—a phenomenon that has become more and more important in recent centuries, with the increased power of mass communications. It helped me understand how political passions (not much different from religious ones, in our secular age) can also run amok. I saw the power of political emotions first hand, of course, growing up in Jersey City, where the Hague Organization in which my father was a leader, regularly staged huge rallies and summoned people to the polls with battle cries that mingled religion, ethnicity and politics.

"The image that has come to dominate my mind, as I look back, is The Path. A committed writer seems to be led down a mysterious path, full of unexpected twists and turns, a sometimes bewildering mix of disappointments an successes. The image flowered almost magically for me in a remarkable dream that preceded my novel, *Loyalties*. I dreamt that I was in Berlin, watching a beautiful blonde woman writhing in bed. I knew she was having a bad dream. Then I was in the dream, watching a submarine with a Knight's head on the conning tower cruising through the Atlantic's depths. Suddenly depth charges explode around the submarine, it tilts to one side and begins to sink. The woman is transported into the submarine's interior, and swims past men thrashing in the rising water until she reaches the conning tower, where her husband, the U-boat's captain, resolutely faces death. Then she is outside the submarine again, watching it sink. Out of the depths swims a gigantic angel, with glaring eyes from a Byzantine painting. The angel takes the dying submarine in its arms. The woman awakes and says: 'The Path. The Angel is part of the Path.' I leaped out of bed and wrote the first chapter of the book, which opens with the dream, in an hour. I still retain the faith that an angel—or perhaps a band of them—has been guiding me down a similar path."

BIOGRAPHICAL/CRITICAL SOURCES:

PERIODICALS

America, November 9, 1963.
American History Review, June, 1980.

Atlantic, September 15, 1975; April, 1981.

Best Sellers, November 1, 1963; October 1, 1967; March 15, 1969; July 15, 1969; September 15, 1969; September 15, 1970; April 15, 1971; February 15, 1972; August 15, 1973; September, 1977; May, 1981.

Booklist, January 1, 1994, Sheilamae O'Hara, review of *Harry S. Truman, President,* p. 815; October 1, 1997, Gilbert Taylor, review of *Liberty!: The American Revolution,* p. 274; September 15, 1998, Margaret Flanagan, review of *The Wages of Fame,* p. 198; October 15, 1999, Gilbert Taylor, review of *Duel,* p. 414; November 15, 1999, Margaret Flanagan, review of *Hours of Gladness,* p. 600.

Boston Herald Traveler, March 21, 1971.

Chicago Daily News, February 27-28, 1971.

Christian Science Monitor, September 23, 1960; November 1, 1963; April 10, 1967.

Commonweal, April 1, 1966; June 26, 1970.

Critic, May-June, 1971; January-February, 1975.

Flint Journal Review, June 3, 2001, David Forsmark, "Review: Historian Rips FDR over Wartime Plans."

Journal of American History, September, 2000, Jeffrey L. Pasley, review of *Duel,* pp. 630-632.

Library Journal, May 1, 1994, p. 136; August, 1997, Barbara Conaty, review of *Remember the Morning,* p. 125; October 1, 1999, Grant A. Fredericksen, review of *Duel,* p. 108.

Los Angeles Times Book Review, February 14, 1971; July 26, 1987, p. 7.

National Review, February 28, 1975.

New York, November 10, 1969.

New York Herald Tribune Book Review, November 13, 1960; December 24, 1961.

New York Review of Books, July 15, 1976.

New York Times, July 19, 1969; March 4, 1971; October 8, 1975.

New York Times Book Review, September 25, 1960; October 1, 1961; November 10, 1963; February 27, 1966; November 15, 1967; June 28, 1968; February 18, 1968; January 12, 1969; May 4, 1969; September 28, 1969; March 4, 1971; December 16, 1973; August 4, 1974; February 22, 1976; May 2, 1976; July 3, 1977; April 12, 1981; June 7, 1992, p. 18; September 13, 1987, pp. 7-8; February 13, 2000, Jean Edward Smith, "The Talented Mr. Burr."

Publishers Weekly, July 4, 1977; March 16, 1992, review of *Over There,* p. 66; April 18, 1994, review of *Loyalties,* p. 44; August 4, 1997, review of *Remember the Morning,* p. 65; October 13, 1997, review of *Liberty!,* p. 63; August 3, 1998, review of

The Wages of Fame, p. 74; September 20, 1999, review of *Duel,* p. 62.

Saturday Review, October 1, 1960; September 30, 1961; November 16, 1963; September 6, 1975.

Springfield (IL) *Republican,* September 25, 1960; September 10, 1961.

Tablet Magazine, September 17, 1970.

Time, July 25, 1969; May 31, 1971.

Tribune Books (Chicago), September 18, 1960; September 24, 1961; August 9, 1987, p. 6.

Virginia Quarterly Review, spring, 1976.

Washington Post Book World, May 26, 1968; March 2, 1969; March 29, 1981; March 10, 1985, p. 1; March 19, 1985, p. 35; July 1, 2001, Richard Pearson, review of *The New Dealers' War,* p. T10.

West Coast Review of Books, January, 1979; March, 1987, p. 36.

OTHER

Salon.com, http://www.salon.com/books/ (September 29, 1999), Katherine Whittemore, review of *Duel.*

*   *   *

FOLLETT, Ken(neth Martin) 1949-
(Martin Martinson, Symon Myles, Bernard L. Ross, Myles Simon, Zachary Stone)

PERSONAL: Born June 5, 1949, in Cardiff, Wales; son of Martin D. (a tax inspector) and Lavinia C. (Evans) Follett; married Mary Emma Ruth Elson, January 5, 1968 (divorced September 20, 1985); married Barbara Broer, November 8, 1985; children (first marriage): Emanuele, Marie-Claire. *Education:* University College, London, B A., 1970. *Religion:* Atheist. *Avocational interests:* Music.

ADDRESSES: Home—P.O. Box 4, Knebworth, Hertfordshire SG3 6UT, England. *Agent*—Writers House, Inc., 21 West 26th St., New York, NY 10010.

CAREER: Trainee journalist and rock music columnist at *South Wales Echo,* 1970-73; *Evening News,* London, England, reporter, 1973-74; Everest Books Ltd., London, England, editorial director, 1974-76, deputy managing director, 1976-77; full-time writer, 1977—.

AWARDS, HONORS: Edgar Award, Mystery Writers of America, 1978, for *Eye of the Needle.*

Ken Follett

WRITINGS:

NOVELS

The Shakeout, Harwood-Smart, 1975.

The Bear Raid, Harwood-Smart, 1976.

The Secret of Kellerman's Studio (juvenile), Abelard, 1976, published with illustrations by Stephen Marchesi as *Mystery Hideout,* Morrow (New York, NY), 1990.

Eye of the Needle (Literary Guild selection), Arbor House (New York, NY), 1978, published in England as *Storm Island,* Macdonald & Jane's, 1978.

Triple, Arbor House (New York, NY), 1979.

The Key to Rebecca, Morrow (New York, NY), 1980.

The Man from St. Petersburg, Morrow (New York, NY), 1982.

Lie down with Lions, Hamilton (London, England), 1985, Morrow (New York, NY), 1986.

The Pillars of the Earth (also see below), Morrow (New York, NY), 1989.

Night over Water, Morrow (New York, NY), 1991.

A Dangerous Fortune, Delacorte (New York, NY), 1993.

Pillars of the Almighty (selections of text from *The Pillars of the Earth*), Morrow (New York, NY), 1994.

A Place Called Freedom, Crown (New York, NY), 1995.

The Third Twin, Crown (New York, NY), 1996.

The Hammer of Eden: A Novel, Crown (New York, NY), 1998.

Code to Zero, Dutton (New York, NY), 2000.

UNDER PSEUDONYM SYMON MYLES

The Big Needle, Everest Books (London, England), 1974, published as *The Big Apple,* Kensington (San Diego, CA), 1975, published under name Ken Follett, Zebra, 1986.

The Big Black, Everest Books (London, England), 1974.

The Big Hit, Everest Books (London, England), 1975.

OTHER

(Under pseudonym Martin Martinsen) *The Power Twins and the Worm Puzzle: A Science Fantasy for Young People,* Abelard, 1976, published under name Ken Follett as *Power Twins,* Scholastic, 1991.

(Under pseudonym Bernard L. Ross) *Amok: King of Legend,* Futura (London, England), 1976.

(Under pseudonym Zachary Stone) *The Modigliani Scandal,* Collins (London, England), 1976, published under name Ken Follett, Morrow (New York, NY), 1985.

(Under pseudonym Zachary Stone) *Paper Money,* Collins, 1977, published under name Ken Follett, Morrow (New York, NY), 1987.

(Under pseudonym Bernard L. Ross) *Capricorn One,* Futura (London, England), 1978.

(With Rene Louis Maurice) *The Heist of the Century* (nonfiction), Fontana Books (London, England), 1978, published as *The Gentlemen of 16 July,* Arbor House, 1980, revised edition published as *Under the Streets of Nice: The Bank Heist of the Century,* National Press Books, 1986.

On Wings of Eagles (nonfiction), Morrow (New York, NY), 1983.

Also author of film scripts *Fringe Banking,* for British Broadcasting Corp., 1978, *A Football Star,* with John Sealey, 1979, and *Lie down with Lions,* for Scott Reeve Enterprises, 1988. Contributor to *New Statesman* and *Writer.*

ADAPTATIONS: Eye of the Needle was adapted for the screen by Stanley Mann. The 1981 United Artists film was directed by Richard Marquand and starred Donald Sutherland and Kate Nelligan. *The Key to Rebecca* was filmed as an Operation Prime Time television miniseries in April, 1985; *On Wings of Eagles* was filmed by Edgar Schenick Productions and broadcast as a television miniseries in 1985. *The Third Twin* was adapted as a 1997 television feature starring Kelly McGillis and Jason Gedrick. *Under the Streets of Nice* was adapted as a sound recording, Dove Audio (Beverly Hills, CA), 1991.

SIDELIGHTS: Ken Follett has blended historical events and action-adventure fiction in a series of best-selling novels, including *Eye of the Needle, Triple, Lie down with Lions,* and *The Pillars of the Earth.* Follett's work has proven immensely successful in the United States, making the native of Wales one of the world's youngest millionaire authors. Follett penned his first bestseller before he turned thirty, and each of his subsequent novels has made a debut with a massive first printing and vast publicity. *Washington Post* correspondent Paul Hendrickson claimed that Follett has earned a reputation as an "international thriller writer with a genius for threading the eye of the literary needle."

"I was a great liver in fantasy worlds from an early age," Follett told the *Washington Post.* The son of an internal revenue clerk, Follett grew up in Cardiff, Wales, and attended the University of London. After graduating with a degree in philosophy in 1970, he worked as a newspaper reporter, first in Cardiff and then in London. He began writing fiction on the side when he needed extra money for car repairs. "It was a hobby for me," he told the *Chicago Tribune.* "You know, some men go home and grow vegetables. I used to go home and write novels. A lucrative hobby. I sold them for far more than you could sell vegetables for."

Follett's early works were published under various pseudonyms. Most of these novels are murder mysteries or crime fiction, based loosely on cases he covered as a reporter for the London *Evening News.* The author admitted in the *Los Angeles Times* that he learned how to write good books "by writing mediocre ones and wondering what was wrong with them." In order to further his knowledge of the book business, Follett joined the staff of Everest Books in 1974. Remembering his decision to move to the publishing house, Follett told the *Chicago Tribune:* "A good deal of it was curiosity to know what made books sell. Some books sell and others don't. All the books I had written up to that point fell into the category of those that did not."

Follett finally got the formula right with his eleventh book, *Eye of the Needle.* He told readers in a *Barnesandnoble.com* interview posted on the *Cicero Chr. Erichsen* Web site that he concentrated on doing three things differently with this book: planning it with care, researching his subject thoroughly, and slowing the book's pace. The result was a popular sensation that catapulted to the top of best seller lists across the globe. The World War II thriller about a ruthless Nazi spy and a crippled pilot's wife received critical raves as well. In the *Washington Post Book World,* reviewer Roderick MacLeish called *Eye of the Needle* "quite simply the best spy novel to come out of England in years," and *Newsweek* correspondent Peter Prescott described the work as "rubbish of the very best sort . . . a triumph of invention over convention." Still in print more than twenty years after its initial publication, *Eye of the Needle,* which won the Edgar Allan Poe Award from the Mystery Writers of America, has since sold more than ten million copies worldwide and been translated into more than twenty-five languages.

With *Eye of the Needle,* Follett established himself as a new sort of thriller writer—one who found a compromise between the serious and the popular. Follett's works have been cited for their special sensitivity to female characters as well as for an overall psychological complexity not often found in adventure stories. As Andrew F. Macdonald and Gina Macdonald noted in the *Dictionary of Literary Biography,* a positive feature of Follett's novels "is his humanizing of his villains. All are well rounded and complete, with credible motives and understandable passions—if anything, they are sometimes so sympathetic that they jeopardize the reader's relationship with the hero." In another *Dictionary of Literary Biography* entry, Michael Adams contended that the author's heroines "are realistically portrayed women who have led fairly ordinary lives but who are capable of heroics when needed." By creating such sympathetic heroines, Follett has been able to lure female readers to novels that traditionally appeal primarily to men.

Follett's forte—in fiction and nonfiction—is the variation upon history. Every human relationship is somehow blighted or molded by the complexities of world politics, and all emotional and sexual entanglements are played out against a backdrop of historical events. Andrew and Gina Macdonald wrote: "Each of [Follett's] best works grows out of news stories and historical events. Cinematic in conception, they follow a hunter-hunted pattern that leads to exciting chase scenes and games of wit and brinkmanship." Several of Follett's books confront the complex issues of Middle Eastern politics, and his novel *Lie down with Lions* offers an ambiguous portrait of the factional strife in Afghanistan. *Time* contributor Michael Demarest claimed that the author's strength remains "an acute sense of geographical place, and the age-old knowledge that character is action. . . . He brilliantly reproduces a distant terrain, complete with sounds and smells and tribal rites."

Adams related some of the reasons for Follett's extraordinary success as a novelist, explaining that in his "exciting, intelligent, generally well-written . . . thrillers, not only are the major characters well developed, but the minor characters are given attention as well. The reader is always able to understand all the characters' political, social, economic, and sexual motives. Follett makes certain that even his villains have sympathetic sides. . . . He also reveals a thorough understanding not only of the history and techniques of espionage but of the intertwining complexities of twentieth-century world politics. Equally important is the skill of his plotting. While spy fiction is frequently complex and bewildering to the reader, Follett's work is consistently clear and easy to follow."

In 1989 Follett made a break with thriller fiction. Since then he has written three massive historical novels, *The Pillars of the Earth, A Dangerous Fortune,* and *A Place Called Freedom. The Pillars of the Earth,* set in twelfth-century England, recounts the four-decades-long construction of a cathedral and the efforts of Prior Philip and his master mason, Tom Builder, to complete the building and keep it from falling into the hands of a rival bishop. Critical reaction to that novel was mixed, perhaps because it was such an unexpected departure for Follett. Gary Jennings in the *Washington Post Book World,* for example, found that "the legions of fanciers of Ken Follett's spy novels will likely be dismayed by his having turned now to historical fiction." Margaret Flanagan in *Booklist* called *The Pillars of the Earth* "a towering triumph of romance, rivalry, and spectacle from a major talent." Margaret Cannon in the Toronto *Globe and Mail,* while acknowledging the book's tendency toward overwriting, admitted that "the period is so good and the cathedrals so marvelous that one keeps reading anyway." Despite some skepticism from critics, *The Pillars of the Earth* became Follett's most popular book.

The historical novel genre has proved compatible with Follett's skills. His subsequent works, which include *A Dangerous Fortune* and *A Place Called Freedom,* weave complicated stories of intrigue in England and the Americas. In *A Dangerous Fortune,* an English

schoolboy's drowning sets off a chain of events that leads to national crisis, as rival bankers seek to undermine each others' positions. "*A Dangerous Fortune* leaves us feeling as though we've visited an age very different from our own, and understand it far better than we did," wrote a *Rapport* correspondent. "Follett's . . . tour through privileged Victorian society . . . won't be easily forgotten." In the *Los Angeles Times Book Review,* Thomas Hines cited *A Dangerous Fortune* for its "eye for the telling historical detail and a fair sense that people from the past weren't like us—and that's precisely what makes them so interesting." *A Place Called Freedom* tells the story of Malachi McAsh, a Scottish miner who rebels against a lifetime of servitude to the brutal local laird. McAsh's quest for freedom leads him to trouble in London and indentured servitude in America, at a time when the very ideals of human liberty are being debated there. A *Publishers Weekly* reviewer noted that in the novel, Follett "adroitly escalates the suspense by mixing intrigue and danger, tinged with ironic complications." The critic concluded that *A Place Called Freedom* is redeemed "by Follett's vigorous narrative drive and keen eye for character."

Between these various historical sagas, Follett completed yet another thriller, *Night over Water.* Set in the last dark days of 1939, the novel recounts the last transatlantic voyage of the opulent Pan American Clipper, its passengers all bent upon various deadly intrigues. According to *Spectator* reviewer Christopher Hawtree, *Night over Water* "marks a return to World War II and top form" for Follett. Hawtree added that the novel provides "a smoothly-controlled bumpy landing. There is no reverse-thrust to this narrative which sedulously leads one into the dark and all that is revealed therein."

Follett chose more up-to-the-minute topics for his next two thrillers. *The Third Twin* spins a dark plot of violence and intrigue around genetic research and human cloning. Deemed "great plane reading" by a reviewer in *Entertainment Weekly,* the book was adapted as a TV miniseries. Also pertinent to themes in late-twentieth-century American culture is *The Hammer of Eden,* in which a charismatic cult leader in California threatens violence when the state plans to build a new power plant on the site of his secret commune. The leader, named Priest, steals a seismic vibrator from a local oil-drilling operation and vows to flatten the entire state with a super earthquake if his demands are not met. "Taut plotting, tense action, skillful writing, and myriad unexpected twists make this one utterly unputdownable," wrote Emily Melton in *Booklist. Library Journal* reviewer V. Louise Saylor, however, cited the novel's reliance on coincidence and its sympathetic portrayal of

Priest as flaws that keep *The Hammer of Eden* below the level of Follett's best work.

Code to Zero marked a return to classic espionage for Follett. Set in 1958, the novel concerns the U.S. Army's attempt to launch the *Explorer 1,* which would have been the country's first rocket in space, during the height of the Cold War. Though some critics objected to Follett's use of amnesia as a major plot device in the novel, others hailed *Code to Zero* as a welcome return to form. A reviewer in *Publishers Weekly* considered it an "absorbing" and "tightly plotted" tale, and *Booklist* contributor Bill Ott praised it as "a classic page-turner on a classic theme." However, Tom LeClair in *Book* found the novel filled with improbabilities and dull writing. Though he also noted Follett's lack of stylistic flair, *New York Times Book Review* contributor John W. Dean suggested that "For most readers, *Code to Zero* will be gripping."

Unlike many of his contemporaries, Follett positively relishes the label "popular writer." He once commented in *Dictionary of Literary Biography:* "I'm not under the illusion that the world is waiting for my thoughts to appear in print. People want to be told a story, and that's what I'm up to. I think of myself as a craftsman more than an artist." Although he likes to read such noted English writers as Thomas Hardy, Jane Austen, and George Eliot, Follett remains satisfied with his own aims and accomplishments. "What I enjoy," he told the *Chicago Tribune,* "is writing a book and then having *millions* of people read it and love it. I wouldn't want to write something that ten people loved; so I'm constrained by what I think are the preferences of my readers. If I'm careful, I'll take them along with me."

BIOGRAPHICAL/CRITICAL SOURCES:

BOOKS

Authors and Artists for Young Adults, Gale (Detroit, MI), 1999.
Contemporary Popular Writers, St. James Press (Detroit, MI), 1997.
Dictionary of Literary Biography, Volume 87: *British Mystery Writers since 1940,* Gale (Detroit, MI), 1989.

PERIODICALS

Book, January, 2001, Tom LeClair, review of *Code to Zero,* p. 78.
Booklist, June 15, 1989; September 1, 1998, Emily Melton, review of *The Hammer of Eden,* p. 5; Oc-

tober 15, 2000, Bill Ott, review of *Code to Zero,* p. 390.
Chicago Tribune, October 14, 1983; October 25, 1987; September 10, 1989.
Chicago Tribune Book World, October 5, 1980.
Detroit Free Press, September 10, 1989.
Entertainment Weekly, October 24, 1997, review of *The Third Twin,* p. 59.
Globe and Mail (Toronto), September 2, 1989.
Guardian, October 29, 2000, "The Great Entertainer" (interview).
Library Journal, July, 1989; January, 1997, Gordon Cheatham, review of audio recording of *The Third Twin,* p. 173; October 1, 1998, V. Louise Saylor, review of *The Hammer of Eden,* p. 132; February 1, 1999, Mark Pumphrey, review of *The Hammer of Eden,* p. 136; August 2000, p. 72; November 1, 2000, Robert Conroy, review of *Code to Zero,* p. 133.
London Review of Books, August 19, 1982, p. 18.
Los Angeles Times, October 1, 1980; June 3, 1990.
Los Angeles Times Book Review, October 7, 1979; September 28, 1980; May 30, 1982; September 11, 1983; February 16, 1986; October 4, 1987, p. 6; December 12, 1993, p. 8.
Nation, April 26, 1980, pp. 504-505.
New Statesman, April 10, 1987.
Newsweek, August 7, 1978; September 29, 1980.
New York, November 10, 1997, John Leonard, review of television miniseries *The Third Twin,* p. 68.
New Yorker, August 21, 1978; August 16, 1982.
New York Times, May 12, 1978; October 3, 1979.
New York Times Book Review, July 16, 1978; September 21, 1980; May 9, 1982; October 23, 1983, pp. 20, 22; January 26, 1986; September 10, 1989; September 29, 1991, p. 22; January 9, 1994, p. 19; January 14, 2001, John W. Dean, review of *Code to Zero.*
People, September 25, 1978.
People Weekly, November 10, 1997, Terry Kelleher, review of television miniseries *The Third Twin,* p. 17.
Publishers Weekly, January 17, 1986; June 30, 1989; July 21, 1989; April 13, 1990, p. 66; July 19, 1991, pp. 44-45; June 5, 1995, pp. 48-49.
Rapport, January, 1994, p. 21; November 9, 1998, J. D. Reed, review of *The Hammer of Eden,* p. 45.
Saturday Review, August, 1978.
Spectator, November 16, 1991, p. 46.
Time, October 30, 1978; November 5, 1979; September 29, 1980; May 3, 1982.
Times Literary Supplement, December 26, 1980; June 4, 1982.
Tribune Books (Chicago), September 10, 1989, p. 7; August 30, 1992, p. 8.

Washington Post, October 11, 1979; September 15, 1980; September 7, 1983; September 21, 1983; June 1, 1985.

Washington Post Book World, April 25, 1982; February 2, 1986, p. 9; August 20, 1989; November 21, 1993, p. 4.

Writer, June, 1979.

OTHER

The Ken Follett Official Web site, http://www.kenfollett.com/ (November 15, 2000).

Cicero Chr. Erichsen, http://www.cicero.dk/forfattere/interviews/ (November 2, 2000), interview with Ken Follett.

*   *   *

FRANKLIN, Caroline 1949-

PERSONAL: Born October 20, 1949, in Halifax, England; daughter of Ronald Victor (a schoolmaster) and Marjorie (a nurse; maiden name, Davies) Evans; married Michael Franklin; children: Geraint, Ieuan. *Ethnicity:* "Welsh." *Education:* Cardiff Institute of Education, Certificate of Education, 1972; University of London, B.A. (with honors), 1983; University of Wales, College of Cardiff, M.A., 1986, Ph.D., 1989. *Politics:* "Socialist/feminist." *Religion:* Church in Wales. *Avocational interests:* Walking, swimming, family activities.

ADDRESSES: Home—6 Hen Parc Ave., Upper Killay, Swansea SA2 7HA, England. *Office*—Department of English, University of Wales, Swansea, Singleton Park, Swansea SA2 8PP, Wales. *E-mail*—c.franklin@ swansea.ac.uk.

CAREER: Schoolteacher in Yorkshire and Worcestershire, England, and in Wales, 1972-84; Trinity College, Carmarthen, Wales, senior lecturer, 1989-94; University of Wales, Swansea, senior lecturer in English, 1995—.

MEMBER: British Association for Romantic Studies, Association of University Teachers, Campaign for Nuclear Disarmament, Greenpeace.

AWARDS, HONORS: Elma Dangerfield Prize, International Byron Society, 1993, and Rose Marie Crawshay Prize, British Academy, 1995, both for *Byron's Heroines.*

WRITINGS:

Byron's Heroines, Oxford University Press (New York, NY), 1992.

(Editor, with P. Garside) *British Women Novelists, 1750-1850,* twelve volumes, Routledge/Thoemmes (London, England), 1992.

(Editor, with Garside) *The Romantics: Women Novelists,* twelve volumes, Routledge/Thoemmes (London, England), 1995.

(Editor) *The Romantics: Women Poets, 1770-1830,* twelve volumes, Routledge/Thoemmes (London, England), 1996.

(Editor) *The Wellesley Series IV: Nineteenth-Century Sources in the Humanities and Social Sciences; British Romantic Poets,* six volumes, Routledge/ Thoemmes (London, England), 1998.

Byron: A Literary Life, Macmillan (London, England), 2000.

Work represented in anthologies, including *Don Juan: Theory in Practice,* edited by Nigel Wood, Open University Press, 1993; and *Romanticism and Colonialism: Writing and Empire, 1770-1830,* edited by Peter Kitson and Tim Fulford, Cambridge University Press (New York, NY), 1998.

SIDELIGHTS: Caroline Franklin once told *CA:* "In *Byron's Heroines* I have attempted to combine a historicist and a feminist approach to Byron's dramatic and narrative poetry. I relate Byron's depictions of women to contemporary ideologies of sexual difference and attempt to assess the political significance of the early nineteenth-century dialectic on the nature of woman. I am currently researching the women writers of the romantic period, now—thanks to modern feminism— being rediscovered."

*   *   *

FREY, Stephen W. 1960-

PERSONAL: Born 1960; married; children: Christina, Ashley. *Education:* University of Virginia, M.B.A., 1987.

ADDRESSES: Home—22 Huntington Dr., Princeton Junction, NJ. *Office*—Westdeutsche Landesbank, 1211 Avenue of the Americas, 24th Floor, New York, NY 10036-8701.

CAREER: Westdeutsche Landesbank, New York, NY, vice president of corporate finance. Worked previously as a corporate lending officer, Irving Trust Company, in the mergers and acquisitions department, J. P. Morgan & Company, and in the corporate group of the French bank, Societe Generale. Co-founder and co-owner of a soft drink distribution company, 1992.

WRITINGS:

The Takeover, Dutton (New York, NY), 1995.
The Vulture Fund, Dutton (New York, NY), 1996.
The Inner Sanctum, Dutton (New York, NY), 1997.
The Legacy, Dutton (New York, NY), 1998.
The Insider, Ballantine Books (New York, NY), 1999.
Trust Fund, Ballantine Books (New York, NY), 2001.

ADAPTATIONS: The film rights for both *The Takeover* and *The Vulture Fund* have been sold to Paramount. *The Legacy* was adapted as an audio book, Penguin, 1998.

SIDELIGHTS: After reading the suspense novels of John Grisham, Tom Clancy, and Scott Turow, Wall Street banker Stephen W. Frey decided he could follow the same course. The result of Frey's first foray into the world of fiction was *The Takeover.* In this Wall Street thriller, the Sevens (a secret society of powerful Harvard Business School alumni) set in motion an elaborate scheme to oust the ultra-liberal U.S. president currently in office because his policies do not support the wealthy. In accomplishing their objective the Sevens put young mergers-and-acquisitions specialist Andrew Falcon in a position to manage the takeover of a major bank. Unbeknownst to Falcon, the Sevens rig the takeover so that the bank will collapse just weeks before the presidential election. By the time Falcon realizes what is going on, it may be too late to save either the bank or himself.

Describing *The Takeover* in a *USA Today* review, John H. Healy wrote that "John Grisham meets Robert Ludlum on Wall Street in this fast-paced novel." A *Publishers Weekly* contributor stated: "Frey's plotting requires leaps of faith, and his characters are cartoonish," yet added that the novel does have all the elements a fan of the thriller genre would enjoy. "Looking to vicariously live the life of a financier on Wall Street?," Healy asked. "This is the roller coaster that will take you there."

A reviewer in *Publishers Weekly* found Frey's fourth novel, *The Legacy,* to be "a strange, lumpy, often ludicrous but finally addictive story that mixes historic tragedy with the personal problems of a would-be Master of the Universe." The protagonist, twenty-nine-year-old Cole Egan, is a Wall Street securities trader who is skirting financial ruin because of shady trading practices and illegal gambling that have left him heavily in debt to the Mafia. Cole's situation seems hopeless when he suddenly inherits, from a father he never knew, a thirty-five-year-old film that shows the assassination of John F. Kennedy from the vantage of the infamous grassy knoll, where many have claimed a second shooter fired at the president. The monetary value of the film seems to promise a solution to Cole's financial woes. The film arouses Cole's curiosity about his father, supposedly a former secret operative. And at the same time, a new cast of heavies, all after the film, suddenly enters the action. "Frey, a slick thriller writer," commented Gilbert Taylor in *Booklist,* "who knows that a contemplative protagonist sells half as well as one on the run, will not allow Egan . . . to ponder his options; he is too frantic dodging bombs, bullets, and knives to think about anything except who's killing people to get the film." Steven Nemmers in *Mystery Reader* concluded: "This is an acceptable but undistinguished book. Stylistically, it's nicely put together and pleasant to read." Catherine Swenson, writing in *Library Journal,* lodged a more positive response, praising the novel's "distinctive characterizations" and "effective level of suspense."

Frey followed *The Legacy* with *The Insider,* the tale of Jay West, a man eager to wheel and deal with the power brokers of Wall Street. When Oliver Mason, head of a major financial firm, offers West a job, the younger man jumps at the chance. However, after a corporate jet explodes and bodies start piling up, West soon begins to understand that both his new position and his new employer are something other than they seemed at first. David Rouse in *Booklist* praised the novel's "crisp style" and observed: "Even though his plot employs a complicated financial scheme, Frey avoids losing his readers by using narration and dialogue that clearly explain the details." Harriet Klausner, a contributor in *Under the Covers,* when reviewing *The Insider,* stated: "The trapping of Jay is brilliantly executed and the financial maneuverings appear intelligent, plausible . . . fully understandable." According to Klausner: "Mr. Frey scores with his best novel to date."

Frey's sixth novel, *Trust Fund,* creates a Kennedyesque political family and involves it in political and financial skullduggery in an attempt to seize the resources of the Internet and control the American military-industrial complex. Patriarch of the family, Jimmy Lee Hancock, donates two million dollars to the conspirators, a secret cadre of congressmen and intelligence agents, so they will support his son Paul for their party's nomination for president. Meanwhile, Paul's brother Bo is responsible for the success of the family's investment firm, Warfield Capital, despite the fact that a third brother, Ted, is ostensibly in charge of the firm and takes the kudos. Bo's reward is to be exiled to Montana, supposedly because of his drinking, but actually to keep him from learning about the firm's increasingly shady dealings. Bo must return to New York to confront both his family's corruption and to battle those who have involved Warfield Capital in their schemes. A reviewer in *Publishers Weekly* stated that "Frey cleverly incorporates the workings of Wall Street, global economics and the wired world into his melodramatic plot. The reader always learns something new about finance from Frey's suspenseful outings."

Despite sometimes mixed critical response, Frey's books have found a ready audience and have consistently appeared on bestseller lists. As *Princeton Packet* staff writer Tony Cantu stated: "Mr. Frey has carved a unique niche in the thriller novel genre. His books deal with the arcane world of business, but their suspenseful settings give the obscure corporate world an accessibility to the layman that has caught on with readers."

BIOGRAPHICAL/CRITICAL SOURCES:

PERIODICALS

Booklist, May 15, 1998, Gilbert Taylor, review of *The Legacy,* p. 1564; August, 1999, David Rouse, review of *The Insider,* p. 1986.
Chicago Tribune, August 20, 1995, section 14, p. 4.
Kirkus Reviews, January 2, 2001, review of *Trust Fund,* p. 1450.
Library Journal, June 15, 1995, p. 93; October 15, 1998, Catherine Swenson, review of *The Legacy,* p. 113.
New York Times Book Review, August 13, 1995, pp. 3, 24.
Publishers Weekly, January 23, 1995, p. 44; June 5, 1995, p. 49; May 18, 1998, review of *The Legacy,* p. 67; November 13, 2000, review of *Trust Fund,* p. 83.
USA Today, August 30, 1995, p. 4B.
Wall Street Journal, September 8, 1995, p. A7.

OTHER

Dateline: News, http://www.pacpub.com/dline/news/ (July 7, 1997), Tony Cantu, "Novel Approach Paying Dividends."
The Mystery Reader Reviews, http://www.themystery reader.com/ (January 4, 2001), Steve Nemmers, review of *The Legacy.*

Under the Covers, http://www.silcom.com/ (January 4, 2001), Harriet Klausner, review of *The Insider.**

*   *   *

FRIEDLANDER, Michael W(ulf) 1928-

PERSONAL: Born November 15, 1928, in Cape Town, South Africa; married Jessica Kramer, July 4, 1958; children: Rachel Friedlander Tickner, David. *Education:* University of Cape Town, B.Sc., 1948, M.Sc. (with first class honors), 1950; University of Bristol, Ph.D., 1955.

ADDRESSES: Office—Department of Physics, Washington University, One Brookings Dr., St. Louis, MO 63130.

CAREER: University of Cape Town, Cape Town, South Africa, junior lecturer in physics, 1951 and 1952; University of Bristol, Bristol, England, research associate in physics, 1954-56; Washington University, St. Louis, MO, assistant professor, 1956-61, associate professor, 1961-67, professor of physics, 1967—. Imperial College of Science and Technology, London, England, visiting professor, 1962-63 and 1971.

MEMBER: American Association of University Professors (member of national council, 1975-78 and 1986-89; vice president, 1978-80), American Association for the Advancement of Science, American Physical Society, American Astronomical Society, History of Science Society.

AWARDS, HONORS: Guggenheim fellow, 1962-63.

WRITINGS:

The Conduct of Science, Prentice-Hall (Englewood Cliffs, NJ), 1972.
Astronomy: From Stonehenge to Quasars, Prentice-Hall (Englewood Cliffs, NJ), 1985.
Cosmic Rays, Harvard University Press (Cambridge, MA), 1986.
At the Fringes of Science, Westview (Boulder, CO), 1995, revised edition, 1998.
A Thin Cosmic Rain: Particles from Outer Space, Harvard University Press (Cambridge, MA), 2000.

Contributor to *Encyclopaedia Britannica* and professional journals.

SIDELIGHTS: Michael W. Friedlander has written *At the Fringes of Science,* a look at unconventional beliefs in the scientific world, and *A Thin Cosmic Rain: Particles from Outer Space,* a popular account of cosmic rays and their effects on human life.

At the Fringes of Science traces the history of unconventional science, telling of the hoaxers and the misguided who have proposed and promoted various ideas over the years. Friedlander documents such unaccepted ideas as those of Immanuel Velikovsky, whose astronomical theories included the proposal that the moon had been formed by breaking off from the earth in distant historical times. He goes on to discuss scientific ideas that once were unproven and untested, such as Einstein's Theory of Relativity, but which became accepted by scientists as time went on. He then explores still-unproven yet possibly valid ideas such as psychic phenomena. Along the way, Friedlander looks at Nazi science, the claims of the Russian scientist Lysenko—whose wild scientific theories were believed to be in keeping with good communist beliefs—and cases of outright fraud perpetrated by scientists seeking fame and fortune. Reviewing the title for the *Skeptical Inquirer,* Barry Markovsky found it to be "an excellent entree into discussions about what science is and what it is not." He concluded: "It is a superb book."

In *A Thin Cosmic Rain* Friedlander presents an overview of scientific investigation into cosmic rays, the constant low-level radiation that comes from outer space and permeates the earth. Cosmic rays make possible the carbon dating system used in archeology. But they may also have damaging effects on human health. In addition to explaining the varying natures and compositions of cosmic rays, Friedlander outlines the origins of some of the most popular theories. A *Publishers Weekly* critic felt that *A Thin Cosmic Rain* "should establish itself as a standard work in the field of cosmic radiation." Reviewing the book for *Booklist,* Gilbert Taylor concluded that it was "a detailed, informative survey of the topic."

BIOGRAPHICAL/CRITICAL SOURCES:

PERIODICALS

Booklist, November 1, 2000, Gilbert Taylor, review of *A Thin Cosmic Rain: Particles from Outer Space,* p. 501.

Book News, August 1, 1995, review of *At the Fringes of Science.*

Physics Today, January, 1996, Harold W. Lewis, review of *At the Fringes of Science,* p. 67.

Publishers Weekly, October 30, 2000, review of *A Thin Cosmic Rain,* p. 56.

Skeptical Inquirer, January-February, 1996, Barry Markovsky, review of *At the Fringes of Science,* p. 49.

Washingtonian, August, 1999, Richard Victory, review of *At the Fringes of Science,* p. 29.

*　　*　　*

FULLBROOK, Kate 1950-

PERSONAL: Born September 7, 1950, in WI; married Edward Fullbrook (a freelance writer), 1972. *Education:* University of Wisconsin, B.A., 1972; Queen Mary College, University of London, M.A., 1976; Newnham College, University of Cambridge, Ph.D., 1981.

ADDRESSES: Office—University of the West of England, St. Matthias Campus, Oldbury Court Road, Fishponds, Bristol BS16 2JP England. *E-mail*—kate.fullbrook@uwe.cc.uk.

CAREER: College of St. Mark and St. John, Plymouth, England, lecturer in English, 1979-83, senior lecturer, 1983-85; Bristol Polytechnic (became University of the West of England), Bristol, England, senior lecturer, 1985-88, principal lecturer in English and head of literary studies department, 1988-96, professor of literary studies and associate dean, Faculty of Humanities, 1996—; writer.

AWARDS, HONORS: Nomination for James Tait Black Memorial Prize for biography, 1993, for *Simone de Beauvoir and Jean-Paul Sartre: The Remaking of a Twentieth-Century Legend.*

WRITINGS:

Katherine Mansfield, Indiana University Press (De Kalb, IN), 1986.

Free Women: Ethics and Aesthetics in Twentieth-Century Women's Fiction, Temple University Press, 1990.

(With husband, Edward Fullbrook) *Simone de Beauvoir and Jean-Paul Sartre: The Remaking of a Twentieth-Century Legend,* Harvester Wheatsheaf (London, England), 1993, Basic Books (New York, NY), 1994.

(With husband, Edward Fullbrook) *Simone de Beauvoir: A Critical Introduction,* Blackwell (London, England), 1998.

(Editor with Judy Simons, and contributor) *Writing: A Woman's Business,* Manchester University Press (Manchester, England), 1998.

Contributor to anthologies, including *Dictionary of Literary Biography: Volume 14: British Novelists since 1960,* edited by Jay L. Halio, Gale, 1983; *Women Reading Women's Writing,* edited by Sue Roe, Harvester Wheatsheaf, 1987; *Dictionary of British Women Writers,* edited by Janet Todd, Routledge, 1989; *The Fine Instrument: Essays on Katherine Mansfield,* edited by Michel Dupuis and Paulette Michel-Michot, Dangarook, 1989; *Rereading the Canon: Feminist Interpretations of Simone de Beauvoir,* edited by Margaret Simons, Pennsylvania University Press, 1995; *Writing and America,* edited by David Timms and Neil Sammells, Longman, 1996; *Lectures d'une Oeuvre,* edited by Stéphanie Amar-Flood and Saud Thornton, Editions du Temps, 1997; *A Companion to Continental Philosophy,* edited by Simon Critchley, Blackwell, 1998; *British Women Writing Fiction,* edited by Abby Werlock, University of Alabama Press, 2000; and *Man Wird Nichtols Frau Geboren,* edited by Alice Schwarzer, Kieponheuer & Witsch, 2000. Also contributor to periodicals, including *British Book News, Feminist Review, Journal of American Studies, Over Here, Pace, Sunday Tribune, Times Higher Education Supplement, Times Literary Supplement, Symbiosis: A Journal of Anglo-American Literary Relations,* and *Hypatia.*

WORK IN PROGRESS: "With Edward Fullbrook, Christine Delphy, and Sylvie Chaperon, an international collection on Simone de Beauvoir, for the French publisher Syllepse (editorial)."

SIDELIGHTS: Kate Fullbrook, who teaches English at the University of the West of England, is an authority on twentieth-century women writers. Among her publications is *Simone de Beauvoir and Jean-Paul Sartre: The Remaking of a Twentieth-Century Legend,* a critical biography of the relationship and collaboration of the two writers that contends that Beauvoir was the primary force behind the couple's partnership. Written with her husband, Edward Fullbrook, the book asserts that Sartre derived many of the main tenets of his massive existential treatise *Being and Nothingness* from Beauvoir's novel *She Came to Stay.* In addition, the volume speculates on possible reasons that Beauvoir allowed the alleged appropriation of her work and thought by Sartre.

New York Times reviewer Michiko Kakutani, questioning the Fullbrooks's thesis on the originality of Sartre's *Being and Nothingness,* declared that the couple "completely ignore the many autobiographical echoes in [Sartre's] text." Kakutani also contended that "the Fullbrooks never advance a convincing argument for what they see as Beauvoir's calculated decision to conceal

her pivotal role in Sartre's work." Anthony Gottlieb, while conceding in the *New York Times Book Review* that *Simone de Beauvoir and Jean-Paul Sartre* is "intriguing," declared that it "falls well short of its over-ambitious goal." Gottlieb, however, acknowledged the book as a "worthwhile attempt to increase our appreciation of Beauvoir the thinker."

Fullbrook told *CA:* "The response to my and my coauthor's study of Jean-Paul Sartre and Simone de Beauvoir has been exceptionally interesting, in that it has attracted both great enthusiasm and real hostility. I think that this illustrates how difficult it still is to secure for women the recognition which their achievement deserves. The historical record is always being skewed and trying to rectify this, no matter how carefully it is done, elicits powerful resistance. However, this kind of work also equally attracts highly positive responses, and one of the most pleasing developments following from our and other writers' recent studies of Beauvoir is the plan for a multi-volume translation of all of Beauvoir's philosophical writing into English. As a teacher and writer who has always been deeply concerned with the relationship between literature and ethics it is an exciting prospect to know that Beauvoir's work, with all its ethical passion, will soon be made available to English-speaking readers."

BIOGRAPHICAL/CRITICAL SOURCES:

PERIODICALS

Choice, May 1994, p. 1440.
New York Times, January 14, 1994, p. C27.
New York Times Book Review, January 23, 1994, pp. 12-13.
Washington Post Book World, February 6, 1994, p. 13.

*   *   *

FURST, Alan 1941-

PERSONAL: Born February 20, 1941, in New York, NY. *Education:* Oberlin College, A.B., 1962; Pennsylvania State University, M.A., 1967.

ADDRESSES: Home—Box 2345, Sag Harbor, NY 11963.

CAREER: Writer.

AWARDS, HONORS: Fulbright teaching fellowship, 1969-70; Edgar Award nomination, 1976.

WRITINGS:

NOVELS

Your Day in the Barrel, Atheneum (New York, NY), 1976.

The Paris Drop, Doubleday (New York, NY), 1980.

The Caribbean Account, Delacorte (New York, NY), 1981.

Shadow Trade, Delacorte (New York, NY), 1983.

Night Soldiers, Houghton Mifflin (Boston, MA), 1988.

Dark Star, Houghton Mifflin (Boston, MA), 1991.

The Polish Officer, Random House (New York, NY), 1995.

The World at Night, Random House (New York, NY), 1996.

Red Gold, Random House (New York, NY), 1999.

Kingdom of Shadows, Random House (New York, NY), 2001.

OTHER

(With Debbi Fields) *One Smart Cookie: How a Housewife's Chocolate Chip Recipe Turned into a Multimillion-Dollar Business—The Story of Mrs. Field's Cookies,* Simon & Schuster (New York, NY), 1987.

Contributor to periodicals, including *Esquire, Architectural Digest, Elle, GQ,* and *International Herald Tribune.*

SIDELIGHTS: "Alan Furst is an American writer, but his heart belongs to Europe," observed Charles Wilson in the *New York Times Book Review.* Indeed, the world of European intelligence services during the 1930s and 1940s is Furst's special fictional domain. Admired for his careful research and his evocation of period detail, Furst creates factually accurate thrillers involving Soviet, German, French, and British agents staged against a historical backdrop that sweeps from Polish battlefields to Parisian nightlife.

Furst's novels, according to *Boston Globe* critic Richard Dyer, "are full of atmosphere, period detail, action, and suspense. But he is primarily interested in the drama of moral choice." This theme is evident in *Shadow Trade,* which features a former CIA agent, Guyer, now in business for himself after being downsized. Here Furst explores the complex and morally questionable habits and techniques of the spy world, in which everyone has a double who can be tracked down and manipulated by darker forces to achieve their evil goals. In his review for the *Times Literary Supplement,*

Reginald Hill noted that *Shadow Trade* "is intelligent, honest, gripping, and not much for our comfort. . . . Out of this, Furst spins a compelling and original plot without any escapist pyrotechnics."

In *Night Soldiers,* Furst moves briskly from country to country to follow the book's hero, Khristo Stoianev. The begins tragically when the rise of Fascism in Bulgaria kills the teenaged Khristo's brother, and the grieving boy ends up in Moscow undergoing training by the NKVD, a precursor of the KGB. As a tool of the Communists, he is dispatched to Spain to murder fellow party members whom Moscow considers turncoats. But Khristo escapes the dirty task and flees to France. By the end of World War II, Khristo has worked his way to a happier arrangement as a spy for the Western victors. "My goal in *Night Solders* was to write a panoramic novel of the period," Furst told Dyer. Walter Goodman in the *New York Times* observed that "the characters tend to be personifications of their nations, and the book serves as something of a tour guide, especially to towns up and down the Danube." Goodman called *Night Soldiers* "absorbing."

Night Soldiers is especially notable as a chronicle of European espionage, observed Anthony Levitas in *Los Angeles Times Book Review,* because "the action unfolds not in the 1950s or '60s, but in the 1930s and '40s." In Levitas's view, Furst has wisely chosen his time frame "to show that it is here, before the war, that the modern lingua franca of diplomatic duplicity and international terror comes into its own."

In *Dark Star,* which *Los Angeles Times Book Review* contributor G. Y. Dryansky considered "more deeply satisfying than much of the non-thrilling 'serious fiction' around today," Furst confronts the subject of the Soviet purges of the 1930s. Its central character is Andre Szara, a Polish-born Russian Jew who serves the NKVD while working as a foreign correspondent for *Pravda* in Paris. Among the jittery French Jewry is the rich Joseph de Montfried, who appeals to Szara's heritage, asking him to pass along secrets about the German military to the British in exchange for British passports that would then be used to help Jews escape Germany. "The historical background and intelligence information are woven into the novel seamlessly," commented Herbert Mitgang in *New York Times.* "It's as if Mr. Furst obtained documents under a Freedom of Information Act." Mitgang added, however, that readers would need to make a slight leap of faith as the novel approaches its end. *Washington Post* contributor Josephine Wol found the novel "stimulating and satisfying."

In *The Polish Officer,* Capt. Alexander de Milja accepts the daring job of underground spy for his exiled government after Poland falls to the Nazis. De Milja proves adept at varying his disguises, particularly with several European languages under his belt. His tasks include bomb production, propaganda, and smuggling Poland's gold reserves out of the country and out of the hands of the Germans. "Relying more on period detail than on the plot (which ultimately fizzles out) in depicting the tense life of a spy and the delicacy of maintaining one's cover, Furst writes like a confident crafter of the genre," observed Gilbert Taylor in a review in *Booklist.*

Furst's skill as a historian was also recognized by *Chicago Tribune* reviewer Robert Chatain, who wrote: "What we see in Furst's novels is the birth of modern spying, the knotted habits of thinking, tradecraft and expediency that have led several generations of public servants down a path that arguably has done their governments more harm than good."

In *The World at Night,* Furst remains rooted in European history of the 1930s and 1940s. Here his ambivalent hero is Jean-Claude Casson, a Grade-B film producer whose world turns upside down after the Nazis invade his beloved France. Without funds, he comes close to collaborating with German film companies in Paris, but in the end he cannot make himself do it. Eventually he is caught up in the more serious decision of who to spy for, since both sides are actively recruiting him.

Richard Eder in the *Los Angeles Times* noted that the novel "lights up the dark element it moves through," and has "an appreciation of France that is at once passionate, graceful and cold, an evocation of French virtues and vices under terrible testing." Lorraine Kreahling, in a profile of Furst in *New York Times,* lauded the author's "careful portrayal of the banalities and the realities of everyday life [which] allows the reader to experience what it means to have not only one's freedom but also one's middle-class comforts suddenly swept away."

Casson returns in *Red Gold,* set in Nazi-occupied Paris and involving dangerous dealings between the Resistance movement and the French Communists. The novel earned much critical enthusiasm. A contributor in *The Economist* praised the "surprising delicacy" with which Furst showed the spirit of resistance. *Library Journal* reviewer David Keymer considered the novel a "classy thriller, strong on mood and action." Bill Ott, a reviewer in *Booklist* and *American Libraries,* named it one of the "Best Reads of 1999." *New York Times*

Book Review contributor Alan Riding observed that "Furst proves himself a master at capturing the bleak and mean mood of wartime Paris."

Kingdom of Shadows centers on Nicholas Morath, a Hungarian émigré aristocrat living in Paris in the late 1930s whose diplomat uncle recruits him for undercover missions against the Nazis in eastern Europe. A story ensues of forged passports, hidden money, smuggled spies, and assorted assassins and refugees. *Los Angeles Times Book Review* contributor Eugen Weber hailed the novel as "the etching of an era," and claimed that "it's hard to overestimate *Kingdom of Shadows.*" Charles Wilson, in the *New York Times Book Review,* named it Furst's best—as did *Boston Globe* reviewer Michael Kenney. "Mr. Furst's writing has the seductive shimmer of an urban black-and-white Hollywood classic," wrote *New York Times* critic Janet Maslin, who admired the novel's "beguiling sophistication, knowing political overview and utterly assured narrative tone."

Furst, who revealed to Dyer that he admires a wide range of writers including Laurence Sterne, William Saroyan, Mary Renault, Willard Motley, A. J. Liebling, and Joseph Roth, commented that he had to invent the genre of the historical espionage novel himself. Dyer suggested that words from Furst's introduction to *The Three Musketeers* described the author's own approach to writing: The "historical novelist . . . knows that history, eternally surprising, inspiring, disheartening, sometimes described as 'one damn thing after another,' will never fail him. It is all there. And it is all there to be used."

BIOGRAPHICAL/CRITICAL SOURCES:

PERIODICALS

American Libraries, February, 2000, Bill Ott, "Quick Bibs: Books on a Timeless Topic," p. 66.

Booklist, January 1, 1995, p. 802; February 1, 1999, Bill Ott, review of *Red Gold,* p. 964; November 15, 2000, Bill Ott, review of *Kingdom of Shadows,* p. 623.

Boston Globe, January 23, 2001, Michael Kenney, review of *Kingdom of Shadows,* p. E2; March 27, 2001, Richard Dyer, "Cloak and Typewriter: Spy Master Alan Furst Explores Moral Choice in His Period Novels," p. E1.

Chicago Tribune, February 26, 1995, section 14, p. 5; June 23, 1996, section 14, p. 4.

Economist, June 19, 1999, review of *Red Gold,* p. 3.

Library Journal, January, 1999, David Keymer, review of *Red Gold,* p. 148.

Los Angeles Times Book Review, February 21, 1988; April 28, 1991, G. Y. Dryansky, review of *Dark Star,* p. 2; June 2, 1996, p. 2; June 10, 2001, Eugen Weber, review of *Kingdom of Shadows,* p. 18.

New York Times, January 30, 1988, p. 16; June 12, 1991, section C, p. 17; June 5, 1996, section C, p. 18, July 21, 1996, p. 2; January 11, 2001, Janet Maslin, review of *Kingdom of Shadows.*

New York Times Book Review, October 25, 1987; April 28, 1991, section 7, p. 24; September 8, 1996, p. 23; April 11, 1999, Alan Riding, review of *Red Gold;* February 4, 2001, Charles Wilson, review of *Kingdom of Shadows.*

Publishers Weekly, January 18, 1999, review of *Red Gold,* p. 324; November 6, 2000, review of *Kingdom of Shadows,* p. 67,

Time, April 15, 1991, p. 65.

Times Literary Supplement, April 5, 1985, p. 394.

Tribune Books (Chicago), May 26, 1991, p. 7.

Washington Post, January 18, 1988; June 4, 1991, section B, p. 3; June 19, 1996, section C, p. 2.*

G

GATENBY, Greg 1950-

PERSONAL: Born May 5, 1950, in Toronto, Ontario, Canada; son of Roy McKinley (a teacher) and Margaret Helen (a teacher; maiden name, O'Connor) Gatenby. *Education:* York University, B.A., 1972. *Avocational interests:* "When I get the chance I travel. Some favorite spots include Slea Head in western Ireland and a certain beach on Formentera."

ADDRESSES: Home—63 Burnet St., Oakville, Ontario, Canada. *Office*—Harbourfront, 417 Queen's Quay W., Toronto, Ontario, Canada M5V 2Z3. *Agent*—Lucinda Vardey Literary Agency, 36 Maitland St., Suite H-2, Toronto, Ontario, Canada M4Y 1C5.

CAREER: McClelland & Stewart, Toronto, Ontario, Canada, editor, 1972-74; Harbourfront, Toronto, Ontario, Canada, coordinator and host of Harbourfront Reading Series, 1975—; artistic director, Harbourfront International Festival of Authors, 1980—. Founding member of the reconstituted PEN Canadian Center; co-organizer of PEN World Congress, Toronto, 1989; served as board member of Writer's Development Trust; hosted a book show for television and was a book reviewer on CBS Radio.

AWARDS, HONORS: Ontario Arts Council awards, 1974-80; Canada Council awards, 1974-80; Canada Council award, 1978; City of Toronto Arts Award for Literature, 1989; named League of Canadian Poets, honorary lifetime member, 1991; Jack Award, for lifetime promotion of Canada's books and authors, 1994; Arts and Letters Club of Toronto, E. J. Pratt Honorary Lifetime Membership.

WRITINGS:

POETRY

Rondeaus for Erica, Missing Link Press (Toronto, Canada), 1976.
Adrienne's Blessing, Missing Link Press (Toronto, Canada), 1976.
The Brown Stealer, Avalon Editions (Oxford, England), 1977.
The Salmon Country, Black Moss Press (Windsor, Canada), 1978.
Growing Still, Black Moss Press (Windsor, Canada), 1981.

OTHER

(Editor) *Fifty-two Pickup,* Dreadnaught Press (Toronto, Canada), 1976.
(Editor) *Whale Sound: An Anthology of Poems about Whales and Dolphins,* Douglas & McIntyre, Dreadnaught Press (Toronto, Canada), 1977.
(Translator, with Irving Layton and Francesca Valente) Giorgio Bassani, *Selected Poems* (foreword by Northrop Frye), Aya Press (Toronto, Canada), 1980.
(Editor) *Whales Art,* 1981.
(Editor) *Contemporary Canadian Poets,* Intermedia Press, 1980.
(Editor) *Whales, A Celebration,* Little, Brown (Boston, MA), 1983.
(Editor) *The Definitive Notes,* Montblanc (Toronto, Canada), 1991.
(Editor) *The Wild Is Always There,* 1993.
(Editor) *The Very Richness of That Past,* Alfred A. Knopf Canada (Toronto, Canada), 1995.

Toronto, A Literary Guide, Alfred A. Knopf Canada (Toronto, Canada), McArthur (Toronto, Canada), 1999.

Also Canadian editor of *Kudos.*

SIDELIGHTS: Greg Gatenby wears several different hats. Although an author in his own right, with five books of poetry and a literary guidebook to his credit, Gatenby is perhaps best known for his work as an editor, and as a promoter of other writers' work. He has not only hosted the acclaimed Harbourfront Reading Series in Toronto, Ontario, for over a quarter century, but has been instrumental in organizing Toronto's Festival of Authors, considered one of the biggest literary events in the world. "My job is to get people excited about the quality of literature," Gatenby told Clyde Farnsworth of the *New York Times* in a 1994 interview. Describing Gatenby as "a man of Falstaffian girth with a ginger beard [who] barrels to the podium," Farnsworth went on to note that he "makes a point of treating his authors equally . . . [whether they are] unknown poets or Nobel Laureates." Although the majority of readers who have appeared at the Harbourfront Reading Series are Canadian, Gatenby has also attracted writers from around the world, including such notables as Arthur Miller, Anthony Burgess, Susan Sontag, and Saul Bellow. Jim Boothroyd, writing in the *Times Literary Supplement,* described Gatenby as "arguably Canada's greatest literary impresario," while an essayist for *Contemporary Poets* credited him with being "on a friendly and informal basis with innumerable influential authors from almost all the countries of the world."

In his role as an editor, Gatenby has published several volumes having to do with whales and other aquatic creatures such as porpoises and dolphins. Reviewing the 1983 *Whales: A Celebration,* a critic in *New York Times Book Review* stated: "Gatenby has unearthed and commissioned hundreds of pieces of lore, poetry, paintings, sculpture and music. . . . rallying them into a lavish artistic tribute to all cetacea." Among the contributors to the collection, described by a *People Weekly* writer as "a stately, absorbing book," are Plutarch, Carl Sagan, Maxine Kumin, Robert Rauschenberg, Leonard Bernstein, John Cage, and Margaret Atwood. Royalties from *Whales: A Celebration* are donated to the Greenpeace Foundation's "Save the Whales" campaign.

Gatenby also edited *The Wild Is Always There,* a compilation that presents the reactions of numerous foreign authors to Canada. Canadian John Bemrose, reviewing the anthology in *Maclean's,* remarked that "the book's stories, essays, letters, and poems play right up to the national weakness for wanting to know what foreigners think about us. And the collection contains so much good news that it could lead to a swelled head." Bemrose added that *The Wild Is Always There* "is a rich and serious anthology that has much to say about the meaning of Canada in a global (or at least a Western) context." Contributors to the volume include Henry James, Willa Cather, William Faulkner, and Ernest Hemingway.

Gatenby's five books of poetry appeared between 1976 and 1981. Discussing their content, the *Contemporary Poets* essay credited Gatenby with "a poetic voice that is characteristically his own . . . strong and vigorous . . . [and with] a metropolitan temperament ill at ease with local, provincial, and intellectual pieties." The essay went on to note that "there is evidence in his late poetry of a trying truce between the hard-nosed poems that satirize cultural and national concerns and the melodious lyric poems about love and life."

Toronto: A Literary Guide offers the reader fifty-eight walking tours of the city along with information and anecdotes about both Canadian and foreign authors who have lived and stayed there. Gatenby devotes a chapter to each of the neighborhoods he surveys, complete with a map, drawings, and photographs. The book begins its tours in the area known as Muddy York, where Charles Dickens stayed briefly in 1842, and moves on to cover such diverse litterateurs and experiences as horror writer Bram Stoker's tobogganing, young Hemingway's trials as a reporter for the *Toronto Star,* and the career of the influential nineteenth-century political cartoonist John Wilson Bengough. Among the many famous authors discussed are Rudyard Kipling, Margaret Atwood, W. H. Auden, and Jorge Luis Borges. "The result," according to Boothroyd, "is a page-turner: a meticulously researched, intimate, opinionated and surprising book."

Gatenby once told *CA:* "I write because I have to. I believe that poets should be speaking for social and political issues much more than they are at present. I think universities are bad for good writers, and good for bad writers."

BIOGRAPHICAL/CRITICAL SOURCES:

BOOKS

Contemporary Poets, 6th edition, St. James Press (Detroit, MI), 1996.

PERIODICALS

Maclean's, January 3, 1994, John Bemrose, review of *The Wild Is Always There,* p. 60.

New York Times, July 14, 1994, Clyde H. Farnsworth, "Helping Excite Toronto over Books for 20 Years."

New York Times Book Review, November 20, 1983, "In Praise of Leviathan," p. 15.

People Weekly, December 12, 1983, review of *Whales: A Celebration,* p. 34.

Times Literary Supplement (London), September 29, 2000, Jim Boothroyd, "Dickens Was Wrong," p. 13.

OTHER

City of Toronto, http://www.toronto.on.ca/ (January 4, 2001), "2000 Toronto Book Awards Short List."*

*　　*　　*

GAULLE, Charles (Andre Joseph Marie) de
See de GAULLE, Charles (Andre Joseph Marie)

*　　*　　*

GILDER, George F. 1939-

PERSONAL: Born November 29, 1939, in New York, NY; son of Richard Watson and Anne (Alsop) Gilder; married Cornelia Brooke (an historic preservationist), 1976; children: Louisa Ludlow, Mary Ellen Tiffany, Richard Brooke, Cornelia Chapin. *Education:* Harvard University, A.B., 1962. *Politics:* Republican.

ADDRESSES: Home—The Red House, Tyringham, MA 01264.

CAREER: Advance (magazine), editor and co-founder, Cambridge, MA, 1961-62, and Washington, DC, 1962-64; *New Leader,* New York, NY, associate editor, beginning 1965; legislative assistant to Senator Charles McC. Mathias, Washington, DC, 1968-70; Manhattan Institute for Policy Research, New York, NY, program director, 1981—. Speech writer for Nelson A. Rockefeller, 1964, Richard M. Nixon, 1968, Ben C. Toledano, 1972, and Robert Dole, 1976. Founder, *The Gilder*

Technology Report. Military service: U.S. Marine Corps Reserve, 1958-64.

AWARDS, HONORS: Kennedy Institute of Politics fellow, Harvard University, 1971-72; White House Special Presidential Award for "entrepreneurial excellence," 1986, for *The Spirit of Enterprise.*

WRITINGS:

(With Bruce K. Chapman) *The Party That Lost Its Head,* Knopf (New York, NY), 1966.

Sexual Suicide, Quadrangle, 1973, revised and expanded edition published as *Men and Marriage,* Pelican Publishing (Gretna, LA), 1986.

Naked Nomads: Unmarried Men in America, Quadrangle, 1974.

Visible Man, Basic Books (New York, NY), 1978, revised edition, (with Robert B. Hawkins) *Visible Man: A True Story of Post-Racist America,* ICS Press (San Francisco, CA), 1995. (With Robert B. Hawkins) *Visible Man: A True Story of Post-Racist America,* ICS Press (San Francisco, CA), 1995..

(With Robert B. Hawkins) *Wealth and Poverty,* Basic Books (New York, NY), 1981.

The Spirit of Enterprise, Simon & Schuster (New York, NY), 1985, revised edition published as *Recapturing the Spirit of Enterprise,* ICS Press (San Francisco, CA), 1992.

Microcosm: The Quantum Revolution in Economics and Technology, Simon & Schuster (New York, NY), 1989.

Life after Television, Whittle Direct Books (Knoxville, TN), 1990, revised edition, Norton (New York, NY), 1994.

Telecosm: How Infinite Bandwidth Will Revolutionize Our World, Free Press (New York, NY), 2000.

Contributor to *National Review, American Spectator, Commentary, Forbes, Wall Street Journal,* and other periodicals. Editor, *Ripon Forum,* 1971-72; contributing editor, *Forbes;* semiconductors editor, *RE-Lease 1.0,* 1983; columnist for *Forbes ASAP.*

ADAPTATIONS: Several of Gilder's books have been recorded as audio books.

SIDELIGHTS: George F. Gilder has created controversy with his conservative commentary on everything from the biological basis of women's roles as housewives to the moral basis of the capitalist system. He was named "the nation's leading male-chauvinist-pig author" by *Time* magazine in 1974, and M. J. Sobran of the *National Review* called him "a man of free and fresh mind and genial temper whose ideas have a way of making people want to scratch his eyes out." Probably best known for his views on the women's movement, and on supply-side economics, Gilder has also written extensively on the evolution of telecommunications. In addition to his writing, he has appeared on numerous television talk shows and at public lectures to discuss his unique brand of social philosophy and economic theory.

Gilder's book, *Sexual Suicide,* concerns the biological and anthropological bases of sexual behavior in our culture, and how, in his view, contemporary American society is courting cultural disaster by its deviation from the norms established by primitive man. In using the term "sexual suicide," Gilder claims that every impulse we have as social animals is tied closely to our sexual instincts; behaviors that depart from the norm, including homosexuality, the enjoyment of pornography, and promiscuity, are all "indices of sexual frustration." In fact, Gilder continues, these types of behavior "all disclose a failure to achieve profound and loving sexuality. When a society deliberately affirms these failures—contemplates legislation of homosexual marriage, celebrates the women who denounce the family, and indulges pornography as a manifestation of sexual health . . . [then] the culture is promoting a form of erotic suicide. For it is destroying the cultural preconditions of profound love and sexuality: the durable heterosexual relationships necessary to a community of emotional investments."

According to Gilder, the "women who denounce the family"—or feminists—are collectively "promoting in the United States an epidemic of erotic and social disorders." The author reasons that by attempting to make marriage and sexuality more "open," feminists, along with sexologists and pornographers, are "subverting and stifling real sexuality and love, and are undermining civilized society." In an interview with Richard K. Rein in *People* magazine, Gilder reemphasized his stance against the feminist movement. "All the cliches about oppressed women are baloney," he claimed. "Women have the opportunity of motherhood, time to be creative and be individuals, and less pressure to submit their lives to a wretched career. You read these feminist books and you'd think every man is a U.S. senator. The fact is most men work for other men."

"The beauty of Gilder's reasoning" in *Sexual Suicide,* averred Isa Kapp in the *New Leader,* "is that it is so persevering and complete. Yet it rests on the somewhat questionable first premise that because woman's responsibility in procreation is more important and more sensuously satisfying than man's, men feel emotionally deprived. To compensate for this male disadvantage, women must hew to their role and reinforce men in theirs; if they falter, we tumble into social disarray." Kapp disputed this conclusion, remarking that "in real life, few males minimize their part in conceiving babies, and most seem content to remain fond spectators in the process of bearing and nursing them. That men feel in any way inferior is not clear."

"One reads this elaborate, Freud-haunted apology for patriarchy with a depressing sense of déja vu," proffered Judith Adler Hennessee in the *New York Times Book Review.* "Whether men invent a mythology that makes women superior or inferior, the end result is likely to be the same—women belong in the home." Hennessee also remarked that there are "dozens of statements in this book that are preposterous, as well as over-simple generalizations that contain a germ of truth but veer off wildly into fantasy. One searches in vain for some understanding of the individual need for self-fulfillment."

National Review contributor Morton A. Kaplan, however, felt that Gilder's book presents "an interesting and provocative thesis. As a counterpoint to the unisex myth and the belief that biology does not matter either in personal relationships or in the cementing of society, it almost surely points in the direction of truth." While the critic found that Gilder's "insights are often profound, his apothegms often brilliant, and his flair for argument strong," he also criticized the author for his authoritative and impassioned style. "As with the feminists he attacks, one senses a desire to convert the reader rather than to engage his intellect," commented Kaplan. In addition, "where Mr. Gilder does marshal evidence, he shows that he can read better and think more clearly than most of his opponents; on the whole, however, we are left more with Mr. Gilder's conclusions than with the analysis that produced them." Overall, Kaplan found that "as a provocative polemic, designed to stimulate debate, Mr. Gilder's book is effective, and as social commentary its insights touch deep wounds in our society."

In 1986 Gilder authored a revised edition of *Sexual Suicide,* titled *Men and Marriage,* in part to expand upon his theories and in part to replace the original work, which had been removed from print shortly after it first appeared. Even though Gilder's recent works had been best sellers, he found it difficult to find a publisher for the revision; eventually he found a small Louisiana press to print it. In this new edition, according to M. D. Aeschliman in the *National Review,* Gilder "tries to do in expository prose what no major novelist since Tolstoi has succeeded in doing: to paint the virtues and joys of pious and civilized marriage. Gilder has a social imagination, not in the sense of conceiving fictions, but in his capacity for understanding the real implications of individual acts and habits." But Barbara Ehrenreich, writing in the *Los Angeles Times Book Review,* found the work "no less floridly idiosyncratic than the original," criticizing the author's theories and style. In addition, the reviewer accused Gilder of adjusting historical facts to fit his ideas. Speaking of "the pact between the sexes," where women let men rule in order to compensate for their loss of freedom, Ehrenreich wrote that "the odd society that doesn't fit the pattern (such as the Trobianders) is dismissed by Gilder as 'perverse' and even 'retarded.' " In contrast, Aeschliman remarked that the author "never simply opines or asserts; the wealth of statistical documentation he brings to bear is enormously impressive."

Writing in *Commentary,* Terry Teachout expressed a more moderate opinion; while frustrated by the author's outbreaks of "purple" prose, Teachout observed that "the insights on which Gilder's sexual myth are built are genuinely compelling. Time and again one encounters striking passages that are rooted in cool observation rather than in some fantastic construct of a fevered imagination." Nevertheless, the critic felt that the book is made less effective by the author's style: "Gilder is no crank, and had he tempered his rhetoric and written *Men and Marriage* with the skeptical reader firmly in mind, he might well have" convinced the skeptic. Instead, Teachout commented, "Gilder has insisted . . . on preaching only to the converted."

In his 1981 book, *Wealth and Poverty,* which he called a "theology" for capitalism, Gilder attempts to establish a moral basis for the capitalist system, using examples from the economies of primitive tribal societies to illustrate the relationship between gift-giving and the spirit of capitalism. In an article in the *Washington Post Book World* on *Wealth and Poverty,* James K. Glassman said, "If you don't understand the wave of new conservative ideas that has swept this country during the past four or five years—or if you consider those ideas window dressing for jingoism and bigotry—then this is the book to read." *Wealth and Poverty* was publicly endorsed by former President Ronald Reagan and proclaimed "Promethean in its vision" by Reagan's former budget adviser, David Stockman, as quoted in a *New York Times* article.

"The ultimate strength and crucial weakness of both capitalism and democracy are their reliance on individ-

ual creativity and courage, leadership and morality, intuition and faith," wrote Gilder in *Wealth and Poverty.* "Capitalist production entails faith—in one's neighbors, in one's society, and in the compensatory logic of the cosmos. Search and you shall find, give and you will be given unto, supply creates its own demand. It is this cosmology, this sequential logic, that essentially distinguishes the free from the socialist economy."

In the *National Review,* conservative critic Irving Kristol, writing of Gilder's belief in the fundamental morality of capitalism, disagreed with what he called Gilder's "pseudo-anthropological analysis of economic activity as inherently and ineluctably giving birth to a viable morality." Kristol feels that successful commercial activity "[does] not add up to a complete moral code that a society can base itself on." Similarly, Andrew Klaven, discussing *Wealth and Poverty* in the *Saturday Review,* claimed that the book "is rendered nonsensical not by its methodical defense of what is known as conservative, supply-side economics, but by the moral hogwash on which that defense is based." Gilder's particular brand of economics, said Ann Crittenden in the *New York Times,* "comes in an ideological fruitcake that many find hard to swallow."

New York Times Book Review contributor Roger Starr, however, found that *Wealth and Poverty* "offers a creed for capitalism worthy of intelligent people. Mr. Gilder has written the kind of good book that alternately astonishes the reader with new and rather daring insights into familiar problems and bores him with long, tract-like passages to support them." Although the critic was not entirely convinced by Gilder's theories, he admitted that "the book stands as an eloquent defense of the capitalist high ground and the human values that capitalists, despite their bad manners and admitted defects, managed to embody to the benefit of their fellows." And Adam Meyerson, writing in *Commentary,* felt that "despite its flaws . . . *Wealth and Poverty* remains one of the most significant, and gracefully written, works of political economy in years." Concluded the critic: "Hardly a page fails to provoke thought or to challenge some conventional assumption."

Gilder focuses on the role of the entrepreneur in capitalist society in his 1984 book, *The Spirit of Enterprise.* Reprising several themes from *Wealth and Poverty,* the book "celebrates the entrepreneur, that wellspring of progress, the hero, who undertakes enormous risks in the face of impossible odds and brings forth benefits to mankind that far exceed the rise in his personal net worth," summarized Paul Craig Roberts in the *Washington Post Book World.* Detailing the stories of several successful enterprisers, Gilder's book explores the backgrounds of these successes and how they demonstrate the productive capacity of the capitalist system. As Roberts described him, "Gilder is a person who drives economists up the wall. The reason is that he writes about their subject with far more lucidity, insight, enthusiasm, and verve than they do." Other critics objected to this "enthusiasm," however, describing it as "evangelism" instead. Eliot Janeway, for example, criticized in the *New York Times Book Review* that "Gilder is an economic evangelist, and evangelists of every persuasion habitually simplify their struggles and glorify their goals."

Los Angeles Times Book Review contributor Donald G. Campbell thought that Gilder presents a thorough picture of the role of entrepreneurship: "Gilder is a sprightly writer and storyteller with provocative ideas. Those ideas, admittedly, lean heavily to supply-side economics and may dismay some readers, but those ideas still refuse to go away."

Gilder next turned his attention to telecommunications and computers and their impact on society and the economy. *Microcosm: The Quantum Revolution in Economics and Technology,* published in 1989, seeks to explain for lay readers the world of the microchip. Illustrating his subject at atomic and subatomic levels, Gilder also explores the impact of the microchip on humanity, "while advising his readers to yield to it or be crushed," noted Langdon Winner in the *New York Times Book Review.* Winner found that although numerous books had already been written in this vein, "Mr. Gilder manages to revitalize the topic . . . exploring fascinating links between the scientific, technical, economic and philosophical dimensions of his subject. Among his chief concerns, for example, are the widespread beliefs that the mind is actually matter and that computers can be said to have minds. These views he attacks with arguments drawn from neurosurgery, theoretical physics and other fields. Even those who disagree with his conclusions will be challenged by his imaginative grasp of the issues." *Microcosm* was enthusiastically praised in *National Review* by Ronald Bailey, who mused: "A reader invariably emerges from one of George Gilder's books intellectually reinvigorated. . . . His celebration of American capitalism and high technology is dazzling."

Gilder examined the effect of the telecomputer on the broadcasting industry in his 1992 book, *Life after Television.* In it, he notes that the invention of transistors in the 1940s, the microchip in the late 1950s, and the development of fiber-optic cables in the 1970s have all contributed to the demise of the television industry. The television set will someday be replaced completely by the telecomputer, which will in turn revolutionize what people watch and how they do so. Gilder sees the new age as a great advancement, allowing for more intelligent, individualized use of television, but he points out that entrenched financial interests have a stake in seeing that things do not change too drastically. "The age of the telecomputer may be decades away, but even couch potatoes will be stimulated by this thought-provoking essay," commented a *Publishers Weekly* writer.

Gilder probed further into the impact of fiber-optics in *Telecosm: How Infinite Bandwidth Will Revolutionize Our World.* Once again, the author shows how the fiber-optic cable is replacing the microchip as the most important element in economics and technology. He points out that a single fiber, only one-tenth the size of a strand of human hair, can transmit almost as much information per second as the entire Internet transmitted during a month in 1995. The dramatic rise of information and the astounding increase in transmission capabilities open the door to a new era, in Gilder's estimation. As in *Life after Television,* however, he warns that established companies may seek to keep the world mired in the microchip age as long as possible. *Kirkus Reviews*'s commentator found *Telecosm* a somewhat muddled but nevertheless valuable work, advising: "Buried beneath futurist hyperbole and purple prose, here lurks a potentially very interesting—if rather blithely utopian—argument regarding the ascendance of fiber-optics."

For all the controversy and opposition his work has invited, Gilder is still praised by some critics for his social vision. "For all his inflammatory generalizations . . . and intellectual U-turns," commented Hazlitt, Gilder "is a writer with a fine sense of what America has become—and what it still might be." Similarly, Sobran maintained that Gilder is a "dauntlessly original thinker, who is unbiased at reaching traditional conclusions. He says things that were never before necessary to say, and it may be a long time before anyone else says them as well."

BIOGRAPHICAL/CRITICAL SOURCES:

BOOKS

Authors in the News, Volume 1, Gale (Detroit), 1976.
Contemporary Issues Criticism, Volume 1, Gale (Detroit, MI), 1982.
Gilder, George, *Sexual Suicide,* Quadrangle, 1973.
Gilder, George, *Wealth and Poverty,* Basic Books, 1981.

PERIODICALS

Adweek (Eastern edition), August 1, 1994, Andrew Jaffe, review of *Life after Television*, p. 38.

American Anthropologist, number 4, 1976.

Booklist, October 15, 1992, review of *Recapturing the Spirit of Enterprise*, p. 384.

Bookwatch, January, 1993, review of *Recapturing the Spirit of Enterprise*, p. 3.

Business Week, October 12, 1992, review of *Life after Television*, p. 14.

Choice, March, 1993, review of *Recapturing the Spirit of Enterprise*, p. 1205; May, 1994, review of *Wealth and Poverty*, p. 1393.

Commentary, July, 1981; April, 1987.

Commonweal, December 4, 1981.

Contemporary Sociology, September, 1974.

Economist, September 16, 1989, review of *Microcosm: The Quantum Revolution in Economics and Technology*, p. 94.

Far Eastern Economic Review, May 13, 1993, review of *Life after Television*, p. 46.

Forbes, October 21, 1991, James W. Michaels, "Riding the Waves," p. 6; August 31, 1992, Steve Forbes, review of *Life after Television*, p. 24; June 6, 1994, George Gilder, "George Gilder's Telecosm."

Harvard Business Review, January, 1994, review of *Life after Television*, p. 38.

Internet World, December, 1997, Gus Venditto, interview with George Gilder, p. 30.

Kirkus Reviews, July 1, 2000, review of *Telecosm: How Infinite Bandwidth Will Revolutionize Our World*, p. 933.

Library Journal, November 1, 1992, review of *Recapturing the Spirit of Enterprise*, p. 98; September 1, 1995, review of *Visible Man*, p. 213.

Los Angeles Times Book Review, April 19, 1981; December 12, 1984; October 5, 1986.

Nation, February 26, 1983.

National Review, December 21, 1973; May 9, 1975; August 18, 1978; April 17, 1981; February 27, 1987; October 27, 1989, Ronald Bailey, review of *Microcosm: The Quantum Revolution in Economics and Technology*, p. 50; September 14, 1992, David Klinghoffer, review of *Life after Television*, p. 58.

New Leader, December 10, 1973.

Newsweek, February 16, 1981.

New York Times, April 26, 1981; May 16, 1981; November 8, 1986; June 18, 1992, Christopher Lehmann-Haupt, review of *Life after Television*.

New York Times Book Review, December 9, 1973; February 1, 1981; October 21, 1984; October 15, 1989, Langdon Winner, review of *Microcosm: The Quantum Revolution in Economics and Technology*, section 7, p. 15.

People, May 18, 1981.

Playboy, October, 1977.

Production, January, 1990, Gary S. Vasilash, review of *Microcosm: The Quantum Revolution in Economic and Technology*, p. 76.

Public Administration Review, May, 1993, review of *Microcosm*, p. 268.

Publishers Weekly, May 11, 1992, review of *Life after Television*, p. 62; May 23, 1994, review of *Life after Television*, p. 85.

Quarterly Journal of Speech, May, 1997, review of *Life after Television*, p. 230.

Saturday Review, January, 1981.

Society, March, 1993, review of *Life after Television*, p. 92.

Success, June, 1990, Duncan Maxwell Anderson, review of *Life after Television*, p. 56.

Time, December 9, 1974.

Times Literary Supplement, September 13, 1985; May 12, 1995, review of *Life after Television*, p. 10.

Washington Post Book World, February 8, 1981; October 7, 1984.

Washington Star-News, December 13, 1974.

Wilson Quarterly Review, spring, 1993, review of *Life after Television*, p. 73; summer, 1994, review of *Life after Television*, p. 39.

OTHER

Star-Tribune (Minneapolis, MN), http://www.startribune.com/ (September 4, 2000), telephone interview with George Gilder.

Wall St. Access, http://www.wsaccess.com/ (October 11, 1999), Scott Moritz, "George Gilder, Whose Musings Have Made Others Millions, Mulls Starting His Own Fund".*

*   *   *

GINSBURG, Mark B. 1949-

PERSONAL: Born December 9, 1949, in Los Angeles, CA; son of Norman Leslie (a business executive) and Blanche Dorothy (a homemaker and volunteer; maiden name, Burg) Ginsburg; married Barbara Iris Chaisin (an educator), September 5, 1971; children: Jolie Richelle, Kevin Eran, Stefanie Alyse. *Ethnicity:* European-American. *Education:* Dartmouth College, B.A. (summa cum laude), 1972; University of California, Los Angeles, M.A., 1974, Ph.D., 1976. *Politics:* Democratic socialist. *Religion:* "Non-practicing Jew." *Avocational interests:* Bicycling, volleyball, collecting coins and stamps, progressive politics.

ADDRESSES: Home—1125 Wightman St., Pittsburgh, PA 15217. *Office*—Institute for International Studies in Education, School of Education, University of Pittsburgh, 5K01 Posvar Hall, Pittsburgh, PA 15230; fax: 412-624-2609. *E-mail*—mbg@pitt.edu.

CAREER: University of Aston, Birmingham, England, lecturer, 1976-78; University of Houston, Houston, TX, assistant professor, 1979-82, associate professor, 1982-87; University of Pittsburgh, Pittsburgh, PA, associate professor, 1987-89, professor, 1989—, director of Institute for International Studies in Education, 1987-93, 1996—. Pittsburgh Peace Institute, member of board of directors, 1989-97, co-chair, 1991-93; Alliance for Progressive Action, member of board of directors and executive committee, 1992—; Metro Pittsburgh chapter of the Labor Party, member of steering committee, 1996—.

MEMBER: Comparative and International Education Society (past president, 1991-92), American Educational Studies Association (member of board of directors, 1991-94), American Educational Research Association (chairperson of Peace Education Special Interest Group, 1992—), United Faculty of the University of Pittsburgh (vice president, 1990-92, president, 1992—).

WRITINGS:

The Role of the Middle School Teacher, University of Aston (Birmingham, England), 1977.
Contradictions in Teacher Education and Society, Falmer Press (London, England), 1988.
(Editor) *Understanding Educational Reform in Global Context,* Garland Publishing (Hamden, CT), 1991.
(Editor) *The Politics of Educators' Work and Lives,* Garland Publishing (Hamden, CT), 1995.
(Coeditor) *The Political Dimension in Teacher Education,* Falmer Press, 1995.
(Coeditor) *Cuba in the Special Period: Cuban Perspectives, Studies in Third World Societies,* 1997.
(Coeditor) *Cuba: Periodo Especial: Perspectives,* Editorial de Ciencias Sociales (La Habana, Cuba), 1998.

WORK IN PROGRESS: The Eclipse at the End of the Tunnel: The Political Socialization of Educators in Mexico, publication expected in 2002.

GLASSMAN, Joyce
See JOHNSON, Joyce

*   *   *

GOLDSTEIN, Melvyn C.   1938-

PERSONAL: Born February 8, 1938, in New York, NY; son of Harold and Rae (Binen) Goldstein; children: Andre. *Education:* University of Michigan, B.A., 1959, M.A., 1960; University of Washington, Seattle, Ph.D., 1968.

ADDRESSES: Home—50 East 252nd St., Euclid, OH 44132. *Office*—Department of Anthropology, Mather Memorial, Case Western Reserve University, Cleveland, OH 44106. *E-mail*—mcg2@po.cwru.edu.

CAREER: Case Western Reserve University, Cleveland, Ohio, assistant professor, 1968-71, associate professor, 1971-76, professor of anthropology, 1976-91, J. R. Harkness Professor, 1991—, department chair, beginning 1976.

MEMBER: International Mountain Society, American Anthropological Association, Society of Applied Anthropology, Society of Medical Anthropology, Association for Anthropology and Gerontology, Nepal Studies Association.

AWARDS, HONORS: Grants from American Council of Learned Societies, 1973-74, National Institutes of Health, 1976-77, 1980-82, National Endowment for the Humanities, 1980-82, 1982-84, 1989-92, 1992-94, 1994-96, 1995-97, 2000-03, U.S. Department of Education, 1980-82, 1986-87, 1994-97, National Geographic Society, 1980-81, 1986-87, 1992, 1996-97 Smithsonian Institution, 1981-83, National Academy of Sciences China Program, 1985, 1986-87, and Henry J. Luce Foundation, 1997-2000, 2000-04; honorable mention, Joseph Levinson Prize, Association of Asian Studies, 1989, for *A History of Modern Tibet, 1913-1951: The Demise of the Lamaist State.*

WRITINGS:

Modern Spoken Tibetan: Lhasa Dialect, University of Washington Press (Seattle, WA), 1970.
Modern Literary Tibetan: A Grammar and Reader, University of Illinois Press (Champaign, IL), 1973.
Tibetan English Dictionary of Modern Tibetan, Ratner Pustak Bhandar, 1975.
English Tibetan Dictionary of Modern Tibetan, University of California Press (Berkeley, CA), 1984.

A History of Modern Tibet, 1913-1951: The Demise of the Lamaist State, University of California Press (Berkeley, CA), 1989.

Nomads of Western Tibet: The Survival of a Way of Life, University of California Press (Berkeley, CA), 1990.

Essentials of Modern Literary Tibetan: A Reading Course and Reference Grammar, University of California Press (Berkeley, CA), 1991.

The Changing World of Mongolia's Nomads, University of California Press (Berkeley, CA), 1994.

The Snow Lion and the Dragon: China, Tibet, and the Dalai Lama, University of California Press (Berkeley, CA), 1997.

(Editor, with M. Kapstein) *Buddhism in Contemporary Tibet: Religious Revival and National Identity,* University of California Press (Berkeley, CA), 1999.

(With William Siebenschuh and Tashi Tsering) *The Struggle for a Modern Tibet: The Autobiography of Tashi Tsering,* M. E. Sharpe (Armonk, NY), 1999.

A New Tibetan-English Dictionary of Modern Tibetan, University of California Press (Berkeley, CA), 2001.

Contributor to anthropology journals. Editor, *Journal of Cross-Cultural Gerontology.*

*   *   *

GOODMAN, Lizbeth (L.) 1964-

PERSONAL: Born December 15, 1964; U.S. citizen; daughter of Alan (in business) and Beverly Alice (a special education teacher; maiden name, Harrington) Goodman. *Education:* University of Rochester, graduated (magna cum laude), 1986; Washington University, St. Louis, MO, graduated (with high honors), 1987; Cambridge University, graduated, 1992.

ADDRESSES: Agent—c/o Blackwell/Polity Press Author Mail, 108 Cowley Rd., Oxford OX4 1JF, England.

CAREER: Open University, Milton Keynes, England, lecturer in literature, beginning 1990, chairperson of Gender in Writing and Performance Research Group, beginning 1992, and Shakespeare Multimedia Research Group, beginning 1995. Better Half Women's Theatre Cooperative, producer, director, and playwright, 1987-89; Cambridge Footlights National Tour Show, executive producer, 1989, 1990; Footlights Women's

Company, artistic director and executive producer, 1989-90; Agreeable Productions, artistic director and producer, 1992-93; Sphinx (women's theater company), member of board of directors, 1996—; Too Creative Productions, associate producer; coordinator, producer, and presenter of radio and television programs. Harvard University, visiting scholar at Radcliffe College, 1994-95; University of British Columbia, visiting fellow at Centre for Women's Studies and Gender Relations, 1995. Women and Theatre International, member of Magdalena Project; Research Theatre International, member of Embodying Myth Embodying Women Project.

MEMBER: International Theatre Institute, International Shakespeare Association, Women's International Studies Europe, British Theatre Writers Union, Association of University Teachers, New Playwrights Trust, Association of Women in the Arts and Education, Nineteenth-Century American Women Writers, American Association of University Women, Association of Theatre in Higher Education, American Society for Theatre Research, Phi Beta Kappa.

AWARDS, HONORS: Simeon Cheatham Award for Community Service, 1984-86, for volunteer tutoring of children in New York, NY; American Academy of Poets Prize, 1986; St. Louis Community Service Award, 1986-87; grants for England, University of New Hampshire, 1986, and British Universities System, 1987-90; Poet of Merit Award, American Poetry Association, 1989; grants from University of Turin, 1990, 1991, New Bulgarian University, 1991, and University of Calgary, 1991; Distinguished Poets Award, National Library of Poetry, 1992; grants from British Broadcasting Corp., 1993, South African Social Science Research Council and University of Stellenbosch, 1993, Institute of Musical Arts, Bodega, CA, 1993, University of Alberta, 1995-96, British Office of Technology Development, 1996, World Literatures Conference (for Russia), 1996, British Council (for Morocco), 1996, and British Consulate, Los Angeles, CA, 1997.

WRITINGS:

Hands (play), first produced at St. John's School of Pythagoras, 1987.

(Editor, with Frances Bonner, Richard Allen, and others; and contributor) *Imagining Women: Cultural Representations and Gender,* Polity Press (Cambridge, England), 1992.

Contemporary Feminist Theatres: To Each Her Own, Routledge (New York, NY), 1993.

(Editor and contributor) *Literature and Gender,* Routledge (New York, NY), 1996.

(Editor, with W. R. Owens; and contributor) *Shakespeare, Aphra Behn, and the Canon,* Routledge (New York, NY), 1996.

(Editor and author of introduction) *Feminist Stages: Interviews with Women in Contemporary British Theater,* Harwood (New York, NY), 1996.

(Editor, with Jane de Gay) *The Routledge Reader in Gender and Performance,* Routledge (New York, NY), 1998.

Sexuality in Performance: Replaying Theatre and Culture, Routledge (New York, NY), 1999.

(Editor) *Women, Politics, and Performance in South African Theatre Today,* 1999.

Mythic Women, Real Women: Plays and Performance Pieces by Women, Faber (New York, NY), 1999.

(Editor, with Jane de Gay) *Routledge Reader in Politics and Performance,* Routledge (New York, NY), 2000.

(Editor, with Jane de Gay) *Women's Comedy: Cross-Cultural Perspectives on Gender and Humour,* Polity Press (Cambridge, England), 2000.

Television and radio writer. Contributor to books, including *Taking Reality by Surprise: A Handbook for Women Writers,* edited by Susan Sellars, Women's Press (London, England), 1991; *Cross-Cultural Performances,* edited by Marianne Novy, University of Illinois Press (Champaign, IL), 1993; *Analysing Performance,* edited by Patrick Campbell, Manchester University Press (Manchester, England), 1996; and *Caryl Churchill: Contemporary Revisions,* edited by Sheila Rabillard, Blizzard Press (Winnipeg, Manitoba, Canada), 1997. Contributor of articles and poems to journals, including *Landfall, Second Shift, Everywoman, Journal of Gender Studies, Women: A Cultural Review, Literary and Linguistic Computing, Modern Drama,* and *Critical Quarterly.* Editor, *Contemporary Theatre Review,* 1995-96, 1997; member of editorial board, *New Theatre Quarterly,* 1995—, and *International Journal of Transdisciplinary Studies,* 1996—.

SIDELIGHTS: Lizbeth Goodman is a leading scholar in the field of feminist drama. Her study *Contemporary Feminist Theaters: To Each Her Own* examines the growth and development of feminist theater since 1968, focusing mainly on British playwrights and theater groups. Bettina L. Knapp, a reviewer for *World Literature Today,* noted that "what sets Lizbeth Goodman's volume apart from other writings of this type is the emphasis she has placed on personal interviews, performance notes, and unpublished works. Such a thrust lends her book, despite the many many repetitions

which could have been omitted in this eight-chapter study, both dynamism and excitement." Goodman treats sexual politics, the definition of gender, and the different focuses implied by the terms "women's theater" and "feminist theater." Reviewing the book for *Drama Review,* Jill Dolan praised the author's "careful discussions of group process; of performance and production contexts; of the complications of funding and government politics," and more; she found, however, that these discussions "proceed within a weak and repetitive critical frame. . . . Still, she captures the energy and commitment women playwrights . . . bring to the feminist theatre scene in Britain." Knapp concluded: "*Feminist Theatres* is a gold mine for all those interested in feminism and theater."

In *Mythic Women, Real Women,* Goodman assembles a collection of performance pieces which "explores and debunks mythic stereotyping of women," and redresses "the imbalances of the performance canon by reassessing female performers' relationship to their mythic alter egos," explained *Times Literary Supplement* reviewer Jane Montgomery. Along with pieces from mainstream theater, she includes poems and multimedia presentations. Goodman's introduction to the anthology is "challenging" as well as "cogent and thought-provoking," in Montgomery's estimation.

Goodman once told *CA:* "I love to write because writing is such a powerful means of communication. I love to write because the act of writing is performative and the 'product' of writing (the book or other published artifact) is interactive: it plays a part in culture by encouraging active participation and interpretation by all its readers. I love to write because I love to break down boundaries: between categories, stereotypes, language barriers, cultural differences. I aim in all I write to reach people who might not think of themselves as able students, and to offer ideas and encouragement which might lead to further education or enjoyment of reading and cultural activism.

"My work is primarily concerned with the intersections between four fields: gender, performance, media studies, and education. While I have published poetry and worked as a theater writer/director and comedy producer, the bulk of my writing has been for the educational sector. In all I write (whether for print or media publication or multimedia publication on video, audio, CD-ROM, or the Web) I try to be clear: to avoid unnecessary jargon, to convey ideas as simply as possible, providing examples and encouraging students and readers of all kinds to feel empowered by what they read. I offer my writing as a springboard for independent thought, action, or new writing and responses from readers.

"At the Open University, my work has focused on developing a new 'distance learning' model appropriate to the teaching of literature and drama to thousands of students across the United Kingdom, Europe, and Singapore. Embracing the dilemma of needing to teach about live performance by recording it and then sharing it via mediated means, I have worked closely with colleagues in the British Broadcasting Corporation, making programs with some of the world's leading actors. In all this work, my primary aim has been the protection and development of live arts (including theater, music, dance, performance art, installation art, and combined arts) in this era of new technology.

"I love to read fiction and plays and poetry. I love to read. That's why I've made a career of encouraging others to write and to study literature and drama."

BIOGRAPHICAL/CRITICAL SOURCES:

PERIODICALS

Choice, May, 1999, review of *The Routledge Reader in Gender and Performance,* p. 1626.
Drama Review, winter, 1994, Jill Dolan, review of *Contemporary Feminist Theatres: To Each Her Own,* p. 189.
Times Literary Supplement, August 4, 2000, Jane Montgomery, review of *Mythic Women/Real Women,* p. 20.
World Literature Today, spring, 1994, Bettina L. Knapp, review of *Contemporary Feminist Theaters: To Each Her Own,* p. 376.*

*　　*　　*

GOPNIK, Adam 1956-

PERSONAL: Born August 24, 1956, in Philadelphia, PA; son of Irwin (dean of students) and Myrna (a professor of linguistics; maiden name, Shapiro) Gopnik; moved to Montreal, Quebec, Canada, 1967; married Martha Rebecca Parker (a filmmaker), August 15, 1981; children: Luke, Olivia. *Education:* McGill University, B.A., 1980; Institute of Fine Arts (New York, NY), M.A. (art history), 1984. *Avocational interests:* Songwriting, baseball, hockey.

ADDRESSES: Office—c/o *New Yorker,* 4 Times Square, New York, NY 10036-6592.

CAREER: Art historian and critic, editor, and author. *Gentleman's Quarterly* magazine, part-time fashion copy editor, then fiction editor, 1983-85; Alfred A. Knopf (publishing house), New York, NY, editor, 1985-87; *New Yorker,* New York, NY, staff writer, art critic, and editor, 1987-92, co-editor (with Louis Menand) of back-of-book section, 1992-95, correspondent in Paris, 1995-2000. Co-curator of "High and Low" exhibition, Museum of Modern Art, 1990.

AWARDS, HONORS: Moyse traveling fellow, 1980; National Magazine Award for Essay and Criticism; George Polk Award for Magazine Reporting.

WRITINGS:

Voila CarAme, with drawings by Jack Huberman and lettering by Carman Tagle, St. Martin's Press (New York, NY), 1980.
(Editor, with Kirk Varnedoe) *Modern Art and Popular Culture: Readings in High and Low,* Abrams/Museum of Modern Art (New York, NY), 1990.
(With Jane Livingston) *Evidence, 1944-1994: Richard Avedon,* edited by Mary Shanahan, Random House (New York, NY), 1994.
Paris to the Moon, Random House (New York, NY), 2000.
(With Steven A. Nash) *Wayne Thiebaud: A Paintings Retrospective,* Thames & Hudson (New York, NY), 2000.
(With Peter Turnley) *Parisians* (photographs by Peter Turnley), Abbeville Press (New York, NY), 2000.

Contributor of numerous articles to the *New Yorker,* including over one hundred "The Talk of the Town" articles, 1987-92.

WORK IN PROGRESS: Essays on American Masters, including Thomas Eakins; and a novella.

SIDELIGHTS: Adam Gopnik possesses "the quintessential *New Yorker* sensibility," in the opinion of *Saturday Night* magazine contributor Charles Oberdorf. That opinion is shared by the *New Yorker*'s editor, Tina Brown, as well as other colleagues of Gopnik's at the publication. A frequent contributor of articles since the mid-1980s, Gopnik became the magazine's art critic under the editorship of Robert Gottlieb. With the advent of Brown, a Britisher who came over from *Vanity Fair* in 1992 amid much controversy and publicity, he was one of the relatively few staffers to survive the editorial transition. Gopnik had been reading the *New Yorker,* and apparently emulating its style, since age seven, when, he recalled for Oberdorf, he first encountered

James Thurber's *The Thurber Carnival.* Even his marriage was affected, for the better, by the nurturing presence of the *New Yorker:* when he first dated his future wife Martha Rebecca Parker, he was encouraged to find her reading that magazine as she awaited him.

The son of two academicians who moved their family from Philadelphia to Montreal in 1967—they had become infatuated with the city while attending Expo '67—Gopnik grew up with five siblings, four of whom went on to earn doctorates in one field or another. He himself graduated from high school at age fourteen—a move, he told Oberdorf in *Saturday Night,* he would not recommend for his own children. Gopnik then went to McGill University, his parents' place of employment, where all his siblings also did their undergraduate work.

An aficionado of fifteenth-century Italian art, Gopnik enrolled at New York's Institute of Fine Arts for a master's degree in that field, but did not complete his doctoral studies. What got in his way was a part-time summer job in *Gentleman's Quarterly* (*GQ*) magazine's fashion copy department, where one of his primary jobs was to concoct two-word captions for the pictured garments. ("I think my best was 'Chiaroscuro Chic,'" he told Oberdorf in *Saturday Night.*) Through a fluke, he survived an editorial turnover that sank almost the entire office: "The magazine's entire staff had been fired the previous Friday, but because I was only working Tuesdays, Wednesdays, and Thursdays, I hadn't heard. [Art] Cooper [the new editor] must have thought I'd been kept on for some special reason, so he made me fiction editor."

GQ served Gopnik as a steppingstone to an editorial post at Alfred A. Knopf publishers, which in turn brought him into informal contact with *New Yorker* editors. Gopnik had been sending short pieces to that magazine for years, and had received encouraging praise, but no sales; now, though, the editors—Gopnik's lunch companions—solicited material. What he had on hand was an article comparing baseball to Renaissance art, titled "Quattrocento Baseball"; he had originally written it as a wedding gift for a sister, but it also turned out to be just the kind of thing *New Yorker* baseball expert Roger Angell, and Angell's colleagues, loved.

When Gottlieb became chief editor of the magazine in 1987, he hired Gopnik away from Knopf—a move that was, in the opinion of another *New Yorker* editor, Chip McGrath (as reported in *Saturday Night*), "probably the only non-controversial aspect of [Gottlieb's] coming." From that point, Gopnik appeared in "The Talk of the Town" almost weekly on an anonymous basis; his art reviews, with byline, were carried every six or eight weeks.

As an editor, Gopnik was responsible for honing and trimming, among other things, the jazz columns of Whitney Balliett, who has called Gopnik "a good editor. . . . Very bright. Sharp. He spots the weaknesses," and who has also expressed admiration for Gopnik's seemingly complete knowledge of the *New Yorker*'s back-stock, according to Oberdorf in *Saturday Night.* When Brown took over the editorship in 1992, Gopnik's byline became the one found most often per issue. Brown gave this rationale to Oberdorf: "I think he's an incandescent talent . . . incisive, surprising, with a definite point of view." Gaining elbow-room for longer articles, Gopnik received attention for a piece on John James Audubon (the first in an ongoing series on great American artists), an obituary for physicist Richard Feynman, and a "splendid"—using Oberdorf's word—profile of comedian Steve Martin, among other works.

Sometimes torn in his loyalties between writing and editing, Gopnik has said that he prefers the former and, given an ultimatum, would relinquish his editing role; he hopes, however, to continue a two-sided career. As a writer of books, he contributed, in 1980, the text to a humorous series of cartoons by Jack Huberman, *Voila CarAme,* on the subject of Marie Antoinette CarAme, a figure in French gastronomical history. Later book publications have in two major cases been connected to art exhibitions.

In 1990 Gopnik joined with Museum of Modern Art painting and sculpture director Kirk Varnedoe, a friend, to curate an exhibit called "High and Low," which would draw comparisons between fine art and commercial art in the twentieth century, showing how each influenced the other. The show, which was based partly on Gopnik's graduate work, received mixed reviews, and in particular a negative assessment from the *New York Times.* It was popular with audiences, however, and drew positive notices from reviewers in Chicago and Los Angeles. According to *Wilson Library Bulletin* contributor Jean Martin, the show was undone by an absence of surprising insights, and the high-art items overshadowed the low. The book based on the exhibit catalogue was much more successful than the exhibit itself, in Martin's view. It contained nine "provocative" essays by art historians, according to Martin. There was too much "hype" in the prose, a *Publishers Weekly* contributor commented, but the reviewer called the volume "visually riveting" and asserted that it "entertains as it informs." For *Library Journal* reviewer Mary Molinaro, it was "beautifully produced. . . . A treasure for scholars of both modern art and popular culture."

Gopnik's next art book, published in 1994, was the catalogue of a retrospective exhibit of the works of photographer Richard Avedon to which Gopnik and Jane Livingston contributed essays. A *Publishers Weekly* critic noted that Gopnik defends Avedon against charges of coldness and sensationalism: "Gopnik views [Avedon's] work as part of a theatrical tradition in photography, a carefully orchestrated interpretation of late twentieth-century life."

Himself an interpreter of late twentieth-century life, Gopnik apparently relished the opportunity to write about any subject he fancied; unifying and guiding his work was what he termed, in Oberdorf 's report in *Saturday Night,* "the *New Yorker*'s credo, which is that everything in the world can be articulated; that there's nothing so recherche that one intelligent person can't explain it to another." Particularly important to him was the boundary, and the interchange, between high and low art; he sought to bridge the gap between esoteric and popular taste in an art world where the middle ground seemed to be shrinking: where almost every success seemed to be either a mass blockbuster, or the jealous possession of an elite. Gopnik saw his own role, he indicated to Oberdorf, as that of interpreter of high and low alike, for a general, receptive audience of well-educated, reasonable people such as those who read him every week.

In 1995, the *New Yorker* offered Gopnik the opportunity to serve as the publication's Paris correspondent. Gopnik had wanted to live in the French capital since his childhood; now the father of a very young child himself, he realized he was at the perfect moment to do so, before his son reached school age. So Gopnik and his family relocated, and he began writing a series of personal essays reflecting on daily life in Paris, which were published regularly in the *New Yorker*. In these pieces, he compared the experience of becoming a parent to that of learning to live in a foreign culture, as both require new routines, new languages, and new guidelines. His focus, throughout his five-year stay in Paris, was on the details of everyday life there; but through those details, he also illuminated larger issues such as the changing status of French culture and that country's obsession with paperwork. As Gopnik told Thomas Jackson in a *Publishers Weekly* interview, the essays show how the narrator "is completely bedazzled by French commonplace civilization, and then becomes absolutely exasperated by French official culture. And then at the end he realizes that the two things are insep-

arable—that the reason French commonplace civilization is so beautiful is that it exists in the shadow of French official culture. . . . There's a lesson of life there: you take things whole."

Gopnik's essays on his experiences in France were later collected into a volume titled *Paris to the Moon*. Some reviewers of the book found fault with Gopnik's focus on the small details of life. A *Publishers Weekly* reviewer stated that his " 'macro in the micro' style sometimes seems a convenient excuse to write about himself," and *Salon* contributor Chris Lehmann criticized the author's "disconcertingly tiny worldview" and his immersion in the "mundane." But the *Publishers Weekly* commentator went on to say that, when "elegantly woven together with the larger issues facing France, those personal observations beautifully convey a vision of Paris and its prideful, abstract-thinking, endlessly fascinating inhabitants."

New York Times writer Alain de Botton identified Gopnik's attention to seemingly trivial subjects as his particular genius: "The distinctive brilliance of Gopnik's essays lies in his ability to pick up a subject one would never have imagined it possible to think deeply about and then cover it in thoughts, making connections with literature, sociology and philosophy—all treated in a highly readable way. . . . He is truly able to see the whole world in a grain of sand." De Botton concluded that although *Paris to the Moon* is, on the surface, about France, by the end of the book readers have learned "about differences among societies, and so too about our own particularities." *Washington Monthly* contributor Alexandra Starr maintained that *Paris to the Moon* "provides ample ammunition for the argument that Gopnik is one of the finest bellelettrists working today," one whose "work can prove as compelling and memorable as Paris itself."

BIOGRAPHICAL/CRITICAL SOURCES:

PERIODICALS

Booklist, September 15, 2000, Brad Hooper, review of *Paris to the Moon*, p. 206.

Library Journal, February 1, 1991, p. 78; September 15, 2000, Brad Hooper, review of *Paris to the Moon,* p. 206; October 1, 2000, Kathryn Wekselman, review of *Wayne Thiebaud: A Paintings Retrospective,* p. 90.

New Republic, December 24, 1990.

New York Times, October 22, 2000, Alain de Botton, review of *Paris to the Moon.*

Publishers Weekly, November 2, 1990, p. 60; April 18, 1994, p. 52; September 25, 2000, review of *Paris*

to the Moon, p. 104; April 18, 1994, Thomas Jackson, interview with Adam Gopnik, p. 105; July 31, 2000, review of *Wayne Thiebaud: A Paintings Retrospective,* p. 87.
Saturday Night, February, 1994, pp. 18-20, 53-54.
Washington Monthly, October, 2000, Alexandra Starr, review of *Paris to the Moon,* p. 60.
Wilson Library Bulletin, February, 1991, p. 135.

OTHER

Frenchculture, http://www.info-france-usa.org/culture/ (November 29, 2000), review of *Paris to the Moon.*
Salon.com, http://www.salon.com/ (November 29, 2000), Chris Lehmann, "Paris When It Fizzles."*

* * *

GOTTLIEB, Erika (Simon)   1938-

PERSONAL: Born February 26, 1938, in Budapest, Hungary; daughter of Paul (a chemical engineer) and Elizabeth Simon (a translator; maiden name, Nagy) Simon; married Paul Gottlieb (a writer), March, 1961; children: Peter, Julie. *Education:* McGill University, B.L.S., 1961, Ph.D. (English), 1975; Concordia University, Montreal, Quebec, B.A., 1961, M.A., 1969.

ADDRESSES: Home—149 Lytton Blvd., Toronto, Ontario, Canada M4R 1L6. *E-mail*—erikagottlieb@hotmail.com.

CAREER: McGill University, Montreal, Quebec, Canada, teaching fellow, English department; Concordia University, Montreal, Canada, part-time lecturer, 1969-74; Loyola College, Montreal, Canada, lecturer, 1973-74; Dawson College, Montreal, professor, 1974-78; Seneca College, Toronto, Ontario, Canada, professor, 1980-99; ELTE University, Budapest, Hungary, visiting professor, 1992; Ryerson University, Toronto, Ontario, 2000—. Also an artist, whose oils and watercolors have been exhibited at nine solo shows in Montreal and Toronto, and represented in public and private collections in Canada, the U.S., England, Italy, Brazil, Israel, and Hungary.

AWARDS, HONORS: Arthur O. Lewis Award, Society of Utopian Studies Conference, 1988, for best paper; three-year research grant, Social Sciences and Humanities Research Council of Canada, 1994-97; publication grants, Aid to Scholarly Publications, 1979, 1991, 2000.

WRITINGS:

Lost Angels of a Ruined Paradise: Themes of Cosmic Strife in Romantic Tragedy, Sono Nis Press (Victoria, British Columbia, Canada), 1981.
The Orwell Conundrum: A Cry of Despair or Faith in the Spirit of Man?, Carleton University Press (Ottawa, Ontario, Canada), 1992.
Universe of Terror and Trial: Dystopian Fiction East and West, McGill-Queen's University Press (Montreal, Quebec, Canada), 2001.

Author of "Silence into Sound: The Concentric Circles of Joy Kogawa's Obasan," published in *Contemporary Literary Criticism,* Gale (Detroit, Michigan), 1995. Contributor to literary journals and magazines, including *Dalhousie Review, Centennial Review, The Texas Review,* and *Utopian Studies.* Has also published poems and short stories in *Kaleidoscope* and *Szivarvany,* as well as anthologies.

WORK IN PROGRESS: Autobiographical fiction. Criticism of Dystopian drama and cinema.

* * *

GREEN, Brian
See CARD, Orson Scott

* * *

GREER, Steven (Crawford)   1956-

PERSONAL: Born September 25, 1956, in Belfast, Northern Ireland; British citizen; son of James Crawford (an electrical engineering technician) and Marie (a secretary; maiden name, Seymour) Greer; married Susan Heather Haire (a nurse), August 7, 1981; children: Cara Ellen, Lucy Maeve, Alanna Hope. *Ethnicity:* "White European." *Education:* Keble College, Oxford, B.A. (with honors), 1979; London School of Economics and Political Science, London, M.Sc., 1981; Queen's University of Belfast, Ph.D., 1990. *Politics:* "Center Left." *Religion:* Agnostic. *Avocational interests:* "Family activities, listening to music, playing piano, reading, swimming."

ADDRESSES: Home—42 Kennington Ave., Bishopton, Bristol BS7 9ET, England. *Office*—Department of Law, Wills Memorial Bldg., University of Bristol,

Queens Rd., Bristol BS8 1RJ, England; fax: 0117-925-1870. *E-mail*—Steven.Greer@bris.ac.uk.

CAREER: University of Sussex, Brighton, England, lecturer in law, 1985-86; University of Bristol, Bristol, England, lecturer in law, 1986-96, reader in law, 1996—, research fellow in human rights and criminal justice, 1993-94. Occasional consultant to Amnesty International and the Council of Europe.

MEMBER: Society of Public Teachers of Law, Socio-Legal Studies Association, Association of University Teachers.

AWARDS, HONORS: Nuffield Foundation fellow, Oñati International Institute for the Sociology of Law, 1991.

WRITINGS:

(With Anthony White) *Abolishing the Diplock Courts: The Case for Restoring Jury Trial to Scheduled Offences in Northern Ireland,* Cobden Trust (London, England), 1986.
(Editor with Rod Morgan; and contributor) *The Right to Silence Debate,* Bristol Centre for Criminal Justice (Bristol, England), 1990.
Supergrasses: A Study in Anti-Terrorist Law Enforcement in Northern Ireland, Clarendon Press (New York, NY), 1995.

Also author of *The Exceptions to Articles 8 to 11 of the European Convention on Human Rights,* Council of Europe (Strasbourg, France), 1997; and *The Margin of Appreciation: Interpretation and Discretion under the European Convention on Human Rights,* Council of Europe (Strasbourg, France), 2000. Contributor to books, including *Contemporary Research on Terrorism,* edited by P. Wilkinson and A. M. Stewart, Aberdeen University Press (Aberdeen, Scotland), 1987; *Justice under Fire,* edited by A. Jennings, second edition, Pluto Press, 1990; *Preventive Detention and Security Law: A Comparative Survey,* edited by A. Harding and J. Hatchard, Nijhoff (Boston, MA), 1993; *Invading the Private? State Accountability and the New Investigative Methods in Europe,* edited by S. Field and C. Pelser, Ashgate/Dartmouth (Brookfield, VT), 1998; and *Informers,* edited by P. Bean, R. Billingsley and T. Nemitz, Willam Publishing (Cullampton, England), 2000. Contributor of more than fifty articles and reviews to academic journals and other periodicals. Member of editorial board, *Journal of Civil Liberties.*

WORK IN PROGRESS: The European Convention on Human Rights: A Critical Re-Appraisal.

SIDELIGHTS: Steven Greer told *CA:* "My primary motivation in writing is to contribute to public and academic debates about human rights, particularly those which straddle several academic disciplines, e.g. law, political theory, sociology. Although the academic community is my principal readership, I also try to write in a manner which makes my work accessible to a wider audience. The principal advice I would give aspiring writers is not to be satisfied with anything less than their best and to be ruthlessly self-critical in order to reach that goal."

BIOGRAPHICAL/CRITICAL SOURCES:

PERIODICALS

Irish Independent, June 10, 1995.
Irish Times, June 24, 1995.
Times Higher Education Supplement, March 1, 1996.
Times Literary Supplement, September 29, 1995.

*　　*　　*

GRILLO, Ralph David   1940-

PERSONAL: Born April 23, 1940, in Watford, England; son of Ralph (a tradesperson) and Muriel May (Harries) Grillo; married Bronacha Frances Ryan, August 7, 1968; children: Claudia Serafina, Philippa Frances, Ioan Benedict. *Education:* King's College, Cambridge, B.A., 1963, Ph.D., 1968. *Politics:* Green Party. *Religion:* "None." *Avocational interests:* Films, cricket, politics.

ADDRESSES: Home—21 Bradford Rd., Lewes, Sussex, England. *Office*—School of African and Asian Studies, University of Sussex, Falmer, Brighton BN1 9SJ, England; fax: 01273-623572. *E-mail*—r.d.grillo@sussex.ac.uk.

CAREER: Queen's University, Belfast, Northern Ireland, assistant lecturer, 1967-69, lecturer in social anthropology, 1969-70; University of Sussex, Brighton, Sussex, England, lecturer in social anthropology, 1970-78, reader, 1978-88, professor, 1988—.

MEMBER: Association of Social Anthropologists of United Kingdom (honorary secretary, 1978-82), Royal Anthropological Institute.

WRITINGS:

African Railwaymen: Solidarity and Opposition in an African Labour Force, Cambridge University Press (Cambridge, England), 1973.

Race, Class, and Militancy: An African Trade Union, 1939-1965, Chandler Publishing (New York, NY), 1974.

(Editor)

"Nation" and "State" in Europe: Anthropological Perspectives, Academic Press (London, England), 1980.

Ideologies and Institutions in Urban France: The Representation of Immigrants, Cambridge University Press, 1985.

(Editor with Alan Rew) *Social Anthropology and Development Policy* (ASA Monographs 25), Routledge (London, England), 1985.

Ideologies and Institutions in Urban France: The Representation of Immigrants, Cambridge University Press (Cambridge, England), 1985.

Dominant Languages, Cambridge University Press (Cambridge, England), 1989.

(Editor) *Social Anthropology and the Politics of Language,* Routledge (London, England), 1989.

(Editor with Roderick Stirrat) *Discourses of Development: Anthropological Perspectives,* Berg (Oxford), 1997.

Pluralism and the Politics of Difference: State, Culture, and Ethnicity in Comparative Perspective, Clarendon Press (Oxford), 1998.

Contributor to *Africa, Journal of the Royal Anthropological Institute,* and other journals.

SIDELIGHTS: Ralph David Grillo has done fieldwork in East Africa from 1964 to 1965, in the Republic of Ireland, and in France from 1975 to 1976.

BIOGRAPHICAL/CRITICAL SOURCES:

PERIODICALS

Choice, June, 1974, p. 639; December, 1985, p. 640; October, 1990, p. 301.

*   *   *

GYATSO, Tenzin 1935-
(Dalai Lama XIV)

PERSONAL: Born Lhamo Thondup, July 6, 1935, in Taktser, Tibet; given the name Jetsun Jampel Ngawang

Dalai Lama XIV

Losang Yeshi Tenzin Gyatso Sisum Wang-gyur Tsungpa Mepai De Pel Sangpo when enthroned as Dalai Llama, 1940; son of Chokyong (a farmer) and Diki (a farmer) Tsering. *Education:* Studied under Buddhist monks at the monasteries of Sera, Drepung, and Gaden in Tibet; earned Geshe Lharampa degree (Master of Metaphysics; Tibetan degree equivalent to Ph.D. in Buddhist philosophy), 1959. *Religion:* Buddhist. *Avocational interests:* Gardening, repairing machines.

ADDRESSES: Home—Thekchen Choeling, Mcleod Ganj 176219, Dharamsala, Himahal Pradesh, India.

CAREER: Enthroned as fourteenth Dalai Lama of Tibet in Lhasa, 1940; named temporal ruler of Tibet, 1950; worked in China and Tibet to end Chinese domination of Tibet, 1950-59; escaped to India and began self-imposed exile, 1959; established Tibetan government-in-exile in Dharamsala, India; has traveled widely in Asia, Europe, and the United States. Held ceremonial political posts in China, including honorary chairman, Chinese Buddhist Association, 1953-59; delegate to National People's Congress, 1954-59; and chairman, Preparatory Committee for the Autonomous Region of Tibet, 1955-59.

AWARDS, HONORS: Ramon Magsaysay Award for Community Leadership, 1959; Admiral Richard E. Byrd Memorial Award, International Rescue Committee, 1959; Lincoln Award, Research Institute of America, 1960; special medal, Asian Buddhist Council for Peace, 1979; Liberty Torch, Friends of Tibet, 1979; Albert Schweitzer Humanitarian Award, 1987; Dr. Leopold Lucas Award (West Germany), 1988; Raoul Wallenberg Congressional Human Rights Award, Congressional Human Rights Foundation, 1989; citation for perseverance in times of adversity, World Management Council, 1989; Nobel Peace Prize, 1989; Prix de la Memoire (Prize of Memory), Foundation Danielle Mitterrand, 1989; Advancing Human Liberty Award, Freedom House, 1991; Distinguished Peace Leadership Award, Nuclear Age Peace Foundation, 1991; United Earth Prize, 1991; Wheel of Life Award, Temple of Understanding, 1991; Peace and Unity awards, National Peace Conference, 1991; Shiromani Award, 1992; Plakett Award, Norwegian Refugee Council; honorary degrees from universities and honorary citizenships in several countries.

WRITINGS:

The International Position of Tibet, 1959.

My Land and My People (autobiography), McGraw-Hill (New York, NY), 1962, published with new introduction and foreword by Melissa Mathison Ford, Warner (New York, NY), 1997.

An Introduction to Buddhism, Tibet House (New Delhi, India), 1965.

The Opening of the Wisdom-Eye and the History of the Advancement of the Buddhadharma in Tibet, Social Science Association Press of Thailand (Bangkok, Thailand), 1968.

Happiness, Karma, and Mind, Tibet Society (Bloomington, IN), 1969.

The Key to Madhyamika, translated by Gonsar Tuiku and Gavin Kilty, Library of Tibetan Works and Archives (Dharamsala, India), 1974.

The Buddhism of Tibet and the Key to the Middle Way, translated by Jeffrey Hopkins and Lati Rinpoche, Harper (New York, NY), 1975.

The Sadhana of the Inseparability of the Spiritual Master and Avalokiteshvara: A Source of All Powerful Attainments; A Mahayana Method for Accomplishment, translated by Sherpa Tulku, Library of Tibetan Works and Archives (Dharamsala, India), 1975.

Universal Responsibility and the Good Heart: The Message of His Holiness the XIV Dalai Lama of Tibet on His First Visit to the West in 1973, Library of Tibetan Works and Archives (Dharamsala, India), 1976.

Teachings of His Holiness the Dalai Lama, edited and photographed by Marcia Keegan, Clear Light Publications (New York, NY), 1981.

Four Essential Buddhist Commentaries (in English and Tibetan), Library of Tibetan Works and Archives (Dharamsala, India), 1982.

The Collected Statements, Articles, and Interviews of His Holiness the Dalai Lama, Information Office of His Holiness the Dalai Lama (Dharamsala, India), 1982.

Advice from Buddha Shakyamuni: An Abridged Exposition of the Bikkshu's Precepts, translated by Jeremy Russell and Tsepak Rigzin, Library of Tibetan Works and Archives, 1982.

Kindness, Clarity, and Insight, translated by Jeffrey Hopkins, edited by Hopkins and Elizabeth Napper, Snow Lion Publications (Ithaca, NY), 1984.

(With others) *Emerging Consciousness for a New Humankind: Asian Interreligious Concern* (conference papers), Asian Trading Corp. (Bangalore, India), 1985.

Opening the Eye of New Awareness, translated by Donald S. Lopez, Jr. and Jeffrey Hopkins, Wisdom Publications (San Diego, CA), 1985, revised edition, Wisdom (Boston, MA), 1999.

The Kalachakra Tantra: Rite of Initiation for the Stage of Generation: A Commentary on the Text of Kay-drup-ge-lek-bel-sang-bo, translated, edited, and annotated by Jeffrey Hopkins, Wisdom Publications (San Diego, CA), 1985.

Transcendent Wisdom: A Commentary on the Ninth Chapter of Shantideva's Guide to the Bodhisattva Way of Life, translated, edited, and annotated by B. Alan Wallace, Snow Lion Publications (Ithaca, NY), 1988.

The Bodhgaya Interviews: His Holiness the Dalai Lama, edited by Jose Ignacio Cabezon, Snow Lion Publications (Ithaca, NY), 1988.

The Dalai Lama at Harvard: Lectures on the Buddhist Path to Peace, translated and edited by Jeffrey Hopkins, Snow Lion Publications (Ithaca, NY), 1988.

The Union of Bliss and Emptiness: A Commentary on the Lama Choepa Guru Yoga Practice, translated by Thupten Jinpa, Snow Lion Publications (Ithaca, NY), 1988.

Tibet, China, and the World (interviews), Narthang Publications (Dharamsala, India), 1989.

Oceans of Wisdom: Guidelines for Living, introduction by Richard Gere, photographs by Marcia Keegan, Clear Light Publishing, 1989.

Freedom in Exile: The Autobiography of the Dalai Lama, HarperCollins (New York, NY), 1990.

The Meaning of Life, translated by Jeffrey Hopkins, Snow Lion Publications (Ithaca, NY), 1990.

My Tibet, photographs and introduction by Galen Rowell, University of California Press (Berkeley, CA), 1990.

(With Thupten Jinpa) *The World of Tibetan Buddhism: An Overview of Its Philosophy and Practice,* Wisdom Publications (Boston, MA), 1995.

(With others) *MindScience: An East-West Dialogue,* edited by Daniel Goleman and Robert A. F. Thurman, Wisdom Publications (Boston, MA), 1991.

Cultivating a Daily Meditation, Library of Tibetan Works and Archives (Dharamsala, India), 1991.

Violence and Compassion, Doubleday (New York, NY), 1995.

The Power of Compassion, Thorsons (London, England), 1995.

Essential Teachings: His Holiness the Dalai Lama, North Atlantic Books (Berkeley, CA), 1995.

The Path to Enlightenment, edited by Glenn H. Mullin, Snow Lion Publications (Ithaca, NY), 1995.

Beyond Dogma: Dialogues & Discourses, North Atlantic Books (Berkeley, CA), 1996.

The Good Heart: A Buddhist Perspective on the Teachings of Jesus, Wisdom Publications (Boston, MA), 1996.

The Joy of Living and Dying in Peace: Core Teachings of Tibetan Buddhism, Harper (San Francisco, CA), 1997.

(With Alexander Berzin) *The Gelug/Kagyu Tradition of Mahamudra,* Snow Lion Publications (Ithaca, NY), 1997.

Awakening the Mind, Lightening the Heart, Thorsons (London, England), 1997.

The Way to Freedom, Thorsons (London, England), 1997.

The Heart of Compassion: A Dalai Lama Reader, Full Circle (Delhi, India), 1997.

The Four Noble Truths, Thorsons (London, England), 1998.

The Art of Happiness: A Handbook for Living, Riverhead (New York, NY), 1998.

Spiritual Advice for Buddhists and Christians, Martin Rowe, 1998.

The Dalai Lama's Book of Wisdom, Thorsons (London, England), 1999.

The Heart of the Buddha's Path, Thorsons (London, England), 1999.

(With Anne Benson and Fabien Ouaki) *Imagine All the People: A Conversation with the Dalai Lama on Money, Politics, and Life As It Could Be,* Wisdom (Boston, MA), 1999.

The Transformed Mind: Reflections on Truth, Love, and Happiness, Viking (New Delhi, India), 1999.

The Path to Tranquility: Daily Wisdom, Viking (New York, NY), 1999.

Ethics for the New Millennium, Riverhead (New York, NY), 2000.

Stages of Meditation, Snow Lion Publications (Ithaca, NY), 2000.

A Simple Path: Basic Buddhist Teachings by His Holiness the Dalai Lama, Thorsons (London, England), 2000.

(With Jigme Khyentse Rinpoche) *Buddha Heart, Buddha Mind: Living the Four Noble Truths,* translated from the French by Robert R. Barr, Crossroad, 2000.

Transforming the Mind: Teachings on Generating Compassion, Thorsons (London, England), 2000, revised as *The Dalai Lama's Book of Transformation,* 2000.

(With Ricard Matthieu) *The Spirit of Tibet: The Life and World of Khyentse Rinpoche, Spiritual Teacher,* Aperture (New York, NY), 2001.

Live in a Better Way: Reflections on Truth, Love, and Happiness, Viking (New York, NY), 2001.

Margaret Gee, compiler, *Words of Wisdom: Selected Quotes from His Holiness the Dalai Lama,* Andrews McMeel (Kansas City, MO), 2001.

Dzogchen: The Heart Essence of the Great Perfection, translated by Thupten Jinpa and Richard Barron, Snow Lion Publications (Ithaca, NY), 2001.

An Open Heart: Practicing Compassion in Everyday Life, afterword by Khyongla Rato and Richard Gere, Little, Brown (Boston, MA), 2001.

Also author of *A Human Approach to World Peace,* Wisdom Publications (Boston, MA), 1984; *Path to Bliss,* edited by Geshe Thubten Jinpa and Christine Cox, Snow Lion Publications (Ithaca, NY); *Kalachakra: Rite of Initiation,* with Jeffrey Hopkins, Snow Lion Publications; *Short Essays of Buddhist Thought and Practice,* Tibet House (New Delhi, India); and *The Buddha Nature: Death and Eternal Soul in Buddhism.* Contributor to books, including *A Prayer of Words of Truth by His Holiness the Dalai Lama and the Tibetan National Anthem,* 1975; *Living Buddhism* by Andrew Powell, Harmony Books; *Essence of Refined Gold,* by Sonam Gyatso, Dalai Lama III, edited by Glenn H. Mullin, Gabriel/Snow Lion Publications, 1982; and *The Spirit's Terrain: Creativity, Activism, and Transformation,* by Christopher Childs, Beacon Press (Boston, MA), 1998.

SIDELIGHTS: Tenzin Gyatso, the fourteenth Dalai Lama, is the religious and temporal leader of Tibet. A recipient of the Nobel Peace Prize, the Dalai Lama has been deeply involved in political, humanitarian, and spiritual issues, both in his homeland of Tibet and around the world, since the mid-twentieth century, and has struggled to maintain the independent identity of Tibet since its occupation by communist China in 1950. While making public appearances and statements to encourage other countries to recognize Tibet's independence, he has also served as the leader of Tibetan Buddhism, a religion claiming adherents all over the world. It is his role as a spiritual leader that has made the Dalai Lama so familiar to Western audiences. An engaging speaker and writer, he has published numerous books that explain Tibetan Buddhist precepts and practices. His persistent and yet nonviolent attempts to end China's domination of Tibet—inspired by Buddhist philosophy—were recognized in 1989 with the Nobel Prize. The awarding body, as quoted in *Newsweek,* cited the Dalai Lama for promoting "peaceful solutions based upon tolerance and mutual respect in order to preserve the historical and cultural heritage of his people." In *Library Journal,* Pam Kingsbury noted that the Dalai Lama's message "is timeless, hopeful, and inclusive."

Gyatso was born Lhamo Thondup to a modest farming family in northeast Tibet in 1935. At the age of two, his life was dramatically altered when two monks arrived at his home in their search for the reincarnated Dalai Lama. Tibetan tradition holds that the religious and political ruler is the reincarnation of each of his predecessors, a spiritual rather than hereditary line that had its origins in the seventeenth century. When the thirteenth Dalai Lama died in 1933, a search was begun for his successor. Interpretations of several signs, including cloud formations and the visions of a high-ranking monk, led the searchers to the home of the young Lhamo. The child was instantly attracted to the strangers, who were traveling disguised as merchants. As well as fulfilling all the earlier visions, the boy possessed the necessary physical characteristics and successfully distinguished objects belonging to the former Dalai Lama from replicas. When it was officially decided that Lhamo was the Dalai Lama, he was taken to a Buddhist monastery to receive preparation for his position.

At the age of five, Gyatso was named Dalai Lama and installed at the one-thousand-room Potala Palace in the Tibetan capital of Lhasa. In his 1990 autobiography, *Freedom in Exile,* the Dalai Lama describes his early days there. Frequently isolated from his family and other children his age, he played games with the sweepers of the palace, and established friendships with older monks. As well as pursuing his religious studies, the young Dalai Lama was fascinated with science and technology, an interest that led to one memorable incident in which, at the age of thirteen, he "borrowed" one of the palace's automobile—one of the four such vehicles in Tibet—to take a joyride.

Freedom in Exile also discusses the Dalai Lama's early assumption of responsibility and the events of the Chinese invasion in late 1949. In that year Chinese Communist forces, claiming a right to the lands of Tibet, invaded the nation and embarked on a violent crusade to destroy Tibet's identity and culture. Particularly targeted were the country's prominent religious institutions, members of which were subjected to torture and massacres, according to reports cited by the Dalai Lama in his autobiography. Although still a student in his teens at the time of the occupation, the Dalai Lama, on the advice of the royal oracle, was invested with the full political powers of his office, becoming king of Tibet. In this capacity, he immediately began what would become his lifelong struggle: to bring a peaceful solution to the troubles in his homeland.

While he initially attempted to work closely with Chinese officials in Beijing, by 1959 a military confrontation between Chinese soldiers and thousands of Tibetan protestors at the Dalai Lama's summer palace in Tibet forced the leader to realize that he could help his country more by working in opposition to the Chinese. In a daring escape, he was smuggled out through the crowd disguised as a soldier. With a small group of family members and advisers, he set out on horseback across the Himalayan mountains to a self-imposed exile in India. There he established a Tibetan government-in-exile, going on to create dozens of refugee communities for Tibetans fleeing Chinese rule. From this base, the Dalai Lama has attempted to bring attention to the plight of Tibet through public appearances and lectures around the world, as well as through his many writings. In an interview with Daniel Goleman in the *New York Times Book Review,* the Dalai Lama stated that the main purpose of writing *Freedom in Exile* was "to counter Chinese claims and misinformation they spread about Tibet's history, culture and religion, and to tell the truth about Tibetan independence." "The Dalai Lama uses his book," noted Chicago *Tribune Books* reviewer John Maxwell Hamilton, "to elaborate a Five-Point Peace Plan, which calls on Beijing to demilitarize the entire Tibetan plateau, end the inflow of Chinese into his country and respect Tibetans' human rights and democratic freedoms."

Critics praised *Freedom in Exile* for both its inside look at the life of the religious and political leader and its discussion of the modern history of Tibet. "Anyone wanting to understand Tibet today will do well to read this priest-king's tale of coping with the ancient and modern worlds that have shaped him," declared Hamilton. Commenting on the personal side of the book, Caroline Moorehead in her *New Statesman & Society* assessment declared, "Part of the charm of *Freedom in Exile* lies in its very ordinariness, the willingness of the author to offer up some of the minutiae of an extraordinary life without embarrassment." *Los Angeles Times Book Review* contributor Paul Jordan-Smith observed that the force behind the book, which he called "a simple and powerful autobiography," is that "instead of explicit teaching, it offers a simple and heartfelt description of external events." Nonetheless, critics recognized the ultimate motivation of the Dalai Lama's book. "The Dalai Lama's work is a political one," stated Rembert G. Weakland in the *New York Times Book Review.* "This book is a call for freedom."

In the 1990s and into the twenty-first century, the Dalai Lama has published numerous books on the everyday, practical applications of Tibetan Buddhism. He is particularly expansive on happiness and compassion, and he has been praised for seeking common ground between Buddhism and other faiths, including Christianity. According to Christine C. Menefee in *School Library Journal,* the Dalai Lama's "disarmingly conversational style . . . engages readers." Indeed, many of the Dalai Lama's books are based on talks he has given at religious seminars in India, England, and the United States. In *Buddha Heart, Buddha Mind: Living the Four Noble Truths,* for example, eight speeches given by His Holiness in Savoie, France in 1997 are transcribed, providing what a *Publishers Weekly* contributor described as containing "considerable, conplex depth that transcends the implied simplicity of the subtitle . . . by addressing suffering and its cessadion." *Booklist* correspondent Donna Seaman suggested that he has become "one of the world's most important spiritual leaders" on the strength of "his wonderfully lucid writings." Seaman commended the Dalai Lama for filling his books with "ponderable wisdom."

BIOGRAPHICAL/CRITICAL SOURCES:

BOOKS

Chopra, P. N., *Ocean of Wisdom: Life of Dalai Lama,* Chronica Botanica India, 1988.
Dalai Lama, *My Land and My People,* McGraw-Hill (New York, NY), 1962.
Dalai Lama, *Freedom in Exile: The Autobiography of the Dalai Lama,* HarperCollins (New York, NY), 1990.

Gibb, Christopher, *The Dalai Lama: The Leader of the Exiled People of Tibet and Tireless Worker for World Peace,* Gareth Stevens, 1990.
Hicks, R., *Great Ocean: Biography of His Holiness Dalai Lama,* Chronica Botanica India, 1984.
Levenson, Claude B., *The Dalai Lama: A Biography,* Unwin Hyman (London, England), 1988.

PERIODICALS

Booklist, December 15, 1995, Donna Seaman, review of *Violence and Compassion,* p. 669.
Library Journal, April 15, 2000, Mark Woodhouse, review of *Transforming the Mind: Teachings on Generating Compassion,* p. 96; August, 2000, Pam Kingsbury, review of *Ethics for the New Millennium,* p. 183; October 1, 2000, Graham Christian, review of *Stages of Meditation,* p. 110.
Los Angeles Times Book Review, September 30, 1990, p. 4.
New Statesman & Society, September 21, 1990, Caroline Moorehead, review of *Freedom and Exile,* p. 44.
Newsweek, October 1, 1990, p. 69.
New York Times Book Review, September 30, 1990, pp. 3, 49.
Omni, December, 1981, James Reston Jr., "Religion in the Twenty-first Century" (interview), p. 80.
Publishers Weekly, February 9, 1998, review of *The Spirit's Terrain,* p. 87; May 29, 2000, review of *Transforming the Mind,* p. 78; September 11, 2000, review of *A Simple Path: Basic Buddhist Teachings by His Holiness the Dalai Lama,* p. 87; October 30, 2000, review of *Buddha Heart, Buddha Mind,* p. 69; January 29, 2001, review of *Live in a Better Way,* p. 85; March 12, 2001, review of *Dzogchen,* p. 79.
School Library Journal, March, 2000, Christine C. Menefee, review of *Ethics for the New Millennium,* p. 265.
Time International, July 17, 2000, "The Dalai Lama: 'It's Time to Prepare New Leaders,' " p. 22.
Tribune Books (Chicago), September 23, 1990, p. 6.
Utne Reader, January-February, 1997, Andrea Martin, review of *The Good Heart: A Buddhist Perspective on the Teachings of Jesus,* p. 97.
Washington Post Book World, October 21, 1990, pp. 3-4.
Whole Earth Review, fall, 1995, M. J. Pramik, review of *My Tibet,* p. 79.

OTHER

Thorsons Publishers Web site, http://www.thorsons. com/ (April 20, 2001).*

H

HADDIX, Margaret Peterson 1964-

PERSONAL: Born April 9, 1964, in Washington Court House, OH; daughter of John Albert (a farmer) and Marilee Grace (a nurse; maiden name, Greshel) Peterson; married Doug Haddix (a newspaper editor), October 3, 1987; children: Meredith, Connor. *Education:* Miami University, B.A. (summa cum laude), 1986. *Religion:* Presbyterian. *Avocational interests:* Travel.

ADDRESSES: Agent—Tracey Adams, McIntoch & Otis, 353 Lexington Ave., New York, NY 10016.

CAREER: Fort Wayne Journal-Gazette, Fort Wayne, IN, copy editor, 1986-87; *Indianapolis News,* Indianapolis, IN, reporter, 1987-91; Danville Area Community College, Danville, IL, adjunct faculty, 1991-93; freelance writer, 1991-94.

MEMBER: Society of Children's Book Writers and Illustrators, Phi Beta Kappa.

AWARDS, HONORS: Honorable mention, *Seventeen* magazine fiction contest, 1983; fiction contest award, National Society of Arts and Letters, 1988; *American Bestseller* Pick of the Lists selection, Mystery Writers of America's Edgar Allan Poe award nomination, Young Adult Library Services Association (YALSA) Quick Pick for Reluctant Young Adult Readers and Best Book for Young Adults designations, listed as a Notable Children's Trade Books in the Field of Social Studies, National Council for Social Studies/Children's Book Council, Sequoyah Young Adult Book Award, Black-Eyed Susan Award, all 1996-97, and Arizona Young Readers' Award, 1998, all for *Running out of Time;* Children's Book Award (older reader category), International Reading Association, and YALSA Quick Pick for Reluctant Young Adult Readers and Best Book for Young Adults designations, all 1997, Black-Eyed Susan Award, 1998-99, Nebraska Golden Sower Award, 2000, all for *Don't You Dare Read This, Mrs. Dunphrey;* YALSA Best Books for Young Adults and *American Bookseller* Pick of the Lists, both for *Leaving Fishers;* YALSA Top Ten Best Books for Young Adults and Quick Picks Top Ten designations, both 2000, California Young Readers' Medal, Minnesota Maud Hart Lovelace Award, and Nevada Young Readers' Award, all 2001, all for *Among the Hidden; American Bookseller* Pick of the Lists, American Library Association Best Book for Young Adults, American Library Association Quick Pick for Reluctant Young Adult Readers, and International Reading Association Young Adults' Choices List, 2001, all for *Just Ella; American Bookseller* Pick of the Lists, for *Turnabout, The Girl with 500 Middle Names,* and *Among the Imposters;* Junior Library Guild selection, for *Takeoffs and Landings.*

WRITINGS:

YOUNG ADULT FICTION

Running out of Time, Simon & Schuster (New York, NY), 1995.
Don't You Dare Read This, Mrs. Dunphrey, Simon & Schuster (New York, NY), 1996.
Leaving Fishers, Simon & Schuster (New York, NY), 1997.
Among the Hidden ("Among the Hidden" series), Simon & Schuster (New York, NY), 1998.
Just Ella, Simon & Schuster (New York, NY), 1999.
Turnabout, Simon & Schuster (New York, NY), 2000.
The Girl with 500 Middle Names, Simon & Schuster (New York, NY), 2001.

Takeoffs and Landings, Simon & Schuster (New York, NY), 2001.

Among the Imposters ("Among the Hidden" series), Simon & Schuster (New York, NY), 2001.

Contributor of short stories to anthologies, including *Indiannual* and *The Luxury of Tears,* National Society of Arts and Letters, 1989; *On the Edge,* Simon & Schuster (New York, NY), 2000; and *I Believe in Water,* HarperCollins (New York, NY), 2000.

ADAPTATIONS: Just Ella, Leaving Fishers, Don't You Dare Read This, Mrs. Dunphrey, and *Among the Hidden* have all been adapted for audiocassette.

WORK IN PROGRESS: Anya's Wig, a middle-grades novel; and *Among the Betrayed* and *Among the Barons,* further books in the "Among the Hidden" series.

SIDELIGHTS: Award-winning author Margaret Peterson Haddix has written a number of highly praised novels for young adults and juvenile readers that deal with topics from religious cults and futuristic dystopias to modern-day science fiction and reality-based fiction. Haddix's 1995 debut novel, *Running out of Time,* a time-slip story with a twist, has become something of a classic of the form, and was adopted for use in middle school classrooms around the United States. Other novels, both fanciful and realistic, from the pen of Haddix include *Don't You Dare Read This, Mrs. Dunphrey, Leaving Fishers, Among the Hidden, Just Ella, Turnabout, The Girl with 500 Middle Names, Takeoffs and Landings,* and *Among the Imposters.* A former journalist-turned-author, Haddix stumbled into writing for young readers. "In fact," noted a contributor to the *Akron Beacon Journal* in an interview with Haddix, the author "was trying to 'get discovered' as a short-story writer when she fell into the world of children's literature, much as Alice tumbled down the rabbit hole." With the popularity of *Running out of Time,* and with several awards to her credit, Haddix decided that this particular rabbit hole was one worth exploring.

Haddix was born in Washington Court House, Ohio, in 1964, the daughter of a farming father and a mother who worked as a nurse. "I grew up on lots of stories," Haddix once commented, "both from books and in my family. My father in particular was always telling tales to my brothers and sister and me—about one of our ancestors who was kidnaped, about some friends who survived lying on a railroad bridge while a train went over the top of them, about the kid who brought possum meat to the school cafeteria when my father was a boy. So I always thought that becoming a storyteller would

be the grandest thing in the world. But I didn't want to just tell stories. I wanted to write them down."

Through adolescence and on into high school, Haddix maintained her love of both reading and writing. "For a long time, I tried to write two different kinds of stories: real and imaginary," she once said. When the time came for college, Haddix chose Miami University, where she earned a B.A. summa cum laude with both university honors and honors in English. "In college I majored in both journalism and creative writing (and history, just because I liked it). After college, I got jobs at newspapers, first as a copy editor in Fort Wayne, then as a reporter in Indianapolis. It was a lot of fun, especially getting to meet and talk to people from all walks of life, from homeless women to congressmen."

All the time, on weekends and in the evenings, she continued to stretch her writing repertoire, working on short stories. "But this was frustrating," Haddix once observed, "because there was never enough time. So, in 1991, when my husband got a new job in Danville, Illinois, I took a radical step: I quit newspapers. I took a series of temporary and part-time jobs, such as teaching at a community college, and used the extra time to write."

The first large-story idea to percolate in Haddix's imagination was the seed of her first published book, *Running out of Time.* "I'd gotten the idea when I was doing a newspaper story about a restored historical village," Haddix recalled. "I kept wondering what it would be like if there was a historical village where all the tourists were hidden and the kids, at least, didn't know what year it really was." In the event, her first manuscript was quickly accepted by an editor at Simon and Schuster, and Haddix was on her way as a juvenile author.

In *Running out of Time,* thirteen-year-old Jessie Keyser lives with her family in a frontier village in 1840, but when the town's children are stricken with diphtheria, Jessie's mother reveals that it is actually the 1990s, and the village is a tourist exhibit and scientific experiment gone awry. Jessie is, in fact, sent to the outside world to get help; her mother is fearful that the one-time idealistic planners of this "ideal" village may have become evil. In fact, Jessie's mother is right: the idealism of Mr. Clifton, who started the community a dozen years before, has been subverted by researchers who have now introduced an outbreak of diphtheria in order to see what will happen to patients without modern medical care. Out in the real world of the 1990s, Jessie comes into contact with modernity with a vengeance: she has to deal with phones, traffic, flush toilets, and the seductions of fast food.

Reviewers were generally positive in their reception of this first novel. Writing in *School Library Journal,* Lisa Dennis dubbed the book "absorbing" and "gripping," further noting that the "action moves swiftly, with plenty of suspense" as Jessie attempts to make her way through the modern world, looking for help for her family and friends. "The suspense and the cataloguing of differences as they appear to Jessie are the best parts," wrote Mary Harris Veeder in a *Booklist* review of the novel. *Voice of Youth Advocates* critic Ann Welton, however, complained that Jessie's adjustment to the drastic shift in time "is far too smooth, resulting in a lack of narrative tension." Welton did, however, go on to point out that the book had "potential as a model for writing assignments and provides an interesting perspective on American history." In his review of *Running out of Time, Bulletin of the Center for Children's Books* critic Roger Sutton also felt that Jessie's "disorientation upon discovering the modern world would surely have been more pronounced than it seems," but concluded that "many kids . . . will be gripped by the concept, and the book, readable throughout, [is] exciting in spots." Dennis concluded in *School Library Journal* that young readers "will look forward to more stories from this intriguing new author." They did not have long to wait.

"I wrote my second book, *Don't You Dare Read This, Mrs. Dunphrey,* when I was eight months pregnant with my first child, and feeling a little bored," Haddix once explained. "The story should have been very difficult to write, because I had a happy childhood and wonderful parents, and should have had nothing in common with the main character—tough-talking, big-haired Tish, whose parents abandoned her. But I'd once worked on a newspaper series where I talked to more than a dozen abused and neglected kids, and their stories haunted me for years. So writing *Don't You Dare* was almost like an exorcism—I did feel possessed by Tish's spirit. Actually, in a way, everything I've written has felt like that, like being possessed. When I'm writing, I feel like I *must* write."

Critics noted that Haddix relies on a much more familiar set-up for her second novel, placing Tish Bonner, the main character in *Don't You Dare Read This, Mrs. Dunphrey,* in an English class where she is required to keep a journal, giving the reader an insiders' view of her troubles. Since Tish has no one but her journal to confide in as she deals with an absent father, a depressed mother unable to care for her or her younger

brother, and a part-time job where the manager subjects her to sexual harassment, "the tone here shifts only in terms of varying shades of anger," a reviewer observed in *Publishers Weekly.* The same writer further described this second book as a "tough-edged if familiar story of a beleaguered high school girl" who confides all her difficulties in her diary. The title of the book refers to the teacher who has promised to only read finished work inspired by her students' journal entries, and not the individual entries themselves. Tish's predicament goes from bad to worse when she has to shoplift from a local store to feed herself and her brother Matthew, and then she faces eviction from her home, as well. Finally Tish turns over the entire journal to her sensitive teacher who helps the young girl find help.

"Tish's journal entries have an authentic ring in phrasing and tone and will keep readers involved," Carol Schene claimed in *School Library Journal.* The result, according to Schene is a "brief, serious look at a young person who is isolated and faced with some seemingly overwhelming problems." Jean Franklin, writing in *Booklist,* called the book "a brief, gritty documentary novel . . . a natural for reluctant readers." Jamie S. Hansen, writing in *Voice of Youth Advocates,* echoed this sentiment: "The breezy style, short diary-entry format, and melodramatic subject matter will ensure popularity for this title, particularly with reluctant readers."

After becoming the mother of two children, Meredith and Connor, Haddix admitted "amuse[ment] that I felt like I didn't have enough time to write before they were born. It's much harder now. . . . And a lot of times when I'm doing the ordinary things that go along with having two kids, a husband, and a house . . . I'm listening to a voice in my head insisting, 'Write about me!' or suggesting things like, 'What if Dorry's dad confronts her before she goes to the mall?' Now, I'll be the first to admit that it sounds a little weird to have voices talking in my head, but I wouldn't have it any other way."

While Haddix's novels for young adults share little in terms of plot, setting, or theme, critics have commended the author's ability to involve even reluctant readers in the lives of her characters. Thus with her third novel, Haddix moved to yet new themes and settings—this time dealing with religious cults and one youngster's attempts at extricating herself from such a group. In *Leaving Fishers,* Haddix tells the story of young Dorry, whose life has been uprooted both geographically and economically. Suffering from diminished circumstances, Dorry is also upset that she has not been able to make friends at her new school. When Angela, one of several attractive and friendly kids who congregate together, asks her to join her friends at lunch, Dorry is eager to blend in. Her enthusiasm is not much diminished when she learns that these students are all part of a religious group called the Fishers of Men. She is introduced to their parties and retreats, and soon these pizza parties turn into prayer groups. Dorry becomes caught up in the zeal at such retreats and becomes a member of the Fishers. Increasingly, Dorry finds all her time taken up with the cult's activities, and begins to fear that she will go to hell if she does not do everything she is told to do by Angela and her assortment of fellow adherents. Neglecting family and school, Dorry is soon caught in the grips of the Fishers. Only when she discovers herself terrifying young babysitting charges with threats of hell if they do not convert does Dorry finally see what has been happening to her. She shakes off the bonds of the cult, unlike other young practitioners.

"Haddix gives a fine portrayal of a teenager's descent into a cult," wrote *Booklist*'s Ilene Cooper, who further noted that the book was a "good read and an informative one for young people who are constantly bombarded with challenges to their beliefs." Reviewing the same title in *Voice of Youth Advocates,* Beverly Youree felt *Leaving Fishers* "is a definite page-turner, full of excitement and pathos." Youree concluded that "Dorry and readers learn that the world is neither black nor white, good nor bad, but shades of gray." A reviewer for *Kirkus Reviews* called the novel "a chilling portrait of an insecure teenager gradually relinquishing her autonomy to a religious cult," and a "wholly convincing picture of the slow, insidious stages by which Dorry is 'caught'." The same reviewer went on to note that Haddix's novel, "[t]ightly written, with well-drawn characters," is "in no way anti-religious." In the end, indeed, Dorry does not turn against religion, but against the sort of mind-numbing cult that seeks total domination over its believers. She continues her spiritual quest, but on her own terms. "Haddix's even-handed portrayal of the rewards of Christian fellowship and the dangers of a legalistic or black-and-white approach to religion" are, according to a reviewer for *Publishers Weekly,* the "book's greatest strength[s]."

Haddix next turned her hand to a future dystopia à la *1984* or *Brave New World.* With *Among the Hidden,* the novelist tells the story of a future totalitarian regime that strictly observes a two-children-only policy. Luke, twelve, is the third child of a farming family and is thus illegal. When the government starts to cut the woods around the family home to make way for new housing, Luke must hide from view, looking at the world outside

through a small air vent in the attic. From this vantage point, he one day sees a shadowy figure in a nearby house and begins to suspect that this might be another hidden person like himself. One day he breaks into the seemingly empty house only to find Jen, a hidden child with a tough exterior who has been secreted in this neighboring house. Through Jen, Luke learns of an entire subculture of hidden children via chat rooms on the Internet. He learns through such discussions, and through literature given to him by Jen, of the repressive policies of the government. When Jen organizes a rally of other hidden children that ends in bloodshed and her death, Luke must finally make a decision as to how far he will go to defy the government in order to have a life that is worth living.

Critics responded positively to the theme of this futuristic novel, applauding, as did a *Publishers Weekly* contributor, for example, "the unsettling, thought-provoking premise [which] should suffice to keep readers hooked." Susan L. Rogers, writing in *School Library Journal,* observed that, as with Haddix's debut novel, *Running out of Time,* this fourth novel took as its theme the loss of free will. Describing *Among the Hidden* as "exciting and compelling," Rogers remarked that readers "will be captivated by Luke's predicament and his reactions to it." Debbie Earl noted in *Voice of Youth Advocates* that Haddix presents a "chilling vision of a possibly not-too-distant future" in this "bleak allegorical tale."

Among the Imposters is a sequel to *Among the Hidden* which picks up the story of Luke Garner as he is sent to a boarding school under the name of Lee Grant. Hendricks School for Boys is a place of violence and fear, where the terrified students quietly follow orders and Luke suffers nightly hazing at the hands of older boys. He soon discovers that some of the boys, along with girls from a neighboring girls' school, are meeting secretly in the woods to plot their escape. Luke must decide whether to join the plotters in their dangerous plan. Brenda Moses-Allen in the *Voice of Youth Advocates* found the story to be filled with "tension and excitement."

With *Just Ella,* her fifth novel, Haddix presented herself yet another creative challenge: rethinking a traditional fairy tale, and putting, as a *Publishers Weekly* reviewer commented, "a feminist spin on the Cinderella story." Haddix starts her revisionist tale at the point in action where the fairy tale ends. Planning to live happily ever after with her Prince Charming who has saved her from her evil step-family, Ella Brown is sorely disappointed upon arrival at the prince's castle. An energetic and resourceful person, Ella has found her own way to the ball where she met the prince, without the aid of a magical fairy godmother. Now she is sorely in need of such divine intervention, for she discovers her husband-to-be is yawningly boring; neither is a continual diet of needlepoint enough to keep her intellectually challenged. Ella's independent nature is assaulted by the etiquette lessons which Madame Bisset dishes out, but her young tutor, Jed, does talk to her about things that matter, and soon she sees that there is no way she can go through with her planned marriage. But then Ella discovers it is not all that easy to walk away from the prince, for she finds herself locked away in a dungeon when her fiancé gets wind of her resolve. However, with the help of a servant girl she has befriended, Ella manages to tunnel her way to freedom and to a life that has meaning for her.

Once again, readers and critics responded warmly to Haddix's writing and invention. "In lively prose, with well-developed characters, creative plot twists, wit, and drama, Haddix transforms the Cinderella tale into an insightful coming-of-age story," wrote Shelle Rosenfeld in a *Booklist* review. Rosenfeld also commented that *Just Ella* was a "provocative and entertaining novel." The contributor for *Publishers Weekly* concluded that Ella's "straightforward, often gleefully glib narrative breathes fresh life into the tale," while Connie Tyrrell Burns, writing in *School Library Journal,* called the book an "imaginative retelling," and recommended it for older readers who could "enjoy this new take on a strong heroine." "Make room in the canon of retold tales for a spirited, first-person retelling of 'Cinderella',", proclaimed Cynthia Grady in *Voice of Youth Advocates.* "Ella," concluded Grady, "is a thoughtful heroine who overcomes her youthful 'foolishness'." Similarly, Natalie Soto, reviewing the novel in the *Rocky Mountain News,* felt that "Ella is a strong and sensitive character sure to make girls cheer."

Haddix returned to the future with *Turnabout,* a novel set in 2085, when the pavement is made of foam rubber and society favors singles. As with her first novel, this one involves a scientific experiment gone wrong. At the heart of this novel is the question, "What if people could turn back the aging clock?" Haddix explores this question through two characters, Melly and Anny Beth, aged respectively 100 and 103 in the year 2001 and residing in a nursing home. Part of an experiment to "unage," the two are given PT-1, a drug in the Project Turnabout program that will reverse the aging process, allowing the participant to grow younger every year until they reach a self-determined perfect age. At that point, they will receive another injection which will

stop the process. The only problem is that this second shot proves fatal, and now the members of Project Turnabout are doomed to continue "unaging" until they reach zero. The novel switches between the present and 2085 when Melly and Anny Beth are teenagers and must find someone to parent them as they grow increasingly younger. Upping the stakes is a reporter who has gotten wind of the project and is trying to track Melly; this would destroy any chance of privacy these refugees from age have, and they have to flee from unwanted exposure. In the telling, Haddix also offers her own view of what the future will be like, with toothpaste so perfect that dentists are no longer necessary, cars that drive themselves, and a society so smitten with news that individual privacy is a thing of the past.

"The story is irresistible," noted an interviewer for the *Akron Beacon Journal,* and "good reading for adults too." Haddix told this writer that she thought she would have trouble picturing the future. "But then I decided to have some fun with it and not be so concerned. I extrapolated from trends I see in society today and pushed them farther." A contributor for *Publishers Weekly* called *Turnabout* a "thought-provoking science fiction adventure," and further noted that Haddix "keeps the pacing smooth and builds up to a surprising face-off." Debbie Carton, reviewing the novel in *Booklist,* felt that the need for love and protection "is poignantly conveyed, as is the isolation of the elderly in society." Carton also thought that the book "will provoke lively discussion in middle-school book clubs." *School Library Journal* contributor Beth Wright commented that the futuristic setting "is scarily believable," and that the theme of the book would spark "thoughtful discussion about human life and human potential."

Haddix continues to have many works in progress, from sequels to her own works to shorter novels for young readers. Her background in journalism and novels is apparent in her meticulous and informed writing, and her appreciation for and belief in the written word. Yet she is not draconian about forcing children to read, remaining doubtful about the effects of programs that push reading. "Like the library programs where you read so many minutes and win a prize at the end of the summer," Haddix commented in her interview for the *Akron Beacon Journal.* "I like seeing the emphasis on reading, but I'm almost afraid the more we push it, the more [young readers] will think of it like broccoli or spinach, that it doesn't taste good or isn't fun. I'd like to see them pick up a book and read it and not think 'I've read for 15 minutes.' The more they read and begin to enjoy it, the more likely they are to continue."

BIOGRAPHICAL/CRITICAL SOURCES:

PERIODICALS

Akron Beacon Journal, October 12, 2000, p. C3; November 2, 2000, " 'Turnabout' Author at Hudson Store" (interview), p. E10.

Booklist, October 1, 1995, Mary Harris Veeder, review of *Running out of Time,* p. 314; October 15, 1996, Jean Franklin, review of *Don't You Dare Read This, Mrs. Dunphrey,* p. 413; December 15, 1997, Ilene Cooper, review of *Leaving Fishers,* p. 691; September 1, 1999, Shelle Rosenfeld, review of *Just Ella,* p. 123; October 15, 2000, Debbie Carton, review of *Turnabout,* p. 431.

Bulletin of the Center for Children's Books, November, 1995, Roger Sutton, review of *Running out of Time,* p. 91; January, 1997, p. 172; November, 1999, pp. 93-94.

Detroit Free Press, October 20, 2000, p. D8.

Horn Book Guide, spring, 1996, p. 62; spring, 1997, p. 79.

Kirkus Reviews, October 1, 1997, review of *Leaving Fishers,* p. 1532; July 15, 1998, p. 1035.

Publishers Weekly, August 12, 1996, review of *Don't You Dare Read This, Mrs. Dunphrey,* p. 85; November 24, 1997, review of *Leaving Fishers,* p. 75; August 31, 1998, review of *Among the Hidden,* p. 76; January 11, 1999, p. 26; May 24, 1999, p. 81; October 11, 1999, review of *Just Ella,* p. 77; February 7, 2000, p. 87; October 16, 2000, review of *Turnabout,* p. 77.

Rocky Mountain News, September 5, 1999, Natalie Soto, review of *Just Ella,* p. E4.

School Library Journal, October, 1995, Lisa Dennis, review of *Running out of Time,* p. 133; October, 1996, Carol Schene, review of *Don't You Dare Read This, Mrs. Dunphrey,* p. 147; October, 1997, p. 132; September, 1998, Susan L. Rogers, review of *Among the Hidden,* p. 203; September, 1999, Connie Tyrrell Burns, review of *Just Ella,* p. 225; September, 2000, Beth Wright, review of *Turnabout,* p. 230; August, 2001, B. Allison Gray, review of *Takeoffs and Landings,* pp. 182-183.

Times Educational Supplement, May 19, 2000, p. FR123.

Voice of Youth Advocates, December, 1995, Ann Welton, review of *Running out of Time,* p. 302; Jamie S. Hansen, review of *Don't You Dare Read This, Mrs. Dunphrey,* p. 270; February, 1998, Beverly Youree, review of *Leaving Fishers,* p. 386; October, 1998, Debbie Earl, review of *Among the Hidden,* p. 283; December, 1999, Cynthia Grady, review of *Just Ella,* p. 346; August, 2001, Brenda

Moses-Allen, review of *Among the Imposters,* p. 213.

*   *   *

HALE, Keith 1955-

PERSONAL: Born July 3, 1955, in Little Rock, AR; son of Carolyn Jean (Harrell) Hale. *Ethnicity:* "USA Caucasian." *Education:* University of Texas at Austin, B.S.E., 1980; University of Central Arkansas, M.A., 1991; Purdue University, Ph.D., 1994.

ADDRESSES: Office—Department of English, Missouri Valley College, Marshall, MO 65340. *E-mail*—khalemo@hotmail.com.

CAREER: English Language Book Editors, Amsterdam, Netherlands, editor, 1984; Arkansas Writers' Project, Little Rock, AR, editor, 1984-87; University of Guam, assistant professor of English, 1996-2000; Missouri Valley College, Marshall, MO, 2000—.

WRITINGS:

Clicking Beat on the Brink of Nada (novel), Spartacus (Amsterdam, Netherlands), 1983.

Cody (novel), Alyson, 1987.

In the Land of Alexander: Gay Travels, with History and Politics, in Hungary, Yugoslavia, Turkey, and Greece, Alyson, 1990.

(With Jim Holobaugh) *Torn Allegiance: The Story of a Gay Cadet,* Alyson, 1993.

(Editor) *Friends and Apostles: The Correspondence of Rupert Brooke and James Strachey, 1905-1914,* Yale University Press (London, England), 1998.

Contributor to *Dickens Studies Annual,* Volume 29, AMS Press, 2000.

SIDELIGHTS: Keith Hale told *CA* that among his influences are Michael Campbell's *Lord, Dismiss Us,* Andre Gidé's *The Counterfeiters,* Vladimir Nabokov's *Pale Fire,* Thomas Wolfe's *Look Homeward, Aryel,* and the short stories of Bienvenido Santos and Nick Joaquin.

*   *   *

HALPERIN, Mark (Warren) 1940-

PERSONAL: Born February 19, 1940, in New York, NY; son of George W. (a dentist) and Minna (Scherzer)

Halperin; married Barbara Scott (a painter), July 15, 1966; children: Noah. *Education:* Bard College, B.A., 1960; New School for Social Research, graduate study, 1962-64; University of Iowa, M.F.A., 1966.

ADDRESSES: Home—12051 Highway 10, Ellensburg, WA 98926. *Office*—Department of English, Central Washington State College, Ellensburg, WA 98926.

CAREER: Machlett Laboratories, Inc., Stanford, CT, junior physicist, 1960-62; Rockefeller Institute, New York, NY, electron microscope technician, 1963; University of Iowa, Iowa City, IA, electron microscope technician, 1964-66; Central Washington State College, Ellensburg, WA, began as assistant professor, became professor of English, 1966—. University of Arizona, visiting professor, 1977-78; Shimane University, visiting professor, 1986-87; Estonian Institute for Human Science, visiting professor, 1990; Moscow State Linguistic University, Fulbright exchange professor, 1994, 1996, and 1999; participant in writers' workshops and literary seminars in St. Petersburg, Russia.

MEMBER: Yakima River Conservancy (president, 1969-74), Alpine Lakes Protection Society (trustee, 1968-71).

AWARDS, HONORS: U.S. Award, International Poetry Forum, 1975, for *Backroads;* award from Washington State Artist's Trust, 2000.

WRITINGS:

Backroads (poetry), University of Pittsburgh Press (Pittsburgh, PA), 1976.
Gomer (poetry), Sea Pen Press, 1979.
The White Coverlet (poetry), Jawbone Press (Waldron Island, WA), 1979.
A Place Made Fast (poetry), Copper Canyon Press (Port Townsend, WA), 1982.
The Measure of Islands (poetry), Wesleyan University Press (Middletown, CT), 1990.
Time and Distance (poetry), Western Michigan University Press (Kalamazoo, MI), 2001.

Translator of prose and poetry from Russian. Contributor of essays and translations to literary magazines, including *Seattle Review, Prairie Schooner, Northwest Review, Iowa Review, North American Review, Yale Review, Porch,* and *Poetry Northwest.*

WORK IN PROGRESS: A new book of poems; translations.

SIDELIGHTS: Mark Halperin once told *CA:* "I want the kind of balance in my poems that I think of as formal, whether I work in traditional forms or so-called free ones. I would like my poetry to go out to the world rather than in to myself, though this is a matter of emphasis more than exclusion. Without being dour about it, I believe poems are important and the making of them serious. Thus, I expect to be unsure of what it is I'm after, to learn to live in and from that dis-ease."

He later added: "I continue to explore and learn from my explorations. I hope that what I write reflects this, that over some core that reflects is who I am, there is a changing surface. The most significant change in my writing life in the last ten years has been my immersion in Russian."*

*   *   *

HAMILTON, Mollie
See KAYE, M(ary) M(argaret)

*   *   *

HAMMOND, Wayne G(ordon)   1953-

PERSONAL: Born February 11, 1953, in Cleveland, OH; son of Wayne Gordon Sr. (a loan manager) and Luella Belle (a secretary; maiden name, Thauvette) Hammond; married Christina Scull (a librarian), December, 1994. *Education:* Baldwin-Wallace College, B.A. (magna cum laude), 1975; University of Michigan, M.A.L.S., 1976. *Avocational interests:* Collecting books, listening to classical music and jazz, cooking.

ADDRESSES: Home—30 Talcott Rd., Williamstown, MA 01267. *E-mail*—wayne.g.hammond@williams. edu.

CAREER: Williams College, Williamstown, MA, assistant librarian at Chapin Library, 1976—.

AWARDS, HONORS: Clyde S. Kilby grant from Marion E. Wade Center, Wheaton College, Wheaton, IL, 1991; Mythopoeic scholarships for "Inklings studies," Mythopoeic Society, 1993 and 1995.

WRITINGS:

J. R. R. Tolkien: A Descriptive Bibliography, St. Paul's Bibliographies, 1993.

(With Christina Scull) *J. R. R. Tolkien: Artist and Illustrator,* HarperCollins (New York, NY), 1995.

(Editor with Christina Scull) *J. R. R. Tolkien, Roverandom,* HarperCollins (New York, NY), 1999.

Arthur Ransome: A Bibliography, Oak Knoll Press (New Castle, DE), 2000.

Contributor to periodicals, including *Mythlore* and *Trade Bindings Research Newsletter.* Designer and editor, *Samuel Butler Newsletter,* 1980-94.

WORK IN PROGRESS: J. R. R. Tolkien: A Companion and Guide, with Christina Scull, for HarperCollins (New York, NY), completion expected in 2002.

SIDELIGHTS: Wayne G. Hammond once told *CA:* "My chief interest in writing is bibliography, as an adjunct to biography and an aid to scholarship. A bibliography should be not merely a list of works, but a readable book with intelligent, well-written commentary, well laid out and printed. As a book designer as well as a writer, I am always aware of the visual effect of the printed page on the reader, and on how it can influence perceptions by its appearance."

* * *

HANSEN, Karen V. 1955-

PERSONAL: Born April 23, 1955, in Chico, CA; daughter of Edwin L. (a maintenance worker) and Esther C. (Kanten) Hansen; married Andrew L. Bundy, February 16, 1985; children: Benjamin, Evan. *Ethnicity:* "Scandinavian-American." *Education:* University of California, Santa Barbara, B.A. (with high honors), 1977, M.A., 1979; University of California, Berkeley, Ph.D., 1989. *Religion:* "None."

ADDRESSES: Home—27 Winsor Ave., Watertown, MA 02472. *Office*—Department of Sociology, M5071 Brandeis University, Waltham, MA 02454-9110; fax: 781-736-2653. *E-mail*—khansen@brandeis.edu.

CAREER: Foote, Cone & Belding/Honig, San Francisco, CA, project director, 1980-81; URSA Institute, San Francisco, research associate, 1981-84; University of California, Berkeley, acting instructor in sociology, 1988; Brandeis University, Waltham, MA, assistant professor, 1989-95, associate professor of sociology, 1995—, Marver and Sheva Bernstein Faculty Fellow, 1993-94. Radcliffe College, fellow at Bunting Institute, 1991-92, visiting scholar at Henry A. Murray Research

Center, 1994-96; Harvard University, Andrew W. Mellon Faculty Fellow in Women's Studies, 1991-92.

MEMBER: American Sociological Association, Sociologists for Women in Society, Coordinating Committee on Women in the Historical Profession, Social Science History Association, Eastern Sociological Society.

AWARDS, HONORS: Woodrow Wilson grant, 1988; National Endowment for the Humanities grant, 1991, fellowship, 1999; grants from American Philosophical Society, 1992, American Sociological Association and National Science Foundation, 1992-93, and Emigration Fund of 1975, Norwegian Royal Ministry of Foreign Affairs, 1998.

WRITINGS:

(Editor, with Ilene Philipson, and contributor) *Women, Class, and the Feminist Imagination: A Socialist-Feminist Reader,* Temple University Press (Philadelphia, PA), 1990.

A Very Social Time: Crafting Community in Antebellum New England, University of California Press (Berkeley, CA), 1994.

(Editor, with Anita Ilta Garey) *Families in the U.S.: Kinship and Domestic Politics,* Temple University Press (Philadelphia, PA), 1998.

Contributor to books, including *The Social Construction of Gender: Theories, Research, and Practice,* edited by Judith Lorber and Susan A. Farrell, Sage Publications (Beverly Hills, CA), 1990; *Men's Friendships,* edited by Peter Nardi, Sage Publications (Beverly Hills, CA), 1992; and *Public and Private in Thought and Practice: Perspectives on a Grand Dichotomy,* edited by Krishan Kumar and Jeff Weintraub, University of Chicago Press (Chicago, IL). Contributor of articles and reviews to academic journals, including *Social Science History, Gender and History, Qualitative Sociology, Historical New Hampshire, Socialist Review,* and *Agricultural History.* Member of editorial board, *Journal of Family History.*

WORK IN PROGRESS: Networks of Care: Family, Work, and Children; The Reservation Frontier: Dakota Encounters with Scandinavian Homesteaders, 1900-1930.

SIDELIGHTS: Karen V. Hansen told *CA:* "Supported by the Center for Working Families at the University of California, Berkeley, *Networks of Care: Family, Work, and Children* investigates the networks of care developed and utilized by working parents for their school-aged children. Based in northern California, this study explores the connections between care-giving, kinship, and childhood by conducting oral histories with members of care-giving networks. By intensively analyzing four extensive networks across the economic spectrum, it investigates whom parents tap to help rear their children and by what criteria the network members are deemed worthy of their trust. The study also explores what entitlements and responsibilities children have in the network. It then examines how the care by extended family members and non-family persons is integrated into family systems of meaning and myths.

"The Reservation Frontier: Dakota Encounters with Scandinavian Homesteaders, 1900-1930 examines three decades of cross-cultural exchange between the Dakota Sioux and Scandinavian immigrant homesteaders. Norwegians in particular came to the Dakotas because of the promise of 'free' land. In fact, the land on which they homesteaded had been appropriated from the Dakota through the Land Allotment Act of 1904, passed by the U.S. Congress.

"This project uses primary source materials to explore the conflict and cooperation that evolved between individuals living on the Devils Lake Sioux Indian Reservation in North Dakota, with this momentous transfer of land as a backdrop. In particular, it investigates the ways that the two peoples, both extremely poor and embattled by Progressive Era Americanization efforts, managed their extensive trade relationships with each other, struggled with public schooling in the lives of their children, and lived as neighbors."

*   *   *

HARARY, Keith 1953-

PERSONAL: Born February 9, 1953, in New York, NY; son of Victor (in sales) and Lillian (in sales; maiden name, Mazur) Harary; married Darlene Moore (a writer), October 22, 1985. *Education:* Duke University, B.A. (magna cum laude), 1975; Union Institute, Ph.D., 1986.

ADDRESSES: Office—Institute for Advanced Psychology, P.O. Box 4109, Burbank, CA 91503. *Agent*—Roslyn Targ, Roslyn Targ Literary Agency, Inc., 105 West 13th St., New York, NY 10011. *E-mail*—kh@iapglobal.org.

CAREER: American Society for Psychical Research, research consultant, 1971-72; Institute for Parapsychol-

ogy, research consultant, 1972; Psychical Research Foundation, research associate, 1973-76; Maimonides Medical Center, research associate in psychiatry, 1976-79; Human Freedom Center, director of counseling, 1979; SRI International, research consultant, 1980-82; Atari Corp., design consultant, 1983-85; Institute for Advanced Psychology, Burbank, CA, president and research director, 1986—. Durham Mental Health Center, crisis and suicide counselor, 1972-76; Dorothea Dix State Psychiatric Hospital, research intern, 1974;. Antioch University, adjunct professor, 1985, 1986; guest lecturer at Smithsonian Institution, Esalen Institute, United Nations, and at universities and colleges, including University of Edinburgh, Stanford University, Duke University, University of North Carolina, University of California at Berkeley, Los Angeles, and Santa Barbara, and Syracuse University; lecturer at conferences, including U.S.S.R. Academy of Sciences and Swiss Industries Fair. *Omni,* producer and host of "Brainstorms," a weekly Internet interview series, 1995-98, producer of live Internet series "Inside Cult Consciousness," 1997; guest on more than 200 television and radio shows, including *Phil Donahue Show, 20/20, 60 Minutes, Oprah Winfrey Show, CNN News, Michael Jackson Show* (radio), and *Barry Farber Show* (radio). Creator and designer of "reflective method" of personality assessment; Sears, Roebuck and Co., Inc., media spokesperson and psychological consultant for the promotion "Right Stuff Personality Profile," 1997; Budget Rent-a-Car, national media spokesperson and psychological consultant for the promotion "Drive Your Alter Ego," 1997-98; consultant to Philadelphia International Airport and Microsoft Corp. Underwater archaeological investigator for an expedition exploring and recovering shipwreck artifacts from an old Spanish galleon in West Palm Beach, FL, 1988; field investigator for an archaeological research team exploring historical sites in American wilderness areas, 1988-90.

MEMBER: American Psychological Society, American Psychological Association, Association for Media Psychology, American Society for Psychical Research (member of board of directors, 1993—).

AWARDS, HONORS: International Mercury Award in public relations, 1997, for "Drive Your Alter Ego" promotional campaign.

WRITINGS:

(With Russell Targ) *The Mind Race: Understanding and Using Psychic Abilities,* Random House (New York, NY), 1984.

(With Pamela Weintraub) *The Creative Sleep Program,* St. Martin's (New York, NY), 1989.

(With Pamela Weintraub) *The Free Flight Program,* St. Martin's (New York, NY), 1989.

(With Pamela Weintraub) *The Erotic Fulfillment Program,* St. Martin's (New York, NY), 1990.

(With Pamela Weintraub) *The Higher Consciousness Program,* St. Martin's (New York, NY), 1990.

(With Pamela Weintraub) *The Total Recall Program,* St. Martin's (New York, NY), 1991.

(With Pamela Weintraub) *The Whole Mind Program,* St. Martin's (New York, NY), 1991.

(With Eileen Donohue) *Who Do You Think You Are?: Explore Your Many-sided Self with the Berkeley Personality Profile,* Harper (San Francisco, CA), 1994.

Also author of two manuals: *Suicidal Calling as Crisis-Coping Behavior* and *Suicide Intervention: Answering the Cry for Help.* Contributor to reference books and anthologies, including *Psychic Powers,* Time-Life (Alexandria, VA), 1987; *Psychic Voyages,* Time-Life (Alexandria, VA), 1988; *Psychic Dreaming,* Warner Books (New York, NY), 1991; and *Phantastische Phanomene,* Herbig, 1993. Author of "The Omni Mind Brain Laboratory," a monthly Internet column, *Omni,* 1995-98. Contributor of articles on experimental psychology, psychical research, philosophy of science, ethics, and counseling to periodicals, including *Journal of the American Society for Psychical Research, Research in Parapsychology, Skeptical Inquirer, Psychology Today,* and *Cosmopolitan.* Scientific editor, *Psi Research,* 1983-86; editor at large, *Omni,* 1995-98.

WORK IN PROGRESS: Continued work on an autobiography; a clinical anthology on reported psychic experiences; several journal articles on a new approach to personality testing.

SIDELIGHTS: Keith Harary once told *CA:* "My current thinking about experimental research on reported psychic experiences and the clinical treatment of those who have such experiences is that we frequently allow our perspective to be clouded by stereotypical attitudes and misconceptions. We invite those who share the intimate details of their psi experiences to lose their perspective along with the rest of us. Perhaps the most familiar example of this destructive tendency is our eagerness to label selected individuals as 'psychic,' and the ardent manner in which many people embrace and even compete for the dubious honor of this questionable label.

"I call for a more balanced and scientific treatment of these experiences. To label anyone a psychic is to deny the limits of our understanding and pretend to have answers to questions that have yet to be asked. That the mind is capable of remarkable feats is undeniable. Exploring the implications of this realization does not require resorting to extremes. It should encourage us to create a middle ground—one that defines human potential in human terms. If a higher perceptual, communicative and thinking capability exists within us, then it cannot be consigned to the realm of the psychic and paranormal. It must be understood within the context of normal experience and achievable human potential and considered within the emerging framework of mainstream science. Rather than approaching this exploration as a conflict between an occult versus a materialistic ideology, we may then embrace a balanced vision of human potential and investigate the mysteries of nature with a truly open mind."

*   *   *

HARRELL, Anne
See NEGGERS, Carla A(malia)

*   *   *

HART, Martin
See 't HART, Maarten

*   *   *

HATTERSLEY, Roy (Sydney George) 1932-

PERSONAL: Born December 28, 1932, in Sheffield, England; son of Frederick Roy and Enid (Brackenbury) Hattersley; married Edith Mary Loughran, 1956. *Education:* University of Hull, B.Sc.

ADDRESSES: Office—c/o *The Guardian,* 119 Farringdon Rd., London ECIR 3ER, England.

CAREER: Journalist and health service executive, 1956-64; Sheffield City Council, Sheffield, England, member of council and chairman of housing and public works committees, 1957-65; Parliament, London, England, Labour member of House of Commons for Sparkbrook Division of Birmingham, 1964-97, Parliamentary private secretary to minister of pensions and national insurance, 1964-67, joint Parliamentary secre-

Roy Hattersley

tary to ministry of labor, 1967-68, and department of employment and productivity, 1968-69, minister of defense for administration, 1969-70, Labour party spokesman on defense, 1972, on education and science, 1972-74, and on the environment, 1979, minister of state at Foreign and Commonwealth Office, 1974-76, secretary of state for prices and consumer protection, 1976-79, opposition spokesman on home affairs, 1980-83 and 1987-c. 1992, and on treasury affairs, 1983-87, deputy leader of Labour Party, 1983-92, life peer and member of the House of Lords, 1997—.

Visiting fellow at Institute of Politics, Harvard University, 1971 and 1972. Director of Campaign for a European Political Community, 1966-67. Consultant to International Business Machines Corp. (IBM).

MEMBER: Reform Club.

AWARDS, HONORS: Member of Privy Council, 1975.

WRITINGS:

NONFICTION

The Overload Performance of Powder Couplings: The Prevention of the Fire Hazard, Safety in Mines Research Establishment, 1957.

Nelson, Saturday Review Press (New York, NY), 1974.

Goodbye to Yorkshire, Gollancz (London, England), 1976.

Press Gang, Robson Books (London, England), 1983.

A Yorkshire Boyhood, Hogarth (London, England), 1983, Oxford University Press (New York, NY), 1984.

Choose Freedom: The Future for Democratic Socialism, M. Joseph (London, England), 1987.

Economic Priorities for a Labour Government, edited by Doug Jones, St. Martin's Press (New York, NY), 1987.

In That Quiet Earth, Macmillan (London, England), 1991.

Between Ourselves, Pan Books (London, England), 1994.

(Author of introduction) John Tilley, *Churchill's Favourite Socialist: A Life of A. V. Alexander,* Holyoak Books (Manchester, England), 1995.

Who Goes Home?: Scenes from a Political Life, Little, Brown (London, England), 1995.

Fifty Years On: A Prejudiced History of Britain since the War, Abacus (London, England), 1998.

Blood and Fire: William and Catherine Booth and Their Salvation Army, Doubleday (New York, NY), 2000.

FICTION

The Maker's Mark, Simon & Schuster (New York, NY), 1990.

Skylark's Song, Pan (London, England), 1994.

Buster's Diaries: The True Story of a Dog and His Man (for children), illustrated by Chris Riddell, Warner Books (New York, NY), 2000.

OTHER

Columnist for newspapers, including *Guardian,* 1981—, *Lustie,* 1980-81 and 1988—, and *Punch,* 1982-88. Contributor to journals.

SIDELIGHTS: Roy Hattersley, a longtime Labour Party leader and member of the British Parliament, has amassed a large body of writings that covers not only his life and political ideology but the lives of other prominent people, such as British naval hero Horatio

Nelson and Salvation Army founders William and Catherine Booth, and the political history of the United Kingdom. A versatile writer, Hattersley has also worked as a journalist and has authored a children's book. His *Buster's Diaries: The True Story of a Dog and His Man* is a canine exposé revealing the challenges of being a well-loved mutt living in London that *School Library Journal* contributor Robert Saunderson praised as a "gem."

In *Fifty Years On: A Prejudiced History of Britain since the War,* Hattersley looks at British politics in the latter half of the twentieth century and expresses dismay at the course of events. Hattersley deplores the right-wing policies put in place by Margaret Thatcher, England's prime minister during the 1980s, and her Conservative Party, but he is also critical of his own party. He had once fought to keep his party from going too far left for his tastes, but he feels it eventually went too far to the right, as evidenced by some conservative stands embraced by Labour's Tony Blair, who became prime minister in 1997. Additionally, Hattersley thinks the United Kingdom became too closely involved with the United States after World War II and ignored its relations with the rest of Europe.

"Hattersley's poignant look back takes the reader through the great political debates of postwar Britain, all of which, in the end, were a nation trying (at times unsuccessfully) to come to terms with its own inexorable decline," observes Michael Cox in *Foreign Policy.* Robert Pearce, writing in *History Today,* finds some factual errors and a dearth of historical perspective in the book, but concedes that "these are minor faults in what is a delightfully entertaining reminder of what we have half-forgotten. Everything here . . . is presented with verve and skill."

Blood and Fire: William and Catherine Booth and Their Salvation Army chronicles the lives and work of the founders of this long-lived religious institution and social reform movement. The Booths, both born in 1829, met and married in the 1850s. Stubbornly devoted to their beliefs and each other, in 1865 they set up an organization called Christian Mission. In 1878 it became the Salvation Army, a group complete with military-style ranks and uniforms. The Booths espoused a radical belief that poverty and other social problems were to blame for immoral behavior, and their ministry sought to serve the physical as well as the spiritual needs of the poor, providing food and shelter along with preaching. They especially reached out to the "undeserving poor," a category including problem drinkers, prostitutes, small-time criminals, and other less

than exemplary types, who were shunned by some other social reformers in favor of those more "deserving" of help. Catherine Booth also held a radical (for her time) belief that women were equal to men and qualified to fill leadership roles in the organization. She and her husband carried on their Salvation Army work while producing eight children, who were sometimes neglected by their zealous, driven parents.

"It is a fascinating story that Hattersley . . . has to tell about the personal as well as the public lives of the Booths," relates Gertrude Himmelfarb in the *New York Times Book Review,* calling *Blood and Fire* "admirable and unhagiographal." A *Publishers Weekly* reviewer applauds Hattersley, particularly for showing how prominent a role Catherine Booth played in the Salvation Army, "without anachronistically turning her into a modern feminist." Similarly, Marvin Olasky notes in the *National Review* that Hattersley makes clear that the Salvation Army "triumphed because of (and despite) the unofficial leadership of Catherine Booth . . . a scandal to some because of biblical teaching about male spiritual leadership." Olasky also points out Hattersley's emphasis on "Booth's willingness to offend in a righteous cause. He had little inhibition—at one point insisting that Cecil Rhodes kneel down with him to pray in a crowded railway car." Himmelfarb, while generally praising the book, takes issue with some of Hattersley's points: "Hattersley sees the originality and great achievement of the Booths to be their rejection of the idea of the 'deserving' poor. But that idea was neither as relentlessly moralistic nor as pervasive as he suggests. . . . Moreover, the Salvation Army also had its moral agenda. Indeed, in some ways it was more moralistic and puritanical than the others." It also bothers Himmelfarb that Hattersley makes "little attempt to establish the connection, let alone a causal relationship, between [the Booths'] social and religious agendas." Failing to make this connection, she says, "deprives them of what might have been their best claim to our attention and a place in the pantheon of eminent Victorians."

BIOGRAPHICAL/CRITICAL SOURCES:

BOOKS

Hattersley, Roy, *A Yorkshire Boyhood,* Hogarth (London), 1983, Oxford University Press (New York, NY), 1984.

Hattersley, Roy, *Who Goes Home?: Scenes from a Political Life,* Little, Brown (London, England), 1995.

PERIODICALS

Booklist, May 15, 2000, review of *Blood and Fire,* p. 1704; August, 2000, review of *Buster's Diaries,* p. 2099.

Economist, April 28, 1990, "The Constitution Revisited," p. 65; November 15, 1997, review of *Fifty Years On,* p. S3.

Foreign Policy, spring, 1998, Michael Cox, review of *Fifty Years On,* p. 172.

History Today, July, 1998, Robert Pearce, review of *Fifty Years On,* p. 61.

National Review, September 11, 2000, Marvin Olasky, review of *Blood and Fire,* p. 62.

New Statesman, October 6, 1972.

New Statesman & Society, June 8, 1990, p. 37; July 5, 1991, p. 56; March 4, 1994, John Cole, "Doing the Next Best Thing," p. 14; December 9, 1994, Ian Aitken, "Hey Preachers, Leave Them Kids Alone," p. 12; November 3, 1995, Ian Aitken, review of *Who Goes Home?,* p. 12.

New York Times Book Review, July 9, 2000, Gertrude Himmelfarb, "First Save the Body, Then the Soul."

Publishers Weekly, July 5, 1991, review of *The Maker's Mark,* p. 135; May 15, 2000, review of *Blood and Fire,* p. 110.

School Library Journal, April, 2001, Robert Saunderson, review for *Buster's Diaries,* p. 171.*

*   *   *

HEMPHILL, Paul   1936-

PERSONAL: Born February 18, 1936, in Birmingham, AL; son of Paul (a truck driver) and Velma Rebecca (an employee of the U.S. government; maiden name, Nelson) Hemphill; married Susan Milliage Olive, September 23, 1961 (divorced, 1975); married Susan Farran Percy (a writer and former editor of *Atlanta*), November 6, 1976; children: (first marriage) Lisa, David, Molly; (second marriage) Martha. *Ethnicity:* "Caucasian." *Education:* Auburn University, B.A., 1959.

ADDRESSES: Agent—David Black, 156 Fifth Ave., Ste. 608, New York, NY 10010.

CAREER: Sportswriter for newspapers in Birmingham, AL, Augusta, GA, and Tampa, FL, 1958-64; *Atlanta Journal,* Atlanta, GA, columnist, 1965-69; freelance writer, 1969—; *San Francisco Examiner,* San Francisco, CA, columnist, 1976. Visiting lecturer at University of Georgia, fall, 1973; writer-in-residence, journal-

ism, at Florida A & M University, 1975; writer-in-residence, Brenau College, 1984-92. Commentator on *All Things Considered,* National Public Radio; guest on *Today* and *McNeill-Lehrer Report* television shows. *Military service:* Alabama Air National Guard, active duty, 1961-62; served in France.

AWARDS, HONORS: Nieman fellow at Harvard University, 1968-69; literary achievement award, Georgia Writers Association, 1970, for *The Nashville Sound: Bright Lights and Country Music; Leaving Birmingham,* nominated for Pulitzer Prize; several books selected for *New York Times* book-of-the-year list.

WRITINGS:

Long Gone (novel), Viking (New York, NY), 1979.

The Nashville Sound: Bright Lights and Country Music, Simon & Schuster (New York, NY), 1970.

(Ghostwriter) Ivan Allen, Jr., *Mayor: Notes on the Sixties* (autobiography), Simon & Schuster (New York, NY), 1971.

The Good Old Boys (collection of Hemphill's newspaper columns), Simon & Schuster (New York, NY), 1974.

Too Old to Cry (collection of Hemphill's newspaper columns), Viking (New York, NY), 1981.

The Sixkiller Chronicles, Macmillan (New York, NY), 1985.

Me and the Boy: Journey of Discovery—Father and Son on the Appalachian Trail (autobiographical), Macmillan (New York, NY), 1986.

King of the Road, Houghton (Boston, MA), 1989.

Leaving Birmingham: Notes of a Native Son (memoir), Viking (New York, NY), 1993.

The Heart of the Game: The Education of a Minor-League Ballplayer, Simon & Schuster (New York, NY), 1996.

Wheels: A Season on NASCAR's Winston Cup Circuit, Simon & Schuster (New York, NY), 1997.

The Ballad of Little River: A Tale of Race and Restless Youth in the Rural South, Free Press (New York, NY), 2000.

Author of columns appearing in *San Francisco Examiner, Baltimore Sun, USA Today, Atlanta Constitution, Sport,* and *Country Music.* Contributor to periodicals, including *Life, Playboy, Cosmopolitan, Mademoiselle, Atlantic, New York Times Magazine, True, Sports Illustrated, Southern,* and *TV Guide.* Senior editor, *Atlanta* (magazine), 1981. The "Hemphill Collection" is housed at Auburn University Library.

ADAPTATIONS: Long Gone was adapted for HBO television, 1987.

SIDELIGHTS: Paul Hemphill once told *CA:* "As it happened, I observed my sixtieth birthday in February of 1996 frantically running from pit road to the garage area to the infield of Daytona International Speedway on my first official day of research on the grueling 31-race Winston Cup stock car racing circuit. I remember asking myself at some point that day, 'What the hell am I doing here?'

"I was there for the same reasons that had driven me to write my ten previous published books. This stuff interested me, seemed to be something I could live with for a while, and might be worth putting down so that at some distant point someone might find the book in a library and say, 'Well, now, that's interesting, what they were doing with cars back there at the end of the twentieth century.'

"So that's how I look at myself as a writer. It certainly wasn't to make a lot of money, which I haven't. I've always felt that writers ought to live out there across the American outback—just private citizens who had this secret eccentricity to write—and every day sit down as though composing a letter to the world, saying, 'Here's what went on around here yesterday.' With every one of my books whether fiction or nonfiction, that has been my intention.

"Writing can be a noble profession, I think, but only when it is driven by a desire to leave an honest record of one's times for those who follow. A writer is in deep trouble when he writes for money and fame. Those, like his bodily remains, will turn to ashes. The real record he leaves, in the libraries, will live forever."

In his life and in his writing, Hemphill is committed to the South. Upon reviewing Hemphill's complete body of work in an essay for the *Dictionary of Literary Biography Yearbook: 1987,* Stephen Whited finds that Hemphill "has consistently produced some of the most carefully pictured views of southern American life." Although Hemphill moved west at one point in his life, he is back in the midst of the foothills he calls home: "Yes, right here on this dinky little old street that hardly anybody in Atlanta knows about, I have found it. I'm home," Hemphill told a *Goodlife* interviewer.

As both a journalist and a fiction author, Hemphill's writings have emerged from the Southern experience. His first book, *The Nashville Sound: Bright Lights and Country Music,* is a journalistic overview of the rising popularity of country and western music. Christopher Lehmann-Haupt of the *New York Times* writes that Hemphill describes this phenomenon "delightfully, by

mixing together history and spot interviews and on-the-scene reportage in a book that reads as smoothly and sparklingly as a bluegrass breakdown." Craigg McGregor similarly comments on the book in his *New York Times Book Review* article: "Hemphill describes the scene in a racy, impressionistic style, mixing profiles of singers . . . with on-the-spot accounts of Friday night at Tootsie's Orchid Lounge, Saturday night at the Grand Ole Opry and several nights on the road with Bill Anderson and the Po' Boys. . . . His book is like a huge pop star collage." Even so, Whited maintains that *The Nashville Sound* is "more than a collection of star biographies. Hemphill gives the reader an understanding of how the country music business is run, what it had to overcome, who (Chet Atkins) make it what it is today, when it all got started, and where it all came from."

In a later autobiographical work called *Me and the Boy: Journey of Discovery—Father and Son on the Appalachian Trail,* Hemphill presents his rendering of the several-hundred-mile hike through southern Appalachia that he and his son undertook. The purpose of the journey was for Hemphill to amend his relationship with the nineteen-year-old David, whom he had abandoned almost ten years earlier because of divorce. The two set out to walk the entire 2,100 miles of the Appalachian Trail, from Georgia to Maine, but were beset with problems from the start. As Dennis Drabelle in the *Washington Post Book World* records: "In some ways the hike was a fiasco. Paul's knees gave out early and often, David sulked and usually hiked miles ahead of his father, and they covered only about a fourth of the total mileage," not to mention the fact that Hemphill's drinking developed a strain between the two. However, as both Drabelle and *Chicago Tribune Book World* reviewer Paul Perry explain, what arises between father and son during the latter part of the journey and book is a "greater understanding of each other and a sort of acceptance that, in an imperfect world, we have no reason to expect perfection from one another," writes Perry. Whited views the eventual reconciliation between father and son as the re-establishment of "the bond between generations, between Hemphill and his son, between Hemphill and his father, between Hemphill and his heritage."

Southern heritage is the focal point of Hemphill's novel *The Sixkiller Chronicles,* as well. Whereas *Los Angeles Times* reviewer Frank Levering is of the opinion that literature often reduces Southern culture to stereotypes and one-dimensionality, he claims "Hemphill has grasped many of the essentials and much of the cussed complication of this elusive, contemporary culture."

Accordingly, Hemphill takes the reader into the lives of three generations of the Clay family as they venture out from the mountains of their heritage in Sixkiller Gap and then return. Although Levering feels Hemphill has not succeeded in actually conveying specificity of place, he nevertheless feels "the central drama of a man trying to raise his son, preserve his land, express his values . . . and ensure their continuity in succeeding generations remains as potent as good corn liquor." In turn, critic Bruce Cook for the *Detroit News* charges that "the people in [*The Sixkiller Chronicles*] breathe life and whoop and holler just like real people. You want to spend more time with them, know all about them, discover what they have been up to in the years [Hemphill] leaves unchronicled. . . . Hemphill is growing stronger with each novel he writes. One or two books down the line he may well emerge as the next truly important Southern novelist."

Yet Hemphill continued to work mostly in the nonfiction genre. His 1996 book *The Heart of the Game: The Education of a Minor-League Ballplayer* was a highly praised account of one season in the life of an aspiring young ballplayer. It also related Hemphill's search for the real spirit of baseball in a year when millionaire players went on strike against billionaire team owners, cancelling most of the season and changing the public's perception of the sport forever. As a young man, Hemphill had a short stint as a minor-league hopeful, and he sees a reflection of his younger self in his subject, Marty Malloy. Malloy is a clean-living, talented young man playing for the Durham Bulls, a farm team for the Atlanta Braves. "The story-line is promising: how does a baseball-obsessed youngster not only manage to climb the sport's treacherous ladder but also learn to live on his own, far from his close-knit family?," reported a reviewer for *Economist*. *Booklist* commentator Wes Lukowsky praised Hemphill for allowing readers to get to know and care deeply about Marty, and for providing "fascinating details on the workings of a modern baseball organization, which is a curious mix of computers, faxes, and tobaccy-chewin' old-timers." Daniel W. Ross concurred in *Aethion*: "*The Heart of the Game* does offer a vivid portrait of minor-league baseball, of the dreams and aspirations that once seemed part of all baseball. The book reminds us that baseball will never be the same again; although attendance has picked up since the 1994 strike, something very essential in the game has been irretrievably lost."

Hemphill used a similar approach to look at stock car racing in his 1997 book, *Wheels: A Season on NASCAR's Winston Cup Circuit*. Hemphill "breathtakingly" shows the "relentless" nature of the 31-race season,

according to a *Publishers Weekly* reviewer, who also praised the author's contrast between the wealthy, elitist forces behind the sport with the fans, characterized by the author as "white, racist, ostentatiously patriotic but waving the Confederate flag, fundamentalist Protestants, hell-raising drinkers and womanizers." Wes Lukowsky endorsed *Wheels* in *Booklist*: "From the first race of the 1995 season-ending banquet at a post Manhattan hotel, Hemphill re-creates the unique mix of danger, excitement, courage, and technology that draws participants and fans alike to stock-car racing. But as always in an account such as this, it's the people who matter, and car racing is rich in both character and characters."

BIOGRAPHICAL/CRITICAL SOURCES:

BOOKS

Dictionary of Literary Biography Yearbook: 1987, Gale (Detroit, MI), 1988.
Hemphill, Paul, *Me and the Boy: Journey of Discovery—Father and Son on the Appalachian Trail,* Macmillan, 1986.
Leaving Birmingham: Notes of a Native Son, Viking, 1993.

PERIODICALS

Aethion, fall, 1998, Daniel W. Ross, review of *The Heart of the Game: The Education of a Minor-League Ballplayer.*
Atlanta Journal-Constitution, November 7, 1993; April 28, 1996, p. L13.
Atlantic, January, 1990, Phoebe-Lou Adams, review of *King of the Road,* p. 101.
Birmingham News, September 19, 1993; April 28, 1996.
Booklist, September 1, 1993, review of *Leaving Birmingham: Notes of a Native Son,* p. 12; March 15, 1996, Wes Lukowsky, review of *The Heart of the Game: The Education of a Minor-League Ballplayer,* p. 1234; June 1, 1997, Wes Lukowsky, review of *Wheels: A Season on NASCAR's Winston Cup Circuit,* p. 1644.
Boston Globe, September 15, 1993.
Chicago Tribune Book World, October 7, 1979; May 11, 1986.
Cosmopolitan, February, 1981, Jane Clapperton, review of *Too Old to Cry,* p. 22.
Detroit News, July 7, 1985.
Economist, September 14, 1996, review of *The Heart of the Game: The Education of a Minor-League Ballplayer,* p. S4.

Forbes, July 7, 1980, Malcolm S. Forbes, review of *Long Gone,* p. 23; March 1, 1982, review of *Too Old to Cry,* p. 27.

Goodlife, June-July, 1985.

Greensboro News & Record, March 31, 1996.

Library Journal, February 1, 1981, Anthony O. Edmonds, review of *Too Old to Cry,* p. 365; April 1, 1985, Dennis Pendleton, review of *The Sixkiller Chronicles,* p. 158; May 1, 1986, Roger W. Fromm, review of *Me and the Boy: Journey of Discovery-Father and Son on the Appalachian Trail,* p. 116; September 15, 1989, James B. Hemesath, review of *King of the Road,* p. 135; August, 1993, review of *Leaving Birmingham: Notes of a Native Son,* p. 114; February 1, 1996, Morey Berger and Paul Kaplan, review of *The Heart of the Game: The Education of a Minor-League Ballplayer,* p. 78; June 15, 1997, review of *Wheels: A Season on NASCAR's Winston Cup Circuit,* p. 76.

Los Angeles Times, September 18, 1985; December 10, 1989, p. 2.

Miami Herald, November 30, 1975.

New Republic, June 27, 1970.

Newsweek, August 20, 1979.

New York Review of Books, November 4, 1971.

New York Times, April 27, 1970; January 26, 1981; April 18, 1996.

New York Times Book Review, July 19, 1970; September 22, 1974; January 18, 1981, Dan Wakefield, review of *Too Old to Cry,* p. 7; May 5, 1985, Richard Goodman, review of *The Sixkiller Chronicles,* p. 24; January 7, 1990, Mark Goodman, review of *King of the Road,* p. 18; September 19, 1993, review of *Leaving Birmingham: Notes of a Native Son,* p. 30; May 5, 1996, review of *The Heart of the Game: The Education of a Minor-League Ballplayer,* p. 23.

Playboy, February, 1981, review of *Too Old to Cry,* p. 32.

Publishers Weekly, November 28, 1980, Genevieve Stuttaford, review of *Too Old to Cry,* p. 41; February 22, 1985, review of *The Sixkiller Chronicles,* p. 151; March 14, 1986, Genevieve Stuttaford, review of *Me and the Boy: Journey of Discovery-Father and Son on the Appalachian Trail,* p. 91; September 22, 1989, Sybil Steinberg, review of *King of the Road,* p. 38; July 19, 1993, review of *Leaving Birmingham: Notes of a Native Son,* p. 242; February 12, 1996, review of *The Heart of the Game: The Education of a Minor-League Ballplayer,* p. 67; May 12, 1997, review of *Wheels: A Season on NASCAR's Winston Cup Circuit,* p. 66.

Southern Living, May, 1985, review of *The Sixkiller Chronicles,* p. 156.

Washington Post, August 27, 1979; February 14, 1981; April 20, 1986.

Washington Post Book World, April 7, 1985.

Writer's Digest, October, 1980, Maxine Rock, "Paul Hemphill vs. the Typewriter," p. 36.*

*   *   *

HIMMELFARB, Gertrude 1922-

PERSONAL: Born August 8, 1922, in New York, NY; daughter of Max (a manufacturer) and Bertha (Lerner) Himmelfarb; married Irving Kristol (a professor and editor), January 18, 1942; children: William, Elizabeth. *Education:* Attended Jewish Theological Seminary, 1939-42; Brooklyn College (now Brooklyn College of the City University of New York), B.A., 1942; University of Chicago, M.A., 1944, Ph.D., 1950; attended Girton College, Cambridge, 1946-47.

ADDRESSES: Office—The Graduate Center, City University of New York, 365 Fifth Ave., New York, NY 10016.

CAREER: Independent scholar, 1950-65; City University of New York, professor of history at the university's Brooklyn College, 1965-78, distinguished professor of history at the university's Graduate School, 1978-88, professor emerita of history, 1988—. National Humanities Center, member of board of trustees, 1976—; National Endowment for the Humanities, council member, 1982—; Library of Congress, council of scholars, 1984—; Woodrow Wilson Center, member of board of trustees, 1985-96; British Institute of the United States, member of board of directors, 1985—; Institute for Contemporary Studies, member of board of directors, 1986—; Ethics and Public Policy Center, associate scholar, 1986—; American Enterprise Institute, council of academic advisers member, 1987—; National Endowment for the Humanities, Jefferson lecturer, 1991; Library of America, board of advisors, 1992—; American Council of Trustees and Alumni, council of scholars, 1995—. Member of Presidential Advisory Commission on Economic Role of Women.

MEMBER: British Academy (fellow), American Academy of Arts and Sciences, Society of American Historians, American Historical Association, Royal Historical Society (fellow), American Philosophical Society.

AWARDS, HONORS: American Association of University Women fellowship, 1951-52; American Philosophical Society fellowship, 1953-54; Guggenheim fellowships, 1955-56, 1957-58; Rockefeller Foundation grants, 1962-63, 1963-64; National Endowment for the Humanities senior fellowship, 1968-69; American Council of Learned Societies fellowship, 1972-73; Phi Beta Kappa visiting scholarship, 1972-73; Woodrow Wilson Center fellowship, 1976-77; Rockefeller Humanities fellowship, 1980-81.

WRITINGS:

Lord Acton: A Study in Conscience and Politics, University of Chicago Press (Chicago, IL), 1952, reprinted, ICS Press (San Francisco, CA), 1993.

Darwin and the Darwinian Revolution, Doubleday (Garden City, NY), 1959, revised edition, P. Smith (Gloucester, MA), 1967, reprinted, I. R. Dee (Chicago, IL), 1996.

Victorian Minds: Essays on Nineteenth-Century Intellectuals, Knopf (New York, NY), 1968, reprinted, I. R. Dee (Chicago, IL), 1995.

On Liberty and Liberalism: The Case of John Stuart Mill, Knopf (New York, NY), 1974, reprinted, ICS Press (San Francisco, CA), 1990.

The Idea of Poverty: England in the Early Industrial Age, Knopf (New York, NY), 1984.

Marriage and Morals among the Victorians, and Other Essays, Knopf (New York, NY), 1986, reprinted as *Marriage and Morals among Victorians: Essays,* I. R. Dee (New York, NY), 2001.

The New History and the Old, Harvard University Press (Cambridge, MA), 1987.

Poverty and Compassion: The Moral Imagination of the Late Victorians, Knopf (New York, NY), 1991.

On Looking into the Abyss: Untimely Thoughts on Culture and Society, Knopf (New York, NY), 1994.

The De-Moralization of Society: From Victorian Virtues to Modern Values, Knopf (New York, NY), 1995.

One Nation, Two Cultures: A Moral Divide, Knopf (New York, NY), 1999.

EDITOR

Lord Acton, *Essays on Freedom and Power,* Free Press (New York, NY), 1948.

Thomas R. Malthus, *On Population,* Modern Library (New York, NY), 1960.

John Stuart Mill, *Essays on Politics and Culture,* Doubleday, 1962.

John Stuart Mill, *On Liberty,* Penguin (Baltimore, MD), 1975.

Also, Tocqueville, *Memoir on Pauperism,* 1997.

OTHER

Contributor to books, including *Chapters in Western Civilization,* Columbia University Press (New York, NY), 3rd edition (Himmelfarb was not included in earlier editions), edited by Bernard Wishy and others, 1962; *The Burke-Paine Controversy,* edited by R. H. Browne, Harcourt (New York, NY), 1963; *British Imperialism,* edited by Robin Winks, Holt (New York, NY), 1963; *The Rise of Science in Relation to Society,* edited by Leonard M. Marsak, Macmillan (New York, NY), 1964; *Ideas in History: Essays in Honor of Louis Gottschalk,* edited by Richard Herr and Harold T. Parker, Duke University Press (Durham, NC), 1965; *Landmarks in Western Culture,* edited by Donald N. Baker and G. W. Fasel, Prentice-Hall (Englewood Cliffs, NJ), 1967; *Civilization Past and Present,* edited by T. W. Wallbank and others, Scott, Foresman (New York, NY), 6th edition (Himmelfarb was not included in earlier editions), 1969; *The Emergence of British Parliamentary Democracy in the Nineteenth Century,* edited by John B. Conacher, Wiley (New York, NY), 1971; *The Victorian City: Images and Realities,* edited by Michael Wolff and H. J. Dyos, Routledge (London, England), 1973; *Art, Politics, and the Will,* edited by Quentin Anderson and others, Basic (New York, NY), 1977; *Points of Light: New Approaches to Ending Welfare Dependency,* edited by Tamar Ann Mehuron, University Press of America (Lanham, MD), 1990; *Work and Welfare,* by Robert M. Solow, edited by Amy Gutmann, Princeton University Press (Princeton, NJ), 1998.

Contributor to journals and periodicals including *Journal of Contemporary History, Victorian Studies, Journal of British Studies, Journal of Modern History, American Historical Review, Commentary, Encounter, American Scholar, New Republic, New York Times, Wilson Quarterly* and *Harper's.* Member of editorial board of *Albion, American Historical Review, American Scholar, Journal of British Studies, Jewish Social Studies, Reviews in European History,* and *This World.*

SIDELIGHTS: Gertrude Himmelfarb is well known as an authority on Victorian England and as a cultural historian whose interests in the past translate into suggestions for the present. She has "occupied a unique place in the historical profession and among American scholars," stated *Encyclopedia of World Biography,* noting that the conservative scholar's "political views and her work [have often been] controversial and subjected to harsh criticism." "Universally recognized and respected for the depth of her scholarship, her gift of analysis, and the incisiveness of her argument, she was justly described by another eminent American historian of Victorian Britain as 'the most eminent American scholar to have written acutely on the history of Victorian ideas.''

As a writer, Himmelfarb "is almost as much a critic of historiography as a historian—a critic, too, with a strong revisionist impulse, an urge to correct (with some asperity) the errors of her predecessors," according to John Gross in the *Observer.* Many of her books focus upon the history of thought in Victorian England, a period which she defines as extending from the late eighteenth century (and the life of Edmund Burke) to the early twentieth century (ending roughly around the time of John Buchan). In these texts she covers a variety of noteworthy figures, including Thomas Malthus, John Stuart Mill, Thomas Macauley, Walter Bagehot, and Jeremy Bentham, while also discussing such historical issues as the Reform Act of 1867 and Social Darwinism.

With an emphasis on the many ambiguities in philosophy which were present in the Victorian Age, Himmelfarb nevertheless manages to unify the whole with what she calls the "moral imagination" of the Victorians (a phrase that Burke first coined). This is a general term which Gross defined as "a set of characteristic Victorian convictions—a belief in human dignity, a respect for human complexity, a sense of common responsibility based on sympathetic insight rather than textbook rules." Although she is able to tie her subjects together with this motif, she does not fall into the trap of "smoothing over contradictions or bringing [a person's] thought into an erroneous uniformity," observed Thomas Lask of the *New York Times.* Himmelfarb feels that modern critics tend to form a consensus on how history is to be treated based upon whatever school of criticism is popular at the time, and that this seriously clouds their ability to analyze facts properly. *New Statesman* contributor A. S. Byatt phrased the historian's attitude this way: "She deprecates current intellectual fashions of simplicity and commitment, pointing out that subtleties, complications, and ambiguities—once the mark of serious thought—are now taken to signify a failure of nerve." This attitude has drawn both positive and negative reactions from her colleagues and critics.

For example, in a review of Himmelfarb's *Victorian Minds, Carleton Miscellany* contributor Robert E. Bonner wrote, "The problem is that the intelligent historian here changes garb rapidly and often becomes a scourge of ideologues past and, by implication, present. The result is at best misconceived or misdirected history or

criticism, and at worst is history in the service of a particular modern American 'liberal' orthodoxy." On the other hand, Robert A. Nisbet, in *Commentary,* observed that Himmelfarb's "knowledge of the century is vast, but it rarely if ever swamps her judgment . . . which remains . . . precise and discriminating."

Continuing to break down the walls of pat historical interpretation, the historian brings to our attention in *The Idea of Poverty* not only the subject of England's nineteenth-century Poor Laws, but also how the very concept of poverty changed over time to include an ever narrower segment of the population. She shows us, according to *Times Literary Supplement* reviewer Harold Perkin, how the awareness of the poverty problem and its relation to ideas about poverty changed over time. Perkin asserted that the scholar "cuts through the mouldy rags of interpretation which have been piled upon the poor and their interpreters for generations."

Marriage and Morals among the Victorians, and Other Essays also offers an analysis of the Victorian Age, this time with an emphasis on the sense of morality of the period. *New York Times Book Review* contributor Neil McKendrick felt that Himmelfarb "offers a more sympathetic response than is usual to late Victorian morality." This book has drawn some negative criticism from reviewers like Rosemary Ashton of the *Times Literary Supplement* who noted, "If one has a complaint, it is that [the idea of a 'precarious' late Victorian morality] is less argued than assumed, that Himmelfarb spends more time disapproving than approving." Overall, however, critics tended to agree with McKendrick that *Marriage and Morals among the Victorians and Other Essays* "is an important book that deserves a wide readership."

Himmelfarb's criticism of modern historians has unfolded in two volumes of essays, *The New History and the Old* and *On Looking into the Abyss: Untimely Thoughts on Culture and Society.* In both books she attacks the prevalent acceptance of social history (a science that studies the history of ordinary people and ignores politics), as well as the recent trends of postmodernist historiography. Her fear here, *Los Angeles Times Book Review* contributor Paul Johnson summarized, is that "when traditional history is completely displaced, what takes over is often not history at all but forms of covert left-wing propaganda." It is not, as Himmelfarb herself proclaims, that she objects "to social history as such," but she does dispute "its claims of dominance, superiority, even 'totality.' "

On Looking into the Abyss crystallizes the author's argument for a return to "the Enlightenment principles [of] reason, truth, justice, morality, reality." Emphasizing the traditional concepts of morality and virtue, Himmelfarb takes to task post-modernist and deconstructionist historians, whose work she deplores as not only inaccurate but potentially harmful to the future of the discipline. "Himmelfarb rejects the postmodernists and their claim to being taken seriously," declared David Kirkwood in *Society*. "She rejects them not only because of their obscurantism, their propensity for dealing with dissent by McCarthy-ite tactics, but mainly for their denial of moral reality and, hence, moral responsibility. . . . Historians have the moral obligation not to impose their values upon their subjects—reading history backwards. But the past must be judged, and historians must make moral judgments, if the present generation is to learn from history."

As controversial as its predecessor, *On Looking into the Abyss* drew most of its praise from conservative essayists, who have consistently applauded Himmelfarb's viewpoint. "Fortunate he who, peering apprehensively into the dread Abyss, finds beside him, peering too and holding his hand, the intrepid, benign, and reassuring figure of Professor Himmelfarb," wrote Colin Welch in the *National Review*. "Reviewing these present splendid essays, I could start by testifying to their formidable erudition and wide range; to the prodigious mastery of areas of dark knowledge which many of us don't have or wish we didn't; to their polemic power and capacity to make clear what is obscure or complex; and so on. But when all is said and done, it is [Himmelfarb's] own character that, like the emperor's head on the Thaler, gives these essays much of their value."

Perhaps one of Himmelfarb's most influential books to date is *The De-Moralization of Society: From Victorian Virtues to Modern Values*. First published in 1995, the book demonstrates that, by use of the Poor Law and other methods to shame the indigent, Victorian England controlled not only the number of persons applying for government relief, but also saw reductions in crime and illegitimate births. She further argues that the absence of morality today—and the substitution of a non-judgmental set of individual "values"—has led to a demoralization and its attendant ills of crime, welfare dependency, and single-parent families. Again the critical response to the book depended upon the reviewer's political leanings.

"It is a delicate matter how a tract for the times gets read," maintained David Bromwich in the *New Republic*. "So often, its reception will depend on the partiali-

ties of the spirit in which it is read. A hardening of antipathy toward the poor, and toward every effort of social amelioration: these are traits of American life in the 1990s that many sharers of the mood would like to sweeten with the name of virtue. And, less from its explicit argument than from a certain shading of style and the ease of the past-and-present structure, I cannot help wondering whether the effect of this pleasant and informative book will not be to act as a great simplifier." Conversely, *National Review* contributor Christie Davies called *The De-Moralization of Society* "an excellent, detailed, and insightful account of the creation, maintenance, and (in our time) decline of the Victorian virtues of work, thrift, self-reliance, self-respect, neighborliness, and patriotism." Davies added, "Gertrude Himmelfarb's latest study of the Victorians is, like all her work in this field, a delight to read—clear, erudite, sensible, logical, and creative. . . . Professor Himmelfarb's is also a moral text, for it not only dissects and praises the morality of Victorian Britain, but also shows in great statistical detail how far present-day Britain and America fall short of the Victorian ideal. It points the way to a possible renewal of society to cure our current demoralization."

In her 1999 release, *One Nation, Two Cultures: A Moral Divide,* Himmelfarb elaborates on her assessment of the moral state of modern American society. *One Nation, Two Cultures* "exhibits the same felicity of expression, sobriety, and intelligence as her previous works," applauded Edward S. Shapiro, who opined in *World & I,* "Himmelfarb's ultimate goal has not been merely to dissect the intellectual and moral premises underlying Anglo-American culture of the past two centuries. Rather, she has sought to refute the various historiographical theories preaching determinism, whether derived from economic, psychological, or sociological premises. For her, the motivating forces in history have been the choices made by individuals, particularly statesmen and intellectuals, and these have frequently involved moral questions regarding values and behavior."

Unlike many of her previous works, in *One Nation, Two Cultures* Himmelfarb does not focus on the Victorian era, "though her warm regard for Victorian civic virtue permeates it," noted a *Booklist* review. Instead, Himmelfarb devotes her text to describing and contrasting what she sees as two distinct segments of the American population, the "dominant" group, whose values and behavior have sprung forth from the liberal trends set in the 1960s, and the minority group, which is comprised of the remaining twenty-five percent (or thereabouts) and holds more definitive, traditional attitudes.

One Nation, Two Cultures is, according to Terry Teachout in *National Review,* "a concise, clear-eyed look at the culture war and what it really means." As Paul Johnson highlighted in *Commentary,* Himmelfarb addresses "the moral consequence of capitalism, the diseases of democracy, civil society, the family and its enemies, the problems of legislating morality, religion as a political institution, and, especially, America's two cultures—the one hedonistic, the other puritanical—and the 'ethics gap' between them."

The manners of the dominant group have, in Himmelfarb's opinion, led America into a state filled with ailments stemming from moral decline. Although not without optimism in her book, she delineates Americas woes, evidenced, as Shapiro related, by "declining educational standards and . . . increasing sexual promiscuity, abortions, divorce, crime, drug usage . . . welfare dependency. . . . [and] illegitimacy." *Publishers Weekly* maintained that *One Nation, Two Cultures* is "substantive" and "well-articulated," and Himmelfarb's "arguments are forceful and sophisticated, but dovetail cleanly with contemporary rightist rhetoric." As Shapiro remarked, "She writes in the great tradition of republican moralists, who recognized that a republic was dependent on, more than anything else, the moral content of the lives of its citizens."

"Himmelfarb's pithy, provocative book celebrates the minority and its ethos as a promising remedy for the many 'diseases' afflicting the country," commented *New Leader* contributor Tamar Jacoby, who assessed, "In a way this is an appealing vision, not only because it is pleasingly schematic . . . but more important because it suggests an easy answer to our moral quandaries. Traditional values are all we need, it implies, and the backbone to live by them, Unfortunately, skilled as she is in marshaling both statistics and moral arguments, in the end Himmelfarb does not persuade. On the contrary, the more she makes her case, the more unduly hopeful it seems and the more dauntingly the moral challenges posed by modernist loom in contrast. Yet, overly simple and certain as her thesis may be, she remains an unusually thoughtful guide to reviving and encouraging a moral sensibility today. It is almost as if her book were good in spite of itself, or in spite of what she perceives to be its central, saving message."

What Himmelfarb argues is "a division between two cultures," Shapiro maintained, "is an exaggeration." For Shapiro, Himmelfarb's arguments are just "the latest, and certainly not the last, chapter in the perennial struggle between indulgence and restraint that has characterized human nature as well as American history."

Teachout acknowledged that what Himmelfarb asserts is not novel, but maintained that her style of presentation makes *One Nation, Two Cultures* stand apart from other works. Teachout lauded, "Once or twice in a generation—if that often—a very wise person writes a very pithy book that compresses everything that needs to be said about a given topic into the briefest of compasses. . . . [A work that] change[s] minds, and lives. *One Nation, Two Cultures* is such a book." Likewise, Paul Johnson complimented in *Commentary,* "Of all those who write about the moral condition of America, Gertrude Himmelfarb is the best—partly because she is a historian, able to dip into deep reserves of knowledge to bring up parallels and precedents; partly because she has a strong taste for hard evidence and makes impressive use of statistics; partly because she is cool-headed and refuses to become hysterical about the awfulness of things and finally because she writes well and succinctly."

BIOGRAPHICAL/CRITICAL SOURCES:

BOOKS

Encyclopedia of World Biography, 2nd edition, Gale (Detroit, MI), 1998.

PERIODICALS

America, March 18, 1995, p. 27.
Booklist, October 1, 1999, review of *One Nation, Two Cultures,* p. 311.
Carleton Miscellany, fall, 1968, Robert E. Bonner, review of *Victorian Minds.*
Commentary, November, 1968; April, 1994, p. 63; May, 1995, p. 66; January, 2000, Paul Johnson, review of *One Nation, Two Cultures,* p. 66.
Harper's, July, 1995, p. 72.
Insight on the News, March 6, 1995, p. 27.
Los Angeles Times Book Review, September 27, 1987.
National Catholic Reporter, April 14, 1995, p. 17.
National Review, April 18, 1994, p. 48; April 3, 1995, p. 63; November 22, 1999, Terry Teachout, "We Lost. Now What?," p. 51.
New Leader, December 13, 1999, Tamar Jacoby, review of *One Nation, Two Cultures,* p. 6.
New Republic, May 15, 1995, David Bromwich, review of *The De-Moralization of Society,* p. 28.
New Statesman, December 6, 1968.
New York Times, February 28, 1986.
New York Times Book Review, March 23, 1986, Neil McKendrick, review of *Marriage and Morals among the Victorians, and Other Essays.*
Observer, October 6, 1968.

Publishers Weekly, January 10, 1994, p. 52; November 1, 1999, review of *One Nation, Two Cultures,* p. 67.

Reason, June, 1995, p. 52.

Society, November-December, 1994, David Kirkwood, review of *On Looking into the Abyss,* pp. 78, 83.

Times Literary Supplement, May 25, 1984; July 25, 1986; January 15, 1988.

USA Today, September, 1995, p. 96.

World & I, May, 2000, Edward S. Shapiro, "A Modern Jeremiad: Culture, Not Economics, Lies at the Heart of What Ails America," pp. 275-279.*

*   *   *

HIRSCH, Edward 1950-

PERSONAL: Born January 20, 1950, in Chicago, IL; son of Kurt and Irma (Ginsburg) Hirsch; married Janet Landay (a museum curator), May 29, 1977; children: Gabriel. *Education:* Grinnell College, B.A., 1972; University of Pennsylvania, Ph.D., 1979.

ADDRESSES: Home—1528 Sul Ross, Houston, TX 77006. *Office*—Department of English, University of Houston, 4800 Calhoun, Houston, TX 77204.

CAREER: Wayne State University, Detroit, MI, assistant professor, 1979-82, associate professor of English, 1982-85; University of Houston, Houston, TX, associate professor, 1985-88, professor of English, 1988—. Member of the education advisory committee of the Guggenheim Foundation. Member of the advisory board of the American Poetry and Literary Project.

MEMBER: Modern Language Association of America, Poetry Society of America, Authors League of America, Authors Guild, PEN, Phi Beta Kappa.

AWARDS, HONORS: Watson fellow, 1972-73; Academy of American Poets awards, 1975-77; Amy Lowell traveling fellow, 1978-79; Ingram Merrill Award, Ingram Merrill Foundation, 1978-79, for poetry; American Council of Learned Societies fellow, 1981; National Endowment for the Arts creative writing fellowship, 1982; National Book Critics Circle Award nomination, 1982, for *For the Sleepwalkers;* Peter I. B. Lavan Younger Poets Award, Academy of American Poets, 1983; Delmore Schwartz Memorial Poetry Award, New York University, 1985; Guggenheim poetry fellowship, 1985-86; National Book Critics Circle Award, 1987, for *Wild Gratitude;* Rome Prize, Ameri-

can Academy and Institute of Arts and Letters, American Academy in Rome, 1988; William Riley Parker Prize, Modern Language Association, 1992; Lyndhurst Prize, 1994-96; American Academy of Arts and Letters literature award, 1998; MacArthur fellow, 1998.

WRITINGS:

POETRY

For the Sleepwalkers, Knopf (New York, NY), 1981.
Wild Gratitude, Knopf (New York, NY), 1986.
The Night Parade, Knopf (New York, NY), 1989.
Earthly Measures, Knopf (New York, NY), 1994.
On Love, Knopf (New York, NY), 1998.

OTHER

(Author of introduction and selector) *Transforming Vision: Writers on Art,* Little, Brown (Boston, MA), 1994.

How to Read a Poem: And Fall in Love with Poetry, Harcourt (San Diego, CA), 1999.

Responsive Reading, University of Michigan Press (Ann Arbor, MI), 1999.

Contributor of articles, stories, poems, and reviews to periodicals, including *New Yorker, Poetry, American Poetry Review, Nation, New Republic, New York Times Book Review,* and *Paris Review.*

SIDELIGHTS: "I would like to speak in my poems with what the Romantic poets called 'the true voice of feeling,' " Edward Hirsch once told *CA.* "I believe, as Ezra Pound once said, that when it comes to poetry, 'only emotion endures.' " Described by Peter Stitt in *Poetry* as "a poet of genuine talent and feeling," Hirsch has been highly acclaimed for his poetry collections, *For the Sleepwalkers* and *Wild Gratitude. For the Sleepwalkers* was nominated for the National Book Critics Circle Award in 1981, and *Wild Gratitude* won the award in 1987. The two books contain vignettes of urban life and numerous tributes to artists, which, according to David Wojahn in the *New York Times Book Review,* "begin as troubled meditations on human suffering [but] end in celebration." *New Republic* contributor Jay Parini wrote that in *For the Sleepwalkers,* "Hirsch inhabits, poem by poem, dozens of other skins. He can become Rimbaud, Rilke, Paul Klee, or Matisse, in each case convincingly." "I admire Edward Hirsch," declared Phoebe Pettingell in the *New Leader,* "for his mystical vision, for the mastery he has . . . attained—and for his daring."

While many reviewers have applauded Hirsch's poetry, declaring that it exhibits tenderness, intelligence, and musicality that goes beyond mere technique, they have also recognized in his highly rhetorical style the propensity to "cross the borderline between effectiveness and excess," as Stitt asserted. For instance, Wojahn maintained that "Hirsch's tenderness [in *Wild Gratitude*] sometimes threatens to become merely ingratiating," and Hugh Seidman, in a *New York Times Book Review* article, thought that Hirsch's first work, *For the Sleepwalkers,* is "a poetry of narcissistic invention employing exaggerated tone and metaphor," an excess that Seidman believed is typical of much contemporary American poetry. Nevertheless, Parini insisted that Hirsch's poems "easily fulfill Auden's request that poems be, above all else, 'memorable language,' " and Carolyn Kizer declared in the *Washington Post Book World* that Hirsch's "great strength lies in his descriptive powers." As Hirsch "learns to administer with lighter touch his considerable linguistic fertility," claimed Stitt, "he will surely grow into one of the important writers of our age."

The poems in Hirsch's third book, *The Night Parade,* continue with themes presented in his first two works, but stray from his stylistic and formal techniques, perhaps indicating a transitional period. Hirsch told *CA:* "Many of these poems are more meditative and narrative, linking the personal to the historical, contemplating the nature of family stories and expanding outward from there to consider the history and development of Chicago as a city." He added, "The passionate clarity of [my] style has not always met with critical approval." In the *New York Times Book Review,* Stephen Dobyns remarked, "Despite several marvelous poems, *The Night Parade* doesn't seem as strong as his previous book. Too many poems become sentimental or seem willed rather than to come from the heart." Pat Monaghan in *Booklist,* however, praised Hirsch's "sure sense of the line between emotion and sentimentality." *New York Review of Books* critic Helen Vendler felt that "when Hirsch is not being historically stagy, he is being familially prosaic, as he recalls stories told by his parents," but she also thought Hirsch "capable of quiet, believable poems." She cited the poem "Infertility" from Hirsch's *The Night Parade* as the most believable poem of the book, and suggested, "This poem, I suspect, will turn up in anthologies. It touches a particular connection between religious longing and secular pessimism that belongs both to the hope and desolation it commemorates and to the moment of scientific possibility and disappointment in which we live."

In his fourth collection of poems, *Earthly Measures,* Hirsch offers a collection focused on religious issues and imagery. Hirsch told *CA:* "If I were to describe [*Earthly Measures*], I would say that it is 'god hungry.' *Earthly Measures* is very much about what the soul does after hungering after God and He does not come. What does one do to fill the subsequent emptiness? The book begins in the dark wood with landscapes of ash and emptiness and hell. Throughout the book are elegies which point toward the loss of presence, power, and direction. The emptiness contains infertility but it is not defined by it. About halfway through the book it takes a turn—not toward celebration exactly, but a sort of agonized reconciliation. The tutelary figures are Simone Weil, Leopardi, and Hoffmansthal. The poems take the transformative and even redemptive powers of art seriously. Art stands against the emptiness. The book is about a soul-journey. It begins in 'Uncertainty' and concludes with an homage to the 17th century Dutch painters and their feeling for 'Earthly Light.' It is a pilgrim's progress struggling toward the light."

Reviewers had mixed opinions of *Earthly Measures,* with some critics praising the "god hungry" nature of the work and others terming the collection insufficiently nuanced. Writing in the *New York Times Book Review,* Patricia Hampl remarked, "The absence of God and the abundant presence of human desire reign over his book and form a passionately important inquiry into the nature of worship." Robert B. Shaw, commenting in *Poetry,* likewise praised the poems in the collection for being "accessible in subject, direct in phrasing, open in their expression of emotion, graced with a finely-tuned lyricism." Yet, Shaw noted, "the neo-Romantic tone and coloration makes for a sameness . . . so that the subjects lose something of their individuality in an all-purpose luminous haze." *Washington Post Book World* contributor Eric Murphy Selinger also lamented the lyrical romanticism of the poems, declaring that "Hirsch is better off when his voice has a bitter or critical edge." Hampl, though, commended Hirsch for his achievement in *Earthly Measures,* concluding, "These are poems of immense wonder and rigor. To say they are religious poems is only to recognize their grandeur and generosity, and their heartbreaking longing."

In the collection *On Love,* Hirsch takes the voice of some two dozen poets from the past, including such diverse writers as D. H. Lawrence, Charles Baudelaire, and Jimi Hendrix. He creates an imaginary conversation between them in which they discuss the subject of love. The verses in *On Love* prove "without question" that Hirsch is "heir to all the great poets of the past," in the opinion of Donna Seaman of *Booklist,* who added that when writing about his own life, Hirsch achieves "lyric poems nearly incandescent in their sensuality." The reviewer for *Publishers Weekly* noted that when reading Hirsch's work, "one is always aware of a formidable intelligence; wide reading, and an ambition to connect the poet's own achievement with the great poetry of the past." While acknowledging the "controlled, precise, formally ambitious" quality of Hirsch's verse, the *Publishers Weekly* reviewer faulted the poet's use of "a highly artificial premise, made more so by the incredibly strict forms." Yet Thomas F. Merrill in *Library Journal* called *On Love* "often stunning" for its "complex evocations of the adopted voices as well as Hirsch's own insight."

Hirsch has also written prose works that have met with critical acclaim. In *How to Read a Poem: And Fall in Love with Poetry,* he collected verses from diverse times and places and then suggested ways to understand and appreciate the works. "The book is scholarly but very readable and incorporates interesting anecdotes from the lives of the poets," noted Ellen Sullivan in *Library Journal. Booklist's* Donna Seaman declared: "Hirsch, a truly gifted poet and scholar, brings the full heat of his literary passion to this enlightening and deeply moving journey into the heart of poetry. . . . Hirsch's magnificent text is supported by an extensive glossary and superb international reading list."

BIOGRAPHICAL/CRITICAL SOURCES:

BOOKS

Contemporary Literary Criticism, Gale (Detroit, MI), Volume 31, 1985, Volume 50, 1988.
Dictionary of Literary Biography, Volume 120: *American Poets since World War II, Third Series,* Gale (Detroit, MI), 1992.

PERIODICALS

AB Bookman's Weekly, November 28, 1994, review of *Earthly Measures,* p. 2281.
American Libraries, December, 1994, review of *Earthly Measures,* p. 1040; April, 1999, review of *How to Read a Poem: And Fall in Love with Poetry,* p. 93.
American Scholar, spring, 1999, review of *How to Read a Poem: And Fall in Love with Poetry,* p. 140.
Bloomsbury Review, March, 2000, interview with Edward Hirsch, pp. 15-16.
Booklist, March 15, 1989, p. 1243; February 15, 1994, Donna Seaman, review of *Earthly Measures,* p. 1053; January 15, 1995, review of *Earthly Measures,* p. 855; May 1, 1998, Donna Seaman, review of *On Love,* p. 1495; March 15, 1999, Donna Seaman, review of *How to Read a Poem: And Fall in Love with Poetry,* p. 1273; January 1, 2000, review of *How to Read a Poem: And Fall in Love with Poetry,* p. 812.
Choice, January, 2000, review of *How to Read a Poem: And Fall in Love with Poetry,* p. 925.
Christian Science Monitor, December 9, 1994, review of *Transforming Vision: Writers on Art,* p. 11.
Commonweal, December 1, 1995, review of *Earthly Measures,* p. 20.
DoubleTake, issue 6, review of *How to Read a Poem: And Fall in Love with Poetry.*
Five Points, winter, 2000, interview with Edward Hirsch, pp. 58-74.
Georgia Review, summer, 1982.
Hudson Review, winter, 1995, review of *Earthly Measures,* p. 673.
Image, fall, 2000, interview with Edward Hirsch, pp. 52-69.
Kenyon Review, spring, 2000, interview with Edward Hirsch, pp. 54-69.
Kirkus Reviews, June 1, 1998, review of *On Love,* p. 778; April 1, 1999, p. 465.
Library Journal, March 1, 1994, review of *Earthly Measures,* p. 90; June 15, 1998, Thomas F. Merrill, review of *On Love,* p. 82; May 1, 1999, Ellen Sullivan, review of *How to Read a Poem: And Fall in Love with Poetry,* p. 77.
Nation, September 13, 1981, p. 14; September 27, 1986, p. 285; December 26, 1994, review of *Earthly Measures,* p. 814.
New Leader, March 8, 1982, Phoebe Pettingell, review of *For the Sleepwalkers.*
New Republic, April 14, 1982, Jay Parini, review of *For the Sleepwalkers,* p. 37.
New Yorker, May 23, 1994, review of *Earthly Measures,* p. 101.
New York Review of Books, August 17, 1989, p. 26; July 16, 1998, review of *On Love,* p. 41.
New York Times, August 3, 1994, p. C19.
New York Times Book Review, September 13, 1981, p. 14; June 8, 1986, p. 38; January 28, 1990, p. 26; May 15, 1994, review of *Earthly Measures,* p. 26; June 5, 1994, review of *Earthly Measures,* p. 34; December 4, 1994, review of *Earthly Measures,* p. 78; July 4, 1999, review of *How to Read a Poem: And Fall in Love with Poetry,* p. 17.
Poetry, May, 1986; December, 1994, Robert B. Shaw, review of *Earthly Measures,* p. 158; March, 1999, review of *On Love,* p. 357.
Publishers Weekly, January 3, 1994, review of *Earthly Measures,* p. 72; May 25, 1998, review of *On Love,*

p. 84; March 29, 1999, review of *How to Read a Poem: And Fall in Love with Poetry,* p. 100.

Rattle, summer, 2000, interview with Edward Hirsch, pp. 139-154.

Tribune Books (Chicago), February 1, 1987, p. 2; August 6, 1989, p. 5.

Voice Quarterly Review, autumn, 1994, review of *Earthly Measures,* p. 133.

Wall Street Journal, April 2, 1999, review of *How to Read a Poem: And Fall in Love with Poetry,* p. W6.

Washington Post Book World, July 6, 1986, p. 8; May 22, 1994, review of *Earthly Measures,* p. 11; January 10, 1999, review of *On Love,* p. 11.

World Literature Today, winter, 1999, review of *On Love,* p. 160.

Yale Review, July, 1998, review of *On Love,* p. 160.

* * *

HONEYMAN, Brenda
See CLARKE, Brenda (Margaret Lilian)

* * *

HUSTON, Nancy 1953-
(Annécie Rosiers, a pseudonym)

PERSONAL: Born September 16, 1953, in Calgary, Alberta, Canada; daughter of James (a professor) and Mary Louise Engels (a clinical psychologist; maiden name, Kester) Huston; married Tzvetan Todoro (a scholar and writer), May, 1981; children: Léa, Alexandre. *Education:* Sarah Lawrence College, B.A., 1975; L'Ecole des Hautes Etudes en Sciences Sociales, Diploma, 1977.

ADDRESSES: Home and Office—4, rue Lacépède 75005 Paris, France. *Agent*—Mary Kling, La Nouvelle Agence, 7 rue Corneille, 75006 Paris, France.

CAREER: Writer. University of Columbia, Paris, France, professor of French feminist theory, 1976, 1983-89, professor of composition and stylistics, 1990-91, professor of French literature, 1992-93; Académie Commerciale Internationale, Chambre de Commerce, Paris, professor of English, 1976-78; Institut Supérieur Libre des Carrières Artistiques, Paris, professor of French literature, 1977-78; Centre de Formation Permanente et de Perfectionnement, Ministère des Finances, Paris, professor of English, 1978-85; Sarah Lawrence College, Paris, professor of literature and semiology, 1983-86. Fiction writer-in-residence, Women's Institute for Continuing Education, American University, Paris, 1989; visiting professor, Department of Romance Languages and Literatures, Harvard University, 1994; writer-in-residence, l'Abbaye de Royaumont, 1994. Member of radio-plays reading committee for France-Culture (French national radio), 1987-90.

AWARDS, HONORS: Prix Binet-Sangle, French Academy, 1980, for *Dire et interdire: Eléments de jurologie;* Prix Contrepoint, 1981, for *Les Variations Goldberg, Romance;* United Nations Peace Prize, 1981, for *Fragments of a Warrior's Discourse;* Prix Canada-Suisse, Prix Luciole, and Governor-General's Award for best French-language novel, all 1993, all for *Cantique des plaines;* Prix "L" de Limoges and Prix Louis Hemon de L'Académie du Languedoc, both 1944, both for *La Virevolte;* Prix Goncourt des lycéens, Prix du Livre-Inter, and Prix des lectrices d'Elle, and shortlisted for Prix Goncourt, Prix Femina, and Prix du Governeur-Général, all 1996, all for *Instruments des ténèbres;* Prix des Libraires, Prix des lyceens de Chartres, and Prix des lectrices de ELLE, all 1998, all for *L'Empreinte de l'ange;* Prix Halif, Royal Academy of French Language and Literature, 1998; Chevalier de l'ordre des arts et des lettres, 1999; nominations for Giller Prize and Governor-General's Award for English Translation, both 1999, both for *The Mark of the Angel;* Prix Marianne, 1999, for *Nord Perdu;* Prix Aliénor-d'Aquitaine, 1999, for *Prodige;* named Chevalier des Arts et des Lettres, 1999; Honoris Causa doctorate, University of Montreal, 2000. An international colloquium, "Nancy Huston: Vision and Division," was held at the Université de la Sorbonne, April 27-28, 2001.

WRITINGS:

Jouer au papa et à l'amant: De l'amour des petites filles (nonfiction), Ramsay (Paris, France), 1979.

Dire et interdire: Eléments de jurologie (nonfiction), Payot (Paris, France), 1980.

Les Variations Goldberg, Romance (novel), Seuil (Paris, France), 1981, translation published as *The Goldberg Variations,* NuAge Editions (Montreal, Canada), 1998.

Mosaïque de la pornographie: Marie-Thérèse et les autres (nonfiction), Denoël (Paris, France), 1982.

(With Samuel Kinser) *A l'amour comme à la guerre,* Seuil (Paris, France), 1984.

Histoire d'Omaya (novel), Seuil (Paris, France), 1985, translation published as *The Story of Omaya,* Women's Press (London, England), 1987.

(Editor, with Patrizia Magli) *Le Donne e i segni: Scrittura, linguaggio, identità nel segno della differenza femminile,* Ancona (Italy), 1985.

(With Leïla Sebbar) *Lettres parisiennes: Autopsie de l'exil,* Barrault (Paris, France), 1986.

Trois fois septembre (novel), Seuil (Paris, France), 1989.

Journal de la création (nonfiction), Seuil (Paris, France), 1990.

(With daughter Léa Huston) *Véra Veut la Vérité* (juvenile; also see below), Ecole des Loisirs, 1992.

(Translator, under pseudonym Annécie Rosiers) Molly Gloss, *The Jump-off Creek,* Ecole des Loisirs, 1992.

Cantique des plaines, Actes Sud (Arles, France), translated as *Plainsong,* HarperCollins, 1993.

(With Léa Huston) *Dora demande des détails* (juvenile), Ecole des loisirs, 1993.

La Virevolte (novel), Actes Sud (Arles, France), 1994, translation published as *Slow Emergencies,* Little, Brown (Canada), 1997, Vintage (New York, NY) and Steerforth Press (South Royalton, VT), 2001.

(Translator) Jane Lazarre, *Le Noeud Maternel,* Edition de l'Aube, 1994, reprinted as *Misères et splendeur de la maternitè,* 2001.

Tombeau de Romain Gary (nonfiction; also see below), Actes Sud (Arles, France), 1995.

Désirs et réalités: textes choisis 1979-1993 (nonfiction), Leméac (Montreal, Quebec, Canada), 1995.

Pour un Patriotisme de l'ambiguïté (nonfiction), Fidès (Quebec, Canada), 1995.

Instruments des ténèbres, Actes Sud (Arles, France), 1996, translation published as *Instruments of Darkness,* Little, Brown (Boston, MA), 1997.

In Deo (also see below), Editions du Silence (Montreal, Quebec, Canada), 1997.

(Translator) Eva Figes, *Spectres,* Actes Sud (Arles, France), 1996.

L'Empreinte de l'ange, Actes Sud (Arles, France), 1998, translation published as *The Mark of the Angel,* Steerforth Press (South Royalton, VT), 1999.

(Translator) Ethel Gorham, *My Tailor Is Rich,* Actes Sud (Arles, France), 1998.

(With Yves Angelo) *Voleur de vie* (screenplay; based on the novel by Steinnun Sigurdardottir), 1998.

Nord perdu (nonfiction), 1999.

Prodige: Polyphonie, Actes Sud (Arles, France), 1999, translation published as *Prodigy: A Novella,* McArthur (Toronto, Canada), 2000.

(With Léa Pool) *Emporte-moi* (screenplay; title means "Set Me Free"), 1999.

Limbes/Limbo: Un hommage à Samuel Beckett (produced in Lyon, France, 2000), Actes Sud (Arles, France), 2000.

(Translator) Goran Tunström, *Un Prosateur à New York,* Actes Sud (Arles, France), 2000.

(Translator) *The Strong of Heart* (screenplay, based on the novel *Les ames fortes* by Jean Giono), 2001.

Dolce agonia: Roman, Actes Sud (Arles, France), 2001, translation published as *Dolce agonia: A Novel,* Steerforth Press (South Royalton, VT), 2001.

Visages de l'aube, photography by V. Winckler, Actes Sud (Arles, France), 2001.

RADIO SCRIPTS

Fragments of a Warrior's Discourse, France-Culture, 1981.

(With Raymond Bellour) *Scènes littéraires, scènes de ménage,* France-Culture, 1986.

Zeta Zuni Rag, France-Culture, 1988.

Terre du Berry: Mère et fille de George Sand, France-Culture, 1988.

Vies à vif, France-Culture, 1989.

Accords mortels, France-Culture, 1990.

Ile en exil, France-Culture, 1990.

Véra veut la vérité, France-Culture, 1992.

Vies à vif, France-Culture, 1992.

Romain Gary, L'Insaisi, France-Culture, 1993.

Choses dites et défaites, France-Culture, 1993.

Passions instrumentales, France-Culture, 1993.

Tombeau de Romain Gary, Radio Canada, 1995.

Créer, procréer: les voies de l'immortalité, France-Culture, 1995.

(With Mariana Loupan) *Tonino Guerra, milles poètes,* France-Culture, 1996.

Etranges Français, France-Culture, 1997-1998.

In Deo, SRC/CBC, 1999.

Also author of short stories and essays, published in various anthologies, including *Women and Men's Wars,* edited by Judith Hicks Stiehm, Pergamon Press (New York, NY), 1982; *Le Donne e i Signi, il lavoro editoriale,* edited by Patrizia Magli, Ancona (Italy), 1985; *The Female Body in Western Culture,* edited by Susan Suleiman, Harvard University Press, 1986; and *Far from Home: Writing and Exile,* edited by Susan Suleiman, Duke University Press, 1996. Contributor to journals and magazines, including *Les Temps Modernes, Histoires d'Elles, Le Genre Humain, Lettre internationale* (France), *Poetics Today, Women's Studies International Quarterly, Salmagundi, Harper's, Sun, Vancouver Review,* and *Descant* (Canada). Translator of short fiction and nonfiction works of writers such as

Jacques Rey Charlier, Andrea Dworkin, Rosellen Brown, Pierette Fleutiaux, James Tate, Roland Barthes, Francois Flahault, Roman Jakobson, Raymond Bellour, Denis Hollier, Thierry Kuntzel, Mary MacCarthy, Richard Rodriguez, Tzvetan Todorov, Elizabeth Young-Bruehl, and Maurice Olender, from French to English or vice versa.

Huston's articles and books have been translated into Czech, Slovak, Serbo-Croat, Polish, German, Hungarian, Dutch, Spanish, Hebrew, Italian, Bulgarian, Greek, Turkish, Chinese, Japanese, Finnish, Norwegian, Swedish, Portuguese, and Russian.

SIDELIGHTS: Canadian-born Nancy Huston has won acclaim and commercial success as a prolific writer in both Canada and France. She writes in English and French, and translates her own novels. Huston went to Paris as a university student in the early 1970s. After studying for a time with esteemed semiologist Roland Barthes, she began a writing career that has encompassed both fiction and nonfiction, and she has won or been nominated for numerous awards in both France and Canada. In the latter country, this has been somewhat controversial, with many Canadians feeling that the nation's awards should be reserved for authors who live and work in Canada. Even so, she has received praise in Canada, France, and the United States as a creator of strong plots and characters, something that, according to some observers, is often lacking in French literature. Since World War II, "French literature has been dominated by people talking about ideas, but they're not great storytellers," noted Huston's first U.S. publisher, Chip Fleischer of Steerforth Press, in an interview with *Publishers Weekly.*

One of Huston's much-lauded works is *Plainsong,* which won the Canadian Governor General's award in French translation as *Cantique des plaines* in 1993. It tells the life story of a man named Paddon Sterling through his granddaughter, Paula. The novel begins, shortly after Paddon's death, with Paula who has inherited a sheaf of papers which carry her grandfather's scribblings. Paula pieces together the life of a man with ambitions who is gradually beaten down by the realities of harsh prairie life. Paula discovers that Paddon was involved in an affair that lasted fifteen years and changed the way in which he viewed the world. Paddon's lover later succumbed to a disease that eroded her memory, forcing him to accept the realities of his life. "Besides offering an account of prairie history that strips away the reader's complacency, it takes on one of the world's oldest literary subjects—how time and life slide inexorably through a man's fingers," noted

Joan Thomas writing in the *Globe and Mail.* Sandra Martin commented in *Quill & Quire* that "the novel is compelling and sometimes haunting."

Huston made her U.S. debut with *The Mark of the Angel.* The protagonist, Saffie, is a mysterious young woman who immigrates from Germany to Paris in 1957 and finds work as housekeeper to a gifted classical musician named Raphael, whom she eventually marries. They have a son together, but Saffie remains an enigma. A simple errand, however, changes her life: Saffie takes Raphael's flute to a repairman, Andras, who turns out to be a Hungarian Jew and Holocaust survivor. Saffie opens up to him about her sufferings during the World War II and her agonized speculations about her family's affiliation with the Nazis. In spite of not knowing anything about each other apart from their respective nationalities, Saffie and Andras become lovers, but their affair is further complicated by Andras's role in aiding Algeria's rebellion against France's colonial rule. *Brown Daily Herald* reviewer Gabrielle Johnson stated that "the two embark on a passionate affair that is interrupted only by the marked differences in their cultures." Johnson also suggested that "through the love story of Saffie and Andras, Huston makes the connection between the political and the personal. She asks the question, 'Which truths are we required to pay attention to?' " "*The Mark of the Angel* is dark and moving, at once love story, war tale and psychological thriller," added *Denver Post Online*'s Jean Charbonneau.

"Once [Huston] establishes her story's central ironies, the narrative achieves relentless velocity," a *Publishers Weekly* critic remarked. *Library Journal*'s Barbara Hoffert lauded Huston's writing style as "strong, ironic, and refreshingly original." *Time* commentator Katherine Govier applauded Huston's "refusal to judge the searchers for love, even for their terrible betrayals," and summed up the novel as "elegant and somber." Bill Ott, critiquing for *Booklist,* felt "the story of Saffie and Andras hits a perfect melancholy note and sustains it superbly." *Library Journal*'s Shirley E. Havens called *The Mark of the Angel* a "hauntingly elegant U.S. debut novel." David Valdes Greenwood, reviewing the novel for the *Boston Phoenix* Web site, wrote, "The tension gets so profound that one is afraid to turn the page, fearful for these characters. Huston achieves this effect with more than just a good story and good characters. Her language is beautiful, with startling juxtapositions of imagery . . . and musical phrasing." He added, "As the noose grows tighter around our trio of adults and the boy in their keeping, we begin to realize that the long-armed horrors of war will ever continue reaching out for new lives to claim, for new horrors to set in motion. From that terrible truth, Huston has made a chilling and beautiful work of art." Jessica Aldred, a contributor to an online review for *Lifewise,* noted that Huston "weaves her beautifully-written novel *The Mark of the Angel* with threads that are both universal and complex: Love, infidelity, trust, and betrayal." Charbonneau, in *Denver Post Online,* praised Huston's style as being "crisp and clean," and called her writing "powerful." He described the novel as containing a "rapid back-and-forth movement between present and past, alternating episodes of sadness, violence, tragedy, romance and horror." He summed up *The Mark of the Angel* as an "engaging, intelligent novel."

Slow Emergencies, winner of two international awards, and published in the United States in 2001, is a tale about a woman's preference for a profession as a ballet star over her family life with her husband and two daughters, and the resulting consequences. *Booklist's* Vanessa Bush called Huston's prose "eloquent and poetic," concluding that Huston "masterfully portrays the convergence of artistry of dance, parenting, and human relationships." Lisa Nussbaum, a reviewer for *Library Journal,* called it a "haunting story about an uncommon subject," while a *Publishers Weekly* reviewer observed, "Huston produces a sensitive, sweeping account of the difficulty of reconciling maternal and artistic callings."

Reba Leiding, reviewing Huston's 2001 book *Dolce agonia: A Novel* for *Library Journal,* commended the author, pointing out that "Huston deftly marshals . . . [the] crowd of characters, her clear prose leading the reader into the characters' individual and collective histories."

BIOGRAPHICAL/CRITICAL SOURCES:

PERIODICALS

Advocate, May 23, 2000, Jan Stuart, review of *Set Me Free,* p. 88.

Booklist, September 15, 1999, Bill Ott, review of *The Mark of the Angel.*

Boston Phoenix, September 16, 1999, David Valdes Greenwood, "Innocence Lost."

Brown Daily Herald, October 26, 1999, Gabrielle Johnson, "Author Nancy Huston Reads Her Work at Bookstore."

Globe and Mail (Toronto, Canada), November 6, 1993, p. C9; December 1, 2000, Vanessa Bush, review of *Slow Emergencies,* p. 693.

Denver Post, October 3, 1999, Jean Charbonneau, "Many-sided Psychological Thriller Skillfully Shaped," p. I8.

Library Journal, October 15, 1999, Barbara Hoffert, review of *The Mark of the Angel,* p. 106; February 1, 2000, Shirley E. Havens, review of *The Mark of the Angel,* p. 140; December, 2000, Lisa Nussbaum, review of *Slow Emergencies,* p. 189; July, 2001, Reba Leiding, review of *Dolce agonia: A Novel,* p. 123.

Maclean's, June 9, 1997, Judith Timson, review of *Instruments of Darkness,* p. 75.

Publishers Weekly, May 17, 1999, John F. Baker, "Get Me Rewrite," p. 16; August 2, 1999, review of *The Mark of the Angel,* p. 70; August 30, 1999, Judith Rosen, "Will Steerforth, Vintage Make Their 'Mark'?," p. 22; October 30, 2000, review of *Slow Emergencies,* p. 44.

Quill & Quire, September, 1993, p. 59.

Time, November 8, 1999, Katherine Govier, "Sex and Violence."

Times Literary Supplement, February 18, 2000, Bryan Cheyette, "A Flattened History," p. 23.

OTHER

Lifewise, http://www.argonauts.on.ca/ (September 10, 2001), Jessica Aldred, "Timeless and Thought-provoking Prose."

Sunday Times, http://www.suntimes.co.za/ (September 10, 2001), review of *The Mark of the Angel.**

J

JAMES, Amalia
See NEGGERS, Carla A(malia)

*   *   *

JANES, J(oseph) Robert   1935-

PERSONAL: Born May 23, 1935, in Toronto, Ontario, Canada; son of Henry F. (in public relations) and Phyllis (an artist; maiden name, Hipwell) Janes; married Gracia Joyce Lind (a social and environmental activist and project coordinator), May 16, 1958; children: Anne Janes Stewart, Peter, Catherine, Janes Damianoff, John. *Education:* University of Toronto, B.A.Sc. (mining engineering), 1958, M.Sc. (geology), 1967; further graduate studies in geology at McMaster University, Queen's University, and Brock University.

ADDRESSES: Home and Office—P.O. Box 1590, 261 King St., Niagara-on-the-Lake, Ontario, Canada L0S 1J0. *E-mail*—jrjanes@sympatico.ca.

CAREER: Mobil Oil of Canada, petroleum engineer in Alberta and Saskatchewan, 1958-59; Ontario Research Foundation, Toronto, Ontario, Canada, research engineer in minerals beneficiation, 1959-64; high school geology, geography and mathematics teacher in Toronto, Ontario, Canada, 1964-66; Ontario Research Foundation, field researcher in geology, 1966; Brock University, St. Catharines, Ontario, Canada, lecturer in geology, 1966-67; Ontario Science Centre, Toronto, Ontario, Canada, earth scientist, 1967-68; Brock University, lecturer in geology, 1968-70; full time writer, 1970—. Consulting field geologist; lacrosse coach.

MEMBER: International Crime Writers, Crime Writers of Canada, Crime Writers of America, Crime Writers Association (U.K.), Historical Novel Society (U.K.).

AWARDS, HONORS: Grants from J. P. Bickell Foundation, Canada Council, and Ontario Arts Council; thesis award from Canadian Institute of Mining and Metallurgy, 1958.

WRITINGS:

NONFICTION

Geology and the New Global Tectonics, Macmillan (Toronto, Ontario, Canada), 1976.
The Great Canadian Outback, Douglas & McIntyre (Vancouver, Canada), 1978.
(With J. D. Mollard) *Airphoto Interpretation and the Canadian Landscape,* Canadian Government Publishing Centre, Supply and Services Canada (Hull, Quebec), 1984.

NOVELS

The Toy Shop, General Publishing, 1981.
The Watcher, General Publishing, 1982.
The Third Story, General Publishing, 1983.
The Hiding Place, Paperjacks, 1984.
The Alice Factor, Stoddart (Toronto, Ontario, Canada), 1991.
Mirage, D. I. Fine (New York, NY), 1992, published as *Mayhem,* Constable (London, England), 1992, Soho Press (New York, NY), 1999.
Carousel, Constable (London, England), 1992, D. I. Fine (New York, NY), 1993.
Kaleidoscope, Constable (London, England), 1993, Soho Press (New York, NY), 2001.

Salamander, Constable (London, England), 1994, Soho Press (New York, NY), 1998.

Mannequin, Constable (London, England), 1994, Soho Press (New York, NY), 1998.

Dollmaker, Constable (London, England), 1995, Soho Press (New York, NY), in press.

Stonekiller, Constable (London, England), 1995, Soho Press (New York, NY), 1997.

Sandman, Constable (London, England), 1996, Soho Press (New York, NY), 1997.

Gypsy, Constable (London, England), 1997.

Madrigal, Victor Gollancz (London, England), 1999.

Beekeeper, Orion Books (London, England), 2001.

Flykiller, Orion Books (London, England), in press.

Some works translated into German, Japanese, and Turkish.

FOR CHILDREN

Geology (television script), first broadcast by Metro Educational Television Authority, 1966.

Rocks, Minerals, and Fossils, Holt, 1973.

Earth Science, Holt, 1974.

The Odd-Lot Boys and the Tree-Fort War, Scholastic Inc., 1976.

(With C. Hopkins and J. D. Hoyes) *Searching for Structure,* Books One and Two, Holt, 1977.

Theft of Gold, Scholastic Inc., 1980.

Danger on the River, Clarke, Irwin (Toronto, Ontario, Canada), 1982.

Spies for Dinner, Collins of Canada, 1984.

Murder in the Market, Collins of Canada, 1985.

Theft of Gold has been translated into Norwegian.

OTHER

Author of fifteen resource kits comprising teaching guides and slide sets for Holt, 1972. Contributor of articles and stories to Canadian magazines and newspapers, including *Canadian, Canadian Children's Annual, Toronto Globe and Mail,* and *Winnipeg Free Press.*

SIDELIGHTS: J. Robert Janes has written many types of books, including nonfiction and children's mysteries, but he is best known for his series of historical novels which are also detective-mystery, psychological thrillers that are set in German-occupied France during the Second World War. That series began with *Mirage* (also published as *Mayhem)* and includes *Kaleidoscope, Mannequin, Stonekiller, Beekeeper,* and numerous other titles. The novels feature a pair of protago-

nists: Jean-Louis St-Cyr, a member of the Parisian Sûreté Nationale, and Hermann Kohler, a reluctant member of the Gestapo. While officially-sanctioned atrocities and corruption seethe around them, the two overcome their differences and even become friends as they join forces to battle common crime in Paris, Lyon, Avignon and elsewhere in Occupied France. Murder is usually tangled with kinky sex in these stories, which have been praised as much for their portrayal of complex relationships as for their suspenseful plotting.

In *Mirage,* the crime involves a murder in the Fountainbleau Forest. Kohler dismisses it as an accident, perhaps the victim was connected to the Résistance, but St-Cyr has his doubts. Complications ensue when Kohler is pressured to drop the case, and St-Cyr discovers that his wife has left him for a German Army officer. A reviewer for *Publishers Weekly* complained that the atmosphere in the story was mostly provided by having the characters utter phrases such as "Gott in Himmel" and "Ah, mon Dieu," but concluded that *Mirage* was, ultimately, "a fast-moving and absorbing story." Janes followed *Mirage* with *Carousel,* another fast-paced murder mystery with a cast that includes a sinful priest and a Nazi necrophiliac.

Salamander, another installment in the series, was praised by Kathy Sorci in *Library Journal* for creating "a distinct picture of the decadence and dissolution of Nazi-occupied France focusing on the victims as well as the oppressors." This time, the mismatched detective team must chase an arsonist who killed 183 people in a movie theater, then went on to set other devastating blazes. Sorci noted that "St-Cyr and Kohler mistrust each other, and their complicated dance to solve the crime without giving any advantage to the other is interesting to watch." A *Publishers Weekly* writer cautioned that "as in previous books in the series, sex— twisted and perverted at times—plays a large part in the investigation. One example of Janes's artistry: in a city starved for food, he spends three richly ironic pages describing the remains of a Christmas Eve feast in an exclusive bordello without slowing down the action or lessening the power of his terrible vision of a world full of large and small crimes." David Pitt, a *Booklist* reviewer, called *Salamander* "an exceedingly clever novel that should appeal to World War II buffs as well as mystery readers."

Mannequin features a particularly grim story involving a series of mutilations and murders of young women. This book prompted a *Publishers Weekly* commentator to remark: "Janes offers, in hundreds of authentic details, a searing picture of the misery, frequent opportunism and shifty uncertainties of the German occupation and, in his two protagonists, a believable bonding of improbable allies. The wind-up is genuinely spine-crawling." Sex crimes also figure prominently in *Sandman,* where St-Cyr and Kohler search for the "Sandman," who has raped and murdered several young girls. "The humanity of Kohler and St-Cyr, and their devotion to their task, transcends both the grimness of the crimes and the decadence of those thriving during the occupation," mused a *Publishers Weekly* reviewer. "Harsh but addictive, this [book] is an acquired taste that lingers long after the last page is read."

Janes once told *CA:* "For [many] years I've been a full-time writer, and on this tenuous living my wife and I raised four children. Generally I work all the time—that is to say, while I used to have hobbies and holidays, I have not had them in a very long time. Virtually everything I do is connected with my writing, the project I'm on, the one I'm about to begin, and those I want to do but can never seem to get the time for. I'm not complaining. This is simply the way it is. For others it will be vastly different.

"I write for kids and adults, both fiction and nonfiction, though in the last sixteen years I've concentrated almost totally on my adult fiction. While *The Alice Factor* is an international thriller about diamonds in the Second World War, *Mirage* and all the adult novels since are a series of detective-mystery, psychological thrillers set in occupied France in late 1942-43. My two detectives, one French from the Sûreté Nationale, one Bavarian from the Kripo of the Gestapo, are from opposite sides of the war. They are thrown together in the battle against common crime when officially-sanctioned crime was rampant. They get on because they have to and become friends in spite of it all. The novels are great fun with a fantastic background, and truly wonderful characters, because that's what it's all about. They have lots of suspense and pace. They're thrillers, really.

"Occasionally I'm asked why I gave up well-paying jobs for the constant stress of never knowing if and when I'd be paid and if it would be enough to meet the bills. There isn't any answer except that I've always wanted to write stories. This desire shows in my nonfiction too, but I have found that the writing of nonfiction is diametrically opposed to that of fiction. It interferes so much I am no longer tempted to do it, though I sometimes ask, 'What if?,' and may yet have to go back to it.

"I was the middle son of three boys and no doubt that helped because, being lonely and left to myself a lot, I used and developed my imagination. Mother was a very fine artist, very creative, a superb cook, and the epitome of what the Great Depression and small-town Ontario could teach a person. That, too, helped so much, for she made me see things as an artist would. My father was once a reporter on the *Toronto Star* and the *Northern Miner,* though most of his working life was spent seven days a week at his firm of Public Relations Services Ltd., behind the King Edward Hotel. He didn't want me to write fiction but missed the series and *The Alice Factor.*

"I think story all the time and want only to work in that medium. In a sense, then, one crosses a threshold and wishes only to be totally involved in the work. It feeds itself and expands until the time is filled and there is no longer time enough for all one wants to do."

BIOGRAPHICAL/CRITICAL SOURCES:

PERIODICALS

Booklist, June 1, 1998, p. 1733.
Library Journal, May 1, 1993, p. 116; May 1, 1997, p. 144; June 15, 1998, p. 107.
New York Times Book Review, November 23, 1997, pp. 23; July 5, 1998, p. 16; November 29, 1998, p. 24; August 8, 1999.
Publishers Weekly, August 10, 1992; March 22, 1993, p. 71; February 24, 1997, p. 66; September 8, 1997, p. 61; May 4, 1998, p. 207; August 17, 1998, p. 51.

*   *   *

JOHNSON, Joyce 1935-
(Joyce Glassman)

PERSONAL: Born September 27, 1935, in New York, NY; daughter of Daniel (a bookkeeper) and Rosalind (a homemaker; maiden name, Ross) Glassman; married James Johnson (a painter), December 12, 1962 (died 1963); married Peter Pinchbeck, November 21, 1965 (divorced 1971); children: (second marriage) Daniel. *Education:* Attended Barnard College, 1951-55, and New School for Social Research. *Religion:* Jewish.

ADDRESSES: Home—595 West End Ave., New York, NY 10024. *Office—Vanity Fair,* 350 Madison Ave., New York, NY 10024. *Agent*—Berenice Hoffman Literary Agency, 215 West 75th St., New York, NY 10023.

CAREER: William Morrow & Co., New York, NY, associate editor, 1965-67; Dial Press, New York, NY, senior editor, 1967-70, executive editor, 1977-84; McGraw-Hill Book Co., New York, NY, senior editor, 1970-77; Atlantic Monthly Press, New York, NY, senior editor, 1984-86; *Vanity Fair* (magazine), New York, NY, contributing editor, 1987—. Adjunct professor of creative writing, Columbia University Graduate Writing Program, 1983-87.

MEMBER: PEN.

AWARDS, HONORS: John Gardner Fellow, Breadloaf Writers Conference, 1983; National Book Critics Circle Award for biography/autobiography, 1983, for *Minor Characters;* co-recipient of O. Henry Award (first prize), 1987, for short story "The Children's Wing."

WRITINGS:

(Under name Joyce Glassman) *Come and Join the Dance* (novel), Atheneum (New York, NY), 1962.
Bad Connections (novel), Putnam (New York, NY), 1978.
Minor Characters: A Young Woman's Coming-of-Age in the Beat Orbit of Jack Kerouac (autobiography), Houghton (Boston, MA), 1983.
In the Night Café (novel), Dutton (New York, NY), 1989.
What Lisa Knew: The Truths and Lies of the Steinberg Case, Putnam (New York, NY), 1990.
(With Jack Kerouac, and author of introduction and commentary) *Door Wide Open: A Beat Love Affair in Letters, 1957-58,* Viking (New York, NY), 2000.

Also author of short story "In the Children's Wing," 1987. Contributor to *New Yorker, Harper's,* and *Vanity Fair.*

SIDELIGHTS: Joyce Johnson drew inspiration for her own writing career from her association with the Beat generation authors and artists. Having courted a Bohemian lifestyle from her early teens, Johnson became Jack Kerouac's lover at age twenty-one and the widow of artist James Johnson in 1963. Her experiences as a "beatnik," a single working mother, and an emerging artist in her own right inform all of her work, especially her National Book Critics Circle Award-winning memoir *Minor Characters: A Young Woman's Coming-of-Age in the Beat Orbit of Jack Kerouac.* Far from being

eclipsed by her famous lover's reputation, Johnson has been praised for the style and substance of her writings, many of which explore the atmosphere of Bohemian Manhattan in the late 1950s and 1960s. "Joyce Johnson is a fine writer," declared Diana O'Hehir in the *Washington Post Book World.* "Not a minor character at all but a major player, she turns out to have been one of the ones who make it all happen."

Johnson grew up in a middle-class household in New York City. The only child of a woman of refined tastes reputedly frustrated by modest means, Johnson became the outlet for her mother's daunted desires and was groomed to become a great classical composer. By age fourteen Johnson began secretly escaping to Greenwich Village after school, fascinated by the artists, political radicals, and vagabonds who frequented the Waldorf Cafeteria. She continued the dual existence of dutiful daughter and rebellious would-be writer through most of her college years, eventually becoming acquainted with the ex-Columbia University students who would become the nucleus of the counterculture Beat movement.

Rejecting social conventions and material values, Beat Generation artists looked to intense experience and beatific illumination for life's meaning, expressing their epiphanies in new ways in their creative work. Poets evoked the rhythms of simple speech or progressive jazz; such novelists as Jack Kerouac chronicled their restless quests for new sensations and experiences. When Joyce was twenty-one she met Kerouac and they began an uneasy romance that coincided with publication of Kerouac's seminal novel, *On the Road.* Johnson—then known as Joyce Glassman—was admitted into the Beat generation's inner circle, a witness to the convergence of people and ideas that ignited a radical cultural shift, ushering in the iconoclastic 1960s.

During those years Johnson supported herself by working as a secretary, but she yearned to be a writer and published her first novel before she turned thirty. The necessity of self-support continued, however, eventually leading her into a successful career as a book editor and a contributing editor to *Vanity Fair* magazine. Having established herself professionally, Johnson resumed writing books in the 1970s and is today best known for her fiction and nonfiction concerning the Beats.

Johnson's novel *Bad Connections* examines the bittersweet dimensions of feminism as it affected women in the 1970s. Protagonist Molly seems to be the typical independent contemporary woman—a successful magazine editor, divorced, raising her young son alone. Still, she replaces her unsatisfactory marriage with equally unsatisfactory relationships with selfish and abusive men. In a review for the *Village Voice,* Ellen Willis observed that Molly "is no fool; she knows that putting up with [these men] is both self-destructive and, ah, politically incorrect. But she can't help it." Unlike early feminist novels, pervaded with a breathless sense of discovery, the critic continued, *Bad Connections* is a postfeminist work "whose stance is more complicated and ambivalent." Willis explained, "Caught in the middle of a historic transformation, feminists must negotiate all sorts of painful and confusing gaps between their ideas and their feelings, their consciousness and their actions, their vision and the stubborn limits of their culture." Adding that "Molly's intelligence and self-deprecating irony make her both interesting and likeable . . . not pathetic," Willis found *Bad Connections* to be "often funny, sometimes cathartically angry, always skillful in rendering the small, excruciating moments that add up to the misery of love gone bad."

Harper's contributor Helen Yglesias also acknowledged the protagonist's "dispiriting" capitulation to "lonely liberation" in *Bad Connections.* Yglesias nonetheless praised Johnson's storytelling skills, concluding that the novel "is controlled, smooth, deftly written; it evokes scene and character with admirable sure swiftness. . . . Joyce Johnson's touches are all true." "Joyce Johnson is a writer of wit and perception . . . and she has a keen eye for the irony of modern life," affirmed Peter Andrews in the *New York Times Book Review.* " 'Bad Connections' is a small-scale book filled with small-scale moments that linger in the mind as Molly eventually declares an armistice with her life." Andrews added that this "fine novel of the alienated woman . . . establishes Joyce Johnson as a writer of considerable talent."

Minor Characters is Johnson's autobiographical account of her years as a member of the Beat community. According to *Atlantic* contributor James Atlas, the memoir provides a unique insider's look at "that over-chronicled phenomenon the Beats . . . suppl[ying] a context for events reported elsewhere without elaboration." Johnson describes her sheltered childhood and her transformation into a seeker of adventure and authentic living, culminating in her intense, if one-sided, romance with Kerouac. Showing Kerouac before and after the publication of his famous novel, Johnson reveals a troubled, private man unable to deal with the critical acclaim and general popularity of *On the Road.* "I wanted to give a picture of Jack as he was as a person," stated Johnson in a *Publishers Weekly* interview

with Sybil S. Steinberg. "I felt I could give a better sense of him by zeroing in on a little piece of his life."

Minor Characters is more than a portrait of Kerouac and other Beat figures, however. To quote Helen Chasin in the *New York Times Book Review,* "[Johnson's] portrayal of growing up bright and sensitive in Manhattan is the true heart of the book." Johnson recalls her sheltered childhood and her eventual rebellion as a youth. She also re-examines the validity of the advice she received from her Barnard College writing instructor—anyone who wanted to be a writer should climb aboard a freight train and travel the continent. "*Minor Characters* is a vigorous, stimulating meditation on why Joyce Glassman wanted Jack Kerouac, wanted him, in her early twenties, more than anything else in the world," noted *Village Voice Literary Supplement* contributor Laurie Stone. "The anecdotes recalled from childhood, the cast of characters selected for inclusion, all work to unravel this question. It gives the book its shape and sustained power."

Critics particularly applauded Johnson's reflections on the idealistic, gifted young women who—like her—were "minor characters" in the great dramas lived by the likes of Jack Kerouac and Allen Ginsberg, prohibited from joining center stage themselves. As Johnson demonstrates in *Minor Characters,* women of that time were tacitly encouraged to put their own ambitions aside in order to nurture their lovers. Beat female companions either abandoned their own artistic goals, turning to men, household, and children, or they "tended to crash-land," Stone related, like Johnson's best friend, Elise Cowen, who took her own life. Stone felt that Cowen's "restless, inspiring ghost rides through the prose, her despair speak[ing] with particular eloquence of the dead-endedness for women in this time." The critic added, "If she attaches herself to an active, creative man, Joyce believes, then she can smell the life that counts and watch it with fascinated eyes. She imagines this will satisfy her. . . . But . . . Joyce discovers that cheering ringside and sponging the performer are not all they're cracked up to be." Stone added, "Part of Johnson's purpose in *Minor Characters* is to show where she's moved since her affair with Kerouac. . . . After 25 years the small feminist battling away inside Joyce Glassman has evidently grown up and grown wise." "Her acquiescent quiet was [the men's] loss as well as her own," reflected Chasin. "Joyce Johnson too had stories, and hers are not only interesting and vivid but in several respects have more dimension than the adventure tales and clubhouse philosophizing that captured America's imagination in the late 50's."

In his *Chicago Tribune Book World* review of *Minor Characters,* William O'Rourke decided that it is precisely Johnson's paradoxical position as both Beat spectator and participant that makes her "all the more judicious. . . . In fact . . . [*Minor Characters*] is one of the best memoirs of the period I have read—for its lack of posturing if nothing else." An *Antioch Review* critic, too, appreciated Johnson's "sharply honest portraits," praising her "clear vision and . . . remarkable fortitude in recalling people and places, and, above all, her own experience." *Nation* correspondent Todd Gitlin wrote, "The beauty of Johnson's book is that all the characters are for real. No one is either sentimentalized or brutalized by caricature. . . . *Minor Characters* glows with affection, as well as regret and pain for the waste of strong energies and high spirits in the Beat circles." Feeling that "it is to her credit that [Kerouac] lives with such boyish good nature in her memory," Seymour Krim commended Johnson's "refusal to be petty" in a *Washington Post Book World* review, adding, "Any anger that this even-tempered New York writer and book editor may once have felt towards the swashbuckling pirates of the Bohemian '50s has long since evaporated. . . . It has been distilled into knowing, unsentimental compassion for Joyce Johnson's neglected sisters. . . . No . . . battle cries ever get in the way of her homage." Chasin offered a similar observation. "Joyce Johnson's enthusiastic loyalty to her days of heightened intensity has not prevented her from getting past them to realize her aim of giving up silence," the critic concurred. "The result makes for compelling reading." According to Christopher Lehmann-Haupt in the *New York Times,* Johnson "has brought to life what history may ultimately judge to have been minor characters, but who were to her own generation major enough to shape its consciousness."

In 1989 Johnson published a second novel, *In the Night Café,* about an aspiring New York actress named Joanna and her bittersweet romance with a self-destructive artist, Tom Murphy. Leaving his wife and children to come to the city during the early 1960s and paint expressionist abstracts, Tom eventually succumbs to apathy and alcohol and dies, overcome with guilt over the son he has abandoned, just as his father deserted him long ago. Diana O'Hehir described *In the Night Café* as "a search by the steady and reliable partner for the causes of the other person's dislocation," as Joanna replays details of Tom's lifelong search for a father's love, of their courtship, brief marriage, and Tom's death, and of the subsequent visit from Tom's young son, clinging to Joanna's every word, hungry to know his father. While later remarrying and having a boy of her own, Johnson's protagonist cannot relinquish her attachment to Tom or lay to rest these images of forsaken children. Joanna speaks for the author, who closes the novel with the episode published as her 1987 short story "In the Children's Wing," a recollection of her own son's extended hospital stay and of the parentless, visitorless young patient who, huddled in a nearby bed, watches others' well-wishers. "What gives . . . [*In the Night Café*] its framework is the theme of the abandoned child," observed Anne Tyler in Chicago's *Tribune Books.* "[It] is bracketed, you might say, by stories of lonely children."

O'Hehir wrote that *In the Night Café* character Tom Murphy "has behind him the vigorous unsettled ghost of Jack Kerouac and the vigorous inquiring voice of Johnson telling their story." The critic deemed *In the Night Café* "an intense, strong love story, direct and moving," adding, "The narrative moves abruptly and skillfully, compelling vast leaps across time. . . . The swift narrative movement is handled with grace, the tone throughout simple and observant, details memorable. The small exact detail is one of the ways Johnson's simple narration enlists the reader." Likewise admiring Johnson's "special gift for evoking other times . . . pounc[ing] upon exactly the right detail, the single sight or smell or sound that could bring a whole era flooding back into memory," Tyler related that this "uncommon deftness and restraint" typifies Johnson's characterization as well, with people conveyed in "a single stroke, allowing us to color in the rest—and therefore to invest ourselves more deeply."

New York Times Book Review contributor Phillip Lopate suggested that *In the Night Café* "displays a gift for social history, for getting the period details right and not resorting to distortions of nostalgia." "Indeed," he added, "one can read this novel as the ethos of the beat, starving-artist 50's reproaching the swinging, opportunistic 60's." The critic further stated, "Ms. Johnson has staked out a territory all her own: the shy, observant young woman of that era, standing in a corner at the party, sensitive to humiliation, drawn to the handsome, tragically self-destructive male artist." Lopate concluded, "The novel's penultimate section, 'The Children's Wing,' . . . is Joyce Johnson's finest achievement as a writer."

Johnson's *What Lisa Knew: The Truth and Lies of the Steinberg Case* is a nonfiction account of one of New York City's most horrific crimes. In November of 1987, six-year-old Lisa Steinberg was pronounced dead in a New York hospital, the victim of severe and repeated beatings. What was unique about Lisa Steinberg's death was her socioeconomic level and the status of her parents: her father, Joel Steinberg, was a well-known attorney, and her mother, Hedda Nussbaum, had been a children's books editor at Random House. Johnson's account explores the patterns of drug abuse and masochism that marked the relationship between Steinberg and Nussbaum, as well as the illegal manner in which Lisa and another baby were adopted by the unmarried couple.

In his *New York Times Book Review* piece on *What Lisa Knew,* Robert Coles declared, "As this patient, shrewd storyteller worked her way through what she calls the 'blanks and blind alleys' of an attempted biographical study, the weight of psychological banality obviously became oppressive and stifling to her. One by one certain words start making a credible appearance in her text—'choice,' 'will,' 'evil,' 'responsibility.' At such moments . . . Ms. Johnson becomes the aroused chronicler of a moral tale. . . . Her novelist's eye for detail and character portrayal serve her and us well—nowhere better than during those moments when she reminds us that some New Yorkers possessed both moral intuition and moral energy in response to their fleeting encounters with young Lisa."

In 2000 Johnson published her collected correspondence with Kerouac titled *Door Wide Open: A Beat Love Affair in Letters, 1957-1958.* The letters of both Johnson and Kerouac are contained in the volume, and although their romance lasted a mere twenty-two months, they wrote each other often during that time. A *Kirkus Reviews* critic felt that the work "provides an intimate glimpse of [Kerouac]." According to Vince Passaro in the *New York Times Book Review,* "Kerouac was already on the way downhill, unsuccessfully fighting off alcoholism, an iron-clawed mother, wandering habits of attention and a befuddled, sentimental, ever more queerly hybridized collection of religious views. His letters to Johnson over the two years of their love affair display all these problems in abundance." Furthermore, Passaro maintained, this collection reveals that Johnson "by 1957 was already a better writer than [Kerouac] was. Her prose in these letters shows her to be calmer, more astute, more honest, more in control of the tone and meter of her language, and, in her way, more exploratory, if not of experience and sensation, then at least of herself and the people around her." Passaro continued, "Her strengths beside Kerouac's growing weaknesses explode some treasured myths not only about him and the male-run Beat society but about American writing in general, with its muscle and its energy and its emphasis on experience over intelligence."

BIOGRAPHICAL/CRITICAL SOURCES:

PERIODICALS

Antioch Review, summer, 1983, review of *Minor Characters.*

Atlantic, February, 1983, James Atlas, review of *Minor Characters.*

Chicago Tribune, April 17, 1987.

Chicago Tribune Book World, March 6, 1983, William O'Rourke, review of *Minor Characters.*

Harper's, August, 1978, Helen Yglesias, review of *Bad Connections.*

Kirkus Reviews, June 1, 2000, review of *Door Wide Open: A Beat Love Affair in Letters, 1957-58,* p. 785.

Los Angeles Times, January 31, 1983.

Ms., March, 1983.

Nation, May 28, 1983, Todd Gitlin, review of *Minor Characters.*

New Yorker, May 2, 1983.

New York Times, January 14, 1983, Christopher Lehmann-Haupt, "Books of the Times," p. 24.

New York Times Book Review, December 10, 1978, Peter Andrews, review of *Bad Connections;* January 16, 1983, Helen Chasin, "The Girl in the Boy Gang," p. 9; April 30, 1989, Phillip Lopate, "Bohemia Died, but Life Went On," p. 11; April 8, 1990, Robert Coles, "The Death of a Child," p. 1; July 23, 2000, Vince Passaro, "Kerouac Wore Khakis."

People, June 8, 1987.

Publishers Weekly, January 14, 1983; February 17, 1984; December 5, 1986; May 1, 2000, review of *Door Wide Open: A Beat Love Affair in Letters 1957-1958,* p. 56.

Spectator, February 9, 1985.

Times Literary Supplement, June 3, 1983.

Tribune Books (Chicago), April 16, 1989, Anne Tyler, review of *In the Night Café.*

Village Voice, July 3, 1978, Ellen Willis, review of *Bad Connections.*

Village Voice Literary Supplement, April, 1983, Laurie Stone, review of *Minor Characters.*

Washington Post, January 10, 1984.

Washington Post Book World, February 6, 1983, Diana O'Hehir, review of *Minor Characters;* April 2, 1989, Diana O'Hehir, review of *In the Night Café.**

JOHNSON, Loch K. 1942-

PERSONAL: Given name is pronounced "lock"; born February 21, 1942, in Auckland, New Zealand; immigrated to the United States, 1946, naturalized citizen, 1969; son of Roland (in the military) and Kathleen (a homemaker) Johnson; married Leena Sepp (a librarian), March 22, 1969; children: Kristin Elizabeth. *Education:* University of California, Davis, A.B., 1965; University of California, Riverside, M.A., 1967, Ph.D., 1969. *Politics:* "Democrat." *Religion:* Presbyterian. *Avocational interests:* Painting, drawing, long distance running.

ADDRESSES: Home—150 Sunnybrook Dr., Athens, GA 30605. *Office*—Department of Political Science, 104 Baldwin, University of Georgia, Athens, GA 30602; fax: 706-542-4421. *E-mail*—johnson@ uga.cc.uga.edu.

CAREER: Visiting assistant professor of political science at University of North Carolina, 1970-71; Ohio University, Athens, OH, associate professor of political science, 1971-75; U.S. Senate, Washington, DC, staff member of Intelligence Committee and Foreign Relations Committee, 1975-77; U.S. House of Representatives, Washington, DC, staff director of Sub-committee on Oversight Intelligence, 1977-79; University of Georgia, Athens, GA, associate professor, 1979-85, professor of political science, 1985-90, Regents professor, 1990—. Member of national advisory board of Center for National Policy; local political campaign coordinator.

MEMBER: International Studies Association (president, Southern Region, 1993), American Political Science Association (secretary, 1994-95).

AWARDS, HONORS: Haynes Foundation fellow, 1966; U.S. Congressional fellow, 1969; named Outstanding Teacher by Pi Sigma Alpha, University of Georgia, 1980, 1981; Outstanding Honors Professor, University of Georgia, 1981, 1982, 1985; co-awarded with Charles S. Bullock III, "Best Paper on Women and Politics" Award, Southern Political Science Association, 1984; certificate of distinction, National Intelligence Study Center, 1986, for *A Season of Inquiry: The Senate Intelligence Investigation;* Creative Research Medal, University of Georgia, 1990; V. O. Key Award, 1993, for *Runoff Elections in the United States.*

WRITINGS:

The Making of International Agreements, New York University Press (New York, NY), 1984.

A Season of Inquiry: The Senate Intelligence Investigation, University Press of Kentucky (Lexington, KY), 1985.

(Editor, with Paul F. Diehl) *Through the Straits of Armageddon: Arms Control Issues and Prospects,* University of Georgia Press (Athens, GA), 1987.

(Editor, with Karl F. Inderfurth) *Decisions of the Highest Order: Perspectives on the National Security Council,* Brooks/Cole (Belmont, CA), 1988.

America's Secret Power: The CIA in a Democratic Society, Oxford University Press, 1989.

America as a World Power: Foreign Policy in a Constitutional Framework, McGraw-Hill (New York, NY), 1990, 2nd edition, 1995.

(With Charles S. Bullock III) *Runoff Elections in the United States* ("Thorton H. Brooks Series in American Law and Society"), University of North Carolina Press (Chapel Hill, NC), 1993.

Secret Agencies: U.S. Intelligence in a Hostile World, Yale University Press (New Haven, CT), 1996.

Bombs, Bugs, Drugs, and Thugs: Intelligence and America's Quest for Security, New York University Press (New York, NY), 2000.

Also contributor to professional journals.

SIDELIGHTS: Loch K. Johnson told *CA:* "My writing revolves around executive-legislative relations and ways to maintain the balance between national security and civil liberties. I have a special interest in the conduct of American foreign policy and the proper role of Congress in this process. Much of my research and writing grows out of my work as an investigator for Congress into the operations of the Central Intelligence Agency. I am searching for the right mix of the openness necessary for a democratic society and the secrecy necessary for some forms of intelligence activity."

BIOGRAPHICAL/CRITICAL SOURCES:

PERIODICALS

New York Times Book Review, December 21, 1986.

*   *   *

JUDD, Denis (O'Nan) 1938-

PERSONAL: Born October 28, 1938, in Byfield, England; son of Denis Allen (proprietor of a garage and bus business) and Joan (Shrimpton) Judd; married Dorothy Janet Woolf, July 10, 1964; children: Kate Emma,

Luke Benedict, Benjamin Keir, Jacob Joseph. *Education:* Magdalen College, Oxford, B.A. (with second class honors), 1961; College of St. Mark and St. John, London, postgraduate certificate in education, 1962; Birkbeck College, London, Ph.D., 1967. *Politics:* Socialist (Labour Party). *Religion:* Atheist. *Avocational interests:* Foreign holidays, the visual arts, theater ("especially the Royal Shakespeare Company"), cinema, sports, good food, family.

ADDRESSES: Home—20 Mount Pleasant Rd., London NW10 3EL, England. *Office*—Department of History and Philosophy, University of North London, London NW5, England. *Agent*—David Higham Associates Ltd., 5-8 Lower John St., London W1R 4HA, England. *E-mail*—d.judd@unl.ac.uk.

CAREER: University of North London, London, England, lecturer, 1964-68, senior lecturer, 1968-72, principal lecturer, 1972—, professor of history, 1990—, head of history, 1975—.

MEMBER: Historical Association, Royal Historical Society (fellow).

WRITINGS:

Balfour and the British Empire: A Study in Imperial Evolution, St. Martin's (New York, NY), 1968.

The Victorian Empire: A Pictorial History, Praeger (New York, NY), 1970.

Posters of World War Two, Wayland (East Sussex, England), 1972.

The British Raj (juvenile), Wayland (East Sussex, England), 1973.

Livingstone in Africa (juvenile), Wayland (East Sussex, England), 1973.

The Life and Times of George V, Weidenfeld & Nicolson (London, England), 1973.

The House of Windsor, Macdonald & Janes (London, England), 1973.

Someone Has Blundered: Calamities of the British Army in the Victorian Age, Arthur Baker, 1973, new edition, Windrush Press, 1999.

Edward VII: A Pictorial Biography, Macdonald & Janes, 1975.

Palmerston, Weidenfeld & Nicolson (London, England), 1975.

The Crimean War, Hart-Davis (London, England), 1975.

The Royal Victorians: A Pictorial Biography, St. Martin's (New York, NY), 1975.

Eclipse of Kings: European Monarchies in the Twentieth Century, Macdonald & Janes, 1976.

The Adventures of Long John Silver, St. Martin's (New York, NY), 1977.

Radical Joe: A Life of Joseph Chamberlain, Hamish Hamilton (London, England), 1977.

The Boer War, Hart-Davis, 1977.

Return to Treasure Island, M. Joseph (London, England), 1978.

Prince Philip: Duke of Edinburgh, M. Joseph (London, England), 1980, Atheneum (New York, NY), 1981.

Lord Reading: A Biography of Rufus Isaacs, Weidenfeld & Nicolson (London, England), 1982.

King George VI, M. Joseph (London, England), 1982, F. Watts (New York, NY), 1983.

(With P. Slinn) *The Evolution of the Modern Commonwealth,* Macmillan (New York, NY), 1982.

Alison Uttley: The Life of a Country Child, M. Joseph (London, England), 1986, revised edition, Sutton Publishing, 2001.

Further Tales of Little Grey Rabbit (juvenile), illustrated by Margaret Tempest, Collins (London, England), 1989.

(Author of preface) Peter Neville, *A Traveller's History of Ireland,* Interlink Publishing Group, 1993.

(Editor) Valerio Lintner, *A Traveller's History of Italy,* updated edition, Interlink Publishing Group, 1993.

Jawaharlal Nehru, University of Wales Press, 1993.

(Editor) *A British Tale of Indian & Foreign Service: The Memoirs of Sir Ian Scott,* Radcliffe Press, 1999.

Empire; the British Imperial Experience from 1765 to the Present, HarperCollins, 1996, new edition, Phoenix, 2001.

Also author of "traveller's histories" of France, Spain, Paris, Japan, England, Russia, and Scotland. Contributor to periodicals, including *History, Times Literary Supplement, Journal of Imperial and Commonwealth History, History Today, Sunday Telegraph, New Statesman and Society, Independent, BBC History Magazine, Mail on Sunday,* and *English Historical Review.*

SIDELIGHTS: Denis Judd has written extensively about the British royal family and about the personalities and events that have shaped modern England. His biography of Prince Philip details the life of a man whom a reviewer for *Punch* believed is "likely to remain something of a mystery." *Prince Philip: Duke of Edinburgh* follows the fortunes of the prince from his birth on the family dining room table as the son of Princess Alice of Battenberg and Prince Andrew of Greece, to his marriage to Elizabeth, future Queen of England, and beyond.

BIOGRAPHICAL/CRITICAL SOURCES:

PERIODICALS

Los Angeles Times, May 11, 1981.
New Statesman, May 5, 1982.
Punch, October 22, 1980.
Times (London, England), March 31, 1990.
Times Literary Supplement, November 13, 1970; November 2, 1973; January 18, 1974; December 5, 1975; January 30, 1976; May 13, 1977; July 2, 1982; December 31, 1982; January 7, 1983; December 5, 1986, p. 1378.
Washington Post Book World, June 7, 1981.

K

KACK-BRICE, Valerie 1950-

PERSONAL: Born April 27, 1950, in Portland, OR; children: Patrick. *Ethnicity:* "Caucasian." *Education:* Cleveland State University, B.A.; University of Washington, Seattle, M.S.W.; California Institute of Integral Studies, Ph.D.

ADDRESSES: Home—10350 Smith Rd., Grass Valley, CA 95949. *Office*—1265 High St., Auburn, CA 95603; fax: 530-272-7632. *E-mail*—kackbrice@hotmail.com.

CAREER: Private practice of psychotherapy in Auburn, CA, 1985—.

MEMBER: National Association of Social Workers, Board of Certified Diplomates in Social Work.

WRITINGS:

The Emotion Handbook, N. W. Publishing, 1992.
(Editor) *For She Is the Tree of Life,* Conari Press (Emeryville, CA), 1995.

WORK IN PROGRESS: Conscious Relationships: From Ending through Beginning.

SIDELIGHTS: Valerie Kack-Brice told *CA:* "I write for my mental and emotional health, and to serve others. My daily experiences in private practice heavily influence my writing. Most importantly, I try to see the whole person and to offer support for the wounded aspects of the self, as well as the spiritual yearnings of the individual."

KAYE, M(ary) M(argaret) 1909-
(Mollie Hamilton, Mollie Kaye)

PERSONAL: Born August 21, 1908, in Simla, India; married Godfrey John Hamilton (an army officer), 1942 (died, 1985); children: Carolyn. *Education:* Attended schools in England.

ADDRESSES: Agent—David Higham Associates, 5-8 Lower John St., London W1R 4HA, England.

CAREER: Writer; painter.

MEMBER: Royal Society of London (fellow).

WRITINGS:

HISTORICAL NOVELS

Shadow of the Moon, Messner (New York, NY), 1956, expanded edition, St. Martin's (New York, NY), 1979.
Trade Wind, Coward (New York, NY), 1963, revised edition, St. Martin's (New York, NY), 1981.
The Far Pavilions, St. Martin's (New York, NY), 1978.

MYSTERIES

Six Bars at Seven, Hutchinson (London, England), 1940.
Death Walked in Kashmir, Staples Press (London, England), 1953, published as *Death in Kashmir,* St. Martin's (New York, NY), 1984.
Death Walked in Berlin, Staples Press (London, England), 1955, published as *Death in Berlin,* St. Martin's (New York, NY), 1983.

Death Walked in Cyprus, Staples Press (London, England), 1956, published as *Death in Cyprus,* St. Martin's (New York, NY), 1984.

Later than You Think, Longman (London, England), 1958, published under pseudonym Mollie Hamilton, Coward, 1959, published as *It's Later than You Think,* World (Manchester, England), 1960, published as *Death in Kenya,* St. Martin's (New York, NY), 1983.

House of Shade, Coward, 1959, published as *Death in Zanzibar,* St. Martin's (New York, NY), 1983.

Night on the Island, Longman (New York, NY), 1960, published as *Death in the Andamans,* St. Martin's (New York, NY), 1985.

Three Complete Novels (contains *Death in Kenya, Death in Zanzibar,* and *Death in Cyprus*), Wings (New York, NY), 1994.

CHILDREN'S BOOKS; UNDER PSEUDONYM MOLLIE KAYE

Potter Pinner series *(Potter Pinner Meadow,* illustrated by Margaret Tempest, *Black Bramble Wood, Willow Witches Brook,* and *Gold Gorse Common)* Collins, 1937-45.

(And illustrator) *The Animals' Vacation,* New York Graphic Society, 1964.

Thistledown, Quartet, 1982.

(And illustrator) *The Ordinary Princess,* Kestrel (London, England), 1980, Doubleday (New York, NY), 1984.

OTHER

The Far Pavilions Picture Book, Bantam (New York, NY), 1979.

(Editor) Emily Bayley and Thomas Metcalf, *The Golden Calm: An English Lady's Life in Moghul Delhi,* Viking (New York, NY), 1980.

(Editor) Rudyard Kipling, *Moon of Other Days: M. M. Kaye's Kipling: Favourite Verses,* Hodder & Stoughton (London, England), 1988, Salem House, 1989.

(Editor and author of foreword) Rudyard Kipling, *Picking up Gold and Silver: Stories,* St. Martin's (New York, NY), 1989, published as *Picking up Gold and Silver: A Selection of Kipling's Short Stories,* Macmillan (London, England), 1989.

(Author of foreword) Rudyard Kipling, *The Complete Verse,* Kyle Cathie (London, England), 1990.

The Sun in the Morning: My Early Years in India and England, St. Martin's (New York, NY), 1990, published as *The Sun in the Morning: The Autobiography of M. M. Kaye,* Curley (South Yarmouth, MA), 1992.

Golden Afternoon: Volume II of the Autobiography of M. M. Kaye, St. Martin's Press (New York, NY), 1998, published as *Golden Afternoon: Being the Second Part of "Share of Summer," Her Autobiography,* Viking (London, England), 1997.

Also author of *Strange Island,* Thacker. Author of the radio play, *England Wakes,* 1941.

ADAPTATIONS: *The Far Pavilions* was produced as a mini-series by Home Box Office in 1984.

SIDELIGHTS: Previously a successful author of children's books and mysteries, M. M. Kaye set these genres aside to concentrate on the historical romance novel, *The Far Pavilions.* After fourteen years and a grueling battle against cancer, Kaye finished the book that has been compared to *Gone with the Wind* and other classics of the genre.

The Far Pavilions gives readers a detailed look at life in colonial India. It is a subject on which she is well qualified to write, for she was born in Simla, India, into a British family that had already lived in that country for two generations. Although she was educated in England, Kaye returned to India after her schooling and married a British army officer. While she was thus a part of the ruling class in colonial India, Kaye's writing has been especially praised for its even-handed portrayal of both the native Indians and the English colonists. Brigitte Weeks wrote in the *Washington Post Book World* that *The Far Pavilions* is so powerful, its "readers . . . cannot ever feel quite the same about either the Indian subcontinent or the decrepit history of the British Empire."

The Far Pavilions has been compared to Rudyard Kipling's *Kim.* Like Kipling's novel, Kaye's book features a young British boy, Ash, who is orphaned, then raised as an Indian and a Hindu. Ash is sent to live with aristocratic relatives in England when his parentage is finally revealed. Later, he returns to India as a soldier and finds himself torn between his two heritages. While some critics dismiss Kaye's plot as standard romantic-adventure fare, others praise her for skillfully combining Ash's adventures with an accurate historical account of the events between the Indian Mutiny and the Second Afghan War. Furthermore, emphasized *Spectator* contributor Francis King, Kaye possesses a "gift for narrative"; he found *The Far Pavilions* "absorbing" in spite of its more than nine hundred pages. A *New Yorker* writer concurred that Kaye is "a topnotch storyteller and historian . . . she holds the reader in thrall."

But critics most often point to Kaye's comprehensive vision of nineteenth-century India as the key to her novel's success. *Times Literary Supplement* reviewer Theon Wilkinson explained: "[Kaye] writes with the conviction that events must be told in their fullness or not at all, that ever[y] facet of information touching the characters must be embraced; and *The Far Pavilions* is a great oriental pot-pourri from which nothing is left out: Indian lullabies; regimental bawdy songs; regimental history, wars and campaigns; weddings; funerals; poisonous plants—a tribute to much painstaking research, some drawn from original diaries and journals. . . . The length of the book is a challenge but the effort is rewarded." And Rahul Singh wrote in *Punch,* "There is none of the romantic sentimentality that saw India as a country of snake charmers and bejewelled princes, with the faithful Gunga Din thrown in. Nor the view of it as one vast, multiplying, putrefying sewer for which there was no possible hope. Ms. Kaye sees India as many Indians do, and for this one must applaud her."

Before publishing *The Far Pavilions,* Kaye had written two other books similar to it. *Shadow of the Moon* dramatizes the events of the Indian Mutiny of 1857 through the story of an orphaned Anglo-Spanish heiress sent to India to marry a man she doesn't know but to whom she has been betrothed since childhood. *Trade Wind* is set in Zanzibar instead of India, but like *Shadow of the Moon* and *The Far Pavilions,* it examines two cultures in conflict while telling the exciting story of a young abolitionist from Massachusetts who is kidnaped by a handsome slave trader when she travels to Zanzibar. Neither book was particularly successful when first published, but when reissued after the publication of *The Far Pavilions,* both *Shadow of the Moon* and *Trade Wind* became best-sellers. Like *The Far Pavilions,* they have been praised for their fine descriptions of exotic settings.

Reviewing *Shadow of the Moon* for the *New York Herald Tribune,* David Tilden stated that the book is "filled with excitement and suspense, but the story of India itself will have even greater fascination for many readers . . . Kaye pictures its welter of races, religions, ideals and superstitions; its fragrances and stench, beauty and horror." While also praising Kaye's portrait of India and its history, Nicholas Shrimpton in the *New Statesman* found her characterizations wanting, particularly with regard to the hero of the book, Alex Winter. According to Shrimpton: "When his [Alex's] mighty brain isn't predicting the next hundred years of Indian history, his mighty body is wrestling with sharks or saving the Raj single-handed. If you can tolerate a bionic tailor's dummy for a hero, however, the local colour is

terrific." In marked contrast, Walter Shapiro, reviewing *Trade Wind* for the *Washington Post Book World,* had no problem with Kaye's characterizations, or anything else about the book. While granting that its story line might seem conventional, he feels that *Trade Wind* "transcends such easy labels as romance or exotic historical novel. It is a sophisticated treat for those traditional readers who favor good writing, subtle character development, clever plotting and a slightly ironic narrative tone."

Assessing *The Far Pavilions, Shadow of the Moon,* and *Trade Wind* for *Twentieth-Century Romance and Historical Writers,* Pamela Cleaver stated: "All three books are long and move at a stately pace. . . . descriptions are graphic and lyrical, the characters lively and well-drawn. . . . the final outcome of these romances is predictable, the twists and turns of the plot are not. The writing is of a high quality and the books are extremely enjoyable." She further advised: "If you want to be immersed in the sights, sounds, and scents of the gorgeous East, to understand the thoughts of mid-Victorian men and women, to enjoy lush, melodramatic romance against a background of authentic history, then read M. M. Kaye's historical romances."

Though overshadowed by the success of her historical fiction, Kaye's mystery novels nevertheless comprise a significant portion of her creative output. Overall critical response to her mysteries in large part parallels the response to her historicals: universal acclaim for the physical and social environments she has crafted, a more mixed response with regard to her plots and characterizations. *Later than You Think* (reprinted in the United States as *Death in Kenya*) takes place in Kenya shortly after the Mau-Mau uprising. Anthony Boucher, writing in the *New York Times,* described the book as "a perfectly conventional whodunit of the feminine persuasion . . . redeemed by its setting." Likewise, a reviewer for the *Times Literary Supplement* felt that Kaye's imagination in the book is more taken with the "Kenya scene and the love-interest . . . than . . . the detective-work necessitated by the plot." Reviewing *House of Shade* (reprinted in the United States as *Death in Zanzibar*) for the *Spectator,* Christopher Pym echoed such sentiments. He describes the book as a "long, and long-drawn-out murder story distinguished by its Zanzibar setting . . . with some of the appeal of a good travel brochure."

Kaye also enjoyed considerable success with the two-part publication of her memoirs. *The Sun in the Morning: My Early Years in India and England* was published in 1990, followed by *Golden Afternoon* in 1997.

Several reviewers cautioned that Kaye's memoirs were hardly a representative picture of life in India during the Raj. Her story is highly personal and she does not reflect on the political issues of the day. A *Contemporary Review* writer called *The Sun in the Morning* "a pleasant tale of an India that never was—except as an elderly lady recalls a privileged childhood, and as the passing of the years dims all discordant notes. . . . Kaye can—though rarely—add a touch of acid. But for the most part this is 'roses everywhere', a tale of sugar and spice and all things sweet-scented." *Publishers Weekly*'s Genevieve Stuttaford concurred that *The Sun in the Morning* is "written with gushing, romantic enthusiasm," but found much to recommend in this "kaleidoscopic story of a long-lost innocence just before and after World War I." Kaye's glowing memories of India stand in sharp contrast to the grim picture she paints of her exile to England. *The Sun in the Morning* ends with the family anticipating a return to India. Kaye's young adult years there are related in *Golden Afternoon*, which also details the Kayes' sojourn in China. Raleigh Trevelyan, a writer for *Time Literary Supplement*, advised that "the book ends with a promise to return to her beloved India: the subject, one hopes, of volume three of these memoirs."

BIOGRAPHICAL/CRITICAL SOURCES:

BOOKS

Contemporary Literary Criticism, Volume 28, Gale (Detroit), 1984.

Twentieth-Century Romance and Historical Writers, St. James Press (Detroit), 1994.

PERIODICALS

Chapter One, May-June, 1979.

Christian Science Monitor, November 13, 1978.

Contemporary Review, February, 1991, review of *The Sun in the Morning: My Early Years in India and England,* p. 112.

Cosmopolitan, December,1 980, Jane Clapperton, review of *The Golden Calm,* p. 20; August, 1981, Jane Clapperton, review of *Trade Wind,* p. 24; June, 1984, Carol E. Rinzler, review of *Death in Cyprus,* p. 54.

Detroit News, October 7, 1979.

Economist, December 26, 1981, review of *Thistledown,* p. 106.

Horn Book, November, 1984, Nancy C. Hammond, review of *The Ordinary Princess,* p. 758.

Library Journal, June 15, 1981, review of *Trade Wind,* p. 1322; April 1, 1983, review of *Death in Zanzi-*

bar, p. 761; October 1, 1990, V. Louise Saylor, review of *The Sun in the Morning: My Early Years in India and England,* p. 96; May 15, 1991, Jeffrey R. Luttrell, review of *Rudyard Kipling: The Complete Verse,* p. 83.

Los Angeles Magazine, September, 1981, Mark Wheeler, review of *Trade Wind,* p. 259.

Los Angeles Times, November 2, 1980; October 9 1984; May 23, 1986.

Maclean's, September 24, 1979.

National Review, May 16, 1980, Christina Steadman, review of *Shadow of the Moon,* p. 616.

New Statesman, October 1, 1979; October 12, 1979; November 14, 1980, Rosemary Stones, review of *The Ordinary Princess,* p. 20.

Newsweek, September 11, 1978.

New York, April 23, 1984, John Leonard, review of *The Far Pavilions,* p. 91.

New Yorker, October 9, 1978; September 24, 1979; March 2, 1981, review of *The Golden Calm,* p. 126; July 27, 1981, review of *Trade Wind,* p. 86.

New York Herald Tribune Book Review, September 1, 1957; September 20, 1959.

New York Times, October 26, 1958, p. 57; December 3, 1978; March 25, 1979.

New York Times Book Review, November 18, 1979; August 31, 1980, review of *Shadow of the Moon,* p. 19; March 4, 1984, review of *Death in Zanzibar,* p. 34; December 16, 1984, Richard Smith, review of *Death in Kashmir,* p. 26; August 25, 1985, Miriam Berkley, review of *Death in Berlin,* p. 16; August 17, 1990, Genevieve Stuttaford, review of *The Sun in the Morning: My Early Years in India and England,* p. 57; September 30, 1990, Geoffrey C. Ward, review of *The Sun in the Morning: My Early Years in India and England,* p. 14.

Parents' Magazine, November, 1984, Alice Siegel, review of *The Ordinary Princess,* p. 56.

People, November 20, 1978; May 16, 1983, review of *Death in Zanzibar,* p. 16.

Publishers Weekly, June 25, 1979; August 15, 1980, review of *The Golden Calm,* p. 49; May 8, 1981, Barbara A. Bannon, review of *Trade Wind,* p. 249; June 3, 1983, review of *Death in Kenya,* p. 64; August 3, 1984, review of *Death in Kashmir,* p. 55; April 26, 1985, Sybil Steinberg, review of *Death in Berlin,* p. 69; April 4, 1986, Sybil Steinberg, review of *Death in the Andamans,* p. 52; August 17, 1990, review of *The Sun in the Morning: My Early Years in India and England,* p. 57; October 25, 1999, p. 55.

Punch, November 14, 1979.

School Library Journal, March, 1985, Linda Amers-Boman, review of *The Ordinary Princess,* p. 168.

Sewanee Review, summer, 1980.

Spectator, April 12, 1957; July 24, 1959, p. 118; September 9, 1978.

Teen, December, 1980, Linda E. Watson, review of *Shadow of the Moon,* p. 45.

Time, April 16, 1984, Richard Stengel, review of *The Far Pavilions,* p. 70.

Times Literary Supplement (London, England), April 19, 1957; August 22, 1958, p. 469; September 22, 1978, November 21, 1980; March 26, 1982; December 19, 1997, Raleigh Trevelyan, review of *Golden Afternoon,* p. 23.

Washington Post, September 11, 1979; April 21, 1984.

Washington Post Book World, September 10, 1978; July 12, 1981; November 11, 1984.*

*   *   *

KAYE, Mollie
See KAYE, M(ary) M(argaret)

*   *   *

KING, Larry 1933-

PERSONAL: Born Lawrence Harvey Zeiger, November 19, 1933, in Brooklyn, NY; son of Edward (a restaurant owner) and Jennie (Gitlitz) Zeiger; married Alene Akins (a Playboy bunny), 1961 (divorced, 1963), remarried, 1967 (divorced, 1971); married Mickey Sutphin, 1964 (divorced, 1966); married Sharon Dorl (a math teacher), September 25, 1976 (divorced, 1982); married Julie Alexander (a headhunter), October 7, 1989 (marriage ended); married Shawn Southwick (a country singer and actress), September 5, 1997; children: Andy (adopted), Chaia, Chance Armstrong, Larry Jr., Cannon. *Politics:* Independent. *Religion:* Jewish.

ADDRESSES: Office—1755 South Jefferson Davis Hwy., Arlington, VA 22202. *Agent*—Bill Adler, 551 Fifth Ave., New York, NY 10018.

CAREER: WAHR-AM, Miami, FL, janitor, 1957, morning disc jockey, 1957-58; WKAT-AM, Miami, FL, drive-time disc jockey, 1958, host of interview show from Pumpernik's Restaurant, 1958-62; WIOD-AM, Miami, FL, host of Pumpernik's interview show, 1962, host of interview show broadcast from a houseboat, 1963-71; freelance writer and broadcaster, 1972-75; interview show host, 1975-78; Mutual Broad-

Larry King

casting System, Arlington, VA, host of *The Larry King Show,* 1978—. Television talk-show host, WLBW-TV, Miami, FL, 1963, and WTVJ-TV, Miami, FL, 1964; WJLA-TV, Washington, DC, host of *Larry King: Let's Talk,* 1985; Cable News Network (CNN), host of *Larry King Live!,* 1985—. Color commentator on radio and television for baseball, football, and hockey teams in Miami, New Orleans, LA, Baltimore, MD, and Washington, DC; anchor for CNN's telecast of the Goodwill Games, 1990.

MEMBER: American Federation of Television and Radio Artists.

AWARDS, HONORS: Man of the Year, City of Hope, 1977; Peabody Award, University of Georgia, 1982; Jack Anderson Investigative Reporting Award, 1985, Radio Award, National Association of Broadcasters, 1985, Best Radio Talk Show Host, *Washington Journalism Review,* 1986, all for *The Larry King Show;* ten CableACE Awards, for *Larry King Live!;* Annual Cable Excellence Awards, 1987, 1988, 1989, for *Larry*

King Live!, 1990, for excellence in cable television; Father of the Year, National Father's Day Council, 1988; Broadcaster of the Year, International Radio and Television Society, 1989; Emerson Hall of Fame and Broadcasters Hall of Fame, 1992; named talk show host of the year, National Association of Radio Talk Show Hosts, 1993; Scopus Award, American Friends of Hebrew University, 1994; Man of the Year, American Heart Association, 1992; Golden Plate Award, American Academy of Achievement, 1996; Mahoney Award, Harvard University, 2000; Franklin Delano Roosevelt Award, March of Dimes, 2000, for efforts on behalf of volunteerism; Unity Award for excellence, Lincoln University of Missouri, 2001; public service award, American Foundation for Suicide Prevention, 2001; honorary degrees from George Washington University, New England Institute of Technology, and Pratt Institute.

WRITINGS:

(With Emily Yoffe) *Larry King by Larry King,* Simon & Schuster (New York, NY), 1982.

(With Peter Occhiogrosso) *Tell It to the King,* Putnam (New York, NY), 1988.

(With B. D. Colen) *"Mr. King, You're Having a Heart Attack": How a Heart Attack and Bypass Surgery Changed My Life,* Delacorte (New York, NY), 1989.

(With Peter Occhiogrosso) *Tell Me More,* Putnam (New York, NY), 1990.

(With Marty Appel) *When You're from Brooklyn, the Rest of the World Is Tokyo,* Little, Brown (Boston, MA), 1992.

(With Mark Stencel) *On the Line: The New Road to the White House,* Harcourt (New York, NY), 1993.

(With Bill Gilbert) *How to Talk to Anyone, Anytime, Anywhere: The Secrets of Good Communication,* Crown (New York, NY), 1994.

The Best of Larry King Live: the Greatest Interviews, Turner Publishing (Atlanta, GA), 1995.

(With Chaia King) *Daddy Day, Daughter Day,* illustrated by Wendy Christensen, Dove Kids (Los Angeles, CA), 1997.

(With Pat Piper) *Future Talk: Conversations about Tomorrow with Today's Most Provocative Personalities,* HarperCollins (New York, NY), 1998.

(With Rabbi Irwin Katsof) *Powerful Prayers,* Renaissance Books (Los Angeles, CA), 1998.

(With Pat Piper) *Anything Goes!: What I've Learned from Pundits, Politicians, and Presidents,* Warner Books (New York, NY), 2000.

(Compiler) *Love Stories of World War II,* Crown (New York, NY), 2001.

Former columnist for *Miami Beach Sun-Reporter, Miami Herald, Miami News,* and *Sporting News;* weekly columnist for *USA Today,* 1983—.

SIDELIGHTS: Larry King has the ear of the American people. As the radio host of the *Larry King Show* on the Mutual Broadcasting System and the television host of *Larry King Live!* on the Cable News Network, he reached more than three million listeners and another million viewers nightly by 2000. One of the most respected figures in radio history and a highly regarded television interviewer, King has talked on the air with some of the most provocative and influential figures in American politics, arts, business, and sports. He has drawn on this wide experience to write several books of anecdotes, reminiscences, and opinions, as well as more personal books about his heart attack, being a parent, and prayer.

In interviewing authors, politicians, entertainers, athletes, and other celebrities, King likes to put himself in the position of his audience, playing the role of an interested layman. To achieve this, he avoids learning too much about the person featured on that night's program. As he told John Pekkanen in a *People* profile, "This way the audience and I can learn together. . . . I never ask a question when I know the answer." The result, *Nightline*'s Ted Koppel told Zoglin, is that "Larry listens to his guests. . . . He pays attention to what they say. Too few interviewers do that." King also avoids reading the books being promoted by his author guests. "I've got to be curious about it," he explained to Dennis McDougal of the *Los Angeles Times,* "and how am I going to be curious if I've read it?" His audience appreciates the approach and so do his guests, often opening up in ways they would not with news reporters or other talk-show hosts.

King's commitments make for a busy work week. Vic Sussman outlined King's schedule in a *Washington Post* feature: "At 8:15 every weekday evening King is at the CNN Washington TV studio ready for 'Larry King Live' at 9. By 10:15 he's at Mutual Broadcasting System's studio in Crystal City preparing to broadcast his 11 p.m.-to-2 a.m. 'Larry King Show'. . . . And on Wednesdays he spends the afternoon writing his weekly column for *USA Today.*" King also finds time to collaborate with co-writers on his several books.

The story of King's rise from a troubled Jewish kid in Brooklyn to one of the top personalities in radio and television is a tale in itself. As Larry Zeiger, he left Brooklyn for Miami, Florida in 1957 to pursue his dream of becoming a radio disc jockey. He started by sweeping floors for WAHR-AM in Miami because it was the only job he could land. When the morning disc jockey quit, the station manager called on the young janitor to step in, suggesting only that he change his last name to King. On May 1, 1957, Larry King began his career on the air. During the next few years, he established himself as one of Miami's leading radio show hosts. He hosted an interview show from a local restaurant, first for WKAT and then for WIOD. He interviewed a wide variety of guests, sometimes ordinary people, sometimes local talent, and sometimes nationally known personalities. The list included Bobby Darin, Lenny Bruce, Don Rickles, Jackie Gleason, Jimmy Hoffa, and Ed Sullivan. Over the next decade, King became a celebrity himself.

But his fortune did not keep pace with his fame, and King began to spend beyond his means and to gamble. In 1971, he lost his job in a scandal that involved his debts, and allegations of larceny made by Louis Wolfson, a Miami financier who claimed he had employed King as a courier for money intended for Jim Garrison, the New Orleans district attorney investigating the John F. Kennedy assassination. King was never prosecuted because the statute of limitations had expired, but no one in Miami wanted to employ him. He spent the next few years working at odd jobs, and then returned to Miami and WIOD when new management at the station offered to give him another chance.

In 1978, the Mutual Broadcasting System hired him to take his late-night interview and phone-in show to a national audience. *The Larry King Show* debuted on twenty-eight stations in 1978 and had spread to more than three hundred within a decade. The format for the show is this: King interviews a guest, listeners call in to ask the guest questions, and then after the guest leaves, King presides over "Open Line America," a phone-in forum for graduate students, shift workers, insomniacs, and other people of the night. "In picking guests," King told Alvin P. Sanoff in a *U.S. News and World Report* interview, "we look for someone passionate, with an ability to be brief and analytical and with the facts to back up what they believe. We also want some anger in a guest—not unbridled anger but somebody mad at the system." King added his television show, *Larry King Live!* on CNN, to his schedule in 1985. It quickly became one of the top-rated shows on cable and spread to reach more than 120 countries.

In his years on the national scene, King has interviewed some of America's most influential, intelligent, intriguing, and egotistical personalities. He has written about many of these encounters in such books as *Tell It to the*

King and *Tell Me More.* His recap of the 1992 presidential campaign, *On the Line: the New Road to the White House,* received considerable attention. The campaign itself was marked by several unusual elements, including businessman Ross Perot's announcement of his candidacy on King's television show. King's insights into the campaign and its personalities, according to Ronnie Dugger in the *New York Times Book Review,* are a "mismash of banal political analysis" and reveal the author's reluctance to provoke any real controversy. A reviewer for *Publishers Weekly* also felt that the book "offers few new insights," but relished it as a "brisk recap" and a "lively account" of an unusual political race.

Political insights also inform *Anything Goes!: What I've Learned from Pundits, Politicians, and Presidents.* Though King writes about his encounters with such celebrities as Marlon Brando, the Dalai Lama, and Judge Lance Ito, many reviewers found the book's comments on politicians to be the heart of the book. While *New York Times* writer Peter Marks criticized the book's superficiality, he appreciated its humorous episodes. "Essentially," he wrote, "it is a chatty, slapped-together scrapbook of an extraordinarily successful decade in the life of a profoundly unflappable talk show host who has a knack for getting almost everyone to agree to spend an hour with him on CNN." Ilene Cooper in *Booklist* expressed similar disappointment in the book's lack of originality and insight. A contributor to *Kirkus Reviews,* however, deemed *Anything Goes* a "light but likable commentary on politics and the media" during the Clinton years; a reviewer for *Publishers Weekly* considered the book "breezy" and "entertaining."

A discussion about future trends forms the basis of *Future Talk: Conversations about Tomorrow with Today's Most Provocative Personalities.* In this book, King questions 48 specialists in various fields, from education and arts to technology, about what may await society in the twenty-first century. His interviewees include Bill Gates and Esther Dyson on technology; Lester Thurow on business and economics; Tim Russert on politics; and Dr. David Satcher and Dr. Everett Koop on medical research and health care. *Futurist* reviewer Jeffrey H. Epstein observed that "by asking common questions that many people would ask, King teases out powerful and thoughtful comments from his subjects." Praising King for his ability to ask "the sort of futuristic questions that elicit information one wants to know about," a *Publishers Weekly* contributor deemed the book "interesting and eminently worth pondering."

Though King claims he is not a religious person, he teamed up with Rabbi Irwin Katsof of New York City to write *Powerful Prayers*. As with many of King's previous books, this one incorporates a multitude of celebrity interviews into the larger theme of a book on prayer. *Library Journal* reviewer Leroy Hommerding appreciated the "bold questions" the authors pose in the book as well as the "provocative, often entertaining" discussions about incorporating faith and spirituality into contemporary life. Though *Booklist* contributor Ray Olsen found King's questions and comments somewhat "commonplace," he concluded that *Powerful Prayers* "is not a bad inspirational book at all."

The secret of King's success, many believe, is his genuineness. "Unlike more confrontational interviewers," wrote a contributor to *U.S. News and World Report*, "King listened intently to guests and drew questions not from a prepared checklist but from what he heard. One of his great assets was his ability to check his own ego at the studio door, ensuring that his visitors' views, not his own, got aired." As Thomas J. Meyer characterized him in a *New York Times Magazine* profile, "He doesn't pose as an intellectual, just as a curious man who likes to ask questions. In a society that has grown skeptical of didactic experts and suspicious of the mass media, King is Everyman with a microphone, the average Joe with a talk show of his own."

BIOGRAPHICAL/CRITICAL SOURCES:

BOOKS

King, Larry, with Emily Yoffe, *Larry King by Larry King,* Simon & Schuster (New York, NY), 1982.

King, Larry, with B. D. Colen, *"Mr. King, You're Having a Heart Attack": How a Heart Attack and Bypass Surgery Changed My Life,* Delacorte (New York, NY), 1989.

King, Larry, *When You're from Brooklyn, the Rest of the World Is Tokyo,* Little, Brown (Boston, MA), 1992.

PERIODICALS

Advertising Age, October 18, 1982; July 11, 1983, p. M18.

Baltimore Evening Sun, February 19, 1989.

Booklist, October 15, 1994, Ilene Cooper, review of *How to Talk to Anyone, Anytime, Anywhere: The Secrets of Good Communication,* p. 370; February 15, 1998, Ilene Cooper, review of *Future Talk: Conversations about Tomorrow with Today's Most Provocative Personalities,* p. 946; September 1,

1998, Ray Olson, review of *Powerful Prayers: Conversations on Faith, Hope, and the Human Spirit with Today's Most Provocative People,* p. 4; October 15, 2000, Ilene Cooper, review of *Anything Goes!: What I've Learned from Pundits, Politicians, and Presidents,* p. 387.

Electronic News, February 27, 1995, Robert Sobel, review of *How to Talk to Anyone, Anytime, Anywhere,* p. 46.

Entertainment Weekly, November 18, 1994, Vanessa V. Friedman, review of *How to Talk to Anyone, Anytime, Anywhere,* p. 98.

Esquire, February 1995, Douglas Rushkoff, "Host Hogs," p. 32.

Futurist, June/July 1998, Jeffrey H. Epstein, review of *Future Talk,* p. 59.

Good Housekeeping, October, 1989, pp. 131, 215-216.

Insight on the News, September 28, 1998, Dave Boyer, review of *Powerful Prayers,* p. 41.

Kirkus Review, October 15, 2000, review of *Anything Goes!,* p. 1466.

Library Journal, September 15, 1998, Leroy Hommerding, review of *Powerful Prayers,* p. 86.

Los Angeles Times, April 21, 1988.

New York Times, November 5, 2000, Peter Marks, review of *Anything Goes!*

New York Times Book Review, December 26, 1993, Ronnie Dugger, review of *On the Line: The New Road to the White House,* p. 12; November 5, 2000, Peter Marks, "Be My Guest: Larry King Has Ways of Making People Talk," p. 18.

New York Times Magazine, May 26, 1991.

People, March 10, 1980, pp. 49-56; May 11, 1987; October 23, 1989, pp. 115-117.

Publishers Weekly, November 8, 1993, review of *On the Line,* p. 67; October 17, 1994, review of *How to Talk to Anyone, Anytime, Anywhere,* p. 75; February 16, 1998, review of *Future Talk,* October 23, 2000, review of *Anything Goes!,* p. 68.

Sports Illustrated, July 29, 1985, p. 58.

Time, July 22, 1985, p. 71; June 1, 1998, Joel Stein, "Q&A: Larry King," p. 88; September 17, 2001, Joel Stein, "Long . . . Live . . . the . . . King!," p. 109.

U.S. News and World Report, January 16, 1984, pp. 55-56; January 15, 1990, pp. 54-55.

Washington Post, September 14, 1982, p. B11; May 17, 1988.

OTHER

BookPage.com, http://www.bookpage.com/ (January 6, 2001), James L. Dickerson, "Backstage and on the Page with the King of Television Talk."

CNN.com, http://www.cnn.com/ (October 4, 2001), "Larry King."

Salon.com, http://www.salonmag.com/ (November 21, 2000), Amy Reiter, review of *Anything Goes!**

*   *   *

KONING, Hans 1924-
(Hans Koningsberger)

PERSONAL: Original name, Hans Koningsberger; name legally changed in 1977; born July 12, 1924, in Amsterdam, Netherlands; came to United States in 1951; son of Daniel and Elizabeth (Van Collem) Koningsberger; married Henriette Waterland; married Elizabeth Sutherland Martinez, March, 1952; married Katherine Scanlon, September, 1963; children: (first marriage) Ellen; (second marriage) Tessa Sutherland; (third marriage) Christina, Andrew. *Education:* Attended University of Amsterdam, 1939-41, University of Zurich, 1941-43, and Sorbonne, University of Paris, 1945.

ADDRESSES: Agent—Frances Goldin, 57 East 11th St., New York, NY 10003.

CAREER: Editor of Amsterdam, Netherlands weekly, 1947-50; radio director in Indonesia, 1950-51; freelance writer. *Military service:* British Liberation Army, 1943-45; became sergeant.

AWARDS, HONORS: Two-time recipient of fellowship for creative writers, National Endowment for the Arts, for fiction.

WRITINGS:

UNDER NAME HANS KONINGSBERGER

Modern Dutch Painting: An Introduction, Netherlands Information Service, c. 1955, 3rd edition, 1960.

The Golden Keys (young adult historical novel), Rand McNally (Chicago, IL), 1956.

The Affair (novel), Knopf (New York, NY), 1958.

(Translator) Carlo Coccioli, *Manuel the Mexican,* Simon & Schuster (New York, NY), 1958.

(Translator) Maria Dermout, *Ten Thousand Things,* Simon & Schuster (New York, NY), 1958.

(Translator) Maria Dermout, *Yesterday,* 1960.

An American Romance (novel), Simon & Schuster (New York, NY), 1960.

A Walk with Love and Death (novel; also see below), Simon & Schuster (New York, NY), 1961.

Hermione (play), first produced in Stockholm, Sweden, 1963.

I Know What I'm Doing (novel), Simon & Schuster (New York, NY), 1964.

Love and Hate in China (travel), McGraw (New York, NY), 1966.

The World of Vermeer, 1632-1675, Time-Life (Alexandria, VA), 1967.

The Revolutionary (novel; also see below), Farrar, Straus (New York, NY), 1967.

Along the Roads of the New Russia (travel), Farrar, Straus (New York, NY), 1968.

The Future of Che Guevara, Doubleday (New York, NY), 1971.

UNDER NAME HANS KONING

The Almost World, Dial (New York, NY), 1972.

Death of a Schoolboy (historical novel), Harcourt (New York, NY), 1974.

The Petersburg-Cannes Express (novel), Harcourt (New York, NY), 1975.

A New Yorker in Egypt (travel), Harcourt (New York, NY), 1976.

Columbus; His Enterprise: Exploding the Myth, Monthly Review Press (New York, NY), 1976.

Amsterdam, Time-Life, 1977.

America Made Me (novel), Gollancz, 1979.

The Kleber Flight, Atheneum (New York, NY), 1981.

De Witt's War (novel), Pantheon (New York, NY), 1983.

Acts of Faith, Gollancz, 1986.

Nineteen Sixty-Eight: A Personal Report, Norton (New York, NY), 1987.

The Conquest of America: How the Indian Nations Lost Their Continent, Monthly Review Press, 1993.

Pursuit of a Woman on the Hinge of History, Brookline (Boston, MA), 1998.

OTHER

Also author of screenplays, based on his novels of the same titles, including *A Walk with Love and Death,* Twentieth Century-Fox, 1969, *The Revolutionary,* United Artists, 1970, and *Death of a Schoolboy,* Miran Films, 1983, and of the screenplay *The Wind in the Pines,* 1961. Author of *Aquarel of Holland,* published in 1950, and *The Iron Age,* published in 1990. Author of plays *The Blood-Red Café,* 1957, *A Day in the Life of Alexander Herzen,* 1978, and *A Woman of New York,* 1984. Editor and translator of *Modern Dutch Poetry,* Netherlands Information Service. Contributor to *New York Times, New Yorker, Harper's,* and other periodicals.

WORK IN PROGRESS: Zeeland, or *Elective Concurrences,* a novel about the interlocking fates of a French printer, condemned to death (yet escaping) after the fall of the Paris Commune in 1871, and his American grandson, a Commando sergeant in the British Army in 1941, escaping from the Germans.

SIDELIGHTS: Hans Koning is a critically favored and often political author of plays, screenplays, travel books, young adult books, and novels. A native Netherlander, Koning has also translated the works of Dutch writers into English. With the exception of a self-imposed ten-year exile in protest of the Vietnam War, Koning has made the United States his home since 1951. Newgate Callendar of the *New York Times Book Review* calls Koning "a cosmopolite with a wry, realistic attitude toward life."

On July 31, 2000, in the *New York Times* series, "Writers on Writing," Koning pleads for "committed literature." "I keep aiming toward . . . a novel for our time," he writes, "dealing with an essential theme and an essential message (but) in a subterranean, carefully hidden way, a message like a snake in the grass, as Trollope put it." Professor William Ferguson, in his *New York Times* review of Koning's latest novel, *Pursuit of a Woman on the Hinge of History,* writes about his hero, "Here comes Everyman." Since November 1999, Koning has hosted a radio program about books and book publishing on Radio WPKN, Bridgeport, CT, discussing with his guests the future of "the serious novel."

Koning's travel books have been praised by reviewers for their authentic depictions, compelling style, and personal touch. *Love and Hate in China,* according to Eliot Fremont-Smith in the *New York Times,* "is particularly sensitive and intelligent, and, quite aside from the extra-literary importance of the subject, it is personal travel-writing in the grand tradition, a compact and beautiful book." *Along the Roads of the New Russia* recounts Koning's 1967 travels so vividly, according to Thomas P. Whitney's review for the *New York Times Book Review,* that his "reader will complete his literary journey . . . with a sense of how it really feels to take such a trip." In *Best Sellers,* David Bianco comments on the merits of Koning's *A New Yorker in Egypt.* "Meticulously avoiding the tourist path," the critic writes, "the author travels on native trains, stays in out-of-the-way places, and wanders in and out of native slums and villages. . . . Politically sophisticated and socially aware, Hans Koning has put together a very readable, up-to-date account of Egypt today." Eric Pace asserts in the *New York Times Book Review* that the book "pro-

vides a graceful, impressionistic sketch" of the Egypt its author saw in 1975.

With *Columbus; His Enterprise: Exploding the Myth,* Koning turns to the history of his adoptive country for a different kind of travel book. In recounting the explorer's arrival in the New World, Christopher Hill explains in the *New York Review of Books,* "the author consciously and deliberately emphasizes the negative aspects of the conquest, the greed, cruelty, and treachery of the conquistadores, their utter contempt for the rights of the native peoples." For Hill and others, "this makes fascinating reading." In 1993, *Monthly Review Press* published a sequel to the Columbus book titled *The Conquest of America.*

Like his nonfiction, Koning's novels often trace politically charged paths. According to Paul Berman in the *Village Voice Literary Supplement,* Koning's "favorite topic is dreamy-eyed young revolutionaries on the verge of throwing a bomb." For many critics, these revolutionaries are sympathetic characters, their stories compellingly told. Of Koning's *I Know What I'm Doing,* a novel published in 1964, a *Times Literary Supplement* reviewer remarks: "The spareness of Mr. [Koning's] style is remarkably successful in showing the extreme thinness of his heroine's emotional life." *Death of a Schoolboy,* the tale of Gavrilo Princip, the student who assassinated Archduke Franz Ferdinand of Austria in 1914, elicits this comment from *Atlantic* reviewer Phoebe Adams: "The author succeeds brilliantly in making Princip and his friends convincing and their story provocative and significant in contemporary terms. There is nothing long ago and far away about the tale." Likewise, Callendar finds that *The Petersburg-Cannes Express,* a story about two young leftists who attempt to kidnap a Russian official in 1900, "is part an exercise in nostalgia, part a sly look at Czarist Russia and turn-of-the-century Europe, part a train ride, and altogether a delightful break from the usual mystery or espionage novel."

Koning's *The Revolutionary* received a mixed response. Some critics found its depiction of an anonymous man ("A.") in an anonymous Socialist state too spare to be compelling. According to Peter Berek's review for the *Nation,* the problem stems from the good intentions of its author: "In his praiseworthy desire to keep our attention focused on the notion of a revolutionary temperament or set of mind, rather than on the details of any particular time and place, [Koning] has given up most of the resources of the conventional realistic novel." Berek concludes that there is an "honesty of imagination" to Koning's vision as revealed in the novel, adding: "Perhaps [it] is more important than some partial failures of craft."

The Kleber Flight, published after Koning's return to the United States from his exile to London, features David Chandler Lum, a "middle-aged American protagonist," in the words of *New York Times* critic Christopher Lehmann-Haupt. While Lehmann-Haupt questions the resolution of the "moral dilemma" the novel raises, he adds that "when all is said and done, there is reason to be glad for David Lum's existence as a literary character." In a review for the *Nation* of several thrillers published in 1983, Robert Lekachman puts *De Witt's War,* a novel set in Holland at the time of Hitler, "at the top of my hit parade for the novelty of the setting, Hans Koning's ironic character sketches and the infallible grip of a well-told contest against massive odds."

Koning's *Nineteen Sixty-Eight: A Personal Report* explores the activity of a nonfictional revolutionary—the author himself. Abe Peck deems the book "an impressionistic which-side-are-you-on memoir" and calls Koning "an unrepentant radical" in a review for the Chicago *Tribune Books.* As such, it appears that Koning's nonfiction is fulfilling similar goals to those he sets for his novels: "In my fiction of the last few years," he told *CA,* "I am trying to be 'political' in the sense of reflecting the crucial issues of our days. . . ; I am trying to do this without writing propaganda or message novels; I'm aiming for novels which will do this and yet remain literature. Such novels are often called 'downbeat' and have a hard life on the current literary scene which is becoming ever more commercial and entertainment-minded, but it seems crucial to me that the modern American novel gets away from the purely individualistic issues . . . and deals with our common fate."

BIOGRAPHICAL/CRITICAL SOURCES:

PERIODICALS

Atlantic, August 4, 1974.
Atlantic Monthly, July 1996, September 1997.
Best Sellers, April, 1977.
Booklist, March 1, 1988, p. 1095; October 15, 1991, p. 371.
Books, June, 1989, p. 11; August, 1989, p. 19; November, 1989, p. 21.
Books & Bookmen, March, 1986, p. 31.
Christian Science Monitor, June 3, 1988, p. B3.
Commonweal, March 1, 1968.
Contemporary Review, September, 1992, p. 136.
History Today, May, 1992, p. 58.

Interracial Books for Children Bulletin, Volume 14, number 7, 1983, p. 35.
Journal of American History, September, 1988, p. 678.
Kirkus Reviews, September 1, 1987, p. 1294; January 1, 1988, p. 9.
Library Journal, November 1, 1987, p. 110; March 1, 1988, p. 77; August, 1991, p. 120.
Listener, June 1, 1989, p. 27.
London Review of Books, May 8, 1986, p. 20; March 17, 1988, p. 10.
Nation, October 16, 1967, p. 376; September 17, 1983, p. 214.
National Observer, November 13, 1967.
New Republic, January 27, 1973, p. 29.
New Statesman, February 21, 1986, p. 26.
New Statesman and Society, September 20, 1991, p. 43.
New Yorker, May 6, 1974, p. 142; June 9, 1975, p. 126.
New York Herald Tribune Book Review, June 8, 1958; April 10, 1960.
New York Review of Books, January 4, 1968, p. 21; November 25, 1976, p. 43.
New York Times, May 25, 1958; May 18, 1966; October 27, 1976; November 16, 1981; January 6, 1985; October 15, 1987, p. 23; October 12, 1992, p. 1.; December 22, 1997; July 31, 2000, p. 1 (arts).
New York Times Book Review, July 31, 1966, p. 7; October 15, 1967; November 17, 1968; March 25, 1973; April 7, 1974; August 24, 1975; January 23, 1977, p. 4; January 4, 1998.
Observer (London, England), March 2, 1986, p. 29; November 10, 1991, p. 59.
Publishers Weekly, October 2, 1987, p. 92; February 12, 1988, p. 72; May 17, 1991, p. 62; September 22, 1997.
Saturday Review, May 28, 1960; July 23, 1966, p. 52; August 26, 1967, p. 35; October 7, 1967, p. 43; October 30, 1976, p. 48.
Social Studies, January, 1992, p. 27.
Spectator, February, 1977, p. 24.
Time, May 26, 1958.
Times Literary Supplement, March 10, 1966, p. 185; September 28, 1967; November 17, 1968; April 7, 1974; August 24, 1975; January 23, 1977; June 17, 1977, p. 740; April 25, 1986, p. 453; December 30, 1988, p. 1439.
Tribune Books (Chicago, IL), October 25, 1987, p. 1.
Village Voice Literary Supplement, October, 1983, p. 3.*

KONINGSBERGER, Hans
  See KONING, Hans

*   *   *

KRAMER, Hilton 1928-

PERSONAL: Born March 25, 1928, in Gloucester, MA; son of Louis and Tillie (Banks) Kramer; married Esta Teich, December 6, 1964. *Education:* Syracuse University, B.A., 1950; attended New School for Social Research (now New School University), 1950, Columbia University, 1950-51, Harvard University, 1951, and Indiana University, 1951-52.

ADDRESSES: Office—*New Criterion,* P.O. Box 5194, FDR Station, New York, NY 10150.

CAREER: Arts Digest, New York, NY, associate editor and features editor, 1954-55; *Arts Magazine,* New York, NY, managing editor, 1955-58, editor, 1958-61; *Nation,* New York, NY, art critic, 1962-63; *New Leader,* New York, NY, art critic and associate editor, 1964-65; *New York Times,* New York, NY, art news editor, 1965-82; *New Criterion* (monthly review), New York, NY, editor, 1982—. Visiting professor of criticism at Yale University School of Drama, 1973-74.

MEMBER: Phi Beta Kappa, Century Association Club of New York City.

AWARDS, HONORS: D.Hum., Syracuse University, 1976.

WRITINGS:

(Editor) *Perspectives on the Arts,* Art Digest (New York, NY), 1961.
(Author of introductory text) Milton Avery, *Paintings, 1930-1960,* Yoseloff, 1962.
(Author of essay) Gaston Lachaise, *The Sculpture of Gaston Lachaise,* Eakins (New York, NY), 1967.
The Age of the Avant-Garde: An Art Chronicle of 1956-1972, Farrar, Straus (New York, NY), 1973.
(Author of text) Richard Lidner, *Richard Lidner,* New York Graphic Society (New York, NY), 1975.
Revenge of the Philistines: Art and Culture, 1972-1984, Farrar, Straus (New York, NY), 1984.
(Editor and author of introduction) *The New Criterion Reader: The First Five Years,* Free Press (New York, NY), 1988.
(Editor, with Roger Kimball) *Against the Grain: The New Criterion on Art and Intellect at the End of the Twentieth Century,* Ivan R. Dee (New York, NY), 1995.
(Editor, with Kimball) *The Future of the European Past,* Ivan R. Dee (New York, NY), 1997.
(Editor, with Kimball; and author of introduction) *The Betrayal of Liberalism: How the Disciples of Freedom and Equality Helped Foster the Illiberal Politics of Coercion and Control,* Ivan R. Dee (Chicago, IL), 1999.
The Twilight of the Intellectuals: Culture and Politics in the Era of the Cold War, Ivan R. Dee (New York, NY), 1999.

Author of texts for exhibition catalogs, including those of Ben Benn and Julio Gonzalez. Contributor to periodicals, including *Partisan Review, Commentary, New Republic, New York Review of Books, Art in America,* and *Artforum.*

SIDELIGHTS: Hilton Kramer is one of the nation's best known critics—"a percipient, sophisticated and highly intelligent observer of the contemporary art scene," to quote Richard Wollheim in the *New York Times Book Review.* From the pages of the *New York Times,* and more recently from his own publication, the monthly *New Criterion,* Kramer has covered the art world for more than three decades. His views on art and culture are controversial, but few fellow writers would argue that he presents his opinions in a forthright and readable style. As Wollheim put it, Kramer "writes about matters that are sometimes difficult and often elusive with enviable fluency, and he has for these purposes formed a style which, bypassing elegance, is descriptively powerful and at times rises to real eloquence."

In *Commentary,* Michael J. Lewis described Kramer's aims as a critic. "Since the early 1950s, when his essays and reviews began appearing in *Arts Magazine, Partisan Review, The Nation,* and *Commentary,* Kramer has been a principled and discriminating champion of modern art," Lewis stated. "His hallmark as a critic is a scrupulous, often exquisite, concern for the aesthetic primacy of the object itself—that is, for the formal properties of a work of art—and secondarily for its place within the art of its time. But as every aspect of art, from its making and display to its criticism and historiography, has in the past generation become relentlessly politicized, Kramer too has turned to politics, and to the larger culture of ideas in which contemporary art has become, willy-nilly, a 'player.' " Indeed, since founding the *New Criterion* in 1982, Kramer has written about wider cultural and political issues and has made his mark as a neoconservative journalist.

In *The Age of the Avant-Garde,* Kramer presents selected articles and reviews that he wrote during the years 1956 to 1972. The essays examine such topics as art exhibits, new books and artists, and events concerning the world of art. According to James Ackerman in the *New York Review of Books,* Kramer transcends the limitations of his genre: he "has accomplished a lot in pieces on more than 125 nineteenth-and twentieth-century artists; the articles are consistently informative, acute, and helpful to the reader." The reviewer added: "Kramer is probably the best art journalist of our time; he knows his subject in depth, understands his audience, and is scrupulously fair as well as courageous in his attacks on wrongdoing and sham." Yet Ackerman also noted that it is precisely Kramer's "scholarly openness and thoroughness" that firmly gives him the label "art historian" rather than "art critic," for rarely does the author espouse a "definable philosophical or critical position" in his writings. "Kramer faults [writer] Clement Greenberg for taking a critical stand that excludes other viewpoints and that narrows his perception of recent art and its evolution," Ackerman wrote, "but no criticism is possible without a particular point of view, and that is why Greenberg's reviews of art exhibitions are still challenging thirty years later, while the commentaries in this collection, informative as they are, have lost their primary function, have ceased to be news, and read like random passages from an encyclopedia of modern art."

Nevertheless, other critics preferred Kramer's careful, conservative assessments of artists and their creations in *The Age of the Avant-Garde.* "Art fares best without fanaticism," asserted Roger Shattuck, writing in the *New York Times Book Review.* "A critic's taste is his least important contribution," Vivien Raynor seconded this view in a *Washington Post Book World* review. She concluded: "It would be out of character for [Kramer] to subscribe to a philosophy based on technique. Seeing art as a metaphor for life, he measures it according to humanistic principles. The content of a work is, on the whole, more important to him than its surface; that is, he is willing to sacrifice some stylistic felicity if he feels the artist is struggling to illuminate some common human experience."

In *The Revenge of the Philistines: Art and Culture, 1972-1984,* Kramer argues that the great traditions in modernist art have been deliberately eroded by such movements as Camp, Pop Art, and revivals of second-rate artistic movements of the past, such as Art Deco. This collection of essays and reviews reveals Kramer's strong aversion to postmodernism and his view that the standards once held to the visual arts have been jetti-soned in favor of kitsch that will sell to uninformed but wealthy patrons. Noting that Kramer "earned a name for incorruptibility in a field much afflicted by mutual back-scratching," *New Republic* contributor Robert Hughes praised *The Revenge of the Philistines* for its "full parade of Kramer's strengths and weaknesses as a critic." Hughes quickly added: "One is glad to have them all, since quite a lot of Kramer's journalism does transcend the hurried and ephemeral nature of his medium. . . . Kramer has never been afraid of going against the grain—indeed, of hacking right into it when he needs to."

The works Kramer has written and edited since 1987 consist of collections of material previously published in the *New Criterion.* His co-editor, Roger Kimball, is another noted editor/contributor at the magazine, and the collections they have produced together concern themselves with assaults on liberalism and the challenges presented to high culture by an age of materialistic ennui. In a *New York Times Book Review* of *The New Criterion Reader: The First Five Years,* David M. Oshinsky noted that the magazine "offered itself as an alternative to [a] 'leftward drift' in our cultural life." Oshinsky went on to observe that of the essays in the book, "the clear majority of them are lively, learned and original." *National Review* correspondent David Lipsky found the essays in *The New Criterion Reader* to be, "in the present climate essentially indispensable."

Kramer's own more recent views are collected in *The Twilight of the Intellectuals: Culture and Politics in the Era of the Cold War.* The essays in this work, among other themes, seek to redress certain distortions of viewpoint on Cold War-era intellectuals and on the distinct threat posed by Soviet Communism, especially in the Stalin era. *Commentary* contributor Michael J. Lewis commended the book for its "trenchant and powerfully argued essays," observing of Kramer: "At bottom, what engages him chiefly is not his subjects' positions on this or that issue but their personal response to the great challenges of their age. Another way of putting this is to say that he is interested mostly in how we as individuals exercise moral choice."

BIOGRAPHICAL/CRITICAL SOURCES:

PERIODICALS

Commentary, June, 1999, Michael J. Lewis, review of *The Twilight of the Intellectuals: Culture and Politics in the Era of the Cold War,* p. 65.
Nation, November 30, 1985, J. Hoberman, review of *The Revenge of the Philistines: Art and Culture, 1972-1984,* p. 590.

National Review, March 28, 1986, Terry Teachout, review of *The Revenge of the Philistines: Art and Culture, 1972-1984,* p. 58; February 5, 1988, David Lipsky, review of *The New Criterion Reader: The First Five Years,* p. 54.

New Republic, April 14, 1986, Robert Hughes, review of *The Revenge of the Philistines: Art and Culture, 1972-1984,* p. 28.

Newsweek, June 17, 1974; February 13, 1995, Peter Plagens, "Kramer versus Everybody," p. 80.

New York, February 13, 1995, Charles Kaiser, "He Bites," p. 72.

New York Review of Books, February 7, 1974.

New York Times, January 12, 1974.

New York Times Book Review, January 6, 1974; November 17, 1985, Richard Wollheim, "Modernism: Smothered by Its Friends," p. 11; April 10, 1988, David M. Oshinsky, "No to 'Leftward Drift,' " p. 35; April 4, 1999, Allen D. Boyer, review of *The Twilight of the Intellectuals: Culture and Politics in the Era of the Cold War.*

Reason, March, 2001, Loren Lomasky, review of *The Betrayal of Liberalism: How the Disciples of Freedom and Equality Helped Foster the Illiberal Politics of Coercion and Control,* p. 61.

Washington Post Book World, January 6, 1974.*

L

LADURIE, Emmanuel Le Roy
See LE ROY LADURIE, Emmanuel (Bernard)

* * *

LANCASTER, Jane F(airchild) 1940-

PERSONAL: Born November 7, 1940, in Hamilton, MS; daughter of John Grover Fairchild (a cotton and peach grower) and Cleo Irvin Crosby (a homemaker); married Hollie Harwell Lancaster, Jr. (in agribusiness), April 2, 1960; children: Phillip Anthony, Fonda Kay. *Education:* Mississippi State University, B.S., 1966; Mississippi University for Women, M.A., 1969; Mississippi State University, Ph.D., 1986. *Politics:* Independent. *Religion:* Baptist. *Avocational interests:* Piano, organ, collecting Native American pottery.

ADDRESSES: Home and Office—40191 Highway 373, Hamilton, MS 39746.

CAREER: Amory High School, Amory, MS, teacher of social studies and department head, 1969-73; homemaker and civic volunteer, Hamilton, MS, 1973-81; Mississippi State University, teaching fellow, 1981-86; self-employed historian and author, 1986—. Served for 25 years as church organist and pianist; former Sunday School and Bible School teacher; historian for Agri-Belles; chair of Hamilton Bicentennial Wagon Train.

MEMBER: Southern Historical Association, Monroe County Historical Society (past director), Southern Association of Women Historians.

AWARDS, HONORS: Graduate fellowship from Mississippi University for Women, 1968-69; Garner fellowship, 1981-84; graduate fellowship from Mississippi State University, 1985-86; *Removal Aftershock: The Seminoles' Struggles to Survive in the West, 1836-1866* was nominated for eleven national and regional awards.

WRITINGS:

Removal Aftershock: The Seminoles' Struggles to Survive in the West, 1836-1866, University of Tennessee Press (Knoxville, TN), 1994.

Author of a booklet, "Hamilton Take Your Place in History as the First County Seat of Monroe," 1975; contributor to books and encyclopedias, including *Encyclopedia of African-American Civil Rights,* Greenwood Press (Westport, CT), 1991; contributor of articles and reviews to periodicals, including *Ostomy Quarterly, Florida Historical Quarterly, Journal of Mississippi History, Mississippi Quarterly, Journal of Southern History, Historical Dictionary of the Gilded Age,* and *Journal of American History.*

WORK IN PROGRESS: Two articles, "The Legacy of Alexander Stephens," and "The Cherokees in North Carolina, 1775-1835"; a novel, titled *The Adventures of Orchid Rose: Elementary School Years in Tombighee, Mississippi, 1940s;* a translation of *Le Grande Nation,* by Jacques Godechot; research on nineteenth- and twentieth-century U.S. and Native American relations.

SIDELIGHTS: Jane F. Lancaster's 1994 volume *Removal Aftershock: The Seminoles' Struggles to Survive in the West, 1836-1866* chronicles the staunch determination of the Seminole Indians to survive after they were driven from their homeland in Florida during the years between 1834 and 1859 and forced to reestablish themselves in the western territory. Upon their arrival in the West, the Seminoles were immediately faced with great opposition; they were federally ordered to merge with their long-time foes, the Creek Indians, thus losing their unique identity. Also, the land to which they were sent was unsuitable for habitation, with improper housing and shelter from the cold, plus a shortage of food and other necessary supplies. These offenses violated many of the promises made to the Seminoles by the United States government, which engineered the move west.

The lack of provisions, harsh weather, and tribal enemies were not the only problems facing the Seminoles, however. Another matter of concern Lancaster describes is the integration into their culture of "Seminole blacks," the result of the mixing of peoples of Seminole and African ancestry. These people were pursued by both white settlers and the Creeks, who claimed them as runaway slaves and sought their return. To avoid enslavement, some Seminole blacks migrated to Mexico, establishing a maroon colony, as had been done by runaway slaves during the seventeenth and early eighteenth centuries. Their legacy is recreated by Lancaster in *Removal Aftershock.*

Lancaster also explains in depth the devastating and divisive effect of the U.S. Civil War on the Seminoles; some aligned with the Confederates, others with the Union. Many Seminoles lost their lives fighting in the war, and the tribe as a whole lost control of some two million acres of land, leaving them with possession of only 200,000 acres. Nevertheless, Lancaster explains, the strong will and determination of the Seminoles caused them to overcome their adversity.

Removal Aftershock has been deemed a valuable addition to literature on Native Americans. James Covington, reviewing the volume in *Florida Historical Quarterly,* declared: "Dr. Lancaster has written a useful and important book with flowing, well-directed narration, excellent maps, and adequate illustrations." *Georgia Historical Quarterly* reviewer James M. Denham concurred, asserting: "With excellent maps, illustrations of prominent Seminoles, informative tables, a good bibliography—and best of all—a smooth, crisp writing style that will attract both general readers and scholars alike, this handsome volume is a brief but excellent addition to the growing literature on the Seminoles."

Lancaster told *CA:* "Most of my writing as a historian has been nonfiction. After doing research, which is checked infinite times for accuracy, I lean toward organizing in narrative form. Using the computer, each line is usually rewritten several times. I strive for truth and accuracy that will hopefully educate.

"The history of relations between the United States and Native Americans has been my primary interest. Due to its complexities, the public has been somewhat uninformed in this area. My writing will hopefully help fill some of the 'potholes' in this bibliographic record. When the topic is a fascinating one, such as the Seminole Indians, the writing will automatically be easier.

"Writing is an outlet that allows the writer to leave his or her own monument that signifies that he or she was on the planet and that also educates or entertains."

BIOGRAPHICAL/CRITICAL SOURCES:

PERIODICALS

Florida Historical Quarterly, April, 1995.
Georgia Historical Quarterly, summer, 1995.

*   *   *

LANDIS, Geoffrey A(lan)   1955-

PERSONAL: Born May 28, 1955, in Detroit, MI; son of John Lloyd and Patricia S. Landis. *Education:* Massachusetts Institute of Technology, B.S., B.E.E., 1980; Brown University, M.S., M.E.E., Ph.D., 1988.

ADDRESSES: Office—NASA Glenn Research Center 302-1, 21000 Brookpark Rd., Cleveland, OH, 44135.

CAREER: Physicist and writer. Spire Corporation, Bedford, MA, staff scientist, 1977-82; Solar Energy Research Institute, Golden, CO, research associate, 1986-87; National Aeronautics and Space Administration (NASA) Lewis Research Center, Cleveland, OH, research associate, 1988-90; Ohio Aerospace Institute, Brook Park, OH, adjunct professor, 1990-92, senior research associate, 1995-2000, senior scientist, 2000—; Sverdup Technology, Brook Park, OH, physicist, 1994-95; NYMA, Inc., Brook Park, senior engineer, 1994-95. National Association of Rocketry, PA, trustee, 1978-81; Spacemodeling World Championships, Jambol, Bulgaria, member of U.S. team, 1978; Vision-21 Conference, Cleveland, technology chair, 1990, 1993.

MEMBER: American Physical Society, American Institute of Aeronautics and Astronautics, Science Fiction Writers of America, Artemis Society, Mars Society.

AWARDS, HONORS: Nebula Award, Science Fiction Writers of America, 1990; Hugo award for best science fiction short story, 1992; Locus award for best first novel, 2001.

WRITINGS:

Myths, Legends, and True History (short stories), Pulphouse Publishing (Eugene, OR), 1991.
(Editor) *Vision-21, Space Travel for the Next Millennium,* NASA, Scientific and Technical Information Division (Washington, DC), 1991.
(Editor) *Vision-21, Interdisciplinary Science and Engineering,* NASA, Scientific and Technical Information Division (Washington, DC), 1993.
Mars Crossing (novel), Tor Books (New York, NY), 2000.
Impact Parameter: And Other Quantum Realities (short stories), Golden Gryphon Books (Urbana, IL), 2001.

Contributor to the anthology *Future Boston: The History of a City 1990-2100.* Author of over sixty published science-fiction short stories; contributor of over two hundred articles to professional journals.

SIDELIGHTS: Geoffrey A. Landis is a scientist who has worked on the Mars Pathfinder project which sent a roving vehicle to Mars that sent back photographs and analyses of the planet, as well as numerous other projects for NASA. This work has informed his science fiction writing, particularly in the subgenre of "hard" science fiction, which emphasizes technology. "There's certainly a lot of crossover in my life between science and science fiction," he told a *Locus* magazine interviewer. "Some very hard-SF stories revolve around a scientific plot." These, he said, include "A Walk in the Sun," dealing with the challenges of using solar power to run a lunar base, and "Ripples in the Dirac Sea," which involves quantum mechanics and teleportation. "Somebody had to invent teleportation, and why couldn't it be me?" he told *Locus.*

Mars Crossing, Landis's first novel, is also an example of hard science fiction. The book's astronauts are on Earth's third mission to Mars; the first two have been failures. This mission appears doomed as well; an accident kills one of the crew and disables the spacecraft, leaving the five survivors in search of a way home. They begin a journey across the planet, bound for an abandoned craft that they hope to use to get back to Earth. This craft, however, does not have the capacity to carry all of them, and it appears one crew member is willing to kill to assure his (or her) place on the vehi-

cle. "Unlike many hard-SF writers, Landis hasn't forgotten the human element," remarked a *Publishers Weekly* reviewer, pointing out that the "techno-lingo" is mixed with a "mystery structure and liberal dollops of suspense" that should appeal to a broad spectrum of readers. A *Kirkus Reviews* contributor, though, found the novel's scientific elements more praiseworthy than the mystery: "When focused on the planet, the engineering, and the epic trek, Landis writes evocatively and with authority; the melodramatic baggage—dark pasts, evil deeds, sinister plots—just drags along behind, raising the dust." *Science Fiction Chronicle* writer Don D'Ammassa, on the other hand, thought *Mars Crossing* "hard SF at its best," with "all the realism and accuracy you'd expect from the author." D'Ammassa also praised Landis's "glorious descriptions of the surface of Mars" and his narration of "the growing tensions among the characters." And *Analog*'s Tom Easton called the book "an excellent job in a classic vein" and "a ripping good yarn."

BIOGRAPHICAL/CRITICAL SOURCES:

PERIODICALS

Analog, January, 2001, Tom Easton, review of *Mars Crossing.*
Kirkus Reviews, November 1, 2000, review of *Mars Crossing,* p. 1523.
Locus, January, 2000, "Geoffrey A. Landis: Hands-on Science."
Publishers Weekly, November 27, 2000, review of *Mars Crossing,* p. 59.
Science Fiction Chronicle, February, 2001, Don D'Ammassa, review of *Mars Crossing.*

OTHER

Geoffrey Landis Web site, http://www.sff.net/people/ (October 4, 2001).

*   *   *

LARGE, David C(lay) 1945-

PERSONAL: Born August 13, 1945, in Scottfield, IL; son of Henry Ranney (a physician) and Lois (Altman) Large; married Jacque Lysons, October 10, 1966 (divorced, 1977); married Margaret Wheeler (a teacher), May 24, 1980; children: Joshua. *Education:* University of Washington, Seattle, B.A., 1967; University of California, Berkeley, M.A., 1969, Ph.D., 1974. *Avocational interests:* Long distance running, racquetball, backpacking, skiing, fly fishing, wine tasting and collecting, reading contemporary fiction.

ADDRESSES: Home—721 West Koch, Bozeman, MT 59715. *Office*—Department of History and Philosophy, 2-155 Wilson Hall, PO Box 172320, Montana State University, Bozeman, MT 59717-2320. *E-mail*—uhild@montana.edu.

CAREER: Smith College, Northhampton, MA, assistant professor of history, 1973-78; Yale University, New Haven, CT, assistant professor of history, 1978-83; Montana State University, Bozeman, MT, assistant professor of history, 1983-88, professor of history, 1988—; writer.

MEMBER: American History Association, Conference Group of Central European Historians, Phi Beta Kappa.

AWARDS, HONORS: Woodrow Wilson fellowship, 1967; Ford Foundation fellowship, 1968-71; Fulbright fellowship, 1972; Morse fellowship from Yale University, 1982; National Endowment for the Humanities fellowship, 1986; German Marshall Fund fellowship, 1990.

WRITINGS:

(With Felix Gilbert) *The End of the European Era: 1890 to the Present,* W. W. Norton (New York, NY), 1970, fifth edition, revised and updated, 2002.

The Politics of Law and Order: A History of the Bavarian Einwohnerwehr, American Philosophical Society, 1980.

(As David C. Large; editor, with William Weber) *Wagnerism in European Culture and Politics,* Cornell University Press, 1984.

Between Two Fires: Europe's Path in the 1930s, W. W. Norton (New York, NY), 1990.

(Editor) *Contending with Hitler: Varieties of German Resistance in the Third Reich,* Cambridge University Press (New York, NY), 1992.

Germans to the Front: West German Rearmament in the Adenauer Era, University of North Carolina Press (Chapel Hill, NC), 1996.

Where Ghosts Walked: Munich's Road to the Third Reich, W. W. Norton (New York, NY), 1997.

Berlin, Basic Books (New York, NY), 2000.

Contributor to periodicals, including *Journal of the History of Ideas.* Also contributor with Felix Gilbert to the "History of Modern Europe" series, Volume 6: *The End of the European Era, 1890 to the Present,* 1991.

WORK IN PROGRESS: What Do We Do Now?, one family's struggle to escape the Holocaust, for Basic Books, 2003.

SIDELIGHTS: Historian David C. Large, a specialist in late nineteenth- and twentieth-century Germany, has written extensively about the politics and culture of the period. Among the works for which he achieved renown is *Wagnerism in European Culture and Politics,* a collection of essays he edited with William Weber, which examines the significance of opera composer Richard Wagner's music and thought in the development of modern Europe. D. J. R. Bruckner, writing in the *New York Times,* stated that "this exploratory examination of the extraordinary wave of Wagnerism that washed over Europe for generations is a salutary undertaking," and he added that the volume "is rich in suggestions and insights and, while the essays are a bit uneven, most are very good reading." James Joll, a contributor in *New York Review of Books,* said that *Wagnerism in European Culture and Politics* "provides a valuable introduction to an important . . . aspect of European cultural history during the last quarter of the nineteenth century." *Times Literary Supplement* reviewer Peter Heyworth noted that the collection compiled by Large and Weber "contains much fascinating information not readily available elsewhere."

The End of the European Era, 1890 to the Present, a study that Large co-wrote with Felix Gilbert, has gone into four revisions since its first publication in 1970. Among Large's other works is *Between Two Fires: Europe's Path in the 1930s,* an analysis of lesser-known events which exerted substantial influence on European culture and politics. In this book, Large examines such subjects as the Stavisky scandal, in which the French government was implicated in the deeds of a swindler; the Austrian civil war of 1934, in which right- and left-wing extremists clashed; and a protest march conducted by unemployed shipyard workers in England in 1936. "To the amateur historian," observed Frank J. Prial in the *New York Times Book Review,* "much of the value of Mr. Large's book is his recounting of events that everyone has heard of but knows little about." Prial, in acknowledging Large's "sense of drama," concluded that the historian "knows how to write: he recognizes a good quotation or anecdote."

Large's works relating to Hitler have also earned critical respect. *Contending with Hitler: Varieties of German Resistance in the Third Reich,* a collection of conference papers he edited and for which he wrote a discussion of resistance in post-war Germany, was hailed by *History Today* reviewer Ian Kershaw as a work that would "prove a valuable basis for discussions of the key issues." In *Where Ghosts Walked: Munich's Road to the Third Reich,* Large traces the city's history from 1880 through the birth and growth of Nazism to the fall of the Third Reich. Deeming Large a "fine historian and gifted writer," *Booklist* reviewer Jay Freeman called the book "a valuable if not definitive analysis of the origins of the Nazi movement."

Berlin, a history of the metropolis that Large considers the "signature city" of the twentieth century, covers the period from 1871 to 1990. As Large points out, Berlin during this era was the emblem of modernism as well as the symbol, as the Nazi capital, of some of the worst human injustices in history. In 1961, the city was divided by the Berlin Wall and became a literal symbol of the Iron Curtain. "Since the fall of the wall and the end of the Great Divide," Large writes, "Berlin has come to represent humanity's aspirations for a new beginning, tempered by caution deriving from the traumas of the recent past."

Berlin was praised as an informative, insightful, and readable work. A *Publishers Weekly* contributor commended it as a "lively, rich and engaging work full of [Large's] passion for his subject." Freeman, in another *Booklist* review, hailed *Berlin* as an "outstanding saga of a metropolis and of its role in history." In the *New York Times Book Review,* Christopher Lehmann-Haupt admired Large's insights into the complexity of his subject—especially regarding Berlin's unique cultural milieu—and considered the book a "witty," "occasionally caustic," and absorbing work.

BIOGRAPHICAL/CRITICAL SOURCES:

PERIODICALS

Booklist, October 15, 1997, Jay Freeman, review of *Where Ghosts Walked: Munich's Road to the Third Reich,* p. 383; October 15, 2000, Jay Freeman, review of *Berlin,* p. 415.
History Today, November, 1993, Ian Kershaw, review of *Contending with Hitler: Varieties of German Resistance in the Third Reich,* p. 55; September 1994, Geoffrey Swain, review of *The End of the European Era, 1890 to the Present,* p. 58.
Kirkus Reviews, October 15, 2000, review of *Berlin,* p. 1466.
New York Review of Books, January 31, 1985, pp. 9-10.
New York Times, January 5, 1985.

New York Times Book Review, February 25, 1990, p. 30; December 26, 2000, Christopher Lehmann-Haupt, review of *Berlin.*
Publishers Weekly, November 6, 2000, review of *Berlin,* p. 84.
Times Literary Supplement, May 17, 1985, p. 538; October 12, 1990, p. 1095.
Washington Post Book World, April 8, 1990, p. 10.

*   *   *

LEE, Tanith 1947-

PERSONAL: Born September 19, 1947, in London, England; daughter of Bernard and Hylda (Moore) Lee. *Education:* Attended secondary school in London, England; studied at an art college. *Avocational interests:* Past civilizations (Egyptian, Roman, Incan), psychic powers (their development, use, and misuse), music.

ADDRESSES: Office—c/o Macmillan London Ltd., 4 Little Essex St., London WC2R 3LF, England.

CAREER: Writer. Has also worked as a librarian.

AWARDS, HONORS: August Derleth Award, 1980; World Fantasy Convention Award, 1983.

WRITINGS:

NOVELS

Volkhavaar, DAW (New York, NY), 1977.
Electric Forest, Doubleday (Garden City, NY), 1979.
Kill the Dead, DAW (New York, NY), 1980.
Sabella; or, The Blood Stone, DAW (New York, NY), 1980.
Day by Night, DAW (New York, NY), 1980.
Lycanthia; or, The Children of Wolves, DAW (New York, NY), 1981, Legend (London), 1990.
Sometimes, after Sunset (includes *Sabella* and *Kill the Dead*), Doubleday (New York, NY), 1981.
The Silver Metal Lover, DAW (New York, NY), 1982.
Sung in Shadow, DAW (New York, NY), 1983.
Days of Grass, DAW (New York, NY), 1985.
Dark Castle, White Horse, DAW (New York, NY), 1986.
A Heroine of the World, DAW (New York, NY), 1989.
The Blood of Roses, Century, 1990.
Heart-Beast, Headline (London, England), 1992, Dell (New York, NY), 1993.
Elephantasm, Headline (London, England), 1993.
Eva Fairdeath, Headline (London, England), 1994.

Reigning Cats and Dogs, Headline (London, England), 1995.

The Gods Are Thirsty, Overlook (Woodstock, NY), 1996.

Islands in the Sky, Random House, (New York, NY), 1999.

White as Snow, introduction by Terri Windling, Tor (New York, NY), 2000.

Vivia, Trafalgar Square, 2000.

"BIRTHGRAVE" SERIES

The Birthgrave, DAW (New York, NY), 1975.

Vazkor, Son of Vaskor, DAW (New York, NY), 1978, published as *Shadowfire,* Futura (London, England), 1979.

Quest for the White Witch, DAW (New York, NY), 1978.

"BLOOD OPERA" SERIES

Dark Dance, Dell (New York, NY), 1992.

Personal Darkness, Little, Brown (London, England), 1993, Dell (New York, NY), 1994.

Darkness, I, Little, Brown (Boston, MA), 1994.

"CLAIDI JOURNALS" SERIES; JUVENILE NOVELS

Wolf Tower, Dutton Children's Books, 2000.

Wolf Star, Dutton Children's Books, 2000.

"DARK CASTLE" SERIES; JUVENILE NOVELS

The Castle of Dark, Macmillan (London, England), 1978.

Prince on a White Horse, Macmillan (London, England), 1982.

"DON'T BITE THE SUN" SERIES

Don't Bite the Sun, DAW (New York, NY), 1976, reprinted, Starmont House (Mercer Island, WA), 1987.

Drinking Sapphire Wine, DAW (New York, NY), 1977, published with *Don't Bite the Sun,* Hamlyn (London, England), 1979.

"DRAGONFLIGHT" SERIES; JUVENILE NOVELS

Black Unicorn, illustrated by Heather Cooper, Atheneum (New York, NY), 1991.

Gold Unicorn, Atheneum (New York, NY), 1994.

Red Unicorn, Tor (New York, NY), 1997.

"SECRET BOOKS OF PARADYS" SERIES

The Book of the Damned (short stories), Unwin (London, England), 1988, Overlook Press (Woodstock, NY), 1990.

The Book of the Beast, Unwin (London, England), 1988, Overlook Press (Woodstock, NY), 1991.

The Book of the Dead (short stories), Overlook Press (Woodstock, NY), 1991.

The Book of the Mad, Overlook Press (Woodstock, NY), 1993.

"SECRET BOOKS OF VENUS" SERIES

Faces Under Water, Overlook Press (Woodstock, NY), 1998.

Saint Fire, Overlook Press (Woodstock, NY), 2000.

"TALES FROM THE FLAT EARTH" SERIES

Night's Master, DAW (New York, NY), 1978.

Death's Master, DAW (New York, NY), 1979.

Delusion's Master, DAW (New York, NY), 1981.

Delirium's Mistress, DAW (New York, NY), 1986.

Night's Sorceries (short stories), DAW (New York, NY), 1987.

Tales from the Flat Earth: Night's Daughter (short stories), Doubleday (New York, NY), 1987.

"WARS OF VIS" SERIES

The Storm Lord, DAW (New York, NY), 1976.

Anackire, DAW (New York, NY), 1983.

The Wars of Vis (contains *The Storm Lord* and *Anackire*), Doubleday (New York, NY), 1984.

The White Serpent, DAW (New York, NY), 1988.

JUVENILE NOVELS

The Dragon Hoard, Farrar, Straus (New York, NY), 1971.

Animal Castle, Farrar, Straus (New York, NY), 1972.

Companions on the Road, Macmillan (London, England), 1975.

The Winter Players, Macmillan (London, England), 1976.

East of Midnight, Macmillan (London, England), 1977, St. Martin's (New York, NY), 1978.

Shon the Taken, Macmillan (London, England), 1979.

Madame Two Swords, illustrated by Thomas Canty, Donald M. Grant (West Kingston, RI), 1988.

SHORT STORY COLLECTIONS

The Betrothed, Slughorn Press (Sidcup, Kent, England), 1968.

Princess Hynchatti and Some Other Surprises (juvenile), Macmillan (London, England), 1972, Farrar, Straus (New York, NY), 1973.

Unsilent Night, NESFA Press (Cambridge, MA), 1981.

Cyrion, DAW (New York, NY), 1982.

Red as Blood; or, Tales from the Sisters Grimmer, DAW (New York, NY), 1983.

The Beautiful Biting Machine, Cheap Street (New Castle, VA), 1984.

Tamastara; or, The Indian Nights, DAW (New York, NY), 1984.

The Gorgon and Other Beastly Tales, DAW (New York, NY), 1985.

Dreams of Dark and Light: The Great Short Fiction of Tanith Lee, Arkham House (Sauk City, WI), 1986.

Forests of the Night, Unwin, 1989.

Nightshades: Thirteen Journeys into Shadow, Headline (London, England), 1993.

NONFICTION

Women as Demons: The Male Perception of Women through Space and Time, Women's Press (London, England), 1989.

PLAYS

Bitter Gate (radio play), BBC Radio, 1977.

Red Wine (radio play), BBC Radio, 1977.

Death Is King (radio play), 1979.

The Silver Sky (radio play), 1980.

Sarcophagus (television play), "Blake's Seven" series, 1980.

Sand (television play), "Blake's Seven" series, 1981.

SIDELIGHTS: Tanith Lee's many works of fiction reveal a dark and erotic imagination at work in the fields of horror, science fiction, and fantasy. Through novels, short story collections, and series such as "The Secret Books of Paradys" and "Tales from the Flat Earth," Lee grapples with such perplexing questions as the fate of the universe, the individual's ability to control events, and the nature of morality. Her work has been cited by critics for its vivid imagery and unique cast of larger-than-life characters. *Voice Literary Supplement* reviewer Peter Stampfel called Lee the "Princess Royal of Heroic Fantasy and Goddess-Empress of the Hot Read," and states that her writing "dazzles and intoxicates."

Lee was born, raised, and educated in London. She began her writing career with books for children, such as *The Dragon Hoard* and *Animal Castle.* Her first novel for adults, *The Birthgrave,* appeared in 1975. Since then she has published at least one novel or story collection a year, and many years she produces multiple works. "I intend my books for anyone who will enjoy them," Lee commented. "Frankly, I write for me, I can't help it. My books are expressions of my private inner world. I love the idea that other people may read and perhaps relish them, but that, if it happens, is a delightful by-product."

Lee has never shied away from depictions of the bizarre. Whether human or god, her heroes and heroines struggle against the madness and morbidity of their worlds. Their travails allow the author to expose human society and its failures as well as the ambiguities in the relationship between behavior and morality. Some of her novels and stories, such as the well-known *Red as Blood; or, Tales from the Sisters Grimmer,* turn popular fairy tales upside down to reveal darker and more diabolic suggestions. Myths and legends also form the basis of the "Tales from the Flat Earth" series, which includes *Night's Master, Death's Master,* and *Delirium's Mistress.* In the *Washington Post Book World,* Michael Swanwick described such works as "darkly, lushly romantic stuff, with silvery veins of eroticism and sinister beauty. . . . Her prose practically shimmers on the page."

Another well-known Lee series is "The Secret Books of Paradys," a selection of linked works that include stories, novellas, and novels. These books reveal the depraved lives of characters in a fictitious French town, variously named Paradys, Paradis, and Paradise. The parallel cities and their various malignant characters allow the author to ruminate on the frailties of modern society, especially in relationship to its younger members and its artists. Reviewing Tanith's 1993 "Paradys" series release, *The Book of the Mad,* in *Los Angeles Times Book Review,* Sue Martin noted: "This is Gothic writing at the extreme end of weirdness." The critic maintains that the writing succeeds because "its dream-drenched, spaced-out characters are compelling as they flit ghost-like on their errands." A *Washington Post Book World* reviewer found in *The Book of the Mad* that Lee "has given us a map to the outer limits of imagination, and then dares us to find our way home." *Locus* contributor Faren Miller argued that the "Secret Books of Paradys" series reveals a writer at the height of her powers. Miller observed: "[Lee] began as a good writer, developed into an elegant, ironic stylist, and has now matured still further to become one of our very best authors of short fiction."

In 1998 Lee launched a new series, "The Secret Books of Venus," with *Faces Under Water.* Set in an alternate fifteenth-century Venice, the novel tells the tale of a young patrician, Furian, who has turned his back on his family's wealth to perform various odd jobs around the city. He finds a mask floating in the canal that had belonged to a drowned magician. Shortly thereafter the gondolier who accompanied Furian is murdered, and Furian finds himself pursued by ruffians. Meanwhile he has fallen in love with Eurydiche, a woman of incomparable beauty whose face remains forever locked in a single expression. When Furian discovers that Eurydiche's father is head of the Guild of Mask Makers, the two plot lines begin to dovetail. A reviewer for *Publishers Weekly* praised Lee's "jeweled prose" and concluded: "This is a fast start to what promises to be an exciting, innovative fantasy series." The second volume, *Saint Fire,* is set in an alternate medieval Italy a few hundred years before *Faces Under Water.* It concerns a young slave girl, Volpa, who possesses the ability to spontaneously generate fire from her red hair. Volpa incinerates a man who tries to rape her. When word of her talent spreads, Volpa is soon adopted by Fra Danielus, a priest who grooms her for war against the invading infidels. Salle Estes of *Booklist* commented: "Lee's sensual and evocative storytelling imparts a dreamlike quality to this tale of transcendent faith and human passion." A *Publishers Weekly* critic praised *Saint Fire* for its "evocative imagery and memorable characters." As the first two novels in this projected four-book series turned on themes of water and fire, the forthcoming volumes will involve earth and air, to complete the four basic alchemical elements.

Another aspect of Lee's work has involved the retelling of classic myths and fairy tales, often providing surprising twists on the original stories in terms of characterization, plot resolution, and moral content. Her "Tales from the Flat Earth" series takes place in a fantasy world rife with demons, wizards, and swordplay. Rendered in an episodic fashion reminiscent of *The Thousand and One Nights,* this series incorporates many classic myths and legends. Reviewing the second volume, *Death's Master,* in *The Scope of the Fantastic,* Michael R. Collings noted that Lee's successful use of "archaic, exotic, and elevated" language made readers feel as if they were "suddenly being immersed in an unfamiliar world." In a like vein, Michael Stamm of *Fantasy Review* credited Lee's prose as "very rich, reminiscent of Clark Ashton Smith's."

White as Snow uses the classic fairy tale of Snow White as its starting point. However, in Lee's version readers are first introduced to the original story's evil queen, Princess Arpazia, when she is a young girl. Arpazia is raped by Draco, a barbarian conqueror who also murders Arpazia's sister. Draco subsequently marries Arpazia and forces her to travel with him on his military campaigns. The child of their union is abandoned by Arpazia, both in fact and for the most part in memory. Unable to face the realities of her life, Queen Arpazia retreats into solitude and spends most of her time staring into a magic mirror admiring her own beauty. When a rival appears in the mirror's reflection Arpazia fails to recognize her own daughter, Coira, and has the young girl kidnapped. A *Publishers Weekly* reviewer concluded that "with its melancholy shading, Lee's new twist on an old tale is sure to engage fans of dark fantasy." In contrast, a writer for *Kirkus Reviews* remarked: "What with the illogical plot and largely unsympathetic characters, even Lee's stylish prose can't breathe new vitality into the familiar old tale."

Except for a six-year hiatus in the mid-1980s, Lee has continued to pen numerous books for children and young adults throughout her career, including several series. In an overview of Lee's writings for a young audience, an essayist in the *St. James Guide to Young Adult Writers* stressed the author's ability to address "themes such as the search for identity, coping with inept and uncaring authority figures, abandonment, loneliness, and many other issues that face adolescent readers." While finding that Lee's language is at times too sophisticated for younger readers, the same writer concluded: "This weakness . . . is overshadowed by the generally dynamic nature of her prose." Reviewing one of Lee's early juvenile novels, *East of Midnight,* in *Times Literary Supplement,* Peter Hammond stated: "Whereas the interchange of minds is rather circumstantial for magic, the world of women-kings who ride lions and dispose of their weak male consorts every five years flashes with ideas. It also touches deeper themes of love, sex, and honor, and reaches a moving climax." Lee's *Red Unicorn,* a 1997 entry in her juvenile "Dragonflight" series, fared less well with reviewers. Estes found this tale of a young princess's travails in parallel universes to be the weakest of the series and to contain "only flashes of the wit found in the first two books," and a reviewer in *Publishers Weekly* noted: "The whole novel seems carelessly tossed off and not what you'd expect from a World Fantasy Award winner."

In 2000 Lee began an new juvenile series, the "Claidi Journals," with *Wolf Tower.* The novel introduces Claidi, a young slave girl who runs away into a supposed wasteland with Neiman, a young man who has literally fallen from the sky in a hot air balloon. The pair experience various adventures in their travels, confront fierce beasts, and are ultimately befriended by a gypsy-like tribe of bandits. Although Claidi is drawn to Argul, the tribe's nineteen-year-old leader, she decides to accompany Neiman to his home city where the Wolf Tower of the title can be found. Yet the world to which Neiman takes Claidi turns out to be far sadder and more authoritarian than anything she expected. Kathleen Isaacs in *School Library Journal* found Lee's "fantasy world . . . clearly and humorously described; its varied cultures . . . both amusing and believable." Isaac also felt that Claidi was "a likable heroine with whom fantasy readers can easily identify."

Lee once commented in *CA:* "I began to write, and continue to write, out of the sheer compulsion to fantasize. I can claim no noble motives, no aspirations that what comes galloping from my Biro will overthrow tyranny, unite nations or cause roses to bloom in the winter snow. I just want to write, can't stop, don't want to stop, and hope I never shall.

"As a writer who has been lucky enough to make writing her profession, I am most undisciplined and erratic. One day I will commence work at four in the afternoon and persevere until four the next morning. Sometimes I start at four in the morning, and go on until physical stamina gives out. Sometimes I get stuck on some knotty problem, (how do you describe the emotions of a man who finds he is a god? What will he do now he knows? Is there any point in his doing anything? Yes. What?) and worry about said problem for days, pen poised, eyes glazed. Frequently I race through 150 pages in a month, and then stick for three months over one page. It's a wonder to me I get anything done. But I do, so presumably it's all right.

"I admire far too many writers to make a list. I'm always discovering new ones to admire. Some operate in the Fantasy/Science Fiction field; a lot don't. I think I can say that I've been influenced by everything I've read and liked. But I'm influenced by symphonies and concertos, too, by paintings and by films. And sometimes by people. A character. A sentence."

Don't Bite the Sun has been translated into Swedish. Several other books are "in the pipeline" for Italy, France, and Germany.

BIOGRAPHICAL/CRITICAL SOURCES:

BOOKS

Authors and Artists for Young Adults, Volumes 7-26, Gale (Detroit, MI), 1992-99.

St. James Guide to Young Adult Writers, 2nd edition, St. James Press (Detroit, MI), 1999.

PERIODICALS

Booklist, June 1, 1997, Sally Estes, review of *Red Unicorn,* p. 1685; April 15, 2000, Sally Estes, review of *Wolf Tower,* p. 1543.

Books and Bookmen, May, 1972.

Fantasy Macabre, Volume 4, 1983.

Fantasy Review, April, 1985, Michael E. Stamm, review of *Death's Master,* p. 25; April, 1986, p. 25.

History Today, December, 1975.

Kirkus Reviews, November 1, 2000, review of *White as Snow,* p. 1523.

Library Journal, November 15, 1999, Jackie Cassada, review of *Saint Fire,* p. 101.

Locus, January, 1989, pp. 15, 17; August, 1991, p. 15; February, 1992, p. 57; June, 1993, p. 57; November, 1993, p. 54; February, 1994, pp. 36-37; June, 1994, p. 63.

Los Angeles Times Book Review, June 6, 1993, p. 11.

Observer (London), November 26, 1972; February 15, 1976; November 28, 1976.

Publishers Weekly, July 21, 1989, p. 55; October 26, 1990, p. 58; January 1, 1992, p. 50; May 19, 1997, review of *Red Unicorn,* p. 70; June 8, 1998, review of *Faces Under Water,* p. 51; October 19, 1999, review of *Saint Fire,* p. 75; November 20, 2000, review of *White as Snow,* p. 51.

Review of Contemporary Fiction, fall, 1993, pp. 238-239.

School Library Journal, June, 2000, Kathleen Isaacs, review of *Wolf Tower,* p. 148.

Spectator, April 22, 1972; November 11, 1972.

Times Literary Supplement (London), July 14, 1972; November 3, 1972; April 2, 1976; October 1, 1976; October 21, 1977, Peter Hunt, review of *East of Midnight,* p. 1246.

Voice Literary Supplement, October, 1981, p. 6.

Voice of Youth Advocates, February, 1990, p. 372; December, 1991, p. 324.

Washington Post Book World, July 27, 1986, p. 4; May 30, 1993, p. 9.

Wilson Library Bulletin, April, 1992, pp. 96-97.*

LEONARD, Thomas M. 1937-

PERSONAL: Born November 8, 1937, in Elizabeth, NJ; son of Edward C. (in sales) and Amelia T. (a homemaker; maiden name, Chap) Leonard; married Yvonne Ann Marie Clements (self-employed), August 13, 1960; children: Thomas, Robert, Randall, Edward, David, Stacy. *Education:* Mount St. Mary's College, Emmitsburg, MD, B.S., 1959; Georgetown University, M.A., 1963; American University, Washington, DC, Ph.D., 1968. *Politics:* "No preference." *Religion:* Catholic. *Avocational interests:* Travel (Central America).

ADDRESSES: Home—1104 Pond View Court, Fruit Cove, FL 32259. *Office*—Department of History, University of North Florida, Jacksonville, FL 32224.

CAREER: Weston Instruments, Newark, NJ, sales expediter, 1959-60; Baltimore County Board of Education, Towson, MD, social studies teacher, 1960-63; St. Joseph College (closed in 1973), Emmitsburg, MD, associate professor of history, 1963-73; University of North Florida, Jacksonville, FL, professor of history, 1973—, distinguished professor, 1985—, director, international studies program, 1992—. Visiting professor in Mexico and Argentina. Consultant to Florida State Department of Education and to Jacksonville Chamber of Commerce's Caribbean Task Force. Member of Florida advisory board that links the State University System of Florida to the National University System of Costa Rica.

MEMBER: Belize Studies Association (president, 1993-95), American Historical Association, Latin American Studies Association, Association of Third World Studies (president, 1999-2000), Society for Historians of American Foreign Relations, First Coast International Affairs Forum (president, 1986-90), Southeast Council on Latin American Studies president, 1992-93), Florida College Teachers of History Association (president, 1981-82), Phi Kappa Phi, Knights of Columbus, Loyal Order of the Moose.

WRITINGS:

(Editor) *Proceedings: Communications Media and Their Responsibilities to the Public,* University of North Florida, 1977.
Day by Day: The Forties, edited by Richard Burbank and Steven L. Goulden, Facts on File (New York, NY), 1977.
United States and Central America, 1944-1949: Perceptions of Political Dynamics, University of Alabama Press (University, AL), 1984.

Central America and United States Policies, 1820s-1980s: A Guide to Issues and References, Regina Books (Claremont, CA), 1985.
(With Cynthia Crippen and Marc Aronson) *Day by Day: The Seventies,* Facts on File, 1988.
Central America and the United States: The Search for Stability, University of Georgia Press (Athens, GA), 1991.
Panama and the United States: Guide to Issues and Sources, Regina Books, 1993.
Guide to Archival Material in the United States on Central America, Greenwood Press (Westport, CT), 1994.
(Editor) *United States and Latin America, 1850-1903,* University of Alabama Press, 1999.
Castro and the Cuban Revolution, Greenwood Press, 1999.
James K. Polk: A Clear and Unquestionable Destiny, Scholarly Resources, 2000.

Contributor to books, including *Political Profiles: The Truman Years,* edited by Eleanora W. Schoenebaum, Facts on File, 1978; *Political Profiles: The Nixon Years,* edited by Schoenebaum, Facts on File, 1979; *Guide to American Foreign Relations since 1700,* edited by Richard Dean Burns, American Bibliographical Center-Clio Press (Santa Barbara, CA), 1982; *The Church and Society in Latin America,* edited by Jeffrey A. Cole and Richard Greenleaf, Tulane University Press (New Orleans, LA), 1983; *Growth and Conflict: America, 1898-1945,* edited by John M. Carroll, Kendall/Hunt (Dubuque, IA), 1986; *The Perils of Limited War: Vietnam, Central America and the Limited Arms Race,* edited by Howard Jones, University of Alabama Press, 1988; *Central America: Historical Perspectives on the Contemporary Crisis,* edited by Ralph Lee Greenwood, Jr., Greenwood Press, 1988; *Oral Tradition and Oral History in Africa and the Diaspora,* edited by E. J. Alagoa, University of Lagos, 1990; *Historia General de Guatemala,* five volumes, edited by Jorge Lujan Munoz, Fundacion Para La Cultura y El Desarrollo, 1993-95; *Hispanic Almanac,* edited by Nicolas Kanellos, Gale, 1993; *Latin America in Transition,* edited by Robert P. Watson and Donald C. Simmons, Troy State University Press (Troy, AL), 1994; *Democracy in Latin America,* edited by Phillip Kelly, Westview Press, 1999; *American National Biography,* edited by John A. Garraty, Oxford University Press, 1999; and *Beyond the Ideal: Pan-Americanism in Inter-American Relations,* edited by David Sheinin, Greenwood Press, 2000.

Contributor to *Encyclopedia of Arms Control and Disarmament,* edited by Richard Dean Burns, Scribner

(New York, NY), 1993, and *Encyclopedia of Latin America History,* edited by Barbara Tennenbaum, Scribner (New York, NY), 1996.

Contributor to periodicals, including *University Review, Americas, East European Quarterly, Interdisciplinary Essays, Hemisphere, Journal of Caribbean Studies, Journal of Third World Studies, Latin American Research Review, Mid America, SECOLAS Annals, Towson State Journal of International Affairs, Revista Interamericana* (Puerto Rico), *Revista Mexicana del Caribe* (Mexico), *Revista Relaciones Internacionales* (Costa Rica), *Southeast Latin Americanist, Tiltai* (Lithuania), *Valley Forge Journal,* and *War and Diplomacy Proceedings.*

WORK IN PROGRESS: United States and Central America During World War II.

SIDELIGHTS: Thomas M. Leonard told *CA:* "I enjoy researching to determine the attitudes and perceptions U.S. policy makers had toward Central America. Their attitudes and perceptions contributed significantly to policy decisions."

BIOGRAPHICAL/CRITICAL SOURCES:

PERIODICALS

American Historical Review, October, 1985.
Hispanic American History Review, May, 1986.
History: Review of New Books, February, 1985.
Journal of American History, June, 1985.
Times Literary Supplement, June 16, 1978.

*   *   *

LE ROY LADURIE, Emmanuel (Bernard)   1929-

PERSONAL: Born July 19, 1929, in Moutiers en Cinglais, France; son of Jacques (an agriculturalist and government minister) and Leontine (Dauger) Le Roy Ladurie; married Madeleine Pupponi (a physician), July 9, 1956; children: Francois, Anne. *Education:* École Normale Superieure, Paris, agrégé de l'université, 1953, docteur des lettres, 1956. *Politics:* "Centre-Gauche." *Religion:* Catholic.

ADDRESSES: Home—88 rue d'Alleray, 75015 Paris, France. *Office*—Collège de France, 11 place Marcelin-Berthelot, 75231 Paris Cedex 05, France; fax: 01-44-27-12-40. *E-mail*—EM.Ladurie@wanadoo.fr.

CAREER: Lycée de Montpellier, Montpellier, France, teacher, 1955-57; Centre National de la Recherche Scientifique, Paris, France, researcher, 1957-60; Faculté des Lettres de Montpellier, Montpellier, France, assistant professor, 1960-63; École Pratique des Hautes Études, Paris, France, master assistant professor, 1963-65, director of studies, 1965-69; Faculté des Lettres de Paris, lecturer, 1969; Sorbonne, Université de Paris, Paris, France, lecturer, 1970-71; Université de Paris-VII, Paris, professor of geography and social sciences, 1971-73; Collège de France, Paris, France, professor of history of modern civilization, 1973—, became honorary professor. Bibliotheque Nationale, Paris, France, general administrator, 1987-94, president of science council, 1994; commandeur of Légion d'Honneur, 1996, and l'ordre des Arts et Lettres; L'Institute (Académie des Sciences Morales et Politiques), member; affiliated with American Philosophical Society, and l'Académie Polonaise des Sciences, 2000.

AWARDS, HONORS: Named chevalier of the French Legion of Honor; silver medal, Centre National de la Recherche Scientifique, 1966; fellow, British Academy, 1984; honorary member, l'Académie des Sciences Américaines, 1984; medal of the Center for French Civilization and Culture, New York University, 1985; Prix de la Fondation "Pierre Lafue," 2000; honorary degrees from the universities of Geneva, 1978, Michigan, 1981, Leeds, 1982, East Anglia, 1985, Leicester, 1986, York, 1986, Durham, 1987, Hull, 1990, Dublin, 1992, Albany, Montréal, 1993, Haïfa, 1993, Oxford, 1993, Pennsylvania, 1995, and H.E.C. Paris, 1999, as well as Carnegie Mellon University, 1987.

WRITINGS:

NONFICTION; IN ENGLISH TRANSLATION

Les Paysans de Languedoc, Mouton, 1966, translation with introduction by John Day published as *The Peasants of Languedoc,* consulting editor, George Huppert, University of Illinois Press (Champaign, IL), 1974.
Histoire du Climat depuis l'An Mil, Flammarion (Paris, France), 1967, translation by Barbara Bray, with revisions and updated material, published as *Times of Feast, Times of Famine: A History of Climate since the Year 1000,* Doubleday (New York, NY), 1971, 2nd edition, 1983.
(With Joseph Goy) *Les Fluctuations de produits de la dime: Conjoncture decimale et dominiale de la fin du moyen age au XVIIIe siècle,* Mouton/DeGruyter (Berlin, Germany), 1972, translation by Susan

Burke published as *Tithe and Agrarian History from the Fourteenth to the Nineteenth Centuries: An Essay in Comparative History,* Cambridge University Press, 1982.

Le Territoire de l'Historien (essays), Gallimard (Paris, France), Volume I, 1973, Volume II, 1978, translation of Volume I by Ben and Sian Reynolds published as *The Territory of the Historian,* University of Chicago Press (Chicago, IL), 1979, translation of Volume II by Ben Reynolds and Sian Reynolds published as *The Mind and Method of the Historian,* University of Chicago Press (Chicago, IL), 1981.

Montaillou: Village occitan de 1294 à 1324, Gallimard (Paris, France), 1975, translation by Barbara Bray published as *Montaillou: The Promised Land of Error,* Braziller (New York, NY), 1978, published as *Mantaillou: Cathars and Catholics in a French Village, 1294-1324,* Scolar (London, England), 1978.

(With Michael Morineau) *Histoire économique et sociale de la France,* Volume I: *De 1450 à 1660,* Volume II: *Paysannerie et croissance,* Gallimard (Paris, France), 1976, translation by Alan Sheridan published as *The French Peasantry, 1450-1660,* University of California Press (Berkeley, CA), 1987.

Le Carnaval de Romans: De la Chandeleur au mercredi des Cendres, 1579-1580, Gallimard (Paris, France), 1979, translation by Mary Feeney published as *Carnival in Romans,* Braziller (New York, NY), 1979, as *Carnival: A People's Uprising at Romans, 1579-1580,* Scolar (London, England), 1980.

L'Argent, l'amour, et la mort en Pays d'Oc, Seuil (Paris, France), 1980, translation by Alan Sheridan published as *Love, Death, and Money in the Pays d'Oc,* Braziller (New York, NY), 1982.

La Sorcière de Jasmin (with a reproduction of the original 1842 bilingual edition of the "Françouneto de Jasmin"), Seuil (Paris, France), 1983, translation by Brian Pearce published as *Jasmin's Witch,* Braziller (New York, NY), 1987.

L'État royal: De Louis XI a Henri IV, 1460-1610, Hachette (Paris, France), 1987, translation by Juliet Vale published as *The Royal French State: 1460-1610,* Blackwell (Oxford, England), 1994.

IN FRENCH

Histoire de Languedoc, Presses Universitaires de France (Paris, France), 1962.

Le Climat des XIe et XVIe siècles: Series comparées, Armand Colin, 1965.

Introduction cartographique à une ecologie quantitative de la France traditionnelle, XVIIe-XIXe siecles, 1966.

(With Jean Paul De Saive and J. P. Goupert) *Mèdecins, climat, et epidemies à la fin du 18e siècle,* Mouton/DeGruyter, 1972.

(With Hugues Neveux and Jean Jacquart) *L'Age classique des paysans, 1340-1789,* Seuil (Paris, France), 1975.

Aix-en-Provence, L'Arc [Versailles, France], 1976.

(With others) *Inventaire des campagnes,* 1980.

(With others) *Histoire de la France urbaine, Tome III,* 1981.

Paris-Montpellier PC-PSU, 1945-1963, Gallimard (Paris, France), 1982.

Parmi les historiens, 1983.

(With Orest Ranum) *Pierre Prion, scribe: Memoires d'un écrivain de campagne au XVIIIe siècle,* Gallimard (Paris, France), 1985.

L'Ancien Régime: De Louis XIII à Louis XV, 1610-1770, Hachette (Paris, France), 1991.

Le Siècle des Platter, (1499-1628), Le Mendicant et le professeur, 1995.

L'Historien, le chiffre et le texte, 1997.

Saint-Simon, le système de la Cour, 1997.

Le voyage de Thomas Platter, 2000.

Histoire de la France des Régions, 2001.

Also, author of *Histoire de la France rurale.*

SIDELIGHTS: One of the most celebrated historians of the Western world, Emmanuel Le Roy Ladurie is associated with the Annales school of thought. The Annales group, or Annalistes, derive their name from the journal *Annales,* which was established in 1929 by French historians who wanted to change the focus of historical analysis and to break away from the traditional view of the history of events. They felt that concentrating on major political actions and powerful people provided too little information about the way most people lived at any given time; instead, they wanted to analyze history in terms of quantitative, material data, and to focus on ordinary communities.

Le Roy Ladurie's collection of essays *Le Territoire de l'historien,* the first volume of which was originally published in 1973, reflects the Annaliste attitudes embraced by the author during the 1960s and early 1970s. As in other of his early writings, Le Roy Ladurie stresses the use of computerized information and statistical analysis of everything from weather patterns and crop production to disease and the distribution of taxes. The message of these essays is "harsh and clear," Lawrence Stone of the *New York Review of Books* explained in response to the 1979 translation of Volume I of *Le Territoire de l'historien:* "Narrative history, the history of events, political history, and biography are dead. The methodology of history must now be strictly quantitative; . . . it must concern itself with long-term shifts in the material bases of life; it must focus on the masses, not the elite. . . . It will be true 'scientific history,' based at bottom on the relationship of population to food supply."

Some of the conclusions of this approach were considered untenable by reviewers like Stone. For instance, one outcome of *Le Territoire de l'historien* is the idea of "l'histoire immobile," which holds that from 1300 until the economic upswing of the eighteenth century, European history did not change. Stone deemed this conclusion "nonsense" and "a gross oversimplification" that ignored five centuries of significant ideological, moral, and social developments. The critic also explained that *Le Territoire de l'historien,* as a collection of Le Roy Ladurie's early essays and articles, reflected an outdated Annaliste approach, and represented "neither the current central interests and methods of the new historians, nor those of the author himself." Rather, Stone remarked, Le Roy Ladurie's more recent works reflected "a wholly different intellectual universe. . . . Gone are the computers, the graphs, and the statistical tables. Gone too is the obsession with long-term structures." In his more recent works Le Roy Ladurie turned to individual communities, their attitudes, values, customs, and beliefs.

Montaillou: Village occitan de 1294 à 1324 and *Le Carnaval de Romans: De la Chandeleur au mercredi des Cendres, 1579-1580,* Le Roy Ladurie's best-known books, are products of their author's shift in concentration. In these books Le Roy Ladurie retains his original Annaliste focus on the ordinary masses and still includes economic information in his analyses, yet he balances quantitative measures with sociological ones. These two works, according to a *New Republic* article by Eugen Weber, represent Le Roy Ladurie "at his storytelling best, squeezing life and local color out of dusty documents." In *Montaillou,* for instance, the author reconstructs the fourteenth-century lives of the villagers of Montaillou, a small town in southern France. The analysis consists of two parts: the first the author calls "the ecology of Montaillou" and in it he deals with the material aspects of the village and its inhabitants; in the second part, "an archaeology of Montaillou," Le Roy Ladurie writes about the attitudes, practices, mores, and perceptions of the villagers. The result is, according to *New York Review of Books* critic Keith Thomas, "a wholly successful demonstration of the his-

torian's capacity to bring together almost every dimension of human experience into a single satisfying whole."

A bestseller in France, *Montaillou* appealed to both scholars and the general public. Critics cited the licentious character of the village as a major reason for the book's popularity. They noted that the villagers, most of them followers of the Cathar or Albigensian heresy, lived by the motto "since everything is forbidden, everything is allowed." Unaffected by religious qualms, the villagers led promiscuous lives. The network of Church spies and closet heretics, who manipulated people with threats of exposure to the Inquisition, only encouraged the exchange of sexual favors.

Prurient appeal aside, *Montaillou*'s critical and public acclaim was largely due to the author's methodology and style. Thomas hailed Le Roy Ladurie's work as "witty and sophisticated, fertile and inventive, [bubbling] over with ideas and comparisons, though sometimes with a faint touch of slickness." Stone noted Le Roy Ladurie's "sheer brilliance in the use of a unique document to reconstruct in fascinating detail a previously totally unknown world." The document Stone cited is a verbatim account of interrogations conducted by inquisitor Jacques Fournier, then bishop of Pamiers, later Pope Benedict XII. In Fournier's attempt to eradicate heresy, he questioned twenty-five Montaillou villagers and recorded their comments in their own words. The result is an extensive account of the villagers' values, lifestyles, and conceptions of the world. Fournier's ledgers are so thorough and detailed, noted Stone, that they "enabled Le Roy Ladurie to bring the Middle Ages to life in a way that has probably never been achieved before by any historian."

In *Carnaval de Romans* Le Roy Ladurie again approaches his historical subject, this time a small southeastern French town in the sixteenth century, with a view to both the socio-economic situations and the mental attitudes of its inhabitants. In addition, the author takes advantage of semiotics, or the interpretation of symbols, in order to read festival rituals in terms of the political, economic, and social preoccupations of the town of Romans. Moreover, as William H. McNeill noted in the *Chicago Tribune Book World,* "by focusing on the microcosm of a small town, [Le Roy] Ladurie illuminates the complex conflicts of the age: noble vs. commoner . . . rich vs. poor within the town itself, and most massive of all, peasant vs. everyone else in society."

These conflicts, as *Le Carnaval de Romans* reveals, came to a head in 1580 during the Mardi Gras (Shrove Tuesday) festivities in Romans. Every year the town divided itself into "kingdoms" of common folk and elites for the pre-Lenten Carnival rituals. In the Romans Carnival of 1580 the artisans' "kingdom" chose the master draper, Paumier, as its festival king. Paumier also happened to be the leader of a coalition of craftsmen and peasants who objected to what they considered an unjust tax burden. According to Le Roy Ladurie, the coincidence of Paumier's political and festival leaderships drew attention to the disputes between Paumier's supporters and the tax-exempt nobles of Romans. As a result, Paumier's followers' actions during Carnival took on more than ritual significance. Indeed, the nobles became convinced that a violent revolt was imminent. To prevent an attack, Judge Guerin, the legal and festival leader of the nobles, seized the city gates and had Paumier shot. The judge then tried and executed more than a thousand villagers.

According to Stone, the main interest of *Le Carnaval de Romans*'s story "lies in the interplay of real social conflicts, described with acuity and learning at the beginning and end of the book, and the symbolism of the carnival parades, feasts, and masquerades, which forms the core." But the symbolism, and Le Roy Ladurie's interpretations of its meaning, drew a mixed reaction from reviewers, including Stone. Critics observed that the author seemed biased in his portrayal of Judge Guerin as an evil villain in the midst of a clear-cut class war. Stone, for instance, found the Guerin described by Le Roy Ladurie "too evil to be convincing," especially in light of "evidence that there was a real threat of radical violence from Paumier and his friends [and] the even greater threat that they might open the city gates to their peasant allies prowling outside." Stone also remarked: "Once overenthusiastic in his acceptance of computerized 'scientific' history, Le Roy Ladurie is now overenthusiastic in his acceptance of folklore and semiotics. As a result, some of his ingenious interpretations of the symbolic meaning of the events of the carnival seem a little far-fetched."

Even so, Stone deemed *Le Carnaval de Romans* "a dazzling psychodrama," asserting: "Whether the data has been correctly interpreted is another matter, but maybe one that, in the last resort, does not matter too much." What does matter, Stone contended, is "the fascination of the story and the author's dexterous interweaving of a brilliant analysis of social conflicts on the one hand with a more dubious but intriguing interpretation of the parades, masquerades, and feasts of carnival time on the other."

Like *Montaillou* and *Le Carnaval de Romans, La Sorcière de Jasmin,* which was first published in 1984 and translated into English as *Jasmin's Witch* in 1987, relied heavily upon folklore and the everyday life of villagers in a small community in southern France. In *Jasmin's Witch* Le Roy Ladurie bases his investigation of the phenomenon of witchcraft on an obscure poem written in the Gascon dialect during the 1840s by a barber whose pen name was Jasmin. The poem had been transmitted orally for several generations before Jasmin committed it to paper. It told the story of Francouneto, a beautiful young woman who lived in the small community of Roquefort. When Francouneto spurned a soldier to marry another man, the soldier hired a sorcerer to spread the rumor that any man who married Francouneto would die. Alarmed because two former suitors had broken limbs while courting Francouneto, the community began to accuse her of other suspicious activities, including causing hailstorms and interfering with the villagers' sexual potency and fertility. Eventually, Francouneto herself began to wonder whether she might be a witch. Then her true love married her and survived, thereby proving that the curse was a wicked plot and convincing the villagers to surrender their belief in witches.

One of the most important aspects of this work, according to Jeffrey B. Russell, writing in the *Los Angeles Times Book Review,* is its potential to spur other historians to explore seemingly unpromising events and unearth new kinds of historical material. "With the Annaliste's nose for a good story behind the story," wrote Russell, "[Le Roy] Ladurie visited the region around Agen to see whether there was any historical basis for Jasmin's poem. Here the book is at its best. Using his understanding of religion, folklore, and language, he works back to a historical Francouneto who lived not in the 1500s as in Jasmin's poem but about 1660-1690." Russell suggested that *Jasmin's Witch* is "most successful as a work in historical detection," and for that reason he likened it to Umberto Eco's *Name of the Rose.*

Calling Le Roy Ladurie an "original" as well as "entertaining" writer, Laurence Wylie, who reviewed *Jasmin's Witch* for the *Washington Post Book World,* also praised him for his unsurpassed knowledge of the history of southwestern France. However, Wylie complained about the effort required to digest the various materials with which Le Roy Ladurie makes his case. "Le Roy Ladurie's style is not obscure," noted Wylie, "on the contrary it is almost conversational. But he expects his reader to follow and retain all the details and to arrive with him at a conclusion. He seems to ignore our need for clarification, but that is apparently the habit of most French intellectuals today." Nonetheless, Wylie was impressed by the author's "brilliant archival and anthropological research," which he said was most clearly evident in the second half of *Jasmin's Witch.* Concluded Wylie: "Le Roy Ladurie is the Sherlock Holmes of the scholarly world."

BIOGRAPHICAL/CRITICAL SOURCES:

PERIODICALS

Chicago Tribune Book World, November 4, 1979.
Guardian Weekly, March 22, 1987.
Los Angeles Times Book Review, October 18, 1981; July 26, 1987, p. 13.
New Republic, July 27, 1987, pp. 38-41.
New Statesman, June 13, 1980.
New Yorker, February 1, 1982.
New York Review of Books, October 12, 1978; November 8, 1979; February 28, 1985, p. 32.
New York Times Book Review, August 6, 1978; September 2, 1979; November 4, 1979; November 25, 1979; November 9, 1980; December 12, 1982.
Time, August 21, 1978; January 7, 1980.
Times Literary Supplement, February 16, 1973; March 6, 1981; May 28, 1982; July 2, 1982; February 24, 1984; July 3, 1987, p. 725.
Village Voice, November 30, 1982.
Washington Post Book World, January 12, 1975; August 20, 1978; December 3, 1978; September 2, 1979; November 4, 1979; September 27, 1981; December 19, 1982; August 30, 1987, pp. 10-12.*

*   *   *

LEVERE, Trevor H(arvey) 1944-

PERSONAL: Born March 21, 1944, in London, England; son of Godfrey and Vicki (Mendes da Costa) Levere; married Jennifer Tiesing (a teacher), July 30, 1966; children: Kevin Christopher, Rebecca Catherine. *Education:* New College, Oxford, B.A., 1966, D.Phil., 1969. *Religion:* Jewish. *Avocational interests:* Bird-watching, music, reading.

ADDRESSES: Home—Toronto, Ontario, Canada. *Office*—Institute for the History and Philosophy of Science and Technology, Victoria College, University of Toronto, 91 Charles Street West, Toronto M5S 1K7, Ontario, Canada. *E-mail*—trevor.levere@utoronto.ca.

CAREER: University of Toronto, Toronto, Ontario, Canada, assistant professor, 1969-74, associate profes-

sor, 1974-81, professor of the history of science, 1981—, director of history of science program, 1981-86, 1993-98.

MEMBER: International Academy of the History of Science (corresponding member), Royal Society of Canada (fellow), Canadian Society for the History of Science, History of Science Society, Royal Geographical Society (fellow), British Society for the History of Science, Dutch Society of Sciences (foreign member).

AWARDS, HONORS: Killam fellow, 1975-77, Guggenheim fellow, 1983-84.

WRITINGS:

Affinity and Matter, Clarendon Press, 1971.
(With G. L'E. Turner) *Martinus Van Marum,* Volume IV, Noordhoff International, 1973.
(Editor, with R. Jarrell) *A Curious Field-Book,* Oxford University Press, 1973.
Poetry Realized in Nature: Samuel Taylor Coleridge and Early Nineteenth-Century Science, Cambridge University Press (Cambridge, England), 1981.
(Editor) *Editing Texts in the History of Science and Medicine,* Garland Publishing (New York, NY), 1982.
(Editor, with W. Shea) *Nature, Experiment, and the Sciences,* Kluwer, 1990.
Science and the Canadian Arctic: A Century of Exploration, 1818-1918, Cambridge University Press (Cambridge, England), 1993.
Chemists and Chemistry in Science and Society, 1750-1878, Variorum, 1994.
(Editor, with F. L. Holmes) *Instruments and Experimentation in the History of Chemistry,* MIT Press (Cambridge, MA), 2000.
Transforming Matter: A History of Chemistry from Alchemy to the Buckyball, John Hopkins University Press (Baltimore, MD), 2001.

WORK IN PROGRESS: Research on the history of chemistry from the eighteenth through the nineteenth centuries; research on science and romanticism, and scientific apparatus.

SIDELIGHTS: Trevor H. Levere told *CA:* "My first degree was in chemistry, but I had a lively historical interest and was delighted to find that history of science enabled me to combine my interests. I have been fortunate in working at a university that encourages me to pursue research and writing. My principal current project involves looking at historical chemical apparatus, as well as manuscripts and publications from the eighteenth and nineteenth centuries, to gain some understanding of the practice of science and the interplay between ideas and instruments."

* * *

LIFSHIN, Lyn (Diane) 1944-

PERSONAL: Born July 12, 1944, in Burlington, VT; daughter of Ben and Frieda (Lazarus) Lipman; married Eric Lifshin, 1963 (divorced 1978). *Education:* Syracuse University, B.A., 1960; University of Vermont, M.A., 1963; also attended Brandeis University and State University of New York—Albany.

ADDRESSES: Home—2142 Apple Tree Lane, Niskayuna, NY 12309-4714; and 2719 Baronhurst Dr., Vienna, VA 22181; fax: 703-242-0127. *E-mail*—onyxvelvet@aol.com.

CAREER: Poet and writing instructor. State University of New York—Albany, teaching fellow, 1964-66; educational television writer, Schenectady, NY, 1966; State University of New York, Cobleskill, NY, instructor, 1968, 1970; writing consultant to New York State Mental Health Department, Albany, NY, 1969, and to Empire State College of the State University of New York, 1973; poet-in-residence, Mansfield State College, 1974, University of Rochester, 1986, Antioch Writers' Conference, 1987, and Glenwood College, 1994 and 1998; Union College, part-time instructor, 1980-85; has also taught at Cornell University, Dartmouth College, University of Chicago, University of New Mexico, and Syracuse University.

AWARDS, HONORS: Hart Crane Award; Bread Loaf scholarship; Harcourt Brace poetry fellowship; Boulder poetry award; San Jose Bicentennial Poetry Award; Yaddo fellowships, 1970, 1971, 1975, 1979, and 1980; MacDowell fellowship, 1973; Millay Colony fellowships, 1975 and 1979; New York Creative Artists Public Service grant, 1976; Jack Kerouac Award, 1984, for *Kiss the Skin Off; Centennial Review* poetry prize, 1985; Madeline Sadin Award, *New York Quarterly,* 1986; *Footwork* (magazine) Award, 1987; Bring Back the Stars Award, 1987; Esterceffler Award, 1987, for poem "Hiroshima"; Peterson Award, 1999, for *Cold Comfort,* and 2001, for *Before It's Light.*

WRITINGS:

POETRY COLLECTIONS

Why Is the House Dissolving?, Open Skull Press (San Francisco, CA), 1968.

Femina 2, Abraxas Press (Madison, WI), 1970.

Leaves and Night Things, Baby John Press (West Lafayette, IN), 1970.

Black Apples, New Books, 1971, revised edition, Crossing Press (Trumansburg, NY), 1973.

Lady Lyn, Morgan Press (Milwaukee, WI), 1971.

I'd Be Jeanne Moreau, Morgan Press (Milwaukee, WI), 1972.

The Mercurochrome Sun, Charas Press (Tacoma, WA), 1972.

Tentacles, Leaves, Hellric Publications (Bellmont, MA), 1972.

Moving by Touch, Cotyledon Press (Traverse City, MI), 1972.

Undressed, Cotyledon Press (Traverse City, MI), 1972.

Love Poems, Zahir Press (Durham, NH), 1972.

Lyn Lifshin, Zahir Press (Durham, NH), 1972.

Poems by Suramm and Lyn Lifshin, Union Literary Committee (Madison, WI), 1972.

Forty Days, Apple Nights, Morgan Press (Milwaukee, WI), 1973.

Museum, Conspiracy Press (Albany, NY), 1973.

The First Week Poems, Zahir Press (Durham, NH), 1973.

All the Women Poets I Ever Liked Didn't Hate Their Fathers, Konglomerati Press (Gulfport, FL), 1973.

The Old House on the Croton, Shameless Hussy Press (San Lorenzo, CA), 1973.

Poems, Konglomerati Press (Gulfport, FL), 1974.

Selected Poems, Crossing Press (Trumansburg, NY), 1974.

Thru Blue Post, New Mexico, Basilisk Press (Fredonia, NY), 1974.

Blue Fingers, Shelter Press (Milwaukee, WI), 1974.

Mountain Moving Day, Crossing Press (Trumansburg, NY), 1974.

Plymouth Women, Morgan Press (Milwaukee, WI), 1974.

Walking thru Audley End Mansion Late Afternoon and Drifting into Certain Faces, M.A.G Press (Long Beach, CA), 1974.

Shaker House, Tideline Press (New York, NY), 1974.

Blue Madonna, Shelter Press (Milwaukee, WI), 1974.

Green Bandages, Hidden Springs (Genesco, NY), 1975.

Upstate Madonna: Poems, 1970-1974, Crossing Press (Trumansburg, NY), 1975.

Old House Poems, Capra Press (Santa Barbara, CA), 1975.

Paper Apples, Wormwood Review Press (Stockton, CA), 1975.

North Poems, Morgan Press (Milwaukee, WI), 1976.

Shaker House Poems, Sagarin Press (Chatham, NY), 1976.

Naked Charm, Fireweed Press, 1976, revised edition published as *Op 15 Second Ed,* Illuminati (Los Angeles, CA), 1984.

Some Madonna Poems, White Pine Press (Buffalo, NY), 1976.

Crazy Arms, Ommation Press (Chicago, IL), 1977.

The January Poems, Waters Journal of the Arts (Cincinnati, OH), 1977.

More Waters, Waters Journal of the Arts (Cincinnati, OH), 1977.

Pantagonia, Wormwood Review Press (Stockton, CA), 1977.

Mad Girl Poems, Out of Sight Press (Wichita, KS), 1977.

Leaning South, Red Dust (New York, NY), 1977.

Lifshin & Richmond, Bombay Duck (Oakland, CA), 1977.

Poems with John Elsberg, Fiasco (Filey, Yorkshire, England), 1978.

Blue Dust, New Mexico, Basilisk Press (Fredonia, NY), 1978.

Glass, Morgan Press (Milwaukee, WI), 1978.

Early Plymouth Women, Morgan Press (Milwaukee, WI), 1978.

35 Sundays, Ommation Press (Chicago, IL), 1979.

More Naked Charm, Illuminati (Los Angeles, CA), 1979.

Doctors, Mudborn (Santa Barbara, CA), 1979.

Men and Cars, Four Zoas Press (Ware, MA), 1979.

Lips on the Blue Rail, Lion's Breath (San Francisco, CA), 1980.

Doctors and Doctors of English, Mudborn Press (Santa Barbara, CA), 1981.

Colors of Cooper Black, Morgan Press (Milwaukee, WI), 1981.

In the Dark with Just One Star, Morgan Press (Milwaukee, WI), 1982.

Want Ads, Morgan Press (Milwaukee, WI), 1982.

Mad Girl, Blue Horse Publications, 1982.

Lobsters and Oatmeal, Pinchpenny (Boston, MA), 1982.

Finger Prints, Wormwood Review Press (Stockton, CA), 1982.

Reading Lips, Morgan Press (Milwaukee, WI), 1982.

Hotel Lifshin, Poetry Now (Eureka, CA), 1982.

Leaving the Bough, New World Press (New York, NY), 1982.

Madonna Who Shifts for Herself, Applezaba (Long Beach, CA), 1983.

The Radio Psychic Is Shaving Her Legs, Planet Detroit (Detroit, MI), 1984.

Matinee, Ommation Press (Chicago, IL), 1984.

Remember the Ladies, Ghost Dance Press (East Lansing, MI), 1985.

Kiss the Skin Off, Cherry Valley Editions (Silver Spring, MD), 1985.

Blue Horses Nuzzle Thursday, Illuminati (Los Angeles, CA), 1985.

Camping Madonna at Indian Lake, M.A.F (Portlandville, NY), 1986.

(With others) *Eye of the Beast,* Vergin Press (El Paso, TX), 1986.

Madonna (bound with *Vergin' Mary* by Belinda Subraman), Vergin Press (El Paso, TX), 1986.

Red Hair and the Jesuit, Trout Creek Press (Parkdale, OR), 1987.

Raw Opals, Illuminati (Los Angeles, CA), 1987.

Rubbed Silk, Illuminati (Los Angeles, CA), 1987.

The Daughter May Be Let Go, Clock Radio Press (Harbor Beach, FL), 1987.

Many Madonnas, Kindred Spirit Press (St. John, KS), 1988.

Dance Poems, Ommation Press (Chicago, IL), 1988.

(With Belinda Subraman) *Skin Divers,* Krax (Leeds, Yorkshire, England), 1989.

The Doctor Poems, Applezaba (Long Beach, CA), 1989.

Blood Road, Illuminati (Los Angeles, CA), 1989.

Under Velvet Pillows, Four Zoas Press (Ashvelot Village, NH), 1989.

Reading Lips, Morgan Press (Milwaukee, WI), 1989.

Not Made of Glass: Poems, 1968-1988, edited by Mary Ann Lynch, introduction by Laura Chester, Combinations Press (Greenfield Center, NY), 1989.

(With Belinda Subraman) *The Innocents,* Buzzard's Roost Press, 1991.

Sulphur River Lifshin Edition, Sulphur River, 1991.

The Jesuit Is Dying, Big Head Press, 1992.

Tammy Says, Big Head Press, 1992.

Apple Blossoms, Ghost Dance Press (East Lansing, MI), 1993.

Marilyn Monroe, Quiet Lion Press (Portland, OR), 1994.

Feathers on the Water, Tazzerine Press, 1994.

Parade, Wormwood Review Press (Stockton, CA), 1994.

Shooting Kodachromes in the Dark, Penumbra Press, 1994.

Blue Tattoo, Event Horizon (Desert Hot Springs, CA), 1995.

The Mad Girl Drives in a Daze, JVC Books, 1995.

Pointe Shoes, JVC Books, 1995.

Mad Girl Poems, Morgan Press (Milwaukee, WI), 1995.

Color and Light, Lilliput Press, 1996.

Mad Girls, Dead Men, Lilliput Press, 1996.

Madonna and Marilyn, Taggerzine Press, 1996.

Cold Comfort: Selected Poems, 1970-1996, Black Sparrow Press (Santa Rosa, CA), 1997.

Jesus Alive in the Flesh, Future Tense Press, 1997.

My Mother's Fire, Glass Cherry, 1997.

Before It's Light, Black Sparrow Press (Santa Rosa, CA), 1999.

OTHER

(Editor) *Tangled Vines: A Collection of Mother and Daughter Poems,* Beacon Press (Boston, MA), 1978, new edition, Harcourt (San Diego, CA), 1992.

(Editor) *Ariadne's Thread: A Collection of Contemporary Women's Journals,* Harper (New York, NY), 1982.

(Editor) *Lips Unsealed,* Capra, 1990.

Lyn Lifshin Reads Her Poems (recording), Women's Audio Exchange, 1977.

Offered by Owner (recording with booklet of poems), Natalie Slohm Associates (Cambridge, NY), 1978.

Some Voices, 1993.

The 375th Poem about Me Comes in the Mail, Impetus Press, 1994.

Mint Leaves at Yappo (prose), Writers Digest (Cincinnati, OH), 1994.

Hints for Writers (prose), Writers Digest (Cincinnati, OH), 1995.

On the Outside (autobiography), 1995.

Also author of *The Jesuit Poems, Between My Lips, White Horse Café, The Radio Shrink, Sunday Poems, More Madonnas, He Wants His Meat, Appletree Lane, Sotto Voce,* and *Mad Windows.* Contributor to anthologies, including, *New American and Canadian Poetry,* edited by John Gill, Beacon Press, 1971; *Writing While Young and Seeing thru Shucks,* Ballantine (New York, NY), 1972; *Rising Tides,* Simon & Schuster (New York, NY), 1973; *Psyche,* Dell (New York, NY), 1974; *In Youth,* Ballantine (New York, NY), 1974; *Pictures That Storm inside My Head,* Avon (New York, NY), 1975; *I Hear My Sisters Saying,* Crowell (New York, NY), 1976; *Six Poets,* Vagabond (Ellensburg, WA), 1978; *Editor's Choice,* Spirit That Moves Us (Jackson Heights, NY), 1980; *Woman: An Affirmation,* Heath (Lexington, MA), 1980; *Contents under Pressure,* edited by Fred H. Laughter, Moonlight Publications, 1981; *Poetry: Sight and Insight,* Random House (New

York, NY), 1982; and *Deep Down,* Dutton (New York, NY), 1988. Contributor to several hundred publications, including *Chicago Review, Rolling Stone, Ms., Chelsea, American Poetry Review,* and *Massachusetts Review.* Manuscript collection held at the University of Texas, Austin.

SIDELIGHTS: One of the most prolific contemporary poets in the United States, Lyn Lifshin has contributed to hundreds of anthologies and appeared in "virtually every poetry and literary magazine," as she once told *CA.* A critic for the *San Francisco Review of Books* calls Lifshin "one of the most distinctive, prolific, and widely published poets of all time . . . and very popular with readers." In addition to publishing more than ninety collections of her own work, an autobiography, and a "how-to" book for other writers, she is also recognized for editing several critically acclaimed collections of women's writings and for her many poetry readings and writing workshops. Essayist Joseph Bruchac in *Contemporary Poets* contends that the very quantity of Lifshin's output has sometimes had a negative effect in terms of "overshadow[ing] the true range and significance of her work."

A typical Lifshin poem is small, consisting of a few words per line and rarely more than thirty lines in length. Her poems, Gerald Burns comments in the *Southwest Review,* are "long thin things." Enjambed phrases intensify the single emotion or event with which each poem is concerned, and humor is never far from the surface. Lifshin's poems, a writer for the *San Francisco Review of Books* believes, are "a quick, fun read, and [she] seems to strive for that effect." Kenneth Funsten of the *Los Angeles Times Book Review* explains that Lifshin "writes poems both spontaneous and sure of their mark." A critic for the *North American Review,* speaking of the speed with which a Lifshin poem can be read, calls her "Queen of the quickies." Bruchac finds irony in the fact that although Lifshin's poems are seldom more than a page, their cumulative "result is a body of work which is impressive in its size, almost epic in proportion." He also observes that "she seems to reach many of the final versions of her poems not so much by rewriting and reworking a single poem as by producing a series of poems which gradually—or even cumulatively—reach the desired effect."

Lifshin began to read "very, very early" and was writing by the age of three. She "skipped several grades in elementary school," where she was "unable . . . to do long division but . . . [was] pretty good at writing poetry." She grew up in Vermont, not far from the home of American poet laureate Robert Frost, who used to shop at her grandfather's department store. "I used to see Frost," Lifshin noted in the *Contemporary Authors Autobiography Series,* "wandering around Middlebury in baggy green pants, carrying strawberries." Lifshin continued writing poetry as she grew up, and when she first began publishing in literary magazines in the late 1960s her father showed one of her poems to Frost. "Very good sayeth Robert Frost," Frost wrote upon it, telling her father that he liked its striking images.

Lifshin's first poetry collection, *Why Is the House Dissolving?,* appeared in 1968. According to Hugh Fox in the *Greenfield Review* it is "a scathing, angry, iconoclastic, shocking, vituperative book." Part of this early anger was caused by Lifshin's failure to pass her oral examination for a doctorate degree in English literature, Fox believes. This anger led her to reject formal, academic writing—and the formal academic world, to which she has never returned—in favor of personal poetry. "She maintains," Fox writes, "a high degree of *voluminous spontaneity* . . . [because she] doesn't see poetry as academic watch-making, but rather [as] an important expression of a primal interior *howl.*"

Speaking to Fox about her views on poetry, Lifshin explained that in the Eskimo language "the words 'to breathe' and 'to make a poem' are the same. I mean poetry is that central, essential, as much a part of me as breathing is." She told Theodore Bouloukos II in *Albany* that "when a great deal of time goes by and I haven't written, I begin to feel edgy. I think it's probably like somebody who has an addiction or an obsession." Writing in *Contemporary Poets,* Lifshin commented: "It seems to me that the poem has to be sensual . . . before it can be anything else. So rhythm matters a lot to me, more, or at least first. Before images even." She went on to single out "old black and country blues rhythms" as particularly influential on her voice. She likes to think of her poems as "strong, tight, real, startling, tough, tender, sexy, physical, controlled." In an online interview for *Amazon.com,* she revealed herself as an eclectic and nearly obsessive reader, and noted that her tastes and consequently the influences on her writing range widely from Dylan Thomas to Emily Dickinson to Charles Bukowski.

Similar to haiku and other short poetic forms, Lifshin's lean and concise poems are especially suited for re-creating a single moment or emotion, or describing a particular place. Her best work, many critics believe, is found in her poems about historical subjects. Some of these pieces are collected in *Shaker House Poems,* in which Lifshin writes about the women of the Shaker religious communities of early America, having visited many of the original historical settlements. A *Choice* critic remarks, Lifshin "very successfully captures the spirit, the mood, the mystique of the Shakers, through magnificently crafted poems, terse as needlework." Her collection *Leaning South* contains poems about sites in New England and about the early Eskimo culture of the Arctic. Peter Schjeldahl, reviewing the book for the *New York Times Book Review,* finds the Eskimo poems to be especially well done. These poems, Schjeldahl writes, evoke "in fantasy, but with a lot of anthropological detail, the world of the ancient Eskimos. Here [Lifshin's] clipped line takes on a chantlike undertone, as of native voices themselves singing from the beyond, that is very pleasing." Fox explains that what Lifshin is doing in her historical poems is "creating a psycho-historical large canvas that traces the evolution of woman within the Occident."

Lifshin's feminist concerns are also evident in her popular "Madonna" poems, each of which describes a modern female archetype in a terse, often humorous manner. Titles in the series include *Madonna Who Shifts for Herself, Many Madonnas,* and *More Madonnas.* Speaking to Bouloukos, Lifshin explained: "Sometimes to be a little more flippant or satirical I use the Madonna as a metaphor. I'm relying on some of my own feelings and reactions which are often totally fictionalized and fantastic." A critic for the *Small Press Review* says of the Madonna poems: "Many have the quick, throwaway humor of the epigram, the pun," but also possess "the irony and resentment that provides much of the energy of Lifshin's poetry." Bruchac notes a greater depth and emotional impact in Lifshin's contemporary feminist poems, contending that "one would be hard-pressed to find another writer who has done as thorough a job of evoking the despair of a woman caught in the traps which social restrictions and marriage create for women." Yet more than dealing exclusively with a feminist perspective, Bruchac stresses that "few have written more bitingly or more tenderly about modern sexual mores" than Lifshin. "In her poems of sexuality," he states, "both the emotional and physical relationships between men and women are laid bare."

In addition to writing poetry, Lifshin teaches classes and workshops in journal and diary writing. She keeps a diary herself and has drawn upon its entries for some of her poems. In 1982 she edited *Ariadne's Thread: A Collection of Contemporary Women's Journals,* which presents a wide spectrum of women's emotions and ideas on such subjects as relationships, work, families, death, and birth. "Most of the journals," Ursula Hegi writes in the *Los Angeles Times,* "are spontaneous, fascinating, and often painfully honest. . . . Lifshin has woven a living tapestry of women's voices—often angry and sad, sometimes joyful and content, yet never self-pitying."

Lifshin has emerged as one of the most recognized woman poets in the United States. She has given many hundreds of poetry readings and participated in mixed media theater performances as well. In 1988 Karista Films released a documentary on Lifshin, *Not Made of Glass,* which shows her typical working day, a visit she made to the Yaddo artist colony, and a reading she gave at a local coffeehouse. Lifshin also appears on the *First American Poetry Disc,* a Laserdisc recording of readings given by contemporary American poets. Her manuscripts are being collected by the University of Texas at Austin and by Temple University.

A *Choice* reviewer claims that Lifshin "has slowly moved up among the ranks of her peers . . . until . . . she comes practically to the top." Janice Eidus notes in the *Small Press Review* that Lifshin "continues to explore her poetic obsessions with her unique poetic voice and her unique sensibility." Speaking of Lifshin's writing career, Fox describes it as "an artistically rich embattled journey into the fragile clarity of the Here and Now." Citing her rejection and condemnation of formal academia, a significant distinction among contemporary poets of renown, along with the ever-increasing range of subject matter she has addressed with intensity and honesty in her writing, Bruchac sees Lifshin as "a risk taker. . . . Continually searching for meaning and identity. . . . One whose journey takes us along and teaches us as we go."

BIOGRAPHICAL/CRITICAL SOURCES:

BOOKS

Contemporary Authors Autobiography Series, Volume 10, Gale (Detroit, MI), 1989.
Contemporary Poets, 6th edition, St. James Press (Detroit, MI), 1996.
Contemporary Women Poets, St. James Press (Detroit, MI), 1998.
Fox, Hugh, *Lifshin: A Critical Study,* Whitiston Press (Troy, NY), 1985.

PERIODICALS

Albany, December, 1986.
Booklist, April 1, 1978; July 15, 1978; April 15, 1990; January 1, 1991.
Bookwatch, January, 1991.
Choice, March, 1977; December, 1978.
Greenfield Review, summer-fall, 1983.

Library Journal, June, 1971; December, 1972; June 1, 1976.
Little Magazine, summer-fall, 1972.
Los Angeles Times, October 18, 1982.
Los Angeles Times Book Review, September 23, 1984; October 13, 1985.
Minneapolis Star, April 18, 1972.
Ms., September, 1976; July, 1978; July, 1983.
New York Times Book Review, December 17, 1978.
North American Review, fall, 1978; March, 1985.
Northeast, fall-winter, 1971-72.
Poetry Now, spring, 1980.
Review of Contemporary Fiction, fall, 1990.
Road Apple Review, summer-fall, 1971.
San Francisco Review of Books, spring, 1985; fall, 1985.
Small Press Book Review, March, 1991.
Small Press Review, September, 1983; March, 1984; January, 1985; May, 1990.
Southwest Review, winter, 1983.
Utne Reader, spring, 1990.
Village Voice, September 24, 1979.
Windless Orchard, summer, 1972.
Wormwood Review, Volume XII, number 3, 1971.
Writers Digest, September, 1994.

OTHER

Lyn Lifshin Web site, http://www.lynlifshin.com.
Lynch, Mary Ann, *Lyn Lifshin: Not Made of Glass* (film), Women Make Movies, 1990.*

*   *   *

LILES, Maurine Walpole 1935-

PERSONAL: Born January 31, 1935, in Floresville, TX; daughter of Horace Louis and Nancy Louisa (McDade) Walpole; married John H. Liles (a physician), July 27, 1965. *Education:* Texas Christian University, B.S.; holds teaching certificate.

ADDRESSES: Home—1405 South 3rd St., Floresville, TX 78114. *E-mail*—willer2@aol.com.

CAREER: Author. Has taught in private and public schools.

WRITINGS:

Rebecca of Blossom Prairie (historical novel; first in trilogy), illustrated by Maggie Fields and Mark Mitchell, Eakin Press (Austin, TX), 1990.

Kitty of Blossom Prairie (historical novel; second in trilogy), illustrated by Pat Finney, Eakin Press (Austin, TX), 1992.

The Boy of Blossom Prairie Who Became Vice-President (historical novel; third in trilogy), illustrated by Pat Finney, Eakin Press (Austin, TX), 1993.

Sam and the Speaker's Chair (biography), illustrated by Pat Finney, Sunbelt Media, 1994.

Willer and the Piney Woods Doctor (historical novel), illustrated by Pat Finney, Eakin Press (Austin, TX), 1995.

The Littlest Vaquero of Spanish Texas, illustrated by Pat Finney, Eakin Press (Austin, TX), 1996.

Doña María, La Ranchera, illustrated by Mark Mitchell, Eakin Press (Austin, TX), 2000.

SIDELIGHTS: Maurine Walpole Liles once told *CA:* "I dress as the pioneer character Rebecca in my early works when I visit schools to tell the children stories from my books."

BIOGRAPHICAL/CRITICAL SOURCES:

PERIODICALS

School Library Journal, June, 1993, p. 108.

*   *   *

LINDSEY, (Helen) Johanna 1952-

PERSONAL: Born March 10, 1952, in Frankfurt, Germany; daughter of Edwin Dennis (a professional soldier) and Wanda (a personnel management specialist; maiden name, Donaldson) Howard; married Ralph Lindsey (an estimator), November 28, 1970 (deceased); children: Alfred, Joseph, Garret. *Education:* Attended high school in Kailua, Hawaii.

ADDRESSES: Home—Ahuimanu Hills, 47-598 Puapoo Place, Kaneohe, HI 96744.

CAREER: Writer, 1975—.

AWARDS, HONORS: Historical romance writer of the year award, 1984, and numerous Reviewer's Choice Awards, *Romantic Times;* bronze award, *West Coast Review of Books,* for *So Speaks the Heart;* Waldenbooks Best Historical, 1986-91; Outstanding Achiever award, 1991, and numerous Favorite Author Awards and Silver Pen Awards, *Affaire de Coeur.*

WRITINGS:

HISTORICAL ROMANCES

Captive Bride, Avon Books (New York, NY), 1977.

A Pirate's Love, Avon Books (New York, NY), 1978.

Fires of Winter, Avon Books (New York, NY), 1980.

Paradise Wild, Avon Books (New York, NY), 1981.

Glorious Angel, Avon Books (New York, NY), 1982.

So Speaks the Heart, Avon Books (New York, NY), 1983.

Heart of Thunder, Avon Books (New York, NY), 1983.

A Gentle Feuding, Avon Books (New York, NY), 1984.

Brave the Wild Wind, Avon Books (New York, NY), 1984.

Tender Is the Storm, Avon Books (New York, NY), 1985.

Love Only Once, Avon Books (New York, NY), 1985.

When Love Awaits, Avon Books (New York, NY), 1986.

A Heart So Wild, Avon Books (New York, NY), 1986.

Hearts Aflame, Avon Books (New York, NY), 1987.

Secret Fire, Avon Books (New York, NY), 1987.

Tender Rebel, Avon Books (New York, NY), 1988.

Silver Angel, Avon Books (New York, NY), 1988.

Defy Not the Heart, Avon Books (New York, NY), 1989.

Savage Thunder, Avon Books (New York, NY), 1989.

Warrior's Woman, Avon Books (New York, NY), 1990.

Gentle Rogue, Avon Books (New York, NY), 1990.

Once a Princess, Avon Books (New York, NY), 1991.

Prisoner of My Desire, Avon Books (New York, NY), 1991.

Man of My Dreams, Avon Books (New York, NY), 1992.

Angel, Avon Books (New York, NY), 1992.

The Magic of You, Avon Books (New York, NY), 1993.

Keeper of the Heart, Avon Books (New York, NY), 1993.

Love Me Forever, Morrow (New York, NY), 1995.

Until Forever, Avon Books (New York, NY), 1995.

Say You Love Me, Morrow (New York, NY), 1996.

You Belong to Me, Avon Books (New York, NY), 1996.

All I Need Is You, Avon Books (New York, NY), 1997.

The Present: A Malory Holiday Novel, Avon Books (New York, NY), 1998.

Joining, Avon Books (New York, NY), 1999.

Home for the Holidays, Morrow (New York, NY), 2000.

The Heir, Morrow (New York, NY), 2000.

Heart of a Warrior, Morrow (New York, NY), 2001.

SIDELIGHTS: "Since I was old enough to appreciate a good novel, I've been a romantic," Johanna Lindsey told Kathryn Falk in *Love's Leading Ladies*. After years of being an avid reader of historical romances, Lindsey began writing them herself. Her books have appeared on the *New York Times* Paperback Best-Seller List and have sold over forty million copies. In addition to being successful, Lindsey feels she is well suited to her profession: "I enjoy happy-ending love stories more than any other type of reading. Romance is what comes out of me."

Lindsey's books are noted for their accurate portrayal of historical periods and foreign settings. Critics have commented favorably on the author's attention to historical detail and her ability to evoke her exotic locations. Lindsey relies primarily on library research to achieve this realism. "I take care of research before I begin my story, once a century and a continent are decided upon," Lindsey explained to Falk. Despite the realism of her fiction, Lindsey has never traveled to the foreign settings she depicts. "I would love to visit the areas that I write about," she told Falk, "but unfortunately, the only traveling I do is to the library." Lindsey also has created several generations of an English noble family, the Malorys, who figure in such books as *Say You Love Me, The Present: A Malory Holiday Novel, Tender Rebel, Gentle Rogue, Love Only Once,* and *The Magic of You.*

After her success with more than thirty paperback titles, Lindsey published her first hardcover title, *Love Me Forever,* in 1995. Set in nineteenth-century England, it concerns a "feisty, intelligent heroine" and "devastatingly brawny Highlander," as a *Kirkus Reviews* critic described them. Lindsey's historical backdrop plays foil to a romantic tale in which the lovers aren't quite ready for each other, but through shared adventure, eventually find true love. A *Publishers Weekly* reviewer called the tale "giddy entertainment."

Lindsey's subsequent works have a variety of settings. *All I Need Is You* is a Wild West story about a woman masquerading as a man. *Joining* has the participants in an arranged marriage unexpectedly finding real love against a background of political intrigue in medieval England. It features the "intriguing characters" and "mini history lessons" readers have come to expect from Lindsey, noted *People* reviewer Cynthia Sanz. *The Heir,* which takes place in the nineteenth century, centers on a plain but vivacious young woman who wins the heart of her more conventionally attractive friend's fiancé, a Scottish nobleman. Of this novel, *Booklist* critic Patty Engelmann commented, "Lindsey

achieves the requisite happy ending with wit and charm." *Home for the Holidays* is set at Christmastime in Regency-era England, where a young man seeking to avenge his brother's death falls in love with the daughter of his intended victim. A *Publishers Weekly* reviewer thought this "a shallow but genre-appropriate tale" that nonetheless showed the mark of Lindsey's "practiced hand." *Booklist* contributor Diana Tixier Herald found it "not as powerful or passionate" as much of Lindsey's work, but predicted "her fans will devour it happily just the same."

In an essay for *Twentieth-Century Romance and Historical Writers,* Barbara E. Kemp summarized Lindsey's career by saying, "Although the explicit sensuality and frequent abusiveness found in Lindsey's work may disturb some readers, her well thought out, fast moving stories appeal to many more. In her skilled hands, the standard battle of strong-willed individuals comes to life. Anchored by authentic descriptions and historical detail and focusing on the turbulent passions in the battle of the sexes, her books are among the best of the sensuous historical novels." Discussing the impact of writing on her life, Lindsey told Falk that, "other than a change in family finances, and the pride of accomplishment, success hasn't changed my life." Yet, she admitted to Falk that her profession is important to her. "I would be literally *lost* if I had to give it up," Lindsey explained.

BIOGRAPHICAL/CRITICAL SOURCES:

BOOKS

Falk, Kathryn, *Love's Leading Ladies,* Pinnacle Books (New York, NY), 1982.
Twentieth-Century Romance and Historical Writers, third edition, St. James Press (Detroit, MI), 1994.

PERIODICALS

Affaire de Coeur, January, 1984.
Booklist, September 1, 1995; September 15, 1998, Donna Seaman, review of *All I Need Is You,* p. 211; April 1, 2000, Patty Engelmann, review of *The Heir,* p. 1413; November 1, 2000, Diana Tixier Herald, review of *Home for the Holidays,* p. 493; April 1, 2001, Diana Tixier Herald, review of *Heart of a Warrior.*
Kirkus Reviews, July 15, 1995; November 1, 2000, review of *Home for the Holidays,* p. 1509.
People, August 23, 1999, Cynthia Sanz, review of *Joining,* p. 49.
Publishers Weekly, July 11, 1980; March 25, 1983; October 10, 1994; September 11, 1995, p. 75; October

30, 2000, review of *Home for the Holidays,* p. 48; April 23, 2001, review of *Heart of a Warrior.**

*   *   *

LITTLEFIELD, Bill 1948-

PERSONAL: Born July 13, 1948, in Montclair, NJ; son of William and Sally Littlefield; married Mary Atlee, January 16, 1982; children: Amy, Alison. *Education:* Yale University, B.A., 1970; Harvard University, Ed.M., 1973.

ADDRESSES: Home—47 Gay St., Needham, MA 02492. *Office*—Curry College, Milton, MA 02186; and WBUR-FM Radio, 890 Commonwealth Ave., Boston, MA 02215.

CAREER: Curry College, Milton, MA, professor, 1976—. WBUR-FM Radio, host and writer of *Only a Game* radio program; freelance writer.

MEMBER: American Association of University Professors, PEN-New England.

AWARDS, HONORS: Named one of Boston's "Literary Lights," Boston Public Library Associates, 1994; *Champions: Stories of Ten Remarkable Athletes* was named a "best book for young adults" by American Library Association and a "book for the teen age" by New York Public Library; five Associated Press Awards for radio commentaries.

WRITINGS:

Prospect, Houghton (Boston, MA), 1989.
Champions: Stories of Ten Remarkable Athletes, illustrated by Bernie Fuchs, Little, Brown (Boston, MA), 1993.
Baseball Days: From the Sandlots to the Show, photographs by Henry Horenstein, Little, Brown (Boston, MA), 1993.
Keepers: Radio Stories from "Only a Game" and Elsewhere, Peninsula Press, 1998.
(Editor) *Best American Sports Writing,* Houghton (Boston, MA), 1998.
The Circus in the Woods, Houghton (Boston, MA), 2001.

Contributor to periodicals.

SIDELIGHTS: An author of fiction and nonfiction works about sports, Bill Littlefield received wide praise for his book for young sports fans, *Champions: Stories of Ten Remarkable Athletes.* Not simply a record of important heroes and heroines in sports, *Champions* retells true stories of courageous athletes who overcame discrimination and physical handicaps to become the best in their sport. Littlefield writes about people who overcame poverty to play World Cup soccer (Pele), challenged racial barriers to play professional baseball (Satchel Paige and Roberto Clemente), beat down male chauvinism to establish women's professional tennis (Billie Jean King), defied all odds by becoming a world-class skier with only one leg (Diana Golden), and much more. In this way, noted *School Library Journal* contributor Renee Steinberg, Littlefield "conveys to youngsters the importance of focusing on goals and consistently working toward reaching them."

Littlefield once commented: "Storytelling is the act that connects my activities. As a writer, I've invented the stories of fictional characters, recounted the tales of old baseball scouts and young ballplayers, and retold for young readers the stories of great athletes. As a teacher, I help writing students make their own stories and literature students appreciate the timeless stories that apply to us all. Storytelling is also at the heart of my work as host and writer for WBUR's *Only a Game,* the weekly public radio sports show. I tell stories endlessly to my younger daughter, Alison, who tells me which characters to include.

"Storytelling is fun, and it's also the activity by which we give our lives shape and meaning. People like to tell their stories to folks inclined to listen, and I'm one of those folks. I can't imagine not doing any of the things I'm doing in the storytelling line."

BIOGRAPHICAL/CRITICAL SOURCES:

PERIODICALS

Booklist, September 1, 1993, p. 48; November 1, 1993, p. 535; March 15, 1994, p. 1357.
Bulletin of the Center for Children's Books, October, 1993, p. 51.
Horn Book, November, 1993, p. 755.
Horn Book Guide, spring, 1994, p. 147.
Kirkus Reviews, August 1, 1993, p. 1005.
Newsweek, December 6, 1993, p. 76.
Publishers Weekly, July 12, 1993, p. 81.
Quill & Quire, March, 1994, p. 77.
School Library Journal, September, 1993, Renee Steinberg, review of *Champions: Stories of Ten Remarkable Athletes,* p. 244.
Tribune Books (Chicago, IL), December 12, 1993, p. 3.
Voice of Youth Advocates, December, 1993, p. 322.

Washington Post Book World, December 5, 1993, p. 26.

*   *   *

LUSTIG, Arnost 1926-

PERSONAL: Born December 21, 1926, in Prague, Czechoslovakia (now Czech Republic); immigrated to U.S. in 1970, and became a citizen; son of Emil and Therese (Lowy) Lustig; married Vera Weislitz, July 24, 1949; children: Josef, Eva. *Ethnicity:* "Czech Jew." *Education:* College of Political and Social Sciences (Prague, Czechoslovakia), M.A., 1951, Ing. degree, 1954.

ADDRESSES: Home—4000 Tunlaw Rd. NW Apt. 825, Washington, DC 20007. *Office*—Department of Literature, American University, Washington, DC 20016.

CAREER: Radio Prague, Prague, Czechoslovakia, Arab-Israeli war correspondent, 1948-49; Czechoslovak Radio Corp., correspondent in Europe, Asia, and North America, 1950-68; Barrandov Film Studios, Prague, screenwriter, 1960-68; writer in Israel, 1968-69; Jadran Film Studio, Zagreb, Yugoslavia, screenwriter, 1969-70; University of Iowa, Iowa City, IA, member of International Writers Program, 1970-71, visiting lecturer, 1971-72; American University, Washington, DC, professor of literature, 1973—. Correspondent for literary magazines in Czechoslovakia, 1950-58; head of the Czechoslovak film delegation to the San Sebastian Film Festival, 1968; member of the jury, Karlovy Vary International Film Festival, 1968 and 1996; visiting professor, Drake University, 1972-73; guest of the Biennale in Venice, Italy, 1977; member of the jury, International Neustadt Prize for Literature, 1980; Terezin Memorial, board of directors member; lecturer in film and literature at universities in Eastern Europe, Israel, Japan, Canada, and the United States.

MEMBER: Authors Guild, Authors League of America, PEN, Film Club (Prague), Academy of Television and Film (Prague), Franz Koflad Society in Prague (honorary president).

AWARDS, HONORS: First prize, Mlada Fronta publishing house, 1962, for *Diamonds of the Night;* best short story, (Meanjian) University of Melbourne, 1962, for "Lemon"; first prize, Czechoslovak Radio Corp., 1966, for radio play *Prague Crossroads;* first prize, Monte Carlo Film Festival, 1966, for television film *A*

Prayer for Katerina Horovitzova; Klement Gotwald State Prize, 1967, nomination for National Book Award, 1974, and B'nai B'rith Award, 1974, all for *A Prayer for Katerina Horovitzova;* first prize, Czechoslovak Radio Corp., 1967, for radio play *A Man the Size of a Postage Stamp;* second prize, San Sebastian Film Festival, 1968, for *Dita Saxova;* Jewish National Book Award, 1980, for *Dita Saxova,* and 1987, for *The Unloved: From the Diary of Perla S.;* Emmy Award, outstanding screenplay, 1985, for documentary *Precious Legacy;* D. of Hebrew Letters, Spertus College, 1986; Korel Cajek Prize, PEN Club, Prague, 1997.

WRITINGS:

Ulice ztracenych bratri, Mlada fronta, 1949.
Muj znamy Vili Feld (novel), Mlada fronta, 1949.
Dita Saxova (novel), Ceskoslovensky spisovatel, 1962, Harper (New York, NY), 1980, translation by George Theiner published as *Dita Sax,* Hutchinson (London, England), 1966.
Nikoho neponizis, Nase vojsko, 1963.
Modlitba pro Katerinu Horovitzovou (novel), Ceskoslovensky spisovatel, 1964, translation by Jeanne Nemcova published as *A Prayer for Katerina Horovitzova,* Harper (New York, NY), 1973.
Bile brizy na podzim, Ceskoslovensky spisovatel, 1966.
Horka vune mandli, Mlada fronta, 1968.
Milacek, Ceskoslovensky spisovatel, 1969.
Z deniku sedmnactilete Perly Sch. (novel), Sixty-Eight Publishers, 1979, translation by Vera Kalina-Levine published as *The Unloved: From the Diary of Perla S.,* Arbor House (New York, NY), 1985.
Indecent Dreams (three novellas), Northwestern University Press (Evanston, IL), 1988.
Street of Lost Brothers (short stories), with a foreword by Jonathan Brent, Northwestern University Press (Evanston, IL), 1990 (also see below).
Tma nema stin, Ceskoslovensky spisovatel, 1991.
(With Milan Kundera and Josef Skvorecky) *Velka trojka,* Galaxie, 1991.
Colette, 1992.
Tanga, 1993.
Beautiful Green Eyes, 1995, Horville Press (London, England), 2001.
Children of the Holocaust, translated by Jeanne Nemcova and George Theiner, Northwestern University Press (Evanston, IL), 1995.
Dobry'den, fone Lustig, Aequitas Publishing, (Prague, Czech Republic), 2000.
Odpovédi, H & H Publishing (Prague, Czech Republic), 2000.
Lea from Leuvoorslen, Eminent (Prague, Czech Republic), 2000.

House of Echo Returned, Northwestern University Press (Evanston, IL), in press.

COLLECTED WORKS

Noc a nadeje (short stories), Nase vojsko, 1958, translation by George Theiner published as *Night and Hope* (also see below), Dutton (New York, NY), 1962.

Demanty noci (short stories), Mlada fronta, 1958, translation by Iris Urwin published as *Diamonds of the Night* (also see below), Artia, 1962, new translation by Jeanne Nemcova, Inscape, 1977.

Darkness Casts No Shadow, translation by Jeanne Nemcova, Inscape, 1977.

Night and Hope, Inscape, 1977, translation by George Theiner, Northwestern University Press, 1985.

Collected Works (more than six volumes), Hynek Publishing (Prague, Czech Republic), 1995—.

Bitter Smell of Almonds: Dita Saxove, Indecent Dreams, Street of Lost Brothers, Northwestern University Press, 2001.

SCREENPLAYS

Transport from Paradise (adapted from *Night and Hope*), Studio Barrandov (Prague, Czechoslovakia), 1963.

Diamonds of the Night (adapted from *Darkness Casts No Shadow*), Studio Barrandov (Prague, Czechoslovakia), 1964.

Dita Saxova, Studio Barrandov (Prague, Czechoslovakia), 1968.

TELEPLAYS

The Blue Day, T.V. Prague, 1960.

A Prayer for Katerina Horovitzova, T.V. Prague, 1965.

(With Ernest Pendrell) *Terezin,* American Broadcasting Companies (ABC-TV), 1965.

Stolen Childhood, TV-Rome, 1966.

OTHER

Author of the novel *Vrásné zelené vci,* Peron Publishers (Prague, Czechoslovakia); of the short filmscript *Bit to Eat,* 1962; of text for Otmar Macha's symphonic poem, "Night and Hope," 1961, and of texts for cantatas, "The Beadl from Prague," 1984, "Precious Legacy," 1984, and "The Street of Lost Brothers," 1991; of radio scripts for Radio Prague, including *Prague Crossroads,* 1966, and *A Man the Size of a Postage Stamp,* 1967; and of commentary to documentary *The Triumph of Memory,* 1989. Editor, *Mlady svet* (magazine),

1958-60. Participated in a documentary film *Fighter,* 2000.

Lustig's works have been translated into more than twenty languages, including German, Spanish, Japanese, Polish, Hebrew, Hindi, Esperanto, French, Estonian, Italian, Norwegian, and Yiddish.

SIDELIGHTS: According to Johanna Kaplan in the *New York Times Book Review,* Czech author Arnost Lustig is "the too-little-known author of over half a dozen works of fiction," including the critically acclaimed *A Prayer for Katerina Horovitzova,* which was nominated for a National Book Award in 1974. *Dita Saxova* and *The Unloved: From the Diary of Perla S.,* both won Lustig the National Jewish Book Award in addition to the honors he had garnered for film and television scripts. Elizabeth Kastor, writing in the *Washington Post* pronounced the author's body of work "grim fables of concentration camps and World War II," yet noted that Lustig's friends consider the survivor of Theresienstadt, Auschwitz, and Buchenwald an optimist. This optimism is one of the qualities that has distinguished Lustig among writers of Holocaust literature; a writer for the *Los Angeles Times Book Review* asserted that "in Arnost Lustig's works, it's the courage, dignity and bravery of characters in the foreground that one remembers." Discussing the nature of Lustig's characters in the *Washington Post Book World,* Curt Leviant commented that "under the sentence of death, his people freeze time, preserve [decency]. They luminesce like light crystals in the dark."

Lustig once told *CA:* "Every writer has a duty to be as good as he can as a writer, to tell stories he likes in the best way he can. . . . I like stories about brave people, about how they survived under the worst circumstances. I like people who are fighting for their fate, and who are better in the end, richer, in a sense, than they were in the beginning. I think that each writer has a certain duty—to imagine himself in theory as perhaps the last human being alive under certain circumstances and that perhaps his testimony will be the last one. He is obliged to deliver that testimony."

Lustig's novels and stories often deliver the testimony of the Holocaust's arguably saddest victims: children—usually adolescent girls—who, unlike their creator, do not survive the camps. According to Kastor, the "bleak, hallucinatory *Darkness Casts No Shadow*" is Lustig's "most autobiographical book," the story of two young boys who briefly escape their fate during a train wreck on their way to being transferred from one camp to the next. The similarity to Lustig's own experience ends with the boys' eventual recapture and death. Kaplan called the novel "a harsh, suspenseful anti-fairy tale . . . [that] must surely be counted a hidden classic."

Dita Saxova is the story of a young survivor of Nazi death camps who tries to come to grips with living, after having expected to die for so long. Stephen Goodwin, writing in the *Washington Post,* called the book "a meditative novel." Though Goodwin admitted that he often found Dita's thoughts difficult to follow and often too much like Lustig's, he said that "when Dita's voice does sound, there is no mistaking its ring of truth, [wisdom] and felt experience. At such moments I don't have to understand Dita; she is mysterious and she is real, and I have only to listen." Goodwin's criticism of what Kastor termed the "elliptical puzzle" of Lustig's writing is not uncommon; *Los Angeles Times* book critic Richard Eder expressed a similar opinion about the writing in *The Unloved.* In defense of Lustig's style, Kastor asserted that "the confusion is endemic to the material: With a subject like Lustig's, narrative sense cannot always be maintained."

A Prayer for Katerina Horovitzova concerns another young woman thrust into the Holocaust. Katerina is a nineteen-year-old Polish dancer who becomes embroiled in a scheme to escape the fate of being sent to a concentration camp. Soon it becomes apparent that her rescuers are really only after the money of the captives and have no intention of sparing them or her from the atrocities of the death camps. Jasper Rees of the London *Times* maintained that the story "has the hard and fast simplicity of a parable." Furthermore, Rees continued, "The world Lustig has recreated is a pure vision of the inferno." Lustig's worlds often evoke hellish imagery. Joseph Coates, critic for the Chicago *Tribune Books,* wrote of Lustig's collection of stories *Street of Lost Brothers:* "It is Lustig's achievement not merely to bring the reader into the various special hells of the Holocaust but also to make them seem commonplace, as indeed they were and are to those who inhabit them."

Lustig's *The Unloved* is the testimony of a seventeen-year-old girl imprisoned at Theresienstadt who sells her body for whatever small tokens the prisoners can amass. Ursula Hegi said in the *New York Times Book Review* that Lustig "has written a stunning and unsentimental novel, celebrating moments of normality amid corruption and death." Jonathan Brent of the Chicago *Tribune Books* declared that "Perla's diary is a dreamily erotic, desultory record of [the] process of inward brutalization." He described *The Unloved* as "an eloquent and moving testament to the enduring worth of the individual and the inexhaustible human need to realize this worth in action."

The protagonist of each of the three novellas in *Indecent Dreams* is again a young woman; according to Richard Lourie in the *Washington Post Book World,* "the tales are also strongly united by their structure and atmosphere. In each a mood is built, gathering like a storm, and only in the final moments is that energy discharged in the lightning of violence." Kaplan summarized the artistry of Lustig's work as a whole: "A world so entirely bound by suffering can be painful to enter, but Mr. Lustig, searching out a code of honor in this most defiled, inhuman sphere, has come upon a maximalist human canvas. His view is oddly invigorating and his work invites a maximal audience: it will quarrel, it will recognize, it will marvel and yes, of course, sometimes it will have to look away."

Lustig had been a prominent writer in Prague, in the former Czechoslovakia, before the Soviet invasion of 1968. As he once told *CA:* "Once everything was lost, when the country was invaded, I was declared by the last congress of the Communist party an 'enemy of the state,' and an 'imperialist agent,' a 'Zionist.' They said all my books and films were paid for by some world conspiracy." When conditions in Czechoslovakia became intolerable and writing was no longer possible, Lustig and his family moved to the United States in an effort "to be outside and keep writing, and to be free, and to keep some hope."

BIOGRAPHICAL/CRITICAL SOURCES:

PERIODICALS

Best Sellers, October 15, 1973.
Booklist, November 1, 1973.
Choice, fall, 1974.
Kirkus Reviews, August 1, 1973.
Los Angeles Times, October 23, 1985.
Los Angeles Times Book Review, December 29, 1985, p. 9.
New York Times Book Review, October 21, 1973; March 18, 1979, p. 21; January 19, 1986, p. 20; June 19, 1988, p. 1; July 22, 1990, p. 32.
Proteus, spring, 1974.
Publishers Weekly, February 21, 1977; March 13, 1987.
Southwest Review, winter, 1974.
Times (London, England), November 1, 1990, Jasper Rees, review of *A Prayer for Katerina Horovitzova.*
Tribune Books (Chicago, IL), November 24, 1985, p. 40; December 16, 1990, p. 3.
Washingtonian, May, 1977.

Washington Post, January 11, 1980; August 9, 1988.
Washington Post Book World, June 12, 1977, p. 1; January 12, 1986, p. 10; June 19, 1988, p. 10.*

M

MacCARTHY, Fiona 1940-

PERSONAL: Born January 23, 1940, in London, England; daughter of Gerald (an army officer) and Yolande (de Belabre) MacCarthy; married David Mellor (a designer), August 19, 1966; children: Corin, Clare. *Education:* Oxford University, M.A., 1961.

ADDRESSES: Home and Office—The Round Building, Hathersage, Sheffield, Yorkshire S32 1BA, England.

CAREER: Guardian, London, England, features writer, 1963-69; *Evening Standard,* London, England, features writer, 1969-72; freelance writer, 1972—; *Times,* London, England, reviewer of books, 1981-92; *Observer,* London, England, reviewer of books, 1992—.

AWARDS, HONORS: Royal Society of Arts Bicentennial Medal, 1987; honorary fellowship, Royal College of Art, 1990; D.Litt., University of Sheffield, 1996; senior fellowship, Royal College of Art, 1997; fellow, Royal Society of Literature, 1997.

WRITINGS:

All Things Bright and Beautiful: Design in Britain, University of California Press (Santa Cruz, CA), 1972.
A History of British Design: 1830 to Today, Allen & Unwin (London, England), 1979.
The Simple Life: C. R. Ashbee in the Cotswolds, University of California Press, 1981.
The British Tradition in Design: From 1880, Humphries (London, England), 1981.
British Design since 1880: A Visual History, Humphries (London, England), 1982.
(Author of introduction and cataloguer) *The Omega Workshops,* [London, England], 1984.

(Author of introduction and cataloguer, with Patrick Nuttgens) *Eye for Industry: Royal Designers for Industry, 1936-1986,* Humphries/Royal Society of Arts, 1986.
Eric Gill: A Lover's Quest for Art and God, Dutton (New York, NY), 1989, published as *Eric Gill,* Faber and Faber (London, England), 1989.
William Morris: A Life for Our Time, Faber and Faber (London, England), 1994, Knopf (New York, NY), 1995.
Telling the Tale of Topsy: William Morris's Biographers: The 1993 Kelmscott Lecture, William Morris Society, 1996.
Stanley Spencer, Yale University Press (New Haven, CT), 1997.

WORK IN PROGRESS: "A new biography of Lord Byron," for John Murray (London, England) and Farrar, Straus (New York, NY), 2002.

SIDELIGHTS: Fiona MacCarthy told *CA:* "For a century or more, from William Morris onwards, there has been an easily identifiable strain in society in Britain concerned with the improvement of the objects which we use and live with. This movement for reform has, through the years, developed certain ideas on the designer's social role as well as recognizable criteria on aesthetics.

"The intensely idealistic early twentieth-century phase of British design history especially fascinates me. This was the background to my book on C. R. Ashbee, arts and crafts architect and designer, and friend of Frank Lloyd Wright. This was a subject that aroused great public interest: the search for the ideal of a creative life is very much still with us. I have since then developed the theme in two much larger scale biographies of Eric

Gill and William Morris, whose ideas about proper human occupation and the relation of art to society are of immense importance to us now. I like to write about *big* subjects, enjoying the challenge of providing a readable, accessible narrative from a mountain of research."

BIOGRAPHICAL/CRITICAL SOURCES:

PERIODICALS

New York Times Book Review, May 7, 1989, p. 11.
Times (London, England), April 23, 1980; April 29, 1982; January 26, 1989; March 13, 1989; November 10, 1994.
Times Literary Supplement, November 9, 1984, p. 1280; February 17-23, 1989, p. 160; November 25, 1994, p. 3.
Washington Post Book World, April 9, 1989, p. 3.

*   *   *

MACU, Pavel
   See MAGOCSI, Paul Robert

*   *   *

MAGOCSI, Paul Robert   1945-
   (Pavel Macu, Philip Michaels)

PERSONAL: Surname is pronounced "*Ma*-go-chee"; born January 26, 1945, in Englewood, NJ; son of Alexander B. (a printer and proofreader) and Anna (a caterer; maiden name, Lengyel) Magocsi; married, wife's name, Maria (a professional dancer), 1971; children: Cindy, Danik, Natalie. *Ethnicity:* "Carpatho-Rusyn." *Education:* Rutgers University, B.A., 1966, M.A., 1967; Princeton University, M.A., 1969, Ph.D., 1972. *Religion:* Protestant.

ADDRESSES: Home—424 Brunswick Ave., Toronto, Ontario, Canada M5R 2Z4. *Office*—Department of History, University of Toronto, Toronto, Ontario, Canada M5S 3G3; fax: 416-978-5566.

CAREER: Harvard University, Cambridge, MA, senior research fellow, 1971-80, lecturer, 1979-80; University of Toronto, Toronto, Ontario, professor of history, 1980—. Carpatho-Rusyn Research Center, president, 1978—; Hebrew University of Jerusalem, visiting pro-

fessor, 1989; Multicultural History Society of Ontario, chief executive officer and director, 1990-97.

MEMBER: American Association for the Advancement of Slavic Studies.

AWARDS, HONORS: Harvard University Society of Fellows, 1976; award from Yeshiva University, 1978; Bernard M. Fry Award from *Government Publications Review,* 1988, for the article "Are the Armenians Really Russians?—Or How the U.S. Census Bureau Classifies America's Ethnic Groups"; fellow, 1996, Royal Society of Canada.

WRITINGS:

Let's Speak Rusyn—Bisidujme po-rus'ky: Presov Region Edition, Transworld Publishers (Englewood, NJ), 1976.
The Shaping of a National Identity: Subcarpathian Rus', 1848-1948, Harvard University Press (Cambridge, MA), 1978.
Let's Speak Rusyn—Hovorim po-rus'ky: Transcarpathian Edition, Transworld Publishers (Fairview, NJ), 1979.
(Editor) *The Ukrainian Experience in the United States: A Symposium,* Ukrainian Research Institute, Harvard University (Cambridge, MA), 1979.
Wooden Churches in the Carpathians/Holzkirchen in der Karpaten: The Photographic Legacy of Florian Zapletal, Wilhelm Braumueller Universitats Verlag (Vienna, Austria), 1982.
The Rusyn-Ukrainians of Czechoslovakia: An Historical Survey, Wilhelm Braumueller Universitats Verlag (Vienna, Austria), 1983.
Galicia: A Historical Survey and Bibliographic Guide, University of Toronto Press (Toronto, Ontario, Canada), 1983.
Our People: Carpatho-Rusyns and Their Descendants in North America, Multicultural History Society of Ontario (Toronto, Ontario, Canada), 1984, 3rd revised edition, 1994.
Ukraine: A Historical Atlas (cartography by Geoffrey Matthews), University of Toronto Press (Toronto, Ontario, Canada), 1985.
Ucrainica in the University of Toronto Library: A Catalog of Holdings, two volumes, University of Toronto Press (Toronto, Ontario, Canada), 1985.
Carpatho-Rusyn Studies: An Annotated Bibliography, Volume 1: *1975-1984,* Garland Publishing (New York, NY), 1988.
The Russian Americans, Chelsea House (New York, NY), 1989.

(Editor) *Morality and Reality: The Life and Times of Andrei Sheptyts'kyi,* Canadian Institute of Ukrainian Studies (Edmonton, Alberta, Canada), 1989.

The Carpatho-Rusyn Americans, Chelsea House, 1989.

(Editor) *The Persistence of Regional Cultures: Rusyns and Ukrainians in Their Carpathian Homeland and Abroad,* Columbia University Press (New York, NY), 1993.

The Rusyns of Slovakia: An Historical Survey, Columbia University Press (New York, NY), 1993.

Historical Atlas of East Central Europe, University of Washington Press (Seattle, WA), 1993, second revised edition, 2001.

History of Ukraine, University of Toronto Press (Toronto, Ontario, Canada), 1996.

(Editor) *Encyclopedia of Canada's Peoples,* University of Toronto Press (Toronto, Ontario, Canada), 1999.

Of the Making of Nationalities There Is No End, two volumes, Columbia University Press (New York, NY), 1999.

Contributor of more than three hundred articles to scholarly journals. Some writings appear under the pseudonyms Pavel Macu and Philip Michaels.

WORK IN PROGRESS: Encyclopedia of Rusyn History and Culture.

*   *   *

MAHARIDGE, Dale (Dimitro) 1956-

PERSONAL: Born October 24, 1956, in Cleveland, OH; son of Steve (a toolmaker) and Joan (Kopfstein) Maharidge. *Education:* Attended Cleveland State University, 1974-76, and Cuyahoga Community College, 1976. *Politics:* Democrat. *Religion:* "None."

ADDRESSES: Office—Department of Communications, Stanford University, Building 120, Stanford, CA 94305-2050. *Agent*—Watkins/Loomis Agency, 133 East 35th St., New York, NY 10016. *E-mail*—maharidg@leland.stanford.edu.

CAREER: Machinery worker in Cleveland, OH, 1971-76; freelance writer, 1977; *Gazette,* Medina, OH, staff writer, 1977-78; freelance writer, 1978-80; *Sacramento Bee,* Sacramento, CA, journalist, 1980-91; Columbia University, New York, NY, assistant professor, 1991-92; Stanford University, Stanford, CA, lecturer, "Lokey" visiting professor; writer.

MEMBER: Sierra Club.

AWARDS, HONORS: San Francisco Press Club, first place award for feature articles, 1982 and 1987; United Press International, California-Nevada, award for best series, 1984; World Hunger Award, New York, NY, 1987; Lucius W. Nieman fellowship from Harvard University, 1988; Pulitzer Prize for general nonfiction, 1990, for *And Their Children after Them;* Pope Foundation award for mid-career achievement, 1994; Freedom Forum Professors' Publishing Program grant, 1995.

WRITINGS:

NONFICTION; WITH PHOTOGRAPHS BY MICHAEL WILLIAMSON

Journey to Nowhere: The Saga of the New Underclass, Dial/Doubleday, 1985, reissued with an introduction by Bruce Springsteen, Hyperion, 1996.

And Their Children after Them: The Legacy of "Let Us Now Praise Famous Men," James Agee, Walker Evans, and the Rise and Fall of Cotton in the South, foreword by Carl Mydans, Pantheon, 1989.

The Last Great American Hobo, Prima, 1993.

The Coming White Minority: California, Multiculturalism, and America's Future, Times Books, 1996, revised edition, Vintage Books, 1999.

OTHER

Yosemite: A Landscape of Life, photographs by Jay Mather, Yosemite Association/Sacramento Bee, 1990.

Contributor to periodicals, including *California Journal, Cleveland Press, Cleveland Plain Dealer, Elyria Chronicle Telegram, George, Mother Jones, Nation, New York Times,* and *Rolling Stone.*

WORK IN PROGRESS: Several movie projects in development. Working on a novel about blue-collar life, involving factory workers in Cleveland and a nearby fictional city involved in a violent steel mill strike. This will be a "social novel" that speaks to contemporary issues as well as an autobiographical work.

SIDELIGHTS: Dale Maharidge is a prize-winning journalist who is probably best known for his books on America's underprivileged, several of which he produced in collaboration with *Sacramento Bee* co-worker and photographer Michael Williamson. First among these publications is *Journey to Nowhere: The Saga of the New Underclass.* This volume concerns contemporary hobos, many of whom sleep under freeway overpasses and travel by hopping aboard moving trains. In researching *Journey to Nowhere,* Maharidge and Williamson spent six months over a three-year period consorting with hobos, even enduring the same hardships. "We realized early on that maybe we had been stupid," Williamson later conceded to *Chicago Tribune* columnist Bob Greene. "There the two of us were, living in these freight cars in the middle of the country, and there were a lot of thoughts of the office and of home." Williamson added, though, that the research was worthwhile. "The exuberance of covering a story like that is so intense," he told Greene. "We knew that we had probably found the best economic story in the country." Upon publication in 1985, *Journey to Nowhere* was hailed by Bert Atkinson in the *New York Times Book Review* as a work of "sensitivity, grace and power."

Maharidge and Williamson followed *Journey to Nowhere* with *And Their Children after Them: The Legacy of "Let Us Now Praise Famous Men," James Agee, Walker Evans, and the Rise and Fall of Cotton in the South.* This work focuses on the descendants of the cotton farmers depicted in Agee and Evans' classic document of life in the Deep South during the Depression. Jonathan Yardley, writing in the *Washington Post Book World,* affirmed that *And Their Children after Them* held "few surprises" and that the book delineates the manner by which the increased development of farming machinery had diminished livelihood of tenant farmers. Yardley was unimpressed with Maharidge's text, however, contending, "Maharidge's sympathy for these people is admirable, but the prose in which he pays tribute to them is not."

Reviewer Ronald B. Taylor, writing in the *Los Angeles Times Book Review,* also provided a somewhat mixed assessment. He conceded that *And Their Children after Them* "leave[s] us a bit wiser perhaps, but wishing for a more unified work with a thoughtful ending." Taylor was favorably inclined, though, toward Maharidge's "straightforward" journalism, particularly as it applied to his portrayal of the destitution of these families, including the Ricketts. Comparing *And Their Children after Them* to the earlier *Let Us Now Praise Famous Men,* Taylor affirmed, "Maharidge digs much deeper into the degradation of the Ricketts family."

Joseph Coates, writing in Chicago *Tribune Books,* provided a more enthusiastic assessment of *And Their Children after Them.* He compared the volume to Agee and Evans' earlier work and determined that Maharidge and Williamson had produced "a companion volume that is as strong in its own way (though more conventional), fully as compassionate, and, to all appearances,

a better job of reporting." Coates found that *And Their Children after Them* "widens the scope of the earlier book," and he observed that Maharidge and Williamson had succeeded in producing "both a multigenerational, documentary saga and an expose."

Another supporter of *And Their Children after Them* was the *New York Times*'s Herbert Mitgang, who proclaimed that the Maharidge-Williamson work "reaches into this country's heart of darkness." Mitgang acknowledged that *And Their Children after Them* "says a good deal about America's poor and lower middle class," and he added, "it is a tragically human story more telling than a thousand polls."

In 1991 Maharidge left the *Sacramento Bee,* where he had worked since 1980. He spent a year teaching in the Graduate School of Journalism at Columbia University in New York City, and in 1992 he accepted the post of visiting Chandler Chair lecturer at Stanford University, teaching courses in journalism, social issues, and magazine writing. In 1993 Maharidge and Williamson once again joined forces to produce *The Last Great American Hobo,* their third volume of collaborative work focusing on issues of poverty in the United States.

Maharidge published *The Coming White Minority: California, Multiculturalism, and America's Future* in 1996, and a revised edition in 1999. In his book, Maharidge addresses the fact that some time after 2050, the United States population will be less than half white. California has already experienced this cultural shift, and Maharidge centers the book around four Californians—Latino, black, white, and Asian—using their lives as a platform to discuss life in a truly multicultural society. In 1996, *Journey to Nowhere* was reissued, with an introduction by Bruce Springsteen. Springsteen had read *Journey to Nowhere,* and the book served as inspiration for two songs, "Youngstown" and "New Timer," on Springsteen's 1995 album *The Ghost of Tom Joad.*

Maharidge told *CA:* "In my poverty books, I've practiced what I call 'documentary journalism,' which means I like to get close to those I write about, and then translate their world to the reader. (If you are not close enough to hurt with those you document, you've not gotten close enough.) For *Journey to Nowhere,* Michael Williamson and I spent six months, over the course of three years, riding freight trains, camping under bridges, living on the road.

"As far as I've been able to determine, *Journey to Nowhere* was the first contemporary book on the homeless. A database search shows almost two hundred other 'homeless' books followed ours. Of those that I've seen, all are failures, including our book. *Journey to Nowhere* had both positive and negative reviews, but none were entirely correct. The truth was off to the side. That book, done in youthful naiveté, was successful in that we showed cause and effect, how people become homeless. But the failure was one of moral realism. We 'canonized' poverty. We didn't show the full range of the human condition, just the parts that made the reader feel sorrow for our subjects.

"That was the start of a decade-long quest of what became a trilogy of books on poverty, as we sought not only moral realism but to have an impact on social conditions that appalled us. In *And Their Children after Them,* we looked at old poverty, but still felt we had more to learn and say. That led us to *The Last Great American Hobo,* the book I am most proud of, the one that had the least media attention. It's impossible to explain in a short space, but we were able to get closest to an understanding about poverty in this story about a nearly eighty-year-old hobo who had been riding the rails since the Great Depression.

"Perhaps, however, one can never understand. All I know is that each book took a chunk out of our lives. One sets out to educate Americans about poverty in the hope that in some small way, conditions will be changed. Then comes the realization that people don't seem to care. This, along with the horror of the lives one documents, takes a toll. I can't speak for Michael, but I plan to never again write a nonfiction book about poverty. Ultimately, it's not the bitterness that makes me say this, but the fact that I have said all I can say."

Maharidge told *CA* later, "Within days after writing the preceding five years ago, and sending it off to *CA,* the phone rang with a call from someone working for Bruce Springsteen. Bruce, I was told, had used *Journey to Nowhere* as inspiration for two songs on the *Ghost of Tom Joad* release: 'New Timer,' and 'Youngstown.'

"Michael Williamson and I met with Bruce and he was immensely supportive. Bruce told us he bought the book many years earlier, and pulled it off his shelf one sleepless night, inspiring him. He asked what he could do to get our book back in print. He agreed to write an introduction, and despite my fears of reimmersing in the world of poverty, Michael and I again hit the road, retracing our own footsteps for an update.

"In Youngstown, we talked to the same disenfranchised former steelworkers—the ones who were not prema-

turely dead from suicide or depression-related health problems. We met with the few remaining active steelworkers, who had just endured a bitter strike. One of them gave us a bomb left from their arsenal. We went across the nation, walking the same hobo jungles. It was one of the hardest things I have ever done. What stunned us was the increase in the numbers of people on the street, in supposed good times. We had a form of closure with the project, when at the end of that trip, we exploded the steelworker's bomb on an empty portion of old Route 66 in California.

"Having Bruce Springsteen interpret our work was a wonderful experience. In a few dozen words, he captured what took me a third of a book to explain, about the horror of Youngstown. The experience taught me a very important thing as an author: you never know who is reading your work. A book like *Journey,* which had less than spectacular sales during both of its press runs, can have impact far beyond publication, that the dead bones of your baby can be resurrected and live again. As Bruce and the E Street Band now perform the rocking version of 'Youngstown,' many thousands of fans are being exposed to something they otherwise might not hear about, even if they never find out about the original book. Truly, this exhibits the power of an idea, morphing from one art form to another.

"Then I spent the 1990s working on a different kind of social non-fiction—race and class. *The Coming White Minority* is about California now being a white minority society, mirroring what will (in not too many decades) happen to the nation. I did not take a left or right stance: I took a realistic position. Too many of these kinds of books are reactionary. I focused on four people and their families, from the major racial backgrounds, and how they are living their lives in this changed culture. My overriding goal was to show how this new society can and must work. There is no alternative."

BIOGRAPHICAL/CRITICAL SOURCES:

PERIODICALS

Chicago Tribune, May 14, 1985.
Los Angeles Times Book Review, May 5, 1985, p. 1; July 2, 1989, p. 8.
News Photographer, June, 1985.
New York Times, June 17, 1989, Herbert Mitgang, review of review of *And Their Children after Them: The Legacy of "Let Us Now Praise Famous Men," James Agee, Walker Evans, and the Rise and Fall of Cotton in the South,* p 13L.

New York Times Book Review, March 17, 1985, Bert Atkinson, *Journey to Nowhere: The Saga of the New Underclass,* p 26.

Tribune Books (Chicago, IL), April 30, 1989, pp. 1, 4.

Village Voice, August 29, 1989.

Washington Post, April 13, 1990.

Washington Post Book World, May 14, 1989, Jonathan Yardley, review of *And Their Children after Them,* p. 3.

West Coast Review of Books, January, 1989.*

*　　*　　*

MAINWARING, Marion

PERSONAL: Born in Boston, MA; daughter of Herbert James and Marion (Imrie) Mainwaring. *Education:* Simmons College, B.S., 1943; Radcliffe College, Ph.D., 1949.

ADDRESSES: Agent—c/o University Press of New England, 23 South Main St., Hanover, NH 03755-2055.

CAREER: Harvard University, Cambridge, MA, tutor and teaching fellow, 1947-49; Mount Holyoke College, South Hadley, MA, instructor in English, 1949-52; Houghton Mifflin Co., Boston, MA, reader and editor in Boston, MA, and London, England, 1958—; freelance writer. Newspaper correspondent in the Balkans, 1962-63; foreign research editor for the Adams Papers, Harvard University Press and Massachusetts Historical Society, 1964-65; survey director, Massachusetts Council on the Arts and Humanities, 1967; foreign correspondent in Paris, France, and Athens, Greece, for *Boston Herald-Traveler,* 1968—; translator and writer, UNESCO, Paris, 1972—.

WRITINGS:

Murder at Midyears, Macmillan (New York, NY), 1953.

Murder in Pastiche, Macmillan (New York, NY), 1954, reprinted as *Murder in Pastiche: Or, Nine Detectives All at Sea,* Rowan Tree (Boston, MA), 1989.

John Quincy Adams and Russia: A Sketch of Early Russian-American Relations, Quincy *Patriot Ledger* (Quincy, MA), 1965.

(Translator) Ivan Turgenev, *Youth and Age: Three Short Novels by Turgenev,* Hart-Davis (London, England), 1968, Farrar, Straus (New York, NY), 1969.

Cultural Needs and Cultural Resources of the Commonwealth of Massachusetts, Commonwealth of Massachusetts, 1968.

(Editor and translator) Ivan Turgenev, *The Portrait Game,* Chatto & Windus (London, England), 1973, Horizon Press (New York, NY), 1974.

(Author of portion of manuscript) Edith Wharton, *The Buccaneers: A Novel,* Viking (New York, NY), 1993.

Mysteries of Paris: The Quest for Morton Fullerton, University Press of New England (Hanover, NH), 2000.

Contributor to popular magazines and academic journals. Editor, 125th anniversary edition of the *Patriot Ledger,* Quincy, MA, 1962.

SIDELIGHTS: Marion Mainwaring combined her skills as a fiction writer and scholar to complete *The Buccaneers,* a novel by Edith Wharton that was left unfinished at Wharton's death. Although an edition of *The Buccaneers* was published in the 1930s, the work had never been completed. Armed with Wharton's outline and a wealth of knowledge about the celebrated writer, Mainwaring not only completed the story but also delicately revised Wharton's prose throughout the text. "This new *Buccaneers* may not be the novel Wharton herself would have written, but it is certainly a lively, engaging piece of fiction, and its fascination is only enhanced by the peculiar collaboration that engendered it," declared Wendy Steiner in the *New York Times Book Review.* Steiner went on to praise Mainwaring's "fearless ventriloquism" in a "fairy-tale novel, miraculously returned to life." *New Republic* contributor Andrew Delbanco took exception to the project, calling it "a pastiche—the larger part composed by a writer devoted to precision and rhetorical tact, the smaller part by a writer whose ear is uncertain and who cannot leave the original work alone." Conversely, a *Publishers Weekly* reviewer felt that the novel "is so smooth and so assured that [the collaboration] will likely go undetected by the reader."

Mainwaring's research for *The Buccaneers* and other Wharton projects led her to develop an interest in Morton Fullerton, an expatriate American with whom Wharton carried on an extramarital affair at mid-life. *Mysteries of Paris: The Quest for Morton Fullerton* offers a biography of Fullerton, as well as a commentary on Mainwaring's obsession with uncovering the truth about the man. Indeed, Fullerton was found to be an outrageous scoundrel by the standards of his time, although he was a close associate not only of Wharton but also of Henry James. In his *Library Journal* review of *Mysteries of Paris,* Robert L. Kelly noted that the work "displays an interesting style . . . in revealing [Mainwaring's] meticulous research." A *Kirkus* reviewer concluded: "As a double character study and tale of hands-on archival research, this is . . . fascinating stuff."

BIOGRAPHICAL/CRITICAL SOURCES:

PERIODICALS

Atlantic, October, 1993, Phoebe-Lou Adams, review of *The Buccaneers,* p. 131.

Booklist, December 15, 2000, Mary Carroll, review of *Mysteries of Paris: The Quest for Morton Fullerton,* p. 781.

Christian Science Monitor, March 4, 1968.

Kirkus Reviews, December 15, 2000, review of *Mysteries of Paris: The Quest for Morton Fullerton,* p. 1743.

Library Journal, December, 2000, Robert L. Kelly, review of *Mysteries of Paris: The Quest for Morton Fullerton,* p. 132.

National Observer, September 1, 1969.

New Republic, October 25, 1993, Andrew Delbanco, review of *The Buccaneers,* p. 31.

New Statesman, May 25, 1973.

New York Herald Tribune Book Review, October 25, 1953; August 15, 1954.

New York Times, August 15, 1954.

New York Times Book Review, October 17, 1993, Wendy Steiner, "Finishing Off Edith Wharton," p. 7.

Publishers Weekly, May 24, 1993, Elizabeth Devereaux, "Austen's First, Wharton's Last," p. 44; June 28, 1993, review of *The Buccaneers,* p. 57.

Times Literary Supplement, August 10, 1968.

Washington Post, November 25, 1973.*

*　　*　　*

MALONE, Hank 1940-

PERSONAL: Born May 5, 1940, in Detroit, MI; son of Charles J. (a mechanical engineer) and Helen (a hospital administrator; maiden name, Waselewski) Malone; married Anita Rodman, 1962 (divorced, 1973); married E. Sharon Kissane, April 25, 1981; children: Alex Scott. *Education:* B.A. (English); Wayne State University, B.A. (philosophy), 1962; M.S.W. (clinical social work); M.S.W. (community organization). *Avocational interests:* "Astronomy, travel, politics, jazz, photography, books, mid-century furniture, archaeology."

ADDRESSES: Home and Office—1220 J Nakomis Dr., N.E., Albuquerque, NM 87112. *E-mail*—hanksharon@ aol.com.

CAREER: Department of Social Work and Urban Studies, Wayne State University, Detroit, MI, part-time faculty member, 1967-71; American Broadcasting Company, Southfield, MI, talk-radio host, 1970-74; Department of Mental Health, City of Highland Park, Highland Park, MI, director, 1976-85; Metrotag, P.C., Livonia, MI, clinical psychotherapist, 1985-95. *Military service:* Army Reserves, 1957-61.

MEMBER: Poetry Society of America, New England Poetry Club, MENSA.

AWARDS, HONORS: Grant, National Endowment for the Arts, 1966; grant, American Academy of Arts, 1967; nominated for the Pushcart Prize, 1986.

WRITINGS:

Survival, Evasion, and Escape: Poems, La Jolla Poets' Press (La Jolla, CA), 1985.

Footstrikes and Spondees: Poems, Parkville (Utica, MI), 1993.

New Mexico Haiku (poems), Poetic License Press (Westland, MI), 1995.

Experiencing New Mexico (essays), Poetic License Press (Westland, MI), 1998.

James Dickey—On the Eve of the Millennium (poems), Poetic License Press (Westland, MI), 1999.

WORK IN PROGRESS: The Science Hipsters, "a nonfiction prose memoir of 1950's adolescence," expected completion, fall 2001.

SIDELIGHTS: Hank Malone told *CA:* "I've been writing on and off, more or less continuously since age ten, starting with short science fiction tales. My motives have changed somewhat since then, yet maybe they really haven't.

"Writing has always been a place I could curl up to, alone, and yet be with everything in the world of my imagination. I bring everything to writing—my politics, my humor, my passion, my rage, my fumbling, and my sense of the surreal. Frequently the stews I brew of all this satisfies me.

"Much of my writing has a definite social conscience at work, and sometimes a moralism I must take care to rein in. Someone said I write with a 'sociological imagination' haunting my lines.

"Writers who continue as a regular presence in my life include Camus, Kenneth Patchen, Jim Dickey and Charles, as well as Edward Abbey, Neruda, and surely one of the most neglected novelists of current fiction, Sam Astrachan, who is grappling always with great themes, large and complex ideas. He is an American writer who lives and writes in France. I am a first generation American. I seem always drawn to the best work of exiles, and first-generation Americans.

"I tend to write daily, if only jotting in this or that journal, mostly short prose, poetry, aphorisms. I am a night writer. When I sit down, I am always writing with pen on a pad of paper, . . . no first-draft computer-writing for me. . . . I am usually in the work for a couple of hours. When I have no large projects moving, I find myself dashing off haiku. I can write a string of haiku, thirty or forty at a time, in a kind of surreal subterranean glaze.

"I am far more interested in people than the other works of nature, like oceans or mountains. People are far more crazy and wicked than mountains, but they yield so much more intrigue, and sometimes they yield great victories.

"I am political and yet, my work is without doctrine. Sometimes I pull the monumental, with luck, out of the details of everyday life. One poem starts with an estate sale, for instance, and ends up at the tip of the Milky Way galaxy."

*   *   *

Greil Marcus

MARCUS, Greil (Gerstley) 1945-

PERSONAL: Born June 19, 1945, in San Francisco, CA; son of Gerald Dodd (an attorney) and Eleanore (a homemaker; maiden name, Hyman) Marcus; married Jenelle Bernstein (a shopkeeper), June 26, 1966; children: Emily Rose, Cecily Helen. *Education:* University of California at Berkeley, B.A., 1966, M.A., 1967. *Avocational interests:* Paleolithic culture.

ADDRESSES: Office—c/o Author Mail, Henry Holt & Co., 115 West 18th St., New York, NY 10011. *Agent*—Wendy Weil Agency, 232 Madison Ave., New York, NY 10016.

CAREER: Author and critic. *Rolling Stone,* San Francisco, CA, associate editor, 1969-70, book editor, 1975-80. Teacher of American studies at University of California at Berkeley, 1971-72. Director of Pagnol & Cie, operators of Chez Panisse restaurant, Berkeley, CA, 1979—.

MEMBER: National Book Critics Circle (director, 1983-89).

AWARDS, HONORS: Nominated for National Book Critics Circle Award for criticism, 1976, for *Mystery Train: Images of America in Rock 'n' Roll Music.*

WRITINGS:

(With Jan Hodenfield and Andrew Kopkind) *Woodstock,* photographs by Baron Wolman, Joseph Sia, and Mark Vargas, Straight Arrow Publishers, 1969.

(Editor) *Rock and Roll Will Stand* (essays), Beacon Press (Boston, MA), 1969.

(With Michael Goodwin) *Double Feature: Movies and Politics,* Outerbridge & Lazard, 1972.

Mystery Train: Images of America in Rock 'n' Roll Music, Dutton (New York, NY), 1975, revised 4th edition, Plume (New York, NY), 1997.

(Contributor) Jim Miller, editor, *The Rolling Stone Illustrated History of Rock and Roll,* Random House (New York, NY), 1976, revised edition, 1980.

(Editor) *Stranded: Rock and Roll for a Desert Island* (essays), Knopf (New York, NY), 1979, revised edition with foreword by Robert Christgau, Da Capo Press (New York, NY), 1996.

(Editor) Lester Bangs, *Psychotic Reactions and Carburetor Dung,* Knopf (New York, NY), 1987.

Lipstick Traces: A Secret History of the Twentieth Century, Harvard University Press (Cambridge, MA), 1989.

Dead Elvis: A Chronicle of a Cultural Obsession, Doubleday (New York, NY), 1991.

Ranters and Crowd Pleasers: Punk in Pop Music, Doubleday (New York, NY), 1993, published as *In the Fascist Bathroom: Writings on Punk, 1977-1992,* Penguin (New York, NY), 1994.

The Dustbin of History, Harvard University Press (Cambridge, MA), 1995.

Invisible Republic: Bob Dylan's Basement Tapes, Holt (New York, NY), 1997, published as *The Old, Weird America: The World of Bob Dylan's Basement Tapes,* Picator (New York, NY), 2001.

Double Trouble: Bill Clinton and Elvis Presley in a Land of No Alternatives, Holt (New York, NY), 2000.

There Is No Eye: John Cohen Photographs, Power-House (New York, NY), 2001.

(Contributor) Ahmet Ertegun and others, *"What'd I Say": The Atlantic Story; Fifty Years of Music,* Welcome Rain, 2001.

Author of biweekly column "Undercover" for *Rolling Stone,* 1975-80; author of monthly columns "Real Life Rock" for *New West Magazine,* 1978-82, and *Music Magazine* (Tokyo, Japan), 1978-73, "Speaker to Speaker" for *Artforum,* 1983-87, and "Real Life Rock Top Ten" for *Village Voice,* 1989-90, *Artforum,* 1990-97, and *Salon.com,* 1999—. Contributor of essays and criticism on music, film, books, and politics to periodicals, including *Creem, Rolling Stone, New York Times, New York Times Book Review, Los Angeles Times, Newsday, New Musical Express, Village Voice, New Yorker, Journal of Country Music,* and *TriQuarterly.*

SIDELIGHTS: Greil Marcus is one of the most highly regarded writers on rock and roll music. Since beginning his career as an editor of the popular music magazine *Rolling Stone,* Marcus has written articles and reviews on music, books, politics, and other subjects for several leading publications. His work has appeared, for example, in the *New York Times, New Yorker, Creem,* and *Newsday,* and he has been a columnist for *New West Magazine, Artforum,* and the *Village Voice.* In addition, he has contributed essays to books, including *The Rolling Stone Illustrated History of Rock and Roll,* and has written and edited numerous books of his own. *Mystery Train: Images of America in Rock 'n' Roll Music,* which was nominated for a National Book Critics Circle award and drew international attention, has been widely praised as one of the most important rock and roll books ever written. As Marcus's career has progressed, his work has evolved from simple music criticism to true cultural commentary, exemplified in his book *Double Trouble: Bill Clinton and Elvis Presley in the Land of No Alternatives.*

Marcus begins *Mystery Train* with short essays on two "ancestors" of rock and roll, 1950s singer Harmonica Frank and 1930s bluesman Robert Johnson, that serve as a "backdrop," as Marcus explains, for the text that follows. Mark Crispin Miller of the *New York Review of Books* noted that, for Marcus, Harmonica Frank personifies what was to become the exuberant side of rock and roll, while Johnson represents an alternative, horror-filled, Puritan element in the music. After painting this backdrop, Marcus divides his discussion of America and its music into four chapters, each of which focuses on, but is not limited to, a performer or group whose work or career exhibits, Marcus suggests, " 'a range and a depth that seem to crystalize naturally in visions and versions of America: its possibilities, limits, openings, traps.' "

Marcus first presents chapters on such musicians as the Band, Sly Stone, and Randy Newman. Marcus then turns to "the knockout section of the book," as Frank Rich, writing in the *Village Voice,* described the book's longest chapter—the "Presliad," which concerns Elvis Presley. Rich asserted that the writing in this section "reaches a pitch of ecstasy, horror, and understanding that diminishes the prose of the book's previous chapters as effectively as Elvis diminishes the subjects of those chapters."

Rich judged the writing to be "forceful, enthusiastic, almost driven" throughout *Mystery Train.* He and Miller both deemed the book "brilliant" in places; Miller called it "impressive . . . well-informed, and frequently hilarious" and found "more of rock's spirit" in *Mystery Train* than in rock music itself. John Rockwell of the *New York Times* called Marcus "a writer of rare perception and a genuinely innovative thinker" and concluded that Marcus's "blend of love and expertise should be read by anybody who cares about America or its music."

Marcus's next book, *Stranded: Rock and Roll for a Desert Island,* is a collection of essays that respond to a question he poses: If you were stranded on a desert island, what is the one record album you would want to have with you? Respondents include rock writers Dave Marsh, Grace Lichtenstein, Ellen Willis, Robert Christgau, Simon Frith, Ed Ward, and others. Marcus himself admits that the premise is "absurd," but Laurence Gonzales of the *New York Times Book Review* found the essays to be "by turns thoughtful, compelling, sexy, hilarious, quirky—and surprisingly true to the basic impulse of rock-and-roll."

Marcus probes the political significance of various countercultural movements in *Lipstick Traces: A Secret History of the Twentieth Century.* The book "is no sedate academic record of libertarian revolt but a bold blending of anecdote, personal confession and cultural analysis, cutting backward and forward from Sid Vicious of the Sex Pistols to the Surrealists," advised *New York Times Book Review* contributor Terry Eagleton. "Treading a precarious line between eleoquence and pretentiousness . . . [the] book is impressively adept at bringing alive some of the dramatic moments of the history it charts."

Elvis Presley's place in American culture is examined in two of Marcus's books, *Dead Elvis: A Chronicle of a Cultural Obession* and *Double Trouble: Bill Clinton and Elvis Presley in the Land of No Alternatives. Dead Elvis* is a collection of eighteen essays on Presley's life, death, and legend, his legend continuing to grow in the years after he passed away. Marcus ponders what Americans' obsession with the dead singer reveals about the national psyche. "It is a great story—gripping, touching, ultimately tragic," declared Terry Teachout in the *New York Times Book Review.* In *Double Trouble,* the author explores what he perceives to be a unique intersection of political and popular culture. In 1991 Bill Clinton won a spot on the presidential ballot and Elvis Presley won a place on a U.S. postage stamp. Shortly thereafter, Clinton appeared on a late-night talk show playing one of Elvis's signature songs, "Heartbreak Hotel," on his saxophone. In Marcus's opinion, that appearance marked the crucial turning point in Clinton's campaign, leading to victory. *Double Trouble* draws parallels between Presley and Clinton: their poor Southern roots, legendary charm, and the way they both rose to fame only to fall into rather tawdry declines. Not every essay included in *Double Trouble* focuses on Presley, Clinton, or their relationship; a *Kirkus Reviews* contributor noted that "frequently the President and the King exist only as ghostly presences amid Marcus's ruminations" on varied subjects. Reviewing the book for *Library Journal,* David Szatmary judged it "a written equivalent of MTV: slick, entertaining, pithy, and insubstantial." Yet a writer for *Publish-*

ers Weekly rated *Double Trouble* a meaningful effort, stating: "With this book, Marcus . . . continues his legacy of scholarly pop journalism and his persistent effort to document pop culture's influence on history."

Marcus once told *CA:* "The critics who inspired me to start writing or who have kept me going, suggesting less how to practice criticism than what it might be worth, include Pauline Kael, D. H. Lawrence, Leslie Fiedler, Harold Rosenberg, Manny Farber, and Walter Benjamin. What they have in common, I think, is the ability to go in any direction at any time; I try to do that, perhaps too self-consciously.

"When I first began writing, I was interested in continuity: in constructing a rock 'n' roll tradition, and connecting it to the mainstream of American culture. In recent years I have found myself more interested in discontinuities—in the broadest sense, in cultural relationships between phenomena that, given the way we usually see the world, should not be related at all. Over the years, though, I suppose my ambition has been to reconstruct a conversation that took place between people who never met, be they blues singer Robert Johnson and Jonathan Edwards, or Johnny Rotten and the dadaist Richard Huelsenbeck. Culture to me is a field of surprise; I work in it in order to be surprised, and to communicate that sense of surprise to others, because a life infused with surprise is better than a life that is not."

BIOGRAPHICAL/CRITICAL SOURCES:

PERIODICALS

American Book Review, April, 1996, review of *The Dustbin of History,* p. 10; May, 1998, review of *Invisible Republic,* p. 21.

Booklist, May 15, 1993, review of *Ranters and Crowd Pleasers,* pp. 1667, 1681; October 1, 1995, review of *The Dustbin of History,* p. 247; May 1, 1997, Gordon Flagg, review of *Invisible Republic,* p. 1473.

Books and Culture, May, 1998, review of *Invisible Republic,* p. 16.

Choice, March, 1996, review of *The Dustbin of History,* p. 1206; December, 1997, review of *Invisible Republic,* p. 646.

Contemporary Review, August, 1997, review of *The Dustbin of History,* p. 107.

Come-All-Ye, fall, 1993, review of *Mystery Train,* p. 10.

Commentary, June, 1970; July, 1980.

Dissent, spring, 1998, review of *Invisible Republic,* p. 100.

Entertainment Weekly, May 9, 1997, Ken Tucker, review of *Invisible Republic,* p. 75; May 22, 1998, review of *Invisible Republic,* p. 63.

History Today, October, 1995, review of *The Dustbin
of History,* p. 53.

Journal of American Studies, December, 1993, review
of *Dead Elvis,* p. 417.

Journal of Popular Culture, winter, 1996, review of
The Dustbin of History, p. 257.

Kirkus Reviews, March 1, 1997, review of *Invisible Republic,* p. 358; July 1, 2000, review of *Double
Trouble: Bill Clinton and Elvis Presley in the Land
of No Alternatives,* p. 940.

Library Journal, April 15, 1993, review of *Ranters and
Crowd Pleasers,* p. 92; November 15, 1995, review
of *The Dustbin of History,* p. 90; May 1, 1997, review of *Invisible Republic,* p. 105; August, 2000,
David Szatmary, review of *Double Trouble,* p. 107.

Los Angeles Times Book Review, May 25, 1997, review
of *Invisible Republic,* p. 3.

Mother Jones, September, 2000, Ana Marie Cox, review of *Double Trouble.*

Nation, August 25, 1997, review of *Invisible Republic,*
p. 44.

New Statesman, May 30, 1997, review of *Invisible Republic,* p. 54.

New York, May 5, 1997, p. 81.

New York Review of Books, February 3, 1977; April 9,
1998, review of *Invisible Republic,* p. 45.

New York Times Book Review, April 9, 1989, review of
*Lipstick Traces: A Secret History of the Twentieth
Century,* p. 12; November 3, 1991, review of *Dead
Elvis: A Chronicle of a Cultural Obsession;* June
14, 1998, review of *Invisible Republic,* p. 32.

New Statesman & Society, June 11, 1993, review of *In
the Fascist Bathroom,* p. 40; January 12, 1996, review of *The Dustbin of History,* p. 39.

New York Times, June 14, 1975.

New York Times Book Review, February 10, 1980; December 20, 1992, review of *Dead Elvis,* p. 24; January 28, 1996, review of *The Dustbin of History,*
p. 20; May 4, 1997, review of *Invisible Republic,*
p. 12.

Observer, October 25, 1992, review of *Dead Elvis,* p.
63; June 13, 1993, review of *Lipstick Traces,* p. 62;
August 1, 1993, review of *In the Fascist Bathroom,*
p. 52; June 25, 1994, review of *In the Fascist Bathroom,* p. 21; May 25, 1997, review of *Invisible Republic,* p. 16; July 27, 1997, review of *Invisible Republic,* p. 15.

Popular Music and Society, spring, 1997, review of
Mystery Train, p. 121.

Publishers Weekly, March 15, 1993, review of *Ranters
and Crowd Pleasers,* p. 77; March 7, 1994, review

of *Ranters and Crowd Pleasers,* p. 67; September
18, 1995, review of *The Dustbin of History,* p. 119;
March 17, 1997, review of *Invisible Republic,* p.
62; August 28, 2000, review of *Double Trouble,* p.
69.

Saturday Night, March, 1970.

Times Literary Supplement, June 14, 1996, review of
The Dustbin of History, p. 12; July 18, 1997, review of *Invisible Republic,* p. 12.

Utne Reader, March, 1993, review of *Mystery Train*
and *Ranters and Crowd Pleasers,* p. 111; May,
1997, review of *Invisible Republic,* p. 84.

Voice Quarterly Review, spring, 1996, review of *The
Dustbin of History,* p. 57.

Village Voice, May 26, 1975; January 21, 1980; October 5, 1993, review of *Ranters and Crowd
Pleasers,* p. 68.

Washington Post Book World, November 29, 1992, review of *Dead Elvis,* p. 12; August 22, 1993, p. 13.

Wilson Quarterly, summer, 1993, review of *Mystery
Train,* p. 30.*

*   *   *

MARGOLIS, Jonathan   1955-

PERSONAL: Born June 6, 1955, in London, England;
son of Maurice (in business) and Sylvia (a journalist)
Margolis; married, wife's name Susan (a television reporter), May 9, 1976; children: Ruth, David, Eleanor.
Education: University of Nottingham, B.A. (with honors). *Politics:* Labour. *Religion:* Jewish.

ADDRESSES: Home—Richmond, England. *Agent*—
Jane Gelfman, John Farquharson Ltd., 250 West 57th
St., New York, NY 10107.

CAREER: Freelance writer.

WRITINGS:

Hothouse People, Pan Books (London, England), 1987.
Cleese Encounters, St. Martin's Press (New York, NY),
1992.
(With Gabrielle Morris) *The Commuter's Tale,* Chap-
mans (London, England), 1992.
Freddie Star Ate My Hamster, Orion (London, En-
gland), 1994.
The Big Yin: The Life and Times of Billy Connolly,
Chapmans (London, England), 1994.
Lenny Henry, Orion, (London, England), 1996.
Bernard Manning, Orion (London, England), 1997.
Michael Palin: A Biography, Orion (London, England),
1997.

Uri Geller: Magician or Mystic?, Welcome Rain (New York, NY), 1999.

A Brief History of Tomorrow: The Future, Past and Present, St. Martin's Press (New York, NY), 2000.

Television critic for *Mail on Sunday,* 1991-92; columnist for the *Sunday Times,* 1992—. Contributor to *Time.*

SIDELIGHTS: Jonathan Margolis's body of work is diverse, including biographies of Monty Python troupe members John Cleese and Michael Palin as well as psychic Uri Geller, plus an exploration of which visions of the future have come to pass—and which haven't—in *A Brief History of Tomorrow: The Future, Past and Present.* And as a frequent contributor to *Time* magazine, he "often investigates the more peculiar facets of life," noted a *Time* profile in 2000.

Monty Python's comedy certainly investigated life's peculiarities—and found peculiarity in the mundane. John Cleese has been one of the highest-profile members of the Python group, having followed the *Monty Python's Flying Circus* television show with another successful series, *Fawlty Towers,* and appearances in numerous films. "John Cleese is arguably one of the funniest people now living," commented Gahan Wilson in a piece on Margolis's biography *Cleese Encounters* for the *New York Times Book Review.* Wilson thought, however, that Margolis's "thoroughly depressing portrait of Mr. Cleese's childhood . . . ends up robbing the later account of Mr. Cleese's many triumphs—the lovely silly walk, Basil Fawlty, the movies 'Clockwise' and 'The Life of Brian'—of an awful lot of the fun, and much of the funniness." Wilson did allow that the book was "a trove of information for anyone interested in its subject."

In *A Brief History of Tomorrow: The Future, Past and Present,* Margolis looks at past soothsayers' projections and also what futurologists predict at the dawn of the twenty-first century. He shows that some forecasts have been bizarrely optimistic, such as the expectation that cars would fly or a network of canals would link distant nations; some overly dire, like the prediction that oil supplies would be depleted by the end of the 1980s; and some just plain silly, as perceived by modern sensibilities, including a British newspaper's comment in 1900 that within a hundred years female harpists would no longer be considered scandalous. Margolis also points out the prognostications that have proved accurate, such as that people would drive on limited-access highways or use a satellite communications network. He rounds out the book by interviewing a variety of thinkers and putting forth some ideas about the future, which

are "both well-presented and disturbingly familiar," according to *Entertainment Weekly*'s L. S. Klepp. Throughout, Margolis emphasizes that concepts of what lies ahead are colored by present realities. "This is a clever look at how the world could have been, how it might be and how it won't be," observed a *Publishers Weekly* reviewer. A *Kirkus Reviews* critic deemed the book "shallow and glib," but "a light and lively survey" just the same. *Booklist* contributor Gilbert Taylor related that Margolis provides "a cornucopia of lively commentary about everything from artificial intelligence to genetic engineering to global warming" and praised the author's "sensible perspective."

BIOGRAPHICAL/CRITICAL SOURCES:

PERIODICALS

Booklist, November 15, 2000, Gilbert Taylor, review of *A Brief History of Tomorrow: The Future, Past and Present,* p. 592.

Entertainment Weekly, December 8, 2000, L. S. Klepp, review of *A Brief History of Tomorrow: The Future, Past and Present,* p. 92.

Kirkus Reviews, October 15, 2000, review of *A Brief History of Tomorrow: The Future, Past and Present,* p. 1467.

New York Times Book Review, November 15, 1992, Gahan Wilson, "The Man with the Silly Walk."

Publishers Weekly, July 5, 1999, review of *Uri Geller: Magician or Mystic?,* p. 47; October 30, 2000, review of *A Brief History of Tomorrow: The Future, Past and Present,* p. 63.

Time, March 6, 2000, "To Our Readers," p. 4; March 13, 2000, "Contributors," p. 4.*

*   *   *

MARSH, Joan F.   1923-

PERSONAL: Born November 24, 1923, in New York, NY; daughter of John William Ferguson, Jr. and Ruth Shaffer Jones; married Richard S. T. Marsh (an attorney), November 27, 1946; children: Sidney M. Moon, Jane M. Allis, Jesse Burgess Thomas, Peter Ferguson. *Ethnicity:* "Caucasian." *Education:* Attended Holton-Arms School. *Politics:* Republican. *Religion:* Congregationalist. *Avocational interests:* Grandchildren, golf, historical research, hiking, travel.

ADDRESSES: Home—101 East Kirke St., Chevy Chase, MD 20815.

CAREER: Writer. British Admiralty Delegation, Washington, DC, 1943-44; Foreign Economic Administration, Washington, DC, 1944-45; Video Ed Productions, Inc., Hyattsville, MD, research editor, 1983-85.

MEMBER: Chevy Chase Historical Society (president, 1989-93), Montgomery County Historical Society (member of board of directors, 1987-89, 1993-95).

WRITINGS:

Martha Washington, Franklin Watts (Danbury, CT), 1993.

Also author of educational videotapes, including *Seventeenth-Century Maryland,* 1984, *Eighteenth-Century Maryland to the Revolution,* 1985, and *Eighteenth-Century Maryland, Aaron's Story,* 1985. Research contributor to *The City of Washington,* Knopf, 1977.

WORK IN PROGRESS: "Working on a children's biography of Ninian Beall, a seventeenth-century Maryland immigrant who patented the land the White House stands on."

SIDELIGHTS: Joan F. Marsh told *CA:* "My interest in historical research was stimulated by the work I did on the Native Americans of the Washington, D.C., area for *The City of Washington,* an illustrated history of the city published by Alfred A. Knopf. Some years later I scripted educational videotapes on Maryland history. The chance reading of a fictional biography of Martha Washington started me wanting to learn more about this impressive lady. I found out that she was not a dumpy, boring housewife Washington married for her money, but a courageous, capable, and well-disciplined woman who was an invaluable partner for her husband. I think the children who read *Martha Washington* will agree.

"Another interest of mine is the history and culture of Native Americans. I really enjoy reading and studying about the past, and sharing some of the wonderful stories I find with young people."

BIOGRAPHICAL/CRITICAL SOURCES:

PERIODICALS

Booklist, June 1, 1993, p. 1823.
Library Talk, January, 1994, p. 37.
School Library Journal, July, 1993, p. 93.

MARTINSON, Martin
  See FOLLETT, Ken(neth Martin)

*   *   *

McELROY, Wendy

PERSONAL: Born in Canada.

ADDRESSES: Office—c/o St. Martin's Press, 175 Fifth Ave., New York, NY 10010. *E-mail*—mac@zetetics.com.

CAREER: Writer. Knowledge Products, Nashville, TN, former script writer and editor.

MEMBER: Feminists for Free Expression (president of Canadian branch).

WRITINGS:

(Editor) *Freedom, Feminism, and the State: An Overview of Individualist Feminism,* foreword by Lewis Perry, Cato Institute (Washington, DC), 1982, 2nd edition, Holmes & Meier, 1991.
(Compiler) *Liberty, 1881-1908: A Comprehensive Index,* M. E. Coughlin (St. Paul, MN), 1982.
(Contributor of scripts) *The Audio Classics Series,* Knowledge Products (Nashville, TN), 1985-86.
(Coeditor) *The United States Constitution* (eight audio cassettes), Knowledge Products (Nashville, TN), 1987.
(Series editor) *The United States at War* (24 audio cassettes), Knowledge Products (Nashville, TN), 1990.
(Series editor) *The World's Political Hot Spots* (24 audio cassettes), Knowledge Products (Nashville, TN), 1991.
XXX: A Woman's Right to Pornography, St. Martin's Press (New York, NY), 1995.
Sexual Correctness: The Gender-Feminist Attack on Women, McFarland (Jefferson, NC), 1996.
(Coeditor) *The World of Philosophy* (24 audio cassettes), Knowledge Products (Nashville, TN), 1996.
(Coeditor) *Secrets of the Great Investors* (24 audio cassettes), Knowledge Products (Nashville, TN), 1996.
Queen Silver: The Godless Girl, Prometheus Books (Amherst, NY), 1998.
The Reasonable Woman: A Guide to Intellectual Survival, Prometheus Books (Amherst, NY), 1998.

(With Carl Watner) *Dissenting Electorate: Those Who Refuse to Vote and the Legitimacy of Their Opposition,* McFarland (Jefferson, NC), 2001.

Individualist Feminism of the Nineteenth Century: Collected Writings and Biographical Profiles, McFarland (Jefferson, NC), 2001.

(Editor) *Women and Liberty,* Ivan R. Dee, 2001.

Contributor to anthologies, including *Facets of Liberty: A Libertarian Primer,* Freeland Press (Santa Ana, CA), 1985; *Equal Opportunities: A Feminist Fallacy,* Institute of Economic Affairs (London, England), 1992; *Bagatorials,* Simon & Schuster (New York, NY), 1994; *Feminist Interpretations of Ayn Rand,* Pennsylvania State University Press (Philadelphia, PA), 1999; and *I Must Speak Out: The Best of the Voluntaryist, 1982-1999,* Fox & Wilkes (San Francisco, CA), 1999. Contributor of articles to *Humanist, National Review, Free Market, Freedom Daily, Independent Review, Libertarian Enterprise, Reason, LewRockwell.com,* and other periodicals. Co-founder, *Voluntaryist;* associate editor, *Free Inquiry;* contributing editor, *Liberty, New Libertarian, Free Inquiry,* and *Ideas on Liberty.*

SIDELIGHTS: Wendy McElroy writes about women's issues from a libertarian perspective—that is, one that puts the rights of the individual over the rights of the state. Her provocative stands on such issues as pornography have put her at odds with the feminist mainstream.

In *Freedom, Feminism, and the State: An Overview of Individualist Feminism,* McElroy chose essays from a number of writers over the last two centuries, and offers background information on each of her essayists, including such famous figures as Emma Goldman and Susan B. Anthony. In her introduction to the collection, McElroy defines individualist, or libertarian, feminism as primarily interested in protecting the rights of the individual over his or her own body; thus, reforming the laws governing birth control and marriage took priority over suffrage for this group of feminists, some of whose writings are collected in this volume. Reviewer Pat Shockley in *Humanist* described the essays in this anthology as "lucid and thought-provoking," and praised the editor for her clear organization of material, which includes both famous and forgotten workers for women's rights. Although *Public Administration Review* contributor Siegrun F. Fox called the libertarian stance toward the government "one-sided" and questioned the inclusion of such non-libertarian thinkers as Goldman, she nonetheless praised McElroy for including essays on women and their relation to the state that other anthologies have excluded. Shockley concluded:

"*Freedom, Feminism, and the State* is for the person who wishes to question and to rethink basic values, be they feminist or socialist, and who wishes to know more."

In *XXX: A Woman's Right to Pornography,* McElroy seeks to free pornography from the stigma that society, and many feminists, attach to it. The author interviewed producers of pornographic films, as well as actors, to discover how the industry treats its female workers, whether their performances are coerced, and whether the violence they sometimes portray is ever real. "While her account is hardly definitive and does not pretend to be," Ellen Willis observed in the *New York Times Book Review,* "it offers a believable impression of a subculture populated not by the villains and victims of [anti-pornography feminist] Catharine MacKinnon's imagination but by businesspeople, artists and entertainers for whom porn is not just work but 'an attitude or life style.' "

XXX: A Woman's Right to Pornography is also an analysis of what Willis calls "the feminist pornography wars," a history of the battles among feminists over the issue of pornography. According to McElroy, anti-pornography movements throughout history have been an attempt to restrict the freedom of women rather than to protect them from exploitation. In addition, McElroy castigates the anti-pornography wing of the feminist movement for its collaboration with conservatives in the effort to control female sexuality. "*XXX* makes a persuasive case for a sexually libertarian feminism," remarked Willis, who nonetheless took issue with McElroy's equation of the terms "radical feminist" and "anti-pornography feminist," and who faulted McElroy's version of the history of the feminist movement in North America. For these reasons, she deemed *XXX: A Woman's Right to Pornography* as "a lively, intelligent, irritating book." Writing in the *Libertarian Enterprise,* Louis James found *XXX* to be "an amazing book" that "debunks myths, challenges preconceptions, provides intellectual ammunition, amuses, and shines bright light on issues that have languished in a darkness few dare enter."

McElroy turned to biography in her book *Queen Silver,* the life story of a personal friend of hers and a long-time activist for feminist and libertarian causes. Queen Silver became a worldwide phenomenon in the late 1910s and early 1920s, touring the country as a child lecturer on such topics as evolution and relativity. By the mid-1920s she left the lecture circuit and began publishing a free-thought magazine and working for the Industrial Workers of the World (IWW), an anarchist workers' organization. By the 1930s Silver withdrew from political life to care for her ailing mother, not returning to politics until the early 1970s. McElroy's account of Queen Silver's life is based on her own memories of her friend as well as personal papers which Silver bequeathed to her upon her death. The book, noted Mari Jo Buhle in *Isis,* "is not a scholarly biography." Rather, McElroy reconstructs "the nearly forgotten story of Silver in remarkable detail and with obvious affection." The reviewer for the *Utne Reader* found the book to be a "fascinating biography."

McElroy's writings on libertarian feminism have garnered attention for the author's well-reasoned arguments in support of the rights of individuals over their own bodies. While not all critics agree on the necessity of her attack on the mainstream feminist movement's collectivist stance, which sees women as an "oppressed class" needing governmental action in order to achieve its goals, McElroy's writings are often considered persuasive and thought-provoking renderings of a stand on feminist issues that is rarely heard.

BIOGRAPHICAL/CRITICAL SOURCES:

PERIODICALS

Foreword, November, 1999, review of *Queen Silver: The Godless Girl.*

Humanist, May-June, 1984, Pat Shockley, review of *Freedom, Feminism, and the State: An Overview of Individualist Feminism,* p. 38.

Isis, December, 2000, Mari Jo Buhle, review of *Queen Silver,* p. 820.

Knight-Ridder/Tribune News Service, September 13, 1995, Joy Thompson, "Pornography Degrades Women," p. 913.

Libertarian Enterprise, October, 1995, Louis James, review of *XXX: A Woman's Right to Pornography;* October 15, 1996, Don L. Tiggre, review of *Sexual Correctness: The Gender-Feminist Attack on Women.*

Los Angeles Times, November 1, 2000, review of *Queen Silver.*

New York Times Book Review, September 10, 1995, Ellen Willis, review of *XXX,* p. 24.

Personal Psychology, summer, 1999, review of *The Reasonable Woman: A Guide to Intellectual Survival,* p. 524.

Public Administration Review, September-October, 1987, Siegrun F. Fox, review of *Freedom, Feminism, and the State,* pp. 436-440.

Social Forces, March, 1985, p. 892.

Utne Reader, May-June, 2000, review of *Queen Silver.*

OTHER

Wendy McElroy's Web site, http://www.zetetics.com/mac/wendy.html/ (May 21, 2001).*

*   *   *

McGANN, Jerome J(ohn)   1937-

PERSONAL: Born July 22, 1937, in New York, NY; son of John Joseph (a printer) and Marie V. (maiden name, Lecouffe) McGann; married Anne P. Lanni (a teacher), August 20, 1960; children: Geoffrey, Christopher, Jennifer. *Education:* LeMoyne College, B.S., 1959; Syracuse University, M.A., 1962; Yale University, Ph.D., 1966.

ADDRESSES: Office—Department of English, 219 Bryan Hall, P.O. Box 400121, University of Virginia, Charlottesville, VA 22904-4121. *E-mail*—jjm2f@virginia.edu.

CAREER: University of Chicago, Chicago, IL, assistant professor, 1966-69, associate professor, 1969-72, professor of English, 1972-75; Johns Hopkins University, Baltimore, Md., professor of English, 1976-80; Bread Loaf School of English, professor, 1978-1980; California Institute of Technology, Dreyfus Professor of Humanities, 1980-86; University of Southern California, adjunct professor of English, 1983-86; University of Virginia, Commonwealth Professor, 1986-93, John Stewart Bryan University Professor, 1993—; Royal Holloway College, University of London, Thomas Holloway Professor of Victorian Media and Culture, 1999—; Institute of English Studies, University of London, senior research fellow, 1999—; University College, London University, senior research fellow, 2000—. Visiting professor at the University of California at Berkeley, Berkeley, CA, 1994, and Northwestern University, Chicago, IL, 1997. Serves on the editorial boards of numerous journals; general editor of *Virginia Victorian Studies.* Institute for Advanced Technology in the Humanities, University of Virginia, Charlottesville, VA, editor and contributor to online media project and *The Complete Writings and Pictures of Dante Gabriel Rossetti,* a hypermedia research archive.

MEMBER: Modern Language Association of America, Byron Society (board of directors), Keats-Shelley Association, Society for Textual Scholarship, Tennyson Society, North American Society for the Study of Romanticism.

AWARDS, HONORS: American Academy of Arts and Sciences fellow; Fulbright fellow, 1965-66; Fels Foundation fellow, 1965-66; American Philosophical Society fellow, 1967; Guggenheim fellow, 1970-71 and 1976-77; Melville Cane Award, American Poetry Society, 1973, for *Swinburne: An Experiment in Criticism;* National Endowment for the Humanities fellow, 1974-76 and 1987-89; Distinguished Scholar Award, Byron Society, 1989; Distinguished Scholar Award, Keats-Shelley Association of America, 1989; Institute for Advanced Technology in the Humanities fellow, 1992-93, associate fellow, 1993; Wilbur Cross Medal, Yale University Graduate School, 1994; D.H.L. (honorary), University of Chicago, 1996.

WRITINGS:

Fiery Dust: Byron's Poetic Development, University of Chicago Press (Chicago, IL), 1968.

Swinburne: An Experiment in Criticism, University of Chicago Press (Chicago, IL), 1972.

Don Juan in Context, University of Chicago Press (Chicago, IL), 1976.

The Romantic Ideology, University of Chicago Press (Chicago, IL), 1983.

A Critique of Modern Textual Criticism, University of Chicago Press (Chicago, IL), 1983, reprinted with a new preface and introduction, University Press of Virginia (Charlottesville, VA), 1992.

The Beauty of Inflections: Literary Investigations in Historical Method and Theory, Oxford University Press (New York, NY), 1985.

Social Values and Poetic Acts: The Historical Judgment of Literary Work, Harvard University Press (Cambridge, MA), 1988.

Towards a Literature of Knowledge, University of Chicago Press (Chicago, IL), 1989.

The Textual Condition, Princeton University Press (Princeton, NJ), 1991.

Black Riders: The Visible Language of Modernism, Princeton University Press (Princeton, NJ), 1993.

The Poetics of Sensibility: A Revolution in Literary Style, Oxford University Press (New York, NY), 1996.

Byron and Wordsworth, University of Nottingham (Nottingham, England), 1999.

Dante Gabriel Rossetti and the Game That Must Be Lost, Yale University Press (New Haven, CT), 2000.

Radiant Textuality: Literature After the World Wide Web, Palgrave (New York, NY), 2001.

EDITOR

Edward Bulwer-Lytton, *Pelham,* University of Nebraska Press (Lincoln, NE), 1972.

Lord Byron: The Complete Poetical Works (seven volumes), Oxford University Press (New York, NY), 1980-1993.

(And author of introduction) *Historical Studies and Literary Criticism,* University of Wisconsin Press (Madison, WI), 1985.

Textual Criticism and Literary Interpretation, University of Chicago Press (Chicago, IL), 1985.

(With Alice Levine) *The Manuscripts of the Younger Romantics: Byron* (five volumes), Garland (New York, NY), 1985-1988.

George Gordon Byron, *Byron,* Oxford University Press (New York, NY), 1986.

Victorian Connections, University Press of Virginia (Charlottesville, VA), 1989.

The New Oxford Book of Romantic Period Verse, Oxford University Press (New York, NY), 1993.

George Gordon Byron, *Lord Byron: Selected Poetry,* Oxford University Press (New York, NY), 1997.

(With Daniel Reiss), Letitia Elizabeth Landon, *Letitia Elizabeth Landon: Selected Writings,* Broadview Press (Peterborough, Ontario, Canada), 1997.

Lord Byron: The Major Works ("World's Classics" series), Oxford University Press (New York, NY), 2000.

PLAYS

(Adapter) George Gordon Byron, *Cain,* produced in Chicago, IL, 1968.

(Adapter) William Blake, *Marriage of Heaven and Hell,* produced in Chicago, IL, 1970.

POETRY

Air Heart Sermons, Pasdeloup Press (Stratford, Ontario, Canada), 1976.

(With Janet Kauffman) *Writing Home,* Coldwater Press (Hudson, MI), 1977.

(With James Kahn) *Nerves in Patterns,* X Press (Los Angeles, CA), 1979.

Four Last Poems, Pasdeloup Press (Stratford, Ontario, Canada), 1996.

Contributor to numerous academic and literary journals, including *London Review of Books, Studies in Romanticism, Victorian Studies, Modern Language Quarterly,* and *Critical Inquiry.*

WORK IN PROGRESS: Dante Gabriel Rossetti: Collected Works, Yale University Press; *Dialogues of the*

Mind With Itself: Literature Without Touchstones; Byron and Romanticism, Cambridge University Press.

SIDELIGHTS: Jerome J. McGann's *Lord Byron: The Complete Poetical Works* was the first comprehensive critical edition of the works of British Romantic poet Lord Byron to be produced during the twentieth century. It contains nearly fifty never-before-published poems in addition to some 350 more familiar titles. Thanks to McGann's diligence, even a substantial number of these underwent some significant changes; the author uncovered many old manuscripts and printers' proofs that have led to textual revisions in some cases. Described by *New York Times* writer Richard Eder as "not merely a Byron scholar but a Byron enthusiast," McGann made the establishment of an accurate record of the poet's work his primary goal.

Accompanying the poems are McGann's observations on the text itself and his comments on the historical context. Unlike the generation of critics who preceded him, McGann believes strongly that important insights can be gained by examining not just the internal structure of a poem, but the external influences on the poet as well—especially, perhaps, in Byron's case. "You can't read him without being involved in his connections," the scholar explained to Eder. "His interest was not words but what they stand for, as in Auden: a window to reality. He can't write the equivalent of a well-wrought urn; each of his poems is deeply involved in its times." In short, concluded Eder, "studying texts and editions, for [McGann], is not an object in itself but a way or reaching some of the most essential values in literature."

In reviewing McGann's *The Textual Condition* in *Modern Language Quarterly,* Stephen Parrish noted that in addition to his large projects, McGann publishes a small book nearly every year. Parrish called them "wonderfully provocative and written with an inventive flair that we should probably begin to define as vintage McGann." Much of *The Textual Condition* had previously appeared in print or as lectures. Parrish said that in the two new chapters on Ezra Pound "as in the older material, an easy informality often prevails."

Studies in the Novel contributor Michael Wutz said that "McGann's acclaimed *A Critique of Modern Textual Criticism* has recuperated textual and bibliographic scholarship from the margins of accepted critical work and identified him as one of the most distinguished practitioners in the field." Wutz wrote that in *Black Riders: The Visible Language of Modernism* McGann "demonstrates anew what innovative scholarship and close attention to the material practices of a culture—in the manner of a 'new historicism'—can contribute to our understanding of literary history." Wutz noted that McGann bases his ideas on theory of William Morris that "poetry and art are fundamentally crafts, practical forms of making," and said that "*Black Riders* broadly argues that 'twentieth-century poetry in English is a direct function and expression of the Renaissance of Printing that began in the late nineteenth century.'" The book also focuses on "the daunting task of investigating the relationship between 'imaginative writing, knowledge, truth,' with the intention of recovering in poetry 'models (touchstones even?) of knowing and truth-telling elsewhere lost.'" Wutz concluded by calling *Black Riders* "a rewarding book for all scholars interested in re-visioning the history of modernism."

McGann edited *The New Oxford Book of Romantic Period Verse,* exploring the range of verse published in England from 1785 to 1832. Included are writings by all the major and minor Romantic poets, as well as satirical, political, regional, and sentimental verse. The material is organized chronologically, rather than by author, and McGann includes the work of female poets who traditionally have not been given their due, including Ann Yearsley, Laeticia Elizabeth Landon, Felica Dorothea Hemans, and Mary Tighe.

Modern Language Quarterly contributor David Collings wrote that *The New Oxford Book of Romantic Period Verse* "complements" McGann's *The Poetics of Sensibility: A Revolution in Literary Style,* partly because of his inclusion in the new volume of authors such as Charlotte Smith, Felicia Hemans, and Ann Batten Cristall, "making available not only neglected poems but also ways of understanding them." McGann includes the work of such authors as Sylvia Plath, Laura Riding, Lyn Hejinian, and Veronica Forrest-Thomson. Collings said that "putting aside political and historical interpretation, [McGann] pursues an aggressively literary criticism of neglected aesthetic traditions while occasionally aligning aspects of the latter with certain trends in recent English and American poetry . . . thereby crafting a critical project sufficiently evocative of modernist criticism to make his revisionary claim credible." Collings noted that in earlier volumes, particularly *The Romantic Ideology,* McGann "challenged the antihistorical aesthetic norms of 'romanticism'; here he partly completes and partly eclipses that argument by describing and celebrating alternative literary practices of the period, the poetry of sensibility and sentiment. Despite its apparent modesty, this book bristles with important implications for the study of late eighteenth- and early nineteenth-century British literature and is a telling sign that 'new historicism' has given way to another project: the wholesale redescription of the period on the basis of a much more comprehensive canon."

Criticism reviewer Benjamin Friedlander called *The Poetics of Sensibility* "uncommonly rich and lively. . . . Rarely does a scholar bring so precise an understanding of current issues in poetry and poetics to a study of the past, and never (so far as I can recall) to a past as repudiated as this one." Friedlander continued, "If, by chance, we experience a renaissance of eighteenth-century possibilities, a poetic rebirth akin to the Metaphysical revival of the Modernist era, our debt to McGann will be as great as our earlier debt to Eliot—an irony no less precious than the poetry itself."

Isobel Armstrong commented in the *Times Literary Supplement* that in each of his books, McGann "has ambitiously revised accepted ways of reading." Armstrong said his *Dante Gabriel Rossetti and the Game That Must Be Lost* "is no exception. He cuts through many obstacles in order to write a poetics of Rossetti's work and imagination, and to affirm Rossetti as the disciplined artist committed to fundamental brainwork. . . . Jerome McGann has restored Rossetti's greatness as a poet and painter and forged the principles of an alternative modernism that challenges the institutional forms of modernism." McGann is editor of the University of Virginia's Institute for Advanced Technology in the Humanities online archive, *The Complete Writings and Pictures of Dante Gabriel Rossetti.*

BIOGRAPHICAL/CRITICAL SOURCES:

PERIODICALS

American Historical Review, June, 1987, review of *Historical Studies and Literary Criticism,* p. 782.

Choice, December, 1996, review of *The Poetics of Sensibility: A Revolution in Literary Style,* p. 615.

Comparative Literature, winter, 1988, review of *Historical Studies and Literary Criticism,* p. 69.

Criticism, spring, 2000, Benjamin Friedlander, review of *The Poetics of Sensibility,* p. 255.

London Review of Books, December 19, 1985, review of *The Beauty of Inflections: Literary Investigations in Historical Method and Theory,* p. 11; March 16, 1989, review of *Social Values and Poetic Acts: The Historical Judgment of Literary Work,* p. 17; October 26, 1989, review of *Towards a Literature of Knowledge,* p. 21; June 9, 1994, review of *Black Riders: The Visible Language of*

Modernism, p. 21; October 20, 1994, review of *The New Oxford Book of Romantic Period Verse,* p. 33.

Modern Language Quarterly, June, 1989, A. C. Goodson, review of *Social Values and Poetic Acts,* p. 197; September, 1992, Stephen Parrish, review of *The Textual Condition,* p. 365; June, 1998, David Collings, review of *The Poetics of Sensibility,* p. 270.

Modern Philology, November, 1985, review of *The Romantic Ideology,* p. 204; May, 1996, review of *Black Riders,* p. 549; May, 1999, review of *The Poetics of Sensibility,* p. 534.

New Statesman & Society, April 16, 1993, Jonathan Bate, review of *The New Oxford Book of Romantic Period Verse,* p. 39.

New York Review of Books, December 17, 1987, Charles Rosen, review of *Lord Byron: The Complete Poetical Works,* p. 22; June 10, 1993, Anne Barton, reviews of *Lord Byron* (Volume 7), and *The Manuscripts of the Younger Romantics: Lord Byron* (Volumes 1, 2, 3, and 4), p. 30.

New York Times, March 27, 1980, Richard Eder, review of *Lord Byron: The Complete Poetical Works.*

Observer (London), April 18, 1993, review of *The New Oxford Book of Romantic Period Verse,* p. 61; June 25, 1994, review of *The New Oxford Book of Romantic Period Verse,* p. 21.

Sewanee Review, April, 1987, reviews of *The Beauty of Inflections,* p. 36, and *The Romantic Ideology,* p. 276.

South Carolina Review, fall, 1991, review of *Victorian Connections,* p. 169.

Southern Humanities Review, spring, 1987, reviews of *Textual Criticism and Literary Interpretation,* p. 174, and *Historical Studies and Literary Criticism,* p. 177.

Studies in the Novel, summer, 1995, Michael Wutz, review of *Black Riders,* p. 228.

Times Educational Supplement, May 7, 1993, review of *The New Oxford Book of Romantic Period Verse,* p. 9.

Times Literary Supplement, May 30, 1986, review of *Historical Studies and Literary Criticism,* p. 599; October 10, 1986, review of *The Beauty of Inflections,* p. 1141; December 16, 1988, review of *Social Values and Poetic Acts,* p. 1399; October 13, 1989, review of *Towards a Literature of Knowledge,* p. 1134; June 26, 1992, review of *The Textual Condition,* p. 23; September 17, 1993, review of *Black Riders,* p. 13; March 18, 1994, review of *The New Oxford Book of Romantic Period Verse,* p. 8; December 27, 1996, review of *The Poetics of Sensibility,* p. 11; November 17, 2000, Isobel Armstrong, "Blessed Damozels," p. 19.

Victorian Studies, winter, 1991, review of *Victorian Connections,* p. 255; winter, 1994, review of *The Textual Condition,* p. 317.

Village Voice Literary Supplement, November, 1983.

Virginia Quarterly Review, spring, 1986, review of *The Beauty of Inflections,* p. 337; autumn, 1986, review of *Historical Studies and Literary Criticism,* p. 116; summer, 1988, review of *Social Values and Poetic Acts,* p. 79; autumn, 1990, review of *Victorian Connections,* p. 118; winter, 1990, review of *Towards a Literature of Knowledge,* p. 10; winter, 1997, review of *The Poetics of Sensibility,* p. 12.

OTHER

Complete Writings and Pictures of Dante Gabriel Rossetti (Institute for Advanced Technology in the Humanities, University of Virginia), http:// jefferson.village.virginia.edu/rossetti (July 13, 2001).

Jerome McGann Web site, http://jefferson.village. virginia.edu/ (July 13, 2001).

Selected Papers on the Theory of Textuality and Media, 1995-2000 (Institute for Advanced Technology in the Humanities, University of Virginia), http:// jefferson.village.virginia.edu:2020/resources.html (July 13, 2001).

*   *   *

MEVES, Christa   1925-

PERSONAL: Born March 4, 1925, in Neumünster, Germany; daughter of Carl and Else (Rohweder) Mittelstaedt; married Harald Meves (a doctor), December 18, 1946; children: two daughters. *Ethnicity:* "German." *Education:* Received degrees from University of Breslau, 1943, University of Kiel, 1948, University of Hamburg, 1949, and Psychotherapeutic Institute of Hannover and Göttingen, 1955. *Religion:* Catholic.

ADDRESSES: *Home*—Albertstrasse 14, 29525 Uelzen 1, Germany; fax: 0581/2366. *E-mail*—email@christa-meves.de.

CAREER: Child psychotherapist in private practice, Uelzen, Germany, 1960—.

AWARDS, HONORS: Wilhelm Bölsche medal, 1974; Prix Amade, 1976; gold medal of Herder-Verlags, 1977; niedersächsischer Verdienstorden first-class, 1978; Konrad-Adenauer prize, 1979; Sonnenscheinme-

daille der Aktion Sorgenkind, 1982; medal of merit, 1984; Bundesverdienstkreuz first-class, 1985; Preis der Stiftung Abendländische Beginnuing, 1995; Preis für Wissenschaftliche Publizistik, 1996; Pries der Vereinigung, 2000, for *Bürger fragen Journalisten.*

WRITINGS:

Die Schulnöte unserer Kinder: Wie Eltern ihnen vorbeugen und abhelfen können, Furche-Verlag, 1969, 17th edition, Gütersloher Verlagshaus Mohn, 1981, revised edition (with Dieter Günter) published as *Neue Schulnöte,* Verlag Herder, 1990, 26th edition, Resch Verlag, 1995.

Mut zum Erziehen: Erfahrungen aus der psychagogischen Praxis, Furche-Verlag, 1970, reprinted as *Mut zum Erziehen: Seelische Gusundheit; Wie können wir sie unseren Kindern vermitteln?,* Güterslohe Verlagshaus, 1976, revised edition, Verlag Herder, 1990, 26th edition, Christiana Verlag, 1996.

Erziehen lernen aus tiefenpsychologischer Sicht (title means "Learning to Educate"), Bayerischer Schulbuch-Verlag, 1971, revised edition, 1973, reprinted as *Erziehen lernen aus tiefenpsychologischer Sicht: Ein Kursbuch für Ellern und Erzieher,* Herder-Verlag, 1985, 14th edition, Resch Verlag, 1997.

Verhaltensstörungen bei Kindern (title means "Disorders in the Behavior of Children"), Piper-Verlag, 1971, 10th edition revised, 1991.

Wunschtraum und Wirklichkeit (title means "Illusion and Reality"), Herder-Verlag, 1972, 14th edition, Christiana Verlag, 1997.

Die Bibel antwortet uns in Bildern: Tiefenpsychologische Textdeutungen im Hinblick auf Lebensfragen heute, Herder-Verlag, 1973, translation by Hal Taussig published as *The Bible Answers Us with Pictures,* Westminster Press, 1977, 15th edition revised, Verlag Lingenbink, 2000.

Ehe-Alphabet (title means "Alphabet of Marriage"; also see below), Herder-Verlag, 1973, 36th edition, Christiana Verlag, 1997.

Ich will leben (Briefe an Martina): Probleme des Jugendalters (title means "I Want to Live!"), Verlag Weißes Kreuz, 1974, 23rd edition, 1994.

Wer paßt zu mir? Der Lebenspartner—Wahl oder Qual? (title means "Who Is Suited to Me?"), Verlag Weißes Kreuz, 1974, 7th edition, Resch Verlag, 2000.

Ninive darf nicht untergehen: Verantwortung für die Zukunft (title means "Ninive Must Not Die!"), Verlag Weißes Kreuz, 1977, 12th edition revised published as *Europa darf nicht untergehen* (title means "Europe Must Not Die!").

Antrieb—Charakter—Erziehung: Werden wir ein Volk von Neurotikern? (title means "Shall We Become a Nation of Neurotics?"), Fromm-Verlag, 1977, 3rd revised edition, 1984.

Ich habe ein Problem: Lebensfragen junger Menschen, Verlag Weißes Kreuz, 1978, 5th edition, 1984.

(With H. D. Ortlieb) *Macht Gleichheit glücklich?,* Verlag Herder, 1978, 4th edition, 1984.

(With Jutta Schmidt) *Anima-Verletzte Mädchenseele: Die Frau zwischen Verfremdung und Entfaltung,* Verlag Weißes Kreuz, 1979.

Kleines ABC für Seelenhelfer: Grundregeln für die Begegnung mit Ratsuchenden und Patienten, Herder-Verlag, 1980, 6th revised edition published as *ABC der Lebeusberatung,* Brunnen Verlag, 1992, revised edition, Hänssler Verlag, 1997.

Unsere Kinder wachsen heran: Wie wir ihnen halfen können, Herder-Verlag, 1981, revised edition, 1985, reprinted, Hänssler Verlag, 2001.

Das große Fragezeichen: Merkwürdige Erlebniße von Astrid, Andreas, Monika, Peter, Maria, Thomas und Alexander, Verlag Weißes Kreuz, 1981.

Das Geringste gilt: Ansprachen und Aufsätze, Verlag Weißes Kreuz, 1981.

(With Joachim Illies) *Dienstanweisüngen für Obertenfel,* Verlag Herder, 1981, 5th edition, 1986.

Problemkinder brauchen Hilfe: ABC der Verhaltensstörungen für Eltern (also see below), Herder-Verlag, 1981, 9th edition revised, Christiana Verlag, 1995.

Das Großeltern-ABC: Was man wissen mus, um mit Kindern und Enkeln glücklich zu werden (also see below), Herder-Verlag, 1983, 11th edition revised, Christiana Verlag, 1999.

(With H. D. Ortlieb) *Die ruinierte Generation,* Verlag Herder, 1982, 3rd edition, 1984.

Was unsere Liebe vermag: Eine Lebenskunde, Herder-Verlag, 1983, reprinted as *Was unsere Liebe vermag: Hilfe für bedrängte Eltern,* Herder-Verlag, 1984.

Der Mensch hinter seiner Maske: Aufsätze zu seelischen Grundphänomenen (title means "Men after Their Masks"), Verlag Weißes Kreuz, 1985.

Lebensrat von A-Z: Ehepartner, Kinder, Großeltern (contains *Ehe-Alphabet, Großeltern-ABC,* and *Problemkinder brauchen Hilfe*), Herder-Verlag, 1985, 5th edition, 1991.

Nußschalen im Ozean: Von der Hoffnung, ans Ufer zu kommen, Verlag Weißes Kreuz, 1985.

Ohne Familie geht es nicht: Ihr Sinn und ihre Gestaltung, Verlag Weißes Kreuz, 1985.

Aus Vorgeschichten lernen: Vom Massenelend vermeidbarer seelischer Erkrankungen, Herder-Verlag, 1985, revised edition published as *Wie das Gestern das Hente bestimmt,* Hänssler Verlag, 2001.

Plädoyer für das Schamgefühl: Und weilere akiülle Beiträge, Verlag Weißes Kreuz, 1985.

Kraft, aus der Du leben kannst: Geburtstagsbriefe an die Enkel, Herder-Verlag, 1986, 4th edition, 1990, revised edition, Hänssler Verlag, 1998.

Ermutigung zur Freude, Verlag Herder, 1987, 2nd edition, 1988.

Wurzeln des Glücks, Verlag Herder, 1987.

Positiv gesehen, Verlag Herder, 1987, 3rd edition, 1991.

Es geht um unsere Kinder, Brunnen Verlag, 1988, 2nd edition, 1989.

Der alte Glaube und die neue Zeit, Verlag Herder, 1988, 3rd edition, 1990.

Ein neues Vaterbild, Christiana Verlag, 1989.

Im Schutzmantel geborgen, Verlag Herder, 1989.

Glücklich ist, wer anders lebt, Verlag Herder, 1989.

Eltern-ABC, Verlag Herder, 1990, 3rd edition revised, Christiana Verlag, 1997.

Zeitloses Maß in maßloser Zeit, Verlag Herder, 1991.

Die Bibel hilft heilen, Verlag Herder, 1992.

Kurswechsel, Verlag Herder, 1992.

Kindgerechte Sexualerziehung, Verlag Weißes Kreuz, 1992, 10th edition revised, Hänssler Verlag, 2001.

Wenn ihr werdet wie die Kinder, Verlag Herder, 1993.

Wahrheit befreit, Christiana Verlag, 1993, 4th edition, 1999.

Alte Narben—neue Nöte, Verlag Herder, 1994.

(With Andrea Dillon) *Hochsommer,* Christiana Verlag, 1994, 2nd edition, 1996.

Mit Kindern leben—Hilfe für bedrängte Eltern, Christiana Verlag, 1999.

Wahrheit befreit, Christiana Verlag, 1989, 4th edition, 1999.

(With Andrea Dillon) *Aber ich will dich verstehen!,* Resch Verlag, 1996.

(With Andrea Dillon) *Weise uns Herr deinen Weg,* Christiana Verlag, 1996.

(With Andrea Dillon) *In die Freiheit gerufen,* Hänssler Verlag, 1997.

Ich will mich ändern, Hänssler Verlag, 1997.

Ohne Liebe geht es nicht-Mutterprobleme, Hänssler Verlag, 1997.

Wandlung durch Widerstand, Christiana Verlag, 1997.

"Trotzdem: Mut zur Zukunft!," Resch Verlag, 1998.

(With Joachim Illies) *Liebe und Aggression,* Resch Verlag, 1999.

Mein Leben-Herausgefordert vom Zeitgeist, Resch Verlag, 1999, 2nd edition, 2000.

Unser Leben braucht Schutz-Bewältigungsstrategien für den Alltag, Hänssler Verlag, 1999.

Auf Dich kommt es an!—Antworten für Jugendliche, MM-Verlag, 1999, 3rd edition, 2001.
(With Thomas Schirrmacher) *Ausverkaufte Würde-Der Pornographieboom und seine psychischen Folgen,* Hänssler Verlag, 2000.
Wie bleiben wir menschlich? Beziehungskonflikte und ihre Lösungswege, Christiana Verlag, 2000.

Also author of *"ABC der Lebensberatung,"* Hänssler Verlag; *Antworten Sie gleich!,* Christiana Verlag; *Charaktertypen-Wer paßt zu wem?,* Resch Verlag; *Danke-mit einem lieben Gruß,* skv; *Das große Fragezeichen,* Christiana Verlag; (with E. Buddenbrock) *Denen im Dunkeln Trost,* Verlag Weißes Kreuz; (with Andrea Dillon) *Ein jeder Tag hat Sinn für dich,* skv; *Europa darf nicht untergehen,* Christiana Verlag; *Freude-für die glücklichen Eltern,* skv; *Glückwünsche-zum neuen Lebensjahr,* skv; *In den Ferien fing es an,* Verlag Weißes Kreuz; *Manipulierte Maßlosigkeit,* Christiana Verlag; (with D. Günter) *Schulnöte-vorbeugen und abhelfen,* Resch Verlag; *Trost-in Zeiten der Trauer,* skv; *Und so ihr nicht werdet wie die Kinder,* skv; *"Wer Wind sät,"* Christiana; and *Werden wir ein Volk von Neurotikern?,* Fromm. Contributor of numerous articles to journals. Co-editor of weekly magazine, *Rheinischer Merkur* (title means "Rhenanian Gazette"), 1978—. Also editor of *Fründerkein Christa Meves,* 1982—, *Vorsitzende der Vereius VFAeu,* and *Uelsen (Verantwarting für di Familie),* 1995—.

WORK IN PROGRESS: A revised edition of *Unsere Kinder wachsen heran: Wie wir ihnen helfen können,* to be published by Hänssler Verlag.

SIDELIGHTS: Christa Meves told *CA:* "In the early 1960s, I proposed a new theory regarding the development of disorders in children's behavior, based on scientific experiments. In collaboration with Konrad Lorenz and Joachim Illies, both scientists at different Max Planck Institutes, I concluded that children being cared for under extremely unnatural circumstances would develop severe and irreversible psychic disorders, subsequently handicapping their adult lives. The results would be neurotic depression, manifested in eating disorders, drug addiction and/or criminal behavior.

"In view of the limited literature dealing with the psychic development of infants being nursed (breast-feeding six months at least!) and raised in non-traditional environments, I wrote my first book outlining my specific scientific theory, *Verhaltensstoerungen bei Kindern* ('Disorders in the Behavior of Children'). My next work dealt with conclusions drawn from my theories which were applicable to the practical educa-

tion of children, *Erziehen lernen aus tiefenpsychologischer Sicht* ('Learning How to Educate from the Point of Depth-Psychology'). In subsequent years, I published numerous books as well as articles in various journals and magazines.

"The educational climate in West Germany during the late '60s and early '70s reflected a strong tendency towards a Marxist ideology, with a reluctant hostility towards 'old fashioned' family values in general. Despite this, or perhaps as a result of it, an increasing number of parents and teachers began to subscribe to my theories. During this same period, I also began publishing ten- and twenty-year projections of long term psychic disorders (also in sexual behavior) likely to result from abandonment of the traditional family values in nursing and raising infants.

"Psychic disorders have taken on epidemic proportions in almost all western industrialized nations, exactly as I had projected years ago. Despite this adverse development, no change has been forthcoming in the basic educational process, nor has there been a significant social shift back to traditional family values. Since this may, as well, reflect an increasing loss of faith, my most recent books and articles have delved deeper into theological as well as philosophical ramifications."

BIOGRAPHICAL/CRITICAL SOURCES:

OTHER

Christa Meves Web site, http://www.christa.meves.de (October 11, 2001).

*   *   *

MEYERS, Jeffrey 1939-

PERSONAL: Born April 1, 1939, in New York, NY; son of Rubin and Judith Meyers; married Valerie Froggatt (a teacher), October 12, 1965; children: Rachel. *Education:* University of Michigan, B.A., 1959; attended University of Pennsylvania, University of Edinburgh, and Harvard Law School; University of California, Berkeley, M.A., 1961, Ph.D., 1967. *Politics:* Socialist. *Religion:* None. *Avocational interests:* Travel (Asia, Africa, the Near East, Europe), tennis.

ADDRESSES: Home—84 Stratford Road, Kensington, CA 94707.

CAREER: University of California, Los Angeles, assistant professor of English, 1963-65; University of Maryland, Far East Division, Tokyo, Japan, lecturer in English, 1965-66; Tufts University, Boston, MA, assistant professor of English, 1967-71; writer in London, England, 1971-74; Christie's, London, in rare books department, 1974; University of Colorado, Boulder, professor of English, 1975-92; writer. Visiting professor, University of Kent, Canterbury, 1979-80, and University of Massachusetts, Amherst, 1982-83.

MEMBER: Royal Society of Literature (fellow).

AWARDS, HONORS: Fellowships from American Council of Learned Societies, 1970, and Huntington Library, 1971; Fulbright fellowship, 1977-78; Guggenheim fellowship, 1978.

WRITINGS:

Fiction and the Colonial Experience, Rowman & Littlefield (Totowa, NJ), 1973.

The Wounded Spirit: A Study of "Seven Pillars of Wisdom," Martin, Brian & O'Keeffe (London, England), 1973, revised as *The Wounded Spirit: T. E. Lawrence's "Seven Pillars of Wisdom,"* St. Martin's (New York, NY), 1989.

T. E. Lawrence: A Bibliography, Garland Publishing (New York, NY), 1974.

A Reader's Guide to George Orwell, Thames & Hudson (London, England), 1975, Littlefield & Adams (Totowa, NJ), 1977.

(Editor and author of introduction and notes) *George Orwell: The Critical Heritage,* Routledge & Kegan Paul (Boston, MA), 1975.

Painting and the Novel, Barnes & Noble (New York, NY), 1975.

Catalogue of the Library of the Late Siegfried Sassoon, Christie's (London, England), 1975.

A Fever at the Core: The Idealist in Politics, Barnes & Noble (New York, NY), 1976.

George Orwell: An Annotated Bibliography of Criticism, Garland Publishing (New York, NY), 1977.

Homosexuality and Literature, 1890-1930, Athlone Press (London, England), McGill-Queen's University Press (Montreal, Canada), 1977.

Married to Genius, Barnes & Noble (New York, NY), 1977.

Katherine Mansfield: A Biography, Hamish Hamilton (London, England), 1978, New Directions Publishing (New York, NY), 1980.

(Editor and author of introduction) Katherine Mansfield, *Four Poems,* Eric & Joan Stevens (London, England), 1980.

The Enemy: A Biography of Wyndham Lewis, Routledge (London, England), 1980, Routledge (Boston, MA), 1982.

(Editor) *Wyndham Lewis: A Revaluation: New Essays,* Athlone Press (London, England), 1980.

D. H. Lawrence and the Experience of Italy, University of Pennsylvania Press (Philadelphia, PA), 1982.

(Editor and author of introduction and notes) *Hemingway: The Critical Heritage,* Routledge (Boston, MA), 1982.

(Editor and author of introduction and chapter) *The Craft of Literary Biography,* Schocken (New York, NY), 1985.

(Editor and author of introduction) *D. H. Lawrence and Tradition,* University of Massachusetts Press (Amherst, MA), 1985.

Disease and the Novel, 1880-1960, St. Martin's (New York, NY), 1985.

Hemingway: A Biography, Harper & Row (New York, NY), 1985.

(Editor and author of introduction) Roy Campbell, *Wyndham Lewis,* University of Natal Press (Pietermaritzburg, South Africa), 1985.

(Editor and author of introduction and chapter) *The Legacy of D. H. Lawrence: New Essays,* St. Martin's (New York, NY), 1987.

Manic Power: Robert Lowell and His Circle, Arbor House (New York, NY), 1987.

(Editor and author of introduction and notes) *Robert Lowell: Interviews and Memoirs,* University of Michigan Press (Ann Arbor, MI), 1988.

(Editor and author of introduction and chapter) *The Biographer's Art: New Essays,* New Amsterdam Books (New York, NY), 1989.

The Spirit of Biography (selected essays), UMI Research Press (Ann Arbor, MI), 1989.

(Editor) *T. E. Lawrence: Soldier, Writer, Legend: New Essays,* St. Martin's (New York, NY), 1989.

D. H. Lawrence: A Biography, Knopf (New York, NY), 1989.

(Editor) *Graham Greene: A Revaluation: New Essays,* St. Martin's (New York, NY), 1990.

Joseph Conrad: A Biography, Scribner (New York, NY).

Edgar Allan Poe: His Life and Legacy, Scribner, 1992.

Scott Fitzgerald: A Biography, HarperCollins (New York, NY), 1994.

Edmund Wilson: A Biography, Houghton (Boston, MA), 1995.

Robert Frost: A Biography, Houghton (Boston, MA), 1996.

(Editor) *Early Frost: The First Three Books,* Ecco Press (Hopewell, NJ), 1996.

Bogart: A Life in Hollywood, Houghton (Boston, MA), 1997.

Gary Cooper: American Hero, Morrow (New York, NY), 1998.

Orwell: Wintry Conscience of a Generation, Norton (New York, NY), 2000.

Privileged Moments: Encounters with Writers, University of Wisconsin Press (Madison, WI), 2000.

Hemingway: Life into Art, Cooper Square (New York, NY), 2000.

Contributor to books, including *Essays by Divers Hands,* volume 44, edited by A. N. Wilson, Boydell & Brewer, 1986; and periodicals, including *London Magazine, Sewanee Review,* and *Virginia Quarterly Review.*

Meyers's books have been translated into French, German, Italian, Japanese, Hebrew, Korean, Polish, and Portuguese.

SIDELIGHTS: Jeffrey Meyers is a prominent and prolific biographer of literary and film figures. The frequency with which his books appear led critic James Atlas, in the *New York Times Book Review,* to call him "indefatigable" and his output "prodigious." Meyers, who has likened his work to that of an investigative journalist, turned to literary biography after a significant career in literary criticism. "Meyers began writing primarily as a literary critic who used biography to explicate texts," explained Mark Allister in *Dictionary of Literary Biography,* "and he has since become primarily a biographer who occasionally interprets literature." Allister saw Meyers's use of information on writers' lives in his critical works as foreshadowing his emergence as an author of full-fledged biographies. Whatever its antecedents, Meyers's career as a biographer has drawn a great deal of attention. As Paul Marx put it in the *Houston Chronicle,* "It would be hard to find someone who knows more about 20th-century British and American culture than Jeffrey Meyers."

Meyers's penchant for telling life stories became further apparent in two group biographies. *A Fever at the Core: The Idealist in Politics* deals with people involved in both the arts and political activism, while *Married to Genius* looks at the marriages of several authors. One of these authors was the influential British short-story writer and poet Katherine Mansfield, who subsequently became the subject of Meyers's first full-length biographical work. *Katherine Mansfield: A Biography* provides details of Mansfield's life that had been covered either superficially or not at all by her previous biographers, including her complex relations with her husband, John Middleton Murry. While Murry had depicted Mansfield and their relationship in only the most flattering manner, Meyers discusses Mansfield's numerous love affairs with both men and women, as well as her husband's infidelities and coldness. Some reviewers found the book cruel to Mansfield, while others contended that Murry was unfairly portrayed as evil. Still others praised Meyers's extensive research—he interviewed every person acquainted with Mansfield—and felt that his work casts new light on this literary life.

In the Mansfield book, Meyers did not write extensively about the times in which she lived, nor did he provide much opinion on her work. However, *The Enemy: A Biography of Wyndham Lewis,* "is rich in such details," according to Allister. Lewis produced many works of poetry, fiction, and nonfiction (in addition to numerous paintings and drawings), but is not as well known as his early-twentieth-century contemporaries, such as T. S. Eliot, D. H. Lawrence, and Ezra Pound, and is frequently confused with another writer, D. B. Wyndham Lewis. Lewis's reputation also has suffered because of his early support of Adolf Hitler, although he later turned against Hitler. Meyers's biography, several reviewers said, contributes to a greater understanding of Lewis. The book is "richly informative, fair, lively, and in every good sense disinterested," wrote Denis Donoghue in the *New York Review of Books.* Bernard Bergonzi in the *Times Literary Supplement* noted that Meyers is by no means a Lewis partisan, but has written a biography that is "solid and well documented, without being pointlessly massive or tediously long." However, while Bergonzi found Meyers's evaluation of Lewis's writings "cautious and sensible," he also considered it "quietly dismissive of a good part of the oeuvre."

For his next biographical work, Meyers chose as his subject a writer far more famous than Mansfield or Lewis—one of the giants of twentieth-century American literature, Ernest Hemingway. *Hemingway: A Biography* was the first full-fledged biography of the writer to appear since Carlos Baker's *Ernest Hemingway: A Life Story* in 1969. Meyers made an effort to gather material that had not been included in Baker's book; among his finds was a Federal Bureau of Investigation dossier on Hemingway, indicating the agency's head, J. Edgar Hoover, wished to destroy Hemingway's standing as a writer (Hoover thought Hemingway was a communist). Christopher Lehmann-Haupt, a reviewer for the *New York Times,* declared Meyers's book well organized, "a relief . . . after Professor Baker's shapeless gathering of a million facts." Meyers, according to Lehmann-Haupt, "is able to illuminate what he considers the major turning points of Hemingway's life" and produce "an absorbing tragic portrait." In *Voice Literary Supplement,* Mario Vargas Llosa noted that the book "adds to as well as corrects" the Baker work and "is the most complete biography" of Hemingway.

Raymond Carver, writing in the *New York Times Book Review,* held a different view: "There's little in this book that Carlos Baker . . . didn't say better. Mr. Baker, despite his blind spots, was far more sympathetic to the work and, finally, more understanding of the man." Carver also asserted: "Adulation is not a requirement for biographers, but Mr. Meyers's book fairly bristles with disapproval of his subject." Carver noted that Meyers devotes much space to Hemingway's large ego (which Meyers claims affected his work adversely), excessive drinking, and ill treatment of his loved ones. *Los Angeles Times Book Review* contributor Irving Marder did not object to Meyers's discussion of Hemingway's personal failings, but saw other flaws in the book: "One is a style so graceless and so imprecise that, at crucial points, there is only ambiguity." Vargas Llosa, while admiring the book's thoroughness, argued that Meyers does not really explain how Hemingway was able to distill the events of his life and various aspects of his personality into literature. Lehmann-Haupt was bothered by Meyers's dismissal of the possibility that Hemingway's ultra-masculine persona was a reaction to insecurity about his sexual identity. "This peculiar bias . . . leaves a gaping hole at the very heart of his otherwise impressive treatment," Lehmann-Haupt concluded.

Meyers returned to group biography with *Manic Power: Robert Lowell and His Circle.* He deals with Lowell and three other poets who were his contemporaries: John Berryman, Randall Jarrell, and Theodore Roethke, adding an epilogue on Sylvia Plath. All had significant personal problems that informed their poetry. Mark Allister considered the book successful as biography, less so as a study of the poets' art. *Times Literary Supplement* critic Michael Hofmann, however, lambasted Meyers's work as "witless, censorious, treacherous and sloppy."

British writer D. H. Lawrence, whose art and life had figured in some of Meyers's previous works, was the author's next biographical subject. In *Times Literary Supplement,* Julian Symons called *D. H. Lawrence: A Biography* a "robust, energetic book" and "probably the best biography" of the controversial Lawrence, once vilified for the sexual explicitness of his novels, later condemned as displaying a supremacist attitude toward women. *New York Review of Books* critic Noel Annan praised Meyers's work in sorting out the various ver-

sions of events in Lawrence's life and referred to the book as "dispassionate . . . a cool, not cold, analysis." Paul Delany, writing for *London Review of Books,* found Meyers's assertion that Lawrence's problems in life were due to his relationship with his mother far too facile, but termed the book as a whole "readable, judicious and authoritative." Christopher Hawtree's *Spectator* review criticized the book as having "a perfunctory air" and "lacking all rhythm and underplaying much of the subject's existence." Nancy Mairs, in the *Los Angeles Times Book Review,* lauded Meyers for illuminating the relationship between Lawrence's life and his work, while finding Lawrence's work too plentiful to allow the biographer to do so in all cases. The book, though, is an "admirable introduction" to Lawrence, Mairs maintained.

Joseph Conrad: A Biography, featuring the Polish-descended seaman who became a highly regarded British novelist, fulfills the need for a book "that makes overall sense of the myriad, often contradictory, facts of Conrad's life," according to Jay Parini in the *Los Angeles Times Book Review.* Parini declared the book's second half "beautifully focused on the author's life of writing," providing insight into the creative process that produced such works as *Heart of Darkness* and *Lord Jim.* The critic also praised Meyers's account of Conrad's little-known love affair with Jane Anderson, an American newspaper reporter. To Peter Kemp of the *Times Literary Supplement,* however, the story of the relationship is "wonky erotic conjecture"; he found Meyers's evidence that the affair was consummated quite unconvincing. Kemp also saw little that sheds new light on any other aspect of Conrad's life or work: "Meyers is happiest with the obvious," he asserted. J. A. Bryant, Jr., while calling the book "neatly crafted" in *Sewanee Review,* termed it "most interesting when [Meyers] is presenting the details of Conrad's life, least interesting when he is reviewing or analyzing the novels." Joyce Carol Oates, writing for *New York Times Book Review,* pronounced *Joseph Conrad* "never less than a workmanlike amalgam of known and new material; at its best, it is sensitively written, and clearly inspired by a great admiration for its subject."

Edgar Allan Poe: His Life and Legacy brought a reaction from some critics that was similar to a reaction to the Conrad book: that it fills a void. This book and Kenneth Silverman's *Edgar Allan Poe: Mournful and Never-Ending Remembrance,* published shortly before Meyers's work, are entries in the "relatively new field" of mature, balanced, Poe biographies, wrote Lloyd Rose in the *Washington Post Book World.* Previously, Rose claimed, biographers tended either to damn or to idealize Poe, known both for his self-destructive way of life and his still-popular stories and poems of the supernatural. According to Rose, "Meyers is sympathetic but dispassionate towards his subject, which strikes me as exactly the right approach towards such a difficult man." Chicago *Tribune Books* reviewer Colin Harrison termed Meyers's chronicle a "solid, thoughtful biography" and *New Statesman and Society* contributor Robert Carver described the book as "elegantly written, important and endlessly fascinating." Carver praised Meyers's insights into Poe's work and his influence as well as his life. In the *Times Literary Supplement,* Arthur Krystal considered both Meyers's and Silverman's books "admirably executed" but allowed that "it is Meyers who, untempted by psychoanalytic theories, better conveys Poe's . . . literary travails." But Erik Rieselbach, in *American Spectator,* compared Meyers's work unfavorably to Silverman's. Meyers "includes almost nothing that can't be found more fully discussed in Silverman," Rieselbach contended.

Meyers chronicled the life of another self-destructive writer in *Scott Fitzgerald: A Biography.* Merle Rubin, reviewing the book for *Christian Science Monitor,* observed that the work "focuses on the aspects of [Fitzgerald's] personality that made it hard for him to achieve his full potential as an artist"; these aspects include his alcoholism and his troubled marriage to Zelda Sayre. While Meyers, according to Rubin, does not fully reconcile Fitzgerald's flaws with his virtues, the biographer manages to "allow the pathos and curious heroism of his subject to merge for themselves." Some other reviewers found Meyers's portrayal of Fitzgerald less tolerant, even unkind. The book has an "all but sneering tone," to quote John Updike in the *New Yorker.* Updike added that Meyers, "like the practitioners of celebrity-centered tabloid journalism, shows his subjects no respect." Similarly, Michiko Kakutani of *New York Times* faulted Meyers for taking "a snide, patronizing tone" and pronounced the biography "an ugly and superfluous book about a major American artist who deserves a better biographical fate." Kakutani saw value in Meyers's discussion of how Fitzgerald was influenced by numerous writers (including two of Meyers's previous subjects, Poe and Conrad), but on the whole she felt that the book gives short shrift to Fitzgerald's writing, especially to his "masterpiece, *The Great Gatsby.*"

Brad Leithauser, in *New York Review of Books,* expected that Meyers will "take some knocks for focusing so insistently on Fitzgerald's dissipations" but deemed such a focus justified: "Fitzgerald's ruinous life-style . . . was not something tangential or supplemental to his work." Fitzgerald's novels and short stories are based to a great degree on his own experiences, Leithauser noted, and Fitzgerald's nemesis—liquor—figures largely in the makeup of his two most famous characters—the bootlegger Gatsby and the alcoholic psychiatrist, Dick Diver, of *Tender Is the Night.* Leithauser maintained that Meyers has drawn "an appealingly pitiful portrait" and, while offering little in the way of new interpretations of Fitzgerald's life or work, has provided "an encyclopedic enumeration of the real-life counterparts that stood behind Fitzgerald's creations."

Meyers's next subject was a contemporary and friend of Fitzgerald's, Edmund Wilson, who was a literary critic, essayist, historian, poet, fiction writer, and general man of letters. *Edmund Wilson: A Biography* was the first full-scale biography of Wilson. According to Elizabeth Hardwick in *New Yorker,* Wilson wrote so extensively about himself that his voluminous diaries and journals are daunting competition for any biographer. Perhaps not surprisingly, then, Hardwick did not find Meyers's work wholly satisfactory. "Meyers has brought together the grand flow of Wilson's work and life, including all the flirtations, the drinking, and the marital discord," she stated. "But he has not been able to recreate in his own pages the subject's brilliant mind and spirit."

In *New York Times Book Review,* James Atlas also noted the challenge that Wilson's autobiographical writings pose, but concluded that "somehow Mr. Meyers has produced a highly engaging book. Lively, well proportioned, insightful about the life and work, his brisk narrative puts it all together." *New York Times* reviewer Christopher Lehmann-Haupt considered the book "fascinating" and worthwhile in its assessment of Wilson's literary significance, but the reviewer was "leery of a tendency on Mr. Meyers's part to emphasize the negative" in his subject's personal life. "Perhaps because [Meyers] wrote this intensely detailed book in a single year . . . he was unable to bring to his story a perspective that might have prevented some of his material from coming across as nasty gossip," Lehmann-Haupt commented.

In 1996, Meyers came out with *Robert Frost: A Biography,* which some reviewers deemed a necessary corrective to Lawrance Thompson's highly unflattering biography of this major American poet. Michiko Kakutani in her *New York Times* piece called Meyers's work "a judicious book that serves as a welcome antidote to Thompson's angry screed and to [Meyers's] own earlier exercises in literary destruction." In the *New York Times Book Review,* however, Miranda Seymour contended that Meyers "is not at his thorough and disciplined best in this book . . . [He] seems to have been unable to get under his subject's skin. The Frost he offers is no less an egotistical monster than the man described by Thompson." The critic also questioned the value of Meyers's detailed recounting of Frost's extramarital affair with Kathleen Morrison. Joseph Parisi, a critic for Chicago *Tribune Books,* declared the biography balanced: Meyers, he said, does not hesitate to point out Frost's personal flaws, but also gives "sympathetic explanations" for them. Parisi judged the book's discussion of Frost's poems to be somewhat superficial, but Kakutani praised many of the insights Meyers offers—such as his discussion of the life experiences Frost reflected in one of his best-known poems, "The Road Not Taken." *Robert Frost,* Kakutani added, "is by far Mr. Meyers's most persuasive and thoughtful biography yet."

Meyers fared better with the reviewers upon the publication of his movie star biographies *Gary Cooper: American Hero* and *Bogart: A Life in Hollywood.* Both books tackle difficult subjects: accomplished actors whose off-screen behavior was in turns inscrutable and inconsistent. In her *New York Times Book Review* assessment of *Bogart,* Jeanine Basinger praised the book as "competent, readable and well researched," but she concluded that "Bogart somehow eludes all his biographers and maintains his mystery, possibly because mystery is what movie stardom is all about." Lehmann-Haupt suggested that the appeal of *Bogart* lies in a "simple nostalgia for a dramatic form in which, for all the moral ambiguity of the characters Bogart played, the issues of good and evil were clearer. This, at any rate, is the main appeal of reading about Bogart at length in [this] . . . exhaustive [biography]." In *Salon.com* Jonathan Lethem commended *Gary Cooper* as "crisply written [and] persuasively researched" but further noted: "The on-screen Cooper still resonates, but if the man himself had greater levels of complication, Meyers hasn't found a way to penetrate them." Conversely, *Booklist* correspondent Mike Tribby applauded Meyers's "deft, unshakably evenhanded portrait of an unforgettable star."

In 2000 Meyers published a biography of the notable British novelist George Orwell, author of *Animal Farm* and *1984.* "Ideally a biography of Orwell would be consistent with its subject's unassuming intelligence, and Jeffrey Meyers's admirable *Orwell: Wintry Conscience of a Generation* is that," stated Richard Bernstein in the *New York Times.* Bernstein added that the book "illuminates the ruggedly individualistic Orwell without calling attention to the illuminator." In the Memphis, Tennessee *Commercial Appeal,* Roger K. Miller also separated Meyers's work from previous biographies of Orwell, noting: "Meyers's effort is leagues ahead of all of them, precisely because it so convincingly demonstrates [the] essence of Orwell's character and relates it to his life and work." Paul Marx commended Meyers for the extent of his research, which included interviewing "just about every Orwell contemporary who had had significant contact with him." The critic added: "Meyers' judgment of Orwell's life, therefore, must be given great credence." A *Publishers Weekly* contributor likewise found Meyers to be "admirably objective in depicting Orwell's complex personality and literary importance." Bernstein concluded: "Meyers's fine biography is a reminder of the uniqueness of [Orwell], . . . of just how much he lived, and of how morally and intellectually cauterizing was his thought."

BIOGRAPHICAL/CRITICAL SOURCES:

BOOKS

Brian, Denis, *The True Gen: An Intimate Portrait of Hemingway by Those Who Knew Him Best,* Grove Press (New York, NY), 1988.
Contemporary Literary Criticism Yearbook, 1985, Volume 39, Gale (Detroit, MI), 1986.
Dictionary of Literary Biography, Volume 111: *Twentieth-Century American Literary Biographers,* Gale (Detroit, MI), 1991.
Donoghue, Denis, *England, Their England: Commentaries on English Language and Literature,* Knopf (New York, NY).
Hamilton, Ian, *The Trouble with Money and Other Essays,* Bloomsbury (London, England), 1988.
Moss, Howard, *Whatever Is Moving,* Little, Brown (Boston, MA), 1981.
Powell, Anthony, *Miscellaneous Verdicts: Writings on Writers, 1946-1989,* Heinemann (London, England), 1990.
Seldon, Anthony, and Joanna Pappworth, *By Word of Mouth: "Elite" Oral History,* Methuen (London, England), 1983.

PERIODICALS

American Spectator, March, 1993, pp. 58-59.
Bloomsbury Review, October-November, 1991, pp. 14-15; November-December, 1995, p. 12.
Booklist, February 1, 1997, Bill Ott, review of *Bogart: A Life in Hollywood,* p. 906; May 1, 1998, Mike Tribby, review of *Gary Cooper: American Hero,* p. 1488.
Christian Science Monitor, August 7, 1990, p. 13; April 22, 1991, p. 13; May 10, 1994, p. 15.

Commercial Appeal (Memphis, TN), November 19, 2000, Roger K. Miller, "Orwell Biography Eclipses Previous Ones," p. H3.

Denver Post: Empire Magazine, March 9, 1986, pp. 8-9.

Economist (US), May 17, 1997, review of *Bogart: A Life in Hollywood,* p. S12; November 4, 2000, "Writers' Lives—The Hard School," p. 94.

Entertainment Weekly, April 11, 1997, L. S. Klepp, review of *Bogart: A Life in Hollywood,* p. 78.

Houston Chronicle, November 12, 2000, Paul Marx, " 'Wintry Conscience': Jeffrey Meyers Writes a Fine Biography of a Fascinating Man," p. 17.

Journal and Constitution (Atlanta, GA), May 8, 1994, p. N10.

London Review of Books, January 24, 1991, pp. 22-23; November 10, 1994, pp. 25-26.

Los Angeles Times Book Review, May 23, 1982, p. 16; December 8, 1985, p. 2, 6; July 22, 1990, pp. 1, 13; June 23, 1991, p. 10.

Nation, June 12, 1995, pp. 840-844.

National Review, November 20, 2000, Ronald Radosh, "The Heretic."

New Statesman and Society, October 16, 1992, pp. 39-40.

New Yorker, May 3, 1989, pp. 166-167; June 27, 1994, pp. 186-194; May 8, 1995, pp. 85-89.

New York Review of Books, April 29, 1982, pp. 28-30; January 17, 1991, pp. 10-14; August 11, 1994, pp. 14-16.

New York Times, April 15, 1994, p. C29; May 1, 1995, p. C15; May 17, 1995, p. C18; October 21, 1995, p. C22; April 23, 1996, p. C16; April 17, 1997, Christopher Lehmann-Haupt, "Fundamental Things Apply: Bogart Stars in a Biographical Double Feature"; October 11, 2000, Richard Bernstein, " 'A Kind of Saint' with Thin Patience for the Saintly."

New York Times Book Review, November 17, 1985, pp. 3, 51-52; April 14, 1991, pp. 15-16; April 30, 1995, pp. 6-7; May 19, 1996, p. 8; April 20, 1997, Jeanine Basinger, "Double Bogie," p. 7; June 22, 1998, Jeff Brown, review of *Gary Cooper: American Hero,* p. 39.

Observer, June 9, 1985, p. 25.

Publishers Weekly, September 27, 1985, p. 90; September 18, 1987, p. 166, May 22, 1995, pp. 38-39; February 17, 1997, review of *Bogart: A Life in Hollywood,* p. 202; July 10, 2000, review of *Orwell: Wintry Conscience of a Generation,* p. 52.

Sewanee Review, summer, 1992, pp. 461-66.

Spectator, September 1, 1990, p. 30; June 4, 1994, p. 37.

Times Literary Supplement, October 31, 1980, pp. 1215-16; July 19, 1985, p. 795; October 18, 1985, pp. 1171-72; December 13, 1985, pp. 1415-16; August 1, 1986, pp. 837-38; May 26-June 1, 1989, p. 578; September 7-13, 1990, p. 940; November 15, 1991, pp. 3-4; October 16, 1992, p. 28.

Tribune Books (Chicago, IL), October 18, 1992, pp. 1, 7; May 29, 1994, pp. 3, 10; May 26, 1996, pp. 1, 11.

Voice Literary Supplement, March, 1986, pp. 6-7.

Washington Post Book World, September 6, 1992, pp. 3, 7.

OTHER

Salon.com, http://www.salon.com/books/sneaks/ (June 3, 1998), Jonathan Lethem, review of *Gary Cooper: American Hero.*

*   *   *

MICHAELS, Philip
  See MAGOCSI, Paul Robert

*   *   *

MILES, Barry   1943-

PERSONAL: Born February 21, 1943, in Cheltenham, Gloucestershire, England; son of Albert and May (Bartlett) Miles. *Education:* Gloucestershire College of Art, national diploma in design, 1963; Institute of Education, London, A.T.D., 1964.

ADDRESSES: *Home*—15 Hanson St., No. 2, London W1P 7LL, England. *Agent*—Andrew Wylie, The Wylie Agency, 250 West Fifty-seventh St., New York, NY 10107.

CAREER: Better Books (bookshop), London, England, manager, 1965; Indica Books and Gallery, London, England, owner and manager, 1966-70; founder and sometime editor of *International Times,* 1966-70; Zapple Records, London, England, label manager, 1969; *New Musical Express,* London, England, journalist, 1976-78; Omnibus Press, London, England, editor-in-chief, 1976-78 and 1980-83; *Time Out* (magazine), London, England, editor, 1979; writer and editor. Producer of record albums, including *Allen Ginsberg at Better Books,* 1965; *Lawrence Ferlinghetti at Better*

Books, 1965; *Allen Ginsberg, Lawrence Ferlinghetti, Gregory Corso, and Andrei Voznesenski at the Architectural Association,* Lovebooks, 1965; *Listening to Richard Brautigan,* Harvest, 1970; *William Blake's Songs of Innocence and Experience Tuned by Allen Ginsberg,* MGM Records, 1970; *Lawrence Ferlinghetti,* Fantasy Records, 1971; *The Master Musicians of Jajouka,* Adelphi Records, 1975; and *Charles Olson: Maximus IV.V.VI.,* Folkways Records, 1976.

MEMBER: Groucho Club (London, England).

AWARDS, HONORS: Ordre de la Grande Gidouille, College of Paraphysics, Paris, France, 1965, for promoting the work of Alfred Jarry.

WRITINGS:

A Catalogue of the William S. Burroughs Archive, Covent Garden Press, 1973.

(With Pearce Marchbank) *The Illustrated Rock Almanac,* Paddington Press, 1977.

Bob Dylan, Big O Books (London, England), 1978.

(Compiler) *The Beatles in Their Own Words,* Delilah/Putnam, 1978.

(Compiler) *Bob Dylan in His Own Words,* edited by Marchbank, Quick Fox Books (New York, NY), 1978.

(Compiler with Joe Maynard) *William S. Burroughs: A Bibliography, 1953-1973: Unlocking Inspector Lee's Word Hoard,* University Press of Virginia, 1978.

Pink Floyd, Quick Fox Books (New York, NY), 1980.

(Compiler) *David Bowie in His Own Words,* Omnibus, 1980.

The Rolling Stones: An Illustrated Discography, Omnibus, 1980.

(Compiler) *John Lennon in His Own Words,* Quick Fox Books (New York, NY), 1981.

Pink Floyd: The Illustrated Discography, Omnibus, 1981.

David Bowie: The Black Book, Omnibus, 1981.

The Pretenders, Wise, 1981.

The Clash, Wise, 1981.

The Ramones, Wise, 1981.

The Jam, Wise, 1981.

Talking Heads, Wise, 1981.

(Compiler) *Mick Jagger in His Own Words,* Delilah/Putnam, 1982.

(Editor) Allen Ginsberg, *Howl: Original Draft Facsimile, Transcript and Variant Versions, Fully Annotated by Author, With Contemporaneous Correspondence, Account of First Public Reading, Legal*

Skirmishes, Precursor Texts, and Bibliography, Viking-Penguin, 1986.

Ginsberg: A Biography, Simon & Schuster, 1989.

The Work of William S. Burroughs, W. H. Allen, 1991.

Two Lectures on the Work of Allen Ginsberg, Contemporary Research Press (Dallas, TX), 1993.

William Burroughs: El hombre invisible: A Portrait, Hyperion (New York, NY), 1993.

(With Charles Perry) *I Want to Take You Higher: The Psychedelic Era, 1965-1969* (essays), edited by James Henke and Parke Puterbaugh, Chronicle (San Francisco, CA), 1997.

Paul McCartney: Many Years from Now, Holt (New York, NY), 1997.

Jack Kerouac, King of the Beats: A Portrait, Holt (New York, NY), 1998.

The Beat Hotel: Ginsberg, Burroughs, and Corso in Paris, Grove (New York, NY), 2000.

(Editor, with James Grauerholz) William S. Burroughs, *Naked Lunch,* Grove Press (New York, NY), 2001.

Also (Compiler) *Zappa in His Own Words,* 1992; *Frank Zappa: A Visual Documentary,* 1993; and *Rolling Stones: A Visual Documentary,* 1994. Editor and author of biographical introductions for songbooks published by Wise, including *Eric Clapton,* 1975, *The Rolling Stones File,* 1976, *Linda Ronstadt,* 1978, *Emmylou Harris,* 1978, *Gram Parsons,* 1978, *Carly Simon,* 1978, *The Best of the Byrds,* 1978, *Pink Floyd: The Early Years,* 1978, *The Clash,* 1978, *Elvis: Sun Sessions,* 1978, *Elvis: Ballads,* 1978, *Elvis: Movies,* 1978, *Elvis: Religious Songs,* 1978, *Elvis: Rock and Roll,* 1978, *The Beatles Singles: 1962-70,* 1978, *Cat Stevens,* 1978, *James Taylor,* 1978, *Janis Ian,* 1978, *Joan Baez,* 1978, and *Judy Collins,* 1978. Author of introductions to French editions of William S. Burroughs's works, including *Exterminateur!,* 1974, and *Le Metro Blanc,* 1976. Author of introduction and coeditor, *Merseybeat: The Beginning of the Beatles,* Omnibus, 1978.

Work represented in numerous anthologies, including *Special Pop Anthology,* Alban Michel (Paris, France), 1967; *Notes from the New Underground,* edited by Jessie Kornbluth, Viking, 1968; *Some of IT Anthology,* edited by David Z. Mairowitz, Knuller Publishing (London, England), 1969; *Underground Graphics,* edited by Graham Keen and Michael La Rue, Academy Editions, 1970; *The Rolling Stone Reader,* edited by Ben Fong-Torres, Bantam, 1974; *Rolling Stones '76,* edited by Karl Dallas, Cumbergrove Books (London, England), 1976; *The Illustrated NME Encyclopedia of Rock,* edited by Nick Logan and Bob Woofinden, Hamlyn Publishing Group, 1976; *Zappa: An Anthology,* Babylon

Books (Manchester, England), 1976; *Bananas Anthology,* edited by Emma Tennant, Quartet Books, 1977; and *Elvis: The Memorial Album,* edited by Pearce Marchbank, Omnibus, 1978. Assistant editor, *Bananas,* 1978.

WORK IN PROGRESS: An inventory of Pablo Picasso's "Vollard Suite."

SIDELIGHTS: In publishing *Ginsberg: A Biography,* Barry Miles became the first biographer of one of America's foremost then living poets and social activists. Miles, a rock music journalist and an editor and author of many books on countercultural poets and musicians, had known Allen Ginsberg for twenty years before writing his 1989 biography; he had previously produced recordings of Ginsberg's poetry readings and edited the 1986 annotated version of his poem *Howl.* For this project, Ginsberg provided Miles with unlimited access to his archives and was forthcoming about his life in their many interviews. The result, according to *Tribune Books* contributor Barry Silesky, is such a colorful and provocative chronicle of Ginsberg's life that even readers already familiar with the poet's exploits "will find themselves shaking their heads with some amazement as the incidents pile up."

Miles's task was monumental as the first biographer of this historically, politically, and artistically significant life. Ginsberg, born in 1926, grew up under the divided influence of his father, a respected poet and teacher committed to socialist politics, and his mother, a diagnosed paranoid neurotic who was in and out of mental hospitals and was finally lobotomized. *New York Times Book Review* contributor Paul Berman, in a critique of Miles's biography, summarized Ginsberg's childhood as one in which he "accustomed himself to living in the world of sanity and the world of madness at the same time." This ability to negotiate both worlds continued into his later years. At Columbia University Ginsberg held the respect of notable professors while he befriended semi-intellectual, and often semi-crazy, nonconformists with whom he had many risky and illegal adventures (including one in which he was arrested in a car full of stolen goods). Ginsberg embraced the genius he found in other people's madness, and rather than follow in the political footsteps of his father as expected, he turned to poetry-writing and social activism to promote his vision of individual freedom.

After the now-legendary reading of his poem *Howl* to an enraptured audience in Berkeley, California, in the 1950s, Ginsberg's marriage of poetry and public agitation became a powerful force in turbulent times, Miles maintains. He explained in the biography that Ginsberg's support of "free love," psychedelic drug-induced mind expansion, unsuppressed self-expression, and Buddhist mysticism, as well as his defiance of police and other authority figures, outraged many but captivated an increasingly rebellious group of American youth. With novelists Jack Kerouac and William S. Burroughs and poets Lawrence Ferlinghetti and Gregory Corso, Ginsberg founded and cultivated the "Beat Generation," a group of alienated youth who sought to break down repressive artistic and social conventions in the 1950s. A decade later Ginsberg was entrenched in his increasingly prominent role as cult leader, and was viewed, *Los Angeles Times Book Review* contributor Todd Gitlin wrote in his assessment of the biography, as "a major personification of the spirit of the '60s."

Ginsberg: A Biography, according to Silesky, is "a mountain of anecdotal information," chronicling not only the events of Ginsberg's life but also the rise of the Beat Generation and hippie culture. Other reviewers agreed that the book is very successful in evoking social and political movements and provides a look at Ginsberg which is, in Silesky's words, "simply fascinating." *Globe and Mail* contributor Miriam Waddington, while praising Miles's animated writing, complained, however, that "the shape of [Ginsberg's] life is lost in a loose accumulation of anecdote, conversation and journal excerpt." Reviewers also found Miles to be fairly uncritical of the poet and his work. Nevertheless, with this abundance of material, much of it straight from the source, critics agreed that *Ginsberg: A Biography* effectively presents the voice of its subject. Gitlin concluded that "Miles' sketch is enthralling—Ginsberg himself sees to that, leaving traces of humor and vehemence everywhere, continuing his life in the open."

In *William Burroughs: El Hombre Invisible* Miles covers the life of the controversial writer (1914-1997) and author of *Naked Lunch* (1959) from his beginnings in St. Louis, Missouri to his settling in Lawrence, Kansas in 1984. Miles discusses Burroughs's sexuality, drug addiction, career, and influence on modern culture. A *Publishers Weekly* reviewer felt Miles was at his best "when considering the genesis and intermingling of Burroughs's fiction and nonfiction."

Miles wrote the authorized biography of his long-time friend and Beatle, *Paul McCartney: Many Years from Now* based on hundreds of hours of interviews conducted over five years. *Maclean's* reviewer Nicholas Jennings felt that the core of the biography "is an examination of McCartney's relationship with Lennon as both friend and collaborator. The author includes a song-by-song analysis of every tune the two wrote together." Miles's extensive quotes by McCartney reflect his admiration and love for Lennon. Jennings felt that the quotes provide "a sense of intimacy and immediacy."

Miles traces McCartney's career with the Beatles from their beginnings in Liverpool playing in a church basement to their rise as the stars of British pop and the swinging London scene. Miles tells how McCartney's relationship with actress Jane Asher led to the formation of the Indica Bookshop and Gallery with John Dunbar, Miles, and Asher, where Lennon first met Yoko Ono. McCartney became a pothead when introduced to marijuana by Bob Dylan, who had first used it with journalist Al Aronowitz, who had been introduced to it by Allen Ginsberg. McCartney initiated Mick Jagger in the use of marijuana. Miles tells that the "you" in *Got to Get You into My Life* referred to marijuana. He also notes the narrator of *Norwegian Wood* is referring to pine paneling he burns after being rejected by a young woman. *Ob-La-Di Ob-La-Da* means "life goes on" in the Yoruba language, a phrase McCartney learned from a Nigerian conga player. Jennings commented that Miles fails to provide much detail on McCartney's marriage to Linda.

"Miles delves into the making of each Beatles album in a fascinating way," wrote Jeffrey L. Perlah in *Billboard.* "An especially interesting section of the book deals with the making of *Sgt. Pepper's Lonely Hearts Club Band,* a record in which the band members tried to show their alter-egos and diversity." Perlah said that "Lennon's eventual heroin abuse, his falling out with McCartney just before the Beatles's breakup, and the infighting over business control of the band will make you sad, but the overall tone of this book is uplifting." Peter Ames Carlin said in *People Weekly* that *Paul McCartney* "is a must read for anyone interested in the Beatles, the 1960s or, for that matter, modern culture itself."

Library Journal contributor William Gargan called *Jack Kerouac, King of the Beats: A Portrait* Miles's "unflattering" biography of Kerouac (1922-1969), in which he views the Beat author as "insensitive, selfish, and cowardly." Miles drew from interviews conducted in his writing of the Ginsberg biography in portraying the author of *On the Road* (1957). Ann Douglas of the *New York Times Book Review* commented that "the highest praise a biographer can offer his subject is extensive research, a commodity in short supply here. Nor

does Miles display much understanding of the life or the work he is examining. Instead, he frequently trivializes the risks Kerouac took with his vagrant lifestyle and his writing. *King of the Beats,* as the book's title has it, was an epithet bestowed on Kerouac by a hostile press, one Kerouac loathed and used only ironically. Indeed, it is hard to see what motive Miles may have had for this undertaking, beyond cashing in on the Kerouac revival now under way."

Kerouac was born to working-class French-Canadian parents in Lowell, Massachusetts. He entered Columbia on a football scholarship in 1940 but dropped out in 1942. It was in 1944 that he met the other Beats in New York City. Kerouac's first novel *The Town and the City* was published in 1950. He wrote *On the Road* in 1951, but it was rejected for years before he found a publisher. Many assumed the protagonist, Dean Moriarty, was Kerouac, but, in fact, Kerouac had fashioned this character after Neal Cassady, who left his wife and child to travel with Kerouac. Kerouac suffered under media criticism of *On the Road* and his spontaneous writing style and was abusing alcohol much of the time. Douglas compared Kerouac to significant figures in other media—Charlie Parker, Jackson Pollock, and Marlon Brando—in his attempt "to create an explosively lyrical, charismatic style."

Mick Brown pointed out for *Literary Review* online that Kerouac avoided military service when he was diagnosed as schizophrenic, "although this seems inadequate to describe the cornucopia of his psychological problems. . . . A misogynist, he was unable to sustain any sort of emotional commitment to a woman." Brown noted that Kerouac had been married three times, but that he was closest to his mother, "Memere," "to whom he would return like a faithful retriever after each of his frenetic excursions on the road. Memere was a monster: a foul-mouthed, virulent racist and anti-Semite who banned Kerouac's Jewish friends, including the saintly Allen Ginsberg, from the house, and who did everything she could to sabotage her son's relationship with women." Kerouac had sexual relationships with many men, including Burroughs, Ginsberg, and Gore Vidal, but he never was a partner of Cassady, although he admired him.

Kerouac's daughter, Jan, whose paternity he denied, fell into addiction and prostitution. Miles feels Kerouac was responsible. Miles called Kerouac "a great writer, but when it came to the human values of compassion, tenderness and care for others he failed miserably. As a human being, he was insensitive, selfish, and cowardly." By the time Kerouac died of alcoholism, he was filled with self-loathing and had adopted the anti-Semitic prejudices of his parents. Douglas wrote that "there is no sense in this book of how extreme, chronic alcoholism brings out the worst, but not necessarily the truest, aspects of the drinker's personality, a fact Kerouac repeatedly acknowledged, describing himself . . . as 'a maniacal drunkard,' a 'scared . . . dumbhead loudmouth.' "

Douglas pointed out that despite his abuse, many of Kerouac's lovers and friends remained loyal. Douglas noted that Miles did not interview either writer Joyce Johnson or musician David Amram, both Jewish, who have said that they never experienced anti-Semitism in their friendships with Kerouac. Kerouac vowed to never be a hypocrite, a vow he kept. Toward the end of his life, his style fell out of favor, but he predicted in 1965 that "some great catastrophe is going to make people wake up again."

In *The Beat Hotel: Ginsberg, Burroughs, and Corso in Paris* Miles documents the years when the three Beat writers lived in a bohemian Left Bank rooming house during a period when many writers and artists flocked to Paris to experience sexual and creative freedom. It was during the six years (1957-1963) at 9 rue Git-le-Coeur that Burroughs completed *Naked Lunch* and where he was nearly arrested for dealing heroin. Ginsberg began *Kaddish* and wrote *To Aunt Rose, The Lion for Real,* and *At Apollinaire's Grave,* and Corso wrote *Bomb.* Burroughs's "cut-up" method influenced the next generation of artists, according to Miles, and the trio opened the door to the use of drugs, including psychedelics, sexual freedom, gay rights, and legalized pornography. A *Publishers Weekly* reviewer wrote that the hotel, "closed for nearly four decades now, still symbolizes the fruitful ground of collaborative creation among the Beats."

Miles told *CA:* "All my work has been essentially editorial—promoting the work of people I admire through bookselling, journalism, editing, and/or publishing their work or writing bibliographies and/or biographies about them. I enjoy working in the area between high art and popular culture, between academic bibliography and underground or rock-and-roll journalism."

BIOGRAPHICAL/CRITICAL SOURCES:

PERIODICALS

Billboard, December 6, 1997, Jeffrey L. Perlah, review of *Paul McCartney: Many Years from Now,* p. 86.
Booklist, August, 1993, Aaron Cohen, review of *William Burroughs: El Hombre Invisible,* p. 2029.

Globe and Mail (Toronto, Ontario, Canada), November 18, 1989.
Kirkus Reviews, June 1, 1993, review of *William Burroughs: El Hombre Invisible.*
Library Journal, July, 1993, William Gargan, review of *William Burroughs: El Hombre Invisible,* p. 81; October 1, 1998, William Gargan, review of *Jack Kerouac, King of the Beats,* p. 86.
Los Angeles Times Book Review, February 15, 1987; October 29, 1989.
Maclean's, December 29, 1997, Nicholas Jennings, review of *Paul McCartney: Many Years from Now,* p. 106.
New York Times Book Review, October 1, 1989; January 24, 1999, Ann Douglas, "On the Road, Again."
People Weekly, December 22, 1997, Peter Ames Carlin, review of *Paul McCartney: Many Years from Now,* p. 33.
Publishers Weekly, June 14, 1993, review of *William Burroughs: El Hombre Invisible,* p. 58; October 5, 1998, review of *Jack Kerouac, King of the Beats,* p. 66; June 19, 2000, review of *The Beat Hotel,* p. 70.
Times Literary Supplement, March 9, 1990.
Tribune Books (Chicago, IL), September 3, 1989.
USA Today, July, 1995, Steven G. Kellman, review of *Howl,* p. 96.
Vogue, June, 1993, Edmund White, review of *William Burroughs: El Hombre Invisible,* p. 92.

OTHER

Literary Review, http://www.litreview.com/ (August 18, 2000).*

*   *   *

MOI, Toril   1953-

PERSONAL: Born 1953, in Norway. *Education:* University of Bergen, Mag.Art., 1980, Dr.Art., 1985.

ADDRESSES: Office—Literature Program, Duke University, Durham, NC 27708-0670.

CAREER: Writer and educator. Oxford University, Oxford, England, lecturer, 1983-85; University of Bergen, Norway, director of Centre for Feminist Research in the Humanities, then adjunct professor of comparative literature, 1985-88; Duke University, Durham, NC, professor of literature and romance studies, 1989-98,

James B. Duke Professor of Literature and Romance Studies, 1999—.

AWARDS, HONORS: John Simon Guggenheim Fellow, 2001.

WRITINGS:

Sexual/Textual Politics: Feminist Literary Theory, Methuen (New York, NY), 1985.
Feminist Literary Theory and Simone de Beauvoir, Basil Blackwell (Oxford, England), 1990.
Simone de Beauvoir: The Making of an Intellectual Woman, Basil Blackwell (Oxford, England), 1994.
What Is a Woman?: And Other Essays, Oxford University Press (New York, NY), 1999.

EDITOR

The Kristeva Reader, Columbia University Press (New York, NY), 1986.
French Feminist Thought: A Reader, Basil Blackwell (Oxford, England), 1987.
(With Janice A. Radway) *Materialist Feminism,* Duke University Press (Durham, NC), 1994.

Contributor of essays to books, including *In Dora's Case: Feminism—Psychoanalysis—Hysteria,* edited by Charles Bernheimer and Claire Kahane, Columbia University Press, 1985; *Gender and Theory: Dialogues on Feminist Criticism,* edited by Linda Kauffman, Basil Blackwell, 1989; and *Between Feminism and Psychoanalysis,* edited by Teresa Brennan, Routledge, 1989. Contributor as a translator and reviewer to journals, including *Vinduet, Edda, Kontrast, Signs, Buchnell Review, New Literary History, Diacritics,* and *French Studies.*

WORK IN PROGRESS: A book on Henrik Ibsen; work on feminism and feminist theory.

SIDELIGHTS: Norwegian-born feminist theorist Toril Moi is the author of several books on feminist literary theory. Her 1985 work, *Sexual/Textual Politics: Feminist Literary Theory,* reviews the two most widely utilized approaches to feminist literary theory: Anglo-American empirical studies and French poststructuralist *écriture.* Moi's ability to present complex theoretical discussions in a lucid and objective manner have won her praise from academics and critics alike. Unique in her approach is Moi's attempt to reveal the theoretical assumptions underlying both forms of criticism and compare and contrast these assumptions with the social and political feminist agenda.

In *Sexual/Textual Politics* Moi discusses the work of many of the major feminist critics of the twentieth century. She begins with Virginia Woolf, whom she hails as the founder of the discipline. Elaine Showalter, Mary Ellman, Kate Millet, Ellen Moers, Sandra Gilbert, and Susan Gubar are each critiqued in the book's first section, as Moi "uncovers the 'gaps,' 'absences,' and fissures in their texts through which ideology can be glimpsed," according to *Women's Review of Books* reviewer Ellen Cronan Rose. While praising French theorists—which include Hélène Cixous, Luce Irigaray, and Julia Kristeva—as the true heirs of Woolf because of their grounding in theoretical, as opposed to empirical, discourse, this "does not blind Moi to the shortcomings of their writings," judged Pamela McCallum in *Signs:* "On the contrary, she aims at a critique and reevaluation of their texts in the light of a more committed sexual/textual politics." While noting that some would take issue with Moi's critical appraisal of certain literary theorists, Rose concluded that "*Sexual/Textual Politics* commands our respect. . . . because of its unflinching integrity. Intended as an 'introduction to feminist literary theory,' this book exemplifies feminist theory-making at its rigorous best."

In addition to *Sexual/Textual Politics,* Moi has authored a number of other books introducing the work of renowned feminist literary theorists. *Feminist Theory and Simone de Beauvoir* and *Simone de Beauvoir: The Making of an Intellectual Woman* cover the career of a woman whom Moi considers "the most important feminist intellectual of the twentieth century." As with all of Moi's writing, these books are engaging narratives easily traversed by the novice reader. Meryl Altman, a reviewer in *Women's Review of Books,* found *Simone de Beauvoir* to be "a lovely, articulate, informative book, firm-minded but sympathetic, responsibly historical, attentive to textual detail." Altman credited the book with teaching her "more than almost any other . . . about how literary criticism could still be made to do feminist work." At the same time, Altman noted the complete lack of "theory with a capital T" in Moi's examination of Beauvoir, leading the critic to surmise "whether there could be two Toril Mois."

In 1999 Moi published *What Is a Woman?: And Other Essays,* a collection containing two new and lengthy essays on Simone de Beauvoir, along with a retrospective of nine shorter essays drawn in roughly reverse chronological order from throughout Moi's career. Altman characterized *What Is a Woman?* as a "complex huge doorstop of a book [536 pages] . . . really two books, the first a substantive new piece of work exploring Beauvoir's continuing value for feminism, the other a loosely connected set of essays ranging from Tristan and Iseult to Pierre Bourdieu." The theories of Sigmund Freud as they apply to contemporary feminist thought also figure prominently in the retrospective section of the book.

Moi's stated aim with the Beauvoir essays, the first of which gives the work its title, is to provide a functional definition of what it means to be a woman without employing either essentialist metaphysics or biological determinism. These essays also, according to Moi, represent an attempt to move beyond poststructuralism in feminist literary theory. A reviewer in *Kirkus Reviews* commented that "readers who can stay with Moi's densely argumentative style—she spends over a hundred pages analyzing the first three paragraphs of *The Second Sex*—will be rewarded with a cutting-edge view of contemporary feminist critique in its continuing struggle to establish just what its subject is." Central to this critique are Moi's rejection of the sex/gender distinction as indispensable to feminist theory and her affirmation of the personal, as well as the philosophical, as a legitimate approach to feminist studies. Rather than hampering feminist thought with preconceived political or theoretical rules, Moi proposes a feminism of freedom that harkens back to Beauvoir's philosophy. "It would be impossible to exaggerate the sense of relief this book gave me," stated Altman, referring to the fact that Moi "argues persuasively" that "compared to what passes for feminist theory now, existentialism looks pretty darn good." Altman's extensive praise for the collection was tempered by what she saw as its failure to suggest how feminist groups can form and initiate change in society.

Moi's interest in broadening the public's understanding of feminist literary theory has also prompted her to edit several anthologies of criticism, including *The Kristeva Reader, French Feminist Thought: A Reader,* and *Materialist Feminism.*

BIOGRAPHICAL/CRITICAL SOURCES:

PERIODICALS

Arizona Quarterly, winter, 1989.
Bloomsbury Review, November, 1989, p. 30.
English Journal, March, 1991, p. 89.
Kirkus Reviews, December 15, 1999, review of *What Is a Woman? And Other Essays.*
London Review of Books, May 18, 2000, Lorna Sage, "Mother's Back," pp. 37-38.
Modern Fiction Studies, Volume 34, number 3, 1988.
Prose Studies, September, 1987.
Signs, summer, 1987, p. 822.

Times Literary Supplement, May 26, 2000, Elizabeth Fallaize, "De Beauvoir Embodied," p. 31.
Women's Review of Books, February, 1986, p. 17; January, 1996, p. 9; October, 2000, Meryl Altman, "Reality Check," pp. 6-7.*

* * *

MOMEN, Moojan 1950-

PERSONAL: Given name is pronounced "Moozhaane"; born January 25, 1950, in Tabriz, Iran; British citizen; son of Sedratu'llah (an airplane pilot) and Gloria (a fashion designer; maiden name, Iman) Momen; married Wendi Worth (a publisher), June 12, 1971; children: Sedrhat (son), Carmel (daughter). *Ethnicity:* "Iranian." *Education:* St. John's College, Cambridge, B.A., 1971, M.A., 1974; Guy's Hospital, London, B.Chir., 1974, M.B., 1975. *Politics:* "None." *Religion:* Baha'i.

ADDRESSES: Agent—c/o George Ronald Publishers, 46 High St., Kidlington, Oxford OX5 2DN, England. *E-mail*—momen@northill.demon.co.uk.

CAREER: Guy's and St. Olave's Hospitals, London, England, house officer, 1974-75; Plymouth General Hospital, Plymouth, England, senior house officer, 1976-78; general medical practitioner, 1980—. Afnan Library Trust, London, England, trustee, 1983—; Landegg Academy, Switzerland, member of the Faculty of Graduate Studies, Department of Religion, 1997—.

MEMBER: British Society for Middle East Studies, British Society for Persian Studies, Society for Iranian Studies, Association for Baha'i Studies, Fellow of the Royal Asiatic Society.

WRITINGS:

Dr. J. E. Esslemont, Baha'i Publishing Trust (London, England), 1975.
(Translator) Muhammad Labib, *The Seven Martyrs of Hurmuzak,* George Ronald (Oxford, England), 1981.
The Babi and Baha'i Religions, 1844-1944: Some Contemporary Western Accounts, George Ronald (Oxford, England), 1981.
(Editor and contributor) *Studies in Babi and Baha'i History,* Volume I, Kalimat Press (Los Angeles, CA), 1982, volume II (with Juan R. Cole), 1984.

Introduction to Shi'i Islam: The History and Doctrines of Twelver Shi'ism, Yale University Press (New Haven, CT), 1985.

(Editor) *Selections From the Writings of E. G. Browne on the Babi and Baha'i Religions,* George Ronald (Oxford, England), 1987.

(Editor) *Studies in Honor of the Late Hasan M. Balyuzi,* Volume 5: *Studies of the Babi and Baha'i Religions,* Kalimat Press (Los Angeles, CA), 1988.

Hinduism and the Baha'i Faith, George Ronald (Oxford, England), 1990.

Buddhism and the Baha'i Faith, George Ronald (Oxford, England), 1995.

(Editor) *Scripture and Revelation,* George Ronald (Oxford, England), 1998.

The Phenomenon of Religion: A Thematic Approach, Oneworld (Oxford, England), 1999.

Islam and the Baha'i Faith, George Ronald (Oxford, England), 2000.

Also author of *The Works of Shaykh Ahmad al-Ahsa'i: A Bibliography* (Baha'i Studies Monograph, no. 1), Newcastle, 1991. Contributor to books, including *Studies in Babi and Baha'i History,* volume III, edited by Peter Smith, Kalimat Press (Los Angeles, CA), 1986; *Islamic Fundamentalism* (Royal Asiatic Seminar Papers No. 1), edited by R. M. Burrell, Royal Asiatic Society, 1989; *Central Asia Tradition and Change,* edited by S. Akiner, Kegan Paul International (London, England), 1991; *Iranian Refugees and Exiles Since Khomeni,* edited by Asghar Fathi, Mazda Publications (London, England), 1991; *Islam in the Contemporary World,* edited by Theodore Gabriel, Vikas (New Delhi, India), 2000; *Encyclopaedia Iranica;* and *Encyclopedia of the Modern Islamic World.* Also contributor to scholarly journals, including *Iran, International Journal of Middle East Studies, Past and Present,* and *Religion,* and contributor of book reviews to *Bulletin of the British Society for Middle Eastern Studies, American Historical Review, Middle East Journal, Journal of the Royal Asiatic Society, Iranian Studies, Journal of Semitic Studies, Journal of Baha'i Studies,* and *Baha'i Studies Review.*

WORK IN PROGRESS: "Research on Baha'i social history, and on comparative religion."

SIDELIGHTS: Moojan Momen explained to *CA* that he began writing because "I felt there was no adequate, scholarly book on the history of the Baha'i faith. My interest in the subject was increased because most previous works on the Baha'i faith had been written polemic either for or against the religion. Though I am a Baha'i myself, I hope that my own books are suffi-

ciently objective to be useful additions to the knowledge of the subject.

"My first books are the result of research undertaken in the Public Records Office and elsewhere while I was assisting H. M. Balyuzi in his own research. My book on Shi'i Islam came about because the roots of the Baha'i faith are in Shi'ism, and there was no comprehensive survey of this aspect of Islam. Using this as a basis, I have now expanded into the area of comparative religion and my book, *The Phenomenon of Religion,* is an attempt to use my knowledge of Islam and the Baha'i faith to gain an understanding of the various ways in which the religious impulse of humanity manifests itself.

"The Baha'i faith began in the middle of the nineteenth century in Iran. Its roots are in Shi'i Islam, although it claims to be a world religion completely independent of Islam. Its founder took the title Baha'u'llah (meaning Glory of God) and claimed that he was the fulfillment of the messianic prophecies of all religions: Islam, Christianity, Judaism, Zoroastrianism, etc. Baha'u'llah was exiled from Iran and, after successive banishments, finally came to Akka in Palestine.

"Baha'u'llah's central teaching is that all the religions of the world have been part of an evolutionary and progressive process culminating in the present age which is the age in which God intends to establish the unity of the world. This will occur upon the basis of such social teachings as universal education, equality between men and women, and a world government. However, it also requires the spiritual development of the individual in order that he or she can initiate and participate in this process.

"The Baha'i faith has no priesthood and is administered by elected bodies. It has few rituals but has a number of personal laws such as daily private prayer. It has now spread to most parts of the world with large communities of Baha'is in many parts of the Third World: India, Africa, South America, and the Pacific."

BIOGRAPHICAL/CRITICAL SOURCES:

PERIODICALS

America, May 3, 1986.
Books and Religion, January, 1986.
Library Journal, October-December, 1985.
Listener, July 18, 1985.
Perspective, Volume 110, no. 6, 1985.
Times Higher Education Supplement, September 20, 1985.

Times Literary Supplement, October 4, 1985.*

*   *   *

MORI, Kyoko 1957-

PERSONAL: Born March 9, 1957, in Kobe, Japan; immigrated to the United States, 1977; naturalized U.S. citizen, 1984; daughter of Hiroshi (an engineer) and Takako (a homemaker; maiden name, Nagai) Mori; married Charles Brock (an elementary school teacher), March 17, 1984 (divorced). *Education:* Rockford College, B.A., 1979; University of Wisconsin—Milwaukee, M.A. 1981, Ph.D., 1984. *Politics:* Democrat, feminist. *Avocational interests:* Fiber arts (knitting, spinning, weaving), running, birdwatching.

ADDRESSES: Home—Cambridge, MA. *Office*—Department of English, Harvard University, Barker Center, 12 Quincy, Cambridge, MA 02138. *Agent*—Ann Rittenberg, 14 Montgomery Pl., Brooklyn, NY 11215.

CAREER: Saint Norbert College, De Pere, WI, associate professor of English and writer-in-residence, beginning 1984; Harvard University, Cambridge, MA, Briggs-Copeland Lecturer in Creative Writing; writer.

MEMBER: Modern Language Association of America, Associated Writing Programs.

AWARDS, HONORS: Editors' Prize, *Missouri Review,* 1992, for poem "Fallout"; American Library Association Best Book for Young Adults, *New York Times* Notable Book, *Publishers Weekly* Editors' Choice, Council of Wisconsin Writers Best Novel, and Elizabeth Burr award for best children's book of the year, Wisconsin Library Association, all 1993, all for *Shizuko's Daughter;* Paterson Poetry Center Best Books for Young Adults, Council of Wisconsin Writers Best Novel, American Library Association Best Book for Young Adults, and Children's Books of Distinction Award, *Hungry Mind Review,* 1996, all for *One Bird.*

WRITINGS:

Shizuko's Daughter, Holt (New York, NY), 1993.
Fallout (poems), Ti Chucha Press, 1994.
The Dream of Water: A Memoir, Holt (New York, NY), 1995.
One Bird, Holt (New York, NY), 1995.
Polite Lies: On Being a Woman Caught between Cultures (essays), Holt (New York, NY), 1998.

Kyoko Mori

Stone Field, True Arrow, Holt (New York, NY), 2000.

Contributor of short stories to books, including *When I Was Your Age: Original Stories about Growing Up,* edited by Amy Erlich, Candlewick Press (New York, NY), 1999; contributor to periodicals, including *Apalachee Quarterly, Beloit Poetry Journal, Crosscurrents, Kenyon Review—New Series, Prairie Schooner,* and *South-East Review.* Contributor of poems to periodicals, including *Missouri Review, Paterson Review, American Scholar,* and *Denver Quarterly.* Contributor of articles to *Writer.*

WORK IN PROGRESS: A novel; poems.

SIDELIGHTS: In several of her prose works, award-winning novelist and poet Kyoko Mori poignantly describes the devastating pain that haunts a young person who must deal with the death of a beloved parent. After coping with the suicide of her mother when Mori was still a preteen, she was then forced to watch her once secure way of life become drastically altered through the tirades of a selfish, patriarchal, and unfeeling father and an insensitive and equally selfish stepmother. This abiding sense of loss, which deprived Mori of both family and community and which has imbued much of her written work, would eventually prompt her to voluntarily give up yet another tie with her youth: her country.

Attending an American college on a scholarship program, she felt more in sync with the relaxed, less emotionally inhibited culture of the United States than she did with the strictures in place in Japanese society. Since her college days, Mori has made her home in the United States, where she has written and published several critically acclaimed novels for young adults, the poignant memoir *The Dream of Water,* and *Polite Lies: On Being a Woman Caught between Cultures,* a book of essays.

Mori was born on the main island of Honshu, in the city of Kobe, Japan, in 1957. Located near both mountains and water, "Kobe is a very beautiful, sophisticated city," she once noted, "but it is also close to nature." The daughter of an engineer and his wife, she was born with both hips displaced, and spent her first year in leg harnesses to correct her gait. Fortunately, that condition was corrected and Mori was soon able to accompany her mother on walks in the mountains and enjoy the visits to the country home of her grandparents that the family made before she began school. She was inspired with an early love of reading and a love of beauty by her mother. A sensitive and creative woman, Takako Mori made a cultured home for her children, reading to both Kyoko and her younger brother, Jumpei, from the time both children were small. Tragically, Takako would commit suicide when Mori was twelve, a victim of depression and, perhaps, the repressive Japanese society that relegated women to a subservient status in relation to their husbands.

While, like most Japanese children, Mori had an early exposure to a few English words and phrases, she began a serious study of the language and its literature when she was twelve. She was immediately struck with the emotional content of much Western writing in comparison with the restraint of its Japanese counterpart; English would be her major in college and she now writes exclusively in her adopted language. "In my teenage years I read a lot of English books in English," she explained in an interview for *Authors and Artists for Young Adults* (*AAYA*). "Before then I don't remember that much what I read, because I don't think that in Japan they really have books written for teenagers. You have to read 'literature'—some 'Great Book' by some guy who died fifty years ago or something. And that was fine; I liked some of that. But to be thirteen and to be a girl and to read that is not necessarily a good experience because [much of Japanese literature] was so male and with such different aesthetics than my everyday life." While she was drawn to the beauty of the language she was exposed to in the books she read in

school, Western books such as *Jane Eyre* and *Anne of Green Gables* captured her imagination.

In her junior year of high school, Mori was given the opportunity to study at a school in Mesa, Arizona, for a year as an exchange student. "It was a revelation for me," she once commented. "For the first time in my life I was away from the social constrictions of my society. In Japan there is so much pressure from family. You can't do . . . [certain things] because it will bring shame to your family." After returning to her home, Mori decided to intensify her studies in English; during her first two years of college in Japan she majored in the subject. "After my year in the United States, I began to think of English as my writing language. So much of Japanese aesthetics is involved in not saying what you want to. To talk about yourself in Japanese is considered rude. So English became a much better language for me as a writer." Her focus on writing in English became so intensive that Mori decided to finish her college education in the United States. She earned a scholarship to Rockford College in 1977 and graduated from that school two years later. She went on to complete her master's degree and Ph.D. and establish a career as a writer and educator.

Shizuko's Daughter, Mori's first published book, was released in 1993. Based on a group of short stories that she wrote for her doctoral dissertation, the book tells the story of Yuki, a young girl who returns from a music lesson one day to discover her mother dead by her own hand. "People will tell you that I've done this because I did not love you," reads the suicide note Shizuko leaves for her daughter. "Don't listen to them. When you grow up to be a strong woman, you will know that this is for the best." During the six years that follow, Yuki must learn to deal with the changes in her life that follow her mother's death: the remarriage of her father, the gradual estrangement of grandparents, and her deep feelings of responsibility and guilt over her mother's unhappiness. Calling the book a "jewel," *New York Times Book Review* contributor Liz Rosenberg felt *Shizuko's Daughter* to be "one of those rarities that shine out only a few times in a generation. It begins and ends with a dream, with a death, yet it is not dreamy or tragic."

Shizuko's Daughter wasn't intended to be a young adult novel to begin with. But as Mori began to revise and edit her initial manuscript with the advice of her editor, she realized that conforming it to certain conventions of the genre ultimately made it a better novel: "Because the way I had it before, I time-skipped around a lot.

Straightening that out made it a more straightforward book, which is what it needed to be."

One Bird, which Mori published in 1995, is even more concise than the author's first book. In the novel, fifteen-year-old Megumi watches as her mother packs her suitcase and leaves the house of her husband, Megumi's father. Unable to go with her mother because to do so would be neither "appropriate" in Japanese society nor financially possible, Megumi is forced to deal with the vacuum left by her mother's abrupt departure, a vacuum that her distant father avoids filling by staying with an out-of-town mistress for long periods of time. During the course of the novel, her emotions and reactions shift from those of a little girl to those of a young woman through the support of a woman veterinarian whom she meets while attempting to care for a small bird. Ultimately, Megumi is able to creatively find a solution to her problem, a solution whereby she and her mother can spend at least part of the year together. "Kyoko Mori's second novel . . . is so lively and affecting that one imagines its readers will be too engaged by its heroine's situation to notice how much— and how painlessly—they are learning about another culture," according to *New York Times Book Review* critic Francine Prose. Noting that the book is filled with "small, radiant schemes and glints of observation," Prose added that *One Bird* shows that teen feelings and attitudes toward life are universal.

As Mori once noted, writing for teens requires that authors rely more on character and plot than on imagery and style. "Both [*Shizuko's Daughter* and *One Bird*] had to be more straightforward, and in a way I think that this made them better books, because sometimes it is so easy to rely on your ability to write and, when you get to some crucial moment in the narrative, try to get through it through fine writing and strong imagery. And I see this as something that I am tempted to do because I am also a poet.

"But I think what you do well is also your downfall," Mori added. "And I think that when you're a poet as well as a fiction writer, there is always the temptation to do something poetic at a crucial moment. Writing for teens, you're not allowed to do that. You have to be straightforward and direct in developing the characters and manipulating the plot."

One Bird and *Shizuko's Daughter* are essentially the same story, seen from different points of view, according to Mori. "One is a tragic version of the story about an isolated teenager and the other is a more humorous version," the author explained. "In *One Bird,* I think

there is an inherent sense of humor and resilience that Megumi doesn't take herself that seriously, not in the way that the teen in *Shizuko's Daughter* has to take herself seriously." Mori characterizes the books as "two flavors of the same thing," admitting that "maybe I needed to do that to grow up. I think that even though I didn't write those books to grow up, it became a process of that. When I first wrote *Shizuko's Daughter,* it was a way of admitting the pain in my life perhaps. And then when I wrote *One Bird,* it was a way of being able to look at that same story with more irreverence. And humor."

In 1990, with the manuscript for *Shizuko's Daughter* circulating among publishers, Mori decided to go to Japan on sabbatical "because it was the only foreign country where I speak the language," she once explained to *AAYA.* She planned to keep a journal, out of which poems normally sprang, and then begin work on a new novel. While she was in Japan, visiting parts of the country that she had never seen as a child and spending time with beloved relatives, she thought to herself, "I'm kind of gathering material and waiting for that novel to form." Finding the time to keep a journal record of her thoughts and reflections was not difficult: "I couldn't sleep in Japan because I was jet-lagged," Mori recalled. "I kept waking up; I couldn't fall asleep, . . . but in a way this was good because it gave me a lot of time to write. In the middle of the night I can't sleep; what else am I going to do? I can only read so much."

After returning to her home in Wisconsin and writing several poems based on her experiences in her native country, Mori realized that an autobiography, rather than a novel, was to be the literary outcome of her trip. "I knew in Japan that the trip was so specific to my family that I couldn't see how I could write it as a novel," the writer explained. "I would be translating these facts in an uncreative way rather than transforming them. So I decided that I would do this as a nonfiction, autobiographical narrative." Mori realized from the start of her new project that she had a wealth of literary models, including *The Woman Warrior* by Maxine Hong Kingston, that read like novels but are nonfiction. The result of her creative efforts was *The Dream of Water: A Memoir.*

In *The Dream of Water,* the reader is drawn into the narrator's reality, but that reality is as compelling as a work of fiction due to Mori's ability to imbue her relatives and her setting with qualities that transcend the mundane and everyday. Each person she meets on her trip is linked to past memories, and past and present interweave on both a physical and emotional plain. Her beloved grandfather is dead, and she is left with only memories and the journals a relative saved for Mori after his death. The house where she lived when her mother committed suicide is gone, replaced by a parking lot, and yet the memories that empty space conjures up render it almost ghostlike. Called "deeply private" by *Booklist* contributor Donna Seaman, Mori's memoir unfolds with "dignity and cathartic integrity, chronicling not only her struggle with grief, anger, and guilt" and her growing understanding of the differences between Japanese and U.S. culture, but the author's ability to ultimately "finally feel at home in both worlds."

"I always wanted to be a writer," Mori once said. "When you're a kid, though, you have all these different aspirations, from the firefighter all the way to the great composer, all at the same time. While I had a series of these dreams, being a writer was always on the list. So every year it would be a different list, but the recurring one was that I wanted to be a writer." In grade school she did a lot of writing, but it was actually her mother and grandfather who inspired her to take her writing seriously. "My grandfather wrote journal entries every morning," Mori recalled, looking back at the visits she made to her grandparents' house as a young child. "When I would go and stay with his family, he would get up and write in his diary. And that really inspired me. Writing was a serious thing. It was something my grandfather did every morning." Mori, who now teaches creative writing at Saint Norbert College in De Pere, Wisconsin, considers herself to be a fairly disciplined writer. "I'm not disciplined all the way in my life," she admitted, "but there are three or four things I'm very disciplined about: running is one of them, and writing. Those are things that I don't have a hard time getting to."

A poet as well as a prose writer, Mori's craft follows certain stages, beginning with thoughts jotted down in journal entries, then poetry, and finally into prose. "I don't see the poems as just a process," she explained; "I see them as finished products. But once I do about ten poems, I start thinking, 'There's something I could do with this.' There's a collective thought that kind of forms in that process that leads me to do a longer prose project." Such is the process that Mori has used with each of her longer prose works. "The only time that I really think about audience is in terms of developing the plot as well as the imagery, so it has more to do with technique in the end than with the story itself," the author added.

Until Mori started teaching creative writing, she believed anyone could write, on some level at least. "And that's still true," she admitted. "I think that anyone can write better than he or she is doing *now*. But as I teach more I start thinking that talent really does play a valuable part in this. There are kids who, without trying, write something so much better than the kid who is trying so hard who is a good student. It really has to do with the way they can see.

"But some of the most talented students are not the best disciplined. [While] I think I can motivate them to be disciplined because they have something to work with, they have to put something out there before I can give them direction." She maintains that the better English majors, those who "read and analyze things and write clearly in an expository manner," don't always write the best stories or poems. "They just don't seem to have the 'eye,' " she surmises. "And that, to me, is much more frustrating than working with a talented but undisciplined student whom I have to nag by saying, 'Your rewrite is due in a week,' because I can usually get that student to do it. And if it's two days late, it's okay."

In 1998, Mori published a series of twelve essays wherein she contrasts living in the Midwest and living in Japan, titled *Polite Lies: On Being a Woman Caught between Cultures.* She produced *Stone Field, True Arrow,* her first novel for adults, in 2000. The book tells the story of Maya Ishida, a Japanese-American who left Japan as a child to live with her distant, academic mother in the U.S. Maya, who is married to a schoolteacher and works as a weaver, begins to re-evaluate the events of her past and her present relationships after she learns of her Japanese father's death. While *Library Journal*'s Shirley N. Quan felt that the novel "appears to carry one too many story lines," a *Publishers Weekly* reviewer found Mori's text "graceful in its simplicity of language." Writing in the *New York Times Book Review,* Jeff Waggoner praised *Stone Field, True Arrow* as a "quiet, heartbreaking novel that has as much to say about art as it does about longing."

In addition to an active teaching schedule and a daily schedule given structure by her disciplined attitude towards running and writing, Mori continues to produce books, poems, and short fiction. In 1999, she contributed the autobiographical short story "Learning to Swim" to *When I Was Your Age: Original Stories about Growing Up,* a collection for young adult readers.

BIOGRAPHICAL/CRITICAL SOURCES:

BOOKS

Authors and Artists for Young Adults, Volume 25, Gale (Detroit, MI), 1998.

PERIODICALS

Booklist, January 1, 1995, Donna Seaman, "Poets Remembered," p. 794; December 1, 1997, review of *Polite Lies,* pp. 590-592; June 1, 1998, Stephanie Zvirin, review of *Shizuko's Daughter,* p. 1717; July, 2000, Michelle Kaske, review of *Stone Field, True Arrow,* p. 2008.
Bulletin of the Center for Children's Books, May, 1993, p. 291; January, 1996, p. 161.
English Journal, September, 1994, p. 87.
Horn Book, May, 1993, p. 291.
Kirkus Reviews, November 1, 1997, review of *Polite Lies,* p. 1628.
Library Journal, July, 2000, Shirley N. Quan, review of *Stone Field, True Arrow,* p. 141.
Los Angeles Times Book Review, April 9, 1995, p. 6.
New York Times Book Review, August 22, 1993, Liz Rosenberg, review of *Shizuko's Daughter,* p. 19. February 5, 1995, p. 13; November 12, 1995, Francine Prose, review of *One Bird,* p. 50; March 8, 1998, p. 19; November 5, 2000, Jeff Waggoner, review of *Stone Field, True Arrow.*
Publishers Weekly, January 25, 1993, p. 87; November 7, 1994, p. 54; November 3, 1997, review of *Polite Lies,* p. 71; August 14, 2000, review of *Stone Field, True Arrow,* p. 329.
School Library Journal, September, 1997, Patricia Lothrop-Green, review of *The Dream of Water,* p. 129.
Voice of Youth Advocates, October, 1993, p. 217; February, 1996, p. 374; August, 1997, Hilary S. Crew, review of *One Bird,* pp. 173-176.
Wilson Library Bulletin, January, 1994, p. 117.

*   *   *

MORROW, Patrick David   1940-

PERSONAL: Born October 1, 1940, in Inglewood, CA; son of Patrick Francis (an appraiser and writer) and Marilyn (a writer and teacher; maiden name, Keefe) Morrow; married Judith R. Spenceley, June 28, 1964 (divorced April 9, 1975); married Mary Elizabeth Vehrs (a special education teacher), August 19, 1975 (divorced September 1, 1980); married Joyce Rothschild (a professor), June 14, 1984; children: (first marriage) Milan Elizabeth, Christopher Patrick; stepchildren: (third marriage) Paul Hotchkiss. *Education:* Attended Sacramento State College (now California State University at Sacramento), 1958-61; University of Southern California, B.A., 1963; University of Washington, Seattle, M.A., 1965, Ph.D., 1969; also attended University of California at Berkeley, and Free University of Seattle. *Politics:* Democrat. *Religion:* Jewish. *Avocational interests:* Music, canasta, and gardening.

ADDRESSES: Home—719 Burke Place, Auburn, AL 36830. *Office*—Department of English, Auburn University, Auburn, AL 36849. *E-mail*—morrow@auburn.edu.

CAREER: Professional musician, 1957-62; U.S. Veterans Administration, Property Management Division, Sacramento, CA, technical writer, 1963; University of Washington, Seattle, instructor in English, 1968-69; University of Southern California, Los Angeles, assistant professor of English and American studies, 1969-75; Auburn University, Auburn, AL, associate professor, 1975-81, professor of English, 1981—. Visiting associate professor at University of New Mexico, summer, 1972; visiting lecturer at Idaho State University, summer, 1974; Fulbright senior lecturer at University of Canterbury, Christchurch, New Zealand, 1981; lecturer in American studies at universities in New Zealand, Australia, and Samoa, 1981. French interpreter for Eighth Winter Olympic Games (Squaw Valley, CA), 1960. Volunteer worker with mentally disabled and handicapped children.

MEMBER: Modern Language Association of America, American Studies Association, Popular Culture Association, Western American Literature Association (member of executive council, 1972—), American Association of Australian Literary Studies, South Atlantic Modern Language Association.

AWARDS, HONORS: Egan Foundation fellowships, 1971, 1974; Leo S. Bing Fellowship from University of Southern California, 1971; National Endowment for the Humanities grant, 1974-75, for curriculum development and publication; grant from the National Endowment for the Arts, 1975; Auburn University faculty fellowships, 1978, 1979; Fulbright grants for research in New Zealand, Australia, and Oceania, 1981, 1989, 1995.

WRITINGS:

(Translator, editor, and author of introduction) *Porcelain Butterfly: Five French Symbolist Poets in Translation* (bilingual text), Red Hill Press, 1971.

Bret Harte (pamphlet), Boise State University, 1972.

(Contributor) Edward F. Heenan, editor, *Mystery, Magic, and Miracle: Religion in a Post-Aquarian Age,* Prentice-Hall, 1973.

Radical Vistas: Eight Essays on American Literature, Fault Press, 1974.

Bret Harte, Literary Critic, Popular Press of Bowling Green State, 1979.

(Editor) *Growing Up in North Dakota,* University Press of America, 1979.

Tradition, Undercut, and Discovery: Eight Essays on British Literature, Rodopi (Amsterdam, Netherlands), 1980.

(Editor) *Seventeen North Dakota Tales,* Center for Western Studies (Sioux Falls, SD), 1985.

The Popular and the Serious in Select Twentieth-Century American Novels, Edwin Mellen (Lewiston, NY), 1992.

Katherine Mansfield's Fiction, Bowling Green State University Press (Bowling Green, OH), 1993.

Post-Colonial Essays on South Pacific Literature, Edwin Mellen (Lewiston, NY), 1998.

Contributor to academic journals. Member of editorial board of *Western American Literature, Journal of American Culture, Journal of Popular Culture,* and *Popular Music and Society;* associate editor, then co-editor, of *Southern Humanities Review,* 1976-83.

WORK IN PROGRESS: Photo Ops: Essays in Literary Criticism (tentative title); and a book on the intersection of anthropological theory and literary theory, with Angel Fournelle.

SIDELIGHTS: Patrick David Morrow analyzes the work of Katharine Mansfield in *Katherine Mansfield's Fiction,* published in 1993. Mansfield, who was active as a writer around the turn of the twentieth century, was a British citizen born in New Zealand. Morrow's book looks at her less-well-known as well as unfinished writing, in addition to her best-known works. Morrow examines the relationship between popular and serious fiction in *The Popular and the Serious in Select Twentieth-Century American Novels.* He presents his theories on the formulaic and unexpected aspects of classics such as *The Great Gatsby* and *The Sun Also Rises,* as well as the work of William Faulkner, popular westerns, and postmodern writer Richard Brautigan.

Morrow spent some time living in the South Pacific, and his experiences there informed his 1998 publication, *Post-Colonial Essays on South Pacific Literature.* In it, he presents a "lively, provocative, and delightfully informal study" of literature in Australia and Fiji, and also New Zealand. Nicholas Birns, a writer for *National Forum,* identified Morrow as "one of the pioneers of the study of South Pacific literature in this country." *Post-Colonial Essays on South Pacific Literature* "gives the reader a sense of the excitement of discovering a whole body of writing far beyond the restrictive canon of traditional Anglo-American masterworks," continued Birns, who concluded: "Morrow is a strikingly unpretentious writer, admitting personal failings and limitations in a way that will at once charm and jolt those accustomed to reading contemporary academic monographs. Morrow's casual style is often deceptive, though, as he addresses matters of deep seriousness."

Morrow once told *CA:* "I consider myself primarily a critic—of life, culture, human relationships, and art. To me the primary function of criticism is explication and not attack. My ideal critic strives to make clear what is obscure, not to pass moral judgments from on high. I strive for the personal voice and vision that the shared experience of reader and writer under these terms makes all concerned better able to understand life and cope with it." He later added: "I wanted to write from my early twenties but of course all I was interested in writing was the sorts of common *angsts* that many people of that age have. Believe me that I was stunned when in my first graduate class at the University of Washington the professor said right away that one could get an A in his class only if one wrote a publishable paper! *Gulp.* But I soon learned how to do this, and discovered that while my creative writing was sort of a silent disaster, I could learn how to write academic essays—and lots of them. While at Auburn a colleague quite correctly accused me of writing literary criticism as journalism, but that's my bag and I have learned to accept it. Oh yes, along the way I also learned to do other things, such as textually edit Bret Harte's shallow but baroque literary criticism and a sort of critical biography of Katherine Mansfield, but what I really do is write essays.

"Actually, I am quite a slow writer, and usually require many revisions and drafts. I need additional time for serious thinking and reconsideration. I also have no idea of what my primary motivation for writing is; reading and writing are both very hard work, but until you have really written something about a given subject, you don't understand that subject.

"Mostly my inspiration has come from the hand of life that fate dealt me. At first that was British literature, then American lit, followed by a very lucky break of getting Fulbright grants to study literature in the South Pacific. I very much like mostly being here in Auburn because it's an interesting place for a native Californian to live, and it's an easy place to negotiate if you happen to have multiple sclerosis, as indeed I do. The disease usually doesn't kill you but it does make you progressively more dependent. I also have the amazing luck of having a very smart and loyal wife, also a teacher at Auburn, named Dr. Joyce Rothschild. What I do now is mostly teach (I learned early not to make my writing a main source of income, although I have earned a bit of money from writing) our early Great Books course, and courses in colonialism and postcolonialism."

BIOGRAPHICAL/CRITICAL SOURCES:

PERIODICALS

English Literature in Transition 1880-1920, issue 3, 1994, review of *Katherine Mansfield's Fiction,* p. 387.

National Forum, summer, 1998, Nicholas Birns, review of *Post-Colonial Essays on South Pacific Literature,* p. 42.

Research & Reference Book News, November, 1993, review of *Katherine Mansfield's Fiction,* p. 43.

Western American Literature, summer, 1993, review of *The Popular and the Serious in Select Twentieth-Century American Novels,* p. 179.

*　　*　　*

MURAKAMI, Haruki　1949-

PERSONAL: Born January 12, 1949, in Ashiya City, Japan; son of high-school literature teachers; married Yoko Takahashi (a fellow university student), 1971. *Education:* Waseda University, Tokyo, Japan, B.A. (drama), 1975.

ADDRESSES: Agent—c/o International Creative Management, Inc., 40 West 57th St., New York, NY 10019.

CAREER: Japanese novelist and short-story writer. Co-owner and manager, with wife Yoko Takahashi, of jazz bar Peter Cat, Tokyo, Japan, 1974-81; full-time writer, 1981—. Princeton University, visiting fellow in East Asian studies, 1991; Tufts University, writer-in-residence, 1993-95.

AWARDS, HONORS: Gunzo Award for first novel, 1979, for *Hear the Wind Sing;* Noma Award for new writers, 1982, for *A Wild Sheep Chase;* Junichiro Tanizaki Prize, 1985, for *Hard-Boiled Wonderland and the End of the World;* Yomiuri Literary Prize, 1996, for *The Wind-Up Bird Chronicle;* Kuwabara Takeo Award, 1999, for *Yakusoku Sareta Basho de.*

WRITINGS:

NOVELS

Kaze no uta o kike, Kodansha (Tokyo, Japan), 1979, translation by Alfred Birnbaum published as *Hear the Wind Sing,* Kodansha International (Tokyo, Japan), 1987.

1973-nen no pinboru, Kodansha International (Tokyo, Japan), 1980, translation by Alfred Birnbaum published as *Pinball, 1973,* Kodansha International (Tokyo, Japan), 1985.

Hitsuji o megaru boken, Kodansha International (Tokyo, Japan), 1982, translation by Alfred Birnbaum published as *A Wild Sheep Chase,* Kodansha International (New York, NY), 1989.

Sekai no owari to hado-boirudo wandarando, Shinchosha (Tokyo, Japan), 1985, translation by Alfred Birnbaum published as *Hard-Boiled Wonderland and the End of the World,* Kodansha International (New York, NY), 1991.

Noruwei no mori, Kodansha International (Tokyo, Japan), 1987, translation by Alfred Birnbaum published as *Norwegian Wood,* Kodansha (Tokyo, Japan), 1989, translated by Jay Rubin, Vintage Books (New York, NY), 2000.

Dansu dansu dansu, Kodansha International (Tokyo, Japan), 1988, two volumes, translation by Alfred Birnbaum published as *Dance Dance Dance: A Novel,* Kodansha International (New York, NY), 1994.

Nejimaki-dori kuronikuru, Shinchosha (Tokyo, Japan), 1994, translation by Jay Rubin published as *The Wind-Up Bird Chronicle: A Novel,* Knopf (New York, NY), 1997.

South of the Border, West of the Sun, translation by Philip Gabriel, Knopf (New York, NY), 1999.

The Sputnik Sweetheart, translation by Philip Gabriel, Knopf (New York, NY), 2001.

OTHER

Murakami Haruki zensakuhin 1979-1989 (collection), eight volumes, Kodansha International (Tokyo, Japan), 1990-91.

The Elephant Vanishes: Stories, translation by Jay Rubin and Alfred Birnbaum, Knopf (New York, NY), 1993.

Andaguraundo, Kodansha International (nonfiction), 1997, published as *Yakusoku Sareta Basho de,* Bungeishunju, 1998, translated as *Underground: The Tokyo Gas Attack and the Japanese Psyche,* Harvill (London, England), 2000, Vintage Books (New York, NY), 2001.

After the Earthquake: Stories (originally published as *Kami no kodomotachi wa mina odoru*), translated by Jay Rubin, Knopf (New York, NY), in press.

Also contributor of short stories to periodicals, including "UFO in Kushiro," translated by Jay Rubin and published in *New Yorker,* 2000; "Thailand," translated by Jay Rubin and published in *Granta,* 2001; and "Honey Pie," translated by Jay Rubin and published in *New Yorker,* 2001.

Contributor of writings to collections, including "On Meeting My 100-Percent Woman One Fine April Morning," translation by K. Flanagan and T. Omi published in *New Japanese Voices: The Best Contemporary Fiction from Japan,* Atlantic Monthly Press (New York, NY), 1991; "TV People," translation by Birnbaum published in *Monkey Brain Sushi: New Taste in Japanese Fiction,* 1991; and "Sleep," published in *The Literary Insomniac: Stories and Essays for Sleepless Nights,* Doubleday (New York, NY), 1996.

Has translated works by Raymond Carver, F. Scott Fitzgerald, John Irving, Grace Paley, Paul Theroux, Truman Capote, Mark Strand, Tim O'Brien, and Tobias Wolff into Japanese.

SIDELIGHTS: Murakami Haruki has been known for most of his career as the leading representative of a hip generation of Japanese who grew up in the post-war years, were disenchanted with their traditional culture, and sought freedom by emulating U.S. pop culture. Ostentatiously refusing to participate in political action, Murakami became known for his cool demeanor, his wearing of sunglasses, and his fashionable casual clothes. He was repeatedly called the Japanese Jay McInerney or the Japanese Bret Easton Ellis, not only for his cool, but also for his ability to attract masses of new-generation youth while alienating older readers.

Born in a suburb of Kobe in 1949, the son of a literature teacher, Murakami felt alienated at an early age from the authoritarian strictures and familial closeness of Japanese culture. Like many Japanese of his era, he turned to U.S. culture for inspiration and escape. He

told reviewer Jay McInerney in a 1992 interview for the *New York Times Book Review* that the infatuation for things American was not a love of the United States per se, but that American culture, from a distance, appeared "so shiny and bright that sometimes it seemed like a fantasy world."

As an adolescent, Murakami read Western literature, turning to such authors as Raymond Chandler, F. Scott Fitzgerald, and Ray Bradbury. He entered Waseda University in Tokyo in 1968, earning his degree in 1975. It was a time of violent student protest, an activity that disillusioned Murakami despite his sympathy with rebellion and with the goals of the protesters. In 1971, while still a student, he married fellow student Yoko Takahashi, who has remained his closest companion ever since, serving as his first reader and most trusted critic. The couple opened a jazz bar in 1974; Yoko's role was to meet the public, while Murakami did physical work such as dishwashing and reading novels in his spare time.

It was during his bar-keeping years that Murakami had a sudden inspiration to write; he described this "revelation" to Ian Buruma, in a 1996 *New Yorker* profile. On an April day, 1978, Murakami was in the bleachers of Jingu Stadium, watching a baseball game between the Yakult and Hiroshima teams, when an American, Dave Hilton, came to the bat and hit a double. Buruma reported, "In that instant, Murakami realized that he could write a novel. He still doesn't know why; he just knew." He began writing the novel in English, at his kitchen table after bar hours, but later put it into Japanese and submitted it, as *Kaze no uta o kike,* for a prestigious first-novel prize, the Gunzo Award. (Submitting unpublished manuscripts is common for first novelists in Japan.) The novel won the prize and sold more than 200,000 hardback copies. Murakami pioneered a new Japanese writing style consciously different from the usual style of Japanese high literature. Brand names and references to American pop culture abound in what Ian Buruma described in the *New Yorker* as "a mixture of science fiction, hard-boiled cool, and metaphysics." A second novel, titled in English, *Pinball, 1973,* has similar traits and a similar atmosphere of alienation.

Murakami turned to full-time writing in 1981 and produced his third novel, *A Wild Sheep Chase.* This postmodernist work features a nearly anonymous narrator and a cast of characters who are known by nicknames; the short chapters and the narrator's pose as a detached Japanese Everyman mark the novel's trendy attitude; and the plot, which concerns a search for a mysterious supernatural sheep, shows typical influences of the science fiction genre. This novel, the first of Murakami's books to be translated into English, was an alternate selection of the Literary Guild. Reviewing it in Chicago's *Tribune Books,* Alan Cheuse thought it was "a greatly entertaining piece of fiction that will remind U.S. readers of the first time they read Tom Robbins or how much they miss Thomas Pynchon." In *Booklist,* Jill Sidoti called it "a fine book, one to be read through, contemplated, and then reread," and who predicted that readers would find in the book a release from mediocrity. More skeptical about Murakami's style, his plot, and his Western proclivities was Fumiko Kometani in the *Los Angeles Times Book Review,* who nevertheless assured readers that Murakami was "immensely readable, his pages as easily consumable as bar peanuts."

Murakami's next novel, titled in English *Hard-Boiled Wonderland and the End of the World,* extends the science-fiction trappings. It tells two separate, alternating tales in the manner of William Faulkner's *Wild Palms,* with the difference that in Murakami's novel, the two tales gradually converge and unite. *Hard-Boiled Wonderland* takes place in a secret part of the Japanese subway system where the narrator, a survivor of a top-secret neurosurgical experiment, waits for death. *The End of the World* takes place behind high walls which no one can see over, in a dying land where unicorns roam and where the narrator works in a library as a reader of dreams (which are stored in animal skulls). A *Los Angeles Times Books Review* contributor felt the science-fictional expositions were "the least successful parts of the book" and that Murakami's plotting was not his strength: "He is better at asides and excursions." Of the plot, the reviewer claimed, "We get no sense of adventure, much less of tension; it is like one of the duller journeys in the Land of Oz." The critic continued, "Murakami's gift is for ironic observations that hint at something graver. At his best, he is wry, absurd, and desolate." Of the author's handling of theme, the reviewer observed, "Murakami's allegory is persuasive, but the means he uses to work it out are awkward and often unconvincing." Some other critics felt differently; for instance, a *Kirkus Reviews* commentator called the novel "a stunning combination of the contemporary and brash with elegiac allegory, all topped off by a strong measure of cyberpunk." The book was a major success in Japan, winning the much-sought-after Tanizaki Prize.

Murakami's fifth and most realistic novel, *Norwegian Wood* (named after the Beatles song), sold over two million hard cover copies in Japan. The protagonist, Toru, a college student, has a passive disposition that Brooke Horvath, in *Review of Contemporary Fiction,* traced back to the hero of the classic *Tale of Genji.* The student loses a friend to suicide, gains the friend's girlfriend, then loses her to a rehabilitation center before her suicide; a second girlfriend consoles him and urges him to get on with life. Horvath found this novel "less startling" than Murakami's earlier work, "a quieter novel, but no less rewarding." Yoshio Iwamoto wrote in *World Literature Today* that Murakami "captures with an unerring ear the ambience of the sixties for a sizable segment of the population in a lyrically simple and clean prose, in turns appealingly sad and humorous." Murakami's Japanese publishers deliberately delayed the appearance of this novel's English translation because they wanted to present him as a cutting-edge talent rather than as a traditional realist. *Norwegian Wood* was finally published in English in the United States in 2000; an earlier translation had been published in his native country for Japanese studying English. "Though it may feel uncharacteristically straightforward to his American following, *Norwegian Wood* bears the unmistakable marks of Murakami's hand," reported Janice P. Nimura in the *New York Times Book Review.* As in his other works, his Japanese characters and setting are "strikingly Westernized," and his narrator is "low-key," she explained. Also, "Although what Toru narrates never ventures into the surreal, his story proves that 'ordinary' love is no less rich and strange," she related, adding that "in some ways, the landscape of *Norwegian Wood* is as disconcerting as that of Murakami's weirdest work. There are no real homes here, only more or less humane institutions: schools, universities, hospitals. Safe havens don't exist, and love is never truly unconditional." *Threepenny Review* contributor Francie Lin compared *Norwegian Wood* to Murakami's other work by calling it "a more interior, less antic type of narrative that deals with the same notion of alternative realities without recourse to overt fantasy. . . . The gap between one world and another is a matter of time rather than place. The central tragedies of *Norwegian Wood* are caused by a kind of failure of the imagination: the people who die are the ones who cannot envision themselves in the future, as if the future were not something organic and inevitable but a construct of the mind."

Murakami's 1988 novel, *Dance Dance Dance* (also named after a Western pop song) sold over a half million hard cover copies in Japan in its first six months in the bookstores. A sequel to *A Wild Sheep Chase,* it presents the narrator of that novel as a public relations writer living in Tokyo. The plot, again a murder mystery with science-fiction leanings, involves several murders, most centrally that of a likable young prostitute named Mei. *New York Times Book Review* critic

Donna Rifkind felt "the book never quite decides what it wants to be," although she expressed admiration for both comic and poetic passages in the text. *Times Literary Supplement* contributor Alexander Harrison remarked, "As well as acute intelligence, the novel has a relentless pace and verve which would run the world's best blockbuster out of breath." Praising the style for "fluid brilliance" and the "strong" characterizations as "based on acute observation," Harrison noted that while much influenced by such Western writers as Raymond Chandler, Murakami paid them homage "before blowing them away. . . . Although the text has its share of postmodern devices, the final effect is neither tricksy nor impenetrable. Philip Kerr, Paul Auster and Nicholson Baker could all take tuition from Haruki Murakami, and so indeed could Jackie Collins."

Although primarily a novelist, Murakami has written many short stories, first published in book form in English in *The Elephant Vanishes.* The seventeen stories are all narrated in the first person, but they span the spectrum between realism and fantasy, usually occupying an intriguing middle ground. Two of the stories, in English translation, were included in year's-best fantasy annuals. Reviewer Gary K. Wolfe of *Locus* appreciated "the edge of sheer *weirdness* that makes all Murakami's stories unique and challenging." Wolfe considered "The Dancing Dwarf," a "surrealistic fairy tale," the best in the volume. In the *Los Angeles Times Book Review,* David L. Ulin praised as "exquisite and affecting" the story "On Seeing the 100-Percent Girl One Beautiful April Morning" and commended the book's "striking sense of playfulness." Said Ulin, "What all of Murakami's stories have in common is the idea that we live in a world without equilibrium." This quality contributed, in that reviewer's mind, to making the book "one of the most consistently universal volumes of fiction you'll ever come across." David Leavitt, writing in the *New York Times Book Review,* had complimentary remarks for many of the individual stories, including the "haunting" title story, but commented that the book as a whole presented "a Japan characterized by a peculiar spiritual torpor. Bizarre events take place regularly, but fail to generate much reaction or curiosity. . . . All the stories . . . take place in parallel worlds not so much remote from ordinary life as hidden within its surfaces: secret alleys that afford unexpected—and unsettling—views."

For a decade, while writing his works of Japanese-style alienation, Murakami lived abroad, first in Greece and Italy, then for several years in the United States, where for a time he taught at Princeton University and at Tufts University. The experience of living in the West seemed to draw him closer, spiritually, to Japan. As he told *New Yorker* writer Ian Buruma, "In Japan, I wanted personal independence. . . . I wanted to be free. In America, I felt free. But Americans take individual independence and freedom for granted. So the question for me was where to go from there. I felt confused."

His confusion resolved itself startlingly during a 1995 trip to China, where he visited Nomonham, a World War II battle site in the Mongolian desert. Here, after the Japanese initiated a senseless aggression against the Chinese, the Chinese in turn massacred them. Carrying his own food in bags because of an aversion to Chinese food, Murakami explored the site; then, in his hotel room, he experienced a revelation equivalent to his 1978 sensation at the baseball park. This time, he felt that the hotel room was undergoing an earthquake. His next novel, published in English in 1997 as *The Wind-Up Bird Chronicle,* features, among other things, a searingly graphic account of the war as remembered by its participants. It was a turnaround for the writer toward political statement. "The most important thing," Murakami told Buruma, "is to face our history, and that means the history of the war." The novel was also an occasion for Murakami to examine his Japanese-ness and to explore the meaning of that concept: "I used to hate it, but now I want to find out what is important to me about Japan," he confided to Buruma. The balance between political engagement and personal introspection, Buruma wrote, could well deepen Murakami's fiction. The *New Yorker* reviewer added, "If Murakami can pull it off, he might become the most important Japanese writer of his age."

In *The Wind-Up Bird Chronicle,* the narrator, Toru Okada, is a directionless young man who has a series of strange, dreamlike experiences while searching for his missing cat and for his wife, who leaves him soon after the cat vanishes. He visits psychics, befriends a melancholy teenage girl, and hears rumors of evil deeds done by his brother-in-law, an ambitious politician. At one point, sitting in a dry well, he finds the entrance to a hotel room, which is visited by characters that include a seductress who endows him with miraculous powers and soldiers who recall horrific events of the war, such as seeing friends skinned alive. "These Bocaccio-like interpolations contain some of the best writing in the book," commented Jamie James in the *New York Times Book Review.* James thought *The Wind-Up Bird Chronicle* "marks a significant advance in Murakami's art. He has stripped away much of the pop ornamentation that in his earlier novels veered perilously near to product placement." *New York Times* reviewer Michiko Kakutani noted that this book differs from Murakami's earlier work because it "not only limns its hero's efforts to achieve self-understanding, but also aspires to examine Japan's burden of historical guilt and place in a post-World War II world. The mechanical cry of the wind-up bird that the book's hero sporadically hears is the sound of history winding its spring, the setting into motion of events that will reverberate through public and private lives." Kakutani found Murakami's effort "only intermittently successful," though, remarking that the novel "has some powerful scenes of antic comedy and some shattering scenes of historical power, but such moments do not add up to a satisfying, fully fashioned novel." The book is "fragmentary and chaotic," and it promises answers to the many questions it raises but ultimately does not provide them, Kakutani wrote, adding that it "often seems so messy that its refusal of closure feels less like an artistic choice than simple laziness." James, however, while allowing that the book "does have its flaws," maintained that "what Murakami lacks in finesse, is more than compensated by the brilliance of his invention." James concluded, "Visionary artists aren't always neat: who reads Kafka for his tight construction? In *The Wind-Up Bird Chronicle* Murakami has written a bold and generous book, and one that would have lost a great deal by being tidied up."

The next Murakami work to appear in the United States, *South of the Border, West of the Sun,* deals with the marks left by an adolescent romance on its participants, who are reunited after many years of separation. The man, Hajime, finds that all the women he meets as an adult lack "something that was waiting just for me." When he encounters Shimamoto, his childhood sweetheart, he becomes obsessed with her. "Murakami contemplates the way in which memory not only lingers but gives rise to overwhelming longing for the unreclaimable past," related Mary Hawthorne in the *New York Times Book Review.* Ultimately, the couple "are incapable of resurrecting the lost perfection of their youth," Hawthorne reported, adding, "This wise and beautiful book is full of hidden truths, but perhaps this is its most essential one, unbearable though it may be to contemplate." *Threepenny Review*'s Lin thought *South of the Border, West of the Sun* something of a companion piece to *Norwegian Wood,* "as the latter is about youth looking forward and the former about age looking back." *Time International* reviewer Hilary Roxe observed that the characters "never know what they're looking for and certainly never find it, but . . . are interesting enough to make their search seem worthwhile," and Lin noted that Murakami's narration has "a kind of restrained candor that gives the novel a quality of private testimony." Richard Bernstein, writing in the

daily *New York Times,* called the book "a delicate and affecting fable" and "a probing meditation on human fragility, the grip of obsession and the impenetrable, erotically charged enigma that is the other."

Obsession and other-ness are at the core of *Sputnik Sweetheart,* in which a young woman writer, Sumire, makes herself over, emulating a beautiful, successful businesswoman, Miu, in an effort to win Miu's love. During a trip to a Greek island, Sumire realizes that Miu does not return her passion—and then Sumire disappears. A man known only as "K," who narrates the story and has an unrequited desire for Sumire, soon arrives from Japan to investigate. "Murakami does hint at a solution," remarked Daniel Zalewski in the *New York Times Book Review.* "And that solution is breathtakingly freaky." Miu, it seems, believes that she has been "split in two"; she once observed a duplicate of herself making love with a man whose advances she had spurned. Perhaps Sumire's knowledge of this phenomenon, Zalewski noted, has enabled her to go to " 'the other side' to find 'the lost part of Miu.' "

The concept of "the other side" also informs Murakami's first nonfiction book, *Underground: The Tokyo Gas Attack and the Japanese Psyche,* about the poison gas attack launched on a Tokyo subway by members of the Aum Shinrikyo cult in 1995. He interviews both survivors of the attack and members of the cult. One survivor describes the Aum Shinrikyo followers as being "from another dimension." "In many ways, the cult members are sinister doppelgängers to his own characters," Zalewski related. "Like Sumire, they've decided to 'live in a fiction.' " He concluded, "One can imagine the shudder that went through Japan's best novelist when an Aum member made this sad confession to him: 'My consciousness had gone over to the other side and I couldn't get back.' "

Reflecting on Murakami's body of work, Lin observed, "Despite the discrete concerns of each work, he essentially writes about one thing: there is, in his books, a familiar world full of the living specifics of music, weather, books, food, marriage, and sex; and then there is its shadow, invariably dark and dreamlike, which intrudes upon the original with intent to harm. The intersection of the familiar and the menacing forms the core of Murakami's interest. Coupled with sheer nerve, this obsession spawns a kind of fantasy literature that has no real precedent." And Jamie James pointed out in the *New York Times Book Review* that "Western critics searching for parallels have variously likened [Murakami] to Raymond Carver, Arthur C. Clarke, Don DeLillo, Philip K. Dick, Bret Easton Ellis and

Thomas Pynchon—a roster so ill-assorted as to suggest that Murakami may in fact be an original."

BIOGRAPHICAL/CRITICAL SOURCES:

PERIODICALS

Booklist, September 15, 1989, Jill Sidoti, review of *A Wild Sheep Chase,* p. 114.

Kirkus Reviews, July 1, 1991, review of *Hard-Boiled Wonderland and the End of the World,* p. 816.

Locus, August, 1993, Gary K. Wolfe, review of *The Elephant Vanishes,* pp. 25, 50.

Los Angeles Times Book Review, October 15, 1989, Foumiko Kometani, review of *A Wild Sheep Chase,* p. 1; September 15, 1991, review of *Hard-Boiled Wonderland and the End of the World,* p. 3; April 4, 1993, p. 3.

New Yorker, December 23, 1996, pp. 60-71.

New York Times, October 31, 1997, Michiko Kakutani, "On a Nightmarish Trek through History's Web," section E, p. 44; February 17, 1999, Richard Bernstein, "An Obsessive Attraction That Cripples Two Lives," section E, p. 8.

New York Times Book Review, March 28, 1993, pp. 10-11; January 2, 1994, Donna Rifkind review of *Dance Dance Dance,* p. 9; November 2, 1997, Jamie James, "East Meets West," p. 8; February 14, 1999, Mary Hawthorne, "Love Hurts," p. 8; September 24, 2000, Janice P. Nimura, "Rubber Souls"; June 10, 2001, Daniel Zalewski, "Lost in Orbit."

Review of Contemporary Fiction, fall, 1993, Brooke Horvath, review of *Norwegian Wood,* pp. 228-29.

Threepenny Review, summer, 2001, Francie Lin, "Break on Through."

Time International, March 1, 1999, Hilary Roxe, "An Enchanting Futile Quest," p. 56.

Times Literary Supplement, March 18, 1994, Alexander Harrison, review of *Dance Dance Dance,* p. 12.

Tribune Books (Chicago), November 11, 1989, Alan Cheuse, review of *A Wild Sheep Chase,* p. 6.

World Literature Today, spring, 1988, p. 335; winter, 1992, Yoshio Iwamoto, review of *Norwegian Wood,* pp. 207-08.

OTHER

Entry reviewed by Jun Kim Perrin, assistant to Haruki Murakami.

*   *   *

MYLES, Symon
   See FOLLETT, Ken(neth Martin)

N

NABOKOV, Vladimir (Vladimirovich) 1899-1977
(V. Sirin)

Vladimir Nabokov

PERSONAL: Name pronounced "Vla-*dee*-meer Nah-*boak*-off "; born April 23, 1899, in St. Petersburg, Russia; came to United States, 1940; naturalized U.S. citizen, 1945; died of a viral infection, July 2, 1977, in Montreux, Switzerland; son of Vladimir Dmitrievich (a jurist and statesman) and Elena Ivanovna (Rukavishnikov) Nabokov; married Vera (Evseevna) Slonim, April 15, 1925; children: Dmitri. *Education:* Attended Prince Tenishev School, St. Petersburg, 1910-17; Trinity College, Cambridge, B.A. (with honors), 1922. *Religion:* "Non-churchgoing Greek Catholic."

CAREER: Novelist, poet, dramatist, literary critic, translator, essayist, and lepidopterist.

Left Russia with his family in 1919; lived in Berlin, Germany, writing, teaching English and tennis, and composing crossword puzzles (the first such puzzles in Russian) for *Rul* (daily émigré newspaper), 1922-37; lived in Paris, France, 1937-40; Stanford University, Palo Alto, CA, instructor in Russian literature and creative writing, summer, 1941; Wellesley College, Wellesley, MA, resident lecturer in comparative literature and instructor in Russian, 1941-48; Museum of Comparative Zoology, Harvard University, Cambridge, MA, research fellow in entomology, 1942-48; Cornell University, Ithaca, NY, became professor of Russian literature, 1948-59. Visiting lecturer, Harvard University, 1952.

MEMBER: Writers Guild (Los Angeles).

AWARDS, HONORS: Guggenheim fellowships for creative writing, 1943 and 1952; National Institute of Arts and Letters grant in literature, 1951; prize for literary achievement, Brandeis University, 1964; Medal of Merit, American Academy of Arts and Letters, 1969; National Medal for Literature, 1973; *Lectures on Literature* was nominated for a National Book Critics Circle Award, 1980.

WRITINGS:

NOVELS; IN RUSSIAN UNDER PSEUDONYM V. SIRIN UNTIL 1940

Mashen'ka, Slovo (Berlin, Germany), 1926, translated by the author and Michael Glenny as *Mary,* McGraw (New York, NY), 1970, reprinted, Ardis Press (Ann Arbor, MI), 1985.

Korol', dama, valet, Slovo (Berlin, Germany), 1928, Ardis Press (Ann Arbor, MI), 1979, translated by the author, translation revised by son, Dimitri Nabokov, in collaboration with the author as *King, Queen, Knave* (also see below), McGraw (New York, NY), 1968.

Zashchita Luzhina, Slovo (Berlin, Germany), 1930, Ardis Press (Ann Arbor, MI), 1979, translated by the author and Michael Scammell as *The Defense,* Putnam (New York, NY), 1964.

Podvig (originally published in *Sovremennye Zapiski* [Parisian-based Russian émigré journal], 1932), Ardis Press (Ann Arbor, MI), 1979, translated by Dimitri Nabokov in collaboration with the author as *Glory* (also see below), McGraw (New York, NY), 1971.

Kamera Obskura (originally published in *Sovremennye Zapiski* [Parisian-based Russian émigré journal], 1932, Ardis Press (Ann Arbor, MI), 1978, translated by W. Roy as *Camera Obscura,* J. Long, 1936, translated by the author as *Laughter in the Dark,* Bobbs-Merrill (New York, NY), 1938, revised edition, New Directions (New York, NY), 1960.

Otchayaniye (originally published serially in *Sovremennye Zapiski* [Parisian-based Russian émigré journal], 1934), Petropolis (Berlin, Germany), 1936, Ardis Press (Ann Arbor, MI), 1978, translated by the author as *Despair,* J. Long, 1937, revised edition, Putnam (New York, NY) 1966.

Dar (originally published serially in *Sovremennye Zapiski* [Parisian-based Russian émigré journal], 1937-38), Izdatelstvo Imeni Chekhova (New York, NY), 1952, translated by Dimitri Nabokov and Michael Scammell in collaboration with the author as *The Gift* (also see below), Putnam (New York, NY), 1963.

Priglashenie na Kazu', Dom Knigi (Paris, France), 1938, Ardis Press (Ann Arbor, MI), 1979, translated by Dimitri Nabokov in collaboration with the author as *Invitation to a Beheading* (also see below), Putnam (New York, NY), 1959.

Soglyadatay, Russkiya Zapiski (Paris, France), 1938, Ardis Press (Ann Arbor, MI), 1978, translated by

Dimitri Nabokov in collaboration with the author as *The Eye,* Phaedra, 1965.

The Real Life of Sebastian Knight, New Directions (New York, NY), 1941, reprinted, Penguin (New York, NY), 1964.

Bend Sinister, Holt (New York, NY), 1947, with a new introduction by the author, Time-Life (New York, NY), 1981.

Lolita (also see below), Olympia Press (Paris, France), 1955, Putnam (New York, NY), 1958, reprinted, Berkley Publishing (New York, NY), 1984, Russian translation by the author, Phaedra, 1966.

Pnin, Doubleday (Garden City, NY), 1957, reprinted, R. Bentley (Cambridge, MA), 1982.

Pale Fire, Putnam (New York, NY), 1962, 2nd edition, Lancer (New York, NY), 1966.

Ada or Ardor: A Family Chronicle, McGraw (New York, NY), 1969.

Transparent Things, McGraw (New York, NY), 1972.

Look at the Harlequins, McGraw (New York, NY), 1974.

Five Novels (includes *Lolita, The Gift, Invitation to a Beheading, King, Queen, Knave,* and *Glory*), introduction by Peter Quennell, Collins (London, England), 1979.

A Way in the World, Random House (New York, NY), 1994.

Also author of unfinished novel *Solus Rex,* partially published in *Sovremennye Zapiski,* 1940, and, as *Ultima Thule,* in *Novy Zhurnal* (New York, NY), 1942.

STORIES; WORKS IN RUSSIAN UNDER PSEUDONYM V. SIRIN UNTIL 1940

Vozurashchenie Chorba (title means "The Return of Chorb"), Slovo (Berlin, Germany), 1929, Ardis Press (Ann Arbor, MI), 1983.

Nine Stories, New Directions (New York, NY), 1947.

Vesna v Fial'te, Drugie Rasskazy (also see below; title means "Spring in Fialta and Other Stories"), Izdatelstvo Imeni Chekhova, 1956, published as *Vesna Fiualte: Spring in Fialte,* Ardis Press (Ann Arbor, MI), c. 1978.

Nabokov's Dozen: A Collection of Thirteen Stories, Doubleday (Garden City, NY), 1958, published as *Spring in Fialta,* Popular Library (New York, NY), 1959, published as *Nabokov's Dozen: Thirteen Stories,* Penguin (Harmondsworth, England) 1971.

Nabokov's Quartet (four stories, three translated from the Russian by Dimitri Nabokov), Phaedra, 1966.

A Russian Beauty and Other Stories, translated from the Russian by Dimitri Nabokov and Simon Karlinsky in collaboration with the author, McGraw (New York, NY), 1973.

Tyrants Destroyed and Other Stories, translated from the Russian by Dimitri Nabokov in collaboration with the author, McGraw (New York, NY), 1975.

Details of a Sunset and Other Stories, McGraw (New York, NY), 1976.

The Enchanter, translated by Dimitri Nabokov from original unpublished Russian manuscript, Putnam (New York, NY), 1986.

Dimitri Nabokov, editor, *The Stories of Vladimir Nabokov,* Knopf (New York, NY), 1995.

POETRY; WORKS IN RUSSIAN UNDER PSEUDONYM V. SIRIN UNTIL 1940

Poems (in Russian), privately printed (St. Petersburg, Russia), 1916.

(With Andrei Balashov) *Two Paths,* privately printed (Petrograd, Russia), 1918.

Gorny Put' (title means "Heavenly Way"), Grani (Berlin, Germany), 1923.

Grozd' (title means "The Grape"), Gamayun (Berlin, Germany), 1923.

Stikhotvoreniya, 1920-1951, Rifma (Paris, France), 1952.

Poems, Doubleday (Garden City, NY), 1959.

Poems and Problems, McGraw (New York, NY), 1970.

Stikhi, Ardis Press (Ann Arbor, MI), 1979.

PLAYS; WORKS IN RUSSIAN UNDER PSEUDONYM V. SIRIN UNTIL 1940

Smerti (verse play; title means "Death"), published in *Rul,* 1923.

Dedushka (verse play; title means "The Grandfather"), published in *Rul,* 1923.

Polius (verse play; title means "The Pole"), published in *Rul,* 1924.

Tragedia gospodina Morna (title means "The Tragedy of Mr. Morn"), excerpts published in *Rul,* 1925.

Tshelovek iz SSSR (five-act play; title means "The Man from the USSR"; also see below; first produced in Berlin, 1926), excerpts published in *Rul,* 1927.

Sobytie (three-act comedy; title means "The Event"; first produced in Paris, 1938; produced in New York, 1941), published in *Russkiya Zapiski,* 1938.

Izobretenie Val'sa, published in *Russkiya Zapiski,* 1938, translated by Dimitri Nabokov in collaboration with the author as *The Waltz Invention* (three-act, first produced by Hartford Stage Co., Hartford, CT, 1969), Phaedra, 1966.

The Man from the USSR, and Other Plays, translated from the Russian by Dimitri Nabokov, Harcourt/Bruccoli Clark (New York, NY), 1984.

P'esy (collected plays), Ardis Press (Ann Arbor, MI), 1987.

Also author of *Skital'tsy,* a pretended translation of the first act of a nonexistent eighteenth-century English play, 1923, and of *Agasfer,* poetic accompaniment to a symphony, c. 1923.

NONFICTION

Nikolai Gogol (critical biography), New Directions (New York, NY), 1944, corrected edition, 1961.

Notes on Prosody: From the Commentary to His Translation of Pushkin's "Eugene Onegin," Bollingen Foundation, 1963, published as *Notes on Prosody and Abram Gannibal: From the Commentary to the Author's Translation of Pushkin's "Eugene Onegin,"* Princeton University Press (Princeton, NJ), 1964.

Strong Opinions (essays), McGraw (New York, NY), 1973.

Letters from Terra: Vladimir Nabokov zu Ehren, edited by Uwe Friesel, Rowohlt, 1977.

The Nabokov-Wilson Letters: Correspondence between Vladimir Nabokov and Edmund Wilson, 1940-1971, edited, annotated, and with an introductory essay by Karlinsky, Harper (New York, NY), 1979, revised and expanded as *Dear Bunny, Dear Volodya: The Nabokov-Wilson Letters, 1940-1971,* University of California Press (Berkeley, CA), 2001.

Lectures on Literature, edited by Fredson Bowers, introduction by John Updike, Harcourt/Bruccoli Clark (New York, NY), 1980.

Lectures on Ulysses: Facsimile of the Manuscript, foreword by A. Walton Litz, Bruccoli Clark (New York, NY), 1980.

Lectures on Russian Literature, edited and with an introduction by Fredson Bowers, Harcourt/Bruccoli Clark (New York, NY), 1980.

(With others) J. E. Rivers and Charles Nicol, editors, *Nabokov's Fifth Arc: Nabokov and Others on His Life Work,* University of Texas Press (Austin, TX), 1982.

Fredson Bowers, editor, *Lectures on Don Quixote,* Harcourt/Bruccoli Clark (New York, NY), 1983.

Perepiska s sestrol (correspondence), Ardis Press (Ann Arbor, MI), 1985.

Brian Boyd and Robert Michael Pyle, editors, *Nabokov's Butterflies: Unpublished and Uncollected*

Writings, translated by Dimitri Nabokov, Beacon Press (Boston, MA), 2000.

TRANSLATOR INTO ENGLISH

Three Russian Poets: Selections from Pushkin, Lermontov, and Tyutchev, New Directions (New York, NY), 1945, reprinted, Folcroft Press (Folcroft, PA), 1969.

(And author of introduction and commentary) *The Song of Igor's Campaign: An Epic of the Twelfth Century,* Vintage (New York, NY), 1960, reprinted, McGraw (New York, NY), 1975.

Raghubir Singh, *Bombay: Gateway of India,* Aperture (Millerton, NY), 1994.

(And editor and author of commentary) Alexander Pushkin, *Eugene Onegin: A Novel in Verse,* four volumes, Bollingen, 1964, revised edition, 1975.

TRANSLATOR INTO RUSSIAN; UNDER PSEUDONYM V. SIRIN

Romain Rolland, *Nikolka Persik* (translation, from the French, of *Colas Breugnon*), Slovo (Berlin, Germany), 1922.

Lewis Carroll, *Anya v Strane Chudes* (translation, from English, of *Alice in Wonderland*), Gamaiun (Berlin, Germany), 1923, reprinted, Ardis Press (Ann Arbor, MI), 1982.

AUTOBIOGRAPHY

Conclusive Evidence: A Memoir, Harper (New York, NY), 1951, published as *Speak Memory: Memoir,* Gollancz (London, England), 1951, revised and translated by the author as *Drugiye Berega,* Izdatelstvo Imeni Chekhova (New York, NY), 1954, English-language edition expanded as *Speak Memory: An Autobiography Revisited,* Putnam (New York, NY), 1966, reprinted, Knopf (New York, NY), 1994.

OTHER

(Author of introduction and notes) Mikhail Lermontov, *Hero in Our Time,* translation by Dimitri Nabokov, Doubleday (Garden City, NY), 1958, reprinted, 1982.

Lolita: A Screenplay (based on his novel of the same title; produced by Metro-Goldwyn-Mayer under the direction of Stanley Kubrick, 1962), McGraw (New York, NY), 1961.

Nabokov's Congeries (reader), edited by Page Stegner, Viking (New York, NY), 1968.

The Portable Nabokov, selected and with a critical introduction by Page Stegner, Viking (New York, NY), 1968.

Dimitri Nabokov and Matthew J. Bruccoli, editors, *Vladimir Nabokov: Selected Letters, 1940-1977,* Harcourt (New York, NY), 1989.

Novels and Memoirs, 1941-1951, Library of America, 1996.

Novels, 1955-1962, Library of America, 1996.

Novels, 1969-1974, Library of America, 1996.

Also author of *Vozvrashchenie Chorba,* 1930, and of a sound recording, *Vladimir Nabokov: An Intimate Self-Portrait of a Great Writer,* Center for Cassette Studies. Collected works published by Ardis Press as *Sobranie sochinenii.* Contributor to Russian émigré journals in Berlin, Paris, and New York, and to periodicals; contributor of papers on lepidoptera to scientific journals, including the *Bulletin of the Museum of Comparative Zoology.*

ADAPTATIONS: Laughter in the Dark was adapted by Edward Bond as a feature film, Woodfall Films, 1969; and *King, Queen, Knave* was adapted as a film, David Wolper-Maran Productions, 1972. *Invitation to a Beheading* was dramatized by Russell McGrath and produced in New York, 1969; *Lolita, My Love,* a musical play based on Nabokov's novel *Lolita,* was produced on Broadway, 1971.

SIDELIGHTS: Vladimir Nabokov, a Russian émigré who began writing in English after his forties, is considered one of the most brilliant writers of the twentieth century. A trilingual author, equally competent in Russian, English, and French, Nabokov wrote prodigiously during the course of his seventy-eight years, producing a body of work that, when collected, was estimated to fill forty volumes. Though he began as a poet, Nabokov quickly branched into writing in numerous genres, including fiction, drama, autobiography, translations, essays, literary criticism, and even, on occasion, scientific studies of butterflies and collections of chess problems. His writing remains so distinctive that several critics deem him not part of any family but a species unto himself, and often cite *Lolita,* Nabokov's best-known work, as a prime example of truly original invention. "He is a major force in the contemporary novel," critic Anthony Burgess asserted in *The Novel Now: A Guide to Contemporary Fiction.* In a *New Republic* article John Updike also acknowledged Nabokov's tremendous impact on twentieth-century literature, citing the Russian writer as one of the few writers "whose books, considered as a whole, give the happy impression of an *oeuvre,* of a continuous task carried forward variously, of a solid personality, of a plenitude of gifts exploited knowingly. His works are an edifice whose every corner rewards inspection. Each . . . yields delight and presents to the aesthetic sense the peculiar hardness of a finished, fully meant thing. His sentences are beautiful out of context and doubly beautiful in it. He writes prose the only way it should be written—that is ecstatically. In the intensity of its intelligence and reflective joy, his fiction is unique . . . and scarcely precedented in American literature."

Despite an awareness of his technical brilliance and verbal facility, readers have sometimes been bewildered by the complexity of Nabokov's writing. "Virtually all of the foremost literary critics in the United States and England have written about Nabokov, with enthusiasm often bordering on awe," noted Andrew Field in *Nabokov: His Life in Art.* "But their eloquence, where one wants and would expect explication, betrays the fact that they are at least as ill at ease with Nabokov as they are fascinated by him." Critic Alfred Kazin, for instance, after reading *Ada or Ardor: A Family Chronicle,* wrote in the *New York Times:* "For some weeks now I have been floundering and traveling in the mind of that American genius Vladimir Vladimirovich Nabokov." In that novel, as in almost all his works, Nabokov intentionally laced the narrative with obscure literary allusions and trilingual puns which pivot on an understanding of Russian—and to a lesser degree French—language and culture. Though helpful, even a broad knowledge of European literature would not make Nabokov's creations entirely clear for, as an artist, he enjoyed playing tricks on his readers.

A consummate gamesman, Nabokov reveled in what Field called "artistic duplicity" and apparently conceived of writing as an elaborate interplay between author and reader. In the literature courses he taught at Cornell, reprinted in *Lectures on Literature,* Nabokov instructed his students "to read books for the sake of their form, their visions, their art" and cautioned them "to share not the emotions of the people in the book but the emotions of its author—the joys and difficulties of creation." Projected into almost all his narratives—including those, like *Lolita,* which seem to revolve around a traditional plot—are "thinly disguised bits of literary criticism and . . . a variety of literary games involving allusion to and parody and citation of other men's writings," noted *New York Times Book Review* contributor Simon Karlinsky. Alfred Appel, also writing in the *New York Times Book Review,* described Nabokov as "the most allusive and linguistically playful writer in English since [James] Joyce." *Hollins Critic* contributor R. H. W. Dillard cautioned that Nabokov

"is clearly and always the . . . serious and deceptive artist with whom we must play the game."

In addition to the difficulties presented by Nabokov's artistic deceptions, the circumstances of his checkered past further cloud his writing. Long after Nabokov had adopted English as his chosen language, his earlier writings remained untranslated and thus available only in their original Russian form. These early poems, reviews, essays, and fictions were published in Russian émigré newspapers, first in Berlin, Germany and, later, in Paris when that city became the center of émigré culture. While it was theoretically possible for displaced Russians to follow both the Berlin and Paris journals, few in practice did. The difficulties for American readers were further compounded, for without easy access to either source, they had no real context in which to place his work. "None of my American friends have read my Russian books and thus every appraisal on the strength of my English ones is bound to be out of focus," Nabokov wrote in a passage reprinted by Field. Field himself postulated that "if the substantial body of Nabokov's Russian writing and the best critical articles about him had been translated before 1950, it is extremely unlikely that *Lolita* or *Pale Fire* would have been nearly as misunderstood as they were." In later years, Nabokov partially remedied the problem by working in close cooperation with his son Dmitri to translate his books.

Before the Bolshevik revolution of 1917 that precipitated his family's flight, Nabokov led a charmed life in one of Russia's noble families. His father was a distinguished lawyer and one of the country's few political liberals, opposed to both Tsarist absolutism and the revolutionary Bolsheviks. It was the elder statesman's custom to take a daily bath in a portable rubber tub, and this habit was adopted by his favorite son, who considered the warm water a catalyst of creative inspiration. From his father, Vladimir also seems to have inherited his belief in patrician democracy—"My father was an old-fashioned liberal, and I do not mind being labeled an old-fashioned liberal, too," he said in a *Paris Review* interview—an interest in the criminal mind, a capacity for sustained work, and a passionate love of butterflies. Because his father wrote under the name Vladimir Nabokov, young Vladimir adopted a pseudonym, V. Sirin. His mother, "equally aristocratic" according to Samuel Schuman in *Vladimir Nabokov: A Reference Guide,* "was most distinguished in her son's memory by a finely developed and artistic sensitivity, sharing many of the novelist's acute reactions to sense impressions, especially reactions to color and sound." Nabokov recorded his impressions in *Speak Memory,* considered by many to be one of the finest autobiographies in the English language.

Vladimir was the eldest and, by all accounts, the most precocious of the five Nabokov children. He was adored by his parents, and they considered his education a matter of utmost concern. During his early childhood, which was divided between St. Petersburg and Vyra, the family's country estate, he was privately tutored by a governess who taught him to speak English, the first language he learned. When he was twelve Nabokov enrolled in the liberal Tenishev Academy in St. Petersburg, and there, during his six-year stay, he privately printed two books of poetry. In 1916, the same year his first chapbook, *Poems,* appeared, Nabokov inherited an estate worth several million dollars from his "Uncle Ruka."

Unfortunately, this prosperity would be short-lived. Just three years later the entire Nabokov family was forced to abandon their home and take refuge in the southern portion of Russia known as the Crimea. As they waited for the restoration of political order and the opportunity to return, unrest spread and the family again decamped, hurriedly boarding a boat bound for England. "The flight into exile resulted in the loss of most of the Nabokov fortune and, much more importantly for Vladimir, the loss of a homeland, a culture, and a language," Schuman observed. "That set of losses was perhaps the single most crucial event in the artist's lifetime—the role of the exile and the vitality of memory remained dominant motifs in Nabokov's work for the next half-century." Field reported in *Vladimir Nabokov: His Life in Part* that one of the author's 1920 poems "refers to that trip into exile of the previous year as 'sailing to nowhere.' "

Nabokov spent the years from 1919 to 1922 studying Romance and Slavic languages at Cambridge and writing Russian poetry. He was an indifferent scholar until his father was assassinated at a political rally in Berlin in March, 1922. After that traumatic event, Nabokov "returned for his last term with the determination to do well and took his degree with honors," according to Donald E. Morton in his book, *Vladimir Nabokov.* After graduation, Nabokov moved to Berlin, the heart of the émigré community, and began contributing poems and prose to *Rul* ("Rudder"), a Russian-language daily his father had helped to found. For many years Nabokov entertained hopes of returning to Russia and continued to write primarily in Russian, a choice "made easier by the fact that I lived in a closed emigré circle of Russian friends and read exclusively Russian newspapers, magazines and books," Nabokov recalled in *Strong Opin-*

ions. In 1925 he married Vera Evseevna Slonim, who became his lifelong companion and literary assistant, and in 1926 his first novel, *Mashen'ka* (later translated as *Mary*), appeared.

While the original Russian version of *Mary* received little attention, after Nabokov's reputation burgeoned and the work was translated into English, it received closer scrutiny. "In it," noted a *Virginia Quarterly Review* contributor, "we find some pleasing confirmations of what we have assumed to be Nabokov's themes." *Mary* details what life was like for the residents of a Berlin boardinghouse in the early 1920s, and is a nostalgic tale of a young émigré's longing for the love he left behind in Russia. As the story opens, the protagonist, Ganin, meets a fellow boarder in a stalled elevator and learns that the man is anticipating the arrival of his Russian wife in six days. Halfway through the novel, Ganin realizes that his friend's wife is none other than his beloved Mary. He plots to interrupt the marital liaison and meet her in her husband's stead. At the last moment, however, he realizes that she will not be the same girl he remembers, and he departs, leaving her waiting alone at the station.

According to *New York Times* reviewer John Leonard, "the heroine would appear to be as much Mother Russia as the girl Mary; they are coextensive." Morton expressed a similar view, noting that "the absent girl is a symbol of the exiles' longing for their lost homeland." Guy Davenport maintained in *National Review* that *Mary* "is about a man who has two minds, one containing an imaginary world, the other well-focused on reality. The characters, except for the lovely (and unseen) Mary, are all Nabokovian marginal people inhabiting interims and delusions. Practically all of the later themes are here." Writing in the *New York Times Book Review,* Mark Slonim identified two of those themes as "the powers of memory and imagination," and went on to suggest that, for Nabokov, these attitudes are "the lifegiving source of all creative acts and . . . the very foundations of art. Of course, Nabokov has traveled a long road and changed greatly since his twenties when he wrote *Mary,* but throughout his work he has never failed to assert the basic truth that forms the core of his first novel."

In addition to their contributions to his thematic development, the early fictions also shaped Nabokov's literary technique. "It was in his Russian novels . . . that he developed his art of incorporating literary allusion and reference as an inherent device of fictional narration," explained Simon Karlinsky in the *New York Times Book Review.* Nabokov's second novel, *Korol', dama, valet* (translated as *King, Queen, Knave*), marks the first appearance of this device. "It is . . . the first of his novels to have a plot and character serve as vehicles for the real subject, which is form, style and the strategies of total creation," noted Eliot Fremont-Smith in the *New York Times.* In this story, one of several Nabokovian variations on the eternal love triangle, a vain and selfish woman named Martha diabolically plots with her bumbling young lover, Franz, to kill her unsuspecting husband and Franz's uncle, Dreyer.

Field has traced the inspiration for this story to an obscure Hans Christian Andersen tale of the same name, in which a pack of cards fights a revolution. "While Nabokov's story apparently has little to do with Andersen's, it is presumably no accident that the novel has thirteen chapters, the number of cards in a suit. The characters are two-dimensional, like cards, and the variations on a conventional plot suggest that the novel is one permutation of dealing a hand," wrote Charles Nicol in the *Atlantic.* Another acknowledged literary source for the novel is Gustave Flaubert's *Madame Bovary,* which *King, Queen, Knave* burlesques. *New York Times Book Review* contributor Philip Toynbee noted that "with both women one has the same oppressive sense of fate hanging heavily over their heads." The force controlling Martha's fate is, of course, the author, and Nabokov uses this power to manipulate the narrative in unexpected ways. Although he patterns his tale on a situation common to many novels, "nothing ends as it's supposed to," according to *Washington Post* reviewer Geoffrey Wolff. Wolff thought the novel "abounds in comic incongruities: Martha is cold, selfish, aloof and beautiful, yet Nabokov has her slip into passionate love with a bumbling, graceless post-adolescent hayseed. Their rendezvous are made in a grubby comic-opera parody of a clerk's garret as it might be imagined in a nineteenth-century Russian novel."

With each new novel published, Nabokov garnered increased attention within the émigré community; still unknown to the public at large, however, he was forced to supplement his writing income with outside work. Between 1922 and 1937 he earned a living by tutoring, translating, performing as an extra in films, and, as his reputation spread, by giving literary readings of his poems and prose. The Berlin years were still a time of material impoverishment, as Field noted in *Vladimir Nabokov: His Life in Part:* "In September 1935 after Nabokov was praised in print for the first time in the United States . . . [he] wrote to his mother:—'In *The New York Times* they write "our age has been enriched by the appearance of a great writer," but I don't have

a decent pair of trousers, and I quite don't know what I shall wear to Belgium where PEN has invited me to read.' "

Further hardships followed. In 1937 Nabokov left Berlin for Paris, accompanied by his wife Vera, who was Jewish, and Dmitri, his only child. In escaping the hostile political climate of Nazi Germany, Nabokov was also shifting to what appeared to be a more stimulating ambience, for Paris had superseded Berlin as the émigré lodestar. Despite its status as a Russian cultural center, Paris proved disappointing, for even here émigré writing seemed ingrown and stale. Increasingly, Nabokov found himself without a proper audience for his Russian work. Writing of émigré Paris in the late 1930s, Field described this decline: "The literature existed, but it had no resonance, or at best one so circumscribed that it could be calculated not even in thousands but in hundreds of readers. The old combinations by which a livelihood might be put together in ways more or less directly connected with literature were less possible now."

Around this time, Nabokov began to experiment with English, translating his Russian novel *Otchayanie* into the English *Despair* in 1937. Initially hesitant about his command of the language, Nabokov requested the assistance of a professional to proofread his work. H. G. Wells was recommended but never materialized; a second candidate bowed out, declaring himself unsuited to the work. Finally, an Englishwoman agreed to make corrections, but when her list of recommendations was completed, Nabokov found it spurious. "All of this stuff is completely insignificant, for any Russian reader can find just as many birthmarks on any page of any of my Russian novels, and any good English writer commits just as many grammatical imprecisions," he wrote in a letter to Vera, quoted in *Vladimir Nabokov: His Life in Part.* The book was published exactly as he wrote it, an event significant in the writer's life, according to Field, "because it is part of that process of metamorphosis which was in a few years to . . . make him an English writer. After he had done that translation, he knew he could do it." Indeed, his very next book, *The Real Life of Sebastian Knight,* was written in English and marks the demise of the pseudonymous V. Sirin and the emergence of Vladimir Nabokov, an American writer.

Regarded as one of Nabokov's lesser accomplishments, *The Real Life of Sebastian Knight* struck *New Republic* correspondent Conrad Brenner as "the most perverse novel you are ever likely to encounter. This book is quite openly a literary trick, astounding in [its] sleek deceitful contours." Filled with autobiographical tidbits and typically Nabokovian allusions to chess, *The Real Life of Sebastian Knight* chronicles the narrator's search for the "essence" of his half-brother, the titular Sebastian Knight—a Russian émigré writer who died an early death in relative obscurity. The brothers had been out of touch for years, but V., the narrator, remains convinced of Sebastian's genius and sets out to write a biography that will insure his brother's critical stature and refute a second-rate biography Sebastian's former secretary has published. Rather than clarifying the details of Sebastian's life, however, V.'s search only raises more questions. The book draws to a close with V. retrospectively visiting Sebastian on his death bed and wondering whether perhaps he is himself Sebastian Knight, or whether Sebastian might be a third person unknown to them both.

While composed largely in the sunlit bathroom of Nabokov's Paris flat, *Sebastian Knight* was published in the United States in 1941, a year after Nabokov and his family arrived in New York City, in flight from Hitler's terror. During the first years of his U.S. residency, Nabokov worked in obscurity at several part-time jobs. His knowledge of butterflies won him a coveted position as a research fellow at Harvard's Museum of Comparative Zoology, and he also received a guest lectureship at Wellesley College, though he was never offered tenure, partly because his anti-Soviet sentiments were suspect during the Russo-American alliance of World War II. Nabokov lived in rented quarters and never purchased his own home, but he eventually settled at Cornell University in Ithaca, New York, where he was considered an inspiring if somewhat eccentric teacher. He delivered his lectures from carefully prepared diagrams and notes, many of which were been published posthumously in *Lectures on Literature.*

Nabokov might have continued quietly lecturing to what he once called, in *Playboy,* "the great fraternity of C-minus, backbone of the nation," but for the publication of a novel that would make his name an unpronounceable household word. "The first little throb of *Lolita* went through me late in 1939 or early in 1940 in Paris, at a time when I was laid up with a severe attack of intercostal neuralgia," Nabokov wrote in an appendix to the novel. The inspiration was a newspaper story about the first ape to have produced a drawing, a pathetic sketch of the bars of his cage. The text had no direct connection to the story that followed, but nonetheless resulted in what Nabokov called "a prototype" of *Lolita;* namely, a Russian tale of fifty typewritten pages. Unhappy with the story, Nabokov abandoned the work (later rediscovered, translated, and posthumously published as *The Enchanter*), but "around 1949, in Ith- aca, upstate New York, the throbbing, which had never quite ceased, began to plague me again." By then, how- ever, "the thing was new and had grown in secret the claws and wings of a novel." Within a few years, Nabokov had completed *Lolita.*

The publishing history of this extraordinary book has been documented in thousands of words by writers on both sides of the Atlantic. Completed in 1954, Nabokov's manuscript was rejected by each of the four U.S. publishers to whom he submitted it. A book that chronicled the seduction of a twelve-year-old girl by a middle-aged man was regarded as a publishing risk, though certain editors did offer some recommendations. "Grotesque improvements were suggested. . . . such as that Lolita be changed into a boy," stated F. W. Dupee in *Encounter.* Rather than compromise his art, Nabokov turned to Olympia Press, a Paris-based publisher best known for pornography. Banned in France along with other "obscene" Olympia publications, *Lolita* surfaced in America, where it was deemed unobjectionable by U.S. Customs agents. This ironic turn of events captured the attention of the international press, who headlined the story at home and abroad. Before long, the French ban was rescinded, the book was brought out in hardback by the respectable G. P. Putnam & Sons, and *Lolita* began its ascent on the bestseller lists.

The novel purports to be the true confession of a middle-aged debaucher who chooses the pseudonym Humbert Humbert because it "expresses the nastiness best." Jailed for the murder of his rival, Humbert seeks to purge himself by recounting his tale, though the reader is warned in a mock preface by an obtuse Freudian psychiatrist that Humbert can never be absolved. Nor is his tone "the characteristic whine of the penitent," but rather, as *New Yorker* contributor Donald Malcolm observed, "an artful modulation of lyricism and jocularity that quickly seduces the reader into something very like willing complicity." In eloquent detail, Humbert describes his lust for that species of prepubescent girls he calls "nymphets" and for twelve-year-old Dolores Haze in particular. In order to he near his beloved Lolita, as Dolores is called, Humbert marries her mother, then finds his dream fulfilled when she dies in an auto accident, leaving him as the child's guardian. He is somewhat chagrined to discover, on their first night alone, that Lolita is a more experienced lover than he. "Their weird affair—which carries them on a frenzied motel-hopping trek around the [North] American continent—is climaxed by Lolita's escape with a playwright and Humbert's eventual revenge on his rival," Charles Rolo wrote in the *Atlantic.*

With its theme of perversion, *Lolita* provoked a moralistic outcry from some conservative critics, such as a *Catholic World* reviewer who believed the "very subject matter makes it a book to which grave objection must he raised." A *Kirkus Reviews* critic also recommended that it be banished from the open shelves: "That a book like this could be written—published here—sold, presumably over the counters, leaves one questioning the [country's] ethical and moral standards. . . . Any librarian surely will question this for anything but the closed shelves." A *Library Journal* critic urged equal caution, noting that "thousands of library patrons conditioned to near-incest by 'Peyton Place' may take this in stride. However, better read before buying. Although the writer prides himself on using no obscene words, he succeeds only too well in conveying his meaning without them."

For every critic who attacked the book, there were dozens who applauded it, however. *San Francisco Chronicle* contributor Lewis Vogler deemed the novel "an authentic work of art which compels our immediate response," and Conrad Brenner called it "a work clearly foreshadowed in the body of [Nabokov's] prose, and the high water mark of his career as *agent provocateur.*"

While Nabokov paid little notice to most interpretations of *Lolita,* he reacted strongly against readers who envisioned the story as a satiric criticism of his adopted land. "Whether or not critics think that in *Lolita* I am ridiculing human folly leaves me supremely indifferent. But I am annoyed when the glad news is spread that I am ridiculing America," he told Alvin Toffler in *Playboy.* In another interview excerpted in the *Washington Post,* Nabokov asserted that "America is the only country where I feel emotionally and mentally at home." Nonetheless, with the proceeds from *Lolita,* Nabokov moved to the Palace Hotel in Switzerland, abandoning his teaching completely and devoting his time to writing and collecting butterflies. His reasons, he told Toffler, were "purely private"—for one thing, most of his family remained in Europe, for another, he was comfortable with the ambience there.

In Montreux, the sixty-year-old Nabokov continued to write, often standing at a lectern in his room and recording his thoughts in longhand on specially ordered index cards. One of his first projects was to resume work on a novel that had been interrupted by the war. Published as *Pale Fire,* this difficult work demonstrates the increased emphasis on form and structure that dominated Nabokov's later fiction. "More than any other of his books, *Pale Fire* lives up to his dictum that 'Art is never

simple. . . . Because, of course, art at its greatest is fantastically deceitful and complex,' " John Hagopian reported in the *Dictionary of Literary Biography.* This complexity frustrated many would-be readers and led *New York Times Book Review* contributor George Cloyne to dismiss *Pale Fire* as a "curiosity . . . one more proof of Mr. Nabokov's rare vitality. Unluckily it is not much more than that." *Christian Science Monitor* contributor Roderick Nordell was less circumspect, judging the book "a prodigal waste of its author's gifts."

Pale Fire consists of a 999-line poem in four cantos, composed by the late John Shade, an American poet recently assassinated by a madman's bullet, and a foreword, commentary, and index contributed by Dr. Charles Kinbote, an émigré scholar of dubious sanity. Since Kinbote's footnotes are keyed to various lines in the poem, the reader cannot simply read the book from cover to cover, but must continually flip back and forth from the commentary to the verse. "This is not the drudgery it may sound, for every vibration of the pages carries the reader to a fresh illumination, a further delight," wrote Donald Malcolm in the *New Yorker.* "But on the other hand, it is not reading in the ordinary sense. It more nearly resembles the manipulation of a pencil along a course of numbered dots until the hidden picture stands forth, compact, single, and astonishing." Noted Mary McCarthy in the *New Republic:* "When the separate parts are assembled, according to the manufacturer's directions, and fitted together with the help of clues and cross-references, which must be hunted down as in a paperchase, a novel on several levels is revealed."

For some critics, this elaborate mechanism tended to overshadow the story. "Indeed the structure is so witty, and so obtrusive, that it threatens constantly to become its own end; and we are made to attend so closely to it that the novel itself seems wholly subordinate to its mode of enclosure," *Nation* contributor Saul Madoff contended. Writing in the *Saturday Review,* William Peden was equally unenthusiastic, noting: "For [those] who feel that a container is more important than the contents within it, 'Pale Fire' will perhaps be considered a masterpiece. But for us less sophisticated mortals it must be reckoned with as withdrawn from humanity, grotesque and definitely diseased, as monstrous as a three-headed calf."

Faced with the same material, Mary McCarthy reached a very different conclusion. She called *Pale Fire* "a Jack-in-the-box, a Faberge gem, a clockwork toy, a chess problem, an infernal machine, a trap to catch reviewers, a cat-and-mouse game, a do-it-yourself novel. . . . This centaur-work of Nabokov's, half poem, half prose, this merman of the deep, is a creation of perfect beauty, symmetry, strangeness, originality, and moral truth. Pretending to be a curio, it cannot disguise the fact that it is one of the very great works of art of this century, the modern novel that everyone thought dead and that was only playing possum."

In his seventieth year, Nabokov produced his last major work, *Ada or Ardor: A Family Chronicle,* a sexually explicit tale of incest, twice as long as any other novel he had written and, according to John Leonard in the *New York Times,* "fourteen times as complicated." An immediate best-seller, *Ada or Ardor* evoked a wide array of critical response, ranging from strong objections to the highest praise. While the value of the novel was debated, *Ada or Ardor* was universally acknowledged as a work of enormous ambition, the culmination of all Nabokov had attempted to accomplish in his writing over the years. "*Ada* is the fullest realization of the program for the novel articulated in 1941 in Nabokov's first English book, *The Real Life of Sebastian Knight,*" explained Robert Alter in *Commentary.* Like the character Sebastian who described his attempt to "use parody as a kind of springboard for leaping into the highest region of serious emotion," Nabokov, through his bristling word play, attempted to illuminate "in new depth and breadth the relation between art, reality, and the evanescent ever-never presence of time past."

On the surface, *Ada or Ardor* chronicles the incestuous love affair between Van Veen and his cousin (soon revealed to be his sister) Ada, who fall in love as adolescents, embark upon a blissful sexual odyssey, are pulled apart by social taboo and circumstance, only to be reunited in late middle age, at which time they prosper together until both are in their nineties. "Nabokov sums up these amorous doings in a mock dust-jacket blurb that closes *Ada* by describing only the book's most superficial aspects," observed a *Time* reviewer. "Long before he gets around to that, though, a suspicion has set in that the surface love story is as different from the real Ada as a bicycle reflector is from a faceted ruby." Van's memoir of his love affair with Ada, ostensibly "Van's book," is actually an anagram for "Nabokov's," and "once the creator's name has been uttered, *Ada*'s profoundest purpose comes into view. . . . Ada is the supreme fictional embodiment of Nabokov's lifelong, bittersweet preoccupation with time and memory," the *Time* reviewer concluded.

Although Nabokov continued writing well into the 1970s, his last books are considered minor additions to his oeuvre. However, *The Stories of Vladimir Nabokov* would prove a fitting coda to his work. Translated with the help of the author's son Dmitri and published in 1995, *Stories* spans the twentieth century. The first of its sixty-five entries dates from 1921—a year before the then-twenty-one-year-old Cambridge student's father was killed—while the most recent, "Lance," dates from 1952, a few years prior to Nabokov's publication of *Lolita.* Eleven of the early works, including 1921's "The Wood-Sprite," Nabokov's first published short story, appear in English translation for the first time; thirteen were never before been collected. As Anthony Lane remarked in the *New Yorker, Stories* "offers a startling, cloudless view of a writer's development." Rather than slowly developing from a novice talent, Nabokov proved in his early fictions to be "a young man who is not only gifted, and serenely confident in that gift, but more than able to hold his own against the sage celebrity that he finally became," according to Lane.

Calling the collected short fiction "some of the most nape-tingling prose and devilish inventions in 20th-century letters," R. Z. Sheppard praised the collection in *Time* as "a welcome edition to the shelves of old admirers and a chance for entry-level fans to sample the author's delights." The theme of happiness runs throughout the book, as it did through all the author's work, according to Tatyana Tolstaya in the *Los Angeles Times Book Review.* "Even the saddest, most tragic stories—about death, loss, and betrayal—are written so that the reader is left with the distinct foretaste of happiness, as if happiness were the genuine lining, the inside of being, which shines through the gloomy patchwork of reality," the critic maintained. "Those who know Nabokov the novelist and have forgotten that Nabokov the story writer exists now have a precious gift."

Works by Nabokov continued to be published decades after his death due to the translation efforts of his son Dmitri. *Nabokov's Butterflies: Unpublished and Uncollected Writings,* released in 2000, demonstrates Nabokov's vast scientific knowledge of butterflies and moths, as well as his passion for discovering new species. Indeed, several species of butterfly in the American West bear the author's name because Nabokov was the first to find and describe them. London *Times* contributor Mark Ridley stated: "The anthology is more of a source-book than one to read cover-to-cover, but, if it is read as a whole, it provides a picture not only of Nabokov's scientific contributions but also of the relation between his science, his writing and his life. . . . One point that the editors wish to make is that Nabokov was not some lightweight dabbler, but a scientist who can be judged by professional standards." A *Publishers Weekly* reviewer styled the work "a volume devotees will delight to browse in and scholars will want to own."

Upon Nabokov's death at seventy-eight, *New York Times* contributor Alden Whitman concluded his obituary with these words: "Anyone so bold as to venture explanations might attempt to show how Mr. Nabokov's fiction was the refinement through memory and art of his own experience as a man who lost both father and fatherland to violent revolution, who adopted another culture, who mastered its language as few of its own have mastered it and who never forgot his origins. But one hesitates to undertake such explorations. Mr. Nabokov . . . would scoff at such extra-esthetic adventures. . . . But as long as Western civilization survives, his reputation is safe. Indeed, he will probably emerge as one of the greatest artists our century has produced."

BIOGRAPHICAL/CRITICAL SOURCES:

BOOKS

Appel, Alfred, Jr., editor, *The Annotated Lolita,* McGraw (New York, NY), 1970.

Appel, Alfred, Jr., and Charles Newman, editors, *Nabokov: Criticisms, Reminiscences, Translations, and Tributes,* Northwestern University Press (Evanston, IL), 1970.

Appel, Alfred, Jr., *Nabokov's Dark Cinema,* Oxford University Press (Oxford, England), 1972.

Bader, Julia, *Crystall Land: Artifice in Nabokov's English Novels,* University of California Press (Berkeley, CA), 1972.

Berdjis, Nassim Winnie, *Imagery in Vladimir Nabokov's Last Russian Novel, Its English Translation, and Other Prose Works of the 1930s,* Peter Lang (New York, NY), 1995.

Blot, Jean, *Nabokov,* Editions du Seuil (Paris, France), 1995.

Burgess, Anthony, *The Novel Now: A Guide to Contemporary Fiction,* Norton (New York, NY), 1967.

Clancy, Laurie, *The Novels of Vladimir Nabokov,* Macmillan (New York, NY), 1984.

Concise Dictionary of American Literary Biography: The New Consciousness, 1941-1968, Gale (Detroit, MI), 1987.

Connolly, Julian, editor, *Invitation to a Beheading: A Critical Companion,* Northwestern University Press (Evanston, IL), 1997.

Contemporary Literary Criticism, Gale (Detroit, MI), Volume 1, 1973, Volume 2, 1974, Volume 3, 1975, Volume 6, 1976, Volume 8, 1978, Volume 11, 1979, Volume 15, 1980, Volume 23, 1983, Volume 44, 1987, Volume 46, 1988, Volume 64, 1991.

Dembo, L. S., editor, *Nabokov: The Man and His Work,* University of Wisconsin Press (Madison, WI), 1967.

Dennison, Sally, *[Alternative] Literary Publishing,* University of Iowa Press (Iowa City, IA), 1984.

Dictionary of Literary Biography, Volume 2: *American Novelists since World War II,* Gale (Detroit, MI), 1978.

Dictionary of Literary Biography Documentary Series, Volume 3, Gale (Detroit, MI), 1983.

Dictionary of Literary Biography Yearbook: 1980, Gale (Detroit, MI), 1981.

Field, Andrew, *Nabokov: His Life in Art,* Little, Brown (Boston, MA), 1967.

Diment, Galya, *Pniniad: Vladimir Nabokov and Marc Szeftel,* University of Washington Press (Seattle, WA), 1997.

Field, Andrew, *V. N.: The Life and Art of Vladimir Nabokov,* Crown (New York, NY), 1986.

Fowler, Douglas, *Reading Nabokov,* Cornell University Press (Ithaca, NY), 1974.

Grabes, H., *Fictitious Biographies: Vladimir Nabokov's English Novels,* Mouton (Hawthorne, NY), 1977.

Grayson, Jane, *Nabokov Translated: A Comparison of Nabokov's Russian and English Prose,* Oxford University Press (Oxford, England), 1976.

Hyde, G. M., *Vladimir Nabokov: America's Russian Novelist,* Marion Boyars (New York, NY), 1978.

Jenkins, Greg, *Stanley Kubrick and the Art of Adaptation: Three Novels, Three Films,* McFarland (Jefferson, NC), 1997.

Johnson, Kurt, *Nabokov's Blues: The Scientific Odyssey of a Literary Genius,* McGraw-Hill (New York, NY), 2001.

L'Affaire Lolita, Olympia Press, 1959.

Lee, L. L., *Vladimir Nabokov,* Twayne (Boston, MA), 1976.

Lokrantz, Jessie Thomas, *The Underside of the Weave: Some Stylistic Devices Used by Vladimir Nabokov,* Acta Universitatis Upsaliensis, 1973.

Long, Michael, *Marvell, Nabokov: Childhood and Arcadia,* Clarendon Press (Oxford, England), 1984.

Mason, Bobbie Ann, *Nabokov's Garden: A Guide to Ada,* Ardis Press (Ann Arbor, MI), 1974.

Morton, Donald E., *Vladimir Nabokov,* Ungar (New York, NY), 1974.

Moynahan, Julian, *Vladimir Nabokov,* University of Minnesota Press (Minneapolis, MN), 1971.

Packman, David, *Vladimir Nabokov: The Structure of Literary Desire,* University of Missouri Press (Columbia, MO), 1982.

Proffer, Carl, *Keys to Lolita,* Indiana University Press (Bloomington, IN), 1968.

Proffer, Carl, editor, *A Book of Things about Vladimir Nabokov,* Ardis Press (Ann Arbor, MI), 1973.

Rampton, David, *Vladimir Nabokov: A Critical Study of the Novels,* Cambridge University Press (Cambridge, England), 1984.

Roth, Phyllis A., *Critical Essays on Vladimir Nabokov,* G. K. Hall (Boston, MA), 1984.

Rowe, William W., *Nabokov's Deceptive World,* New York University Press (New York, NY), 1971.

Schuman, Samuel, *Vladimir Nabokov: A Reference Guide,* G. K. Hall (Boston, MA), 1979.

Stegner, Page, *Escape into Aesthetics: The Art of Vladimir Nabokov,* Morrow (New York, NY), 1966.

Stegner, Page, *Nabokov's Congeries,* Viking (New York, NY), 1971.

Toker, Leona, *Nabokov: The Mystery of Literary Structure,* Cornell University Press (Ithaca, NY), 1989.

Wood, Michael, *The Magician's Doubts: Nabokov and the Risks of Fiction,* Princeton University Press (Princeton, NJ), 1995.

Zimmer, Dieter E., *A Guide to Nabokov's Butterflies and Moths,* D. E. Zimmer (Hamburg, Germany), 1996.

PERIODICALS

American Scholar, summer, 1994, p. 379.

Atlantic, September, 1958; June, 1968; June, 1969.

Booklist, March 15, 2000, Donna Seaman, review of *Nabokov's Butterflies: Unpublished and Uncollected Writings,* p. 1304.

Catholic World, October, 1958.

Centennial Review, summer, 1980, pp. 360-383.

Christian Science Monitor, May 31, 1962; May 8, 1969; December 4, 1995, p. 15.

Commentary, August, 1969; January, 1990, pp. 52-54; January, 1996, p. 68.

Dalhousie Review, winter, 1980-81, pp. 605-621.

Encounter, October, 1958, pp. 9-19; February, 1959; January, 1965; February, 1966.

Essays in Criticism, April, 1974, pp. 169-184.

Geste (*Lolita* special issue), March, 1959.

Harper's, May, 2001, Michael Scammell, "The Servile Path," p. 52.

Hollins Critic, June, 1966.

Kirkus Reviews, June 5, 1958.

Library Journal, August, 1958.

Los Angeles Times Book Review, February 4, 1996, p. 2.

Modern Fiction Studies, autumn, 1979, pp. 463-469; spring, 1986, pp. 115-126.

Nation, August 30, 1958; June 16, 1962; January 17, 1966.

National Review, July 15, 1969; November 17, 1970; December 11, 1995, p. 131.

New Mexico Humanities Review, no. 31, 1989, pp. 71-76.

New Republic, June 23, 1958; June 4, 1962; September 26, 1964; April 3, 1965; January 20, 1968; June 28, 1969; November 20, 1995, pp. 42-45.

Newsweek, November 6, 1995, p. 90.

New Yorker, November 8, 1958; September 22, 1962; August 2, 1969; December 4, 1995, pp. 108-114.

New York Times, January 12, 1968; May 13, 1968; May 1, 1969; October 7, 1970; August 24, 1989; October 5, 1989.

New York Times Book Review, May 27, 1962; May 15, 1966; January 15, 1967; July 2, 1967; May 12, 1968; May 4, 1969; June 14, 1970; October 25, 1970; April 18, 1971; October 1, 1989; October 29, 1995, p. 7.

Paris Review, summer-fall, 1967.

Playboy, January, 1964; December, 1995, p. 35.

Publishers Weekly, March 13, 2000, review of *Nabokov's Butterflies: Unpublished and Uncollected Writings,* p. 74.

San Francisco Chronicle, August 24, 1958.

Saturday Review, August 16, 1958; May 26, 1962; January 7, 1967; January 28, 1967.

Science, October 6, 2000, May Berenbaum, review of *Nabokov's Butterflies,* p. 57.

Time, July 28, 1967; May 17, 1968; May 23, 1969; November 2, 1970; December 21, 1970; October 30, 1995, p. 96.

Times Literary Supplement, August 2, 1996; August 4, 2000, Mark Ridley, "Humbert's Humming-Birds," pp. 3-4.

Tribune Books (Chicago, IL), September 24, 1989.

Twentieth Century Literature, December, 1975, pp. 428-437; summer, 2000, James Tweedie, "Lolita's Loose Ends: Nabokov and the Boundless Novel," p. 150.

Virginia Quarterly Review, winter, 1971.

Washington Post Book World, November 19, 1995, pp. 1, 11.*

NEGGERS, Carla A(malia) 1955-
  (Anne Harrell, Amalia James)

PERSONAL: Born August 9, 1955, in Belchertown, MA; daughter of Leonardus C. (a machinist) and Florine (a teacher; maiden name, Harrell) Neggers; married Joe B. Jewell (a United Methodist minister), July 23, 1977; children: Katherine Rye, Zachary Wynne. *Education:* Boston University, B.S. (magna cum laude), 1977. *Avocational interests:* Reading, counted cross-stitch embroidery, exercise, cooking, gardening.

ADDRESSES: Home—P.O. Box 826, Quechee, VT 05059. *Office*—Denise Marcil Literary Agency, Inc., 685 West End Ave., New York, NY 10025. *E-mail*—cneggers@aol.com.

CAREER: American Heart Association, Boston, MA, public relations associate, 1975-77; staff writer, L. W. Robbins Associates, 1977; freelance writer, 1978—. Presents writers' workshops; guest on television and radio programs.

MEMBER: International Women's Writing Guild, Romance Writers of America, Authors Guild, Authors League of America.

AWARDS, HONORS: Reviewer's Choice Award nominations, *Romantic Times,* 1983, for best Bantam Loveswept, 1986 and 1987, both for best Harlequin Temptation, 1988, for best romance series writer; Reviewer's Choice Award, *Romantic Times,* 1985, for *The Uneven Score,* 1988, for *All in a Name.*

WRITINGS:

(Under pseudonym Amalia James) *Midsummer Dreams,* Bantam (New York, NY), 1982.
(Under pseudonym Amalia James) *Tangled Promises,* Bantam (New York, NY), 1982.
(Under pseudonym Amalia James) *Dream Images,* Bantam (New York, NY), 1983.
Dancing Season, Avon (New York, NY), 1983.
Matching Wits, Bantam (New York, NY), 1983.
Outrageous Desire, Dell (New York, NY), 1983.
Heart on a String, Bantam (New York, NY), 1983.
A Touch of Magic, Bantam (New York, NY), 1984.
Delinquent Desire, New American Library (New York, NY), 1984.
The Venus Shoe, Avon (New York, NY), 1984.
The Knotted Skein, Avon (New York, NY), 1984.
Southern Comfort, Dell (New York, NY), 1984.
The Uneven Score, Avon (New York, NY), 1985.
Apple of My Eye, Dell (New York, NY), 1985.
Interior Designs, Dell (New York, NY), 1985.

Captivated, Harlequin (New York, NY), 1986.
Trade Secrets, Harlequin (New York, NY), 1987.
Claim the Crown, Harlequin (New York, NY), 1987, reissued, Mira, 1997.
Family Matters, Harlequin (New York, NY), 1988.
All in a Name, Harlequin (New York, NY), 1988.
A Winning Battle, Harlequin (New York, NY), 1989.
Finders Keepers, Harlequin (New York, NY), 1989.
(Under pseudonym Anne Harrell) *Minstrel's Fire,* Berkley Publishing (New York, NY), 1989.
(Under pseudonym Anne Harrell) *Betrayals,* Berkley Publishing (New York, NY), 1990.
Within Reason, Harlequin (New York, NY), 1990.
That Stubborn Yankee, Harlequin (New York, NY), 1991.
Wisconsin Wedding, Harlequin (New York, NY), 1992.
Tempting Fate, Berkley Publishing (New York, NY), 1993.
Bewitching, Harlequin (New York, NY), 1993.
Trying Patience, Harlequin (New York, NY), 1993.
Night Watch, Harlequin (New York, NY), 1993.
(With Jayne Ann Krentz, Linda Lael Miller, Linda Howard and Kasey Michaels) *Everlasting Love,* Pocket Books (New York, NY), 1995.
(With Anne Stuart and Rebecca Brandewyne) *New Year's Resolution: Husband,* Harlequin (New York, NY), 1996.
Finding You, Pocket Books (New York, NY), 1996.
The Groom Who (Almost) Got Away, Silhouette (New York, NY), 1996.
A Rare Chance, Pocket Books (New York, NY), 1996.
Just Before Sunrise, Pocket Star (New York, NY), 1997.
Night Scents, Pocket Books (New York, NY), 1997.
White Hot, Pocket Books (New York, NY), 1998.
Kiss the Moon, Mira, 1999.
On Fire, Mira, 1999.
The Waterfall, Mira, 2000.
The Carriage House, Mira, 2001.
The Cabin, Mira, 2002.

SIDELIGHTS: Carla A. Neggers has enjoyed a successful career as a romance/romantic suspense novelist. According to a *Publishers Weekly* reviewer, she is known "for creating likeable, believable characters and [for] her keen recognition of the obstacles that can muddle relationships." Neggers's novels are set in the present day, and her heroines are modern women in the sense that they have strong identities and the ability to carry themselves gracefully through trying emotional situations and even life-threatening events. Although they may ally themselves to men, the alliance becomes more of a partnership than a matter of seeking protection.

Neggers grew up in a large family in rural Massachusetts. Even as a child she would steal away to write stories, and she completed her first novel at the age of twenty-three. In an interview with *BookTalk,* she said that many of her tales begin with a "what if " scenario, sometimes based on her own experiences. The suspense in *The Carriage House,* for instance, grew from her own stay in a carriage house with a trapdoor leading to a dirt basement. The heroine of *The Carriage House* finds a skeleton in just such a basement at the outset of the novel. On the *Whitestone* Web site, Harriet Klausner stated that Neggers, who lives with her husband and children in Vermont, "is renowned for her romance novels that capture the essence of New England living."

Neggers once told *CA:* "I began writing romances in 1981 after my first novel, a romantic suspense, had been rejected sixteen times. Romantic suspense, it seemed, was out. So over a spicy lunch in Manhattan my agent suggested I try writing a book without a corpse in it. This hadn't really occurred to me. 'Try a straight romance,' she said. To which I said, 'You mean a formulaic story about a pretty, virginal, innocent twenty-year-old who's swept off her feet by a tall, dark, macho, handsome and worldly forty-year-old man? *Yuck!*' She asked me if I'd ever read a series romance. I admitted I hadn't. So she, being a patient woman, loaded me up with books and told me to call her.

"I read the books and realized the market was much more open to new ideas and new twists than I'd ever imagined. The heroines weren't all virgins! They were *over twenty-five!* They had *careers!* The heroes weren't all brooding violent types! Sure, there were books that I despised, but weren't there mysteries I despised? Why should I have to like every romance? So I said to myself: 'if I can write a romance with characters I like and situations I find amusing, I'll do it.' So I wrote, I sold, and I've been having lots of fun being a 'romance writer.'

"Meanwhile, of course, I'm still partial to my corpses, and when publishers started thinking about bringing back romantic suspense, there I was with my much-rejected novel. I revised it and sold it to Avon, who had rejected it way back when. So I always tell new writers to *persevere.*

"I write because I like to create characters and tell stories. Not all my stories are light-hearted romances or mysteries. Some will sell, some won't. But I know I have to stretch myself and take risks. . . . as a writer and as a person."

BIOGRAPHICAL/CRITICAL SOURCES:

PERIODICALS

Boston Herald, January 23, 1983.
Boy Meets Girl, January 28, 1983.
Los Angeles Times Book Review, October 14, 1984; January 6, 1985.
Publishers Weekly, February 15, 1993, review of *Tempting Fate,* p. 234; February 5, 1996, review of *Finding You,* p. 83; February 10, 1997, review of *Just Before Sunrise,* p. 81; June 1, 1998, review of *White Hot,* p. 48B; January 25, 1999, review of *Kiss the Moon,* p. 93; October 4, 1999, review of *On Fire,* p. 71; April 24, 2000, review of *The Waterfall,* p. 67; November 27, 2000, review of *The Carriage House,* p. 60.

OTHER

Amazon.com, http://www.amazon.com/ (February 27, 2001), interview with Neggers.
BookTalk, http://www.booktalk.com/ (March 6, 2001), "Carla Neggers: Biography."
Whitestone Books, http://www.whitestone.com/reviews/ (March 6, 2001), Harriet Klausner, reviews of *The Waterfall* and *The Carriage House.**

*   *   *

NICOLSON, Nigel 1917-

PERSONAL: Born January 19, 1917, in London, England; son of Harold George (a politician, diplomat, and writer) and Victoria (a writer; maiden name, Sackville-West) Nicolson; married Philippa Janet d'Eyncourt, 1953 (divorced, 1970); children: Adam, Juliet (Mrs. James Macmillan Scott), Rebecca (Mrs. Guy Phillips). *Education:* Attended Eron College, 1930-35, and Oxford University, 1936-39. *Politics:* Conservative. *Avocational interests:* Archaeology.

ADDRESSES: Home—Sissinghurst Castle, Cranbrook, Kent TN17 2AB, England.

CAREER: Writer. Weidenfeld & Nicolson Ltd. (publisher), London, England, director, 1946-92. Conservative member of English Parliament, 1952-59; chairman of United Nations Association, 1960-67. *Military service:* Grenadier Guards, 1939-45; served in Tunisian and Italian campaigns; became captain.

MEMBER: Royal Society of Literature (fellow), Society of Antiquaries (fellow), Beefsteak Club.

AWARDS, HONORS: Whitbread Prize, 1977, for *Mary Curzon;* Order of the British Empire, 2000.

WRITINGS:

The Grenadier Guards, 1939-1945, Gale & Polden, 1949.

People and Parliament, Weidenfeld & Nicholson (London, England), 1958, reprinted, Greenwood Press (Westport, CT), 1974.

Lord of the Isles: Lord Leverhulme in the Hebrides, Weidenfeld & Nicolson (London, England), 1960, reprinted, Acair (Stornoway, England), 2000.

Great Houses of Britain, photographs by Kerry Dundas, Putnam (New York, NY), 1965.

Great Houses of the Western World, photographs by Ian Graham, Putnam (New York, NY), 1968, published as *Great Houses,* Weidenfeld & Nicolson (London, England), 1968.

Portrait of a Marriage, Atheneum (New York, NY), 1973, reprinted, University of Chicago Press (Chicago, IL), 1998.

Alex: The Life of Field Marshal Earl Alexander of Tunis, Atheneum (New York, NY), 1973.

The Himalayas, Time-Life (New York, NY), 1975.

Mary Curzon, Harper & Row (New York, NY), 1977.

The National Trust Book of Great Houses of Britain, Weidenfeld & Nicolson (London, England), 1978.

Napoleon 1812, Harper & Row (New York, NY), 1985.

(With son, Adam Nicolson) *Two Roads to Dodge City: Two Colorful English Writers, Father and Son, Chronicle Their Wonderful Journeys Across America,* Harper & Row (New York, NY), 1987.

Kent, photographs by Patrick Sutherland, Harmony House (New York, NY), 1988.

The World of Jane Austen, photographs by Stephen Colover, Weidenfeld & Nicolson (London, England), 1991.

Long Life (memoirs), G. P. Putnam's Sons (New York, NY), 1998.

Virginia Woolf ("Penguin Lives" series), Viking (New York, NY), 2000.

EDITOR

Diaries and Letters of Harold Nicolson, Atheneum (New York, NY), Volume I: *1930-1939,* 1966, Volume II: *The War Years: 1939-1945,* 1967, Volume III: *The Later Years: 1945-1962,* 1968.

(With Joanne Trautman) *The Letters of Virginia Woolf,* Harcourt (New York, NY), Volume I: *The Flight of the Mind: 1888-1912,* 1975, Volume II: *The Question of Things Happening: 1912-1922,* 1976, Volume III: *A Change of Perspective: 1923-1928,*

1978, Volume IV: *A Reflection of the Other Person: 1929-1931,* 1979, Volume V: *The Sickle Side of the Moon: 1932-1935,* 1979, Volume VI: *Leave the Letters Till We're Dead: 1936-1941,* 1980.

Vita and Harold: The Letters of Vita Sackville-West and Harold Nicolson, G. P. Putnam's Sons (New York, NY), 1992.

ADAPTATIONS: The three-part BBC television series *Portrait of a Marriage,* cosponsored by WGBH, Boston, and aired on PBS's *Masterpiece Theatre,* was an adaptation of *Portrait of a Marriage* and *Vita and Harold: The Letters of Vita Sackville-West and Harold Nicolson.*

SIDELIGHTS: Nigel Nicolson was a member of Parliament and founder, with George Weidenfeld, of the publishing house of Weidenfeld & Nicolson. He is also a journalist, lecturer, and world traveler. Nicolson's *Portrait of a Marriage* recounts the nearly fifty-year union of his father, Harold Nicolson, and his mother, Victoria Sackville-West, known to friends as Vita. The book is based on the diary/autobiography of Vita undertaken when she was twenty-eight years old, married for eight years, and already the mother of two sons. She began simply: "Of course I have no right whatsoever to write down the truth about my life, involving as it does the lives of so many other people, but I do so urged by a necessity of truth-telling, because there is no other soul who knows the complete truth." Nigel Nicolson explains in his book that his mother's diary was "a confession, an attempt to purge her mind and heart of a love that had possessed her, a love for another woman, Violet Trefusis." Trefusis, a writer, was the daughter of Alice Keppel, the last mistress of Edward VII.

Although Violet was not the only woman Vita became involved with—another was Virginia Woolf—theirs was "a passion that [was] so intense it [was] like the grip of death," related Eliot Fremont-Smith in *New York.* He went on to note that "in her diary, Vita sees herself as two people (and her son does likewise): a rational, safe, well-born, intelligent, *good* person, wanting and needing her husband as 'safe harbor' and wanting to love him and deserve his amazingly steady devotion; and a rebellious, creative, independent free spirit, supremely sensual, ready to risk all to satisfy the gift-curse craving the gods implanted in her soul, the essence of herself."

Harold Nicolson's homosexuality was, reportedly, a loosely guarded secret. In fact, Harold and Vita often chided each other for their indulgences: she for her "muddles," and he for his "fun." And the marriage thrived, according to a contributor in *Times Literary Supplement,* for "neither of them felt in the least threatened by what, in both cases, was dismissed as idle peccadilloes, for they knew that they were indissolubly linked by a unique bond of affection, which only strengthened with time." Fremont-Smith concluded that "one comes away from *Portrait of a Marriage* not exactly liking these people . . . but with a sense of having known them in their souls, of having seen the raw insides of the intensity of their passions. It is all exhausting and haunting, not pleasant, perhaps, but an experience that reverberates, of a sort provided by very few books." A reviewer for the *Times Literary Supplement* praised Nicolson for his handling of the delicate subject matter in *Portrait of a Marriage,* writing that "he demonstrates an enlargement of sympathy without evading painful realities."

Nicolson again revealed the mind of a woman in *The Letters of Virginia Woolf.* This six-volume work includes correspondences from the time Virginia was six years old until her suicide at age fifty-nine. Although the first volume, covering the period from 1888 to 1912, does not portray the famous literary figure of her later years, it nevertheless "provides the undeniable fascination of watching her become that woman," reported Christopher Porterfield in *Time.* Volume II, subtitled *The Question of Things Happening,* chronicles two of her bouts with insanity and an attempted suicide. Woolf's correspondents at this time included her beloved sister Vanessa, one-time lover Violet Dickenson, future brother-in-law Clive Bell, and the writers Lytton Strachey and Roger Fry.

Letters from the three-year love affair of Virginia and Vita Sackville-West constitute the majority of the third volume. "I doubt there can be other love letters in the language quite like the ones printed here," remarked Claire Tomalin in *New Statesman.* "They can be read without a twinge; open, unembarrassed tributes from one woman to another for her beauty and seductiveness, direct appeals to her to come and hold her in her arms."

The next volume is also dominated by a figure of Virginia's affection, Ethel Smyth, a woman described by various writers as "vehement, impetuous, egotistic," and "a loudmouth." "An old woman of seventy-one has fallen in love with me," Virginia wrote in 1930. "It is like being caught up by a giant crab." Although Smyth did not at first appeal to Woolf, their relationship grew both in openness and intensity as Virginia poured out some of the most emotional letters of her life. She wrote openly of sex, madness, and other topics Virginia would not readily reveal to others. But their affair

soured, and whereas Virginia's letters to Vita were described as gentle, passionate, and moving, even when the two had broken off their relationship, her letters to Smyth were coarse and at times cruel. In one letter, for example, she condemned Smyth as "the rough-haired burr-tangled Cornish pig . . . an uncastrated pig . . . a wild boar, or a savage sow," and in another she railed against the older woman, calling her "a damned Harlot—hoary harpy—or an eldritch shriek of egotism—a hail storm of inconsecutive and inconsequent conceit."

The fifth volume, *The Sickle Side of the Moon,* contains letters written when Woolf was in her early fifties. Though distressed by the deaths of several close friends, including Strachey and Fry, she remained generally in good spirits and continued her literary endeavors. Reviews of this volume and of Nicolson's editing were decidedly more mixed than in previous volumes. A reviewer in *Economist* commented that "the editing is as good as ever, which is high praise." On the other hand, Jane Marcus held the work in low esteem, writing that "this is Nigel Nicolson's fifth time around with Virginia Woolf and he still hasn't got the hang of it. He flails and flounders, clutches at anything to prove his previous statements . . . and so muddles the actual facts with his own steadfastly incorrect opinions that the reader can only wonder: Why should anyone edit the letters of anyone he holds in such contempt?" She acknowledged, however, that "while obviously not a labor of love, [the work] might have been a labor of respect."

In 1973, Nicolson wrote *Alex: The Life of Field Marshal Earl Alexander of Tunis,* a biography of World War II hero Earl Alexander. Montgomery's commander in chief at Alamein, Alex, as he was referred to, conquered the whole of Italy, toppling Mussolini's regime and taking Rome. Nicolson, according to several reviewers, was the best person to write Alex's biography, having served under him in the Tunisian and Italian campaigns. "This is an important biography," said Alun Chalfont, "written with sympathy and perception." The reviewer added that the "portrait is strongly drawn and convincing."

In 1986, Nicolson and his son, Adam, drove across the United States. They took separate cars and went their separate ways, with Nicolson taking the southern route and visiting stately mansions and historic landmarks, and Adam covering the American West, with stops in Las Vegas and Berkeley. They document their travels in *Two Roads to Dodge City: Two Colorful English Writers, Father and Son, Chronicle Their Wonderful Journeys Across America.*

Time reviewer Pico Iyer said the two writers "breeze through their missions with the jaunty patrician charm of the charmed. The cross fire of their letters—a burst from Nigel, a counterburst from Adam—is the British equivalent of the nautical exchanges between William F. Buckley, Jr. and his son Christopher."

Nicolson chose a selection of letters from the more than ten thousand written between his parents and published them as *Vita and Harold: The Letters of Vita Sackville-West and Harold Nicolson*. A *Publishers Weekly* reviewer wrote that "the sound of their own voices in these enchanting letters gives fresh and privileged insight into exceptional lives and times." Anthony Burgess wrote in the *Atlantic* that "mostly the tone is one of quiet delight that both have a haven to steer to after excursions that have proved stormy, and not only on the sea of sex. The letters, especially Harold's, cover a period of English history that contained two wars and a painful interim. . . . Harold was in the middle of things, from Versailles to Nuremberg; Vita was mostly at an unchanging center of digging and planting. His letters are, on the ground of their subject matter, the more interesting. He was, moreover, the better letter writer." From the letters, a great deal is revealed about their international circle of friends that included leaders of government and society and prominent literary figures. Among them were Winston Churchill, Charles De Gaulle, the Shah of Iran, Anne and Charles Lindbergh, Somerset Maugham, Sinclair Lewis, and James Joyce. Burgess concluded by writing that "to American readers, this collection must have the quality of a museum. Ancient presumptions and prejudices are fossilized, and a way of privileged life shown in medallions. Love comes through, however, and as a testament of love superficially bizarre but fundamentally exemplary this volume stands as a monument."

A three-part television movie based on *Portrait of a Marriage, Vita and Harold,* and a reprinted version of Violet Trefusis's 1952 autobiography *Don't Look Round* was produced by the BBC in London and cosponsored by the WGBH Foundation of Boston. *Nation* contributor Charlotte Innes wrote that "it says something about our society's confusion over sexual matters that most critics of the TV series and the books have treated the homosexuality of the three principles as peripheral, and the forty-eight-year marriage of Harold and Vita as the natural core around which everything else revolved. . . . Adding to the distorted picture, critics are taking at face value Vita, Harold, and Violet's own acceptance of convention, born of the period in which they lived." Innes noted that Alistair Cooke, host of the PBS presentation "echoed Nigel's

and Vita and Harold's language, labeling the Vita-Violet affair an 'infatuation' and a 'tumultuous interlude' that 'almost shattered the marriage.' Quoting Harold, Cooke described Violet as 'that dreadful woman' and Vita as an irresponsible wife who 'neglected' her husband and 'abandoned' her two sons. Cooke failed to say that as a diplomat abroad and then as a journalist in London, Harold spent far more time away from home than Vita did in pursuit of Violet, and that the children were packed off to boarding school at an early age in the traditional English upper-class manner."

Cooke said that although Harold was "a homosexual all his life," it was "in a mild way." "In fact," said Innes, "Harold had lifelong relationships with many gay men, such as Raymond Mortimer and Ivor Novello. But his role in public life required him to exercise discretion since, under British law, male (though) not female homosexuality was illegal until 1967." Innes commented that the cosponsor, the WGBH Foundation of Boston, made cuts in the American version, and that "contrary to WGBH's insistence that the cuts were made for pacing, the lesbian scenes had been singled out."

Long Life, Nicolson's memoir, is filled with the names of the famous people who influenced him from an early age. It was Woolf who suggested that he write letters and keep a diary, because "nothing has really happened until you have described it." In primary school, Nicolson was taught by future poet laureate C. Day-Lewis, and as a student, he attended a lecture by Goebbels in Nazi Germany. He vacationed with Aldous Huxley and later rented a house to Charles Lindbergh. He had as dinner guests Greta Garbo, Prince Charles, and Princess Grace of Monaco, and bought three islands off the coast of Scotland. He served in Parliament and in the British army. *Washington Post* reviewer Michael Dirda wrote that "in the most moving chapter of *Long Life,* Nicolson relates the betrayal of thousands of White Russians and Yugoslav rebels who had sought asylum at the war's end with the British in Carinthia. Orders came down to deliver these men to their enemies, the Soviet army and Marshal Tito's partisans, but to tell them they were being transported to Italy." Dirda concluded by calling the memoir "that rare thing: a very agreeable one." *Library Journal* contributor Ronald Ray Ratliff called it "a marvelous memoir of a rich, multifaceted life."

Library Journal reviewer Diane Gardner Premo called Nicolson's biography *Virginia Woolf* "beautifully written," and said Nicolson "does not allow his fond recollections to cloud his view of his subject's troubled life." Nicolson recalls his childhood memories of Woolf and analyzes her novels, noting that he may have inspired the character James in *Mrs. Dalloway.* He also provides insight into Woolf 's own childhood and youth. A *Publishers Weekly* reviewer said his personal accounts "enliven Nicolson's respectful position between various, often hotly contended views of Woolf as writer, feminist, and Bloomsburian."

BIOGRAPHICAL/CRITICAL SOURCES:

BOOKS

Nicolson, Nigel, *Long Life,* G. P. Putnam's Sons (New York, NY), 1998.

Nicolson, Nigel, *Portrait of a Marriage,* Atheneum (New York, NY), 1973.

Nicolson, Nigel, and Adam Nicolson, *Two Roads to Dodge City: Two Colorful English Writers, Father and Son, Chronicle Their Wonderful Journeys Across America,* Harper & Row (New York, NY), 1987.

PERIODICALS

Atlantic, July, 1992, Anthony Burgess, review of *Vita and Harold: The Letters of Vita Sackville-West and Harold Nicolson,* p. 87.

Booklist, April 15, 1992, Donna Seaman, review of *Vita and Harold,* p. 1496; February 15, 1998, Frank Caso, review of *Long Life,* p. 974.

Chicago Tribune Book World, April 22, 1979; November 4, 1979.

Christian Science Monitor, December 22, 1975; March 6, 1987, review of *Two Roads to Dodge City: Two Colorful English Writers, Father and Son, Chronicle Their Wonderful Journeys Across America,* p. 4.

Contemporary Review, September, 1997, review of *Mary Curzon,* p. 165.

Economist, March 31, 1973; September 20, 1975.

History Today, January, 1986, David Chandler, review of *Napoleon 1812,* p. 55; January, 1998, Peter Burley, review of *Napoleon 1812,* p. 55.

Insight on the News, September 7, 1992, Richard Grenier, "An Imperfect View of Marriage," p. 23.

Library Journal, November 1, 1976; March 1, 1987, Roger W. Fromm, review of *Two Roads to Dodge City,* p. 75; June 1, 1992, Lesley Jorbin, review of *Vita and Harold,* p. 126; March 1, 1998, Ronald Ray Ratliff, review of *Long Life,* p. 88; December, 2000, Diane Gardner Premo, review of *Virginia Woolf,* p. 130.

London Magazine, October, 1967.

Los Angeles Times, March 26, 1979.

Los Angeles Times Book Review, December 22, 1985, review of *Napoleon 1812,* p. 6; November 7, 1993, review of *The World of Jane Austen,* p. 8.

Ms., February, 1974.

Nation, September 28, 1992, Charlotte Innes, review of *Vita and Harold,* p. 337.

National Review, December 19, 1986, J. O. Tate, review of *Napoleon 1812,* p. 51.

New Statesman, October 13, 1967, Claire Tomalin, review of *The Letters of Virginia Woolf,* Volume III.

Newsweek, November 17, 1975; January 9, 1978.

New York, October 8, 1973, Eliot Fremont-Smith, review of *Portrait of a Marriage.*

New Yorker, October 29, 1973; July 18, 1977; January 27, 1986, review of *Napoleon 1812,* p. 98.

New York Review of Books, March 23, 1967; November 15, 1973; July 15, 1976; November 19, 1992, Robert Craft, review of *Vita and Harold,* p. 26.

New York Times, December 27, 1977.

New York Times Book Review, June 11, 1967; November 10, 1974; November 23, 1975; November 14, 1976; January 8, 1978; March 25, 1979; April 22, 1979; September 26, 1982, review of *The Letters of Virginia Woolf,* Volume VI, p. 39; January 26, 1986, Peter Paret, review of *Napoleon 1812,* p. 24; April 12, 1987, Karal Ann Marling, review of *Two Roads to Dodge City,* p. 47; July 26, 1992, Denis Donoghue, review of *Vita and Harold,* p. 3; August 22, 1993, Diane Cole, review of *The World of Jane Austen,* p. 16; March 15, 1998, R. W. B. Lewis, review of *Long Life,* p. 7; December 17, 2000, Aoibheann Sweeney, "Back to Bloomsbury; Nigel Nicolson's Biography of Virginia Woolf Is Partly a Family Portrait and Memoir," p. 19.

Publishers Weekly, January 30, 1987, Genevieve Stuttaford, review of *Two Roads to Dodge City,* p. 377; May 18, 1992, review of *Vita and Harold,* p. 50; January 12, 1998, review of *Long Life,* p. 49; September 25, 2000, review of *Virginia Woolf,* p. 95.

Saturday Night, October, 1968.

Spectator, March 1, 1997, review of *Mary Curzon,* p. 32; August 23, 1997, review of *Long Life,* p. 30.

Time, January 19, 1976, Christopher Porterfield, review of *The Letters of Virginia Woolf,* Volume I; May 4, 1987, Pico Iyer, review of *Two Roads to Dodge City,* p. 103; January 19, 1998, review of *Long Life,* p. 49.

Times Literary Supplement, November 2, 1973; September 19, 1975; September 24, 1976; November 11, 1977; December 12, 1986, review of *Two Roads to Dodge City,* p. 1398; July 4, 1997, review of *The World of Jane Austen,* p. 31; July 11, 1997, review of *Mary Curzon,* p. 32; September 12, 1997, review of *Long Life,* p. 31.

Wall Street Journal, August 20, 1992, Willard Spiegelman, review of *Vita and Harold,* p. A9; March 17, 1998, Penelope Fitzgerald, review of *Long Life,* p. A16.

Washington Post Book World, March 1, 1998, Michael Dirda, "Keeping Good Company," pX4; February 7, 1999, review of *Portrait of a Marriage,* p. 6.

World Literature Today, summer, 1993, Daniel P. King, review of *Vita and Harold,* p. 615.

Yale Review, spring, 1976.

* * *

NUSSBAUM, Martha Craven 1947-

PERSONAL: Born May 6, 1947, in New York, NY; daughter of George (an attorney) and Betty (a homemaker; maiden name, Warren) Craven; married Alan Jeffrey Nussbaum, August, 1969 (divorced, November, 1987); children: Rachel Emily. *Education:* Attended Wellesley College, 1964-66; New York University, B.A., 1969; Harvard University, M.A., 1971, Ph.D., 1975.

ADDRESSES: Home—10 Chester St., Cambridge, MA 02140. *Office*—University of Chicago Law School, 1111 East 60th St., Chicago, IL 60637-2776. *E-mail*—martha—nussbaum@law.uchicago.edu.

CAREER: Harvard University, Cambridge, MA, assistant professor, 1975-80, associate professor of philosophy and classics, 1980-83; Wellesley College, Wellesley, MA, visiting associate professor of philosophy and classics, 1983-84; Brown University, Providence, RI, associate professor, 1984-85, professor of philosophy, classics, and comparative literature, 1985-87, David Benedict Professor, 1987-88, university professor, 1988-95; World Institute for Development Economics Research (WIDER), Helsinki, Finland, research advisor, 1986-93; Alexander Rosenthal Lecturer, Northwestern University, 1991; University of Chicago, Chicago, IL, 1995—, Ernst Freund Professor of Law and Ethics (appointed to the law school, philosophy department, divinity school), associate in classics, affiliate of the Committee on Southern Asian Studies, board member of the Center for Gender Studies.

MEMBER: American Philosophical Association (national board member; executive committee, Eastern division, 1985-87; chair of committee on international cooperation, 1989-92; chair, committee on status of women, 1994-97; presidents, central division, 1999-00), American Philological Association, PEN.

AWARDS, HONORS: Harvard University, junior fellow, 1972-75; Princeton University, humanities fellow, 1977-78; Guggenheim Foundation fellow, 1983; National Institutes of Health fellow, 1986-87; All Souls College, Oxford, England, visiting fellow, 1986-87; National Endowment for the Humanities fellow, 1986-87; Brandeis Creative Arts Award, nonfiction, 1990; Spielvogel-Diamonstein Prize, International PEN, 1991, for *Love's Knowledge;* Ness Book Award, Association of American Colleges and Universities, 1998, for *Cultivating Humanity: A Classical Defense of Reform in Liberal Education;* book award, North American Society for Social Philosophy, 2000, for *Sex and Social Justice;* Distinguished Alumni Award, New York University, 2000. Honorary degrees received from Kalamazoo College, Grinnell College, Williams College, St. Andrews University, Katholieke Universiteit Leuven, Whitman College, University of Toronto, University for Humanist Studies (Utrecht, the Netherlands), Bard College, Wabash College, SUNY-Brockport, and Queen's University, Ontario.

WRITINGS:

(And translator) Aristotle, *Aristotle's De Motu Animalium,* Princeton University Press (Princeton, NJ), 1978.

The Fragility of Goodness: Luck and Ethics in Greek Tragedy and Philosophy, Cambridge University Press (New York, NY), 1986, revised edition, 2001.

Non-Relative Virtues: An Aristotelian Approach ("WIDER Working Papers" series), World Institute for Development Economics Research (Helsinki, Finland), 1987.

Nature, Function, and Capability: Aristotle on Political Distribution ("WIDER Working Papers" series), World Institute for Development Economics Research, United Nations University (Helsinki, Finland), 1987.

(With Amartya Sen) *Internal Criticism and Indian Rationalist Traditions* ("WIDER Working Papers" series), World Institute for Development Economics Research, United Nations University (Helsinki, Finland), 1987.

Love's Knowledge: Essays on Philosophy and Literature, Oxford University Press (New York, NY), 1990.

The Therapy of Desire: Theory and Practice in Hellenistic Ethics, Princeton University Press (Princeton, NJ), 1994.

Poetic Justice: The Literary Imagination and Public Life, Beacon Press (Boston, MA), 1995.

For Love of Country: Debating the Limits of Patriotism, edited by Joshua Cohen, Beacon Press (Boston, MA), 1996.

The Feminist Critique of Liberalism (Lindley Lecture), University of Kansas, Department of Philosophy (Lawrence, KS), 1997.

Cultivating Humanity: A Classical Defense of Reform in Liberal Education, Harvard University Press (Cambridge, MA), 1997.

Plato's Republic: The Good Society and the Deformation of Desire (Bradley Lecture), Library of Congress (Washington, DC), 1998.

Sex & Social Justice, Oxford University Press (New York, NY), 1999.

Women and Human Development: The Capabilities Approach ("The Seeley Lectures"), Cambridge University Press (New York, NY), 2000.

(With others) *The Human Embrace: The Love of Philosophy and the Philosophy of Love,* Pennsylvania State University Press (University Park, PA), 2000.

Upheavals of Thought: The Intelligence of Emotions, Cambridge University Press (New York, NY), 2001.

Women and Human Development: The Capabilities Approach ("The Seeley Lectures," no. 3), Cambridge University Press (New York, NY), 2001.

EDITOR

(With Malcolm Schofield) *Language and Logos: Studies in Ancient Greek Philosophy Presented to G. E. L. Owen,* Cambridge University Press (New York, NY), 1982.

G. E. L. Owen, *Logic, Science, and Dialectic: Collected Papers in Greek Philosophy,* Cornell University Press (Ithaca, NY), 1986.

With A. Rorty) *Essays on Aristotle's De Anima,* Oxford University Press (New York, NY), 1992.

(With Amartya Sen) *The Quality of Life* ("WIDER Studies in Development Economics" series), Oxford University Press (New York, NY), 1993.

(With Jacques Brunschwig) *Passions and Perceptions: Studies in Hellenistic Philosophy of Mind: Proceedings of the Fifth Symposium Hellenisticum,* Cambridge University Press (New York, NY), 1993.

(With Jonathan Glover), *Women, Culture, and Development: A Study of Human Capabilities,* Oxford University Press (New York, NY), 1995.

(With David M. Estlund) *Sex, Preference, and Family: Essays on Law and Nature,* Oxford University Press (New York, NY), 1997.

(With Cass R. Sunstein), *Clones and Clones: Facts and Fantasies About Human Cloning,* Norton (New York, NY), 1998.

(With Saul M. Olyan) *Sexual Orientation and Human Rights in American Religious Discourse,* Oxford University Press (New York, NY), 1998.

(With others) Susan Moller Okin, *Is Multiculturalism Bad For Women?,* Princeton University Press (Princeton, NJ), 1999.

Contributor to periodicals and journals.

SIDELIGHTS: Martha Craven Nussbaum is a professor of law and ethics who has written or edited a long list of books dealing with her interests, which include philosophy. Among those she has edited is *The Quality of Life,* the proceedings of a conference held in Helsinki, Finland in 1988, and sponsored by the United Nation's World Institute for Development Economics Research (WIDER), for which Nussbaum served as a research advisor. Nussbaum's own paper on gender issues is included, as is that of her coeditor Amartya Sen.

Nussbaum's *The Therapy of Desire: Theory and Practice in Hellenistic Ethics* examines the rise of ethical philosophy in Hellenistic Greek society (323 to 31 B.C.) in which a shift in the political order led to new ways of thinking about the connections between the individual and the city-state. *Insight on the News* contributor Mark Miller noted that "Empires ebbed and flowed and generals fought over territory stretching from the Balkans to the Hindu Kush, but the ancient Greeks became disaffected, losing concern for the polis as their power to govern it slipped away." Greek culture changed as poets turned from writing about heroes, warriors, and gods, and began to write about the pleasures of life. According to Miller, Nussbaum writes "Hellenistic ethics was more than an abstract system of rational thought, as much philosophy had been up to that time. It was a practical plan for living the so-called 'good life'—a medical cure for diseases of the soul." *New Republic* contributor Peter Green wrote that "for every philosophical sect, as Nussbaum emphasizes, 'the medical analogy is not simply a decorative metaphor; it is an important tool both of discovery and of justification.' Rival theorists competed for attention in the same way their medical exemplars did; and anyone who has studied the extraordinary history of the ancient medical schools—Dogmatists, Empiricists, Methodists, and Pneumatists, roughly corresponding in theory to Stoics, Epicureans, Skeptics, and Eclectics—will know just how tangled and complex a skein Nussbaum has set out to unravel." *America* reviewer Daniel J. Harrington said Nussbaum "brings light to an important chapter in the history of philosophy."

In reviewing Nussbaum's *Poetic Justice: The Literary Imagination and Public Life, Nation* reviewer Lennard J. Davis remarked that "the vexed question for novelists and readers has always been, is the novel an essential part of the public, political life, or does it simply provide an escape from that life? Are we better citizens for reading novels, or are novel readers really dandified shirkers lounging about in the overstuffed chairs of indifference?" Davis wrote that Nussbaum "is on the side of those who claim that the novel provides us with a valuable way of seeing the world, as useful as factual documents, economic analyses, or utilitarian blueprints. Indeed, she claims that the novel goes these quantitative approaches one better because the novel 'constructs empathy and compassion in ways highly relevant to citizenship.' " Francis A. Beer wrote in *American Political Science Review* that *Poetic Justice* "presents a partisan and compelling case for literature as a significant . . . mode of political analysis. Such literary analysis of politics draws from a rich tradition that includes the philosophy of Paul Ricoeur, the anthropology of Mircea Eliade and Claude Levi-Strauss, the history of William McNeill. . . . It is consistent with renewed interest and attention being given to narrative form in the psychology of Jerome Bruner, the artificial intelligence of Roger Shank, the public policy analysis of Emery Roe." *Journal of Economic Issues* contributor Kevin Quinn said "this book, and Nussbaum's work generally, ought to be required reading for the economist, as it constitutes a well-worked-out critique of a conception of rationality, and more particularly of public rationality, that the mainstream of the profession at any rate has made its stock-in-trade."

Nussbaum and Judith Glover edited *Women, Culture, and Development: A Study of Human Capabilities. Ethics* writer Neera K. Badhwar said the collection of papers "elaborates and defends the capabilities approach, focusing on the widespread ill-functioning of women in developing countries and the issue of cultural relativism versus universalism." Badhwar felt the most valuable parts of the book to be "the analyses of human capabilities and functioning and of gender justice, and the revealing philosophical and sociological studies of quality of life in specific countries." *Journal of Economic Issues* contributor Eiman Zein-Elabdin also found the issues of culture, development, and justice essential, and added that, "more importantly, [the book] uncovers some of the philosophical underpinnings of economic theory and policy in the area of development.

For Love of Country: Debating the Limits of Patriotism leads with Nussbaum's essay, "Patriotism and Cosmopolitanism," which first appeared in the *Boston Review*. In the piece, Nussbaum argues for cosmopolitanism, or world citizen status. Fifteen essays by authors who agree or disagree with her view follow the essay. Of those who disagree, Hilary Putnam felt the time isn't right; Elaine Scarry raises constitutional issues; and Richard Falk stresses the need for addressing market-driven globalism. Other contributors include Nathan Glazer, Benjamin Barber, and Gertrude Himmelfarb. Nussbaum maintains that each person's country of birth is an accident and that there are many opportunities to morally act as a world citizen, even without a world state. She believes that we should reach beyond American values and embrace the range of human values, which will provide insight into global problems. *Foreign Affairs* contributor Francis Fukuyama felt that universal rights cannot be considered "without being aware that some regimes support while others systematically deny rights." "Readers will wonder whether some of the respondents have a clue about what Nussbaum proposes in this exciting compendium," wrote a *Publishers Weekly* reviewer. *Booklist* contributor Ray Olson called *For Love of Country* a "slim but demanding volume."

In reviewing *Cultivating Humanity: A Classical Defense of Reform in Liberal Education* in *America,* writer Joseph A. Appleyard said that Nussbaum "does a great service in this book, both to those inside higher education who are trying to steer their way through this muddle and to the general public interested in how to think about the contemporary issues that generate so much of the argument: multiculturalism, race, ethnicity, gender, and sexuality. Calmly, lucidly, and without ducking any of the difficult questions, she proposes that a truly liberal education for today's world has to teach students how to think critically about these topics and their relationship to the intellectual traditions that underlie U.S. culture." *Ethics* contributor Marilyn Friedman wrote "as Nussbaum points out, education which emphasizes group-based identities may well be divisive in the short run. Intergroup antagonisms could be temporarily intensified. We might, however, need temporary divisiveness in order for some among us to be motivated to make the demanding sacrifices that are needed to bring about, in the long run, the just community of world citizens in which all are recognized and treated by all as equals in moral worth."

Commonweal contributor Dennis O'Brien said "unlike most philosophers setting out to prove a case, Nussbaum actually cites empirical evidence. She has personally tracked the practices of liberal arts teachers in . . . varied settings. . . . At each of these institutions, she salutes individuals and/or programs which challenge students to think openly and creatively, to resist the 'idols of the marketplace,' to make up their own minds. The new—supposedly anticlassical—curricula do exactly what one hopes the liberal arts will accomplish: liberation of the human mind." Nussbaum feels universities should promote world citizenship. "Infusing world citizenship into the curriculum is a much larger project than the designing of one or two required courses," wrote *Public Interest* contributor David Frum. "Its goals can and should pervade the curriculum as a whole, as multinational, minority, and gender perspectives can illuminate the teaching of many standard parts of the curriculum, from American history to economics to art history to ancient Greek literature."

Nussbaum, with Cass R. Sunstein, is editor of *Clones and Clones: Facts and Fantasies About Human Cloning,* a collection of essays, poetry, and short fiction on the subject. Opinions of each of the editors are presented, with contributions in the categories of science, commentary, ethics and religion, law and public policy, and fiction and fantasy. Included are contributions by Winston Churchill, biologist Richard Dawkins, poet C. K. Williams, essayist Jay Gould, and Ian Wilmut who created Dolly, the sheep cloned in 1997. Two-thirds of the contributions are original. "The spectrum of authors and their varying perspectives in fact and fiction are assets to anyone who hopes to understand this broad issue and its vast cultural implications," wrote a *Publishers Weekly* reviewer. *Chemistry and Industry* writer Gearoid Tuohy remarked that "in particular, many of the articles dealing with the legislative issues of human cloning make informative reading. Unfortunately, you will have to read the whole book to find the very limited number of pieces that add more light than heat." Mary Midgley, who reviewed the book for the *Hastings Center Report,* commented on two papers she called "excellent," Miller's "Sheep, Joking, Cloning, and the Uncanny," and Wendy Doniger's "Sex and the Mythological Clone." Midgley said these contributions "survey the mysterious symbolism of Doppelgangers, a theme that surely underlies much of the confusion surrounding this project." *Foreign Affairs* contributor Eliot A. Cohen called the volume "a worthy exploration of a discomfiting topic."

Sexual Orientation and Human Rights in American Religious Discourse, edited by Nussbaum and Saul M. Olyan, represents the proceedings of a conference held at Brown University in 1995, at which opposing viewpoints on homosexuality were presented by religious thinkers. *Journal of Religion* writer Eric Bain-Selbo said "this remarkable collection of essays serves up a generous feast of reflection about homosexuality in American culture. Within the collection one can get a significant introduction to religious thought on the subject, an intriguing sampling of approaches to theological ethics, a smattering of political positions concerning sexual issues, a heaping portion of legal theory, and even some insightful cultural criticism on the side." *National Review* contributor Gerard V. Bradley called the essay by Rabbi David Novak "a highlight," and noted that the book "concludes with thoughtful essays by legal scholars Andrew Koppelman and Michael McConnell." James Waller wrote in *Lambda Book Report* that the book "is a laudable attempt to replace passionate diatribes and name-calling with measured, civil intercourse. The essays are all theologically learned, and, together, they're immensely revealing about what's at stake."

In a review of *Sex & Social Justice,* a *Publishers Weekly* contributor said that "among academic stars, Nussbaum is one of the brightest," and called Nussbaum's prose "remarkably clear given the density of the content and the rigor of her thinking." Nussbaum's fifteen essays are divided into two sections, "Justice" and "Sex." She addresses women's rights, with emphasis on women in India and Bangladesh, lesbian and gay rights, and sexual experience. Lisa Sowle Cahill and George M. Anderson wrote in *America* that the essays "recapitulate Nussbaum's essential philosophical approach. . . . Nussbaum sees herself as both a liberal and an Aristotelian. Her brand of liberalism derives from Kant's requirements of equality and equal respect and places a high emphasis on critical reason. From Aristotle she takes the conviction that human beings have certain basic needs and capabilities, preconditions of happiness and well-being. . . . An important contribution is Nussbaum's insistence that the emotions are not irrational passions, but connections to others that nuance and give texture to the moral life."

Nussbaum further studies the status of women around the world, particularly in India, in *Women and Human Development: The Capabilities Approach. Booklist* reviewer Mary Carroll said the book is "not an easy read, but an appropriate acquisition where feminist theory and writers such as Rorty, Rawls, and Posner circulate."

BIOGRAPHICAL/CRITICAL SOURCES:

BOOKS

Pyle, Andrew, editor, *Key Philosophers in Conversation: The Cogito Interviews,* Routledge, 1999.

PERIODICALS

America, April 8, 1995, Daniel J. Harrington, review of *The Therapy of Desire: Theory and Practice in Hellenistic Ethics,* p. 26; May 23, 1998, Joseph A. Appleyard, review of *Cultivating Humanity: A Classical Defense of Reform in Liberal Education,* p. 29; February 12, 2000, Lisa Sowle Cahill, George M. Anderson, "Normative and Not," p. 20.

American Political Science Review, December, 1993, Douglas Rae, review of *The Quality of Life,* p. 1006; September, 1996, Francis A. Beer, review of *Poetic Justice: The Literary Imagination and Public Life,* p. 636.

Booklist, August, 1996, Ray Olson, review of *For Love Country: Debating the Limits of Patriotism,* p. 1863; April 15, 2000, Mary Carroll, review of *Women and Human Development: The Capabilities Approach,* p. 1506.

Chemistry and Industry, March 6, 2000, Gearoid Tuohy, "The River of Heraclitus," p. 185.

Choice, October, 1994, review of *The Quality of Life,* p. 300; January, 1995, review of *The Therapy of Desire,* p. 801; September, 1996, review of *Poetic Justice,* p. 118; October, 1998, review of *Cultivating Humanity,* p. 370; January, 1999, review of *Clones and Clones: Facts and Fantasies About Human Cloning,* p. 910.

Christian Science Monitor, March 13, 1998, review of *Clones and Clones,* p. B5.

Commonweal, April 10, 1998, Dennis O'Brien, review of *Cultivating Humanity,* p. 26; December 4, 1998, review of *Cultivating Humanity,* p. 26.

Economist, November 14, 1998, review of *Clones and Clones,* p. 11.

Ethics, October, 1992, Jesse Kalin, review of *Love's Knowledge: Essays on Philosophy and Literature,* pp. 135-151; October, 1994, James P. Sterba, review of *The Quality of Life,* pp. 198-201; January, 1995, Deborah K. W. Modrak, review of *Essays on Aristotle's De Anima,* pp. 413-416; April, 1995, Richard Kraut, review of *The Therapy of Desire,* pp. 613-625; July, 1997, Neera K. Badhwar, review of *Women, Culture, and Development: A Study of Human Capabilities,* p. 725; April, 2000, Marilyn Friedman, "Educating for World Citizenship," p. 586; October, 2000, Hilary Charlesworth, "Martha Nussbaum's Feminist Internationalism," p. 64.

Foreign Affairs, March-April, 1997, Francis Fukuyama, review of *For Love of Country,* p. 173; September-October, 1998, Eliot A. Cohen, review of *Clones and Clones,* p. 149.

Hastings Center Report, July, 1994, review of *The Quality of Life,* p. 48; May, 1996, review of *Women, Culture, and Development,* p. 45; March, 2000, Mary Midgley, review of *Clones and Clones,* p. 41.

Insight on the News, August 1, 1994, Mark Miller, review of *The Therapy of Desire,* p. 29.

Journal of Economic Issues, September, 1997, Kevin Quinn, review of *Poetic Justice,* p. 847, Eiman Zein-Elabdin, review of *Women, Culture, and Development,* p. 849.

Journal of Philosophy, February, 1994, review of *Love's Knowledge,* p. 105; August, 1997, review of *Poetic Justice,* p. 431.

Journal of Religion, July, 1993, Louis A. Ruprecht, Jr., review of *Love's Knowledge,* p. 463; January, 2001, Eric Bain-Selbo, review of *Sexual Orientation and Human Rights in American Religious Discourse,* p. 168.

Lambda Book Report, February, 1999, James Waller, review of *Sexual Orientation and Human Rights in American Religious Discourse,* p. 25.

Library Journal, March 15, 1994, Terry Skeats, review of *The Therapy of Desire,* p. 74; March 15, 1996, Gene Shaw, review of *Poetic Justice,* p. 71; December, 1998, Linda V. Carlisle, review of *Sex & Social Justice,* p. 140.

London Review of Books, October 20, 1994, review of *The Therapy of Desire,* p. 25; October 17, 1996, review of *Poetic Justice,* p. 13; March 6, 1997, review of *For Love of Country,* p. 22; November 16, 2000, Elizabeth Spelman, "How Do They See You?" pp. 11, 13.

Nation, July 15, 1996, Lennard J. Davis, review of *Poetic Justice,* p. 40.

National Review, February 9, 1998, E. Christian Kopff, review of *Cultivating Humanity,* p. 56; December 7, 1998, Gerard V. Bradley, review of *Sexual Orientation and Human Rights in American Religious Discourse,* p. 73.

New Republic, September 5, 1994, Peter Green, review of *The Therapy of Desire,* p. 38; March 8, 1999, review of *Sex & Social Justice,* p. 33.

New Scientist, December 12, 1998, review of *Clones and Clones,* p. 53.

New Statesman, November 28, 1997, review of *Cultivating Humanity,* p. 49; October 9, 1998, review of *Clones and Clones,* p. 45.

New York Times Book Review, February 10, 1991; June 19, 1994, Richard Jenkins, review of *The Therapy of Desire,* p. 11; April 7, 1996, Morris Dickstein, review of *Poetic Justice,* p. 19; September 8, 1996, review of *The Therapy of Desire,* p. 36; January 4, 1998, James Shapiro, review of *Cultivating Hu-*

manity, p. 18; September 6, 1998, David Papineau, review of *Clones and Clones,* p. 11; March 14, 1999, Alan Ryan, review of *Sex & Social Justice,* p. 16.

Philosophy in Review, June, 1998, review of *Cultivating Humanity,* p. 216.

Public Interest, spring, 1998, David Frum, review of *Cultivating Humanity,* p. 105.

Publishers Weekly, June 10, 1996, review of *For Love of Country,* p. 93; July 28, 1997, review of *Cultivating Humanity,* p. 60; July 13, 1998, review of *Clones and Clones,* p. 70; December 21, 1998, review of *Sex & Social Justice,* p. 45; September 13, 1999, review of *Is Multiculturalism Bad For Women?,* p. 70.

Times Literary Supplement, April 10, 1992, review of *Love's Knowledge,* p. 6; September 11, 1992, review of *Essays on Aristotle's De Anima,* p. 27; June 24, 1994, review of *The Therapy of Desire,* p. 9; March 15, 1996, review of *Poetic Justice,* p. 9; December 27, 1996, review of *For Love of Country,* p. 8; January 23, 1998, review of *Cultivating Humanity,* p. 12.

Washington Post Book World, November 25, 1990; October 26, 1997, Timothy P. Duffy, review of *Cultivating Humanity,* p. 16.

OTHER

Philosophy Arena, http://www.philosophyarena.com/ (March 6, 2001), interview taken from *Key Philosophers in Conversation: The Cogito Interviews,* edited by Andrew Pyle, Routledge, 1999.*

*   *   *

NUWER, Hank
    See NUWER, Henry Joseph

*   *   *

NUWER, Henry Joseph   1946-
    (Hank Nuwer)

PERSONAL: Born August 19, 1946, in Buffalo, NY; son of Henry Robert (a truck driver and delivery man) and Teresa (an assembly-line worker and maid; maiden name, Lysiak) Nuwer; married Alice M. Cerniglia, December 28, 1968 (divorced, 1980); married N. Jenine Howard (an editor), April 9, 1982; children: (first mar-

riage) Henry Christian; (second marriage) Adam Robert Drew. *Ethnicity:* "Polish and Alsatian." *Education:* Buffalo State College, B.S., 1968; New Mexico Highlands University, M.A., 1971; Ball State University, Ph.D. equivalency, 1987. *Politics:* Democrat. *Religion:* Roman Catholic. *Avocational interests:* Quarter horses, tropical fish, stamp collecting, baseball, fishing.

ADDRESSES: Home—3220 West 39th St., Indianapolis, IN 46228. *Office*—Communications Department, Anderson University, Box 2016, 110 East 5th St., Anderson, IN 46012. *Agent*—Kevin and Jayne Moore, 1210 Coit Ct., Waunakee, WI 53597. *E-mail*—Nuwer@attglobal.net.

CAREER: Freelance writer, 1969—. Professional speaker on hazing and nonfiction writing, 1990—. *Chic Magazine,* editorial staff, 1976-77; Clemson University, Clemson, SC, assistant professor, 1982-83; Ball State University, Muncie, IN, assistant professor, 1985-89; Rodale Press, Emmaus, PA, senior editor; *Arts Indiana Magazine,* Indianapolis, IN, editor-in-chief, 1993-95; University of Richmond, Richmond, VA, associate professor of journalism, 1995-97; Indiana University, Indianapolis, IN, adjunct professor of journalism, 1995—; Anderson University, Anderson, IN, adjunct professor of journalism, 1998—. Consultant, NBC television movie, *Moment of Truth: Broken Pledges,* 1994; correspondent for *Onhealth.com,* online magazine, 1998—; has appeared on national television shows, including *CNN Headline News, NBC Nightly News,* and *Fox on Education,* to discuss hazing; advisor to National Collegiate Athletic Association study on hazing in college athletic groups, 1999.

MEMBER: Society of Professional Journalists, Investigative Reporters and Editors.

AWARDS, HONORS: National Magazine Advisor of the Year, College Media Advisors, 1988; Distinguished Alumni, Buffalo State College, 1999.

WRITINGS:

UNDER NAME HANK NUWER

(With William Boyles) *The Deadliest Profession* (novel), Playboy Press (Chicago, IL), 1980.
(With William Boyles) *A Killing Trade* (novel), Playboy Press (Chicago, IL), 1981.
(With William Boyles) *The Wild Ride* (novel), Playboy Press (Chicago, IL), 1981.
(With William Boyles) *Blood Mountain* (novel), Playboy Press (Chicago, IL), 1982.

(With Carole Shaw) *Come Out, Come Out, Wherever You Are* (nonfiction), R & R Press, 1982.

(Editor, with Robert G. Waite) *Rendezvous at the Ezra Pound Centennial Conference,* 1986.

Strategies of the Great Football Coaches, F. Watts (New York, NY), 1987.

Strategies of the Great Baseball Managers, F. Watts (New York, NY), 1988.

Rendezvousing with Contemporary Authors, Idaho State University Press, 1988.

Recruiting in Sports, F. Watts (New York, NY), 1989.

Steroids, F. Watts (New York, NY), 1990.

Broken Pledges: The Deadly Rite of Hazing, Longstreet Press (Atlanta, GA), 1990.

Sports Scandals, F. Watts (New York, NY), 1994.

How to Write Like an Expert about Anything, Writers Digest (Cincinnati, OH), 1995.

The Legend of Jesse Owens (juvenile; biography), F. Watts (New York, NY), 1998.

Wrongs of Passage: Fraternities, Sororities, Hazing, and Binge Drinking, Indiana University Press (Bloomington, IN), 1999.

High School Hazing: When Rites Become Wrongs (juvenile), F. Watts (New York, NY), 2000.

To the Young Writer, F. Watts (New York, NY), in press.

Contributor to periodicals, including *Saturday Review, Harper's, Inside Sports, Nation, Outside, Success,* and *Sport.* Author of chapters for *Prevention Magazine Health Books.* Manuscript collection: Special Collections/Archives, Butler Library, 1300 Elmwood Ave., Buffalo State College, Buffalo, NY, 14222.

ADAPTATIONS: Broken Pledges was adapted for an NBC television movie, *Moment of Truth: Broken Pledges,* 1994.

WORK IN PROGRESS: To the Young Athlete, a book of interviews with athletes who can serve a role models for young adults. A book about hazing in the military, with emphasis on the Russian military; a book about the tense relationship between college students and administrators; a book about women's education; a book about Japanese-American women living in Japan during World War II. A collection of essays.

SIDELIGHTS: The author or coauthor of sixteen books, including novels, sports books, and "how to write" books, Henry Joseph Nuwer, who writes as Hank Nuwer, is best known for his writings on the practice of hazing, a ritual initiation into fraternities and other organizations that can often involve humiliation, sexual abuse, and physical violence. *Broken Pledges: The*

Deadly Rite of Hazing provides a detailed account of many of these rites, including stories of those who were injured or killed during initiations. Since the appearance of *Broken Pledges,* Nuwer has been viewed as one of America's leading experts on the subject of hazing, speaking on the topic at numerous colleges and universities as well as appearing on national television.

As Nuwer told Linda Star in an interview in *Education World,* "Collegiate hazing has resulted in at least 59 fraternity deaths and one athletic death since the 1970s, when [forced consumption of] alcohol became a big part of the rituals." Nuwer added that a recent survey had indicated the use of alcohol and illegal drugs had now become common in initiations into organizations at the high school level. Linking the increased violence found in initiation rites to violence in the media and society in general, Nuwer went on to reject the argument that hazing can be a character-building experience. "Hazing doesn't breed character, " he stated. "It breeds deception, and it gives bullies an opportunity to get their licks in while, at the same time, getting the group's approval."

Wrongs of Passage: Fraternities, Sororities, Hazing, and Binge Drinking continues and updates the exploration Nuwer had begun with *Broken Pledges.* Writing in *Library Journal,* Danna C. Bell-Russel described *Wrongs of Passage* as "extremely well researched, with lots of interviews with victims of hazing and the parents of those who have died," and went on to recommend it highly for both academic libraries and the offices of student activity coordinators. The book includes a history of hazing in fraternities and past efforts to discourage it, along with Nuwer's own ideas about prevention. On the heels of *Wrongs of Passage,* Nuwer published *High School Hazing: When Rites Become Wrongs,* which shifts its focus to hazing in the nation's high schools and aims at a high school audience. Critic Randy Meyer of *Booklist* found the organization of the book to be "too loose" and its narrative "repetitive at times," but concluded by commending Nuwer's passion for his subject and finding the author's suggestions for dealing with hazing to be "a real call to action." Key among Nuwer's solutions to the problem are more serious legal penalties for offenders, clearly defined school policies, and counseling for both the perpetrators and the victims of hazing.

Nuwer has penned several other books aimed at the high school level, including a biography of 1936 Olympic gold medalist Jesse Owens, *The Legend of Jesse Owens,* and *To the Young Writer,* a collection of nine interviews with established contemporary authors. Reviewing the former volume in *Booklist,* Roger Leslie stated: "This densely detailed biography occasionally sags under the weight of redundancy, but it shows obvious reverence for Owens and the dignity with which he faced his tribulations." Leslie also felt that the book could provide inspiration for readers in its depiction of how Owens, a grandson of slaves who was born into poverty, overcame racism "by simply being true to himself." Included in *To the Young Writer* are interviews with poet Rebecca Kai Dotlich, novelist Phyllis Reynolds Taylor, and journalist Patrick O'Driscoll. Nuwer told Star that one of his primary aims with *To the Young Writer* was to provide role models for teenagers. He plans a similar book for young people containing interviews with prominent athletes.

Nuwer once commented in *CA:* "My first books and magazine articles were humorous, frivolous, satirical and adventurous pieces that reflected both the times in the seventies and early eighties and my own thrill-seeking tendencies. I wrote about playing minor-league baseball on assignment, accompanying a part-time bounty hunter on his appointed rounds, visiting herders in remote sheep camps out West, and flying the unfriendly skies of Idaho with a rescue pilot. From 1983 to 1990, I began thinking of myself more as a journalist and less and less as an entertainer, writing mainly about health, fitness, and sports. My work after 1990 tends to be serious and spiritual: personal essays, a book examining deaths resulting from fraternity initiations, a history of women's education, and investigative journalism.

"Buffalo State College teacher and author Fraser Drew has been my lifelong mentor. Since 1982 my wife Jenine, an editor, has not only served as a trusted editor but also as a friend and counselor. In the seventies and eighties I heeded advice from authors Jesse Stuart, Gian-Carlo Bertelli, Robert Laxalt, Ron Rash, Mark Steadman, Richard Etulain, Jim Harrison, and David Mamet. An editor at Longstreet Press named Jane Hill, and Poynter Institute for Media Studies writing coaches

Roy Clark and Donald Fry, helped me discipline my writing style. In the mid-nineties Indiana author Susan Neville, a regular contributor to *Arts Indiana Magazine* which I then edited, inspired me to write personal essays.

"The major career satisfaction I've had as a journalist is that my *Broken Pledges* has helped illuminate the problem of hazing to help eliminate deaths by hazing. As a teacher I feel fulfilled because some of my own students have become authors and editors."

BIOGRAPHICAL/CRITICAL SOURCES:

PERIODICALS

Booklist, January 1, 1999, Roger Leslie, review of *The Legend of Jesse Owens,* p. 851; April 1, 2000, Randy Meyer, review of *High School Hazing: When Rites Become Wrongs,* p. 1450.
Boston Globe, October 2, 1990.
Chicago Tribune, March 22, 1994.
Denver Post Contemporary Magazine, November 9, 1980.
Library Journal, September 1, 1999, Danna C. Bell-Russel, review of *Wrongs of Passage: Fraternities, Sororities, Hazing, and Binge Drinking,* p. 219.
Los Angeles Times Book Review, April 16, 1981.
New York Times, January 27, 1993; December 21, 1994.
Wall Street Journal, November 18, 1994.

OTHER

University of Ricmond Web site, http://www.richmond.edu/ (April 1997), "Bio: Hank Nuwer."
Education World, http://www.educationworld.com/ (September 9, 2000), Linda Starr, "An *Education World* E-Interview with Hank Nuwer, Author of *High School Hazing: When Rites Become Wrongs.*"*

O

O'BRIEN, Edna 1932-

PERSONAL: Born December 15, 1932, in Tuamgraney, County Clare, Ireland; daughter of Michael and Lena (maiden name, Cleary) O'Brien; married Ernest Gébler (an author), 1952 (divorced, 1964); children: Sasha, Carlos (sons). *Education:* Attended Pharmaceutical College of Ireland. *Avocational interests:* Reading, remembering.

ADDRESSES: Office—Fraser & Dunlop Scripts Ltd., 91 Regent St., London W1, England. *Agent*—c/o Curtis Brown Group Ltd., Haymarket House, 28-29 Haymarket, London SW1Y 4SP, England.

CAREER: Novelist, short story writer, playwright, and screenwriter. City College, New York, NY, creative writing teacher.

MEMBER: American Academy of Arts and Letters (honorary).

AWARDS, HONORS: Kingsley Amis Award, 1962; *Yorkshire Post* Book of the Year Award, 1970, for *A Pagan Place; Los Angeles Times* Book Prize, 1990, for *Lantern Slides; Los Angeles Times* Book Award for Fiction, 1992, for *Time and Tide.*

WRITINGS:

NOVELS

The Country Girls (also see below), Knopf (New York, NY), 1960.

The Lonely Girl (also see below), Random House (New York, NY), 1962, published as *The Girl with Green Eyes,* Penguin (London, England), 1964.

Girls in Their Married Bliss (also see below), J. Cape (London, England), 1964.

August Is a Wicked Month (also see below), Simon & Schuster (New York, NY), 1965.

Casualties of Peace (also see below), J. Cape (London, England), 1966.

A Pagan Place, (also see below), Weidenfeld & Nicolson (London, England), 1970, Houghton Mifflin (Boston, MA), 2001.

Zee and Company, (also see below), Weidenfeld & Nicolson (London, England), 1971.

Night, Knopf (New York, NY), 1972.

Johnny I Hardly Knew You (also see below), Weidenfeld & Nicolson (London, England), 1977, published as *I Hardly Knew You,* Doubleday (New York, NY), 1978.

Seven Novels and Other Short Stories, Collins (London, England), 1978.

The Country Girls Trilogy and Epilogue (contains *The Country Girls, The Lonely Girl,* and *Girls in Their Married Bliss*), Farrar, Straus (New York, NY), 1986, published as *The Country Girls Trilogy: Second Epilogue,* Dutton (New York, NY), 1989.

The High Road (novel), Farrar, Straus (New York, NY), 1988.

Time and Tide, Farrar, Straus (New York, NY), 1992.

House of Splendid Isolation, Farrar, Straus (New York, NY), 1994.

An Edna O'Brien Reader (contains *August Is a Wicked Month, Casualties of Peace,* and *Johnny I Hardly Knew You*), Warner Books (New York, NY), 1994.

Down by the River, Weidenfeld & Nicolson (London, England), 1996.

Wild Decembers, [London, England], 1999, Houghton Mifflin (Boston, MA), 2000.

SHORT STORIES

The Love Object, J. Cape (London, England), 1968.

A Scandalous Woman, and Other Stories, Harcourt (New York, NY), 1974.

Mrs. Reinhardt, and Other Stories, Weidenfeld & Nicolson (London, England), 1978, published as *A Rose in the Heart,* Doubleday (New York, NY), 1979.

Returning, Weidenfeld & Nicolson (London, England), 1982.

Stories of Joan of Arc, 1984.

A Fanatic Heart: Selected Stories of Edna O'Brien, foreword by Philip Roth, Farrar, Straus (New York, NY), 1984.

Lantern Slides: Stories, Farrar, Straus (New York, NY), 1990.

JUVENILE

The Dazzle, illustrated by Peter Stevenson, Hodder & Stoughton (London, England), 1981.

A Christmas Treat (sequel to *The Dazzle*), illustrated by Stevenson, Hodder & Stoughton (London, England), 1982.

The Expedition, Hodder & Stoughton (London, England), 1982.

The Rescue, illustrated by Stevenson, Hodder & Stoughton (London, England), 1983.

Tales for the Telling: Irish Folk and Fairy Stories, illustrated by Michael Foreman, Atheneum (New York, NY), 1986.

PLAYS

A Cheap Bunch of Nice Flowers (produced in London, England, 1962), Ungar (New York, NY), 1963.

(With others) *Oh! Calcutta!,* produced in New York, 1969), Grove (New York, NY), 1969.

A Pagan Place (produced in the West End, 1972), Knopf (New York, NY), 1970.

The Ladies, produced in London, 1975.

The Gathering, produced in Dublin, Ireland, 1974, produced in New York at Manhattan Theatre Club, 1977.

Virginia (produced in Stratford, Ontario, Canada, 1980, produced in London and New York, 1985), Harcourt (New York, NY), 1981, revised edition, 1985.

Flesh and Blood, produced in Bath, 1985, produced in New York, 1986.

Madame Bovary (based on the novel by Gustave Flaubert), produced at the Palace, Watford, England, 1987.

Our Father, produced in London, 1999.

SCREENPLAYS

The Girl with Green Eyes (based on O'Brien's novel *The Lonely Girl*), Lopert, 1964.

(With Desmond Davis) *I was Happy Here,* 1965, revised, 1979.

Three into Two Won't Go, Universal, 1969.

X Y and Zee (based on O'Brien's novel *Zee and Company*), Columbia, 1972.

(With others) *The Tempter,* 1975.

A Woman at the Seaside, 1979.

The Wicked Lady, 1979.

The Country Girls, 1984.

TELEVISON PLAYS

The Wedding Dress, 1963.

The Keys to the Café, 1965.

Give My Love to the Pilchards, 1965.

Which of These Two Ladies Is He Married To?, 1967.

Nothing's Ever Over, 1968.

Then and Now, 1973.

Mrs. Reinhardt, from Her Own Story, 1981.

OTHER

Mother Ireland, photographs by Fergus Bourke, Harcourt (New York, NY), 1976.

Arabian Days, photographs by Gerard Klijn, Horizon Press (New York, NY), 1977.

The Collected Edna O'Brien (miscellany), Collins (London, England), 1978.

(Editor) *Some Irish Loving: A Selection,* Harper (New York, NY), 1979.

James and Nora: A Portrait of Joyce's Marriage, Lord John Press (Northridge, CA), 1981.

Vanishing Ireland, photographs by Richard Fitzgerald, J. Cape (London, England), 1986, Potter (New York, NY), 1987.

On the Bone (poetry), Greville Press, 1989.

James Joyce (biography; "Penguin Lives" series), Viking (New York, NY), 1999.

Also contributor to magazines, including *New Yorker, Ladies' Home Journal,* and *Cosmopolitan,* and to various English journals.

ADAPTATIONS: Works adapted for audio include *Wild Decembers* (four cassettes), read by Suzanne Bertish, Houghton Mifflin.

SIDELIGHTS: Irish author Edna O'Brien is "renowned for her anguished female characters, lonely Catholic girls in search of adventure, or single, older women in wretched affairs with married men," wrote Richard B. Woodward in *New York Times Magazine.* "A poet of heartbreak, she writes most tellingly about the hopeless, angry passion that courts self-ruin." Her women are loving, but frustrated, betrayed, lonely, and struggling to escape the role society has assigned them, while her male characters are cruel, cold, drunken, and irresponsible. The divorced mother of two, O'Brien knows about struggle, heartbreak, and pain firsthand. She has used her personal experiences, especially her childhood in Ireland, as sources for many of her works, drawing on her memories to evoke the emotions of her readers. An author of novels, short stories, plays, biographies, and children's books, she is a prolific writer, often considered controversial, who appeals to many audiences.

O'Brien was born in Tuamgraney, County Clare, a small, rural, devoutly Catholic village of about 200 people in the west of Ireland. Raised on a farm, she grew up in an area where everyone knew everyone else's secrets, business, and problems. She claims this has helped her in her writing, telling Amanda Smith in *Publishers Weekly,* "I had sort of a limitless access to everyone's life story. For a writer, it's a marvelous chance." Educated first at the local national school and then in a convent, she escaped rural life by attending Pharmaceutical College in Dublin. In 1952, she eloped with Czech-Irish author Ernest Gébler. They moved first to County Wicklow, and then to London, where O'Brien has remained. They divorced after twelve years of marriage, and she raised their two sons alone.

Books were scarce in O'Brien's childhood, and it wasn't until she was in Dublin that she began to take an interest in them. *Introducing James Joyce* by T. S. Eliot was among her first purchases, and she recalled in *Lear's* that "reading it was the most astonishing literary experience of my life. . . . What I learned from that brief extract from *A Portrait of the Artist as a Young Man* was that as a writer one must take one's material from life, from the simple, indisputable, and often painful world about one, and give it somehow its transfiguration, but at the same time shave all excess and untruth from it, like peeling a willow. What I did not know, although I must have sensed it, was that this would bring me into conflict with parents, friends, and indeed the Irish establishment."

Conflict and writing seemed to go hand in hand for O'Brien throughout her career. The birth of her first published novel, *The Country Girls,* heralded the death of her marriage. Written at the age of twenty-six and published in 1960, *The Country Girls* broke new ground in Irish literature, giving a frank speaking voice

to women characters. The subject matter and especially the daringly graphic sexual scenes caused this book, and the six that followed, to be banned in Ireland. The first novel in what became a trilogy, *The Lonely Girl* and *Girls in Their Married Bliss* completed the set. The three novels were collected in *The Country Girls Trilogy and Epilogue,* published in 1986.

"It's a difficult trip, this coming of age," wrote Mary Rourke in the *Los Angeles Times Book Review* of *The Country Girls Trilogy and Epilogue.* "Two girls set adrift, misdirected, lost at sea. O'Brien tells it with love and outrage, compassion and contempt." The stories revolve around two young women, the "country girls" Kate and Baba, who search for love and sex in a series of tragicomic adventures after being expelled from their convent school. Kate Brady, the daughter of a drunken father, was raised in poverty. She is the shy, naive but pretty woman who begins her adventure by having an affair with an older, married man. Baba Brennan, the daughter of the village veterinarian, is the tough, sassy character willing to live as freely as a man. Through affairs, marriages, more affairs, children, and psychotherapy, Baba and Kate remain friends.

"Miss O'Brien's outlook is intemperate, like Irish weather. She's fond of blarney, but a bleak, literary kind, more in the mood of the later Yeats than of Celtic charm," commented Anatole Broyard, writing in the *New York Times Book Review.* "She has no patience with the ordinary, the soothing monotony of innocent small events." Feelings of loss, conflict, and disappointment in love pervade each novel of *The Country Girls Trilogy and Epilogue* as the girls try to reach their dreams. *Village Voice* contributor Terrence Rafferty observed that "the psychological insights are sharp, the descriptions graceful and resonant" in *The Country Girls Trilogy and Epilogue.* At the conclusion of the trilogy, both women are disillusioned, neither one having reached her dreams or found love or happiness. What began in *The Country Girls* ends far from "married bliss."

O'Brien added the epilogue to *The Country Girls Trilogy* when the stories were released in one volume. Rafferty explained that it "brings the story full circle, back to earth, in a tragedy that would be unbearable were it not for the exuberance of the writing, the hope engendered by language that goes on and on." The epilogue is presented as Baba's soliloquy, a retrospective view of both women's lives. Mourning the deceased Kate, raging against the men who took advantage or abused them in some way, blaming men for Kate's death, and remembering the happier times, Baba concludes the trilogy with emotional force. Broyard, commenting on the whole collection, noted, that "everyday scenes . . . are the truest and best parts of Miss O'Brien's work. Reading them, we wonder whether love and sex, for which she has become an ambivalent apologist, are her natural subject after all—or just a burlesque to keep the genuine terrors at bay."

Many of O'Brien's short stories have also been assembled and published as collections, including *A Fanatic Heart.* Covering two decades of her career, the twenty-nine stories in this collection explore the themes of childhood, love, and loss, all from a woman's perspective. "Most of the stories in *A Fanatic Heart* are set down in languorous, elegiac prose," commented Michiko Kakutani in the *New York Times,* adding that "they're enlivened by Miss O'Brien's earthy humor and her sense of place." She writes of relationships, exile, and betrayal, drawing the reader in by seeming to reveal herself. Tales such as "My Mother's Mother," describing the "ghastly" death of her grandfather one night while saying the Rosary, evoke O'Brien's native Ireland. Others explore the temptations of the flesh in strictly-reared young women, as in "The Connor Girls," or contrast girls with carousing drunks, as in "Irish Revel." Still others concern affairs, mental breakdown, and entrapment in bad marriages. In the *Los Angeles Times Book Review* Charles Champlin commented, "She writes with a graceful, poetical simplicity, a soft and mesmerizing brogue audible in every cadence." *Washington Post Book World* contributor Jonathan Yardley concluded by saying, "It's all there: the violence, the superstition, the craziness, the drink, the brooding religion, the terrorized women. O'Brien's Ireland is as hard and unremitting a place as O'Connor's South. Yet longings her women feel for love and peace, for a kind connection with another human being, give these stories a tenderness that is both surprising and enriching."

O'Brien presents another side of Ireland in *Tales for the Telling: Irish Folk and Fairy Stories,* a book for children published in 1986. Twelve stories reveal a land of fairy folk, giants, castles, princes and princesses, magic, and heroes. A fierce wolf and a young boy dance to the magic tune of fife music in one tale, and another tells of a giant who betters an opponent with help from his cunning wife. O'Brien writes her stories in standard English, using the characters' conversations to express their Irish descent. "In the dialogue she revels in the glories of local dialect," wrote Elizabeth MacCallum in the Toronto *Globe and Mail,* "and in her descriptive passages she evokes wondrous visions." Another critic, *Times Literary Supplement* contributor Patricia Craig,

remarked that O'Brien's stories correspond rather closely to those published in *Donegal Fairy Stories* written by Seumas MacManus, but commented that O'Brien's tales "are notable for their decorativeness and sturdy vocabulary." In the opinion of E. F. Bleiler, writing in *Washington Post Book World,* "O'Brien does convey the flavor of Ireland. . . . The book as a whole is pleasant to look at and into, but not very exciting." Diane Roback wrote in *Publishers Weekly* that the "color-rich, vigorous paintings" by Michael Foreman complement "a collection for the entire family [that] fires the imagination."

O'Brien examines more than Ireland in her various writings. In two stage plays she focuses on Virginia Woolf and Gustave Flaubert's Madame Bovary. "O'Brien . . . knows how to create climax, epiphany and incandescence by compression," observed Jack Kroll in *Newsweek,* discussing the play *Virginia.* The story of Woolf, one of the Bloomsbury group and a prominent literary figure, the play encompasses her life from her birth in 1882 to her suicide in 1942. Woolf's "intense subjective style" is echoed throughout the piece, often transcending "chronological narrative," wrote Lawrence Christon in the *Los Angeles Times.* "*Virginia* is virtually a monologue," Christon continued, noting that the play "is top-heavy with talk."

Madame Bovary is similar to *Virginia,* particularly in its use of time and narration. O'Brien claims the title character as her own creation rather than an adaptation of Flaubert's novel. The story of love, marriage, boredom, adultery, and death by suicide, O'Brien's work, however, closely follows Flaubert's piece. The drama takes place in Emma Bovary's mind, even juggling the events as if they were really memories happening in her head, giving the audience clear access to her thoughts and emotions. *Observer* contributor Michael Ratcliffe remarked, "Edna O'Brien has turned Flaubert's novel into a tasteful melodrama whose tragic ironies shine sharp and bright." But, Ratcliffe noted, the "dramatic narrative unfolds in a series of sketches and jerks. . . . Time-leaps and chronology are not always clear." Irving Wardle, writing in the London *Times,* pointed out that "the action unrolls as if by flashes of lightning. . . . the effect is to present an ever-strengthening sequence of hopes and defeats in which grand emotions are brought tumbling down."

While continuing to publish books for children, short stories, and plays, O'Brien waited ten years after *Johnny I Hardly Knew You* before publishing another novel. The long-awaited volume, *The High Road,* concerns Anna, a middle-aged, successful Irish writer recovering from the breakup of an affair. She escapes to an unidentified Spanish island, hoping to take time to write in her diary and repair her broken heart. But she becomes involved with the other inhabitants, eventually having an affair with another woman. The story ends in tragedy, with the death of Anna's lover. "This is a disorderly novel about the disorder of human needs and the grotesqueries of appetite, how unsuitable, how inappropriate our longings often are, how difficult it is to find even a moment of pure unspoiled happiness," said Carol Shields in the Toronto *Globe and Mail.* Many critics seemed to share this viewpoint, with *Publishers Weekly* contributor Sybil Steinberg calling *The High Road* "a disappointing narrative." "At its best O'Brien's prose is, as usual, eloquent and passionate, but it cannot disguise the fundamental confusion of this strange little book," wrote Jonathan Yardley in the *Washington Post.* "There are enough bright moments in it to reward O'Brien's most devoted followers, but few other readers are likely to take any pleasure in trying to make connections between characters that O'Brien herself never makes."

"Raise a jar to Edna O'Brien herself, back among us from foreign parts . . . the black mood of *The High Road* all but dispelled," wrote Elaine Kendall in the *Los Angeles Times* in her discussion of *Lantern Slides: Stories.* "She is at her best again, telling of people and places close to her heart." O'Brien returns to the short story with *Lantern Slides.* "Though she covers little new ground here, she also digs deeper into the old ground than ever before, unearthing a rich archeology," commented David Leavitt in the *New York Times Book Review.* The stories focus on women and their relationships—with lovers, fathers, husbands, and children. Insanity, jealousy, and fear are only some of the emotions O'Brien calls into play in her tales. In "Brother," an incestuous relationship causes one woman to plot the death of her new sister-in-law. Another story explores the feelings between a mother and her son during a Mediterranean vacation in the company of his girlfriend. The title story, "Lantern Slides," was highly praised by many critics, Leavitt labeling it the "collection's masterpiece." Describing a birthday party held for a woman whose husband has deserted her, the tale reveals the guests individually, discussing their problems as it moves along.

Regarding the whole collection, Victoria Glendinning wrote in the London *Times* that "this is good writing; and good thinking." *Times Literary Supplement* contributor Louise Doughty praised *Lantern Slides,* writing that "the same precision with which she portrays landscape is applied to human emotions; there isn't a single

character in these stories who is unconvincing. O'Brien continues to display acute powers of observation in a prose that is always neat and often immaculate."

Time and Tide features a hard-luck protagonist who faces one disaster after another. First, Nell endures physical abuse at the hands of her husband; when she summons the courage to leave him, she has to battle for custody of their two sons. Although free of her husband, Nell continues to experience tragedy: the death of a son, drug addiction, a nervous breakdown, and failed romances. "O'Brien transforms what could have been a depressing or, at best, maudlin tale into a revelation," commented Gale Harris in *Belles Lettres.* Writing in the *Times Literary Supplement,* however, Patricia Craig averred that "throughout the bulk of O'Brien's narrative, clarity gets lost in a fuzz of emotions." Still, Craig noted that "parts of *Time and Tide* are wonderfully clear-toned and powerfully imagined."

O'Brien's next novel, *House of Splendid Isolation,* departed somewhat from the author's usual terrain. The story of an IRA terrorist who takes an elderly woman hostage, the novel directly engages the contemporary political struggles in Northern Ireland. While McGeevy, the terrorist, is the character that sets the plot in motion, it is his elderly captive, Josie O'Meara, whose remembered passions and setbacks make up the heart of the story. Writing in the *New York Times Book Review,* John L'Heureux maintained that the novel's two distinct components are not successfully fused. "Uncomfortable with her story of the terrorist and the lady, Ms. O'Brien seeks refuge in easy symbolism, and her art is swallowed up in rhetoric." Still, noted L'Heureux, O'Brien excels in portraying Josie's world: "The author is comfortable here. She understands the blindness and desperation of these characters and she gets inside them with devastating effects." Focusing on the author's achievement in telling the story of modern Ireland, Chicago *Tribune Books* reviewer Andy Solomon remarked, "Moving beyond her stunningly wrought landscapes of private heartbreak and haunted agony, in this novel O'Brien shows us the land that forged her vision."

O'Brien's confessional tone and use of the first person in many of her novels has led to speculation concerning the distance between her life and her fiction. In the *Dictionary of Literary Biography,* Patricia Boyle Haberstroh quotes an interview between Ludovic Kennedy and O'Brien, wherein the author said her life and her work are "quite close, but they're not as close as they seem. . . . I think writing, especially semi-autobiographical writing, is the life you might have liked to have had." In an interview with Woodward,

O'Brien concluded: "All I know is that I want to write about something that has no fashion and that does not pander to any period or to a journalistic point of view. I want to write about something that would apply to any time because it's a state of the soul." O'Brien also discussed her writing in *Lear's,* noting that "the need to write becomes as intrinsic as the need to breathe. I believe that the hidden reason is to do with time and emotion and the retrieval of both. It is as if the life lived has not been lived until it is set down in this unconscious sequence of words."

O'Brien's novel *Down by the River* is based on the actual case of an Irish girl who became pregnant by a friend of her father, and the theme of the book is the abortion issue in Ireland. In the novel, the girl, Mary, becomes pregnant as a result of her father's sexual abuse. The story begins with the father assaulting her for the first time, an act he repeats with more frequency and violence after Mary's mother dies. After returning from London with a neighbor who helps her with the termination of her pregnancy, Mary and the friend are arrested. Her life is torn apart by politicians and anti-abortion advocates who don't know that Mary's father was responsible for the pregnancy. Jose Lanters wrote in *World Literature Today* that *Down by the River* makes the point "about the involvement of church and state in what are often very painful and tragic personal circumstances."

New York Times Book Review contributor Brooke Allen called *Wild Decembers* a "beautiful and lush novel." Joseph Brennan and his younger sister, Breege, live in a remote area of western Ireland. Joseph's mother had begged him to stay when he made one attempt at leaving, and now he and his sister live alone in Cloontha, immersed in their ancient culture and farming practices. Mick Buglar arrives from Australia to claim his inheritance, the neighboring farm. The two families have had a generational feud over grazing rights and boundaries, but the two men become friends, with Joseph teaching Mick the old ways, and Mick introducing him to modern practices, like the first tractor to be used on their mountain. Their differences surface when disputes over property rights develop, and the friendship suffers. Joseph is also upset by the relationship that is developing between Breege and Mick. Mick's fiancée, Rosemary, is waiting for him to build their home, after which she will travel from Australia, but Mick realizes she will never adapt to the desolate land. "O'Brien's evocative prose shows the chilling hold that history and the dead clamp on the living," wrote Paul Gray in *Time.*

Allen said that "O'Brien's prose is her own and firmly under control, an apt instrument for the precise, poetic recollection of a distant world. With the instincts of an orchestra conductor, she builds from muted subtleties to crescendos of linguistic color." Allen continued that "O'Brien is a past master at mixing up such lyrical flights with tonic doses of sexual humor. In *Wild Decembers* this takes the shape of two lascivious sisters, Reena and Riat, who have feathered their nest with hush money from the local men they ensnare. Reena and Rita are a little too out there, too bawdily O'Brienesque, to ring quite true in this essentially somber tale—yet who can confidently accuse any novelist of exaggeration when the truth is so often supremely bizarre?"

"O'Brien allows the inevitable tragedy to play itself out, evincing the pity and terror of classical drama," said a *Publishers Weekly* reviewer. Molly Winans wrote in *Commonweal* that "O'Brien's eye is most often trained on turbulent sorrow, and her gaze is fearless. Each character is torn so many ways. . . . Breege and Bugler's love for each other is itself a question without an answer. Happiness rarely enters in, and then only tinged by dread—Bugler, already engaged to a beautiful woman, has no reason to court trouble with the immensely shy sister of a man who hates him—and still, the very existence of Breege and Bugler's love gives us hope. . . . The hope it introduces is thrilling and clean." *Booklist* reviewer Grace Fill called O'Brien's writing "dark, but not without humor, and rich in dramatic imagery of the Irish countryside, as she probes the inner landscape of the human heart."

World of Hibernia contributor John McCourt wrote that in *James Joyce,* O'Brien "puts her critical heritage, her vast experience as a novelist and short-story writer, and her dazzling linguistic skills to excellent use in this biography, which will be remembered for its panache, verve, readability, and its humane understanding of Joyce and of the Irish world that formed him." *Booklist* reviewer Mary Carroll noted that O'Brien "also provides thoughtful appreciations of Joyce's major works." *Contemporary Review* contributor John McGurk said that O'Brien reveals "Joyce's love/hate relationship with Dublin and Ireland, with the 'Rock of Rome,' the English Crown, the legal profession: and between home and exile, then his other innermost conflicts between lust and love; order and chaos, family restrictions and the free-booting spirit at odds with the tenacity with which he pursued his life as a writer."

New York Times Book Review contributor Robert Sullivan called *James Joyce* "a hardheaded hagiography in which [O'Brien] spends a lot of time knocking Joyce around, especially the early Joyce, the Joyce who would run into you at the pub, go on about his imminent greatness, pity you, and then hit you up for a couple of quid on his way out." "After she's roughed Joyce up," wrote Sullivan, "she raises his hand in the air and proclaims him a genius. . . . Not since Anthony Burgess has anyone so gorgeously sung such praise for a man whose work, let's fact it, can seem incomprehensible to the noninfatuated. . . . The chapters on *Ulysses* and then *Finnegan's Wake* are explanatory marvelings at the respective books' literary merits but also at Joyce's obsession with his craft, in the face of every conceivable obstacle." Sullivan concluded by saying that "O'Brien's triumph is that while celebrating Joyce and his ecstatic quest to lay image on counterimage . . . she has drawn the desperation and sadness of the man whose name means joy."

BIOGRAPHICAL/CRITICAL SOURCES:

BOOKS

Concise Dictionary of British Literary Biography, Volume 8: *Contemporary Writers, 1960-Present,* Gale (Detroit, MI), 1992.

Contemporary Literary Criticism, Gale (Detroit, MI), Volume 3, 1975, Volume 5, 1976, Volume 8, 1978, Volume 13, 1980, Volume 36, 1986, Volume 65, 1991.

Contemporary Novelists, sixth edition, St. James Press (Detroit, MI), 1996.

Dictionary of Literary Biography, Volume 14: *British Novelists since 1960,* Gale (Detroit, MI),1983.

Eckley, Grace, *Edna O'Brien,* Bucknell University Press (Lewisburg, PA), 1974.

Feminist Writers, St. James Press (Detroit, MI), 1996.

Staley, Thomas F., editor, *Twentieth-Century Woman Novelists,* Barnes & Noble (Totowa, NJ), 1982.

PERIODICALS

America, April 15, 1995, p. 35.

Atlantic Monthly, July, 1965.

Belles Lettres, fall, 1992, p. 2.

Booklist, January 1, 1998, review of *Down by the River,* p. 731; October 1, 1999, Mary Carroll, review of *James Joyce,* p. 338; February 1, 2000, Grace Fill, review of *Wild Decembers,* p. 996.

Books, June, 1965.

Books and Bookmen, December, 1964.

Chicago Tribune Book World, December 9, 1984, p. 31.

Commonweal, May 5, 2000, Molly Winans, "A Dark Tale, Told in Singing Prose," p. 19.

Contemporary Review, July, 2000, John McGurk, "Edna O'Brien on James Joyce," p. 56.

Entertainment Weekly, April 14, 2000, "The Week," p. 68.

Globe and Mail (Toronto), December 17, 1988; December 31, 1988.

Lear's, July, 1992, pp. 62-65.

Library Journal, October 1, 1999, Shelley Cox, review of *James Joyce,* p. 92.

Los Angeles Times, April 3, 1979; May 1, 1986; December 16, 1988; June 8, 1990.

Los Angeles Times Book Review, June 30, 1985, p. 1; January 19, 1986, p. 4; April 27, 1986, p. 4; September 2, 1990, p. 9; October 31, 1999, review of *James Joyce,* p. 10.

Ms., November, 1988, pp. 76, 78.

National Observer, June 21, 1965.

New Statesman & Society, April 15, 1994, p. 41.

Newsweek, March 18, 1985, p. 72.

New Yorker, June 27, 1994, p. 195.

New York Review of Books, June 3, 1965; August 24, 1967; January 31, 1985, p. 17; December 16, 1999, John Banville, "The Motherless Child," p. 48.

New York Times, November 12, 1984; March 1, 1985; May 30, 1990.

New York Times Book Review, March 26, 1967; February 9, 1969; September 22, 1974; June 27, 1978; February 11, 1979; November 18, 1984, pp. 1, 38; May 11, 1986, p. 12; March 1, 1987, p. 31; November 20, 1988, p. 11; June 25, 1990, p. 9; June 26, 1994, p. 7; March 22, 1998, review of *Down by the River,* p. 32; January 9, 2000, Robert Sullivan, "Oh Joist, Poor Joist," p. 6; April 9, 2000, Brooke Allen, "The Last of His Kind," p. 7.

New York Times Magazine, March 12, 1989.

Observer, February 8, 1987.

People Weekly, April 17, 1978; May 1, 2000, Jean Reynolds, review of *Wild Decembers,* p. 41.

Publishers Weekly, November 28, 1986, p. 71; December 26, 1986, p. 30; September 9, 1988, p. 122; April 25, 1994, p. 56; January 31, 2000, review of *Wild Decembers,* p. 77; June 5, 2000, review of *Wild Decembers,* p. 61.

Saturday Review, June 5, 1965; March 25, 1967.

Spectator, October 9, 1999, review of *Wild Decembers,* p. 42.

Studies in Short Fiction, summer, 1993, Kiera O'Hara, "Love Objects: Love and Obsession in the Short Stories of Edna O'Brien," pp. 317-325; spring 1995, Jeanette Roberts Schumaker, "Sacrificial Women in Short Stories by Mary Lavin and Edna O'Brien," pp. 185-197.

Time, April 17, 2000, Paul Gray, "Perils of the Rustic Life: *Wild Decembers* Portrays a Simmering Irish Feud," p. 82.

Times (London), February 6, 1987; October 14, 1988; October 27, 1988; June 7, 1990.

Times Literary Supplement, April 23, 1982, p. 456; January 9, 1987, p. 46; October 28, 1988, p. 1212; June 8, 1990, p. 616; September 18, 1992, p. 23; April 22, 1994, p. 22.

Tribune Books (Chicago), November 20, 1988, p. 6; May 27, 1990, p. 1; July 24, 1994, p. 1.

Variety, December 13, 1999, Matt Wolf, review of *Our Father,* p. 119.

Village Voice, July 1, 1985, p. 61.

Vogue, September 1, 1971.

Wall Street Journal, March 31, 2000, Kate Flatley, review of *Wild Decembers,* p. 10.

Washington Post, November 2, 1988.

Washington Post Book World, August 21, 1994, p. 3.

World Literature Today, winter, 1998, Jose Lanters, review of *Down by the River,* p. 135.

World of Hibernia, fall, 1999, John McCourt, "Edna O'Brien: *James Joyce,*" p. 92.

OTHER

Salon.com, http://www.salon.com/ (December 2, 1995), "Lit Chat."*

*   *   *

OLAFSSON, Ólaf
  See ÓLAFSSON, Ólafur Jóhann

*   *   *

ÓLAFSSON, Ólafur Jóhann 1962-
   (Ólaf Ólafsson)

PERSONAL: Born September 26, 1962, in Reykjavik, Iceland; son of Ólafur Jóhann (a writer) and Anna (Jonsdottir) Sigurdsson; married Anna Olafsdottir (a homemaker), September 12, 1986; children: Ólafur Jóhann, Jr. *Education:* Brandeis University, graduated (summa cum laude), 1985.

ADDRESSES: Home—New York, NY. *Office*—Random/Pantheon Books, 299 Park Ave., New York, NY 10171.

CAREER: Sony Corporation, San Jose, CA, New York, NY, began as researcher, became vice president of spe-

cial projects, 1985-91, founded and became president and chief executive officer of division, Sony Interactive Entertainment, 1991-98; Advanta Corporation, Spring Hill, PA, president, 1998-99; Time Warner Digital Media, vice chair, 1999—. Author.

MEMBER: Phi Beta Kappa.

WRITINGS:

Absolution, Pantheon (New York, NY), 1994.
Lávarour Heims, Veka-Helgafell (Reykjavik, Iceland), 1996.
Slóo Fiorildanna, Vaka-Helgafell (Reykjavik, Iceland), 1999, translated as *The Journey Home,* Pantheon Books (New York, NY), 2000.

Also author of *Marketplace of the Gods* and *The Economist.*

SIDELIGHTS: Ólafur Jóhann Ólafsson is a best-selling novelist in his native Iceland. He is also vice chairman of Time Warner Digital Media and the founder of Sony Interactive Entertainment. Reviewing Ólafsson's *The Journey Home,* a critic for the online publication *Mostly Fiction* remarked: "The fact that this is the same Ólaf Ólafsson as the businessman came as a big surprise to me. . . . I brashly assumed that he had friends in the business world that would indifferently publish his novel no matter its quality. . . . But, I wasn't very far into the novel when I had a feeling that this was the real thing. I read it from start to finish in nearly one sitting."

Ólafsson came to the United States in 1982 to study physics at Brandeis University. After graduating, he went to work for the Sony Corporation in 1985 as a researcher and was quickly promoted to the position of vice president in charge of special projects. In 1991 Ólafsson founded a new division, alternately known as Sony Electronic Publishing and Sony Interactive Entertainment, for the company. During his seven-year tenure as the division's president and chief executive officer, he was responsible for launching the popular 32-bit PlayStation video game platform. Meanwhile he continued to write novels in Icelandic that were published in Iceland, a few also finding their way into translation in the United States.

The Journey Home is set in the 1960s in England and Iceland and tells the story of Disa, a restaurateur and chef at Ditton Hall, an English country home that has been converted to a hotel. Disa's life, which she shares in a common-law marriage with the local squire, is both successful and complacent. All of this changes when she is diagnosed with a terminal illness and given a year to live. Disa decides she must return to her native Iceland to find the answers to an unresolved episode from her past. Disa's journey is interspersed with her memories of the past, her youth in Iceland, her training as a cook in prewar London, and her passionate love affair with a Jewish boy who returned to Germany in 1938 in an attempt to save his parents from the Nazis. The previously cited critic for *Mostly Fiction* observed: "This is the best kind of book to read. Quietly and almost poetically it reveals insight into Disa's past and yet at the same time raises new mysteries."

In spite of Disa's terminal illness, R. Z. Sheppard in *Time* found *The Journey Home* to be "not a morose novel but one lifted by love, friendship and cooking." Cathleen A. Towey in *Library Journal* commented that "Disa is not always likable but is always believable, and though the novel starts simply, it unfolds as an intricate tale of a strong and complex woman." Neal Wyatt in *Booklist* concluded: "The directness of Ólafsson's prose and the honesty of Disa's tale involve the reader in her testimony. Searing in its quietness, overwhelming in its intent, this novel of silence stands witness to the heroic nature of life."

BIOGRAPHICAL/CRITICAL SOURCES:

PERIODICALS

American Banker, March 10, 1998, Heather Timmons, "Advanta Hires Sony Playstation Chief as President," p. 7.
Entertainment Weekly, July 14, 1995, Albert Kim, "They Might Be Giants," p. 58.
Billboard, November 6, 1999, "Time Warner," p. 70.
Booklist, October 1, 2000, Neal Wyatt, review of *The Journey Home,* p. 324.
Library Journal, September 15, 2000, Cathleen A. Towey, review of *The Journey Home,* p. 113.
Publishers Weekly, October 30, 2000, review of *The Journey Home,* p. 45.
Time, December 11, 2000, R. Z. Sheppard, review of *The Journey Home,* p. 115.

OTHER

Mostly Fiction, http://www.mostlyfiction.com/ (November 19, 2000), "*The Journey Home* by Ólaf Ólafsson."*

OLSON, Gary A. 1954-

PERSONAL: Born December 12, 1954, in Waterbury, CT; son of Joseph David (a metal worker and writer) and Charlotte (a clerk; maiden name, Anderson) Olson; married, wife's name Marlyne (a recreation therapist), June 3, 1978 (divorced, 1993). *Education:* Kings College (Wilkes-Barre, PA), B.A. (cum laude), 1976; University of Connecticut, M.A., 1978; Indiana University of Pennsylvania, Ph.D., 1980. *Politics:* Democrat.

ADDRESSES: Home—3909 Turkey Oak Drive, Valrico, FL 33594. *Office*—Department of English, University of South Florida, 4202 East Fowler Ave., CPR 107, Tampa, FL 33620-5550. *E-mail*—olson@chuma.cas.usf.edu.

CAREER: Indiana University of Pennsylvania, Indiana, director of Writing Center, 1978-80; Shelton State Community College, Tuscaloosa, AL, adjunct instructor in literature, 1980; University of Alabama, University, AL, instructor in English and director of Writing Center, 1980-82; University of North Carolina—Wilmington, assistant professor of English, 1982-85, director of developmental writing, 1982-83, director of Center for Writing, 1982-84; University of South Florida, Tampa, FL, assistant professor, 1985-87, associate professor, 1987-92, professor of rhetoric and composition, 1992—, associate of Institute for Interpretive Human Studies, 1991—; St. Thomas University, Miami, FL, coordinator of Writing Across the Curriculum, 1988. Roxbury Publishing, member of board of consulting editors, 1993—; consultant to Federal Trade Commission. Has also served in a number of academic administrative positions.

MEMBER: Council of Editors of Learned Journals, Association of Teachers of Advanced Composition (president, 1994—), Conference on College Composition and Communication (member of executive committee, 1992-95), Rhetoric Society of America (member of board of directors, 1990-95), South Atlantic Modern Language Association (chairperson of Advanced Writing Section, 1992), Southeastern Writing Center Association (founding president, 1981-83; vice president, 1983-84), Alabama Council of Teachers of English (member of board of directors, 1982).

AWARDS, HONORS: Certificate of Appreciation for "outstanding contribution to the professional growth of the English teachers of North Carolina," 1983; President's Award for Outstanding Achievement for directing a record-breaking faculty-staff scholarship campaign in the College of Arts and Letters, 1988; Research and Creative Scholarship Award, University of South Florida Division of Sponsored Research, 1990; Undergraduate Teaching Enhancement Award, for outstanding teaching on the undergraduate level, 1990; Certificate of Recognition from Suncoast chapter, Society for Technical Communication, 1991-92, 1993; International Award from Council of Editors of Learned Journals, for *Journal of Advanced Composition,* 1993; TIP Award, University of South Florida, for outstanding teaching on the undergraduate level, 1993, 1996; Award for Outstanding Contribution to Scholarship in Rhetoric and Composition from Association of Teachers of Advanced Composition; Research and Creative Scholarship Award from University of South Florida Division of Sponsored Research, and International Award for Distinguished Retiring Editor, all 1994.

WRITINGS:

(With Richard Ray and James DeGeorge) *Style and Readability in Technical Writing,* Random House (New York, NY), 1983.

Writing Centers: Theory and Administration, NCTE Publications (Urbana, IL), 1984.

(With Richard Ray and James DeGeorge) *Style and Readability in Business Writing,* Random House (New York, NY), 1984.

(Editor with Richard Ray and James DeGeorge) *The Process Reader,* Prentice-Hall (Englewood Cliffs, NJ), 1985.

(Editor with Elizabeth Metzger and Evelyn Ashton-Jones) *Advanced Placement English: Theory, Politics, and Pedagogy,* Boynton Cook (Upper Montclair, NJ), 1989.

(Editor with Evelyn Ashton-Jones) *The Gender Reader,* Allyn & Bacon (Newton, MA), 1990.

(Editor with Irene Gale) *(Inter)Views: Cross-Disciplinary Perspectives on Rhetoric and Literacy,* Southern Illinois University Press (Carbondale, IL), 1991.

Philosophy, Rhetoric, Literary Criticism, Southern Illinois University Press (Carbondale, IL), 1994.

(Editor with Sidney Dobrin) *Composition Theory for the Postmodern Classroom,* State University of New York Press (Albany, NY), 1994.

(With Elizabeth Hirsh) *Women Writing Culture,* State University of New York Press, 1995.

(Editor with Julie Drew) *Landmark Essays on Advanced Composition,* Hermahoras/Erlbaum, 1996.

(Editor with Todd Taylor) *Publishing in Rhetoric and Composition,* State University of New York Press, 1997.

(Editor with Elizabeth Metzger and Evelyn Ashton-Jones) *Advanced Placement English: Theory, Poli-*

tics and Pedagogy, 1st edition, 1989, Boynton Cook (Upper Montclair, NJ), 2nd edition, 1998.

(With Lynn Worsham) *Race, Rhetoric, and the Post-colonial,* State University of New York Press, 1999.

(Editor with Merry Perry and Evelyn Ashton-Jones) *The Gender Reader,* 2nd edition, Allyn and Bacon (Newton, MA), 2000.

(With Lynn Worsham and S. Dobrin) *The Kinneavy Papers: Theory and the Study of Discourse,* State University of New York Press, 2000.

Contributor to books, including *Teaching Advanced Composition: Why and How,* edited by Katherine H. Adams and John L. Adams, Heinemann, 1990; *Writing and Publishing for Academic Authors,* edited by Joseph Moxley, University Press of America (Lanham, MD), 1991; and *Gender in Academe,* edited by Sara Deats and Lagretta Lenker, Rowman & Littlefield (Totowa, NJ), 1994; *Literacy as Social Exchange,* edited by Maureen Hourigan, State University of New York Press, 1994; *There's No Such Thing as Free Speech: And It's a Good Thing Too,"* edited by Stanley Fish, Oxford University Press (New York, NY), 1994; *Rhetoric: Concepts, Definitions, and Boundaries,* edited by William Covino and David Jolliffe, Allyn and Bacon (Newton, MA), 1995; *Teachers, Discourses, and Authority in the Postmodern Composition Classroom,* edited by Xin Liu Gale, State University of New York Press, 1996; *Constructing Knowledges: The Politics of Theory-Building and Pedagogy in Composition,* edited by Sidney Dobrin, State University of New York Press (Albany), 1997; *Ethical Considerations in the Composition Classroom,* edited by F. Gale and James L. Kinneavy, Lang (New York, NY), 1999; *Post-Process Theory: New Directions for Composition Research,* edited by Thomas Kent, Southern Illinois University Press (Carbondale, IL), 1999; *(Re)Visioning Composition Textbooks: Conflicts of Culture, Ideology, and Pedagogy,* edited by Fredric Gale and Xin Liu Gale, State University of New York Press (Albany), 2000; and *Words in the Wilderness: Critical Literacy in the Borderlands,* edited by Stephen Gilbert Brown, State University of New York, 2000.

Contributor of numerous articles to academic journals. Served many editorial roles, including editor, *SWCA Newsletter,* 1981-83; associate editor, *Technical Communication,* 1983-87; guest editor, *Teaching English in the Two-Year College,* winter, 1984; *Journal of Advanced Composition,* associate editor, 1984-85, editor, 1985-94, editor emeritus, 1994—. Also member of editorial board, *Writing on the Edge: A Multiperspective on Writing,* 1988—, *Journal of Business and Technical*

Communication, 1990—, *Rhetoric Society Quarterly,* 1990—, Council of Editors of Learned Journals E-Journal, 1997—, *Writerly/Readerly Texts: Essays on Literature, Literary/Textual Criticism, and Pedagogy,* 1998—, *Review of Education/Pedagogy/Cultural Studies,* 1998—.

WORK IN PROGRESS: Editing *The Critical Reader,* with Ashton Jones and Irene Ward, for McGraw (New York, NY). Two books under contract, *Rhetoric and Composition as Intellectual Work,* for Southern Illinois University Press (Carbondale, IL), and *Rhetoric and Interpretation: Stanley Fish and the Production of Discourse,* for State University of New York Press.

SIDELIGHTS: Gary A. Olson told *CA:* "My academic discipline, rhetoric and composition, is in part a very young field (about thirty years old) and in part the re-emergence of one of the first intellectual disciplines (rhetoric). Scholars in the field investigate all aspects of written discourse. Rhetoric and composition is a thoroughly interdisciplinary field, drawing on work from anthropology, linguistics, literary criticism, philosophy, psychology, sociology, and numerous other disciplines. My work over the last fifteen years has involved helping to expand the boundaries of the discipline by encouraging intellectual dialogues across disciplines. I have done this principally through my service as editor of the *Journal of Advanced Composition* and my work in conducting scholarly interviews with prominent intellectuals outside my field, addressing issues central to the field itself."*

*   *   *

ORE, Rebecca 1948-
(Rebecca Brown)

PERSONAL: Born 1948, in Louisville, KY. *Education:* Columbia University, B.A. 1979; University of North Carolina at Charlotte, M.A., 1980; attended State University of New York, Albany, 1980-82.

ADDRESSES: Home—P.O. Box 129, Critz, Virginia, 24082-0129. *Agent*—Donald Maas, 160 West 95th St., New York, NY, 10025. *E-mail*—rebeccabrownore@ msn.com.

CAREER: Poet and novelist. Editorial assistant, New York City, 1968-72; part-time secretary, San Francisco, CA, 1975-76; *The Patriot,* reporter, Patrick County,

VA, 1976-77; office assistant, New York, NY, 1977-78; science-fiction writer, 1983—.

AWARDS, HONORS: Philip K. Dick Award, Best Original Science Fiction Paperback, 1988, 1990.

WRITINGS:

The Illegal Rebirth of Billy the Kid, Tor (New York, NY), 1991.
Alien Bootlegger (short stories), Tor (New York, NY), 1993.
Slow Funeral, Tor (New York, NY), 1994.
Gaia's Toys, Tor (New York, NY), 1995.
Outlaw School, EOS (New York, NY), 2000.

"DISCOVERIES" TRILOGY

Becoming Alien, Tor (New York, NY), 1988.
Being Alien, Tor (New York, NY), 1989.
Human to Human, Tor (New York, NY), 1990.

Contributor of stories to periodicals, including *The Magazine of Fantasy and Science Fiction.*

POETRY; UNDER REBECCA BROWN

Mouse Works, Siamese Banana Press (New York, NY), 1971.
The Bicycle Trip and Poems, Telephone Books (New York, NY), 1974.
For the Eighty-second Airborne, Adventures in Poetry Press (New York, NY), 1976.
The Barbarian Queen, Telephone Press (Guilford, CT), 1981.

SIDELIGHTS: Some of Rebecca Ore's earliest efforts as a writer were reading her poetry during the 1970s at venues like San Francisco State University and New York City's poetry hub, St. Mark's Place. Although she began her writing career as a poet, playwright, and author of memoirs, Ore has become best known for her science-fiction novels, including *Becoming Alien, Gaia's Toys,* and *Slow Funeral.* For these and other books, she has been placed by some critics at the forefront of the contemporary science-fiction scene in America.

Ore has authored several science fiction novels. One of her most ambitious works is a trilogy for Tor's Ben Bova "Discoveries" series. The first novel in the three-part series, *Becoming Alien,* is, according to reviewer Roland Green in *Booklist,* "a superior variation on the theme of alien contact." In the story, a teenager becomes friends with the lone survivor of a spaceship that has crashed. As a reward, the alien takes the boy, Tom "Red Clay" Gentry, to his home planet for training as a planetary explorer.

Being Alien, the second book in the trilogy, was called "challenging entertainment in the grand tradition" by *Locus* reviewer Faren Miller. In this episode, Tom returns to Earth and settles in a futuristic Berkeley, California. The setting provides a humorous touch, and the book is peopled with interesting characters. The overarching theme, though, is xenophobia—the fear of anything strange or foreign. *Being Alien* charts these waters in detail, creating crises that, according to Miller, "have an emotional depth and maturity that's rare in light adventure fiction."

The third book of the trilogy, *Human to Human,* begins a few years after the end of *Being Alien.* Tom, who has taken up with a woman named Marianne, has a seven-year-old child named Karl. When an alien Sharwani family moves in with Tom and Marianne, hostile Sharwanis attack Karl and kill one of Tom's friends. Tom retaliates in an all-too-human manner, killing a Sharwani. Reviewer Tom Easton in *Analog* summarized that the events in *Human to Human* give Ore "a chance to tell us which two human groups might be least xenophobic," and the novel itself was "an excellent ending to the trilogy."

Ore followed her trilogy with *The Illegal Rebirth of Billy the Kid,* a story that takes place in the mid- to late-twenty-first century. Genetic engineers have mastered cloning, and one particular scientist, the evil Simon Boyle, has managed to construct a chimera-like version of Billy the Kid, the famous nineteenth-century western gunslinger. Boyle uses Billy as a gigolo to earn money and, disguised as Pat Garrett, Boyle shoots Billy dead after each lovemaking session. One female client escapes with Billy, and thus begins a series of events that places Billy in danger and leads him to seek out other chimera-beings. The plot gives Ore a good deal of room to explore truth, violence, myths, and the nature of societal change through the eyes of a legendary nineteenth-century figure. "It all sounds gloomy, drab and rather dumb," wrote reviewer John Clute in *Washington Post Book World,* but "it is nothing of the sort."

In *Slow Funeral,* protagonist Maude Fuller is living in California and collecting government benefits by feigning insanity. When Maude leaves her safe enclave to return home to Bracken County, Virginia to see her dying grandmother, she encounters conflicts within the family and finds her hometown plagued by ancient magic.

Eventually, Maude is forced to summon her own innate magical powers in an attempt to thwart the efforts of aunt Betty and her husband Luke. Sybil S. Steinberg in *Publishers Weekly* said that *Slow Funeral* "offers a colorful depiction of Appalachian life and culture."

Gaia's Toys depicts the world of the near future as a grim, heartless place that presents new and creative obstacles for a set of heroes. Allison Dodge, the story's narrator, is an eco-terrorist who is tricked by her superiors and then kidnapped by government operatives led by the villainous Mr. Kearney. Willie Hunsucker is a hapless welfare recipient who, like other welfare recipients, has had his brain hard-wired for menial computer use by the government in exchange for the financial assistance provided to him. Dorcas Rae, a genetics expert, finds herself working on a project that would train wasps to sting humans who are angry or engaged in conflict. These three characters must work together to defeat Kearney's sinister plan to drug humans into meekness and compliance. *Gaia's Toys,* declared reviewer Carl Hays in *Booklist,* places Ore "in the ranks of such leading-edge science fiction talent as William Gibson and Neal Stephenson."

In her next novel, *Outlaw School,* Ore portrays a near-future world that is technologically advanced and rigidly defined by class, a society where individual life options are severely limited and strict conformity is required of all. Growing up in this society, young middle-class Jane attends a school where she is expected to act less bright, less verbal, and less sure of herself than those who are considered her social superiors. Jane has few choices in life. She can either plan on marriage, which first involves becoming a Judas girl and having a surveillance device implanted in one of her eyes so potential husbands can keep tabs on her, or she can submit to a course of state-approved drug control that will dampen her thought processes and keep her submissive. When Jane breaks the rules by becoming pregnant, she is banished to a psychiatric rehabilitation center where recalcitrant patients must undergo forced virtual reality sessions known as "cyberia." Jane discovers she is expected to assist the center's doctors in restraining patients in order to help pay for her own stay and treatment. Although Jane never sees her baby, who is taken away from her at birth, she eventually gains a powerful ally in a rich philanthropist named Ocean. With Ocean's help, Jane leaves the rehabilitation center and becomes an illegal teacher at the Outlaw School of the book's title. Jane's students are outcasts such as herself, misfits, malcontents, and those rejected by the system. The information Jane imparts to them has not been approved by the state. Inevitably, the government News

Agency, a kind of thought police, becomes award of Jane' illegal activities.

Reviewing *Outlaw School* online in *Bookbrowser,* Harriet Klausner found Jane to be "a fabulous protagonist who dares to dream," and went on to conclude: "Not for everyone because the plot is somber grey, Rebecca Ore paints a hellish technological future with upper class big brother in full control." A critic in *Kirkus Reviews* adds: "Shelve this one alongside *1984* and *The Color Purple:* it's that good. It's also unremittingly harrowing. Read it anyway."

BIOGRAPHICAL/CRITICAL SOURCES:

BOOKS

St. James Guide to Science-Fiction Writers, St. James Press (Detroit, MI), 1996.

PERIODICALS

Analog, November, 1987, p. 131; August, 1989, pp. 176-178; October, 1990, pp. 182-183; March, 1991, pp. 179-180; January, 1994, p. 307; December, 1994, p. 163; December, 1995, p. 162.
Booklist, November 15, 1987, p. 542; July, 1995, p. 1866.
Kirkus Reviews, May 15, 1994, p. 673; May 15, 1995, p. 677; November 1, 2000, review of *Outlaw School,* p. 1524.
Library Journal, June 15, 1994, p. 99.
Locus, November, 1989, pp. 15, 59; March, 1991, pp. 15, 61.
Magazine of Fantasy and Science Fiction, June, 1987, p. 53; January, 1995, p. 30; January, 1996, p. 26.
Publishers Weekly, December 25, 1987, p. 70; July 4, 1994, p. 56; June 26, 1995, p. 90.
Voice of Youth Advocates, June, 1988, pp. 96-97.
Washington Post Book World, June 30, 1991, p. 5.

OTHER

Bookbrowser, http://www.bookbrowser.com/Reviews/ (November 5, 2000), Harriet Klausner, review of *Outlaw School.**

*   *   *

ORLEAN, Susan 1955-

PERSONAL: Born October 31, 1955, in Cleveland, OH; daughter of Arthur (a real estate developer) and Edith (a bank officer; maiden name, Gross) Orlean; married John Gillespie (investment banker), September 15, 2001. *Education:* University of Michigan, B.A. (with honors), 1976.

ADDRESSES: Home—New York, NY. *Office*—*The New Yorker,* 4 Times Square, New York, NY 10036. *Agent*—Richard S. Pine, Arthur Pine Associates Inc., 250 West 57th St., New York, NY 10019.

CAREER: Boston Phoenix, Boston, MA, staff writer, 1983-86; *Boston Globe,* Boston, MA, columnist, 1986-87; *Rolling Stone,* New York, NY, contributing editor, 1987—; *New Yorker,* New York, NY, staff writer, 1987—. Freelance writer, 1987—. Also worked as reporter for *Wilamette Week,* Portland, OR.

MEMBER: Authors Guild, PEN.

AWARDS, HONORS: PEN/New England Discovery Award, Pen American Center, 1984; *New York Times* Notable Book, for *Saturday Night,* 1990; six Sigma Delta Chi Distinguished Service awards for reporting, Society of Professional Journalists.

WRITINGS:

Red Sox and Bluefish: Meditations of What Makes New England New England, Faber & Faber (Winchester, MA), 1987.
Saturday Night, Knopf (New York, NY), 1990.
The Orchid Thief: A True Story of Beauty and Obsession, Random House (New York, NY), 1998.
The Bullfighter Checks Her Makeup: My Encounters with Extraordinary People, Random House (New York, NY), 2000.

Contributor of articles to periodicals, including the *New Yorker, Rolling Stone, Vogue,* and *Esquire.*

SIDELIGHTS: Inspired by and derived from her feature articles in such publications as the *New Yorker* and *Rolling Stone,* Susan Orlean's books have explored various aspects of life in contemporary America. According to Ted Conover, writing in *New York Times Book Review:* "Given a stack of 30 long features from the nations' magazines, a reader could quickly find the one written by Susan Orlean. It would have a narrow focus. . . . It would be stylishly written, whimsical yet sophisticated, quirkily detailed and full of empathy for a person you might not have thought about empathetically before. . . . It would be lightly first person. . . . yet the whole would feel somehow suffused with her (Orlean's) personality."

Red Sox and Bluefish: Meditations of What Makes New England New England, Orlean's first collection of essays, details some of the unique characteristics of life in New England, including its distinctive language, drivers, and cuisine. Praised for its effective combination of wit and wisdom, the work initially appeared as a series of essays in the *Boston Globe.*

In her second book, *Saturday Night,* Orlean chronicles her travels throughout the United States—including stops in Portland, Oregon, New York City, Miami Beach, Florida, and Elkhart, Indiana—to discover the range of activities pursued by typical Americans on a Saturday night. The practices explored in her book run the gamut from cruising, bowling, and watching television, to dating, dining, and drinking, to gambling, thieving, and murdering. Orlean's study, which blends her observations with information obtained from academic authorities on human behavior, also speculates on why many people cannot stay home on a Saturday night and why most individuals practice ordinary activities with more intensity on a Saturday night. The work was called "convivial, amusing and informative" by David Finkle in the *Chicago Tribune,* while Orlean was described as making "mostly splendid use of the conglomeration of those moments that can steer people through the sameness of a week," by Scott Simon in *New York Times Book Review.*

In 1994 Orlean's attention was drawn to a newspaper item that described the theft of two hundred rare orchid plants from the Fakahatchee Strand State Preserve in the swampland of southern Florida. The flowers had been taken by John Laroche and several Seminole Indians to supply a nursery that Laroche ran for the Seminoles. Laroche, a self-taught botanist, had not only convinced the Seminoles to hire him, but assured them that they had a legal right to pick orchids from land that had once belonged to them. Orlean met and interviewed Laroche, attended the trial, and penned an article titled "Orchid Fever" in *New Yorker.* Increasingly fascinated by the subculture of orchid lovers, some of whom will pay up to a $1,000 for a single plant, Orlean returned to Florida and continued her research, expanding the article into *The Orchid Thief: A True Story of Beauty and Obsession.* This was Orlean's first book-length narrative; her earlier books collected shorter pieces. Describing the process of writing *The Orchid Thief* to Dave Weich in *Powell's Books Interviews,* Orlean stated: "I'd come across a report of a crime that was so peculiar, that touched so many seemingly incongruous places, communities, and subjects, that writing the book was largely a matter of unpacking those elements. In the process, each element became a story in itself,

much more interesting and involved than I would have ever imagined."

In *The Orchid Thief* Laroche emerges as a disturbed personality who monomaniacally pursues one passion after another—photography, turtles, fossils, orchids, designing Web sites—and who has deluded himself into thinking he is smarter than anyone else. Yet as Orlean related to Weich, the book delves into more than the trial and conviction of Laroche. In the course of her narrative, Orlean discusses the passion for orchid collecting that swept through Victorian England, the fanaticism of contemporary orchid afficionados, the Seminoles' ongoing battle with the U.S. Government for control of their tribal lands, and the destruction of Florida's swamps by land developers. Orlean even treks into the swamps herself, in an unsuccessful search for a ghost orchid. Conover remarked that *The Orchid Thief 's* "true subject" is neither orchids nor Laroche, but the "monomania of collectors." Brian Lym in *Library Journal* observed that Orlean's "narrative forays underscore a central theme—the costs and consequences of the single-minded pursuit of an ideal or passion." Donna Seaman in *Booklist* concluded: "In prose as lush and full of surprises as the Fakahatchee itself, Orlean connects orchid-related excesses of the past with exploits of the present so dramatically an orchid will never be just an orchid again."

The Bullfighter Checks Her Makeup: My Encounters with Extraordinary People delivers exactly what its subtitle promises. Extraordinary people for Orlean are not always famous ones. Compiled mostly from a series of profiles that the author penned for the *New Yorker,* the collection's twenty subjects include designer Bill Blass, figure skater Tanya Harding, a New York cab driver who is also the king of the Ashanti—a tribe from Ghana—residing in the United States, Orlean's own hairdresser, Hawaiian surfer girls, the female bullfighter of the title, and a typical ten-year-old boy from New Jersey. A writer in *Kirkus Reviews* commented: "Some essays work better than others, but in general the collection is marred only by a few too many run-on sentences and the occasional quick ending. . . . Well-paced and good-humored; a page turner." Lodging a more enthusiastic response was Seaman, who stated: "Orlean's curiosity, faith in improvisation, fundamental respect and fondness for humankind, and a ready sense of humor inform each of these well-crafted pieces."

BIOGRAPHICAL/CRITICAL SOURCES:

PERIODICALS

Booklist, December 1, 1998, Donna Seaman, review of *The Orchid Thief,* p. 634; October 1, 2000, Donna Seaman, review of *The Bullfighter Checks Her Makeup,* p. 387.
Chicago Tribune, May 28, 1990.
Economist (US), March 27, 1999, "Lifting Orchids," p. 87.
Kirkus Reviews, November 1, 2000, review of *The Bullfighter Checks Her Makeup,* p. 1533.
Knight-Ridder/Tribune News Service, January 13, 1999, Chuck McCartney, review of *The Orchid Thief,* p. K7163.
Library Journal, January, 1999, Brian Lym, review of *The Orchid Thief,* p. 126.

New York Times, April 26, 1990; January 4, 1999, Christopher Lehmann-Haupt, "Seeing with New Eyes in a World of Exotic Obsession."
New York Times Book Review, May 6, 1990, p. 9; January 3, 1999, Ten Conover, "Flower Power."
Publishers Weekly, November 23, 1998, review of *The Orchid Thief,* p. 51; November 13, 2000, review of *The Bullfighter Checks Her Makeup,* p. 92.
Time, January 25, 1999, John Skow, review of *The Orchid Thief,* p. 80.
Washington Post Book World, April 22, 1990, p. 3.

OTHER

MetroActive Books, http://www.metroactive.com/papers/ (March 4, 1999), Traci Hukill, "Flower Power."
Powell's Books Interviews, http://www.powels.com/authors/ (January 6, 2001), Dave Weich, "Susan Orlean's Orchid Adventures."

P-R

PAOLUCCI, Anne (Attura)

PERSONAL: Born in Rome, Italy; naturalized U.S. citizen; daughter of Joseph and Lucy (Guidoni) Attura; married Henry Paolucci. *Education:* Barnard College, B.A.; Columbia University, M.A., Ph.D.; also attended University of Perugia and the University of Rome.

ADDRESSES: Office—c/o Author Mail, Griffon House Publications, P.O. Box 81, Whitestone, NY 11357.

CAREER: Rye Country Day School, Rye, NY, English teacher, 1955-57; The Brearley School, New York, NY, English teacher, 1957-59; City College of the City University of New York, New York, NY, assistant professor of English and comparative literature, 1959-69; St. John's University, Jamaica, NY, university research professor, beginning in 1969, professor of English, beginning in 1975, department chair, 1982-91, director of Doctor of Arts program in English, 1982-93. Queens College of the City University of New York, distinguished (adjunct) visiting professor, 1982; special lecturer, universities of Bologna, Catania, Messina, Palermo, Milan, Innsbruck, and Pisa, 1965-67, University of Bari, 1967, University of Urbino, summers, 1966 and 1967, Renaissance Institute at the Ashland Shakespeare Festival (Oregon), summers, 1974 and 1975, Chinese University of Hong Kong, 1979, Australian National University, Monash University, Deakin University, University of Adelaide, University of Queensland (St. Lucia), Flinders University, and Latrobe University, Australia, 1979; Fulbright lecturer in American drama at University of Naples, 1965-67; visiting fellow, Humanities Research Centre, Australian National University, 1979; guest speaker (with Edward Albee), Ohio Northern University, 1990.

Member of American Commission to Screen Fulbright Applicants for the United States, 1966, 1967; founder of American Playwrights' and Producers' Showcase, 1967; special guest of Yugoslav Ministry of Culture, 1972; member of board of directors, World Centre for Shakespeare Studies, beginning in 1972; founder and executive director, Council on National Literatures, beginning in 1974; consultant to National Endowment for the Humanities, beginning in 1977; member of advisory board, UNESCO's Commission of Technological and Cultural Transformation, beginning in 1978; member of North American advisory council, Shakespeare Globe Theatre Center, beginning in 1981; member of fellowship board, National Graduate Fellows Program (appointed by President Reagan), 1985-86; member of National Council on Humanities, beginning in 1986; City University of New York, Board of Trustees member, beginning in 1996, Board of Trustee chair, beginning in 1997. Organized and hosted television series *Magazines in Focus,* NYC-Television, 1972-73, and *Successful Women: Before, during, and after Women's Lib,* American Broadcasting Corporation, 1973; theatrical producer and director.

MEMBER: International Shakespeare Association, International Comparative Literature Association, Renaissance Institute of Japan, Byron Society of America and England (founding member of advisory board, beginning in 1973), American Institute of Italian Studies (board of advisors, beginning 1977), American Society of Italian Legions of Merit (board of directors; chairman of cultural committee, beginning 1990), American Comparative Literature Association, PEN American Center, Renaissance Society of America, Modern Language Association of America (member of executive committee, 1975-77), Shakespeare Association of America, Hegel Society of America, Dante Society of

America (member of council, 1974-76; vice president, 1976-77), Pirandello Society of America (founding member and vice president, 1968-79; president, beginning in 1979), American Society of Italian Legions of Merit (board of directors, beginning in 1990), National Society of Literature and the Arts, Alpha Psi Omega.

AWARDS, HONORS: Artemesia award, *Quicksilver* (literary magazine), 1961, for "Poetry Reading"; first Woodbridge Honorary Fellow, Columbia University, 1961-62; New York State grants, 1963, 1964, 1964-65; writer-in-residence at Yaddo Colony, 1965; voted one of the ten best teachers, City College of the City University of New York, 1969; award from Italian-American Women of Achievement, 1970; drama award, Medieval and Renaissance Conference at Western Michigan University, 1972, for play *Minions of the Race;* received notable rating, *New York Times,* 1972, for *Magazines in Focus* television series; Woman of the Year award, Herman Henry Scholarship Foundation, 1973; Woman of the Year award, Woman's Press Club of New York, 1974; American Council of Learned Societies grant, 1978; City-Wide Italian Week Award, 1982; leadership award, Association of Teachers of New York, 1983; honored by Pirandello Society of America's 25th anniversary awards dinner, 1983; named one of ten outstanding Italian ambassadors in Washington, 1986; named Cavaliere of the Italian Republic, 1986; Gold Medal, National Italian American Foundation, 1990; awards from Consortium of Italian-American Associations, and American-Italian History Association, both 1991; Columbus Award, Catholic Charities, 1991.

WRITINGS:

NONFICTION

(Translator) *Machiavelli's "Mandragola,"* Liberal Arts Press, 1957.

(Translator) Henry Paolucci and James Brophy, *Pierre Duhem on Galileo,* Twayne (Boston, MA), 1962.

(With husband, Henry Paolucci) *Hegel on Tragedy,* Anchor Books (New York, NY), 1962.

A Short History of American Drama, University of Urbino Press, 1966.

Eugene O'Neill, Arthur Miller, Edward Albee, University of Urbino Press, 1967.

Commenti critici sur Giulio Cesare, Macbeth, Amleto, Otello, (title means "Critical Commentary on Julius Caesar, Macbeth, Hamlet, Othello"), University of Urbino Press, 1967.

From Tension to Tonic: The Plays of Edward Albee, Southern Illinois University Press (Carbondale,

IL), 1972, new edition, Griffon House (Whitestone, NY), 2000.

Pirandello's Theater: The Recovery of the Modern Stage for Dramatic Art, Southern Illinois University Press (Carbondale, IL), 1974.

(Editor and author of introduction) *Canada,* Griffon House (Whitestone, NY), 1977.

(Editor and author of introduction) *Dante's Influence on American Writers,* Griffon House (Whitestone, NY), 1977.

(Editor with Ronald Warwick) *India: Review of National Literatures,* Bagehot Council, 1979.

(With husband, Henry Paolucci) *Dante and the "Quest for Eloquence" in India's Vernacular Languages,* Griffon House (Whitestone, NY), 1984.

(Editor with Jennifer Stone) Mary Reynolds, *Pirandello: Annual Volume of Review of National Literature Essays on the Fiction and Plays of Luigi Pirandello, Nobel Laureate,* Bagehot Council, 1986.

(Editor) *Contemporary Literary Theory: An Overview,* Bagehot Council, 1987.

(Editor with husband, Henry Paolucci) *Columbus; Modern Views of Columbus and His Time: Essays, Poems, Reprints,* Griffon House (Whitestone, NY), 1990.

(Editor) *Henry Paolucci: Selected Writings on Literature and the Arts, Science and Astronomy, Law, Government, and Political Philosophy,* Griffon House (Whitestone, NY), 1999.

Also editor, with Donald Puchala, of *Problems in National Literary Identity and the Writer as Social Critic: Selected Papers of the Fourth Annual NDEA Seminar on Foreign Area Studies, Columbia University, February 28-29, 1980,* Bagehot Council.

PLAYS

The Short Season (three acts), first produced in New York, NY at Cubiculo, 1970.

Minions of the Race, (one act), first produced in Kalamazoo, MI, at Western Michigan University, 1972.

(Translator) Mario Appollonio, *The Apocalypse according to J. J. [Rousseau]* (three acts), first produced in New York, NY at Classic Theater, 1976.

Incidents at the Great Wall, (one act), first produced with *Minions of the Race* in New York, NY at the Churchyard Theater, 1976.

Cipango!: A One-Act Play in Three Scenes about Christopher Columbus (produced in New York, NY, 1987), Griffon House (Whitestone, NY), 1985.

The Actor in Search of His Mask (one act; produced in Italian translation, Genoa, Italy, 1987), Griffon House (Whitestone, NY), 1987.

In the Green Room with Machiavelli, Griffon House (Whitestone, NY), 2000.

SOUND RECORDINGS

Political Idealism and Political Realism: Dante and Machiavelli, Everett/Edwards, 1975.

Classical and Modern Tragedy: From Aeschylus to Shakespeare and Beyond, Everett/Edwards, 1975.

Masks in Focus: Dissolution of Character in Pirandello's Plays, Everett/Edwards, 1975.

Toward a New Theory of Comparative Literature, Everett/Edwards, 1975.

Also editor of forty-cassette series on China, for Everett/Edwards.

POETRY

Poems Written for Sbek's Mummies, Marie Menken, and Other Important Persons, Places, and Things, Griffon House (Whitestone, NY), 1977.

Riding the Mast Where It Swings, Griffon House (Whitestone, NY), 1980.

Tropic of the Gods, Griffon House (Whitestone, NY), 1980.

Gorbachev in Concert (and Other Poems), Bagehot Council, 1991.

Queensboro Bridge (and Other Poems), Griffon House (Whitestone, NY), 1995.

OTHER

Eight Short Stories (fiction), Griffon House (Whitestone, NY), 1977.

Sepia Tones: Seven Short Stories (fiction), Rimu Publishing/Griffon House (Whitestone, NY), 1986.

Also, author of *Terminal Degrees* (fiction), Griffon House (Whitestone, NY). Contributor of numerous poems, stories, articles, and reviews to magazines, including *American Pen, Ararat, Literature East and West, Poem, South Carolina Review, Kenyon Review, Quicksilver, Shakespeare Quarterly,* and *Pacific Quarterly.* Founder and editor, *Review of National Literatures* and *CNL/Report,* both beginning 1970, and *CNL/Quarterly World Report,* beginning 1978; member of editorial board of *Barnard Alumnae,* 1969-71, and *Pirandello Newsletter,* 1972; member of advisory board of *Italian-Americana,* beginning 1973, *America-Latina,* beginning 1975, and *Gradiva,* beginning 1977.

SIDELIGHTS: Though she became a United States citizen in her youth, Anne Paolucci has remained an amazingly energetic participant in civic, scholarly, educational, and media events that celebrate her Italian heritage. Commenting on her busy schedule in a *New York Daily News* profile, Paolucci admitted to sometimes writing around the clock without realizing it. "I just wish I had thirty hours in the day," she said of her hectic lifestyle. "It's a lot of work, but I enjoy it. I have fun."

In 1979 Paolucci's travels took her to Australia, where in addition to lecturing at a number of universities she found inspiration for her second book of poems, *Riding the Mast Where It Swings.* The centerpiece of this collection is a ten-page sequence titled "Tropic of the Gods" which is dedicated "to my Australian friends." The poem attempts to capture the brooding presence of the Australian landscape, the American speaker's response to it, and echoes of the world culture from ancient Egypt through the Renaissance to such modernist poets as Ezra Pound and T. S. Eliot. It concludes: "Oblivion is a large silence / Beyond art." Other sequences in the collection deal with the Italian-American experience through the medium of bilingual poetry.

Italian-American experiences surface once again in Paolucci's 1986 volume of short stories, *Sepia Tones.* While the title refers to the brown-and-white tint of the old photographs which accompany the stories, it also expresses a dominant tone of nostalgia in the stories themselves. Set in New York City and in the farm country of southern Italy, the stories are partially linked by recurring characters and setting. Reviewing the volume for the *New York Times Book Review,* Nancy Forbes praised the quality of "Rara," the story of a terminally ill priest, and "The Oracle Is Dumb or Cheat," a tale of two young lovers choosing between heritage and freedom. However, some of the other stories, Forbes felt, suffered from the author's unwillingness to give away the characters' unpleasant secrets; but the volume as a whole, she comments, "helps dispel the silence" about the Italian-American experience.

Paolucci told *CA:* "I was appointed in 1996 by New York State Governor George Pataki to the Board of Trustees of the City University of New York (200,000+ students), and in 1997 was asked to serve as the first chairwoman of that board."

BIOGRAPHICAL/CRITICAL SOURCES:

BOOKS

Paolucci, Anne, *Riding the Mast Where It Swings,* Griffon House (Whitestone, NY), 1980.

PERIODICALS

New York Daily News, November 22, 1978, profile of Anne Paolucci.
New York Times Book Review, February 16, 1986, Nancy Forbes, review of *Sepia Tones,* p.16.

*   *   *

PARKS, Rosa (Louise Lee) 1913-

PERSONAL: Born February 4, 1913, in Tuskegee, AL; daughter of James (a carpenter) and Leona (a teacher; maiden name, Edwards) McCauley; married Raymond Parks (a barber and civil rights activist), December 18, 1932 (died, 1977). *Education:* Attended Alabama State College (now Alabama State University).

ADDRESSES: Office—c/o Congressman John J. Conyers, Jr., 231 West Lafayette, 305 Federal Bldg., Detroit, MI 48226; 313-894-3566. *E-mail*—general@rosaparks.org.

CAREER: Civil rights activist and speaker. National Association for the Advancement of Colored People (NAACP), Montgomery, AL, secretary, 1943-56, and youth advisor; office of U.S. Congressman John Conyers, Jr., Detroit, MI, administrative assistant, receptionist, secretary, 1965-88; African Methodist Episcopal Church (AME), became deaconess, 1964, affiliated with St. Matthew AME Church, Detroit, MI; Rosa and Raymond Parks Institute for Self-Development (youth assistance organization), founder with Elaine Eason Steele, 1987. Worked variously in her early career as a seamstress, housekeeper, hotel supervisor, and life insurance agent.

MEMBER: National Association for the Advancement of Colored People, Southern Christian Leadership Conference, Detroit and Women's Public Affairs Committee, Women's Public Affairs Committee of 100.

AWARDS, HONORS: The Southern Christian Leadership Conference sponsors annual Rosa Parks Freedom Award, beginning in 1963; Rosa Parks Boulevard and Rosa Parts Art Center, both Detroit, MI, 1969; honored by Women's Missionary Society, AME Church at Quadrennial Conventions, 1971; Spingarn Medal, National Association for the Advancement of Colored People (NAACP), 1979; Women in Community Service awards Rosa Parks Award, beginning in 1979; Martin Luther King, Jr. Award, 1980; Service Award, *Ebony,* 1980; Martin Luther King, Jr. Nonviolent Peace Prize, 1980; Eleanor Roosevelt Women of Courage Award, Wonder Woman Foundation, 1984; Medal of Honor for contribution to American ethnic diversity, celebration of Statue of Liberty's 100th birthday, 1986; Martin Luther King, Jr. Leadership Award, 1987; Adam Clayton Powell Jr. Legislative Achievement Award, 1990; *Parents' Choice* Award, 1992, and Hungry Mind Award, 1993, for *Rosa Parks: My Story;* Rosa Parks Peace Prize, 1994; Medal of Freedom awarded by U.S. President William Jefferson Clinton, 1996; State of Michigan published Act no. 28 of 1997 designating the first Monday following February 4 as Mrs. Rosa Parks's Day; dedication of Rosa L. Parks Learning Center, Botsford Commons, 1998; International Freedom Conductor's Award, National Underground Railroad Freedom Center, 1998; attended "State of the Union Address" by President Clinton, 1999; Congressional Gold Medal of Honor, 1999; named as one of the 100 most influential people of the 20th Century, *Time* magazine; Rosa Parks Library and Museum, Troy State University, opened in 2000; Image Award for Best Supporting Actress, NAACP, for role in *Touched by an Angel* television episode "Black like Monica"; Image Award for Outstanding Literary Work, NAACP, for *Dear Mrs. Parks: A Dialogue with Today's Youth;* has received keys to many cities and more than forty-three honorary doctorate degrees from various institutions, including Mount Holyoke College, 1981, Shaw College, and Soka University (Tokyo, Japan).

WRITINGS:

(With James Haskins) *The Autobiography of Rosa Parks as Told to James Haskins,* Dial, 1990, published as *Rosa Parks: My Story,* 1992, and *Rosa Parks: Mother to a Movement,* 1992.
(With James Haskins) *I Am Rosa Parks* (for preschoolers), 1996.

Also, with Gregory J. Reed, *Quiet Strength* and *Dear Mrs. Parks: A Dialogue with Today's Youth.*

SIDELIGHTS: Rosa Parks's contribution to the civil rights movement is legendary: When she was arrested for refusing to give up her seat on a Montgomery, Alabama, city bus for a white man, the movement to end segregation in the United States was galvanized. More than thirty years after this pivotal event, Parks collaborated with James Haskins, the noted biographer of African American historical and sports figures, to write *Rosa Parks: My Story.* Helen E. Williams maintained in *School Library Journal* that in this work Parks "corrects some media-created distortions" relating to the bus incident. In addition, a *Publishers Weekly* reviewer noted that Parks's autobiography enables its readers "to put this historic moment into a broader context."

Parks's story begins in rural Alabama, where she was born in 1913. Her father, a carpenter, and her mother, a teacher, separated when she was just two years old; Parks's mother took her and her younger brother to live with their maternal grandparents in Pine Level, Alabama. Parks attended the Montgomery Industrial School for Girls and Booker T. Washington High School, but dropped out of the latter before completion to help take care of her mother when she fell ill. Parks also attended Alabama State College for a short time.

Throughout her childhood, Parks experienced the pain and fear caused by hate, injustice, and segregation. Raymond Parks, a barber, shared her concerns, and the couple married in 1932. Raymond was working to encourage black people to register to vote and was a member of the National Committee to Save the Scottsboro Boys, formed in support of a group of young black men who had been accused of raping white women. He supported Parks when she became more active in the struggle against segregation. In addition to working for the Montgomery Voters League, she signed on as one of the first female members of the Montgomery Chapter of the National Association for the Advancement of Colored People (NAACP) and was elected secretary of the branch in 1943.

During the 1950s, Parks worked as a seamstress at the Montgomery Fair department store and had to ride a segregated bus to get to work. Like other black people who rode the bus, Parks was forced to abide by the law that reserved the first ten seats for whites and mandated that blacks give up their own seats if necessary to accommodate white passengers. Black riders also had to enter the bus by the back door; on one occasion in 1943, Parks was ejected from the bus for failing to do so.

On December 1, 1955, Parks was sitting with three others at the front of the black section of a bus when a white man boarded. As there were no seats available in the white section, the driver told Parks and the others in her row to move. Initially, no one complied, but the other passengers vacated their seats when the driver insisted that they not make trouble for themselves. Parks, however, remained seated even after the driver threatened to call the police to force her to move. When the police arrived, they arrested Parks and took her to jail. As Parks explained in her autobiography, she did not intend to change history that December evening. "If I

had been paying attention, I wouldn't even have gotten on the bus."

Nevertheless, other leaders of the nascent Civil Rights Movement rallied around the injustice of Parks's arrest. Attorney Clifford Durr, his wife Virginia, who was a civil rights activist, and E. D. Nixon, who had served as branch president of the NAACP, bailed Parks out of jail for one hundred dollars, and Nixon suggested that Parks appeal her case. Parks agreed, despite her family's valid concerns for her personal safety. When Jo Ann Robinson, the president of the Women's Political Council, who had been planning a boycott of the segregated buses, heard the news of Parks's arrest, she distributed pamphlets stating that the boycott would begin. The ministers of the city's black congregations lent their support, creating the Montgomery Improvement Association and electing the young Reverend Martin Luther King, Jr. its president.

The boycott continued for three hundred eighty-one days. In *Rosa Parks: My Story,* Parks describes how the black community worked together to sustain the effort and find alternative ways to get to work, as well as how some whites attempted to threaten them into compliance. Finally, the United States District Court and the United States Supreme Court ruled in favor of the Montgomery Improvement Association's suit against segregated seating, and the buses were legally integrated.

Although ultimately successful, Parks's determined protest was not without cost to herself and her family. Harassed continuously, Parks lost her position as an assistant tailor; her husband, who also lost his job, suffered a nervous breakdown. The couple could not find work anywhere near Montgomery. In August, 1957, they moved to Detroit, Michigan, where Rosa's brother lived. Parks was hospitalized briefly for stomach ulcers and the family's financial situation remained unstable until Parks began work as a staff assistant to U.S. Congressman John Conyers in 1965.

Parks worked at Congressman Conyers' office as an assistant and receptionist until her retirement in 1988. America's appreciation for her is reflected in the long list of awards and honors she has received, among them a seventy-seventh birthday celebration in the nation's capitol attended by prominent entertainers, government dignitaries, and a host of notable black leaders. Parks continues to accept such honors with grace, and despite recent heart trouble, gives speeches reminding Americans of the need to promote freedom throughout the world.

BIOGRAPHICAL/CRITICAL SOURCES:

BOOKS

Greenfield, Eloise, *Rosa Parks,* illustrated by Eric Marlow, Crowell, 1973.

Macdonald, Fiona, *Working for Equality,* Hampstead Press, 1987.

Parks, Rosa, and James Haskins, *Rosa Parks: My Story,* Dial, 1992.

Smith, Jessie Carney, editor, *Epic Lives: One Hundred Black Women Who Made a Difference,* Visible Ink Press, 1993.

PERIODICALS

Bulletin of the Center for Children's Books, February, 1992, p. 166.

Ebony, February, 1988, pp. 68-70.

Kirkus Reviews, December 15, 1991, p. 1597.

New York Times Book Review, February 2, 1992, p. 30.

Publishers Weekly, November 29, 1991, review of *Rosa Parks: My Story,* p. 53.

School Library Journal, February, 1992, Helen E. Williams, review of *Rosa Parks: My Story,* p. 104.

Smithsonian, May, 1993, p. 145.

Voice of Youth Advocates, June, 1992, p. 131.

*   *   *

PERETTI, Frank E. 1951-

PERSONAL: Born January 13, 1951, in Lethbridge, Alberta, Canada; son of Gene E. (a minister) and Joyce E. (a homemaker; maiden name, Schneider) Peretti; married Barbara Jean Ammon (a homemaker), June 24, 1972. *Education:* Attended University of California, Los Angeles. *Politics:* Conservative. *Religion:* Christian. *Avocational interests:* Carpentry, sculpturing, bicycling, hiking, banjo making, flying a private plane.

ADDRESSES: Home—Kingston, ID. *Office*—c/o W Publishing Group, P.O. Box 141000, Nashville, TN 37214. *Agent*—Blanton Harrell Entertainment, 25 Music Square West, Nashville, TN 37203.

CAREER: Ordained minister; associate pastor of community church, 1978-84; K-2 Ski Factory, production worker (ski maker), 1985-88; writer and public speaker, 1988—. Has played banjo with a bluegrass group, toured with a pop band, and performed as an actor in Bible videos for children.

WRITINGS:

NOVELS

This Present Darkness (also see below), Crossway Books (Wheaton, IL), 1986.

The Door in the Dragon's Throat (for children), Crossway Books (Wheaton, IL), 1986.

Escape from the Island of Aquarius (for children), Crossway Books (Wheaton, IL), 1986.

The Tombs of Anak (for children), Crossway Books (Wheaton, IL), 1987.

Trapped at the Bottom of the Sea (for children), Crossway Books (Wheaton, IL), 1988.

Tilly, Crossway Books (Wheaton, IL), 1988.

Piercing the Darkness (also see below), Crossway Books (Wheaton, IL), 1989.

All Is Well, illustrated by Robert Sauber, Word (Dallas, TX), 1991.

Prophet, Crossway Books (Wheaton, IL), 1992.

The Oath, Word Publications (Nashville, TN), 1995.

The Secret of the Desert Stone, Word Publications (Nashville, TN), 1996.

The Deadly Curse of Toco-Roy, Word Publications (Nashville, TN), 1996.

The Legend of Annie Murphy, Word Publications (Nashville, TN), 1997.

The Visitation, Word Publications (Nashville, TN), 1999.

Hangman's Curse, Tommy Nelson (Nashville, TN), 2000.

This Present Darkness and *Piercing the Darkness,* Crossway Books (Wheaton, IL), 2000.

The Wounded Spirit (memoir), Word Publications (Nashville, TN), 2000.

OTHER

Author of the radio drama *Tilly.* Contributor to Christian periodicals.

SIDELIGHTS: Frank E. Peretti is among the most popular contemporary writers of Christian fiction. "Mr. Peretti's publisher acclaims him the successor to C. S. Lewis; the *Darkness* novels have sold millions. Yet the author's name is virtually unknown outside the Christian community," wrote Jared Lobdell in the *National Review.* The son of a minister and an ordained minister himself, Peretti writes evangelical stories that celebrate the divine power of God and prayer. In his writing, inspired by conservative Christian theology, angels vanquish demons and good always prevails over evil.

Peretti's first novel, *This Present Darkness,* features protagonist Pastor Hank Busche and his heroic efforts to save a small college town from the Legions of Hell. The demons, in the guise of the Universal Consciousness Society, conspire to purchase the college and then subjugate humankind with the help of a Satanist professor, a New Age minister, a corrupt multinational corporation, and a police chief. Their sinister plot culminates in dramatic defeat when Pastor Busche summons an army of angels to repel the demons. The sequel, *The Piercing Darkness,* similarly involves cataclysmic confrontation between good and evil, this time precipitated by demonic litigation leveled against a small Christian school by liberals and representatives of the New Age movement. Both novels quickly became best-sellers and established the author's popularity.

In 1995 Peretti produced *The Oath,* an allegorical novel set in a Northwestern mining town. The story involves wildlife biologist Steve Benson, who arrives to care for his sister-in-law after his brother is killed and she is mauled by a mysterious animal. Benson tracks the strange beast and eventually discovers that it is a voracious dragon that brands and devours sinful members of the isolated community. After committing adultery and falling from grace, Benson is forced to confront the dragon himself. He begs forgiveness, experiences a dramatic conversion, and defeats the demon monster. Criticizing the savage misogyny underlying the death of Benson's adulterous lover, who is butchered by the dragon for her part in their sin, *Nation* reviewer Donna Minkowitz wrote, "In *The Oath,* morality literally means saving your own skin, and no one does any good for any other reason than self-preservation." Despite the overt theological message, as Martha Duffy noted in *Time,* the pacing and suspense of this novel "has brought his genre closer to mainstream pop fiction."

While still classifiable as a religious thriller, *The Visitation* marked a departure from the successful formula Peretti had established with his previous novels. "While he maintains his vintage trademark of fast action and multiple scene changes," observed Etta Wilson in *Book Page,* "signs of a more thoughtful maturity appear in this new novel." *The Visitation* contains no graphic battle scenes between armed legions of angels and demons. Instead, drawing on his own experiences as a Christian minister, Peretti explores more personal issues. "I'm not writing about spiritual warfare here," the author told Wilson. "This book is more the story of a crisis of faith. It deals with the deeper unspoken things that most Christians face at one time or another and points back to the heart of the reader, rather than being a battle out there somewhere."

The Visitation also marked a departure in style for Peretti, as it was the first novel he chose to write in the first person, exclusively from the protagonist's viewpoint. Set in the small farming community of Antioch, Washington, the book opens with the conflicts faced by Travis Jordan, a widower and former pastor who believes he has failed at his profession and who has also begun to lose his faith. Meanwhile, a long-haired olive-skinned drifter named Brandon Nichols has appeared in town. Brandon appears to be capable of performing medical miracles, including returning the ability to walk to a Vietnam veteran formerly confined to a wheelchair. Some embrace Brandon as a resurrected Christ figure, yet there are also indications that the power behind his miracles may have darker origins. Travis, with the help of the young pastor who has replaced him, must investigate Brandon's origins and history to determine if he is ultimately a force for good or evil. Reviewing the novel in *Christianity Today,* Susan Wise Bauer remarked that "Peretti has taken a light-year's leap toward realism in his depiction of the divine." Bauer went on to praise the book's suspense, dialogue, and character development. "A fine Peretti effort," commented John Mort of *Booklist,* "distinguished for its honest considerations of religious excess."

Peretti's first nonfiction book, *The Wounded Spirit,* was inspired by the 1999 shootings at Columbine High School that left thirteen people dead. Peretti explores the causes of youth violence and suggests some possible solutions by relating experiences from his own childhood and young adult years. Born with a condition known as cystic hygroma which caused his lymph nodes to swell, Peretti as a youth was often afflicted with a severely swollen tongue and a large lump on his neck. Because of these differences he was branded as an outsider, suffering the jibes and taunts of fellow students, much as Eric Harris and Dylan Klebold, the perpetrators of the Columbine tragedy, had been teased and ostracized for their differences. It was a high school gym teacher who finally came to Peretti's aid, merely by being there as someone with whom a troubled young man could speak about his problems. Peretti urges those who hurt others to be kinder and more aware of the effects of their actions. He also encourages those who are injured by the pettiness and insensitivity of others to speak out about their pain, rather than letting resentments build. Reviewing *The Wounded Spirit* in *Publishers Weekly,* a critic stated: "This book is full of painful stories, but also memorable moments of hope, as Peretti recounts instances when a peer or a teacher stood up for him. This remarkable memoir will inspire readers to undertake similar acts of courageous compassion."

Peretti has also written several books for children, including *The Door in the Dragon's Throat* and *Escape from the Island of Aquarius*. Both are exotic adventure stories featuring Dr. Jake Cooper and his children; the first involves a treasure hunt in the Middle East, the second a manhunt for a missionary missing amongst a satanic cult in the South Pacific.

Commenting on the appeal of Peretti's novels, Lobdell wrote, "Whatever their genre may be, it is not 'fantasy.' In the minds of the author and his readership, these Powers and Principalities are altogether real as the powers of prayer and 'watchcare.'" Though noting the underdeveloped personalities of his characters and the unsurprising melodramatic plots of his stories, Lobdell added, "Still, Mr. Peretti deserves his sales, and many readers will get exactly what they want from his books." Duffy observed, "Like most successful Christian novelists, he practices what he preaches as a devout Evangelical." According to Peretti, as quoted in *Time*, "Part of being a Christian is that you share your faith. . . . My writing is message centered."

BIOGRAPHICAL/CRITICAL SOURCES:

PERIODICALS

Booklist, June, 1999, John Mort, review of *The Visitation*, p. 1743.
Bookstore Journal, January, 1988, p. 163.
Christianity Today, April 29, 1996, p. 24; August 9, 1999, Susan Wise Bauer, review of *The Visitation*, p. 70.
Library Journal August, 1989, p. 165; October 15, 1989, p. 50; November 1, 1991, p. 68; September 1, 1995, p. 158.
Nation, February 19, 1996, p. 25.
National Review, August 20, 1990, p. 45.
Publishers Weekly, May 15, 1995, p. 15; August 17, 1998, Carol Chapman Stertzer, "Frank Peretti," p. S28; July 31, 2000, Marcia Nelson, "Post-Columbine Reflections, p. 44; October 30, 2000, review of *The Wounded Spirit*, p. 68; October 30, 2000, Jana Riess, "*PW* Talks with Frank Peretti," p. 69.
School Library Journal, February, 1986, p. 89; May, 1986, p. 96.
Time, November 13, 1995, p. 105.
Voice Literary Supplement, July, 1990, p. 15.

OTHER

Book Page, http://www.bookpage.com/ (January 6, 2001), Etta Wilson, "Maturity Marks Frank Peretti's *The Visitation*."

Steeling the Mind of America, http://www.steeling the mind.com/ (January 6, 2001), "Steeling Speaker, Frank Peretti page."*

*   *   *

PHILLIPS, Gary   1955-

PERSONAL: Born August 24, 1955, in Los Angeles, CA; son of Dikes (a mechanic) and Leonelle (a librarian; maiden name, Hutton) Phillips. *Education:* Attended San Francisco State University, 1972-73; California State University, Los Angeles, B.A., 1978.

ADDRESSES: Office—1102 S. Crenshaw Blvd., Los Angeles, CA 90014. *Agent*—David Smith, DHS Literary, 2528 Elm St., Ste. 350, Dallas, TX 75226.

CAREER: Writer. Worked as a union organizer, community activist, campaign political director, and teacher of incarcerated youths.

WRITINGS:

MYSTERY NOVELS

Violent Spring (first book in "Ivan Monk" series), West Coast Crime (Portland, OR), 1994.
Perdition, U.S.A. (second book in "Ivan Monk" series), John Brown Books (Salem, OR), 1996.
Bad Night Is Falling (third book in "Ivan Monk" series), Berkley Prime Crime, (New York, NY), 1998.
The Jook, Really Great Books (Los Angeles, CA), 1999.
Only the Wicked (fourth book in "Ivan Monk" series), Write Way Publishing (Aurora, CO), 2000.
High Hand (first book in "Martha Chainey" series), Kensington Books (New York, NY), 2000.
Shooter's Point (second book in "Martha Chainey" series), Kensington Books (New York, NY), 2001.

Author of the short stories "Dead Man's Shadow," *Spooks, Spies, and Private Eyes: Black Mystery, Crime and Suspense Fiction*, edited by Paula Woods, Doubleday (New York, NY), 1995; and "Boom, Boom," *New Mystery Magazine*, and "The Sleeping Detective," for *The Shamus Game*, edited by Robert J. Randisi, Signet (New York, NY), 2000. Author of articles and commentaries on pop culture and politics in periodicals, including *L.A. Times, San Francisco Examiner, Miami Herald*, and other newspapers.

WORK IN PROGRESS: Freedom's Fight, "a historical novel about black folks and the World War II years," for Tor (New York, NY), expected 2002; *Culprits,* a screenplay; more "Monk" stories,, edgier crime stories, including a four-part crime story comic book called *Shot Callerz,* for ONI Comics; and nonfiction (with narratives of current and past events).

SIDELIGHTS: Gary Phillips is known for his mystery tales featuring Los Angeles-based private investigator Ivan Monk—tales that deal with a variety of political and social issues as well as crime-solving. Phillips introduced the shrewd, physically imposing Monk in *Violent Spring,* a 1994 publication set during the turbulent, post-riot period after the acquittal in 1992 of Los Angeles police officers involved in the videotaped beating of African-American motorist Rodney King.

The story begins during a public event—the groundbreaking ceremony for a new mall opening at the "riot epicenter"—to promote social healing, which goes awry when the corpse of a Korean shop owner is unearthed in front of the media. Other Korean merchants hire Monk to find the murderer. During his investigation, Monk fails to endear himself to the F.B.I. and the Los Angeles police, both of whose members are reluctant to cooperate, and his obligatory contact with various street people and gang members proves equally laborious.

Monk soon comes to realize that certain individuals who are wealthy and powerful stand to profit further from the racial and economic divisions in Los Angeles. One of the few subjects on which blacks and whites—rich and poor—seem to agree is that Monk himself is not to be trusted. Such suspicion renders Monk's task doubly difficult. Marvin Lachman, writing in *Armchair Detective,* stated that Phillips undermines the effectiveness of *Violent Spring* by incorporating social commentary with crime solving. "Political and social issues are legitimate fare for the mystery," Lachman acknowledged, "but they must not overwhelm the elements of escape fiction that cause us to dip into this genre rather than the mainstream." Lachman termed *Violent Spring* "a literary hybrid."

Phillips followed *Violent Spring* with *Perdition, U.S.A.,* in which Monk probes the violent demise of several African-Americans in the impoverished town of Pacific Shores. Monk initially dismisses the killings as gang related, but he soon comes to find that the gang members in the area are being exploited by those in power. "By the time he's finished," wrote Michael Harris in the *Los Angeles Times Book Review,* "Monk has dealt with gar-

ment sweatshops, a phony-watch sales ring, a band of 'multiracial skinheads' . . . and a plot to assassinate a liberal U.S. senator." Harris ranked *Perdition, U.S.A.* among "*why*dunits—mystery novels with a progressive political slant," and he praised Monk as "an asset to the series—flawed, human and angry, but [also] level-headed, brainy *and* brawny."

Bad Night Is Falling, the next Monk mystery, deals, like its predecessors, with social, racial, and class issues. It finds Monk investigating a firebombing at a housing project that killed three members of a Mexican-American family. Members of a Black Muslim group providing security for the complex are suspected—wrongly, they say—of the bombing; they hire Monk to clear their names. Meanwhile, Monk's romantic interest, Judge Jill Kodama, is threatened with loss of her position because of her doubts about mandatory-sentencing laws. *Booklist* critic Wes Lukowsky deemed the novel "solid hard-boiled fare" in the tradition of such mystery writers as Ross Macdonald. A *Publishers Weekly* reviewer found it marred at times by "sloppy writing and/or editing," but thought the plot "compelling" and the characters well-drawn. Lukowsky concluded by calling the book "a thoughtful and intelligent mystery."

After publishing a non-series mystery, *The Jook,* Phillips brought Monk back in *Only the Wicked.* Monk's cousin, Kennesaw Riles, is murdered after the funeral of a friend with whom he had played baseball in the Negro Leagues. As Monk investigates, he journeys to Mississippi, where he meets a renowned blues musician and tangles with a white supremacist group. The novel is "full of neighborhood activity, baseball and jazz history, and general comments on the human condition," reported Rex Klett in *Library Journal. Booklist* contributor Bill Ott thought the book had "too much backstory passed off as conversation" but was "an otherwise gripping tale," with historical information well integrated into the plot and an appealing hero in Monk.

High Hand is the first book in a series featuring Martha Chainey, a rarity among crime-fiction protagonists because the protagonist is an African-American woman. She is a former Las Vegas entertainer now delivering money for a mobster. When she is robbed of $7 million she was supposed to drop off, she receives orders to track down the thieves and get the money back within seventy-two hours. In the course of this hazardous assignment, she becomes involved with an Indian tribe operating a gambling casino. "Phillips never loses a moment's momentum while riffing on politics, diversity, and the Tao of Vegas," remarked a *Kirkus Reviews* critic. A *Publishers Weekly* reviewer deemed *High Hand* a "sordid tale," with Chainey placed in sexually humiliating situations, but noted that the book has a "fast-moving, uncomplicated plot." The reviewer did praise Phillips's use of historical material about African Americans in Las Vegas, as did *Booklist*'s Ott. Ott added that the novel combines "the cartoon appeal of the best blaxspoitation flicks" with "three-dimensional characters living in an all-too-real world," and he summed it up as "a fine debut" for the series. The *Kirkus Reviews* critic found the book flawed by occasional misuse of words but "otherwise brilliant," with a fascinating heroine. "Here's hoping Phillips buffs up his prose," the critic concluded, "because Chainey's too good to give up."

Phillips once told *CA:* "What better time to be a writer? How else can we try to capture the strangeness, the fear and the hope in all of us?"

BIOGRAPHICAL/CRITICAL SOURCES:

PERIODICALS

Armchair Detective, summer, 1994, Marvin Lachman, review of *Violent Spring,* p. 305.
Booklist, February 1, 1994, p. 997; May 1, 1998, Wes Lukowsky, review of *Bad Night Is Falling,* p. 1506; September 1, 2000, Wes Lukowsky, review of *The Jook,* p. 72; August, 2000, Bill Ott, review of *Only the Wicked,* p. 122; October 15, 2000, Bill Ott, review of *High Hand,* p. 425.
Kirkus Reviews, September 15, 2000, review of *High Hand,* p. 1320.
Library Journal, September 1, 2000, Rex Klett, review of *Only the Wicked,* p. 255.
Los Angeles Times Book Review, June 2, 1996, p. 6.
Publishers Weekly, May 26, 1997, p. 83; May 4, 1998, review of *Bad Night Is Falling,* p. 206; September 25, 2000, review of *High Hand,* p. 90.

OTHER

Gary Phillips's Home Page, http://www.gdphillips.com/ (October 9, 2001).

*   *   *

PIERS, Robert
    See ANTHONY, Piers

POUNDS, Norman John Greville   1912-

PERSONAL: Born February 23, 1912, in Bath, England; son of John Greville and Camilla Martha Minnie (Fisher) Pounds; married June 31, 1938. *Education:* Cambridge University, B.A., 1934, M.A., 1940; University of London, B.A., 1942, Ph.D., 1944. *Avocational interests:* Travel, music (especially chamber music), archaeology.

ADDRESSES: Office—Department of History, Indiana University, Bloomington, IN 47401.

CAREER: Cambridge University, Fitzwilliam College, Cambridge, England, lecturer and tutor, 1944-50; Indiana University at Bloomington, IN, professor of geography, 1950-59, university professor of history and geography, 1959-77, university professor emeritus, 1977—, chairman of department of East European studies, chairman of department of geography, 1962-65. Visiting professor, University of Wisconsin, 1949-50; Rose Morgan Professor, University of Kansas, 1958-59; Borah Lecturer, University of Idaho, 1961. Visiting lecturer, Austrian Academy of Sciences, 1975.

MEMBER: Royal Geographical Society, Economic History Society, Royal Archaeological Institute (president, 1987-90), Society of Antiquaries of London (fellow), Cambridge Antiquarian Society (president, 1992-94).

AWARDS, HONORS: "Brown Derby Award" from Indiana University chapter of Sigma Delta Chi, for teaching; Senior Class Distinguished Teaching Award, Indiana University, 1969; Sagamore of the Wabash award, governor of Indiana, for services to education, 1989; Honorary Fellow, Fitzwilliam College (Cambridge, England).

WRITINGS:

An Historical and Political Geography of Europe, Harrap (London, England), 1947.
An Introduction to Economic Geography, J. Murray (London, England), 1951, 4th edition, 1970.
Ruhr: A Study in History and Economic Geography, Faber (London, England), 1952, Indiana University Press (Bloomington, IN), 1953.
Europe and the Mediterranean, McGraw (New York, NY), 1953, 2nd edition published as *Europe and the Soviet Union,* 1966.
North America, J. Murray (London, England), 1955, 3rd edition, 1971.

U.S.A.: Its Geography and Growth, J. Murray (London, England), 1955, 3rd edition, 1962.

(With Emlyn Jones) *Beyond the Oceans: Eurasia, Africa, Australia,* Rand McNally (Chicago, IL), 1956.

(Editor, with Edward Cooper) *World Geography,* 5th edition (Pounds was not associated with earlier editions), South-Western (Cincinnati, OH), 1957, 8th edition (with J. W. Taylor), 1974.

(With Nicholas Spulber) *Resources and Planning in Eastern Europe,* Indiana University Press (Bloomington, IN), 1957.

(With W. Parker) *Coal and Steel in Western Europe,* Indiana University Press (Bloomington, IN), 1957.

The Upper Silesian Industrial Region, Indiana University Press (Bloomington, IN), 1958.

The Geography of Iron and Steel, Hutchinson (London, England), 1959, 5th revised edition, 1971.

Hungary, Bulgaria and Rumania, Doubleday (Garden City, NY), 1961.

(Editor) *Geographical Essays on Eastern Europe,* Indiana University Press (Bloomington, IN), 1961, reprinted, Greenwood Press (Westport, CT), 1972.

The Earth and You, Rand McNally (Chicago, IL), 1962.

Divided Germany and Berlin, Van Nostrand (New York, NY), 1962.

Political Geography, McGraw (New York, NY), 1963, 2nd edition, 1972.

An Atlas of Middle Eastern Affairs, Praeger (New York, NY), 1963, revised edition, 1964.

The Economic Pattern of Modern Germany, J. Murray (London, England), 1963, Rand McNally (Chicago, IL), 1964.

An Atlas of European Affairs, Praeger (New York, NY), 1964.

Poland between East and West, Van Nostrand (New York, NY), 1964.

(Editor) *Europe: With Focus on Germany,* Fideler (Grand Rapids, MI), 1965.

Eastern Europe, Aldine (Hawthorne, NY), 1969.

(With V. L. Benes) *Poland,* Praeger (New York, NY), 1970.

An Historical Geography of Europe, Cambridge University Press (Cambridge, England), Volume I: *450 B.C.-A.D. 1330,* 1973, Volume II: *1500-1840,* 1979, Volume III: *1800-1914,* 1985, all volumes reprinted, 1990.

An Economic History of Medieval Europe, Longman (London, England), 1974, 2nd edition, 1994.

Success in Geography: Human and Regional, J. Murray (London, England), 1976.

World Geography, Silver Burdett Co. (Morristown, NJ), 1980.

Hearth & Home: A History of Material Culture, Indiana University Press (Bloomington, IN), 1989.

The Medieval Castle in England and Wales: A Social and Political History, Cambridge University Press (New York, NY), 1990.

The Culture of the English People: Iron Age to the Industrial Revolution, Cambridge University Press (New York, NY), 1994.

A History of the English Parish: The Culture of Religion from Augustine to Victoria, Cambridge University Press (New York, NY), 2000.

Contributor to *France,* edited by Virginia Creed, Fideler (Grand Rapids, MI), 1974; and *Germany,* edited by Gerhart Heinrich Seger, Fideler (Grand Rapids, MI), 1978. Also contributor to professional journals.

SIDELIGHTS: Norman John Greville Pounds, a cultural historian and geographer, spent the bulk of his career teaching at Indiana University. While there he established himself as an expert on the geography of Europe, and during the 1960s and early 1970s he wrote a great deal about Eastern Europe behind the Iron Curtain. Pounds is perhaps best known for his three-volume *An Historical Geography of Europe,* a work that "stands above reproach," according to P. K. O'Brien in the *Times Literary Supplement.* Since becoming a professor emeritus in 1977, Pounds has added to his academic credentials by writing cultural histories of England in which he explores the connections between the material culture and social relationships.

Pounds's writings on the history of material culture began with *Hearth & Home: A History of Material Culture* and continued with the more ambitious *The Culture of the English People: Iron Age to the Industrial Revolution.* The latter work surveys 2,000 years of material culture in England, with special concentration on housing, furniture, food preparation, and medicine. In his *History Today* review of *The Culture of the English People,* Peter Laslett wrote: "This is a brave and valuable book; the outcome of a long and successful career working at its subject matter and expounding it. It provides in judicious, quite readable form just that which the reader of history, and to a considerable extent the writer of it, needs to know as cultural 'background' to her chosen topic or his, where the word 'background' should be held to slough off its faintly patronising garb." Laslett further praised the book for "the outstanding achievement of marrying material culture with [the] intellectual, ideological and aesthetic." *Journal of Modern History* contributor Moira Donald noted that *The Culture of the English People* "is innovative insofar as it broadens the notion of culture to include as central to the study of premodern traditions and social relationships the material world in which those rituals and relations operated. The book is extremely wide-ranging and has the merit of linking physical, literary, and statistical evidence in a coherent and persuasive manner."

In *A History of the English Parish: The Culture of Religion from Augustine to Victoria,* Pounds concentrates on the archaeological and documentary records of English parish churches to build "a vivid picture of the regular life of the parish," to quote Colin Cunningham in the *Times Literary Supplement.* Cunningham added: "Above all, [the] book is packed with fascinating detail; and this story is emphatically one of details. Often they are of no more than local relevance, but they are none the less integral to the tapestry of parish life."

BIOGRAPHICAL/CRITICAL SOURCES:

PERIODICALS

Antiquity, June, 1995, Elaine Grummit, review of *The Culture of the English People: Iron Age to the Industrial Revolution,* p. 431.
Historian, winter 1996, Olivia Remie Constable, review of *An Economic History of Medieval Europe,* p. 448.
History Today, September, 1995, Peter Laslett, review of *The Culture of the English People: Iron Age to the Industrial Revolution,* p. 55.
Journal of Modern History, September, 1997, Moira Donald, review of *The Culture of the English People: Iron Age to the Industrial Revolution,* p. 573.
Journal of Social History, spring 1996, review of *The Culture of the English People: Iron Age to the Industrial Revolution,* p. 728.
Observer Review, July 17, 1994, Keith Thomas, "Most People Were Ill, Most of the Time."
Times Literary Supplement, July 25, 1980; April 25, 1986, P. K. O'Brien, review of *An Historical Geography of Europe,* Volume III: *1800-1914,* p. 44; September 20, 1991, R. B. Dobson, review of *The Medieval Castle in England and Wales: A Social and Political History,* p. 27; October 14, 1994, Keith Wrighton, review of *The Culture of the English People: Iron Age to the Industrial Revolution,* p. 6; September 1, 2000, Colin Cunningham, "Rats in the Belfry, Squeaking in the Choir," p. 32.

PRINGLE, Peter   1940-

PERSONAL: Born June 28, 1940, in England; son of Herbert John (an air force officer) and Leslie (White) Pringle. *Education:* Oxford University, B.A. (with honors), 1962. *Avocational interests:* Cooking, walking, sailing, flying, collecting fossils.

ADDRESSES: Office—London *Independent,* 405 East 42nd St., New York, NY 10017.

CAREER: London Sunday Times, London, England, reporter, 1968-75, New York City bureau chief, beginning 1975. Washington correspondent for London *Observer.* New York City correspondent for London *Independent.*

WRITINGS:

(With others) *Insight on Middle East War,* Viking (New York, NY), 1974.
(With others) *Insight on Portugal,* Deutsch (London, England), 1974.
(With Peter Cole) *Can You Positively Identify This Man?: George Ince and the Barn Murder,* Deutsch (London, England), 1975.
(With James Spigelman) *The Nuclear Barons,* Holt (New York, NY), 1981.
(With William Arkin) *S.T.O.P.: The Secret U.S. Plan for Nuclear War,* Norton (New York, NY), 1983.
(With Nigel Hawkes, Geoffrey Lean, David Leigh, Robin McKie, and Andrew Wilson) *The Worst Accident in the World: Chernobyl—The End of the Nuclear Dream,* William Collins (London, England), 1986, Vintage Books (New York, NY), 1987.
Cornered: Big Tobacco at the Bar of Justice, Holt (New York, NY), 1998, published in England as *Dirty Press: Big Tobacco at the Bar of Justice,* Aurum (London, England), 1998.
(With Philip Jacobson) *Those Are Real Bullets: Bloody Sunday, Derry, 1972,* Grove Press (New York, NY), 2001.

SIDELIGHTS: British journalist Peter Pringle has written nonfiction books, usually in collaboration, on a variety of topics, including nuclear energy and weapons, lawsuits against the tobacco industry, and strife in Northern Ireland. *The Nuclear Barons* by Pringle and James Spigelman aims to provide a thorough history of nuclear energy in terms of both its military and commercial development. According to *Nation* reviewer Jessica Mitford, Pringle and Spigelman's "valiant effort" has succeeded: "For the general reader, *The Nu-*

clear *Barons* is an excellent overview; for those who want to probe deeper, a valuable research tool with meticulous notes and bibliography. A felicitous collaboration." Mitford thought Pringle and Spigelman at their best when describing the expansion of nuclear power from weaponry into the commercial arena, a description that also includes the authors' recollection of "the extravagant hopes once held out for this source of energy . . . [and] the Machiavellian attempts to suppress data pointing to its dangers." In the *Washington Post Book World*, Gregg Easterbrook directed his attention to Pringle and Spigelman's argument that "making electricity from atoms never made much sense, either economically or technologically. Yet utility executives and government officials the world over have longed for it, like boys dreaming of hot rods. They've sunk hundreds of billions of dollars into it, then often looked the other way when their dream machines produced more grief than power. . . . [Pringle and Spigelman] attribute most of nuclear power's appeal to the lure of 'Big Science.' . . . It is here that Pringle and Spigelman are most convincing, where so many critiques of the nuclear industry falter. They understand that human foibles and well-intentioned blunders, not sinister conspiracies, lie at the heart of the nuclear mess." Mitford, while impressed with *The Nuclear Barons* on the whole, was disturbed by what she called its ironic conclusion, the fact that Pringle and Spigelman feel there may be no alternatives to nuclear power. She felt that the authors should spend time discussing alternate sources of energy. If they did, she wrote, "I should be first in line to buy such a book by these authors."

Pringle's *Cornered: Big Tobacco at the Bar of Justice* details the history of the multi-state lawsuit against tobacco companies that led the industry to agree in 1997 to pay the states $369 billion to help cover the cost of treating smoking-related illnesses. "The dramatic events that led to the settlement make for a remarkable story, and Pringle gets the human details just right," commented a *Publishers Weekly* reviewer. *New York Times Book Review* contributor Laura Mansnerus remarked, "There are many threads to be pulled together, and Peter Pringle pulls them nicely." She voiced reservations, however, about his "conclusion that the system works." She allowed that in the tobacco suit, "the system did work in that it promised to accomplish something that many people want accomplished," but she observed, "Pringle does not ask what a corporation's obligation to public health consists of, or how much we want any arm of government to protect us from ourselves." Still, Pringle's narration of the legal battle won praise from several other reviewers. "It is meticulously researched yet reads like a novel," wrote Eris Weaver in *Library Journal*, while *Booklist*'s Mary Carroll added that "Pringle recounts this extraordinarily complex story gracefully." *Business Week* reviewer David Greising called the book "a deftly written, comprehensive account," and thought that Pringle's "particular strength is his use of detail and shrewd character judgments to humanize the story."

Pringle and Philip Jacobson discuss one of the most traumatic events in the troubled history of Northern Ireland in *Those Are Real Bullets: Bloody Sunday, Derry, 1972,* which details British soldiers' killing of thirteen Irish civilians during a civil rights march in the city of Derry. The authors use interviews and government documents to support their position that British political and military leaders planned and sanctioned the attack. Pringle and Jacobson describe the tragedy "in wrenching fashion," noted a *Kirkus Reviews* critic, while providing a broader context with background on the persistent Irish-British, Catholic-Protestant strife in Northern Ireland. The book is "a lucid and bitter chronicle of yet another day that lives in infamy," the critic concluded.

BIOGRAPHICAL/CRITICAL SOURCES:

PERIODICALS

Booklist, February 15, 1998, Mary Carroll, review of *Cornered: Big Tobacco at the Bar of Justice,* p. 956.

Business Week, February 23, 1998, David Greising, "War and Peace on the Tobacco Front," p. 23.

Globe and Mail (Toronto), August 9, 1986.

Insight on the News, July 6, 1998, Kenneth Smith, review of *Cornered: Big Tobacco at the Bar of Justice,* p. 36.

Kirkus Reviews, November 1, 2000, review of *Those Are Real Bullets: Bloody Sunday, Derry, 1972,* pp. 1534-1535.

Library Journal, March 1, 1998, Eris Weaver, review of *Cornered: Big Tobacco at the Bar of Justice,* p. 108.

Nation, May 8, 1982, Jessica Mitford, review of *The Nuclear Barons.*

New York Times Book Review, January 31, 1982; March 15, 1998, Laura Mansnerus, "The Suing of Mr. Butts," p. 34.

Publishers Weekly, January 19, 1998, review of *Cornered: Big Tobacco at the Bar of Justice,* p. 366.

Spectator, February 20, 1982.

Washington Post Book World, September 20, 1981, Gregg Easterbrook, review of *The Nuclear Barons.**

RAAB, Lawrence 1946-

PERSONAL: Born May 8, 1946, in Pittsfield, MA; son of Edward Louis and Marjorie (maiden name, Young) Raab; married Judith Ann Michaels, December 29, 1968; children: Jennifer. Education: Middlebury College, B.A., 1968; Syracuse University, M.A., 1972.

ADDRESSES: Home—139 Bulkley St., Williamstown, MA 01267. Office—Department of English, Williams College, Williamstown, MA 01267. E-mail—lawrence.e.raab@williams.edu.

CAREER: American University, Washington, DC, instructor in English, 1970-71; New York State Council for the Arts, Syracuse, instructor at poetry workshop for children, 1972; University of Michigan, Ann Arbor, lecturer in English, autumn, 1974; Bread Loaf Writer's Conference, Middlebury, VT, staff assistant, 1974-76; Williams College, Williamstown, MA, lecturer in English (Morris Professor of Rhetoric), 1976—. Has given poetry readings at colleges and universities throughout the United States.

MEMBER: Phi Beta Kappa, Blue Key.

AWARDS, HONORS: Woodrow Wilson fellowship, 1968; CINE Eagle from Council on International Nontheatrical Events, 1968, for film Or I'll Come to You; Academy of American Poets prize, 1972, for "The Wolf 's Journey"; creative writing grant from National Endowment for the Arts, 1972-73; National Endowment for the Arts fellow, 1972 and 1984; Robert Frost fellow at Bread Loaf Writers' Conference, 1973; junior fellow of University of Michigan Society of Fellows, 1973-76; Creative Writing fellowship, Massachusetts Council on the Arts, 1982; Bess Hokin prize from Poetry magazine, 1983; National Book Award nomination, 1993, for What We Don't Know about Each Other; Charity Randall Citation, International Poetry Forum, 2000. Residencies at Yaddo, 1979-80, 1982, 1984, 1986-90, 1994, 1996, 1998, 2001, and at Mac-Dowell Colony, 1993, 1995, 1997, 2000.

WRITINGS:

POETRY

Mysteries of the Horizon, Doubleday (New York, NY), 1972.
The Collector of Cold Weather, Ecco Press (New York, NY), 1976.
Other Children, Carnegie-Mellon University Press (Pittsburgh, PA), 1986.
What We Don't Know about Each Other, Penguin Books (New York, NY), 1993.
(With Stephen Dunn) Winter at the Caspian Sea, Palanquin Press (Aiken, SC), 1999.
The Probable World, Penguin Books (New York, NY), 2000.

Work represented in anthologies, including The Norton Anthology of Poetry, third edition, Norton, 1983; The Best American Poetry 1992, edited by Charles Simic, Collier, 1992; The Best American Poetry 1993, edited by Louise Gluck, Scribner/Collier, 1993; A Book of Luminous Things, edited by Czeslaw Milosz, Harcourt, 1996; and The Best American Poetry 2000, edited by Rita Dove, Collier, 2000. Author of film scripts The Distances, 1967, and Or I'll Come to You, 1968. Also author of The Birds (adaptation of a play by Aristophanes), first produced in Ann Arbor, MI, at Power Center, April, 1975. Also author of Dracula (libretto for an opera adapted from the novel by Bram Stoker), as yet unpublished and unproduced. Contributor of poems, essays, reviews, and translations from the French, to literary journals, including Poetry, Paris Review, Kayak, Shenandoah, and Prairie Schooner, and to popular magazines, including New Yorker, Atlantic Monthly, and American Scholar. Editor of Frontiers, 1967 and 1968; member of editorial board of Alkahest, 1968.

WORK IN PROGRESS: New and Selected Poems, for Penguin Books (New York, NY), 2003.

SIDELIGHTS: Free-verse poet Lawrence Raab has published six volumes of his work, which uses simple, everyday language to explore a wide range of large, complicated issues. In What We Don't Know about Each Other, for instance, observations of the natural world, including dogs, birds, and trees, lead to speculations about the supernatural, such as angels, ghosts, and extraterrestrial life. "While such topics prompt mediocre poets into clichés, Raab's highly lyrical meditations are so concrete that readers are sucked into his magical netherworld," remarked a Publishers Weekly reviewer. Poetry contributor Thomas M. Disch found the collection, and Raab's body of work, not to his liking. Raab's "language is as flat as Kansas in August," Disch commented, although he allowed that Raab had received so much acclaim that his "esthetic respectability is an established fact."

The Probable World again shows Raab using unpretentious language to discuss "big ideas," a phrase that provides the title of a poem in which he notes, "We watch the news, we read the papers, afraid, sometimes, of what we understand." In a poem about spirituality, he looks for guidance but finds none: "Week by week we were on our own." And he contemplates death by writing, "Think of the truck out of control. . . . Think of the terrorist planting his bomb. Not one of us is spared such imaginings." A *Publishers Weekly* critic thought Raab failed to fully exploit his "potentially volatile subjects," saying the collection had "only occasionally compelling narrative motifs" and a verse style that is "neither formally demanding nor linguistically playful." *Booklist* contributor Donna Seaman, however, praised this volume's poems as "simultaneously gentle and robust," filled with "down-to-earth wisdom and quiet passion." Matthew Flamm, writing in the *New York Times Book Review,* found in the collection "transcendent moments . . . in language that's plain as day." Raab is "a graceful writer," with "no interest in stylistic variation," Flamm commented, adding, "But he does have a voice that puzzles over everything, and that rescues *The Probable World* from monotony."

BIOGRAPHICAL/CRITICAL SOURCES:

PERIODICALS

Booklist, March 15, 2000, Donna Seaman, review of *The Probable World,* p. 1319.
New York Times Book Review, July 23, 2000, Matthew Flamm, review of *The Probable World,* p. 16.
Poetry, February, 1994, Thomas M. Disch, review of *What We Don't Know about Each Other,* p. 285.
Publishers Weekly, June 14, 1993, review of *What We Don't Know about Each Other,* p. 66; April 17, 2000, review of *The Probable World,* p. 72.
Wall Street Journal, April 21, 2000, David Lehman, review of *The Probable World.*

*   *   *

RAMSAY, Jay
See CAMPBELL, (John) Ramsey

*   *   *

ROOM, Adrian   1933-

PERSONAL: Born September 27, 1933, in Melksham, England; son of Richard Geoffrey and Cynthia (West) Room. *Education:* Received degree with honors from Exeter College, Oxford, England, 1957; Oxford University, diploma in education, 1958.

ADDRESSES: Home—173 The Causeway, Petersfield, Hampshire GU31 4LN, England.

CAREER: Milton Abbey School, Blandford, England, teacher, 1958-60; Cambridge University, King's College, Cambridge, England, senior language teacher and housemaster, 1960-69; Anglo-American Sixth Form College, Faringdon, England, 1969-71; freelance teacher, researcher, and writer, 1971-74; Ministry of Defense, lecturer, 1974-80, senior lecturer in Russian, 1980-83; full-time writer, 1984—. *Military service:* Royal Naval Reserve, Special Branch, 1952-79, retiring as lieutenant commander.

MEMBER: Association of Teachers of Russian (founding member), Royal Geographical Society (fellow), Names Society (vice president).

AWARDS, HONORS: Winner of Russian short story translation prize from Translators Association, 1985.

WRITINGS:

Place-names of the World, Rowman and Littlefield (Totowa, NJ), 1974, revised as *Placenames of the World: Origins and Meanings of the Names for over 5,000 Natural Features, Countries, Capitals, Territories, Cities, and Historic Sites,* McFarland (Jefferson, NC), 1997.
Great Britain: A Background Studies Dictionary (English-Russian), Russian Language (Moscow, Russia), 1978.
Room's Dictionary of Confusibles, Routledge & Kegan Paul (London, England), 1979, published as *The Penguin Dictionary of Confusibles,* Penguin Books (New York, NY), 1980.
Place-Name Changes since 1900: A World Gazetteer, Scarecrow Press (Metuchen, NJ), 1979, revised as *Place-Name Changes 1900-1991,* Scarecrow Press (Metuchen, NJ), 1993.
Room's Dictionary of Distinguishables, Routledge & Kegan Paul (London, England), 1980.
Dictionary of Trade Name Origins, Routledge & Kegan Paul (London, England), 1981, revised as *NTC's Dictionary of Trade Name Origins,* NTC (Lincolnwood, IL), 1991, revised as *Trade Name Origins,* NTC (Lincolnwood, IL), 1997.
Naming Names: A Book of Pseudonyms and Name Changes with a Who's Who, McFarland (Jefferson, NC), 1981, 2nd edition revised as *Dictionary of Pseudonyms and Their Origins, with Stories of Name Changes,* 1989.
Room's Classical Dictionary: The Origins of the Names of Characters in Classical Mythology, Routledge & Kegan Paul (Boston, MA), 1983.
Dictionary of Cryptic Crossword Clues, Routledge & Kegan Paul (Boston, MA), 1983.

A Concise Dictionary of Modern Place-Names in Great Britain and Ireland, Oxford University Press (New York, NY), 1983.

Guide to British Place-Names, Longman (London, England), 1985.

Dictionary of Confusing Words and Meanings, Routledge & Kegan Paul (London, England), 1985.

A Dictionary of Irish Place-Names, Appletree Press (Belfast, Northern Ireland), 1986, revised edition, 1994.

Dictionary of Translated Names and Titles, Routledge & Kegan Paul (Boston, MA), 1986.

A Dictionary of True Etymologies, Routledge & Kegan Paul (Boston, MA), 1986.

Dictionary of Changes in Meaning, Routledge & Kegan Paul (New York, NY), 1986.

Dictionary of Coin Names, Routledge & Kegan Paul (New York, NY), 1986.

Dictionary of Britain, Oxford University Press (New York, NY), 1986.

Dictionary of Astronomical Names, Routledge & Kegan Paul (New York, NY), 1988.

Dictionary of Contrasting Pairs, Routledge & Kegan Paul (New York, NY), 1988.

Dictionary of Place-Names in the British Isles, Bloomsbury (London, England), 1988.

Dictionary of World Place Names Derived from British Names, Routledge & Kegan Paul (New York, NY), 1989.

Bloomsbury Dictionary of Dedications, Bloomsbury (London, England), 1990, reprinted as *Tuttle Dictionary of Dedications,* Tuttle (Boston, MA), 1992.

(With Leslie Dunkling) *The Guinness Book of Money,* Facts on File (New York, NY), 1990.

NTC's Dictionary of Word Origins, NTC (Lincolnwood, IL), 1991, revised as *The Fascinating Origins of Everyday Words,* NTC (Lincolnwood, IL), 1997.

Brewer's Dictionary of Names, Cassell (New York, NY), 1992, published as *Cassell Dictionary of Proper Names,* Cassell (New York, NY), 1994.

Corporate Eponymy: A Biographical Dictionary of the Persons behind the Names of Major American, European, and Asian Businesses, McFarland (Jefferson, NC), 1992.

Dictionary of Place Names, Bloomsbury (London, England), 1993.

The Naming of Animals: An Appellative Reference to Domestic, Work, and Show Animals, Real and Fictional, McFarland (Jefferson, NC), 1993.

African Place Names: Origins and Meanings of the Names for over 2,000 Natural Features, Towns, Cities, Provinces, and Countries, McFarland (Jefferson, NC), 1994.

Dictionary of First Names, Cassell (London, England), 1995.

An Alphabetical Guide to the Language of Name Studies, Scarecrow Press (Lanham, MD), 1996.

Literally Entitled: A Dictionary of the Origins of the Titles of over 1,300 Major Literary Works of the Nineteenth and Twentieth Centuries, McFarland (Jefferson, NC), 1996.

Place Names of Russia and the Former Soviet Union: Origins and Meanings of the Names for over 2,000 Natural Features, Towns, Regions, and Countries, McFarland (Jefferson, NC), 1996.

Who's Who in Classical Mythology, NTC (Lincolnwood, IL), 1997.

Brewer's Dictionary of Phrase and Fable, 16th edition, HarperResource (New York, NY), 1999, published in England as *Brewer's Modern Dictionary of Phrase and Fable,* Cassell (London, England), 2000.

Dictionary of Great Britain, Russkii Iazyk (Moscow, Russia), 1999.

Dictionary of Word Histories, Cassell (London, England), 1999.

Cassell's Foreign Words and Phrases, Cassell (London, England), 2000.

A Dictionary of Art Titles: The Origins of the Names and Titles of 3,000 Works of Art, McFarland (Jefferson, NC), 2000.

A Dictionary of Music Titles: The Origins of the Names and Titles of 3,500 Musical Compositions, McFarland (Jefferson, NC), 2000.

(Editor) *Dictionary of Confusable Words,* Fitzroy Dearborn Publishers (Chicago, IL), 2000.

Scriptwriter for British Broadcasting Corporation (BBC). Contributor to *Everyman's Encyclopaedia.* Also contributor to newspapers and journals.

SIDELIGHTS: Adrian Room is a "top toponymist and onomastician," in the words of *Library Journal* reviewer Carol Spielman Lezak in a piece on his *Dictionary of Pseudonyms and Their Origins, with Stories of Name Changes.* A toponymist is one who studies place names; an onomastician studies the origins and meanings of words. Room has indeed been a productive worker in these and related fields, with roughly forty volumes on place, personal names, business, and other names, as well as words in general, to his credit.

Critics have described some of Room's works as useful to almost any reader, others as designed for a specialized audience. They have praised many of his works as having significant educational value. *Placenames of the World: Origins and Meanings of the Names for over*

5,000 Natural Features, Countries, Capitals, Territories, Cities, and Historic Sites is "an easy-to-use, straightforward, useful reference source," a *Booklist* reviewer reported. Of *African Place Names: Origins and Meanings of the Names for over 2,000 Natural Features, Towns, Cities, Provinces, and Countries, RQ* contributor M. Elaine Hughes remarked, "For those who have a need of this type of information this book is absolutely essential." *Literally Entitled: A Dictionary of the Origins of the Titles of over 1,300 Major Literary Works of the Nineteenth and Twentieth Centuries* "offers interesting information on the most frequently used words in titles and the sources most often quoted," related a *Booklist* reviewer.

Also, some reviewers have noted that Room's books are not only informative but entertaining. For example, an *Economist* critic thought that *The Guinness Book of Money*, "rather than a dry reference work . . . is an ideal bedside—or toiletside—companion." Lezak observed that the *Dictionary of Pseudonyms and Their Origins, with Stories of Name Changes* is "filled with fascinating tidbits of information gleaned from copious research," including reasons people have adopted pseudonyms. *Corporate Eponymy: A Biographical Dictionary of the Persons behind the Names of Major American, European, and Asian Businesses* "gives insight into the identities of people behind products ranging from hamburgers to automobiles to chain stores," wrote Diane Turner in *RQ*. And although a *Booklist* reviewer found *The Naming of Animals: An Appellative Reference to Domestic, Work, and Show Animals, Real and Fictional* to be a "curious work" with a "sizable quantity of esoteric information," the reviewer added that "it makes for fascinating reading for animal lovers."

Room once told *CA:* "Words, with which we communicate, are of extreme importance and are constantly absorbing. Why do we use the words that we do? Where do the words come from? Why does our speech not match our writing? How do the words of one language differ from another in the way they are used to communicate? In my everyday professional work and in my books I try to deal with some of these questions, aiming to go behind the standard dictionaries and reference works—and if possible beyond them. Especially fascinating, and in my view under-rated and under-promoted, are names. Names are words, of course, but what makes a name a name? Where do our own names come from? How do we set about naming places? What motivates people to change their names? How do trade names originate? Name-study is rarely taught as an academic subject, but why not? Place-names, for a start,

contain a mine of information about history, language, geography, demography, psychology, and the human race as a whole. Most of my writing is consciously name-oriented, and I aim to bridge the gap between the conventional dictionary and encyclopedia, which may have little information on names, and the specialist who works on onomastics. At the same time I aim to popularize name-study as a worthwhile and highly rewarding topic."

BIOGRAPHICAL/CRITICAL SOURCES:

PERIODICALS

Booklist, February 1, 1994, review of *The Naming of Animals: An Appellative Reference to Domestic, Work, and Show Animals, Real and Fictional,* p. 1027; May 1, 1996, review of *Literally Entitled: A Dictionary of the Origins of the Titles of over 1,300 Major Literary Works of the Nineteenth and Twentieth Centuries,* p. 1530; June 1, 1997, review of *Placenames of the World: Origins and Meanings of the Names for over 5,000 Natural Features, Countries, Capitals, Territories, Cities, and Historic Sites,* p. 764; July, 2000, Mary Ellen Quinn, reviews of *A Dictionary of Art Titles: The Origins of the Names and Titles of 3,000 Works of Art* and *A Dictionary of Music Titles: The Origins of the Names and Titles of 3,500 Musical Compositions,* p. 2056; October 15, 2000, Mary Ellen Quinn, review of *Brewer's Dictionary of Phrase and Fable,* p. 480; November 15, 2000, review of *Dictionary of Confusable Words,* p. 666.
Economist, December 22, 1990, review of *The Guinness Book of Money,* p. 118.
Library Journal, May 15, 1997, Elizabeth Connor, review of *Place-Names of the World,* p. 73; October 1, 1998, Carol Spielman Lezak, review of *Dictionary of Pseudonyms and Their Origins, with Stories of Name Changes,* p. 78.
RQ, spring, 1993, Diane Turner, review of *Corporate Eponymy: A Biographical Dictionary of the Persons behind the Names of Major American, European, and Asian Businesses,* p. 421; summer, 1994, Jeris Cassel, review of *Place-Name Changes 1900-1991,* p. 562; winter, 1994, M. Elaine Hughes, review of *African Place Names: Origins and Meanings of the Names for over 2,000 Natural Features, Towns, Cities, Provinces, and Countries,* p. 234.
Times Educational Supplement, May 18, 1984.
Times Literary Supplement, May 20, 1983; September 29, 2000, Adrian Tahourdin, "Raise a Glass to Canon Kir," p. 12.*

ROSS, Bernard L.
    See FOLLETT, Ken(neth Martin)

S-U

SALVATORE, R(obert) A(nthony) 1959-

PERSONAL: Born 1959, in Leominster, MA; married; wife's name, Diane; children: Bryan, Geno, Caitlin. *Education:* Fitchburg State College, B.S., 1981, B.A., 1989. *Avocational interests:* Softball, hockey, music, particularly Mozart.

ADDRESSES: Home—Massachusetts. *Agent*—Scott Siegel, P.O. Box 20340, New York, NY 10017.

CAREER: Fantasy writer. Worked at various jobs to support writing habit, 1982-90. Creator, with others, of game modules for "Fantasy Realms" computer game, TSR, 1999.

WRITINGS:

"FORGOTTEN REALMS" SERIES

The Crystal Shard (first volume of "Icewind Dale" trilogy; also see below), TSR (Lake Geneva, WI), 1988.

Streams of Silver (second volume of "Icewind Dale" trilogy; also see below), TSR (Lake Geneva, WI), 1989.

The Halfling's Gem (third volume of "Icewind Dale" trilogy; also see below), TSR (Lake Geneva, WI), 1990.

Homeland (first volume of "Dark Elf " trilogy; also see below), TSR (Lake Geneva, WI), 1990.

Exile (second volume of "Dark Elf " trilogy; also see below), TSR (Lake Geneva, WI), 1990.

Sojourn (third volume of "Dark Elf " trilogy; also see below), TSR (Lake Geneva, WI), 1991.

Canticle (first volume of "Cleric Quintet"; also see below), TSR (Lake Geneva, WI), 1991.

In Sylvan Shadows (second volume of "Cleric Quintet"; also see below), TSR (Lake Geneva, WI), 1992.

The Legacy (first volume of "Legacy of the Drow"; also see below), TSR (Lake Geneva, WI), 1992.

Night Masks (third volume of "Cleric Quintet"; also see below), TSR (Lake Geneva, WI), 1992.

The Fallen Fortress (fourth volume of "Cleric Quintet"; also see below), TSR (Lake Geneva, WI), 1993.

Starless Night (second volume of "Legacy of the Drow"; also see below), TSR (Lake Geneva, WI), 1993.

The Chaos Curse (fifth volume of "Cleric Quintet"; also see below), TSR (Lake Geneva, WI), 1994.

Siege of Darkness (third volume of "Legacy of the Drow"; also see below), TSR (Lake Geneva, WI), 1994.

Passage to Dawn (fourth volume of "Legacy of the Drow"; also see below), TSR (Lake Geneva, WI), 1996.

The Dark Elf Trilogy (contains *Homeland, Exile,* and *Sojourn*), TSR (Lake Geneva, WI), 1998.

The Silent Blade, TSR (Lake Geneva, WI), 1998.

The Spine of the World, TSR (Lake Geneva, WI), 1999.

The Cleric Quintet (contains *Canticle, In Sylvan Shadows, Night Masks, The Fallen Fortress,* and *The Chaos Curse*), TSR (Lake Geneva, WI), 1999.

Servant of the Shard, Wizards Publishing (Renton, WA), 2000.

The Icewind Dale Trilogy (contains *The Crystal Shard, Streams of Silver,* and *The Halfling's Gem*), Wizards Publishing (Renton, WA), 2001.

Legacy of the Drow (contains *The Legacy, Starless Night, Siege of Darkness,* and *Passage to Dawn*), Wizards Publishing (Renton, WA), 2001.

"SPEARWIELDER'S TALE" SERIES

The Woods out Back, Ace Books (New York, NY), 1993.

The Dragon's Dagger, Ace Books (New York, NY), 1994.

Dragonslayer's Return, Ace Books (New York, NY), 1995.

"CRIMSON SHADOW" TRILOGY

The Sword of Bedwyr, Warner Books (New York, NY), 1995.

Luthien's Gamble, Warner Books (New York, NY), 1996.

The Dragon King, Warner Books (New York, NY), 1996.

"DEMON WARS" SERIES

The Demon Awakens, Ballantine Books (New York, NY), 1997.

The Demon Spirit, Ballantine Books (New York, NY), 1997.

The Demon Apostle, Ballantine Books (New York, NY), 1999.

Mortalis, Ballantine Books (New York, NY), 2000.

Ascendance, Ballantine Books (New York, NY), 2001.

OTHER NOVELS

Echoes of the Fourth Magic, Roc (New York, NY), 1990.

The Witch's Daughter, Roc (New York, NY), 1991, updated, 1999.

Tarzan: The Epic Adventures (based on a character by Edgar Rice Burroughs), Ballantine Books (New York, NY), 1997.

The New Jedi Order: Vector Prime (part of "Star Wars" series), Del Rey Books (New York, NY), 1999.

Bastion of Darkness (part of "Chronicles of Ynis Aielle" series), Ballantine Books (New York, NY), 2000.

Sea of Swords, Wizards Publishing (Renton, WA), 2001.

WORK IN PROGRESS: More books in the "Demon Wars" series.

SIDELIGHTS: Writing fantasy novels that appeal to a young adult audience, R. A. Salvatore has taken inspiration from sources such as the legend of Robin Hood and the writings of J. R. R. Tolkien. He excels at crafting battle scenes that are integral to much of his work.

His "Forgotten Realms" novels are set in a world that is used in the Advanced Dungeons and Dragons role-playing game. Another series, the "Spearwielder's Tale," follows a man from this world into a "faerie" land. The prolific writer has also penned a number of other novels outside of these series. Featuring three-dimensional characters and non-stereotypical plots, Salvatore's work often "reaches beyond the traditions of the genre to establish new standards," commented an essayist for the *St. James Guide to Young Adult Writers,* who added, "Readers continue to return to Salvatore novels since he is known for strong, perceptive prose and entertaining stories that speak to the emotions and the senses."

Salvatore's first novel, *The Crystal Shard,* was also his first in the "Forgotten Realms" sequence. The story revolves around a murderous apprentice who comes to power using the magical crystal shard named in the title. In a review for *Voice of Youth Advocates,* Ruth Cline remarked, "There are many gruesome death scenes, violent battles, unexplained appearances of weird characters and coincidences in the plot." The book is perhaps most notable for introducing the character of the dark elf Drizzt, who takes center stage in some of the author's later works. "Young adult readers will find many qualities in Drizzt to identify with as the young hero struggles with moral and spiritual conflicts," noted the *St. James Guide to Young Adult Writers* contributor.

Drizzt appears in sub-trilogies made up of *Streams of Silver, The Halfling's Gem, Homeland, Exile, Sojourn,* and *The Legacy.* Born to a cruel race of subterranean dark elves and a powerful family, the House Do'Urden, Drizzt tries to break with the predatory behavior of his relations. The various tales tell of his attempts to hide his true feelings from his evil mother and siblings, and of his discovery of peace-loving elves, dwarves, and humans. In the bestseller *The Legacy,* Drizzt is hunted by his sister Vierna, an evil priestess who seeks to use him in her religious rituals. A *Rapport* reviewer called *The Legacy* "an adventure story with a heart. . . . Whether you've gamed in the 'Forgotten Realms' or not, you'll feel a great familiarity with its territory and a fondness for many of its inhabitants." A *Rapport* critic deemed the subsequent installment *Siege of Darkness* a "powerful tale of intrigue and danger."

Also within the "Forgotten Realms" series is Salvatore's "Cleric Quintet," a five-volume series that follows the adventures of the priest Cadderly. Using his increasingly effective magical powers, Cadderly fights evil forces, including a living dead phenomenon called

"Ghost." Leslie S. J. Farmer reviewed the third volume, *Night Masks,* in *Kliatt,* and commented that battles "dominate the story to the detriment of character development." Regarding the next Cleric entry, *The Fallen Fortress,* Farmer found it "not breathtaking wizardry, but . . . pleasantly entertaining." About *The Chaos Curse,* Cleric book five, Farmer commented that it had "the tightest plot and clearest writing." She noted that the "Cleric Quintet" took several years to write and concluded that the series "may prove to be a standard set within the fantasy genre."

Salvatore departed from the "Forgotten Realms" formula to create his "Spearwielder's Tale" series, beginning with *The Woods out Back.* In this tale, Englishman Gary Leger leads a humdrum life until he is kidnapped into a "Faerie" world by the leprechaun Mickey McMickey, who involves him in aquest to repair an ancient magical spear. Together with the elf Kelsey Gil-Ravadry, they are thwarted in this effort by the sorceress Ceridwen. A *Publishers Weekly* contributor found the story to be flawed, and stated that it "does not adequately explain for what purposes Kelsey wants the spear or why Ceridwen opposes him." Roland Green, writing in *Booklist,* called the author a "seasoned fantasist" but found no surprises "nor anything badly done." *Voice of Youth Advocates* reviewer Deborah L. Dubois enjoyed the book's "clever" premise and suggested that "adventure and fantasy fans will enjoy this tale and will look forward to further adventures."

With *The Sword of Bedwyr,* Salvatore inaugurated yet another fantasy series. The "Robin Hood-like" character of Luthien Bedwyr—"Crimson Shadow"—is an exiled nobleman who surreptitiously leads his people in a rebellion against the foreign power that has taken hold of Eriador, his homeland. A *Library Journal* reviewer called the novel "a fast-paced series opener." A *Publishers Weekly* critic noted that "Salvatore describes and choreographs battle scenes better than any other contemporary fantasist." *Booklist* reviewer Roland Green found the book "briskly paced, with touches of wry wit . . . easy to recommend."

Reviewing the sequel, *Luthien's Gamble,* a *Publishers Weekly* contributor stated that the "battle scenes are robust, but [Salvatore's] fantasy is dully derivative." Similarly, a *Kirkus Reviews* critic noted that the book is "aimed at readers who want maximum agitation with minimum cogitation." The *St. James Guide to Young Adult Writers* essayist, though, praised the inclusion of romantic complications involving Luthien and two young women who fight beside him, saying, "the resulting love-triangle adds a subplot of conflict for the young hero, bringing depth to the storyline yet never turning into romantic triviality." A *Publishers Weekly* reviewer called the trilogy's conclusion, *The Dragon King,* "pseudo-Tolkien" with "plenty of sound and fury but precious little fire." *Booklist* contributor Green, however, wrote that "Salvatore reliably delivers intelligent, fast-moving, entertaining fantasy."

The Demon Awakens gave Salvatore the opportunity to enter new territory, the world of the demon dactyl Bestesbulzibar. The dactyl leads an assault on Corona, where young Elbryan and his girlfriend, Pony, live. The pair are orphaned during the conflict, find a magical amethyst, and join in an answering attack on the dactyl. According to *Booklist* reviewer Green, this is Salvatore's "most ambitious book to date. . . . It is not superlatively original," but "it is certainly very readable." Elbryan and Pony defeat the dactyl in the follow-up *The Demon Spirit,* only to find in *The Demon Apostle* that the dactyl lives on in the form of a monk, Father Abbot Markwart. The latter "may be Salvatore's strongest fantasy to date," observed a *Publishers Weekly* critic, praising the author's development of characters and historical background in an action-filled story. Similarly, in a *Library Journal* review of this book, Jackie Cassada noted that "Salvatore excels in worldbuilding and creating complex, introspective characters" who possess ample "wit and determination." In *Mortalis,* Pony is on her own, Elbryan having been killed, and she must seek to end a deadly plague caused by the demon dactyl. A *Publishers Weekly* commentator thought this entry "filled with far more angst than action," but still providing "enough adventure . . . to keep it moving at a happy pace." *Library Journal*'s Cassada echoed her earlier complimentary words about Salvatore, pointing out his "skill at creating a richly complex world peopled with well-rounded characters."

BIOGRAPHICAL/CRITICAL SOURCES:

BOOKS

Pringle, David, *St. James Guide to Fantasy Writers,* St. James Press (Detroit, MI), 1996.

St. James Guide to Young Adult Writers, 2nd edition, St. James Press (Detroit, MI), 1999.

PERIODICALS

Booklist, October 15, 1993, p. 422; August, 1994, p. 2030; January 15, 1995, p. 901; October 1, 1996, Roland Green, review of *The Dragon King,* p. 326; May 1, 1997, Roland Green, review of *The Demon Awakens,* p. 1483; March 15, 1998, Roland Green, review of *The Demon Spirit,* p. 1207; March 1, 1999, Candace Smith, review of *The Demon Apostle,* p. 1161.

Kirkus Reviews, December 1, 1995, pp. 1673-1674; September 1, 1996, p. 1282; March 15, 1997, p. 423.

Kliatt, November, 1992, Leslie S. J. Farmer, review of *Night Masks,* p. 19; November, 1993, p. 18; March, 1994, p. 20; November, 1994, Leslie S. J. Farmer, review of *The Chaos Curse,* p. 24; January, 1995, p. 19; November, 1995, p. 20; March, 1997, Hugh M. Flick, Jr., review of *Luthien's Gamble,* p. 21.

Library Journal, November 15, 1993, p. 118; December, 1994, p. 139; February 15, 1996, p. 179; April, 1997, p. 124; March 15, 1998, Jackie Cassada, review of *The Demon Spirit,* p. 99; March 15, 1999, Jackie Cassada, review of *The Demon Apostle,* p. 113; June 15, 2000, Jackie Cassada, review of *Mortalis,* p. 120.

Locus, April, 1990, p. 39; November, 1993, Scott Winnett, review of *The Woods out Back,* pp. 56-57.

Publishers Weekly, June 28, 1993, p. 61; September 6, 1993, review of *The Woods out Back,* p. 88; January 2, 1995, review of *The Sword of Bedwyr,* p. 63; January 29, 1996, review of *Luthien's Gamble,* p. 88; October 12, 1996, review of *The Dragon King,* pp. 74-75; March 9, 1998, review of *The Demon Spirit,* p. 53; September 28, 1998, review of *The Silent Blade,* p. 78; February 22, 1999, review of *The Demon Apostle,* p. 70; June 5, 2000, review of *Mortalis,* p. 77; October 2, 2000, review of *Servant of the Shard,* p. 63.

Rapport, Volume 17, 1992, p. 26; May, 1995, p. 20.

Voice of Youth Advocates, August, 1988, Ruth Cline, review of *The Crystal Shard,* p. 140; February, 1994, Deborah L. Dubois, review of *The Woods out Back,* p. 385; April, 1995, Dorothy M. Thompson, review of *The Sword of Bedwyr,* p. 39.

OTHER

R. A. Salvatore's Web site, http://www.rasalvatore.com (January 21, 2001).*

*   *   *

SCHOR, Juliet B. 1955-

PERSONAL: Born November 9, 1955; married Prasannan Parthasarathi (an economist); children: Krishnan, Sulakshana. *Education:* Wesleyan University, B.A. (magna cum laude), 1975; University of Massachusetts, Ph.D., 1982.

ADDRESSES: Home—Newton, MA. *Office*—Department of Sociology, McGuinn 505, Boston College, 140 Commonwealth Ave., Chestnut Hill, MA 02459. *Agent*—Gerard McCauley, Box 844, Katonah, NY 10536. *E-mail*—juliet.schor@bc.edu.

CAREER: Williams College, Williamstown, MA, assistant professor of economics, 1981-83; Columbia University, New York, NY, assistant professor of economics at Barnard College, 1983-84; Harvard University, Cambridge, MA, assistant professor, 1984-89, associate professor of economics, 1989-92, senior lecturer in economics, beginning 1992, research affiliate for center for European studies, beginning 1986, head tutor of committee on degrees in women's studies, 1991-92, director of studies for women's studies program, beginning 1992; University of Tilburg, professor in the economics of leisure, beginning 1995; Boston College, Chestnut Hill, MA, professor of sociology, 2001—. Center for Popular Economics, founder and staff economist, 1978-90; United Nations, World Institute for Development Economics Research (WIDER), research adviser for Project on Global Macropolicy, 1985-91; Economic Policy Institute, member of research advisory council, 1986—; Wesleyan University, member of board of trustees, 1988-91; member of the International Advisory Board for the "Project on Social-Economic Security" of the International Labour Organization; member of The Parenting Task Force of the National Parenting Association. South End Press, founder and editor, 1977-79; member of editorial board, *International Journal of Applied Economics,* 1992—, and *Journal of Consumer Culture;* board member and founding member of the Center for a New American Dream.

AWARDS, HONORS: Teaching fellowship from University of Massachusetts, 1976-79; Distinguished Teacher Award, University of Massachusetts, 1978; Research fellowship from Brookings Institution, 1980-81; Guggenheim fellowship, 1995.

WRITINGS:

(With Daniel Cantor) *Tunnel Vision: Labor, the World Economy, and Central America* (PACCA series on the domestic roots of U.S. foreign policy), South End Press (Boston, MA), 1987.

(With Gerald A. Epstein) *Macropolicy in the Rise and Fall of the Golden Age* ("WIDER Working Papers" series), World Institute for Development Economics Research of United Nations University (Helsinki, Finland), 1988.

(Editor, with Stephen A. Marglin) *The Golden Age of Capitalism: Reinterpreting the Postwar Experience* ("Studies in Development Economics" series), Oxford University Press (New York, NY), 1990.

(Editor, with Tariq Banuri) *Financial Openness and National Policy Autonomy: Opportunities and Constraints* ("Studies in Development Economics" series), Oxford University Press (New York, NY), 1992.

(Editor, with Jong-Il You) *Capital, the State, and Labour: A Global Perspective,* Edward Elgar (Brookfield, VT), 1995.

The Overworked American: The Unexpected Decline of Leisure, Basic Books (New York, NY), 1991.

A Sustainable Economy for the 21st Century, Seven Stories Press (New York, NY), 1998.

The Overspent American: Upscaling, Downshifting, and the New Consumer, Basic Books (New York, NY), 1998, reprinted as *The Overspent American: Why We Want What We Don't Need,* HarperPerennial (New York, NY), 1999.

Do Americans Shop Too Much?: A New Democracy Forum with Juliet Schor, foreword by Ralph Nader, edited by Joshua Cohen and Joel Rogers, Beacon Press (Boston, MA), 2000.

(Editor, with Douglas Holt) *The Consumer Society Reader,* New Press (New York, NY), 2000.

Economic columnist, *Z* (magazine), 1987—. Contributor of articles to periodicals and to books, including *The North, the South and the Environment,* edited by V. Bhaskar and Andrew Glyn, Earthscan, 1995, and *The Ethics of Consumption and Global Stewardship,* edited by David Crocker, 1995.

WORK IN PROGRESS: Working on a project about sustainable consumption.

SIDELIGHTS: In *The Overworked American: The Unexpected Decline of Leisure,* Juliet B. Schor chronicles the tendency of U.S. citizens to spend increasing amounts of time working at the expense of involving themselves in such nonprofessional activities as volunteer service, rest, and self-improvement. According to Schor, the trend to work longer hours began in the 1970s after the length of the average work week fell to thirty-nine hours. Since that point, Americans have been increasing the amount of time that they devote to work. At the time of the book's publication in the early 1990s, Americans were working an average of forty-seven hours a week. If the pattern were to hold over the

next 20 years, according to Schor, "the average person would be on the job 60 hours a week—for an annual 3,000 hours a year."

The tendency to overwork has contributed to a number of problems in American society. Schor notes that overworked employees are sleeping less and experiencing higher levels of stress. She also documents the effect that overworking has on families: parents no longer have the time to provide their children with proper attention and care. Additionally, the author contends that Americans are less willing to involve themselves in learning new skills—such as training to play a musical instrument or acting in local theater troupes—because such nonprofessional activities take time and effort that employees are reluctant to spend after a hard day in the office. People, therefore, devote their free time to such activities as shopping at the mall or watching television, which require minimal energy.

Schor offers various reasons for the tendency to spend more time working. The advance of technology has created higher standards for Americans who work, whether it be in the home or in the office. Schor acknowledges that such efficient labor-saving devices as washing machines and vacuum cleaners have created higher expectations for homemakers who are spending more time in maintaining a pleasant living environment. She also remarks that, with the invention of portable computers and communications equipment, employers presume that their workers are no longer confined by the normal office hours or environment.

In *The Overworked American* Schor also notes that the capitalist system, in which the economy is primarily determined by private parties rather than controlled by the government, has also played a major role in increasing the amount of time spent in professional capacities. The author remarks that it is less expensive to have fewer people work more hours—even if the employees are compensated for overtime—than it is to hire more people. Extra employees require corporations to pay for costly medical benefits. Additionally, Schor asserts that by keeping the number of workers low, employers contribute to higher unemployment which, in turn, gives businesses the justification to keep wages down.

Schor also analyzes trends that have contributed to the fluctuation of the American work week throughout history. During the 1930s, economists and members of trade unions led the push for shorter working hours. In the years that followed World War II, some argued that the normal forty-hour work week should be reduced to thirty-five hours. At the time, industries were realizing substantial financial growth, according to Schor. In the 1950s, economic experts began to worry that Americans would eventually be spending too much time in nonprofessional pursuits. But as the economy began to stagnate in the early 1970s, Schor notes that workers found themselves in a position where they had to work harder in order to maintain the same standard of living that they had come to depend on. Schor charges that since the mid-twentieth century, Americans have become increasingly fixated on buying material goods in order to provide themselves with a measure of happiness in life. The focus on consumption has resulted, in the author's opinion, in negative patterns of working harder in order to have more money to spend on manufactured products.

To remedy the situation, Schor suggests that all salaried white-collar workers should only be responsible for spending a set number of hours in the office. (One of her contentions is that management takes advantage of salaried employees by paying them a fixed income, while coercing them to work extra hours.) Those who work overtime, in Schor's opinion, should then be provided with additional compensation. But rather than paying out overtime money in all cases, companies should consider offering compensatory time to employees who work more than the required number of hours. After a person has worked enough overtime, they should be allowed time away from the office based on the number of hours that they have accumulated.

While Schor realizes that many employers will be reluctant to take her advice, she cites numerous examples of situations in which shortening the work week has resulted in no drop-off—and in some cases a rise—in productivity. In an interview with *Newsweek,* she pointed out that both Medtronic, Inc. in Minneapolis and the Kellogg Company in Battle Creek, Michigan, discovered that reducing the number of hours in the workplace boosted the efficiency of their workers. In *The Overworked American* the author also provides examples of numerous countries—predominantly in Western Europe—that have preserved their working and living standards without compromising the length of the work week.

Several reviewers were impressed with Schor's scholarship. Troy Segal of *Business Week* acknowledged that "solid reasoning and thorough numbers-crunching mark her work." And though he felt that readers might be overwhelmed by the statistics presented in the beginning of the book, Segal encouraged those unfamiliar with the subject to "bear with it: *The Overworked American* becomes a fascinating blend of social observation and economic theory as it discusses the causes of the work crunch." In the *New York Times Book Review,* Robert Kuttner also commended Schor's work, remarking that "her training as an economist, happily, has alerted her to this widely overlooked pocketbook issue, but without deadening either her ear for the English language or her social conscience. Her book is systematic enough to satisfy the scholar, yet it is witty and engaging for the lay reader."

Schor's *The Overspent American: Upscaling, Downshifting, and the New Consumer* was reprinted as *The Overspent American: Why We Want What We Don't Need.* Schor notes that beginning in the postwar period, American consumers were concerned with keeping up with "the Joneses," other families in the neighborhood who generally had similar incomes and lifestyles. She suggests that our "reference groups" now tend to be more affluent coworkers and professionals, and upscale fictional characters featured in television shows. Janet T. Knoedler said in the *Journal of Economic Issues* that Schor "explores the use of the media in creating and exploiting the symbolic attributes of certain goods. Upscale versions of what once were fairly ordinary and serviceable products—ranging from the ubiquitous sport utility vehicles to fancy coffee—are sold to us through a constant barrage of media images and powerful status symbols embedded in products. As a result, standards for what are deemed to be the socially necessary versions of food, shelter, and clothing are continuously being ratcheted up, with the result that we feel compelled to constantly replace or update our possessions so as not to be left behind."

Schor notes the escalating number of bankruptcies in the United States and the declining savings rate, which are in part the result of our consumption of "stuff" that we seldom need or use. John de Graaf noted in *Amicus Journal* that "our annual output of trash would fill a convoy of garbage trucks long enough to reach halfway to the moon." De Graaf wrote that Schor "offers a set of principles to lead us to a more frugal, environmentally friendly society. Many of these, including tips for 'controlling desire,' getting people together to agree to voluntary restraints on 'competitive consumption,' creating community lending centers for 'products that are not in use all the time,' and negotiating with employers for reduced work hours, are eminently practical and could have great impact." Schor emphasizes the benefits of consumer education on saving and budgeting, cooperative agreements on sums spent for gifts between coworkers and family members, and less television viewing. Schor found in her studies that people spend an average of $208 more a year for every hour they said they spent watching television. She told a *People Weekly* interviewer that, on average, her sample watched eleven and a half hours of television each week, "which meant they spent $2,400 more than they would have if they turned off their TVs." When asked if she felt commercials encourage overspending, Schor replied that "it's not the ads so much; people are conditioned to resist them. It's the programs. With few exceptions, programs today tend to show characters who lead incredibly affluent lifestyles they would never be able to afford in reality. Ordinary sitcom families own million-dollar houses. That's the big difference from *The Dick Van Dyke Show,* where the Petries lived much more modestly. Research shows that the more TV people watch, the more likely they are to overestimate what the average American has." Schor said that with people spending so much time working, they spend more to have others do those things for which they no longer have time, including food preparation, housework, and gardening. This becomes a vicious cycle as they must work even longer hours to pay for these services.

Schor also proposes luxury taxes on high-end status symbols and the elimination of the tax deductions businesses are allowed to take for advertising. *Fortune* contributor N. Gregory Mankiw felt that "the problem is that what looks conspicuous to one person is just a good value to another. Is a Mercedes a status symbol or simply a safe and comfortable car? Do parents send their children to Ivy League schools to give them a good education or to one-up their colleagues at work? I am not ready to give Congress the mandate to decide which types of consumption are laudable and which are not."

Jennifer Kingson-bloom interviewed Schor for *American Banker.* Kingson-bloom said, "You call banks 'credit pushers,' making it sound almost like a drug problem." Schor replied, "They are giving credit cards to kids in high school, kids in college, who they know are going to run up balances. . . . I resent the fact that the companies have spent so much money on solicitations and so much money lobbying Congress to get the bankruptcy laws changed. They're trying to put repayments ahead of child support and alimony—I find that reprehensible. They're giving credit to people who have bad credit histories or have gone into bankruptcy before. There seem to be virtually no standards at this point for receiving credit cards."

David George noted in *Review of Social Economy* that Schor "does not ignore the plight of the segment of our population that has seen its economic condition erode in recent years. Her focus nonetheless remains on that large middle that has seen its material conditions im-

prove." *Progressive* contributor John Buell wrote that Schor "provides a concise exposition of the theory of consumption. She then applies it to our contemporary market economy. She argues that the urge to consume has caused a range of social and personal problems. She concludes by suggesting that overconsumption is not an iron cage. There are personal and social ways out of the bind."

Schor interviewed a broad spectrum of people, including "downshifters," who have chosen to work less and enjoy life more. Some have lost jobs, but others have chosen to change their lifestyle to one of voluntary simplicity. Buell concluded by saying that "in Schor's world, individuals would enjoy a lot more freedom. They would have some control over how much they work, and the get-and-spend treadmill would no longer overwhelm their lives. People need space to express an individuality not colonized by the demands of consumer culture. . . . It is time to slow things down. Schor has a number of creative ideas about how to step off the treadmill." An *Entertainment Weekly* reviewer said that "there's something endearing about an economist who admits to giving up an expensive makeup habit. . . . This is the stuff from which revolutions are made."

Monroe Friedman wrote in the *Journal of Socio-Economics* that "while Schor's book lacks a rigorous intellectual treatment of the issues it discusses, it nonetheless raises some provocative questions in a manner which many Americans are likely to find engaging and thought provoking. And it provides flesh-and-blood models of individuals and families who have made the downshifting transition successfully. If their stories help consumers find a more humane and personally fulfilling way of life, the book will have served a useful purpose." A *Publishers Weekly* reviewer said *The Overspent American* "offers trenchant commentary on Americans' overspending lifestyle and lack of savings."

In *Do Americans Shop Too Much?: A New Democracy Forum with Juliet Schor,* the author focuses on declining neighborhoods, the stock market, and television, as components of "competitive consumption" responsible for Americans' excessive stress levels and lack of leisure time in their private lives, as well as the environmental damage to our lives in general. The foreword is written by Ralph Nader, and the volume includes responses from critics, including Robert Frank, author of *Luxury Fever.*

Schor and Douglas Halt collected twenty-eight essays that deal with "the nature and evolution of consumer society" for *The Consumer Society Reader.* Included are selections from the writings of Thorstein Veblen, Betty Friedan, Theodor Adorno, and John Kenneth Galbraith, as well as from the more recent works of Pierre Bourdieu, bell hooks, Thomas Frank, Bill McKibben, and Janice Radway. A *Publishers Weekly* reviewer felt the anthology to be "an ideal introduction to consumer theory."

BIOGRAPHICAL/CRITICAL SOURCES:

PERIODICALS

Alternatives Journal, winter, 2001, "The Big Questions" (interview), p. 25.

American Banker, July 6, 1998, Jennifer Kingson-bloom, "Eyes On Credit: Banks Blamed in Consumer Overspending" (interview), p. 19.

Amicus Journal, summer, 1999, John de Graaf, review of *The Overspent American: Why We Want What We Don't Need,* p. 41.

Business Week, February 17, 1992, Troy Segal, review of *The Overworked American: The Unexpected Decline of Leisure,* p. 18; July 5, 1993, review of *The Overworked American,* p. 13; May 25, 1998, Keith H. Hammonds, review of *The Overspent American,* p. 17; June 28, 1999, review of *The Overspent American,* p. 15.

Christian Science Monitor, April 4, 1995, Shelley Donald Coolidge, "Work and Spend Cycle Makes Company Slaves," p. 9.

Economic Journal, January, 1997, review of *Capital, the State, and Labour: A Global Perspective,* p. 284.

Entertainment Weekly, May 22, 1998, "Shopping Mauled," p. 65; April 23, 1999, review of *The Overspent American,* p. 57.

Fortune, May 11, 1998, N. Gregory Mankiw, review of *The Overspent American,* p. 40.

Glamour, July, 1998, Karen Houppert, "Why Americans Overspend," p. 80.

International Journal of Manpower, July, 1996, Malcolm Sawyer, review of *Capital, the State, and Labour,* p. 114.

Journal of Economic Issues, September, 1999, Janet T. Knoedler, review of *The Overspent American,* p. 747.

Journal of Economic Literature, March, 1996, review of *Capital, the State, and Labour,* p. 242; March, 1999, review of *The Overspent American,* p. 241.

Journal of Socio-Economics, March-April, 1999, Monroe Friedman, review of *The Overspent American,* p. 200.

Kirkus Reviews, April 15, 1998, review of *The Overspent American,* p. 566.

Library Journal, May 15, 1998, Patrick J. Brunet, review of *The Overspent American,* p. 94.

Los Angeles Times Book Review, September 6, 1998, review of *The Overspent American,* p. 8.

Multinational Monitor, September, 1998, "*The Overspent American:* An Interview with Juliet Schor," p. 21.

Newsweek, February 17, 1992, pp. 42-43; June 1, 1998, Jolie Solomon, "The Land of the Spree," p. 70.

New Yorker, July 13, 1998, review of *The Overspent American,* p. 75; January 25, 1999, John Cassidy, review of *The Overspent American,* p. 90.

New York Times Book Review, February 2, 1992, Robert Kuttner, review of *The Overworked American,* p. 1; June 6, 1993, review of *The Overworked American,* p. 56; June 21, 1998, Peter T. Kilborn, review of *The Overspent American,* p. 34.

People Weekly, August 17, 1998, "Dough Nuts," p. 93.

Progressive, October, 1998, John Buell, review of *The Overspent American,* p. 40.

Publishers Weekly, January 18, 1993, review of *The Overworked American,* p. 467; April 13, 1998, review of *The Overspent American,* p. 63; April 10, 2000, "Current Affairs," p. 90; June 26, 2000, "August Publications," p. 68.

Review of Social Economy, winter, 1998, David George, review of *The Overspent American,* p. 554.

Social Science Quarterly, December, 1993, review of *The Overworked American,* p. 922.

Times Literary Supplement, July 10, 1998, review of *The Overspent American,* p. 5.

Virginia Quarterly Review, spring, 1999, review of *The Overspent American,* p. 64.

Wall Street Journal, May 21, 1998, Cynthia Crossen, review of *The Overspent American,* p. 15.

Washington Monthly, July-August, 1998, "Keeping up with the Trumps: How the Middle Class Identifies with the Rich" (excerpt from *The Overspent American*), p. 34.

Working Woman, February, 2000, Dana Asher, "Speaking Volumes on the Dollar," p. S19.

SCOTT, Melissa 1960-

PERSONAL: Born August 7, 1960, in Little Rock, AR; partner of Lisa A. Barnett (a writer), since 1979. *Education:* Harvard, Radcliffe College, B.A. (magna cum laude), 1981; Brandeis University, Ph.D., 1992.

ADDRESSES: Agent—Richard Curtis, Richard Curtis Agency, 171 East 74th St., Suite 2, New York, NY 10021.

CAREER: Writer. Worked as an usher, teller, answering service operator, teaching assistant, stock person, secretary, and receptionist. Founder and contributing editor of *Wavelengths,* a review of science fiction of interest to a gay/lesbian/bisexual readership.

AWARDS, HONORS: John W. Campbell Memorial Award, World Science Fiction Society, 1986, for *Conceiving the Heavens: Creating the Science Fiction Novel;* Lambda awards for Best Science Gay/Lesbian Fiction/Fantasy Novel, Lambda Book Report, 1994, for *Trouble and Her Friends,* and 1995, for *Shadow Man.*

WRITINGS:

SCIENCE FICTION NOVELS

The Game Beyond, Baen (New York, NY), 1984.
Five-Twelfths of Heaven (first novel in "Silence Leigh" trilogy), Baen (New York, NY), 1985.
A Choice of Destinies, Baen (New York, NY), 1986.
Silence in Solitude (second novel in "Silence Leigh" trilogy), Baen (New York, NY), 1986.
The Empress of Earth (third novel in "Silence Leigh" trilogy), Baen (New York, NY), 1987.
The Kindly Ones, Baen (New York, NY), 1987.
(With Lisa A. Barnett) *The Armor of Light* (first novel in "Nico Rathe" trilogy), Baen (New York, NY), 1988.
The Roads of Heaven (the "Silence Leigh" trilogy; contains *Five-Twelfths of Heaven, Silence in Solitude,* and *The Empress of Earth*), Doubleday (Garden City, NY), 1988.
Mighty Good Road, Baen (New York, NY), 1990.
Dreamships, Tor (New York, NY), 1992.
Burning Bright, Tor (New York, NY), 1993.
Trouble and Her Friends, Tor (New York, NY), 1994.
(With Lisa A. Barnett) *Point of Hopes* (second novel in "Nico Rathe" trilogy), Tor (New York, NY), 1995.
Proud Helios (part of the *Star Trek: Deep Space Nine* series), Pocket (New York, NY), 1995.
Shadow Man, Tor (New York, NY), 1995.
Night Sky Mine, Tor (New York, NY), 1996.
Dreaming Metal, Tor (New York, NY), 1997.

The Shapes of Their Hearts, Tor (New York, NY), 1998.
The Jazz, Tor, 2000.
(With Lisa A. Barnett) *Point of Dreams* (third novel in "Nico Rathe" trilogy), Tor (New York, NY), 2001.

OTHER

Territorial Rites (novel), Silhouette (New York, NY), 1984.
Conceiving the Heavens: Creating the Science-Fiction Novel (nonfiction), Heinemann (Portsmouth, NH), 1997.

SIDELIGHTS: Melissa Scott writes science fiction that is informed by her educational background in history and by her identity as a lesbian. She uses her stories to focus on such issues as the impact of technology on society, the role of gender in the formation of identity, and the consequences of creating boundaries among societies with different ideologies. Reviewers have consistently praised Scott's ability to create comprehensive, believable worlds.

Scott's initial foray into the genre was with *The Game Beyond,* in which people compete in a gaming tournament to decide who will rule a planetary community, She then wrote *Five-Twelfths of Heaven,* the first book in a trilogy featuring spaceship pilot Silence Leigh, a woman who struggles against the male-dominated society of which she is a part. In the first story, financial hardship causes her to lose ownership of a spaceship left to her by her grandfather. Denis Balthasar, her guardian on her home planet, asks her to be a pilot on a voyage to Earth in his craft, Sun-Treader. The novel focuses on the relationships among Leigh, Balthasar, and spaceship engineer Chase Mago as they try to reach their destination.

Silence in Solitude, the second book of the trilogy, focuses on Leigh's struggle to facilitate communication between Earth and the rest of the interstellar community, in order to prove herself as a pilot. *The Empress of Earth* concludes the trilogy, as Silence and two husbands endeavor to save the Earth from rule by the villainous Rose Worlders. The novel details an entire technology inspired by the science of the Middle Ages and the beliefs of Aristotle. When Silence displays her magical abilities, the people of Earth regard her as a savior. Complimenting the author's use of the invented science, Don Sakers noted in the *Wilson Library Bulletin,* "The mystical technology is so well conceived and exhaustively thought-out that by the end one finds oneself convinced that it is real."

In *The Kindly Ones,* Scott depicts lunar communities on the moons Orestes and Electra. Survivors of a space disaster form a society in which the inhabitants are expected to follow a code of honor, and where people who disobey are relegated to the community of "ghosts," forbidden to speak to the "living." The plot revolves around the development of the Necropolis, a den of hedonism formed by the outcasts; on attempts by the living and the ghosts to communicate through Trey Maturin, a medium with the ability to convey messages between the two groups; and on the weakening of the society when the rulers of the communities begin to quarrel.

Scott collaborated with her partner, Lisa A. Barnett, on *The Armor of Light,* which is set in England in the 1590s. *The Armor of Light* was not the first novel to make use of Scott's background in history. *A Choice of Destinies,* published earlier, reveals how history could have been altered if Alexander the Great had chosen to conquer the Roman Empire instead of India. In *The Armor of Light,* Scott and Barnett employ such historical figures as playwright Christopher Marlowe and explorer Sir Walter Raleigh, as they tell the story of England at a critical time in its history. In the novel, a royal astronomer predicts the ruin of England unless King James of Scotland inherits the throne. Sir Philip Sidney is dispatched by Queen Elizabeth to ensure that evil forces do not prevent James from ruling England. Don Sakers in *Wilson Library Bulletin* called *The Armor of Light* "a beautifully written, artfully crafted fantasy set in Elizabethan England."

In *Mighty Good Road,* Scott develops a planetary system connected by a transportation system that allows for rapid travel from one station stop to another. The novel focuses on a mission to salvage some important cargo from an airwreck over one of the planets. When the leader of the effort to retrieve the equipment begins to ponder the circumstances of the crash, the company that commissioned the rescue mission turns against the contractors.

Dreamships also focuses on a rescue mission. In this novel, pilot Reverdy Jian and partner Imre Vaughn are charged with the task of tracking down their employer's brother. They are guided by Manfred, an extremely intelligent on-board guidance system. Their programmed overseer, in fact, so closely approximates humanity that it raises the question of whether Manfred deserves the same rights as humans have. Although Tom Easton of *Analog Science Fiction and Fact* felt Scott occasionally provided too many details of the subterranean community from which the protagonists hail, he called *Dreamships* "thoughtful and ingenious."

Burning Bright features Quinn Lioe, a pilot who lands on a planet where virtual-reality gaming is a serious preoccupation of the inhabitants and visitors. When Lioe involves herself in directing the Game with her own imagined scenarios, she alters the political climate of the Burning Bright community, including as participants a number of people who are involved in power struggles outside of the gaming environment. As the novel progresses, Lioe threatens the fabric of Burning Bright by daring to construct a scenario that will conclude the Game. In *Voice of Youth Advocates,* Katharine L. "Kat" Kan prompted young adult readers to make an effort to read the novel, stating that "readers will have to pay close attention to what they read, but they will be rewarded with a highly satisfying adventure with lots to think about after."

In *Trouble and Her Friends,* lesbian lovers Cerise and Trouble are expert computer hackers who use their abilities to steal corporate secrets and sell them. Both Cerise and Trouble are equipped with the "brainworm," a technological enhancement that allows them to receive sensations when connected to computer networks. When Congress threatens to put a stop to the use of the brainworm, Trouble ends her life as a criminal. But she is pulled back into the criminal underworld when another hacker begins using "Trouble" as an alias. Because the imposter named Trouble has invaded the company for which Cerise now works, the stable lives that the former hackers have created for themselves are threatened. The two join forces to upset the scheme of the imposter.

Scott collaborated again with Lisa A. Barnett on *Point of Hopes,* a novel set in a futuristic city at the time of its annual celebration. The inhabitants of the city are anticipating a major astronomical event that will mark the ascendancy of a new monarch to the throne. Coincidentally, the children of the city are vanishing. The protagonist, Nico Rathe, is called upon to solve the mystery.

After writing *Proud Helios,* a novel for the *Star Trek: Deep Six Nine* series, Scott began exploring issues of gender in science fiction with the novel *Shadow Man,* in which the author develops a galaxy that identifies five distinct genders. The use of drugs to ease the effects of faster-than-light travel has contributed to the development of the new genders. A planet in the system whose inhabitants are conservative and self-righteous has outlawed all but two genders—male and female.

When Warreven Stiller is identified as androgynous, however, the ideologies held by the people of the planet are threatened.

In *Night Sky Mine,* galactic police are called upon to investigate the mysterious abandonment of an asteroid owned by the Night Sky Mine company. Central to the plot are the contributions of an orphan found in a mining shaft years before the incident under investigation. Scott's fictional universe is also populated with computer programs that compete with one another, reproduce, and mutate, just like organisms.

Booklist reviewer Bonnie Johnston wrote that in *The Shapes of Their Hearts,* Scott "gives us a story full of deviousness and of characters for whom delicate subterfuge is a way of life." Gabril Aurik, a prophet who claims to have received a message from God, takes his sect, the Seeking Children, and establishes a new society they call Eden, away from human cloning and DNA manipulation. When Aurik is close to death, he records his experiences, visions, emotions, and memories on a braintape, called the Memoriant, to guide the Children. Religious leaders of the sect use direct links to the brains of the Children to receive the word of God, but something corrupts the tape, and their behavior turns violent toward those who do not share their religious beliefs, as they come under the influence of a form of artificial intelligence. The outcasts live away from the believers, and a *Publishers Weekly* reviewer said that "Scott's colorful setting is Eden's grungy Freeport, where hyperrock Steel musicians scarf greasy fries." Anton Sien Hsia Tso, a clone involved in the drug-making business, may be the only hope for halting the influence of the mutated Memoriant. Pamela Keesey said in *Lambda Book Report* that "this engaging story is as much about people and the way they feel, think, and believe as it is about the complexities of technology in a world where God is a self-aware computer program."

The Jazz is set in the near future and features protagonist Tin Lizzy, who creates content for the jazz, an Internet art form made up of truths, lies, and variations of both. Lizzy works with a teenage boy named Keyz, whose talent has progressed to the point where Lizzy knows something drastic has happened. Keyz tells her that the quality of his work has skyrocketed because he is using a secret experimental program he stole from a film studio. The two are pursued by Gardner Gerretty, the head of the studio, who also was responsible for Lizzy's having done jail time years earlier. In a *Locus* interview, Scott, who was working on *The Jazz* at the time, said that the story is "turning out to be structured

rather like *The Wizard of Oz.*" A *Publishers Weekly* reviewer called Scott "one of the best writers around in portraying what life online may really be like in the future."

In *Point of Dreams,* the sequel to *Point of Hopes,* authors Scott and Barnett provide ample background so that readers can enjoy it without having read the first two books of the trilogy. The city of Astreiant is putting on a production called a masque, based on The Alphabet of Desire, a book of magic that draws on flowers and plants. Nico Rathe is called in when dead bodies are found on the stage. *Booklist* contributor Roland Green wrote that "at heart, this fantasy novel is a mystery." A *Publishers Weekly* reviewer said the authors "have produced a page-turner that is sure to win them new fans." In a *Library Journal* review, Jackie Cassada called *Point of Dreams* "a fascinating and exotic tale."

Throughout her career, Scott has featured strong female protagonists in stories that explore, among other issues, situations brought about by the introduction of technology to communities. Her stories have earned recognition for the attention that Scott pays to developing intricate and believable universes. In addition to earning the praise of reviewers, Scott has proven herself a favorite with fans, and was the winner of a 1986 Joseph Campbell Award, given by the reading public to the best new science fiction writer of the year.

Scott told *CA:* "I have always been most interested in the intersection of technology and society—of the hard and soft sciences—and I think that is reflected in my science fiction. I am fascinated by technology and its developments—and I enjoy the challenge of playing by the rules of the genre, getting the science as 'right' as possible—but I'm more interested in the effects of that technology on characters and imagined societies than in the development of some new machine or program. In other words, I tend to set my novels fifty years after a great breakthrough, and consider its aftereffects, rather than write the story of the discovery itself. My academic training (as a historian specializing in early modern Europe) meant that I was exposed to the work of the new group of social and cultural historians, from Michel Foucault to Natalie Zemon-Davis and Simon Schama, and the tools I learned for analyzing past cultures have proved invaluable for creating future ones. (In fact, my dissertation ended up being oddly similar to my science fiction, in that it was concerned with the effects of a technological change—the development of gunpowder weapons—and the unintended consequences of the model created to make use of it.)

"Of course, since I'm a novelist rather than a futurist, all of this has to be expressed through plot and character. It's very hard to talk about the creative process without making it sound either stilted ('this developed from my interest in . . .') or mystical ('this character/place appeared . . .'), especially when both statements are always at least partially true. I tend to spend a great deal of time on the settings of my novels, cultural and social as well as physical, and to let both the plot and the characters grow organically from that process. I find that as I work out the details, particularly the ways that technology influences or upsets social norms (and vice versa), the inevitable contradictions that emerge are the most fruitful sources for the characters and their stories. I enjoy the complexity and messiness of the real world, and believe that one of the real challenges of any fiction is to model that complexity without losing sight of the structure that makes a good novel.

"It's also fairly obvious that I'm one of the few lesbians writing about queer characters whose science fiction is published by the so-called mainstream science fiction houses. I began writing about queer women first out of the usual impulse: I wanted to read about people who were 'like me,' and almost no one else was doing it. As I've gotten older, however, I've begun to realize that behind that superficially naive statement is something actually quite useful. Even in science fiction, there is a limited budget for novelty, both for the writer and for the reader; if one is creating something new in one part of the novel, other parts must of necessity be drawn from that which is familiar. In most of my novels, the technological and social changes are the new things and, as a result, I draw on the people and culture in which I live to make up the balance. It's that culture, my own culture, people like me, that provides the emotional background of my novels. Certainly my fascination with masks, identity, and roles comes from living in a culture that is deeply concerned, seriously and in play, with just these issues.

"I was drawn to science fiction largely because of the radical (in a nonpolitical sense) nature of the genre: here is a form of writing that starts from the premise that change is inevitable. Good or bad, it will happen, and the writer's job is to imagine plausible change and depict its possible consequences for people and their worlds. I've been lucky in being able to blend my own various interests into stories that catch readers' imaginations. Because, of course, science fiction, like any other fiction, is ultimately about the story, about the communication between writer and reader, the moment in which the reader is fully, deeply, and willingly part of the writer's world. Without the story, characters,

plot, and setting, the writer has no right to ask for that participation; with it, the writer can take the reader into worlds s/he would never otherwise have considered."

BIOGRAPHICAL/CRITICAL SOURCES:

PERIODICALS

Analog Science Fiction and Fact, October, 1992, pp. 164-165; October, 1993, pp. 162-163; November, 1998, Tom Easton, review of *The Shapes of Their Hearts,* p. 132; November, 2000, Tom Easton, review of *The Jazz,* p. 133.

Booklist, June 1, 1985, pp. 1373-1374; October 15, 1986, p. 327; September 1, 1987, p. 31; November 1, 1987, p. 437; October 15, 1988, p. 368; June 1, 1995, p. 1737; November 1, 1995, p. 458; May 15, 1998, Bonnie Johnston, review of *The Shapes of Their Hearts,* p. 1607; February 15, 2001, Roland Green, review of *Point of Dreams,* p. 1122.

Kirkus Reviews, May 1, 1992, p. 577; March 1, 1993, p. 266; March 15, 1994, p. 350; October 1, 1995, pp. 1387-1388; June 15, 1996, p. 865; May 15, 1998, review of *The Shapes of Their Hearts,* p. 701.

Kliatt, September, 1990, p. 24; May, 1995, p. 18.

Lambda Book Report, September, 1998, Pamela Keesey, review of *The Shapes of Their Hearts,* p. 35.

Library Journal, March 15, 1985, pp. 74-75; June 15, 1995, pp. 97-98; October 15, 1995, p. 91; August, 1996, p. 119; June 15, 1998, Jackie Cassada, review of *The Shapes of Their Hearts,* p. 111; February 15, 2001, Jackie Cassada, review of *Point of Dreams,* p. 204.

Locus, January, 1999, "Melissa Scott: Of Masks and Metaphors."

New York Times Book Review, August 2, 1992, Gerald Jonas, review of *Dreamships,* p. 19; August 13, 1995, Gerald Jonas, review of *Shadow Man,* p. 30.

Publishers Weekly, May 9, 1986, p. 250; July 31, 1987, p. 73; May 4, 1992, p. 45; April 4, 1994, p. 61; June 26, 1995, p. 91; July 22, 1996, p. 230; April 27, 1998, review of *The Shapes of Their Hearts,* p. 50; May 15, 2000, review of *The Jazz,* p. 93; January 8, 2001, review of *Point of Dreams,* p. 52.

Science Fiction Chronicle, January, 1985, p. 34; September, 1986, p. 43; December, 1998, review of *The Shapes of Their Hearts,* p. 49.

Voice of Youth Advocates, June, 1985, p. 140; October, 1985, pp. 269-270; February, 1988, p. 291; April, 1988, p. 42; April, 1989, p. 46; December, 1990, p. 302; October, 1993, p. 234; April, 1998, review of *Dreaming Metal,* pp. 14, 60.

Wilson Library Bulletin, May, 1988, pp. 86-87; February, 1989, p. 94; November, 1994, p. 103.

OTHER

Melissa Scott Web site, http://www.rscs.net/üms001/mainpage.html (March 6, 2001).*

*   *   *

SEDLEY, Kate
  See CLARKE, Brenda (Margaret Lilian)

*   *   *

SHEPARD, Neil 1951-

PERSONAL: Born January 29, 1951; son of Stanley (a plastics salesman) and Reba (a homemaker; maiden name, Miller) Shepard; married Mary Spagnol, 1982 (divorced, 1986); married Kate Riley (an anthropologist and writer), September 15, 1990; children: Anna. *Education:* Attended St. Peter's College, Oxford, England, 1972; University of Vermont, B.A., 1973; Colorado State University, M.A., 1976; Ohio University, Ph.D., 1980. *Avocational interests:* Hiking, birding, travel, jazz piano.

ADDRESSES: Home—2051 Clay Hill Rd., Johnson, VT 05656. *Office*—Department of Writing and Literature, Johnson State College, Johnson, VT 05656. *E-mail*—shepard@badger.jsc.vsc.edu.

CAREER: Louisiana State University, Baton Rouge, LA, instructor in English, 1980-82; Rider College, Lawrenceville, NJ, assistant professor of English, 1982-85; Johnson State College, Johnson, VT, professor of creative writing and literature, 1985—, chairman of department, 1987-91. Vermont Studio Center, director of writing program, 1989-97; presenter of community writing workshops, 1985-87. Member of Johnson Town Planning Commission, 1989-90. Visiting professor, Shanghai International Studies University, Shanghai, China, 1991; visiting writer, Chautauqua Institution, 2001.

MEMBER: Associated Writing Programs.

AWARDS, HONORS: Mid-List Press first book of poetry award, 1992; state arts fellowships from New Jersey, 1984, Pennsylvania, 1985, and Vermont, 1986; Arts Colony fellowships to MacDowell and Virginia Center for Creative Arts, both 1998.

WRITINGS:

Scavenging the Country for a Heartbeat, Mid-List Press (Minneapolis, MN), 1992.
I'm Here Because I Lost My Way, Mid-List Press (Minneapolis, MN), 1998.

Contributor of poems to anthologies, including *Anthology of Magazine Verse & Yearbook of American Poetry, 1983, 1986, 1995, 1996, 1997, 1999, Texas Review: A New England Sampler, 1988,* and Jay Parini and Robert Pack, editors, *The Poetry of New England,* 2001. Contributor of articles, reviews, and poetry to periodicals, including *Southern Review, Denver Quarterly, Poetry East, Antioch Review, Poetry Now, Paris Review, Triquarterly, Seneca Review, Southwest Review,* and *Poetry Northwest.* General editor and poetry editor, *Green Mountains Review,* 1987—.

WORK IN PROGRESS: The Language Tree, a volume of poems; nonfiction books on teaching experiences in China and on travels in the South Pacific, specifically the Marquesas Islands.

SIDELIGHTS: Neil Shepard is a Vermont-based poet and author whose wide travels in America and abroad inform his writings. In a *Poet & Critic* review of Shepard's *Scavenging the Country for a Heartbeat,* J. P. White observed that the poet's work "takes as its central theme the zigzag meandering of the individual heart in search of an inner and outer homeland." Naton Leslie likewise noted in the *Mid-American Review* that Shepard's poems show that "place is as much internal as it is external, that poetic journey is a traveling which occurs in time as much as space, on emotion as much as on highways." Shepard's poetry has been praised for its evocation of nature and memory, as well as for its treatment of the small epiphanies that reveal the universal in the personal. "Neil Shepard's . . . poems roam and caress the universe, the earth, the self," maintained Melissa Studdard Williamson in *Chelsea,* adding that "they attempt to make sense of a life and of life." Williamson concluded that Shepard's work "is spiritual enough to be placed on the altar as an offering, but reasonable enough to be offered to humanity rather than to the gods."

Shepard once told *CA:* "I grew up in Leominster, a small mill town in central Massachusetts, advertised on highway billboards as the 'Pioneer Plastics City.' In the summers, I escaped to a family home on the Maine coast where the salt air, amusement park lights, and polyglot of languages on the boardwalk first enlarged my notion of the world and whetted my appetite for travel.

"I attended colleges in Vermont, Colorado, Ohio, and Oxford, England, and traveled widely in the United States and abroad, hitchhiking throughout the American West and much of Europe. An avid hiker and amateur naturalist, I trekked through the American and Canadian Rockies, the Cascades, Smokies, Blue Ridge, most of the ranges in the Northeast, and mountains in Switzerland, Austria, Germany, Greece, Norway, New Zealand, Tahiti, and China. I am also a musician. I enjoy playing jazz and blues piano and guitar, and I attribute much of the lyricism in my poems to my early musical training.

"I came late to literature, enrolling in my freshman year at the University of Vermont as a pre-medical student. In my sophomore year, I had a 'spontaneous conversion' experience in chemistry class where, while fixating on the twenty-foot chart of the periodic table, I suddenly began daydreaming the lines of poems. By the end of class, I had determined to change my major.

"My interest in the sciences continues, however, mostly as an amateur birder and stargazer. My interests in music and modern dance have led me into the realm of multi-disciplinary performance pieces; my poems have been set to classical music and choreographed to modern dance."

Shepard told *CA:* "I'm attracted to poems as musical structures, both their rhythmic and sonic possibilities, and I'm interested in how this music lives within and beyond the deepest semantic features of the poem. As for specific issues of content, I favor poems with embedded narratives and dramatic contexts. Some of my poems are acts of recovery, triage missions into the past; other poems want to move beyond the small circle of self and the small moment of time I find myself in, toward an expansion of spirit. As Ibsen has said it, 'I write to make clear to myself and others the temporal and eternal questions.'

"My first creative writing teacher was David Huddle, poet and short story writer at University of Vermont. The strongest influence on my early poetry, however, was the charismatic Colorado poet, Bill Tremblay, whose love of jazz and Beat poetry, whose insistence on metaphoric magic, prophecy, and song, all struck their mark in me. His working-class, mill town, Massachusetts background also resembled my own. During my doctoral years at Ohio University, Stanley Plumly

and Paul Nelson did what they could to smooth my rough edges.

"Other influences on my poetry include my many years playing piano and guitar; my love of jazz (bebop and post-bebop), soul, and classical music; world-wide treks in the mountains, from China to New Zealand to Norway to Switzerland to the American Rockies. . . . I have lived abroad several times: once in Oxford, England, where the dons at Christ Church College and St. Peter's College convinced me of the virtues of the life of the mind; once in Shanghai, China, where I taught English language and literature, and, in return, was taught about contemporary Chinese surrealist poetry; once in the Marquesas Islands of French Polynesia, where my wife, Kate Riley, was conducting her field work in linguistic anthropology. Eventually, I wrote the Marquesan poems that appear in my second book, *I'm Here because I Lost My Way.*

"I write about what moves me. My elegiac impulse leads me to write about love-lost rather than love-found; about deaths, in one form or another, that point toward rebirths, in one form or another; about the intersection of politics, history and family history; about the natural world, world-wide travel, political and social disaffections. I suppose all of this brands me an 'autobiographical' writer, but like every self-respecting poet, my allegiances are to the imaginative, rather than to the biographical, truth.

"These days, I'm interested in language experiments—manipulating the minims of sense and maxims of nonsense—though I still insist on an embedded narrative and dramatic context. I'm interested in misdirections and odd digressions, and in getting humor—that constant in my daily, 'walking around' life—into the poems, the majority of which are serious, tragic, highminded pieces. I appreciate Dean Young, Bob Hicok, and Billy Collins, all of whose poetry evokes deep laughter."

BIOGRAPHICAL/CRITICAL SOURCES:

PERIODICALS

Chelsea, Volume 67, 1999, Melissa Studdard Williamson, review of *I'm Here because I Lost My Way.*
Mid-American Review, Volume XV, numbers 1-2, Naton Leslie, review of *Scavenging the Country for a Heartbeat,* pp. 252-255.
Poet & Critic, fall, 1993, J. P. White, review of *Scavenging the Country for a Heartbeat,* pp. 42-45.

SHOBIN, David 1945-

PERSONAL: Born May 2, 1945, in Baltimore, MD; son of Jack (a dentist) and Gertrude (Goldberg) Shobin; married Sharyn Sokoloff, January 16, 1975; children: Rick, Jon, Jill. *Education:* University of Pennsylvania, B.A., 1965; University of Maryland, M.D., 1969. *Religion:* Jewish.

ADDRESSES: Office—498 Route 111, Smithtown, NY 11787. *Agent*—Henry Morrison, P.O. Box 235, Bedford Hills, NY 11787.

CAREER: Montefiore Hospital and Medical Center, Bronx, NY, intern, 1969-70; New York Medical College/Flower Fifth Avenue Hospital, New York, NY, resident in obstetrics and gynecology, 1971-75; private practice of obstetrics and gynecology in Smithtown, NY, 1975—. Diplomate of American Board of Obstetrics and Gynecology; assistant clinical professor at State University of New York at Stony Brook. *Military service:* U.S. Army Reserve, Medical Corps, 1970-80; became captain.

MEMBER: American College of Obstetrics and Gynecology (fellow), Writers Guild of America, Alpha Omega Alpha.

WRITINGS:

The Unborn, Linden Press (New York, NY), 1981.
The Seeding, Linden Press (New York, NY), 1983.
The Obsession, Bantam Books (New York, NY), 1985.
The Center, St. Martin's Press (New York, NY), 1997.
Terminal Condition, St. Martin's Press (New York, NY), 1998.
The Provider, St. Martin's Press (New York, NY), 2000.
The Cure, St. Martin's Press (New York, NY), 2001.

ADAPTATIONS: The Unborn is under contract for production by Edwards/Orgliana Productions and Cinema Group.

SIDELIGHTS: David Shobin is a physician and the author of a number of medical thrillers. In *Terminal Condition,* Todd Langford is chief resident in the emergency room of a New York hospital, dealing with an escalating case load and death rate. With the help of Jordan Parker-Ross, a medical student, Todd investigates a head trauma patient with the ability to sense when lies are being told. The trail leads them to a mob boss and the discovery that patients are being used to conduct research. A *Publishers Weekly* reviewer called the atmosphere "believable," but felt that readers may find that Shobin's medical terminology "hinders the pace of his thriller." Steve Nemmers wrote for the *Mystery Reader* online that "this is a violent suspense novel. It has bloody medical scenes, guns, and hand-to-hand combat. The action sequences of the hospital and on the streets are very well constructed."

In *The Provider,* a disproportionate number of babies in the intensive care unit are dying, and obstetrician Brad Hawkins comes to the realization that they were all covered by the same HMO, AmeriCare. After some initial distrust, Brad and AmeriCare employee Morgan Robinson work together to discover that the company is employing drastic measures to increase its bottom line. Morgan is also fending off the advances of the mentally unstable Hugh Britten, an AmeriCare board member who collects skeleton specimens. A *Publishers Weekly* contributor said Shobin "nicely integrates his physician background into vivid descriptions of hospital routines."

The Cure refers to Restore Tabs, an herbal supplement made from marine plants and tested on poor women, that is said to slow the aging process and increase female sex drive. The supplement contains high estrogen levels and is causing cancers and deaths among its users, including a thirteen-year-old hysterectomy patient. Steve McLaren is the handsome doctor who has become a mouthpiece for Ecolabs, the company that produces Restore Tabs, as a favor to his friend Ted DiGiorgio, who founded the company. Steve becomes suspicious of the nutritional tablet when his patients begin to experience adverse reactions. His pursuit of the truth leads him to the discovery of the identities of the supplement's unscrupulous producers and distributors. *Library Journal* reviewer Linda M. G. Katz pointed out the educational aspect of *The Cure,* saying that it "raises issues about natural and herbal supplements as well as the regulatory loopholes that govern their availability." "Shobin's style and characterization skills help keep the yarn lively and believable," wrote William Beatty in *Booklist.*

Shobin told *CA:* "My genre as a novelist is medical melodrama."

BIOGRAPHICAL/CRITICAL SOURCES:

PERIODICALS

Booklist, January 1, 2001, William Beatty, review of *The Cure,* p. 922.
Kirkus Reviews, December 15, 2000, review of *The Cure,* p. 1715.

Library Journal, July, 1982, review of *The Seeding,* p. 1347; January 1, 2001, Linda M. G. Katz, review of *The Cure,* p. 158.

Publishers Weekly, December 19, 1980, Barbara A. Bannon, review of *The Unborn,* p. 38; June 4, 1982, review of *The Seeding,* p. 60; October 19, 1998, review of *Terminal Condition,* p. 76; January 10, 2000, review of *The Provider,* p. 49; January 1, 2001, review of *The Cure,* p. 67.

Washington Post Book World, September 5, 1982.

OTHER

Mystery Reader, http://www.themysteryreader.com/ (October 10, 2001), Steve Nemmers, review of *Terminal Condition.*

*   *   *

SIEGELBAUM, Lewis H. 1949-

PERSONAL: Born January 28, 1949, in New York, NY; son of Morton and Blanche Siegelbaum; children: Sami, Sasu. *Education:* Columbia University, B.A., 1970; St. Antony's College, Oxford, D.Phil., 1975. *Politics:* "Left progressive." *Avocational interests:* Tennis, movies.

ADDRESSES: Home—453 Rosewood Ave., East Lansing, MI 48823. *Office*—Department of History, Michigan State University, East Lansing, MI 48824. *E-mail*—siegelba@msu.edu.

CAREER: La Trobe University, Melbourne, Australia, began as lecturer, became senior lecturer in history, 1975-83; Michigan State University, East Lansing, MI, assistant professor, 1983-85, associate professor, 1985-87, professor of history, 1988—, chair of department, 1999—.

MEMBER: American Historical Association, American Association for the Advancement of Slavic Studies.

WRITINGS:

The Politics of Industrial Mobilization in Russia, 1915-1917: A Study of the War-Industries Committees, St. Martin's Press (New York, NY), 1984.

Stakhanovism and the Politics of Productivity in the USSR, 1935-1941, Cambridge University Press (New York, NY), 1988.

The Soviet State and Society between Revolutions, 1918-1929, Cambridge University Press (New York, NY), 1992.

(Editor, with William G. Rosenberg) *Social Dimensions of Soviet Industrialization,* Indiana University Press (Bloomington, IN), 1993.

(Editor, with Ronald Grigor Suny) *Making Workers Soviet: Power, Class, and Identity,* Cornell University Press (Ithaca, NY), 1994.

(Editor, with Daniel J. Walkowitz) *Workers of the Donbass Speak: Survival and Identity in the New Ukraine, 1989-1992,* State University of New York Press (Albany, NY), 1995.

(Editor, with Andrei Sokolov) *Stalinism as a Way of Life: A Narrative in Documents,* Yale University Press (New Haven, CT), 2000.

SIDELIGHTS: Lewis H. Siegelbaum is a scholar of Russian history whose *Stalinism as a Way of Life: A Narrative in Documents,* co-edited with Andrei Sokolov, gathers together some 157 documents from Soviet archives for the 1930s. These documents include letters written by Soviet citizens to their government officials and to local newspapers, and reports written by government officials to their superiors. Letter-writers complained about living conditions, about the hardships of collective farming, and what they considered injustices and violations of Soviet legality. According to the critic for *Kirkus Reviews, Stalinism as a Way of Life* reveals "the mass of popular resistance to Soviet rule." The book provides what Leonard Benardo in the *New York Times Book Review* called "a wide-angle lens on the decade's dizzying events." Benardo praised Siegelbaum and Sokolov for having "performed a worthwhile service." Similarly, Richard Pipes in the *New Republic* wrote: "Siegelbaum has performed a major service by selecting and translating these materials which depict the day-to-day conditions of life under Stalin. . . . They indicate more convincingly than ever that Soviet citizens were the helpless victims of a totalitarian regime driven primarily by a lust for power."

Siegelbaum told *CA:* "The Soviet Union is gone but it lives on in many unexpected ways, for better and for worse."

BIOGRAPHICAL/CRITICAL SOURCES:

PERIODICALS

American Historical Review, April, 1994, William B. Husband, review of *The Soviet State and Society between Revolutions, 1918-1929,* p. 613.

Booklist, November 15, 2000, Gilbert Taylor, review of *Stalinism as a Way of Life: A Narrative in Documents,* p. 608.

Kirkus Reviews, October 15, 2000, review of *Stalinism as a Way of Life,* p. 1469.

New Republic, December 18, 2000, Richard Pipes, "The Evil of Banality," p. 35.

New York Times Book Review, November 19, 2000, Leonard Benardo, review of *Stalinism as a Way of Life,* p. 75.

Times Literary Supplement, December 9, 1988, p. 1366.

*   *   *

SILBERMAN, Neil Asher 1950-

PERSONAL: Born June 19, 1950, in Boston, MA; son of Saul J. (a manufacturer) and Barbara (Kimball) Silberman; married Ellen Glassburn, November 30, 1976; children: Maya. *Education:* Wesleyan University, Middletown, CT, B.A., 1972; attended Hebrew University of Jerusalem, 1974-76.

ADDRESSES: Home—Ohain, Belgium. *Office*—Ename Center for Public Archaeology, 13-15 Abdijstraat, B-9700 Oudenaarde, Belgium. *Agent*—Carol Mann Agency. *E-mail*—neil.silberman@enamecenter. org.

CAREER: Israel Department of Antiquities and Museums, Jerusalem, Israel, staff archaeologist, 1972-74; University of Haifa, Haifa, Israel, staff archaeologist on Akko Excavation Project, 1974-76. Coordinator of International Programs, Ename Center for Public Archaeology and Heritage Presentation, 1998—; *Archaeology* (magazine), contributing editor.

WRITINGS:

Digging for God and Country: Exploration, Archaeology, and the Secret Struggle for the Holy Land, 1799-1917, Knopf (New York, NY), 1982.

Between Past and Present: Archaeology, Ideology, and Nationalism in the Modern Middle East, Henry Holt (New York, NY), 1989.

A Prophet from amongst You: The Life of Yigael Yadin: Soldier, Scholar, and Mythmaker of Modern Israel, Addison Wesley (Reading, MA), 1993.

The Hidden Scrolls: Christianity, Judaism, and the War for the Dead Sea Scrolls, G. P. Putnam's Sons (New York, NY), 1994.

(Editor, with Mark P. Leone) *Invisible America: Unearthing Our Hidden History,* Henry Holt (New York, NY), 1995.

(Editor, with David Small) *The Archaeology of Israel: Constructing the Past, Interpreting the Present,*

Sheffield Academic Press (Sheffield, England), 1997.

(With Richard A. Horsley) *The Message and the Kingdom: How Jesus and Paul Ignited a Revolution and Transformed the Ancient World,* Grosset/Putnam (New York, NY), 1997.

Heavenly Powers: Unraveling the Secret History of the Kabbalah, Grosset/Putnam (New York, NY), 1998.

(With Israel Finkelstein) *The Bible Unearthed: Archaeology's New Vision of Ancient Israel and the Origin of Its Sacred Texts,* Free Press (New York, NY), 2001.

SIDELIGHTS: In *Digging for God and Country: Exploration, Archaeology, and the Secret Struggle for the Holy Land, 1799-1917,* Neil Asher Silberman discusses the burgeoning international and archaeological interest in Palestine at the turn of the nineteenth century and details the subsequent political struggles for the possession of the area's religious treasures. The book contains descriptions of various national expeditions to the Holy Land and profiles major personalities involved in exploring the area's trade routes, mapping the lands for later conquest, and establishing the field of biblical archaeology. Sam Hall Kaplan of the *Los Angeles Times* judged *Digging for God and Country* "a fascinating tale well told." "To understand some of the emotions archaeology in the Holy Land engenders," he continued, "is to understand some of the problems besetting the region today."

In *Between Past and Present: Archaeology, Ideology, and Nationalism in the Modern Middle East,* Silberman studies the links between archaeological research and social and political trends. His investigation focuses on Israel, Egypt, Yugoslavia, Greece, Turkey, Cyprus and North Yemen. *New York Times Book Review* contributor Catherine Vanderpool felt that the reason for the author's selection of countries lies "in the historical background: all are centers of ancient and creative civilizations that in later history underwent phases of external conquest and subjugation, followed by—in most cases—a period of domination by Western Europe." Vanderpool wrote that Silberman "is most cogent in his discussion of Israel, which fits in with the overall framework."

A Prophet from amongst You: The Life of Yigael Yadin: Soldier, Scholar, and Mythmaker of Modern Israel is a biography of the Israeli archaeologist and director of the Masada excavations of the 1960s. As the title reflects, Yadin (1917-1984) was also a teacher and military man. He led the underground militia, served under

David Ben-Gurion during Israel's war for independence, and headed the Israeli delegations to the peace conferences in Rhodes and Lausanne. He was the first chief of staff of the Israeli Defense Forces during peacetime. In 1952, Yadin left politics to teach. In a *New York Times Book Review* article, Susan Shapiro called Silberman "a respectful and careful chronicler."

A *Kirkus Reviews* contributor wrote that in *The Hidden Scrolls: Christianity, Judaism, and the War for the Dead Sea Scrolls,* Silberman "presents both a stunning indictment of the small cadre of scholars who controlled access to the scrolls for decades and a marvelous revisionist reconstruction of the ancient community that produced the Scrolls. . . . His depiction . . . is terrific." Silberman puts forth his view that the Dead Sea Scrolls are more than a collection of the religious manuscripts of an isolated monastic community. He feels they are the written documentation of Jewish protest and the call for a holy war against Roman rule that resulted in the unsuccessful rebellion of A.D. 66. Silberman concludes that the messiah of the Scrolls is not a spiritual leader, but rather a political figure who will lead the holy war. In writing this study, Silberman interviewed two dozen Scroll scholars, and he provides the history of the discovery of the Scrolls in 1946 by a young Bedouin shepherd, and the fight to liberate the Scrolls from the experts who have exerted control over the documents. A *Publishers Weekly* reviewer called *The Hidden Scrolls* a "provocative report." Ilene Cooper wrote in *Booklist* that it is "interesting reading, whether or not one agrees with Silberman's conclusions."

The Archaeology of Israel: Constructing the Past, Interpreting the Present is a collection of essays that came out of a conference on the archaeology of Israel which brought together scholars from various disciplines and different perspectives. Silberman and coeditor David Small provide the introduction and an overview of the proceedings and contributions. Keith Whitelam wrote in *Antiquity* that "the opening presentations are sensitive to the politics of scholarship, and particularly the politics of archaeology, while Silberman makes an eloquent case for the ways in which all scholarship is implicated, whether closely or not, in politics. . . . The volume, with its different voices and perspectives, as well as significant silences, illustrates that the social and political location of scholarship, its constructions of the past, and its consequences for contemporary perceptions of identity or land are the proper object of scholarly analysis."

Silberman wrote *The Message and the Kingdom: How Jesus and Paul Ignited a Revolution and Transformed the Ancient World* with Richard A. Horsley, who teaches religion at the University of Massachusetts. *Booklist* reviewer Steve Schroeder called it "a riveting account of the emergence of Christianity and the sociopolitical world in which it was born." Eugene O. Bowser wrote in *Library Journal* that "in this scholarly, well-written book, the authors view everything through a political filter, even religious motivation." Silberman and Horsley consider whether the messages of Jesus and Paul were limited to spirituality or whether they more directly applied to the lives of the people living under Roman rule. They draw on archaeological evidence, such as the funeral urn of Joseph Caiaphas, the high priest at Jesus's trial. A *Publishers Weekly* reviewer called *The Message and the Kingdom* "a riveting page-turner that opens a new window on the origins of Christianity."

A *Publishers Weekly* contributor called *Heavenly Powers: Unraveling the Secret History of the Kabbalah* "part detective story and part cultural history." Silberman follows the mystical tradition from its beginnings with the visions of Ezekiel, to its movement through the Roman and Byzantine empires, to France, Spain, and finally the land that is now Israel. He writes of the Kabbalah's popularity with New Age followers and of its relevance in modern times. A *Booklist* reviewer said that Silberman "manages to put this very complicated topic into a readable framework that encompasses time, place, and ideology."

Silberman wrote *The Bible Unearthed: Archaeology's New Vision of Ancient Israel and the Origin of Its Sacred Texts* with Israel Finkelstein, director of Tel Aviv University's excavations at Megiddo (ancient Armageddon). *Library Journal* contributor Marianne Orme wrote that they "attempt to sort out what archaeology tells us about who wrote the Bible." The volume was called "a contentious study that will dismay advocates of a literal interpretation of the Bible," by a *Publishers Weekly* reviewer. The authors draw on digs in Israel, Jordan, Egypt, Lebanon, and Syria, in concluding that the early books of the Bible were first codified hundreds of years after the core events which they were describing took place. These first writings came during the time of King Josiah (639-609), when the text was edited "to further religious reform and territorial ambitions." They find no historical records to reenforce the Biblical accounts of Abraham, Joseph, Moses, and the Exodus. The authors conclude that the accounts of David and Solomon contained in the Bible are out of proportion to their actual power and importance. David is described as merely a tribal chief, and the story of Joshua and the walls of Jericho are viewed as "a romantic mirage." Bryce Christensen, writing in *Booklist,* called *The Bible Unearthed* "a significant, if controversial, contribution to cross-disciplinary studies of history and religion."

BIOGRAPHICAL/CRITICAL SOURCES:

PERIODICALS

American Journal of Archaeology, January, 1991, review of *Between Past and Present: Archaeology, Ideology, and Nationalism in the Modern Middle East,* p. 173.

Antiquity, September, 1990, Peter Gathercole, review of *Between Past and Present,* p. 696; December, 1998, Keith Whitelam, review of *The Archaeology of Israel: Constructing the Past, Interpreting the Present,* p. 951.

Archaeology, September, 1983, review of *Digging for God and Country: Exploration, Archaeology, and the Secret Struggle for the Holy Land, 1799-1917,* p. 73; November, 1990, Douglas V. Campana, Pamela J. Crabtree, review of *Between Past and Present,* p. 80; March, 1994, William G. Dever, review of *A Prophet from amongst You: The Life of Yigael Yadin: Soldier, Scholar, and Mythmaker of Modern Israel,* p. 59.

Booklist, September 15, 1989, review of *Between Past and Present,* p. 141; October 15, 1994, Ilene Cooper, review of *The Hidden Scrolls: Christianity, Judaism, and the War for the Dead Sea Scrolls,* p. 376; October 1, 1997, Steve Schroeder, review of *The Message and the Kingdom: How Jesus and Paul Ignited a Revolution and Transformed the Ancient World,* p. 284; October 1, 1998, review of *Heavenly Powers: Unraveling the Secret History of the Kabbalah,* p. 295; January 1, 2001, Bryce Christensen, review of *The Bible Unearthed: Archaeology's New Vision of Ancient Israel and the Origin of Its Sacred Texts,* p. 880.

Choice, April, 1991, review of *Digging for God and Country,* p. 1281; July, 1994, review of *A Prophet from amongst You,* p. 1781.

Christian Science Monitor, March 4, 1998, Judy Huenneke, review of *The Message and the Kingdom,* p. 14.

Kirkus Reviews, August 15, 1989, review of *Between Past and Present,* p. 1231; October 15, 1993, review of *A Prophet from amongst You,* p. 1318; August 15, 1994, review of *The Hidden Scrolls,* p. 1108; September 15, 1998, review of *Heavenly Powers,* p. 1366.

Kliatt, March, 1997, review of *The Hidden Scrolls,* p. 28.

Library Journal, October 1, 1989, Joan W. Gartland, review of *Between Past and Present,* p. 106; October 1, 1994, Craig W. Beard, review of *The Hidden Scrolls,* p. 84; September 15, 1995, Robert A. Curtis, review of *Invisible America: Unearthing Our Hidden History,* p. 81; November 1, 1997, Eugene O. Bowser, review of *The Message and the Kingdom,* p. 79; October 15, 1998, review of *Heavenly Powers,* p. 75; December, 2000, Marianne Orme, review of *The Bible Unearthed,* p. 150.

Los Angeles Times, June 29, 1982, Sam Hall Kaplan, review of *Digging for God and Country;* January 7, 1990, review of *Between Past and Present,* p. 7.

Nation, November 11, 1996, review of *A Prophet from amongst You,* p. 25.

New York Times Book Review, November 12, 1989, Catherine Vanderpool, "Politics among the Ruins," p. 66; August 28, 1994, Susan Shapiro, "In Short: Nonfiction," p. 16; December 25, 1994, Anthony J. Saldarini, review of *The Hidden Scrolls,* p. 21; December 22, 1996, review of *The Hidden Scrolls,* p. 20.

Publishers Weekly, August 11, 1989, Genevieve Stuttaford, review of *Between Past and Present,* p. 446; October 26, 1990, review of *Between Past and Present,* p. 64; August 29, 1994, review of *The Hidden Scrolls,* p. 57; September 15, 1997, review of *The Message and the Kingdom,* p. 69; October 26, 1998, review of *Heavenly Powers,* p. 61; November 27, 2000, review of *The Bible Unearthed,* p. 72.

Religious Studies Review, January, 1985, review of *Digging for God and Country,* p. 67; January, 1998, review of *The Archaeology of Israel,* p. 56.

Southern Humanities Review, spring, 1998, review of *The Hidden Scrolls,* p. 191.

Washington Post Book World, October 29, 1989, review of *Between Past and Present,* p. 5.

*   *   *

SIMON, Christopher Fitz
  See FITZ-SIMON, Christopher

*   *   *

SIMON, Myles
  See FOLLETT, Ken(neth Martin)

SINGER, Peter (Albert David) 1946-

PERSONAL: Born July 6, 1946, in Melbourne, Australia; son of Ernest (a businessman) and Cora (a doctor; maiden name, Oppenheim) Singer; married Renata Diamond (a teacher), December 16, 1968; children: Ruth, Marion, Esther. *Education:* University of Melbourne, B.A. (with honors), 1967, M.A., 1969; University College, Oxford, B.Phil., 1971. *Politics:* Australian Greens. *Religion:* "None."

ADDRESSES: Office—University Center for Human Values, Louis Marx Hall, Princeton University, Princeton, NJ 08544; fax: 609-258-1285. *E-mail*—psinger@Princeton.EDU.

CAREER: Oxford University, University College, Oxford, England, lecturer in philosophy, 1971-73; New York University, New York, NY, visiting assistant professor of philosophy, 1973-74; La Trobe University, Bundoora, Victoria, Australia, senior lecturer in philosophy, 1975-76; Monash University, Clayton, Victoria, Australia, professor of philosophy, 1977-99; Centre for Human Bioethics, Clayton, Australia, director, 1983-91, deputy director, 1992-99; Princeton University, Princeton, NJ, Ira W. DeCamp Professor of Bioethics, 1999—. Senate candidate for The Greens, Victoria, at the 1996 Australian federal election.

AWARDS, HONORS: Best nonfiction book published in Australia, National Book Council of Australia, 1994, for *Rethinking Life and Death.*

WRITINGS:

Democracy and Disobedience, Clarendon Press, 1973, Oxford University Press (New York, NY), 1974.
(Editor, with Thomas Regan) *Animal Rights and Human Obligations,* Prentice-Hall (Englewood Cliffs, NJ), 1975, 2nd edition, 1989.
Animal Liberation: A New Ethics for Our Treatment of Animals, Random House (New York, NY), 1975, 2nd edition, 1990.
Practical Ethics, Cambridge University Press (New York, NY), 1979, 2nd edition, 1993.
Marx, Oxford University Press, 1980.
The Expanding Circle: Ethics and Sociobiology, Farrar, Straus (New York, NY), 1981.
(Editor, with William Walters) *Test-Tube Babies,* Oxford University Press (Oxford, England), 1982.
Hegel, Oxford University Press (Oxford, England), 1983.
(With Deane Wells) *The Reproduction Revolution: New Ways of Making Babies,* Oxford University Press, 1984, 2nd edition published as *Making Babies: The New Science and Ethics of Conception,* Scribner's (New York, NY), 1985.
(Editor) *In Defence of Animals,* Blackwell (New York, NY), 1985.
(With Helga Kuhse) *Should the Baby Live? The Problem of Handicapped Infants,* Oxford University Press (Oxford, England), 1985.
(Editor) *Applied Ethics,* Oxford University Press (Oxford, England), 1986.
(With Lori Gruen) *Animal Liberation: A Graphic Guide,* Camden Press (London, England), 1987.
(With Jim Mason) *Animal Factories,* Harmony Books (New York, NY), 1990.
(Editor) *Embryo Experimentation,* Cambridge University Press (Cambridge, England), 1990.
(Editor) *A Companion to Ethics,* Oxford University Press (Oxford, England), 1991.
(With Barbara Dover and Ingrid Newkirk) *Save the Animals,* 1991.
How Are We to Live?, Text (Melbourne, Australia), 1993, Prometheus (Buffalo, NY), 1994.
(Editor) *Ethics,* Oxford University Press (Oxford, England), 1994.
(Editor, with Paola Cavalieri) *The Great Ape Project: Equality beyond Humanity,* St. Martin's Press (New York, NY), 1994.
Rethinking Life and Death, Text (Melbourne, Australia), 1994, St. Martin's Press (New York, NY), 1995.
The Greens, Text (Melbourne, Australia), 1996.
(Editor, with Helga Kuhse) *A Companion to Bioethics,* Blackwell Publishers (Malden, MA), 1998.
Ethics into Action: Henry Spim and the Animal Rights Movement, Rowman & Littlefield (Latham, MD), 1998.
(Editor, with Helga Kuhse) *Bioethics: An Anthology,* Blackwell Publishers (Malden, MA), 1999.
A Darwinian Left: Politics, Evolution, and Cooperation, Yale University Press (New Haven, CT), 2000.
Writings on an Ethical Life, Ecco Press (New York, NY), 2000.

Coeditor of *Bioethics,* 1986-99. Contributor to *New York Review of Books* and to philosophy journals.

WORK IN PROGRESS: A biography of his maternal grandfather, David Oppenheim, a teacher and onetime associate of Sigmund Freud who died in a Nazi concentration camp in 1943; a work on globalization and ethics.

SIDELIGHTS: Few philosophers have attracted as much public notice as Peter Singer. His appointment as Ira W. DeCamp Professor of Bioethics at Princeton University's Center for Human Values late in 1998 provoked outrage across the country. Singer's critics demonstrated on campus and inundated the school's alumni and student newspapers with written protests. Millionaire alumnus Steve Forbes, then a Republican candidate for president, announced that he would withhold future contributions to the university while Singer remained on the faculty. *U.S. News & World Report* ran a headline associating Singer with the "Final Solution" of Nazism, and a headline in the *Washington Post* referred to his "PHILOSOPHY OF DEATH." The controversy centered on arguments, which Singer has presented in such books as *Practical Ethics, Should the Baby Live?,* and *Rethinking Life and Death,* advocating euthanasia and a rethinking of what he considers to be outdated attitudes toward the sanctity of human life. "I'm a philosopher," Singer explained to *Los Angeles Times* writer Josh Getlin. "And that's someone who makes others uncomfortable. Someone who asks them to consider the unthinkable."

Indeed, Singer has been called the most influential philosopher of his generation. His books have been translated into eighteen languages and are widely used in college courses in the United States and Europe. He has served as president of the International Association of Bioethics and as editor of its official journal, *Bioethics.* His work, according to a statement from the university's president in the *Princeton Weekly Bulletin,* considers "difficult and provocative topics and in many cases challenges long-established ways of thinking—or ways of avoiding thinking—about them," and "is intellectually astute, morally serious and open to engagement with others" while examining "important questions with integrity, rigor and originality."

Singer maintains that many of his critics take his "unthinkable" views out of context and grossly misrepresent his work. "My entire philosophy is shaped by an abhorrence of suffering and cruelty," he told *Psychology Today* interviewer Jill Neimark. In fact, it was Singer's sensitivity to the suffering of animals that first introduced the Australian philosopher to a wide readership. While teaching at England's Oxford University in the early 1970s, Singer encountered a group of people who were vegetarians, not because of any personal distaste for meat, but because they felt, as Singer later wrote, that "there was no way in which [maltreatment of animals by humans] could be justified ethically." Impressed by their arguments, the young philosopher soon joined their ranks. Out of his growing concern for the

rights of animals came the book, *Animal Liberation: A New Ethics for Our Treatment of Animals,* a study of the suffering inflicted upon animals in the name of scientific experimentation and food production.

In this widely influential book, Singer used the term "speciesism" to define "a prejudice or attitude of bias toward the interests of members of one's own species and against those of members of other species." Speciesism, he argues, is at the root of human cruelty to other animals. For example, Singer believes that many of the experiments performed on laboratory animals are unnecessary because, in the words of *New York Times Book Review* critic C. G. Luckhardt, they often "duplicate experiments already performed, . . . tell us what we already know, . . . cause medical problems in animals that could for the most part be avoided by humans, . . . and create data that are useless because inapplicable to humans." It is also unnecessary for humans to eat meat, the author maintains, especially when it means that animals must suffer during nearly every stage of their lives in order to provide us with protein that can be obtained from other sources. As Luckhardt concluded in his summary of Singer's position, our treatment of animals is ultimately immoral because "there is every reason to believe, and no good reason to deny, that animals feel pain. . . . Whatever reasons we have for not inflicting pain on innocent and helpless humans extend equally well to animals."

Luckhardt praised Singer for writing a work of philosophy that is so "refreshing and well-argued; as a book intended for the mass market it is quite unhysterical yet engagingly written. [His] documentation is unrhetorical and unemotional, his arguments tight and formidable, for he bases his case on neither personal nor religious nor highly abstract philosophical principles, but on moral positions most of us already accept. The strength of this book lies in shifting the burden of argument to those who would maintain that animals ought to be excluded from our sphere of moral concern."

John Naughton of *Listener* called *Animal Liberation* "a sombre, challenging and somewhat harrowing book, which deserves to be widely read and 'inwardly digested,' if that is not too gruesome a phrase . . . [Singer] is supported in [his] claims, not by the gooey affirmations of little old ladies, but by the sober deliberations of some of the most eminent scientists in Britain." Though Naughton found that Singer "occasionally rides roughshod over his opponents," he declared that *Animal Liberation* "is one of the most thoughtful and persuasive books that I have read in a long time."

Despite assessments of the book that were otherwise quite favorable, both *Spectator*'s Nick Totton and *Village Voice*'s Richard Goldstein detected a hint of naivete in Singer's philosophy. Totton observed: "Mr. Singer's main shortcoming as a propagandist is that he believes in the naked light of human reason. He is a philosopher, and a utilitarian at that; for him, a logical demonstration that meat-eating or vivisection increases the overall quotient of sentient suffering on this planet is conclusive. . . . [His] arguments are lucid, but really quite beside the point: they depend firstly on the axiom that there is a network of ethical values somehow built into the universe, and secondly upon the fond hope that conformity with such values is the primary intention of human beings."

Goldstein also noted a tendency towards what he termed "social obliviousness" in *Animal Liberation*. He contended that Singer ignores considerations such as the major changes that would need to occur in institutions, economics, labor, and individual behavior for people to give up eating meat and the general confusion this would create in our society. Nevertheless, Goldstein concluded, "I am willing to forgive Peter Singer his social obliviousness and more. [*Animal Liberation*] is an important book, first, because it reveals . . . the rough beast of self-interest which motivates all human society. Second, because it offers its solutions . . . in a spirit of mercy so touching and disquieting that one can only marvel at the persistent power of compassion. And third, because it questions, unintentionally perhaps, the sectarian organization of the world's people into competing states, and the brutality we extend to all those (animals, and the people who are denied the protein we feed to animals) beyond the pale."

"I want us to have a graduated moral approach to all sentient beings, related to their capacities to feel and suffer," Singer explained when Neimark asked him to sum up his views on speciesism. "If the being has self-awareness, we ought to give it even more rights. I'm not a biological egalitarian. I do not think that all nonhuman animals have the same claim to protection of their lives as humans do. I don't think it's as bad to kill a simple animal, like a frog or a fish, as it is to kill a normal human being. You have to ask yourself what actually makes it worse to kill one being rather than another, and the best answer I can come up with is one's sense of self, that you are alive and have a past and future."

Responding to criticism that this view de-emphasizes the value of human life, Singer added "You really have to question human superiority. What justifies the things we do to animals? What justifies keeping a person in a vegetative coma alive?" Noting that Aristotelian and Judeo-Christian philosophies justify human dominance over animals, he suggested that "Once you get away from those two worldviews, there just isn't a basis for drawing a sharp moral boundary between us and them." Since the publication of *Animal Liberation,* which by 2000 had sold more than 500,000 copies, the animal rights movement has increased in power and influence. Singer expresses satisfaction that some of the most egregious practices he condemned in the book have been discontinued.

Though his advocacy of animal liberation brought Singer into the public eye, his views on the relative value of human lives, most forcefully expressed in *Practical Ethics,* form the core of his most controversial thought. In this book, Singer grapples with such questions as the permissibility of ending lives filled with suffering or meaninglessness, and states outright that "Killing a disabled infant is not morally equivalent to killing a person. Very often it is not wrong at all." These two sentences may be the most frequently quoted of all Singer's statements, but he maintains that they are generally misunderstood. His argument, he explains, is not that all disabled infants should be put to death, or that the state should have any authority to decide upon such an action. Rather, Singer writes that the parents of severely disabled newborns should have the right to decide whether the child should live or die. Administering a lethal injection to such a child, Singer argues, is morally preferable to the common, but not openly acknowledged practice, of withholding life-sustaining treatments. As he commented to Neimark, "a lot of this goes on all the time and it's kind of ironic that all this flak I get is really just for saying, Hey, wait a minute, let's look at what we're doing and see if we can find a coherent ethic for it."

Despite this justification, Singer's views remain highly controversial. He was booed off the podium in 1991 when he attempted to speak about infanticide at the University of Zurich; he has also received death threats and been physically assaulted. "Those incidents in Europe made me most uncomfortable," he told Getlin. "They gave me a sense of what fanaticism is, what it feels like to be on the receiving end of such behavior. Those people wanted to shut me up, to keep me from publishing." Yet Singer has continued to write books that confront some of the thorniest moral and ethical dilemmas of our time, including those arising from new medical and reproductive technologies. In *Making Babies: The New Science and Ethics of Conception,* a book he co-authored with Deane Wells, he examines the issue of test-tube babies, surrogate motherhood, sperm banks, and cloning. Praising the authors for their "calm and sensitivity," Lionel Tiger of *New York Times Book Review* wrote, "With almost triumphant sobriety, Mr. Singer and Mr. Wells offer a plausible and practical context within which to approach each general issue . . . without losing sight of a good physician's sense of responsibility to individual patients."

Rae Goodell, reviewing the book in *Washington Post Book World,* commented that while the authors welcome and encourage the unprecedented changes occurring in human reproduction, they cast an unfavorable eye toward unbridled progress and recommend that national bioethics committees be appointed to study and regulate the progress and use of new reproductive technologies. "Singer and Wells ask that each stage of development be carefully evaluated before proceeding to the next, and that basic ethical and environmental standards be set," Goodell wrote, continuing that "the restrictions that Singer and Wells would place on reproduction technologies are relatively few and remarkably lenient, however. Embryos could be harvested for spare organs until the embryos were old enough to be sentient, and cloning would be permitted if limited, say, to 'one replica per person.' "

Tabitha Powledge in *Nation* disagreed with the authors' discussion of the private and public control of genetic engineering. "It is a mystery why Singer and Wells appear unable to see that the [government] committee's veto power effectively removes the decision from parents, where the authors say it ought to be." Powledge also identified what she considered another weakness in the work. While congratulating the authors for a "clear, jargon-free model of how to present philosophical arguments to a general audience," Powledge discerned an "insidious" aspect to the book. "It pretends to be a disinterested, dispassionate examination of I.V.F. [in vitro fertilization], although it is actually promulgating a strong utilitarian point of view. . . . It all but ignores the issues of justice and equality which I.V.F. raises."

In *Rethinking Life and Death: The Collapse of Our Traditional Ethics,* Singer returns to themes introduced in *Practical Ethics.* He argues that decisions based on Judeo-Christian notions of the value of human life are outmoded due to twentieth-century advances in medicine and technology. These have in turn created new moral conflicts, such as determining how long to keep someone in a vegetative state alive through technical means. He urges the adoption of a more utilitarian approach to moral issues. Singer's solution, according to

Los Angeles Times reviewer Judith Gingold, is to discard "the Old Testament account of man as a special being created in God's image, with dominion over the rest of nature. Instead, Singer bases his ethic on a Darwinian view of man as one among other animal species, one who shares many emotional and psychological features with his fellow creatures, and who is a part of nature rather than its conqueror." In this vein, Singer argues that the worth of human and non-human life needs to be examined against items such as self-awareness, rationality, and the conscious desire for life and the ability to enjoy it. He then recommends adding new commandments to the traditional Judeo-Christian set, including allowing for a person's will to live or die, bringing only wanted children into the world, and not discriminating against other species. Singer acknowledges there may be many different remedies, and encourages people to begin rethinking and searching for solutions.

Rethinking Life and Death received mixed reviews. *Washington Post Book World*'s George Weigel contended that Singer's solutions "would mean nothing less than the end of humanism in either its Judeo-Christian or Enlightenment-secular form," concluding that, "Far from pointing the way out of today's moral dilemmas, Singer's book is a roadmap for driving down the darkest of moral blind alleys, at the end of which, however spiffed-up and genteel, is Dr. Mengele: The embodiment of the triumph of power over principle, in the manipulation of life and death by the 'fit' at the expense of the 'unworthy.' " In contrast, Gingold praised Singer's ideas as "coherent, lucid and fresh, and presented in a non-didactic voice that resonates with good will." A reviewer in *Publishers Weekly* noted that *Rethinking Life and Death* contains "brilliant essays," while Singer "makes a forceful case for his new ethic."

In his analysis of political issues, *The Darwinian Left: Politics, Evolution, and Cooperation,* Singer contends that the Left is "in need of a new paradigm," incorporating awareness of the biological basis of human behavior. Both Jenny Teichman in *New Criterion* and Larry Arnhart in *National Review* argued that, though Singer identifies his views as Darwinian, they are not based on evolutionary theory at all. "Singer's mistake," Arnhart wrote, "is to assume that we can organize our moral lives around norms derived from abstract reasoning without guidance from our natural emotions. . . . Darwinian social theory provides scientific confirmation for what conservatives already know by common sense: Despite the variability of our moral judgments in different circumstances, enduring standards of right and wrong are rooted in our natural instincts. Singer's confused attempt to justify a Darwinian Left therefore actually helps us to see the potential justification for a Darwinian Right." *Salon.com* reviewer Ralph Brave, however, welcomed the book as "one of the few genuinely stimulating meditations on the topic, and one whose perspectives have implications far beyond the considerations of the Left."

Singer has also attracted considerable attention for his views about obligations toward the poor. His 1999 essay in the *New York Times* Sunday magazine, "The Singer Solution to World Poverty," presents this argument in simple terms: we act immorally when we spend money on luxuries, because that money could instead be used to save the lives of starving children. A person who kills a child to sell his or her organs for transplant is no different, he suggests, from people who spend excess money on household remodeling, new clothes, and gourmet meals rather than donating it to famine relief organizations. Singer offers a precise dollar amount: "An American household with an income of $50,000 spends around $30,000 annually on necessities. . . . Therefore, for a household bringing in $50,000 a year, donations to help the world's poor should be as close as possible to $20,000. The $30,000 required for necessities holds for higher incomes as well. So a household making $100,000 could cut a yearly check for $70,000. Again, the formula is simple: whatever money you're spending on luxuries, not necessities, should be given away. . . . If that makes living a morally decent life extremely arduous, well, then that is the way things are." Singer states that he gives twenty percent of his own income to Oxfam and has donated royalties from his books to other charities.

Peter Berkowitz, writing for *The New Republic,* responded to Singer's *New York Times* article with skepticism. "Having casually invested intuition with moral authority," Berkowitz wrote, "Singer overlooks that in living the moral life we find ourselves subject to the authority of multiple and competing intuitions." Pointing out that Singer violates his own ethic by continuing to support his mother, who has Alzheimer's disease, Berkowitz concluded that "it is hard to imagine a more stunning rebuke to the well-heeled and well-ensconced academic discipline of practical ethics than that its most controversial and influential star, at the peak of his discipline . . . should reveal, only as the result of a reporter's prodding, and only in the battle with his own elderly mother's suffering, that he has just begun to appreciate that the moral life is complex."

Concerned that the publicity surrounding his Princeton appointment had resulted in a widespread misunder-

standing of his work, Singer wrote *Writings on an Ethical Life* to set the record straight. The book, which clarifies his basic philosophy and teachings, drew spirited response. Many critics, including Roger Scruton in *New Statesman,* identified serious flaws and inconsistencies in Singer's theses, and complained that his arguments are oversimplified. Several others, however, found *Writings on an Ethical Life* a work of brilliance and courage. A reviewer for *Publishers Weekly* hailed it as a work that "makes a significant contribution to ethical discussions in modern society," and praised Singer as "one of the most innovative, sensitive and honest philosophers of morality in today's world." J. B. Schneewind, in *New York Times Book Review,* wrote that Singer's aim "is to make us better people, not better moral philosophers" and concluded, "If you read this book, it may change your life." Joyce Carol Oates, according to a report by *Publishers Weekly* contributor Bridget Kinsella, has promoted *Writings on an Ethical Life* as an important book that should be widely read and discussed.

Among his fellow philosophers, Singer has both adamant critics and staunch supporters. Getlin writes that Peter Unger, distinguished professor at New York University, considers Singer "one of the most influential ethicists and philosophers of the last thirty to forty years."

As a writer in *Economist* stated, "Until Peter Singer came on the scene, philosophical discussion of moral questions in the twentieth century Anglophone world was limited on the whole to refined speculation about the meaning of the main moral ideas such as goodness, duty and virtue. . . . Almost single-handedly [Singer] took moral philosophy back to an earlier tradition of direct engagement with the world, and in doing so has made . . . substantial contributions to ethical debate."

BIOGRAPHICAL/CRITICAL SOURCES:

BOOKS

Singer, Peter, *Animal Liberation: A New Ethics for Our Treatment of Animals,* Random House, 1975.
Singer, Peter, *Practical Ethics,* Cambridge University Press, 1979, 2nd edition, 1993.
Singer, Peter, *Writings on an Ethical Life,* Ecco Press, 2000.

PERIODICALS

Animals' Agenda, March-April, 1999, Jill Howard Church, "Philosophical Differences," p. 8.
Bloomsbury Review, March, 1999, review of *Ethics into Action,* p. 21.

Booklist, November 15, 2000, Mary Carroll, review of *Writings on an Ethical Life,* p. 589.

Commentary, April, 2001, Damon Linker, "Rights for Rodents," p. 41.

Current, February, 2000, Peter Berkowitz, review of *A Darwinian Left: Politics, Evolution, and Cooperation,* p. 29.

Economist, November 11, 2000, review of *Writings on an Ethical Life,* p. 108.

Kirkus Reviews, October 15, 2000, review of *Writings on an Ethical Life,* p. 1469.

Library Journal, January, 1999, Peggie Partello, review of *Ethics into Action: Henry Spira and the Animal Rights Movement,* p. 140.

Listener, June 17, 1976.

Los Angeles Times, January 8, 2001, Josh Getlin, "The Philosopher as Provocateur," p. E-1.

Los Angeles Times Book Review, September 24, 1995, p. 2.

Melbourne Weekly, December 10, 1995, p. 4.

Nation, August 17-24, 1985; July 5, 1999, Benjamin Kunkel, review of *Ethical Vegetarianism: From Pythagoras to Peter Singer,* p. 32.

National Review, April 2, 2001, Larry Arnhart, review of *A Darwinian Left.*

New Criterion, October, 2000, Jenny Teichman, review of *A Darwinian Left,* p. 64.

New Jersey Monthly, October, 2000, Shannon Mullen, "The World According to Peter Singer," p. 84.

New Republic, May 29, 1976; February 7, 1981; January 10, 2000, Peter Berkowitz, review of *A Darwinian Left,* p. 27.

New Statesman, May, 1997, review of *Rethinking Life and Death,* p. 128; January 22, 2001, Roger Scruton, review of *Writings on an Ethical Life,* p. 55.

Newsweek, September 13, 1999, George Will, "Life and Death at Princeton: Professor Peter Singer Is Pro-Choice and He Is the Abortion-Rights Movement's Worst Nightmare," p. 80.

New York Review of Books, May 15, 1980; June 29, 2000, Ian Hacking, review of *Ethics into Action,* p. 20.

New York Times Book Review, January 4, 1976; March 1, 1981; June 23, 1985; May 7, 1995; December 17, 2000, J. B. Schneewind, review of *Writings on an Ethical Life,* p. 24.

New York Times Magazine, September 5, 1999, Peter Singer, "The Singer Solution to World Poverty."

Philosophical Review, January, 1997, review of *How Are We to Live?,* p. 125.

Psychology Today, January, 1999, Jill Neimark, "Living and Dying," p. 56.

Publishers Weekly, March 6, 1995, p. 53; November 27, 2000, review of *Writings on an Ethical Life,* p.

68; December 11, 2000, Bridget Kinsella, "Modern Times, Murky Issues," p. 22; August 3, 1998, review of *Ethics into Action,* p. 65; November 27, 2000, review of *Writings on an Ethical Life,* p. 68.

Reason, December, 2000, Ronald Bailey, "The Pursuit of Happiness," p. 29.

Scientific American, June, 2000, Leigh Van Halen, review of *A Darwinian Left,* p. 110.

Spectator, June 5, 1976.

Times Literary Supplement, January 15, 1982; August 9, 2000, Mary Douglas, review of *Ethical Vegetarianism.*

Village Voice, March 22, 1976.

Washington Post Book World, June 7, 1981; August 18, 1985; January 30, 1994; March 26, 1995, pp. 1, 11.

OTHER

Princeton Weekly Bulletin, http://www.princeton.edu/ (December 7, 1998), "The President's Page: The Appointment of Professor Singer."

Salon.com, http://www.salon.com/books/ (January 9, 2001), Ralph Brave, review of *A Darwinian Left.*

* * *

SIRIN, V.
See NABOKOV, Vladimir (Vladimirovich)

* * *

STEAD, C(hristian) K(arlson) 1932-

PERSONAL: Surname rhymes with "head"; born October 17, 1932, in Auckland, New Zealand; son of James Walter (an accountant) and Olive (a music teacher; maiden name, Karlson) Stead; married Kathleen Elizabeth Roberts, January 8, 1955; children: Oliver William, Charlotte Mary, Margaret Hermione. *Education:* University of New Zealand, B.A., 1954, M.A., 1955; University of Bristol, Ph.D., 1961; University of Auckland, D. Litt., 1982.

ADDRESSES: Home and Office—37 Tohunga Cres., Parnell, Auckland 1, New Zealand.

CAREER: University of New England, Australia, lecturer in English, 1956-57; University of Auckland, Auckland, New Zealand, lecturer, 1960-61, senior lecturer, 1962-64, associate professor, 1964-67, professor of English, 1967-86, professor emeritus, 1986—. Full-time writer, 1986—. Chair of New Zealand Literary Fund Advisory Committee, 1972-75; chair of New Zealand Authors' Fund Committee, 1989-91.

MEMBER: New Zealand PEN (Auckland Branch chair, 1986-89; national vice-president, 1988-90).

AWARDS, HONORS: Michael Hiatt Baker Scholar, University of Bristol, England, 1957-59; Katherine Mansfield Prize, 1960, for a short story; Nuffield travelling fellowship, 1965; Winn-Mansen Menton fellowship, 1972; Jessie Mackay Award for Poetry, 1972; Katherine Mansfield fellow, Menton, France, 1972; New Zealand Book Award for Poetry, 1975; honorary research fellow, University College, London, 1977; New Zealand Literary Fund Award for fiction, 1982; Commander of the Order of the British Empire (C.B.E.) for services to New Zealand literature, 1984; New Zealand Book Awards for fiction, 1985, for *All Visitors Ashore,* and 1994, for *The Singing Whakapapa;* QEII Arts Council Scholarship in Letters, 1988-89; Queen's Medal for services to New Zealand Literature, 1990; elected Fellow of the Royal Society of Literature (FRSL), 1995; D.Litt., University of Bristol, 2001.

WRITINGS:

POETRY

Whether the Will Is Free, Blackwood (London, England), 1964.
Crossing the Bar, Oxford University Press (Oxford, England), 1972.
Quesada: Poems 1972-74, The Shed (Auckland, New Zealand), 1975.
Walking Westward, The Shed (Auckland, New Zealand), 1979.
Geographies, Oxford University Press (Oxford, England), 1982.
Poems of a Decade, Pilgrims South Press (New Zealand), 1983.
Paris, Oxford University Press (Oxford, England), 1984.
Between, Auckland University Press (Auckland, New Zealand), 1988.
Voices, GP Books (New Zealand), 1990.
The Right Thing, 1999.

FICTION

Smith's Dream, Longman (London, England), 1971.
Five for the Symbol (stories), Longman (London, England), 1981.
All Visitors Ashore, Collins (London, England), 1984.

The Death of the Body, Collins (London, England), 1986, HarperCollins (New York, NY), 1993.
Sister Hollywood, St. Martin's Press (New York, NY), 1989.
The End of the Century at the End of the World, Harvill (London, England), 1992.
The Singing Whakapapa, Penguin (New York, NY), 1994.
Villa Vittoria, Penguin (New York, NY), 1997.
The Blind Blonde with Candles in Her Hair (stories), Penguin (New York, NY), 1999.
Talking about O'Dwyer, Penguin (New York, NY), 2000.
The Secret History of Modernism, Harvill (London, England), 2001.

CRITICISM

The New Poetic: Yeats to Eliot, Hutchinson (London, England), 1964, revised edition, University of Pennsylvania Press (Philadelphia, PA), 1987.
In the Glass Case: Essays on New Zealand Literature, Oxford University Press (Oxford, England), 1981.
Pound, Yeats, Eliot, and the Modernist Movement, Rutgers University Press (New Brunswick, NJ), 1986.
Answering to the Language: Essays on Modern Writers, Auckland University Press (Auckland, New Zealand), 1989.
The Writer at Work, Otago University Press, 2000.

EDITOR

(And contributor) *World's Classics: New Zealand Short Stories,* 2nd series (Stead was not associated with earlier series), Oxford University Press (Oxford, England), 1966, 3rd edition, 1975.
Measure for Measure: A Casebook, Macmillan, 1971, revised edition, 1973.
Letters and Journals of Katherine Mansfield, Allen Lane (London, England), 1977.
Collected Stories of Maurice Duggan, Oxford University Press (Oxford, England), 1981.
(With Elizabeth Smither and Kendrick Smithyman) *The New Gramophone Room: Poetry and Fiction,* University of Auckland (Auckland, New Zealand), 1985.
Faber Book of Contemporary South Pacific Stories, Faber, 1993.

Also contributor of poetry and fiction to numerous anthologies, including *The Penguin Book of New Zealand Verse,* edited by Allen Curnow, Penguin, 1960; *New Zealand Poetry,* edited by Vincent O'Sullivan, Oxford University Press (Oxford, England); and *From a Room of Their Own,* edited by Michael Gifkins, [Auckland, New Zealand], 1993. Contributor of criticism to numerous anthologies, including *Literary History and Literary Criticism,* edited by Leon Edel, [New York, NY], 1965; *Contemporary Literary Criticism,* edited by Sharon K. Hall, Gale (Detroit, MI), 1986; and *The Writing of New Zealand,* edited by Alex Calder, [Auckland, New Zealand], 1993. Many of Stead's works have been translated into other languages, including French, German, Swedish, Spanish, Portuguese, and Croatian.

Manuscript collection held in the Alexander Turnbull Library of the National Library of New Zealand, Wellington.

ADAPTATIONS: The novel *Smith's Dream* was adapted for a film directed by Roger Donaldson and released as *Sleeping Dogs* in 1977; the short story "A Fitting Tribute" was adapted for television by Hibiscus Films in 1987.

SIDELIGHTS: C. K. Stead is a prominent New Zealand poet, critic, and novelist whose fiction in particular has begun to find an international audience. Born and raised in New Zealand, and a professor of English at the University of Auckland for twenty-six years, Stead has won awards for his poetry and his fiction, including the prestigious C.B.E. in 1984. Both his verse and his fiction are highly confessional, but they also reveal a writer fascinated with metafictions and the beauty of the English language. To quote Stephen Oxenham in *World Literature Today,* Stead "has contributed hugely to contemporary New Zealand literature, its study, its teaching, its controversies, along with its creation."

In novels such as *All Visitors Ashore* and *Talking about O'Dwyer,* Stead weaves New Zealand history, collegiate erudition, and human frailty into stories that wrestle with cultural politics and race. Paul Sharrad in *World Literature Today* found a "New Zealand mythos" in Stead's oeuvre as the author meditates upon "changes the world has brought to both Europe and his homeland."

Stead once commented in *CA:* "Fiction and poetry are arts whose material is language. A beautiful soul, immense erudition, something important to say—none of these will help if you lack that basic talent with the language. Good writing offers a grammatical dance, a verbal music. But because part of its function is to refer, or to 'mean,' language points beyond itself. One of the greatest and least obtrusive of the writer's skills is to recreate a world we know already. Where I feel my fiction is working best the reader should be aware simulta-

neously of a language which has on it the stamp of this writer and no other, and yet which is producing what someone called 'the shock of recognition,' almost as if language had nothing to do with it."

Stead added, "If there is inevitably a strong regional element in my work, it alone is not enough to explain what I write or what I look for in writing. Those schools and that university I attended gave me access to something more than my own region; or perhaps I should say they taught me that I had access to it in the language I grew up speaking. That larger 'something' is the whole European culture we inherit along with our language and history. I value it; and I don't like a shallow nationalism which inclines to say it is something second hand and geographically irrelevant.

"I began writing at the age of thirteen and under the influence of English writers—first Rupert Brooke and John Buchan, then Keats and Wordsworth, Dickens and Sir Walter Scott. Later I discovered the New Zealand poets and fiction writers who were mapping our own country in literature; and as a student I began to read the Americans. In those days New Zealand was still emerging from its colonial phase and it seemed necessary to insist on our independence—political, cultural and literary. Now I think we believe in our independence, and it may be more important that we remember kinship and history."

BIOGRAPHICAL/CRITICAL SOURCES:

PERIODICALS

Los Angeles Times, August 20, 1990.
Publishers Weekly, June 8, 1990, Sybil Steinberg, review of *Sister Hollywood,* p. 45; August 30, 1993, review of *The Death of the Body,* p. 89.
Times (London, England), August 28, 1986; June 22, 1989.
Times Literary Supplement, July 5, 1985; August 29, 1986; October 10, 1986; August 11, 1989; February 22, 1991.
World Literature Today, fall 1996, Stephen Oxenham, review of *All Visitors Ashore,* p. 1034; winter 2001, Paul Sharrad, review of *Talking about O'Dwyer,* p. 110.

OTHER

C. K. Stead, http://www.vuw.ac.nz/nzbookcouncil/writers/steadck.htm/ (February 1, 2001), author entry from *The Oxford Companion to New Zealand Literature.*

STEIN, Kevin 1954-

PERSONAL: Born January 1, 1954, in Anderson, IN; son of Joseph and Mary Rita (Kelly) Stein; married Debra Lang (a registered nurse), May 26, 1979; children: Kirsten Anne, Joseph Kevin. *Education:* Ball State University, B.S. (summa cum laude), 1976, M.A., 1978; Indiana University, M.A. (creative writing), 1982, Ph.D. (American literature), 1984.

ADDRESSES: Home—6127 West Legion Hall Rd., Dunlap, IL 61525. *Office*—English Department, Bradley University, 1501 West Bradley Ave., Peoria, IL 61625-0258; fax: 309-677-2330. *E-mail*—kstein@ bradley.edu.

CAREER: Ball State University, Muncie, IN, instructor, 1978-79; Indiana University, Bloomington, IN, associate instructor, 1980-84; Bradley University, Peoria, IL, assistant professor, 1984-88, associate professor, 1988-94, professor of English, 1994—, Caterpillar Professor of English, 2000—; writer.

MEMBER: Modern Language Association, Illinois Writers.

AWARDS, HONORS: Fellowship, Illinois Arts Council, 1986; chapbook award, Illinois Writers, 1986, for *A Field of Wings;* Frederick Bock Prize, *Poetry,* 1987; literary award, Illinois Arts Council, 1987 and 1991; Stanley Hanks Chapbook Award, 1988, for *The Figure Our Bodies Make;* Faculty Member of the Year, Bradley University, 1989; fellowship, National Endowment for the Arts, 1991; Devins Award for Poetry, University of Missouri Press, 1992, for *A Circus of Want;* fellowship, Illinois Arts Council, 1996; poetry prize, *Indiana Review,* 1998.

WRITINGS:

POETRY

A Field of Wings, Illinois Writers Inc. (Normal, IL), 1986.
The Figure Our Bodies Make, St. Louis Poetry Center (St. Louis, MO), 1988.
A Circus of Want, University of Missouri Press (Columbia, MO), 1992.
Bruised Paradise, University of Illinois Press (Urbana, IL), 1996.
Chance Ransom, University of Illinois Press (Urbana, IL), 2000.

Contributor to periodicals, including *Black Warrior Review, Boulevard, Colorado Review, Crab Orchard Review, Crazyhorse, Denver Quarterly, Gettysburg Review, Indiana Review, Kenyon Review, Missouri Review, North American Review, Ploughshares, Poetry, Poetry Northwest, Quarterly West, Shenandoah, Southern Review,* and *TriQuarterly.*

OTHER

James Wright: The Poetry of a Grown Man (literary criticism), Ohio University Press (Athens, OH), 1988.
Private Poets, Worldly Acts: Public and Private History in Contemporary American Poetry (essays), Ohio University Press (Athens, OH), 1996.
(Editor with G. E. Murray) *Illinois Voices: An Anthology of Twentieth-Century Poetry,* University of Illinois Press (Urbana, IL), 2001.

Contributor of essays to periodicals, including *American Poetry Review, Boulevard, College Literature, Concerning Poetry, Indiana Review, Iowa English Journal, Massachusetts Review, Mississippi Review, Poetry East,* and *Ohio Review.* Editor, *Illinois Writers Review,* 1988-92; associate poetry editor, *Crazyhorse,* 1992-94.

SIDELIGHTS: Kevin Stein is a poet who is primarily concerned with the nature of significance and appreciation. Sally Thomas, writing in *Quarterly West,* declared that "Stein's poems represent the part of the story that can be told: what we can see, know, and say, all we can mean when we say we love our lives." Thomas noted that in the volume *A Circus of Want* Stein explores "what it means to live in a universe in which life is not easily lovable, and beauty and despair are often the same thing."

Stein told *CA:* "My work in recent years has been increasingly fueled by the belief that poets face a dual obligation not only to write their own poems but also to write thoughtfully about others' work. Doing so, they give back to the art something larger than themselves. Not surprisingly—though happily—doing so also helps poets avoid the solipsism so often debilitating to artists whose world narrows to something no broader than the coffee cup in which their own reflection looms waiting to return their lips' kiss. No doubt my own poetry has been deepened by the study of James Wright's work and its characteristic 'furious and unceasing growth.' Additionally, the study of others' poetry often interrogates my easy assumptions about what a poem is and might become, as I discovered examining Lowell, Rich, O'Hara, Wright, Levine, Komunyakaa, Dove, Forché, and Wojahn in researching the essays of *Private Poets,*

Worldly Acts. The inventive ways these poets found to intersect private and public history have come to inform my own poems in a fashion I'd simply not expected.

"As a result, a number of poems in my recent collection *Chance Ransom* render intersecting planes of high and low art, pop culture and staid history, as well as racial, social, and economic dialogues played out in forms ranging from rock lyric to history text. Nothing pleases me more than to imagine the poem as a field of possibility welcoming on even terms profound philosophical inquiry and crass commercial marketing. The work is both agent and end product of this discourse. Thus, understanding how words simultaneously construct and express out lives asks that we're alert to a world in which The La-Z-Boy, Bob Marley, and Martin Heidegger prove variously (and equally) instructive.

"One result of this notion is my escalating use of the musical phrase. More and more I've worked to flesh my lines with assonance, consonance, and scores of slant and exact rhymes. I've purposefully enhanced the sonic qualities of my poems beyond the typical possibilities offered by shopworn end-rhyme. It's a way to update the furniture of the traditional meditative lyric or narrative poem I'm so fond of. It's also a way to make music exhibit qualities of thought and to make thought itself aspire to the passionate fluidity of music. In my view, the current version of the meditative poem often overlooks the pleasurable play of sound, music, and rhythm in favor of the play of mind. Similarly, the conventional narrative overlooks the same pleasures in favor of story. Why not slow down, turn up the treble, and see what discoveries of mind and story that music itself might offer? Why not enable music to do more than simply embellish thought and story but actually to generate both? Such a poem is surely more fun for the poet to write and, I trust, more fun for the reader to read."

Earlier Stein told *CA:* "What most interests me is the way our lives continually surprise us, how the common may suddenly glint with uncommon light or darken with horror. How these quotidian events change our lives, or fail to. How what matters comes to matter, or matter not at all. It is precisely this mysterious process, through which we sort our lives and apply to their vagaries intellectual or emotional significance, that fascinates me. My poems, and to some extent my critical essays, reflect that, for what else is an essay if not a sorting out of what attracts or repels us as readers?

"I've always been interested in muting the line between lyric and narrative poetry, a fictional boundary created and maintained by writerly convention. A number of poems in *A Circus of Want* experiment with ways to invoke elements of story with an essentially lyric form and, conversely, ways to make lyrical the telling of a story. This enables the speaker to follow meditative tangents along the way, to delay and transgress. Recently, I've worked with the dramatic monologue in poetry. Doing so offers me—because dramatic monologue is seemingly out of fashion—the enviable opportunity to be radical using traditional forms. I worked from a small packet of my great-great-grandfather's personal papers: a few letters, his immigration documents, a note absolving him of chicken thievery, some bills and receipts. I researched county historical records where he settled in Richmond, Indiana, in the 1850s, and found mention of him and his family in microfilmed copies of old newspapers. The result, a series of twelve or so dramatic monologues spoken in his voice, are part fact and part fiction, some measure real and much more imagined, an invented flesh of history stitched over skeletal facts.

"Those writers whom I find most compelling are characterized by what James Wright called a 'furious and unceasing growth.' I admire those writers who, while not abandoning all they've learned to do, journey into the unknown spreading before them like Arctic tundra and see in its vast emptiness only possibility. Not nothingness but something they've yet to discover. That fierce embracing of aesthetic change first attracted me to Wright and led to my critical study, *James Wright: The Poetry of the Grown Man.* In the process of my research, however, I was startled by the continuity of themes beneath the surface of Wright's stylistic alterations. The need for change and the will for order provided a useful, generative tension throughout his career. For the last two years, I've focused on poets whose work demands an intersection of public and private 'history,' poets such as Wright, Philip Levine, and Yusef Komunyakaa. I'm thinking, for example, of the importance of work and workers in Wright's poetry, or the significance of the Spanish Civil War in Levine's. Given the day's vertiginous theory and ideology, it's more necessary than ever for writers to enter the dialogue by examining and responding to the work of others. Silence, while protective, amounts to the worst sort of abnegation."

BIOGRAPHICAL/CRITICAL SOURCES:

PERIODICALS

American Literature, March, 1998, Kirk Nesset, review of *Private Poets, Worldly Acts,* p. 210.

Colorado Review, fall, 1998, Donald Revell, review of *Bruised Paradise* and *Private Poets, Worldly Acts,* pp. 173-79.

Quarterly West, winter, 1992, pp. 232-36.

Tar River Poetry, spring, 1999, Elizabeth Dodd, review of *Bruised Paradise,* pp. 51-53.

OTHER

Poetic Voices, http://www.poeticvoices.com/ (February, 2000), Robin Travers, "Featured Poet: Kevin Stein."

* * *

STONE, Zachary
See FOLLETT, Ken(neth Martin)

* * *

't HART, Maarten 1944-
(Martin Hart)

PERSONAL: Born November 25, 1944, in Maassluis, the Netherlands. *Education:* Attended University of Leiden.

ADDRESSES: *Office*—c/o De Arbeiders, Herengracht 372, 1016 CH. Amsterdam, Netherlands.

CAREER: Writer and scientist. University of Leiden, Leiden, the Netherlands, worked as research ethologist.

WRITINGS:

NOVELS

(Under name Martin Hart) *Stenen voor een Ransuil,* De Arbeiderspers (Amsterdam, the Netherlands), 1971.

Ilk had een Wapenbroeder, De Arbeiderspers (Amsterdam, the Netherlands), 1973.

Een vlucht Regenwulpen, De Arbeiderspers (Amsterdam, the Netherlands), 1978, translation by J. W. Arriëns published as *A Flight of Curlews,* Allison & Busby (New York, NY), 1986.

De Aansprekers: Roman van Vader en Zoon, De Arbeiderspers (Amsterdam, the Netherlands), 1979, translation by J. W. Arriëns published as *Bearer of*

Bad Tidings: A Story of Father and Son, Allison & Busby (New York, NY), 1984.

De Droomkoningin, De Arbeiderspers (Amsterdam, the Netherlands), 1980.

De Kroongetuige, De Arbeiderspers (Amsterdam, the Netherlands), 1983.

De Jacobsladder, De Arbeiderspers (Amsterdam, the Netherlands), 1986.

Het Uur tussen Hond en Wolf, De Arbeiderspers (Amsterdam, the Netherlands), 1987.

De Steile Helling, De Arbeiderspers (Amsterdam, the Netherlands), 1988.

Onder de Koren maat (title means "Under a Bushel"), De Arbeiderspers (Amsterdam, the Netherlands), 1991.

Het Woeden der Gehele Wereld, De Arbeiderspers (Amsterdam, the Netherlands), 1993.

De Nakomer, De Arbeiderspers (Amsterdam, the Netherlands), 1996.

De Vlieger, De Arbeiderspers (Amsterdam, the Netherlands), 1998.

SHORT FICTION; COLLECTIONS, EXCEPT WHERE INDICATED

Het Vrome Volk, De Arbeiderspers (Amsterdam, the Netherlands), 1975.

Mamoet op Zondag, De Arbeiderspers (Amsterdam, the Netherlands), 1977.

Laatste Zomernacht (novella), De Arbeiderspers (Amsterdam, the Netherlands), 1977.

De Dorstige Minnaar, Bulkboek, 1978.

De Zaterdagvliegers, De Arbeiderspers (Amsterdam, the Netherlands), 1981.

Alle verhalen, De Arbeiderspers (Amsterdam, the Netherlands), 1982.

De Ortolaan, Stichting voor de Collectieve Propaganda van het Nederlandse Boek (Amsterdam, the Netherlands), 1984.

De Huismeester, De Arbeiderspers (Amsterdam, the Netherlands), 1985.

De Unster, De Arbeiderspers (Amsterdam, the Netherlands), 1989.

De gevaren van joggen, De Arbeiderspers (Amsterdam, Netherlands), 1999.

Author of short stories, including "Avondwandeling," 1976; and "De Draagmoeder," 1987.

ESSAYS

De Kritische Afstand: Aggressieve aantekeningen over mens en dier, De Arbeiderspers (Amsterdam, the Netherlands), 1976.

(With Midas Dekkers) *Natuurlijke historie,* 1976.

De Som van Misverstanden, De Arbeiderspers (Amsterdam, the Netherlands), 1978.

Ongewenste Zeeris, De Arbeiderspers (Amsterdam, the Netherlands), 1979.

De Vrouw Bestaat Niet, De Arbeiderspers (Amsterdam, the Netherlands), 1982.

Het Eeuwige Moment, De Arbeiderspers (Amsterdam, the Netherlands), 1983.

Een Dasspeld uit Toela, De Arbeiderspers (Amsterdam, the Netherlands), 1990.

Een Havik onder Delft: Polemische pakeslagen en andere kritische beschouwingen, De Arbeiderspers (Amsterdam, the Netherlands), 1992.

(With H. Br. Corstius) *Het gebergte: De tweeënvijftig romans van S. Vestdijk,* Nijgh & van Ditmar (Amsterdam, the Netherlands), 1996.

Wie God verlaat heeft niets te vrezen: De Schrift betwist, De Arbeiderspers (Amsterdam, the Netherlands), 1997.

OTHER

Ratten (nonfiction), Wetenschappelijke Uitgeverij (Amsterdam, Netherlands), 1973, translation by Arnold Pomerans published as *Rats,* Allison & Busby (New York, NY), 1982.

De stekelbaars (nonfiction), 1978.

Het Roerkan nog Zesmaal om (autobiography), De Arbeiderspers (Amsterdam, the Netherlands), 1984.

Mijn vaderstad: Een literaire wandeling door het Maassluis van Maarten 't Hart, 1999.

Ein Schwarm: Regenbrachvögel, Taschenbuch, 1999.

Een deerne in lokkend postuur: Persoonlijke kroniek (autobiography), De Arbeiderspers (Amsterdam, the Netherlands), 1999.

Johann Sebastian Bach, 2000.

English translations of 't Hart's writings appear under the name Martin Hart.

BIOGRAPHICAL/CRITICAL SOURCES:

PERIODICALS

World Literature Today, summer, 1992, Henri Kops, review of *Onder de Koren maat,* p. 528.

OTHER

SchrijversNet, http://www.schrijversnet.nl/ (August 23, 2000).

University of Hull Web Site, http://www.hull.ac.uk/ (August 23, 2000).*

THOMAS, David H(urst)   1945-

PERSONAL: Born May 27, 1945, in Oakland, CA; son of David Hurst (in real estate) and Barbara L. (a teacher) Thomas; married Trudy Carter, March, 1969. *Education:* University of California, Davis, B.A., 1967, M.A., 1968, Ph.D., 1971. *Politics:* Liberal. *Religion:* Protestant. *Avocational interests:* Automobile restoration, carpentry.

ADDRESSES: Home—West Nyack, NY. *Office*—Department of Anthropology, American Museum of Natural History, Central Park West at 79th St., New York, NY 10024.

CAREER: City College of the City University of New York, New York, NY, assistant professor of anthropology and chairman of department, 1971-72; American Museum of Natural History, New York, NY, assistant curator, 1972-76, associate curator, 1977-82, curator of department of anthropology, 1982—. Adjunct curator, Department of Anthropology, Florida Museum of Natural History, Gainesville, FL, 1987—. Adjunct professor, Columbia University and City University of New York, 1991—. Member of advisory board: *New Directions in Archaeology, Journal of Archaeological Method and Theory, Journal of Quantitative Anthropology, Advances in Archaeology Method and Theory,* and *North American Archaeologist.* National Museum of the American Indian, Smithsonian Institution, founding trustee, 1990-95.

MEMBER: International Union of Pre-and Proto-Science, American Anthropological Association, Society for American Archaeology, National Science Foundation (panel for archaeology), National Academy of Sciences, New York Academy of Sciences, Society of Systematic Zoology.

AWARDS, HONORS: Choice Magazine Awards, Outstanding Scholarly Book of 1989, for *Columbian Consequences,* Volume 1, and Outstanding Scholarly Book of 1990, for *Columbian Consequences,* Volume 2; Presidential Recognition Award, Society for American Archaeology, 1991; Best Western Nonfiction Historical Book of 1993, Western Writers of America, for *The Native Americans;* honorary doctorate, University of the South, 1995.

WRITINGS:

(Contributor) David L. Clarke, editor, *Models in Archaeology,* Methuen (New York, NY), 1972.

Predicting the Past: An Introduction to Anthropological Archaeology, Holt (New York, NY), 1974.

(With Edwin H. McKee) *An Aboriginal Rock Alignment in the Toiyabe Range, Central Nevada,* American Museum of Natural History (New York, NY), 1974.

Figuring Anthropology: First Principles of Probability and Archaeology, Holt (New York, NY), 1976.

(With others) *Prehistoric Piñon Ecotone Settlements of the Upper Reese River Valley, Central Nevada,* American Museum of Natural History (New York, NY), 1976.

Rich Man, Poor Men: Observations on Three Antebellum Burials from the Georgia Coast, American Museum of Natural History (New York, NY), 1977.

(With others) *The Anthropology of St. Catherines Island,* American Museum of Natural History (New York, NY), 1978.

Archaeology, Holt (New York, NY), 1979, revised edition, Harcourt Brace College Publishers (Fort Worth, TX), 1998.

(With Thomas N. Layton) *The Archaeology of Silent Snake Springs, Humboldt County, Nevada,* American Museum of Natural History (New York, NY), 1979.

(Editor, with Shuzo Koyama) *Affluent Foragers: Pacific Coasts East and West,* National Museum of Ethnology (Suita, Osaka, Japan), 1981.

(With Lorann S. A. Pendleton) *The Fort Sage Drift Fence, Washoe County, Nevada,* American Museum of Natural History (New York, NY), 1983.

The Archaeology of Monitor Valley, American Museum of Natural History (New York, NY), 1983.

(Editor and author of introduction) *A Great Basin Shoshonean Source Book,* Garland (New York, NY), 1986.

(Editor and author of introduction) *A Blackfoot Source Book: Papers,* Garland (New York, NY), 1986.

St. Catherines: An Island in Time, Georgia Endowment for the Humanities (Atlanta, GA), 1988.

(Editor) *Columbian Consequences,* three volumes, Smithsonian Institution Press (Washington, DC), Volume 1: *Archaeological and Historical Perspectives on the Spanish Borderlands West,* 1989, Volume 2: *Archaeological and Historical Perspectives on the Spanish Borderlands East,* 1990, Volume 3: *The Spanish Borderlands in Pan-American Perspective,* 1991.

(Editor and author of introduction) *Ethnology of the Indians of Spanish Florida,* Garland (New York, NY), 1991.

Archaeology: Down to Earth, Harcourt Brace College Publishers (Fort Worth, TX), 1991, revised edition, 1999.

(Editor and author of introduction) *The Missions of Spanish Florida,* Garland (New York, NY), 1991.

(Author of text, with others) *The Native Americans: An Illustrated History,* Turner Publications (Atlanta, GA), 1993.

Exploring Ancient Native America: An Archaeological Guide, Macmillan (New York, NY), 1994.

(Consulting editor, with Lorann S. A. Pendleton) *Native Americans,* Time-Life Books (Alexandria, VA), 1995.

Skull Wars: Kennewick Man, Archaeology, and the Battle for Native American Identity, Basic Books (New York, NY), 2000.

Exploring Native North America, Oxford University Press (New York, NY), 2000.

Also author of *The Illustrated History of Humankind,* 5 volumes, 1993-94. Contributor to anthropology and archaeology journals. Associate editor of *Journal of Human Ecology,* 1972—.

WORK IN PROGRESS: A second volume in Oxford University Press series "Places in Time," on major colonial era archaeology sites.

SIDELIGHTS: David H. Thomas, the curator of the anthropology department at the American Museum of Natural History in New York City, is a nationally recognized expert on the archaeology of ancient Native America. Thomas has participated in field work at numerous sites in Georgia, Florida, and the American West. In addition, he has led tours through and written books about important Native American archaeological sites. The author's prominence in his profession has been demonstrated by two contributions to the Oxford University Press series titled "Places in Time," one volume on Native America and another, in press, on colonial-era America. *Exploring Native North America,* the first of Thomas's volumes for "Places in Time," was described by Sean George in *School Library Journal* as a "thorough but sophisticated book" and "an excellent resource for serious students." In *Booklist,* Vanessa Bush likewise found *Exploring Native North America* to be "accessible to a broad readership." Bush concluded that the work is a "well-illustrated and well-researched look at fascinating American cultures."

In an interview with *Scanet.org,* Thomas noted that archaeologists working on Native American sites need to have sensitivity to the culture and humanity of Native Americans, past and present. "Archaeologists have special responsibilities," he explained, "not only to recover and interpret evidence of the human past, but also to insure that the past is not used for malevolent purposes in the present. This is not an easy task because it requires that individual archaeologists balance and sort out the sometimes conflicting realities." He added: "This, it seems to me, is perhaps the greatest challenge facing the archaeologists of the twenty-first century."

BIOGRAPHICAL/CRITICAL SOURCES:

PERIODICALS

Booklist, August, 2000, Vanessa Bush, review of *Exploring Native North America*, p. 2107.

Library Journal, April 1, 2000, John Burch, review of *Skull Wars: Kennewick Man, Archaeology, and the Battle for Native American Identity*, p. 115.

Publishers Weekly, March 13, 2000, review of *Skull Wars: Kennewick Man, Archaeology, and the Battle for Native American Identity*, p. 72.

School Library Journal, October, 2000, Sean George, review of *Exploring Native North America*, p. 197.

OTHER

Scanet.org, http://www.scanet.org/thomas.html/ (February 2, 2001), "An Interview with David Hurst Thomas."*

* * *

THOMPSON, Julian F(rancis) 1927-

PERSONAL: Born November 16, 1927, in New York, NY; son of Julian Francis (a playwright; in business) and Amalita (Stagg) Thompson; married Polly Nichy (an artist), August 11, 1978. *Education:* Princeton University, A.B., 1949; Columbia University, M.A., 1955.

ADDRESSES: Agent—Curtis Brown Ltd., 10 Astor Place, New York, NY 10003.

CAREER: Lawrenceville School (private school), Lawrenceville, NJ, history teacher, athletic coach, and director of lower school, 1949-61; Changes, Inc. (alternative high school), East Orange, NJ, director, 1971-77; writer, 1979—.

MEMBER: Authors Guild, Authors League of America, PEN American Center.

WRITINGS:

YOUNG ADULT NOVELS

The Grounding of Group Six, Avon (New York, NY), 1983, reissued, Holt (New York, NY), 1997.

Facing It, Avon (New York, NY), 1983.

A Question of Survival, Avon (New York, NY), 1984.

Discontinued, Scholastic (New York, NY), 1985.

A Band of Angels, Scholastic (New York, NY), 1986.

Simon Pure, Scholastic (New York, NY), 1987.

The Taking of Mariasburg, Scholastic (New York, NY), 1988.

Goofbang Value Daze, Scholastic (New York, NY), 1989.

Herb Seasoning, Scholastic (New York, NY), 1990.

Gypsyworld, Holt (New York, NY), 1992.

Shepherd, Holt (New York, NY), 1993.

The Fling, Holt (New York, NY), 1994.

Philo Fortune's Awesome Journey to His Comfort Zone, Hyperion (Westport, CT), 1995.

The Trials of Molly Sheldon, Holt (New York, NY), 1996.

Ghost Story, Holt (New York, NY), 1997.

Brothers, Knopf (New York, NY), 1998.

Terry and the Pirates, Atheneum (New York, NY), 2000.

SIDELIGHTS: Julian F. Thompson writes novels for young adults that reflect his own respect for people in that age group. Thompson tackles important topical subjects—including pedophilia, militia groups, and the gulf between most parents and their teens—but he does so with a blend of humor and suspense that make his messages easier to accept. In one of his best-known novels, *The Grounding of Group 6*, he presents a harrowing tale of wealthy teens sent to a boarding school where, at their parents' orders, they are to be killed. As frightening as the scenario seems, Thompson injects the story with enough hilarity to soften the subject matter.

Other Thompson novels are more serious, but these too reveal the secret lives of teenagers. In *Ghost Story* a girl named Anna receives an otherworldly visitor who warns her to stay away from a neighbor who wants to make videos of her. And in *Brothers*, a caring teen named Chris journeys across the country to save his mentally ill brother from a fringe militia group. A *Publishers Weekly* correspondent praised *Brothers* for its "hard look at the differences between nonconformity, disturbed behavior and fanaticism."

Terry and the Pirates is meant to be humorous throughout. In an effort to avoid being sent to boarding school, a girl named Terry stows away on a yacht—only to find that it is being piloted not by its millionaire owner but by his son. Soon enough the two teens are in deep water as a storm overtakes them and Terry is thrown upon a desert island populated by latter-day pirates. *Booklist* reviewer Roger Leslie declared that Thompson "earns solid laughs" for "the comic twists and intentionally absurd plot." In *Publishers Weekly,* a contributor noted that the "fast-paced and pleasingly far-fetched adventure story . . . will elicit hearty laughter."

Thompson once told *CA:* "For years, it's seemed to me that, after poisonous snakes and rabid German Shepherds, many Americans detest and fear teenagers as much as they do anything else in the natural world. Politicians and editorial writers are constantly advising or lambasting them, municipalities pass laws that ban them from their streets at certain hours, and many parents say that other people's sons and daughters (and even their own, sometimes) are noisy, moody, disrespectful, sloppy, and unfocused. Kids make easy targets: they have few legal rights, are generally short of cash, and either can't vote or are disinclined to do so. And most adults are convinced that the current batch is a lot worse than they were, at the same age.

"When I was in my teens, it seemed to me that many teachers and parents and other people who had 'authority' over me didn't have a clue about what it felt like to be me. It was as if they'd skipped the age that I was then, or if they hadn't, that they'd experienced that time of life completely differently. Whenever I came upon a grown-up who seemed to understand me, I felt relief and gratitude in equal measure, and I think that same thing is true for many kids today.

"So when I started writing books, I decided I'd try to tell stories in which kids, most kids, are presented positively, as they go through the process of defining themselves and their beliefs. I'm still grateful to the reviewer who said a book of mine combined 'romantic realism' and 'surrealistic black humor'; indeed, I think they all do. My protagonists tend to be idealists, but like almost all people their age they have an interest in sex, sometimes use mild vulgarities when talking to their friends, and often adopt, at least temporarily, anti-establishment attitudes. They aren't dopes, and they don't talk or act like dopes. I like to think my readers are as intelligent as they are.

"My characters, in fact, reflect the opinions and attitudes and humor of the hundreds of teenagers I got to know well during the thirty years I spent as a teacher, coach, and counselor in settings as diverse as a state re-

formatory and a selective private boarding school. They are thoughtful, imaginative, easily amused, often suspicious, and very much involved in trying to become the kinds of adults that their own teenaged kids will be able to respect and love, some day."

BIOGRAPHICAL/CRITICAL SOURCES:

PERIODICALS

Booklist, November 1, 1998, Roger Leslie, review of *Brothers,* p. 485; November 1, 2000, Roger Leslie, review of *Terry and the Pirates,* p. 526.
Publishers Weekly, February 17, 1997, review of *Ghost Story,* p. 220; November 23, 1998, review of *Brothers,* p. 68; October 30, 2000, review of *Terry and the Pirates,* p. 76.
School Library Journal, October, 2000, Miranda Doyle, review of *Terry and the Pirates,* p. 172.

*   *   *

TREVOR, William
See COX, William Trevor

*   *   *

UNDERCLIFFE, Errol
See CAMPBELL, (John) Ramsey

*   *   *

UTLEY, (Clifton) Garrick   1939-

PERSONAL: Born November 19, 1939, in Chicago, IL; son of Clifton Maxwell (a journalist) and Frayn (a journalist; maiden name, Garrick) Utley; married, wife's name Gertje, May 25, 1973. *Education:* Carleton College, B.A., 1961; Free University in Berlin, graduate study, 1962-63.

ADDRESSES: Office—Cable News Network (CNN), 5 Penn Plaza, 21st Floor, New York, NY 10001.

CAREER: National Broadcasting Corporation (NBC News), television correspondent in Brussels, Belgium, 1963-64, Vietnam, 1964-65, Chicago, IL, and New York, NY, 1966, Berlin, Germany, 1966-68, chief of bureau in Paris, France, 1968-71, U.S. presidential campaign correspondent, 1972, chief European correspondent, 1973-79, U.S. presidential campaign correspondent, 1980, chief foreign correspondent, 1982-87, U.S. presidential campaign correspondent, 1988, anchor of news program *Sunday Today,* 1987-92, weekend news anchor, anchor of news programs *Meet the Press, First Tuesday,* and *NBC Magazine;* American Broadcasting Company (ABC), chief foreign correspondent, 1993-96; Cable News Network (CNN), contributor in New York, NY bureau, 1997—. *Military service:* U.S. Army, 1961-62.

AWARDS, HONORS: Edward R. Murrow Award, Overseas Press Club, 1984, for reports on Soviet-American relations; George Foster Peabody Award, 1986, for contributions to program, *Vietnam: Ten Years Later.*

WRITINGS:

Globalism or Regionalism? United States Policy on Southern Africa, International Institute for Strategic Studies (London, England), 1979.
You Should Have Been Here Yesterday: A Life in Television News, Public Affairs (New York, NY), 2000.

SIDELIGHTS: Garrick Utley has covered news in seventy countries during his career as a broadcast journalist. He has reported on the Vietnam War, the Soviet Union's invasion of Prague, Czechoslovakia in 1968, the Yom Kippur War in 1973 in Israel, and countless other events. In *You Should Have Been Here Yesterday: A Life in Television News,* he chronicles his career and also analyzes the medium. "He includes vivid descriptions of career highlights," reported a *Publishers Weekly* reviewer, adding that especially "chilling" is Utley's discussion of his interview in 1977 with Albert Speer, a former high-ranking official in Nazi Germany. The book makes clear, the reviewer noted, that Utley loves his work and that he is committed to high-quality

journalism, although television sometimes falls short of his standards. "Utley is candid about [television's] limitations and tendency to superficiality," remarked Vanessa Bush in *Booklist.* Utley sees threats to high-quality foreign coverage; networks, seeking higher profits, are sometimes unwilling to spend money on it, and some viewers' have a lack of interest in news from overseas. However, he also thinks economic globalization is helping to turn this situation around, stimulating a demand for foreign news that networks will try to satisfy. Utley's analysis of the news business is the "most important" aspect of the book, in the opinion of the *Publishers Weekly* reviewer, who termed the work as a whole "low-key but engrossing." In *Columbia Journalism Review,* James Boylan stated of *You Should Have Been Here Yesterday:* "It is notably clear; it moves swiftly from point to point; it tells you the major facts." Boylan said the memoir resembles "a good television reporter's story."

BIOGRAPHICAL/CRITICAL SOURCES:

BOOKS

Almanac of Famous People, sixth edition, Gale (Detroit, MI), 1998.

PERIODICALS

Booklist, November 1, 2000, Vanessa Bush, review of *You Should Have Been Here Yesterday: A Life in Television News,* p. 494.
Columbia Journalism Review, November, 2000, James Boylan, review of *You Should Have Been Here Yesterday: A Life in Television News,* p. 82.
Library Journal, February 1, 2001, Susan M. Colowick, review of *You Should Have Been Here Yesterday: A Life in Television News,* p. 104.
Publishers Weekly, October 30, 2000, review of *You Should Have Been Here Yesterday: A Life in Television News,* p. 64.*

V

VAN WORMER, Laura (Eleanor) 1955-

PERSONAL: Born November 11, 1955, in Pittsburgh, PA; daughter of Benjamin Francis (a business executive) and Margaret (a homemaker; maiden name, Garner) Van Wormer. *Education:* Attended University of Arizona, 1974-75; Syracuse University, B.S., 1978. *Religion:* Presbyterian.

ADDRESSES: Agent—c/o Mira Books, Author Mail, P.O. Box 5190, Buffalo, NY 14240-5190.

CAREER: Doubleday & Co., Inc., New York, NY, began as secretary, became editor, 1978-84; writer, 1984—. Commissioned game creator for Maruca Industries, 1986.

MEMBER: Authors Guild.

WRITINGS:

NOVELS

Riverside Drive, Doubleday (New York, NY), 1988.
West End, Doubleday (New York, NY), 1989.
Benedict Canyon, Crown Publishers (New York, NY), 1992.
Any Given Moment, Crown Publishers (New York, NY), 1995.
Jury Duty, Crown Publishers (New York, NY), 1995.
Just for the Summer, Mira Books (Don Mills, Ontario, Canada), 1997.
Talk, Mira Books (Don Mills, Ontario, Canada), 1998.
Exposé, Mira Books (Don Mills, Ontario, Canada), 1999.
The Last Lover, Mira Books (Don Mills, Ontario, Canada), 2000.

OTHER

Dallas: The Complete Ewing Family Saga, 1860-1985, Doubleday (New York, NY), 1985.
Knots Landing: The Saga of Seaview Circle, Doubleday (New York, NY), 1986.

SIDELIGHTS: Laura Van Wormer is "a master of romantic suspense," in the words of *New York Times Book Review* contributor Mary-Ann Tirone Smith. "Romantic suspense," Smith explained in a piece on Van Wormer's novel *Exposé,* "is a genre that requires the first-person narration of a suspicious death by a clever, witty, and attractive female protagonist-sleuth. The sleuthing, though, is secondary to her main concern, the quest for true love." Diane Cole, critiquing *The Last Lover* for the *New York Times Book Review,* noted further that Van Wormer "specializes in creating smart heroines with glamorous jobs and a knack for solving complicated murder mysteries."

Van Wormer had appropriate experience for creating these appealing women and their suspenseful plots. She "honed her storytelling skills in the world of nighttime soaps," Emily Jenkins related in a *Publishers Weekly* profile of the author. As Van Wormer once commented: "I majored in broadcasting in college, feeling that until I had lived long enough to have something to say as a novelist, I could try writing for television. I didn't. I got a job in trade book publishing instead and eventually became an editor. I left editing in 1984 to start learning how to write again. This was made possible when Lorimar hired me to write and photo-edit a fictional 'biography' of the Ewing family of the long-running, nighttime soap *Dallas.* As a student of television and a devotee of 'the father of soap opera,' Victorian serial novelist Anthony Trollope, I had enormous fun with the project, and the following year, wrote the 'biography' of the whole *neighborhood* of 'Knots Landing.' These two projects covered the rent while I was laboring on my first novel, and they also taught me a good deal about handling simultaneous plot lines—which was a very good thing, since *Riverside Drive* has no less than six.

"*Riverside Drive* is about five families who share the same cleaning woman, and what occurs when something happens to her and the households begin to interact. *West End* is about six workaholics who establish a new television network. Their professional lives are remarkably successful, but their personal lives are remarkably a mess. It is accurate to say the first is about extended family in the neighborhood and the second, about extended family in the workplace."

Van Wormer followed those books with *Benedict Canyon,* which focuses on a book editor trying to persuade a mercurial television actress to submit her autobiography. The editor, Kate Weston, and the star, Lydia Southland, become devoted, if unlikely, friends, and both go through a variety of work- and love-related problems, as do Lydia's various hangers-on. "Too many characters battle too many trendy addictions," commented *People* reviewer Susan Toepfer, but a *Publishers Weekly* critic deemed the book "Van Wormer's most accomplished story yet." *Any Given Moment* also deals with the worlds of literature and Hollywood, as an entertainment tycoon tries to drive a small literary agency out of business. A *Publishers Weekly* reviewer described this as "a clever but somewhat romanticized story," while *Booklist*'s Denise Perry Donavin reported that it "explores some sensitive turf and exhibits more depth of characterization" than Van Wormer's previous work.

Jury Duty is a tale of romantic entanglements and legal deliberations among a group of jurors assigned to a high-profile society murder trial in Manhattan, with the main focus being on Libby Winslow, a once-successful novelist whose career has been going downhill, who is attracted to two men on the jury. Although "some of the plot lines never get untangled," the novel "is at least as entertaining as Court TV," observed Carol Peace Robins in the *New York Times Book Review.* Ilene Cooper, writing in *Booklist,* thought the book "a fast-paced and appealing piece of storytelling." The protagonist of *Just for the Summer* is, in at least one way, the opposite of Libby—Mary Liz Scott is successful enough to have retired from investment banking at thirty-three. To plan the rest of her life, she goes to spend a summer in the wealthy community of East Hampton on Long Island,

where Mary Liz, who once wanted to be a detective, gets a chance to do just that, investigating the mysterious death and confused financial dealings of her godmother's husband. "Alas, the plot is often confusing rather than complex," remarked a *Publishers Weekly* reviewer, adding that the novel "goes tepid when it should sizzle." In the *New York Times Book Review,* Bruno Maddox called the novel "unashamedly trashy." *Booklist* contributor Melanie Duncan, however, dubbed *Just for the Summer* "a romantic thriller perfect for relaxing at the beach."

Talk revolves around a TV talk-show host, Jessica Wright, who has success and fame but longs for love. She has a secret admirer in newsman Will Rafferty; she also has a dangerous one in a fan who is stalking her. He eventually kills Jessica's secretary and kidnaps Jessica herself. "The convoluted plot initially moves briskly but then gets bogged down in the details of the abduction," a *Publishers Weekly* commentator reported. *Booklist*'s Duncan, though, praised *Talk* as having "enough intrigue, drama, and tangled relationships to give Jerry Springer pause." Lynn Karpen, writing in the *New York Times Book Review,* thought the stalker "somewhat stereotypical" but Jessica "anything but a cookie-cutter heroine," "wisecracking but vulnerable," and "a truly winning creation." Karpen also observed, "If there ever was a book for summer reading, this is it."

The heroine of *Exposé,* Sally Harrington, has left a desirable job writing for a magazine in Los Angeles to return to her small hometown in Connecticut, where her mother is recovering from cancer. She becomes a reporter for the local newspaper, meanwhile freelancing a profile of television executive Cassy Cochran for a slick national magazine. But she begins to suspect the magazine's publisher has unsavory motives, and she also investigates a murder in her hometown, seeing in it a possible link to her father's supposedly accidental death twenty years earlier. Further complications come as Sally is torn between her feelings for two men—a high-powered New York book editor and her childhood sweetheart, who is now a prosecuting attorney. In the *New York Times Book Review,* Mary-Ann Tirone Smith related that *Exposé* "briskly renders all the necessary ingredients (sex, love, a glamorous professional life, a crime—in that order) while ignoring issues of import (the situation in Kosovo, the political races)." Smith added that Sally's sleuthing "takes a back seat to the pre-emptive predicaments of workplace and heart." Catherine Sias, critiquing for *Booklist,* deemed the novel "lighthearted and amusing, suspenseful and romantic, and told with wit and insight."

Sally returns in *The Last Lover*. She's still working for the Connecticut newspaper but has a second job on a national news TV network based in New York, and she is romantically involved with Spencer Hawes, the book editor who vied for her affections in *Exposé*. When she and Spencer visit Los Angeles, film star Lilliana Martin sets out to seduce him. Spencer and Lilliana disappear, and then her former lover, a union leader believed to have ties to organized crime, is murdered. The police and the mob think Sally is the perpetrator—so to prove her innocence and also get a great story, she goes about finding the real culprit. "All this might sound like a bit much, but Van Wormer keeps a firm hand on the material and does a brisk job of sending up the publishing, news and movie industries," Diane Cole related in the *New York Times Book Review*. *Booklist* reviewer Sias described the book as "an enjoyable, fast-paced mystery" enlivened by "unexpected plot twists and likable characters."

BIOGRAPHICAL/CRITICAL SOURCES:

PERIODICALS

Booklist, December 1, 1994, Denise Perry Donavin, review of *Any Given Moment,* p. 656; October 15, 1995, Ilene Cooper, review of *Jury Duty,* p. 364; April 1, 1997, Melanie Duncan, review of *Just for the Summer,* p. 1269; July, 1998, Duncan, review of *Talk,* p. 1832; June 1, 1999, Catherine Sias, review of *Exposé,* p. 1744; September 1, 2000, Sias, review of *The Last Lover,* p. 70.

Library Journal, Samantha J. Gust, review of *The Last Lover,* p. 100.

New York Times Book Review, July 10, 1988; April 9, 1995, Malachy Duffy, review of *Any Given Moment;* February 18, 1996, Carol Peace Robins, review of *Jury Duty;* July 20, 1997, Bruno Maddox, "Beached"; August 9, 1998, Lynn Karpen, review of *Talk;* August 22, 1999, Mary-Ann Tirone Smith, "Love, Death and Lunch at the Four Seasons"; November 12, 2000, Diane Cole, review of *The Last Lover.*

People, October 23, 1989, Susan Toepfer, review of *West End,* p. 33; May 25, 1992, Toepfer, review of *Benedict Canyon,* p. 36; February 5, 1996, Pam Lambert, review of *Jury Duty,* p. 41.

Publishers Weekly, January 20, 1992, review of *Benedict Canyon,* p. 46; November 21, 1994, review of *Any Given Moment,* p. 67; October 16, 1995, review of *Jury Duty,* p. 40; April 17, 1997, review of *Just for the Summer,* p. 52; June 15, 1998, review of *Talk,* p. 41; June 14, 1999, review of *Exposé,* p. 45; August 16, 1999, Emily Jenkins, "Laura Van Wormer: Serious Glitz," p. 55; October 16, 2000, review of *The Last Lover,* p. 52.*

W-Z

*   *   *

*   *   *

*   *   *

WOLFE, Thomas (Clayton) 1900-1938

PERSONAL: Born October 3, 1900, in Asheville, NC; died of tubercular meningitis, September 15, 1938, in Baltimore, MD; son of William Oliver (a stonecutter) and Julia Elizabeth (a boardinghouse proprietor; maiden name, Westall) Wolfe. *Education:* University of North Carolina, Chapel Hill, B.A., 1920; Harvard University, M.A., 1922, graduate study, 1923.

CAREER: Writer. New York University, New York, NY, instructor in English at Washington Square College, intermittently, 1924-30. Worked in naval shipyards, Newport News, VA, 1918.

MEMBER: National Institute of Arts and Letters.

AWARDS, HONORS: Worth Prize, 1919, for essay *The Crisis in Industry;* Guggenheim fellowship, 1930; Scribner's Magazine Prize, 1932, for *A Portrait of Bascom Hawke.*

WRITINGS:

The Crisis in Industry (essay), University of North Carolina (Chapel Hill, NC), 1919, reprinted, 1978.

The Return of Buck Gavin: The Tragedy of a Mountain Outlaw (play; first produced by Carolina Playmakers, March, 1919), published in *Carolina Folk-Plays, Second Series,* edited by Frederick H. Koch, Holt (New York, NY), 1924.

Third Night (play), first produced by Carolina Playmakers, December, 1919.

The Mountains: A Play in One Act (produced by 47 Workshop at Harvard University, Boston, MA, 1921), edited with an introduction by Pat M. Ryan, University of North Carolina Press (Chapel Hill, NC), 1970.

Welcome to Our City (play; first produced in 1923), abridged version published in *Esquire,* October, 1957, published as *Welcome to Our City: A Play in Ten Scenes,* edited with an introduction by Richard S. Kennedy, Louisiana State University Press (Baton Rouge, LA), 1983.

Look Homeward, Angel: A Story of the Buried Life (novel), Scribner (New York, NY), 1929, published under same title with textual variations, Heinemann (London, England), 1930, published with introduction by Maxwell E. Perkins, illustrations by Douglas W. Gorsline, Scribner (New York, NY), 1952, reprinted, 1995.

A Portrait of Bascom Hawke (novella), published in *Scribner's Magazine,* 1932.

Of Time and the River: A Legend of Man's Hunger in His Youth (novel), Scribner (New York, NY), 1935, reprinted, 1999.

From Death to Morning (short stories), Scribner (New York, NY), 1935, reprinted, 1970.

The Story of a Novel (essay), serialized in *Saturday Review of Literature,* December, 1935, published in one volume with certain modifications, Scribner (New York, NY), 1936, published with *Writing and Living* as *The Autobiography of an American Novelist,* edited by Leslie Field, Harvard University Press (Cambridge, MA), 1983.

A Note on Experts: Dexter Vespasian Joyner (fragment), House of Books (New York, NY), 1939.

The Web and the Rock (novel), Harper (New York, NY), 1939, reprinted, Perennial Library (New York, NY), 1986.

You Can't Go Home Again (novel), Harper, 1940 (New York, NY), reprinted, Perennial Library (New York, NY), 1973.

The Hills Beyond (contains a novel fragment, the play *Gentleman of the Press* [also see below], and short stories, including "The Lost Boy" [also see below] and "The Web of Earth"), biographical note by Edward C. Aswell, Harper (New York, NY), 1941, reprinted, New American Library (New York, NY), 1968.

Gentlemen of the Press (play), Black Archer Press (Chicago, IL), 1942.

Mannerhouse: A Play in a Prologue and Three Acts (produced by the Yale University dramatic association, 1949), Harper (New York, NY), 1948, reprinted, edited by Louis D. Rubin, Jr., and John L. Idol, Jr., Louisiana State University Press (Baton Rouge, LA), 1985.

What Is Man?, [Chicago, IL], 1942.

A Western Journal: A Daily Log of the Great Parks Trip, June 20-July 2, 1938, University of Pittsburgh Press (Pittsburgh, PA), 1951, reprinted, 1967.

Thomas Wolfe's Purdue Speech: Writing and Living, edited with an introduction and notes by William Braswell and Leslie Field, Purdue University Studies (West Lafayette, IN), 1964, published as *Writing and Living* with *The Story of a Novel* as *The Autobiography of an American Novelist,* edited by Leslie Field, Harvard University Press (Cambridge, MA), 1983 (also see below).

The Notebooks of Thomas Wolfe, edited by Richard S. Kennedy and Paschal Reeves, two volumes, University of North Carolina Press (Chapel Hill, NC), 1970.

Return, Thomas Wolfe Memorial (Asheville, NC), 1976.

A Prologue to America, Croissant (Athens, OH), 1978.

The Streets of Durham (play), introduction by Richard Walser, Wolf's Head Press, 1982.

The Autobiography of an American Novelist: The Story of a Novel [and] *Writing and Living,* edited by Leslie Field, Harvard University Press (Cambridge, MA), 1983.

The Hound of Darkness (play), edited with foreword by John L. Idol, Jr., Thomas Wolfe Society (Akron, Ohio), 1986.

Thomas Wolfe's Composition Books: The North State Fitting School, 1912-1915, North Caroliniana Society (Chapel Hill, NC), 1990.

The Good Child's River, University of North Carolina Press (Chapel Hill, NC), 1991.

The Lost Boy (novella), University of North Carolina Press (Chapel Hill, NC), 1992.

The Starwick Episodes, edited by Richard S. Kennedy, Louisiana State University Press (Baton Rouge, LA), 1994.

The Party at Jack's (novella), edited by Suzanne Stutman and John L. Idol, Jr., University of North Carolina Press (Chapel Hill, NC), 1995.

O Lost: A Story of the Buried Life (novel; original manuscript of *Look Homeward, Angel),* text established by Arlyn Bruccoli and Matthew J. Bruccoli, University of South Carolina Press (Chapel Hill, SC), 2001.

CORRESPONDENCE

Thomas Wolfe's Letters to His Mother, Julia Elizabeth Wolfe (facsimile edition), edited with an introduction by John Skally Terry, Scribner (New York, NY), 1943, revised edition newly edited from the original manuscript by C. Hugh Holman and Sue Fields Ross, published as *The Letters of Thomas Wolfe to His Mother,* University of North Carolina Press (Chapel Hill, NC), 1968.

The Correspondence of Thomas Wolfe and Homer Andrew Watt, edited by Oscar Cargill and Thomas Clark Pollock, New York University Press (New York, NY), 1954.

Letters, collected and edited with introduction and explanatory text by Elizabeth Nowell, Scribner (New York, NY), 1956, abridged version with selection by Daniel George published as *Selected Letters of Thomas Wolfe,* Heinemann (London, England), 1958.

"Dear Mabel": Letters of Thomas Wolfe to His Sister, Mabel Wolfe Wheaton, edited by Mary Lindsay Thornton, published in *South Atlantic Quarterly,* autumn, 1961, reprinted, [Durham, NC], 1961.

Beyond Love and Loyalty: The Letters of Thomas Wolfe and Elizabeth Nowell; Together With "No More Rivers," a Story, edited by Kennedy, University of North Carolina Press (Chapel Hill, NC), 1983.

My Other Loneliness: Letters of Thomas Wolfe and Aline Bernstein, edited by Suzanne Stutman, University of North Carolina Press (Chapel Hill, NC), 1983.

Holding On For Heaven: The Cables and Postcards of Thomas Wolfe and Aline Bernstein, edited by Stutman, Thomas Wolfe Society, 1985.

To Loot My Life Clean: The Thomas Wolfe-Maxwell Perkins Correspondence, edited by Matthew J. Bruccoli and Park Bucker, University of South Carolina Press (Chapel Hill, NC), 2001.

SELECTED WRITINGS

The Face of a Nation: Poetical Passages From the Writings of Thomas Wolfe, selected and edited with introduction by John Hall Wheelock, Scribner (New York, NY), 1939.

A Stone, A Leaf, A Door: Poems by Thomas Wolfe, selected and arranged in verse by John S. Barnes, foreword by Louis Untermeyer, Scribner (New York, NY), 1945, recent edition, 1991.

The Portable Thomas Wolfe, edited by Maxwell Geismar, Viking (New York, NY), 1946, published as *The Portable Thomas Wolfe: Selections From the Works of Thomas Wolfe,* Heinemann (London, England), 1952.

Short Novels, edited with an introduction and notes by Holman, Scribner (New York, NY), 1961.

The Thomas Wolfe Reader, edited with an introduction and notes by Holman, Scribner (New York, NY), 1962.

K-19: Salvaged Pieces, edited with an introduction by John L. Idol, Jr., Thomas Wolfe Society, 1983.

The Complete Short Stories of Thomas Wolfe, edited by Francis E. Skipp, foreword by James Dickey, Scribner (New York, NY), 1987.

OTHER

Contributor of short stories, essays, and book reviews to periodicals, including *Scribner's Magazine, New Yorker, New York Evening Post, Saturday Review of Literature, Saturday Evening Post, Harper's Bazaar, Atlantic Monthly, American Mercury, Redbook,* and *Vogue.* Editor of *Tar Heel,* literary magazine of University of North Carolina at Chapel Hill, c. 1917.

Wolfe's writings have been translated into French, German, Spanish, Russian, Polish, and Hungarian. The William B. Wisdom collection of Wolfe's letters, manuscripts, inscribed works, galley and page proofs, notebooks, and school papers is gathered at the Houghton Library at Harvard University. A smaller collection of both printed and manuscript materials is housed at the Library of the University of North Carolina and a collection of printed materials and some letters is gathered at the Pack Memorial Public Library in Asheville, NC.

ADAPTATIONS: Look Homeward, Angel was adapted as a three-act comedy-drama by Ketti Frings, first produced in New York at the Ethel Barrymore Theater in 1957, and published by Scribner in 1958; it won the Pulitzer Prize, was made into a motion picture, and was adapted by Frings and Peter Udell as the musical comedy *Angel,* published by S. French in 1979. *Mannerhouse* was translated into French and adapted for the stage by Georges Sion and first produced as *Le Manoir* at the Theatre National de Belgique in 1957. The text from *Of Time and the River* has been set to music by Hugh W. Aitken, titled *Of Wandering Forever.*

SIDELIGHTS: American novelist Thomas Wolfe is best remembered for his four sprawling novels, *Look Homeward, Angel, Of Time and the River, The Web and the Rock,* and *You Can't Go Home Again,* all of which burst with youthful exuberance and reveal an unquenchable thirst for experience. "I will go everywhere and see everything," the young Wolfe wrote to his mother, as cited in the *Dictionary of Literary Biography.* "I will meet all the people I can. I will think all the thoughts, feel all the emotions I am able, and I will write, write, write." His massive books, crammed with sensual detail and romantic sensibility, made Wolfe a popular writer during his lifetime. Critics praised the energy and exuberance of his work, even as they found fault with its artistic flaws. As Terry Roberts pointed out in *Southern Literary Journal,* when Wolfe died in 1938, "his literary reputation was equal in the United States to that of Faulkner, Hemingway, and Fitzgerald." Since then, critical assessments of Wolfe's achievements have been somewhat less positive. Though some dismiss his work as adolescent and undisciplined, however, others maintain that Wolfe's best books reveal signs of a mature literary genius.

Wolfe's novels read as a fictional chronicle of his life. He was born October 3, 1900, in the Blue Ridge Mountain resort town of Asheville, North Carolina, a town which he would romanticize and call Altamont in *Look Homeward, Angel* and *Of Time and the River,* and Old Catawba in *The Web and the Rock* and *You Can't Go Home Again.* He was the youngest of six surviving children born to Julia Elizabeth Westall, a cold, overprotective, and parsimonious woman who avidly purchased property but forced her children to wear shoes they had long outgrown, and William Oliver Wolfe, an uproarious Pennsylvania tombstone cutter who recited Shakespeare. From 1906 on, the couple lived apart, with W. O. and one daughter sharing the apartment behind his shop and Julia and the rest of the children residing at the boardinghouse she owned and operated.

Wolfe portrays himself through *Look Homeward, Angel*'s Eugene Gant as a child who identified with the heroes of his adventure stories and history books. He attended public elementary school in Asheville but, deemed a promising student, he entered a private school there in 1912 at the request of its supervisors, Mr. and Mrs. J. M. Roberts (the Leonards in *Look Homeward, Angel*). Though basically uninspiring teachers, the Robertses introduced him to the arts and classical literature and encouraged him to write. At his mother's urging—she grudgingly paid his private-school tuition but willingly financed college—Wolfe entered the University of North Carolina at Chapel Hill at age fifteen, intending to pursue a career as a dramatist. As a freshman Wolfe lost his virginity in a brothel, and the following year he had an affair with one of his mother's boarders, who was five years his senior. He would later write about their bittersweet romance in the Laura James episodes in *Look Homeward, Angel,* which critics have claimed capture perfectly the passion and angst of adolescent love.

In March, 1919, Wolfe's first play, the melodrama *The Return of Buck Gavin: The Tragedy of a Mountain Outlaw,* was staged by the university's Carolina Playmakers. Encouraged by its success, Wolfe entered Harvard University as a graduate student in 1920 to study playwriting under George Pierce Baker, at his famous 47 Workshop. The Workshop performed two of Wolfe's plays, *The Mountains* and *Welcome to Our City,* but attempts to secure New York producers for the verbose dramas were unsuccessful. Needing money after graduating with a master's degree, Wolfe taught English at Washington Square College of New York University intermittently between 1924 and 1930.

In the fall of 1924 Wolfe took his first trip to Europe. He spent time in Germany and in France, where he met writers Sinclair Lewis and F. Scott Fitzgerald and a former Harvard classmate, Kenneth Raisbeck. Wolfe would later record their escapades in Parisian bistros and brothels in the Francis Starwick episodes in *Of Time and the River.* After his return to New York, while again seeking a producer for one of his plays, Wolfe met Aline Bernstein, a wealthy set designer with the New York Theatre Guild. Although Bernstein was married, a mother, and nearly twenty years his senior, she and Wolfe carried on a tempestuous affair over the next

five years. Wolfe dedicated *Look Homeward, Angel* to her, and she was the model for Esther Jack of *The Web and the Rock.*

Wolfe resumed teaching for a short while, and then joined Bernstein in England's Lake District in June, 1926. There she convinced him to forsake drama for novel writing, which she thought was better suited to his sweeping descriptive style. Wolfe began writing *Look Homeward, Angel* in London, and after he returned to the United States he shared a Manhattan apartment with Bernstein, who supported him while he worked full time on his novel. After he finished the book in 1928 he submitted it to several publishing houses. Each rejected it because, according to Wolfe in *The Story of a Novel,* in its original form it "was so amateurish, autobiographical, and unskilful that a publisher could not risk a chance on it." Sensitive to adverse criticism, a despondent Wolfe set sail for Europe. But while in Germany he received word that Scribner's editor, Maxwell Perkins, who worked with Ernest Hemingway and F. Scott Fitzgerald, was interested in his novel. Perkins recognized Wolfe's genius but also believed that the ponderous manuscript was unmanageable. Under his direction, some 60,000 words were trimmed from the text, including obscenities and passages of explicit sexual content. According to *New Republic* contributor Daniel Aaron, Wolfe was eager to have the book published and "did not protest the good intentions of his editors"; indeed, Aaron added, the young writer "was more than pleased with [the novel's] transformation. To many people, he wrote Perkins, it would be a 'modest success.' To him, it was 'touched with wonder,' a 'miracle.' "

Look Homeward, Angel traces protagonist Eugene Gant's childhood and young adulthood, which were marked by his turbulent relationships with family and society. The episodic and frankly autobigraphical novel climaxes with the death of Eugene's beloved brother, and with Eugene vowing to seek artistic and spiritual fulfillment within himself. The novel met with an enthusiastic reception and many hailed Wolfe as a writer of great promise. " 'Look Homeward, Angel' is as interesting and powerful a book as has ever been made out of the drab circumstances of provincial American life," Margaret Wallace observed in the *New York Times Book Review.* "It is at once enormously sensuous, full of the joy and gusto of life, and shrinkingly sensitive, torn with revulsion and disgust. Mr. Wolfe's style is sprawling, fecund, subtly rhythmic and amazingly vital." Some detractors felt that the novel lacked structure and was self-indulgent and unabashedly lyric. "Whenever Mr. Wolfe feels like it, which is fairly often, he launches into episodes, descriptions and proclamations of his own that could be cut out without impairing the architectural unity of his book," Geoffrey T. Hellman commented in a *New Republic* review. "Such deletions, however, would rob it of its gusto, and anyone in favor of making them is the sort of person who thinks that 'Moby Dick' would be a good book if it weren't for Mr. Melville's digressions."

Look Homeward, Angel's autobiographical content angered residents of Asheville. They were provoked by its thinly disguised and often unflattering characterizations, and many Southerners were appalled by passages that indicted southern society in general. "Years later," Wolfe wrote of Eugene in one such passage, "when he could no longer think of the barren spiritual wilderness, the hostile and murderous entrenchment against all new life—when their cheap mythology, their legend of the charm of their manner, the aristocratic culture of their lives, the quaint sweetness of their drawl, made him writhe—when he could think of no return to their life and its swarming superstition without weariness and horror, so great was his fear of the legend, his fear of their antagonism, that he still pretended the most fantastic devotion to them, excusing his Northern residence on grounds of necessity rather than desire." Shaken by their hostility—one indignant local wrote the author that she longed to see his "big overgoan karkus" dragged across the public square—Wolfe did not return to Asheville for seven years.

The royalties from *Look Homeward, Angel* allowed Wolfe to leave his teaching post in February, 1930. The following month he received a Guggenheim fellowship and sailed to Europe, where he could live relatively cheaply and write uninterrupted. Although in Paris Wolfe associated with many American expatriates, including Lewis, Fitzgerald, and Hemingway, he did not share their political interests and rejection of American society. On the contrary, Wolfe "discovered" his America. "During that summer in Paris," Wolfe explained in *The Story of a Novel,* "I think I felt this great homesickness more than ever before, and I really believe that from this emotion, this constant and almost intolerable effort of memory and desire, the material and structure of the books I now began to write were derived." Knowing that European nations possessed long literary traditions and believing that the foundation of American literature was still being laid, Wolfe vowed to leave his mark on the fledgling tradition by capturing the American experience in his subsequent novels.

In 1931 Wolfe began work on his second novel, in which he aimed to describe America's greatness as ex-

perienced by one man. After severing his ties with Bernstein when their affair became wearisome, Wolfe found a cheap flat in Brooklyn, living on canned beans, coffee, cigarettes, and the proceeds of a few short stories, while he wrote the new novel. Throughout 1934 Wolfe and Perkins edited the immense manuscript, with Perkins generally excising long passages and Wolfe rewriting transitions even longer than the originals. Finally Perkins sent the novel to the typesetter without Wolfe's knowledge, believing it to be complete; an aghast Wolfe insisted that he needed six more months to make it less episodic. Nervous about the novel's reception, Wolfe set sail for Europe a week before the 912-page *Of Time and the River* was published in March, 1935.

Of Time and the River covers the years 1920 to 1925, and opens with Eugene, now an aspiring novelist, on a northbound train anticipating life in Boston. The book then follows him to England, France, and Germany, where his homesickness becomes apparent in his vivid memories and idyllic descriptions of American life. The novel ends with Eugene returning home on an ocean liner and falling in love with Esther Jack, a character based on Wolfe's former mistress, Aline Bernstein.

Once again, critical reaction was mixed. *Of Time and the River* was faulted for its episodic nature—whole segments of the story seemed disconnected—and its apparent "formlessness." Some reviewers, however, maintained that the "formlessness" was intentional and that Wolfe, instead of ordering the novel around a sequence of events, unified it around a series of sense impressions, thereby capturing the diversity of the American experience and of life itself. While various reviewers condemned the book for its excessive emotion, others claimed that the rhapsodic, elegiac style complemented the book's loose structure.

Malcolm Cowley's *New Republic* assessment of the book was representative of general critical opinion. "Thomas Wolfe at his best is the only contemporary American writer who can be mentioned in the same breath with [Charles] Dickens and [Fyodor] Dostoevsky," he wrote. "But the trouble is that the best passages are scattered, that they occur without logic or pattern, except the biographical pattern of the hero's life, and they lack the cumulative effect, the slow tightening of emotions to an intolerable pitch, that one finds in great novels." Cowley also pointed out that "the author's style goes flabby as soon as attention is taken away from the outside world and concentrated on the hero's yearning and hungering soul." William Styron's impressions were similar. In *Harper's,* he wrote: "That furrow-browed, earnest sense of discovery in which the reader participates willingly in *Look Homeward, Angel* loses a great deal of its vivacity when the same protagonist has begun to pass into adulthood." Thomas C. Moser stated in *The American Novel,* "The older [Eugene] becomes, the less interesting the central character. When Wolfe writes badly, the subject is almost always Eugene."

Many others, however, were deeply moved by Wolfe's energy. *New York Post* contributor Herschel Brickell, for one, announced that "you can't, if you are of ordinary stature and vitality, believe completely in [Wolfe's] gigantic world of shadow shapes, where everything is magnified and intensified, but you will be fascinated just the same, swept along on the tides of his passions, carried away with the gargantuan appetite of a man who wishes to swallow life whole when most of us are content to chew a tiny fragment in our frightened and dyspeptic way." Bernard DeVoto was exasperated by Wolfe's lack of rhetorical restraint. He complained in a notorious *Saturday Review* critique, "Genius Is Not Enough," that all of Eugene's experiences are portrayed with equal intensity: "If the death of one's father comes out emotionally even with a ham-on-rye, then the art of fiction is cockeyed." *Of Time and the River* was nonetheless a best-selling novel, and Wolfe cemented his literary reputation later in 1935 with the publication of a short story volume, *From Death to Morning,* which Perkins culled from manuscript discarded from *Look Homeward, Angel* and *Of Time and the River.*

For a writer's conference in July of 1935, Wolfe composed a lecture that was later published as *The Story of a Novel,* in which he discusses his writing theories as well as his close working relationship with Perkins. DeVoto, in his *Saturday Review* article, questioned Wolfe's craftsmanship and editorial judgment, claiming that his writing was formless autobiography chopped up and rearranged by Perkins. "Works of art cannot be assembled like a carburetor," the critic stated, adding, "They must be grown like a plant." Stung by this criticism, Wolfe broke with Perkins and signed with Harper's in December 1937, where his editor was to be Edward C. Aswell.

In 1936 Wolfe took his seventh and last trip to Europe. He spent much of his time in Germany, where he was much celebrated, his success due in part to fine translations of his works by the German writer Hermann Hesse. Wolfe was dismayed, however, at the changes that had taken place in Germany since Adolf Hitler's rise to power. Upon returning to the United States,

Wolfe discussed the new Germany in a *New Republic* essay titled "I Have a Thing to Tell You." He wrote that the dark forests, with "their legendary sense of magic and time," were replaced by the "dark Messiah" Hitler and his Nazi followers. The following year Wolfe, no longer vilified, visited his native Asheville. Though he was disheartened by the many changes he encountered—a land boom had brought industry, commerce and corruption to the town—he rented a cottage nearby where he wrote during the summer of 1937.

During the first part of 1938 Wolfe wrote in seclusion in Brooklyn, and then accepted an invitation to tour the national parks in the West. En route he stopped at Purdue University, where he delivered a speech that would later be published as *Writing and Living.* He admitted the egocentric nature of his youthful writings, and stated that he had only recently realized his responsibility to society. In his new novels, he said, he planned to address more common human problems and to include his growing knowledge of worldwide political and economic situations. To symbolize his new literary direction, he changed his protagonist from recognizable alter-ego Eugene Gant to George "Monk" Webber.

Wolfe resumed his trip across America, but while in Seattle in July he contracted pneumonia. When his condition worsened he returned east to Baltimore, where doctors diagnosed tuberculosis of the brain. Wolfe had unknowingly contracted tuberculosis in his youth, the pneumonia had activated old tubercular scars in his lungs, and the tuberculosis then found its way to his brain through his bloodstream. After a series of operations Wolfe died on September 15, 1938, only a few weeks before his thirty-eighth birthday.

Before Wolfe set out for the west he had entrusted Aswell with a packing crate of manuscript eight feet high, containing thirty-five notebooks and other papers recording his impressions of America and Europe. He had also provided Aswell with extensive outlines and summaries for his works, and within three years, Aswell edited—many say overedited—much of the material, extracting from it the novels *The Web and the Rock* and *You Can't Go Home Again,* as well as the volume *The Hills Beyond,* a collection of short stories, a play, and a novel fragment.

The Web and the Rock carries forward Wolfe's story through protagonist George Webber, a successful novelist whose works resemble Wolfe's own. The first half of the book parallels *Look Homeward, Angel*— although it is written in a more detached tone—as the story of a small-town southern boy arriving in the North eager to experience life. The book's second half, which stands as a sequel to *Of Time and the River,* is devoted to George's affair with his muse, the sophisticated Esther Jack, and features luxuriant passages describing their lovemaking, feasts, and quarrels and reconciliations.

George and Esther's love affair ultimately collapses, precipitated by events surrounding a swank dinner party the couple host for the New York literati and various socialites at their Park Avenue apartment. A fire breaks out in their building, and as the guests evacuate, the superficial sophisticates mix with elevator operators, fire fighters, and street people, in a sharp commentary on the gap between the rich and poor in Depression-era America. Rejecting Esther and the privileged life she represents, George flees to Europe, but he cannot find solace there, for in Germany Hitler has risen to power, dashing all romantic images of that nation. Thus at the end of *The Web and the Rock,* George learns that time and change can only corrupt.

George is also disappointed when he returns to his native North Carolina in Wolfe's next novel, *You Can't Go Home Again.* Having avoided his home town throughout much of the burgeoning 1920s, George discovers that newfound wealth has debased many of its natives. Regardless of the corruption, *You Can't Go Home Again* ends with an optimistic cry of faith for all Americans: "I believe that we are lost here in America but I believe we shall be found." Although Americans cannot recapture the innocence they lost during the 1920s, Wolfe maintains, they must have faith in the future, when all Americans will be able to fulfill their potential through honest work, and live—as he professed to be doing—the American dream. "Though he used his life and art interchangeably," wrote Alfred Kazin in *On Native Grounds,* "they were, taken together, a reflection of Wolfe's conviction that he himself was a prime symbol of American experience and of a perpetual American ambition."

The Web and Rock and *You Can't Go Home Again* drew mixed reviews. While critics commended the author for passages revealing his heightened sensitivity to the plight of the oppressed, many noticed that Wolfe's more restrained style often fell flat. Most were struck by the disconcerting mixture of brilliant and poor writing in the novels (recent studies of the original texts show that Aswell combined early and late writings in these works). Stephen Vincent Benet, nevertheless, acknowledged Wolfe's growth as a writer and as a social being in his *Saturday Review of Literature* critique of

You Can't Go Home Again: "There is . . . a mature line. George Webber does grow up."

Aswell also edited Wolfe's posthumous collection, *The Hills Beyond,* which contains some of Wolfe's finest short stories, including "The Lost Boy," a moving account of his brother's death, and "The Web of Earth," a monologue in which Wolfe's mother relates her life story. Also included is a 150-page novel fragment—from which the work takes its title—which was to be a history of George Webber's maternal ancestors. Wolfe planned to tell the story of America through the descendants of one man and his twenty children, including a lawyer, politician, teacher, and businessman. Although Wolfe asked his mother to send him their family tree as a basis for the work, none of the characters were derived from people he knew. Some critics maintained that *The Hills Beyond* features some of Wolfe's most restrained and controlled writing, as well as some of his least exciting. Others, such as J. Donald Adams, admired Wolfe's more objective, dispassionate style. Critiquing the volume in the *New York Times Book Review,* Adams noted: "It contains some of his best, and certainly his most mature, work. The unfinished novel from which the book takes its title would, I think, have surpassed in creative power those other four on which his reputation must rest."

Two publications from the mid-1990s—*The Starwick Episodes* and *The Party at Jack's*—reconstruct fragments of Wolfe's earlier works. *The Starwick Episodes* grew out of portions of *Of Time and the River* which had been deleted by the author's editor. English scholar and Wolfe expert Richard S. Kennedy drew parallels between scenes of Eugene's friendship with the homosexual Starwick and the real-life relationship between Wolfe and ill-fated playwright Kenneth Raisbeck. In *The Party at Jack's*—material originally published as a novella in *Scribner's Monthly* and in a different form as part of *You Can't Go Home Again*—editors Suzanne Stutman and John L. Idol, Jr. piece together what is believed to be the most complete version of the story from Harvard University's Houghton Library manuscript collection. "It is clear," noted J. R. Morris in *World Literature Today,* "that this is 'the new Wolfe,' more aware of the society around him and determined to deal with social issues and important events of his day. The verbosity is still a problem, but some of the writing is among Wolfe's best." Donald Newlove, writing in Chicago *Tribune Books,* called the writing "fearless" and added, "Wolfe says to hell with you [the reader] if you don't like all my special effects."

Though Wolfe's reputation has waned since his death, the publication in 2001 of *O Lost: A Story of the Buried Life* reopened critical debate on his merits as a novelist. The book presents a text of *Look Homeward, Angel* that editors Arlyn Bruccoli and Matthew J. Bruccoli maintain is Wolfe's original manuscript; it restores some 60,000 words that Perkins cut and, in the opinion of many critics, reveals a stronger and more vibrant artistic voice than is present in the novel that Perkins edited. "*Look Homeward, Angel* is less panoramic in its sweep than *O Lost,*" admitted Aaron, though he went on to suggest that "it could be plausibly entertained that [Perkins's] cuts reduced the book's girth and corrected its sprawl without stifling its vitality." Roberts saw *O Lost* as evidence that, contrary to the common opinion that Wolfe wrote only about himself, he was really interested in exploring multiple points of view. And a contributor to *Kirkus Reviews* noted that "this unabridged version is lumbering and ungainly. It's also filled with gorgeous incidental visionary writing."

Also shedding considerable light on the creative process surrounding Wolfe's first novel are his letters to Perkins, published in *To Loot My Life Clean: The Thomas Wolfe-Maxwell Perkins Correspondence*. Wolfe's letters, according to Aaron, reveal the extent to which Wolfe depended on Perkins and show both the author's intense literary ambition and his deep doubts about his achievement and his reputation.

While Wolfe's detractors have seen him as an undisciplined writer, none can dismiss his epic, exuberant, and unaffected celebration of American and European life. "[I intend] to use myself to the top of my bent," Wolfe wrote in *You Can't Go Home Again*. "To use everything I have. To milk the udder dry, squeeze out the last drop, until there is nothing left." "My admiration for Wolfe is that he tried his best to get it all said," William Faulkner wrote to Richard Walser, editor of *The Enigma of Thomas Wolfe*. "He was willing to throw away style, coherence, all the rules of preciseness, to try to put all the experience of the human heart on the head of a pin."

BIOGRAPHICAL/CRITICAL SOURCES:

BOOKS

Adams, Agatha Boyd, *Thomas Wolfe: Carolina Student,* University of North Carolina Press (Chapel Hill, NC), 1950.

Austin, Neal F., *A Biography of Thomas Wolfe,* Beachman, 1968.

Bassett, John Earl, *Thomas Wolfe: An Annotated Critical Bibliography,* Scarecrow (Metuchen, NJ), 1996.

Berger, Brian F., *Thomas Wolfe: The Final Journey,* Willamette River Press, 1984.

Bernstein, Aline, *The Journey Down,* Knopf (New York, NY), 1938.

Bloom, Harold, editor, *Thomas Wolfe,* Chelsea House (New York, NY), 1987.

Boyd, Madeleine, *Thomas Wolfe: The Discovery of a Genius,* edited by Aldo P. Magi, Thomas Wolfe Society, 1981.

Concise Dictionary of American Literary Biography: The Age of Maturity, 1929-1941, Gale (Detroit, MI), 1989.

Dictionary of Literary Biography, Volume 9: *American Novelists, 1910-1945,* Gale (Detroit, MI), 1982, Volume 102: *American Short Story Writers, 1910-1945, Second Series,* Gale (Detroit, MI), 1991.

Dictionary of Literary Biography Documentary Series, Volume 2, Gale (Detroit, MI), 1982.

Dictionary of Literary Biography Yearbook: 1985, Gale (Detroit, MI), 1986.

Donald, David Herbert, *Look Homeward: A Life of Thomas Wolfe,* Little, Brown (Boston, MA), 1987.

Encyclopedia of World Biography, 2nd edition, Gale (Detroit, MI), 1998.

Evans, Elizabeth, *Thomas Wolfe,* Ungar (New York, NY), 1984.

Field, Leslie A., editor, *Thomas Wolfe: Three Decades of Criticism,* New York University Press (New York, NY), 1968.

Field, Leslie A., *Thomas Wolfe and His Editors,* University of Oklahoma Press (Norman, OK), 1987.

Griffin, John Chandler, *Memories of Thomas Wolfe: A Pictorial Companion to "Look Homeward, Angel,"* Summerhouse Press (Columbia, SC), 1996.

Gurko, Leo, *Thomas Wolfe: Beyond the Romantic Ego,* Crowell (New York, NY), 1975.

Holman, C. Hugh, *The Loneliness at the Core: Studies in Thomas Wolfe,* Louisiana State University Press (Baton Rouge, LA), 1975.

Holman, C. Hugh, *Thomas Wolfe,* University of Minnesota Press (Minneapolis, MN), 1960.

Holman, C. Hugh, editor, *The World of Thomas Wolfe,* Scribner (New York, NY), 1962.

Johnson, Elmer D., *Of Time and Thomas Wolfe: A Bibliography with a Character Index of His Works,* Scarecrow (Metuchen, NJ), 1959.

Johnson, Elmer D., *Thomas Wolfe: A Checklist,* Kent State University Press (Kent, OH), 1970.

Johnston, Carol, *Thomas Wolfe: A Descriptive Bibliography,* University of Pittsburgh Press (Pittsburgh, PA), 1987.

Johnston, Carol, *Of Time and the Artist: Thomas Wolfe, His Novels, and the Critics,* Camden House (Columbia, SC), 1995.

Kazin, Alfred, *On Native Grounds: An Interpretation of Modern American Prose Literature,* Harcourt (New York, NY), 1970.

Kennedy, Richard S., editor, *Thomas Wolfe: A Harvard Perspective,* Croissant (Athens, OH), 1983.

Kennedy, Richard S., *The Window of Memory: The Literary Career of Thomas Wolfe,* University of North Carolina Press (Chapel Hill, NC), 1962.

Magi, Aldo P. and Richard Walser, editors, *Thomas Wolfe Interviewed: 1929-1938,* Louisiana State University Press (Baton Rouge, LA), 1985.

Marx, Samuel, *Thomas Wolfe and Hollywood,* Croissant (Athens, OH), 1980.

Nowell, Elizabeth, *Thomas Wolfe: A Biography,* Doubleday (New York, NY), 1960.

Philipson, John S., editor, *Critical Essays on Thomas Wolfe,* G. K. Hall (Boston, MA), 1985.

Philipson, John S., *Thomas Wolfe: A Reference Guide,* G. K. Hall (Boston, MA), 1977.

Reeves, Paschal, editor, *Thomas Wolfe: The Critical Reception,* David Lewis, 1974.

Reeves, Paschal, editor, *Studies in Look Homeward, Angel,* Merrill, 1970.

Rubin, Louis D., Jr., editor, *Thomas Wolfe: A Collection of Critical Essays,* Prentice-Hall (Englewood Cliffs, NJ), 1973.

Steele, Richard, *Thomas Wolfe: A Study in Psychoanalytic Literary Criticism,* Dorrance (Bryn Mawr, PA), 1976.

Turnbull, Andrew, *Thomas Wolfe,* Scribner (New York, NY), 1967.

Twentieth-Century Literary Criticism, Gale (Detroit, MI), Volume 4, 1981, Volume 13, 1984, Volume 29, 1988.

Walser, Richard, *Thomas Wolfe, Undergraduate,* Duke University Press (Durham, NC), 1977.

Walser, Richard, *Thomas Wolfe: An Introduction and Interpretation,* Barnes & Noble (New York, NY), 1961.

Walser, Richard, editor, *The Enigma of Thomas Wolfe: Biographical and Critical Selections,* Harvard University Press (Cambridge, MA), 1953.

Watkins, Floyd C., *Thomas Wolfe's Characters,* University of Oklahoma Press (Norman, OK), 1957.

PERIODICALS

American Heritage, October 1992, review of *Look Homeward, Angel: A Story of the Buried Life,* p. 99.

American Literature, June 1992 review of *The Good Child's River,* p. 426; March 1995, review of *The Starwick Episodes,* p. 188; December 1995, review of *The Party at Jack's,* p. 899.

American Review, April, 1935.

American Scholar, autumn, 1995, p. 624.

Atlantic Monthly, January, 1940.

Booklist, October 15, 1991, review of *The Good Child's River,* p. 412.

Carolina Quarterly, winter 1993, review of *The Lost Boy,* p. 74.

Choice, April 1992, review of *The Good Child's River,* p. 1230; November 1995, review of *The Party at Jack's,* p. 469.

Christian Century, July 10, 1991, review of *Look Homeward, Angel,* p. 676.

Christian Science Monitor, September 30, 1991, review of *The Good Child's River,* p. 13.

English Journal, December 1991, review of *The Hills Beyond,* p. 90.

Harper's, April, 1968.

Harvard Library Bulletin, autumn, 1947.

Harvard Magazine, September-October, 1981, pp. 48-53, 62.

Kirkus Reviews, August 1, 1991, review of *The Good Child's River,* p. 969; September 15, 1992, review of *The Lost Boy,* p. 1156; March 15, 1995, review of *The Party at Jack's,* p. 344; October 1, 2000, review of *O Lost: A Story of the Buried Life,* p. 1384.

Kliatt Young Adult and Paperback Book Guide, May, 1996, review of *Look Homeward, Angel* (audio version), p. 45.

Library Journal, June 15, 1991, review of *A Stone, a Leaf, a Door: Poems by Thomas Wolfe,* p. 110; September 15, 1991, review of *The Good Child's River,* p. 115; November 1, 1991, review of *The Hills Beyond,* p. 116; October 1, 1992, review of *The Lost Boy,* p. 121; April 1, 1995, review of *The Party at Jack's,* p. 127; November 15, 1997, review of *From Death to Morning* (audio version), p. 91; September 15, 1999, review of *The Web and the Rock,* p. 117; October 1, 2000, Michael Rogers, review of *To Loot My Life Clean: The Thomas Wolfe-Maxwell Perkins Correspondence,* p. 96.

Los Angeles Times Book Review, November 3, 1991, review of *The Good Child's River,* p. 7; November 8, 1992, review of *The Lost Boy,* p. 6; August 28, 1994, review of *The Lost Boy,* p. 11.

Modern Fiction Studies, autumn, 1965.

New Republic, December 18, 1929; March 20, 1935, September 28, 1938; February 5, 2001, Daniel Aaron, review of *O Lost* and *To Loot My Life Clean: The Thomas Wolfe-Maxwell Perkins Correspondence,* p. 37.

New York Herald Tribune, September 16, 1938.

New York Post, March 8, 1935; June 22, 1939.

New York Times, September 16, 1938.

New York Times Book Review, October 27, 1929; October 26, 1941; October 29, 1995, review of *The Party at Jack's,* p. 42.

Publishers Weekly, December 24, 1938; August 30, 1991, review of *The Good Child's River,* p. 67; August 24, 1992, review of *The Lost Boy,* p. 63; July 25, 1994, review of *The Lost Boy,* p. 48; August 22, 1994, review of *The Starwick Episodes,* p. 43; March 6, 1995, review of *The Party at Jack's,* p. 61.

Reference and Research Book News, December 1994, review of *The Starwick Episodes,* p. 39.

Saturday Review of Literature, April 25, 1936; September 21, 1940.

School Library Journal, April 1993, review of *The Lost Boy,* p. 150.

Southern Literary Review, fall, 2000, Terry Roberts, "Resurrecting Thomas Wolfe," p. 27.

Studies in Short Fiction, summer, 1993, review of *The Lost Boy,* p. 142.

Texas Studies in Literature and Language, autumn, 1959, pp. 425-445.

Times Literary Supplement, January 2, 1969.

Tribune Books (Chicago, IL), May 21, 1995, review of *The Party at Jack's,* p. 6.

Washington Post Book World, December 29, 1991, review of *The Good Child's River,* p. 7.

World Literature Today, spring 1992, review of *The Good Child's River,* p. 346; winter 1994, review of *The Lost Boy,* p. 142; autumn, 1995, review of *The Party at Jack's,* p. 805.

Yale Review, October, 1980, pp. 79-84.

OTHER

The Thomas Wolfe Society Web site, http://www. thomaswolfe.org/ (September 17, 2001).

The Thomas Wolfe Web site, http://library.uncwil.edu/ wolfe/ (September 17, 2001).*

ZIMMER, Carl 1966-

PERSONAL: Born July 13, 1966, in New Haven, NJ; son of Richard (a lawyer) and Marfy (a farmer; maiden name, Goodspeed) Zimmer. *Education:* Yale University, B.A., 1987.

ADDRESSES: Agent—Eric Simonoff, Janklow & Nesbit Associates, 598 Madison Ave, New York, NY 10022. *E-mail*—zimmer@panix.com.

CAREER: Journalist. *Discover* magazine, senior editor, 1994-99; freelance writer, 1999—.

MEMBER: National Association of Science Writers.

AWARDS, HONORS: Everett Clark Award for science journalism; American Institute of Biological Sciences Media Award, 1997; Pan-American Health Organization Award for excellence in International Health Reporting, 1999.

WRITINGS:

At the Water's Edge: Macroevolution and the Transformation of Life, Free Press (New York, NY), 1998.
Parasite Rex: Inside the Bizarre World of Nature's Most Dangerous Creatures, Free Press (New York, NY), 2000.
Evolution: The Triumph of an Idea, HarperCollins (New York, NY), 2001.

Contributor to periodicals, including *National Geographic, Science, Audubon, Natural History,* and *Wired.*

ADAPTATIONS: Evolution: The Triumph of an Idea was the companion piece for the PBS series *Evolution,* 2001.

SIDELIGHTS: Carl Zimmer, a science journalist, and at the time senior editor for the magazine *Discover,* published his first book, *At the Water's Edge: Macroevolution and the Transformation of Life,* in 1998. Though he was often occupied with work for the magazine, Zimmer found the time to expand the breadth of his work in creating the book. In an interview with *Amazon.com,* Zimmer explained that *At the Water's Edge* was just a natural culmination of his work and interests. "I've been writing since I was a kid, but writing about science became my passion when I started working at *Discover* magazine," Zimmer said. "Sometimes a subject needs more space than a magazine can allow, and that's when I turn to writing books."

At the Water's Edge is an in-depth study of the Darwinian concept of macroevolution, a theoretical explanation of how entire species change or evolve in an attempt to adapt to other environments. More specifically, Zimmer examines how primitive organisms first left the world's seas to adapt to life on land, and then, millions of years later, how certain land mammals adapted again to go back to the seas. In what Zimmer calls "two of the most beautiful opportunities for studying macroevolution," he explains how, 350 to 400 million years ago, those early fishes crawled out of the seas and evolved into tetrapods, and then forty to fifty million years ago, some terrestrial mammals decided to go back to the water and eventually evolved into the world's whales and other marine mammals. In the beginning of his book, Zimmer writes an introductory survey concerning the rise of evolutionary thinking, beginning with Darwin and his work. He explains how and why Darwin's theories were so greatly opposed in the beginning, largely because many people were appalled by the idea that man was descended from apes.

In *At the Water's Edge* Zimmer ponders what the reaction would have been had Darwin explained to people that they really were descendants of fish. "Yet the transition from apelike ancestors to humans was a late, minor change in our kaleidoscopic descent. At least an ape can walk and breathe air. At least it has hair and thumbs," Zimmer writes in the book. "For real alienation, go back to a fish. Who can see a kindred spirit in those flat button eyes? The flattened or elongated body, nothing more than a mouth driven forward by muscle?" According to Zimmer, Darwin was well aware of this and once wrote to a friend, "Our ancestor was an animal which breathed water, had a swim bladder, a great swimming tail, an imperfect skull, and undoubtedly was an hermaphrodite! Here is a pleasant genealogy for mankind."

In the first half of the book, Zimmer concentrates on how the fishes left the water and were able to travel despite the strains of gravity. They first evolved into tetrapods, and then into all land animals including mammals. The rest of the book focuses on the rise of whales, porpoises, and other marine mammals, all of which evolved from well-adapted land mammals. Despite the fact that these animals did not have the aid of gills or fins, they still transformed themselves to live an aquatic life. Zimmer considers this adaptation an incredible evolutionary feat. To back up his claims Zimmer utilizes a wide array of evidence. First, he interviewed many preeminent scientists as they worked in the field and in their laboratories. In his search he traveled all over the world, including such places as Greenland,

Brussels, Pakistan, and Australia, and in his writing he takes the reader along for the ride. He combines evidence from several different fields of study including paleontology, genealogy, biology, and anatomy. The reader also gets a good look at how scientists work and theorize.

The critical response to *At the Water's Edge* was generally positive. Jean E. Crampon, reviewing the book for *Library Journal,* called it an "excellent discussion of macroevolution" that was "very readable." A contributor to *Publishers Weekly* was also impressed with the book. "More than just an informative book about macroevolution itself, this is an entertaining history of ideas written with literary flair and technical rigor," the contributor wrote. Calling it a "tale of high-stakes scientific sleuthing," Bryce Christensen of *Booklist* thought *At the Water's Edge* was filled with "marvelously lucid writing." *Quarterly Review of Biology* critic John A. Ruben remarked that Zimmer's "easygoing, almost folksy, book represents one of the best popular resources available to help remedy the notion that evolutionary theory suffers from a dearth of easily taught, easily understood facts about macroevolution."

Zimmer's follow-up, *Parasite Rex: Inside the Bizarre World of Nature's Most Dangerous Creatures,* deals with "the enormous variety of one- and many-celled organisms that live on and inside other animals and plants," as a *Publishers Weekly* reviewer put it. Zimmer analyzes the various parasites and how they affect their hosts, for ill and, sometimes, good: Zimmer makes the case that parasites can protect against allergies and certain diseases of the digestive tract, and suggests that they can alter their hosts' emotional and sexual behavior. Many parasites, however, are cringe-inducing. Zimmer "introduces readers to some of nature's most sinister characters: nematodes that cause blindness, worms that swell up a scrotum until it fills a wheelbarrow, 60-foot-long tapeworms and deadly creatures so tiny they hitchhike on the back of a fly," reported Jill Wolfson in the online magazine *Salon.* The book led the *Publishers Weekly* reviewer to state, "One of the year's most fascinating works of popular science is also its most disgusting." *Forbes* contributor Susan Adams commented of parasites, "Loathsome they may be, but these creatures deserve a little respect. . . . In fact, parasites are powerful, complex, highly evolved organisms." Adams called Zimmer's book "spellbinding," while *Library Journal* critic Margaret Henderson observed that it "makes parasitology interesting and accessible to everyone." *Booklist*'s Gilbert Taylor concluded that *Parasite Rex* is "a well-organized and well-presented survey of parasites' life cycles and the debilitations they cause."

Zimmer's 2001 book, *Evolution: The Triumph of an Idea,* discusses the subject of evolution and other related contentious topics, such as Charles Darwin and his attempts at propounding the theory of evolution before society. A *Publishers Weekly* reviewer praised Zimmer for having done "a superb job of providing a sweeping overview of most of the topics critical to understanding evolution, presenting his material from both a historical and a topical perspective."

BIOGRAPHICAL/CRITICAL SOURCES:

PERIODICALS

Booklist, March 1, 1998, Bryce Christensen, review of *At the Water's Edge: Macroevolution and the Transformation of Life,* p. 1078; August, 2000, Gilbert Taylor, review of *Parasite Rex: Inside the Bizarre World of Nature's Most Dangerous Creatures,* p. 2090; December 1, 2000, Hazel Rochman, review of *Parasite Rex,* p. 734.

Forbes, September 18, 2000, Susan Adams, "Those Resourceful Bugs."

Library Journal, February 1, 1998, Jean E. Crampon, review of *At the Water's Edge,* p. 108; June 1, 2000, Margaret Henderson, review of *Parasite Rex: Inside the Bizarre World of Nature's Most Dangerous Creatures,* p. 190.

New York Times Book Review, May 3, 1998, Philip Gingerich, review of *At the Water's Edge,* p. 22.

Publishers Weekly, February 9, 1998, review of *At the Water's Edge,* pp. 83-84; July 10, 2000, review of *Parasite Rex,* p. 52; August 6, 2001, review of *Evolution: The Triumph of an Idea,* p. 71.

Quarterly Review of Biology, June, 1999, John A. Ruben, review of *At the Water's Edge,* p. 222.

Sciences, September, 2000, Laurence A. Marschall, review of *Parasite Rex,* p. 44.

OTHER

Amazon.com, http://www.amazon.com/ (August 8, 2001), interview with Zimmer.

Carl Zimmer's Web site, http://www.carlzimmer.com/ (January 7, 2001).

Salon.com, http://www.salon.com/ (September 26, 2000), Jill Wolfson, "You're a Good Host."